World
Business
Rankings
Annual

ISSN 1096-2840

1998

World Business Rankings Annual

Lists of International Companies, Products, Services, and Activities Compiled from a Variety of Published Sources.

**Compiled by
Robert Lazich,
Editorial Code & Data Inc.
and
Brooklyn Public Library
Business Library Staff**

GALE

DETROIT · NEW YORK · TORONTO · LONDON

Robert S. Lazich, *Editor*

Editorial Code & Data Inc. Staff

David Smith, *Contributing Editor*
Joyce Piwowarski, *Programmer/Analyst*
Kenneth J. Muth, *Manager, Technical Operations*

Gale Research Staff

Lynn M. Pearce, *Coordinating Editor*
Mary Beth Trimper, *Production Director*
Cynthia Baldwin, *Product Design Manager*
Barbara J. Yarrow, *Graphic Services Supervisor*
C. J. Jonik, *Desktop Publisher*

The paper used in this publication meets the minimum requirements of American National Standard for Information Sciences—Permanence Paper for Printed Library Materials, ANSI Z39.48-1984.

ISBN 0-7876-1880-2
ISSN 1096-2840
10 9 8 7 6 5 4 3 2 1

Printed in the United States of America

Contents

Introduction

World Business Rankings Annual (*WBRA*) is a diverse compilation of international rankings data. More than 2,500 tabular entries are included. Entries show companies, brands, markets, and other business categories in some kind of rank order—by dollars or other currencies, unit counts, percentage, or some other measure.

WBRA is a new publication in Gale's well-known *Business Rankings Annual* series. Until the publication of *WBRA*, *Business Rankings Annual* included international data to greater or lesser extent depending on the availability of space. User requests led Gale to expand the international coverage of *Business Rankings Annual*. Thus *WBRA* was born. This publication gives the user a much wider and more comprehensive view of business markets across the globe. In this day and age of vast, interlocking global economic activity, the editors hope that *WBRA* will provide a welcome addition to available data.

Method of Compilation

WBRA was drawn from more than 260 periodicals and other sources. About one-third of the entries were collected by the staff of the Business Library of the Brooklyn Public Library, the compilers of *Business Rankings Annual*, as part of the overall effort in preparing that book. All other entries were obtained by the editors using a variety of techniques, including library visits, review of publications normally received by Editorial Code and Data, Inc., online searches, etc. All potential entries were reviewed by the editors for suitability. Once an entry was selected, it was categorized, assigned a Standard Industrial Classification (SIC) code, and prepared for inclusion. In the case of entries with more than ten items, the top ten items were selected. If an entry had fewer than ten entries, all items were selected. Preparation of each entry included the writing of introductory descriptions and the source note.

Coverage and Sources

WBRA covers the entire range of economic activity from Agricultural Production through and including selected government activities. The range of coverage can be overseen, based on subject, in the *Outline of Contents* or, based on industrial classification, in the *SIC Index*.

This first edition of *WBRA* features data from 262 sources, including periodicals, government reports, online databases, or data obtained using online searches. Most entries were drawn from serials and periodicals published between January, 1995 and the end of September, 1997.

Data extracted were often parts of much more comprehensive discussions of the subject in the source, with the tabulation published in *WBRA* serving as illustrative material. The user is encouraged to consult the original source when doing in-depth investigations.

Organization and Categorization of Entries

WBRA begins with an *Outline of Contents*. The body of the book follows, with entries arranged alphabetically, as discussed below. An *Index*, *Geographical Index*, and *SIC Index* follow. The *Bibliography* completes the work.

Subject Categorization. *WBRA* presents entries grouped by subject. Subjects are arranged alphabetically. Headings used are those familiar to users of *Business Rankings Annual*. Most are taken from the Library of Congress (LC) subject headings, for example: Banks and Banking. When LC did not offer an appropriate or sufficiently up-to-date heading, Wilson's *Business Periodicals Index* and Information Access Corporation's *Business Index* were used to find categories already in use in the field. *See* and *See also* references are provided throughout the body of the book. All subjects used appear in the *Outline of Contents*. It is possible to scan the list of headings quickly to determine the exact form of the subject term that has been used.

Geographical Categorization. Entries are also categorized by geography, where appropriate. Using the *Geographical Index*, entries can be located by country, region, state, or city. The basis of the geographical categorization is usually clearly visible in the entry itself: the entry is either about activities in a country or a region or countries/states/regions/cities are listed in the body of the entry itself.

SIC Categorization. *WBRA* entries are classified by SIC to enable users accustomed to the SIC coding system to find entries using the *SIC Index*. The SIC codes, however, do not actually appear in the entries.

Arrangement of Entries. An entry may feature an international ranking or cover a particular market in a city, country, or region. In most cases, the tables are company rankings. However, some tables feature brand, country, and product rankings. Entries thought to be most in demand by business people, analysts, librarians, students, and the public were selected; for each entry, this volume typically provides at least "the top ten" on the list, along with important details about the ranking. Some entries contain fewer than 10 listees; these tables were included because they were deemed to be particularly interesting or informative. A *Sample Entry* is provided following this Introduction.

Indexes

WBRA featues three indices as follows:

Index. *WBRA*'s main index shows all names and geographical entities arranged alphabetically. Geographical entities are also listed separately in the *Geographical Index* (see below) for user convenience. Beneath each such index item (in **bold** type), are references to subjects and entries (by number). For example:

> **Ahold**
> Corporations—Netherlands 1014
> Retail Trade 2180, 2184
> Supermarkets—Europe 2348

In the example above, the company Ahold is shown under three subjects and in four separate entries.

Geographical Index. This index shows all geographical entities mentioned in *WBRA*, including regions, countries, states, and cities. Entities are arranged in alphabetical order. Beneath each item are refrences to subjects and entries (by number). For example:

> **Geneva, Switzerland**
> Computer Industry 704
> Hotels and Motels—Europe 1611
> Institutional Investments 1669

In this example, Geneva is shown to appear in three entries under three subject categories.

SIC Index. This index features 4-digit SIC categories. Each SIC item is followed by a listing of subjects under that SIC; entry references (by number) are also shown. Arrangement of the index is by SIC number. Headers are provided for the 2-digit level (but without an SIC number); thus **REAL ESTATE** serves as a header for *SIC 6512 Nonresidential building operators* and *SIC 6531 Real estate agents and managers*. Example:

7363 Help supply services
Employment Agencies 1218
Temporary Help Services Agencies 2396

The above item shows that two entries are classified as SIC 7363. They are under two separate subject categories.

Bibliography

A complete listing of the more than 260 original sources used to compile *WBRA* is provided in the *Bibliography*. Information cited includes:

- publication name
- publisher
- address, telephone, and fax number
- frequency of publication
- price
- ISSN if applicable

Acknowledgments

Many people and organizations contributed data, suggestions, and advice in the compilation of *WBRA*. The editorial staff thanks them all for their help and guidance. Special thanks are due to the staff of the Business Library of the Brooklyn Public Library. With their access to some fourteen hundred periodicals, eighteen newspapers, and numerous directories, company reports, and statistical annuals, their contributions to this book are invaluable.

Comments and Suggestions

Although every effort has been made to ensure the accuracy and timeliness of the data in *WBRA*, errors and omissions may occur. Notification of changes or additions deemed appropriate by users of this edition are appreciated. Comments and suggestions for the improvement of *WBRA* are welcome. Please contact:

> *World Business Rankings Annual*
> Gale Research
> 835 Penobscot Building
> Detroit, MI 48226-4094
> Phone: (313) 961-2242
> Toll-free: 800-347-GALE
> Fax: (313) 961-6815

Sample Entry

[1] *1581*

[2] **TOP ACCESSORIES BRANDS BY BRAND VALUE** [4]

[3] **Ranked by:** Brand value, in millions of U.S. dollars. **Remarks:** Value was calculated using capital, ratio of capital to company sales, earnings, and corporate tax rate of the country where the parent company is located. See source for details. **Number** [5] **listed:** 6

1. Louis Vuitton (LVMH) with $6,137 million
2. Hermes (Hermes), $1,178
[6] 3. Gucci (Gucci Group), $717
4. Ray-Ban (Bausch & Lomb), $530
5. Swatch (SMH Corp.), $369
6. Coach (Sara Lee), $271

[7] **Source:** *Financial World*, World's Most Valuable Brands (annual), July 8, 1996, p. 56.

[1] Sequential entry number.

[2] **Ranking title** - A descriptive phrase, identifying the contents of the list cited. These titles may be taken verbatim from the original source or, if need be, assigned by the rankings editor to categorize the list more effectively.

[3] **Ranked by**: Indicates the criteria that establish the hierarchy, with specifics of date and unit of measurement, if given.

[4] **Remarks**: Provides additional details relating to the list from the source material.

[5] **Number listed**: Notes the number of listees in the ranking source.

[6] **Items in the list**. The top 10 items (or fewer if fewer are available) are shown. In many cases the listing also includes data substantiating the rankings, as the dollar figures above show.

[7] **Source**: Gives complete bibliographic details. For periodicals, notes title, date, and page number. For books, lists author/editor and publisher as well.

Outline of Contents

World Business Rankings Annual

Accessories

★1★

TOP ACCESSORIES BRANDS BY BRAND VALUE
Ranked by: Brand value, in millions of U.S. dollars.
Remarks: Value was calculated using capital, ratio of capital to company sales, earnings, and corporate tax rate of the country where the parent company is located. See source for details. **Number listed:** 6
1. Louis Vuitton (LVMH) with $6,137 million
2. Hermes (Hermes), $1,178
3. Gucci (Gucci Group), $717
4. Ray-Ban (Bausch & Lomb), $530
5. Swatch (SMH Corp.), $369
6. Coach (Sara Lee), $271

Source: *Financial World,* World's Most Valuable Brands (annual), July 8, 1996, p. 56.

★2★

TOP APPAREL BRANDS BY BRAND VALUE
Ranked by: Brand value, in millions of U.S. dollars.
Remarks: Value was calculated using capital, ratio of capital to company sales, earnings, and corporate tax rate of the country where the parent company is located. See source for details. **Number listed:** 14
1. Levi's (Levi Strauss) with $7,376 million
2. Nike (Nike), $7,267
3. Reebok (Reebok International), $2,726
4. Hanes (Sara Lee), $1,694
5. Benetton (Benetton Group), $1,564
6. Fruit of the Loom (Fruit of the Loom), $1,333
7. Wrangler (VF Corp.), $1,266
8. Lee (VF Corp.), $1,045
9. Adidas (Adidas), $1,028
10. Liz Claiborne (Liz Claiborne), $868

Source: *Financial World,* World's Most Valuable Brands (annual), July 8, 1996, p. 56.

Accidents

★3★

COMMERCIAL JET TRANSPORT ACCIDENTS BY PHASE OF OPERATION
Ranked by: Number of accidents. **Remarks:** Accidents may involve more than one phase. **Number listed:** 11
1. Landing with 586 accidents
2. Approach, 271
3. Takeoff, 265
4. Climb, 104
5. Cruise, 82
6. Taxi, 80
7. Descent, 47
8. Go-around, 26
9. Ground event, 16
10. Engine start, 4

Source: *Aviation Week & Space Technology*, August 18, 1997, p. 23.

Accounting Firms

★4★

LARGEST ACCOUNTING FIRMS IN ISRAEL, 1995
Ranked by: Number of total staff at the end of 1995.
Remarks: Data for Somekh Chaikin are from July 1996. Notes number of offices, partners, professionals, and most recent year's fee income. **Number listed:** 10
1. Kesselman & Kesselman with 354 total staff
2. Braude Bavly, 350
3. Somekh Chaikin, 317
4. Kost Levary & Forer, 291
5. Igal Brightman, 257
6. HHSL Haft & Haft, 216
7. Almagor & Co., 196
8. Luboshitz Kasierer, 181
9. Fahn Kanne, 119
10. Shlomo Ziv, 116

Source: *The Accountant*, January 1997, p. 14.

★5★

LARGEST ACCOUNTING FIRMS IN MEXICO

Ranked by: Number of employees. **Number listed:** 10

1. Deloitte & Touche/Galaz, Gomez, Morfin, Chavero, Yamazaki with 2,000 employees
2. Coopers & Lybrand/Roberto Casas Alatriste, 1,500
3. Mancera, S.C. Ernst & Young, 1,500
4. Price Waterhouse, 1,381
5. EDS/AT Kearney, 1,287
6. Arthur Andersen, 1,066
7. KPMG Cardenas Dosal, 1,000
8. Andersen Consulting, 310
9. Mckinsey & Co., 146
10. Booz Allen & Hamilton, 50

Source: *Mexico Business*, May 1996, p. 56.

★6★

TOP ACCOUNTING FIRMS BY PROFITS PER PARTNER, 1996

Ranked by: Profits per partner, in British pounds (£).
Remarks: Notes figures for 1995. **Number listed:** 5

1. KPMG with £207,198
2. Ernst & Young, £200,474
3. Pannell Kerr Foster, £107,924
4. Neville Russell, £98,024
5. BDO Stoy Hayward, £92,000

Source: *Accountancy - International Edition*, July 1997, p. 16.

★7★

TOP ACCOUNTING FIRMS BY REVENUE PER PARTNER, 1996

Ranked by: Revenue per partner, in millions of U.S. dollars. **Number listed:** 6

1. Andersen Worldwide with $3.638 million
2. Price Waterhouse, $1.517
3. Ernst & Young, $1.447
4. Deloitte & Touche, $1.356
5. Coopers & Lybrand, $1.296
6. KPMG, $1.180

Source: *The New York Times*, September 23, 1997, p. C2.

★8★

TOP ACCOUNTING FIRMS BY REVENUE PER PROFESSIONAL, 1996

Ranked by: Revenue per professional, in millions of U.S. dollars. **Number listed:** 6

1. Ernst & Young with $0.145 million
2. Deloitte & Touche, $0.135
3. Andersen Worldwide, $0.134
4. KPMG, $0.123
5. Price Waterhouse, $0.120
6. Coopers & Lybrand, $0.117

Source: *The New York Times*, September 23, 1997, p. C2.

★9★

TOP ACCOUNTING FIRMS BY TOTAL EMPLOYEES, 1996

Ranked by: Employees. **Number listed:** 6

1. Andersen Worldwide with 91,572
2. KPMG, 78,725
3. Coopers & Lybrand, 74,000
4. Ernst & Young, 68,452
5. Deloitte & Touche, 63,450
6. Price Waterhouse, 55,853

Source: *The New York Times*, September 19, 1997, p. C3.

★10★

TOP ACCOUNTING FIRMS BY TOTAL REVENUE, 1996

Ranked by: Revenue, in millions of U.S. dollars. **Number listed:** 6

1. Anderson Worldwide with $9,499 million
2. Ernst & Young, $7,800
3. KPMG, $7,458
4. Coopers & Lybrand, $6,805
5. Deloitte & Touche, $6,500
6. Price & Waterhouse, $5,018

Source: *The New York Times*, September 23, 1997, p. C2.

★11★

TOP INTERNATIONAL ACCOUNTING NETWORKS, 1995

Ranked by: Fee income, in millions of U.S. dollars.
Remarks: Also notes percent change, number of offices, partners, and professional staff. **Number listed:** 25

1. Arthur Andersen with $8,100 million
2. KPMG, $7,500
3. Ernst & Young International, $6,870
4. Coopers & Lybrand International, $6,200
5. Deloitte Touche Tohmatsu, $5,950
6. Price Waterhouse, $4,460
7. BDO International, $1,230
8. Grant Thornton International, $1,200
9. Moores Rowland International, $922
10. RSM International, $871

Source: *Accountancy - International Edition*, August 1996, p. 14.

Accounting Firms – Australia

★12★

LEADING ACCOUNTING FIRMS AND ASSOCIATIONS IN AUSTRALIA, 1996

Ranked by: Fee income, in millions of Australian dollars (A$). **Number listed:** 10

1. Andersen Worldwide with A$407.0 million
2. Coopers & Lybrand, A$348.0
3. Price Waterhouse, A$333.6

4. KPMG, A$329.0
5. Ernst & Young, A$316.0
6. Deloitte Touche Tohmatsu, A$219.0
7. Horwath & Horwath, A$42.7
8. Pannell Kerr Forster, A$37.6
9. Grant Thornton, A$35.2
10. Bird Cameron, A$29.7

Source: *The Accountant*, October 1996, p. 13.

Accounting Firms – Canada

★ 13 ★
LEADING ACCOUNTING AND AUDITING FIRMS IN CANADA BY FEE INCOME
Ranked by: Fee income, in millions of Canadian dollars (C$). **Number listed:** 36
1. KPMG with C$492.5 million
2. Deloitte & Touche, C$441.0
3. Ernst & Young, C$382.0
4. Coopers & Lybrand, C$298.8
5. Price Waterhouse, C$251.0
6. Doane Raymond Grant Thornton, C$204.6
7. Arthur Andersen, C$130.0
8. BDO Dunwoody, C$128.0
9. Summit International, C$71.6
10. Collins Barrow, C$27.7

Source: *The Accountant*, July 1996, p. 11.

★ 14 ★
LEADING ACCOUNTING AND AUDITING FIRMS IN CANADA BY STAFF, 1995
Ranked by: Total staff. **Remarks:** Notes number of offices, partners, professional staff, and administrative staff for 1994 and 1995. **Number listed:** 36
1. KPMG with 4,688
2. Deloitte & Touche, 4,519
3. Ernst & Young, 3,248
4. Coopers & Lybrand, 2,687
5. Price Waterhouse, 2,300
6. Doane Raymond Grant Thornton, 2,279
7. Arthur Andersen, 1,444
8. BDO Dunwoody, 1,428
9. Summit International, 671
10. Collins Barrow, 364

Source: *The Accountant*, July 1996, p. 12.

Accounting Firms – Denmark

★ 15 ★
LEADING DANISH ACCOUNTING AND AUDITING FIRMS BY FEE INCOME, 1996
Ranked by: Fee income, in millions of Danish krone (DKr). **Number listed:** 10
1. KPMG with DKr761.0 million
2. Deloitte & Touche, DKr699.0
3. Coopers & Lybrand, DKr570.0
4. Ernst & Young, DKr440.0
5. Price Waterhouse/Seier-Petersen, DKr325.0
6. BDO ScanRevision, DKr309.0
7. Arthur Andersen, DKr270.0
8. Mortensen & Beierholm, DKr146.0
9. Revisorsamarbejdet Kreston, DKr90.0
10. Grant Thornton/Grothen & Perregaard, DKr84.0

Source: *The Accountant*, March 1997, p. 14.

★ 16 ★
LEADING DANISH ACCOUNTING FIRMS BY STAFF, 1996
Ranked by: Total staff. **Number listed:** 10
1. KPMG with 761.0
2. Deloitte & Touche, 699.0
3. Coopers & Lybrand, 570.0
4. Ernst & Young, 440.0
5. Price Waterhouse/Seier-Petersen, 325.0
6. BDO ScanRevision, 309.0
7. Arthur Andersen, 270.0
8. Mortensen & Beierholm, 146.0
9. Revisorsamarbeidet Kreston, 90.0
10. Grant Thornton/Grothen & Perregaard, 84.0

Source: *The Accountant*, March 1997, p. 14.

Accounting Firms – Ireland

★ 17 ★
IRELAND'S ACCOUNTING FIRMS
Ranked by: Fee income, in millions of Irish pounds (IR£). **Number listed:** 20
1. KPMG with IR£39.9 million
2. Arthur Andersen, IR£20.0
3. BDO Simpson Xavier, IR£9.6
4. Grant Thornton, IR£5.5
5. IFAC, IR£4.2
6. Farrell Grant Sparks, IR£2.9
7. Bastow Charleton, IR£2.8
8. Moores Rowland, IR£2.1
9. VF Nathan, IR£2.0

10. McGrath & Co, IR£1.9
Source: *Accountancy - International Edition*, September 1996, p. 12.

Accounting Firms – Japan

★ 18 ★
LEADING ACCOUNTING FIRMS IN JAPAN, 1996
Ranked by: Fee income, in millions of yen (¥).
Remarks: Notes number of offices, partners, and professional staff, as well as figures for 1995. Fee income for Chuo Audit Corporation and Showa Ota were unavailable. **Number listed:** 13
1. Arthur Andersen with ¥41,041.3 million
2. Tohmatsu & Co., ¥29,034.0
3. KPMG, ¥13,889.0
4. Aoyama Audit Corporation, ¥11,000.0
5. Gen Group, ¥1,003.0
6. Central Audit Corporation, ¥976.7
7. Horwath & Co., ¥685.0
8. Actus Audit Corporation, ¥635.0
9. Jeffreys Henry International, ¥541.0
10. HLB International, ¥363.0
Source: *Accountancy - International Edition*, December 1996, p. 12.

Accounting Firms – Singapore

★ 19 ★
TOP SINGAPORE ACCOUNTING FIRMS BY FEE INCOME, 1995
Ranked by: Fee income, in millions of Singapore dollars (S$). **Number listed:** 12
1. Teo Foong & Wong with S$4.0 million
2. Soh Wong & Partners, S$3.8
3. Moore Stephens, S$3.0
4. Cheong Khee San & Co., S$2.8
5. Ng Lee & Associates, S$2.3
6. Loke Lum & Partners, S$2.0
7. Chan Ma/Chan Soh & Co., S$1.8
8. IA International, S$1.8
9. Ang & Co/Lee Boon Song & Co., S$1.7
10. Diong T.P. & Co., S$1.5
Source: *The Accountant*, September 1996, p. 12.

★ 20 ★
TOP SINGAPORE ACCOUNTING FIRMS BY TOTAL STAFF, 1996
Ranked by: Total staff. **Remarks:** Notes number of offices, partners, professional staff, and administrative staff for 1995 and 1996. **Number listed:** 25
1. Ernst & Young with 728

2. KPMG Peat Marwick, 721
3. Price Waterhouse, 700
4. Coopers & Lybrand, 620
5. Arthur Andersen, 597
6. Deloitte & Toche, 458
7. Foo Kon & Tan, 150
8. Chio Lim & Associates, 119
9. Patrick Tay Kim Chuan, 73
10. Soh Wong & Partners, 68
Source: *The Accountant*, September 1996, p. 25.

Accounting Firms – South Africa

★ 21 ★
LEADING ACCOUNTING FIRMS IN SOUTH AFRICA, 1996
Ranked by: Fee income, in millions of Rands (R).
Remarks: Figure for Price Waterhouse is for 1995. Notes percent increase, number of partners, offices, and professional staff. **Number listed:** 17
1. Deloitte & Touche with R414.0 million
2. Coopers & Lybrand, R335.0
3. Arthur Andersen, R275.0
4. Ernst & Young, R262.0
5. KPMG, R244.0
6. Price Waterhouse, R161.0
7. Kessel Feinstein, R83.6
8. Fisher Hoffman Sithole, R73.8
9. BDO Spencer Steward, R41.3
10. Moores Rowland, R37.5
Source: *Accountancy - International Edition*, April 1997, p. 8.

Accounting Firms – United Kingdom

★ 22 ★
BRITAIN'S TOP ACCOUNTING FIRMS, 1996
Ranked by: Fees, in millions of British pounds (£).
Remarks: KPMG was the only Big Six firm to make data available at the time of publication. Also notes number of partners, total professional staff, U.K. offices, ratio of fees to partners, and ratio of fees to total professional staff. **Number listed:** 30
1. KPMG with £588.8 million
2. Grant Thornton, £120.1
3. BDO Stoy Hayward, £100.3
4. Pannell Kerr Forster, £83.7
5. Clark Whitehill, £60.2
6. Kidsons Impey, £55.6
7. Moore Stephens, £45.8
8. Robson Rhodes, £42.0
9. Smith & Williamson, £37.5

10.   Neville Russell, £35.5
Source: *Accountancy - International Edition*, July 1996, p. 12.

Acquisition, Corporate
See: **Corporate Acquisitions and Mergers**

Advertisements
See: **Advertising**

Advertisers

★ 23 ★
TOP ADVERTISERS IN CHINA, 1995
Ranked by: Ad spending, in thousands of U.S. dollars.
Number listed: 10
1.   Procter & Gamble Co. with $4,535.0 thousand
2.   Xiaobavang C&E Study, $4,007.3
3.   Kongful Feast Wine, $2,943.7
4.   Motorola, $2,827.5
5.   Triatop Shampoo, $2,557.7
6.   Changshou Changle Wine, $2,320.6
7.   Intel Corp., $2,284.2
8.   Taita Oral Solution, $2,212.9
9.   505 Healthcare Products, $2,211.2
10.   DeBeers Mines, $2,206.0
Source: *Advertising Age International*, Top Global Ad Markets (annual), May 1997, p. 10.

★ 24 ★
TOP ADVERTISERS IN SOUTH KOREA, 1995
Ranked by: Ad spending, in thousands of U.S. dollars.
Number listed: 10
1.   Samsung Electronics Co. with $192,392 thousand
2.   LG Group, $171,371
3.   Lotte Group, $120,867
4.   Hyundai Group, $110,477
5.   Daewoo Group, $58,037
6.   HaiTai Group, $57,237
7.   Kia Motors, $51,087
8.   Pacific Chemical, $44,239
9.   Woori Motor Sales, $43,714
10.   Oriental Brewery, $41,187
Source: *Advertising Age International*, Top Global Ad Markets (annual), May 1997, p. 10.

★ 25 ★
TOP ADVERTISERS IN THE UNITED KINGDOM, 1995
Ranked by: Ad spending, in thousands of U.S. dollars.
Number listed: 10
1.   Unilever with $351,186 thousand
2.   Procter & Gamble Co., $257,632
3.   U.K. government, $139,815
4.   General Motors Corp., $139,486
5.   Mars Inc., $136,040
6.   British Telecom, $128,086
7.   Ford Motor Co., $125,634
8.   Dixons Stores Group, $112,788
9.   PSA Peugeot-Citroen SA, $110,878
10.   Kellogg Co., $109,661
Source: *Advertising Age International*, Top Global Ad Markets (annual), May 1997, p. 8.

★ 26 ★
TOP AUTOMOBILE ADVERTISERS IN AUSTRIA
Ranked by: Ad spending, in millions of U.S. dollars.
Number listed: 3
1.   Volkswagen AG with $14,638 million
2.   Renault SA, $10,631
3.   General Motors Co., $9,026
Source: *Automotive News*, July 22, 1996, p. 40.

★ 27 ★
TOP AUTOMOBILE ADVERTISERS IN CANADA
Ranked by: Ad spending, in millions of U.S. dollars.
Number listed: 10
1.   General Motors Corp. with $89,236 million
2.   Chrysler Corp., $38,307
3.   Ford Motor Co., $28,537
4.   Toyota Motor Corp., $18,904
5.   Honda Motor Co., $14,760
6.   Nissan Motor Co., $12,715
7.   Hyundai Group, $12,093
8.   Mazda Motor Corp., $10,209
9.   Volkswagen AG, $7,950
10.   Volvo AB, $3,842
Source: *Automotive News*, July 22, 1996, p. 40.

★ 28 ★
TOP AUTOMOBILE ADVERTISERS IN COLOMBIA
Ranked by: Ad spending, in millions of U.S. dollars.
Number listed: 3
1.   General Motors Corp. with $7,868 million
2.   Mazda Motor Corp., $6,514
3.   Renault SA, $2,589
Source: *Automotive News*, July 22, 1996, p. 40.

★ 29 ★

TOP AUTOMOBILE ADVERTISERS IN FRANCE
Ranked by: Ad spending, in millions of U.S. dollars.
Number listed: 3
1. PSA Peugeot-Citroen with $297,023 million
2. Renault SA, $190,664
3. Volkswagen AG, $102,446

Source: *Automotive News*, July 22, 1996, p. 40.

★ 30 ★

TOP AUTOMOBILE ADVERTISERS IN GERMANY
Ranked by: Ad spending, in millions of U.S. dollars.
Number listed: 3
1. Volkswagen AG with $257,296 million
2. General Motors Corp., $152,903
3. PSA Peugeot-Citroen, $105,975

Source: *Automotive News*, July 22, 1996, p. 40.

★ 31 ★

TOP AUTOMOBILE ADVERTISERS IN GREAT BRITAIN
Ranked by: Ad spending, in millions of U.S. dollars.
Number listed: 3
1. PSA Peugeot-Citroen SA with $115,280 million
2. Ford Motor Co., $112,759
3. General Motors Corp., $103,210

Source: *Automotive News*, July 22, 1996, p. 40.

★ 32 ★

TOP AUTOMOBILE ADVERTISERS IN GREECE
Ranked by: Ad spending, in millions of U.S. dollars.
Number listed: 3
1. Hyundai Group with $6,331 million
2. PSA Peugeot-Citroen SA, $5,438
3. Toyota Motor Corp., $4,768

Source: *Automotive News*, July 22, 1996, p. 40.

★ 33 ★

TOP AUTOMOBILE ADVERTISERS IN ITALY
Ranked by: Ad spending, in millions of U.S. dollars.
Number listed: 3
1. Fiat SpA with $196,447 million
2. Volkswagen AG, $59,814
3. PSA Peugeot-Citroen SA, $56,193

Source: *Automotive News*, July 22, 1996, p. 40.

★ 34 ★

TOP AUTOMOBILE ADVERTISERS IN MEXICO
Ranked by: Ad spending, in millions of U.S. dollars.
Number listed: 5
1. General Motors Corp. with $7,418 million
2. Nissan Motor Co., $6,401
3. Chrysler Corp., $5,919
4. Ford Motor Co., $5,507
5. Volkswagen AG, $5,489

Source: *Automotive News*, July 22, 1996, p. 40.

★ 35 ★

TOP AUTOMOBILE ADVERTISERS IN SAUDI ARABIA
Ranked by: Ad spending, in millions of U.S. dollars.
Number listed: 3
1. Toyota Motor Corp. with $7,073 million
2. Ford Motor Co., $2,351
3. Nissan Motor Co., $2,089

Source: *Automotive News*, July 22, 1996, p. 40.

★ 36 ★

TOP AUTOMOBILE ADVERTISERS IN SOUTH AFRICA
Ranked by: Ad spending, in millions of U.S. dollars.
Number listed: 3
1. Toyota Motor Corp. with $12,367 million
2. Mazda Motor Corp., $8,032
3. Volkswagen AG, $5,614

Source: *Automotive News*, July 22, 1996, p. 40.

★ 37 ★

TOP AUTOMOBILE ADVERTISERS IN SOUTH KOREA
Ranked by: Ad spending, in millions of U.S. dollars.
Number listed: 3
1. Daewoo Group with $108,666 million
2. Hyundai Group, $102,341
3. Kia Motors, $39,456

Source: *Automotive News*, July 22, 1996, p. 40.

★ 38 ★

TOP AUTOMOBILE ADVERTISERS IN SWEDEN
Ranked by: Ad spending, in millions of U.S. dollars.
Number listed: 3
1. Volvo AB with $24,701 million
2. Saab AB, $13,988
3. Volkswagen AG, $8,548

Source: *Automotive News*, July 22, 1996, p. 40.

★ 39 ★

TOP AUTOMOBILE ADVERTISERS IN TAIWAN
Ranked by: Ad spending, in millions of U.S. dollars.
Number listed: 3
1. Toyota Motor Corp. with $24,434 million
2. Kingcar Enterprises Co., $24,405
3. Ford Motor Co., $22,780

Source: *Automotive News*, July 22, 1996, p. 40.

★ 40 ★

TOP AUTOMOTIVE ADVERTISERS IN AUSTRALIA
Ranked by: Ad spending in millions of U.S. dollars.
Number listed: 3
1. Toyota Motor Corp. with $30,899 million
2. Ford Motor Co., $21,857
3. General Motors Corp., $21,514

Source: *Automotive News*, July 22, 1996, p. 40.

★ 41 ★
TOP AUTOMOTIVE ADVERTISERS IN HONG KONG
Ranked by: Ad spending, in millions of U.S. dollars.
Number listed: 3
1. Nissan Motor Co. with $6,426 million
2. Daimler--Benz AG, $5,233
3. Mitsubishi Motor Co., $3,989
Source: *Automotive News*, July 22, 1996, p. 40.

★ 42 ★
TOP AUTOMOTIVE ADVERTISERS IN INDIA
Ranked by: Ad spending, in millions of U.S. dollars.
Number listed: 3
1. Bajaj Auto with $4,880 million
2. Honda Motor Co., $2,505
3. Ford Motor Co., $125
Source: *Automotive News*, July 22, 1996, p. 40.

★ 43 ★
TOP AUTOMOTIVE ADVERTISERS IN JAPAN
Ranked by: Ad spending, in millions of U.S. dollars.
Number listed: 3
1. Toyota Motor Corp. with $424,822 million
2. Nissan Motor Co., $334,818
3. Mitsubishi Motor Co., $325,132
Source: *Automotive News*, July 22, 1996, p. 40.

Advertisers – Brazil

★ 44 ★
TOP ADVERTISERS IN BRAZIL, 1995
Ranked by: Ad spending, in thousands of U.S. dollars.
Number listed: 10
1. Unilever with $130,018 thousand
2. Casas Bahia Comercial, $119,296
3. Globex Utilidades, $87,397
4. Volkswagen AG, $78,822
5. General Motors Corp., $77,442
6. Cia. Antarctica Paulista Ind., $62,092
7. Cia. Bras de Distribuicao, $61,912
8. Fiat SpA, $58,491
9. Nestle SA, $54,782
10. Coca-Cola Co., $54,247
Source: *Advertising Age International*, Top Global Ad Markets (annual), May 1997, p. 8.

★ 45 ★
TOP SPENDING ADVERTISERS IN BRAZIL, 1995
Ranked by: Advertising spending, in millions of U.S. dollars. **Number listed:** 10
1. Gessey Lever with $130.0 million
2. Casas Bahia, $119.3
3. Ponto Frio, $87.4

4. Volkswagen, $78.8
5. General Motors, $77.4
6. Antarctica, $62.1
7. Pao de Acucar, $61.9
8. Fiat, $58.5
9. Nestle, $54.8
10. Coca-Cola, $54.2
Source: *Business Latin America*, August 26, 1996, p. 6.

Advertisers – Europe

★ 46 ★
TOP ADVERTISERS IN EUROPE, 1995
Ranked by: Ad spending, in thousands of U.S. dollars.
Number listed: 15
1. Procter & Gamble Co. with $1,753,080 thousand
2. Unilever, $1,564,301
3. Nestle SA, $954,955
4. PSA Peugeot-Citroen SA, $866,084
5. Volkswagen AG, $671,716
6. Mars Inc., $625,307
7. L'Oreal, $583,616
8. General Motors Corp., $583,385
9. Philip Morris Cos., $579,368
10. Renault SA, $552,835
Source: *Advertising Age International*, Special Issue: Europe, May 1997, p. I3.

Advertisers – France

★ 47 ★
TOP ADVERTISERS IN FRANCE, 1995
Ranked by: Ad spending, in thousands of U.S. dollars.
Number listed: 10
1. PSA Peugeot-Citroen SA with $346,474 thousand
2. Nestle SA, $306,708
3. L'Oreal, $297,259
4. Danone, $277,376
5. Renault SA, $204,538
6. Unilever, $172,056
7. Philips NV, $168,906
8. Procter & Gamble Co., $158,275
9. Auchan, $145,480
10. Fiat SpA, $133,077
Source: *Advertising Age International*, Top Global Ad Markets (annual), May 1997, p. 8.

Advertisers – Germany

★ 48 ★
TOP GERMAN ADVERTISERS, 1995
Ranked by: Ad spending, in thousands of U.S. dollars.
Number listed: 10
1. Procter & Gamble Co. with $653,111 thousand
2. Unilever, $332,072
3. Nestle SA, $278,386
4. Volkswagen AG, $268,708
5. Henkel Group, $235,008
6. Ferrero SpA, $220,145
7. Metro Group, $210,125
8. Philip Morris Co., $209,079
9. Mars Inc., $203,703
10. Deutsch Telekom, $195,700

Source: *Advertising Age International*, Top Global Ad Markets (annual), May 1997, p. 8.

Advertisers – Italy

★ 49 ★
TOP ADVERTISERS IN ITALY, 1995
Ranked by: Ad spending, in thousands of U.S. dollars.
Number listed: 10
1. Ferrero SpA with $136,889 thousand
2. Fiat SpA, $135,675
3. Unilever, $96,070
4. Procter & Gamble Co., $84,802
5. Nestle SA, $82,182
6. PSA Peugeot-Citroen SA, $67,004
7. Volkswagen AG, $58,957
8. L'Oreal, $58,303
9. Telecom Italia, $57,168
10. Barilla SpA, $55,787

Source: *Advertising Age International*, Top Global Ad Markets (annual), May 1997, p. 10.

Advertisers – Japan

★ 50 ★
TOP AD CATEGORIES IN JAPAN, 1996
Ranked by: Ad spending, in thousands of U.S. dollars.
Number listed: 10
1. Food, drink & confectionery with $4,859,065 thousand
2. Service & leisure, $3,760,886
3. Cosmetics & toiletries, $2,451,306
4. Education & related sectors, $2,344,418
5. Automotive, $1,990,498
6. Publishing, $1,852,731
7. Retail & distribution, $1,673,000
8. Pharmaceuticals, $1,493,269
9. Housing/real estate, $1,323,832
10. Finance & insurance, $1,219,319

Source: *Advertising Age International*, Top Global Ad Markets (annual), May 1997, p. I7.

★ 51 ★
TOP JAPANESE ADVERTISERS, 1995
Ranked by: Ad spending, in thousands of U.S. dollars.
Number listed: 10
1. Toyota Motor Corp. with $757,546 thousand
2. Kao Corp., $525,950
3. Nissan Motor Corp., $498,881
4. Matsushita Electric Industrial Co., $455,780
5. Matsushita Motor Co., $437,599
6. Suntory, $423,370
7. Daiei, $402,113
8. Honda Motor Co., $388,536
9. NEC Corp., $352,335
10. Sony Corp., $350,776

Source: *Advertising Age International*, Top Global Ad Markets (annual), May 1997, p. I7.

Advertisers – Latin America

★ 52 ★
TOP ADVERTISERS IN LATIN AMERICAN PRINT, 1997
Ranked by: Ad spending, in millions of U.S. dollars.
Number listed: 25
1. Ford passenger cars with $2.62 million
2. DirectTV satellite service, $2.18
3. Folha de Sao Paulo newspaper, $2.10
4. O Estado de Sao Paulo newspaper, $2.00
5. Iberia Airlines, $1.84
6. Volkswagen passenger cars, $1.62
7. BMW passenger cars, $1.56
8. Caixa Economica Federal Bank, $1.50
9. Gradiente audio and video systems, $1.39
10. Credicard credi card services, $1.30

Source: *Advertising Age International*, Special Issue: Latin America, September 1997, p. i2.

★ 53 ★
TOP CREDIT CARD ADVERTISERS IN LATIN AMERICA, 1997
Ranked by: Ad spending for January to June 1997, in millions of U.S. dollars. **Number listed:** 10
1. Credicard with $1.30 million
2. Diners Club, $1.06
3. American Express, $.85
4. Banco do Brasil, $.47
5. Visa, $.46

6. Itau, $.42
7. Varig, $.32
8. MasterCard, $.25
9. American Airlines, $.24
10. MasterCard Gold, $.24

Source: *Advertising Age*, September 1997, p. i30.

Advertisers – Taiwan

★ **54** ★
TAIWAN'S LARGEST ADVERTISERS, 1995
Ranked by: Advertising expenditures, in millions of U.S. dollars. **Remarks:** Includes leading advertising industries. **Number listed:** 20
1. Ford Motor Co., Ltd. with $58.3 million
2. Procter & Gamble Taiwan Ltd., $37.1
3. Ho Tai Motor Co., Ltd., $36.8
4. Yulon Motor Co., Ltd., $30.6
5. King Car Ford Industrial Co., Ltd., $28.1
6. Unilever, $24.3
7. The Best Actress Esthetics Int'l Co., $21.5
8. Chinese Automobile Co., Ltd., $20.1
9. President Enterprises Corp., $20.0
10. Madenform Esthetics Int'l Co., $17.9

Source: *National Trade Data Bank*, June 19, 1996, p. ISA960301.

Advertising

★ **55** ★
AD SPENDING IN CHILE, 1995
Ranked by: Ad spending, distributed as a percent of 246.7 million pesos spent. **Number listed:** 6
1. Cinema with 67.0%
2. Television, 15.3%
3. Dailies (newspapers), 11.7%
4. Radio, 2.6%
5. Outdoor, 2.2%
6. Magazines, 1.2%

Source: *El Mercurio*, July 4, 1996, p. 4.

★ **56** ★
ADVERTISING IN JAMAICA, 1996
Ranked by: Share of advertising placement for the first six months of 1996, in percent. **Number listed:** 3
1. Print with 53.6%
2. Radio, 23.3%
3. TV, 23.1%

Source: *The Gleaner*, July 26, 1996, p. 5.

★ **57** ★
ADVERTISING IN POLAND, 1996
Ranked by: Market share, in percent. **Remarks:** Notes 1995 figures. **Number listed:** 4
1. TV with 48.8%
2. Press, 37.5%
3. Radio, 8.7%
4. Outdoor, 5.0%

Source: *The Warsaw Voice*, May 12, 1996, p. 11.

★ **58** ★
GLOBAL ADVERTISING EXPENDITURES, 1996
Ranked by: Main media expenditures, in billions of U.S. dollars. **Remarks:** Notes data for 1995 and forecasts 1997 to 1999. "Main Media" includes television, print, radio, cinema, and outdoor venues. **Number listed:** 5
1. North America with $105 billion
2. Europe, $82
3. Asia/Pacific, $78
4. Latin America, $21
5. Other, $6

Source: *Financial Times*, December 16, 1996, p. 11.

★ **59** ★
LARGEST ADVERTISING SPENDERS IN INDONESIA
Ranked by: Spending, in millions of U.S. dollars. **Remarks:** Spending is broken down by radio, newspaper, magazines, and radio markets. **Number listed:** 10
1. Food & beverages with $162.0 million
2. Personal care, $150.9
3. Medicines, $134.7
4. Automotive, $60.9
5. Real estate, $51.6
6. Banks, $50.7
7. Household, $50.6
8. Public companies, $48.3
9. Cigarettes, $43.9
10. Print media, $42.6

Source: *National Trade Data Bank*, May 9, 1996, p. IMI960509.

★ **60** ★
LEADING TV CHANNELS IN MALAYSIA BY AD REVENUE, 1996
Ranked by: Share of ad revenue for the year ending June 1996, in percent. **Number listed:** 4
1. TV3 with 41%
2. TRM2, 31%
3. RTM1, 17%
4. MV, 11%

Source: *Far Eastern Economic Review*, February 6, 1997, p. 51.

★ 61 ★
TOP AD CATEGORIES IN BRAZIL, 1996
Ranked by: Ad spending, in thousands of U.S. dollars.
Number listed: 10
1. Real estate with $692,097 thousand
2. Department stores, $630,296
3. Automotive, $562,268
4. Pension funds/private security funds, $259,839
5. Installment services, $252,219
6. Office equipment & machines, $237,878
7. Hypermarkets/supermarkets, $233,102
8. Magazine publishing, $185,245
9. Sound recordings & audio tapes, $178,730
10. Other retail sectors, $414,308

Source: *Advertising Age International*, Top Global Ad Markets (annual), May 1997, p. 8.

★ 62 ★
TOP AD CATEGORIES IN CHINA, 1996
Ranked by: Ad spending, in thousands of U.S. dollars.
Number listed: 10
1. TV/video equipment & accessories with $57,870.73 thousand
2. Chinese wines & spirits, $53,289.73
3. Haircare, $51,081.01
4. Skincare, $45,607.84
5. Air conditioners & dehumidifiers, $41,186.74
6. Residential real estate, $32,923.78
7. Communications equipment & service, $32,530.97
8. Tonics & vitamins, $29,349.59
9. Toothpaste & oral hygiene, $26,387.87
10. Chinese over-the-counter medicines, $26,031.48

Source: *Advertising Age International*, Top Global Ad Markets (annual), May 1997, p. 10.

★ 63 ★
TOP AD CATEGORIES IN FRANCE, 1996
Ranked by: Ad spending, in thousands of U.S. dollars.
Number listed: 10
1. Food with $1,369,602 thousand
2. Distribution, $1,223,834
3. Transport, $1,206,563
4. Services, $998,791
5. Cosmetics & toiletries, $867,357
6. Culture & leisure, $691,537
7. Publishing, $662,176
8. Media & information, $472,538
9. Travel & tourism, $416,580
10. Beverages, $388,946

Source: *Advertising Age International*, Top Global Ad Markets (annual), May 1997, p. 8.

★ 64 ★
TOP AD CATEGORIES IN GERMANY, 1996
Ranked by: Ad spending, in thousands of U.S. dollars.
Number listed: 10
1. Automotive with $1,487,835 thousand
2. Mass media, $1,292,687
3. Retail organizations, $959,435
4. Pharmaceuticals, $634,883
5. Chocolate & confectionery, $605,258
6. Banks, $497,727
7. Computer hardware, software & services, $493,755
8. Beer, $448,191
9. Special mail-order companies, $384,340
10. Office equipment & machines, $269,097

Source: *Advertising Age International*, Top Global Ad Markets (annual), May 1997, p. 8.

★ 65 ★
TOP AD CATEGORIES IN ITALY, 1996
Ranked by: Ad spending, in thousands of U.S. dollars.
Number listed: 10
1. Publishing with $1,629,560 thousand
2. Automotive, $1,607,540
3. Confectionery, $1,503,070
4. Clothing, $1,297,020
5. Services, $877,670
6. Cosmetics, $854,410
7. Retail/distribution, $684,180
8. Telecommunications, $600,690
9. Beverages, $586,180
10. Toiletries, $572,980

Source: *Advertising Age International*, Top Global Ad Markets (annual), May 1997, p. 10.

★ 66 ★
TOP AD CATEGORIES IN SOUTH KOREA, 1996
Ranked by: Ad spending, in thousands of U.S. dollars.
Number listed: 10
1. Food/beverages with $862,929 thousand
2. Electrical/electronics products, $677,265
3. Leisure, $676,526
4. Clothes, $407,354
5. Publishing, $382,021
6. Pharmaceuticals, $330,026
7. Retail/wholesale distribution, $273,050
8. Cosmetics, $271,889
9. Construction, $233,399
10. Household goods, $217,897

Source: *Advertising Age International*, Top Global Ad Markets (annual), May 1997, p. 10.

★ 67 ★

TOP AD CATEGORIES IN THE UNITED KINGDOM, 1996

Ranked by: Ad spending, in thousands of U.S. dollars.
Number listed: 10
1. Retail with $1,758,573 thousand
2. Automotive, $1,324,089
3. Financial, $1,113,526
4. Food, $826,887
5. Office automation, $737,672
6. Cosmetics & toiletries, $557,411
7. Travel/holidays & transport, $549,092
8. Leisure equipment, $539,057
9. Mail-order, $538,936
10. Alcoholic beverages, $466,252

Source: *Advertising Age International*, Top Global Ad Markets (annual), May 1997, p. 8.

★ 68 ★

TOP ADVERTISING FIRMS IN CANADA, 1995

Ranked by: Market share based on revenue, in percent.
Number listed: 11
1. BBDO Canada with 5.5%
2. Cossette Communication-Marketing, 4.9%
3. MacLaren McCann Canada, 4.0%
4. Young & Rubicam Group of Cos., 3.2%
5. Leo Burnett Company, 2.6%
6. Ogilvy & Mather, 2.6%
7. FCB Canada, 2.5%
8. Publicis-BCP, 2.5%
9. Vickers & Benson Advertising, 1.7%
10. Palmer Jarvis Communications, 1.6%

Source: *Marketing Magazine*, May 26, 1997, p. 14.

Advertising Agencies

★ 69 ★

LARGEST ADVERTISING FIRMS IN MEXICO

Ranked by: Billings, in millions of U.S. dollars. **Number listed:** 10
1. McCann-Erickson Mexico with $88.0 million
2. J. Walter Thompson Mexico, $65.0
3. Young & Rubicam Mexico, $54.0
4. Leo Burnett Mexico, $51.4
5. BBDO Mexico, $42.9

Source: *Mexico Business*, May 1996, p. 54.

★ 70 ★

TOP ADVERTISING ORGANIZATIONS WORLDWIDE, 1996

Ranked by: Worldwide gross income, in millions of U.S. dollars. **Remarks:** Notes gross income for 1995 and capitalized volume for 1995-1996. **Number listed:** 50
1. WPP Group (London) with $3,419.9 million

2. Omnicom Group (New York), $3,035.5
3. Interpublic Group of Cos. (New York), $2,751.2
4. Dentsu (Tokyo), $1,929.9
5. Young & Rubicam (New York), $1,356.4
6. Cordiant (London), $1,169.3
7. Grey Advertising (New York), $987.8
8. Havas Advertising (Levallois-Perret, France), $974.3
9. Hakuhodo (Tokyo), $897.7
10. True North Communications (Chicago), $889.5

Source: *Advertising Age*, Agency Report (annual), April 21, 1997, p. S14.

Advertising Agencies – Australia

★ 71 ★

TOP ADVERTISING AGENCIES IN AUSTRALIA, 1996

Ranked by: Gross income, in thousands of U.S. dollars.
Remarks: Notes percent change from 1995. **Number listed:** 31
1. George Patterson Bates with $84,120 thousand
2. Clemenger BBDO, $65,235
3. Mattingly & Partners Australia, $59,975
4. DDB Australia Worldwide, $51,839
5. McCann-Erickson Advertising, $26,919
6. J. Walter Thompson, $25,523
7. Leo Burnett Connaghan & May Pty., $23,650
8. Ammirati Puris Lintas Australia, $22,134
9. Neville Jeffress, $22,000
10. Grey Australia, $17,285

Source: *Advertising Age*, Agency Report (annual), April 21, 1997, p. S26.

Advertising Agencies – Belgium

★ 72 ★

TOP ADVERTISING AGENCIES IN BELGIUM, 1996
Ranked by: Gross income, in thousands of U.S. dollars.
Remarks: Notes percent change from 1995. **Number listed:** 27
1. McCann-Erickson Co. S.A. with $21,913 thousand
2. HHD O&M, $20,874
3. BBDO Belgium, $19,349
4. DDB/Belgium, $15,322
5. Euro RSCG, $12,516
6. Ammirati Puris Lintas Belgium, $12,127
7. Young & Rubicam Belgium, $11,271
8. Publicis, $11,017

9. Grey, $10,902
10. Lowe Troost, $10,815

Source: *Advertising Age*, Agency Report (annual), April 21, 1997, p. S26.

Advertising Agencies – Brazil

★ 73 ★
TOP ADVERTISING AGENCIES IN BRAZIL, 1996
Ranked by: Gross income, in thousands of U.S. dollars.
Remarks: Notes percent change from 1995. **Number listed:** 30

1. McCann-Erickson Publicidade Ltda with $87,715 thousand
2. Duailibi, Petit, Zaragoza Propaganda, $63,046
3. Young & Rubicam do Brasil, $62,368
4. J. Walter Thompson, $61,000
5. Fischer, Justus Comunicacao Total, $56,480
6. Standard, O&M, $51,106
7. DM9 Publicidade, $48,600
8. Almap/BBDO, $43,368
9. W/Brasil Publicidade, $41,995
10. Ammirati Puris Lintas Brazil, $37,814

Source: *Advertising Age*, Agency Report (annual), April 21, 1997, p. S26.

Advertising Agencies – Chile

★ 74 ★
TOP ADVERTISING AGENCIES IN CHILE, 1996
Ranked by: Gross income, in thousands of U.S. dollars.
Remarks: Notes percent change from 1995. **Number listed:** 15

1. BBDO de Chile with $12,989 thousand
2. McCann-Erickson S.A. de Publicidad, $11,687
3. Prolam/Young & Rubicam, $8,109
4. Leo Burnett - Chile, $6,524
5. Ammirati Puris Lintas Chile S.A., $5,987
6. J. Walter Thompson, $5,247
7. Northcote & Asociados, $5,016
8. Porta Publicidad, $4,647
9. Grey Chile, $3,890
10. Zegers DDB Worldwide, $2,854

Source: *Advertising Age*, Agency Report (annual), April 21, 1997, p. S28.

Advertising Agencies – Costa Rica

★ 75 ★
TOP ADVERTISING AGENCIES IN COSTA RICA, 1996
Ranked by: Gross income, in thousands of U.S. dollars.
Remarks: Notes percent change from 1995. **Number listed:** 12

1. Garnier/BBDO with $2,925 thousand
2. McCann-Erickson Centroamericana, $1,931
3. Jimenez, Blanco & Quiros, $1,664
4. Asesores/Young & Rubicam, $1,170
5. APCU-Thompson, $931
6. Leo Burnett - Costa Rica, S.A., $742
7. Modernoble Publicidad, $718
8. FCB de Costa Rica, $658
9. DDB Needham Costa Rica, $491
10. Publimark S.A., $437

Source: *Advertising Age*, Agency Report (annual), April 21, 1997, p. S28.

Advertising Agencies – Denmark

★ 76 ★
TOP ADVERTISING AGENCIES IN DENMARK, 1996
Ranked by: Gross income, in thousands of U.S. dollars.
Remarks: Notes percent change from 1995. **Number listed:** 19

1. Grey Communications Group with $34,711 thousand
2. Bates Gruppen Denmark, $24,760
3. Young & Rubicam Copenhagen, $19,663
4. BBDO Denmark, $14,363
5. DDB Denmark, $10,606
6. Scan-Ad Gruppen, $9,188
7. Ammirati Puris Lintas Denmark, $7,785
8. McCann-Erickson A/S, $7,145
9. Ogilvy & Mather, $7,113
10. Saatchi & Saatchi Advertising, $5,965

Source: *Advertising Age*, Agency Report (annual), April 21, 1997, p. S28.

Advertising Agencies – Europe

★ 77 ★
LARGEST ADVERTISING AGENCIES IN EUROPE
Ranked by: Sales, in thousands of U.S. dollars. **Remarks:** Also notes previous year's rank, type of industry, percent change in sales, and percent change in local currencies.
Number listed: 100

1. WPP Group Plc with $10,175,621 thousand

2. Havas SA, $9,125,038
3. Cordiant Plc, $6,478,726
4. Aegis Group Plc, $5,281,055
5. Publicis SA, $4,199,979
6. Euro RSCG, $2,471,730
7. Interpublic Ltd., $2,107,704
8. Publitalia 80 Concessionaria Pubblicita S.P.A., $1,639,848
9. Publicitas Holding SA, $1,608,676
10. SIPRA Societa' Italiana Pubblicita' S.P.A., $968,080

Source: *Europe's 15,000 Largest Companies* (annual), Dun & Bradstreet, 1997, p. 676.

Advertising Agencies – France

★ 78 ★
TOP ADVERTISING AGENCIES IN FRANCE, 1996
Ranked by: Gross income, in thousands of U.S. dollars.
Remarks: Notes percent change from 1995. **Number listed:** 39
1. Euro RSCG France with $301,081 thousand
2. Publicis Conseil, $199,325
3. DDB/France, $146,412
4. BDDP France, $130,975
5. McCann-Erickson S.A., $67,963
6. Ogilvy & Mather, $66,764
7. CLM/BBDO-La Compagnie, $63,475
8. Young & Rubicam France, $60,147
9. Ammirati Puris Lintas France Group, $55,765
10. D'Arcy Masius Benton & Bowles, $40,448

Source: *Advertising Age*, Agency Report (annual), April 21, 1997, p. S30.

Advertising Agencies – Germany

★ 79 ★
TOP ADVERTISING AGENCIES IN GERMANY, 1996
Ranked by: Gross income, in thousands of U.S. dollars.
Remarks: Notes percent change from 1995. **Number listed:** 39
1. BBDO Group with $161,284 thousand
2. Grey Gruppe Deutschland, $110,119
3. Publicis, $77,474
4. Ammirati Puris Lintas Deutschland, $75,677
5. Ogilvy & Mather, $73,310
6. Young & Rubicam, $72,764
7. J. Walter Thompson, $67,626
8. Springer & Jacoby, $61,786
9. McCann-Erickson Deutschland GmbH, $60,633

10. Scholz & Friends, $54,484
Source: *Advertising Age*, Agency Report (annual), April 21, 1997, p. S30.

Advertising Agencies – Greece

★ 80 ★
TOP AD FIRMS IN GREECE
Ranked by: Gross earnings, in thousands of Greek drachma (GDr). **Number listed:** 10
1. Spot/Thompson S.A. with GDr5,550.2 thousand
2. BBDO Athens, GDr3,326.1
3. Olympic DDB/Needham, GDr2,777.6
4. Bold/Ogilvy & Mather, GDr2,364.0
5. McCann-Erickson, GDr2,290.0
6. Adel/SSA, GDr2,270.0
7. Lintas, GDr2,039.0
8. Leo Burnett, GDr1,587.0
9. Producta/TBWA, GDr1,440.0
10. Dot & Daash, GDr1,006.3
Source: *Trade With Greece*, Summer 1996, p. 73.

Advertising Agencies – Guatemala

★ 81 ★
TOP ADVERTISING AGENCIES IN GUATEMALA, 1996
Ranked by: Gross income, in thousands of U.S. dollars.
Remarks: Notes percent change from 1995. **Number listed:** 11
1. Leo Burnett - Comunica, S.A. with $3,437 thousand
2. Publicidad McCann-Erickson, $2,394
3. BBDO/Guatemala, $2,132
4. Eco Young & Rubicam, $1,747
5. Publicentro, $945
6. Tobar & Conde Publicad, $818
7. APCU-Thompson, $706
8. Creacion SSAW, $677
9. FCB Publicidad, $536
10. WO/O&M, $430
Source: *Advertising Age*, Agency Report (annual), April 21, 1997, p. S31.

Advertising Agencies – Hong Kong

★ 82 ★

TOP ADVERTISING AGENCIES IN HONG KONG, 1996

Ranked by: Gross income, in thousands of U.S. dollars.
Remarks: Figures are estimates. Notes percent change from 1995. **Number listed:** 28

1. Ogilvy & Mather with $21,543 thousand
2. DY & R Hong Kong, $19,574
3. Leo Burnett, $18,012
4. JWT-Hong Kong, $17,735
5. DDB Worldwide, $14,449
6. Bates Hong Kong, $13,501
7. D'Arcy Masius Benton & Bowles, $11,113
8. Grey Hong Kong, $10,936
9. McCann-Erickson, $10,003
10. Euro RSCG Partnership Hong Kong, $9,322

Source: *Advertising Age*, Agency Report (annual), April 21, 1997, p. S31.

Advertising Agencies – India

★ 83 ★

TOP AD FIRMS IN INDIA

Ranked by: Gross income, in millions of rupees (Rs).
Number listed: 10

1. Hindustan Thomson Associates Ltd. with Rs901.65 million
2. Lintas India Ltd., Rs676.70
3. Mudra Communications Ltd., Rs467.77
4. Ogilvy & Mather, Rs394.04
5. Ulka Advertising, Rs345.20
6. Trikaya Grey Advertising, Rs252.60
7. R K Swamy/BBDO Advertising, Rs245.48
8. Contract Advertising, Rs227.45
9. MAA Communications Bozell Ltd., Rs196.11
10. Rediffusion-Dentsu, Young & Rubicam, Rs180.32

Source: *The Statesman*, December 29, 1996, p. 11.

Advertising Agencies – Ireland

★ 84 ★

TOP ADVERTISING AGENCIES IN IRELAND, 1996

Ranked by: Gross income, in thousands of U.S. dollars.
Remarks: Notes percent change from 1995. **Number listed:** 9

1. Wilson Hartnell Group with $9,063 thousand
2. DDFH&B, $4,142
3. Peter Owens, $3,978
4. Saatchi & Saatchi Advertising, $2,612
5. McCann-Erickson Limited, $2,538
6. Bates Ireland, $2,304
7. O'Connor & O'Sullivan, $1,898
8. Campbell Grey, $1,313
9. Gaffney McHugh Advertising, $286

Source: *Advertising Age*, Agency Report (annual), April 21, 1997, p. S32.

Advertising Agencies – Italy

★ 85 ★

TOP ADVERTISING AGENCIES IN ITALY, 1996

Ranked by: Gross income, in thousands of U.S. dollars.
Remarks: Notes percent change from 1995. **Number listed:** 38

1. Armando Testa Group with $57,265 thousand
2. Young & Rubicam Italia, $47,272
3. BGS/D'Arcy Masius Benton & Bowles, $45,936
4. McCann-Erickson Italiana, $38,290
5. Saatchi & Saatchi Advertising, $37,579
6. J. Walter Thompson, $34,168
7. Milano & Grey, $26,832
8. Publicis, $20,926
9. Ammirati Puris Lintas Milan, $19,526
10. Leo Burnett Co., $18,953

Source: *Advertising Age*, Agency Report (annual), April 21, 1997, p. S32.

Advertising Agencies – Japan

★ 86 ★

TOP AD FIRMS IN JAPAN

Ranked by: Market share, in percent. **Number listed:** 6

1. Dentsu with 21.4%
2. Hakuhodo, 11.0%
3. Tokyu Agency, 3.1%
4. Daiko Advertising, 3.0%
5. Asatsu, 2.9%
6. Other, 58.6%

Source: *Nikkei Weekly*, August 5, 1996, p. 10.

★ 87 ★

TOP ADVERTISING AGENCIES IN JAPAN, 1996

Ranked by: Gross income, in thousands of U.S. dollars.
Remarks: Figures are estimates. Notes percent change from 1995. **Number listed:** 61

1. Dentsu Inc. with $1,614,665 thousand
2. Hakuhodo Inc., $827,598
3. Daiko Advertising, $256,721
4. Tokyu Agency, $214,000

5. Asatsu Inc., $199,385
6. McCann-Erickson, $130,266
7. Yomiko Advertising, $125,919
8. Dai-Ichi Kikaku, $125,434
9. I&S Corp., $124,647
10. Asahi Advertising, $106,686

Source: *Advertising Age*, Agency Report (annual), April 21, 1997, p. S32.

Advertising Agencies – Malaysia

★ 88 ★
TOP ADVERTISING AGENCIES IN MALAYSIA, 1996
Ranked by: Gross income, in thousands of U.S. dollars.
Remarks: Notes percent change from 1995. **Number listed:** 22

1. Bates Malaysia with $13,680 thousand
2. Dentsu, Young & Rubicam, $7,798
3. Ogilvy & Mather, $7,782
4. McCann-Erickson Sdn. Berhad, $7,348
5. Leo Burnett Advertising Sdn. Bhd., $7,251
6. J. Walter Thompson, $5,037
7. Grey Malaysia, $4,847
8. Ammirati Puris Lintas Malaysia, $4,769
9. Naga DDB, $4,672
10. Batey Ads Malaysia, $3,672

Source: *Advertising Age*, Agency Report (annual), April 21, 1997, p. S33.

Advertising Agencies – Netherlands

★ 89 ★
TOP ADVERTISING AGENCIES IN THE NETHERLANDS, 1996
Ranked by: Gross income, in thousands of U.S. dollars.
Remarks: Figures are estimates. Notes percent change from 1995. **Number listed:** 30

1. BBDO Nederland with $51,497 thousand
2. PMS&vW/Y&R, $40,626
3. E-Company, $39,264
4. Publicis, $37,232
5. Ogilvy & Mather, $32,940
6. Result DDB, $31,491
7. PPGH/JWT, $30,869
8. Ammirati Puris Lintas Netherlands, $22,635
9. McCann-Erickson BV, $18,054
10. Grey, $17,788

Source: *Advertising Age*, Agency Report (annual), April 21, 1997, p. S34.

Advertising Agencies – Norway

★ 90 ★
TOP ADVERTISING AGENCIES IN NORWAY, 1996
Ranked by: Gross income, in thousands of U.S. dollars.
Remarks: Notes percent change from 1995. **Number listed:** 17

1. Bates Gruppen with $29,164 thousand
2. JBR McCann, $18,875
3. Leo Burnett A/S, $12,755
4. GCG Norway, $11,305
5. Publicis, $9,695
6. D'Arcy Masius Benton & Bowles, $9,109
7. Ogilvy & Mather, $7,346
8. New Deal DDB, $7,039
9. Young & Rubicam/BM Norway, $4,427
10. BBDO Oslo, $4,141

Source: *Advertising Age*, Agency Report (annual), April 21, 1997, p. S34.

Advertising Agencies – Quebec

★ 91 ★
TOP AD FIRMS IN QUEBEC
Ranked by: Revenues. No specific dollar values provided. **Remarks:** Notes principal clients. **Number listed:** 15

1. Cossette Communication-Marketing
2. Publicis-BCP
3. Marketel
4. PNMD Communication
5. Allard et associes
6. Groupaction/JWT
7. Palm Publicite-Marketing
8. Le Groupe Everest
9. Saint-Jacques, Vallee, Young & Rubicam
10. FCB Direct Montreal

Source: *Le Devoir*, February 9, 1997, p. C2.

Advertising Agencies – Romania

★ 92 ★
TOP ADVERTISING AGENCIES IN ROMANIA, 1996
Ranked by: Gross income, in thousands of U.S. dollars.
Remarks: Notes percent change from 1995. **Number listed:** 15

1. Plus Advertising Romania with $3,679 thousand
2. B.V. McCann-Erickson Advertising, $2,911
3. Graffiti/BDDO, $1,796
4. Bates Centrade Saatchi & Saatchi, $1,776

5. Leo Burnett & Target/Bucharest, $1,347
6. OFC International/DMB&B, $920
7. Ogilvy & Mather, $881
8. Y&R/Media Pro & Partners, $685
9. Focus Advertising, $541
10. Grey, $486

Source: *Advertising Age*, Agency Report (annual), April 21, 1997, p. S35.

Advertising Agencies – Spain

★ 93 ★
TOP ADVERTISING AGENCIES IN SPAIN, 1996
Ranked by: Gross income, in thousands of U.S. dollars.
Remarks: Figures are estimates. Notes percent change from 1995. **Number listed:** 29
1. Bassat with $42,827 thousand
2. Tapsa Advertising, $36,700
3. McCann-Erickson, S.A., $36,105
4. Grey Espana, $35,842
5. BBDO Espana, $35,286
6. Bates Advertising Holding, $35,276
7. Euro RSCG, $33,578
8. J. Walter Thompson, $33,110
9. Young & Rubicam, $29,932
10. Tandem DDB, $25,196

Source: *Advertising Age*, Agency Report (annual), April 21, 1997, p. S36.

Advertising Agencies – Switzerland

★ 94 ★
TOP ADVERTISING AGENCIES IN SWITZERLAND, 1996
Ranked by: Gross income, in thousands of U.S. dollars.
Remarks: Notes percent change from 1995. **Number listed:** 18
1. Advico Young & Rubicam with $30,277 thousand
2. Wirz Werbeberatung, $19,411
3. Seiler DDB, $18,016
4. Euro RSCG Switzerland, $16,951
5. Publicis, $15,834
6. McCann-Erickson S.A., $15,052
7. GGK Basel, $13,889
8. Grendene, $12,202
9. Bosch & Butz, $9,991
10. Ammirati Puris Lintas Zurich, $8,489

Source: *Advertising Age*, Agency Report (annual), April 21, 1997, p. S36.

Advertising Agencies – Taiwan

★ 95 ★
TAIWAN'S LARGEST ADVERTISING AGENCIES, 1995
Ranked by: Billings, in millions of U.S. dollars.
Remarks: Includes leading advertising industries.
Number listed: 10
1. Taiwan Advertising Co., Ltd. with $77.0 million
2. Eastern Advertising Co., Ltd., $29.0
3. International Advertising Agency Ltd., $22.1
4. Regal International Advertising Inc., $22.0
5. Harvest Advertising Co., Ltd., $21.2
6. Ideology Advertising Agency, $20.7
7. Brain Advertising Co., Ltd., $20.1
8. Look Advertising Co., Ltd., $13.4
9. Target Advertising Agency Ltd., $11.1
10. Interface Advertising Agency Ltd., $9.6

Source: *National Trade Data Bank*, June 19, 1996, p. ISA960301.

Advertising Agencies – Thailand

★ 96 ★
TOP AD FIRMS IN THAILAND, 1996
Ranked by: Billings, in thousands of baht (Bt). **Number listed:** 10
1. Ammirati Puritas Lintas with Bt4,200 thousand
2. Ogilvy & Mather Group, Bt4,009
3. Spa Advertising, Bt2,000
4. Prakit & FCB Plc, Bt1,900
5. Leo Burnett, Bt1,824
6. Far East Advertising Plc, Bt1,800
7. J Walter Thompson, Bt1,700
8. Dentsu, Young & Rubicam, Bt1,500
9. McCann-Erickson, Bt1,500
10. Dentsu Thailand, Bt1,200

Source: *Bangkok Post*, January 9, 1997, p. 12.

Advertising Agencies – Turkey

★ 97 ★
TOP ADVERTISING FIRMS IN TURKEY, 1995
Ranked by: Turnover, in millions of Turkish lira (TL).
Number listed: 18
1. Cenajans/Grey with TL1,500 million
2. Guzel Sanatlar, TL1,400
3. Lowe Adam, TL713
4. Grafika Lintas, TL678
5. Manajans-Thompson, TL629
6. Y&R Reklam, TL613

7.   Yorum, TL603
8.   Pars/McCann-Erickson, TL559
9.   Penajans-DMB&B, TL546
10. Saatchi & Saatchi, TL494

Source: *National Trade Data Bank*, February 12, 1996, p. IMI960212.

Advertising Agencies – United Kingdom

★ 98 ★
BRITAIN'S TOP AD FIRMS
Ranked by: Billings, in millions of British pounds (£).
Number listed: 10
1.   Abbott Mead Vickers BBDO with £306.81 million
2.   J. Walter Thompson, £278.15
3.   Ogilvy & Mather, £254.63
4.   BMP DDB, £237.00
5.   Saatchi & Saatchi, £224.34
6.   DMB&B, £186.86
7.   Publicis, £186.46
8.   M&C Saatchi, £174.95
9.   Lowe Howard-Spink, £169.54
10. Bates Dorland, £168.38

Source: *The Observer*, March 2, 1997, p. 6.

Advertising – Canada

★ 99 ★
TOP ADVERTISING CATEGORIES IN CANADA, 1995
Ranked by: Ad spending, in millions of Canadian dollars.
Remarks: Notes figures for 1994 and 1993. **Number listed:** 25
1.   Retail with C$891.1 million
2.   Automotive, C$514.4
3.   Food, C$395.7
4.   Business equipment and services, C$395.0
5.   Entertainment, C$300.9
6.   Financial services and insurance services, C$213.7
7.   Restaurants, catering services, and nightclubs, C$186.9
8.   Travel and transportation, C$182.1
9.   Local automotive dealers, C$137.4
10. Cosmetics and toiletries, C$126.9

Source: *Marketing*, October 28, 1996, p. 24.

Advertising Expenditures

★ 100 ★
LEADING MEDIUMS FOR AD SPENDING IN SOUTH AFRICA, 1995
Ranked by: Ad spending, distributed in percent. **Number listed:** 5
1.   Print with 43.8%
2.   Television, 39.6%
3.   Radio, 12.6%
4.   Outdoor, 3.2%
5.   Cinema, 0.8%

Source: *National Trade Data Bank*, June 30, 1997, p. IMI970630.

★ 101 ★
TOP AD SPENDERS IN ASIA-PACIFIC PRINT, 1995
Ranked by: Spending, in millions of U.S. dollars.
Remarks: Also notes number of pages. **Number listed:** 25
1.   Thai International Airways with $6.89 million
2.   Singapore Airlines, $6.59
3.   Rolex Watches, $5.90
4.   Hongkong Bank, $5.58
5.   Volkswagen, $5.36
6.   Tag Heuer Watches, $4.62
7.   Toyota, $4.61
8.   Philip Morris' Marlboro Cigarettes, $3.88
9.   Cathay Pacific Airways, $3.64
10. Heineken Beer, $3.58

Source: *Advertising Age International*, July 1997, p. I22.

★ 102 ★
TOP AD SPENDERS IN EUROPEAN PRINT, 1995
Ranked by: Spending, in millions of U.S. dollars.
Remarks: Also notes number of pages. **Number listed:** 25
1.   Singapore Airlines with $6.90 million
2.   Tag Heuer Watches, $5.31
3.   Thai International Airways, $4.82
4.   Rolex Watches, $4.40
5.   AT&T, $3.16
6.   Carlsberg Beer, $3.15
7.   Saab, $2.99
8.   Air France, $2.87
9.   American Airlines, $2.87
10. Opel, $2.77

Source: *Advertising Age International*, July 1997, p. I27.

★ 103 ★
TOP AD SPENDERS IN INTERNATIONAL PRINT, 1995
Ranked by: Spending, in millions of U.S. dollars.
Remarks: Also notes number of pages. **Number listed:** 25

1. AT&T International Long Distance with $4.24 million
2. Deutsche Telekom, $3.52
3. American Express, $3.43
4. Philips NV, $3.27
5. Sheraton Hotels International, $2.98
6. AIG, $2.60
7. Citibank NA, $2.43
8. Singapore Airlines, $2.21
9. LG Group, $2.00
10. ING Bank, $1.99

Source: *Advertising Age International*, July 1997, p. I20.

★ 104 ★
TOP AD SPENDERS IN LATIN AMERICAN PRINT, 1995
Ranked by: Spending, in millions of U.S. dollars.
Remarks: Also notes number of pages. **Number listed:** 25

1. Ford Motor Co. with $3.01 million
2. Citibank's Creditcard, $2.95
3. Volkswagen, $2.90
4. Galaxy Satellite, $2.69
5. Visa Credit Card Services, $2.67
6. IBM, $2.61
7. Chevrolet, $2.48
8. Diners Club International, $2.28
9. O Estado de Sao Paulo Newspaper, $1.91
10. H. Stern Jewelers, $1.84

Source: *Advertising Age International*, July 1997, p. I25.

Advertising, Magazine

★ 105 ★
TOP BRANDS BY AD SPENDING IN THE UNITED KINGDOM, 1995
Ranked by: Ad spending, in millions of British pounds (£). **Number listed:** 10

1. Franklin Mint Plates with £3.7 million
2. Benson & Hedges, £2.5
3. Marlboro, £2.0
4. Silk Cut, £1.9
5. Dateline, £1.8
6. Britannia Music, £1.6
7. Freemans Catalogue, £1.6
8. Bernard Matthews, £1.5
9. Persil (Finesse), £1.5
10. Kays Catalogue, £1.4

Source: *Marketing*, August 22, 1996, p. 9.

Aerosols

★ 106 ★
AEROSOL PRODUCTION IN JAPAN, 1996
Ranked by: Production, in millions of units. **Remarks:** Also notes production for 1988-1995. **Number listed:** 19

1. Hair care products other than hair spray with 158,398 million units
2. Personal deodorants, 72,861
3. Hair spray, 66,629
4. Space insecticides, 44,522
5. Automotive products, 43,763
6. Room fresheners, 31,229
7. Medicinals and pharmaceuticals, 22,715
8. Shaving foams, 22,218
9. Other personal products, 27,659
10. Other household products, 24,694

Source: *Spray Technology & Marketing*, July 1997, p. 38.

★ 107 ★
TOP AEROSOL CATEGORIES IN THE UNITED KINGDOM, 1996
Ranked by: Production, in millions of units. **Remarks:** Also notes production for 1988-1995. **Number listed:** 18

1. Deodorants/body sprays with 330.0 million units
2. Pharmaceuticals, 200.0
3. Hair spray, 190.0
4. Shaving lathers, 155.0
5. Antiperspirants, 130.0
6. Air fresheners, 106.0
7. Mouses, 65.0
8. Waxes/polishes, 44.0
9. Automotive, 33.0
10. Insecticides, 33.0

Source: *Spray Technology & Marketing*, July 1997, p. 39.

Aerospace Industries

★ 108 ★
LARGEST AEROSPACE COMPANIES, 1995
Ranked by: Revenue, in millions of U.S. dollars. **Remarks:** Notes profits and global rank. **Number listed:** 8

1. Lockheed Martin (United States) with $22,853 million
2. United Technologies (United States), $22,802
3. Boeing (United States), $19,515
4. AlliedSignal (United States), $14,346

5. McDonnell Douglas (United States), $14,346
6. Aerospatiale (France), $10,073
7. Textron (United States), $9,973
8. British Aerospace (United Kingdom), $9,060

Source: *Fortune,* The Global 500: World's Biggest Corporations (annual), August 5, 1996, p. F-15.

★ 109 ★
LARGEST AEROSPACE DEFENSE COMPANIES BY COMPETITIVENESS, 1996

Ranked by: Competitiveness, based on the sum of percentage increases and/or decreases in operating earnings, return on net assets, working capital productivity, independent research & development, and product or employee productivity. **Remarks:** Provides data for each of the performance measures used to calculate competitiveness. **Number listed:** 15

1. McDonnell Douglas Corp. with 2,941.60
2. Daimler-Benz AG -Spon ADR, 2,733.11
3. Boeing Co., 1,489.57
4. British Aerospace PLC, 1,200.31
5. Lockheed Martin Corp., 951.10
6. United Technologies Corp., 321.11
7. Honeywell Inc., 312.41
8. Northrop Grumman Corp., 263.92
9. AlliedSignal Inc., 235.39
10. Textron Inc., 86.81

Source: *Aviation Week & Space Technology*, Industry Report Card on Competitiveness, June 9, 1997, p. 57.

★ 110 ★
MOST COMPETITIVE AEROSPACE COMPANIES WORLDWIDE, 1996

Ranked by: Competitiveness, based on the sum of percentage increases and/or decreases in operating earnings, return on net assets, working capital productivity, independent research & development, and product or employee productivity. **Remarks:** Provides data for each of the performance measures used to calculate competitiveness. **Number listed:** 66

1. Stanford Telecommunications with 40,946.81
2. Orbital Sciences Corp., 23,411.07
3. Wyman-Gordon Co., 19,494.29
4. Miltope Group Inc., 8,517.06
5. EDO Corp., 7,706.62
6. Canadian Marconi Co., 6,131.71
7. Dynamics Research Corp., 5,410.53
8. Alliant Techsystems Inc., 4,794.12
9. Fairchild Corp., 3,115.26
10. Heroux Inc., 3,066.07

Source: *Aviation Week & Space Technology*, Industry Report Card on Competitiveness, June 9, 1997, p. 53.

★ 111 ★
TOP AEROSPACE FIRMS IN AUSTRALIA

Ranked by: Turnover, in millions of Australian dollars (A$). **Number listed:** 5

1. ADI Ltd. with A$500.9 million
2. Australian Submarine Corp., A$400.0
3. Transfield Defense Systems, A$400.0
4. British Aerospace Australia, A$150.0
5. Siemens Plessey, A$75.0

Source: *Interavia*, August 1996, p. 51.

★ 112 ★
TOP AEROSPACE FIRMS WORLDWIDE, 1995

Ranked by: Sales, in millions of U.S. dollars. **Number listed:** 20

1. Lockheed Martin with $27.4 million
2. Boeing, $22.9
3. McDonnell Douglas, $14.0
4. Aerospatiale, $9.9
5. United Technologies, $9.1
6. Hughes Electronics, $9.0
7. British Aerospace, $8.9
8. Daimler-Benz, $8.2
9. Raytheon, $7.4
10. Northrop Grumman, $6.8

Source: *The Sunday Times*, September 8, 1996, p. 6.

Aerospace Industries – Export-Import Trade

★ 113 ★
CANADIAN AEROSPACE EXPORTS, 1995

Ranked by: Distribution, in percent. **Number listed:** 6

1. Electronic parts with 35%
2. Fixed-wing aircraft, 24%
3. Aircraft engines & parts, 20%
4. Aircraft systems & parts, 13%
5. Helicopters, 5%
6. Flight simulators, 3%

Source: *Financial Times*, May 1, 1997, p. 15.

Afghanistan – see under individual headings

Africa – see under individual headings

Agricultural Chemicals

★ 114 ★

TOP INSECTICIDE MAKERS IN SPAIN

Ranked by: Market share, in percent. **Number listed:** 6
1. Cruz Verde (Sara Lee) with 31.2%
2. Zelnova, 13.9%
3. Johnson's Wax, 13.4%
4. Benckiser, 10.5%
5. Bayer, 9.5%
6. Other, 21.5%

Source: *National Trade Data Bank*, June 26, 1996, p. IMI960618.

Agriculture

★ 115 ★

THAILAND'S AGRIBUSINESS LEADERS, 1994

Ranked by: Revenue, in millions of bahts (Bt). **Remarks:** Includes profits and assets. **Number listed:** 100
1. Bangkok Produce Merchandising with Bt15,944.66 million
2. Charoen Pokphand Feedmill, Bt13,698.52
3. Soon Hua Seng Rice, Bt6,772.43
4. C.P. Intertrade, Bt6,512.58
5. Bangkok Feedmill, Bt5,067.65
6. Sri Trang Agro-Industry, Bt4,428.84
7. Soon Hua Seng, Bt4,359.76
8. Thai Hua Rubber, Bt4,348.69
9. Bangkok Livestock Processing, Bt4,205.91
10. Thai Prawn Culture Center, Bt4,016.12

Source: *Business Review*, December 1995, p. 157+.

Agriculture – Asia

★ 116 ★

TOP AGRICULTURE, FISHING, FORESTRY, AND PLANTATION COMPANIES IN ASIA

Ranked by: Sales, in thousands of U.S. dollars. **Remarks:** Also notes profit as a percent of sales. **Number listed:** 67
1. Sumitomo Forestry Co. Ltd. with $6,781,174 thousand
2. Nippon Suisan Kaisma Ltd., $4,550,805
3. Osaka Uoichiba Co. Ltd., $4,506,320
4. Sime Darby Bhd., $3,699,960
5. Perlis Plantations Bhd., $2,404,987
6. Nichiro Gyogyo Kaisha Ltd., $2,296,407
7. Kyokuyo Co. Ltd., $1,700,990
8. Multi-Purpose Holdings Bhd., $1,131,547
9. Pokka Corp., $1,120,776

10. Hoko Fishing Co. Ltd., $1,007,271

Source: *Asia's 7,500 Largest Companies* (annual), Dun & Bradstreet, 1997, p. 71+.

Agriculture – Europe

★ 117 ★

TOP AGRICULTURE, FORESTRY, AND FISHING COMPANIES IN EUROPE

Ranked by: Sales, in millions of European Currency Units (ECUs). **Remarks:** Also notes the number of employees. **Number listed:** 86
1. Dalgety Plc with 5,229 million ECUs
2. Varkensonderzoekcentrum Nieuw-Dalland BV, 1,531
3. Arla Ek For, 1,507
4. AMF Austria Milch- und Fleischvermarktung Registrierte GmbH, 1,425
5. Valio Oy, 1,408
6. Sodra Skogsagarna, Ek For, 776
7. Stora Skog AB, 730
8. Julius Meinl Nahrungsmittel Produktions-Gesellschaft M.B.H., 700
9. Assidoman Skog & Tra AB, 659
10. Lohmann & Co. A.G., 609

Source: *Duns Europa* (annual), vol. 4, Dun & Bradstreet, 1997, p. 205+.

Air Cargo

See: **Air Freight Service**

Air Conditioning Industry

★ 118 ★

JAPAN'S TOP AIR CONDITIONER MAKERS

Ranked by: Market share, in percent. **Number listed:** 6
1. Matsushita Electric Industrial with 18.0%
2. Mitsubishi Electric, 13.0%
3. Toshiba, 13.0%
4. Sanyo Electric, 11.0%
5. Hitachi, 10.0%
6. Other, 35.0%

Source: *Nikkei Weekly*, July 22, 1996, p. 8.

★ 119 ★

LARGEST AIR CONDITIONER MAKERS IN EGYPT, 1995

Ranked by: Market share, in percent. **Remarks:** Notes production capacity for each firm. **Number listed:** 6
1. Miraco-Carrier with 53.0%

2. Power, 18.0%
3. Philco, 12.0%
4. Koldair, 10.0%
5. Trane, 4.0%
6. Gibson, 3.0%

Source: *National Trade Data Bank*, August 12, 1996, p. ISA 960701.

★ 120 ★

LEADING MANUFACTURERS OF ROOM AIR-CONDITIONERS IN CHINA, 1995
Ranked by: Units shipped. **Number listed:** 10

1. Chunlan with 1,142,000 units
2. Geli, 703,000
3. Meide, 421,400
4. Kelong, 267,900
5. Haier, 265,100
6. Huabao, 195,600
7. Sharp, 192,700
8. Hitachi, 780,200
9. Aite, 170,700
10. Feilu, 155,500

Source: *Appliance Manufacturer*, February 1997, p. G-17.

★ 121 ★

TOP AIR CONDITIONER MAKERS IN GERMANY
Ranked by: Market share, in percent. **Number listed:** 7

1. De Longhi with 31.0%
2. Bosch, 18.0%
3. Rowenta, 14.0%
4. Stiebel Eltron, 11.0%
5. AEG, 9.0%
6. Polenz, 9.0%
7. Other, 8.0%

Source: *Wirtschaftswoche*, July 25, 1996, p. 48.

★ 122 ★

WHO PURCHASES AIR CONDITIONERS IN COLOMBIA
Ranked by: Percent distribution. **Number listed:** 9

1. Industrial companies with 45.0%
2. Residential, 15.0%
3. Office buildings, 12.0%
4. Banks and financial companies, 10.0%
5. Hotels, 9.0%
6. Hospitals, 7.0%
7. Department stores and retail stores, 0.5%
8. Restaurants, 0.5%
9. Others, 0.1%

Source: *National Trade Data Bank*, June 24, 1997, p. ISA970501.

Air Couriers
See: **Air Freight Service**

Air Freight Service

★ 123 ★

INTERNATIONAL EXPRESS FREIGHT MARKET, 1996
Ranked by: Market share based on shipments, in percent. **Number listed:** 9

1. FedEx with 34.0%
2. DHL, 31.5%
3. United Parcel Service, 10.3%
4. TNT, 7.8%
5. Freight forwarders, 6.0%
6. Airborne, 3.0%
7. USPS-Express Mail, 1.9%
8. Airlines-retail, 1.5%
9. Other couriers, 4.0%

Source: *Air Cargo World*, June 1997, p. 35.

★ 124 ★

LARGEST CARGO AIRPORTS IN ARGENTINA, 1994
Ranked by: Cargo transported, in tons. **Number listed:** 30

1. Ezeiza with 139,313 tons
2. Aerospace, 21,840
3. Mendoza, 3,178
4. Cordoba, 2,954
5. Com. Rivadavia, 2,483
6. Rio Grande, 1,477
7. Tucuman, 1,313
8. Neuquen, 1,247
9. Rio Gallegos, 1,122
10. Salta, 890

Source: *National Trade Data Bank*, July 16, 1996, p. ISA960501.

★ 125 ★

TOP AIR CARGO CARRIERS WORLDWIDE, 1995
Ranked by: Metric tons transported in 1995. **Number listed:** 25

1. Lufthansa with 918,000 metric tons
2. Federal Express, 693,000
3. Korean Air Lines, 641,000
4. Air France, 640,000
5. Singapore Airlines, 586,000
6. KLM, 551,000
7. Cathay Pacific, 522,000
8. British Airways, 510,000
9. Japan Airlines, 504,000
10. Northwest Airlines, 386,000

Source: *World Trade*, August 1997, p. 62.

★ 126 ★
TOP AIR EXPORTING COUNTRIES, 1995
Ranked by: Pounds of cargo exported, in billions. **Remarks:** A total of 40.9 billion pounds were shipped in 1995. Data exclude domestic service. **Number listed:** 10

1. Germany with 5.94 billion pounds
2. U.S., 4.89
3. France, 4.04
4. Italy, 3.88
5. U.K., 3.06
6. Netherlands, 2.54
7. Hong Kong, 2.26
8. Japan, 1.11
9. Spain, 0.90
10. China, 0.90

Source: *International Business*, February 1997, p. 6.

★ 127 ★
TOP AIR FREIGHT CARRIERS BY TON-KILOMETERS, 1995
Ranked by: Scheduled freight, in ton-kilometers performed. **Remarks:** Provides international and domestic data. **Number listed:** 50

1. Federal Express with 6,983 million ton-kilometers
2. Lufthansa, 5,833
3. Air France, 4,420
4. Korean Air Lines, 4,305
5. Japan Airlines, 3,781
6. Singapore Airlines, 3,666
7. KLM, 3,612
8. British Airways, 3,253
9. Northwest Airlines, 2,839
10. Cathay Pacific, 2,790

Source: *World Air Transport Statistics* (annual), 1996, p. 42.

★ 128 ★
TOP AIR FREIGHT CARRIERS BY TONS CARRIED, 1995
Ranked by: Scheduled freight, in tons carried. **Remarks:** Provides international and domestic data. **Number listed:** 50

1. Federal Express with 3,421 thousand tons
2. Lufthansa, 979
3. Korean Air Lines, 851
4. Japan Airlines, 838
5. Northwest Airlines, 719
6. Air France, 657
7. American Airlines, 638
8. Singapore Airlines, 586
9. KLM, 551
10. United Airlines, 529

Source: *World Air Transport Statistics* (annual), 1996, p. 40.

★ 129 ★
TOP CARGO AIRPORTS WORLDWIDE, 1996
Ranked by: Cargo traffic, in metric tons. **Number listed:** 28

1. Memphis, TN (MEM) with 173,829 metric tons
2. Los Angeles, CA (LAX), 143,451
3. Miami, FL (MA), 139,287
4. New York, NY (JFK), 133,964
5. Hong Kong (HKG), 131,200
6. Tokyo, Japan (NRT), 127,228
7. Frankfurt, Germany (FRA), 121,146
8. Louisville, KY (SDF), 115,836
9. Seoul, South Korea (SEL), 111,468
10. Chicago, IL (ORD), 104,882

Source: *Asiaweek*, October 11, 1996, p. 12.

Air Pollution

★ 130 ★
LEADING EMITTERS OF CARBON DIOXIDE
Ranked by: Annual emissions, in millions of metric tons per year. **Number listed:** 10

1. United States with 4.80 million
2. China, 2.60
3. Russian Federation, 2.10
4. Japan, 1.06
5. Germany, 0.87
6. India, 0.76
7. Ukraine, 0.61
8. United Kingdom, 0.56
9. Canada, 0.41
10. Italy, 0.41

Source: *The Wall Street Journal*, May 27, 1997, p. A20.

Airlines

★ 131 ★
AIRLINE MARKET IN SOUTH AFRICA
Ranked by: Market share, in percent. **Number listed:** 3

1. South African Airways with 65.0%
2. Sun Air, 20.0%
3. Comair, 15.0%

Source: *The Economist*, September 28, 1996, p. 80.

★ 132 ★
BUSIEST AIRLINE ROUTES
Ranked by: Millions of passengers per year. **Number listed:** 10

1. Tokyo/Sapporo with 7.43 million passengers
2. Tokyo/Fukuoka, 5.95
3. London/Paris, 3.37
4. Tokyo/Osaka, 3.34

5. New York/Chicago, 2.84
6. Honolulu/Maui, 2.68
7. New York/Los Angeles, 2.50
8. Hong Kong/Taipei, 2.39
9. London/New York, 2.39
10. Tokyo/Naha, 2.31
Source: *Financial Times*, October 25, 1996, p. 14.

★ 133 ★
CANADA'S LEADING AIRLINES, 1996
Ranked by: Market share based on sales, in percent.
Number listed: 3
1. Air Canada with 57%
2. Canadian Airlines International, 42%
3. Others, 1%
Source: *Marketing Magazine*, May 26, 1997, p. 17.

★ 134 ★
LARGEST AIRLINES, 1995
Ranked by: Revenue, in millions of U.S. dollars.
Remarks: Notes profits and global rank. **Number listed:**
8
1. AMR (United States) with $16,910 million
2. Japan Airlines, $15,013
3. UAL (United States), $14,943
4. Lufthansa Group (Germany), $13,886
5. Delta Air Lines (United States), $12,194
6. British Airways (Britain), $12,147
7. All Nippon Airways (Japan), $10,022
8. NWA (United States), $9,085
Source: *Fortune,* The Global 500: World's Biggest Corporations (annual), August 5, 1996, p. F-15.

★ 135 ★
TOP AIRLINES BY INTERNATIONAL PASSENGERS
Ranked by: Passengers carried, in millions. **Number listed:** 10
1. British Airways with 23.9 million passengers
2. Lufthansa, 17.5
3. American Airlines, 14.9
4. Air France, 13.8
5. KLM, 11.6
6. United Airlines, 11.3
7. Singapore Airlines, 9.9
8. SAS, 9.8
9. Cathay Pacific, 9.7
10. Japan Airlines, 9.4
Source: *Financial Times*, May 9, 1996, p. 18.

★ 136 ★
TOP AIRLINES BY INTERNATIONAL PASSENGERS CARRIED
Ranked by: International passengers, in thousands.
Number listed: 10
1. British Airways with 25,351 thousand passengers

2. Lufthansa, 19,347
3. American Airlines, 16,352
4. Air France, 12,682
5. KLM, 12,172
6. United Airlines, 11,311
7. Singapore Airlines, 10,761
8. Cathay Pacific, 10,375
9. SAS, 10,258
10. Japan Airlines, 10,211
Source: *Financial Times*, January 7, 1997, p. 2.

★ 137 ★
TOP AIRLINES WORLDWIDE, 1997
Ranked by: Results of a survey of assistants and in-house travel agents about their bosses' business trips over the past year. They were asked to nominate their favorite airlines. **Remarks:** See source for details on scoring. Includes best airlines for long and short flights, specific routes, first class travel and overall business accomodations. **Number listed:** 10
1. British Airways with 145
2. Cathay Pacific, 40
3. Singapore Airlines, 40
4. Virgin Atlantic, 35
5. Lufthansa, 29
6. United Airlines, 25
7. Swissair, 17
8. American Airlines, 12
9. KLM-Royal Dutch Airlines, 11
10. SAS, 7
Source: *Euromoney*, Business Travel Survey (biannual), April 1997, p. 143.

★ 138 ★
U.S./EUROPE AIR MARKET
Ranked by: Market share based on total departures, in percent. **Number listed:** 11
1. American Airlines with 14.6%
2. British Airways, 13.7%
3. Delta Airlines, 12.1%
4. United Airlines, 8.1%
5. Lufthansa German Airlines, 6.0%
6. Air France, 4.5%
7. Trans World Airlines, 4.1%
8. KLM-Royal Dutch Airlines, 3.8%
9. Northwest Airlines, 3.7%
10. Virgin Atlantic Airways, 3.1%
Source: *The Wall Street Journal*, May 17, 1996, p. A2.

Airlines – Asia

★ 139 ★
MOST ADMIRED AIRLINES IN ASIA, 1997
Ranked by: Results of a questionnaire sent to more than 9,000 managers and CEOs chosen from the magazine's circulation and evaluated by Asia Market Intelligence, a research firm. **Remarks:** Respondents scored each company in terms of overall admirability, then on six attributes: quality of products, quality of management, contribution to local economy, record as an employer, growth potential and reputation for ethics. Also notes 1996 figures. **Number listed:** 10
1. Singapore Airlines with 8.76
2. Cathay Pacific, 7.58
3. KLM, 7.18
4. All Nippon Airways, 7.12
5. Swissair, 7.07
6. Korean Air, 7.07
7. British Airways, 6.93
8. United Airlines, 6.71
9. Thai Airways International, 6.69
10. Lufthansa, 6.53

Source: *Asian Business,* Most Admired Companies in Asia (annual), May 1997, p. 30.

Airlines – Europe

★ 140 ★
TOP EUROPEAN AIRLINES, 1994
Ranked by: Passengers carried, in thousands. **Remarks:** Also notes operating revenues. **Number listed:** 15
1. British Airways with 30,202
2. Lufthansa, 29,956
3. SAS, 18,775
4. Air France, 15,592
5. Alitalia, 14,536
6. Iberia, 13,356
7. KLM, 11,686
8. Swissair, 8,272
9. Turkish Airlines, 6,856
10. Olympic, 5,813

Source: *International Business,* October 1996, p. 14.

Airplanes

★ 141 ★
FASTEST GROWING AIRCRAFT AND AIRCRAFT PARTS MARKETS OUTSIDE THE U.S., 1993-1995
Ranked by: Average annual growth, in percent. **Number listed:** 10
1. Czech Republic with 100% growth
2. Saudi Arabia, 50%
3. Romania, 30%
4. Costa Rica, 28%
5. Taiwan, 28%
6. India, 25%
7. South Korea, 25%
8. Australia, 20%
9. Chile, 20%
10. China, 20%

Source: *National Trade Data Bank,* March 21, 1995, p. BMR9404.

★ 142 ★
LARGEST AIRCRAFT AND AIRCRAFT PARTS IMPORT MARKETS OUTSIDE THE U.S.
Ranked by: Value of imports, in millions of U.S. dollars. **Number listed:** 10
1. Germany with $10,700.0 million
2. United Kingdom, $10,560.0
3. Japan, $5,055.0
4. Canada, $3,665.0
5. China, $2,800.0
6. South Korea, $2,600.0
7. Saudi Arabia, $2,200.0
8. Italy, $2,000.0
9. Singapore, $1,710.0
10. Malaysia, $1,703.0

Source: *National Trade Data Bank,* March 21, 1995, p. BMR9404.

★ 143 ★
LARGEST AIRCRAFT AND AIRCRAFT PARTS MARKETS OUTSIDE THE U.S.
Ranked by: Total market value, in millions of U.S. dollars. **Number listed:** 10
1. United Kingdom with $11,800.0 million
2. Germany, $10,900.0
3. Japan, $8,994.0
4. Italy, $5,400.0
5. Canada, $4,924.0
6. South Korea, $3,100.0
7. China, $3,000.0
8. Saudi Arabia, $2,200.0
9. Singapore, $2,125.0
10. Malaysia, $1,703.0

Source: *National Trade Data Bank,* March 21, 1995, p. BMR9404.

★ 144 ★
TOP AIRCRAFT MANUFACTURERS IN AUSTRALIA, 1996
Ranked by: Number of aircraft listed on the Australian Civil Aircraft Register as of June 1996. **Number listed:** 30
1. Cessna with 3,317
2. Piper, 1,945
3. Beech, 707
4. Homebuilt, 571
5. Robinson, 245
6. Bell, 200
7. Boeing, 149
8. Mooney, 148
9. Auster, 134
10. Kavanagh Balloons, 132

Source: *National Trade Data Bank*, April 17, 1997, p. ISA970401.

Airports

★ 145 ★
ARGENTINA'S LARGEST AIRPORTS, 1994
Ranked by: Passengers transported. **Number listed:** 30
1. Ezeiza with 4,055,793 passengers
2. Aeroparque, 4,002,278
3. Cordoba, 832,684
4. Mendoza, 579,050
5. Mar del Plata, 398,718
6. Neuquen, 293,106
7. Rio Gallegos, 289,264
8. Iguaza, 277,575
9. Trelew, 247,945
10. Rosario, 243,404

Source: *National Trade Data Bank*, July 16, 1996, p. ISA960501.

★ 146 ★
LARGEST AFRICAN AIRPORTS, 1995
Ranked by: Number of visitors, in millions. **Number listed:** 10
1. Johannesburg, South Africa with 7.31 million visitors
2. Cairo, Egypt, 7.03
3. Lagos, Nigeria, 6.00
4. Alger, Algeria, 3.09
5. Tunis, Tunisia, 2.83
6. Le Cap, South Africa, 2.53
7. Monastir, Tunisia, 2.53
8. Casablanca, Morocco, 2.24
9. Durban, South Africa, 2.06
10. Djerba, Tunisia, 1.55

Source: *Jeune Afrique Economie*, October 14, 1996, p. 26.

★ 147 ★
LARGEST AIRPORTS IN GERMANY, 1995
Ranked by: Passengers transported, in millions. **Number listed:** 15
1. Frankfurt with 38.2 million passengers
2. Dusseldorf, 15.1
3. Munich, 14.9
4. Berlin/Tegel, 8.3
5. Hamburg, 8.2
6. Stuttgart, 5.1
7. Cologne, 4.7
8. Hannover, 4.3
9. Nuremberg, 2.3
10. Leipzig/Halle, 2.1

Source: *National Trade Data Bank*, July 25, 1996, p. IMI960725.

★ 148 ★
MOST POPULAR AIRPORTS FOR INTERNATIONAL TRAVELLERS, 1995
Ranked by: International passengers embarked and disembarked, in thousands. **Remarks:** Also notes figures for 1994. **Number listed:** 25
1. London Heathrow with 46,830
2. Frankfurt, 30,257
3. Hong Kong, 27,424
4. Paris Charles de Gaulle, 25,534
5. Amsterdam Schipol, 24,709
6. Singapore, 21,743
7. Tokyo Narita, 21,488
8. London Gatwick, 20,604
9. New York Kennedy, 16,973
10. Bangkok, 15,119

Source: *ICAO Journal*, July/August 1996, p. 17.

★ 149 ★
TOP AIRPORTS BY TOTAL PASSENGERS
Ranked by: Total passengers. **Remarks:** Notes percent changed. **Number listed:** 50
1. O'Hare International (Chicago) with 67,253,358
2. Hartsfield Atlanta International, 57,734,755
3. Dallas/Fort Worth Airport, 56,490,851
4. Heathrow (London), 54,452,634
5. Los Angeles International, 53,909,223
6. Haneda (Tokyo), 45,822,503
7. Rhein/Main (Frankfurt/Main), 38,179,543
8. San Francisco International, 36,262,745
9. Miami International, 33,235,658
10. Denver International, 31,036,622

Source: *Financial Times*, November 28, 1996, p. VI.

★ 150 ★
TOP AIRPORTS FOR BUSINESS TRAVELLERS, 1996
Ranked by: Airports rated 1 to 10 on overall passenger convenience, based on a March 1996 survey of business travellers asked to rank 43 international cities **Remarks:** Also notes survey results from leisure passengers.
Number listed: 10
1. Singapore Changi Airport with 8.23
2. Manchster Airport (England), 8.09
3. Amsterdam Schiphol Airport, 8.05
4. Raleigh-Durham Airport (North Carolina), 8.00
5. Melbourne International Airport (Australia), 7.73
6. Calgary International Airport, 7.71
7. Sydney International Airport, 7.57
8. Greater Cincinnati International Airport, 7.55
9. International Airport of Montreal-Mirabel, 7.52
10. Houston Intercontinental Airport, 7.44
Source: *World Business*, August 1996, p. 16.

★ 151 ★
TOP AIRPORTS IN CHINA, 1995
Ranked by: Passengers. **Remarks:** Notes percent change.
Number listed: 50
1. Beijing with 15,044,668
2. Guagzhou, 12,574,882
3. Shanghai, 11,076,018
4. Chengdu, 4,155,243
5. Shenzhen, 4,120,697
6. Xiamen, 3,488,179
7. Kunming, 3,365,454
8. Haikou, 2,807,066
9. Xian (Xianyang), 2,429,621
10. Chongqing, 2,332,974
Source: *Air Transport World*, September 1996, p. 1.

★ 152 ★
TOP AIRPORTS WORLDWIDE, 2005
Ranked by: Passengers, forecast in millions. **Number listed:** 10
1. Dallas/Fort Worth (TX) with 81.3 million passengers
2. O'Hare (Chicago, IL), 78.6
3. Heathrow (London, England), 68.1
4. Los Angeles (CA), 60.2
5. Hong Kong, 50.3
6. Rhein/Main (Frankfurt, Germany), 47.9
7. Kimpo (Seoul, South Korea), 43.4
8. Logan (Boston, MA), 42.0
9. San Francisco (CA), 40.5
10. Charles de Gaulle (Paris, France), 39.5
Source: *The World in 1997*, 1997, p. 108.

Airports – Asia

★ 153 ★
AIRPORTS IN ASIAN COUNTRIES
Ranked by: Number of airports. **Number listed:** 29
1. Indonesia with 450 airports
2. India, 352
3. Philippines, 269
4. Iran, 261
5. China, 204
6. Japan, 175
7. Pakistan, 119
8. Malaysia, 115
9. South Korea, 114
10. Thailand, 105
Source: *The World Factbook 1995,* Information obtained from the Internet, http:// www.odci.gov.

Airports – Europe

★ 154 ★
AIRPORTS IN EUROPEAN COUNTRIES
Ranked by: Number of airports. **Number listed:** 36
1. Germany with 660 airports
2. United Kingdom, 505
3. France, 476
4. Bulgaria, 355
5. Sweden, 253
6. Finland, 159
7. Romania, 156
8. Italy, 138
9. Poland, 134
10. Denmark, 118
Source: *The World Factbook 1995,* Information obtained from the Internet, http:// www.odci.gov.

Airports, International

★ 155 ★
AIRPORTS IN FORMER SOVIET COUNTRIES
Ranked by: Number of airports. **Number listed:** 10
1. Russia with 2,517 airports
2. Ukraine, 706
3. Kazakhstan, 352
4. Uzbekistan, 261
5. Belarus, 118
6. Lithuania, 96
7. Azerbaijan, 69
8. Turkmenistan, 64
9. Tajikistan, 59

10. Kyrgyzstan, 54

Source: *The World Factbook 1995,* Information obtained from the Internet, http:// www.odci.gov.

★ **156** ★

AIRPORTS IN LATIN AMERICA AND THE CARIBBEAN

Ranked by: Number of airports. **Number listed:** 10

1. Brazil with 3,467 airports
2. Mexico, 2,055
3. Argentina, 1,602
4. Bolivia, 1,382
5. Colombia, 1,307
6. Paraguay, 929
7. Guatemala, 528
8. Venezuela, 431
9. Chile, 390
10. Peru, 236

Source: *The World Factbook 1995,* Information obtained from the Internet, http:// www.odci.gov.

Algeria – see under individual headings

Aluminum Industry

★ **157** ★

TOP ALUMINUM CONSUMERS, 1996

Ranked by: Demand, in thousands of metric tons. **Number listed:** 6

1. Western Europe with 5,300 thousand metric tons
2. United States, 5,030
3. Japan, 2,400
4. China, 1,950
5. Eastern Europe, 650
6. Other, 4,700

Source: *Engineering & Mining Journal,* 1997 Commodities Review Issue (annual), March 1997, p. WW-11.

Amman Financial Market

★ **158** ★

LARGEST COMPANIES ON THE AMMAN FINANCIAL MARKET, 1995

Ranked by: Market capitalization, in millions of Jordanian dinar (JDi). **Number listed:** 20

1. Arab Bank with JDi1,034.0 million
2. Arab Potash Company, JDi462.2
3. Jordan Cement Factory, JDi223.0

4. Jordan Phosphate Mines, JDi156.2
5. Housing Bank, JDi90.9
6. Jordan National Bank, JDi71.8
7. Jordan Petroleum Refinery, JDi65.9
8. Arab Banking Corporation/Jordan, JDi56.0
9. Jordan Islamic Bank, JDi51.2
10. Dar Al Dawa Development and Investment, JDi46.8

Source: *GT Guide to World Equity Markets* (annual), Euromoney Publications, 1996, p. 463.

★ **159** ★

MOST ACTIVELY TRADED SHARES ON THE AMMAN FINANCIAL MARKET, 1995

Ranked by: Traded value, in millions of Jordanian dinar (JD). **Number listed:** 10

1. Arab Bank with JD40.79 million
2. Jordan Cement Factories, JD26.66
3. Arab International Hotels, JD24.43
4. Jordan Electric Power, JD19.62
5. Jordan National Bank, JD18.47
6. Jordan Hotel and Tourism, JD17.02
7. Arab Pharmaceutical Manufacturing, JD14.20
8. Jordan Islamic Bank, JD13.95
9. Amman Bank for Investment, JD12.92
10. Philadelphia Investment Bank, JD12.74

Source: *GT Guide to World Equity Markets* (annual), Euromoney Publications, 1996, p. 463.

Amsterdam Stock Exchange

★ **160** ★

LARGEST COMPANIES ON THE AMSTERDAM STOCK EXCHANGE, 1995

Ranked by: Market value, in millions of guilders (G). **Number listed:** 20

1. Royal Dutch with G120,188 million
2. Unilever Cert, G36,089
3. ING, G31,365
4. KPN, G27,377
5. ABN AMRO Holding, G23,228
6. Philips Electronics, G19,667
7. AEGON, G18,758
8. PolyGram, G15,336
9. Heineken, G14,284
10. Elsevier, G14,144

Source: *GT Guide to World Equity Markets* (annual), Euromoney Publications, 1996, p. 251.

★ 161 ★
MOST ACTIVELY TRADED SHARES ON THE AMSTERDAM STOCK EXCHANGE, 1995
Ranked by: Turnover, in millions of guilders (G).
Remarks: Also notes volume of shares. **Number listed:** 20

1. Philips Electronics with G53,165 million
2. Royal Dutch, G45,037
3. Unilever Cert, G24,953
4. ING Group Cert, G21,287
5. ABN AMRO Holding, G18,468
6. Akzo Nobel, G16,363
7. Elsevier, G14,932
8. KPN, G14,138
9. KLM, G10,172
10. Wolters-Kluwer Cert, G9,655

Source: *GT Guide to World Equity Markets* (annual), Euromoney Publications, 1996, p. 252.

Amusement Parks – Latin America

★ 162 ★
TOP AMUSEMENT PARKS IN LATIN AMERICA, 1996
Ranked by: Attendance, in thousands of visitors.
Number listed: 10

1. Chapultepec (Mexico City, Mexico) with 2,900 thousand visitors
2. Playcenter (Sao Paulo, Brazil), 2,100
3. Reino Aventuro (Mexico City, Mexico), 2,000
4. Beto Carrero (Santa Catarina, Brazil), 1,600
5. Selva Magica (Guadalajara, Mexico), 1,600
6. Parque da Monica (Sao Paulo, Brazil), 1,200
7. Divertido (Mexico City, Mexico), 1,100
8. Fantasilandia (Santiago, Chile), 620
9. All Star (Sao Paulo, Brazil), 320
10. La Granja Villa (Lima, Peru), 260

Source: *Amusement Business*, Amusement Business Anual Year-End Issue, December 16, 1996, p. 70.

Analysts, Security
See: **Financial Analysts**

Angola – see under individual headings

Apparel Industry
See: **Clothing Trade**

Apparel Stores
See: **Clothing Stores**

Appliances, Household
See: **Household Appliances**

Argentina – see under individual headings

Art Organizations

★ 163 ★
LARGEST AUCTION HOUSES, 1996
Ranked by: Auction sales, in billions of U.S. dollars.
Number listed: 2

1. Christie's with $1.599 billion
2. Sotheby's, $1.602

Source: *The New York Times*, February 11, 1997, p. B1.

Arts Funding

★ 164 ★
SPENDING ON THE ARTS AND MUSEUMS
Ranked by: Per capita spending for selected countries, in U.S. dollars. **Number listed:** 7

1. Sweden with $45.6
2. Germany, $39.4
3. France, $35.1
4. Netherlands, $33.6
5. Canada, $28.5
6. United Kingdom, $16.1
7. United States, $3.3

Source: *Time*, August 7, 1995, p. 64.

Athens Stock Exchange

★ 165 ★
LARGEST COMPANIES ON THE ATHENS STOCK EXCHANGE, 1995
Ranked by: Market value, in millions of Greek drachma (GDr). **Number listed:** 20

1. Hellenic Bottling Company SA with GDr378,943 million
2. Alpha Credit Bank, GDr271,260
3. Commercial Bank of Greece, GDr193,405
4. National Bank of Greece, GDr191,950

5. Ergo Bank SA, GDr171,143
6. Heracles General Cement Co., GDr113,605
7. Intracom SA, GDr109,313
8. Titan Cement Co., GDr101,105
9. Ionian Bank, GDr100,919
10. Papastratos Cigarette Co. SA, GDr92,780

Source: *GT Guide to World Equity Markets* (annual), Euromoney Publications, 1996, p. 154.

★ 166 ★
MOST ACTIVELY TRADED SHARES ON THE ATHENS STOCK EXCHANGE, 1995
Ranked by: Trading value, in millions of Greek drachma (GDr). **Number listed:** 20
1. National Mortgage Bank with GDr60,977 million
2. Alpha Credit Bank SA, GDr51,842
3. Commercial Bank of Greece, GDr48,265
4. Hellenic Bottling Co., GDr48,099
5. Ergo Bank SA, GDr47,602
6. Hellenic Sugar Industry SA, GDr46,771
7. Alte, GDr43,983
8. Michaniki, GDr39,937
9. National Bank of Greece, GDr32,979
10. Selonda Aquaculture, GDr30,942

Source: *GT Guide to World Equity Markets* (annual), Euromoney Publications, 1996, p. 154.

Athletic Shoes

★ 167 ★
LEADING MANUFACTURERS OF SPORT SHOES OPERATING IN INDONESIA
Ranked by: Share of total production, in percent. **Number listed:** 5
1. Nike with 40%
2. Reebok, 20%
3. Adidas, 15%
4. Fila, 15%
5. Other, 10%

Source: *National Trade Data Bank*, June 20, 1997, p. IMI970603.

★ 168 ★
NON-LEATHER FOOTWEAR MARKET IN INDIA
Ranked by: Market share, in percent. **Number listed:** 4
1. Bata with 52.03%
2. Liberty, 21.84%
3. Carona, 2.67%
4. Other, 23.46%

Source: *Business Today*, April 22, 1996, p. 64.

Auditing Services

★ 169 ★
TOP AUDITORS IN SINGAPORE, 1996
Ranked by: Number of clients. **Number listed:** 10
1. Ernst & Young with 56 clients
2. KPMG Peat Marwick, 51
3. Price Waterhouse, 50
4. Coopers & Lybrand, 42
5. Deloitte & Touche, 36
6. Arthur Andersen, 11
7. Foo Kon & Tan, 7
8. BDO Binder, 3
9. Ng Lee & Associates, 2
10. TS Tray & Associates, 2

Source: *The Accountant*, September 1996, p. 12.

Australian Stock Exchange

★ 170 ★
LARGEST COMPANIES ON THE AUSTRALIAN STOCK EXCHANGE, 1995
Ranked by: Market value, in millions of Australian dollars (A$). **Number listed:** 20
1. BHP with A$36,789 million
2. National Australia Bank, A$17,277
3. News Corporation, A$13,900
4. CRA, A$11,797
5. Westpac, A$11,292
6. WMC, A$9,582
7. ANZ Bank, A$9,125
8. Amcor, A$5,584
9. Coco-Cola Amatil, A$5,274
10. Commonwealth Bank, A$5,214

Source: *GT Guide to World Equity Markets* (annual), Euromoney Publications, 1996, p. 44.

★ 171 ★
MOST ACTIVELY TRADED SHARES ON THE AUSTRALIAN STOCK EXCHANGE, 1995
Ranked by: Turnover, in millions of Australian dollars ($A). **Number listed:** 20
1. BHP with A$15,735 million
2. News Corporation, A$7,970
3. National Australia Bank, A$7,897
4. Western Mining Corporation, A$6,239
5. CRA, A$5,891
6. ANZ Bank, A$4,001
7. Westpac Bank, A$3,678
8. MIM Holdings, A$2,369
9. Pacific Dunlop, A$2,237

10. Amcor, A$2,147
Source: *GT Guide to World Equity Markets* (annual), Euromoney Publications, 1996, p. 45.

Austria – see under individual headings

Automated Teller Machines

★ 172 ★
LARGEST ATM NETWORKS IN THAILAND, 1996
Ranked by: Number of ATMs nationwide as of December 31, 1996. **Number listed:** 15
1. BBL with 878 ATMs
2. KTB, 690
3. TFB, 579
4. SCB, 522
5. TMB, 406
6. BAY, 323
7. SCIB, 178
8. BMB, 166
9. TDB, 110
10. FBCB, 76
Source: *Bangkok Post*, March 21, 1997, p. B1.

Automated Teller Machines, Europe

★ 173 ★
AUTOMATED TELLER MACHINES IN EUROPE, 1994
Ranked by: Number of ATMs in each country. **Number listed:** 10
1. Germany with 24,382 units
2. Spain, 23,292
3. United Kingdom, 19,377
4. France, 18,729
5. Italy, 16,475
6. Netherlands, 4,342
7. Turkey, 3,880
8. Portugal, 3,561
9. Switzerland, 3,065
10. Finland, 2,994
Source: *World of Banking*, June/July 1995, p. 26.

Automobile Dealers

★ 174 ★
TOP AUTO DEALERS IN JAPAN
Ranked by: Income, in millions of yen (¥). **Number listed:** 10
1. Autobacs Seven with ¥14,702 million
2. Mercedes-Benz Japan, ¥11,143
3. BMW Japan, ¥11,011
4. Royal, ¥2,434
5. Aichi Toyota Motor, ¥2,199
6. Toyota Corolla Gifu, ¥2,028
7. Volvo Cars Japan, ¥1,926
8. Yokohama Toyopet Motor Sales, ¥1,634
9. Hino Motor Sales, ¥1,589
10. Nagano Toyota Motor, ¥1,570
Source: *Tokyo Business Today*, August 1995, p. 26.

Automobile Dealers – Canada

★ 175 ★
AUTO DEALER SATISFACTION IN CANADA, 1996
Ranked by: Dealers' satisfaction with their franchises, according to the 1996 Dealer Satisfaction Index.
Remarks: No specific criteria were provided. Notes rankings for 1995. **Number listed:** 25
1. Lexus
2. Jaguar
3. Porsche
4. Mercedes-Benz
5. Subaru
6. Saturn-Saab-Isuzu
7. Volvo
8. Jeep-Eagle
9. Plymouth-Dodge
10. Toyota
Source: *Automotive News*, February 3, 1997, p. 8.

Automobile Industry and Trade

★ 176 ★
AUTOMOBILE COMPANIES WITH THE HIGHEST MARKET CAPITALIZATION, 1996
Ranked by: Market capitalization at September 30, 1996, in millions of U.S. dollars. **Number listed:** 10
1. Toyota with $97,926.3 million
2. Ford, $36,968.8
3. General Motors, $36,317.8
4. Daimler-Benz, $29,107.3
5. Honda, $24,847.9
6. Chrysler, $20,856.2

7. Nissan Motor, $20,576.6
8. BMW, $10,681.8
9. Fiat, $10,634.5
10. Volkswagen, $10,512.7

Source: *Financial Times*, January 7, 1997, p. IV.

★ 177 ★
BEST SELLING CARS IN SOUTH AFRICA, 1995
Ranked by: Market share, in percent. **Number listed:** 21

1. Toyota Corolla with 15.9%
2. Volkswagen Citi/Fox, 11.4%
3. Delta Kadett/Astra, 9.9%
4. Volkswagen Golf/Jetta, 9.6%
5. Samcor 323/Laser/Meteor, 8.0%
6. Nissan Sentra/Sabre, 7.0%
7. BMW 3-Series, 6.6%
8. Nissan Fiat Uno, 6.5%
9. Mercedes-Benz Honda Ballade, 5.5%
10. Mercedes-Benz C-Class, 4.5%

Source: *WARD's Automotive International*, June 1996, p. 14.

★ 178 ★
BEST-SELLING AUTOS, 1996
Ranked by: Unit sales. **Remarks:** Also notes 1995 figures. **Number listed:** 10

1. Escort (Ford) with 918,000 units
2. Corolla (Toyota), 883,000
3. Golf (Volkswagen), 731,000
4. Fiesta (Ford), 645,000
5. Accord (Honda), 624,000
6. Punto (Fiat), 601,000
7. Civic (Honda), 570,000
8. Camry (Toyota), 512,000
9. Astra (Opel), 484,000
10. Polo (Volkswagen), 359,000

Source: *Automotive Industries*, June 1997, p. 33.

★ 179 ★
CAR MARKET IN ARGENTINA, 1996
Ranked by: Market share, in percent. **Number listed:** 16

1. VW Gol with 10.0%
2. Fiat Duna, 9.3%
3. Ford Fiesta, 9.0%
4. Renault 9, 8.8%
5. Fiat Spazio, 8.0%
6. VW Pointer, 8.0%
7. Renault 19, 7.2%
8. Peugeot 306, 4.6%
9. Renault Clio, 4.6%
10. Peugeot 504, 4.3%

Source: *National Trade Data Bank*, June 23, 1997, p. ISA970601.

★ 180 ★
CAR REGISTRATIONS IN WESTERN EUROPE, 1996
Ranked by: Units, in millions. **Number listed:** 9

1. Volkswagen Group with 2,203.6 million units
2. General Motors, 1,602.2
3. PSA Peugeot Citroen, 1,528.5
4. Ford Group, 1,484.8
5. Fiat Group, 1,438.7
6. Renault, 1,289.6
7. BMW Group, 804.9
8. Mercedes-Benz, 461.9
9. Volvo, 206.1

Source: *Financial Times*, January 15, 1997, p. 2.

★ 181 ★
LARGEST AUTO ASSEMBLERS IN THAILAND
Ranked by: Production, in units per year. **Number listed:** 14

1. MMC Sittiphol Motor with 126,600 units
2. Toyota Motor (Thailand), 100,000
3. Isuzu Motor Thailand, 76,000
4. Nissan Automobile, 74,900
5. Siam Motor and Nissan, 21,600
6. Honda Cars, 21,000
7. Bangchan General Assembly, 18,000
8. YMC Assembly, 12,000
9. Thai Hino Industry, 9,600
10. Union Cars, 7,200

Source: *Bangkok Post*, May 31, 1996, p. 2.

★ 182 ★
LARGEST AUTO MAKERS BY EMPLOYMENT, 1995
Ranked by: Number of employees. **Remarks:** Includes sales and production figures. **Number listed:** 24

1. GM with 745,000 employees
2. Ford, 346,990
3. VW, 242,285
4. Fiat, 236,800
5. Mercedes-Benz, 197,164
6. Toyota, 142,645
7. Renault, 139,950
8. PSA Group, 139,900
9. Nissan, 139,856
10. BMW, 115,763

Source: *WARD's Automotive International*, August 1996, p. 12.

★ 183 ★
LATIN AMERICAN AUTO SALES, 1995
Ranked by: Units sold. **Remarks:** Notes projected sales for 2000. **Number listed:** 7

1. Brazil with 1,682,555 units
2. Argentina, 322,793
3. Mexico, 187,703
4. Chile, 148,654
5. Colombia, 138,381

6. Venezuela, 87,151
7. Peru, 41,766

Source: *Inbound Logistics*, November 1996, p. 16.

★ **184** ★
LEADING CAR AND TRUCK PRODUCERS WORLDWIDE, 1996

Ranked by: Units produced. **Remarks:** Figure for General Motors is estimated. **Number listed:** 19

1. General Motors with 8,400,000
2. Ford Motor Co., 6,750,000
3. Toyota Motor Corp., 4,756,123
4. Volkswagen AG, 3,976,896
5. Chrysler Corp., 2,860,805
6. Nissan Motor Co., 2,742,000
7. Fiat Group, 2,586,000
8. Honda Motor Co., 2,084,000
9. Mitsubishi Motor Corp., 1,943,000
10. Renault SA, 1,803,733

Source: *Automotive News,* Market Data Fact Book (annual), May 28, 1997, p. 9.

★ **185** ★
LEADING CAR MANUFACTURERS IN MOSCOW

Ranked by: Market share, in percent. **Number listed:** 29

1. VAZ with 19.3%
2. Ford, 11.4%
3. BMW, 9.3%
4. Volkswagen, 8.6%
5. Mercedes, 5.0%
6. Nissan, 4.3%
7. Audi, 3.5%
8. Chevrolet, 3.5%
9. Volga, 2.8%
10. Fiat, 2.1%

Source: *National Trade Data Bank*, March 3, 1997, p. ISA970301.

★ **186** ★
LEADING CAR MANUFACTURERS IN VLADIVOSTOK

Ranked by: Market share, in percent. **Number listed:** 29

1. Toyota with 58.0%
2. Mitsubishi, 16.0%
3. Nissan, 12.0%
4. Honda, 4.8%
5. Isuzu, 3.2%
6. Volga, 1.6%
7. Mazda, 1.2%
8. VAZ, 1.2%
9. Kia, 0.8%
10. Moskvitch, 0.8%

Source: *National Trade Data Bank*, March 3, 1997, p. ISA970301.

★ **187** ★
LEADING VEHICLE MANUFACTURERS IN FRANCE, 1996

Ranked by: Market share of vehicles produced, in percent. **Remarks:** Also notes number of units produced and percent change from 1995. **Number listed:** 7

1. Renault with 45.7%
2. Auto Peugeot, 30.5%
3. Citroen, 22.6%
4. Sevel Fiat, 1.1%
5. Sevel Lancia, 0.1%

Source: *WARD's Automotive International*, June 1997, p. 12.

★ **188** ★
LEADING VEHICLE MANUFACTURERS IN GERMANY, 1996

Ranked by: Market share of vehicles produced, in percent. **Remarks:** Also notes number of units produced and percent change from 1995. **Number listed:** 13

1. Volkswagen with 27.5%
2. Opel, 21.4%
3. Mercedes-Benz, 16.5%
4. BMW, 11.8%
5. Ford, 11.2%
6. Audi, 10.2%
7. MAN, 0.6%
8. Porsche, 0.5%
9. Iveco-Magirus, 0.2%
10. Evo-Bus, 0.1%

Source: *WARD's Automotive International*, June 1997, p. 12.

★ **189** ★
LEADING VEHICLE MANUFACTURERS IN ITALY, 1996

Ranked by: Market share of vehicles produced, in percent. **Remarks:** Also notes number of units produced and percent change from 1995. **Number listed:** 16

1. Fiat with 68.9%
2. Lancia, 9.0%
3. Alfa Romeo, 7.4%
4. Iveco, 4.6%
5. Sevel Fiat, 4.5%
6. Sevel P.S.A., 3.9%
7. Piaggio, 0.9%
8. AutoBianchi, 0.5%
9. Ferrari, 0.2%
10. Astra, 0.1%

Source: *WARD's Automotive International*, June 1997, p. 12.

★ 190 ★

LEADING VEHICLE MANUFACTURERS IN SPAIN, 1996

Ranked by: Market share of vehicles produced, in percent. **Remarks:** Data are estimated. Also notes number of units produced and percent change from 1995. **Number listed:** 12

1. General Motors with 23.1%
2. SEAT, 16.1%
3. Renault, 13.5%
4. Ford, 12.4%
5. VW Audi, 11.4%
6. Citroen, 11.3%
7. Peugeot, 4.1%
8. Nissan, 4.0%
9. Mercedes, 1.9%
10. Suzuki, 1.1%

Source: *WARD's Automotive International*, June 1997, p. 12.

★ 191 ★

LEADING VEHICLE MANUFACTURERS IN THE UNITED KINGDOM, 1996

Ranked by: Market share of vehicles produced, in percent. **Remarks:** Also notes number of units produced and percent change from 1995. **Number listed:** 24

1. Rover with 26.3%
2. Ford, 24.9%
3. Vauxhall, 14.5%
4. Nissan, 12.0%
5. Toyota, 6.1%
6. Honda, 5.5%
7. Peugeot/Talbot, 4.5%
8. Jaguar/Daimler, 2.0%
9. IBC, 1.6%
10. LDV, 0.9%

Source: *WARD's Automotive International*, June 1997, p. 12.

★ 192 ★

LUXURY CAR SALES WORLDWIDE, 1996

Ranked by: Units sold. **Remarks:** Notes U.K. price of most expensive mainstream model. **Number listed:** 5

1. Toyota Lexus LS400 with 69,616 units
2. Mercedes-Benz S Class, 52,140
3. BMW 7 Series, 50,421
4. Cadillac Seville, 37,421
5. Rolls-Royce/Bentley, 1,744

Source: *Financial Times*, January 24, 1997, p. 22.

★ 193 ★

NEW CAR SALES IN EUROPE, 1996

Ranked by: New car sales, in units. **Remarks:** Notes percent change from 1995 and forecasts sales for 1997. **Number listed:** 12

1. Germany with 3,508,300 units

2. France, 2,132,100
3. United Kingdom, 2,025,500
4. Italy, 1,737,300
5. Poland, 366,352
6. Sweden, 183,820
7. Czech Republic, 153,907
8. Romania, 124,638
9. Slovakia, 74,705
10. Hungary, 74,118

Source: *Financial Times*, March 6, 1997, p. 3.

★ 194 ★

NEW VEHICLE SALES IN SLOVAKIA, 1996

Ranked by: Unit sales. **Remarks:** 74,652 new vehicles were sold in 1996. Notes 1995 figures. **Number listed:** 29

1. Skoda with 22,020 units
2. Daewoo, 11,362
3. Volkswagen, 6,966
4. Fiat, 6,683
5. GM-Opel, 4,012
6. Renault, 3,672
7. SEAT, 3,446
8. Hyundai, 2,261
9. Mazda, 1,987
10. Lada, 1,856

Source: *WARD's Automotive International*, March 1997, p. 13.

★ 195 ★

NEW VEHICLE SALES IN SLOVENIA, 1996

Ranked by: Unit sales. **Remarks:** 60,294 new vehicles were sold in 1996. Notes 1995 figures. **Number listed:** 41

1. Renault with 15,663 units
2. Volkswagen, 7,025
3. Hyundai, 4,394
4. Fiat, 3,976
5. GM-Opel, 3,838
6. Ford, 3,633
7. Skoda, 3,419
8. SEAT, 2,030
9. Lada, 1,933
10. Peugeot, 1,609

Source: *WARD's Automotive International*, March 1997, p. 13.

★ 196 ★

NEW ZEALAND'S TOP CAR MAKERS

Ranked by: 1996 first quarter market share, in percent. **Remarks:** Includes unit sales for 1995 and first quarter 1996. **Number listed:** 8

1. Toyota with 18.6%
2. Ford, 15.1%
3. Nissan, 11.0%
4. Holden, 10.6%
5. Honda, 10.6%
6. Mitsubishi, 9.3%

7. Mazda, 4.7%
8. Others, 20.1%
Source: *WARD's Automotive International*, June 1996, p. 4.

★ 197 ★
SOUTHEAST ASIA'S CAR SALES, 1995
Ranked by: Market share, in percent. **Remarks:** Includes unit sales figures. **Number listed:** 12
1. Toyota with 22.1%
2. Isuzu, 12.6%
3. Mitsubishi, 12.2%
4. Nissan, 9.9%
5. Proton, 8.5%
6. Suzuki, 5.8%
7. Daihatsu, 5.6%
8. Honda, 4.2%
9. Mazda, 2.5%
10. Mercedes Benz, 1.9%
Source: *Financial Times*, May 31, 1996, p. 6.

★ 198 ★
TOP CAR MAKERS WORLDWIDE, 1995
Ranked by: Revenues, in billions of French francs (FFr). **Number listed:** 11
1. General Motors (United States) with FFr716.9 billion
2. Ford (United States), FFr551.4
3. Toyota (Japan), FFr432.0
4. Nissan (Japan), FFr314.6
5. VAG Germany, FFr262.0
6. Daimler-Benz (Germany), FFr250.7
7. Chrysler (United States), FFr247.5
8. Honda (Japan), FFr195.1
9. Renault (France), FFr175.5
10. Peugeot-Citroen (France), FFr164.2
Source: *Financial Times*, July 8, 1997, p. 13.

★ 199 ★
TOP CAR MANUFACTURERS IN INDIA
Ranked by: Manufacturing capacity, in thousands of units. **Remarks:** Includes increases planned through 2001 and the likely costs of those increases. **Number listed:** 7
1. Maruti Udyog with 300 thousand units
2. DCM Daewoo, 72
3. Hindustan Motors, 65
4. PAL-Peugeot, 30
5. Premier Autos, 30
6. HM General Motors, 25
7. Telco-Mercedes, 5
Source: *Financial Times*, April 10, 1997, p. 4.

★ 200 ★
TOP CAR MARKETS IN AFRICA, 1996
Ranked by: Units sold. **Remarks:** Also notes 1995 figures. **Number listed:** 20
1. South Africa with 249,800
2. Egypt, 70,000
3. Algeria, 27,000
4. Reunion, 19,500
5. Nigeria, 17,600
6. Libya, 16,800
7. Tunisia, 9,500
8. Morocco, 8,300
9. Ivory Coast, 8,000
10. Ghana, 7,600
Source: *Automotive News*, Market Data Fact Book (annual), 1997, p. 22.

★ 201 ★
TOP CAR MARKETS IN LATIN AMERICA, 1996
Ranked by: Units sold. **Remarks:** Also notes 1995 figures. **Number listed:** 20
1. Brazil with 1,469,700
2. Argentina, 299,200
3. Chile, 85,900
4. Colombia, 85,400
5. Venezuela, 36,600
6. Peru, 32,100
7. Uruguay, 28,400
8. Ecuador, 25,000
9. Panama, 15,300
10. Jamaica, 11,700
Source: *Automotive News*, Market Data Fact Book (annual), 1997, p. 22.

★ 202 ★
TOP CAR MARKETS IN THE ASIA-PACIFIC REGION, 1996
Ranked by: Units sold. **Remarks:** Also notes 1995 figures. **Number listed:** 20
1. Japan with 4,592,000 units
2. South Korea, 1,246,600
3. Australia, 497,500
4. India, 470,000
5. China, 390,000
6. Taiwan, 350,000
7. Malaysia, 273,000
8. Thailand, 162,000
9. Philippines, 91,300
10. New Zealand, 66,000
Source: *Automotive News*, Market Data Fact Book (annual), 1997, p. 22.

★ 203 ★
TOP CAR PRODUCERS WORLDWIDE, 1996
Ranked by: Company shares, in percent. **Remarks:** Global production reached 35 million units. **Number listed:** 11
1. General Motors with 14.3%
2. Ford/Mazda, 12.6%
3. Volkswagen, 10.6%
4. Toyota, 10.3%
5. Fiat, 6.3%
6. PSA, 6.3%
7. Nissan, 6.0%
8. Honda, 5.4%
9. Renault, 5.1%
10. Mitsubishi, 3.1%

Source: *The Economist*, May 10, 1997, p. 23.

★ 204 ★
TOP NATIONS OF ORIGIN FOR AUTO IMPORTS TO JAPAN, 1996
Ranked by: New vehicle registrations. **Remarks:** Also notes figures for 1992-1995. **Number listed:** 11
1. Germany with 184,133
2. United States, 122,559
3. United Kingdom, 30,833
4. Sweden, 24,938
5. France, 10,502
6. Spain, 9,812
7. Italy, 7,059
8. Australia, 1,436
9. Netherlands, 1,423
10. South Korea, 78

Source: *Look Japan*, September 1997, p. 33.

★ 205 ★
VENEZUELA'S TOP CAR BRANDS, 1996
Ranked by: Unit sales for the first nine months of 1996. **Remarks:** Includes 1995 data. **Number listed:** 22
1. GM with 8,865 units
2. Ford, 7,401
3. Toyota, 6,163
4. Fiat, 4,658
5. Chrysler, 2,706
6. Mitsubishi, 1,239
7. Daewoo, 1,175
8. Mazda, 847
9. Honda, 365
10. Lada, 183

Source: *National Trade Data Bank*, October 30, 1996, p. ISA961001.

Automobile Industry and Trade – Asia

★ 206 ★
ASIA'S TOP MOTOR VEHICLE FIRMS, 1995
Ranked by: Sales, in millions of U.S. dollars. **Remarks:** Includes profits profits as a percentage of sales and assets, and overall sales rank. **Number listed:** 20
1. Toyota Motor Corp. with $113,956.4 million
2. Nissan Motor, $64,204.8
3. Honda Motor, $45,207.8
4. Mitsubishi Motors, $37,603.8
5. Mazda Motor Corp., $19,592.7
6. Isuzu Motors, $17,880.8
7. Suzuki Motor, $14,683.5
8. Hyundai Motor, $13,405.4
9. Fuji Heavy Industries, $11,453.5
10. Daihatsu Motor, $8,436.1

Source: *Asiaweek*, The Asiaweek 1,000, November 22, 1996, p. 164.

Automobile Industry and Trade – Brazil

★ 207 ★
AUTOMOTIVE COMPANIES MAKING THE LARGEST INVESTMENTS IN BRAZIL, 1996-2000
Ranked by: Outlays, in millions of U.S. dollars. **Number listed:** 17
1. Fiat with $3,000 million
2. General Motors, $2,800
3. Ford, $2,500
4. Volkswagen, $2,800
5. Hyundai, $1,700
6. Renault, $1,000
7. Asia Motors, $900
8. Mercedes-Benz, $800
9. Honda, $600
10. Toyota, $600

Source: *National Trade Data Bank*, June 19, 1997, p. ISA970601.

★ 208 ★
BRAZIL'S TOP CAR MAKERS, 1995
Ranked by: Unit sales. **Number listed:** 5
1. VW with 470,993 units
2. Fiat, 389,000
3. GM, 286,000
4. Ford, 150,722
5. Others, 75,709

Source: *Financial Times*, January 7, 1997, p. 11.

★ 209 ★
LARGEST AUTO INVESTORS IN BRAZIL, 1995
Ranked by: Investment, in millions of U.S. dollars.
Number listed: 9
1. Ford with $3,500 million
2. Volkswagen, $2,500
3. GM, $2,000
4. Fiat, $1,600
5. Renault, $750
6. Mercedes-Benz, $400
7. Honda, $350
8. Chrysler, $315
9. Toyota, $150
Source: *Automotive News*, November 25, 1996, p. 9.

Automobile Industry and Trade – China

★ 210 ★
AUTOMOBILE MARKET IN CHINA, 1996
Ranked by: Market share, in percent. **Remarks:** Includes production and sales figures. **Number listed:** 9
1. Santana with 52.38%
2. Charade, 22.68%
3. Jetta/Golf, 6.91%
4. Beijing Cherokee, 6.74%
5. Alto, 4.52%
6. Audi, Little Redflag, 3.85%
7. Fukang (Citroen), 1.91%
8. Guangzhou Peugeot, 0.70%
9. Subaru, 0.31%
Source: *Financial Times*, June 25, 1997, p. 13.

Automobile Industry and Trade – Europe

★ 211 ★
CAR SALES IN EUROPE, 1996
Ranked by: Units sold, based on new car registrations.
Remarks: Volkswagen includes Audi, SEAT, and Skoda. General Motors includes Opel/Vauxhall and Saab. Ford includes Jaguar. Fiat includes Lancia and Alfa Romeo. BMW includes Rover. **Number listed:** 9
1. Volkswagen with 2,203,870 units
2. General Motors, 1,602,222
3. PSA Peugeot Citroen, 1,528,534
4. Ford, 1,484,870
5. Fiat Group, 1,438,765
6. Renault, 1,289,677
7. BMW Group, 804,987
8. Mercedes-Benz, 461,939
9. Volvo, 206,111
Source: *Europe*, February 1997, p. 23.

Automobile Industry and Trade – Germany

★ 212 ★
BEST-SELLING ALL-PURPOSE VANS IN GERMANY, 1994
Ranked by: Share of registered models, in percent.
Remarks: Includes data for 1992 and 1993. **Number listed:** 12
1. Renault Espace with 27.6%
2. Chrysler Voyager, 24.1%
3. Mitsubishi Space Wagon, 9.7%
4. Pontiac Transport, 8.0%
5. Toyota Previa, 7.2%
6. Mitsubishi Space Runner, 7.1%
7. Nissan Serena, 6.4%
8. Fiat Ulysse, 3.1%
9. Nissan Prairie, 2.7%
10. Peugot 806, 2.6%
Source: *National Trade Data Bank*, October 18, 1995, p. ISA9508.

★ 213 ★
NEW CAR REGISTRATIONS IN GERMANY, 1995
Ranked by: Number of new car registrations, shown by manufacturer. **Remarks:** Includes share of total registrations for each firm. **Number listed:** 28
1. Volkswagen with 643,055 new registrations
2. Opel, 566,055
3. Ford, 376,179
4. Daimler-Benz, 250,334
5. BMW, 214,702
6. Audi, 205,812
7. Renault, 170,907
8. Fiat, 116,238
9. Peugeot, 87,062
10. Nissan, 85,620
Source: *National Trade Data Bank*, July 15, 1996, p. ISA960601.

Automobile Industry and Trade – Japan

★ 214 ★
JAPANESE CAR MARKET, 1997
Ranked by: Market share for the second quarter of 1997, in percent. **Remarks:** Notes figures for the first quarter of 1989. **Number listed:** 4
1. Toyota with 38.4%
2. Nissan, 19.6%
3. Honda, 11.8%
4. Other, 30.2%
Source: *The Wall Street Journal*, August 12, 1997, p. A10.

★ 215 ★
TOP AUTO MAKERS IN JAPAN
Ranked by: Income, in millions of yen (¥). **Number listed:** 10
1. Toyota Motor with ¥262,090 million
2. Suzuki Motor, ¥32,509
3. Mitsubishi Motors, ¥28,129
4. Honda Motor, ¥21,542
5. Toyoda Automatic Loom Works, ¥9,531
6. Hino Motors, ¥4,831
7. Aichi Machine Industry, ¥3,875
8. Yamaha Motor, ¥3,439
9. Daihatsu Motor, ¥3,032
10. Kyokuto Kaihatsu Kogyo, ¥2,186

Source: *Tokyo Business Today*, August 1995, p. 26.

★ 216 ★
TOP SELLING AUTOMOBILES IN JAPAN, 1996
Ranked by: Unit sales. **Remarks:** Also notes 1995 sales. **Number listed:** 20
1. Toyota Corolla with 282,218
2. Toyota Crown, 139,027
3. Nissan March, 131,830
4. Toyota Starlet, 121,749
5. Toyota Mark II, 118,178
6. Toyota Hiace series, 117,978
7. Honda Odyssey, 110,274
8. Honda CR-V, 102,828
9. Toyota Estima, 102,184
10. Toyota Caldina, 98,720

Source: *Automotive News*, Market Data Fact Book (annual), 1997, p. 20.

Automobile Industry and Trade – Mexico

★ 217 ★
MEXICAN STATES WITH THE MOST VEHICLES
Ranked by: Percent distribution. **Number listed:** 14
1. Mexico City with 25.1%
2. Mexico (State of), 9.1%
3. Jalisco, 6.5%
4. Chihuahua, 5.4%
5. Baja California Norte, 4.9%
6. Nuevo Leon, 4.8%
7. Veracruz, 4.2%
8. Tamaulipas, 3.7%
9. Coahuila, 3.4%
10. Puebla, 3.2%

Source: *National Trade Data Bank*, July 3, 1997, p. ISA970401.

Automobile Industry and Trade – Sweden

★ 218 ★
BEST-SELLING CARS IN SWEDEN, 1996
Ranked by: Units sold. **Number listed:** 10
1. Volvo 800, S/V/C70 with 22,679 units
2. Volvo 900, S/V90, 13,301
3. VW Golf, 9,231
4. Ford Escort, 8,078
5. Saab 900, 7,915
6. Saab 9000, 7,733
7. Volvo S40/V40, 6,756
8. Ford Mondeo, 6,210
9. Opel Astra, 5,826
10. Audi 80/A4, 5,717

Source: *National Trade Data Bank*, May 5, 1997, p. ISA970501.

Automobile Industry and Trade – United Kingdom

★ 219 ★
BRITAIN'S TOP CAR SELLERS, 1996
Ranked by: Market share, in percent. **Number listed:** 13
1. Ford with 19.6%
2. Vauxhall, 14.0%
3. Rover, 10.9%
4. Peugeot, 7.6%
5. Renault, 6.5%
6. Volkswagen, 5.6%
7. Nissan, 4.6%
8. Fiat, 4.2%
9. Citroen, 3.8%
10. Other, 23.2%

Source: *The Observer*, January 5, 1997, p. B1.

Automobile Industry and Trade – Western Europe

★ 220 ★
TOP AUTOMOBILE MANUFACTURERS IN WESTERN EUROPE
Ranked by: Market share, in percent. **Remarks:** "Others" includes Mercedes-Benz, Volvo, and South Korean automakers. **Number listed:** 9
1. Volkswagen with 16.8%
2. GM group, 13.1%
3. PSA group, 12.0%
4. Ford group, 11.9%
5. Fiat group, 11.1%
6. Japanese cars, 10.6%

7. Renault, 10.3%
8. BMW group, 6.3%
9. Others, 7.9%

Source: *Japanese Finance & Industry*, 1996, p. 4.

★ 221 ★

TOP SELLING AUTOMOBILES IN WESTERN EUROPE, 1996

Ranked by: Unit sales. **Remarks:** Also notes 1995 sales. **Number listed:** 20

1. Volkswagen Golf with 637,348
2. Fiat Punto, 552,445
3. Ford Fiesta, 550,588
4. Ford Escort, 459,172
5. Volkswagen Polo, 439,957
6. Opel Astra, 418,090
7. Opel Corsa, 410,582
8. Renault Megane, 380,301
9. Renault Clio, 374,801
10. Peugeot 106, 318,321

Source: *Automotive News*, Market Data Fact Book (annual), 1997, p. 20.

Automobile Leasing and Rental Companies

★ 222 ★

GERMANY'S AUTO RENTAL LEADERS

Ranked by: Market share, in percent. **Number listed:** 6

1. Sixt with 17.0%
2. Europcar, 14.0%
3. Avis, 10.0%
4. Autohansa, 6.0%
5. Hertz, 3.0%
6. Other, 50.0%

Source: *Wirtschaftswoche*, March 7, 1996, p. 73.

★ 223 ★

TOP CAR-LEASING MARKETS WORLDWIDE, 1995

Ranked by: Value, in millions of U.S. dollars. **Remarks:** Includes values for 1994 markets and 1994-1995 growth rates of each market. **Number listed:** 10

1. United States with $62,800 million
2. Germany, $14,495
3. United Kingdom, $10,200
4. Japan, $4,300
5. Brazil, $3,500
6. France, $2,604
7. Australia, $2,305
8. Canada, $1,709
9. Sweden, $1,600
10. Switzerland, $1,600

Source: *Adweek*, April 22, 1996, p. 17.

Automobile Parts

★ 224 ★

ASIA'S TOP AUTO PARTS FIRMS, 1995

Ranked by: Sales, in millions of U.S. dollars. **Remarks:** Includes profits, profits as a percentage of sales and assets, and overall sales rank. **Number listed:** 20

1. Nippondenso with $15,124.5 million
2. Aisin Seiki, $8,807.5
3. Yazaki Corp., $5,225.5
4. Aisin AW, $3,539.2
5. Woori Auto Sales Co., $3,494.6
6. Zexel, $2,764.6
7. Calsonic, $2,514.0
8. NGK Insulators, $2,494.7
9. Toyoda Gosei, $2,433.5
10. NHK Spring, $2,379.6

Source: *Asiaweek*, The Asiaweek 1,000, November 22, 1996, p. 164.

★ 225 ★

BRAZIL'S TOP AUTO COMPONENT IMPORTS, 1995

Ranked by: Value of imports, in millions of U.S. dollars. **Number listed:** 20

1. Gearboxes with $502.09 million
2. Subassemblies, $329.99
3. Spark ignition and internal combustion engines, $299.02
4. Subassemblies and parts for engines, $97.07
5. Ball bearings, $94.56
6. Brakes and servobrakes, $87.31
7. Subassemblies of fuel pumps, $83.40
8. Subassemblies and accessories for vehicle bodies, $74.20
9. Cylinder blocks, valve heads, and crank cases, $60.53
10. Joints and gaskets, $57.18

Source: *National Trade Data Bank*, June 19, 1997, p. ISA970601.

★ 226 ★

LARGEST MOTOR VEHICLE AND PARTS COMPANIES, 1995

Ranked by: Revenue, in millions of U.S. dollars. **Remarks:** Notes profits and global rank. **Number listed:** 26

1. General Motors (United States) with $168,829 million
2. Ford Motor (United States), $137,137
3. Toyota Motor (Japan), $111,052
4. Daimler-Benz (Germany), $72,256
5. Nissan Motor (Japan), $62,568
6. Volkswagen (Germany), $61,489
7. Chrysler (United States), $53,195
8. Fiat (Italy), $46,468

9. Honda Motor (Japan), $44,056
10. Renault (France), $36,895

Source: *Fortune,* The Global 500: World's Biggest Corporations (annual), August 5, 1996, p. F-23.

★ **227** ★

TOP AUTO COMPONENT MAKERS IN FRANCE
Ranked by: Turnover, in millions of French francs (FFr).
Remarks: Data exclude non-automotive business.
Number listed: 10

1. Valeo with FFr16,100 million
2. Bertrand Faurs, FFr9,750
3. ECIA, FFr6,910
4. Sommer Allibert, FFr5,450
5. Sylea, FFr3,500
6. Plastic Omnium, FFr3,060
7. Valfond, FFr2,490
8. Reydel, FFr1,670
9. MGI Coutier, FFr1,460
10. Montupet, FFr1,180

Source: *Financial Times*, April 10, 1996, p. 15.

★ **228** ★

TOP AUTO COMPONENT MAKERS IN GERMANY
Ranked by: Turnover, in millions of deutschmarks (DM). **Remarks:** Data exclude non-automotive business.
Number listed: 10

1. Robert Bosch with DM19,500 million
2. Thyssen, DM8,750
3. Continental, DM8,395
4. Mannesmann, DM5,423
5. ZF, DM5,050
6. Krupp-Hoesch, DM3,950
7. Siemens, DM3,900
8. ITT, DM3,400
9. Hella, DM2,216
10. Mahle, DM2,111

Source: *Financial Times*, April 10, 1996, p. 15.

★ **229** ★

TOP AUTO COMPONENT MAKERS IN JAPAN
Ranked by: Turnover, in millions of yen (¥). **Remarks:** Data exclude non-automotive business. **Number listed:** 10

1. Nippondenso with ¥1,427,000 million
2. Aisin Seiki, ¥786,000
3. Zexel, ¥260,000
4. Calsonic, ¥242,000
5. Koito Manuf., ¥233,000
6. Unisai Jecs, ¥228,000
7. NHK Spring, ¥219,000
8. Tokai Rika, ¥191,000
9. NOK, ¥186,000
10. Press Kogyo, ¥172,000

Source: *Financial Times*, April 10, 1996, p. 15.

★ **230** ★

TOP AUTOMOBILE PARTS MANUFACTURERS IN JAPAN
Ranked by: Income, in millions of yen (¥). **Number listed:** 10

1. Nippondenso Co. with ¥71,486 million
2. Aisin Seiki, ¥10,910
3. Aisin AV, ¥9,665
4. Futaba Industrial, ¥8,949
5. Sango Co., ¥6,074
6. Usui Kokusai Sangyo Kaisha, ¥4,959
7. Araco, ¥4,840
8. Toyota Auto Body, ¥4,558
9. Toyoda Gosei, ¥4,529
10. Calsonic, ¥4,527

Source: *Tokyo Business Today*, August 1995, p. 26.

★ **231** ★

TOP BRAKES AND BRAKES COMPONENTS MANUFACTURERS IN BRAZIL
Ranked by: Annual sales, in millions of U.S. dollars.
Remarks: Notes each company's net worth. **Number listed:** 10

1. Freios Varga with $188,066.7 million
2. ITT Automotive, $116,432.4
3. Allied Signal, $110,104.9
4. Frans-Le, $94,449.0
5. Master, $40,621.0
6. Cobreq, $36,901.0
7. Knorr, $29,290.0
8. Tecalon, $20,028.9
9. Controil Freios, $8,581.0
10. Controil, $6,705.0

Source: *National Trade Data Bank*, June 19, 1997, p. ISA970601.

★ **232** ★

TOP ELECTRIC PARTS MANUFACTURERS IN BRAZIL
Ranked by: Annual sales, in millions of U.S. dollars.
Remarks: Notes each company's net worth. **Number listed:** 10

1. Wapsa with $186,295.0 million
2. Robert Bosch, $156,691.6
3. Arteb, $83,925.0
4. NGK, $67,332.1
5. Electronica Dyna, $28,718.0
6. HL, $27,537.9
7. Shreder V lvulas, $21,819.0
8. Mar lia, $13,526.0
9. Lucas Elect., $13,495.0
10. Wahler, $2,505.6

Source: *National Trade Data Bank*, June 19, 1997, p. ISA970601.

★ 233 ★
TOP ENGINE AND ENGINE COMPONENT MANUFACTURERS IN BRAZIL
Ranked by: Annual sales, in millions of U.S. dollars.
Remarks: Notes each company's net worth. **Number listed:** 11

1. Iochpe-Maxion with $598,293.20 million
2. MWM, $295,959.50
3. Metal Leve, $215,387.00
4. Tekside, $212,938.00
5. Cummins, $180,561.00
6. Sifco, $168,585.00
7. Behr, $23,494.00
8. Irm os Zen, $19,244.09
9. Liebau, $16,700.0
10. Colombia, $14,016.0

Source: *National Trade Data Bank*, June 19, 1997, p. ISA970601.

★ 234 ★
TOP MANUFACTURERS OF AUTO ACCESSORIES IN BRAZIL
Ranked by: Annual sales, in millions of U.S. dollars.
Remarks: Notes each company's net worth. **Number listed:** 10

1. Metagal with $93,384.5 million
2. Kadron, $53,116.0
3. Macisa, $50,170.0
4. Tecnon, $24,333.9
5. Bianco & Savino, $21,500.0
6. Emeege, $14,739.0
7. Rovel, $13,802.0
8. Truffi, $9,670.0
9. J.E. Teixeira, $6,526.0
10. IAM, $6,232.0

Source: *National Trade Data Bank*, June 19, 1997, p. ISA970601.

★ 235 ★
TOP MANUFACTURERS OF BODIES AND BODY COMPONENTS IN BRAZIL
Ranked by: Annual sales, in millions of U.S. dollars.
Remarks: Notes each company's net worth. **Number listed:** 10

1. Brasinca with $120,788.2 million
2. Plascar, $111,167.0
3. Plasticos Mueller, $72,260.0
4. Aethra, $64,952.0
5. Zanettini Barossi, $27,222.0
6. Hammer, $26,126.0
7. Pollone, $23,769.0
8. Comil, $17,569.0
9. Igasa, $4,780.0
10. Lider Viaturas, $3,048.0

Source: *National Trade Data Bank*, June 19, 1997, p. ISA970601.

★ 236 ★
TOP MANUFACTURERS OF PARTS FOR VEHICLE INTERIORS IN BRAZIL
Ranked by: Annual sales, in millions of U.S. dollars.
Remarks: Notes each company's net worth. **Number listed:** 6

1. Coplatex with $114,965.0 million
2. Acill, $76,908.0
3. Resil Minas, $37,421.0
4. Teperman, $29,103.0
5. Plavigor, $28,053.0
6. Grammar, $15,221.3

Source: *National Trade Data Bank*, June 19, 1997, p. ISA970601.

★ 237 ★
TOP MANUFACTURERS OF SHOCK ABSORBERS AND SPRINGS IN BRAZIL
Ranked by: Annual sales, in millions of U.S. dollars.
Remarks: Notes each company's net worth. **Number listed:** 8

1. Cofap with $411,539.1 million
2. Nakata Ind. Com., $104,052.0
3. Hoesch, $84,766.6
4. Monroe, $53,847.0
5. Cundumel Metais, $31,788.0
6. C. Fabrini, $30,612.0
7. Suzuki, $4,181.0
8. Fenamor, $2,656.9

Source: *National Trade Data Bank*, June 19, 1997, p. ISA970601.

★ 238 ★
TOP MANUFACTURERS OF WHEELS IN BRAZIL
Ranked by: Annual sales, in millions of U.S. dollars.
Remarks: Notes each company's net worth. **Number listed:** 4

1. Borlem with $103,891.0 million
2. FPS, $18,922.7
3. Scorro, $8,242.0
4. Jolly, $2,465.8

Source: *National Trade Data Bank*, June 19, 1997, p. ISA970601.

★ 239 ★
TOP PRODUCERS OF AUTO BATTERIES IN BRAZIL
Ranked by: Annual sales, in millions of U.S. dollars.
Remarks: Notes each company's net worth. **Number listed:** 7

1. Microlite with $249,933.0 million
2. Moura Acumuladores, $30,075.0
3. Ipojuca, $20,343.0
4. Nife, $19,979.0
5. Durex, $11,936.0
6. Tudor, $5,452.7

7. Electromoura PE, $2,389.0

Source: *National Trade Data Bank*, June 19, 1997, p. ISA970601.

★ 240 ★

TOP TRANSMISSIONS AND TRANSMISSION COMPONENTS MANUFACTURERS IN BRAZIL

Ranked by: Annual sales, in millions of U.S. dollars.
Remarks: Notes each company's net worth. **Number listed:** 10

1. ZF with $264,547.0 million
2. Clark, $183,286.0
3. Albarus, $174,994.3
4. Rockwell, $102,331.0
5. DHB, $68,482.0
6. Cinpal, $42,409.0
7. Motogear Engrenagens, $32,652.0
8. Rayton, $20,953.0
9. Moto Pe as, $20,556.5
10. Minusa, $18,682.0

Source: *National Trade Data Bank*, June 19, 1997, p. ISA970601.

Automobile Plants

★ 241 ★

LARGEST AUTOMOBILE FACTORIES IN EUROPE

Ranked by: Annual production capacity, in units produced. **Remarks:** Notes models produced. **Number listed:** 40

1. Wolfsburg (Germany, Volkswagen) with 1,100,000
2. Longbridge (United Kingdom, Rover), 550,000
3. Melfi (Italy, Fiat), 500,000
4. Turin-Mirafiori (Italy, Fiat), 500,000
5. Sochaux (France, Peugeot), 425,000
6. Saragossa (Spain, Opel), 420,000
7. Genk (Belgium, Ford), 410,000
8. Anvers (Belgium, Opel), 400,000
9. Barcelona-Martorell (Spain, SEAT), 400,000
10. Mulhouse (France, Peugeot), 400,000

Source: *L'Expansion*, June 11, 1997, p. 101.

★ 242 ★

MOST EXPENSIVE AUTO FACILITIES WORLDWIDE

Ranked by: Investment, in millions of U.S. dollars. Figures are from 1990 to the present. **Number listed:** 21

1. Samsung (Pusan, South Korea) with $4,540 million
2. Volkswagen AG (Sao Paulo, Brazil), $3,000
3. Ford Motor Co./Volkswagen AG (Palmela, Portugal), $2,800
4. Ford Motor Co. (Sao Paulo, Brazil), $2,500

5. Ssangyong (Dalsung, South Korea), $2,411
6. Chain Tai International Ltd. (Lang Chi Island, China), $2,000
7. Ford Motor Co. (Hermosillo, Mexico), $1,500
8. Adam Opel AG (Eisenach, Germany), $1,480
9. First Automobile Corp./Volkswagen AG (Changchun, China), $1,200
10. Hyundai Motor (New Delhi, India), $1,100

Source: *Site Selection*, December 1996, p. 1067.

★ 243 ★

MOST PRODUCTIVE AUTO PLANTS IN EUROPE

Ranked by: Number of vehicles produced annually per worker. **Number listed:** 9

1. Opel Eisenach (Germany) with 71.9 vehicles
2. Fiat Melfi (Italy), 64.3
3. Nissan Sunderland (United Kingdom), 56.7
4. Honda Swindon (United Kingdom), 55.9
5. Opel Saragosse (Spain), 54.0
6. Ford Valence (Spain), 52.9
7. Toyota Burnaston (United Kingdom), 52.1
8. Ford Saarlouis (Germany), 48.1
9. Renault Flins (France), 46.9

Source: *L'Express*, March 13, 1997, p. 30.

Automobile Service Stations

★ 244 ★

LEADING GAS STATIONS IN SPAIN

Ranked by: Number of outlets. **Number listed:** 8

1. Repsol with 1,800 outlets
2. Campsa, 1,750
3. Cepsa/ELF, 1,700
4. Shell, 210
5. Galp, 122
6. Total, 107
7. Mobil Oil, 70
8. Other, 200

Source: http:// www.templeton.ox.ac.uk/www/insts/ oxirm/digest/wint9596/featsp.htm, June 9, 1997, p. 11.

★ 245 ★

LEADING TECHNICAL INSPECTION CENTERS IN FRANCE, 1996

Ranked by: Market share, in percent. **Remarks:** Also notes number of centers and number of inspections performed. **Number listed:** 7

1. Cecomut with 19.6%
2. Autosur, 18.6%
3. Securitest, 17.5%
4. Dekra, 15.8%
5. Autovision, 14.7%
6. Veritas, 11.8%

7. Independent, 1.8%
Source: *National Trade Data Bank*, May 29, 1997, p. ISA970401.

★ 246 ★
SERVICE STATION LEADERS IN THAILAND, 1996
Ranked by: Market share for the third quarter of 1996, in percent. **Number listed:** 17
1. PTT with 15.7%
2. Shell, 10.9%
3. BCP, 10.6%
4. Esso, 8.6%
5. Caltex, 5.9%
6. PA, 4.8%
7. PT, 2.9%
8. Cosmo, 1.8%
9. Susco, 1.5%
10. Other, 37.2%
Source: *Bangkok Post*, January 13, 1997, p. 1.

★ 247 ★
TOP GAS STATION OPERATORS IN ECUADOR
Ranked by: Number of stations. **Remarks:** Includes multinational and domestic firms. **Number listed:** 10
1. Petroleos y Servicios with 205
2. Petrocomercial, 108
3. Petrolgupsa, 64
4. Perolitoral, 47
5. Mobil, 36
6. Shell, 36
7. Texaco, 32
8. Triperol Gas, 13
9. Petrolrios, 6
10. Baneybo, 2
Source: *National Trade Data Bank*, July 18, 1995, p. IMI950717.

★ 248 ★
TOP GAS STATION RETAILERS IN EASTERN GERMANY, 1996
Ranked by: Number of outlets as of January 1, 1996. **Number listed:** 23
1. Elf/Amoco with 466 outlets
2. Aral/Gasolin, 254
3. Dea/Texaco, 145
4. Shell, 127
5. Esso, 113
6. Hem-Hamburg, 84
7. Avia, 73
8. BP, 72
9. Agip, 60
10. Conoco, 47
Source: *National Trade Data Bank*, July 15, 1996, p. ISA960601.

★ 249 ★
TOP GAS STATION RETAILERS IN WESTERN GERMANY, 1996
Ranked by: Number of outlets as of January 1, 1996.
Number listed: 23
1. Aral Gasolin with 2,294 outlets
2. Shell, 1,568
3. Dea/Texaco, 1,503
4. Esso, 1,432
5. BP, 1,331
6. Avia, 842
7. Conoco, 531
8. Agip, 422
9. Fina/Chevron, 371
10. Elf/Amoco, 303
Source: *National Trade Data Bank*, July 15, 1996, p. ISA960601.

Automobiles

★ 250 ★
CAR SALES IN CANADA, 1996
Ranked by: Market share based on unit sales, in percent.
Number listed: 11
1. General Motors Cavalier with 6.6%
2. Honda Civic, 5.6%
3. General Motors Sunfire, 5.5%
4. Ford Escort, 5.2%
5. Chrysler Neon, 4.4%
6. Toyota Corolla, 4.4%
7. Ford Taurus, 3.8%
8. General Motors Grand Am, 3.6%
9. Chrysler Intrepid, 3.5%
10. Honda Accord, 3.1%
Source: *Marketing Magazine*, May 26, 1997, p. 17.

★ 251 ★
TOP AUTO MAKERS IN TURKEY, 1996
Ranked by: Domestic production, in number of commercial and passenger vehicles. **Number listed:** 18
1. Tofas (Fiat) with 117,880
2. Renault, 64,474
3. Otosan (Ford), 25,080
4. T. Traktor, 24,046
5. Uzel, 21,586
6. Toyotasa, 21,382
7. B.M.C., 8,982
8. Otoyol (Iveco), 5,310
9. A.O.S. (Isuzu), 4,954
10. Mercedes Benz, 4,786
Source: *National Trade Data Bank*, January 31, 1997, p. ISA961201.

Aviation – Accidents

★ 252 ★

FLIGHT FATALITIES BY REGION, 1991-1996
Ranked by: Fatal accidents from 1991 to June 30, 1996.
Remarks: Also note total number of flights. **Number listed:** 6
1. Asia with 14
2. Europe, 8
3. North America and Caribbean, 6
4. Africa, 5
5. South and Central America, 5
6. Australia, 0
Source: *Business Travel News*, March 17, 1997, p. 12.

Baby Foods
See: **Infants' Food**

Bahamas – see under individual headings

Bahrain – see under individual headings

Balance of Trade

★ 253 ★

U.S. BUSINESS COMPLAINTS ON UNFAIR TRADE PRACTICES, 1996
Ranked by: Number of complaints. **Remarks:** Figures cover tariffs customs, health regulations, intellectual property, import restrictions and export subsidies.
Number listed: 20
1. Mexico with 21 complaints
2. Chile, 14
3. Argentina, 10
4. Brazil, 10
5. Venezuela, 9
6. Ecuador, 7
7. Colombia, 6
8. Panama, 5
9. Paraguay, 3
10. Peru, 3
Source: *Latin American Weekly Report*, February 25, 1997, p. 104.

Bangladesh – see under individual headings

Bank Advertising

★ 254 ★

TOP BANK ADVERTISERS IN LATIN AMERICAN PRINT, 1997
Ranked by: Ad spending for January to June 1997, in millions of U.S. dollars. **Number listed:** 10
1. Bradesco Bank with $1.17 million
2. Unibanco, $.84
3. Banco Itau, $.74
4. Banco Sudameris Brasil, $.69
5. Banco Safra, $.54
6. Banco Itau SA, $.48
7. Banco do Brasil, $.45
8. Lloyds Bank, $.45
9. Citibank, $.40
10. Banco da Amazonia SA, $.37
Source: *Advertising Age*, September 1997, p. i29.

Bank Credit Cards

★ 255 ★

TAIWAN'S TOP CREDIT CARD ISSUERS BY NUMBER OF CARDS, 1997
Ranked by: Number of cards as of the end of April 1997.
Remarks: Also notes share of total cards. **Number listed:** 6
1. China Trust with 1,319,525 cards
2. Citibank, 1,020,683
3. Standard Chartered, 270,038
4. Chinfon, 220,097
5. Taishin, 219,582
6. ICBC, 187,363
Source: *Financial Times*, October 2, 1997, p. 21.

★ 256 ★

TAIWAN'S TOP CREDIT CARD ISSUERS BY SPENDING PER CARD, 1997
Ranked by: Spending per card during April 1997, in Taiwan dollars (T$). **Remarks:** Data do not include cash advances. **Number listed:** 6
1. Bank of America with T$7,521
2. United World Chinese, T$6,367
3. Shanghai, T$5,297
4. Citibank, T$5,265
5. Pan Asia, T$4,925
6. Dah An, T$4,782
Source: *Financial Times*, October 2, 1997, p. 21.

Bank Loans

★ 257 ★
ARGENTINA'S TOP BANKS BY LOANS
Ranked by: Market share based on loans arranged, in percent. **Remarks:** Shows loans arranged in millions of U.S. dollars. **Number listed:** 10
1. de la Providencia de Buenos Aires with 19.60%
2. de la Nacion Argentina, 14.20%
3. de Galicia y Buenos Aires, 6.08%
4. Rio de la Plata S.A., 5.65%
5. Citibank N.A., 3.87%
6. The First National Bank of Boston, 3.67%
7. Roberts S.A., 2.69%
8. Frances del Rio de la Plata, 2.66%
9. de la Ciudad de Buenos Aires, 2.55%
10. de Credito Argentino S.A., 2.36%

Source: *National Trade Data Bank*, August 26, 1996, p. ISA960201.

★ 258 ★
INDONESIA'S TOP INTERNATIONAL LOANERS
Ranked by: Loans, in millions of U.S. dollars. **Number listed:** 10
1. Citibank with $492.61 million
2. Dai-Ichi Kangyo Bank, $355.64
3. Sakura Bank, $300.72
4. HSBC Investment Bank, $300.50
5. Paribas, $288.50
6. Bank Dagang Negara, $282.91
7. Credit Lyonnais, $267.54
8. Bank Bira, $243.51
9. Deutsche Bank, $241.86
10. Bank of Tokyo-Mitsubishi, $241.09

Source: *Far Eastern Economic Review*, October 3, 1996, p. 72.

Banks and Banking

★ 259 ★
BANKING COMPANIES POSTING THE LARGEST ASSET GAINS, 1995
Ranked by: Asset gains, in percent. **Remarks:** Also notes total assets. **Number listed:** 10
1. Banco Pinto & Sotto Mayor with 240.7%
2. Banco Comercial Portugues, 166.6%
3. First Chicago NBD Bancorp, Inc., 158.5%
4. Merita Group, 98.5%
5. Lloyds TSB Group Inc., 78.8%
6. Fleet Financial Group, Inc., 73.1%
7. First Union Corp., 70.4%
8. Rolo Banca 1473, 60.5%
9. Swiss Bank Corp., 54.1%

10. Union Bank of Switzerland, 47.7%

Source: *American Banker*, August 5, 1996, p. 10.

★ 260 ★
BANKING COMPANIES POSTING THE LARGEST ASSET LOSSES, 1995
Ranked by: Asset losses, in percent. **Remarks:** Also notes total assets. **Number listed:** 10
1. Long-Term Credit Bank of Japan Ltd. with -20.8%
2. Shoko Chukin Bank, -20.4%
3. Nippon Credit Bank, Ltd., -20.3%
4. Toyo Trust & Banking Co. Ltd., -19.8%
5. Hokkaido Takushoku Bank, Ltd., -19.4%
6. Bank of Yokohama, Ltd., -18.6%
7. Zenshinren Bank, -18.6%
8. Daiwa Bank, Ltd., -18.5%
9. Hyakujushi Bank, Ltd., -18.5%
10. Hiroshima Bank, Ltd., -18.3%

Source: *American Banker*, August 5, 1996, p. 10.

★ 261 ★
LARGEST COMMERCIAL BANKING COMPANIES, 1995
Ranked by: Revenue, in millions of U.S. dollars. **Remarks:** Notes profits and global rank. **Number listed:** 64
1. Deutsche Bank (Japan) with $38,420 million
2. Industrial Bank of Japan, $38,229
3. Sanwa Bank (Japan), $34,886
4. Mitsubishi Bank (Japan), $32,702
5. Credit Agricole (France), $32,343
6. Citicorp (United States), $31,690
7. Fuji Bank (Japan), $31,572
8. Dai-Ichi Kangyo Bank (Japan), $30,345
9. Long-Term Credit Bank (Japan), $29,307
10. Credit Lyonnais (France), $28,496

Source: *Fortune,* The Global 500: World's Biggest Corporations (annual), August 5, 1996, p. F-16.

★ 262 ★
LEADING BOOK RUNNERS FOR ASSET-BACKED ISSUES, 1990-1995
Ranked by: Issue amount, in millions of U.S. dollars. **Remarks:** Notes number of issues. **Number listed:** 15
1. Credit Lyonnais with $4,421.03 million
2. Morgan Stanley & Co., $3,945.00
3. Merrill Lynch & Co., $2,839.87
4. J.P. Morgan, $2,586.25
5. Goldman, Sachs & Co., $2,265.80
6. Banque Paribas, $1,568.30
7. Union Bank of Switzerland, $1,503.66
8. Nomura Group, $1,164.55
9. Barclays Bank, $1,151.37
10. Credit Suisse/CS First Boston Group, $946.77

Source: *Institutional Investor*, October 1996, p. 41.

★ 263 ★

LEADING MULTINATIONAL BANKS BY PROFITABILTY

Ranked by: 5-year return on capital, in percent. **Remarks:** Also notes growth, sales, net income, profit margin, and debt to capital ratio. **Number listed:** 8
1. J.P. Morgan & Co. with 11.3%
2. Citicorp, 11.0%
3. First Chicago NBD, 10.9%
4. Chase Manhattan, 9.7%
5. Bankers Trust NY, 9.1%
6. Bank of Boston, 9.0%
7. BankAmerica, 8.1%
8. Republic New York, 7.0%

Source: *Forbes,* Annual Report on American Industry (annual), January 13, 1997, p. 152.

★ 264 ★

LEAST STABLE BANKING COUNTRIES IN THE FAR EAST

Ranked by: Stability of the banking system, rated by Western bankers. "0" is very positive; "5" is average; "10" is very negative. **Number listed:** 12
1. Vietnam with 8.00
2. Indonesia, 6.41
3. China, 6.05
4. Philippines, 5.76
5. India, 5.56
6. South Korea, 4.84
7. Thailand, 4.65
8. Malaysia, 4.63
9. Hong Kong, 4.53
10. Taiwan, 4.50

Source: *Far Eastern Economic Review*, March 6, 1997, p. 63.

★ 265 ★

MOST RESPECTED EUROPEAN BANKS AND FINANCIAL INSTITUTIONS

Ranked by: Survey based on FT 500 list, as well as polls of investment analysts and chief executives of European companies. See source for details. **Number listed:** 3
1. Deutsche Bank
2. Banco Bilbao Vizcaya
2. Barclays

Source: *Financial Times,* Europe's Most Respected Companies (annual), September 24, 1997, p. 2.

★ 266 ★

TOP ARABIC BANKS BY TOTAL CAPITAL

Ranked by: Total capital, in millions of U.S. dollars. **Remarks:** Notes total assets, net profit, and return on equity. **Number listed:** 100
1. Islamic Development Bank with $3,565,079 million
2. National Commercial Bank, $1,941,879

3. Riyad Bank, $1,904,834
4. Arab Banking Corporation, $1,814,000
5. Arab Bank Group, $1,267,900
6. Al Rajhi Banking and Investment Corp., $1,194,888
7. National Bank of Kuwait, $1,157,465
8. Saudi American Bank, $1,088,592
9. Gulf Investment Corporation, $1,001,070
10. National Bank of Dubai, $975,883

Source: *Euromoney*, September 1996, p. 442.

★ 267 ★

TOP ARRANGERS OF INTERNATIONAL LOANS IN THE ASIA PACIFIC REGION

Ranked by: Share of loans, in percent. **Remarks:** Also notes number of issues. **Number listed:** 20
1. Citibank with 5.91%
2. HSBC Investment Bank, 4.66%
3. Union Bank of Switzerland, 3.62%
4. Sanwa Bank, 3.60%
5. ABN AMRO, 3.26%
6. Sumitomo Bank, 2.88%
7. Chase Manhattan, 2.81%
8. Korea Development Bank, 2.44%
9. Bank of Tokyo-Mitsubishi, 2.23%
10. Societe Generale, 2.20%

Source: *Far Eastern Economic Review*, October 3, 1996, p. 46.

★ 268 ★

TOP ASEAN BANKS BY SHAREHOLDER EQUITY

Ranked by: Shareholders' equity, in millions of U.S. dollars. **Remarks:** Also includes equity and asset growth, net profits, total assets, return on equity and differential. **Number listed:** 25
1. Development Bank of Singapore with $4,330 million
2. Bangkok Bank, $3,695
3. Oversea-Chinese Banking Corp, $3,612
4. United Overseas Bank, $3,157
5. Overseas Union Bank, $2,120
6. Thai Farmers Bank, $2,096
7. Malayan Banking, $2,068
8. Krung Thai Bank, $1,785
9. Siam Commercial Bank, $1,402
10. Post Office Savings Bank Singapore, $1,359

Source: *Euromoney*, December 1996, p. 71.

★ 269 ★

TOP BANKING MARKETS IN THE MIDDLE EAST, 1996

Ranked by: Total banking sector deposits as of June 1996, in millions of U.S. dollars. **Remarks:** Bahrain and Kuwait show March figures; Algeria shows December. Notes foreign assets. **Number listed:** 12
1. Saudi Arabia with $64,446 million

2. Egypt, $51,332
3. United Arab Emirates, $35,037
4. Kuwait, $22,404
5. Lebanon, $17,437
6. Morocco, $15,873
7. Algeria, $12,922
8. Jordan, $9,153
9. Tunisia, $7,909
10. Qatar, $7,272

Source: *Middle East*, February 1997, p. 20.

★ 270 ★
TOP BANKS WORLDWIDE, 1995

Ranked by: Assets, in millions of U.S. dollars as of December 31, 1995. **Remarks:** Notes change from 1994, capital, and net income. **Number listed:** 100

1. Sumitomo Bank (Japan) with $505,932 million
2. Dai-Ichi Kangyo Bank (Japan), $505,211
3. Sanwa Bank (Japan), $505,089
4. Deutsche Bank (Germany), $502,199
5. Fuji Bank (Japan), $489,212
6. Mitsubishi Bank (Japan), $483,440
7. Sakura Bank (Japan), $478,026
8. Norinchukin Bank (Japan), $427,076
9. Credit Agricole (France), $385,400
10. Industrial & Commercial Bank (China), $373,490

Source: *The Wall Street Journal*, September 26, 1996, p. R29.

★ 271 ★
TOP DEVELOPMENT BANKS

Ranked by: Total equity, in millions of U.S. dollars. **Remarks:** Also notes assets and gross disbursements. **Number listed:** 50

1. World Bank with $28,300 million
2. European Investment Bank, $21,977
3. Export-Import Bank of Japan, $13,019
4. Japan Development Bank, $10,407
5. Inter-American Development Bank, $9,910
6. Asian Development Bank, $9,653
7. European Bank for Reconstruction & Development, $3,750
8. Korea Development Bank, $2,460
9. Islamic Development Bank, $1,909
10. African Development Bank, $1,740

Source: *The Banker*, May 1997, p. 79.

★ 272 ★
TOP INDIAN SUB-CONTINENT BANKS BY SHAREHOLDER EQUITY

Ranked by: Shareholders' equity, in millions of U.S. dollars. **Remarks:** Also includes equity and asset growth, net profits, total assets, return on equity and differential. **Number listed:** 25

1. Industrial Development Bank of India with $1,889 million
2. State Bank of India, $1,502
3. Bank of India, $770
4. Canara Bank, $551
5. Central Bank of India, $545
6. UCO Bank, $542
7. Bank of Baroda, $503
8. Indian Overseas Bank, $495
9. Syndicate Bank, $410
10. Punjab National Bank, $402

Source: *Euromoney*, December 1996, p. 71.

★ 273 ★
TOP LOCATIONS FOR FOREIGN BANKS IN EUROPE

Ranked by: Number of foreign branches. **Remarks:** Notes that there were 375 foreign banks in the European Union. **Number listed:** 10

1. Germany with 91
2. France, 85
3. Luxembourg, 58
4. Netherlands, 30
5. Belgium, 29
6. Italy, 23
7. Spain, 23
8. Austria, 13
9. Greece, 9
10. Other, 14

Source: *The Banker*, December 1996, p. 47.

★ 274 ★
TOP NATIONS BY BANKING ASSETS, 1994

Ranked by: Assets, in billions of U.S. dollars. **Number listed:** 10

1. Japan with $7,106 billion
2. United States, $3,620
3. Germany, $3,255
4. United Kingdom, $2,257
5. China, $388
6. Korea, $283
7. Hong Kong, $257
8. Thailand, $153
9. Singapore, $115
10. Indonesia, $90

Source: *Financial Times*, April 29, 1996, p. V.

★ 275 ★
TOP WORLD BANKING COMPANIES, 1995
Ranked by: Total assets as of December 31, 1995, in millions of U.S. dollars. **Remarks:** Also notes percent change and equity capital. **Number listed:** 200
1. Deutsche Bank, AG with $502,279 million
2. Sanwa Bank Ltd., $500,026
3. Sumitomo Bank Ltd., $498,917
4. Dai-Ichi Kangyo Bank Ltd., $497,612
5. Fuji Bank, Ltd., $486,351
6. Sakura Bank, Ltd., $477,079
7. Mitsubishi Bank Ltd., $474,045
8. Norinchukin Bank, $428,644
9. Credit Agricole Mutuel, $384,340
10. Industrial Bank of Japan, $360,638
Source: *American Banker*, August 5, 1996, p. 8.

Banks and Banking – Africa

★ 276 ★
TOP BANKS IN AFRICA
Ranked by: Capital, in millions of U.S. dollars. **Remarks:** Also notes location, as well as capital percentage change, dollar amount, rank, and percentage change for assets. **Number listed:** 100
1. Stanbic (South Africa) with $1,804 million
2. Amalgamated Banks of South Africa, $1,709
3. Nedcor (South Africa), $1,115
4. First National Bank Holdings (South Africa), $1,062
5. Investec Bank (South Africa), $537
6. NBS Bank (South Africa), $337
7. United Bank for Africa (Nigeria), $200
8. Mauritius Commercial Bank (Mauritius), $179
9. First Bank of Nigeria, $178
10. Banque Belgolaise Bank (Belgium), $143
Source: *The Banker,* Top 100 African Banks - By Country (annual), December 1996, p. 84.

Banks and Banking – Algeria

★ 277 ★
TOP BANKS IN ALGERIA
Ranked by: Assets, in millions of U.S. dollars. **Remarks:** Also notes paid-up capital. **Number listed:** 3
1. Banque de l'Agriculture et du Developpement Rural with $8,999 million
2. Banque Exterieure d'Algerie, $7,397
3. Banque Nationale d'Algerie, $6,032
Source: *Bankers' Almanac World Ranking* (annual), 1996, p. 125.

Banks and Banking – Argentina

★ 278 ★
LARGEST PRIVATE BANKS IN ARGENTINA
Ranked by: Assets, in billions of U.S. dollars. **Remarks:** Notes main shareholder. **Number listed:** 5
1. Banco Galicia with $8.0 billion
2. Banco Rio, $5.8
3. Banco Grances, $4.2
4. Bansud, $3.0
5. Banco Credito, $2.8
Source: *The Wall Street Journal*, May 28, 1997, p. A15.

★ 279 ★
LEADING BANKS IN ARGENTINA
Ranked by: Market share based on deposits, in percent. **Number listed:** 11
1. Banco Nacion with 13.8%
2. Banco de la Provincia de Buenos Aires, 11.7%
3. Banco de Galicia, 6.7%
4. Banco Rio, 5.0%
5. Citibank, 5.0%
6. Banco Boston, 3.9%
7. Banco Frances, 3.5%
8. Banco de la Ciudad de Buenos Aires, 3.2%
9. Banco Roberts, 2.9%
10. Banco de Credito Argentino, 2.7%
Source: *Financial Times*, June 12, 1997, p. 17.

★ 280 ★
TOP BANKS IN ARGENTINA
Ranked by: Market share based on deposits, in percent. **Remarks:** Shows deposits in millions of U.S. dollars. **Number listed:** 10
1. de la Nacion Argentina with 14.01%
2. de la Providencia de Buenos Aires, 11.31%
3. de Galicia y Buenos Aires, 6.63%
4. Rio de la Plata S.A., 5.71%
5. Citibank N.A., 5.00%
6. The First National Bank of Boston, 4.23%
7. de la Ciudad de Buenos Aires, 3.13%
8. Frances del Rio de la Plata, 3.12%
9. de Credito Argentino S.A., 2.77%
10. Roberts S.A., 2.52%
Source: *National Trade Data Bank*, August 26, 1996, p. ISA960201.

Banks and Banking – Asia

★ 281 ★
LARGEST BANKS IN ASIA, 1995
Ranked by: Tier One capital, in billions of U.S. dollars.
Remarks: Also notes pre-tax profits. Tier One capital is shareholders' equity plus minority interests. **Number listed:** 10
1. Bank of China with $10.9 billion
2. Industrial and Commercial Bank of China, $10.1
3. China Construction Bank, $4.8
4. Agricultural Bank of China, $4.7
5. Bank of Taiwan, $3.3
6. Bangkok Bank, $2.9
7. Hanil Bank, $2.8
8. Bank of Communications (China), $2.4
9. Cho Hung Bank (South Korea), $2.4
10. Korea Exchange Bank (South Korea), $2.4
Source: *The Economist*, April 12, 1997, p. 26.

★ 282 ★
TOP ASIAN BANKS BY ASSETS, 1995
Ranked by: Assets, in thousands of U.S. dollars.
Remarks: Also notes previous year's rank and percent change. **Number listed:** 200
1. Sumitomo Bank Ltd. with $545,043,834 thousand
2. Sanwa Bank Ltd., $540,316,864
3. Dai-Ichi Kangyo Bank Ltd., $535,732,213
4. Fuji Bank Ltd., $518,730,067
5. Sakura Bank Ltd., $513,898,271
6. Industrial Bank of Japan Ltd., $396,681,990
7. Tokai Bank Ltd., $321,697,893
8. Long-Term Credit Bank of Japan Ltd., $315,938,378
9. Asahi Bank Ltd., $287,195,320
10. Daiwa Bank Ltd., $164,399,640
Source: *Asia's 7,500 Largest Companies* (annual), Dun & Bradstreet, 1997, p. 296+.

★ 283 ★
TOP ASIAN BANKS BY SHAREHOLDER EQUITY
Ranked by: Shareholders' equity, in millions of U.S. dollars. **Remarks:** Also includes equity and asset growth, net profits, total assets, return on equity and differential.
Number listed: 100
1. Bank of China with $12,363 million
2. Industrial & Commercial Bank of China, $11,147
3. Hong Kong & Shanghai Banking Group, $11,057
4. National Australian Bank, $8,968
5. Westpac Banking Corp., $6,466

6. Australia & New Zealand Banking Group, $5,048
7. Agricultural Bank of China, $4,903
8. Commonwealth Bank of Australia, $4,844
9. People's Construction Bank of China, $4,810
10. Development Bank of Singapore, $4,330
Source: *Euromoney*, December 1996, p. 68.

★ 284 ★
TOP ASIAN BANKS, 1996
Ranked by: Capital, in millions of U.S. dollars. **Remarks:** Also lists assets and rank by assets. **Number listed:** 200
1. Bank of China with $10,869 million
2. Industrial & Commercial Bank of China, $10,060
3. National Australia Bank, $7,589
4. Westpac Banking Corporation (Australia), $5,348
5. Commonwealth Bank Group (Australia), $5,110
6. China Construction Bank, $4,810
7. Agricultural Bank of China, $4,670
8. DBS Bank (Singapore), $4,331
9. ANZ Banking Group (Australia), $4,155
10. Oversea-Chinese Banking Corporation (Singapore), $3,611
Source: *The Banker,* Top 200 Asians (annual), October 1996, p. 81.

Banks and Banking – Australia

★ 285 ★
TOP AUSTRALIAN BANKS BY SHAREHOLDER EQUITY
Ranked by: Shareholders' equity, in millions of U.S. dollars. **Remarks:** Also includes equity and asset growth, net profits, total assets, return on equity and differential.
Number listed: 25
1. National Australia Bank with $8,968 million
2. Westpac Banking Corp., $6,466
3. Australia and New Zealand Banking Group, $5,048
4. Commonwealth Bank of Australia, $4,844
5. Bank of Melbourne, $794
6. St. George Bank, $758
7. Bank of New Zealand, $726
8. Bank of South Australia, $491
9. NZI Corp., $482
10. Bank of Western Australia, $471
Source: *Euromoney*, December 1996, p. 71.

★ 286 ★

TOP BANKS IN AUSTRALIA

Ranked by: Deposits, as a percent of all deposits in Australian banks. **Number listed:** 6
1. Commonwealth with 20.6%
2. National Australian Bank, 16.0%
3. Westpac, 14.8%
4. ANZ, 12.8%
5. Regionals, 21.6%
6. Other, 14.3%

Source: *Financial Times*, March 25, 1997, p. 19.

★ 287 ★

TOP BANKS IN AUSTRALIA BY LOANS, 1997

Ranked by: Share of loans as of February 1997, distributed in percent. **Number listed:** 4
1. Commonwealth Bank of Australia with 17%
2. National Australia Bank, 17%
3. The Westpac Bank, 14%
4. The ANZ Bank, 13%

Source: *National Trade Data Bank*, May 7, 1997, p. IMI970507.

★ 288 ★

TOP INTERNATIONAL LENDERS IN AUSTRALIA

Ranked by: Share of loans, in percent. **Remarks:** Also notes number of issues. **Number listed:** 10
1. Citibank with 17.59%
2. Westpac, 16.35%
3. Chase Manhattan, 15.65%
4. Commonwealth Bank of Australia, 12.76%
5. BankAmercia, 11.20%
6. ABN AMRO, 9.13%
7. J.P. Morgan, 3.98%
8. National Australia Bank, 3.91%
9. Deutsche Bank, 3.32%
10. ANZ, 2.52%

Source: *Far Eastern Economic Review*, October 3, 1996, p. 80.

Banks and Banking – Austria

★ 289 ★

TOP BANKS BY TIER ONE CAPITAL IN AUSTRIA, 1995

Ranked by: Tier one capital as of December 1995, in millions of Austrian schillings (AS). **Remarks:** Notes total assets, pre-tax assets, number of employees, and number of branches. **Number listed:** 10
1. Bank Austria with AS30,856 million
2. Creditanstalt-Bankverein, AS25,700
3. GiroCredit, AS12,849
4. First Austrian Bank, AS10,255
5. Raiffeissen Zentralbank Osterreich, AS10,120

6. PSK Banking Group, AS9,695
7. Bank fur Arbeit & Wirtschaft, AS9,522
8. Raiffeisenlandesbank Nierosterreich-Wien, AS4,052
9. Oberbank, AS3,945
10. Landes-Hypothekenbank Tirol, AS3,125

Source: *The Banker*, August 1996, p. 32.

Banks and Banking – Bahamas

★ 290 ★

TOP BANKS IN THE BAHAMAS

Ranked by: Assets, in millions of U.S. dollars. **Remarks:** Also notes paid-up capital. **Number listed:** 2
1. Bank of the Bahamas Limited with $156 million
2. Ansbacher (Bahamas) Limited, $83

Source: *Bankers' Almanac World Ranking* (annual), 1996, p. 132.

Banks and Banking – Bangladesh

★ 291 ★

TOP BANKS IN BANGLADESH

Ranked by: Assets, in millions of U.S. dollars. **Remarks:** Also notes paid-up capital. **Number listed:** 13
1. Sonali Bank with $2,840 million
2. Janata Bank, $2,020
3. Agrani Bank, $1,998
4. Bangladesh Krishi Bank, $979
5. International Finance Investment and Commerce Bank Limited, $509
6. National Bank Limited, $501
7. Uttara Bank Ltd., $466
8. Islami Bank Bangladesh Ltd., $465
9. Arab Bangladesh Bank Limited, $366
10. Rajshahi Krishi Unnayan Bank, $349

Source: *Bankers' Almanac World Ranking* (annual), 1996, p. 132.

Banks and Banking – Belarus

★ 292 ★

TOP BANKS IN BELARUS

Ranked by: Assets, in millions of U.S. dollars. **Remarks:** Also notes paid-up capital. **Number listed:** 7
1. Belarussian Joint Stock Commercial Agro-Industrial Bank with $203.00 million
2. Priorbank, $198.00
3. Belarussian Joint Stock Commercial Bank for Industry and Construction, $193.00

4. Belvnesheconombank, $182.00
5. Byelorussian Joint Stock Commercial Bank for Reconstruction and Devel., $128.00
6. Bank "Poisk", $49.00
7. Bank "OLiMP", $4.05

Source: *Bankers' Almanac World Ranking* (annual), 1996, p. 133.

Banks and Banking – Bermuda

★ 293 ★
TOP BANKS IN BERMUDA
Ranked by: Assets, in millions of U.S. dollars. **Remarks:** Also notes paid-up capital. **Number listed:** 3
1. Bank of Bermuda Limited with $7,390 million
2. Bank of N.T. Butterfield & Son Ltd., $4,282
3. Bermuda Commercial Bank Limited, $273

Source: *Bankers' Almanac World Ranking* (annual), 1996, p. 136.

Banks and Banking – Botswana

★ 294 ★
TOP BANKS IN BOTSWANA
Ranked by: Assets, in millions of U.S. dollars. **Remarks:** Also notes paid-up capital. **Number listed:** 4
1. Barclays Bank of Botswana Limited with $436 million
2. Standard Chartered Bank Botswana Limited, $323
3. Stanbic Bank Botswana Limited, $80
4. National Development Bank, $36

Source: *Bankers' Almanac World Ranking* (annual), 1996, p. 136.

Banks and Banking – Brazil

★ 295 ★
TOP BRAZILIAN BANKS BY RETURN ON EQUITY, 1996
Ranked by: Return on equity, in percent. **Remarks:** Includes the top banks ranked by assets. **Number listed:** 6
1. Safra with 23.7% return
2. Itau, 15.4%
3. Bradesco, 15.1%
4. Sudemeris, 14.2%
5. Unibanco, 13.2%
6. Real, 11.4%

Source: *The Wall Street Journal*, March 7, 1997, p. A8.

Banks and Banking – Bulgaria

★ 296 ★
TOP BANKS IN BULGARIA
Ranked by: Tier One capital, in millions of levs (Le). **Remarks:** Also notes total assets, pre-tax assets, number of employees, and number of branches. **Number listed:** 5
1. Bulbank with Le24,754 million
2. State Savings Bank, Le12,481
3. First Private Bank, Le2,146
4. First East International Bank, Le1,659
5. Economic Bank, Le1,467

Source: *The Banker*, October 1996, p. 59.

★ 297 ★
TOP BANKS IN BULGARIA
Ranked by: Assets, in millions of U.S. dollars. **Remarks:** Also notes paid-up capital. **Number listed:** 20
1. BULBANK Ltd. with $4,159 million
2. Bulgarska Narodna Banka, $3,658
3. Bank for Economic Projects, $1,337
4. United Bulgarian Bank Plc., $792
5. Economic Bank, $778
6. First Private Bank Ltd., $586
7. Hebros Bank, $520
8. Trade & Savings Bank plc, $344
9. Expressbank, $335
10. Commercial Bank Biochim, $269

Source: *Bankers' Almanac World Ranking* (annual), 1996, p. 139.

Banks and Banking – Burkina Faso

★ 298 ★
TOP BANKS IN BURKINA FASO
Ranked by: Tier one capital, in millions of U.S. dollars. **Remarks:** Also notes capital percentage change, assets, assets percentage change, pre-tax profits, and performance. **Number listed:** 3
1. B. Int pour le Comm, l'Ind & l'Ag with $12 million
2. Caisse Nat. de Credit Agricole du Burkina, $11
3. Banque Meridien BIAO Burkina, $10

Source: *The Banker,* Top 100 African Banks - By Country, December 1996, p. 86.

Banks and Banking – Burundi

★ **299** ★
TOP BANKS IN BURUNDI
Ranked by: Assets, in millions of U.S. dollars. **Remarks:** Also notes paid-up capital. **Number listed:** 3
1. Banque de Credit de Bujumbura "B.C.B." SARL with $72 million
2. Banque Commerciale du Burundi SARL "BANCOBU", $62
3. Banque Nationale pour le Developpement Economique Sarl, $37

Source: *Bankers' Almanac World Ranking* (annual), 1996, p. 140.

Banks and Banking – Cameroon

★ **300** ★
TOP BANKS IN CAMEROON
Ranked by: Tier one capital, in millions of U.S. dollars. **Remarks:** Also notes capital percentage change, assets, assets percentage change, pre-tax profit, and performance. **Number listed:** 2
1. B. Int pour le Comm & l'Ind du Cameroun with $21 million
2. Credit Foncier du Cameroon, $15

Source: *The Banker,* Top 100 African Banks - By Country (annual), December 1996, p. 86.

Banks and Banking – Canada

★ **301** ★
LARGEST BANKS IN CANADA, 1996
Ranked by: Market share based on deposits as of October 31, 1966, in percent. **Number listed:** 10
1. Royal Bank of Canada with 22.50%
2. CIBC, 17.70%
3. Bank of Montreal, 16.50%
4. Bank of Nova Scotia, 16.40%
5. Toronto Dominion Bank, 12.20%
6. National Bank of Canada, 5.60%
7. Laurentian Bank of Canada, 1.50%
8. Canadian Western Bank, 0.20%
9. Other domestic banks, 0.03%
10. Foreign banks, 7.40%

Source: *Marketing Magazine,* May 26, 1997, p. 18.

Banks and Banking – Cayman Islands

★ **302** ★
TOP BANKS IN THE CAYMAN ISLANDS
Ranked by: Assets, in millions of U.S. dollars. **Remarks:** Also notes paid-up capital. **Number listed:** 2
1. Cayman National Bank Ltd. with $280 million
2. Midland Bank Trust Corporation (Cayman) Limited, $109

Source: *Bankers' Almanac World Ranking* (annual), 1996, p. 142.

Banks and Banking – Central Europe

★ **303** ★
TOP CENTRAL EUROPEAN BANKS
Ranked by: Capital, in millions of U.S. dollars. **Remarks:** Notes percent change. **Number listed:** 100
1. Komercni banka with $988 million
2. Ceska Sporitelna, $752
3. Bank Handlowy w Warszawie, $725
4. Bank Gospordarki Zywnosciowej, $610
5. Ceskoslovenska obchodni banka, $537
6. Investicni a Postovni banka, $494
7. Privredna Banka Zagreb, $437
8. Vseobecna uverova banka, $403
9. Bank Pekao, $391
10. Bulbank, $349

Source: *The Banker,* Top 100 Central Europeans (annual), April 1997, p. 38.

Banks and Banking – Channel Islands

★ **304** ★
TOP BANKS IN THE CHANNEL ISLANDS
Ranked by: Assets, in millions of U.S. dollars. **Remarks:** Also notes paid-up capital. **Number listed:** 43
1. British Bank of the Middle East with $5,002 million
2. Midland Bank International Finance Corporation Limited, $4,059
3. Morgan Grenfell (C.I.) Limited, $3,260
4. Cantrade Private Bank Switzerland (C.I.) Limited, $2,266
5. Standard Chartered Bank (C.I.) Limited, $2,158
6. TSB Bank Channel Islands Limited, $1,829
7. Royal Bank of Canada (Channel Islands) Limited, $1,645
8. Credit Suisse (Guernsey) Limited, $1,579
9. AIB Bank (C.I.) Limited, $1,456

10. ANZ Grindlays Bank (Jersey) Limited, $1,398
Source: *Bankers' Almanac World Ranking* (annual), 1996, p. 142.

Banks and Banking – China

★ 305 ★
TOP FOREIGN BANKS IN CHINA, 1995
Ranked by: Loans, in millions of U.S. dollars. **Remarks:** Also provides figures for assets and profits. **Number listed:** 20
1. HSBC with $1,061.8 million
2. Bank of Tokyo, $1,011.6
3. Sanwa Bank, $938.8
4. Industrial Bank of Japan, $706.6
5. Dai-Ichi Kangyo Bank, $608.1
6. Sumitomo Bank, $593.4
7. Sakura Bank, $589.7
8. Fuji Bank, $546.1
9. Nanyang Commercial Bank, $486.1
10. Bank of East Asia, $459.7

Source: *Asiamoney*, January 1997, p. 16.

Banks and Banking – Congo

★ 306 ★
TOP BANKS IN THE CONGO
Ranked by: Tier one capital, in millions of U.S. dollars. **Remarks:** Also notes capital percentage change, assets, assets percentage change, pre-tax profit, and performance. **Number listed:** 2
1. Banque Internationale de Congo with $9 million
2. Union Congolaise de Banques, $9

Source: *The Banker,* Top 100 African Banks - By Country (annual), December 1996, p. 86.

Banks and Banking – Croatia

★ 307 ★
TOP CROATIAN BANKS
Ranked by: Tier One capital, in percent. **Remarks:** Also notes total assets, pre-tax profits, profit to capital ratio, number of employees, and number of branches. **Number listed:** 10
1. Privredna Banka Zagreb with 2,324%
2. Zagrebacka Banka, 1,669%
3. Varazdinska Banka, 359%
4. Rijecka Banka, 315%
5. Dubrovacka Banka, 305%

6. Croatia Banka, 217%
7. Dalmatinska Banka DD Zadar, 196%
8. Jadranska Banka, 175%
9. Karlovacka Banka, 139%
10. Bjelovarska Banka, 120%

Source: *The Banker*, May 1997, p. 48.

Banks and Banking – Cyprus

★ 308 ★
TOP BANKS IN CYRUS
Ranked by: Assets, in millions of U.S. dollars. **Remarks:** Also notes paid-up capital. **Number listed:** 5
1. Bank of Cyprus Limited with $6,086 million
2. Cyprus Popular Bank Limited, $3,306
3. Hellenic Bank Limited, $872
4. Co-operative Central Bank Ltd., $841
5. Lombard NatWest Bank Ltd., $643

Source: *Bankers' Almanac World Ranking* (annual), 1996, p. 148.

Banks and Banking – Czech Republic

★ 309 ★
CZECH REPUBLIC'S BANKING MARKET, 1995
Ranked by: Share of total banking sector. **Number listed:** 7
1. Komercni Banka with 20%
2. Ceska Sporitelna, 19%
3. IPB, 11%
4. CSOB, 10%
5. Agrobanka, 4%
6. Zivnostenska Banka, 2%
7. Others, 35%

Source: *Financial Times*, October 23, 1996, p. 3.

★ 310 ★
TOP BANKS IN THE CZECH REPUBLIC
Ranked by: Assets, in millions of U.S. dollars. **Remarks:** Also notes paid-up capital. **Number listed:** 19
1. Ceska Sporitelna as with $12,826 million
2. Komercni Banka as, $11,110
3. Investicni a Postovni Banka as, $7,398
4. Ceskoslovenska Obchodni Banka as, $5,537
5. Konsolidacni banka Praha, spu, $3,964
6. Agrobanka Praha Ltd., $1,783
7. Zivnostenska Banka as, $979
8. Pragobanka as, $661
9. Citibank as, $485
10. Moravia Bank as, $447

Source: *Bankers' Almanac World Ranking* (annual), 1996, p. 149.

★ 311 ★
TOP CZECH BANKS
Ranked by: Market share, in percent. **Number listed:** 6
1. Ceska Sportitelna with 34.5%
2. Komercni Banka, 22.6%
3. Investicni A Postovni Banka, 11.5%
4. Ceskoslovenska Obchodni Banka, 7.7%
5. Agrobanka, 4.7%
6. Other, 19.0%

Source: *Global Finance*, July 1996, p. 69.

Banks and Banking – Djibouti

★ 312 ★
TOP BANKS IN DJIBOUTI
Ranked by: Assets, in millions of U.S. dollars. **Remarks:** Also notes paid-up capital. **Number listed:** 3
1. Banque pour le Commerce et l'Industrie-Mer Rouge with $177 million
2. Banque Indosuez Mer Rouge, $122
3. Banque Albaraka Djibouti, $27

Source: *Bankers' Almanac World Ranking* (annual), 1996, p. 151.

Banks and Banking – Dominican Republic

★ 313 ★
TOP BANKS IN DOMINICAN REPUBLIC
Ranked by: Assets, in millions of U.S. dollars. **Remarks:** Also notes paid-up capital. **Number listed:** 4
1. Banco de Reservas de la Republica Dominicana with $883 million
2. Banco Popular Dominicano, $580
3. Banco del Comercio Dominicano SA, $339
4. Banco Dominicano del Progreso SA, $98

Source: *Bankers' Almanac World Ranking* (annual), 1996, p. 151.

Banks and Banking – Ecuador

★ 314 ★
TOP BANKS IN ECUADOR
Ranked by: Assets, in millions of U.S. dollars. **Remarks:** Also notes paid-up capital. **Number listed:** 8
1. Banco del Pacifico SA with $1,690 million
2. Banco del Pichincha CA, $657
3. Filanbanco SA, $499
4. Banco de la Produccion SA, $174
5. Banco Popular del Ecuador, $162
6. Banco Amazonas SA, $130

7. Banco La Previsora, $128
8. Banco Sociedad General de Credito CA, $47

Source: *Bankers' Almanac World Ranking* (annual), 1996, p. 151.

Banks and Banking – Estonia

★ 315 ★
TOP BANKS IN ESTONIA
Ranked by: Assets, in millions of U.S. dollars. **Remarks:** Also notes paid-up capital. **Number listed:** 12
1. Bank of Estonia with $555 million
2. Hansabank Ltd., $166
3. North Estonian Bank, $83
4. Estonian Investment Bank, $59
5. Tallinna Pank, $50
6. Estonian Bank of Industry, $45
7. Estonian Forexbank, $43
8. Virumaa Kommertspank, $25
9. ERA-Bank Ltd., $17
10. EVEA Bank, $16

Source: *Bankers' Almanac World Ranking* (annual), 1996, p. 153.

Banks and Banking – Ethiopia

★ 316 ★
TOP BANKS IN ETHIOPIA
Ranked by: Tier one capital, in millions of U.S. dollars. **Remarks:** Also notes capital percentage change, assets, assets percentage change, pre-tax profits, and performance. **Number listed:** 2
1. Commercial Bank of Ethiopia with $44 million
2. Construction & Business Bank, $9

Source: *The Banker,* Top 100 African Banks - By Country, December 1996, p. 86.

Banks and Banking – Europe

★ 317 ★
TOP BANKS IN EUROPE BY ASSETS
Ranked by: Total assets, in millions of European Currency Units (ECUs). **Remarks:** Also notes number of employees. **Number listed:** 500
1. Deutsche Bank A.G. with 313.122 million ECUs
2. Credit Lyonnais, 272.591
3. ABN AMRO Holding NV, 257.304
4. Schweizerische Bankgesellschaft, 247.580
5. H.S.B.C. Holdings Plc, 241.743

6. Dresdner Bank A.G., 219.906
7. Westdeutsche Landesbank-Girozentrale-Duesseldorf/Muenster, 194.552
8. Schweizerischer Bankverein, 184.525
9. Commerzbank A.G., 183.451
10. Barclays Plc, 179.691

Source: *Duns Europa,* (annual), vol. 4, Dun & Bradstreet, 1997, p. 131.

★ 318 ★
TOP EUROPEAN BANKS
Ranked by: Market capitalization, in billions of U.S. dollars. **Remarks:** Includes net income figures. **Number listed:** 20

1. HSBC with $38.32 billion
2. UBS, $25.28
3. Lloyds TSB, $24.52
4. Deutsche Bank, $22.74
5. ING, $21.90
6. Barclays, $18.38
7. National Westminster, $16.84
8. ABN Amro Holding, $16.37
9. CS Holding, $15.81
10. SBC, $13.49

Source: *Financial Times,* June 17, 1996, p. 23.

Banks and Banking, Foreign

★ 319 ★
TOP FOREIGN BANKS IN JAPAN
Ranked by: Income, in millions of yen (¥). **Number listed:** 10

1. Bank of China with ¥2,814 million
2. Deutsche Bank, ¥2,622
3. Commerzbank, ¥1,413
4. Hanil Bank, ¥716
5. Banco do Brasil S.A., ¥683
6. Barclays Bank, ¥681
7. Shinhan Bank, ¥590
8. Cho Hung Bank, ¥537
9. State Street Bank and Trust, ¥529
10. Toronto-Dominion Bank, ¥430

Source: *Tokyo Business Today,* August 1995, p. 27.

★ 320 ★
TOP FOREIGN BANKS IN LATIN AMERICA, 1996
Ranked by: Assets, in millions of U.S. dollars. **Remarks:** Also provides figures for deposits and loans. **Number listed:** 10

1. Banco Santander (Chile) with $10,225 million
2. CCF Brasil (Brazil), $6,758
3. BBV (Mexico), $6,240
4. Bank of Boston (Brazil), $5,410
5. Citibank (Argentina), $4,237

6. Bank of Boston (Argentina), $4,002
7. Citibank (Brazil), $3,412
8. Citibank (Chile), $3,225
9. ABN Amro Bank (Brazil), $3,209
10. Continental (Peru), $2,478

Source: *Latin Trade,* The Top 50 Banks (annual), July 1997, p. 44.

Banks and Banking, Foreign – Canada

★ 321 ★
TOP FOREIGN BANKS IN CANADA, 1995
Ranked by: Revenue, in thousands of Canadian dollars. **Remarks:** Also notes profit, return on capital, assets, return on assets, and capital ratio. **Number listed:** 11

1. Hongkong Bank of Canada with C$1,431,010 thousand
2. Citibank Canada, C$482,440
3. Union Bank of Switzerland (Canada), C$293,020
4. Societe Generale (Canada), C$182,495
5. Credit Suisse of Canada, C$171,574
6. Banque Nat'l de Paris (Canada), C$163,242
7. Credit Lyonnais Canada, C$130,076
8. Banca Commerciale Italiana, C$126,920
9. Bank of Tokyo-Mitsubishi (Canada), C$121,373
10. Swiss Bank Corp. (Canada), C$113,496

Source: *Globe and Mail,* Globe and Mail Report on Business 1000 (annual), July 1996, p. 157.

Banks and Banking – Gabon

★ 322 ★
TOP BANKS IN GABON
Ranked by: Tier one capital, in millions of U.S. dollars. **Remarks:** Also notes capital percentage change, assets, assets percentage change, pre-tax profit, and performance. **Number listed:** 2

1. B. Int pour le Comm & l'Ind du Gabon with $24 million
2. Union Gabonaise de Banque, $24

Source: *The Banker,* Top 100 African Banks - By Country (annual), December 1996, p. 86.

Banks and Banking – Germany

★ 323 ★
TOP BANKS IN GERMANY, 1995
Ranked by: Assets, in millions of deutschmarks (DM).
Remarks: Also notes net interest income, net commercial income, and operating income for the years 1992 through 1995. **Number listed:** 25
1. Deutsche Bank A.G. with DM721,665 million
2. Dresdner Bank A.G., DM484,482
3. Westdeutsche Landesbank, DM428,622
4. Commerzbank A.G., DM404,167
5. Bayerische Vereinsbank A.G., DM356,543
6. Bayerische Landesbank, DM318,447
7. Bayerische Hypotheken- und Wechsel-Bank A.G., DM298,563
8. DG Bank, DM291,221
9. Bankgesellschaft Berlin A.G., DM281,553
10. Kreditanstalt fur Wiederaufbau, DM249,796
Source: *Germany's Top 500: A Hanbook of Germany's Largest Corporations* (annual), 1997, p. 505.

Banks and Banking – Ghana

★ 324 ★
TOP BANKS IN GHANA
Ranked by: Tier one capital, in millions of U.S. dollars.
Remarks: Also notes capital percentage change, assets, assets percentage change, pre-tax profit, and performance. **Number listed:** 4
1. Ghana Commercial Bank with $46 million
2. Social Security Bank, $25
3. Merchant Bank (Ghana), $11
4. Bank for Housing & Construction, $8
Source: *The Banker,* Top 100 African Banks - By Country (annual), December 1996, p. 86.

Banks and Banking – Greece

★ 325 ★
LEADING GREEK BANKS FOR PROFITS, 1995
Ranked by: Profit, in billions of Greek drachma (GDr).
Remarks: Notes percent change and 1994 profits.
Number listed: 12
1. Alpha Credit with GDr50.7 billion
2. National Bank, GDr41.4
3. Ergobank, GDr37.4
4. Commercial Bank, GDr26.2
5. Mortgage Bank, GDr20.6
6. Ionian Bank, GDr13.6
7. General Bank, GDr6.7

8. Bank of Macedonia-Thrace, GDr3.4
9. National Housing Bank, GDr2.8
10. Piraeus Bank, GDr2.3
Source: *Financial Times*, November 28, 1996, p. II.

Banks and Banking – Greenland

★ 326 ★
TOP BANKS IN GREENLAND
Ranked by: Assets, in millions of U.S. dollars. **Remarks:** Also notes paid-up capital. **Number listed:** 2
1. Bank of Greenland A/S with $277 million
2. Nuna Bank, $209
Source: *Bankers' Almanac World Ranking* (annual), 1996, p. 175.

Banks and Banking – Guatemala

★ 327 ★
TOP BANKS IN GUATEMALA
Ranked by: Assets, in millions of U.S. dollars. **Remarks:** Also notes paid-up capital. **Number listed:** 3
1. Banco Granai & Townson SA with $258 million
2. Banco Agricola Mercantil SA, $173
3. Banco de la Construccion SA, $91
Source: *Bankers' Almanac World Ranking* (annual), 1996, p. 175.

Banks and Banking – Guinea

★ 328 ★
TOP BANKS IN GUINEA
Ranked by: Tier one capital, in millions of U.S. dollars.
Remarks: Also notes capital percentage change, assets, assets percentage change, pre-tax profit, and performance. **Number listed:** 2
1. B. Int pour le Comm & l'Ind de la Guinee with $13 million
2. Societe Generale de Banques en Guinee, $6
Source: *The Banker,* Top 100 African Banks - By Country (annual), December 1996, p. 86.

Banks and Banking – Honduras

★ 329 ★
TOP BANKS IN HONDURAS
Ranked by: Assets, in millions of U.S. dollars. **Remarks:** Also notes paid-up capital. **Number listed:** 5
1. Banco Atlantida SA with $187 million
2. Banco Nacional de Desarrollo Agricola, $110
3. Banco Continental SA, $50

Source: *Bankers' Almanac World Ranking* (annual), 1996, p. 196.

Banks and Banking – Hong Kong

★ 330 ★
TOP BANKS IN HONG KONG
Ranked by: Assets, in millions of U.S. dollars. **Remarks:** Also notes paid-up capital. **Number listed:** 30
1. Hongkong and Shanghai Banking Corporation Limited with $151,641 million
2. Hang Seng Bank Limited, $44,640
3. Bank of East Asia Limited, $12,034
4. Dao Heng Bank Limited, $8,674
5. Nanyang Commercial Bank Ltd., $7,771
6. Po Sang Bank Limited, $5,528
7. Shanghai Commercial Bank Ltd., $5,148
8. Wing Lung Bank Ltd., $5,127
9. Dah Sing Bank Limited, $4,042
10. Hua Chiao Commercial Bank Ltd., $3,823

Source: *Bankers' Almanac World Ranking* (annual), 1996, p. 176.

Banks and Banking – Hungary

★ 331 ★
TOP BANKS IN HUNGARY
Ranked by: Assets, in millions of U.S. dollars. **Remarks:** Also notes paid-up capital. **Number listed:** 22
1. Magyar Nemzeti Bank with $35,565 million
2. Orszagos Takarekpenztar es Kereskedelmi Bank Rt., $8,265
3. Kereskedelmi es Hitelbank Rt, $2,679
4. Magyar Kulkereskedelmi Bank Rt, $2,053
5. Postabank es Takarekpenztar Rt, $1,973
6. Budapest Bank Rt, $1,773
7. CIB Hungaria Bank Rt, $707
8. Inter-Europa Bank Rt., $449
9. Unicbank Rt., $434

10. Magyar Befektetesi es Fejlesztesi Bank Rt., $423

Source: *Bankers' Almanac World Ranking* (annual), 1996, p. 178.

Banks and Banking – Iceland

★ 332 ★
TOP BANKS IN ICELAND
Ranked by: Assets, in millions of U.S. dollars. **Remarks:** Also notes paid-up capital. **Number listed:** 4
1. Landsbanki Islands with $1,564 million
2. Islandsbanki HF, $842
3. Bunadarbanki Islands, $680
4. Icebank Ltd., $108

Source: *Bankers' Almanac World Ranking* (annual), 1996, p. 179.

Banks and Banking – India

★ 333 ★
TOP BANKS BY PROFITS IN INDIA, 1996
Ranked by: Profits, in Rs crore. **Remarks:** Includes 1995 profits. **Number listed:** 29
1. Citibank with Rs crore174.89
2. Standard Chartered Bank, Rs crore102.09
3. HongKongBank, Rs crore90.65
4. ANZ Grindlays Bank, Rs crore59.11
5. Bank of America, Rs crore52.90
6. American Express Bank, Rs crore35.29
7. Bank of Tokyo-Mitsubishi, Rs crore34.29
8. Deutsche Bank, Rs crore23.12
9. ABN-AMRO Bank, Rs crore22.80
10. The British Bank of Middle East, Rs crore18.93

Source: *Business India*, October 21, 1996, p. 158.

★ 334 ★
TOP BANKS IN INDIA
Ranked by: Assets, in millions of U.S. dollars. **Remarks:** Also notes paid-up capital. **Number listed:** 40
1. State Bank of India with $38,834 million
2. Industrial Development Bank of India, $12,148
3. Bank of Baroda, $9,907
4. Bank of India, $9,600
5. Punjab National Bank, $9,138
6. Canara Bank, $8,403
7. Central Bank of India, $6,579
8. Union Bank of India, $5,430
9. Indian Overseas Bank, $5,092

10. Syndicate Bank, $4,551
Source: *Bankers' Almanac World Ranking* (annual), 1996, p. 179.

Banks and Banking – Indonesia

★ 335 ★
TOP BANKS IN INDONESIA
Ranked by: Assets, in millions of U.S. dollars. **Remarks:** Also notes paid-up capital. **Number listed:** 44
1. PT Bank Negara Indonesia (Persero) with $13,977 million
2. PT Bank Bumi Daya (Persero), $11,926
3. Bank Rakyat Indonesia, $11,784
4. PT Bank Ekspor Impor Indonesia, $8,610
5. Bank Central Asia, $8,455
6. PT Bank Pembangunan Indonesia, $6,910
7. Bank Danamon Indonesia, $4,757
8. Bank Internasional Indonesia, $4,244
9. Bank Danang Nasional Indonesia, $4,047
10. Lippo Bank PT, $3,146
Source: *Bankers' Almanac World Ranking* (annual), 1996, p. 181.

★ 336 ★
TOP PRIVATE DOMESTIC BANKS IN INDONESIA, 1995
Ranked by: Assets, in billions of U.S. dollars. **Remarks:** Also notes profits. **Number listed:** 10
1. Bank Central Asia with $11.8 billion
2. Bank Danamon, $6.2
3. BII, $5.7
4. BDNI, $5.5
5. Bank Lippo, $3.4
6. Bank Niaga, $2.9
7. Bank Bali, $2.8
8. Bank Unum Nasional, $2.7
9. Bank Panin, $1.9
10. Bank Duta, $1.5
Source: *National Trade Data Bank*, November 15, 1996, p. IMI961114.

Banks and Banking – Iran

★ 337 ★
TOP BANKS IN IRAN
Ranked by: Assets, in millions of U.S. dollars. **Remarks:** Also notes paid-up capital. **Number listed:** 15
1. Bank Melli Iran with $11,393 million
2. Bank Tejarat, $7,068
3. Bank Saderat Iran, $6,885
4. Bank Mellat, $4,853

5. Bank Sepah, $3,875
Source: *Bankers' Almanac World Ranking* (annual), 1996, p. 182.

Banks and Banking – Isle of Man

★ 338 ★
TOP BANKS ON THE ISLE OF MAN
Ranked by: Assets, in millions of U.S. dollars. **Remarks:** Also notes paid-up capital. **Number listed:** 16
1. Isle of Man Bank Limited with $2,663 million
2. Royal Bank of Scotland, $1,013
3. Bank of Ireland (I.O.M.) Limited, $971
4. Ulster Bank (Isle of Man) Limited, $524
5. Tyndall Bank International Limited, $350
6. Royal Bank of Canada (IOM) Limited, $273
7. Standard Bank Isle of Man Limited, $269
8. Singer & Friedlander (Isle of Man) Ltd., $176
9. Allied Dunbar Bank International Limited, $134
10. Bank of Bermuda (Isle of Man) Limited, $129
Source: *Bankers' Almanac World Ranking* (annual), 1996, p. 183.

Banks and Banking – Italy

★ 339 ★
TOP BANKS IN ITALY, 1995
Ranked by: Tier one capital as of December 1995, in billions of lira (L). **Remarks:** Mediobanca figures are for June 30, 1995. Also notes total assets, pre-tax assets, number of employees, and number of branches. **Number listed:** 10
1. Cariplo with L11,117 billion
2. San Paolo Bank Holding, L10,770
3. BNL-Banca Nazionale del Lavoro, L8,705
4. Banca di Roma, L8,494
5. Banca Commerciale Italiana, L8,110
6. Istitutu Mobiliare Italiano, L7,179
7. Banca Monte dei Paschi di Siena, L6,605
8. Credito Italiano, L4,871
9. Mediobanca, L3,311
Source: *The Banker*, August 1996, p. 26.

Banks and Banking – Ivory Coast

★ 340 ★
TOP BANKS IN THE IVORY COAST
Ranked by: Tier one capital, in millions of U.S. dollars.
Remarks: Also notes capital percentage change, assets, assets percentage change, pre-tax profit, and performance. **Number listed:** 3
1. B. Int pour le Comm & l'Ind Cote d'Ivoire with $54 million
2. Societe Gen. de Banques en Cote d'Ivoire, $47
3. Societe Ivoirienne de Banque, $8

Source: *The Banker,* Top 100 African Banks - By Country (annual), December 1996, p. 3.

Banks and Banking – Jamaica

★ 341 ★
TOP BANKS IN JAMAICA BY ASSETS
Ranked by: Assets, in millions of U.S. dollars. **Remarks:** Also note paid-up capital. **Number listed:** 5
1. National Commercial Bank Jamaica Limited with $1,037.00 million
2. Bank of Nova Scotia Jamaica Limited, $681.00
3. Citizens Bank Limited, $221.00
4. CIBC Jamaica Limited, $194.00
5. CIBC Trust and Merchant Bank Jamaica Limited, $4.69

Source: *Bankers' Almanac World Ranking* (annual), 1996, p. 192.

Banks and Banking – Japan

★ 342 ★
MOST PROFITABLE COMMERCIAL BANKS IN JAPAN
Ranked by: Operating profits, in billions of yen (¥).
Remarks: Notes percent change and value of bad loans.
Number listed: 10
1. Tokyo-Mitsubishi with ¥525.3 billion
2. Dai-Ichi Kangyo, ¥391.3
3. Sumitomo, ¥338.2
4. Fuji, ¥327.1
5. Sanwa, ¥355.3
6. Sakura, ¥281.7
7. Asahi, ¥152.6
8. Tokai, ¥161.8
9. Daiwa, ¥98.2
10. Hokkaido-Takushoku, ¥55.0

Source: *Financial Times,* May 25, 1997, p. 23.

★ 343 ★
TOP BANKS BY SHAREHOLDER EQUITY IN JAPAN
Ranked by: Shareholders' equity, in millions of U.S. dollars. **Remarks:** Also includes equity and asset growth, net profits, total assets return, on equity and differential.
Number listed: 50
1. Bank of Tokyo-Mitsubishi with $36,351 million
2. Dai-Ichi Kangyo Bank, $19,629
3. Sumitomo Bank, $18,735
4. Sanwa Bank, $17,747
5. Sakura Bank, $16,119
6. Fuji Bank, $15,658
7. Industrial Bank of Japan, $12,591
8. Long-Term Credit Bank of Japan, $9,975
9. Asahi Bank, $9,259
10. Tokai Bank, $9,034

Source: *Euromoney,* December 1996, p. 66.

★ 344 ★
TOP BANKS IN JAPAN
Ranked by: Income, in millions of yen (¥). **Number listed:** 10
1. Sumitomo Bank with ¥97,447 million
2. Sanwa Bank, ¥79,349
3. Bank of Tokyo, ¥59,883
4. Long-Term Credit Bank of Japan, ¥57,840
5. Daiwa Bank, ¥57,537
6. Mitsubishi Bank, ¥57,251
7. Mitsubishi Trust & Banking, ¥55,924
8. Fuji Bank, ¥53,077
9. Asahi Bank, ¥47,405
10. Sumitomo Trust & Banking, ¥46,306

Source: *Tokyo Business Today,* August 1995, p. 27.

★ 345 ★
TOP BANKS IN JAPAN BY ASSETS
Ranked by: Assets, in millions of U.S. dollars. **Remarks:** Also notes paid-up capital. **Number listed:** 135
1. Dai-Ichi Kangyo Bank Limited with $626,171 million
2. Sumitomo Bank Limited, $617,053
3. Sakura Bank Limited, $607,245
4. Sanwa Bank Limited, $600,111
5. Fuji Bank Limited, $587,154
6. Norinchukin Bank, $516,015
7. Industrial Bank of Japan Limited, $453,015
8. Long-Term Credit Bank of Japan Limited, $367,132
9. Tokai Bank Limited, $357,182
10. Asahi Bank Ltd., $324,124

Source: *Bankers' Almanac World Ranking* (annual), 1996, p. 192.

Banks and Banking – Kazakhstan

★ 346 ★
TOP BANKS IN KAZAKHSTAN
Ranked by: Assets, in millions of U.S. dollars. **Remarks:**
Also notes paid-up capital. **Number listed:** 4
1. Alem Bank Kazakhstan with $1,374 million
2. Kazakh Corporation Bank "Turanbank", $377
3. Kazakh Central Joint-Stock Bank "Centerbank", $38
4. Eurasian Bank, $19
Source: *Bankers' Almanac World Ranking* (annual), 1996, p. 197.

Banks and Banking – Kenya

★ 347 ★
TOP BANKS IN KENYA
Ranked by: Tier one capital, in millions of U.S. dollars.
Remarks: Also notes capital percentage change, assets, assets percentage change, pre-tax profit, and performance. **Number listed:** 7
1. Kenya Commercial Bank with $93 million
2. National Bank of Kenya, $43
3. Co-operative Bank of Kenya, $18
4. Diamond Trust of Kenya, $18
5. Consolidated Bank of Kenya, $11
6. Trust Bank, $11
7. Commercial Bank of Africa, $10
Source: *The Banker,* Top 100 African Banks - By Country, December 1996, p. 86.

Banks and Banking – Korea, South

★ 348 ★
LEADING INTERNATIONAL LENDERS IN SOUTH KOREA
Ranked by: Loans, in millions of U.S. dollars. **Remarks:**
Also notes loan share and number of issues. **Number listed:** 10
1. Korea Development Bank with $844.57 million
2. Cho Hung Bank, $571.80
3. Citibank, $484.31
4. Commercial Bank of Korea, $469.44
5. Hanil Bank, $300.92
6. Korea Exchange Bank, $274.38
7. Seoul Bank, $169.32
8. Societe Generale, $167.32
9. WestLB, $154.25

10. Bank of Tokyo-Mitsubishi, $151.00
Source: *Far Eastern Economic Review*, October 3, 1996, p. 66.

★ 349 ★
SOUTH KOREA'S MOST TROUBLED BANKS, 1996
Ranked by: Shareholder equity for year end 1996, in billions of U.S. dollars. **Remarks:** Notes value of nonperforming loans and unrealized losses on equity holdings. "Other" includes 14 major banks. **Number listed:** 7
1. Korea Exchange Bank with $2.47 billion
2. Hanil Bank, $2.10
3. Korea First Bank, $2.08
4. Cho Hung Bank, $2.00
5. Commercial Bank of Korea, $1.80
6. Seoul Bank, $1.36
7. Other, $19.65
Source: *The Wall Street Journal*, February 3, 1997, p. A9.

★ 350 ★
TOP BANKS BY OPERATING PROFIT IN KOREA, 1996
Ranked by: Operating profits, in billions of won (W).
Remarks: Notes net profits for 1995 and 1996. **Number listed:** 15
1. Kookmin with W511.8 billion
2. Cho Hung, W497.2
3. Korea First, W443.4
4. Korea Exchange, W418.5
5. Commercial, W395.5
6. Shinhan, W377.2
7. Hanil, W364.0
8. Seoul, W291.4
9. Hana, W99.0
10. KorAm, W76.2
Source: *Financial Times*, January 17, 1996, p. 22.

Banks and Banking – Latin America

★ 351 ★
LARGEST BANKS IN LATIN AMERICA, 1995
Ranked by: Tier one capital, in billions of U.S. dollars.
Remarks: Also notes pre-tax profits. **Number listed:** 10
1. Banco Bradesco (Brazil) with $5.1 billion
2. Banco Itau (Brazil), $3.8
3. Banco do Brasil (Brazil), $3.6
4. Unibanco (Brazil), $2.0
5. Banco de la Nacion (Argentina), $1.9
6. Banco Bamerindus (Brazil), $1.4
7. Banco Real (Brazil), $1.3
8. Banespa (Brazil), $1.3
9. Bancomer (Mexico), $1.2

10. Banco de la Provincia de Buenos Aires
     (Argentina), $1.2
Source: *The Economist*, April 12, 1997, p. 18.

★ 352 ★
LARGEST BANKS IN LATIN AMERICA, 1996
Ranked by: Assets, in millions of U.S. dollars. **Remarks:**
Also provides figures for deposits and loans. **Number listed:** 50
1. Caixa Economica Federal (Brazil) with $90,828
    million
2. Banco do Brasil (Brazil), $78,467
3. Bradesco (Brazil), $33,042
4. Banamex (Mexico), $30,815
5. Bancomer (Mexico), $26,330
6. Itau (Brazil), $24,958
7. Unibanco (Brazil), $23,023
8. Serfin (Mexico), $20,307
9. Banco de la Nacion Argentina (Argentina),
    $14,316
10. HSBC Bamerindus (Brazil), $12,432
Source: *Latin Trade,* The Top 50 Banks (annual), July
1997, p. 41.

Banks and Banking – Latvia

★ 353 ★
TOP BANKS IN LATVIA
Ranked by: Assets, in millions of U.S. dollars. **Remarks:**
Also notes paid-up capital. **Number listed:** 14
1. Bank of Latvia with $897 million
2. Parex Bank, $151
3. Latvian Savings Bank, $123
4. Rigas Komercbanka PLC, $110
5. Land Bank of Latvia, $84
6. Saules Banka, $63
7. Investment Bank of Latvia, $31
8. Capital Bank of Latvia, $28
9. Bank Atmoda, $14
10. Banka Dinastija, $13
Source: *Bankers' Almanac World Ranking* (annual),
1996, p. 200.

Banks and Banking – Lebanon

★ 354 ★
TOP BANKS IN LEBANON
Ranked by: Assets, in millions of U.S. dollars. **Remarks:**
Also notes paid-up capital. **Number listed:** 42
1. Banque du Liban et d'Outre-Mer SAL with
    $1,431 million
2. Banque de la Mediterranee SAL, $1,172

3. Banque Libano-Francaise SAL, $1,032
4. Banque Audi SAL, $986
5. Fransabank SAL, $842
6. Societe Generale Libano-Europeene de Banque
    SAL, $815
7. Byblos Bank SAL, $746
8. Credit Libanais SAL, $583
9. Bank of Beirut and the Arab Countries SAL,
    $530
10. Banque Beyrouth pour le Commerce SAL, $362
Source: *Bankers' Almanac World Ranking* (annual),
1996, p. 201.

Banks and Banking – Lesotho

★ 355 ★
TOP BANKS IN LESOTHO
Ranked by: Assets, in millions of U.S. dollars. **Remarks:**
Also notes paid-up capital. **Number listed:** 3
1. Central Bank of Lesotho with $431 million
2. Lesotho Bank, $231
3. Stanbic Bank Lesotho Ltd., $67
Source: *Bankers' Almanac World Ranking* (annual),
1996, p. 203.

Banks and Banking – Lithuania

★ 356 ★
TOP BANKS IN LITHUANIA
Ranked by: Assets, in millions of U.S. dollars. **Remarks:**
Also notes paid-up capital. **Number listed:** 9
1. Bank of Lithuania with $635 million
2. Agricultural Bank of Lithuania, $197
3. Lithuanian Joint-Stock Innovation Bank, $169
4. Vilniaus Bankas AB, $87
5. Vakaru Bankas, $79
6. Litimpex Bank, $64
7. Bankas Hermis, $41
8. Bank of Commerce and Credit, $13
9. Tauro Bank, $13
Source: *Bankers' Almanac World Ranking* (annual),
1996, p. 204.

Banks and Banking – Luxembourg

★ 357 ★
TOP BANKS IN LUXEMBOURG, 1994
Ranked by: Deposits, in billions of U.S. dollars. **Number listed:** 15
1. Banque Internationale a Luxembourg with $18.23 billion
2. Banque Generale du Luxembourg, $16.69
3. Deutsche Bank Luxembourg, $14.22
4. Banque & Caisse d'Epargne de l'Etat, $14.12
5. Kredietbank Luxembourgeoise, $10.50
6. Banque de Luxembourg, $6.10
7. Union de Banques Suisses, Luxembourg, $6.03
8. Vereinsbank International, $5.77
9. Norddeusche Landesbank Luxembourg, $5.67
10. DG Bank Lumbourg, $5.25

Source: *The Wall Street Journal*, August 23, 1996, p. A6.

Banks and Banking – Macedonia

★ 358 ★
TOP BANKS IN MACEDONIA
Ranked by: Assets, in millions of U.S. dollars. **Remarks:** Also notes paid-up capital. **Number listed:** 4
1. Stopanska Banka AD with $1,653 million
2. Komercijalna Bank AD Skopje, $326
3. TUTUNSKA BANKA AD Skopje, $21
4. Kreditna Banka A.D. Skopje, $18

Source: *Bankers' Almanac World Ranking* (annual), 1996, p. 207.

Banks and Banking – Madagascar

★ 359 ★
TOP BANKS IN MADAGASCAR
Ranked by: Tier one capital, in millions of U.S. dollars. **Remarks:** Also notes capital percentage change, assets, assets percentage change, pre-tax profits, and performance. **Number listed:** 2
1. Banque Malgache de l'Ocean Indien with $7 million
2. Banque Nationale pour le Commerce, $5

Source: *The Banker,* Top 100 African Banks - By Country (annual), December 1996, p. 87.

Banks and Banking – Malawi

★ 360 ★
TOP BANKS IN MALAWI
Ranked by: Tier one capital, in millions of U.S. dollars. **Remarks:** Also notes capital percentage change, assets, assets percentage change, pre-tax profit, and performance. **Number listed:** 3
1. Malawi Savings Bank with $22 million
2. National Bank of Malawi, $12
3. Commercial Bank of Malawi, $11

Source: *The Banker,* Top 100 African Banks - By Country (annual), December 1996, p. 87.

Banks and Banking – Malaysia

★ 361 ★
LEADING COMMERCIAL BANKS IN MALAYSIA, 1995
Ranked by: Total assets, in millions of Malaysian ringgit (MR). **Remarks:** Notes loans, deposits, and shareholders' funds for each bank. **Number listed:** 12
1. Malayan Banking with MR64,135 million
2. Bank Bumiputra, MR30,932
3. Public Bank, MR23,263
4. DCB Bank, MR17,551
5. Bank of Commerce, MR14,625
6. UMBC, MR13,088
7. Perwira Affin Bank, MR9,263
8. Hong Leong Bank, MR7,018
9. Kwong Yik Bank, MR6,748
10. Pacific Bank, MR5,815

Source: *Asiamoney*, October 1996, p. 11.

★ 362 ★
TOP MALAYSIAN BANKS
Ranked by: Assets, in hundreds of millions of Malaysian dollars (M$). **Remarks:** Notes pretax profits. **Number listed:** 10
1. Malayan Banking with M$669.1 hundred million
2. Bank Bumiputra Malaysia, M$364.6
3. DCB/Kwong Yik Bank, M$270.1
4. Public Bank, M$232.6
5. Hongkong Bank, M$217.6
6. Bank of Commerce, M$150.4
7. Standard Chartered Bank, M$147.0
8. Citibank, M$140.0
9. United Malayan Banking, M$130.5
10. OCBC Bank (Malaysia), M$110.1

Source: *Nikkei Weekly*, April 14, 1997, p. 21.

Banks and Banking – Malta

★ 363 ★
TOP BANKS IN MALTA
Ranked by: Assets, in millions of U.S. dollars. **Remarks:** Also notes paid-up capital. **Number listed:** 5
1. Mid-Med Bank Limited with $2,496 million
2. Central Bank of Malta, $2,328
3. Bank of Valletta Limited, $2,274
4. Lombard Bank (Malta) Limited, $129
5. APS Bank Limited, $97

Source: *Bankers' Almanac World Ranking* (annual), 1996, p. 209.

Banks and Banking – Mauritania

★ 364 ★
TOP BANKS IN MAURITANIA
Ranked by: Tier one capital, in millions of U.S. dollars. **Remarks:** Also notes capital percentage change, assets, assets percentage change, pre-tax profit, and performance. **Number listed:** 2
1. Banque Mauritanienne Pour le Commerce Int'l with $10 million
2. Banque Nationale de Mauritanie, $5

Source: *The Banker,* Top 100 African Banks - By Country (annual), December 1996, p. 87.

Banks and Banking – Mauritius

★ 365 ★
TOP BANKS IN MAURITIUS
Ranked by: Tier one capital, in millions of U.S. dollars. **Remarks:** Also notes capital percentage change, assets, assets percentage change, pre-tax profit, and performance. **Number listed:** 5
1. Mauritius Commercial Bank with $179 million
2. State Bank of Mauritius, $119
3. State Bank International, $13
4. Indian Ocean International Bank, $5
5. South East Asian Bank, $5

Source: *The Banker,* Top 100 African Banks - By Country (annual), December 1996, p. 87.

Banks and Banking – Mexico

★ 366 ★
TOP BANKS IN MEXICO
Ranked by: Assets, in millions of U.S. dollars. **Remarks:** Notes deposits and number of branches. **Number listed:** 10
1. Banamex with $30,954.9 million
2. Bancomer, $26,449.7
3. Serfin, $20,399.5
4. Internacional, $10,278.7
5. Mexicano, $8,769.2
6. Promex, $7,179.4
7. Bancrecer, $6,832.2
8. Atlantico, $6,300.7
9. Confia, $4,386.3
10. Mercantil del Norte, $4,097.9

Source: *Mexico Business*, July/August 1997, p. 12.

Banks and Banking – Monaco

★ 367 ★
TOP BANKS IN MONACO
Ranked by: Assets, in millions of U.S. dollars. **Remarks:** Also notes paid-up capital. **Number listed:** 5
1. Credit Foncier de Monaco with $2,005 million
2. Compagnie Monegasque de Banque, $1,983
3. Societe de Banque Suisse (Monaco), $1,127
4. Societe Monegasque de Banque, $324
5. ABC Bancque Internationale de Monaco, $271

Source: *Bankers' Almanac World Ranking* (annual), 1996, p. 210.

Banks and Banking – Namibia

★ 368 ★
TOP BANKS IN NAMIBIA
Ranked by: Assets, in millions of U.S. dollars. **Remarks:** Also notes paid-up capital. **Number listed:** 5
1. First National Bank of Namibia with $458 million
2. Bank of Namibia, $451
3. Standard Bank Namibia Ltd., $405
4. Commercial Bank of Namibia, $297
5. Bank Windhoek Limited, $246

Source: *Bankers' Almanac World Ranking* (annual), 1996, p. 211.

Banks and Banking – Netherlands Antilles

★ 369 ★
TOP BANKS IN THE NETHERLANDS ANTILLES
Ranked by: Assets, in millions of U.S. dollars. **Remarks:** Also notes paid-up capital. **Number listed:** 4
1. Maduro & Curiel's Bank NV with $1,222 million
2. Rabobank Curacao NV, $916
3. Orco Bank NV, $583
4. Banco di Caribe NV, $253
Source: *Bankers' Almanac World Ranking* (annual), 1996, p. 214.

Banks and Banking – New Caledonia

★ 370 ★
TOP BANKS IN NEW CALEDONIA
Ranked by: Assets, in millions of U.S. dollars. **Remarks:** Also notes paid-up capital. **Number listed:** 2
1. Societe Generale Caledonienne de Banque with $360 million
2. Banque de Nouvelle Caledonie (Credit Lyonnais), $223
Source: *Bankers' Almanac World Ranking* (annual), 1996, p. 214.

Banks and Banking – Nigeria

★ 371 ★
TOP BANKS IN NIGERIA
Ranked by: Tier one capital, in millions of U.S. dollars. **Remarks:** Also notes capital percentage change, assets, assets percentage change, pre-tax profit, and performance. **Number listed:** 28
1. United Bank for Africa with $200 million
2. First Bank of Nigeria, $178
3. Union Bank of Nigeria, $79
4. Investment Banking & Trust Company, $49
5. Nigeria International Bank, $49
6. Afribank Nigeria, $43
7. Diamondbank, $38
8. Zenith International Bank, $33
9. Wema Bank, $29
10. NAL Merchant Bank, $20
Source: *The Banker,* Top 100 African Banks - By Country, December 1996, p. 87.

Banks and Banking – Oman

★ 372 ★
TOP BANKS IN OMAN
Ranked by: Assets, in millions of U.S. dollars. **Remarks:** Also notes paid-up capital. **Number listed:** 8
1. Bank Muscat Al Ahli Al Omani SAOG with $883 million
2. Oman International Bank SAOG, $838
3. National Bank of Oman Ltd. SAOG, $745
4. Oman Arab Bank SAO, $426
5. Bank of Oman, Bahrain and Kuwait SAOG, $380
6. Commercial Bank of Oman Ltd., $281
7. Bank Dhofar Al Omani Al Fransi SAOC, $261
8. Oman Development Bank SAO, $136
Source: *Bankers' Almanac World Ranking* (annual), 1996, p. 217.

Banks and Banking – Papua New Guinea

★ 373 ★
TOP BANKS IN PAPUA NEW GUINEA
Ranked by: Assets, in millions of U.S. dollars. **Remarks:** Also notes paid-up capital. **Number listed:** 4
1. Papua New Guinea Banking Corporation with $650 million
2. Bank of South Pacific Limited, $187
3. Rural Development Bank of Papua New Guinea, $64
4. Indosuez Niugini Bank Ltd., $57
Source: *Bankers' Almanac World Ranking* (annual), 1996, p. 218.

Banks and Banking – Paraguay

★ 374 ★
TOP BANKS IN PARAGUAY
Ranked by: Assets, in millions of U.S. dollars. **Remarks:** Also notes paid-up capital. **Number listed:** 7
1. Banco Union SA with $162 million
2. Banco General SA, $156
3. Banco Sudameris Paraguay SA, $90
4. Banco de Inversiones del Paraguay SA, $78
5. Banco del Parana SA, $70
6. Banco Paraguayo Oriental de Inversion y de Fomento SA, $64
7. Bancosur SA de Inversion y Fomento, $36
Source: *Bankers' Almanac World Ranking* (annual), 1996, p. 219.

Banks and Banking – Peru

★ 375 ★
TOP BANKS IN PERU, 1996
Ranked by: Tier one capital, in millions of nuevos soles (NS). **Remarks:** Also notes total assets, capital to assets ratio, profit to capital ratio, number of employees, and number of branches. **Number listed:** 6
1. Banco de Credito del Peru with NS1,165 million
2. Banco Wiese, NS615
3. Banco de la Nacion, NS563
4. Banco Continental, NS533
5. Banco del Nuevo Mundo, NS80
6. Banco Republica, NS40
Source: *The Banker*, May 1997, p. 61.

Banks and Banking – Philippines

★ 376 ★
TOP BANKS IN THE PHILIPPINES
Ranked by: Assets, in billions of Philippino pesos (PP). **Number listed:** 5
1. Metrobank with PP218 billion
2. Philippine National Bank, PP214
3. BPI, PP154
4. Philippine Commercial International Bank, PP118
5. Far East Bank, PP114
Source: *Financial Times*, October 9, 1996, p. 17.

Banks and Banking – Poland

★ 377 ★
TOP BANKS BY EQUITY IN POLAND, 1995
Ranked by: Equity as of June 30, 1995, in millions of zlotys (Zl). **Number listed:** 15
1. BGZ with Zl1,567.90 million
2. Bank Handlowy, Zl1,484.50
3. PKO BP, Zl924.50
4. Pekao SA, Zl662.00
5. Bank Slaski, Zl564.80
6. BPH, Zl479.30
7. Bank Gdanski, Zl453.20
8. Pow. Bank Kredytowy, Zl391.20
9. Bank Zachodni, Zl342.80
10. BRE, Zl311.70
Source: *Financial Times*, September 17, 1996, p. 20.

★ 378 ★
TOP BANKS IN POLAND
Ranked by: Assets, in millions of U.S. dollars. **Remarks:** Also notes paid-up capital. **Number listed:** 32
1. Powszechna Kasa Oszczednosci-Bank Panstwowy with $7,325 million
2. Bank Polska Kasa Opieki SA, $7,040
3. Bank Handlowy w Warszawie SA, $3,649
4. Powszechny Bank Gospodarczy SA w Lodzi, $2,392
5. Powszechny Bank Kredytowy S.A. w Warszawie, $2,331
6. Bank Slaski SA w Katowicach, $2,086
7. Bank Przemyslowo-Handlowy SA, $1,739
8. Bank Gospodarki Zywnosciowej SA, $1,672
9. Polski Bank Inwestycyjny SA, $1,267
10. Wielkopolski Bank Kredytowy Spolka Akcyjna w Poznaniu, $1,153
Source: *Bankers' Almanac World Ranking* (annual), 1996, p. 221.

Banks and Banking – Romania

★ 379 ★
TOP BANKS IN ROMANIA
Ranked by: Assets, in millions of U.S. dollars. **Remarks:** Also notes paid-up capital. **Number listed:** 9
1. Banca Nationala a Romaniei with $7,764 million
2. Banca Agricola SA, $2,520
3. Banca Romana de Comert Exterior SA, $1,819
4. Banca Comerciala Romana SA, $1,690
5. Banca Romana Pentru Dezvoltare SA, $780
6. Banca de Credit Cooperatist "BANKCOOP" SA, $295
7. Banca "DACIA-FELIX" SA, $225
8. Banca Comerciala "Ion Tiriac", $181
9. Bank for Small Industry and Free Enterprise-Mindbank, $42
Source: *Bankers' Almanac World Ranking* (annual), 1996, p. 224.

Banks and Banking – Russia (Republic)

★ 380 ★
TOP RUSSIAN BANKS BY ASSETS, 1996
Ranked by: Assets as of January 1, 1996, in millions of roubles (R). **Remarks:** Includes capital, deposits, and net profits. **Number listed:** 49
1. Sberbank with R119,824,868 million
2. Vneshtorgbank, R26,066,736
3. Agroprombank, R18,622,009

4.　Uneximbank, R17,717,302
5.　Inkombank, R14,686,940
6.　Moskiznesbank, R13,110,620
7.　Rossiyskiy Kredit Bank, R11,982,206
8.　MezhFinKompania, R11,265,122
9.　Imperial, R10,100,994
10.　Mosindustrial Bank, R10,017,547

Source: *The Banker*, April 1996, p. 58.

★ 381 ★
TOP RUSSIAN BANKS BY DEPOSITS, 1996
Ranked by: Deposits as of January 1, 1996, in billions of U.S. dollars. **Number listed:** 10
1.　Sberbank with $13.08 billion
2.　Vneshforgbank, $2.09
3.　Uneximbank, $1.76
4.　Inkombank, $1.65
5.　Agroprombank, $1.09
6.　Mosbusinessbank, $0.68
7.　Moscow Independent Bank, $0.50
8.　Moscow Financial, $0.41
9.　RosCredit, $0.36
10.　Imperial, $0.27

Source: *The Wall Street Journal*, July 12, 1996, p. A9.

Banks and Banking – Senegal

★ 382 ★
TOP BANKS IN SENEGAL
Ranked by: Tier one capital, in millions of U.S. dollars. **Remarks:** Also notes capital percentage change, assets, assets percentage change, pre-tax profit, and performance. **Number listed:** 5
1.　Societe Generale de Banques au Senegal with $13 million
2.　B. Int pour le Comm & l'Ind du Senegal, $12
3.　C. Nationale de Credit Agricole du Senegal, $10
4.　Banque de l'Habitat du Senegal, $7
5.　Banque Sengalo-Tunisienne, $7

Source: *The Banker,* Top 100 African Banks - By Country (annual), December 1996, p. 88.

Banks and Banking – Sierra Leone

★ 383 ★
TOP BANKS IN SIERRA LEONE
Ranked by: Assets, in millions of U.S. dollars. **Remarks:** Notes paid-up capital and rank from previous year. **Number listed:** 3
1.　Barclays Bank of Sierra Leone Limited with $25 million

2.　Standard Chartered Bank Sierra Leone Limited, $25
3.　Sierra Leone Commercial Bank Limited, $16

Source: *Bankers' Almanac World Ranking* (annual), 1996, p. 230.

Banks and Banking – Singapore

★ 384 ★
TOP BANKS IN SINGAPORE BY TOTAL ASSETS, 1995
Ranked by: Total assets as of December 1995, in millions of Singapore dollars (S$). **Remarks:** Also notes Tier One capital, pre-tax profits, number of employees, and number of branches. **Number listed:** 5
1.　DBS Bank with S$49,187 million
2.　Oversea-Chinese Banking Corporation, S$45,469
3.　United Overseas Bank, S$40,565
4.　Overseas Union Bank, S$25,627
5.　Tat Lee Bank, S$8,576

Source: *The Banker*, August 1996, p. 71.

★ 385 ★
TOP INTERNATIONAL LENDERS IN SINGAPORE
Ranked by: Share of loans, in percent. **Remarks:** Also notes number of issues. **Number listed:** 10
1.　Citibank with 20.25%
2.　United Overseas Bank, 15.70%
3.　Overseas Union Bank, 7.39%
4.　Dresdner Bank, 6.45%
5.　Development Bank of Singapore, 6.02%
6.　Keppel Bank, 5.57%
7.　NM Rothschild, 5.36%
8.　Bank of Boston, 3.18%
9.　Commerzbank, 2.93%
10.　Sumitomo Bank, 2.93%

Source: *Far Eastern Economic Review*, August 3, 1996, p. 68.

Banks and Banking – Slovakia

★ 386 ★
TOP BANKS IN SLOVAKIA
Ranked by: Assets, in millions of U.S. dollars. **Remarks:** Also notes paid-up capital. **Number listed:** 12
1.　Narodna Banka Slovenska with $6,547 million
2.　Vseobecna Uverova Banka AS, $4,710
3.　Slovenska sporitelna AS, $4,484
4.　Investicna a rozvojova banka AS, $1,338
5.　Slovenska Pol'nohospodarska Banka, $540
6.　Tatra Banka AS, $369

7.　Priemyselna Banka A.S. Kosice, $339
8.　Postova Banka AS (Post Bank as), $251
9.　Istrobanka AS, $198
10.　Ludova Banka Bratislava AS, $172

Source: *Bankers' Almanac World Ranking* (annual), 1996, p. 232.

Banks and Banking – Slovenia

★ 387 ★
TOP BANKS IN SLOVENIA

Ranked by: Assets, in millions of U.S. dollars. **Remarks:** Also notes paid-up capital. **Number listed:** 17

1.　Nova Ljubljanska banka dd, Ljubljana with $3,539 million
2.　SKB Banka dd, $1,354
3.　Nova Kreditna banka Maribor dd, $671
4.　Spolsna banka Koper dd, Koper, $640
5.　Abanka dd, Ljubljana, $472
6.　Gorenjska banka dd, Kranj, $424
7.　Banka Celje dd, $404
8.　Dolenjska banka dd, $225
9.　Bank Austria dd Lubljana, $166
10.　Banka Vipa dd, $135

Source: *Bankers' Almanac World Ranking* (annual), 1996, p. 232.

Banks and Banking – South Africa

★ 388 ★
TOP BANKS IN SOUTH AFRICA

Ranked by: Tier one capital, in millions of U.S. dollars. **Remarks:** Also notes capital percentage change, assets, assets percentage change, pre-tax profit, and performance. **Number listed:** 8

1.　Stanbic with $1,804 million
2.　Amalgamated Banks of South Africa, $1,709
3.　Nedcor, $1,115
4.　First National Bank Holdings, $1,062
5.　Investec Bank, $537
6.　NBS Bank, $337
7.　Boland Bank, $85
8.　Rand Merchant Bank, $81

Source: *The Banker,* Top 100 African Banks - By Country (annual), December 1996, p. 88.

★ 389 ★
TOP SOUTH AFRICAN BANKS BY TIER ONE CAPITAL

Ranked by: Tier One capital, in millions of rands (R). **Remarks:** Notes total assets, pre-tax profits, number of employees, and number of branches. **Number listed:** 5

1.　Amalgamated Banks of South Africa with R6,804 million
2.　Stanbic, R6,580
3.　First National Bank Holdings, R4,112
4.　Nedcor, R4,068
5.　Investec Bank, R2,139

Source: *The Banker*, August 1996, p. 62.

Banks and Banking – Sri Lanka

★ 390 ★
TOP BANKS IN SRI LANKA

Ranked by: Assets, in millions of U.S. dollars. **Remarks:** Also notes paid-up capital. **Number listed:** 6

1.　Bank of Ceylon with $2,076 million
2.　People's Bank, $1,605
3.　Hatton National Bank Limited, $461
4.　Seylan Bank Limited, $405
5.　Commercial Bank of Ceylon Limited, $356
6.　Sampath Bank Limited, $201

Source: *Bankers' Almanac World Ranking* (annual), 1996, p. 237.

Banks and Banking – Suriname

★ 391 ★
TOP BANKS IN SURINAME

Ranked by: Assets, in millions of U.S. dollars. **Remarks:** Also notes paid-up capital. **Number listed:** 2

1.　Surinaamsche Bank NV with $51 million
2.　Handels-Krediet-en Industriebank NV, $15

Source: *Bankers' Almanac World Ranking* (annual), 1996, p. 237.

Banks and Banking – Swaziland

★ 392 ★
TOP BANKS IN SWAZILAND

Ranked by: Assets, in millions of U.S. dollars. **Remarks:** Also notes paid-up capital. **Number listed:** 4

1.　Barclays Bank of Swaziland Limited with $147 million
2.　Standard Chartered Bank Swaziland Limited, $75

3.   Swaziland Development and Savings Bank, $71
4.   Stanbic Bank Swaziland Limited, $68
Source: *Bankers' Almanac World Ranking* (annual), 1996, p. 238.

Banks and Banking – Taiwan

★ 393 ★
LEADING STATE-OWNED BANKS IN TAIWAN
Ranked by: Assets, in billions of New Taiwan dollars (NT$). **Number listed:** 9
1.   Bank of Taiwan with NT$1,623 billion
2.   Co-operative Bank, NT$1,509
3.   Land Bank, NT$1,131
4.   First Commercial Bank, NT$947.4
5.   Hua Nan Bank, NT$922.9
6.   Chang Hwa Bank, NT$855.3
7.   Taiwan Business Bank, NT$703.4
8.   Chiao Tung Bank, NT$442.7
9.   Farmers Bank, NT$414.4
Source: *Financial Times*, May 9, 1997, p. 25.

★ 394 ★
TOP BANKS IN TAIWAN
Ranked by: Assets, in millions of U.S. dollars. **Remarks:** Notes growth rates. **Number listed:** 13
1.   Taiwan Cooperative Bank with $51,362.5 million
2.   Bank of Taiwan, $44,999.9
3.   First Commercial Bank, $30,137.9
4.   Hua Nan Comm. Bank, $28,712.4
5.   Chang Hwa Comm. Bank, $27,463.6
6.   The Int'l Comm. Bank of China, $11,764.4
7.   Chinatrust Comm. Bank, $10,351.0
8.   Citibank, N.A., $3,433.3
9.   The Chinese Bank, $2,182.1
10. Cosmos Bank, Taiwan, $2,005.6
Source: *National Trade Data Bank*, April 24, 1996, p. ISA960101.

Banks and Banking – Tajikistan

★ 395 ★
TOP BANKS IN TAJIKISTAN
Ranked by: Assets, in millions of U.S. dollars. **Remarks:** Also notes paid-up capital. **Number listed:** 2
1.   National Bank of the Republic of Tajikistan with $1,227 million
2.   Tajik Joint Stock Commercial Industrial and Construction Bank, $177
Source: *Bankers' Almanac World Ranking* (annual), 1996, p. 247.

Banks and Banking – Thailand

★ 396 ★
LARGEST THAI BANKS BY DEPOSITS
Ranked by: Deposits, in millions of baht (Bt). **Remarks:** Includes share of total deposits. **Number listed:** 15
1.   Bangkok Bank with Bt790,685.13 million
2.   Krung Thai Bank, Bt533,337.05
3.   Thai Farmers Bank, Bt520,198.65
4.   Siam Commercial Bank, Bt393,191.09
5.   Bank of Ayudhya, Bt342,756.14
6.   Thai Military Bank, Bt195,276.25
7.   Siam City Bank, Bt168,995.61
8.   First Bangkok City Bank, Bt158,907.49
9.   Bangkok Metropolitan Bank, Bt146,322.55
10. Bangkok Bank of Commerce, Bt110,546.61
Source: *Bangkok Post*, March 3, 1997, p. 14.

★ 397 ★
TOP INTERNATIONAL LENDERS IN THAILAND
Ranked by: Share of loans, in percent. **Number listed:** 10
1.   Union Bank of Switzerland with $9.69
2.   Citibank, $8.25
3.   Fuji Bank, $5.71
4.   ABN AMRO, $5.04
5.   AFC Merchant Bank, $4.12
6.   Societe Generale, $3.42
7.   Sanwa Bank, $3.12
8.   Chase Manhattan, $2.62
9.   BHF-Bank, $2.59
10. Industrial Bank of Japan, $2.54
Source: *Far Eastern Economic Review*, October 3, 1996, p. 76.

Banks and Banking – Togo

★ 398 ★
TOP BANKS IN TOGO
Ranked by: Assets, in millions of U.S. dollars. **Remarks:** Also notes paid-up capital. **Number listed:** 2
1.   Banque Togolaise de Developpement with $78 million
2.   Ecobank-Togo, $47
Source: *Bankers' Almanac World Ranking* (annual), 1996, p. 248.

Banks and Banking – Trinidad and Tobago

★ 399 ★
TOP BANKS IN TRINIDAD AND TOBAGO
Ranked by: Assets, in millions of U.S. dollars. **Remarks:**
Also notes paid-up capital. **Number listed:** 6
1. Republic Bank Limited with $1,206 million
2. Royal Bank of Trinidad and Tobago Limited, $1,200
3. First Citizens Bank Limited, $573
4. Bank of Nova Scotia Trinidad and Tobago Limited, $509
5. Bank of Commerce Tinidad and Tobago Limited, $415
6. Citibank (Trinidad and Tobabgo) Limited, $137
Source: *Bankers' Almanac World Ranking* (annual), 1996, p. 248.

Banks and Banking – Tunisia

★ 400 ★
TOP BANKS IN TUNISIA
Ranked by: Assets, in millions of U.S. dollars. **Remarks:**
Also notes paid-up capital. **Number listed:** 7
1. Banque Nationale Agricole with $2,927 million
2. Societe Tunisienne de Banque SA, $2,137
3. Banque Internationale Arabe de Tunisie SA, $1,487
4. Banque de Tunisie SA, $844
5. Amen Bank, $675
6. Banque de Developpement Economique de Tunisie, $664
7. Banque Arabe Tuniso-Libyenne de Developpement et de Commerce Exterieur, $158
Source: *Bankers' Almanac World Ranking* (annual), 1996, p. 249.

Banks and Banking – Turkey

★ 401 ★
TOP BANKS IN TURKEY
Ranked by: Assets, in millions of U.S. dollars. **Remarks:**
Also notes paid-up capital. **Number listed:** 46
1. Turkiye Cumhuriyet Ziraat Bankasi with $11,907 million
2. Turkiye is Bankasi AS, $6,160
3. Yapi Ve Kredi Bankasi AS, $6,017
4. Turkiye Halk Bankasi AS, $5,049
5. Turkiye Emlak Bankasi AS, $4,427
6. Akbank T.A.S., $3,856

7. Turkiye Vakiflar Bankasi TAO, $3,748
8. Pamukbank TAS, $2,792
9. Turkiye Garanti Bankasi AS, $2,479
10. Turkiye Ihracat Kredi Bankasi AS, $1,870
Source: *Bankers' Almanac World Ranking* (annual), 1996, p. 249.

Banks and Banking – Uganda

★ 402 ★
TOP BANKS IN UGANDA
Ranked by: Assets, in millions of U.S. dollars. **Remarks:**
Also notes paid-up capital. **Number listed:** 7
1. Uganda Commercial Bank with $155.00 million
2. Barclays Bank of Unganda Limited, $72.00
3. Standard Chartered Bank Uganda Limited, $62.00
4. Bank of Baroda (Uganda) Limited, $57.00
5. Greenland Bank Litd., $34.00
6. Gold Trust Bank Ltd., $7.70
7. International Credit Bank Limited, $6.22
Source: *Bankers' Almanac World Ranking* (annual), 1996, p. 251.

Banks and Banking – Ukraine

★ 403 ★
TOP BANKS IN UKRAINE
Ranked by: Assets, in millions of U.S. dollars. **Remarks:**
Also notes paid-up capital. **Number listed:** 6
1. UKREXIMBANK with $696 million
2. Privatbank, $227
3. Ukrainian Credit Bank, $35
4. West-Ukrainian Commercial Bank, $19
5. Banker's House Ukraine, $15
6. ENERGOBANK, $15
Source: *Bankers' Almanac World Ranking* (annual), 1996, p. 251.

Banks and Banking – United Arab Emirates

★ **404** ★

TOP BANKS IN THE UNITED ARAB EMIRATES, 1994-1995

Ranked by: Assets and liabilities, in millions of dirham. **Remarks:** Also notes liabilities, loans and advances, customer deposits, shareholders' equity, net profit, and figures for the previous year. 1995 data not provided for Dubai Islamic Bank. **Number listed:** 17
1. National Bank of Abu Dhabi with 25,415 million
2. National Bank of Dubai, 21,602
3. Emirates Bank International, 15,518
4. MashreqBank, 13,765
5. Abu Dhabi Commercial Bank, 13,483
6. Arab Bank for Investment & Foreign Trade, 4,484
7. Commercial Bank of Dubai, 3,320
8. National Bank of Fujairah, 1786
9. Investbank, 1,521
10. National Bank of Ras al-Khaimah, 1,474

Source: *MEED*, August 2, 1996, p. 8.

Banks and Banking – Uzbekistan

★ **405** ★

TOP BANKS IN UZBEKISTAN

Ranked by: Assets, in millions of U.S. dollars. **Remarks:** Also notes paid-up capital. **Number listed:** 2
1. Uzagroprombank with $2,508.00 million
2. Rustambank, $9.11

Source: *Bankers' Almanac World Ranking* (annual), 1996, p. 271.

Banks and Banking – Venezuela

★ **406** ★

LEADING VENEZUELAN BANKS

Ranked by: Assets at the end of November 1996, in millions of bolivares (B). **Number listed:** 11
1. Provincial with B1,428 million
2. Mercantil, B625
3. Venezuela, B620
4. Industrial, B440
5. Consolidado, B437
6. Union, B404
7. Latino, B224
8. Caribe, B218
9. Banesco, B201

10. Lara, B152

Source: *Business Latin America*, February 10, 1997, p. 2.

Banks and Banking – Vietnam

★ **407** ★

TOP BANKS IN VIETNAM

Ranked by: Assets, in millions of U.S. dollars. **Remarks:** Also notes paid-up capital. **Number listed:** 2
1. Bank for Foreign Trade of Vietnam with $1,238 million
2. Industrial and Commercial Bank of Vietnam, $962

Source: *Bankers' Almanac World Ranking* (annual), 1996, p. 272.

Banks and Banking – Western Samoa

★ **408** ★

TOP BANKS IN WESTERN SAMOA

Ranked by: Assets, in millions of U.S. dollars. **Remarks:** Also notes paid-up capital. **Number listed:** 2
1. Bank of Western Samoa with $54 million
2. Pacific Commercial Bank Ltd., $17

Source: *Bankers' Almanac World Ranking* (annual), 1996, p. 272.

Banks and Banking – Yemen Arab Republic

★ **409** ★

TOP BANKS IN YEMEN ARAB REPUBLIC

Ranked by: Assets, in millions of U.S. dollars. **Remarks:** Also notes paid-up capital. **Number listed:** 2
1. National Bank of Yemen with $260 million
2. International Bank of Yemen YSC, $79

Source: *Bankers' Almanac World Ranking* (annual), 1996, p. 273.

Banks and Banking – Zimbabwe

★ **410** ★

TOP BANKS IN ZIMBABWE

Ranked by: Tier one capital, in millions of U.S. dollars. **Remarks:** Also notes capital percentage change, assets, assets percentage change, pre-tax profit, and performance. **Number listed:** 3
1. Zimbabwe Financial Holdings with $29 million
2. FMB Holdings, $24

3. Merchant Bank of Central Africa, $16

Source: *The Banker,* Top 100 African Banks - By Country (annual), December 1996, p. 88.

Barbados – see under individual headings

Bars and Barrooms – Great Britain

★ 411 ★
LEADING PUB OPERATORS IN THE UNITED KINGDOM
Ranked by: Number of outlets. **Number listed:** 10
1. Intrepreneur with 2,900 outlets
2. Phoenix/Spring Inns, 2,860
3. Whitbread, 2,200
4. Allied Domecq, 1,800
5. Pubmaster, 1,560
6. Bass Taverns, 1,500
7. Greenalls, 1,200
8. Enterprise, 950
9. Scottish & Newcastle, 780
10. Greene King, 670

Source: *Financial Times,* October 28, 1996, p. 7.

Batteries

★ 412 ★
INDIA'S BATTERY MARKET
Ranked by: Market share, in percent. **Number listed:** 3
1. Energizer with 45.0%
2. Duracell, 40.0%
3. Other, 15.0%

Source: *Business India,* June 17, 1996, p. 77.

Beer

★ 413 ★
AUSTRALIA'S IMPORTED BEER MARKET
Ranked by: Market share, in percent. **Number listed:** 10
1. Corona with 34.0%
2. Heineken, 26.0%
3. Miller, 17.0%
4. Steinlager, 5.0%
5. Becks, 3.0%
6. Budweiser, 3.0%
7. Carlsburg, 3.0%
8. Grolsch, 3.0%
9. Peroni, 3.0%

10. Stella Artois, 3.0%

Source: *Beverage World,* April 1996, p. 77.

★ 414 ★
BRITAIN'S TOP BEER MAKERS
Ranked by: Market share, in percent. **Number listed:** 5
1. Scottish Courage with 33.0%
2. Bass, 23.0%
3. Carlsberg-Telley, 17.0%
4. Whitbread, 14.0%
5. Others, 13.0%

Source: *Cornell Hotel and Administration Quarterly,* December 1996, p. 64.

★ 415 ★
CANADIAN BEER MARKET, 1996
Ranked by: Market share based on 16,661,000 packaged hectolitres, in percent. **Remarks:** Also notes 1995 figures. **Number listed:** 11
1. Blue with 12.3%
2. Canadian, 11.1%
3. Budweiser, 7.8%
4. Molson Dry, 5.9%
5. Coors Light, 5.1%
6. Export, 4.7%
7. Kokanee, 2.9%
8. Labatt Genuine Draft, 2.5%
9. Labatt Life, 2.3%
10. Wildcat, 2.2%

Source: *Marketing Magazine,* June 26, 1997, p. 11.

★ 416 ★
JAPAN'S TOP BEER MAKERS
Ranked by: Market share, in percent. **Number listed:** 6
1. Kirin Brewery with 46.8%
2. Asahi Breweries, 26.1%
3. Sapporo Breweries, 18.1%
4. Suntory, 5.6%
5. Orion Breweries, 0.9%
6. Others, 1.5%

Source: *Nikkei Weekly,* August 5, 1996, p. 10.

★ 417 ★
LEADING BEER COMPANIES IN COLOMBIA, 1996
Ranked by: Market share, in percent. **Remarks:** Figures include malt and malted beverages. **Number listed:** 8
1. Bavaria S.A. with 58.3%
2. Cerveceria Aguila S.A., 13.3%
3. Cerveceria Leona S.A., 6.5%
4. Cervunion S.A., 6.0%
5. Malterias de Colombia S.A., 5.9%
6. Cerveceria El Litoral S.A., 5.4%
7. Malterias Unidas S.A., 3.0%
8. Cerveceria Ancla S.A., 0.2%

Source: *National Trade Data Bank,* July 9, 1997, p. ISA970501.

★ 418 ★

LEADING BEER PRODUCERS IN ITALY, 1995

Ranked by: Market share, in percent. **Number listed:** 8

1. Industrie Peroni with 30.0%
2. Heineken, 27.0%
3. Carlsberg Italia, 10.0%
4. Birra Moretti, 9.1%
5. Forst/Menabrea, 5.0%
6. Castelberg, 0.5%
7. Imports, 8.4%
8. Others, 10.0%

Source: *Marketing in Europe*, January 1997, p. 37.

★ 419 ★

TOP BEER BRANDS BY BRAND VALUE

Ranked by: Brand value, in millions of U.S. dollars. **Remarks:** Value was calculated using capital, ratio of capital to company sales, earnings, and corporate tax rate of the country where the parent company is located. See source for details. **Number listed:** 12

1. Budweiser (Anheuser-Busch) with $11,026 million
2. Kirin (Kirin Brewery), $3,691
3. Heineken (Heineken), $2,510
4. Guinness (Guinness), $2,337
5. Miller (Philip Morris), $2,157
6. Asahi (Asahi Breweries), $2,098
7. Busch (Anheuser-Busch), $1,166
8. Molson (Molson Breweries), $1,076
9. Carlsberg (Carlsberg), $897
10. Bass (Bass), $518

Source: *Financial World,* World's Most Valuable Brands (annual), July 8, 1996, p. 56.

★ 420 ★

TOP BEER MAKERS IN BULGARIA

Ranked by: Annual turnover, in millions of U.S. dollars. **Remarks:** Includes figures on production capacity, employment, and market share. **Number listed:** 5

1. Shoumensko Brewery with $8.5 million
2. Varnesk Brewery, $3.9
3. Velikoturnovsko Brewery, $3.4
4. Dobrudjansko Brewery, $3.1
5. Bourgasko Brewery, $3.0

Source: http:// www.itaiep.doc.gov/eebic/industry/ bulbeer.html, July 25, 1997, p. 3.

★ 421 ★

TOP BEER MAKERS IN FRANCE, 1994

Ranked by: Market share, in percent. **Remarks:** Total consumption was 23 million hectolitres. **Number listed:** 4

1. Kronenburg with 43.0%
2. Heineken, 35.0%
3. Interbrew, 10.0%
4. Other, 12.0%

Source: *L'Express*, July 3, 1996, p. 28.

★ 422 ★

TOP BEER MAKERS IN THE PHILIPPINES, 1996

Ranked by: Market share, in percent. **Number listed:** 3

1. San Miguel with 80.0%
2. Asia Brewery, 19.0%
3. Foreign, 1.0%

Source: *Financial Times*, September 26, 1996, p. 16.

★ 423 ★

TOP BEER MAKERS WORLDWIDE, 1995

Ranked by: Global production, in millions of barrels. **Number listed:** 10

1. Anheuser-Busch Inc. with 91.1 million barrels
2. Heineken, 54.7
3. Miller Brewing Co., 46.1
4. Companhla Cervejaria Brahma, 31.0
5. South Africa Breweries Ltd., 31.0
6. Interbrew, 29.9
7. Kirin Brewery Co., 28.7
8. Carlsberg, 26.9
9. Foster's Brewing Group, 22.9
10. Coors Brewing Company, 22.4

Source: *Le Figaro*, September 2, 1996, p. 13.

★ 424 ★

TOP BEER PRODUCERS IN VENEZUELA

Ranked by: Market share, in percent. **Number listed:** 3

1. Polar with 80.0%
2. Brahma, 10.0%
3. Other, 10.0%

Source: *Financial Times*, June 11, 1996, p. 21.

★ 425 ★

TOP IMPORTED BEER BRANDS IN TAIWAN, 1995

Ranked by: Market share, in percent. **Number listed:** 20

1. Miller with 25.2%
2. Michelob, 15.6%
3. Beck's, 15.5%
4. Heineken, 6.2%
5. Kirin, 4.8%
6. San Miguel, 2.6%
7. HB, 2.2%
8. YSH, 2.1%
9. Sapporo, 2.0%
10. Others, 23.8%

Source: *AgExporter*, July/August 1996, p. 24.

Belgium – see under individual headings

Bermuda – see under individual headings

Beverage Industry

★ 426 ★

ALCOHOLIC DRINK SALES IN MEXICO, 1995

Ranked by: Sales, in millions of U.S. dollars. **Number listed:** 4

1. Beer with $1,659.6 million
2. Spirits, $274.3
3. Brandy, $263.0
4. Wine, $108.3

Source: *Beverage Industry*, January 1997, p. 22.

★ 427 ★

BRAZIL'S NATURAL JUICE MARKET

Ranked by: Market share, in percent. **Number listed:** 3

1. Maguary with 41.0%
2. Dafruta, 27.0%
3. Other, 31.2%

Source: *National Trade Data Bank*, May 27, 1996, p. ISA960301.

★ 428 ★

LARGEST BEVERAGE COMPANIES, 1995

Ranked by: Revenue, in millions of U.S. dollars. **Remarks:** Notes profits and global rank. **Number listed:** 6

1. Coca-Cola (United States) with $18,018 million
2. Anheuser-Busch (United States), $12,326
3. Grand Metropolitan (United Kingdom), $11,380
4. Kirin Brewery (Japan), $9,465
5. Suntory (Japan), $8,991
6. Seagram (Canada), $8,935

Source: *Fortune,* The Global 500: World's Biggest Corporations (annual), August 5, 1996, p. F-16.

★ 429 ★

LEADING CATEGORIES IN SPAIN'S NON-ALCOHOLIC DRINKS AND BEER MARKET, 1995

Ranked by: Market share, in percent. **Number listed:** 8

1. Carbonated soft drinks with 44.9%
2. Beer, 28.8%
3. Mineral water, 13.8%
4. Fruit juices, 10.0%
5. Bitter soft drinks, 1.0%
6. Horchata, 0.8%
7. Isotonic drinks, 0.7%
8. Powdered soft drinks, 0.2%

Source: *Marketing in Europe*, January 1997, p. 20.

★ 430 ★

LEADING NON-ALCOHOLIC BEVERAGE PRODUCERS IN COLOMBIA, 1996

Ranked by: Market share, in percent. **Number listed:** 12

1. Panamco-Indega S.A. with 15.6%

2. Postobon S.A., 14.5%
3. Gaseosas Lux S.A., 10.2%
4. Gaseosas Colombianas S.A., 8.8%
5. Industrias Roman S.A., 6.4%
6. Coca-Cola S.A., 6.2%
7. Inversiones Medellin S.A., 5.7%
8. Antioquena de Inversiones S.A., 4.5%
9. Embotelladora Santander S.A., 3.6%
10. Gaseosas de Duitama S.A., 1.6%

Source: *National Trade Data Bank*, July 9, 1997, p. ISA970501.

★ 431 ★

LEADING SOFT DRINK AND JUICE BRANDS BY BRAND VALUE

Ranked by: Brand value, in millions of U.S. dollars. **Remarks:** Value was calculated using capital, ratio of capital to company sales, earnings, and corporate tax rate of the country where the parent company is located. See source for details. **Number listed:** 19

1. Coca-Cola (Coca-Cola) with $43,427 million
2. Pepsi (PepsiCo), $8,895
3. Fanta (Coca-Cola), $3,187
4. Sprite (Coca-Cola), $2,044
5. Schweppes (Cadbury Schweppes), $1,877
6. Dr. Pepper (Cadbury Schweppes), $1,174
7. Gatorade (Quaker Oats), $1,073
8. Evian (Danone), $923
9. 7UP (Pepsico, Cadbury Schweppes), $912
10. Tropicana (Seagram), $828

Source: *Financial World,* World's Most Valuable Brands (annual), July 8, 1996, p. 57.

★ 432 ★

SOFT BEVERAGE MARKET IN THE WEST BANK

Ranked by: Percent distribution. **Number listed:** 4

1. Carbonated with 44.5%
2. Non-carbonated, 27.2%
3. Carbonated juices, 25.4%
4. Natural juices, 3.0%

Source: *National Trade Data Bank*, June 25, 1997, p. IMI970625.

★ 433 ★

TOP BEVERAGE COMPANIES, 1995

Ranked by: Sales, in millions of U.S. dollars. **Remarks:** Notes data for 1994. **Number listed:** 100

1. Coca-Cola Co. with $18,018 million
2. Nestle SA, $13,300
3. PepsiCo Inc., $10,548
4. Anheuser-Busch Inc., $9,600
5. Seagram Co., $6,694
6. Miller Brewing Co., $4,304
7. Cadbury Beverages, $4,270
8. IDV North America, $2,827
9. Quaker Oats Beverages, $1,959

10. Coors Brewing Co., $1,675
Source: *Beverage Industry,* Top 100 (annual), July 1996, p. 28.

★ 434 ★
TOP CIDER MAKERS IN CANADA, 1997
Ranked by: Market share, in percent, for the first seven months of 1997. **Remarks:** Includes market share for the same period in 1996 and notes volume of case sales. **Number listed:** 4
1. Okanagan Cider with 48%
2. Growers Cider, 36%
3. Vibe Cider, 5%
4. Others, 11%
Source: *Marketing Magazine*, August 11, 1997, p. 3.

Beverage Industry – Europe

★ 435 ★
LARGEST BEVERAGE GROUPS IN EUROPE
Ranked by: Turnover, in billions of U.S. dollars. **Remarks:** Includes figures on net income and market capitalization. **Number listed:** 10
1. Allied Domeco with $13.48 billion
2. Grand Metropolitan, $12.12
3. Guinness, $7.07
4. Bass, $6.86
5. LVMH, $5.72
6. Heineken, $5.27
7. Whitbread, $3.73
8. Pernod Ricard, $3.07
9. Scottish & Newcastle, $3.05
10. Carlsberg, $2.87
Source: *Financial Times*, June 17, 1996, p. 24.

Beverage Industry – United Kingdom

★ 436 ★
TOP HOT BEVERAGE BRANDS IN THE UNITED KINGDOM, 1995
Ranked by: Estimated sales, in millions of British pounds (£). **Remarks:** Notes ad agency and spending. **Number listed:** 10
1. Nescafe (Nestle) with £Over 253 million
2. PG Tips (Brooke Bond), £115-120
3. Tetley (Tetley GB), £115-120
4. Gold Blend (Nestle), £75-80
5. Kenco (Kraft Jacob Suchard), £45-50
6. Maxwell House (Kraft Jacob Suchard), £40-45
7. Typhoo (Premier Beverages), £40-45
8. Horlicks (SmithKline Beecham), £30-35
9. Co-op 99 tea (CWS), £15-20

10. Red Mountain (Brooke Bond), £15-20
Source: *Marketing*, July 4, 1996, p. 25.

Beverages & Tobacco
See: **Beverage Industry; Tobacco Industry**

Bhutan – see under individual headings

Bicycles

★ 437 ★
LARGEST BIKE IMPORTERS/EXPORTERS IN TAIWAN, 1994
Ranked by: Total trade, in billions of U.S. dollars. **Remarks:** Notes separate export and import figures. **Number listed:** 85
1. Giant with $304.20 billion
2. Cheng Shin, $197.50
3. Merida, $135.30
4. Taiwan Hodaka, $70.70
5. Wheeler, $49.60
6. Hwa Fong Rubber, $49.30
7. Ideal Bike, $41.60
8. Far Great Plastics, $40.50
9. Sanfa Bicycle, $39.70
10. Sen Tai, $38.60
Source: http:// www.biknet.com.tw/bikint/report/e-1994.htm, March 3, 1997, p. 1.

★ 438 ★
TURKEY'S BIKE MARKET
Ranked by: Market share, in percent. **Number listed:** 3
1. Bisan with 50.0%
2. Beldesan, 25.0%
3. Other, 25.0%
Source: *National Trade Data Bank*, May 27, 1996, p. IMI951214.

Billionaires

★ 439 ★
RICHEST PEOPLE IN THE WORLD
Ranked by: Net worth, in billions of U.S. dollars. **Number listed:** 10
1. William Henry Gates III with $18.0 billion
2. Warren Buffett, $15.3
3. Paul Sacher, $13.1
4. Lee Shau Kee, $12.7

5. Tsai Wan-lin, $12.2
6. Li Ka-shing, $10.6
7. Yoshiaki Tsutsumi, $9.2
8. Paul G. Allen, $7.5
9. Kenneth R. Thomson, $7.4
10. Tan Yu, $7.0

Source: *Forbes*, July 15, 1996, p. 125.

Biotechnology Industries

★ 440 ★
TOP BIOTECHNOLOGY FIRMS WORLDWIDE, 1996
Ranked by: Turnover, in millions of U.S. dollars.
Number listed: 9

1. Amgen with $14.7 million
2. Genentech, $6.9
3. Chiron, $3.1
4. Biogen, $2.7
5. Biochem Pharma, $2.3
6. Centocor, $2.1
7. British Biotech, $1.9
8. Genzyme, $1.9
9. Immex, $1.0

Source: *L'Expansion*, July 23, 1997, p. 60.

Bolivia – see under individual headings

Bolsa de Madrid

★ 441 ★
LARGEST COMPANIES ON THE MADRID STOCK EXCHANGE, 1995
Ranked by: Market value, in billions of pesetas (Ptas).
Number listed: 20

1. Endesa with Ptas1,786.2 billion
2. Telefonica, Ptas1,578.3
3. Repsol, Ptas1,192.5
4. Iberdrola, Ptas1,026.7
5. Banco Bilbao Vizcaya, Ptas992.0
6. Banco Santander, Ptas972.7
7. Gas Natural, Ptas705.2
8. Banco Popular, Ptas646.5
9. Argentaria, Ptas627.5
10. Banesto, Ptas514.6

Source: *GT Guide to World Equity Markets* (annual), Euromoney Publications, 1996, p. 305.

★ 442 ★
MOST ACTIVELY TRADED SHARES ON THE MADRID STOCK EXCHANGE, 1995
Ranked by: Trading value, in millions of pesetas (Ptas).
Number listed: 20

1. Telefonica with Ptas1,074,637 million
2. Repsol, Ptas829,397
3. Endesa, Ptas588,215
4. Banco Santander, Ptas388,015
5. Iberdrola, Ptas374,625
6. Argentaria, Ptas314,477
7. Banco Popular, Ptas264,864
8. Banco Bilbao Vizcaya, Ptas251,375
9. Acerinox, Ptas129,189
10. Banco Central Hispano, Ptas106,787

Source: *GT Guide to World Equity Markets* (annual), Euromoney Publications, 1996, p. 305.

Bombay Stock Exchange

★ 443 ★
LARGEST COMPANIES ON THE BOMBAY STOCK EXCHANGE, 1995
Ranked by: Market value, in billions of rupees (Rs).
Number listed: 20

1. Steel Authority of India with Rs103.52 billion
2. Reliance Industries, Rs97.37
3. Hindustan Lever, Rs91.00
4. State Bank of India, Rs90.77
5. Mahangar Telephone Nigam, Rs90.00
6. Neyveli Lignites, Rs87.69
7. Tata Engineering & Loco Co., Rs83.35
8. Tata Iron & Steel Co., Rs66.45
9. Videsh Sanchar Nigam, Rs65.60
10. ITC, Rs60.95

Source: *GT Guide to World Equity Markets* (annual), Euromoney Publications, 1996, p. 170.

★ 444 ★
MOST ACTIVELY TRADED SHARES ON THE BOMBAY STOCK EXCHANGE, 1995
Ranked by: Turnover, in billions of rupees (Rs). **Number listed:** 20

1. Reliance Industries with Rs70.50 billion
2. Tata Iron & Steel Company, Rs35.80
3. State Bank of India, Rs21.32
4. Thermax, Rs11.72
5. Femnor Minerals, Rs7.36
6. Tata Engineering & Loco Co., Rs6.75
7. Larsen & Tubro, Rs4.31
8. Associated Cement Company, Rs4.06
9. Ahmedabad Electric Co., Rs3.64

10. Great Eastern Shipping Company, Rs3.08

Source: *GT Guide to World Equity Markets* (annual), Euromoney Publications, 1996, p. 170.

Bonds

★ 445 ★

JAPAN'S TOP BOND ISSUERS, 1980-1996

Ranked by: Bond issuance beginning in 1980 and ending October 28, 1996, in millions of U.S. dollars. **Remarks:** Notes number of issues and market share for each issuer. **Number listed:** 30

1. Toyota Motor Corporation with $29,877.20 million
2. Bank of Tokyo-Mitsubishi, $18,118.60
3. Export-Import Bank of Japan, $10,398.95
4. Nippon Telegraph & Telephone Corporation, $10,111.20
5. Sakura Bank, $10,009.04
6. Mitsubishi Corporation, $9,981.87
7. Marubeni Corporation, $8,409.46
8. Tokyo Electric Power Co., $8,225.05
9. Nissan Motor Co., $7,765.51
10. Sumitomo Bank, $7,759.25

Source: *Euromoney*, November 1996, p. 91.

★ 446 ★

LEADING BOND BOOKRUNNERS IN LATIN AMERICA, 1996

Ranked by: Market share, in percent. **Remarks:** Shares are shown based on total issues of $14.73 billion. Notes number of deals conducted by each firm. Offshore issues were credited to countries where issues are located. Sovereign issues were excluded. Data calculated using equal apportionment. **Number listed:** 20

1. J.P. Morgan with 14.96%
2. Morgan Stanley, 9.05%
3. Citicorp Group, 8.55%
4. ING Barings, 8.51%
5. Chase Manhattan Corp., 6.90%
6. ING Barings, 5.78%
7. CS First Boston/Credit Suisse, 5.43%
8. Goldman Sachs, 4.14%
9. Union Bank of Switzerland, 4.07%
10. Salomon Brothers, 4.02%

Source: *Latin Corporate Finance Handbook* (annual), 1997, p. 12.

★ 447 ★

TOP BOND ISSUERS IN ASIA, 1997

Ranked by: Value of issues for the 12 months ending June 1997, in millions of U.S. dollars. **Remarks:** Data do not include Japanese firms. **Number listed:** 50

1. Petroliam Nasional (Malaysia) with $2,214.44 million
2. Cagamas (Malaysia), $1,907.22
3. Asian Pulp & Paper (Indonesia), $1,500.00
4. Nissho Iwai HK (Hong Kong), $1,157.59
5. Korea Electric Power (South Korea), $843.51
6. Tenaga Nasional (Malaysia), $800.00
7. Pan Pacific Industrial Investments (Singapore), $715.00
8. New World China Finance (Hong Kong), $650.00
9. Samsung Electronics (South Korea), $646.59
10. CITIC (Hong Kong), $597.53

Source: *Global Finance*, August 1997, p. 31.

Bonds, International

★ 448 ★

TOP INTERNATIONAL BOND LEAD MANAGERS, 1996

Ranked by: Market share, in percent. **Remarks:** Includes value of transactions. Full credit is given to the bookrunner. **Number listed:** 10

1. Merrill Lynch with 7.62%
2. Morgan Stanley, 5.98%
3. SBC Warburg, 5.37%
4. Goldman Sachs, 5.02%
5. JP Morgan, 4.97%
6. CSFB, 4.15%
7. Deutsche MG, 4.13%
8. Lehman Brothers, 3.97%
9. Nomura, 3.65%
10. UBS, 3.63%

Source: *Financial Times*, January 6, 1997, p. 24.

Book Industries and Trade

★ 449 ★

TOP BOOK MARKETS WORLDWIDE, 1995

Ranked by: Retail sales, in billions of U.S. dollars. **Remarks:** Global retail sales were $80.1 billion. **Number listed:** 10

1. United States with $25.49 billion
2. Japan, $10.47
3. Germany, $9.96
4. United Kingdom, $3.60
5. France, $3.38

6. Spain, $2.99
7. South Korea, $2.80
8. Brazil, $2.53
9. Italy, $2.25
10. China, $1.76

Source: *The Christian Science Monitor*, October 28, 1996, p. 2.

Books

★ 450 ★
BOOK SALES IN LATIN AMERICA, 1995
Ranked by: Sales, in millions of U.S. dollars. **Remarks:** Also notes percent change from 1994. **Number listed:** 7
1. Brazil with $2,526 million
2. Mexico, $822
3. Argentina, $614
4. Chile, $131
5. Venezuela, $90
6. Peru, $72
7. Colombia, $53

Source: *Latin Trade*, October 1997, p. 30.

Booksellers and Bookselling

★ 451 ★
LEADING BOOK RETAILERS IN SINGAPORE
Ranked by: Number of outlets. **Remarks:** There are an estimated 46 book dealers and wholesalers in Singapore. **Number listed:** 4
1. Times the Bookshop with 22 outlets
2. Popular Book Co. PTE. Ltd., 13
3. MPH Bookstores PTE. Ltd., 8
4. Kinokuniya Book Stores of Singapore, 5

Source: *National Trade Data Bank*, May 27, 1996, p. IMI950915.

Bosses
See: **Executives**

Botswana – see under individual headings

Bottled Water

★ 452 ★
BOTTLED WATER MARKET IN GERMANY, 1995
Ranked by: Production, in millions of liters. **Remarks:** Figure for spring water was unavailable. **Number listed:** 4
1. Mineral waters with 7,294 million liters
2. Heilwasser, 295
3. Table waters, 206

Source: *Marketing in Europe*, January 1997, p. 6.

★ 453 ★
LEADING MINERAL WATERS IN POLAND, 1996
Ranked by: Market shares, in percent, for April to May 1996. **Number listed:** 7
1. Aqua Minerale with 12.0%
2. Nateczo-wianka, 11.9%
3. Bonaqua, 11.4%
4. Multivina, 7.7%
5. Mazow-szanka, 7.3%
6. Grodziska, 3.0%
7. Others, 26.0%

Source: *The Warsaw Voice*, July 21, 1996, p. 12.

Bourse de Bruxelles

★ 454 ★
LARGEST COMPANIES ON THE BRUSSELS STOCK EXCHANGE, 1995
Ranked by: Market value, in billions of Belgian francs (BFr). **Number listed:** 20
1. Electrabel with BFr380 billion
2. Petrofina, BFr210
3. Tractebel, BFr168
4. Generale de Banque, BFr160
5. Solvay, BFr133
6. Fortis, BFr130
7. Kredietbank, BFr118
8. BBL, BFr96
9. GBL, BFr95
10. Powerfin, BFr93

Source: *GT Guide to World Equity Markets* (annual), Euromoney Publications, 1996, p. 61.

★ 455 ★
MOST ACTIVELY TRADED SHARES ON THE BRUSSELS STOCK EXCHANGE, 1995
Ranked by: Trading value, in billions of Belgian francs (BFr). **Number listed:** 20
1. Electrabel with BFr51,949 billion
2. Solvay, BFr30,032
3. Generale de Banque, BFr28,678

4. Fortis-AG, BFr27,167
5. Petrofina, BFr24,550
6. Kredietbank, BFr21,892
7. Bekaert, BFr21,084
8. Delhaize-le-Lion, BFr19,874
9. Union Miniere, BFr18,889
10. CBR, BFr17,795

Source: *GT Guide to World Equity Markets* (annual), Euromoney Publications, 1996, p. 61.

Bourse de Paris

★ 456 ★
LARGEST COMPANIES ON THE PARIS STOCK EXCHANGE, 1995

Ranked by: Market value, in billions of French francs (FFr). **Number listed:** 20

1. Elf Aquitaine with FFr97.951 billion
2. LVMH, FFr88.758
3. L'Oreal, FFr80.548
4. Total, FFr77.467
5. Carrefour, FFr76.179
6. Alcatel Alsthom, FFr63.561
7. Eaux (Cie Gle des), FFr57.394
8. Danone, FFr57.392
9. Axa, FFr54.257
10. Air Liquide, FFr53.590

Source: *GT Guide to World Equity Markets* (annual), Euromoney Publications, 1996, p. 131.

★ 457 ★
MOST ACTIVELY TRADED SHARES ON THE PARIS STOCK EXCHANGE, 1995

Ranked by: Average daily turnover, in billions of French francs (FFr). **Number listed:** 20

1. Elf Aquitaine with FFr217.352 billion
2. Alcatel Altsthom, FFr191.793
3. LVMH, FFr166.872
4. Carrefour, FFr146.088
5. Eaux (Cie Gle des), FFr145.079
6. Total, FFr142.747
7. Societe Generale, FFr133.917
8. Saint Gobain, FFr127.127
9. Danone, FFr123.670
10. L'Oreal, FFr109.554

Source: *GT Guide to World Equity Markets* (annual), Euromoney Publications, 1996, p. 132.

Brand Choice

★ 458 ★
BRANDS MOST FAVORED BY BRITISH TEENAGERS

Ranked by: Source provided no ranking criteria. **Number listed:** 10

1. Reebok
2. Cadbury
3. Nike
4. Adidas
5. Coca-Cola
6. Mars
7. Umbro
8. Wackers Crisps
9. Puma
10. Nestle

Source: *Nouvel Economiste*, December 24, 1996, p. 50.

★ 459 ★
BRANDS MOST FAVORED BY FRENCH TEENAGERS

Ranked by: Source provided no ranking criteria. **Number listed:** 10

1. Coca-Cola
2. Hollywood
3. Nike
4. Levi's
5. Adidas
6. McDonald's
7. Nintendo
8. Orangina
9. Sega
10. Mars

Source: *Nouvel Economiste*, December 24, 1996, p. 50.

★ 460 ★
BRANDS MOST FAVORED BY GERMAN TEENAGERS

Ranked by: Source provided no ranking criteria. **Number listed:** 10

1. Levi's
2. Adidas
3. Coca-Cola
4. Nike
5. Volkswagen
6. MTV
7. Diesel
8. Reebok
9. BMW
10. Langnese

Source: *Nouvel Economiste*, December 24, 1996, p. 50.

★ 461 ★
BRANDS MOST FAVORED BY ITALIAN TEENAGERS
Ranked by: Source provided no ranking criteria. **Number listed:** 10

1. Levi's
2. Ray-Ban
3. Radio Dee Jay
4. Adidas
5. Energy
6. Video Music
7. Nike
8. Coca-Cola
9. Smemoranda
10. Swatch

Source: *Nouvel Economiste*, December 24, 1996, p. 50.

★ 462 ★
BRANDS MOST FAVORED BY SPANISH TEENAGERS
Ranked by: Source provided no ranking criteria. **Number listed:** 10

1. Coca-Cola
2. Nike
3. Nintendo
4. Sega
5. Sony
6. Pepsi
7. Radical Fruit Company
8. Adidas
9. Reebok
10. Los Yo Principales

Source: *Nouvel Economiste*, December 24, 1996, p. 50.

Brand Loyalty
See: **Brand Choice**

Brand Name Goods

★ 463 ★
BEST MANAGED BRANDS
Ranked by: Premium to category, in percent. **Remarks:** Data represent the difference between current brand value and the value of a typical company in the same category. See source for details. **Number listed:** 20

1. Gillette with 212%
2. McDonald's, 204%
3. Coca-Cola, 196%
4. Louis Vuitton, 142%
5. Microsoft, 125%
6. Jell-O, 120%
7. Braun, 115%

8. Levi's, 114%
9. GE, 113%
10. Kellogg's, 113%

Source: *Financial World,* World's Most Valuable Brands (annual), July 8, 1996, p. 54.

★ 464 ★
MOST UNDERUTILIZED BRANDS
Ranked by: Discount to category, in percent. **Remarks:** Data represent the difference between current brand value and its potential value. See source for details. **Number listed:** 20

1. Arm & Hammer with 79%
2. Olive Garden, 77%
3. Coors, 77%
4. Keebler, 75%
5. Timberland, 72%
6. Electrolux, 70%
7. Dow, 70%
8. Sega, 70%
9. VO5, 66%
10. Orangina, 64%

Source: *Financial World,* World's Most Valuable Brands (annual), July 8, 1996, p. 55.

★ 465 ★
MOST VALUABLE BRANDS
Ranked by: Brand value, in millions of U.S. dollars. **Remarks:** Value was calculated using capital, ratio of capital to company sales, earnings, and corporate tax rate of the country where the parent company is located. See source for details. **Number listed:** 20

1. Marlboro with $44,614 million
2. Coca-Cola, $43,427
3. McDonald's, $18,920
4. IBM, $18,491
5. Disney, $15,358
6. Kodak, $13,267
7. Kellogg's, $11,409
8. Budweiser, $11,026
9. Nescafe, $10,527
10. Intel, $10,499

Source: *Financial World,* World's Most Valuable Brands (annual), July 8, 1996, p. 53.

Brazil – see under individual headings

Brewing Industry – United Kingdom

★ 466 ★
TOP BEER BRANDS IN THE UNITED KINGDOM, 1995

Ranked by: Estimated sales, in millions of British pounds (£). **Remarks:** Notes ad agency and spending. **Number listed:** 10
1. Stella Artois (Whitbread) with £Over 86 million
2. Carling Black Label (Bass Brewers), £70-75
3. Carlsberg (Carlsberg-Tetley), £55-60
4. Heineken (Whitbread), £55-60
5. Budweiser (Anheuser-Busch), £50-55
6. Tennent's Super (Bass Brewers), £50-55
7. Skol (Carlsberg-Tetley), £45-50
8. Boddingtons (Whitbread), £40-45
9. Guinness Original (Guinness), £40-45
10. McEwan's Export (Scottish & Newcastle), £40-45

Source: *Marketing,* July 4, 1996, p. 25.

Brokers

★ 467 ★
LARGEST BROKERAGES, 1995

Ranked by: Revenue, in millions of U.S. dollars. **Remarks:** Notes profits and global rank. **Number listed:** 4
1. Merrill Lynch (United States) with $21,513 million
2. Lehman Brothers Holdings (United States), $13,476
3. Morgan Stanley Group (United States), $10,949
4. Salomon (United States), $8,933

Source: *Fortune,* The Global 500: World's Biggest Corporations (annual), August 5, 1996, p. F-16.

★ 468 ★
TOP SOUTH KOREAN BROKERAGE FIRMS IN BACK OFFICE, 1996

Ranked by: Points, based on votes cast by over 100 international institutional investors active in the Asian equity markets from five continents. **Number listed:** 5
1. ING Barings with 24
2. CS First Boston, 12
3. SBC Warburg, 9
4. WI Carr, 6
5. Jardine Fleming, 3

Source: *Asiamoney,* Asiamoney Stockbrokers' Poll (annual), October 1996, p. 49.

★ 469 ★
TOP SOUTH KOREAN BROKERAGE FIRMS IN OVERALL RESEARCH, 1996

Ranked by: Points, based on votes cast by over 100 international institutional investors active in the Asian equity markets from five continents. **Number listed:** 9
1. Jardine Fleming with 57
2. ING Barings, 54
3. Peregrine, 30
4. Daewoo, 18
5. Morgan Grenfell, 15
6. SBC Warburg, 12
7. Dongsuh, 9
8. Ssangyong, 9
9. UBS Securities, 9

Source: *Asiamoney,* Asiamoney Stockbrokers' Poll (annual), October 1996, p. 49.

★ 470 ★
TOP SOUTH KOREAN BROKERAGE FIRMS IN SALES, 1996

Ranked by: Points, based on votes cast by over 100 international institutional investors active in the Asian equity markets from five continents. **Number listed:** 8
1. Jardine Fleming with 23
2. ING Barings, 17
3. LG Securities, 14
4. Peregrine, 13
5. Dai Shin, 11
6. SBC Warburg, 10
7. CS First Boston, 8
8. Daewoo, 8

Source: *Asiamoney,* Asiamoney Stockbrokers' Poll (annual), October 1996, p. 49.

★ 471 ★
TOP SOUTH KOREAN BROKERAGE FIRMS IN SPECIALIST RESEARCH, 1996

Ranked by: Points, based on votes cast by over 100 international institutional investors active in the Asian equity markets from five continents. **Number listed:** 10
1. ING Barings with 32.49
2. Jardine Fleming, 26.26
3. Peregrine, 22.93
4. Daewoo, 11.63
5. Morgan Grenfell, 7.68
6. SBC Warburg, 6.84
7. Ssangyong, 6.66
8. Dongsuh, 4.54
9. Nomura, 4.03
10. CS First Boston, 4.01

Source: *Asiamoney,* Asiamoney Stockbrokers' Poll (annual), October 1996, p. 49.

★ 472 ★

TOP SOUTH KOREAN BROKERAGE FIRMS, 1996

Ranked by: Points, based on votes cast by over 100 international institutional investors active in the Asian equity markets from five continents. **Number listed:** 15

1. ING Barings with 127.49
2. Jardine Fleming, 109.26
3. Peregrine, 65.93
4. SBC Warburg, 37.84
5. Daewoo, 37.63
6. Morgan Grenfell, 29.68
7. CS First Boston, 27.01
8. Dongsuh, 20.54
9. WI Carr, 18.41
10. Ssangyong, 17.66

Source: *Asiamoney,* Asiamoney Stockbrokers' Poll (annual), October 1996, p. 49.

Brokers – Asia

★ 473 ★

TOP BROKERAGE FIRMS IN ASIA, 1996

Ranked by: Points, based on votes cast by over 100 international institutional investors active in the Asian equity markets from five continents. **Number listed:** 20

1. Jardine Fleming with 1,561.83 points
2. ING Barings, 1,296.40
3. Credit Lyonnais, 1,022.42
4. Crosby Securities, 742.12
5. SBC Warburg, 734.07
6. WI Carr, 625.83
7. UBS Securities, 551.62
8. Merrill Lynch, 535.84
9. HG Asia, 512.50
10. Peregrine, 484.03

Source: *Asiamoney,* Asiamoney Stockbrokers' Poll (annual), October 1996, p. 33.

Brokers – Australia

★ 474 ★

TOP AUSTRALIAN BROKERAGE FIRMS IN BACK OFFICE, 1996

Ranked by: Points, based on votes cast by over 100 international institutional investors active in the Asian equity markets from five continents. **Number listed:** 8

1. J.B. Were with 24 points
2. County NatWest, 21
3. Macquarie Equities, 9
4. Ord Minnett, 9
5. SBC Warburg, 9
6. ANZ McCaughan, 6

7. BZW, 6
8. First Pacific, 3

Source: *Asiamoney,* Asiamoney Stockbrokers' Poll (annual), October 1996, p. 44.

★ 475 ★

TOP AUSTRALIAN BROKERAGE FIRMS IN OVERALL RESEARCH, 1996

Ranked by: Points, based on votes cast by over 100 international institutional investors active in the Asian equity markets from five continents. **Number listed:** 9

1. J.B. Were with 72 points
2. SBC Warburg, 36
3. First Pacific, 24
4. Bain & Co., 21
5. County NatWest, 21
6. Ord Minnett, 21
7. BZW, 9
8. Macquarie Equities, 6
9. McIntosh & Co., 6

Source: *Asiamoney,* Asiamoney Stockbrokers' Poll (annual), October 1996, p. 44.

★ 476 ★

TOP AUSTRALIAN BROKERAGE FIRMS IN SALES, 1996

Ranked by: Points, based on votes cast by over 100 international institutional investors active in the Asian equity markets from five continents. **Number listed:** 9

1. J.B. Were with 35 points
2. SBC Warburg, 23
3. Country NatWest, 21
4. McIntosh & Co., 14
5. Ord Minnett, 13
6. Bain & Co., 10
7. Macquarie Equities, 9
8. BZW, 4
9. First Pacific, 4

Source: *Asiamoney,* Asiamoney Stockbrokers' Poll (annual), October 1996, p. 44.

★ 477 ★

TOP AUSTRALIAN BROKERAGE FIRMS IN SPECIALIST RESEARCH, 1996

Ranked by: Points, based on votes cast by over 100 international institutional investors active in the Asian equity markets from five continents. **Number listed:** 10

1. J.B. Were with 46.94 points
2. SBC Warburg, 16.31
3. Ord Minnett, 15.27
4. Country NatWest, 14.37
5. First Pacific, 10.30
6. BZW, 9.07
7. McIntosh & Co., 7.38
8. Macquarie Equities, 7.03
9. Bain & Co., 6.89

10. James Capel, 3.07

Source: *Asiamoney,* Asiamoney Stockbrokers' Poll (annual), October 1996, p. 44.

★ 478 ★
TOP AUSTRALIAN BROKERAGE FIRMS, 1996
Ranked by: Points, based on votes cast by over 100 international institutional investors active in the Asian equity markets from five continents. **Number listed:** 13

1. J.B. Were with 177.94 points
2. SBC Warburg, 84.31
3. County NatWest, 77.37
4. Ord Minnett, 58.27
5. First Pacific, 41.65
6. Bain & Co., 37.89
7. Macquarie Equities, 31.03
8. BZW, 28.07
9. McIntosh & Co., 27.38
10. ANZ McCaughan, 7.74

Source: *Asiamoney,* Asiamoney Stockbrokers' Poll (annual), October 1996, p. 44.

Brokers – China

★ 479 ★
TOP CHINESE BROKERAGE FIRMS IN BACK OFFICE, 1996
Ranked by: Points, based on votes cast by over 100 international institutional investors active in the Asian equity markets from five continents. **Number listed:** 6

1. Credit Lyonnais with 48 points
2. Jardine Fleming, 27
3. Crosby, 15
4. HG Asia, 12
5. Peregrine, 12
6. WI Carr, 9

Source: *Asiamoney,* Asiamoney Stockbrokers' Poll (annual), October 1996, p. 44.

★ 480 ★
TOP CHINESE BROKERAGE FIRMS IN OVERALL RESEARCH, 1996
Ranked by: Points, based on votes cast by over 100 international institutional investors active in the Asian equity markets from five continents. **Number listed:** 9

1. Credit Lyonnais with 99 points
2. Jardine Fleming, 51
3. Crosby, 36
4. HG Asia, 27
5. Peregrine, 18
6. SBC Warburg, 6
7. WI Carr, 6
8. ING Barings, 3

9. Nomura, 3

Source: *Asiamoney,* Asiamoney Stockbrokers' Poll (annual), October 1996, p. 44.

★ 481 ★
TOP CHINESE BROKERAGE FIRMS IN SALES, 1996
Ranked by: Points, based on votes cast by over 100 international institutional investors active in the Asian equity markets from five continents. **Number listed:** 6

1. Credit Lyonnais with 35 points
2. Jardine Fleming, 28
3. Peregrine, 25
4. HG Asia, 14
5. WI Carr, 9
6. SBC Warburg, 4

Source: *Asiamoney,* Asiamoney Stockbrokers' Poll (annual), October 1996, p. 44.

★ 482 ★
TOP CHINESE BROKERAGE FIRMS IN SPECIALIST RESEARCH, 1996
Ranked by: Points, based on votes cast by over 100 international institutional investors active in the Asian equity markets from five continents. **Number listed:** 10

1. Credit Lyonnais with 49.51 points
2. Jardine Fleming, 31.75
3. Crosby, 15.63
4. Peregrine, 13.06
5. HG Asia, 6.94
6. WI Carr, 3.44
7. ING Barings, 3.02
8. SBC Warburg, 2.54
9. Merrill Lynch, 2.11
10. UBS, 1.91

Source: *Asiamoney,* Asiamoney Stockbrokers' Poll (annual), October 1996, p. 44.

★ 483 ★
TOP CHINESE BROKERAGE FIRMS, 1996
Ranked by: Points, based on votes cast by over 100 international institutional investors active in the Asian equity markets from five continents. **Number listed:** 15

1. Credit Lyonnais with 231.51 points
2. Jardine Fleming, 137.75
3. Crosby, 69.63
4. Peregrine, 68.06
5. HG Asia, 59.94
6. WI Carr, 27.44
7. SBC Warburg, 12.54
8. Nomura, 7.77
9. ING Barings, 5.02
10. Merrill Lynch, 5.11

Source: *Asiamoney,* Asiamoney Stockbrokers' Poll (annual), October 1996, p. 44.

Brokers – Hong Kong

★ 484 ★
TOP HONG KONG BROKERAGE FIRMS IN BACK OFFICE, 1996
Ranked by: Points, based on votes cast by over 100 international institutional investors active in the Asian equity markets from five continents. **Number listed:** 9

1. Kim Eng with 36 points
2. ING Barings, 30
3. Jardine Fleming, 30
4. BZW, 27
5. Peregrine, 24
6. James Capel, 21
7. Asia Equity, 18
8. HG Asia, 18
9. SBC Warburg, 15

Source: *Asiamoney,* Asiamoney Stockbrokers' Poll (annual), October 1996, p. 44.

★ 485 ★
TOP HONG KONG BROKERAGE FIRMS IN OVERALL RESEARCH, 1996
Ranked by: Points, based on votes cast by over 100 international institutional investors active in the Asian equity markets from five continents. **Number listed:** 10

1. Jardine Fleming with 201 points
2. Credit Lyonnais, 123
3. ING Barings, 81
4. SBC Warburg, 63
5. Crosby, 45
6. Merrill Lynch, 45
7. HG Asia, 30
8. Kim Eng, 27
9. Peregrine, 27
10. BZW, 24

Source: *Asiamoney,* Asiamoney Stockbrokers' Poll (annual), October 1996, p. 44.

★ 486 ★
TOP HONG KONG BROKERAGE FIRMS IN SALES, 1996
Ranked by: Points, based on votes cast by over 100 international institutional investors active in the Asian equity markets from five continents. **Number listed:** 10

1. Jardine Fleming with 79 points
2. Crosby, 43
3. Credit Lyonnais, 42
4. ING Barings, 42
5. Peregrine, 38
6. HG Asia, 37
7. Kim Eng, 34
8. Merrill Lynch, 23
9. Asia Equity, 22

10. James Capel, 21

Source: *Asiamoney,* Asiamoney Stockbrokers' Poll (annual), October 1996, p. 44.

★ 487 ★
TOP HONG KONG BROKERAGE FIRMS IN SPECIALIST RESEARCH, 1996
Ranked by: Points, based on votes cast by over 100 international institutional investors active in the Asian equity markets from five continents. **Number listed:** 10

1. Jardine Fleming with 85.69 points
2. Credit Lyonnais, 58.54
3. SBC Warburg, 37.72
4. ING Barings, 36.23
5. Crosby, 32.16
6. Merrill Lynch, 30.99
7. Kim Eng, 24.89
8. HG Asia, 21.64
9. Peregrine, 19.38
10. Morgan Stanley, 15.01

Source: *Asiamoney,* Asiamoney Stockbrokers' Poll (annual), October 1996, p. 96.

★ 488 ★
TOP HONG KONG BROKERAGE FIRMS, 1996
Ranked by: Points, based on votes cast by over 100 international institutional investors active in the Asian equity markets from five continents. **Number listed:** 15

1. Jardine Fleming with 395.69 points
2. Credit Lyonnais, 229.54
3. ING Barings, 189.23
4. Crosby, 132.16
5. SBC Warburg, 131.72
6. Kim Eng, 121.89
7. Peregrine, 108.38
8. Merrill Lynch, 107.99
9. HG Asia, 106.64
10. BZW, 80.41

Source: *Asiamoney,* Asiamoney Stockbrokers' Poll (annual), October 1996, p. 44.

Brokers – India

★ 489 ★
TOP INDIAN BROKERAGE FIRMS IN BACK OFFICE, 1996
Ranked by: Points, based on votes cast by over 100 international institutional investors active in the Asian equity markets from five continents. **Number listed:** 6

1. Jardine Fleming with 9
2. WI Carr, 9
3. DSP, 6
4. James Capel, 6
5. Kotak Mahindra, 3

6. Peregrine, 3

Source: *Asiamoney,* Asiamoney Stockbrokers' Poll (annual), October 1996, p. 46.

★ 490 ★

TOP INDIAN BROKERAGE FIRMS IN OVERALL RESEARCH, 1996

Ranked by: Points, based on votes cast by over 100 international institutional investors active in the Asian equity markets from five continents. **Number listed:** 8

1. Credit Lyonnais with 30
2. Jardine Fleming, 27
3. Morgan Stanley, 27
4. Peregrine, 24
5. WI Carr, 21
6. UBS Securities, 15
7. CS First Boston, 12
8. SSKI, 12

Source: *Asiamoney,* Asiamoney Stockbrokers' Poll (annual), October 1996, p. 46.

★ 491 ★

TOP INDIAN BROKERAGE FIRMS IN SALES, 1996

Ranked by: Points, based on votes cast by over 100 international institutional investors active in the Asian equity markets from five continents. **Number listed:** 10

1. WI Carr with 33
2. Peregrine, 25
3. Jardine Fleming, 14
4. Morgan Stanley, 12
5. UBS Securities, 11
6. Credit Lyonnais, 8
7. HG Asia, 7
8. ING Barings, 5
9. James Capel, 5
10. SSKI, 5

Source: *Asiamoney,* Asiamoney Stockbrokers' Poll (annual), October 1996, p. 46.

★ 492 ★

TOP INDIAN BROKERAGE FIRMS IN SPECIALIST RESEARCH, 1996

Ranked by: Points, based on votes cast by over 100 international institutional investors active in the Asian equity markets from five continents. **Number listed:** 10

1. Morgan Stanley with 18.60
2. Peregrine, 18.05
3. WI Carr, 9.86
4. CS First Boston, 8.93
5. Jardine Fleming, 8.73
6. Credit Lyonnais, 8.05
7. ING Barings, 7.70
8. James Capel, 6.04
9. Lehman Brothers, 5.31

10. UBS Securities, 4.46

Source: *Asiamoney,* Asiamoney Stockbrokers' Poll (annual), October 1996, p. 46.

★ 493 ★

TOP INDIAN BROKERAGE FIRMS, 1996

Ranked by: Points, based on votes cast by over 100 international institutional investors active in the Asian equity markets from five continents. **Number listed:** 15

1. WI Carr with 72.86
2. Peregrine, 70.05
3. Jardine Fleming, 58.73
4. Morgan Stanley, 57.60
5. Credit Lyonnais, 46.05
6. UBS Securities, 30.46
7. CS First Boston, 21.93
8. ING Barings, 21.70
9. SSKI, 18.99
10. James Capel, 17.04

Source: *Asiamoney,* Asiamoney Stockbrokers' Poll (annual), October 1996, p. 46.

Brokers – Indonesia

★ 494 ★

TOP INDONESIAN BROKERAGE FIRMS IN BACK OFFICE, 1996

Ranked by: Points, based on votes cast by over 100 international institutional investors active in the Asian equity markets from five continents. **Number listed:** 9

1. Jardine Fleming with 24
2. Baring, 15
3. Credit Lyonnais, 15
4. Lippo Securities, 12
5. Daiwa, 9
6. OCBC Sikap, 9
7. GK Goh, 6
8. James Capel, 6
9. Morgan Grenfell, 6

Source: *Asiamoney,* Asiamoney Stockbrokers' Poll (annual), October 1996, p. 46.

★ 495 ★

TOP INDONESIAN BROKERAGE FIRMS IN OVERALL RESEARCH, 1996

Ranked by: Points, based on votes cast by over 100 international institutional investors active in the Asian equity markets from five continents. **Number listed:** 8

1. HG Asia with 57
2. Jardine Fleming, 45
3. Baring, 39
4. WI Carr, 39
5. Credit Lyonnais, 36
6. UBS Securities, 24

7. Merrill Lynch, 21
8. Lippo Securities, 12

Source: *Asiamoney,* Asiamoney Stockbrokers' Poll (annual), October 1996, p. 46.

★ 496 ★
TOP INDONESIAN BROKERAGE FIRMS IN SALES, 1996
Ranked by: Points, based on votes cast by over 100 international institutional investors active in the Asian equity markets from five continents. **Number listed:** 9
1. Baring with 28
2. Credit Lyonnais, 27
3. WI Carr, 21
4. HG Asia, 20
5. Jardine Fleming, 17
6. Daiwa, 9
7. Lippo Securities, 9
8. Merrill Lynch, 9
9. UBS Securities, 9

Source: *Asiamoney,* Asiamoney Stockbrokers' Poll (annual), October 1996, p. 46.

★ 497 ★
TOP INDONESIAN BROKERAGE FIRMS IN SPECIALIST RESEARCH, 1996
Ranked by: Points, based on votes cast by over 100 international institutional investors active in the Asian equity markets from five continents. **Number listed:** 10
1. Baring with 23.26
2. WI Carr, 23.26
3. HG Asia, 22.97
4. Jardine Fleming, 21.49
5. Credit Lyonnais, 19.51
6. UBS Securities, 16.03
7. Merrill Lynch, 11.65
8. Peregrine, 7.85
9. BZW, 7.53
10. Lippo Securities, 5.13

Source: *Asiamoney,* Asiamoney Stockbrokers' Poll (annual), October 1996, p. 46.

★ 498 ★
TOP INDONESIAN BROKERAGE FIRMS, 1996
Ranked by: Points, based on votes cast by over 100 international institutional investors active in the Asian equity markets from five continents. **Number listed:** 15
1. Jardine Fleming with 107.49
2. Baring, 105.26
3. HG Asia, 102.97
4. Credit Lyonnais, 97.51
5. WI Carr, 83.26
6. UBS Securities, 49.03
7. Merrill Lynch, 41.65
8. Lippo Securities, 38.13
9. GK Goh, 25.39

10. Morgan Grenfell, 24.21

Source: *Asiamoney,* Asiamoney Stockbrokers' Poll (annual), October 1996, p. 46.

Brokers – Japan

★ 499 ★
TOP JAPANESE BROKERAGE FIRMS IN BACK OFFICE, 1996
Ranked by: Points, based on votes cast by over 100 international institutional investors active in the Asian equity markets from five continents. **Number listed:** 10
1. Yamaichi with 21
2. BZW, 18
3. Jardine Fleming, 18
4. Schroders, 18
5. James Capel, 15
6. Nikko, 15
7. SBC Warburg, 15
8. Goldman Sachs, 12
9. Merrill Lynch, 12
10. Nomura, 12

Source: *Asiamoney,* Asiamoney Stockbrokers' Poll (annual), October 1996, p. 46.

★ 500 ★
TOP JAPANESE BROKERAGE FIRMS IN OVERALL RESEARCH, 1996
Ranked by: Points, based on votes cast by over 100 international institutional investors active in the Asian equity markets from five continents. **Number listed:** 8
1. Nomura with 114
2. Jardine Fleming, 30
3. Merrill Lynch, 30
4. BZW, 27
5. James Capel, 27
6. SBC Warburg, 27
7. Goldman Sachs, 21
8. Nikko, 18

Source: *Asiamoney,* Asiamoney Stockbrokers' Poll (annual), October 1996, p. 46.

★ 501 ★
TOP JAPANESE BROKERAGE FIRMS IN SALES, 1996
Ranked by: Points, based on votes cast by over 100 international institutional investors active in the Asian equity markets from five continents. **Number listed:** 10
1. Nomura with 40
2. James Capel, 24
3. Yamaichi, 24
4. Merrill Lynch, 17
5. SBC Warburg, 17
6. BZW, 12

7. Daiwa, 12
8. Morgan Grenfell, 12
9. Nikko, 12
10. Salomon Brothers, 12

Source: *Asiamoney,* Asiamoney Stockbrokers' Poll (annual), October 1996, p. 46.

★ 502 ★
TOP JAPANESE BROKERAGE FIRMS IN SPECIALIST RESEARCH, 1996

Ranked by: Points, based on votes cast by over 100 international institutional investors active in the Asian equity markets from five continents. **Number listed:** 10

1. Nomura with 76.95
2. Nikko, 19.32
3. James Capel, 18.43
4. Merrill Lynch, 18.05
5. Yamaichi, 16.01
6. Daiwa, 15.83
7. Goldman Sachs, 15.24
8. BZW, 14.62
9. Jardine Fleming, 13.52
10. Salomon Brothers, 12.76

Source: *Asiamoney,* Asiamoney Stockbrokers' Poll (annual), October 1996, p. 46.

★ 503 ★
TOP JAPANESE BROKERAGE FIRMS, 1996

Ranked by: Points, based on votes cast by over 100 international institutional investors active in the Asian equity markets from five continents. **Number listed:** 15

1. Nomura with 242.95
2. James Capel, 84.43
3. Merrill Lynch, 77.05
4. Yamaichi, 73.01
5. BZW, 71.62
6. SBC Warburg, 70.09
7. Jardine Fleming, 69.52
8. Nikko, 64.32
9. Goldman Sachs, 53.24
10. Daiwa, 42.83

Source: *Asiamoney,* Asiamoney Stockbrokers' Poll (annual), October 1996, p. 46.

★ 504 ★
TOP SECURITIES BROKERS IN JAPAN, 1996

Ranked by: Operating revenue, in billions of yen (¥). **Remarks:** Includes net and recurring profits for 1996 and 1995. **Number listed:** 20

1. Nomura with ¥250.4 billion
2. Daiwa, ¥157.6
3. Nikko, ¥142.4
4. Yamaichi, ¥110.9
5. Kokusai, ¥44.2
6. New Japan, ¥40.7
7. Kankaku, ¥31.8

8. Sanyo, ¥29.8
9. Wako, ¥29.8
10. Okasan, ¥22.7

Source: *Financial Times,* October 23, 1996, p. 22.

Brokers – Malaysia

★ 505 ★
TOP MALAYSIAN BROKERAGE FIRMS IN BACK OFFICE, 1996

Ranked by: Points, based on votes cast by over 100 international institutional investors active in the Asian equity markets from five continents. **Number listed:** 9

1. Rashid Hussain with 60
2. Morgan Grenfell, 39
3. Arab-Malaysian, 27
4. Peregrine, 18
5. Crosby, 15
6. Hwang DBS, 15
7. UBS Securities, 15
8. Jardine Fleming, 12
9. Merrill Lynch, 12

Source: *Asiamoney,* Asiamoney Stockbrokers' Poll (annual), October 1996, p. 49.

★ 506 ★
TOP MALAYSIAN BROKERAGE FIRMS IN OVERALL RESEARCH, 1996

Ranked by: Points, based on votes cast by over 100 international institutional investors active in the Asian equity markets from five continents. **Number listed:** 8

1. Crosby with 90
2. Rashid Hussain, 90
3. ING Barings, 75
4. UBS Securities, 51
5. Merrill Lynch, 36
6. Credit Lyonnais, 33
7. Jardine Fleming, 33
8. James Capel, 30

Source: *Asiamoney,* Asiamoney Stockbrokers' Poll (annual), October 1996, p. 49.

★ 507 ★
TOP MALAYSIAN BROKERAGE FIRMS IN SALES, 1996

Ranked by: Points, based on votes cast by over 100 international institutional investors active in the Asian equity markets from five continents. **Number listed:** 10

1. Rashid Hussain with 58
2. Crosby, 54
3. Morgan Grenfell, 29
4. Phileo Allied, 26
5. ING Barings, 25
6. Merrill Lynch, 24

7. UBS Securities, 23
8. Arab-Malaysian, 22
9. Jardine Fleming, 20
10. Kim Eng, 20

Source: *Asiamoney,* Asiamoney Stockbrokers' Poll (annual), October 1996, p. 49.

★ 508 ★

TOP MALAYSIAN BROKERAGE FIRMS IN SPECIALIST RESEARCH, 1996

Ranked by: Points, based on votes cast by over 100 international institutional investors active in the Asian equity markets from five continents. **Number listed:** 10

1. Rashid Hussain with 64.32
2. Crosby, 52.42
3. ING Barings, 44.65
4. UBS Securities, 28.74
5. Credit Lyonnais, 28.23
6. Merrill Lynch, 25.89
7. Jardine Fleming, 20.27
8. Morgan Grenfell, 18.71
9. Arab-Malaysian, 16.76
10. SBC Warburg, 16.38

Source: *Asiamoney,* Asiamoney Stockbrokers' Poll (annual), October 1996, p. 49.

★ 509 ★

TOP MALAYSIAN BROKERAGE FIRMS, 1996

Ranked by: Points, based on votes cast by over 100 international institutional investors active in the Asian equity markets from five continents. **Number listed:** 14

1. Rashid Hussain with 272.32
2. Crosby, 211.42
3. ING Barings, 153.65
4. UBS Securities, 117.74
5. Morgan Grenfell, 107.71
6. Merrill Lynch, 97.89
7. Jardine Fleming, 85.27
8. Arab-Malaysian, 77.76
9. Credit Lyonnais, 73.23
10. Peregrine, 71.69

Source: *Asiamoney,* Asiamoney Stockbrokers' Poll (annual), October 1996, p. 49.

Brokers – New Zealand

★ 510 ★

TOP NEW ZEALAND BROKERAGE FIRMS IN BACK OFFICE, 1996

Ranked by: Points, based on votes cast by over 100 international institutional investors active in the Asian equity markets from five continents. **Number listed:** 9

1. Doyle Paterson with 18
2. BZW, 12

3. Hendry Hay McIntosh, 12
4. Ord Minnett, 12
5. SBC Warburg, 12
6. Cavill White, 9
7. Country NatWest, 9
8. First NZ Capital, 9
9. ANZ McCaughan, 6

Source: *Asiamoney,* Asiamoney Stockbrokers' Poll (annual), October 1996, p. 49.

★ 511 ★

TOP NEW ZEALAND BROKERAGE FIRMS IN OVERALL RESEARCH, 1996

Ranked by: Points, based on votes cast by over 100 international institutional investors active in the Asian equity markets from five continents. **Number listed:** 9

1. Doyle Paterson with 48
2. JB Were, 36
3. SBC Warburg, 30
4. Ord Minnett, 27
5. First NZ Capital, 15
6. BZW, 9
7. County NatWest, 6
8. Hendry Hay McIntosh, 6
9. ANZ McCaughan, 3

Source: *Asiamoney,* Asiamoney Stockbrokers' Poll (annual), October 1996, p. 49.

★ 512 ★

TOP NEW ZEALAND BROKERAGE FIRMS IN SALES, 1996

Ranked by: Points, based on votes cast by over 100 international institutional investors active in the Asian equity markets from five continents. **Number listed:** 9

1. SBC Warburg with 25
2. First NZ Capital, 19
3. Doyle Paterson, 14
4. Hendry Hay McIntosh, 9
5. Ord Minnett, 9
6. BZW, 5
7. ANZ McCaughan, 3
8. JB Were, 3
9. County NatWest, 1

Source: *Asiamoney,* Asiamoney Stockbrokers' Poll (annual), October 1996, p. 49.

★ 513 ★

TOP NEW ZEALAND BROKERAGE FIRMS IN SPECIALIST RESEARCH, 1996

Ranked by: Points, based on votes cast by over 100 international institutional investors active in the Asian equity markets from five continents. **Number listed:** 10

1. SBC Warburg with 17.27
2. First NZ Capital, 15.42
3. Doyle Paterson, 15.20
4. Ord Minnett, 14.97

5. BZW, 6.95
6. ANZ McCaughan, 5.52
7. Hendry Hay McIntosh, 5.50
8. County NatWest, 4.18
9. JB Were, 3.98
10. Garlick & Co., 0.93

Source: *Asiamoney,* Asiamoney Stockbrokers' Poll (annual), October 1996, p. 49.

★ 514 ★

TOP NEW ZEALAND BROKERAGE FIRMS, 1996

Ranked by: Points, based on votes cast by over 100 international institutional investors active in the Asian equity markets from five continents. **Number listed:** 11

1. Doyle Paterson with 95.20
2. SBC Warburg, 84.27
3. Ord Minnett, 62.97
4. First NZ Capital, 58.42
5. JB Were, 45.98
6. BZW, 32.95
7. Hendry Hay McIntosh, 32.50
8. County NatWest, 20.18
9. ANZ McCaughan, 17.52
10. Cavill White, 9.00

Source: *Asiamoney,* Asiamoney Stockbrokers' Poll (annual), October 1996, p. 49.

Brokers – Pakistan

★ 515 ★

TOP PAKISTAN BROKERAGE FIRMS IN BACK OFFICE, 1996

Ranked by: Points, based on votes cast by over 100 international institutional investors active in the Asian equity markets from five continents. **Number listed:** 3

1. HG Asia with 18
2. WI Carr, 12
3. Credit Lyonnais, 6

Source: *Asiamoney,* Asiamoney Stockbrokers' Poll (annual), October 1996, p. 51.

★ 516 ★

TOP PAKISTAN BROKERAGE FIRMS IN OVERALL RESEARCH, 1996

Ranked by: Points, based on votes cast by over 100 international institutional investors active in the Asian equity markets from five continents. **Number listed:** 7

1. WI Carr with 54
2. Credit Lyonnais, 36
3. ING Barings, 18
4. HG Asia, 12
5. Merrill Lynch, 12
6. Crosby, 6

7. J. Suddyin, 6

Source: *Asiamoney,* Asiamoney Stockbrokers' Poll (annual), October 1996, p. 51.

★ 517 ★

TOP PAKISTAN BROKERAGE FIRMS IN SALES, 1996

Ranked by: Points, based on votes cast by over 100 international institutional investors active in the Asian equity markets from five continents. **Number listed:** 8

1. Credit Lyonnais with 46
2. WI Carr, 36
3. Merrill Lynch, 16
4. HG Asia, 14
5. Crosby, 12
6. J. Suddyin, 12
7. ING Barings, 10
8. UBS Securities, 4

Source: *Asiamoney,* Asiamoney Stockbrokers' Poll (annual), October 1996, p. 51.

★ 518 ★

TOP PAKISTAN BROKERAGE FIRMS IN SPECIALIST RESEARCH, 1996

Ranked by: Points, based on votes cast by over 100 international institutional investors active in the Asian equity markets from five continents. **Number listed:** 9

1. Credit Lyonnais with 23.86
2. WI Carr, 18.50
3. Jardine Flemings, 8.36
4. J. Suddyin, 7.71
5. ING Barings, 6.93
6. HG Asia, 5.30
7. Crosby, 3.56
8. UBS Securities, 0.84
9. Merrill Lynch, 0.81

Source: *Asiamoney,* Asiamoney Stockbrokers' Poll (annual), October 1996, p. 51.

★ 519 ★

TOP PAKISTAN BROKERAGE FIRMS, 1996

Ranked by: Points, based on votes cast by over 100 international institutional investors active in the Asian equity markets from five continents. **Number listed:** 9

1. WI Carr with 120.50
2. Credit Lyonnais, 111.86
3. HG Asia, 49.30
4. ING Barings, 34.93
5. Merrill Lynch, 28.81
6. J. Suddyin, 25.71
7. Crosby, 21.56
8. Jardine Fleming, 8.36
9. UBS, 4.84

Source: *Asiamoney,* Asiamoney Stockbrokers' Poll (annual), October 1996, p. 51.

Brokers – Philippines

★ 520 ★

TOP PHILIPPINE BROKERAGE FIRMS IN BACK OFFICE, 1996

Ranked by: Points, based on votes cast by over 100 international institutional investors active in the Asian equity markets from five continents. **Number listed:** 9

1. Jardine Fleming with 33
2. ING Barings, 30
3. BZW, 12
4. Daiwa, 9
5. Morgan Grenfell, 9
6. SBC Warburg, 9
7. HG Asia, 6
8. JP Morgan, 6
9. UBS Securities, 6

Source: *Asiamoney,* Asiamoney Stockbrokers' Poll (annual), October 1996, p. 51.

★ 521 ★

TOP PHILIPPINE BROKERAGE FIRMS IN OVERALL RESEARCH, 1996

Ranked by: Points, based on votes cast by over 100 international institutional investors active in the Asian equity markets from five continents. **Number listed:** 10

1. ING Barings with 99
2. Jardine Fleming, 66
3. Morgan Grenfell, 33
4. Asia Equity, 27
5. SBC Warburg, 27
6. Crosby, 15
7. UBS Securities, 15
8. All Asia, 9
9. HG Asia, 9

Source: *Asiamoney,* Asiamoney Stockbrokers' Poll (annual), October 1996, p. 51.

★ 522 ★

TOP PHILIPPINE BROKERAGE FIRMS IN SALES, 1996

Ranked by: Points, based on votes cast by over 100 international institutional investors active in the Asian equity markets from five continents. **Number listed:** 10

1. ING Barings with 45
2. Jardine Fleming, 32
3. Morgan Grenfell, 23
4. UBS Securities, 13
5. Asia Equity, 12
6. SBC Warburg, 12
7. Peregrine, 9
8. Pryce, 9
9. Crosby, 7

10. Worldsec, 7

Source: *Asiamoney,* Asiamoney Stockbrokers' Poll (annual), October 1996, p. 51.

★ 523 ★

TOP PHILIPPINE BROKERAGE FIRMS IN SPECIALIST RESEARCH, 1996

Ranked by: Points, based on votes cast by over 100 international institutional investors active in the Asian equity markets from five continents. **Number listed:** 10

1. ING Barings with 59.21
2. Jardine Fleming, 34.99
3. Morgan Grenfell, 15.29
4. SBC Warburg, 14.95
5. HG Asia, 13.43
6. Asia Equity, 12.59
7. UBS Securities, 5.45
8. Crosby, 5.21
9. All Asia, 5.18
10. James Capel, 4.32

Source: *Asiamoney,* Asiamoney Stockbrokers' Poll (annual), October 1996, p. 51.

★ 524 ★

TOP PHILIPPINE BROKERAGE FIRMS, 1996

Ranked by: Points, based on votes cast by over 100 international institutional investors active in the Asian equity markets from five continents. **Number listed:** 15

1. ING Barings with 233.21
2. Jardine Fleming, 165.99
3. Morgan Grenfell, 80.29
4. SBC Warburg, 62.95
5. Asia Equity, 54.59
6. UBS Securities, 39.45
7. HG Asia, 34.43
8. BZW, 28.20
9. Crosby, 27.21
10. All Asia, 20.18

Source: *Asiamoney,* Asiamoney Stockbrokers' Poll (annual), October 1996, p. 51.

Brokers – Singapore

★ 525 ★

TOP SINGAPORE BROKERAGE FIRMS IN BACK OFFICE, 1996

Ranked by: Points, based on votes cast by over 100 international institutional investors active in the Asian equity markets from five continents. **Number listed:** 10

1. GK Goh with 27
2. ING Barings, 27
3. Kim Eng, 18
4. Merrill Lynch, 18
5. UBS Securities, 18

6. WI Carr, 18
7. DBS Securities, 15
8. Jardine Fleming, 15
9. SBC Warburg, 15
10. BZW, 12

Source: *Asiamoney,* Asiamoney Stockbrokers' Poll (annual), October 1996, p. 51.

★ 526 ★
TOP SINGAPORE BROKERAGE FIRMS IN OVERALL RESEARCH, 1996
Ranked by: Points, based on votes cast by over 100 international institutional investors active in the Asian equity markets from five continents. **Number listed:** 10
1. ING Barings with 78
2. UBS Securities, 66
3. Crosby, 57
4. Merrill Lynch, 39
5. Credit Lyonnais, 33
6. James Capel, 33
7. WI Carr, 30
8. BZW, 27
9. Jardine Fleming, 24
10. Kim Eng, 21

Source: *Asiamoney,* Asiamoney Stockbrokers' Poll (annual), October 1996, p. 51.

★ 527 ★
TOP SINGAPORE BROKERAGE FIRMS IN SALES, 1996
Ranked by: Points, based on votes cast by over 100 international institutional investors active in the Asian equity markets from five continents. **Number listed:** 10
1. Crosby with 43
2. ING Barings, 39
3. Kim Eng, 31
4. Merrill Lynch, 28
5. WI Carr, 25
6. GK Goh, 24
7. James Capel, 22
8. Morgan Grenfell, 19
9. Jardine Fleming, 18
10. DBS Securities, 16

Source: *Asiamoney,* Asiamoney Stockbrokers' Poll (annual), October 1996, p. 51.

★ 528 ★
TOP SINGAPORE BROKERAGE FIRMS IN SPECIALIST RESEARCH, 1996
Ranked by: Points, based on votes cast by over 100 international institutional investors active in the Asian equity markets from five continents. **Number listed:** 10
1. Crosby with 41.55
2. ING Barings, 37.75
3. UBS Securities, 33.25
4. Credit Lyonnais, 30.98

5. Kim Eng, 22.84
6. Merrill Lynch, 21.61
7. Jardine Fleming, 17.03
8. BZW, 13.86
9. GK Goh, 13.42
10. WI Carr, 12.58

Source: *Asiamoney,* Asiamoney Stockbrokers' Poll (annual), October 1996, p. 51.

★ 529 ★
TOP SINGAPORE BROKERAGE FIRMS, 1996
Ranked by: Points, based on votes cast by over 100 international institutional investors active in the Asian equity markets from five continents. **Number listed:** 15
1. ING Barings with 181.75
2. Crosby, 153.55
3. UBS Securities, 129.25
4. Merrill Lynch, 106.61
5. Kim Eng, 92.84
6. Credit Lyonnais, 87.98
7. WI Carr, 85.58
8. GK Goh, 79.42
9. James Capel, 74.35
10. Jardine Flemming, 74.03

Source: *Asiamoney,* Asiamoney Stockbrokers' Poll (annual), October 1996, p. 51.

Brokers – Taiwan

★ 530 ★
TOP TAIWAN BROKERAGE FIRMS IN BACK OFFICE, 1996
Ranked by: Points, based on votes cast by over 100 international institutional investors active in the Asian equity markets from five continents. **Number listed:** 7
1. SBC Warburg with 27
2. Jardine Fleming, 18
3. BZW, 9
4. HG Asia, 6
5. ING Barings, 3
6. National Securities, 3
7. WI Carr, 3

Source: *Asiamoney,* Asiamoney Stockbrokers' Poll (annual), October 1996, p. 52.

★ 531 ★
TOP TAIWAN BROKERAGE FIRMS IN OVERALL RESEARCH, 1996
Ranked by: Points, based on votes cast by over 100 international institutional investors active in the Asian equity markets from five continents. **Number listed:** 8
1. ING Barings with 72
2. SBC Warburg, 54
3. Jardine Fleming, 30

4. UBS Securities, 21
5. HG Asia, 15
6. Credit Lyonnais, 9
7. BZW, 6
8. WI Carr, 6

Source: *Asiamoney,* Asiamoney Stockbrokers' Poll (annual), October 1996, p. 52.

★ 532 ★

TOP TAIWAN BROKERAGE FIRMS IN SALES, 1996

Ranked by: Points, based on votes cast by over 100 international institutional investors active in the Asian equity markets from five continents. **Number listed:** 9

1. Jardine Fleming with 22
2. SBC Warburg, 19
3. ING Barings, 15
4. Credit Lyonnais, 13
5. HG Asia, 12
6. BZW, 6
7. Capital Securities, 6
8. WI Carr, 6
9. James Capel, 4

Source: *Asiamoney,* Asiamoney Stockbrokers' Poll (annual), October 1996, p. 52.

★ 533 ★

TOP TAIWAN BROKERAGE FIRMS IN SPECIALIST RESEARCH, 1996

Ranked by: Points, based on votes cast by over 100 international institutional investors active in the Asian equity markets from five continents. **Number listed:** 10

1. ING Barings with 31.25
2. SBC Warburg, 28.97
3. Jardine Fleming, 22.86
4. WI Carr, 13.10
5. UBS Securities, 7.98
6. Credit Lyonnais, 7.90
7. BZW, 6.31
8. China Trust, 4.42
9. James Capel, 4.33
10. HG Asia, 3.97

Source: *Asiamoney,* Asiamoney Stockbrokers' Poll (annual), October 1996, p. 52.

★ 534 ★

TOP TAIWAN BROKERAGE FIRMS, 1996

Ranked by: Points, based on votes cast by over 100 international institutional investors active in the Asian equity markets from five continents. **Number listed:** 15

1. SBC Warburg with 128.97
2. ING Barings, 121.25
3. Jardine Fleming, 92.86
4. HG Asia, 36.97
5. UBS Securities, 31.98
6. Credit Lyonnais, 29.90
7. WI Carr, 28.10

8. BZW, 27.31
9. James Capel, 8.33
10. Capital Securities, 7.78

Source: *Asiamoney,* Asiamoney Stockbrokers' Poll (annual), October 1996, p. 52.

Brokers – Thailand

★ 535 ★

TOP THAILAND BROKERAGE FIRMS IN BACK OFFICE, 1996

Ranked by: Points, based on votes cast by over 100 international institutional investors active in the Asian equity markets from five continents. **Number listed:** 9

1. Jardine Fleming with 21
2. Crosby, 18
3. James Capel, 15
4. Asia Equity, 12
5. Credit Lyonnais, 9
6. Merrill Lynch, 9
7. Morgan Grenfell, 9
8. Nomura, 9
9. UBS Securities, 9

Source: *Asiamoney,* Asiamoney Stockbrokers' Poll (annual), October 1996, p. 52.

★ 536 ★

TOP THAILAND BROKERAGE FIRMS IN OVERALL RESEARCH, 1996

Ranked by: Points, based on votes cast by over 100 international institutional investors active in the Asian equity markets from five continents. **Number listed:** 8

1. Jardine Fleming with 57
2. Crosby, 54
3. Credit Lyonnais, 42
4. WI Carr, 39
5. Asia Equity, 36
6. UBS Securities, 30
7. BZW, 21
8. ING Barings, 18
9. Merrill Lynch, 18

Source: *Asiamoney,* Asiamoney Stockbrokers' Poll (annual), October 1996, p. 52.

★ 537 ★

TOP THAILAND BROKERAGE FIRMS IN SALES, 1996

Ranked by: Points, based on votes cast by over 100 international institutional investors active in the Asian equity markets from five continents. **Number listed:** 10

1. WI Carr with 42
2. Jardine Fleming, 33
3. Asia Equity, 26
4. Credit Lyonnais, 25

5. Merrill Lynch, 20
6. UBS Securities, 19
7. Peregrine, 17
8. Morgan Grenfell, 15
9. Crosby, 12
10. HG Asia, 10

Source: *Asiamoney,* Asiamoney Stockbrokers' Poll (annual), October 1996, p. 52.

★ 538 ★
TOP THAILAND BROKERAGE FIRMS IN SPECIALIST RESEARCH, 1996
Ranked by: Points, based on votes cast by over 100 international institutional investors active in the Asian equity markets from five continents. **Number listed:** 10
1. Asia Equity with 27.99
2. Jardine Fleming, 24.62
3. Crosby, 21.56
4. WI Carr, 20.80
5. Credit Lyonnais, 20.50
6. UBS Securities, 18.81
7. HG Asia, 17.11
8. ING Barings, 16.83
9. Merrill Lynch, 12.29
10. Peregrine, 11.33

Source: *Asiamoney,* Asiamoney Stockbrokers' Poll (annual), October 1996, p. 52.

★ 539 ★
TOP THAILAND BROKERAGE FIRMS, 1996
Ranked by: Points, based on votes cast by over 100 international institutional investors active in the Asian equity markets from five continents. **Number listed:** 15
1. Jardine Fleming with 135.62
2. WI Carr, 107.80
3. Crosby, 105.56
4. Asia Equity, 101.99
5. Credit Lyonnais, 96.50
6. UBS Securities, 76.81
7. Merrill Lynch, 59.29
8. Peregrine, 49.33
9. HG Asia, 45.11
10. BZW, 44.45

Source: *Asiamoney,* Asiamoney Stockbrokers' Poll (annual), October 1996, p. 52.

Brussels Stock Exchange
See: **Bourse de Bruxelles**

Budapest Stock Exchange

★ 540 ★
LARGEST COMPANIES ON THE BUDAPEST STOCK EXCHANGE, 1995
Ranked by: Market capitalization, in billions of forints (Fo). **Number listed:** 10
1. Mol with Fo111.19 billion
2. Richter, Fo44.60
3. OTP, Fo25.37
4. Egis, Fo23.63
5. Pharmavit, Fo14.30
6. Pick, Fo13.82
7. Primagaz, Fo13.12
8. Danubius, Fo10.28
9. Dunaholding, Fo9.35
10. Graboplast, Fo5.80

Source: *GT Guide to World Equity Markets* (annual), Euromoney Publications, 1996, p. 516.

Buenos Aires Stock Exchange

★ 541 ★
LARGEST COMPANIES ON THE BUENOS AIRES STOCK EXCHANGE, 1995
Ranked by: Market value, in millions of U.S. dollars. **Number listed:** 20
1. YPF with $7,589.5 million
2. Telefonica de Argentina, $6,365.3
3. Telecom Argentina, $4,646.3
4. Perez Companc, $3,540.3
5. Transportadora Gas del Sur, $1,914.7
6. Banco Frances, $1,134.8
7. Banco Galicia y Buenos Aires, $1,117.6
8. Citicorp Equity Investments, $917.9
9. Siderca, $904.2
10. Buenos Aires Embotelladora, $764.9

Source: *GT Guide to World Equity Markets* (annual), Euromoney Publications, 1996, p. 35.

★ 542 ★
MOST ACTIVELY TRADED SHARES ON THE BUENOS AIRES STOCK EXCHANGE, 1995
Ranked by: Trading value, in millions of pesos (Pe). **Number listed:** 20
1. Perez Companc with Pe815.2 million
2. YPF, Pe490.2
3. Indupa, Pe386.8
4. Siderca, Pe346.2
5. Telefonica de Argentina, Pe319.8
6. Cia Interamericana de Automoviles, Pe298.8
7. Astra, Pe285.6
8. Acindar, Pe266.5

9. Comercial del Plata, Pe259.5
10. Banco Frances, Pe249.7

Source: *GT Guide to World Equity Markets* (annual), Euromoney Publications, 1996, p. 36.

Building Contractors
See: **Contractors**

Building Materials Industry

★ 543 ★
LARGEST BUILDING MATERIALS MAKERS IN THAILAND
Ranked by: Revenue, in millions of bahts (Bt). **Remarks:** Includes profits and assets. **Number listed:** 103
1. Siam Cement with Bt47,246.62 million
2. Siam City Cement, Bt12,831.49
3. Concrete Product and Aggregate, Bt7,937.38
4. Bangkok Steel Industry, Bt6,402.50
5. BSI Marketing, Bt5,733.58
6. Thai Tinplate Manufacturing, Bt5,319.81
7. Siam Fibre-Cement, Bt4,551.52
8. Thai Central Steel, Bt3,853.30
9. Sahaviriya Steel Industries, Bt3,781.18
10. Siam Steel Pipes Import-Export, Bt3,760.21

Source: *Business Review*, December 1995, p. 169+.

★ 544 ★
TOP BUILDING MATERIALS & CONSTRUCTION COMPANIES, 1996
Ranked by: Market capitalization at September 30, 1996, in millions of U.S. dollars. **Number listed:** 10
1. Saint-Gobain with $11,776.2 million
2. Kajima Corp., $9,178.5
3. Corning, $8,970.0
4. Shimizu Corp., $7,899.8
5. Sekisui House, $7,857.6
6. Daiwa House Industry, $7,402.4
7. Taisei Corp., $6,715.4
8. Tostem Corp., $6,579.9
9. Obayashi Corp., $6,203.5
10. Lafarge, $5,616.1

Source: *Financial Times*, January 7, 1997, p. IV.

Building Materials Industry – Europe

★ 545 ★
LARGEST EUROPEAN CONSTRUCTION MATERIALS GROUPS
Ranked by: Turnover, in billions of U.S. dollars. **Remarks:** Includes figures on net income and market capitalization. **Number listed:** 10
1. Bouygues with $14.10 billion
2. Saint Gobain, $13.52
3. Holzmann, $9.12
4. Holderbank, $6.61
5. Lafarge, $6.39
6. RMC, $6.22
7. Wolseley, $5.71
8. Skanska, $5.64
9. Bilfinger & Berger BAU, $5.58
10. Poliet, $4.36

Source: *Financial Times*, June 17, 1996, p. 24.

Bulgaria – see under individual headings

Burkina Faso – see under individual headings

Burundi – see under individual headings

Buses

★ 546 ★
TOP MANUFACTURERS OF BUS BODIES IN BRAZIL
Ranked by: Annual sales, in millions of U.S. dollars. **Remarks:** Notes each company's net worth. **Number listed:** 6
1. Marcopolo with $238,283.0 million
2. CAIO, $117,089.0
3. Nielson, $104,758.0
4. Caio Norte, $15,495.0
5. Mec nica Auxiliar, $1,079.0
6. Reciferal, $4.0

Source: *National Trade Data Bank*, June 19, 1997, p. ISA970601.

Business Conditions

★ 547 ★
BUSINESS START-UPS IN THE UNITED KINGDOM, 1996
Ranked by: Number of start-ups in each region. **Number listed:** 10
1. South East with 103,000 start-ups
2. Greater London, 54,000
3. South West, 54,000
4. North West, 49,000
5. East Midlands, 43,000
6. West Midlands, 43,000
7. Yorks/Humberside, 40,000
8. East Anglia, 22,000
9. North, 20,000
10. Wales, 20,000
Source: *The Times*, April 18, 1997, p. 37.

Business Consultants

★ 548 ★
BUSINESS CONSULTING MARKET, 1995
Ranked by: Distribution of services offered by 40 largest firms, as a percent of world revenues. **Number listed:** 7
1. Process/operations management with 31.0%
2. Corporate strategy, 17.0%
3. IT strategy, 17.0%
4. Actuarial/benefits, 16.0%
5. Organizational design, 11.0%
6. Financial advisory, 6.0%
7. Marketing/sales, 2.0%
Source: *The Economist*, March 22, 1997, p. 5.

★ 549 ★
TOP CONSULTING FIRMS IN FRANCE, 1995
Ranked by: Consulting business, in millions of francs (FFr). **Number listed:** 10
1. Andersen Consulting with FFr1,100 million
2. Bossard Consultants, FFr565
3. Ernst & Young Conseil, FFr270
4. AT Kearney, FFr250
5. Price Waterhouse Conseil, FFr230
6. McKinsey & Company, FFr225
7. Gemini Consulting, FFr222
8. KPMG Peat Marwick, FFr221
9. Sema Group, FFr220
10. Coopers & Lybrand, FFr212
Source: *Nouvel Economiste*, July 12, 1996, p. 37.

★ 550 ★
TOP MANAGEMENT CONSULTANTS WORLDWIDE, 1996
Ranked by: Revenue, in millions of U.S. dollars.
Remarks: Notes growth rate, staff numbers, and revenue per consultant. **Number listed:** 20
1. Andersen Consulting with $5,300.0 million
2. Ernst & Young, $2,010.4
3. McKinsey & Co., $2,000.0
4. KPMG, $1,836.0
5. Deloitte Touche Tomatsu International, $1,550.0
6. Coopers & Lybrand, $1,422.0
7. Arthur Andersen, $1,379.6
8. Price Waterhouse, $1,200.0
9. Mercer Consulting Group, $1,159.2
10. Towers Perrin, $1,001.3
Source: *Financial Times*, June 19, 1997, p. 4.

Business Consultants – United Kingdom

★ 551 ★
LARGEST U.K. CONSULTING FIRMS IN MANUFACTURING, 1996
Ranked by: Consultants working in manufacturing.
Number listed: 17
1. Andersen Consulting with 300
2. CSC, 220
3. Deloitte & Touche, 200
4. Arthur D. Little, 150
5. IBM, 150
6. Coopers & Lybrand, 100
7. McKinsey, 100
8. A.T. Kearney, 100
9. Price Waterhouse, 90
10. KPMG, 70
Source: *Financial Times*, January 3, 1997, p. 6.

Business Ethics

★ 552 ★
LEAST CORRUPT BUSINESS CULTURES, 1996
Ranked by: Countries rated 1 to 10 on a 1996 survey of business perceptions regarding the level of corruption in each country. **Remarks:** A rating of 10.00 would be given to a country with a corruption-free business culture. Notes 1995 ratings. **Number listed:** 54
1. New Zealand with 9.43
2. Denmark, 9.33
3. Sweden, 9.08
4. Finland, 9.05
5. Canada, 8.96

6. Norway, 8.87
7. Singapore, 8.80
8. Switzerland, 8.76
9. Netherlands, 8.71
10. Australia, 8.60

Source: *Financial Times*, July 26, 1996, p. 3.

Business Schools and Colleges

★ 553 ★

LARGEST ASIA/PACIFIC BUSINESS SCHOOLS

Ranked by: Enrollment. **Number listed:** 25

1. De La Salle University (Manila) with 992
2. Curtin University of Technology (Perth), 583
3. Monash University (Melbourne), 550
4. Nanyang Technological University (Singapore), 550
5. University of Queensland (Brisbane), 490
6. University of Melbourne, 410
7. Indian Institute of Management (Ahmedabad), 394
8. Indian Institute of Management (Bangalore), 378
9. Asian Institute of Management (Manila), 361
10. Indian Institute of Management (Calcutta), 304

Source: *Asia Inc.*, September 1996, p. 32.

Business Travel

★ 554 ★

CANADIAN TRAVEL SPENDING

Ranked by: Share of corporate travel/entertainment dollar, in percent. **Remarks:** Figures are national averages. **Number listed:** 6

1. Airfares with 37%
2. Lodging, 21%
3. Meals, 20%
4. Entertainment, 11%
5. Car rental, 5%
6. Other, 6%

Source: *Globe and Mail*, February 25, 1997, p. C4.

★ 555 ★

LEADING INEXPENSIVE CITIES FOR BUSINESS TRAVEL PER DIEM, 1997

Ranked by: Total cost per diem, in U.S. dollars. **Remarks:** Data include meals in business-class restaurants and lodging in a business-class hotel. **Number listed:** 5

1. Hamilton, Canada with $99
2. Monterrey, Mexico, $129

3. Bordeaux, France, $133
4. Panama City, $135
5. Penang Island, Malaysia, $143

Source: *USA TODAY*, March 18, 1997, p. B1.

★ 556 ★

LEAST EXPENSIVE CITIES FOR BUSINESS TRAVELLERS

Ranked by: Daily expenses for one traveller, in U.S. dollars. **Remarks:** Expenses include four-star hotel accomodation, continental breakfast, laundry, lunch and dinner, alcoholic and soft drinks, incidental costs, and two taxi rides. **Number listed:** 5

1. Bombay (India) with $159
2. Mexico City (Mexico), $161
3. Toronto (Canada), $197
4. Caracas (Venezuela), $232
5. Sydney (Australia), $246

Source: *Site Selection*, March 1997, p. 34.

★ 557 ★

MOST EXPENSIVE CITIES FOR BUSINESS TRAVELLERS

Ranked by: Total cost per diem, in U.S. dollars. **Remarks:** Daily expenses include single-rate lodging in a business-class hotel along with breakfast, lunch, and dinner in a business-class restaurant. **Number listed:** 5

1. Hong Kong with $474
2. Tokyo, $440
3. Moscow, $392
4. Buenos Aires, $383
5. Paris, $377

Source: *Travel Weekly*, May 22, 1997, p. 19.

Business Women

See: **Women Executives**

Buyback of Stocks

See: **Stocks – Repurchase**

Cable Broadcasting

★ 558 ★

EUROPE'S PAY TV MARKET

Ranked by: Market share, in percent. **Number listed:** 6

1. BSkyB (U.K.) with 33.5%
2. Canal Plus (France), 32.8%
3. Canal Plus (Belgium, Spain, Germany, Poland), 19.0%
4. Telepiu (Italy), 6.1%

5.   FilmNet (Benelux), 6.0%
6.   TV1000 (Scandinavia), 2.0%
Source: *The European*, September 19, 1996, p. 27.

★ 559 ★
EUROPEAN COUNTRIES WITH THE MOST CABLE SUBSCRIBERS
Ranked by: Millions of cable subscribers. **Remarks:** Shows population and total number of homes in each country. **Number listed:** 15
1.   Germany with 15.8 million subscribers
2.   Netherlands, 5.7
3.   Belgium, 3.6
4.   Switzerland, 2.3
5.   Poland, 2.1
6.   France, 1.9
7.   Sweden, 1.9
8.   Austria, 1.0
9.   Denmark, 0.9
10. Israel, 0.9
Source: *Financial Times*, June 14, 1996, p. 22.

★ 560 ★
EUROPEAN COUNTRIES WITH THE MOST HOMES PASSED BY CABLE
Ranked by: Millions of homes passed by cable. **Remarks:** Shows population and total number of homes in each country. **Number listed:** 15
1.   Germany with 24.2 million homes
2.   France, 6.3
3.   Netherlands, 6.1
4.   Belgium, 3.8
5.   Poland, 3.0
6.   Czech Republic, 2.2
7.   Sweden, 2.2
8.   Austria, 1.7
9.   Denmark, 1.5
10. Israel, 1.4
Source: *Financial Times*, June 14, 1996, p. 22.

★ 561 ★
TOP CABLE FIRMS IN LATIN AMERICA
Ranked by: Household subscribers, in millions. **Remarks:** Figure for CNN en Espanol is estimated. **Number listed:** 12
1.   CBS TeleNoticias with 10.0 million households
2.   ESPN, 8.0
3.   Cartoon Network, 7.0
4.   MTV, 7.0
5.   Discovery Channel, 6.2
6.   TNT, 6.2
7.   CNNI, 6.1
8.   Canal Fox, 6.0
9.   USA Network, 4.5
10. CNN en Espanol, 3.7
Source: *Latin Trade*, April 1997, p. 42.

★ 562 ★
TOP CABLE LEADERS IN BRITAIN
Ranked by: Homes passed by lain cable, in millions. **Number listed:** 9
1.   TeleWest with 3.9 million homes
2.   Nynex, 2.5
3.   Bell Cablemedia, 2.0
4.   CableTel, 1.9
5.   Diamond, 1.0
6.   Comcast, 0.8
7.   General Cable, 0.8
8.   Videotron, 0.7
9.   Others, 2.2
Source: *Financial Times*, February 28, 1996, p. 7.

Cable Television

★ 563 ★
AUSTRALIA'S PAY TV SERVICES
Ranked by: Number of subscribers. **Number listed:** 4
1.   Optus Vision with 180,000 subscribers
2.   Foxtel, 140,000
3.   Austar, 120,000
4.   Australis, 90,000
Source: *Sydney Morning Herald*, February 15, 1997, p. 85.

★ 564 ★
CABLE TELEVISION MARKET IN THE UNITED KINGDOM
Ranked by: Market share, in percent. **Remarks:** CWC includes Nynex, Bell Cablemedia, and Videotron. **Number listed:** 8
1.   CWC with 33%
2.   TeleWest, 28%
3.   Comcast, 14%
4.   International CableTel, 7%
5.   General Cable, 6%
6.   Telecential, 6%
7.   Diamond Cable, 3%
8.   Other, 3%
Source: *Cable World*, January 13, 1997, p. 26.

Cable Television – Advertising

★ 565 ★
TOP TAIWANESE CABLE TELEVISION CHANNELS BY ADVERTISING REVENUE, 1996
Ranked by: Cable television advertising revenue, as a percent of all channels. **Remarks:** Notes type of programming. **Number listed:** 10
1.   TVBS with 19.2%
2.   Super TV, 11.4%

3. Sanli, 7.1%
4. TVBS-N, 6.1%
5. FSTV, 5.8%
6. Star Chinese, 5.0%
7. TVIS, 3.4%
8. Star Prime, 2.7%
9. Lian Deng, 2.5%
10. CTN, 2.4%

Source: *Financial Times*, September 2, 1997, p. 6.

Cafeterias

See: **Restaurants**

California – see under individual headings

Cameras

★ 566 ★

TOP CAMERA BRANDS IN GERMANY

Ranked by: Market share, in percent. **Number listed:** 8
1. Caruna with 11.0%
2. Canon, 10.0%
3. Olympus, 10.0%
4. Minolta, 6.0%
5. Pentax, 6.0%
6. Nikon, 5.0%
7. Yashica, 5.0%
8. Other, 47.0%

Source: *Wirtschaftswoche*, July 4, 1996, p. 54.

★ 567 ★

TOP CAMERA MAKERS IN JAPAN

Ranked by: Market share, in percent. **Number listed:** 6
1. Canon with 36.4%
2. Minolta, 23.7%
3. Nikon, 16.5%
4. Asahi Optical, 9.5%
5. Kyocera, 4.8%
6. Other, 9.1%

Source: *Nikkei Weekly*, July 22, 1996, p. 8.

★ 568 ★

TOP SELLING TYPES OF CAMERA LENSES IN THE UNITED KINGDOM, 1995

Ranked by: Percent distribution. **Number listed:** 3
1. Fixed with 81.3%
2. Zoom, 16.8%
3. Twin, 1.9%

Source: *Photo Marketing*, August 1997, p. 80.

Cameroon – see under individual headings

Canada – see under individual headings

Candy Industry

★ 569 ★

LEADING CONSUMERS OF CHOCOLATE CONFECTIONERIES, 1994

Ranked by: Per capital consumption, in pounds. **Number listed:** 19
1. Switzerland with 20.4
2. Austria, 19.6
3. Ireland, 17.8
4. Norway, 17.8
5. Germany, 14.9
6. United Kingdom, 14.9
7. Australia, 12.9
8. Denmark, 12.3
9. Belgium, 11.9

Source: *Candy Industry*, State of the Industry Report (annual), July 1997, p. A17.

★ 570 ★

LEADING CONSUMERS OF NON-CHOCOLATE CONFECTIONERIES, 1994

Ranked by: Per capital consumption, in pounds. **Number listed:** 19
1. Denmark with 21.7
2. Germany, 13.5
3. Ireland, 12.8
4. Netherlands, 12.2
5. Belgium, 11.7
6. United States, 11.5
7. Sweden, 11.2
8. United Kingdom, 11.1
9. Finland, 10.2
10. Norway, 9.6

Source: *Candy Industry*, State of the Industry Report (annual), July 1997, p. A17.

★ 571 ★

TOP CONFECTIONERY BRANDS IN THE UNITED KINGDOM, 1995

Ranked by: Estimated sales, in millions of British pounds (£). **Remarks:** Notes ad agency and spending. **Number listed:** 10
1. Kit Kat (Nestle) with £Over 125 million
2. Mars Bar (Mars), £100-105
3. Cadbury's Dairy Milk (Cadbury), £80-85
4. Galaxy (Mars), £75-80

5. Cadbury's Roses (Cadbury), £65-70
6. Twix (Mars), £60-65
7. Quality Street (Nestle), £55-60
8. Snickers (Mars), £50-55
9. Maltesers (Mars), £45-50
10. Fruit 'n Nut (Cadbury), £35-40
Source: *Marketing*, July 4, 1996, p. 25.

★ 572 ★
TOP PRODUCERS OF CHOCOLATE FINISHED GOODS, 1994
Ranked by: Production, in millions of pounds. **Number listed:** 19
1. United States with 2,859.8 million
2. Germany, 1,289.4
3. United Kingdom, 922.0
4. France, 569.7
5. Brazil, 537.9
6. Netherlands, 399.0
7. Italy, 299.8
8. Belgium, 254.9
9. Australia, 246.7
10. Japan, 244.7
Source: *Candy Industry,* State of the Industry Report (annual), July 1997, p. A17.

★ 573 ★
TOP PRODUCERS OF NON-CHOCOLATE FINISHED GOODS, 1994
Ranked by: Production, in millions of pounds. **Number listed:** 19
1. United States with 2,835.1 million
2. Germany, 1,169.9
3. Brazil, 963.4
4. United Kingdom, 745.8
5. Japan, 452.6
6. Spain, 398.8
7. France, 394.4
8. Netherlands, 280.0
9. Italy, 269.2
10. Denmark, 174.6
Source: *Candy Industry,* State of the Industry Report (annual), July 1997, p. A17.

Canned Food Industry

★ 574 ★
LARGEST CANNERIES IN MOLDOVA
Ranked by: Number of employees. **Number listed:** 16
1. Varnita, Bender Cannery with 1,100 employees
2. Cantemir Cannery, 1,000
3. Causeni Cannery, 1,000
4. Cupcini Cannery, 1,000
5. Grigoriopol Cannery, 1,000

6. Oktiabri Cannery, 1,000
7. Coshnita Cannery, 900
8. Glodeni Cannery, 700
9. Calarash Cannery, 600
10. Kamenskii Cannery, 600
Source: *National Trade Data Bank*, February 1, 1996, p. IMI960201.

★ 575 ★
TOP CANNED FOOD BRANDS IN THE UNITED KINGDOM, 1995
Ranked by: Estimated sales, in millions of British pounds (£). **Remarks:** Notes ad agency and spending. **Number listed:** 10
1. Heinz Baked Beans (HJ Heinz) with £Over 102 million
2. Heinz Ready to Serve soup (HJ Heinz), £95-100
3. Heinz Spaghetti (HJ Heinz), £60-65
4. John West Salmon (John West Foods), £35-40
5. Del Monte Canned Fruit (Del Monte), £30-35
6. John West Tuna (John West Foods), £30-35
7. Ambrosia Creamed Rice (CPC), £25-30
8. Baxters Soup (Baxters of Speyside), £25-30
9. Princes Corned Beef (Princes), £25-30
10. Homepride Cooking Sauces (Homepride), £20-25
Source: *Marketing*, July 4, 1996, p. 26.

Capital Equipment Industry
See: **Industrial Equipment Industry**

Capital Market

★ 576 ★
TOP RECEIVERS OF PRIVATE CAPITAL, 1996
Ranked by: Inflow, in billions of U.S. dollars. **Number listed:** 12
1. China with $52.0 billion
2. Mexico, $28.1
3. Indonesia, $17.9
4. Malaysia, $16.0
5. Brazil, $14.7
6. Thailand, $13.3
7. Argentina, $11.3
8. India, $8.0
9. Turkey, $4.7
10. Chile, $4.6
Source: *The Wall Street Journal*, March 24, 1997, p. B9.

Captive Insurance Companies – Bermuda

★ 577 ★
LARGEST CAPTIVES MANAGERS IN BERMUDA, 1996
Ranked by: Premium volume, in millions of U.S. dollars.
Remarks: Notes figures for 1995. **Number listed:** 10
1. Johnson & Higgins Ltd. with $1,653 million
2. International Advisory Services Ltd., $925
3. Aon Risk Services Ltd., $650
4. Alexander Insurance Managers Ltd., $572
5. Marsh & McLennan Management Services Ltd., $500
6. Sedgwick Management Services Ltd., $305
7. Skandia International Risk Management Ltd., $268
8. International Risk Management Ltd., $240
9. AIG Insurance Management Services, $198
10. Mutual Risk Management Ltd., $197
Source: _Business Insurance_, May 14, 1997, p. 12.

Captive Insurance Companies – Cayman Islands

★ 578 ★
LARGEST CAPTIVES MANAGERS IN THE CAYMAN ISLANDS, 1996
Ranked by: Premium volume, in millions of U.S. dollars.
Remarks: Notes figures for 1995. **Number listed:** 10
1. Johnson & Higgins Ltd. with $501.7 million
2. International Risk Management Ltd., $413.0
3. Willis Corroon Management Ltd., $283.0
4. Midland Bank Trust Corp. Ltd., $230.0
5. Cayside Insurance Management Ltd., $90.8
6. Mutual Risk Management Ltd., $87.0
7. Marsh & McLennan Management Services Ltd., $83.0
8. Crusader International Management Ltd., $64.0
9. Caledonian Bank & Trusk Ltd., $55.2
10. Chandler Insurance Management Ltd., $22.3
Source: _Business Insurance_, May 14, 1997, p. 28.

Caracas Stock Exchange

★ 579 ★
LARGEST COMPANIES ON THE CARACAS STOCK EXCHANGE, 1995
Ranked by: Market value, in bolivar millions (Bo).
Number listed: 20
1. Electricidad de Caracas with Bo307,714.96 million
2. Venezolana de Cementos, Bo118,655.43
3. Banco de Venezuela, Bo107,500.00
4. Banco Provincial, Bo103,334.77
5. Siderurgica Venezolana, Bo91,046.76
6. Manufacturas de Papel, Bo51,997.55
7. Mavesa, Bo51,660.00
8. Banco Venezolano de Credito, Bo36,288.00
9. Ceramica Carabobo, Bo26,679.52
10. Corimon, Bo24,411.24
Source: _GT Guide to World Equity Markets_ (annual), Euromoney Publications, 1996, p. 382.

★ 580 ★
MOST ACTIVELY TRADED SHARES ON THE CARACAS STOCK EXCHANGE, 1995
Ranked by: Trading value, in bolivar millions (Bo).
Number listed: 20
1. Electricidad de Caracas with Bo20,463.62 million
2. Vencemos, Bo19,172.08
3. Sivensa, Bo12,655.41
4. Manpa, Bo7,993.71
5. Consolidata de Cementos, Bo7,139.86
6. Banco Venezolano de Credito, Bo5,198.75
7. Vencemos, Bo2,906.09
8. Mantex, Bo2,531.65
9. Mavesa, Bo2,338.71
10. Banco Mercantil, Bo1,831.45
Source: _GT Guide to World Equity Markets_ (annual), Euromoney Publications, 1996, p. 383.

Carpet Industry – United Kingdom

★ 581 ★
TOP CARPET RETAILERS IN THE UNITED KINGDOM
Ranked by: Market share, in percent. **Number listed:** 6
1. Independents with 58.0%
2. Allied, 12.0%
3. Carpetright, 11.0%
4. Department stores, 5.0%
5. Paul Eyres, 3.0%
6. Other, 11.0%
Source: _The Guardian_, July 19, 1996, p. 20.

Carpets

★ 582 ★
BELGIUM'S CARPET MARKET, 1995
Ranked by: Production, in thousands of square meters.
Remarks: Also notes figures for 1991-1994. **Number listed:** 4
1. Tufted with 260,000 thousand square meters
2. Needlefelt, 105,000
3. Woven, 105,000
4. Other, 5,000

Source: *Marketing in Europe*, February 1997, p. 13.

Cars
See: **Automobiles**

Casablanca Stock Exchange

★ 583 ★
LARGEST COMPANIES ON THE CASABLANCA STOCK EXCHANGE, 1995
Ranked by: Market capitalization, in dirham millions (Di). **Number listed:** 20
1. BCM with Di6,456 million
2. ONA, Di5,659
3. SNI, Di4,128
4. BMCE, Di3,900
5. Credit du Maroc, Di2,902
6. Cosumar, Di2,598
7. Brasseries du Maroc, Di2,332
8. Lesieur, Di2,321
9. BNDE, Di2,100
10. Wafabank, Di2,019

Source: *GT Guide to World Equity Markets* (annual), Euromoney Publications, 1996, p. 481.

★ 584 ★
MOST ACTIVELY TRADED STOCKS ON THE CASABLANCA STOCK EXCHANGE, 1995
Ranked by: Turnover value, in dirham millions (Di).
Number listed: 20
1. BCM with Di2,283 million
2. BMCE, Di2,041
3. SNI, Di1,673
4. ONA, Di977
5. Wafabank, Di874
6. Brasseries du Maroc, Di351
7. Lesieur, Di214
8. Credit Eqdom, Di211
9. Credit du Maroc, Di210

10. BMCI, Di204

Source: *GT Guide to World Equity Markets* (annual), Euromoney Publications, 1996, p. 481.

Casinos

★ 585 ★
CASINO LEADERS IN BRITAIN
Ranked by: Number of casinos. **Remarks:** London has 18% of the country's casinos. "Others" include A&S Leisure, Tower Group, and Annabel. **Number listed:** 7
1. Rank with 30 casinos
2. Stakis, 22
3. Stanley Leisure, 21
4. London Clubs, 7
5. Ladbroke, 3
6. Capital Corp., 2
7. Others, 33

Source: *The Guardian*, February 28, 1996, p. 2.

Cat Food
See: **Pet Food**

Catastrophes

★ 586 ★
FREQUENTLY OCCURING TYPES OF DISASTERS, 1971-1994
Ranked by: Percent distribution. **Remarks:** Man-made disasters include industrial and transportation accidents.
Number listed: 8
1. Man-made with 34%
2. High wind, 21%
3. Flood, 19%
4. Earthquake, 8%
5. Drought and famine, 6%
6. Landslide, 3%
7. Volcano, 1%
8. Other, 8%

Source: *The Economist*, September 6, 1997, p. 106.

Catering

★ 587 ★

CATERING MARKET IN SPAIN, 1995

Ranked by: Market share based on sales, in percent. **Remarks:** Also notes number of outlets. Other bars include "take away" businesses. **Number listed:** 5
1. Large cafe-bars with 30.2%
2. Small cafe-bars, 28.3%
3. Restaurants and hotels, 27.0%
4. Discotheques, 5.6%

Source: *Marketing in Europe*, January 1997, p. 97.

★ 588 ★

GLOBAL CATERING MARKET, 1996

Ranked by: Market share, in percent. **Remarks:** The global market is estimated to have turnover of $10 billion. **Number listed:** 8
1. LSG Sky Chefs with 30.0%
2. Gate Gourmet, 13.0%
3. Dobbs, 8.0%
4. Servair/Ogden, 7.0%
5. Alpha, 5.0%
6. Cathay Pacific, 4.0%
7. Singapore Airlines, 2.0%
8. Other, 30.0%

Source: *Interavia*, March 1996, p. 39.

Cayman Islands – see under individual headings

CD-ROM

★ 589 ★

GERMAN CD-ROM MARKET, 1996

Ranked by: Market share, in percent. **Remarks:** Advice programs include financial, tax, and legal counsel. **Number listed:** 15
1. Advice programs with 16.7%
2. Travel, 15.1%
3. Language, 14.3%
4. Computer based training, 10.9%
5. Entertainment, 10.9%
6. Music, 8.5%
7. Children, 7.9%
8. Sports, 4.4%
9. Dictionaries, encyclopedias, and directories, 4.1%
10. Culture, 2.9%

Source: *National Trade Data Bank*, April 18, 1997, p. ISA970401.

Cellular Radio Service Companies

★ 590 ★

GSM MARKET IN SPAIN, 1997

Ranked by: Market share for March 1997, in percent. **Remarks:** "GSM" stands for global service for mobile communication. **Number listed:** 2
1. MoviStar with 63%
2. Airtel, 37%

Source: *National Trade Data Bank*, April 30, 1997, p. IMI970417.

★ 591 ★

LARGEST MOBILE TELEPHONE COMPANIES IN SPAIN, 1997

Ranked by: Clients as of March 1997. **Number listed:** 3
1. MoviLine (Telefonica) with 1,217,000
2. MoviStar (Telefonica), 1,268,000
3. Airtel, 740,000

Source: *National Trade Data Bank*, April 30, 1997, p. IMI970417.

★ 592 ★

TOP AUSTRALIAN LONG-DISTANCE MOBILE COMMUNICATIONS COMPANIES, 1995-1996

Ranked by: Market share, in percent. **Number listed:** 2
1. Telstra with 84%
2. Optus, 16%

Source: http:// www.dca.gov.au/responsi/factsfig.html, April 28, 1997, p. 2.

★ 593 ★

TOP DIGITAL MOBILE COMMUNICATIONS COMPANIES IN AUSTRALIA, 1995-1996

Ranked by: Market share, in percent. **Number listed:** 3
1. Optus with 38%
2. Telstra, 38%
3. Vodafone, 24%

Source: http:// www.dca.gov.au/responsi/factsfig.html, April 28, 1997, p. 1.

Cellular Telephone Equipment Industry

★ 594 ★

DIGITAL CELLULAR PHONE MARKET WORLDWIDE, 1996

Ranked by: Market share, in percent. **Number listed:** 5
1. Ericsson with 55.7%
2. Nokia, 33.0%
3. Motorola, 8.0%
4. Qualcomm, 2.9%
5. Others, 0.4%

Source: *USA TODAY*, April 14, 1997, p. 813.

Cellular Telephone Systems
See: **Cellular Radio Service Companies**

Cellular Telephones

★ 595 ★
CELLULAR PHONE INTERCONNECTION RATES IN SELECTED COUNTRIES
Ranked by: Interconnection rates charged to competitors, in U.S. cents per minute. **Number listed:** 8
1. Italy with 11.8
2. Spain, 6.6
3. Germany, 5.9
4. France, 4.4
5. Sweden, 3.4
6. Greece, 2.1
7. United Kingdom, 1.5
8. United States, 0.8

Source: *The Wall Street Journal*, April 11, 1997, p. A10.

★ 596 ★
CELLULAR PHONE LEADERS IN SPAIN, 1996
Ranked by: Number of cellular phone subscribers in March 1996. **Remarks:** Includes figures for June, September, and December of 1995. Notes the size of the market for each year between 1982 and 1996. **Number listed:** 3
1. Moviline with 1,100,000 subscribers
2. Movistar, 150,000
3. Airttel, 74,000

Source: *Cambio*, April 29, 1996.

★ 597 ★
CELLULAR PHONE MARKET IN JAPAN, 1995
Ranked by: Number of cellular phone subsribers, in thousands. **Number listed:** 5
1. NTT DoCoMo with 3,900 thousand subscribers
2. Cellular Phone Group, 1,600
3. IDO, 990
4. Digital Phone Group, 790
5. Tuka Group, 720

Source: *Computing Japan*, April 1996, p. 11.

★ 598 ★
CELLULAR PHONE PENETRATION IN LATIN AMERICA, 1998
Ranked by: Projected number of subscribers per 100 population. **Number listed:** 8
1. Chile with 5.30
2. Argentina, 4.90
3. Brazil, 4.20
4. Colombia, 3.60
5. Venezuela, 3.50

6. Uruguay, 3.00
7. Mexico, 2.00
8. Peru, 1.70

Source: *Latin Trade*, October 1996, p. 50.

★ 599 ★
GLOBAL MOBILE PHONE MARKET LEADERS, 1994
Ranked by: Market share, in percent. **Remarks:** The worldwide market sold 25 million units. **Number listed:** 6
1. Motorola with 29.0%
2. Nokia, 18.0%
3. Ericsson, 13.0%
4. NEC, 7.0%
5. Siemens, 5.0%
6. Other, 28.0%

Source: *L'Expansion*, January 25, 1996, p. 70.

★ 600 ★
LEADING CELLULAR PHONE COMPANIES IN CANADA, 1997
Ranked by: Market share based on subscribers for the year ending March 31, 1997, in percent. **Number listed:** 2
1. Rogers Cantel with 57%
2. BCE Mobile, 43%

Source: *Marketing Magazine*, May 26, 1997, p. 14.

★ 601 ★
MOBILE PHONE LEADERS IN BRITAIN
Ranked by: Market share, in percent. **Number listed:** 4
1. Cellnet with 44.0%
2. Vodafone, 44.0%
3. One-2-One, 6.0%
4. Orange, 6.0%

Source: *Financial Times*, March 21, 1996, p. 3.

★ 602 ★
MOBILE PHONE MARKET IN LATIN AMERICA
Ranked by: Market share, in percent. **Number listed:** 5
1. Ericsson with 35.0%
2. Northern Telecom, 22.0%
3. Motorola, 18.0%
4. NEC, 15.0%
5. Other, 10.0%

Source: *Latin Trade*, April 1996, p. 28.

★ 603 ★
TOP CELLULAR MARKETS WORLDWIDE, 1996
Ranked by: Number of subscribers as of January 1, 1996, in millions. **Number listed:** 20
1. United States with 33.7 million subscribers
2. Japan, 8.1
3. United Kingdom, 5.4
4. Italy, 3.9
5. Germany, 3.7
6. China, 3.6

7. Australia, 3.1
8. Canada, 2.5
9. Sweden, 1.9
10. South Korea, 1.6

Source: *Financial Times*, October 16, 1996, p. 13.

★ 604 ★

WIRELESS COMMUNICATIONS MARKET IN AUSTRIA

Ranked by: Market share, in percent. **Number listed:** 6

1. Nokia with 33%
2. Ericsson, 26%
3. Philips, 8%
4. Motorola, 7%
5. Bosch, 6%
6. Siemens, 5%

Source: *National Trade Data Bank*, July 15, 1997, p. ISA970601.

Cement Industry

★ 605 ★

LEADING CEMENT COMPANIES IN TAIWAN, 1996

Ranked by: Market share, in percent. **Number listed:** 7

1. Asia Cement with 26%
2. Taiwan Cement, 23%
3. Lucky Cement, 8%
4. Chia Hsin Cement, 7%
5. Hsin Ta Cement, 5%
6. Imports, 10%
7. Other, 21%

Source: *Financial Times*, July 31, 1997, p. 6.

★ 606 ★

LEADING FRENCH CEMENT ENTERPRISES, 1996

Ranked by: Enterprise value to sales ratio. **Number listed:** 8

1. Semapa with 2.27
2. Valderrivas, 2.08
3. Cimpor, 2.04
4. Ciments Francais, 1.48
5. Blue Circle, 1.41
6. Hisalba, 1.28
7. Holderbank, 1.23
8. Lafarge, 1.16

Source: *Financial Times*, October 10, 1996, p. 22.

★ 607 ★

MOST PROFITABLE CEMENT OPERATIONS IN UKRAINE

Ranked by: Profits, in percent. **Number listed:** 4

1. Enakievo with 34.0% profits
2. Ivano-Frankovsk, 29.0%
3. Yugcement, 19.0%

4. Nikolaevskcement, 18.0%

Source: http:// www.alfa.rosmail.com/research/sectors/ reviews/whis15.htm, May 27, 1997, p. 2.

★ 608 ★

TOP CEMENT MAKERS IN JAPAN, 1995

Ranked by: Market share, in percent. **Number listed:** 6

1. Chichibu Onoda Cement with 24.8%
2. Sumitomo Osaka Cement, 18.8%
3. Nihon Cement, 16.9%
4. Mitsubishi Materials, 14.3%
5. Ube Industries, 10.8%
6. Others, 14.6%

Source: *Nikkei Weekly*, July 29, 1996, p. 8.

Ceramic Tiles

See: **Tiles**

Ceramics

★ 609 ★

TOP CERAMICS COMPANIES IN GERMANY, 1994

Ranked by: Turnover, in millions of deutschmarks (DM). **Number listed:** 25

1. Villeroy & Boch AG with DM1,612.0 million
2. Cremer-Gruppe, DM1,460.0
3. Didier-Konzem, DM1,397.0
4. Ideal Standard, DM435.0
5. Keramchemie GmbH, DM414.0
6. Hutschenreuther AG, DM399.0
7. Rosenthal AG, DM362.3
8. Keramag AG, DM293.0
9. Wienerberger Ziegelind, DM226.0
10. Dralonc, DM220.0

Source: *Ceramic Forum International*, 1995, p. 538.

Cereal Products

★ 610 ★

CEREAL MARKET IN LATIN AMERICA

Ranked by: Market share, in percent. **Number listed:** 2

1. Kellogg with 69.0%
2. Other, 31.0%

Source: *Forbes*, October 7, 1996, p. 45.

Cereal Products – United Kingdom

★ **611** ★

TOP CEREAL BRANDS IN THE UNITED KINGDOM, 1995
Ranked by: Estimated sales, in millions of British pounds (£). **Remarks:** Notes ad agency and spending. **Number listed:** 10
1. Kellogg's Corn Flakes (Kellogg) with £Over 109 million
2. Kellogg's Frosties (Kellogg), £65-70
3. Weetabix (Weetabix), £65-70
4. Kellogg's Rice Krispies (Kellogg), £40-45
5. Kellogg's Crunchy Nut Corn Flakes (Kellogg), £35-40
6. Kellogg's Bran Flakes (Kellogg), £25-30
7. Kellogg's Fruit 'N Fibre (Kellogg), £25-30
8. Kellogg's Special K (Kellogg), £25-30
9. Shredded Wheat (Cereal Partners), £25-30
10. Kellogg's Coco Pops (Kellogg), £20-25

Source: *Marketing*, July 4, 1996, p. 26.

Chain Stores, Apparel
See: **Clothing Stores**

Chain Stores, Food
See: **Grocery Trade**

Champagne

★ **612** ★

LEADING CHAMPAGNE BRANDS IN THE UNITED KINGDOM, 1994
Ranked by: Market share based on value, in percent. **Number listed:** 10
1. Moet et Chandon with 22%
2. Lanson, 12%
3. Laurent Perrier, 6%
4. Mumm, 5%
5. Bollinger, 4%
6. Veuve Cliquot, 4%
7. Piper Heidsiek, 3%
8. Mercier, 2%
9. Own label, 31%
10. Others, 11%

Source: *Wines & Vines*, August 1995, p. 13.

Channel Islands – see under individual headings

Charitable Contributions

★ **613** ★

TOP CORPORATE DONORS TO CHARITABLE ORGANIZATIONS IN CANADA, 1995-1996
Ranked by: Cash donations given between April 1, 1995, and March 31, 1996, in millions of Canadian dollars. **Remarks:** Does not include gifts in kind and employee fund raising. **Number listed:** 34
1. Royal Bank of Canada with C$16.0 million
2. Canadian Imperial Bank of Commerce, C$9.0
3. Bank of Montreal, C$6.5
4. Imperial Oil Charitable Foundation, C$6.3
5. Bank of Nova Scotia, C$5.0
6. Bell Canada, C$4.7
7. Glaxo Wellcome Inc., C$4.7
8. Merck Frosst Canada Inc., C$4.0
9. Nova Corp., C$4.0
10. Seagram Co. Ltd., C$4.0

Source: *Globe and Mail*, August 21, 1997, p. B11.

Charities – United Kingdom

★ **614** ★

TOP CORPORATE DONORS IN THE UNITED KINGDOM, 1995-1996
Ranked by: Community contributions, in millions of British pounds (£). **Number listed:** 10
1. British Telecommunications plc with £14.87 million
2. GlaxoWellcome plc, £10.70
3. National Westminster Bank plc, £10.56
4. Marks & Spencer plc, £8.50
5. Barclays plc, £8.40
6. British Petroleum Company plc, £6.10
7. Midland Bank plc, £5.50
8. British Gas plc, £5.00
9. Grand Metropolitan plc, £4.99
10. Shell UK Limited, £4.81

Source: *Investors Chronicle*, March 21, 1997, p. 8.

★ **615** ★

TOP FUNDRAISING CHARITIES IN THE UNITED KINGDOM, 1995-1996
Ranked by: Total voluntary income, in millions of British pounds (£). **Remarks:** Notes rank from previous year. **Number listed:** 10
1. Oxfam with £92.3 million

2. National Trust, £77.0
3. Imperial Cancer Research Fund, £71.0
4. Cancer Research Campaign, £60.2
5. British Heart Foundation, £57.2
6. Royal National Lifeboat Institution, £55.7
7. Barnardos, £47.3
8. Help The Aged, £43.2
9. British Red Cross Society, £38.4
10. Scope, £37.2
Source: *The Guardian*, June 30, 1997, p. 9.

Cheese

★ 616 ★
INDIA'S CHEESE MARKET
Ranked by: Market share, in percent. **Number listed:** 5
1. Amul with 61.4%
2. Vijaya, 14.0%
3. Vadial, 10.5%
4. Verka, 8.8%
5. Other, 5.3%
Source: *Business Today*, August 7, 1996, p. 50.

Chemical Industries

★ 617 ★
CHEMICALS MARKET IN CHINA
Ranked by: Percent distribution. **Number listed:** 11
1. Plastic products with 17%
2. Pharmaceuticals, 15%
3. Organic chemicals, 12%
4. Chemical fibers, 10%
5. Rubber products, 10%
6. Basic chemical raw materials, 9%
7. Chemical fertilers, 9%
8. Household/personal chemicals, 6%
9. Synthetic materials, 4%
10. Pesticides, 2%
Source: *China-Britain Trade Review*, August 1996, p. 8.

★ 618 ★
COUNTRIES MOST SPECIALIZED IN CHEMISTRY
Ranked by: Ratio of each country's chemical industry turnover to gross domestic product divided by the same ratio for all the countries under consideration. **Number listed:** 10
1. Belgium with 2.54
2. Ireland, 1.97
3. Switzerland, 1.53
4. Netherlands, 1.34
5. United States, 1.01
6. France, 1.00

7. Japan, 0.98
8. Germany, 0.97
9. Spain, 0.97
10. United Kingdom, 0.96
Source: http:// www.vbo-feb.be/chemistry/ FICEN5.html, June 2, 1997, p. 3.

★ 619 ★
LARGEST CHEMICALS COMPANIES, 1995
Ranked by: Revenue, in millions of U.S. dollars. **Remarks:** Notes profits and global rank. **Number listed:** 18
1. E.I. du Pont de Nemours (United States) with $37,607 million
2. Hoechst (Germany), $36,409
3. BASF (Germany), $32,258
4. Bayer (Germany), $31,108
5. Dow Chemical (United States), $20,957
6. Ciba-Geigy (Switzerland), $17,509
7. Mitsubishi Chemical (Japan), $17,074
8. Rhone-Poulenc (France), $16,996
9. Imperial Chemical Industries (United Kingdom), $16,206
10. Akzo Nobel (Netherlands), $13,383
Source: *Fortune,* The Global 500: World's Biggest Corporations (annual), August 5, 1996, p. F-16.

★ 620 ★
LEADING CHEMICALS COMPANIES IN SOUTH KOREA, 1996
Ranked by: Sales for the first six months of 1996, in hundred million won (W). **Remarks:** Also notes net profits. **Number listed:** 45
1. LG Chemical with W17,121.6 hundred million
2. Hanwha, W7,786.5
3. Hanwha Chemical, W7,485.9
4. Pacific, W3,385.5
5. Oriental Chemical Ind., W2,700.3
6. Honam Petrochemical, W2,623.4
7. Korea Chemical, W2,411.6
8. Namhae Chemical, W2,073.7
9. Saehan Media, W1,904.5
10. Korea Kumho Petrochemical, W1,734.0
Source: *Business Korea*, October 1996, p. 33.

★ 621 ★
TOP CHEMICAL COMPANIES WORLDWIDE, 1996
Ranked by: Market capitalization at September 30, 1996, in millions of U.S. dollars. **Number listed:** 10
1. DuPont (E I) de Nemours with $49,345.8 million
2. Ciba, $38,133.4
3. Bayer, $26,276.1
4. Hoechst, $21,747.5
5. Monsanto, $21,171.6
6. Dow Chemical, $19,685.2

7. BASF, $19,446.5
8. L'Air Liquide, $11,383.9
9. PPG Industries, $10,142.2
10. Imperial Chemical Industries, $9,560.6
Source: *Financial Times*, January 7, 1997, p. IV.

★ 622 ★
TOP CHEMICAL FIRMS BY R&D SPENDING, 1996
Ranked by: R&D spending, in millions of U.S. dollars.
Remarks: Figures for Dupont exclude Conoco energy business; figures for Degussa include pharmaceutical sector and metal sector spending. Notes company spending plans for 1997 and 1998. **Number listed:** 23
1. Bayer with $2,124 million
2. Rhone-Poulenc, $1,369
3. BASF, $1,283
4. DuPont, $944
5. Dow Chemical, $762
6. Bayer Corp., $623
7. Degussa, $290
8. Elf Atochem, $267
9. PPG Industries, $255
10. Henkel, $233
Source: *Chemical Week*, February 26, 1997, p. 24.

★ 623 ★
TOP CHEMICAL PRODUCERS, 1996
Ranked by: Chemical sales, in millions of U.S. dollars. **Number listed:** 50
1. Dow Chemical with $18,988.0 million
2. DuPont, $18,044.0
3. Exxon, $11,430.0
4. Monsanto, $7,267.0
5. Hoechst Celanese, $6,906.0
6. General Electric, $6,487.0
7. Union Carbide, $6,106.0
8. Amoco, $5,698.0
9. Eastman Chemical, $4,782.0
10. BASF Corp., $4,707.0
Source: *Chemical & Engineering News*, May 5, 1997, p. 22.

★ 624 ★
TOP MAKERS OF STYRENE WORLDWIDE
Ranked by: Capacity, in thousands of metric tons per year. **Number listed:** 11
1. Arco Chemical with 1,145 thousand metric tons
2. Dow, 1,000
3. Cos-Mar, 962
4. Chevron, 772
5. Sterling Chemicals, 772
6. Elf Atochem, 720
7. Huntsman, 644
8. BASF, 510
9. Asahi Chemical, 480

10. Mitsubishi Kagaku, 480
Source: *Chemical Week*, August 31, 1996, p. 53.

Chemical Industries – Asia

★ 625 ★
ASIA'S TOP CHEMICAL FIRMS, 1995
Ranked by: Sales, in millions of U.S. dollars. **Remarks:** Includes profits, profits as a percentage of sales and assets, and overall sales rank. **Number listed:** 20
1. China Petrochemical Corp. with $25,329.7 million
2. Mitsubishi Chemical Corp., $17,520.9
3. Sumitomo Chemical Corp., $10,120.3
4. Dainippon Ink & Chemical, $9,231.7
5. Ube Industries, $6,701.8
6. Shin-Etsu Chemical, $6,115.0
7. Showa Denko, $5,743.9
8. Mitsui Toatsu Chemicals, $5,505.3
9. LG Chemical, $4,299.1
10. Mitsui Petrochemical, $4,167.7
Source: *Asiaweek*, The Asiaweek 1,000, November 22, 1996, p. 158.

★ 626 ★
LARGEST CHEMICALS, PLASTICS, AND PETROLEUM COMPANIES IN ASIA
Ranked by: Sales, in thousands of U.S. dollars. **Remarks:** Notes profits as a percent of sales. **Number listed:** 100
1. Japan Energy Corp. with $18,116,097 thousand
2. Showa Shell Sekiyu KK, $13,992,000
3. Asahi Chemical Industry Co. Ltd., $11,749,223
4. Mitsubishi Oil Co. Ltd., $10,882,029
5. Mitsubishi Kasei Corp., $10,457,417
6. Sekisui Chemical Co. Ltd., $10,437,000
7. Sumitomo Chemical Co. Ltd., $9,241,902
8. Toray Industries Inc., $9,139,281
9. Dainippon Ink & Chemicals Inc., $8,430,466
10. Takeda Chemical Industries Ltd., $7,780,009
Source: *Asia's 7,500 Largest Companies* annual, Dun & Bradstreet, 1997, p. 75.

Chemical Industries – Canada

★ 627 ★
CANADA'S TOP CHEMICAL COMPANIES, 1996
Ranked by: Sales, in millions of Canadian dollars. **Remarks:** Also notes figures for 1994 and 1995. **Number listed:** 17
1. Nova Chemicals with C$3,043 million
2. Agrium, C$2,485
3. Dow Chemical Canada, C$2,281

4. Potash Corp. Saskatchewan, C$1,918
5. DuPont Canada, C$1,827
6. Methanex, C$1,300
7. Imperial Oil, C$875
8. ICI Canada, C$847
9. BASF, C$720
10. Shell Canada, C$606

Source: *Chemical Week*, July 23, 1997, p. 25.

Chemical Industries – Europe

★ 628 ★
LARGEST CHEMICAL FIRMS IN EUROPE
Ranked by: Turnover, in billions of U.S. dollars.
Remarks: Includes figures on net income and market capitalization. **Number listed:** 10

1. Hoechst with $33.93 billion
2. BASF, $30.06
3. Bayer, $28.99
4. Rhone Poulenc, $16.31
5. ICI, $15.51
6. Montedison, $14.98
7. Akzo Nobel, $12.50
8. Henkel, $9.24
9. Degussa, $9.01
10. Solvay, $8.61

Source: *Financial Times*, June 17, 1996, p. 23.

★ 629 ★
TOP CHEMICAL AND ALLIED PRODUCTS COMPANIES IN EUROPE
Ranked by: Sales, in millions of European Currency Units (ECUs). **Remarks:** Also notes number of employees. **Number listed:** 266

1. Hoechst A.G. with 23,683 million ECUs
2. BASF A.G., 20,983
3. Bayer A.G., 20,235
4. Ciba-Geigy A.G., 14,114
5. Rhone-Poulenc S.A., 13,185
6. Glaxo Wellcome Plc, 11,180
7. Imperial Chemical Industries Plc, 10,945
8. Akzo Nobel Coatings International BV, 10,117
9. Akzo Nobel Fibers International BV, 10,117
10. Akzo Nobel N.V., 10,117

Source: *Duns Europa* (annual), vol. 4, Dun & Bradstreet, 1997, p. 223+.

Chemical Industries – Export-Import Trade, International

★ 630 ★
LEADING IMPORTERS OF CHEMICALS TO MEXICO, 1996
Ranked by: Share of import market from January to August, in percent. **Number listed:** 6

1. North America with 67%
2. European Union, 17%
3. Asia, 7%
4. Latin American Integration Association, 3%
5. Central America, 1%
6. Others, 5%

Source: *Chemical Week*, January 8, 1997, p. 31.

Chemical Industries – Japan

★ 631 ★
TOP CHEMICAL COMPANIES IN JAPAN
Ranked by: Income, in millions of yen (¥). **Number listed:** 10

1. Shin-Etsu Chemical with ¥13,150 million
2. Nippon Sanso, ¥9,981
3. Nippon Shokubai, ¥6,213
4. Daido Hoxan, ¥5,571
5. Tokuyama, ¥4,189
6. Toagosei, ¥3,060
7. Teisan, ¥3,030
8. Nissan Chemical Industries, ¥2,756
9. Nitto FC, ¥2,266
10. Dainichiseika Colour & Chemicals, ¥2,189

Source: *Tokyo Business Today*, August 1995, p. 26.

★ 632 ★
TOP CHEMICAL FIRMS IN JAPAN, 1996
Ranked by: Chemical sales for fiscal year 1996, in millions of U.S. dollars. **Remarks:** Notes total sales, net profits, capacity and R&D spending. **Number listed:** 25

1. Mitsubishi Kagaku with $14,499 million
2. Sumitomo Chemical, $7,377
3. Toray, $7,247
4. Asahi Chemical, $5,297
5. Shin-Etsu Chemical, $4,886
6. Dainippon Ink & Chemical, $4,476
7. Sekisui, $4,175
8. Kao, $4,031
9. Toyobo, $3,978
10. Mitsui Sekka, $3,698

Source: *Chemical Week*, January 22, 1997, p. 25.

Chemical Industries – Western Europe

★ 633 ★

TOP CHEMICAL FIRMS IN WESTERN EUROPE, 1995

Ranked by: Sales, in millions of U.S. dollars. **Remarks:** Includes profits. **Number listed:** 50

1. Hoechst (Germany) with $36,320 million
2. BASF (Germany), $32,180
3. Bayer (Germany), $31,032
4. Ciba (Switzerland), $17,944
5. Rhone-Poulenc (France), $17,289
6. ICI (U.K.), $15,948
7. Elf Group (France), $15,882
8. Shell (U.K./Netherlands), $14,348
9. Akzo Nobel (Netherlands), $13,363
10. Sandoz (Switzerland), $13,215

Source: *European Chemical News*, December 1996, p. 10.

Chemicals, Organic

★ 634 ★

TOP ETHYLENE PRODUCERS IN BRAZIL

Ranked by: Capacity, in thousands of metric tons. **Number listed:** 4

1. Copene with 1,200 thousand metric tons
2. Copesul, 615
3. PqU, 390
4. Other, 32

Source: *Chemical Week*, May 4, 1997, p. 13.

Chile – see under individual headings

China – see under individual headings

Chocolate Industry

★ 635 ★

BRITAIN'S TOP CHOCOLATE MAKERS, 1995

Ranked by: Market share, in percent. **Remarks:** Includes chocolate consumption per person. **Number listed:** 5

1. Cadbury with 29.0%
2. Nestle Rowntree, 25.0%
3. Mars, 21.0%
4. Terry Suchard, 4.0%

5. Others, 20.0%

Source: *The Sunday Telegraph*, September 8, 1996, p. 5.

★ 636 ★

CANADIAN CHOCOLATE BAR MARKET, 1997

Ranked by: Market share based on 30.9 million 36-bar equivalents, in percent. **Remarks:** Also notes 1996 figures. **Number listed:** 11

1. Oh Henry! with 7.6%
2. M&M's, 5.6%
3. Caramilk, 5.5%
4. Mars, 5.0%
5. Reese Peanut Butter Cups, 4.4%
6. Kit Kat, 4.4%
7. Smarties, 4.0%
8. Coffee Crisp, 3.9%
9. Aere, 3.8%
10. Closette, 3.2%

Source: *Marketing Magazine*, June 26, 1997, p. 11.

★ 637 ★

CHOCOLATE BAR MARKET IN GERMANY

Ranked by: Market share, in percent. **Number listed:** 7

1. Ferrero with 36.0%
2. Mars, 35.8%
3. Nestle, 6.5%
4. Suchard, 6.4%
5. Schwartau, 6.1%
6. Storck, 4.1%
7. Others, 5.1%

Source: *The Manufacturing Confectioner*, June 1997, p. 9.

★ 638 ★

CHOCOLATE TABLET MARKET IN GERMANY

Ranked by: Market share, in percent. **Number listed:** 7

1. Suchard with 33.2%
2. Ritter Sport, 18.8%
3. Ferrero, 11.4%
4. Stollwerck, 8.4%
5. Nestle, 6.6%
6. Ludwig Schokolade, 5.4%
7. Others, 16.2%

Source: *The Manufacturing Confectioner*, June 1997, p. 9.

★ 639 ★

FASTEST GROWING CHOCOLATE IMPORT MARKETS

Ranked by: Percent increase in imports from 1992-93 to 1994-95. **Remarks:** Lists tons of chocolate imported by country. **Number listed:** 12

1. Brazil with 780% increase
2. Algeria, 486%
3. Nicaragua, 420%
4. Pakistan, 253%
5. Czech Republic, 165%
6. China, 164%

7. Tunisia, 160%
8. Romania, 153%
9. India, 150%
10. Peru, 137%

Source: *The Christian Science Monitor*, February 13, 1997, p. 9.

★ 640 ★
TOP PRALINE PRODUCERS IN GERMANY
Ranked by: Market share, in percent. **Number listed:** 9
1. Ferrero with 39.0%
2. Storck, 14.5%
3. Lindt, 9.3%
4. Nestle, 8.8%
5. Suchard, 5.6%
6. Ludwig, 3.4%
7. Gubor, 3.3%
8. Imhoff, 2.4%
9. Others, 13.7%

Source: *The Manufacturing Confectioner*, June 1997, p. 9.

Cigarette Industry
See Also: Tobacco Industry

★ 641 ★
CANADIAN CIGARETTE MARKET, 1996
Ranked by: Market share based on sales of 54.5 billion cigarettes, in percent. **Remarks:** Also notes 1995 figures. **Number listed:** 11
1. Player's Light Regular with 12.6%
2. du Maurier King Size, 9.4%
3. du Maurier Regular, 5.5%
4. Player's Light King Size, 4.9%
5. Export A Regular, 4.6%
6. Player's Regular, 4.4%
7. du Maurier Light King Size, 3.9%
8. Export A Medium, 3.2%
9. Rothmans Kings, 3.1%
10. du Maurier Light Regular, 2.8%

Source: *Marketing Magazine*, June 26, 1997, p. 11.

★ 642 ★
CHANGE IN SALES OF CIGARETTES WORLDWIDE, 1990-1995
Ranked by: Change in sales of cigarettes from 1990 to 1995, in percent. **Number listed:** 7
1. Middle East with + 17.7% change
2. Asia/Pacific, + 8.0%
3. Eastern Europe, + 5.6%
4. Africa, - 0.1%
5. Western Europe, - 1.7%
6. United States and Canada, - 4.5%
7. Latin America, - 11.3%

Source: *The New York Times*, June 24, 1997, p. A1.

★ 643 ★
CIGARETTE MAKERS IN ST. PETERSBURG, RUSSIA
Ranked by: Market share, in percent. **Number listed:** 6
1. Philip Morris with 32.53%
2. R.J. Reynolds, 18.10%
3. British-American Tobacco, 10.84%
4. Bulgartabak, 10.80%
5. Rothman's, 8.12%
6. Others, 19.62%

Source: *Business in Russia*, February 1997, p. 75.

★ 644 ★
CIGARETTE MARKET WORLDWIDE, 1996
Ranked by: Market share, in percent. **Remarks:** Includes data on unit and dollar sales worldwide, ad spending, and cost. **Number listed:** 5
1. Philip Morris with 16.2%
2. B.A.T., 12.8%
3. R.J. Reynolds, 5.9%
4. Japan Tobacco, 5.1%
5. Rothmans, 4.2%
6. Others, 55.8%

Source: *The Wall Street Journal*, June 23, 1997, p. B1.

★ 645 ★
CIGARETTE SALES WORLDWIDE, 1995
Ranked by: Sales, in billions of cigarettes. **Number listed:** 7
1. Asia with 2,711 billion cigaretttes
2. Eastern Europe, 689
3. Western Europe, 626
4. North America, 541
5. South America, 317
6. Africa, 190
7. Middle East, 181

Source: *The New York Times*, June 24, 1997, p. A9.

★ 646 ★
KOREA'S TOP CIGARETTE BRANDS
Ranked by: Market share, in percent. **Number listed:** 3
1. Virginia Slims with 33.0%
2. Mild Seven Light of Japan, 23.0%
3. Other, 44.0%

Source: *The Wall Street Journal*, January 14, 1997, p. B10.

★ 647 ★
LARGEST FOREIGN CIGARETTE MAKERS IN RUSSIA
Ranked by: Production capacity, in millions of units. **Remarks:** Includes data on number of employees and investment dollars. **Number listed:** 6
1. British American Tobacco with 21,630 million units
2. Petro, 20,770

3. Ligget, 15,900
4. Rothmans, 11,800
5. Yelets, 10,000
6. Philip Morris, 8,200

Source: *Business in Russia*, February 1997, p. 75.

★ 648 ★

LEADING FOREIGN CIGARETTE BRANDS IN SOUTH KOREA, 1996
Ranked by: Market share, in percent. **Remarks:** Notes figures for 1995. **Number listed:** 5
1. Mild Seven with 27.9%
2. Virginia Slims, 24.0%
3. Marlboro, 20.6%
4. Dunhill, 5.1%
5. Finesse, 3.6%
6. Other, 18.8%

Source: *Business Korea*, March 1997, p. 12.

★ 649 ★

TOP CIGARETTE BRANDS IN SWITZERLAND, 1996
Ranked by: Market share, in percent. **Number listed:** 10
1. Marlboro with 24.3%
2. Parisienne, 9.4%
3. Select, 7.3%
4. Muratti, 7.2%
5. Camel, 7.1%
6. Barclay, 7.0%
7. MaryLong, 6.9%
8. Philip Morris, 6.7%
9. Brunette, 4.7%
10. Marocaine, 3.0%

Source: *Tobacco International*, May 1997, p. 55.

★ 650 ★

TOP CIGARETTE BRANDS IN THE NETHERLANDS, 1995
Ranked by: Market share, in percent. **Remarks:** Also notes figures for 1994. **Number listed:** 10
1. Marlboro with 19.9%
2. Camel Filter, 9.3%
3. Barclay, 6.3%
4. Marlboro Lights, 6.3%
5. Peter Stuyvesant, 6.0%
6. Caballero Plain, 5.5%
7. Caballero Filter, 5.2%
8. Pall Mall Export Filter, 3.6%
9. Gladstone Mild, 2.7%
10. Camel Mild, 2.0%

Source: *Tobacco International*, May 1997, p. 62.

★ 651 ★

TOP CIGARETTE BRANDS WORLDWIDE
Ranked by: Brand shares, in percent. **Remarks:** Includes reoccuring profits. **Number listed:** 5
1. Marlboro (Philip Morris) with 8.4%

2. Mild Seven (Japan Tobacco), 2.3%
3. L&M (Philip Morris/Liggett), 1.8%
4. Winston (R.J. Reynolds), 1.6%
5. Camel (R.J. Reynolds), 1.2%
6. Others, 84.7%

Source: *The Wall Street Journal*, June 23, 1997, p. B1.

★ 652 ★

TOP CIGARETTE MARKETS, 1996
Ranked by: Market size, in billions of cigarettes. **Remarks:** Includes data on unit and dollar sales worldwide, ad spending, and cost. **Number listed:** 5
1. China with 1,791 billion cigarettes
2. United States, 488
3. Japan, 335
4. Russia, 180
5. Indonesia, 173

Source: *The Wall Street Journal*, June 23, 1997, p. B1.

★ 653 ★

TOP SELLING CIGARETTE BRANDS IN ITALY, 1996
Ranked by: Cigarettes sold, in thousands. **Remarks:** Also notes data for 1995. **Number listed:** 11
1. MS "Regular" KS with 16,381,973 thousand cigarettes
2. Marlboro "Red" KS, 13,612,247
3. Diana KS, 6,717,491
4. Marlboro Lights KS, 6,693,744
5. Merit KS, 5,935,204
6. MS Mild, 5,474,105
7. Diana Mild KS, 3,582,256
8. Philip Morris Super Lights, 1,900,174
9. Multifilter 100, 1,603,390
10. MS Lights, 1,306,363

Source: *Tobacco International*, May 1997, p. 62.

Cigarette Industry – Germany

★ 654 ★

TOP TOBACCO BRANDS IN GERMANY, 1996
Ranked by: Market share, in percent. **Number listed:** 10
1. Marlboro with 19.7%
2. Marlboro Lights, 9.4%
3. HB, 6.7%
4. West Filter, 6.7%
5. F6, 4.2%
6. Peter Stuyvesant, 3.5%
7. Camel Filter, 3.3%
8. Lord Extra, 3.0%
9. West Lights, 2.8%
10. Lucky Strike, 2.0%

Source: *Tobacco International*, May 1997, p. 52.

    World Business Rankings Annual

Cigarette Industry – Spain

★ 655 ★

TOP SELLING CIGARETTE BRANDS IN SPAIN, 1996
Ranked by: Sales, in millions of packs. **Remarks:** Notes market share and figures for 1995. **Number listed:** 10
1. Fortuna with 844.4 million packs
2. Ducados, 787.6
3. Marlboro, 367.1
4. L&M, 268.5
5. Winston, 147.4
6. Camel, 144.6
7. Gold Coast, 144.2
8. Chesterfield, 140.5
9. Lucky Strike, 114.4
10. Nobel, 112.0

Source: *Tobacco International*, May 1997, p. 60.

Cleaning Products Industry

★ 656 ★

HOUSEHOLD-CLEANING PRODUCT MARKET WORLDWIDE, 1994
Ranked by: Sector share, in percent. **Number listed:** 8
1. Textile with 57%
2. Dishwashing, 12%
3. Polish, 10%
4. Surface, 5%
5. Air fresheners, 5%
6. Lavatory, 4%
7. Insecticides, 4%
8. Others, 3%

Source: *Adweek*, June 12, 1995, p. 23.

★ 657 ★

TOP HOUSEHOLD CLEANING BRANDS IN THE UNITED KINGDOM, 1995
Ranked by: Estimated sales, in millions of British pounds (£). **Remarks:** Notes ad agency and spending. **Number listed:** 10
1. Fairy Excel (Procter & Gamble) with £Over 68 million
2. Domestos (Lever Brothers), £50-55
3. Flash (Procter & Gamble), £40-45
4. Finish dishwater products (Benckiser), £35-40
5. Jif (Lever Brothers), £35-40
6. Glade (SC Johnson), £30-35
7. Mr. Muscle (SC Johnson), £25-30
8. Persil Washing-Up Liquids (Lever Brothers), £15-20
9. Harpic (Reckitt & Colman), £10-15
10. Haze (Reckitt & Colman), £10-15

Source: *Marketing*, July 4, 1996, p. 26.

Client Server Computing

★ 658 ★

TOP CLIENT/SERVER DATABASE MAKERS WORLDWIDE, 1996
Ranked by: Revenue, in millions of U.S. dollars. **Remarks:** Includes 1995 revenues. **Number listed:** 5
1. Oracle with $1,760 million
2. Informix, $522
3. Sybase, $251
4. Microsoft, $170
5. IBM, $95

Source: *Computer Reseller News*, June 2, 1997, p. 138.

Clock and Watch Industry – Export-Import Trade

★ 659 ★

HONG KONG'S TOP MARKETS FOR EXPORTS OF WATCHES AND CLOCKS, 1996
Ranked by: Value of exports, in thousands of Hong Kong dollars (HK$). **Number listed:** 31
1. United States with HK$10,270,138 thousand
2. China, HK$7,909,928
3. Japan, HK$4,700,165
4. Germany, Federal Republic of, HK$2,945,475
5. United Kingdom, HK$1,745,908
6. Switzerland, HK$1,744,247
7. United Arab Emirates, HK$1,686,107
8. Singapore, HK$1,632,088
9. Spain, HK$1,136,821
10. Panama, HK$996,737

Source: http:// www.tdc.org.hk/hkstat/watches.htm, August 25, 1997, p. 2.

Closely Held Corporations – Canada

★ 660 ★

LARGEST PRIVATE COMPANIES IN CANADA, 1995
Ranked by: Revenue for the year ending December 1995, in thousands of Canadian dollars. **Remarks:** Also notes return on capital, profit, assets, and major shareholders. **Number listed:** 1
1. General Motors of Canada with C$30,893,182 thousand
2. Ford Motor Co. of Canada, C$19,100,000
3. Chrysler Canada, C$13,691,000
4. Sun Life Assurance of Canada, C$10,615,000
5. IBM Canada, C$10,310,000
6. Manulife Financial, C$8,874,000
7. McCain Capital Corp., C$7,072,048

8. Amoco Canada Petroleum, C$3,619,000
9. Canada Safeway, C$4,795,900
10. Canada Life Assurance, C$4,670,660

Source: *Globe and Mail,* Globe and Mail Report on Business 1000 (annual), July 1996, p. 141.

Clothing and Dress – Men

★ 661 ★
MEN'S APPAREL SALES IN JAPAN, 1995
Ranked by: Sales, in millions of yen (¥). **Number listed:** 9

1. Jackets with ¥558,140 million
2. Suits, ¥558,140
3. Slacks, ¥513,954
4. Shirts, ¥469,353
5. Sweaters, ¥382,583
6. Shoes, ¥323,000
7. Jumper, ¥265,820
8. Polo shirts, ¥263,398
9. Coats, ¥220,300

Source: *National Trade Data Bank*, November 8, 1996, p. IMI961107.

★ 662 ★
MENSWEAR SALES BY COUNTRY
Ranked by: Value of men's underwear and outerwear sales, in billions of U.S. dollars. **Number listed:** 6

1. Germany with $36.7 billion
2. Spain, $22.9
3. United Kingdom, $15.0
4. France, $13.0
5. Italy, $13.0
6. United States, $8.4

Source: *Business Review*, October 1995, p. 14.

Clothing and Dress – Women

★ 663 ★
WOMEN'S LARGE ARTICLE CLOTHING SALES IN FRANCE
Ranked by: Market share, in percent. **Remarks:** Includes population distribution of women aged 13 and up. **Number listed:** 9

1. Pants/jeans with 25.8%
2. Skirts, 25.1%
3. Dresses, 16.6%
4. Suits, 8.3%
5. Shorts, 7.1%
6. Anoraks, 6.7%
7. Vests, 5.6%
8. Coats and raincoats, 4.0%

9. Other, 0.8%

Source: *National Trade Data Bank*, June 3, 1996, p. ISA960301.

★ 664 ★
WOMEN'S SMALL ARTICLE CLOTHING SALES IN FRANCE
Ranked by: Market share, in percent. **Remarks:** Includes population distribution of women aged 13 and up. **Number listed:** 7

1. Sweaters with 36.2%
2. Polos/T-shirts, 32.4%
3. Blouses, 19.5%
4. Swimsuits, 4.5%
5. Sweatshirts, 2.7%
6. Jogging outfits, 2.1%
7. Other, 2.4%

Source: *National Trade Data Bank*, June 3, 1996, p. ISA960301.

★ 665 ★
WOMENSWEAR SPENDING BY COUNTRY
Ranked by: Per capita expenditure, in U.S. dollars. **Remarks:** The women's clothing market was valued at $670 billion. **Number listed:** 6

1. Germany with $751.1
2. United Kingdom, $657.7
3. United States, $639.5
4. Italy, $543.9
5. France, $530.0
6. Spain, $354.0

Source: *Business Review*, October 1995, p. 14.

Clothing Stores

★ 666 ★
CANADA'S TOP APPAREL STORES
Ranked by: Revenue, in thousands of Canadian dollars. **Remarks:** Includes figures on profits and return on capital. **Number listed:** 6

1. Dylex Ltd. with C$1,692,348 thousand
2. Reitmans, C$360,478
3. Suzy Shier, C$267,485
4. Mark's Work Wearhouse, C$185,924
5. Chateau Stores of Canada, C$159,768
6. Pantorama Industries, C$147,742

Source: *Globe and Mail's Report on Business Magazine*, July 1996, p. 159.

Clothing Trade

★ 667 ★

BEST-SELLING SPORTS APPAREL SALES IN THE UNITED KINGDOM, 1994

Ranked by: Sales, in millions of U.S. dollars. **Remarks:** Reebok leads the sports market with an 18.0% share. **Number listed:** 12

1. Waterproofs/Outdoor clothing with $464 million
2. Track Suits, $432
3. Swimming, $192
4. Football, $112
5. Golf, $104
6. Whites, $72
7. Skiing, $69
8. Aerobics, $67
9. Cycling, $40
10. Athletics/Jogging, $35

Source: *National Trade Data Bank*, January 16, 1996, p. ISA9510.

★ 668 ★

LEADING INTEGRATED MILL COMPANIES IN BRAZIL

Ranked by: Sales, in millions of U.S. dollars. **Remarks:** Includes yarn, fabric, and apparel. **Number listed:** 7

1. Sao Paulo Alpargatas with $767.59 million
2. Tatuape, $376.03
3. Buettner, $57.54
4. Schlosser, $42.80
5. Filobel, $41.65
6. Karibe, $21.96
7. Buddemeyer, $13.71

Source: *National Trade Data Bank*, August 18, 1995, p. ISA9505.

★ 669 ★

LEADING PRODUCERS OF KNITS AND KNITTED ITEMS IN BRAZIL

Ranked by: Sales, in millions of U.S. dollars. **Number listed:** 10

1. Hering Textil with $253.37 million
2. Malwee, $127.93
3. Marisol, $115.39
4. Sulfabril Malhas, $96.80
5. Pettenati, $85.73
6. Dou Tex, $32.06
7. Velonorte, $26.83
8. Sulfabril Nordeste, $12.90
9. Guararapes, $12.44
10. Iracema, $11.50

Source: *National Trade Data Bank*, August 18, 1995, p. ISA9505.

★ 670 ★

LEADING PRODUCERS OF SOCKS IN BRAZIL

Ranked by: Sales, in millions of U.S. dollars. **Number listed:** 7

1. Lupo with $39.46 million
2. Drastosa, $33.50
3. Selene, $25.47
4. Lolypop, $18.35
5. Meias Aco, $10.95
6. William, $7.66
7. Meias Palmira, $0.44

Source: *National Trade Data Bank*, August 18, 1995, p. ISA9505.

★ 671 ★

TOP APPAREL FIRMS WORLDWIDE, 1995-1996

Ranked by: Revenue for the fiscal years ending between November 1995 and March 1996, in billions of U.S. dollars. **Number listed:** 15

1. Levi Strauss (U.S.) with $6.5 billion
2. VF Corporation (U.S.), $5.3
3. Fruit of the Loom (U.S.), $2.4
4. Liz Claiborne (U.S.), $2.3
5. Benetton Group (Italy), $2.1
6. Renown (Japan), $2.1
7. Onward Kashiyama (Japan), $1.9
8. Itokin (Japan), $1.6
9. Marzotto Group (Italy), $1.6
10. Kelwood (U.S.), $1.4

Source: *The Economist*, June 8, 1996, p. 66.

★ 672 ★

TOP GARMENT COMPANIES IN BRAZIL

Ranked by: Sales, in millions of U.S. dollars. **Number listed:** 12

1. Hering Nordeste with $128.52 million
2. Levi Strauss, $46.93
3. Guararapes, $42.75
4. Guadalajara, $31.80
5. Lee Nordeste, $24.46
6. Dudalina, $22.31
7. Staroup, $18.80
8. Vila Romana, $16.44
9. Lee, $15.82
10. Andriello, $15.58

Source: *National Trade Data Bank*, August 18, 1995, p. ISA9505.

★ 673 ★

TOP PRODUCERS OF UNDERWEAR AND BATHING SUITS IN BRAZIL

Ranked by: Sales, in millions of U.S. dollars. **Number listed:** 10

1. De Millus with $80.25 million
2. Du Loren, $62.46
3. Brasileira Moda, $36.00

4.   Zorba, $21.40
5.   N. Grunkraut, $12.29
6.   Morisco, $11.19
7.   Lumiere, $10.94
8.   Sinimbu, $9.81
9.   A. Ferro, $6.54
10. De Millus Roupas, $0.22

Source: *National Trade Data Bank*, August 18, 1995, p. ISA9505.

Clothing Trade – Europe

★ 674 ★
TOP EUROPEAN COMPANIES IN APPAREL AND OTHER FINISHED PRODUCTS
Ranked by: Sales, in millions of European Currency Units (ECUs). **Remarks:** Also notes number of employees. **Number listed:** 81
1.   Triumph International Spiesshofer & Braun with 1,306 million ECUs
2.   Courtaulds Textiles Plc, 1,194
3.   Benetton Group S.P.A., 1,066
4.   Levi Straus & Co. Europe S.A., 807
5.   William Baird Plc, 715
6.   Klaus Steilmann GmbH & Co. Kommanditgesellschaft, 607
7.   Baird Textile Holdings Ltd., 607
8.   Sommer-Allibert Industrie A.G., 560
9.   Escada A.G., 531
10. Miroglio Tessile S.P.A., 528

Source: *Duns Europa* (annual), vol. 4, Dun & Bradstreet, 1997, p. 218+.

Coal Industry

★ 675 ★
THERMAL COAL CONSUMPTION BY CANADIAN PROVINCE
Ranked by: Consumption, in millions of tons. **Number listed:** 6
1.   Alberta with 25.8 million tons
2.   Saskatchewan, 9.7
3.   Ontario, 7.0
4.   Nova Scotia, 2.9
5.   New Brunswick, 1.4
6.   Manitoba, 0.2

Source: *Globe and Mail*, August 19, 1997, p. B6.

★ 676 ★
TOP COAL PRODUCING NATIONS, 1995
Ranked by: Production, in millions of tons. **Number listed:** 12
1.   China with 1,292 million tons
2.   United States, 849
3.   C.I.S., 365
4.   India, 233
5.   South Africa, 197
6.   Australia, 196
7.   Western Europe, 138
8.   Poland, 132
9.   Canada, 39
10. Colombia, 20

Source: *Engineering & Mining Journal*, 1997 Commodities Review Issue (annual), March 1997, p. 58-WW.

Coal Mines and Mining

★ 677 ★
LEADING COAL BASINS IN RUSSIA
Ranked by: Resources, in billions of metric tons. **Remarks:** Shows thermal coal, coking coal, anthracite, and brown coal resources for each basin. **Number listed:** 9
1.   Kuznetsk with 211.5 billion metric tons
2.   Kansk-Achinsk, 78.0
3.   Donbass, 16.6
4.   Far East, 15.7
5.   East Siberia, 13.0
6.   Pechora, 12.4
7.   North East, 12.0
8.   Moscow, 4.4
9.   Urals, 2.5

Source: *Coal*, August 1996, p. CA-1.

Cobalt

★ 678 ★
TOP COBALT PRODUCERS, 1995
Ranked by: Production, in metric tons. **Number listed:** 8
1.   Gecamines with 4,150 metric tons
2.   OMG, 3,610
3.   ZCCM, 2,934
4.   Falconbridge, 2,804
5.   ICCI, 1,730
6.   INCO, 1,362
7.   Sumitomo, 222

8. Other, 2,577

Source: *Engineering & Mining Journal*, 1997 Commodities Review Issue (annual), March 1997, p. WW-11.

Cocoa

★ 679 ★
TOP COCOA BEAN PRODUCERS IN LATIN AMERICA, 1996
Ranked by: Thousands of tons for the first nine months of 1996. **Number listed:** 7
1. Brazil with 200.0 thousand tons
2. Ecuador, 85.0
3. Dominican Republic, 58.0
4. Colombia, 50.0
5. Mexico, 45.0
6. Venezuela, 18.0
7. Costa Rica, 3.0

Source: *Latin American Economy & Business - Quarterly Update*, September 1996, p. 10.

Coffee Industry

★ 680 ★
GERMANY'S COFFEE MARKET
Ranked by: Market share, in percent. **Number listed:** 8
1. Jacobs with 29.8%
2. Andere, 15.4%
3. Tchibo, 15.4%
4. Aldi, 12.1%
5. Melitta, 11.7%
6. Eduscho, 10.5%
7. Dallmeyer, 7.1%
8. Idee (Darboven), 2.3%

Source: *Wirtschaftswoche*, May 2, 1996, p. 90.

★ 681 ★
GERMANY'S TOP COFFEE MAKERS, 1996
Ranked by: Market share for October 1996, in percent. **Number listed:** 8
1. Jacobs with 30.1%
2. Tchibo, 18.1%
3. Melitta, 11.1%
4. Eduscho, 10.6%
5. Aldi, 10.2%
6. Dallmayr, 7.4%
7. Darboven, 2.8%
8. Other, 9.7%

Source: *Der Spiegel*, 1996, p. 86.

★ 682 ★
LEADERS IN THE ITALIAN COFFEE MARKET, 1996
Ranked by: Market share for June to July 1996, in percent. **Number listed:** 8
1. Lavazza with 45.4%
2. Cafe do Brazil, 10.4%
3. General Foods Splendid, 8.4%
4. Segafredo Zanetti, 3.4%
5. Sao Groupo, 2.6%
6. Mauro, 1.7%
7. Private label, 3.7%
8. Other, 22.8%

Source: *Tea & Coffee Trade Journal*, September 1996, p. 78.

★ 683 ★
LEADERS IN THE PUERTO RICAN COFFEE MARKET
Ranked by: Market share, in percent. **Number listed:** 3
1. Jimenez & Fernandez with 60.0%
2. Garrido y Compania Inc., 25.0%
3. Other, 15.0%

Source: *Tea & Coffee Trade Journal*, September 1996, p. 78.

★ 684 ★
LEADING COFFEE PRODUCERS IN POLAND
Ranked by: Market share, in percent. **Number listed:** 5
1. Tschibo Warsaw Ltd. with 22.0%
2. Jacobs, 14.0%
3. Union Coffee Poland, 13.0%
4. Multi Mielno, 9.0%
5. Woseba of Odolanow, 5.0%

Source: *National Trade Data Bank*, March 27, 1997, p. IMI970327.

★ 685 ★
TOP COFFEE BRANDS BY BRAND VALUE
Ranked by: Brand value, in millions of U.S. dollars. **Remarks:** Value was calculated using capital, ratio of capital to company sales, earnings, and corporate tax rate of the country where the parent company is located. See source for details. **Number listed:** 4
1. Nescafe (Nestle) with $10,527 million
2. Jacobs (Philip Morris), $1,453
3. Maxwell House (Philip Morris), $1,383
4. Douwe Egberts (Sara Lee), $904

Source: *Financial World,* World's Most Valuable Brands (annual), July 8, 1996, p. 60.

★ 686 ★
TOP COFFEE CONSUMING COUNTRIES, 1994
Ranked by: Consumption, in millions of bags. **Remarks:** One bag contains 60 kilograms of coffee beans. **Number listed:** 5
1. United States with 18.1 million bags

2. Germany, 10.0
3. Japan, 6.1
4. France, 5.4
5. Italy, 4.8

Source: *The Wall Street Journal*, July 25, 1996, p. B1.

★ 687 ★
TOP DESTINATIONS FOR ITALIAN ROASTED COFFEE EXPORTS, 1995
Ranked by: Coffee exports, in kilograms. **Number listed:** 15

1. France with 14,001,181
2. Germany, 5,483,910
3. Portugal, 1,638,242
4. United States, 1,591,805
5. United Kingdom, 1,027,056
6. Switzerland, 769,149
7. Australia, 760,849
8. Slovenia, 698,220
9. Spain, 620,605
10. Netherlands, 611,649

Source: *Tea & Coffee Trade Journal*, March 1997, p. 15.

Collecting of Accounts

★ 688 ★
FASTEST BILL PAYERS IN EUROPE
Ranked by: Average number of days it takes companies in European countries to pay American exporters. **Number listed:** 17

1. Finland with 24 days
2. Denmark, 35
3. Sweden, 37
4. Germany, 38
5. Austria, 43
6. Netherlands, 46
7. Switzerland, 50
8. United Kingdom, 50
9. Belgium, 52
10. Luxembourg, 56

Source: *Entrepreneur*, November 1996, p. 98.

Collectors and Collecting

★ 689 ★
SPAIN'S COLLECTIBLES MARKET
Ranked by: Sales, in thousands of pesetas. **Number listed:** 6

1. Planeta de Agostini with 25,000
2. RBA Editores, 14,500
3. Salvat, 7,400
4. Orbis Fabbri, 5,600

5. Altaya, 3,300
6. Others, 200

Source: *National Trade Data Bank*, May 27, 1996, p. IMI960329.

Colombia – see under individual headings

Colombo Stock Exchange

★ 690 ★
LARGEST COMPANIES ON THE COLOMBO STOCK EXCHANGE, 1995
Ranked by: Market value, in millions of rupees (Rs). **Number listed:** 20

1. DFCC with Rs9,383 million
2. Hatton National Bank, Rs6,900
3. National Development Bank, Rs3,850
4. Hayles, Rs3,510
5. John Keels Holdings, Rs3,430
6. Commercial Bank of Ceylon, Rs2,625
7. Ceylon Grain Elevators, Rs2,520
8. Ceylon Tobacco, Rs2,485
9. Aitken Spence, Rs2,387
10. Sampath Bank, Rs1,993

Source: *GT Guide to World Equity Markets* (annual), Euromoney Publications, 1996, p. 438.

★ 691 ★
MOST ACTIVELY TRADED SHARES ON THE COLOMBO STOCK EXCHANGE, 1995
Ranked by: Turnover, in millions of rupees (Rs). **Number listed:** 20

1. DFCC with Rs1,296 million
2. National Development Bank, Rs1,028
3. John Keels Holdings, Rs658
4. Aitken Spence and Company, Rs637
5. Hayles, Rs578
6. Vanik Incorporation, Rs420
7. Sampath Bank, Rs412
8. Asia Capital, Rs371
9. Hatton National Bank, Rs282
10. Distilleries Company of Sri Lanka, Rs275

Source: *GT Guide to World Equity Markets* (annual), Euromoney Publications, 1996, p. 439.

Colorado – see under individual headings

Commercials
See: **Radio Advertising; Television Advertising**

Communications Satellites

★ 692 ★
GLOBAL SATELLITE MAKERS, 1990-2000
Ranked by: Market share of prime contracts for 1990-2001, in percent. **Number listed:** 6
1. Hughes Aircraft with 34.1%
2. Space Systems/Loral, 16.5%
3. Lockheed Martin Telecom, 16.0%
4. ESI (Aerospatiale/DASA), 13.8%
5. Matra Marconi, 10.8%
6. Others, 8.8%

Source: *Interavia*, October 1996, p. 44.

Compact Disc Industry

★ 693 ★
TOP COMPACT DISC PLAYERS IN JAPAN
Ranked by: Market share, in percent. **Number listed:** 6
1. Sony Music Entertainment with 17.7%
2. Polygram, 13.6%
3. Toshiba EMI, 13.1%
4. BMG Victor, 8.5%
5. Victor Entertainment, 8.0%
6. Other, 39.1%

Source: *Nikkei Weekly*, July 22, 1996, p. 8.

Companies
See: **Corporations**

Competitiveness

★ 694 ★
LEAST COMPETITIVE COUNTRIES
Ranked by: Competitiveness, based on criteria such as labor markets, fiscal policies, tax and regulatory regimes, and openness to trade and investment. **Remarks:** No specific data were given. **Number listed:** 10
1. Russia
2. Ukraine
3. Zimbabwe
4. Poland
5. Vietnam
6. Greece

7. Venezuela
8. Hungary
9. India
10. South Africa

Source: *The New York Times*, May 21, 1997, p. C3.

★ 695 ★
MOST COMPETITIVE ECONOMIES WORLDWIDE, 1997
Ranked by: Competitiveness. No specific data were given. **Remarks:** Also provides rankings for 1996. **Number listed:** 10
1. Singapore
2. Hong Kong
3. United States
4. Canada
5. New Zealand
6. Switzerland
7. England
8. Taiwan
9. Malaysia
10. Norway

Source: *The Wall Street Journal*, June 4, 1997, p. A13.

★ 696 ★
MOST COMPETITVE COUNTRIES, 1996
Ranked by: Survey results, based on 225 criteria such as labor force quality, management performance, and other statistical data. **Remarks:** Notes 1995 ranking. **Number listed:** 46
1. United States
2. Singapore
3. Hong Kong
4. Japan
5. Denmark
6. Norway
7. Netherlands
8. Luxembourg
9. Switzerland
10. Germany

Source: *Agri Finance*, July 1996, p. 7.

Computer Industry
See Also: Microcomputers

★ 697 ★
BRITAIN'S TOP HOME COMPUTER VENDORS, 1994
Ranked by: Market share, in percent. **Remarks:** Includes 1993 figures, shares of the overall market and sales by outlet. **Number listed:** 10
1. IBM with 10.8%
2. Packard Bell, 9.6%
3. Apple, 9.1%

4. Compaq, 9.1%
5. Dell, 5.7%
6. AST, 3.1%
7. Olivetti, 2.4%
8. Opus, 2.0%
9. Viglen, 1.8%
10. Amstrad, 1.7%

Source: *National Trade Data Bank*, May 1, 1996, p. ISA960501.

★ 698 ★
CHINA'S COMPUTER SALES BY TYPE OF PROCESSOR, 1995
Ranked by: Market share, in percent. **Remarks:** Notes figures for 1994. **Number listed:** 8
1. 486DX2 with 55%
2. Pentium 75, 10%
3. 486SX, 9%
4. 486SX/DX, 8%
5. Pentium 90/100, 6%
6. 486DX4, 5%
7. Pentium 60, 3%
8. Others, 8%

Source: http:// www.china-research.com/ciw/c4-06-96.htm, April 28, 1997, p. 5.

★ 699 ★
COMPUTER MARKET WORLDWIDE, 1997
Ranked by: Distribution of revenue, in percent. **Number listed:** 5
1. Portable computers with 89.0%
2. PC cards, 6.1%
3. Pen computers, 2.1%
4. Palmtops, 2.0%
5. Portable printers, 0.8%

Source: *Computer Reseller News*, May 20, 1996, p. 18.

★ 700 ★
COMPUTER USE IN ECUADOR, 1996
Ranked by: Percent distribution. **Number listed:** 6
1. Banking with 36%
2. Government, 22%
3. Management, 19%
4. Production, 11%
5. Education, 8%
6. Personal, 4%

Source: *National Trade Data Bank*, May 29, 1997, p. IMI970527.

★ 701 ★
GLOBAL PC MARKET, 1996
Ranked by: Estimated market share, in percent. **Number listed:** 6
1. Compaq with 10.1%
2. IBM, 8.6%
3. Packard Bell NEC, 6.1%

4. Apple, 5.2%
5. Hewlett-Packard, 4.1%
6. Others, 65.9%

Source: *Macweek*, February 3, 1997, p. 1.

★ 702 ★
JAPAN'S MAINFRAME COMPUTER MAKERS
Ranked by: Market share, in percent. **Number listed:** 6
1. Fujistu with 25.5%
2. IBM Japan, 23.8%
3. Hitachi, 17.7%
4. NEC, 17.5%
5. Nihon Unisys, 9.8%
6. Other, 5.7%

Source: *Nikkei Weekly*, July 15, 1996, p. 8.

★ 703 ★
LARGEST COMPUTER BRANDS BY BRAND VALUE
Ranked by: Brand value, in millions of U.S. dollars. **Remarks:** Value was calculated using capital, ratio of capital to company sales, earnings, and corporate tax rate of the country where the parent company is located. See source for details. **Number listed:** 8
1. IBM (International Business Machines) with $18,491 million
2. Hewlett-Packard (Hewlett-Packard), $8,111
3. Compaq (Compaq Computer), $4,038
4. Apple (Apple Computer), $2,247
5. Sun (Sun Microsystems), $970
6. Dell (Dell Computer), $743
7. Digital (Digital Equipment), $483
8. 3COM (3COM), $160

Source: *Financial World,* World's Most Valuable Brands (annual), July 8, 1996, p. 61.

★ 704 ★
LARGEST COMPUTER FIRMS IN POLAND, 1995
Ranked by: Profits, in millions of zlotys (Zl). **Remarks:** Includes 1994 profits. **Number listed:** 10
1. Optimus (Nowy Sacz) with Zl419.282 million
2. JTT Computer (Wroclaw), Zl330.617
3. Hewlett-Packard (Warsaw/Geneva), Zl271.559
4. IBM (Warsaw/Vienna), Zl200.257
5. Computer 2000 Polska (Warsaw), Zl139.248
6. ICL Poland Operators (Warsaw/London), Zl137.698
7. Prokom (Gdynia), Zl119.704
8. ComputerLand Poland (Warsaw), Zl102.127
9. Compaq Computer (Warsaw/Munich), Zl86.400
10. ABC Data (Warsaw), Zl75.500

Source: *The Warsaw Voice*, August 11, 1996, p. 13.

★ 705 ★

LARGEST COMPUTER OFFICE EQUIPMENT COMPANIES, 1995

Ranked by: Revenue, in millions of U.S. dollars.
Remarks: Notes profits and global rank. **Number listed:** 8

1. International Business Machines (United States) with $71,940 million
2. Fujitsu (Japan), $38,976
3. Hewlett-Packard (United States), $31,519
4. Canon (Japan), $23,012
5. Compaq Computer (United States), $14,755
6. Digital Equipment (United States), $13,813
7. Ricoh (Japan), $11,532
8. Apple Computer (United States), $11,062

Source: *Fortune,* The Global 500: World's Biggest Corporations (annual), August 5, 1996, p. F-18.

★ 706 ★

LEADING PC MANUFACTURERS IN FRANCE, 1997

Ranked by: Market share for the first quarter of 1997, in percent. **Number listed:** 11

1. Compaq with 12.2%
2. IBM, 10.4%
3. Packard Bell/NEC, 9.3%
4. Hewlett-Packard, 8.4%
5. Toshiba, 5.5%
6. Dell, 5.4%
7. Apple, 4.0%
8. Siemens-Nixdorf, 3.5%
9. Gateway 2000, 2.5%
10. Digital, 2.3%

Source: *National Trade Data Bank,* May 13, 1997, p. IMI970512.

★ 707 ★

LEADING PC VENDORS IN CHINA

Ranked by: Market share, in percent. **Number listed:** 6

1. IBM with 6.9%
2. Legend, 6.9%
3. Hewlett-Packard, 6.7%
4. Compaq, 6.3%
5. AST, 5.4%
6. Other, 67.8%

Source: http:// www.news.com/SpecialFeaturs/ Continued/0,6,11889_3,00.html, July 7, 1997, p. 2.

★ 708 ★

MOROCCO'S TOP PC MARKET

Ranked by: Market share, in percent. **Number listed:** 18

1. IBM with 18.0%
2. Apple, 12.0%
3. Acer, 10.0%
4. Nixdorf, 10.0%
5. Bull, 7.0%
6. Compaq, 7.0%

7. Olivetti, 5.0%
8. AST, 3.0%
9. AT&T/NCR, 3.0%
10. DEC, 3.0%

Source: *National Trade Data Bank,* March 21, 1995, p. ISA9406.

★ 709 ★

PC MARKET IN LATIN AMERICA, 1995

Ranked by: Unit shipments. **Number listed:** 5

1. IBM with 320,000 units
2. Compaq, 300,000
3. Acer, 255,000
4. Hewlett-Packard, 115,000
5. Apple, 110,000

Source: *Latin Trade,* July 1996, p. 12.

★ 710 ★

PC MARKET IN POLAND, 1995

Ranked by: Market share, in percent, of domestic personal computer market. **Remarks:** Notes market share of foreign manufacturers. Foreign firms captured 33% of the market in Poland. IBM was the leading foreign computer manufacturer with a 13.97% share. **Number listed:** 11

1. Optimus with 51.76%
2. Adax, 12.23%
3. NTT, 5.63%
4. Baza, 4.48%
5. Inver, 4.34%
6. Datacom, 2.65%
7. Hector, 2.59%
8. Gulipin, 1.44%
9. Altkom, 0.82%
10. Comptrade, 0.61%

Source: *The Warsaw Voice,* August 11, 1996, p. 12.

★ 711 ★

PERSONAL COMPUTER VENDORS IN NEW ZEALAND, 1995

Ranked by: Market share based on unit shipments, in percent. **Remarks:** Total PC shipments were 204,565 units. Also provides data for 1994. **Number listed:** 21

1. Compaq with 12.5%
2. Apple, 9.3%
3. IBM, 8.3%
4. PC Direct, 8.2%
5. Digital, 7.4%
6. Toshiba, 6.7%
7. Acer, 5.0%
8. Total Peripherals, 4.3%
9. AST, 3.9%
10. PC General, 3.6%

Source: *National Trade Data Bank,* January 8, 1997, p. ISA961201.

★ 712 ★
SLOVENIA'S TOP COMPUTER FIRMS
Ranked by: Turnover, in thousands of tolars (To).
Remarks: Also notes profits, number of employees, income per employee, and profit per employee.
1. Iskra Tel-Podjetje Telekomunikacijskih Sistemov, D.O.O. with To14,618,125 thousand
2. Mladinska Knjiga Birooprema, D.D., To3,077,877
3. Intertrade ITS, D.D., To2,338,895
4. Teling-Teleinformacijski Sistemi In Storitve, D.O.O., To1,965,784
5. Repro, D.O.O., To1,917,818
6. Hermes Plus, D.D., To1,916,697
7. IBM Slovenija, D.O.O., To1,879,455
8. Zalozba Obzorja, P.O., To1,750,970
9. PCX, P.O., To1,501,837
10. SRC Computers, D.O.O., To1,338,296

Source: *Slovenian Business Report*, Spring 1997, p. 30.

★ 713 ★
SLOVENIA'S TOP COMPUTER INDUSTRY EMPLOYERS
Ranked by: Number of employees. **Number listed:** 10
1. Iskra Tel-Podjetje Telekomunikacijskih Sistemov, D.O.O. with 1,049 employees
2. Mladinska Knjiga Birooprema, D.D., 163
3. Zalozba Obzorja, P.O., 156
4. Intertrade ITS, D.D., 142
5. IBM Slovenija, D.O.O., 133
6. Iskra-Sysen, D.D., 110
7. Primorski Tisk, D.D., 92
8. Kefo, D.D., 85
9. Gralan, D.D., 78
10. Metalka MDS Informacijski Inzeniring, P.O., 71

Source: *Slovenian Business Report*, Spring 1997, p. 30.

★ 714 ★
SPAIN'S LARGEST COMPUTER MAKERS, 1994
Ranked by: Sales, in millions of U.S. dollars. **Remarks:** Includes market share and industry sales by segment.
Number listed: 13
1. IBM with $1,511.42 million
2. Hewlett-Packard, $748.59
3. El Corte Ingles, $234.00
4. Digital, $206.00
5. Olivetti, $196.32
6. Fujitsu, $180.54
7. AT&T GIS, $181.08
8. Eritel (Indra), $149.25
9. Andersen Consulting, $145.45
10. Computer 2000, $127.61

Source: *National Trade Data Bank*, September 27, 1995, p. IMI950922.

★ 715 ★
TOP COMPUTER COMPANIES IN ECUADOR
Ranked by: Units sold. **Remarks:** Also notes market shares. **Number listed:** 5
1. IBM with 18,500
2. Compaq, 15,500
3. Acer, 7,900
4. DTK, 5,600
5. Other, 14,500

Source: *National Trade Data Bank*, May 29, 1997, p. IMI970527.

★ 716 ★
TOP COMPUTER MAKERS IN HUNGARY, 1996
Ranked by: Market share for the first six months of 1996, in percent. **Number listed:** 11
1. Albacomp with 14.3%
2. Escom, 7.6%
3. Compaq, 7.5%
4. DTK, 5.4%
5. IBM, 4.4%
6. Packard Bell, 3.6%
7. Mikropro, 3.4%
8. Elender, 3.3%
9. Hewlett-Packard, 3.1%
10. Digital Equipment, 2.7%

Source: *Business Central Europe*, November 1996, p. 6.

★ 717 ★
TOP COMPUTER MAKERS IN POLAND, 1996
Ranked by: Market share for the first six months of 1996, in percent. **Number listed:** 11
1. Optimus with 35.3%
2. JTT, 8.0%
3. Compaq, 6.1%
4. IBM, 4.5%
5. Baza, 3.3%
6. Escom, 3.1%
7. Inwar, 3.0%
8. Highscreen, 2.5%
9. NTT, 2.4%
10. Hewlett-Packard, 2.2%

Source: *Business Central Europe*, November 1996, p. 6.

★ 718 ★
TOP COMPUTER MAKERS IN RUSSIA, 1996
Ranked by: Market share for the first six months of 1996, in percent. **Number listed:** 11
1. Visit with 14.6%
2. IBM, 5.6%
3. R+K, 5.6%
4. Compaq, 3.6%
5. Hewlett-Packard, 3.6%
6. Acer, 3.4%
7. Formoza, 2.7%
8. Compulink/CLR, 2.3%

9. Apple, 1.8%
10. R-Style, 1.6%

Source: *Business Central Europe*, November 1996, p. 6.

★ 719 ★

TOP COMPUTER MAKERS IN THE CZECH REPUBLIC, 1996

Ranked by: Market share for the first six months of 1996, in percent. **Number listed:** 10

1. IBM with 10.4%
2. AutoCont, 7.8%
3. Compaq, 7.3%
4. Dell, 6.8%
5. Escom, 5.5%
6. Vikomt, 5.2%
7. Hewlett-Packard, 5.0%
8. Multisys, 4.4%
9. Tesco, 2.8%
10. Others, 44.8%

Source: *Business Central Europe*, November 1996, p. 6.

★ 720 ★

TOP DESKTOP PC FIRMS WORLDWIDE

Ranked by: Sales, in billions of U.S. dollars. **Remarks:** Includes 1995 sales. **Number listed:** 10

1. Compaq with $11.48 billion
2. Packard Bell NEC, $10.21
3. IBM PC Co., $9.18
4. Apple, $5.98
5. Dell, $5.89
6. Hewlett-Packard, $5.30
7. Gateway 2000, $4.42
8. Fujitsu, $3.91
9. Acer America, $3.77
10. Digital Equipment, $1.90

Source: *Computer Reseller News*, June 2, 1997, p. 122.

★ 721 ★

TOP MAINFRAME PRODUCERS WORLDWIDE

Ranked by: Market share, in percent. **Number listed:** 7

1. IBM with 30.8%
2. Fujitsu, 24.1%
3. Hitachi, 13.3%
4. NEC, 9.7%
5. Amdhal, 4.2%
6. Unisys, 3.3%
7. Others, 14.6%

Source: *Business Today*, May 22, 1996, p. 77.

★ 722 ★

TOP MOTHERBOARD MAKERS, 1996

Ranked by: Sales, in millions of U.S. dollars. **Remarks:** Includes 1995 sales. **Number listed:** 10

1. Intel with $2,000 million
2. Acer America, $700
3. Elite Group, $600

4. First International, $450
5. Asustek Computer, $426
6. Micro-Star, $180
7. Micronics, $171
8. Giga-Byte Technology, $165
9. Soyo Computer, $123
10. DFI, $100

Source: *Computer Reseller News*, Market Leaders (annual), June 2, 1997, p. 136.

★ 723 ★

TOP NOTEBOOK MAKERS BY SALES, 1996

Ranked by: Sales, in millions of U.S. dollars. **Remarks:** Includes 1995 sales. **Number listed:** 10

1. Toshiba with $5,800 million
2. IBM, $3,300
3. Packard Bell NEC, $2,600
4. Compaq, $2,500
5. Texas Instruments, $1,500
6. Apple, $1,200
7. Fujitsu, $1,200
8. Dell, $908
9. Acer America, $508
10. AST Research, $420

Source: *Computer Reseller News*, June 2, 1997, p. 126.

★ 724 ★

TOP NOTEBOOK MAKERS WORLDWIDE

Ranked by: Market share, in percent. **Number listed:** 12

1. Toshiba with 15.0%
2. Compaq, 11.0%
3. NEC, 10.0%
4. IBM, 9.9%
5. Apple, 6.7%
6. Fujitsu, 2.9%
7. Dell, 2.5%
8. AST, 2.1%
9. Texas Instruments, 1.8%
10. ZDS, 1.7%

Source: *PC Week*, March 25, 1996, p. 39.

★ 725 ★

TOP PC FIRMS IN CHINA, 1996

Ranked by: Market share for the first nine months of 1996, in percent. **Number listed:** 10

1. Compaq with 15.82%
2. IBM, 9.90%
3. AST, 6.63%
4. Hewlett Packard, 4.75%
5. Legend, 4.02%
6. Great Wall, 3.43%
7. Dell, 2.94%
8. IBM compatible, 2.17%
9. Others, 8.12%

10. Unknown, 43.13%

Source: *National Trade Data Bank*, November 14, 1996, p. IMI961106.

★ 726 ★
TOP PC MAKERS WORLDWIDE
Ranked by: Market share, in percent. **Number listed:** 13
1. Compaq with 13.1%
2. IBM, 12.3%
3. Apple, 10.1%
4. NEC, 8.1%
5. Dell, 4.0%
6. Toshiba, 3.6%
7. Gateway, 3.5%
8. AST, 3.2%
9. Packard Bell, 3.2%
10. Hewlett-Packard, 3.0%

Source: *Business Today*, May 22, 1996, p. 77.

★ 727 ★
TOP PC VENDORS IN INDIA, 1995-1996
Ranked by: Units sold. **Number listed:** 10
1. PCL with 62,820 units
2. HCL HP, 55,800
3. Wipro, 34,026
4. Unicorp, 18,472
5. TISL, 11,962
6. Modi Olivetti, 10,393
7. Cerebra, 9,455
8. Hewlett-Packard India, 9,346
9. Digital, 7,040
10. DCM Data Systems, 5,765

Source: *National Trade Data Bank*, May 22, 1997, p. ISA970501.

Computer Industry – Australia

★ 728 ★
PC MARKET IN AUSTRALIA, 1996
Ranked by: Units sold, in thousands. **Number listed:** 10
1. Compaq with 123 thousand
2. Apple, 95
3. IBM, 95
4. Ipex, 75
5. Digital, 70
6. Toshiba, 66
7. Acer, 51
8. NEC, 36
9. AST, 32
10. Dell, 32

Source: *National Trade Data Bank*, May 22, 1997, p. IMI970522.

Computer Industry – Canada

★ 729 ★
TOP PERSONAL COMPUTER MAKERS IN CANADA, 1996
Ranked by: Market share based on wholesale revenues, in percent. **Number listed:** 11
1. IBM Canada with 14.8%
2. Compaq Canada, 11.8%
3. Apple Canada, 6.5%
4. AST Canada, 5.2%
5. Dell Computer, 5.0%
6. Toshiba, 4.4%
7. NEC, 4.2%
8. Hewlett-Packard, 2.5%
9. Seanix, 2.5%
10. Sidus Systems, 2.2%

Source: *Marketing Magazine*, May 26, 1997, p. 14.

Computer Industry, International

★ 730 ★
LEADING NATIONS FOR HOME COMPUTER PENETRATION, 1995
Ranked by: Homes with personal computers, in percent.
Remarks: Data include systems used in home offices.
Number listed: 7
1. United States with 39%
2. Australia, 35%
3. Hong Kong, 32%
3. Singapore, 32%
4. Germany, 30%
5. United Kingdom, 25%
6. France, 22%
7. Japan, 21%

Source: *Electronic Business Today*, January 1996, p. 28.

Computer Industry – Japan

★ 731 ★
TOP PC MAKERS IN JAPAN, 1996
Ranked by: Market share, in percent. **Remarks:** Includes figures for 1995. **Number listed:** 6
1. NEC with 32.9%
2. Fujitsu, 21.9%
3. IBM, 11.9%
4. Apple, 11.0%
5. Toshiba, 5.4%
6. Other, 16.9%

Source: *The Wall Street Journal*, January 31, 1997, p. A13.

Source: *National Trade Data Bank*, October 9, 1996, p. ISA960801.

★ 732 ★
TOP WORD PROCESSOR MAKERS IN JAPAN, 1995
Ranked by: Market share, in percent. **Number listed:** 6
1. Sharp with 21.5%
2. NEC, 16.4%
3. Fujitsu, 14.4%
4. Toshiba, 14.2%
5. Casio, 13.6%
6. Other, 19.9%
Source: *Nikkei Weekly*, July 15, 1996, p. 8.

Computer Monitors

★ 733 ★
DESKTOP CRT MONITORS BY SIZE, 1997
Ranked by: Market share, in percent. **Remarks:** "CRT" stands for cathode ray tube. **Number listed:** 5
1. 15-inch with 45.5%
2. 14-inch, 32.5%
3. 17-inch, 19.9%
4. 20-inch, 1.1%
5. 21-inch, 1.0%
Source: *PC Today*, December 1996, p. 81.

★ 734 ★
TOP COMPUTER MONITOR MAKERS, 1996
Ranked by: Sales, in millions of U.S. dollars. **Remarks:** Includes 1995 sales. **Number listed:** 10
1. Samsung with $3,330 million
2. NECT, $2,100
3. LG Electronics USA, $1,400
4. Philips Consumer, $1,350
5. Sony, $1,000
6. ADI Systems, $830
7. Lite-On Technology, $750
8. Tatung, $700
9. Acer America, $687
10. Mag Innovision, $655
Source: *Computer Reseller News*, June 2, 1997, p. 130.

Computer Networks

★ 735 ★
PC SERVER MARKET IN MALAYSIA, 1995
Ranked by: Market share by unit shipment, in percent. **Number listed:** 7
1. Compaq with 17.2%
2. Hewlett-Packard, 14.4%
3. Digital, 13.7%
4. Acer, 13.3%
5. ALR, 8.9%
6. IPC, 1.9%

★ 736 ★
PC SERVER MARKET WORLDWIDE, 1995
Ranked by: Market share, in percent. **Number listed:** 6
1. Compaq with 34.0%
2. IBM, 14.0%
3. Hewlett-Packard, 12.0%
4. Acer, 5.0%
5. DEC, 5.0%
6. Other, 29.0%
Source: *The Wall Street Journal*, May 29, 1996, p. B4.

★ 737 ★
PC SERVER SOFTWARE VENDORS IN CANADA, 1996
Ranked by: Market share, in percent. **Number listed:** 6
1. Compaq with 39.3%
2. IBM, 14.4%
3. Hewlett-Packard, 9.4%
4. Digital, 5.3%
5. Dell, 4.1%
6. Others, 30.3%
Source: *Computing Canada*, May 12, 1997, p. 44.

★ 738 ★
TOP MID-RANGE SERVER PRODUCERS WORLDWIDE
Ranked by: Market share, in percent. **Number listed:** 11
1. IBM with 15.8%
2. Hewlett-Packard, 12.5%
3. Fujitsu, 10.4%
4. NEC, 6.8%
5. AT&T, 5.8%
6. DEC, 5.4%
7. Tandem, 4.6%
8. Toshiba, 4.2%
9. Compaq, 3.6%
10. Siemens-Nixdorf, 2.8%
Source: *Business Today*, May 22, 1996, p. 77.

★ 739 ★
TOP VENDORS OF NON-PC SERVERS IN INDIA
Ranked by: Turnover, in millions of U.S. dollars. **Number listed:** 5
1. HCL HP with $67.88 million
2. Digital, $23.45
3. Wipro, $11.04
4. TISL, $7.60
5. Tata Elxsi, $1.27
Source: *National Trade Data Bank*, May 22, 1997, p. ISA970501.

Computer Printers

★ 740 ★
JAPAN'S INKJET PRINTER MAKERS
Ranked by: Market share, in percent. **Number listed:** 6
1. Seiko Epson with 36.1%
2. Canon, 33.9%
3. NEC, 14.8%
4. Other, 15.2%
Source: *Nikkei Weekly*, July 15, 1996, p. 8.

★ 741 ★
TOP MANUFACTURERS OF COMPUTER PRINTERS IN HUNGARY, 1996
Ranked by: Market share for the first six months of 1996, in percent. **Number listed:** 6
1. Hewlett-Packard with 50.6%
2. Epson, 28.3%
3. Oki, 7.9%
4. Canon, 4.5%
5. Star, 3.5%
6. Others, 5.1%
Source: *Business Central Europe*, November 1996, p. 7.

★ 742 ★
TOP MANUFACTURERS OF COMPUTER PRINTERS IN POLAND, 1996
Ranked by: Market share for the first six months of 1996, in percent. **Number listed:** 6
1. Hewlett-Packard with 56.2%
2. Oki, 18.5%
3. Epson, 10.5%
4. Panasonic, 7.7%
5. Canon, 1.9%
6. Others, 5.2%
Source: *Business Central Europe*, November 1996, p. 7.

★ 743 ★
TOP MANUFACTURERS OF COMPUTER PRINTERS IN RUSSIA, 1996
Ranked by: Market share for the first six months of 1996, in percent. **Number listed:** 6
1. Epson with 64.8%
2. Hewlett-Packard, 27.2%
3. Panasonic, 3.3%
4. Lexmark, 1.7%
5. Star, 0.8%
6. Others, 2.1%
Source: *Business Central Europe*, November 1996, p. 7.

★ 744 ★
TOP MANUFACTURERS OF COMPUTER PRINTERS IN THE CZECH REPUBLIC, 1996
Ranked by: Market share for the first six months of 1996, in percent. **Number listed:** 6
1. Hewlett-Packard with 50.1%
2. Epson, 24.5%
3. Canon, 6.3%
4. Star, 4.9%
5. Panasonic, 4.5%
6. Others, 9.7%
Source: *Business Central Europe*, November 1996, p. 7.

★ 745 ★
TOP PRINTER MANUFACTURERS WORLDWIDE
Ranked by: Market share, in percent. **Remarks:** Data are estimated. **Number listed:** 4
1. Hewlett-Packard with 55%
2. Canon, 25%
3. Epson, 10%
4. Others, 10%
Source: *Business Today*, May 22, 1996, p. 77.

Computer Programmers, International

★ 746 ★
COMPUTER PROGRAMMER SALARIES
Ranked by: Average salary, in U.S. dollars. **Number listed:** 8
1. Japan with $42,316
2. West Germany, $40,124
3. United States, $36,002
4. Hong Kong, $28,211
5. France, $26,311
6. Britain, $25,529
7. Mexico, $14,917
8. India, $1,769
Source: *The Economist*, July 30, 1994, p. 63.

Computer Services Industry
See: **Computer Software Industry**

Computer Software Industry

★ 747 ★
FASTEST GROWING COMPUTER SOFTWARE IMPORT MARKETS OUTSIDE THE U.S., 1993-1995
Ranked by: Average annual growth, in percent. **Number listed:** 10
1. Portugal with 55% growth

2. Guatemala, 50%
3. Brazil, 42%
4. Venezuela, 35%
5. Chile, 30%
6. China, 30%
7. Czech Republic, 30%
8. India, 30%
9. Nigeria, 30%
10. Poland, 30%

Source: *National Trade Data Bank*, March 21, 1995, p. BMR9405.

★ 748 ★

FASTEST GROWING COMPUTER SOFTWARE MARKETS OUTSIDE THE U.S., 1993-1995

Ranked by: Average annual growth, in percent. **Number listed:** 10

1. Guatemala with 50% growth
2. Portugal, 50%
3. Brazil, 42%
4. India, 40%
5. Venezuela, 40%
6. Chile, 30%
7. China, 30%
8. Mexico, 30%
9. Nigeria, 30%
10. Poland, 30%

Source: *National Trade Data Bank*, March 21, 1995, p. BMR9405.

★ 749 ★

INDIA'S TOP SOFTWARE COMPANIES, 1995-1996

Ranked by: Turnover, in millions of U.S. dollars. **Remarks:** Also notes figures from the previous year. **Number listed:** 20

1. TCS with $145.07 million
2. HCL Consulting, $76.05
3. Wipro, $52.67
4. Tata Unisys, $36.05
5. Pentafour, $30.14
6. Silverline, $25.35
7. Infosys, $24.89
8. Fujitsu ICIM, $24.78
9. ECIL, $22.81
10. TISL, $17.33

Source: *National Trade Data Bank*, May 22, 1997, p. ISA970501.

★ 750 ★

JAPAN'S OFFICE SUITE MARKET

Ranked by: Market share, in percent. **Number listed:** 5

1. Microsoft Office with 64.1%
2. Lotus Office, 20.0%
3. Ichitaro Office, 5.8%
4. JustSystem, 5.7%

5. Other, 4.4%

Source: *Investor's Business Daily*, June 20, 1996, p. A8.

★ 751 ★

JAPAN'S SPREADSHEET MARKET

Ranked by: Market share, in percent. **Number listed:** 5

1. Microsoft Excel with 39.6%
2. Lotus 1-2-3 for Windows, 27.8%
3. Sanshiro, 12.4%
4. Lotus 1-2-3 for DOS, 11.0%
5. Other, 9.2%

Source: *Investor's Business Daily*, June 20, 1996, p. A8.

★ 752 ★

LARGEST SOFTWARE CREATORS IN POLAND, 1995

Ranked by: Revenue, in millions of zlotys (Zl) from creating software. **Number listed:** 15

1. Prokom Software Gdynia with Zl35.91 million
2. Softbank SA Warsaw, Zl15.91
3. CSBI Warsaw, Zl9.34
4. CrossComm Poland Gdansk, Zl7.92
5. Computron-Rewiks Warsaw, Zl7.86
6. COIG Katowice, Zl5.24
7. River Cracow, Zl5.10
8. Centrum Informatyki Energetyki Warsaw, Zl4.12
9. Compact Disc Novelty Cracow, Zl3.21
10. Simple Warsaw, Zl3.17

Source: *The Warsaw Voice*, November 10, 1996, p. 13.

★ 753 ★

LARGEST SOFTWARE VENDORS IN ARGENTINA, 1994

Ranked by: Billings, in millions of U.S. dollars. **Number listed:** 10

1. IBM with $55.0 million
2. EDS, $26.0
3. Microsoft, $15.0
4. J.D. Edwards, $13.0
5. Oracle, $11.5
6. Intersoft, $11.0
7. SSA, $9.0
8. Informix, $6.0
9. Novell, $6.0
10. Lotus, $4.5

Source: *National Trade Data Bank*, October 19, 1995, p. ISA9506.

★ 754 ★

LEADING CLIENT OPERATING SYSTEMS BY UNIT SHIPMENTS, 1996

Ranked by: Units shipped, as a percent of global total. **Number listed:** 5

1. Windows 95 with 62.9%
2. Windows 3.x, 17.4%

3.　Mac OS, 5.6%
4.　Windows NT Workstation, 3.0%
5.　Other, 11.1%
Source: *PC Week*, August 11, 1997, p. 14.

★ 755 ★
LEADING COMPUTER SERVICE FIRMS IN TURKEY, 1994
Ranked by: Market share, in percent. **Number listed:** 16
1.　IBM Turk Ltd with 20.0%
2.　Koc Unisys, 14.0%
3.　AT&T Global Information Solutions, 9.0%
4.　Siemens Nixdorf, 8.0%
5.　BIMSA Bilgisayar Islem Merkezi, 7.0%
6.　BILPA - Bilgi Islem Pazarlama A.S., 6.0%
7.　BILTAM Mumessillik Dis Tic. A.S., 2.0%
8.　Bull Bilgisaya Teknoloji A.S., 2.0%
9.　Digital Equipment Turkiye A.S., 2.0%
10.　Garanti Bilgi Islem A.S., 2.0%
Source: *National Trade Data Bank*, September 19, 1996, p. ISA960901.

★ 756 ★
LEADING CONSOLIDATION SOFTWARE APPLICATIONS IN THE UNITED KINGDOM
Ranked by: Percent distribution. **Remarks:** Data refer to software used by 150 British companies with a turnover of more than 200 million British pounds. **Number listed:** 5
1.　Third-party with 40%
2.　Spreadsheets, 28%
3.　Bespoke, 16%
4.　General ledger, 11%
5.　Other, 5%
Source: *Financial Times*, September 3, 1997, p. 8.

★ 757 ★
LEADING CONSOLIDATION SOFTWARE PACKAGES IN THE UNITED KINGDOM
Ranked by: Market share, in percent. **Remarks:** Data refer to software used by 150 British companies with a turnover of more than 200 million British pounds. **Number listed:** 4
1.　Hyperion with 37%
2.　Plus Plan, 23%
3.　Commander FDC, 15%
4.　Other, 25%
Source: *Financial Times*, September 3, 1997, p. 8.

★ 758 ★
LEADING VENDORS OF PC SOFTWARE IN JAPAN
Ranked by: Sales, in millions of U.S. dollars. **Number listed:** 4
1.　Softbank with $1,026 million
2.　Catena, $732
3.　Software Japan, $324

4.　Computer Wave, $149
Source: *National Trade Data Bank*, March 14, 1997, p. ISA960901.

★ 759 ★
OBJECT DATABASE MARKET
Ranked by: Market share, in percent. **Number listed:** 4
1.　Object Design with 27.9%
2.　Versant, 10.5%
3.　GemStone Systems, 7.4%
4.　Objectivity, 7.2%
5.　Other, 47.2%
Source: *Computerworld*, August 19, 1996, p. 43.

★ 760 ★
TOP COMPUTER SOFTWARE IMPORT MARKETS OUTSIDE THE U.S.
Ranked by: Total market value, in millions of U.S. dollars. **Number listed:** 10
1.　Germany with $7,057.0 million
2.　France, $4,789.0
3.　Sweden, $2,300.0
4.　Netherlands, $1,600.0
5.　Austria, $1,529.0
6.　United Kingdom, $1,325.0
7.　Belgium, $1,100.0
8.　Switzerland, $933.0
9.　Denmark, $930.0
10.　Australia, $697.0
Source: *National Trade Data Bank*, March 21, 1995, p. BMR9405.

★ 761 ★
TOP COMPUTER SOFTWARE MARKETS OUTSIDE THE U.S.
Ranked by: Total market value, in millions of U.S. dollars. **Number listed:** 10
1.　Japan with $38,000.0 million
2.　France, $15,863.0
3.　Germany, $9,419.0
4.　United Kingdom, $6,700.0
5.　Netherlands, $4,100.0
6.　Sweden, $3,800.0
7.　Italy, $2,995.0
8.　Austria, $2,548.0
9.　Switzerland, $2,350.0
10.　Belgium, $1,622.0
Source: *National Trade Data Bank*, March 21, 1995, p. BMR9405.

★ 762 ★
TOP MARKETS FOR PERSONAL SOFTWARE IN WESTERN EUROPE
Ranked by: Sales, in millions of U.S. dollars. **Number listed:** 10
1.　U.K./Ireland with $159.7 million

2. Germany/Austria, $154.3
3. France, $70.7
4. Benelux, $53.4
5. Nordic countries, $46.3
6. Italy, $45.4
7. Sweden, $32.3
8. Switzerland, $31.0
9. Spain/Portugal, $22.7
10. Greece, $1.5

Source: *Computer Reseller News*, September 16, 1996, p. 87.

★ 763 ★
TOP MARKETS FOR SALES OF WINDOWS 95 IN ASIA AND OCEANIA, 1995

Ranked by: Units sold in the third quarter of 1995. **Number listed:** 10

1. Australia with 42,000 units
2. New Zealand, 16,967
3. Singapore, 15,667
4. South Korea, 14,167
5. Malaysia, 13,000
6. Taiwan, 10,000
7. India, 9,317
8. Thailand, 5,000
9. Hong Kong, 4,833
10. Philippines, 4,510

Source: *Far Eastern Economic Review*, December 28, 1995, p. 55.

★ 764 ★
TOP PC OPERATING SYSTEMS BY SHIPMENT, 1995

Ranked by: Shipments, in thousands of units. **Number listed:** 7

1. 16-bit Windows/DOS with 33,527 thousand units
2. Windows 95, 19,500
3. Mac OS, 4,650
4. OS/2, 4,205
5. DOS alone, 3,451
6. Windows NT Workstation, 565
7. Other, 2,357

Source: *Software Magazine*, December 1996, p. 127.

★ 765 ★
TOP PRODUCERS OF NT DATABASES, 1995

Ranked by: Market share, in percent, of worldwide license revenue for Windows NT relational databases. **Remarks:** The global market earned $262.6 million. **Number listed:** 6

1. Microsoft with 40%
2. Oracle, 25%
3. Sybase, 6%
4. Computer Associates, 4%
5. Informix, 1%

6. Other, 24%

Source: *Informationweek*, December 23, 1996, p. 56.

★ 766 ★
TOP REGIONS FOR SOFTWARE SALES, 1996

Ranked by: Sales for the first three quarters of 1996, in millions of U.S. dollars. **Remarks:** Also notes percent change from 1995. **Number listed:** 4

1. North America with $6,900 million
2. Europe, $1,600
3. Asia-Pacific, $1,000
4. Latin America, $154

Source: *Smart Computing*, May 1997, p. 92.

★ 767 ★
TOP SOFTWARE BRANDS BY BRAND VALUE

Ranked by: Brand value, in millions of U.S. dollars. **Remarks:** Value was calculated using capital, ratio of capital to company sales, earnings, and corporate tax rate of the country where the parent company is located. See source for details. Brand value for Borland International's Borland brand was "not meaningful." **Number listed:** 10

1. Microsoft (Microsoft Corp.) with $5,634 million
2. Computer Associates (Computer Associates), $774
3. Oracle (Oracle Systems), $445
4. CompuServe (CompuServe), $285
5. Novell (Novell Inc.), $265
6. America Online (America Online), $178
7. Lotus (International Business Machines), $156
8. Sybase (Sybase), $25
9. Intuit (Intuit), $15

Source: *Financial World,* World's Most Valuable Brands (annual), July 8, 1996, p. 61.

★ 768 ★
TOP SOFTWARE COMPANIES WORLDWIDE, 1995

Ranked by: Packaged software revenues, in millions of U.S. dollars. **Remarks:** Notes figures for 1994. **Number listed:** 20

1. Microsoft Corp. with $7,271 million
2. Computer Associates International Inc., $3,196
3. Oracle, $2,558
4. Novell Inc., $1,990
5. SAP AG, $1,350
6. Sybase Inc., $786
7. Adobe Systems Inc., $762
8. Informix Software Inc., $536
9. SAS Institute, $534
10. Symantec Corp., $437

Source: *Financial Times*, December 4, 1996, p. 2.

★ 769 ★
TOP SOFTWARE EXPORTERS IN INDIA, 1995-1996
Ranked by: Revenue, in millions of rupees (Rs).
Remarks: Includes revenue for 1993-1995. **Number listed:** 31
1. Tata Consultancy Services with Rs4,205.2 million
2. HCL Corporation Ltd., Rs2,700.0
3. Wipro Infotech Group, Rs1,639.0
4. Pentafour Software & Exports Ltd., Rs1,020.3
5. Tata Unisys Ltd., Rs940.0
6. Silverline Industries Ltd., Rs814.9
7. Infosys Technologies Ltd., Rs806.5
8. Fujitsu ICIM Ltd., Rs640.0
9. Square D Software Ltd., Rs621.0
10. Patni Computer Systems Ltd., Rs560.0
Source: *Financial Times*, November 6, 1996, p. FT3.

★ 770 ★
TOP SOFTWARE FIRMS IN GERMANY, 1995
Ranked by: Turnover, in millions of deutschmarks (DM). **Number listed:** 10
1. Microsoft with DM800 million
2. SAP, DM722
3. Oracle Deutschland, DM400
4. Computer Associates, DM305
5. CSC Ploenzke, DM298
6. Novell, DM235
7. Sligos Software Products, DM216
8. Alldata, DM208
9. Informix, DM182
10. Bonndata, DM170
Source: *Wirtschaftswoche*, July 4, 1996, p. 43.

★ 771 ★
TOP SOFTWARE MARKETS IN THE PACIFIC RIM
Ranked by: Software revenue, in millions of U.S. dollars. **Number listed:** 9
1. Japan with $757.8 million
2. Singapore, $42.0
3. Taiwan, $37.9
4. Korea, $34.4
5. Hong Kong, $30.7
6. Malaysia, $13.4
7. Thailand, $11.6
8. India/Pakistan, $10.6
9. China, $4.6
Source: *Macweek*, May 27, 1996, p. 6.

★ 772 ★
TOP SOFTWARE SUPPLIERS TO BRAZIL, 1995
Ranked by: Sales, in thousands of U.S. dollars. **Remarks:** Notes distribution channel for each company. **Number listed:** 10
1. IBM with $300,000 thousand
2. Microsoft, $112,000

3. Oracle, $40,000
4. Novell, $28,000
5. SSA, $25,000
6. Informix, $17,000
7. Sybase, $12,000
8. AutoDesk, $7,400
9. Compuware, $6,000
Source: *National Trade Data Bank*, February 20, 1996, p. ISA9601.

★ 773 ★
UNIX MARKET IN FRANCE, 1995
Ranked by: Market share, in percent. **Number listed:** 5
1. Oracle with 45.2%
2. Informix, 19.4%
3. Sybase, 17.1%
4. Computer Associates-Ingres, 6.4%
5. Other, 12.9%
Source: *Le Figaro*, January 13, 1997, p. 11.

★ 774 ★
WEB BROWSING MARKET
Ranked by: Market share, in percent. **Number listed:** 4
1. Netscape with 74.0%
2. America Online, 8.0%
3. Microsoft, 4.0%
4. Other, 14.0%
Source: *Le Figaro*, August 28, 1996, p. 5.

★ 775 ★
WORLD MARKET FOR PACKAGED SOFTWARE, 1995
Ranked by: Sales of packaged software by country/region, in millions of U.S. dollars. **Remarks:** The world market was $86,060,000. **Number listed:** 8
1. United States with $40,000 million
2. Western Europe, $28,970
3. Japan, $8,365
4. Latin America, $1,840
5. Asia, $1,647
6. Canada, $1,613
7. Australia, $1,364
8. Other, $2,279
Source: *U.S. Global Trade Outlook 1995-2000: Toward the 21st Century*, 1995, p. 135.

★ 776 ★
WORLDWIDE DATABASE MARKET, 1996
Ranked by: Market share, in percent. **Number listed:** 5
1. Oracle with 29.8%
2. IBM, 25.6%
3. Informix, 9.3%
4. Sybase, 6.0%
5. Other, 29.3%
Source: *Investor's Business Daily*, June 2, 1997, p. A6.

Computer Software Industry – Canada

★ 777 ★
TOP CANADIAN SOFTWARE COMPANIES, 1995
Ranked by: Software revenues, in millions of Canadian dollars. **Number listed:** 10
1. Corel with C$270.0 million
2. Cognos, C$168.0
3. Eicon, C$74.4
4. Hummingbird, C$67.0
5. Fulcrum, C$43.0
6. M3i, C$21.6
7. Jetform, C$20.0
8. Promis, C$20.0
9. Andyne, C$10.4
10. Speedware, C$10.0

Source: *Marketing*, September 9, 1996, p. 13.

Computer Software Publishers
See: **Computer Software Industry**

Computer Stores

★ 778 ★
TOP COMPUTER RETAILERS IN THE UNITED KINGDOM, 1996
Ranked by: Revenue, in millions of British pounds (£).
Remarks: Notes change in revenues from 1995 in percent. **Number listed:** 6
1. Currys Superstores with £814.2 million
2. Dixons, £577.7
3. PC World, £261.5
4. Curry Highstreet, £187.7
5. The Link, £21.0
6. Others, £38.7

Source: *The Guardian*, July 11, 1996, p. 21.

Condoms

★ 779 ★
TOP CONDOM BRANDS IN CANADA, 1996
Ranked by: Market share based on sales, in percent.
Number listed: 7
1. Trojan with 32.0%
2. Durex Ramses, 23.8%
3. Durex Sheik, 20.5%
4. Ortho Shields, 11.2%
5. Durex Titan, 4.0%
6. Ortho Supreme, 2.8%

7. Ortho Legend, 0.5%
8. Other Julius Schmid brands, 0.6%
9. Others, 4.6%

Source: *Marketing Magazine*, May 26, 1997, p. 12.

Confectionery

★ 780 ★
INDIA'S CONFECTIONERY MARKET
Ranked by: Market share, in percent. **Number listed:** 4
1. Parle & Parry's with 35.0%
2. Nutrine, 30.0%
3. Ravalgaon/Bakeman's, 20.0%
4. Other, 15.0%

Source: *Business Today*, August 7, 1996, p. 50.

★ 781 ★
LEADING CONFECTIONERY BRANDS BY BRAND VALUE
Ranked by: Brand value, in millions of U.S. dollars.
Remarks: Value was calculated using capital, ratio of capital to company sales, earnings, and corporate tax rate of the country where the parent company is located. See source for details. **Number listed:** 11
1. Nestle (Nestle) with $3,634 million
2. Wrigley's (Wm. Wrigley Jr.), $3,157
3. Hershey's (Hershey Foods), $2,931
4. Cadbury's (Cadbury Schweppes), $2,156
5. Trident (Warner-Lambert), $472
6. Tootsie Roll (Tootsie Roll Industries), $264
7. Clorets (Warner-Lambert), $244
8. Chiclets (Warner-Lambert), $157
9. Certs (Warner-Lambert), $91
10. Dentyne (Warner-Lambert), $87

Source: *Financial World,* World's Most Valuable Brands (annual), July 8, 1996, p. 60.

★ 782 ★
TOP KASHI SUPPLIERS IN JAPAN, 1994
Ranked by: Sales, estimated in billions of yen (¥).
Remarks: Data refer to chocolates, biscuits, and sweets. Includes 1993 data. **Number listed:** 25
1. Lotte Shoji with ¥231 billion
2. Meiji Seika, ¥230
3. Ezaki Glico, ¥161
4. Morinaga Seika, ¥156
5. Fujiya, ¥126
6. Bourbon, ¥106
7. Calbee, ¥98
8. Kameda Seika, ¥68
9. Yamakazi Nabisco, ¥48
10. Tohato Seika, ¥38

Source: *The Manufacturing Confectioner*, March 1996, p. 31.

Confectionery Industry – United Kingdom

★ 783 ★
CONFECTIONERY MARKET IN THE UNITED KINGDOM
Ranked by: Market share, in percent. **Number listed:** 8
1. Cadbury with 20%
2. Nestle Rowntree, 20%
3. Mars, 18%
4. Trebor Bassett, 10%
5. Terry's, 4%
6. Wrigley, 2%
7. Warner Lambert, 1%
8. Others, 25%

Source: *The Manufacturing Confectioner*, May 1997, p. 21.

Congo – see under individual headings

Connectors
See: **Electric Connectors**

Construction Equipment Industry

★ 784 ★
EARTHMOVING EQUIPMENT MARKET IN EGYPT
Ranked by: Market share, in percent. **Number listed:** 12
1. Caterpillar with 55.0%
2. Hitachi, 10.0%
3. Komatsu, 10.0%
4. Case, 5.0%
5. John Deere, 5.0%
6. Kawasaki, 3.0%
7. Furukawa, 2.0%
8. JCB, 2.0%
9. Kobelco, 2.0%
10. O & K, 2.0%

Source: *National Trade Data Bank*, March 2, 1996, p. ISA9511.

★ 785 ★
LARGEST CONSTRUCTION EQUIPMENT CATEGORIES IN AUSTRALIA
Ranked by: Number of brands available in each category. **Number listed:** 15
1. Loaders (crawler, skidsteer, wheeled) with 39
2. Pumps, 35
3. Cranes, 31
4. Excavators and face shovels, 22
5. Rollers and compactors (static and vibratory), 18
6. Dump trucks, 15
7. Hammers, 15
8. Engines (industrial), 13
9. Dozers, 11
10. Road planners and recyclers, 9

Source: *National Trade Data Bank*, April 9, 1997, p. ISA970401.

Construction Industry
See Also: **Contractors**

★ 786 ★
LARGEST CONSTRUCTION FIRMS IN GREECE, 1995
Ranked by: Turnover, in millions of Greek drachma (GDr). **Remarks:** Includes 1994 turnover as well as profits before taxes in 1994 and 1995. **Number listed:** 30
1. Aegek S.A. with GDr27,662 million
2. Elliniki Technodomiki S.A., GDr21,383
3. Michaniki S.A., GDr19,170
4. GEK S.A., GDr11,451
5. Ergas A.T.E., GDr11,268
6. Aktor A.T.E., GDr9,167
7. Gnomon A.T.E., GDr9,051
8. K.I. Sarantopoulos S.A., GDr8,980
9. Gener S.A., GDr8,029
10. Technodomi A.B.E.T.T.E., GDr8,022

Source: *Trade With Greece*, Spring 1996, p. 36.

★ 787 ★
TOP CONSTRUCTION COMPANIES IN SOUTH KOREA, 1996
Ranked by: Sales for the first six months of 1996, in hundred million won (W). **Number listed:** 43
1. Hyundai Engineering & Construction with W20,976.3 hundred million
2. Dong Ah Construction Ind., W11,925.1
3. Daelim Ind., W11,321.2
4. LG Construction, W8,322.4
5. Kumho Construction & Engineering, W5,669.1
6. Hanshin Construction, W4,704.0
7. Hanjin Engineering & Construction, W4,330.3
8. Doosan Construction & Engineering, W3,918.9
9. Dongbu Engineering & Construction, W3,657.5
10. Chonggu Housing & Construction, W3,442.1

Source: *Business Korea*, October 1996, p. 40.

Construction Industry – Asia

★ 788 ★
ASIA'S LARGEST CONSTRUCTION FIRMS, 1995
Ranked by: Sales, in millions of U.S. dollars. **Remarks:**
Includes profits, profits as a percentage of sales and
assets, and overall sales rank. **Number listed:** 20
1. Taisei Corp. with $20,278.5 million
2. Shimizu Corp., $19,417.5
3. Kajima Corp., $18,749.2
4. Takenaka Corp., $15,375.5
5. Sekisui House, $13,921.5
6. Obayashi Corp., $13,228.6
7. Kumagai Gumi, $11,589.6
8. Sekisui Chemical, $11,429.0
9. Daiwa House Industry, $11,335.5
10. Nishimatsu Construction, $7,676.2
Source: *Asiaweek*, The Asiaweek 1,000, November 22,
1996, p. 159.

★ 789 ★
LARGEST CONSTRUCTION COMPANIES IN ASIA
Ranked by: Sales, in thousands of U.S. dollars. **Remarks:**
Also notes profit as a percent of sales. **Number listed:**
100
1. Taisei Corp. with $18,518,398 thousand
2. Shimizu Corp., $17,732,087
3. Kajima Corp., $17,121,825
4. Sekisui House Ltd., $12,713,165
5. Obayashi Corp., $11,497,077
6. Kumagai Gumi Corp., $10,583,660
7. Daiwa House Industry Co. Ltd., $10,351,621
8. Fujita Corp., $6,959,776
9. Sato Kogyo Co. Ltd., $6,709,378
10. Toda Corp., $6,226,359
Source: *Asia's 7,500 Largest Companies* (annual), Dun &
Bradstreet, 1997, p. 85+.

Construction Industry – Europe

★ 790 ★
TOP CONSTRUCTION COMPANIES IN EUROPE
Ranked by: Sales, in millions of European Currency
Units (ECUs). **Remarks:** Also notes number of
employees. **Number listed:** 299
1. Total with 21,121 million ECUs
2. Enterprises (Societe Generale D'), 7,036
3. Trackwork Group Ltd., 6,800
4. GTM Entrepose, 6,663
5. Philipp Holzmann A.G., 5,188
6. B.I.C.C. Plc, 4,330
7. Trafalgar House Plc, 3,966
8. Bilfinger + Berger Bauaktiengesellschaft, 3,195

9. Hochtief A.G. Vorm. Gebr. Helfmann, 2,719
10. Spie Batignolles, 2,648
Source: *Duns Europa* (annual), vol. 4, Dun & Bradstreet,
1997, p. 206+.

Construction Industry – Japan

★ 791 ★
TOP CONSTRUCTION FIRMS IN JAPAN
Ranked by: Income, in millions of yen (¥). **Number
listed:** 10
1. Taisei Corp. with ¥84,324 million
2. Daiwa House Industry, ¥77,792
3. Sekisui House, ¥74,407
4. Takenaka Corp., ¥54,886
5. Toda Construction, ¥51,316
6. Daito Trust Construction, ¥48,301
7. Ohbayashi Corp., ¥39,321
8. Nishimatsu Construction, ¥36,169
9. Okumura Corp., ¥26,188
10. Kajima Corp., ¥23,645
Source: *Tokyo Business Today*, August 1995, p. 26.

Consumer Electronics
See: **Home Electronics**

Contact Lenses

★ 792 ★
INDIA'S CONTACT LENSES MARKET
Ranked by: Market share, in percent. **Number listed:** 3
1. Ciba Vision with 70%
2. Bausch & Lomb, 25%
3. Johnson & Johnson, 5%
Source: *Business Today*, May 7, 1997, p. 25.

Container Industry

★ 793 ★
TOP CONTAINER GROUPS WORLDWIDE
Ranked by: Top groups. **Remarks:** The source provides
no criteria for these rankings. **Number listed:** 19
1. Evergreen Marine/Uniglory Marine
2. Maersk Line
3. Nedlloyd/P&O Containers
4. COSCO
5. Sealand
6. Nippon Yusen Kaisha/TSK Line

7. American President Lines
8. Neptune Orient Lines
9. Mitsui O.S.K. Lines
10. Hanjin Shipping

Source: *Marine Log,* Yearbook and Marine Review (annual), June 1997, p. 21.

★ 794 ★
TOP CONTAINER LESSORS WORLDWIDE, 1996
Ranked by: Twenty-foot equivalent units (TEUs) comprising the total fleet as of April 1996, in thousands. **Number listed:** 11

1. Genstar with 1,150 thousand TEUs
2. Transamerica Leasing, 1,000
3. Textainer Group, 410
4. Triton Container Intl., 410
5. Cronos Containers, 280
6. Sea Containers, 270
7. Interpool Inc., 250
8. Xtra Intl. Intermodal, 230
9. Trans Ocean, 170
10. CAI, 130

Source: *The Journal of Commerce,* January 2, 1997, p. B1.

Contractors
See Also: Industry

★ 795 ★
TOP INTERNATIONAL CONTRACTORS BY INTERNATIONAL REVENUE, 1995
Ranked by: International revenue, in millions of U.S. dollars. **Remarks:** Also notes figures for total revenue and new contracts. **Number listed:** 225

1. Mitsubishi Heavy Industries Ltd. with $5,725.4 million
2. SGE, $3,960.0
3. Bouygues S.A., $3,891.0
4. Fluor Daniel Inc., $3,625.0
5. Bechtel Group Inc., $3,165.0
6. GTM-Entrepose, $3,077.0
7. Philipp Holzmann A.G., $2,775.1
8. Hochtief A.G., $2,761.0
9. Fiatimpresit S.P.A., $2,758.0
10. Bilfinger + Berger Bau A.G., $2,675.5

Source: *ENR,* Top 225 International Contractors (annual), August 26, 1996, p. 45+.

★ 796 ★
TOP INTERNATIONAL CONTRACTORS BY TOTAL REVENUE, 1995
Ranked by: Total construction contract revenue, in millions of U.S. dollars. **Remarks:** Also notes figures for international and new contracts. **Number listed:** 225

1. Mitsubishi Heavy Industries Ltd. with $17,427.7 million
2. Shimizu Corp., $15,250.0
3. Taisei Corp., $13,779.0
4. Philipp Holzmann A.G., $13,655.6
5. Kajima Corp., $13,276.0
6. Takenaka Corp., $12,596.0
7. Bouygues S.A., $12,418.0
8. Obayashi Corp., $11,966.0
9. Kumagai Gumi, $9,089.0
10. SGE, $9,050.0

Source: *ENR,* Top 225 International Contractors (annual), August 26, 1996, p. 63.

★ 797 ★
TOP INTERNATIONAL CONTRACTORS IN BUILDING, 1995
Ranked by: Billings. **Remarks:** Specific dollar value is not provided. **Number listed:** 10

1. SGE
2. Hochtief A.G.
3. Bovis Construction Group
4. Bouygues S.A.
5. Skanska A.B.
6. GTM-Entrepose
7. Fiatimpresit S.P.A.
8. EIFFAGE
9. HBG, Hollandshe Beton Groep N.V.
10. Bilfinger + Berger Bau A.G.

Source: *ENR,* Top 225 International Contractors (annual), August 26, 1996, p. 41.

★ 798 ★
TOP INTERNATIONAL CONTRACTORS IN HAZARDOUS WASTE, 1995
Ranked by: Billings. **Remarks:** Specific dollar value is not provided. **Number listed:** 10

1. Jacobs Engineering Group Inc.
2. Philipp Holzmann A.G.
3. Chiyoda Corp.
4. Chengda Chemical Engrg. Corp. of China
5. Samsung Engineering Co. Ltd.
6. Foster Wheeler Corp.
7. Ansaldo S.P.A.
8. Skanska A.B.
9. Kajima Corp.
10. ICF Kaiser International Inc.

Source: *ENR,* Top 225 International Contractors (annual), August 26, 1996, p. 41.

★ 799 ★

TOP INTERNATIONAL CONTRACTORS IN MANUFACTURING, 1995

Ranked by: Billings. **Remarks:** Specific dollar value is not provided. **Number listed:** 10

1. Takenaka Corp.
2. Mitsubishi Heavy Industries Ltd.
3. Dongah Construction Ind. Co. Ltd.
4. Kajima Corp.
5. Phillipp Holzmann A.G.
6. Taikisha Ltd.
7. Shimizu Corp.
8. Dragados y Construcciones S.A.
9. Ansaldo S.P.A.
10. Daewoo Corp. Engineering & Construction

Source: *ENR,* Top 225 International Contractors (annual), August 26, 1996, p. 41.

★ 800 ★

TOP INTERNATIONAL CONTRACTORS IN POWER, 1995

Ranked by: Billings. **Remarks:** Specific dollar value is not provided. **Number listed:** 10

1. Mitsubishi Heavy Industries Ltd.
2. Ansaldo S.P.A.
3. ABB SAE Sadelmi S.P.A.
4. CEGELEC
5. Black & Veatch
6. Taisei Corp.
7. Bechtel Group Inc.
8. Raytheon Engineers & Constructors Intl.
9. Belleli S.P.A.
10. SGE

Source: *ENR,* Top 225 International Contractors (annual), August 26, 1996, p. 41.

★ 801 ★

TOP INTERNATIONAL CONTRACTORS IN SEWER/WASTE, 1995

Ranked by: Billings. **Remarks:** Specific dollar value is not provided. **Number listed:** 10

1. Bechtel Group Inc.
2. Daewoo Corp. Engineering & Construction
3. Tarmac PLC
4. The Parsons Corp.
5. Mitsubishi Heavy Industries Ltd.
6. McConnell Dowell Corp. Ltd.
7. CEGELEC
8. Philipp Holzmann A.G.
9. Morrison Knudsen Corp.
10. Hazama Corp.

Source: *ENR,* Top 225 International Contractors (annual), August 26, 1996, p. 41.

★ 802 ★

TOP INTERNATIONAL CONTRACTORS IN TRANSPORTATION, 1995

Ranked by: Billings **Remarks:** Specific dollar value is not provided. **Number listed:** 10

1. Bouygues S.A.
2. SGE
3. Bilfinger + Berger Bau A.G.
4. GTM-Entrepose
5. Fiatimpresit S.P.A.
6. Nishimatsu Construction Co. Ltd.
7. Hochtief A.G.
8. HBG, Hoolandsche Beton Groep N.V.
9. Hyundai Engineering & Construction Co.
10. Ballast Nedam International B.V.

Source: *ENR,* Top 225 International Contractors (annual), August 26, 1996, p. 41.

★ 803 ★

TOP INTERNATIONAL CONTRACTORS IN WATER, 1995

Ranked by: Billings. **Remarks:** Specific dollar value is not provided. **Number listed:** 10

1. Fiatimpresit S.P.A.
2. IMPREGILO S.P.A.
3. Philipp Holzmann A.G.
4. Dongah Construction Ind. Co. Ltd.
5. SGE
6. GTM-Entrepose
7. Odebrecht S.A.
8. Aoki Corp.
9. Ed. Zublin AG
10. SOLETANCHE

Source: *ENR,* Top 225 International Contractors (annual), August 26, 1996, p. 41.

★ 804 ★

TOP INTERNATIONAL INDUSTRIAL/PETROLEUM CONTRACTORS, 1995

Ranked by: Billings. **Remarks:** Specific dollar value is not provided. **Number listed:** 10

1. Fluor Daniel Inc.
2. JGC Corp.
3. Chiyoda Corp.
4. TECHNIP
5. Bechtel Group Inc.
6. McDermott International Inc.
7. Foster Wheeler Corp.
8. The M.W. Kellogg Co.
9. ABB Lummus Global Inc.
10. Brown & Root Inc.

Source: *ENR,* Top 225 International Contractors (annual), August 26, 1996, p. 41.

Contractors, Foreign – Africa

★ 805 ★
TOP FOREIGN CONTRATORS IN AFRICA, 1995
Ranked by: Dollar amount of foreign contracts.
Remarks: No specific data were provided. **Number listed:** 10
1. Bouygues S.A.
2. Bechtel Group Inc.
3. SGE
4. Bilfinger + Berger Bau A.G.
5. Fiatimpresit S.P.A.
6. HBG, Hollandsche Beton Groep N.V.
7. GTM-Entrepose
8. IMPREGILO S.P.A.
9. Daewoo Corp. Engineering & Construction
10. JGC Corp.
Source: *ENR*, Top 225 International Contractors (annual), August 26, 1996, p. 38.

Contractors, Foreign – Asia

★ 806 ★
TOP FOREIGN CONTRACTORS IN ASIA, 1995
Ranked by: Dollar amount of foreign contracts.
Remarks: No specific data were provided. **Number listed:** 10
1. Mitsubishi Heavy Industries Ltd.
2. Toyo Engineering Corp.
3. JGC Corp.
4. Fluor Daniel Inc.
5. Bilfinger + Berger Bau A.G.
6. Chiyoda Corp.
7. Nishimatsu Construction Co. Ltd.
8. Dongah Construction Ind. Co. Ltd.
9. Shimizu Corp.
10. Hochtief A.G.
Source: *ENR*, Top 225 International Contractors (annual), August 26, 1996, p. 38.

Contractors, Foreign – Canada

★ 807 ★
TOP FOREIGN CONTRACTORS IN CANADA, 1995
Ranked by: Dollar amount of foreign contracts.
Remarks: No specific data were provided. **Number listed:** 10
1. GTM-Entrepose
2. Klewit Construction Group Inc.
3. Ellis-Don Construction Inc.
4. McDermott International Inc.

5. Bouygues S.A.
6. J.S. Alberici Construction Co. Inc.
7. Fluor Daniel Inc.
8. Morrison Knudsen Corp.
9. CEGELEC
10. Wallbridge Aldhinger
Source: *ENR*, Top 225 International Contractors (annual), August 26, 1996, p. 38.

Contractors, Foreign – Europe

★ 808 ★
TOP FOREIGN CONTRACTORS IN EUROPE, 1995
Ranked by: Dollar amount of foreign contracts.
Remarks: No specific data were provided. **Number listed:** 10
1. SGE
2. GTM-Entrepose
3. HBG, Hollandsche Beton Groep N.V.
4. Bouygues S.A.
5. Hochtief A.G.
6. Fiatimpresit S.P.A.
7. Fluor Daniel Inc.
8. Phillipp Holzmann A.G.
9. Brown & Root Inc.
10. Skanska A.B.
Source: *ENR*, Top 225 International Contractors (annual), August 26, 1996, p. 38.

Contractors, Foreign – Latin America

★ 809 ★
TOP FOREIGN CONTRACTORS IN LATIN AMERICA, 1995
Ranked by: Dollar amount of foreign contracts.
Remarks: No specific data were provided. **Number listed:** 10
1. Bechtel Group Inc.
2. Fluor Daniel Inc.
3. Fiatimpresit S.P.A.
4. The M.W. Kellogg Co.
5. IMPREGILO S.P.A.
6. Odebrecht S.A.
7. Foster Wheeler Corp.
8. Dragados y Construcciones S.A.
9. Mitsubishi Heavy Industries Ltd.
10. Snamprogetti S.P.A.
Source: *ENR*, Top 225 International Contractors (annual), August 26, 1996, p. 38.

Contractors, Foreign – Middle East

★ 810 ★
TOP FOREIGN CONTRACTORS IN THE MIDDLE EAST, 1995
Ranked by: Dollar amount of foreign contracts.
Remarks: No specific data were provided. **Number listed:** 10

1. Consolidated Contractors Intl. Co. SAL
2. Chiyoda Corp.
3. Mitsubishi Heavy Industries Ltd.
4. TECHNIP
5. ABB SAE Sadelmi S.P.A.
6. Bechtel Group Inc.
7. Ballast Nedam International B.V.
8. Hyundai Engineering & Construction Co.
9. Ansaldo S.P.A.
10. Jacobs Engineering Group Inc.

Source: *ENR*, Top 225 International Contractors (annual), August 26, 1996, p. 38.

Contractors – United Kingdom

★ 811 ★
TOP CONTRACTORS IN THE UNITED KINGDOM
Ranked by: Contracting turnover, in thousands of British pounds (£). **Number listed:** 20

1. Trafalgar House with £3,300 thousand
2. Amec, £1,770
3. Balfour Beatty, £1,468
4. Bovis, £1,262
5. Tarmac, £1,040
6. Mowlem, £1,110
7. Laing, £948
8. Costain, £702
9. Wimpey, £684
10. Taylor Woodrow, £643

Source: *Management Today*, February 1996, p. 31.

Convenience Stores

★ 812 ★
TAIWAN'S TOP CONVENIENCE STORES, 1996
Ranked by: Number of outlets at the end of 1996.
Remarks: There is one convenience store for every 10,000 people in Taiwan. **Number listed:** 5

1. 7-Eleven with 1,150 outlets
2. President, 650
3. Family Mart, 280
4. Hi-Life, 230
5. OK, 210

Source: *National Trade Data Bank*, November 26, 1996, p. IMI961021.

★ 813 ★
TOP CONVENIENCE STORES IN JAPAN
Ranked by: Income, in millions of yen (¥). **Number listed:** 10

1. 7-Eleven Japan with ¥89,007 million
2. Ito-Yokado, ¥74,021
3. Daiei, ¥26,938
4. Jusco, ¥16,199
5. Nichii, ¥16,064
6. FamilyMart, ¥15,896
7. Seiyu, ¥13,896
8. Izumiya, ¥11,916
9. York-Benimaru, ¥10,535
10. Heiwado, ¥7,509

Source: *Tokyo Business Today*, August 1995, p. 27.

★ 814 ★
TOP FOOD RETAILERS WORLDWIDE, 1996
Ranked by: Sales, in billions of U.S. dollars. **Remarks:** Figures for Metro Group and Aldi are for 1995. **Number listed:** 20

1. Metro Group with $52.4 billion
2. Tengelmann, $33.7
3. Aldi, $32.0
4. Spar International, $30.1
5. Carrefour, $29.6
6. Edeka/AVA, $27.1
7. Leclerc, $26.2
8. Intermarche, $25.9
9. Kroger Co., $25.2
10. Ito-Yokoda, $24.9

Source: *Supermarket News*, June 2, 1997, p. 21.

Cookies and Crackers

★ 815 ★
TOP COOKIES IN GERMANY
Ranked by: Top cookies. **Remarks:** The source provides no criteria for these rankings. **Number listed:** 30

1. Leibniz Butterkeks, 200 g
2. Prinzenrolle Schoko, 400 g
3. Selection, 500 g
4. Leibniz Schokokeks VM
5. Soft Cake Orange Griesson
6. Leibniz Zoo
7. Hannover Waffeln
8. Ohne Gleichen VM
9. ABC
10. Eiswaffeln Tekrum

Source: *The Manufacturing Confectioner*, June 1997, p. 9.

Copenhagen Stock Exchange

★ 816 ★
LARGEST COMPANIES ON THE COPENHAGEN STOCK EXCHANGE, 1995
Ranked by: Market value, in millions of Danish krone (Dkr). **Number listed:** 20
1. Novo Nordisk B with Dkr24,298 million
2. Den Danske Bank, Dkr20,270
3. Tele Danmark B, Dkr19,222
4. Skandia Gr. Insurance (Skr5), Dkr15,353
5. Danisco EM, Dkr14,892
6. Asea B (Skr50), Dkr12,976
7. Unidanmark A, Dkr12,896
8. D/S 1912 B, Dkr11,362
9. D/S Svendborg B, Dkr11,342
10. D/S Svendborg A, Dkr11,253

Source: *GT Guide to World Equity Markets* (annual), Euromoney Publications, 1996, p. 116.

★ 817 ★
MOST ACTIVELY TRADED SHARES ON THE COPENHAGEN STOCK EXCHANGE, 1995
Ranked by: Trading value, in millions of Danish krone (Dkr). **Number listed:** 20
1. Tele Danmark B with Dkr20,037 million
2. Novo Nordisk B, Dkr12,094
3. Unidanmark, Dkr9,644
4. Den Danske Bank, Dkr8,970
5. Tryg-Baltica Forsikring, Dkr8,875
6. Danisco EM, Dkr7,129
7. ISS International B, Dkr5,483
8. Sophus Berendsen B, Dkr5,466
9. Radiometer B, Dkr3,162
10. Carlsberg B, Dkr2,501

Source: *GT Guide to World Equity Markets* (annual), Euromoney Publications, 1996, p. 117.

Copper Industry

★ 818 ★
TOP COPPER CONSUMING COUNTRIES, 1995
Ranked by: Consumption, in thousands of tons. **Number listed:** 5
1. United States with 2,526 thousand tons
2. Japan, 1,415
3. Germany, 1,058
4. China, 912
5. Taiwan, 563

Source: *Japanese Finance and Industry*, 1997, p. 5.

★ 819 ★
TOP COPPER PRODUCERS IN JAPAN, 1995
Ranked by: Market share based on sales of 1,211,000 tons, in percent. **Number listed:** 7
1. Nippon Mining and Metals with 25.8%
2. Mitsubishi Materials, 23.3%
3. Sumitomo Metal Mining, 16.6%
4. Mitsui Mining & Smelting, 13.0%
5. Dowa Mining, 11.1%
6. Furukawa, 7.9%
7. Nittetsu Mining, 2.4%

Source: *Japanese Finance and Industry*, 1997, p. 24.

★ 820 ★
TOP END MARKETS FOR COPPER WORLDWIDE
Ranked by: Percent distribution. **Number listed:** 7
1. General wire with 21%
2. Alloys, 18%
3. Tube, 11%
4. Winding wire, 10%
5. Sheet, 7%
6. Other wire, 25%
7. Other, 8%

Source: *Financial Times*, July 18, 1997, p. 34.

Copying Machines

★ 821 ★
TOP COPY MACHINE MAKERS IN CHILE
Ranked by: Market share, in percent. **Number listed:** 7
1. Xerox with 35.0%
2. Gestetner, 9.0%
3. Dimacofi, 8.0%
4. Elca (Toshiba), 8.0%
5. Lanier, 8.0%
6. Econsa (Canon), 7.0%
7. Other, 25.0%

Source: *National Trade Data Bank*, March 2, 1996, p. ISA9308.

★ 822 ★
TOP COPY MACHINE MAKERS IN JAPAN
Ranked by: Market share, in percent. **Number listed:** 6
1. Ricoh with 31.3%
2. Canon, 28.3%
3. Fuji Xerox, 25.0%
4. Sharp, 8.0%
5. Konica, 5.0%
6. Others, 2.1%

Source: *Nikkei Weekly*, July 22, 1996, p. 8.

★ 823 ★
UZBEKISTAN'S COPY MACHINE MARKET, 1996
Ranked by: Market share as of July 1, 1996, in percent.
Remarks: Includes computer and printer sales. **Number listed:** 9
1. Xerox 5009-5332 with 29%
2. Canon NP 1215, 19%
3. Canon FC 210-230, 11%
4. Canon PC 530, 11%
5. Olivetti Copia, 11%
6. Sharp Z-20-50, 7%
7. Canon PC 300-310, 4%
8. Canon FC 210-230, 4%
9. Konica L0152, 4%
Source: *National Trade Data Bank*, August 12, 1996, p. IMI960805.

Corn

★ 824 ★
CORN PRODUCTION PER HECTARE IN SELECTED COUNTRIES, 1995-1996
Ranked by: Estimated yield of corn per hectare, in metric tons. **Number listed:** 10
1. Canada with 7.249 metric tons
2. United States, 7.121
3. China, 4.919
4. Argentina, 4.100
5. Thailand, 3.246
6. South Africa, 3.091
7. Brazil, 2.360
8. Mexico, 2.286
9. Indonesia, 1.698
10. Philippines, 1.558
Source: *Foreign Agricultural Service*, November 13, 1996, p. 14.

Corporate Acquisition and Merger Services

★ 825 ★
LEADING ADVISORS IN GERMAN TAKEOVER DEALS, 1997
Ranked by: Volume for the first half of 1997, in billions of deutschmarks (DM). **Remarks:** Also notes number of deals. **Number listed:** 10
1. Goldman Sachs with DM26.7 billion
2. SBC Warburg, DM11.3
3. Morgan Stanley, DM6.1
4. Deutsche Morgan Grenfell, DM5.4
5. J.P. Morgan, DM5.4
6. Salomon Brothers, DM3.3
7. Lehman Brothers, DM2.9

8. Dresdner Kleinwort Benson, DM2.7
9. Credit Suisse First Boston, DM2.1
10. Rothschild, DM2.1
Source: *Financial Times*, September 3, 1997, p. 15.

★ 826 ★
TOP MERGER & ACQUISITION ADVISORS IN MEXICO, 1996
Ranked by: Market share, in percent. **Remarks:** Shares are shown based on total deals valued at $7.473 billion. Data refer to all deals completed in 1996 in which the target company is Latin American. Full credit given to advisors. **Number listed:** 10
1. Lehman Brothers with 17.40%
2. J.P. Morgan & Co. Inc., 13.20%
3. Bankers Trust, 8.40%
4. Banco Santander, 5.10%
5. Goldman Sachs & Co., 4.20%
6. Bear, Stearns, 3.80%
7. Merrill Lynch & Co., 2.60%
8. Violy, Byorum & Partners, LLC, 2.10%
9. Salomon Brothers, 1.90%
10. Credit Suisse First Boston, 1.80%
Source: *Latin Corporate Finance Handbook* (annual), 1997, p. 34.

★ 827 ★
TOP MERGERS AND ACQUISITIONS ADVISORS, 1996
Ranked by: Value, in millions of British pounds (£). **Remarks:** Also notes number of deals. **Number listed:** 20
1. Baring Brothers with £11,789 million
2. Lazard Brothers, £11,096
3. SBC Warburg, £10,320
4. Schroders, £9,626
5. NM Rothschild, £9,348
6. Kleinwort Benson, £8,987
7. Hambros Bank, £7,825
8. UBS, £7,671
9. Merrill Lynch, £7,661
10. Goldman Sachs, £7,461
Source: *Financial Times*, December 12, 1996, p. 4.

Corporate Acquisitions and Mergers

★ 828 ★
FOREIGN TAKEOVERS BY COUNTRY, 1996
Ranked by: Value of takeovers, in billions of U.S. dollars. **Number listed:** 10
1. United Kingdom with $38.54 billion
2. France, $10.47
3. Germany, $6.50
4. Italy, $4.72

5. Switzerland, $4.39
6. Netherlands, $3.55
7. Sweden, $2.63
8. Belgium, $1.89
9. Russia, $1.69
10. Spain, $1.67

Source: *The European*, January 23, 1997, p. 21.

★ 829 ★
LARGEST AUTO SUPPLIER MERGERS, 1996
Ranked by: Combined market value of the merged companies, in billions of U.S. dollars. Acquired companies are shown in parentheses. **Number listed:** 12

1. Varity Corp. (Lucas Industries) with $4.800 billion
2. Autoliv AB (Morton International), $3.900
3. Robert Bosch (AlliedSignal Inc.), $1.500
4. Johnson Controls (Prince Corp.), $1.350
5. Cie Generale d'Industrie Partic. (Valeo SA), $1.250
6. Hayes Wheel (MWC Holdings), $1.100
7. Tomkins PLC (Gates Rubber Co.), $1.100
8. TRW Inc. (Magna International), $0.418
9. Lear Corp. (Masland Corp.), $0.385
10. Thomas H. Lee. Co. (Safelite Glass Corp.), $0.350

Source: *Automotive News*, January 20, 1997, p. 18.

★ 830 ★
LARGEST CORPORATE ACQUISTIONS IN THE UNITED KINGDOM, 1997
Ranked by: Value of deals completed between January and June 1997, in millions of British pounds (£). **Remarks:** Acquirers are shown in parentheses. **Number listed:** 8

1. Bell Cablemedia (Cable and Wireless) with £1,729 millions
2. Mortgage Express (Bradford & Bingley Building Society), £1,546
3. Yorkshire Electricity Group (America Electric Power), £1,475
4. East Midlands Electricity (Dominion Resources), £1,329
5. Chubb Security (Williams Holdings), £1,287
6. Coca-Cola & Schweppes Beverages (Coca-Cola Enterprises), £1,243
7. London Electricity (Entergy Corporation), £1,231
8. NYNEX CableComms (Cable and Wireless), £1,021

Source: *The Guardian*, July 8, 1997, p. 2.

★ 831 ★
LARGEST CORPORATE MERGERS AND ACQUISITIONS
Ranked by: Price, in billions of U.S. dollars. **Number listed:** 7

1. Mitsubishi Bank (acquirer), Bank of Tokyo (target) with $33.8 billion
2. Kohlberg Kravis Roberts (acquirer), RJR Nabisco (target), $30.6
3. Sandoz (acquirer), Ciba-Geigy (target), $30.1
4. Mitsui Bank (acquirer), Taiyo Kobe Bank (target), $23.0
5. Guinness (acquirer), Grand Metropolitan (target), $22.3
6. Bell Atlantic (acquirer), Nynex (target), $22.0
7. British Telecommunications (acquirer), MCI Communcations (target), $21.2

Source: *The New York Times*, May 13, 1997, p. D10.

★ 832 ★
LEADING M&A ADVISORS IN LATIN AMERICA, 1996
Ranked by: Market share, in percent. **Remarks:** Shares are shown based on total deals valued at $30.218 billion. Data refer to all deals completed in 1996 in which the target company is Latin American. Full credit given to advisors. **Number listed:** 25

1. J.P. Morgan & Co. Inc. with 17.90%
2. Salomon Brothers, 12.40%
3. Credit Suisse First Boston, 10.50%
4. Rothschild Group, 7.60%
5. Baring Brothers & Co., Ltd., 5.80%
6. Banco Investimentos Garantia, 5.10%
7. Banco Santander, 4.70%
8. Violy, Byorum & Partners, LLC, 4.50%
9. Lehman Brothers, 4.30%
10. Bankers Trust, 4.10%

Source: *Latin Corporate Finance Handbook* (annual), 1997, p. 34.

★ 833 ★
TOP LATIN AMERICAN MERGERS, 1996
Ranked by: Value of deal, in millions of U.S. dollars. **Number listed:** 10

1. Consortium (acquirer), Light (target) with $1,699.6 million
2. Banco Osorno y La Union (acquirer), Banco Santander (target), $830.7
3. White Martins (acquirer), Liquid Carbonic Ind. -South America (target), $724.3
4. Cintra (acquirer), Aeromexico (target), $678.0
5. Cintra (acquirer), Cia. Mexicana de Aviacion (target), $604.4
6. Consortium (acquirer), CERJ (target), $587.4
7. Acesita (acquirer), Cia. Siderurgica de Tubarao (target), $455.1

8. Bank of Montreal (acquirer), Grupo Financiero Bancomer (target), $435.0
9. ICI (acquirer), Bunge Paints (target), $430.0
10. Cemex (acquirer), Cementos Diamante (target), $400.0

Source: *Business Latin America*, December 2, 1996, p. 8.

★ 834 ★
TOP MERGER & ACQUISITION ADVISORS IN BRAZIL, 1996
Ranked by: Market share, in percent. **Remarks:** Shares are shown based on total deals valued at $9.483 billion. Data refer to all deals completed in 1996 in which the target company is Latin American. Full credit given to advisors. **Number listed:** 25

1. Baring Brothers & Co., Ltd. with 18.60%
2. Rothschild Group, 17.90%
3. Credit Suisse First Boston, 16.60%
4. Banco Investimentos Garantia, 16.20%
5. Banco Bozano, Simonsen SA, 10.20%
6. J.P. Morgan & Co. Inc., 10.00%
7. Salomon Brothers, 7.70%
8. Banco Bradesco SA, 7.20%
9. SBC Warburg, 7.20%
10. ABN AMRO, 6.90%

Source: *Latin Corporate Finance Handbook* (annual), 1997, p. 34.

★ 835 ★
TOP MERGER ADVISORS IN FRANCE, 1996
Ranked by: Value of transactions, in billions of French francs (FFr). **Remarks:** Notes number of transactions. **Number listed:** 25

1. Lazard Freres with FFr168.2 billion
2. Banexi - groupe BNP, FFr101.2
3. Goldman Sachs, FFr93.5
4. Paribas, FFr90.7
5. Rothschild & Cie, FFr80.2
6. Morgan Stanley, FFr67.3
7. Societe Generale, FFr53.2
8. JP Morgan, FFr47.7
9. Clinvest - groupe Credit Lyonnais, FFr43.8
10. CCF, FFr29.2

Source: *Financial Times*, June 20, 1997, p. Special Section p. 4.

★ 836 ★
U.S. MERGERS IN EUROPE BY TARGET COUNTRY, 1988
Ranked by: Share of total mergers from 1988 through the first six months of 1996, in percent. **Number listed:** 10

1. United Kingdom with 49%
2. France, 13%
3. Sweden, 8%
4. Germany, 7%

5. Netherlands, 5%
6. Italy, 4%
7. Switzerland, 4%
8. Spain, 2%
9. Belgium, 1%
10. Rest of Europe, 7%

Source: *The European*, November 21, 1996, p. 24.

Corporate Acquisitions and Mergers – Europe

★ 837 ★
TOP M&A ADVISORS IN EUROPE
Ranked by: Value of deals, in millions of British pounds (£). **Number listed:** 20

1. Lazard Houses with £12,003 million
2. Morgan Stanley, £11,065
3. Goldman Sachs, £10,185
4. Credit Suisse First Boston, £9,980
5. J.P. Morgan, £9,386
6. Merrill Lynch, £8,236
7. SBC Warburg, £5,896
8. Lehman Brothers, £4,289
9. Rothschild Group, £3,907
10. Societe Generale, £3,756

Source: *Financial Times*, January 23, 1997, p. 19.

Corporate Acquisitions and Mergers – Germany

★ 838 ★
LARGEST M&A INVESTMENT BANKS IN GERMANY, 1996
Ranked by: Value of transactions, in billions of U.S. dollars. **Remarks:** Notes number of deals conducted by each bank. **Number listed:** 12

1. Goldman Sachs with $17.21 billion
2. Deutsche Morgan Grenfell, $10.64
3. Credit Suisse First Boston, $9.32
4. Dresdner Kleinwort Benson, $8.01
5. Morgan Stanley, $7.47
6. Barings/Dillon Read, $5.56
7. SBC Warburg, $5.26
8. Merrill Lynch, $4.66
9. Lehman Brothers, $4.30
10. Salomon Brothers, $4.00

Source: *The Wall Street Journal*, March 20, 1997, p. A13.

Corporate Acquisitions and Mergers – International Aspects

★ 839 ★

COUNTRIES OF ORIGIN FOR BUYERS OF U.S. COMPANIES, 1996

Ranked by: Number of transactions. **Remarks:** Notes figures for 1992 through 1996. **Number listed:** 50

1. Canada with 103 transactions
2. United Kingdom, 64
3. Netherlands, 30
4. Germany, 25
5. France, 22
6. Japan, 14
7. Sweden, 14
8. Switzerland, 8
9. Ireland, 7
10. Israel, 4

Source: *MergerStat Review* (annual), 1997, p. 82.

★ 840 ★

COUNTRIES OF ORIGIN FOR U.S. ACQUISITIONS BY DOLLAR VALUE, 1996

Ranked by: Dollar value, in millions of U.S. dollars. **Remarks:** Notes figures for 1992 through 1996. **Number listed:** 58

1. United Kingdom with $16,386.0 million
2. Canada, $7,089.9
3. France, $3,338.8
4. Hong Kong, $3,308.0
5. Bermuda, $2,396.5
6. Australia, $2,340.5
7. Brazil, $2,117.5
8. Netherlands, $2,103.3
9. Switzerland, $1,847.0
10. Norway, $1,540.4

Source: *MergerStat Review* (annual), 1997, p. 85.

★ 841 ★

COUNTRIES OF ORIGIN FOR U.S. ACQUISITIONS BY NUMBER OF TRANSACTIONS, 1996

Ranked by: Number of transactions. **Remarks:** Notes figures for 1992 through 1996. **Number listed:** 85

1. United Kingdom with 181 transactions
2. Canada, 151
3. Germany, 79
4. Australia, 51
5. France, 46
6. Netherlands, 30
7. Italy, 28
8. Mexico, 24
9. Argentina, 21
10. Brazil, 21

Source: *MergerStat Review* (annual), 1997, p. 84.

★ 842 ★

DOLLAR VALUE OF U.S. COMPANIES ACQUIRED BY FOREIGN BUYERS, 1996

Ranked by: Dollar value, in millions of U.S. dollars. **Remarks:** Notes figures for 1992 through 1996. **Number listed:** 50

1. United Kingdom with $34,015.46 million
2. Germany, $11,363.00
3. Canada, $8,754.7
4. Netherlands, $7,077.8
5. Japan, $2,913.8
6. France, $2,728.4
7. Australia, $2,556.3
8. Ireland, $843.6
9. South Africa, $400.0
10. Hong Kong, $359.3

Source: *MergerStat Review* (annual), 1997, p. 83.

★ 843 ★

INDUSTRIES ATTRACTING FOREIGN BUYERS OF U.S. COMPANIES BY INDUSTRY DOLLAR VALUE, 1996

Ranked by: Industry dollars value, in millions of U.S. dollars. **Remarks:** Notes figures for 1992 through 1996. **Number listed:** 50

1. Communications with $21,710.6 million
2. Insurance, $6,391.9
3. Retail, $4,851.4
4. Health services, $4,687.0
5. Auto products and accessories, $3,934.5
6. Wholesale and distribution, $3,721.9
7. Printing and publishing, $3,515.0
8. Miscellaneous services, $3,503.5
9. Chemicals, paints and coatings, $3,064.8
10. Broadcasting, $2,492.5

Source: *MergerStat Review* (annual), 1997, p. 72.

★ 844 ★

INDUSTRIES ATTRACTING FOREIGN BUYERS OF U.S. COMPANIES BY NUMBER OF TRANSACTIONS, 1996

Ranked by: Number of transactions. **Remarks:** Notes figures for 1992 through 1996. **Number listed:** 50

1. Wholesale and distribution with 37
2. Computer software, supplies and services, 35
3. Miscellaneous services, 20
4. Drugs, medical supplies and equipment, 17
5. Retail, 15
6. Chemicals, paints and coatings, 15
7. Banking and finance, 13
8. Insurance, 13
9. Leisure and entertainment, 12
10. Food processing, 11

Source: *MergerStat Review* (annual), 1997, p. 71.

★ 845 ★

INDUSTRIES ATTRACTING U.S. BUYERS OF FOREIGN COMPANIES BY INDUSTRY DOLLAR VALUE, 1996

Ranked by: Industry dollar value, in millions of U.S. dollars. **Remarks:** Notes figures for 1992 through 1996. **Number listed:** 50

1. Electric, gas, water, and sanitary services with $15,205.3 million
2. Leisure and entertainment, $3,935.9
3. Miscellaneous services, $3,853.9
4. Energy services, $3,024.7
5. Wholesale and distribution, $1,987.9
6. Drugs, medical supplies, and equipment, $1,979.9
7. Beverages, $1,575.4
8. Industrial and farm equipment and machinery, $1,565.2
9. Mining and minerals, $1,526.8
10. Oil and gas, $1,484.1

Source: *MergerStat Review* (annual), 1997, p. 74.

★ 846 ★

LARGEST ACQUISITIONS OF FOREIGN COMPANIES BY U.S. BUYERS

Ranked by: Price offered, in millions of U.S. dollars. **Number listed:** 5

1. Amoco Corp. (buyer), Dome Petroleum Ltd. (Canada) (seller) with $4,180.0 million
2. Exxon Corp. (buyer), Texaco Canada Inc. (seller), $4,149.6
3. Crown Cork & Seal Co. Inc. (buyer), Carnaudmetalbox S.A. (France) (seller), $4,000.0
4. Philip Morris Companies Inc. (buyer), Jacobs Suchard A.G. (Switzerland) (seller), $3,825.2
5. Private group, led by Wasserstein Perella and Great Atlantic Pacific Tea Co. (buyer), Gateway Corp. (United Kingdom) (seller), $3,280.0

Source: *MergerStat Review* (annual), 1997, p. 163.

★ 847 ★

LARGEST ACQUISITIONS OF U.S. COMPANIES BY FOREIGN BUYERS

Ranked by: Price offered, in millions of U.S. dollars. **Number listed:** 5

1. British Petroleum Co. (United Kingdom) (buyer), Standard Oil Co. (seller) with $7,762.2 million
2. Matsushita Electric Industrial Co. (Japan) (buyer), MCA Inc. (seller), $6,588.8
3. Campeau Corp. (Canada) (buyer), Federated Department Stores Inc. (seller), $6,544.5
4. Grand Metropolitan PLC (United Kingdom) (buyer), Pillsbury Co. (seller), $5,635.6
5. Royal Dutch/Shell Group (Netherlands) (buyer), Shell Oil Co. (seller), $5,467.9

Source: *MergerStat Review* (annual), 1997, p. 162.

Corporate Image

★ 848 ★

IDEAL WESTERN EMPLOYERS AMONG CENTRAL EUROPEANS

Ranked by: Results based on a survey of 1,200 Central European graduates and young professionals. **Remarks:** No specific figures provided. **Number listed:** 10

1. Coca-Cola
2. Procter & Gamble
3. KPMG
4. EBRD
5. McKinsey
6. Citibank
7. Andersen Consulting
8. Microsoft
9. IBM
10. L'Oreal

Source: *Business Central Europe*, August 1997, p. 63.

★ 849 ★

MOST RESPECTED COMPANIES WORLDWIDE

Ranked by: Survey based on FT 500 list, as well as polls of investment analysts and chief executives of European companies. See source for details. **Number listed:** 11

1. Microsoft
2. General Electric
3. Coca-Cola
4. ABB
4. British Airways
4. Nestle
7. Intel
8. British Petroleum
8. Daimler-Benz
8. L'Oreal

Source: *Financial Times,* Europe's Most Respected Companies (annual), September 24, 1997, p. 6.

★ 850 ★

MOST RESPECTED EUROPEAN FIRMS

Ranked by: Survey based on FT 500 list, as well as polls of investment analysts and chief executives of European companies. See source for details. **Number listed:** 31

1. ABB
2. British Petroleum
2. Nestle
4. British Airways
5. Tesco
6. AXA-UAP
7. BMW

8. Carrefour
9. Unilever
10. Daimler-Benz

Source: *Financial Times,* Europe's Most Respected Companies (annual), September 24, 1997, p. 1.

Corporate Philanthropy
See: **Charitable Contributions**

Corporate Reputation
See: **Corporate Image**

Corporations

★ 851 ★
ASIAN COMPANIES CONSIDERED THE MOST ETHICAL AND HONEST, 1997
Ranked by: Results (0-5) of a questionnaire sent to more than 9,000 managers and CEOs chosen from the magazine's circulation and evaluated by Asia Market Intelligence, a research firm. **Remarks:** Respondents scored each company in terms of overall admirability, then on six attributes: quality of products, quality of management, contribution to local economy, record as an employer, growth potential and reputation for ethics. **Number listed:** 10

1. Acer with 4.08
2. Astra International, 4.00
3. Hewlett-Packard, 3.99
4. Pohang Iron & Steel, 3.98
5. Singapore Airlines, 3.92
6. Sony Corporation, 3.90
7. DBS Bank, 3.90
8. Ayala, 3.89
9. Siam Cement, 3.88
10. McDonald's, 3.87

Source: *Asian Business,* Most Admired Companies in Asia (annual), May 1997, p. 27.

★ 852 ★
ASIAN COMPANIES WITH THE GREATEST POTENTIAL FOR GROWTH, 1997
Ranked by: Results (0-5) of a questionnaire sent to more than 9,000 managers and CEOs chosen from the magazine's circulation and evaluated by Asia Market Intelligence, a research firm. **Remarks:** Respondents scored each company in terms of overall admirability, then on six attributes: quality of products, quality of management, contribution to local economy, record as an employer, growth potential and reputation for ethics. **Number listed:** 10

1. Acer with 4.58
2. Bank of China, 4.43
3. Samsung, 4.39
4. Dacom, 4.32
5. Pohang Iron & Steel, 4.28
6. Taiwan Semiconductor Manufacturing, 4.25
7. Astra International, 4.23
8. Indosat, 4.20
9. AT&T (Telecom), 4.20
10. Sony Corporation, 4.20

Source: *Asian Business,* Most Admired Companies in Asia (annual), May 1997, p. 27.

★ 853 ★
CORPORATIONS POSTING THE HIGHEST PROFITS, 1995
Ranked by: Profits, in millions of U.S. dollars. **Remarks:** Notes percent change and global rank. **Number listed:** 50

1. Royal Dutch/Shell with $6,904.6 million
2. General Motors, $6,880.7
3. General Electric, $6,573.0
4. Exxon, $6,470.0
5. Philip Morris, $5,450.0
6. International Business Machines, $4,178.0
7. Ford Motor, $4,139.0
8. HSBC Holdings, $3,885.5
9. Deutsche Telekom, $3,678.8
10. Intel, $3,566.0

Source: *Fortune,* The Global 500: World's Biggest Corporations (annual), August 5, 1996, p. F-13.

★ 854 ★
CORPORATIONS POSTING THE HIGHEST RETURNS ON ASSETS, 1995
Ranked by: Profits as a percent of assets. **Remarks:** Also notes global rank. **Number listed:** 50

1. Intel with 20.4%
2. Glaxo Wellcome, 20.2%
3. Coca-Cola, 19.9%
4. Abbott Laboratories, 17.9%
5. Seagram, 15.9%
6. Merck, 14.0%
7. Johnson & Johnson, 13.4%

8. Samsung Electronics, 13.1%
9. Bristol-Myers Squibb, 13.0%
10. IBP, 12.7%

Source: *Fortune,* The Global 500: World's Biggest Corporations (annual), August 5, 1996, p. F-14.

★ 855 ★
CORPORATIONS POSTING THE HIGHEST RETURNS ON REVENUE, 1995

Ranked by: Profits as a percent of revenue. **Remarks:** Notes global rank. **Number listed:** 50

1. Seagram with 38.1%
2. Roche Holding, 22.9%
3. Glaxo Wellcome, 22.3%
4. Intel, 22.0%
5. Merck, 20.0%
6. Abbott Laboratories, 16.9%
7. Coca-Cola, 16.6%
8. Pfizer, 15.7%
9. National Australia Bank, 15.4%
10. Ameritech, 15.0%

Source: *Fortune,* The Global 500: World's Biggest Corporations (annual), August 5, 1996, p. F-14.

★ 856 ★
CORPORATIONS WITH THE HIGHEST INCREASE IN PROFITS, 1995

Ranked by: Increase in profits over the past year, in percent. **Remarks:** Also notes dollar value of 1995 profits. **Number listed:** 50

1. Fuji Heavy Industries with 1,521.8%
2. Thyssen, 1,486.3%
3. SmithKline Beecham, 1,287.7%
4. Sekisui Chemical, 1,084.4%
5. Mitsubishi Chemical, 662.7%
6. UAL, 584.3%
7. Loews, 559.3%
8. Lufthansa Group, 467.6%
9. Nippon Paper Industries, 411.9%
10. Usinor-Sacilor, 389.6%

Source: *Fortune,* The Global 500: World's Biggest Corporations (annual), August 5, 1996, p. F-13.

★ 857 ★
CORPORATIONS WITH THE HIGHEST INCREASE IN REVENUE, 1995

Ranked by: Increase in revenue over past year, in percent. **Remarks:** Also notes dollar value of 1995 revenue. **Number listed:** 50

1. First Chicago NBD Corp. with 208.6% increase
2. Kimberly-Clark, 87.2%
3. Federated Department Stores, 81.0%
4. Lloyds TSB Group, 77.4%
5. Samsung, 76.2%
6. Lockheed Martin, 74.1%
7. First Union Corp., 69.2%

8. Samsung Electronics, 65.7%
9. VIAG, 63.9%
10. Banco do Brasil, 63.1%

Source: *Fortune,* The Global 500: World's Biggest Corporations (annual), August 5, 1996, p. F-12+.

★ 858 ★
EUROPEAN BUSINESS SECTORS WITH THE HIGHEST GROWTH IN PROFITS, 1997

Ranked by: Forecast growth of profits by sector, in percent. **Remarks:** Also notes forecast for 1998. **Number listed:** 9

1. Banking with 43% growth
2. Construction, 34%
3. Automobiles, 32%
4. Electronics, 26%
5. Telecom services, 23%
6. Pharmaceuticals, 18%
7. Insurance, 16%
8. Media, 10%
9. Oil and gas, 9%

Source: *The Wall Street Journal*, August 6, 1997, p. A10.

★ 859 ★
EUROPEAN NATIONS WITH THE HIGHEST GROWTH IN CORPORATE PROFITS, 1997

Ranked by: Forecast growth of corporate profits, in percent. **Remarks:** Also notes forecast for 1998. **Number listed:** 9

1. Switzerland with 133% growth
2. France, 38%
3. Germany, 24%
4. Netherlands, 18%
5. Spain, 17%
6. Italy, 15%
7. United Kingdom, 8%
8. Belgium, 7%
9. Sweden, 6%

Source: *The Wall Street Journal*, August 6, 1997, p. A10.

★ 860 ★
FASTEST GROWING SLOVENIAN COMPANIES, 1993-1995

Ranked by: Growth index. **Remarks:** Includes data on incomes and profits. **Number listed:** 67

1. TGA trading d.o.o. with 3520.6
2. Suzuki Wolf in Odar d.o.o., 3152.8
3. Comet d.d., 2119.8
4. MTT tovarna tkanin Melje d.o.o., 1795.3
5. Junior d.o.o., 1393.3
6. DM Drogerie markt d.o.o., 1231.1
7. Aquasava d.o.o., 1093.3
8. Avtomagaxin d.o.o., 1090.4
9. Map-trade d.o.o., 1075.3
10. Hyundai auto trade d.o.o., 1050.8

Source: *Slovenian Business Report*, Winter 1996, p. 15.

★ 861 ★
LARGEST COMPANIES IN AUSTRALIA, 1997
Ranked by: Market capitalization on July 31, 1997, in billions of U.S. dollars. **Number listed:** 10
1. B.H.P. with $27.3 billion
2. Australia & New Zealand Bank, $21.1
3. National Australia Bank, $21.1
4. Westpac Banking Corp., $11.7
5. Commonwealth Bank, $11.6
6. Rio Tinto, $10.0
7. News Corp., $9.0
8. Coca-Cola Amatil, $7.7
9. WMC, $6.6
10. Coles Myer, $5.9

Source: *The New York Times*, September 13, 1997, p. 23.

★ 862 ★
LARGEST COMPANIES IN SOUTH KOREA
Ranked by: Sales, in thousands of U.S. dollars. **Number listed:** 100
1. Samsung Co. Ltd. with $24,819 thousand
2. Samsung Electronics Co. Ltd., $20,869
3. Daewoo, $19,367
4. Hyundai Corporation, $14,238
5. LG International, $13,467
6. Hyundai Motor Co. Ltd., $13,328
7. Korea Electric Power Co. Ltd., $12,909
8. Yukong Ltd., $8,499
9. LG Electronics, $8,497
10. Kia Motors Corp., $7,332

Source: *Asia's 7,500 Largest Companies* (annual), Dun & Bradstreet, 1997, p. 65+.

★ 863 ★
LARGEST CORPORATIONS BY ASSETS, 1995
Ranked by: Assets, in millions of U.S. dollars. **Number listed:** 500
1. Sumitomo Bank (Japan) with $524,668.4 million
2. Sanwa Bank (Japan), $520,118.1
3. Dai-Ichi Kangyo Bank (Japan), $515,704.8
4. Fuji Bank (Japan), $508,424.3
5. Deutsche Bank (Germany), $503,077.7
6. Mitsubishi Bank (Japan), $497,394.5
7. Sakura Bank (Japan), $494,687.1
8. Norinchukin Bank (Japan), $431,640.9
9. Credit Agricole (France), $386,584.8
10. Industrial Bank of Japan, $380,726.5

Source: *Fortune,* The Global 500: World's Biggest Corporations (annual), August 5, 1996, p. F-1+.

★ 864 ★
LARGEST CORPORATIONS BY EMPLOYEES, 1995
Ranked by: Number of employees. **Number listed:** 500
1. U.S. Postal Service (United States) with 870,160 employees
2. General Motors (United States), 709,000
3. Wal-Mart Stores (United States), 675,000
4. Pepsico (United States), 480,000
5. Siemens (Germany), 373,000
6. Ford Motor (United States), 346,990
7. Deutsche Post (Germany), 342,413
8. United Parcel Service (United States), 337,000
9. Hitachi (Japan), 331,852
10. Deutsche Bahn (Germany), 312,579

Source: *Fortune,* The Global 500: World's Biggest Corporations (annual), August 5, 1996, p. F-1.

★ 865 ★
LARGEST CORPORATIONS BY PROFITS, 1995
Ranked by: Profits, in millions of U.S. dollars. **Remarks:** Notes percent change from 1994. **Number listed:** 500
1. Royal Dutch/Shell Group (U.K./Netherlands) with $6,904.6 million
2. General Motors (United States), $6,880.7
3. General Electric (United States), $6,573.0
4. Exxon (United States), $6,470.0
5. Philip Morris (United States), $5,450.0
6. International Business Machines (United States), $4,178.0
7. Ford Motor (United States), $4,139.0
8. HSBC Holdings (United Kingdom), $3,885.5
9. Deutsche Telekom (Germany), $3,678.8
10. Intel (United States), $3,566.0

Source: *Fortune,* The Global 500: World's Biggest Corporations (annual), August 5, 1996, p. F-1+.

★ 866 ★
LARGEST CORPORATIONS BY REVENUE, 1995
Ranked by: Revenue, in millions of U.S. dollars. **Remarks:** Notes percent change from 1994. **Number listed:** 500
1. Mitsubishi (Japan) with $184,365.2 million
2. Mitsui (Japan), $181,518.7
3. Itochu (Japan), $169,164.6
4. General Motors (United States), $168,828.6
5. Sumitomo (Japan), $167,530.7
6. Marubeni (Japan), $161,057.4
7. Ford Motor (United States), $137,137.0
8. Toyota Motor (Japan), $111,052.0
9. Exxon (United States), $110,009.0
10. Royal Dutch/Shell Group (U.K./Netherlands), $109,833.7

Source: *Fortune,* The Global 500: World's Biggest Corporations (annual), August 5, 1996, p. F-1+.

★ 867 ★
LARGEST CORPORATIONS BY STOCKHOLDERS' EQUITY, 1995
Ranked by: Stockholders' equity, in millions of U.S. dollars. **Number listed:** 500
1. Royal Dutch/Shell Group (U.K./Netherlands) with $58,986.4 million
2. Toyota Motor (Japan), $49,691.6
3. Japan Postal Service, $47,462.3
4. Nippon Telegraph & Telephone (Japan), $42,240.1
5. Exxon (United States), $40,436.0
6. Electricite de France, $32,617.6
7. Matsushita Electric Industrial (Japan), $31,753.2
8. Hitachi (Japan), $29,907.2
9. General Electric (United States), $29,609.0
10. British Gas (United Kingdom), $29,390.7

Source: *Fortune,* The Global 500: World's Biggest Corporations (annual), August 5, 1996, p. F-1+.

★ 868 ★
LARGEST EASTERN EUROPEAN COMPANIES, 1997
Ranked by: Market capitalization for January 1997, in millions of U.S. dollars. **Number listed:** 20
1. Gazprom (Russia) with $7,931 million
2. Lukoil Oil Co. (Russia), $5,956
3. Unified Energy System (Russia), $3,037
4. SPT Telecom (Czech Republic), $2,949
5. Mosenergo (Russia), $2,289
6. CEZ (Czech Republic), $2,046
7. Surgetneftegaz (Russia), $1,952
8. Komercni Banka (Czech Republic), $1,682
9. Rostelecom (Russia), $1,681
10. Pliva (Czech Republic), $1,378

Source: *Investor's Business Daily,* May 27, 1997, p. B1.

★ 869 ★
LARGEST EUROPEAN COMPANIES, 1997
Ranked by: Market capitalization for January 1997, in billions of U.S. dollars. **Number listed:** 25
1. Royal Dutch/Shell (Netherlands) with $135.4 billion
2. Roche Holding (Switzerland), $72.0
3. British Petroleum (United Kingdom), $58.2
4. Glaxo Wellcome (United Kingdom), $52.3
5. HSBC Holdings (United Kingdom), $50.0
6. Sandoz (Switzerland), $46.3
7. Nestle (Switzerland), $44.7
8. Unilever plc/NV (Netherlands), $43.1
9. ENI (Italy), $41.0
10. Allianz Holding (Germany), $40.5

Source: *Investor's Business Daily,* May 23, 1997, p. B1.

★ 870 ★
LARGEST NET PROFITS EARNERS IN SLOVENIA
Ranked by: Net profits per employee, in thousands of tolars (To). **Number listed:** 20
1. Fundus Ljubljana with To255,103 thousand
2. Atena Ljubljana, To210,314
3. Aktiva PZDU Ljublana, To171,636
4. Nika Brezice, To144,888
5. KMB Infond, To142,417
6. Zdravilisce Rogaska Holding, To141,264
7. Intara S&P Ljubljana, To136,476
8. Krekova druzba Maribor, To120,482
9. Kmecka druzba Ljublana, To111,168
10. Nacionalna financna druzba Lj., To110,321

Source: *Slovenian Business Report,* Fall 1996, p. 14.

★ 871 ★
LARGEST PUBLIC COMPANIES, 1996
Ranked by: Market value as of July 31, 1996, in millions of U.S. dollars. **Remarks:** Notes profits and sales for fiscal year 1995. **Number listed:** 100
1. General Electric with $136,515 million
2. Royal Dutch/Shell, $128,206
3. Coca-Cola, $117,258
4. NTT, $113,609
5. Exxon, $102,161
6. Bank of Tokyo-Mitsubishi, $98,191
7. Toyota Motor, $91,519
8. Philip Morris, $86,424
9. AT&T, $83,960
10. Merck, $78,163

Source: *The Wall Street Journal,* September 26, 1996, p. R27.

★ 872 ★
LARGEST SUB-SAHARAN FIRMS, 1996
Ranked by: Market capitalization, in millions of U.S. dollars. **Number listed:** 18
1. Ashanti Goldfields with $1,252 million
2. Delta Corporation, $911
3. PZ Industries, $394
4. Lonhro Sugar, $345
5. Barclays Bank Zimbabwe, $329
6. Meikles Africa, $278
7. Lever Brothers, $252
8. West African Cement, $249
9. Barclays Bank Kenya, $233
10. Nign Breweries, $221

Source: *Financial Times,* January 24, 1997, p. 43.

★ 873 ★
LATIN AMERICA'S TOP FIRMS BY ASSETS
Ranked by: Net income, in millions of U.S. dollars. **Remarks:** Notes location of company and primary activity. **Number listed:** 25
1. Eletrobras with $88,880 million

2. Telebras, $40,564
3. Itausa, $33,740
4. Petrobras, $33,736
5. Cesp, $23,767
6. CVRD, $16,782
7. Telefonos de Mexico, $14,212
8. Sabesp, $12,467
9. Telesp, $12,212
10. YPF, $12,079

Source: *Latin Trade,* The Top 100 Publicly Traded Companies (annual), September 1997, p. 42.

★ 874 ★

LATIN AMERICA'S TOP FIRMS BY PROFITS

Ranked by: Net income, in millions of U.S. dollars.
Remarks: Notes location of company and primary activity. **Number listed:** 25

1. Telebras with $2,653 million
2. Eletrobras, $2,303
3. Telefonos de Mexico, $1,476
4. Cemex, $980
5. YPF, $817
6. Telesp, $782
7. Petrobras, $643
8. Alfa, $500
9. CVRD, $498
10. Ahmsa, $466

Source: *Latin Trade,* The Top 100 Publicly Traded Companies (annual), September 1997, p. 42.

★ 875 ★

LEADING INDUSTRIES BY ASSETS PER EMPLOYEE, 1995

Ranked by: Assets per employee, in U.S. dollars.
Number listed: 30

1. Diversified financials with $22,504,856
2. Brokerage, $15,171,744
3. Commercial banks, $6,342,593
4. Insurance: life, health (stock), $3,703,870
5. Insurance: property and casualty (stock), $2,911,452
6. Trading, $2,010,095
7. Electric and gas utilities, $1,208,547
8. Engineering, construction, $1,091,618
9. Petroleum refining, $798,019
10. Beverages, $598,513

Source: *Fortune,* The Global 500: World's Biggest Corporations (annual), August 5, 1996, p. F-28.

★ 876 ★

LEADING INDUSTRIES BY INCREASE IN PROFITS, 1995

Ranked by: Increase in profits over past year, in percent.
Number listed: 30

1. Forest and paper products with 223.0% increase

2. Metals, 110.7%
3. Airlines, 90.4%
4. Brokerage, 61.9%
5. Railroads, 52.5%
6. Trading, 50.1%
7. Computers, office equipment, 38.3%
8. Chemicals, 37.5%
9. Industrial and farm equipment, 34.4%
10. Electronics, electrical equipment, 32.8%

Source: *Fortune,* The Global 500: World's Biggest Corporations (annual), August 5, 1996, p. F-29.

★ 877 ★

LEADING INDUSTRIES BY INCREASE IN REVENUE, 1995

Ranked by: Increase in revenue over past year, in percent. **Number listed:** 30

1. Brokerage with 42.3% increase
2. Computers, office equipment, 19.6%
3. Commercial banks, 19.0%
4. Insurance: life, health (stock), 17.3%
5. Electronics, electrical equipment, 16.0%
6. Insurance: property and casualty (stock), 15.9%
7. Pharmaceuticals, 14.9%
8. Forest and paper products, 13.4%
9. Diversified financials, 11.2%
10. Wholesalers, 11.1%

Source: *Fortune,* The Global 500: World's Biggest Corporations (annual), August 5, 1996, p. F-28.

★ 878 ★

LEADING INDUSTRIES BY RETURN ON ASSETS, 1995

Ranked by: Profits as a percent of assets, in percent.
Number listed: 30

1. Pharmaceuticals with 12.7%
2. Scientific, photo, control equipment, 6.9%
3. Beverages, 5.7%
4. Chemicals, 5.0%
5. Forest and paper products, 4.8%
6. Food, 4.6%
7. Publishing, printing, 4.4%
8. Food and drug stores, 4.3%
9. Wholesalers, 3.9%
10. Computers, office equipment, 3.8%

Source: *Fortune,* The Global 500: World's Biggest Corporations (annual), August 5, 1996, p. F-28.

★ 879 ★

LEADING INDUSTRIES BY RETURN ON REVENUE, 1995

Ranked by: Profits as a percent of revenue, in percent.
Number listed: 30

1. Pharmaceuticals with 14.8%
2. Diversified financials, 9.9%
3. Beverages, 6.8%

4. Scientific, photo, control equipment, 6.7%
5. Forest and paper products, 5.8%
6. Brokerage, 5.1%
7. Chemicals, 5.1%
8. Telecommunications, 4.5%
9. Publishing, printing, 3.3%
10. Mail, package, and freight delivery, 3.2%

Source: *Fortune,* The Global 500: World's Biggest Corporations (annual), August 5, 1996, p. F-28.

★ 880 ★
LEADING INDUSTRIES BY REVENUE PER EMPLOYEE, 1995

Ranked by: Revenue per employee, in U.S. dollars.
Number listed: 30

1. Trading with $4,309,684
2. Diversified financials, $1,709,332
3. Brokerage, $1,121,875
4. Engineering, construction, $892,819
5. Petroleum refining, $777,069
6. Insurance: property and casualty (stock), $766,040
7. Insurance: life, health (stock), $724,205
8. Commercial banks, $466,397
9. Electric and gas utilities, $439,625
10. Beverages, $439,530

Source: *Fortune,* The Global 500: World's Biggest Corporations (annual), August 5, 1996, p. F-28.

★ 881 ★
MOST PROFITABLE COMPANIES IN MEXICO

Ranked by: Profit as a percent of sales. **Number listed:** 10

1. Grupo Mexicano de Desarrollo with 78.79%
2. Tolmex, 55.11%
3. Altos Hornos de Mexico, 33.07%
4. Tubos de Acero de Mexico, 32.75%
5. Grupo Industrial Durango, 31.66%
6. Minera del Norte, 29.64%
7. Cemex, 29.03%
8. Grupo Posados, 28.98%
9. Empaques Ponderosqa, 28.23%
10. Apasco, 27.36%

Source: *Mexico Business,* July/August 1997, p. 12.

★ 882 ★
MULTINATIONAL PARENT CORPORATIONS BY COUNTRY

Ranked by: Number of parent corporations based in country. **Number listed:** 5

1. South Korea with 1,049 companies
2. Brazil, 566
3. Hong Kong, 500
4. China, 379
5. India, 187

Source: *India Today,* January 31, 1996, p. 67.

★ 883 ★
TOP BRITISH FIRMS BY TURNOVER, 1996

Ranked by: Turnover, in millions of British pounds (£).
Number listed: 60

1. Shell Transport & Trading with £69,595.0 million
2. British Petroleum, £36,106.0
3. Unilever, £31,516.0
4. Sumitomo Corporation U.K., £14,564.6
5. BT, £14,446.0
6. Mitsui & Co. U.K., £13,333.6
7. J. Sainsbury, £12,627.0
8. Tesco, £12,094.0
9. Hanson, £11,184.0
10. Glaxo Wellcome, £10,490.0

Source: *Financial Times,* January 24, 1997, p. 28.

★ 884 ★
TOP CHAEBOLS IN SOUTH KOREA, 1995

Ranked by: Assets at the end of 1995, in billions of U.S. dollars. **Number listed:** 4

1. Hyundai with $56.5 billion
2. Samsung, $52.6
3. LG, $40.5
4. Daewoo, $40.4

Source: *The Economist,* May 18, 1996, p. 66.

★ 885 ★
TOP COLOMBIAN COMPANIES BY REVENUE, 1996

Ranked by: Revenue, in millions of U.S. dollars.
Remarks: Also notes percent change over 1995. **Number listed:** 10

1. Ecopetrol with $3,888.0 million
2. Mobil de Colombia, $918.4
3. Esso Colombra, $774.8
4. Cadenalco, $763.6
5. Bavaria, $744.8
6. Almacenes Exito, $724.9
7. GM-Colmotores, $645.6
8. Texaco, $627.2
9. Postobon, $610.7
10. Avianca, $607.1

Source: *Latin Trade,* September 1997, p. 48.

★ 886 ★
TOP COMPANIES IN ARGENTINA, 1995

Ranked by: Net sales, in millions of U.S. dollars.
Number listed: 10

1. YPF with $5,935 million
2. Telefonica de Argentina, $2,798
3. Telecom Argentina, $2,034
4. Perez Companc, $1,420
5. Molinos, $1,340
6. Ciadea, $1,306
7. Sevel, $1,217
8. Siderar, $983

9. Siderca, $916
10. Banco de Galicia y Buenos AIres, $895

Source: *Latin Trade,* The Top 100 Publicly Traded Companies (annual), September 1997, p. 36.

★ 887 ★

TOP COMPANIES IN BRAZIL, 1995

Ranked by: Net sales, in millions of U.S. dollars.
Number listed: 10

1. Petrobras with $17,477 million
2. Telebras, $12,018
3. Itausa, $8,587
4. Petrobras Distributora, $6,801
5. Eletrobras, $5,863
6. CVRD, $4,535
7. Ipiranga Distrbuidora, $4,247
8. Eletropaulo, $4,130
9. Odebrecht, $3,845
10. Ipiranga, $3,495

Source: *Latin Trade,* The Top 100 Publicly Traded Companies (annual), September 1997, p. 36.

★ 888 ★

TOP COMPANIES IN CHILE, 1995

Ranked by: Net sales, in millions of U.S. dollars.
Remarks: Quinenco is the name of Luksic Group holdings after September 1996. **Number listed:** 10

1. Copec with $2,957 million
2. Enersis, $2,731
3. CTC, $1,274
4. CMPC, $1,227
5. Endesa, $1,139
6. Quinenco, $952
7. SudAmericana de Vapores, $944
8. Falabella, $897
9. Distribucion & Servicios, $786
10. Chilectra, $647

Source: *Latin Trade,* The Top 100 Publicly Traded Companies (annual), September 1997, p. 36.

★ 889 ★

TOP COMPANIES IN COLOMBIA, 1995

Ranked by: Net sales, in millions of U.S. dollars.
Number listed: 10

1. Bavaria with $833 million
2. Banco Ganadero, $825
3. Cadelnaco, $787
4. Almacenes Exito, $750
5. Banco de Colombia, $737
6. Avianca, $626
7. Banco de Bogota, $568
8. Granahorror, $491
9. Bco. Industrial Colombiano, $460
10. Upac Colpatria, $460

Source: *Latin Trade,* The Top 100 Publicly Traded Companies (annual), September 1997, p. 36.

★ 890 ★

TOP COMPANIES IN MEXICO, 1995

Ranked by: Net sales, in millions of U.S. dollars.
Number listed: 10

1. Telmex with $6,708 million
2. Alfa, $3,541
3. Cemex, $3,374
4. Carso, $3,050
5. Cifra, $2,960
6. Visa, $2,485
7. FEMSA, $2,475
8. Vitro, $2,234
9. Panamco, $1,993
10. Bimbo, $1,918

Source: *Latin Trade,* The Top 100 Publicly Traded Companies (annual), September 1997, p. 36.

★ 891 ★

TOP COMPANIES IN PERU, 1995

Ranked by: Net sales, in millions of U.S. dollars.
Number listed: 10

1. Telefonica del Peru with $1,205 million
2. SPL, $750
3. Banco de Credito de Peru, $531
4. Alicorp, $415
5. Banco Wiese, $391
6. Banco Continental, $379
7. Backus & Johnston, $330
8. Southern Peru Copper, $290
9. Edelnor, $267
10. Credicorp, $252

Source: *Latin Trade,* The Top 100 Publicly Traded Companies (annual), September 1997, p. 36.

★ 892 ★

TOP COMPANIES IN SLOVAKIA, 1995

Ranked by: Sales, in billions of koruna (Sko). **Remarks:** Also notes gross profits. **Number listed:** 10

1. VSZ with Sko49.8 billion
2. Slovensky plynarensky, Sko36.8
3. Kerametal, Sko33.8
4. Slovnaft, Sko32.0
5. Slovenska Elektrarne, Sko26.2
6. Sipox Holding, Sko19.2
7. Benzinol, Sko16.4
8. Zeleznicne SR, Sko15.6
9. Petrimex, Sko12.5
10. ZEZ, Sko11.3

Source: *Business Central Europe,* October 1996, p. 14.

★ 893 ★
TOP COMPANIES IN SOUTH KOREA
Ranked by: Scores (1-7) based on a survey response of over 4,000 professionals throughout Asia. Respondents were asked to rate companies on their quality of services/products offered, long-term management vision, response to customer needs, and financial soundness.
Number listed: 10
1. Samsung Electronics with 6.48
2. Pohang Iron & Steel, 6.38
3. Hyundai Motor, 6.33
4. Samsung Corp., 6.33
5. Samsung Life Insurance, 5.88
6. Korean Air Lines, 5.87
7. Hyundai Heavy Industries, 5.76
8. Hyundai Engineering & Construction, 5.66
9. LG Electronics, 5.54
10. Yukong, 5.50

Source: *Far Eastern Economic Review,* Review 200 (annual), January 2, 1997, p. 48.

★ 894 ★
TOP COMPANIES IN SOUTH KOREA BY PROFITS, 1996
Ranked by: Profits for the first six months of 1996, in hundred million won (W). **Number listed:** 30
1. Samsung Electronics with W4,534.1 hundred million
2. Pohang Iron & Steel, W3,858.3
3. Korea Electric Power, W3,335.2
4. Korea Mobile Telecom, W1,561.3
5. Kookmin Bank, W1,001.0
6. Korea Long Term Credit Bank, W844.8
7. Samsung Display Devices, W835.7
8. Commercial Bank of Korea, W793.1
9. LG Electronics, W782.7
10. Shinhan Bank, W754.6

Source: *Business Korea,* October 1996, p. 10.

★ 895 ★
TOP COMPANIES IN SOUTH KOREA BY SALES, 1996
Ranked by: Sales for the first six months of 1996, in hundred million won (W). **Number listed:** 30
1. Samsung Corp. with W116,172.9 hundred million
2. Hyundai Corp., W95,716.3
3. Daewoo Corp., W91,272.7
4. Samsung Electronics, W87,137.0
5. LG International, W68,672.6
6. Hyundai Motor, W55,557.7
7. Korea Electric Power, W53,418.0
8. Pohang Iron & Steel, W41,739.9
9. Yukong, W39,472.0
10. LG Electronics, W36,769.2

Source: *Business Korea,* October 1996, p. 10.

★ 896 ★
TOP COMPANIES IN VENEZUELA, 1995
Ranked by: Net sales, in millions of U.S. dollars.
Number listed: 10
1. CANTV with $1,455 million
2. Sivensa, $654
3. Electridad de Caracas, $465
4. Vencernos, $340
5. Mavesa, $292
6. Sudamtex de Venezuela, $136
7. Bco. Venezolano de Credito, $67
8. Mantex, $64
9. Vencred, $45
10. Fondo de Valores, $24

Source: *Latin Trade,* The Top 100 Publicly Traded Companies (annual), September 1997, p. 36.

★ 897 ★
TOP FIRMS BY MARKET CAPITALIZATION, 1996
Ranked by: Market capitalization, in millions of U.S. dollars. **Number listed:** 250
1. General Electric Co. with $150,264.2 million
2. Royal Dutch/Shell, $135,350.2
3. Coca-Cola, $126,872.4
4. Nippon Telegraph & Telephone, $119,564.6
5. Exxon Corp, $103,384.0
6. Bank of Tokyo-Mitsubishi, $102,661.1
7. Toyota Motor Corporation, $97,926.3
8. Merck, $85,072.9
9. AT&T Corp, $84,141.3
10. Intel Corp, $78,668.7

Source: *Financial Times,* January 24, 1997, p. 6.

★ 898 ★
TOP FIRMS IN LATIN AMERICA, 1996
Ranked by: Sales, in millions of dollars. **Remarks:** Includes location of firm and main activity. **Number listed:** 100
1. Petrobras with $17,477 million
2. Telebras, $12,018
3. Itausa, $8,587
4. Petrobras Distribuidora, $6,801
5. Telefonas de Mexico, $6,708
6. YPF, $5,863
7. Electrobras, $4,535
8. CVRD, $4,247
9. Ipiranga Distribuidora, $4,130
10. Eletropaulo, $3,845

Source: *Latin Trade,* The Top 100 Publicly Traded Companies (annual), September 1997, p. 40+.

★ 899 ★
TOP JAPANESE FIRMS BY ASSETS
Ranked by: Assets, in billions of yen (¥). **Remarks:** Survey covered 1,751 companies listed on Japan's eight stock exchanges. Fiscal institutions and corporations that changed their accounting year in fiscal 1996 were excluded. **Number listed:** 10
1. Tokyo Electric Power Co. with ¥13.9 billion
2. Nippon Telegraph and Telephone Corp., ¥11.1
3. Toyota Motor Corp., ¥7.1
4. East Japan Railway Co., ¥6.7
5. Kansai Electric Power Co., ¥6.6
6. Nippon Shinpan Co., ¥6.6
7. Orient Corp., ¥6.4
8. Chibu Electric Power Co., ¥6.0
9. Mitsubishi Corp., ¥5.5
10. Mitsui & Co., ¥5.2

Source: *Nikkei Weekly*, July 14, 1997, p. 3.

★ 900 ★
TOP JAPANESE FIRMS BY PRETAX PROFIT
Ranked by: Pretax profit, in billions of yen (¥). **Remarks:** Survey covered 1,751 companies listed on Japan's eight stock exchanges. Fiscal institutions and corporations that changed their accounting year in fiscal 1996 were excluded. **Number listed:** 10
1. Toyota Motor Corp. with ¥620 billion
2. Nippon Telegraph and Telephone Corp., ¥365
3. Mitsubishi Heavy Industries Ltd., ¥192
4. Honda Motor Co., ¥166
5. Matsushita Electric Industrial Co., ¥143
6. Tokyo Electric Power Co., ¥142
7. Japan Tobacco Inc., ¥136
8. Fuji Photo Film Co., ¥125
9. Kansai Electric Power Co., ¥115
10. Sankyo Co., ¥112

Source: *Nikkei Weekly*, July 14, 1997, p. 3.

★ 901 ★
TOP JAPANESE FIRMS BY RETURN ON EQUITY
Ranked by: Return on equity, in percent. **Remarks:** Suvey covered 1,751 companies listed on Japan's eight stock exchanges. Financial institutions and corporations that changed their accounting year in fiscal 1996 were cxcludcd. **Numbcr listcd:** 10
1. Nichiei Co. with 21.2%
2. Kojima Co., 19.9%
3. Advantest Corp., 16.5%
4. DDI Corp., 16.4%
5. Takuma Co., 16.1%
6. Promise Co., 16.0%
7. Acom Co., 15.5%
8. Circle K Japan Co., 15.3%
9. Kawasaki Heavy Industries Ltd., 15.3%
10. Tokyo Electron Ltd., 15.2%

Source: *Nikkei Weekly*, July 14, 1997, p. 3.

★ 902 ★
TOP JAPANESE FIRMS BY SALES
Ranked by: Sales in billions of yen (¥). **Remarks:** Survey covered 1,751 companies listed on Japan's eight stock exchanges. Fiscal institutions and corporations that changed their accounting year in fiscal 1996 were excluded. **Number listed:** 10
1. Itochu Corp. with ¥141 billion
2. Marubeni Corp., ¥134
3. Mitsui & Co., ¥133
4. Sumitomo Corp., ¥127
5. Mitsubishi Corp., ¥118
6. Toyota Motor Corp., ¥91
7. Nissho Iwai Corp., ¥77
8. Nippon Telegraph and Telephone Corp., ¥63
9. Tokyo Electric Power Co., ¥50
10. Matsushita Electric Industrial Co., ¥47

Source: *Nikkei Weekly*, July 14, 1997, p. 3.

★ 903 ★
TOP LATIN AMERICAN FIRMS BY MARKET CAPITALIZATION
Ranked by: Sales, in millions of dollars. **Remarks:** Includes location of company and main activity. **Number listed:** 25
1. Telebras with $24,663
2. Eltrobas, $19,961
3. Petrobras, $17,294
4. Telmex, $14,764
5. Telesp, $11,506
6. YPF, $8,910
7. CVRD, $7,477
8. Telefonica de Argentina, $6,174
9. IMSA, $5,606
10. Cemex, $5,606

Source: *Latin Trade,* The Top 100 Publicly Traded Companies (annual), September 1997, p. 43.

★ 904 ★
TOP MANUFACTURING COMPANIES, 1996
Ranked by: Revenue, in millions of U.S. dollars. **Remarks:** Also notes primary industry, earnings per share, profit margin, profit growth, total equity, and debt to equity ratio. **Number listed:** 1
1. General Motors Corp. with $164,069.0 million
2. Ford Motor Co., $146,991.0
3. Royal Dutch Petroleum Co., $139,082.9
4. Exxon Corp., $134,249.0
5. Mobil Corp., $81,503.0
6. General Electric Co., $79,179.0
7. International Business Machines Corp., $75,947.0
8. British Petroleuem Co. PLC, $75,796.7
9. Hitachi Ltd., $70,677.2

10. Toyota Motor Corp., $70,652.5
Source: *IndustryWeek,* IndustryWeek 1000 (annual), June 9, 1997, p. 50.

★ 905 ★
TOP REVENUE EARNERS IN SLOVENIA, 1994
Ranked by: Revenue, in thousands of tolars (To).
Remarks: Includes number of employees for each firm.
Number listed: 323
1. Lek (Ljubljana) with To33,083 thousand
2. Tobacna Grosist (Ljubljana), To24,848
3. Iskraemeco (Kranj), To11,447
4. Porsche Inter Auto (Ljubljana), To10,963
5. MGA Mali Gospodinjski Aparati (Nazarje), To6,063
6. Kras Commerce (Sezana), To4,602
7. Trimo (Trebnje), To4,218
8. Danfoss Compressors (Crnomelj), To4,088
9. Sugros (Celje), To3,843
10. Jurmes (Sentjur Pri Celju), To3,292
Source: *Slovenian Business Report,* Spring 1996, p. 34+.

★ 906 ★
WORLD'S TOP CORPORATIONS IN PROFITS, 1996
Ranked by: Profits, in billions of U.S. dollars. **Number listed:** 10
1. Royal Dutch/Shell Group with $6.78 billion
2. General Motors, $6.72
3. General Electric, $6.57
4. Exxon, $6.47
5. IBM, $6.02
6. AT&T, $5.52
7. Philip Morris, $5.48
8. Ford Motor, $4.14
9. HSBC Holdings, $3.82
10. Glaxo Wellcome, $3.79
Source: *Business Week,* Global 1,000 (annual), July 8, 1996, p. 46.

★ 907 ★
WORLD'S TOP CORPORATIONS IN RETURN ON EQUITY, 1996
Ranked by: Return on equity, in percent. **Number listed:** 10
1. Glaxo Wellcome with 1,915.0% return
2. General Mills, 302.2%
3. Intimate Brands, 184.8%
4. Avon Products, 149.1%
5. UST, 143.2%
6. Vastar Resources, 130.1%
7. Investor, 104.7%
8. SmithKline Beecham, 78.7%
9. Freeport-McMoran Copper & Gold, 68.5%
10. Schering-Plough, 66.6%
Source: *Business Week,* Global 1,000 (annual), July 8, 1996, p. 46.

★ 908 ★
WORLD'S TOP CORPORATIONS IN SALES, 1996
Ranked by: Sales, in billions of U.S. dollars. **Number listed:** 10
1. General Motors with $168.8 billion
2. Mitsubishi Corp., $164.6
3. Mitsui & Co., $162.1
4. Itochu, $151.1
5. Sumitomo Corp., $149.6
6. Marubeni, $143.8
7. Ford Motor, $137.1
8. Exxon, $107.9
9. Royal Dutch/Shell Group, $107.8
10. Toyota Motor, $99.2
Source: *Business Week,* Global 1,000 (annual), July 8, 1996, p. 46.

★ 909 ★
WORLD'S TOP CORPORATIONS IN SHARE-PRICE GAIN, 1996
Ranked by: Share-price gain over previous year, in percent. **Number listed:** 10
1. Iomega with 1,774% gain
2. Ascend Communications, 590%
3. Cascade Communications, 431%
4. U.S. Robotics, 340%
5. HFS, 314%
6. Republic Industries, 292%
7. Total System Services, 254%
8. America Online, 217%
9. Fore Systems, 209%
10. Gartner Group, 199%
Source: *Business Week,* Global 1,000 (annual), July 8, 1996, p. 46.

★ 910 ★
WORLD'S TOP EMERGING-MARKET COMPANIES, 1996
Ranked by: Market value, in millions of U.S. dollars.
Remarks: Also notes price per share, price to book value ratio, yield, sales, profits, assets, and return on equity.
Number listed: 100
1. Korea Electric Power (Korea) with $23,945 million
2. Telebras (Brazil), $20,740
3. Telekom Malaysia (Malaysia), $18,209
4. Cathay Life Insurance (Taiwan), $16,413
5. Anglo American (South Africa), $15,111
6. Telefonos de Mexico (Mexico), $15,023
7. PT Telekomunikasi Indonesia (Indonesia), $14,205
8. Eletrobras (Brazil), $13,215
9. Tenaga Nasional (Malaysia), $13,050

10. De Beers Consolidated Mines (South Africa), $12,361
Source: *Business Week,* Global 1,000 (annual), July 8, 1996, p. 88.

Corporations – Asia

★ 911 ★
ASIAN COMPANIES BY GROWTH IN POPULARITY, 1997
Ranked by: Change in overall rank from previous year's rank as a result of a questionnaire sent to more than 9,000 managers and CEOs chosen from the magazine's circulation and evaluated by Asia Market Intelligence, a research firm. **Remarks:** Respondents scored each company in terms of overall admirability, then on six attributes: quality of products, quality of management, contribution to local economy, record as an employer, growth potential and reputation for ethics. Also notes 1997 rank. **Number listed:** 10
1. Dong Ah Construction with +107
2. Thai Airways International, +88
3. Daewoo Corporation, +82
4. 3M, +75
5. United Tractors, +74
6. Unilever, +72
7. CITIC, +68
8. Sunkyong, +56
9. Bakrie & Brothers, +53
10. Hutchison Whampoa, +48
Source: *Asian Business,* Most Admired Companies in Asia (annual), May 1997, p. 34.

★ 912 ★
ASIAN COMPANIES BY LOSS OF POPULARITY, 1997
Ranked by: Change in overall rank from previous year's rank as a result of a questionnaire sent to more than 9,000 managers and CEOs chosen from the magazine's circulation and evaluated by Asia Market Intelligence, a research firm. **Remarks:** Respondents scored each company in terms of overall admirability, then on six attributes: quality of products, quality of management, contribution to local economy, record as an employer, growth potential and reputation for ethics. Also notes 1997 rank. **Number listed:** 10
1. Malaysian Airlines with -104
2. Shinawatra Computer, -77
3. Sumitomo Corporation, -75
4. Edaran Otomobil Nasional, -61
5. Yaohan, -59
6. China Steel, -54
7. Formosa Chemical Fibre, -49
8. China Motor, -44

9. Telekom Malaysia, -44
10. Qantas, -40
Source: *Asian Business,* Most Admired Companies in Asia (annual), May 1997, p. 34.

★ 913 ★
ASIAN COMPANIES CONSIDERED THE BEST EMPLOYERS, 1997
Ranked by: Results (0-5) of a questionnaire sent to more than 9,000 managers and CEOs chosen from the magazine's circulation and evaluated by Asia Market Intelligence, a research firm. **Remarks:** Respondents scored each company in terms of overall admirability, then on six attributes: quality of products, quality of management, contribution to local economy, record as an employer, growth potential and reputation for ethics. **Number listed:** 10
1. Samsung with 4.28
2. Astra International, 4.21
3. San Miguel Corporation, 4.12
4. Acer, 4.10
5. Pohang Iron & Steel, 4.10
6. Taiwan Semiconductor Manufacturing, 4.06
7. Hewlett-Packard, 4.02
8. Singapore Airlines, 4.02
9. McDonald's, 4.01
10. LG Group (Lucky Goldstar), 3.96
Source: *Asian Business,* Most Admired Companies in Asia (annual), May 1997, p. 27.

★ 914 ★
ASIAN COMPANIES CONSIDERED THE BEST MANAGED, 1997
Ranked by: Results (0-5) of a questionnaire sent to more than 9,000 managers and CEOs chosen from the magazine's circulation and evaluated by Asia Market Intelligence, a research firm. **Remarks:** Respondents scored each company in terms of overall admirability, then on six attributes: quality of products, quality of management, contribution to local economy, record as an employer, growth potential and reputation for ethics. **Number listed:** 10
1. McDonald's with 4.13
2. Sinapore Airlines, 4.10
3. Samsung, 4.06
4. Astra International, 4.02
5. San Miguel Corp., 3.99
6. Hewlett-Packard, 3.98
7. Ayala, 3.96
8. Boeing, 3.96
9. Acer, 3.95
10. Sony Corporation, 3.94
Source: *Asian Business,* Most Admired Companies in Asia (annual), May 1997, p. 27.

★ 915 ★
ASIAN COMPANIES CONSIDERED THE MOST FINANCIALLY SOUND

Ranked by: Results of a survey asking over 4,000 professionals throughout Asia to rank companies based on high quality of services or products, long-term vision, innovation in responding to customer needs, and which companies were most often emulated. No specific data were provided. **Number listed:** 10

1. Deutsche Bank
2. Citibank
3. UBS
4. Swiss Bank Corp.
5. Chase Manhattan
6. Bank of America
7. Credit Suisse
8. Standard Chartered
9. Coca-Cola
10. Royal Dutch/Shell

Source: *Far Eastern Economic Review*, Review 200 (annual), January 2, 1997, p. 46.

★ 916 ★
ASIAN COMPANIES MAKING THE GREATEST CONTRIBUTIONS TO THE LOCAL ECONOMY, 1997

Ranked by: Results (0-5) of a questionnaire sent to more than 9,000 managers and CEOs chosen from the magazine's circulation and evaluated by Asia Market Intelligence, a research firm. **Remarks:** Respondents scored each company in terms of overall admirability, then on six attributes: quality of products, quality of management, contribution to local economy, record as an employer, growth potential and reputation for ethics. **Number listed:** 10

1. Pohang Iron & Steel with 4.62
2. Samsung, 4.58
3. Hyundai Corporation, 4.47
4. Astra International, 4.45
5. Hongkong Telecom, 4.45
6. Gudang Garam, 4.43
7. Acer, 4.41
8. DBS Bank, 4.24
9. Singapore Telekom, 4.23
10. San Miguel Corp., 4.19

Source: *Asian Business,* Most Admired Companies in Asia (annual), May 1997, p. 27.

★ 917 ★
ASIAN COMPANIES OTHERS TRY TO EMULATE

Ranked by: Results of a survey asking over 4,000 professionals throughout Asia to rank companies based on high quality of services or products, long-term vision, innovation in responding to customer needs, and which companies were most often emulated. No specific data were provided. **Number listed:** 10

1. Coca-Cola

2. Microsoft
3. McDonald's
4. Walt Disney
5. IBM
6. Boeing
7. Xerox
8. BMW
9. Daimler-Benz
10. Rolex

Source: *Far Eastern Economic Review*, Review 200 (annual), January 2, 1997, p. 46.

★ 918 ★
ASIAN COMPANIES POSTING THE GREATEST LOSS

Ranked by: Pre-tax loss, in thousands of U.S. dollars. **Number listed:** 200

1. Haseko Corp. with $1,145,640 thousand
2. Nissan Motor Co. Ltd., $518,834
3. JVC (Victor Co. of Japan Ltd.), $418,165
4. Kenwood Corp., $215,582
5. Tokyu Land Corp., $183,058
6. Sanyo Securities Ltd., $175,427
7. Tokyo Electronic Co. Ltd., $165,786
8. Kanebo Ltd., $149,902
9. Kankaku Securities Co. Ltd., $145,155
10. Pioneer Electronic Corp., $143,339

Source: *Asia's 7,500 Largest Companies* (annual), Dun & Bradstreet, 1997, p. 581+.

★ 919 ★
ASIAN COMPANIES RATED THE BEST IN PRODUCTS AND SERVICES, 1997

Ranked by: Results (0-5) of a questionnaire sent to more than 9,000 managers and CEOs chosen from the magazine's circulation and evaluated by Asia Market Intelligence, a research firm. **Remarks:** Respondents scored each company in terms of overall admirability, then on six attributes: quality of products, quality of management, contribution to local economy, record as an employer, growth potential and reputation for ethics. **Number listed:** 10

1. Singapore Airlines with 4.44
2. Hewlett-Packard, 4.40
3. Sony Corp., 4.33
4. BMW, 4.25
5. 3M, 4.22
6. Daimler-Benz, 4.22
7. Astra International, 4.21
8. Coca-Cola, 4.21
9. San Miguel Corp., 4.21
10. Shangri-La Hotels, 4.20

Source: *Asian Business,* Most Admired Companies in Asia (annual), May 1997, p. 27.

★ 920 ★
ASIAN FIRMS WITH THE BIGGEST LOSSES, 1995
Ranked by: Losses, in millions of U.S. dollars. **Remarks:** Also lists overall sales rank. **Number listed:** 40
1. Haseko with -$2,279.2 million losses
2. Aoki Corp., -$1,054.5
3. Mitsubishi Estate, -$1,052.2
4. Nissan Motor, -$940.0
5. Matsushita Electric Industrial, -$604.6
6. Isetan, -$337.0
7. Kanebo, -$292.6
8. Nissho Iwai Corp., -$266.3
9. Kenwood, -$236.1
10. Nagasakiya, -$182.9
Source: *Asiaweek*, The Asiaweek 1,000, November 22, 1996, p. 130.

★ 921 ★
ASIAN FIRMS WITH THE HIGHEST RETURN ON MARGINS, 1995
Ranked by: Profits, as a percentage of assets. **Remarks:** Also includes overall sales rank. **Number listed:** 40
1. Tab New South Wales with 57.9%
2. Australian Wheat Board, 53.5%
3. Seagate Technology International, 36.4%
4. Dentsu, 29.9%
5. Public Utilities Board, 28.6%
6. Hongkong Telecom, 27.2%
7. Malaysia LNG, 22.6%
8. Federal Flour Mills, 21.6%
9. Hewlett-Packard, Singapore, 20.9%
10. Hyundai Electronics Industries, 20.6%
Source: *Asiaweek*, The Asiaweek 1,000, November 22, 1996, p. 138.

★ 922 ★
ASIAN FIRMS WITH THE LARGEST PROFIT MARGINS, 1995
Ranked by: Profits, as a percentage of sales. **Remarks:** Includes overall sales rank. **Number listed:** 40
1. Cheung Kong with 91.8%
2. Henderson Land Development, 54.7%
3. Australian Wheat Board, 54.7%
4. Sun Hung Kai Properties, 48.8%
5. Singapore Telecom, 37.2%
6. Hong Kong Telecom, 33.8%
7. LG Semicon, 30.9%
8. Telekom Malaysia, 30.0%
9. Chunghwa Telecom, 29.0%
10. Citic Pacific, 28.4%
Source: *Asiaweek*, The Asiaweek 1,000, November 22, 1996, p. 138.

★ 923 ★
LARGEST EMPLOYERS IN ASIA, 1995
Ranked by: Number of employees. **Remarks:** Also lists overall sales rank. **Number listed:** 40
1. China Petrochemical Corp. with 650,000 employees
2. Coal India, 641,000
3. Jiangsu Supplies & Marketing Co-op., 415,929
4. Hitachi Ltd., 331,852
5. Daqing Petroleum Management Bur., 270,853
6. Matsushita Electric Industrial, 265,538
7. China State Construction Engineering, 259,250
8. Jardine Matheson, 220,770
9. Anshan Iron & Steel, 217,700
10. Shengli Oil Field Management, 188,214
Source: *Asiaweek*, The Asiaweek 1,000, November 22, 1996, p. 132.

★ 924 ★
MOST ADMIRED COMPANIES IN ASIA, 1997
Ranked by: Results of a questionnaire sent to more than 9,000 managers and CEOs chosen from the magazine's circulation and evaluated by Asia Market Intelligence, a research firm. **Remarks:** Respondents scored each company in terms of overall admirability, then on six attributes: quality of products, quality of management, contribution to local economy, record as an employer, growth potential and reputation for ethics. Also notes rank from 1996. **Number listed:** 248
1. Singapore Airlines with 8.76
2. San Miguel Corp., 8.51
3. Samsung, 8.47
4. Jollibee, 8.37
5. McDonald's, 8.32
6. Charoen Pokphand, 8.31
7. Sony Corp., 8.26
8. Acer, 8.20
9. Hewlett-Packard, 8.20
10. Boeing, 8.19
Source: *Asian Business,* Most Admired Companies in Asia (annual), May 1997, p. 24.

★ 925 ★
TOP ASIAN COMPANIES
Ranked by: Score (1-7) based on a survey response of over 4,000 professionals throughout Asia. Respondents were asked to rate companies on their quality of services/products offered, long-term management vision, response to customer needs, and financial soundness. **Number listed:** 90
1. Microsoft with 6.21
2. Coca-Cola, 6.16
3. McDonald's, 5.90
4. Motorola, 5.89
5. Walt Disney, 5.81
6. Citbank, 5.73

7. Xerox, 5.64
8. Kodak, 5.63
9. Boeing, 5.61
10. IBM, 5.60

Source: *Far Eastern Economic Review*, Review 200 (annual), January 2, 1997, p. 49.

★ 926 ★

TOP ASIAN COMPANIES BY PROFITABILITY

Ranked by: Profit as a percent of sales. **Number listed:** 500

1. Taiwan Semiconductor Manufacturing Co. Ltd. with 49.7%
2. Jaka Investments Corporation, 49.6%
3. Jaya Real Property, 49.6%
4. Lee Hing Development Ltd., 49.6%
5. Chuang's Consortium International Ltd., 49.4%
6. Shell Electric Manufacturing (Holdings) Co. Ltd., 49.3%
7. Shangri-La Asia Ltd., 48.5%
8. Hongkong Macau (Holdings) Ltd., 48.4%
9. Keck Seng Investment (Hong Kong) Ltd., 48.0%
10. Krungdhep Warehouse Co. Ltd., 48.0%

Source: *Asia's 7,500 Largest Companies* (annual), Dun & Bradstreet, 1997, p. 48+.

★ 927 ★

TOP ASIAN COMPANIES BY SALES

Ranked by: Sales, in thousands of U.S. dollars. **Remarks:** Also notes previous year's rank, type of industry, percent change in sales, and percent change in local currencies. **Number listed:** 7

1. Mitsubishi Corp. with $172,766,300 thousand
2. Mitsui & Co. Ltd., $170,098,873
3. Itochu Corp., $162,548,281
4. Sumitomo Corp., $156,990,893
5. Marubeni Corp., $151,381,631
6. Toyota Motor Corp., $104,065,427
7. Nissho Iwai Corp., $91,728,106
8. Hitachi Ltd., $78,871,941
9. Nippon Telegraph & Telephone Corp., $76,782,310
10. Matsushita Electric Industrial Co. Ltd., $65,969,436

Source: *Asia's 7,500 Largest Companies* (annual), Dun & Bradstreet, 1997, p. 94+.

★ 928 ★

TOP ASIAN COMPANIES IN HIGH QUALITY SERVICES/PRODUCTS

Ranked by: Results of a survey asking over 4,000 professionals throughout Asia to rank companies based on high quality of services or products, long-term vision, innovation in responding to customer needs, and which companies were most often emulated. No specific data were provided. **Number listed:** 10

1. Rolex
2. BMW
3. Rolls-Royce Motor
4. Kodak
5. Volvo
6. Daimler-Benz
7. Xerox
8. IBM
9. Boeing
10. Nestle

Source: *Far Eastern Economic Review*, Review 200 (annual), January 2, 1997, p. 46.

★ 929 ★

TOP ASIAN COMPANIES IN INNOVATIVE RESPONSE TO CUSTOMER NEEDS

Ranked by: Results of a survey asking over 4,000 professionals throughout Asia to rank companies based on high quality of services or products, long-term vision, innovation in responding to customer needs, and which companies were most often emulated. No specific data were provided. **Number listed:** 10

1. McDonald's
2. Nike
3. Microsoft
4. Walt Disney
5. Federal Express
6. Toys 'R' Us
7. Motorola
8. Hewlett-Packard
9. American Express
10. Citibank

Source: *Far Eastern Economic Review*, Review 200 (annual), January 2, 1997, p. 46.

★ 930 ★

TOP ASIAN COMPANIES IN LONG-TERM VISION

Ranked by: Results of a survey asking over 4,000 professionals throughout Asia to rank companies based on high quality of services or products, long-term vision, innovation in responding to customer needs, and which companies were most often emulated. No specific data were provided. **Number listed:** 10

1. Microsoft
2. Boeing
3. Coca-Cola
4. Walt Disney

5. General Electric
6. AT&T
7. IBM
8. Royal Dutch/Shell
9. Citibank
10. British Petroleum

Source: *Far Eastern Economic Review*, Review 200 (annual), January 2, 1997, p. 46.

★ 931 ★

TOP ASIAN FIRMS BY ASSETS, 1995

Ranked by: Assets, in millions of U.S. dollars. **Remarks:** Also lists overall sales rank. **Number listed:** 40

1. Tokyo Electric Power with $149,574.1 million
2. Nippon Telegraph & Telephone, $144,559.6
3. Toyota Motor Corp., $120,587.4
4. Mitsubishi Corp., $104,566.2
5. Hitachi Ltd., $104,225.4
6. Matsushita Electric Industrial, $85,177.9
7. Marubeni Corp., $81,267.3
8. Mitsui & Co., $78,231.8
9. East Japan Railway, $78,096.5
10. Nissan Motor, $75,394.4

Source: *Asiaweek*, The Asiaweek 1,000, November 22, 1996, p. 132.

★ 932 ★

TOP ASIAN FIRMS BY PROFIT PER EMPLOYEE, 1995

Ranked by: Profits per employee, in U.S. dollars. **Remarks:** Also lists overall sales rank. **Number listed:** 40

1. Hong Leong Investment with $9,017,744
2. Australian Wheat Board, $2,112,665
3. Sanshin Electronics, $873,556
4. Yukong International (S), $609,564
5. Cheung Kong, $552,823
6. Malaysia LNG, $446,659
7. Singapore Pools, $430,950
8. Mobil Oil Singapore, $374,623
9. Dentsu, $368,466
10. Amway Japan, $345,329

Source: *Asiaweek*, The Asiaweek 1,000, November 22, 1996, p. 140.

★ 933 ★

TOP ASIAN FIRMS BY PROFITS, 1995

Ranked by: Profits, in millions of U.S. dollars. **Remarks:** Also lists overall sales rank. **Number listed:** 40

1. Samsung Electronics with $3,248.5 million
2. Toyota Motor Corp., $2,732.0
3. Nippon Telephone & Telegraph, $2,266.9
4. Petroliam Nasional, $2,266.0
5. Dentsu, $2,144.5
6. Chunghwa Telecom, $1,722.5
7. Telstra, $1,709.0
8. Hitachi Ltd., $1,507.2

9. Cheung Kong, $1,426.3
10. Sun Hung Kai Properties, $1,415.3

Source: *Asiaweek*, The Asiaweek 1,000, November 22, 1996, p. 130.

★ 934 ★

TOP COMPANIES IN ASIA

Ranked by: Sales, in millions of U.S. dollars. **Number listed:** 50

1. Samsung Electronic Co. with $20,685 million
2. Hyundai Motor Co., $13,210
3. Korea Electric Power Corp., $12,795
4. Indian Oil Corp., $12,777
5. Pohang Iron & Steel Co., $10,500
6. Yukong Ltd., $8,424
7. LG Electronics Co., $8,422
8. Kia Motors Co., $7,268
9. Jardine Strategic Holdings Ltd., $6,437
10. Dairy Farm International Holdings Ltd., $6,235

Source: *Nikkei Weekly*, December 16, 1996, p. 28.

Corporations – Australia

★ 935 ★

TOP COMPANIES IN AUSTRALIA

Ranked by: Score (1-7) based on a survey response of over 4,000 professionals throughout Asia. Respondents were asked to rate companies on their quality of services/products offered, long-term management vision, response to customer needs, and financial soundness. **Number listed:** 10

1. National Australia Bank with 5.86
2. Broken Hill Proprietary, 5.78
3. Woolworths, 5.44
4. Qantas Airways, 5.38
5. News Corp., 5.25
6. ANZ Banking Group, 4.87
7. RTZ-CRA, 4.83
8. Lend Lease, 4.81
9. Western Mining, 4.75
10. Amcor, 4.66

Source: *Far Eastern Economic Review*, Review 200 (annual), January 2, 1997, p. 48.

★ 936 ★

TOP CORPORATIONS IN AUSTRALIA BY MARKET VALUE, 1996

Ranked by: Market value as of May, 31, 1996, in millions of U.S. dollars. **Remarks:** Also notes price per share, price to book value ratio, yield, sales, profits, assets, and return on equity. **Number listed:** 16

1. Broken Hill Proprietary with $29,421 million
2. News Corp., $15,958

3. National Australia Bank, $13,655
4. Westpac Banking, $8,875
5. WMC, $8,430
6. Commonwealth Bank of Australia, $8,066
7. Australia & New Zealand Banking Group, $6,741
8. Coca-Cola Amatil, $5,405
9. CRA, $5,321
10. Amcor, $4,241

Source: *Business Week,* Global 1,000 (annual), July 8, 1996, p. 49.

★ 937 ★

TOP PUBLICLY TRADED CORPORATIONS IN AUSTRALIA, 1995

Ranked by: Revenue, in millions of U.S. dollars.
Remarks: Also notes net income, assets, market value, stock price, employees, and global rank. **Number listed:** 12

1. Broken Hill Proprietary with $13,196 million
2. Coles Myer, $12,468
3. Woolworths, $9,500
4. National Australia Bank, $9,490
5. News Corp., $9,043
6. RTZ-CRA, $7,704
7. ANZ Banking, $7,644
8. Westpac Banking Group, $6,365
9. Commonwealth Bank Group, $6,034
10. Pacific Dunlop, $5,427

Source: *Forbes,* Forbes Foreign Rankings (annual), July 15, 1996, p. 246.

Corporations – Austria

★ 938 ★

LEADING CORPORATIONS IN AUSTRIA BY SALES

Ranked by: Sales, in thousands of U.S. dollars. **Number listed:** 100

1. OMV A.G. with $9,140,913 thousand
2. Porsche Holding O.H.G., $4,468,452
3. Voest-Alpine Stahl A.G., $4,289,714
4. Auricon Beteiligungs A.G., $2,234,895
5. Siemens A.G. Oesterreich, $2,022,233
6. Interspar GmbH, $1,985,978
7. Wiener Stadtwerke, $1,964,563
8. Metro Einkaufsgesellschaft MbH, $1,539,133
9. Shell Austria A.G., $1,416,985
10. Bau Holding A.G., $1,360,395

Source: *Europe's 15,000 Largest Companies* (annual), Dun & Bradstreet, 1997, p. 71.

★ 939 ★

TOP PUBLICLY TRADED CORPORATIONS IN AUSTRIA, 1995

Ranked by: Revenue, in millions of U.S. dollars.
Remarks: Also notes net income, assets, market value, stock price, employees, and global ranking. **Number listed:** 2

1. OMV Group with $5,950 million
2. Creditanstalt, $4,898

Source: *Forbes,* Forbes Foreign Rankings (annual), July 15, 1996, p. 274.

Corporations – Belgium

★ 940 ★

LEADING CORPORATIONS IN BELGIUM BY SALES

Ranked by: Sales, in thousands of U.S. dollars. **Number listed:** 100

1. Petrofina S.A. with $19,136,697 thousand
2. Electrabel S.A., $9,874,579
3. Solvay S.A., $9,288,243
4. GB Inno BM S.A., $7,745,092
5. Belgacom, $4,524,502
6. Delhaize Freres Et Cie - Le Lion S.A., $3,077,767
7. Sidmar N.V., $2,812,836
8. Volvo Cars Europe Industry N.V., $2,498,779
9. Volkswagen Bruxelles S.A., $2,258,148
10. Agfa-Gevaert N.V., $1,916,851

Source: *Europe's 15,000 Largest Companies* (annual), Dun & Bradstreet, 1997, p. 72.

★ 941 ★

TOP CORPORATIONS IN BELGIUM BY MARKET VALUE, 1996

Ranked by: Market value as of May, 31, 1996, in millions of U.S. dollars. **Remarks:** Also notes price per share, price to book value ratio, yield, sales, profits, assets, and return on equity. **Number listed:** 11

1. Electrabel with $11,657 million
2. Petrofina, $6,898
3. Tractebel, $6,099
4. Generale de Banque, $5,194
5. Societe Generale de Belgique, $5,186
6. Fortis A.G., $5,052
7. Solvay, $4,986
8. Kredietbank, $4,280
9. Banque Bruxelles Lambert, $3,595
10. Powerfin, $3,331

Source: *Business Week,* Global 1,000 (annual), July 8, 1996, p. 49.

★ 942 ★

TOP PUBLICLY TRADED CORPORATIONS IN BELGIUM, 1995

Ranked by: Revenue, in millions of U.S. dollars. **Remarks:** Also notes net income, assets, market value, stock price, employees, and global rank. **Number listed:** 12

1. Fortis Group with $22,619 million
2. Delhaize Le Lion Group, $12,499
3. PetroFina, $12,476
4. Tractebel, $10,923
5. Generale Bank Group, $10,706
6. Solvay Group, $9,272
7. Arbed, $8,721
8. Bank Bruxelles Lambert, $7,824
9. GIB Group, $7,760
10. Kredietbank, $7,715

Source: *Forbes,* Forbes Foreign Rankings (annual), July 15, 1996, p. 248.

Corporations – Brazil

★ 943 ★

LARGEST PUBLICLY TRADED, PRIVATE SECTOR COMPANIES IN BRAZIL, 1995

Ranked by: Revenues, in millions of U.S. dollars. **Remarks:** Also notes net income, assets, market value, stock price, and number of employees. **Number listed:** 6

1. Petrobras-Petroleo Brasil with $17,366 million
2. Banco do Brasil, $17,221
3. Telebras, $9,391
4. Banco Bradesco Group, $8,092
5. Banco Itau Group, $6,480
6. Eletrobras, $5,889

Source: *Forbes,* Forbes Foreign Rankings (annual), July 15, 1996, p. 248.

Corporations – Canada

★ 944 ★

FASTEST GROWING CANADIAN COMPANIES BY 5-YEAR PROFIT GROWTH, 1995

Ranked by: 5-year profit growth, in percent. **Remarks:** Data is shown only for those companies listed on the Canadian Stock Exchange. Also notes total profits. **Number listed:** 50

1. Noble China with 836.11%
2. Samoth Capital, 258.42%
3. Stampeder Exploration, 237.06%
4. International Aqua Foods, 187.27%
5. Domco Industries, 143.21%
6. Cott Corp., 142.52%

7. Avcorp Industries, 141.11%
8. Provigo, 125.37%
9. Weldwood of Canada, 119.61%
10. United Canadian Shares, 118.65%

Source: *Globe and Mail,* Globe and Mail Report on Business 1000 (annual), July 1996, p. 93.

★ 945 ★

FASTEST GROWING CANADIAN COMPANIES BY 5-YEAR REVENUE GROWTH, 1995

Ranked by: 5-year revenue growth, in percent. **Remarks:** Data is shown only for those companies listed on the Canadian Stock Exchange. Also notes total revenues. **Number listed:** 50

1. Pan American Silver with 841.37%
2. Gulfstream Resources Canada, 442.39%
3. Stampeder Exploration, 319.03%
4. IntelCom Group, 275.51%
5. MSV Resources, 228.17%
6. Corp. Reg. Invest. Amisk, 214.89%
7. Redaurum, 200.09%
8. Tiomin Resources, 198.04%
9. Eden Roc Mineral, 189.67%
10. Noble China, 185.43%

Source: *Globe and Mail,* Globe and Mail Report on Business 1000 (annual), July 1996, p. 91.

★ 946 ★

LARGEST CANADIAN EMPLOYERS, 1995

Ranked by: Number of employees. **Remarks:** Also notes revenue per employee and profit per employee. **Number listed:** 50

1. BCE Inc. with 121,000
2. George Weston Ltd., 75,000
3. Hudson's Bay Co., 69,000
4. Imasco Ltd., 66,000
5. Northern Telecom, 60,293
6. Loblaw Cos., 60,000
7. Laldlaw Inc., 53,000
8. Bell Canada, 51,503
9. Semi-Tech Corp., 50,000
10. Royal Bank of Canada, 49,011

Source: *Globe and Mail,* Globe and Mail Report on Business 1000 (annual), July 1996, p. 89.

★ 947 ★

TOP CANADIAN COMPANIES BY AFTER-TAX PROFITS, 1995

Ranked by: After-tax profits, in thousands of Canadian dollars. **Remarks:** Data is shown only for those companies listed on the Canadian Stock Exchange. Also notes revenues, assets, shareholders' equity, earnings per share, return on common equity, return on capital, and number of employees. **Number listed:** 10

1. Seagram Co. Ltd. with C$3,406,000 thousand
2. Royal Bank of Canada, C$1,262,000

3. Canadian Imp. Bank of Commerce, C$1,015,000
4. Bank of Montreal, C$986,000
5. Bank of Nova Scotia, C$876,000
6. Thomson Corp., C$799,000
7. Toronto Dominion Bank, C$794,000
8. BCE Inc., C$782,000
9. Nova Corp., C$702,000
10. Alcan Aluminium, C$543,000

Source: *Globe and Mail,* Globe and Mail Report on Business 1000 (annual), July 1996, p. 102.

★ 948 ★

TOP CANADIAN COMPANIES, 1997

Ranked by: Sales, in millions of U.S. dollars. **Remarks:** Also notes net income, assets, and number of employees. **Number listed:** 500

1. BCE Inc. with $28,167.0 million
2. General Motors of Canada Ltd., $27,300.0
3. Ford Motor Co. of Canada Ltd., $25,536.6
4. Northern Telecom Ltd., $17,518.2
5. Chrysler Canada Ltd., $17,060.0
6. Royal Bank of Canada, $16,474.0
7. Canadian Imperial Bank of Commerce, $14,878.0
8. Bank of Montreal, $13,000.0
9. George Weston Ltd., $12,709.0
10. Bank of Nova Scotia, $12,402.0

Source: *Canadian Business,* Performance 500 Issue (annual), June 1997, p. 150.

★ 949 ★

TOP CORPORATIONS BY PROFITS IN CANADA, 1995

Ranked by: Profits, in thousands of Canadian dollars. **Number listed:** 100

1. Seagram Co. Ltd. with C$3,406,000 thousand
2. Royal Bank of Canada, C$1,262,000
3. Cdn. Imp. Bank of Commerce, C$1,015,000
4. Bank of Montreal, C$986,000
5. Bank of Nova Scotia, C$876,000
6. Thomson Corp., C$799,000
7. Toronto Dominion Bank, C$794,000
8. BCE Inc., C$782,000
9. Nova Corp., C$702,000
10. Alcan Aluminium, C$543,000

Source: *Globe and Mail's Report on Business Magazine,* July 1996, p. 102.

★ 950 ★

TOP CORPORATIONS IN CANADA BY MARKET VALUE, 1996

Ranked by: Market value as of May 31, 1996, in millions of U.S. dollars. **Remarks:** Also notes price per share, price to book value ratio, yield, sales, profits, assets, and return on equity. **Number listed:** 25

1. Northern Telecom with $13,900 million
2. Seagram, $12,918
3. BCE (Bell Canada Enterprises), $12,540
4. Barrick Gold, $11,318
5. Thomson, $9,729
6. Imperial Oil, $8,115
7. Royal Bank of Canada, $7,493
8. Alcan Aluminium, $7,386
9. Placer Dome, $7,045
10. Canadian Pacific, $7,017

Source: *Business Week,* Global 1,000 (annual), July 8, 1996, p. 52.

★ 951 ★

TOP PERFORMING CANADIAN STOCKS BY 5-YEAR SHARE APPRECIATION, 1995

Ranked by: 5-year share appreciation, in percent. **Remarks:** Data is shown only for those companies listed on the Canadian Stock Exchange. Also notes return on common equity and market price. **Number listed:** 50

1. Equisure Financial Network with 8,900.00%
2. Pan American Silver, 4,525.00%
3. Stampeder Exploration, 4,185.71%
4. Canabrava Diamond, 4,150.00%
5. Goran Capital, 3,858.33%
6. Cott Corp., 3,327.97%
7. Lytton Minerals, 3,238.46%
8. Spectrum Signal Processing, 3,025.00%
9. Tee-Comm Electronics, 2,619.29%
10. Taseko Mines, 2,578.57%

Source: *Globe and Mail,* Globe and Mail Report on Business 1000 (annual), July 1996, p. 94.

★ 952 ★

TOP PUBLICLY TRADED CORPORATIONS IN CANADA, 1995

Ranked by: Revenue, in millions of U.S. dollars. **Remarks:** Also notes net income, assets, market value, stock price, employees, and global rank. **Number listed:** 16

1. BCE with $17,942 million
2. Royal Bank of Canada, $11,137
3. Canadian Imperial Bank, $9,588
4. George Weston, $9,447
5. Alcan Aluminium, $9,282
6. Seagram, $8,935
7. Bank of Nova Scotia, $8,795
8. Bank of Montreal, $8,790
9. Thomson Corp., $7,225

10. Toronto-Dominion Bank, $6,333
Source: *Forbes,* Forbes Foreign Rankings (annual), July 15, 1996, p. 250.

Corporations – Charitable Contributions
See: **Charitable Contributions**

Corporations – China

★ 953 ★
LARGEST CORPORATIONS IN CHINA, 1995
Ranked by: Revenue, in millions of U.S. dollars. **Remarks:** Notes profits and global rank. **Number listed:** 2
1. Bank of China with $19,278.3 million
2. COFCO, $12,304.8

Source: *Fortune,* The Global 500: World's Biggest Corporations (annual), August 5, 1996, p. F-32.

★ 954 ★
LARGEST OVERSEAS CHINESE PUBLIC COMPANIES BY ASSETS, 1994
Ranked by: Value of Chinese company assets in country, in billions of U.S. dollars. **Number listed:** 7
1. Hong Kong with $173 billion
2. Thailand, $95
3. Singapore, $92
4. Taiwan, $89
5. Malaysia, $49
6. Indonesia, $33
7. Philippines, $8

Source: *California Management Review,* Summer 1996, p. 142.

★ 955 ★
LARGEST OVERSEAS CHINESE PUBLIC COMPANIES BY LOCATION, 1994
Ranked by: Number of Chinese companies in a country. **Number listed:** 7
1. Indonesia with 396 companies
2. Taiwan, 159
3. Hong Kong, 123
4. Malaysia, 83
5. Singapore, 52
6. Thailand, 39
7. Philippines, 8

Source: *California Management Review,* Summer 1996, p. 142.

Corporations – Denmark

★ 956 ★
LEADING CORPORATIONS IN DENMARK BY SALES
Ranked by: Sales, in thousands of U.S. dollars. **Number listed:** 46
1. FDB Faellesforeningen for Danmarks Brugsforeninge with $4,751,539 thousand
2. Tele Danmark A.S., $3,393,107
3. Unidanmark Gruppen Aktieselskab, $3,255,093
4. FLS Industries Aktieselskab, $3,245,111
5. Danisco A.S., $2,914,263
6. The East Asiatic Company Ltd., $2,596,413
7. ISS International Service System Aktiesselskab, $2,591,030
8. Kone Elevator Aktieselskab, $1,714,601
9. Monberg og Thorsen Aktieselskab, $1,416,531
10. Korn og Foderstof Kompagniet (Koncern) Aktiesels, $1,331,556

Source: *Europe's 15,000 Largest Companies* (annual), Dun & Bradstreet, 1997, p. 75.

★ 957 ★
TOP CORPORATIONS IN DENMARK BY MARKET VALUE, 1996
Ranked by: Market value as of May, 31, 1996, in millions of U.S. dollars. **Remarks:** Also notes price per share, price to book value ratio, yield, sales, profits, assets, and return on equity. **Number listed:** 7
1. Tele Danmark with $6,436 million
2. Novo-Nordisk, $5,148
3. Dampskibsselskabet Svenborg, $4,848
4. Dampskibsselskabet AF 1912, $4,757
5. Carlsberg, $3,603
6. Den Danske Bank, $3,309
7. Sophus Berendsen, $3,183

Source: *Business Week,* Global 1,000 (annual), July 8, 1996, p. 52.

Corporations – Europe

★ 958 ★
EUROPE'S LARGEST EMPLOYERS
Ranked by: Number of employees. **Remarks:** Also notes sales. **Number listed:** 10
1. Siemens A.G. with 376,100
2. Deutsche Post A.G., 342,413
3. Deutsche Bahn A.G., 331,552
4. Daimler-Benz A.G., 321,222
5. Unilever Plc, 308,000
6. La Poste, 293,040
7. Philips Electronics NV, 265,100

8. Volkswagen A.G., 242,285
9. Deutsche Telekom A.G., 231,720
10. Nestle S.A., 212,687

Source: *Duns Europa* (annual), vol. 4, Dun & Bradstreet, 1997, p. 141+.

★ 959 ★

EUROPEAN COMPANIES POSTING THE GREATEST LOSS

Ranked by: Loss, in thousands of U.S. dollars. **Number listed:** 100

1. IRI Istituto Per La Ricostruzione Industriale S.P.A. with $6,448,356 thousand
2. Alcatel Alsthom, $5,234,638
3. Daimler-Benz A.G., $3,754,628
4. SNCF-Ste National des Chemins de Fers Francais, $3,390,877
5. Bourgela, $2,267,267
6. Daimler-Benz Aerospace A.G., $1,330,957
7. Ing C. Olivetti & Co. S.P.A., $960,086
8. Coop Farmaceutica Espanola, $925,078
9. Kloeckner-Humboldt-Deutz A.G. (KHD), $829,106
10. Fisons Plc, $720,496

Source: *Europe's 15,000 Largest Companies* (annual), Dun & Bradstreet, 1997, p. 89+.

★ 960 ★

EUROPEAN COMPANIES WITH THE HIGHEST TURNOVER, 1996

Ranked by: Turnover, in millions of U.S. dollars. **Number listed:** 60

1. Royal Dutch/Shell (Netherlands/United Kingdom) with $108,555.6 million
2. Daimler Benz (Germany), $68,785.0
3. Siemens (Germany), $58,963.1
4. Volkswagen (Germany), $58,535.3
5. ENI (Italy), $57,321.7
6. British Petroleum (United Kingdom), $56,318.8
7. Fiat (Italy), $49,231.6
8. Unilever plc/NV (Netherlands/United Kingdom), $49,159.3
9. IRI (Italy), $48,171.2
10. Nestle (Switzerland), $45,858.6

Source: *Financial Times,* FT Top 500 (annual), January 24, 1997, p. 28.

★ 961 ★

LARGEST EMPLOYERS IN EUROPE, 1996

Ranked by: Number of employees. **Remarks:** Includes 1995 rank. **Number listed:** 25

1. Siemens (Germany) with 376,100 employees
2. Daimler-Benz (Germany), 321,222
3. Unilever plc/NV (Netherlands/United Kingdom), 308,000
4. Gazprom (Russia), 300,000

5. Philips (Netherlands), 263,554
6. Volkswagen (Germany), 242,285
7. Fiat (Italy), 240,517
8. Generale des Eaux (France), 221,157
9. Nestle (Switzerland), 220,172
10. ABB Asea Brown Boveri (Sweden), 209,637

Source: *Financial Times,* FT Top 500 (annual), January 24, 1997, p. 19.

★ 962 ★

LARGEST EUROPEAN CORPORATIONS BY MARKET CAPITALIZATION, 1996

Ranked by: Market capitalization, in millions of U.S. dollars. **Remarks:** Also notes turnover and profit. **Number listed:** 500

1. Royal Dutch/Shell (Netherlands/United Kingdom) with $135,350.2 million
2. Roche Holding (Switzerland), $72,031.9
3. British Petroleum (United Kingdom), $58,197.6
4. Glaxo Wellcome (United Kingdom), $52,300.6
5. HSBC Holdings (United Kingdom), $49,952.2
6. Sandoz (Switzerland), $46,302.4
7. Nestle (Switzerland), $44,745.8
8. Unilever plc/NV (Netherlands/United Kingdom), $43,063.2
9. ENI (Italy), $41,006.3
10. Allianz Holding (Germany), $40,494.1

Source: *Financial Times,* FT Top 500 (annual), January 24, 1997, p. 9+.

★ 963 ★

LARGEST EUROPEAN EMPLOYERS, 1996

Ranked by: Number of employees. **Number listed:** 25

1. Siemens with 376,100 employees
2. Daimler-Benz, 321,222
3. Unilever plc/NV, 308,000
4. Gazprom, 300,000
5. Philips, 263,554
6. Volkswagen, 242,285
7. Fiat, 240,517
8. Generale des Eaux, 221,157
9. Nestle, 220,172
10. ABB Asea Brown Boveri, 209,637

Source: *Financial Times,* January 24, 1997, p. 19.

★ 964 ★

LARGEST EUROPEAN INDUSTRIAL COMPANIES, 1995

Ranked by: Sales, in thousands of U.S. dollars. **Remarks:** Also notes previous year's rank, type of industry, percent change in sales, and percent change in local currencies. **Number listed:** 500

1. Daimler-Benz A.G. with $72,346,118 thousand
2. Siemens A.G., $62,015,650
3. Volkswagen A.G., $61,565,709

4. Royal Dutch Petroleum Company (Shell), $59,540,265
5. British Petroleum Co. Plc, $56,065,217
6. Veba A.G., $50,563,823
7. Unilever NV, $49,718,046
8. Nestle SA, $49,086,642
9. Fiat S.P.A., $47,125,748
10. RWE A.G., $44,424,648

Source: *Europe's 15,000 Largest Companies* (annual), Dun & Bradstreet, 1997, p. 92+.

★ 965 ★
TOP EUROPEAN COMPANIES BY PROFITABILITY
Ranked by: Profits as a percent of sales. **Number listed:** 500

1. EDP-Electricidade De Portugal SA with 1,249.6%
2. Repsol SA, 407.8%
3. Reche Y Gilabert SA, 180.0%
4. Kampa-Haus A.G., 166.6%
5. Castrol Ltd., 133.4%
6. Oldham Estate Company Plc, 93.6%
7. News International Plc, 92.5%
8. Group Bruxelles Lambert, 75.8%
9. Volvo Cars Europe Coordination NV, 69.2%
10. Newscorp Investments Ltd., 69.0%

Source: *Europe's 15,000 Largest Companies* (annual), Dun & Bradstreet, 1997, p. 49.

★ 966 ★
TOP EUROPEAN COMPANIES BY PROFITS
Ranked by: Profits, in thousands of U.S. dollars. **Number listed:** 500

1. Deutsche Telekom A.G. with $7,204,639 thousand
2. ENI Group, $5,194,453
3. Royal Dutch Petroleum Company (Shell), $4,975,360
4. Shell Transportation & Trading Co. Plc, $4,953,416
5. British Telecommunications Plc, $4,687,888
6. Nestle SA, $3,902,841
7. Glaxo Wellcome Plc, $3,706,521
8. BAT Industries Plc, $3,701,863
9. Nuclear Electric Plc, $3,038,819
10. British Petroleum Co. Plc, $3,021,739

Source: *Europe's 15,000 Largest Companies* (annual), Dun & Bradstreet, 1997, p. 39.

★ 967 ★
TOP EUROPEAN COMPANIES BY SALES
Ranked by: Sales, in thousands of U.S. dollars. **Number listed:** 500

1. Daimler-Benz A.G. with $72,346,118 thousand
2. Siemens A.G., $62,015,650
3. Volkswagen A.G., $61,565,709

4. Royal Dutch Petroleum Company (Shell), $59,540,265
5. British Petroleum Co. Plc, $56,065,217
6. Veba A.G., $50,563,823
7. Mercedes-Benz A.G., $50,324,879
8. Unilever NV, $49,718,046
9. Nestle SA, $49,086,642
10. Fiat S.P.A., $47,125,748

Source: *Europe's 15,000 Largest Companies* (annual), Dun & Bradstreet, 1997, p. 29.

★ 968 ★
TOP EUROPEAN COMPANIES BY SALES
Ranked by: Sales, in millions of European Currency Units (ECUs). **Remarks:** Also notes number of employees. **Number listed:** 5

1. NV Kon. Nederlandse Petroleum Maatschappij with 86,900 million ECUs
2. Daimler-Benz A.G., 47,001
3. Siemens A.G., 40,290
4. Volkswagen A.G., 39,997
5. British Petroleum Co. Plc, 38,482
6. Unilever Nederland BV, 37,524
7. Unilever NV, 37,524
8. Nestle S.A., 36,418
9. Britoil Plc, 35,295
10. Metro Holding A.G., 35,204

Source: *Duns Europa* (annual), vol. 4, Dun & Bradstreet, 1997, p. 67+.

★ 969 ★
TOP EUROPEAN FIRMS BY TURNOVER, 1996
Ranked by: Turnover, in millions of U.S. dollars. **Number listed:** 60

1. Royal Dutch/Shell with $108,555.6 million
2. Daimler Benz, $68,785.0
3. Siemens, $58,963.1
4. Volkswagen, $58,535.3
5. ENI, $57,321.7
6. British Petroleum, $56,318.8
7. Fiat, $49,231.6
8. Unilever plc/NV, $49,159.3
9. IRI, $48,171.2
10. Nestle, $45,858.6

Source: *Financial Times*, January 24, 1997, p. 28.

Corporations – Finland

★ 970 ★
LARGEST COMPANIES IN FINLAND
Ranked by: Sales, in thousands of U.S. dollars. **Number listed:** 100

1. Neste Oy with $9,979,964 thousand
2. Repola Ltd., $7,645,202

3. Nokia AB Oy, $6,949,702
4. Kesko Oy, $6,088,733
5. Kymmene Oy, $4,960,895
6. Enso-Gutzeit Oy, $4,850,859
7. Outokumpu Oy, $3,904,011
8. Kemira Oy, $2,844,640
9. Yhtyneet Paperitehtaat Oy, $2,809,405
10. Metra, $2,445,073

Source: *Europe's 15,000 Largest Companies* (annual), Dun & Bradstreet, 1997, p. 85.

★ 971 ★
TOP CORPORATIONS IN FINLAND BY MARKET VALUE, 1996

Ranked by: Market value as of May, 31, 1996, in millions of U.S. dollars. **Remarks:** Also notes price per share, price to book value ratio, yield, sales, profits, assets, and return on equity. **Number listed:** 2

1. Nokia with $13,010 million
2. UPM-Kymmene, $5,144

Source: *Business Week,* Global 1,000 (annual), July 8, 1996, p. 54.

★ 972 ★
TOP PUBLICLY TRADED CORPORATIONS IN FINLAND, 1995

Ranked by: Revenue, in millions of U.S. dollars. **Remarks:** Also notes net income, assets, market value, stock price, employees, and global rank. **Number listed:** 4

1. UPM-Kymmene with $12,535 million
2. Neste, $9,924
3. Nokia, $8,430
4. Kesko Group, $6,054

Source: *Forbes,* Forbes Foreign Rankings (annual), July 15, 1996, p. 274.

Corporations, Foreign

★ 973 ★
LARGEST PUBLIC COMPANIES OUTSIDE THE U.S., 1994

Ranked by: Revenue, in millions of U.S. dollars. **Remarks:** Also notes number of employees. **Number listed:** 25

1. Mitsubishi (Japan) with $184,510 million
2. Mitsui & Co. (Japan), $181,661
3. Itochu (Japan), $169,300
4. Sumitomo (Japan), $167,662
5. Marubeni (Japan), $161,184
6. Toyota Motor (Japan), $111,139
7. Royal Dutch/Shell Group (Netherlands/U.K.), $109,853
8. Nissho Iwai (Japan), $97,963

9. Hitachi (Japan), $84,233
10. Nippon Tel. & Tel., $82,002

Source: *Forbes,* Forbes Foreign Rankings (annual), July 15, 1996, p. 242.

★ 974 ★
MAJOR U.S. FIRMS IN GERMANY, 1995

Ranked by: Turnover, in billions of deutschmarks (DM). **Remarks:** Notes each firm's primary business. **Number listed:** 10

1. Adam Opel AG with DM25.9 billion
2. Ford-Werke AG, DM25.0
3. IBM Deutschland GmbH, DM12.2
4. Esso AG, DM9.9
5. Hewlett-Packard GmbH, DM8.8
6. Coca-Cola GmbH, DM7.8
7. Procter & Gamble GmbH, DM6.9
8. Mobil Oil Ag, DM6.3
9. ITT Gesellschaft fur Beteiligungen mbH, DM4.9
10. Kraft Jacobs Suchard, DM4.5

Source: *Euromoney*, February 1997, p. 31.

Corporations – France

★ 975 ★
LARGEST COMPANIES IN FRANCE

Ranked by: Sales, in thousands of U.S. dollars. **Number listed:** 100

1. Elf Aquitaine with $42,464,778 thousand
2. Electricite De France, $38,554,953
3. Alcatel Alsthom, $32,958,184
4. France Telecom, $26,438,400
5. Carrefour SA, $25,172,272
6. Promodes Sa, $20,565,586
7. Lyonnaise Des Eaux, $20,164,604
8. Peugeot (Automobiles) SA, $18,088,531
9. Altus Finance, $17,441,979
10. Rhone-Poulenc SA, $17,338,308

Source: *Europe's 15,000 Largest Companies* (annual), Dun & Bradstreet, 1997, p. 77.

★ 976 ★
TOP CORPORATIONS IN FRANCE BY MARKET VALUE, 1996

Ranked by: Market value as of May, 31, 1996, in millions of U.S. dollars. **Remarks:** Also notes price per share, price to book value ratio, yield, sales, profits, assets, and return on equity. **Number listed:** 43

1. LVMH Moet Hennessy Louis Vuitton with $21,149 million
2. Carrefour, $21,027
3. Elf Aquitaine, $19,578
4. L'Oreal, $18,676

5.   Total, $17,059
6.   Alcatel Alsthom, $13,698
7.   Compagnie Generale Des Eaux, $12,693
8.   L'Air Liquide, $11,511
9.   Axa, $10,739
10. Compagnie de Saint-Gobain, $10,654

Source: *Business Week,* Global 1,000 (annual), July 8, 1996, p. 54.

★ 977 ★

TOP PUBLICLY TRADED CORPORATIONS IN FRANCE, 1995

Ranked by: Revenue, in millions of U.S. dollars. **Remarks:** Also notes net income, assets, market value, stock price, employees, and global rank. **Number listed:** 46

1.   BCE with $17,942 million
2.   Royal Bank of Canada, $11,132
3.   Canadian Imperial Bank, $9,588
4.   George Weston, $9,447
5.   Alcan Aluminium, $9,287
6.   Seagram, $8,935
7.   Bank of Nova Scotia, $8,795
8.   Bank of Montreal, $8,790
9.   Thomson Corp., $7,225
10. Toronto-Dominion Bank, $6,333

Source: *Forbes,* Forbes Foreign Rankings (annual), July 15, 1996, p. 252.

Corporations – Germany

★ 978 ★

LARGEST COMPANIES IN GERMANY

Ranked by: Sales, in thousands of U.S. dollars. **Number listed:** 100

1.   Daimler-Benz A.G. with $72,346,118 thousand
2.   Siemens A.G., $62,015,650
3.   Volkswagen A.G., $61,565,709
4.   Veba A.G., $50,563,823
5.   Mercedes-Benz A.G., $50,324,879
6.   Deutsche Telekom A.G., $46,206,246
7.   RWE A.G., $44,424,648
8.   Edeka Group, $37,169,007
9.   Hoechst A.G., $34,454,272
10. Tengelmann Group, $34,863,410

Source: *Europe's 15,000 Largest Companies* (annual), Dun & Bradstreet, 1997, p. 74+.

★ 979 ★

TOP CORPORATIONS IN GERMANY BY MARKET VALUE, 1996

Ranked by: Market value as of May, 31, 1996, in millions of U.S. dollars. **Remarks:** Also notes price per share, price to book value ratio, yield, sales, profits, assets, and return on equity. **Number listed:** 35

1.   Allianz Holding with $36,942 million
2.   Siemens, $31,369
3.   Daimler-Benz, $28,048
4.   Veba, $25,520
5.   Bayer, $23,553
6.   Deutsche Bank, $23,441
7.   Hoechst, $19,546
8.   RWE, $19,495
9.   BASF, $16,926
10. Munchener Ruck., $14,582

Source: *Business Week,* Global 1,000 (annual), July 8, 1996, p. 54.

★ 980 ★

TOP INDUSTRIAL COMPANIES IN GERMANY, 1995

Ranked by: Turnover, in millions of deutsche marks. **Number listed:** 500

1.   Daimler-Benz A.G. with 103,549 million
2.   Siemens A.G., 88,763
3.   Volkswagen A.G., 88,119
4.   Metro A.G., 75,118
5.   Veba A.G., 72,372
6.   Mercedes-Benz A.G., 72,030
7.   Deutsche Telekom A.G., 66,135
8.   RWE A.G., 63,585
9.   EDEKA Group, 53,200
10. Hoechst A.G., 52,177

Source: *Germany's Top 500: A Handbook of Germany's Largest Corporations* (annual), 1997, p. 1+.

★ 981 ★

TOP PUBLICLY TRADED CORPORATIONS IN GERMANY, 1995

Ranked by: Revenue, in millions of U.S. dollars. **Remarks:** Also notes net income, assets, market value, stock price, employees, and global rank. **Number listed:** 39

1.   Daimler-Benz Group with $72,253 million
2.   Volkswagen Group, $61,487
3.   Siemens Group, $60,673
4.   VEBA Group, $46,278
5.   Allianz Worldwide, $43,486
6.   Deutsche Bank Group, $38,418
7.   Hoechst Group, $36,407
8.   RWE Group, $35,383
9.   BASF Group, $32,257
10. BMW-Bayerische Motor, $32,198

Source: *Forbes,* Forbes Foreign Rankings (annual), July 15, 1996, p. 254.

Corporations – Hong Kong

★ 982 ★
LARGEST COMPANIES IN HONG KONG
Ranked by: Sales, in thousands of U.S. dollars. **Number listed:** 100

1. Peregrine Investments Holdings Ltd. with $10,913,587 thousand
2. Swire Pacific Ltd., $6,939,023
3. First Pacific Company Ltd., $5,295,526
4. Hutchison Whampoa Ltd., $4,529,712
5. Cathay Pacific Airways Ltd., $3,938,441
6. Hong Kong Telecommunications Ltd., $3,802,806
7. Sun Hung Kai Properties Ltd., $2,566,440
8. New World Development Co. Ltd., $2,257,575
9. China Light & Power Co. Ltd., $2,207,824
10. Jardine International Motor Holdings Ltd., $1,882,793

Source: *Asia's 7,500 Largest Companies* (annual), Dun & Bradstreet, 1997, p. 62+.

★ 983 ★
LEADING COMPANIES IN HONG KONG
Ranked by: Scores (1-7) based on a survey response of over 4,000 professionals throughout Asia. Respondents were asked to rate companies on their quality of services/products offered, long-term management vision, response to customer needs, and financial soundness. **Number listed:** 10

1. Hongkong Bank with 5.95
2. Mass Transit Railway Corp., 5.44
3. Cathay Pacific Airways, 5.41
4. Cheung Kong, 5.37
5. Hang Seng Bank, 5.35
6. Swire Pacific, 5.33
7. Hutchison Whampoa, 5.16
8. Sun Hung Kai Properties, 5.16
9. Hongkong Telecom, 5.02
10. China Light & Power, 4.92

Source: *Far Eastern Economic Review,* Review 200 (annual), January 2, 1997, p. 48.

★ 984 ★
TOP CORPORATIONS IN HONG KONG BY MARKET VALUE, 1996
Ranked by: Market value as of May, 31, 1996, in millions of U.S. dollars. **Remarks:** Also notes price per share, price to book value ratio, yield, sales, profits, assets, and return on equity. **Number listed:** 17

1. Sun Hung Kai Properties with $24,397 million
2. Hutchison Whampoa, $23,219
3. Hong Kong Telecommunications, $20,973
4. Hang Seng Bank, $20,158
5. Cheung Kong Holdings, $17,000

6. Swire Pacific, $14,086
7. Henderson Land Development, $12,431
8. China Light & Power, $9,468
9. Citic Pacific, $8,767
10. Wharf (Holdings), $8,369

Source: *Business Week,* Global 1,000 (annual), July 8, 1996, p. 56.

★ 985 ★
TOP PUBLICLY TRADED CORPORATIONS IN HONG KONG, 1995
Ranked by: Revenue, in millions of U.S. dollars. **Remarks:** Notes net income, assets, market value, stock price, employees, and global rank. **Number listed:** 4

1. Jardine Matheson Holdings with $10,636 million
2. Swire Pacific, $6,937
3. Dairy Farm International, $6,236
4. First Pacific, $5,250

Source: *Forbes,* Forbes Foreign Rankings (annual), July 15, 1996, p. 274.

Corporations – India

★ 986 ★
FIRMS WITH THE LOWEST GROWTH IN SALES IN INDIA
Ranked by: Increase in profits, shown in percent. **Remarks:** Lists profits for 1995 and 1996 in Rs crore. **Number listed:** 10

1. Essar Steel with -67.73% increase
2. RCF, -55.54%
3. Jindal Iron, -43.04%
4. Essar Shipping, -34.12%
5. ONGC, -14.88%
6. Indo Gulf Fertilisers, -13.84%
7. GE Shipping, -11.21%
8. ITC, -0.21%
9. Jaiprakash Industries, 1.94%
10. Madras Refineries, 2.08%

Source: *Business India*, October 21, 1996, p. 138.

★ 987 ★
LARGEST COMPANIES IN INDIA
Ranked by: Sales, in thousands of U.S. dollars. **Number listed:** 50

1. Astra International Pt. with $5,103 thousand
2. Telekomunikasi Indonesia, $2,232
3. Indocement Tunggal Prakarsa Pt., $1,724
4. Indofood Sukses Makmur, $914
5. Indah Kiat Pulp & Paper Corp. Pt., $907
6. Hanjaya Mandala Sampoerna, $738
7. Matahari Putra Prima, $626
8. Unilever Indonesia Pt., $586

9. Bakrie & Brothers Bhd., $552
10. Pabrik Kertas Tjiwi Kimia, $543

Source: *Asia's 7,500 Largest Companies* (annual), 1997, p. 63.

★ 988 ★
LARGEST INDIAN-AMERICAN FIRMS, 1995
Ranked by: Revenue, in millions of U.S. dollars.
Remarks: Lists CEO of each firm, year established, number of employees, and its primary industry. **Number listed:** 100

1. Vinmar Group with $467.00 million
2. ATCO Rubber Products, Inc., $121.43
3. Kikomo Ltd., $110.03
4. Mastech Systems Corporation, $103.67
5. ANSTEC, INC., $59.14
6. Attronica Computers, Inc., $50.60
7. System Resources Corp., $47.43
8. DLZ Corporation, $46.46
9. ACRO Service Corp., $39.30
10. Durgam Industries, $37.53

Source: *India Abroad*, August 16, 1996, p. 29.

★ 989 ★
LEADING COMPANIES IN INDIA
Ranked by: Scores (1-7) based on a survey response of over 4,000 professionals throughout Asia. Respondents were asked to rate companies on their quality of services/products offered, long-term management vision, response to customer needs, and financial soundness.
Number listed: 10

1. Hindustan Lever with 6.41
2. Tata Engineering & Locomotive, 6.29
3. Larsen & Toubro, 6.16
4. Tata Iron & Steel Co., 6.15
5. Bajaj Auto, 6.10
6. Titan Watches, 6.03
7. ITC Ltd., 5.77
8. Reliance Industries, 5.75
9. Brooke Bond Lipton India, 5.61
10. MRF Ltd./MRF Tyres, 5.52

Source: *Far Eastern Economic Review,* Review 200 (annual), January 2, 1997, p. 48.

Corporations – Indonesia

★ 990 ★
TOP COMPANIES IN INDONESIA
Ranked by: Scores (1-7) based on a survey response of over 4,000 professionals throughout Asia. Respondents were asked to rate companies on their quality of services/products offered, long-term management vision, response to customer needs, and financial soundness.
Number listed: 10

1. Astra International with 5.96
2. Toyota Astra Motor, 5.78
3. Indosat, 5.60
4. Indofood, 5.32
5. Ciputra Development, 5.29
6. Bank Central Asia, 5.26
7. HM Sampoerna, 5.21
8. Bank Bali, 5.19
9. Gudang Garam, 5.10
10. Bank Niaga, 5.06

Source: *Far Eastern Economic Review,* Review 200 (annual), January 2, 1997, p. 48.

Corporations – Ireland

★ 991 ★
LARGEST COMPANIES IN IRELAND
Ranked by: Sales, in thousands of U.S. dollars. **Number listed:** 87

1. Jefferson Smurfit Group Plc with $4,861,064 thousand
2. CRH Plc, $3,062,990
3. Avonmore Foods Plc, $1,963,920
4. Telecom Eireann, $1,753,724
5. Electricity Supply Board (ESB), $1,565,172
6. Dunnes Stores Ltd., $1,482,609
7. Kerry Group Plc, $1,410,282
8. Fyffes Plc, $1,358,483
9. Aer Lingus Plc, $1,274,887
10. Waterford Foods Plc, $1,138,988

Source: *Europe's 15,000 Largest Companies* (annual), Dun & Bradstreet, 1997, p. 80 +.

Corporations – Italy

★ 992 ★
LARGEST CORPORATIONS IN ITALY
Ranked by: Sales, in thousands of U.S. dollars. **Number listed:** 100

1. Fiat Spa with $47,125,748 thousand
2. ENI Group, $36,673,810

3. Agip Petroli Spa, $23,442,875
4. Telecom Italia SpA, $18,965,208
5. Ferruzzi Finanziaria Spa, $16,765,836
6. Montedison Spa, $15,484,399
7. Fiat Auto Spa, $14,798,702
8. SIP Soc. Ital. Per l'Escercizo Delle Telecomnicz Spa, $14,757,012
9. Italaina Petroli Spa, $9,901,991
10. CIR Spa (Compagnie Industriali Riunite), $7,982,541

Source: *Europe's 15,000 Largest Companies* (annual), Dun & Bradstreet, 1997, p. 79.

★ 993 ★
TOP CORPORATIONS IN ITALY BY MARKET VALUE, 1996
Ranked by: Market value as of May, 31, 1996, in millions of U.S. dollars. **Remarks:** Also notes price per share, price to book value ratio, yield, sales, profits, assets, and return on equity. **Number listed:** 17

1. ENI with $38,189 million
2. Assicurazioni Generali, $19,078
3. Stet, $17,814
4. Telecom Italia Mobile, $16,365
5. Telecom Italia, $15,960
6. Fiat Group, $14,566
7. Istituto Nazionale Delle Assicurazioni, $6,026
8. Alleanza Assicurazioni, $5,526
9. Istituto Bancario San Paolo di Torino, $4,950
10. Istituto Mobiliare Italiano, $4,896

Source: *Business Week,* Global 1,000 (annual), July 8, 1996, p. 56.

★ 994 ★
TOP PUBLICLY TRADED COMPANIES IN ITALY, 1995
Ranked by: Revenue, in millions of U.S. dollars. **Remarks:** Also notes net income, assets, market value, stock price, employees, and global rank. **Number listed:** 14

1. Fiat Group with $46,467 million
2. ENI, $34,924
3. STET, $22,943
4. Generali Group, $20,487
5. Sanpaolo Group, $14,951
6. Montedison Group, $14,842
7. Banca di Roma, $11,634
8. Credito Italiano, $10,322
9. Banca Commerciale Italian, $10,119
10. Finmeccanica, $7,515

Source: *Forbes,* Forbes Foreign Rankings (annual), July 15, 1996, p. 256.

Corporations – Japan

★ 995 ★
LARGEST COMPANIES IN JAPAN
Ranked by: Sales, in thousands of U.S. dollars. **Number listed:** 100

1. Mitsubishi Corp. with $172,766,300 thousand
2. Mitsui & Co. Ltd., $170,098,873
3. Itochu Corp., $162,548,281
4. Sumitomo Corp., $156,990,893
5. Marubeni Corp., $151,381,631
6. Toyota Motor Corp., $104,065,427
7. Nissho Iwai Corp., $91,728,106
8. Hitachi Ltd., $78,871,941
9. Nippon Telegraph & Telephone Corp., $76,782,310
10. Matsushita Electric Industrial Co. Ltd., $65,969,436

Source: *Asia's 7,500 Largest Companies* (annual), Dun & Bradstreet, 1997, p. 64+.

★ 996 ★
TOP COMPANIES IN JAPAN
Ranked by: Scores (1-7) based on a survey response of over 4,000 professionals throughout Asia. Respondents were asked to rate companies on their quality of services/products offered, long-term management vision, response to customer needs, and financial soundness. **Number listed:** 10

1. Sony with 6.08
2. Toyota Motor, 6.00
3. Canon, 5.67
4. Honda Motor, 5.66
5. Nintendo, 5.66
6. NEC, 5.42
7. Matsushita Electric Industrial, 5.38
8. Fujitsu, 5.34
9. Hitachi, 5.27
10. Sega Enterprises, 5.24

Source: *Far Eastern Economic Review,* Review 200 (annual), January 2, 1997, p. 48.

★ 997 ★
TOP CORPORATIONS IN JAPAN BY MARKET VALUE, 1996
Ranked by: Market value as of May, 31, 1996, in millions of U.S. dollars. **Remarks:** Also notes price per share, price to book value ratio, yield, sales, profits, assets, and return on equity. **Number listed:** 227

1. Nippon Telegraph & Telephone with $115,697 million
2. Bank of Tokyo-Mitsubishi, $110,286
3. Toyota Motor, $85,779
4. Fuji Bank, $62,988
5. Sumitomo Bank, $61,891

6. Industrial Bank of Japan, $60,472
7. Dai-Ichi Kangyo Bank, $56,294
8. Sanwa Bank, $55,829
9. Sakura Bank, $37,909
10. Nomura Securities, $37,044

Source: *Business Week,* Global 1,000 (annual), July 8, 1996, p. 56.

★ **998** ★

TOP FOREIGN FIRMS IN JAPAN, 1994
Ranked by: Equity-adjusted sales, in billions of U.S. dollars. **Number listed:** 20
1. IBM (U.S.) with $13.20 billion
2. Ford (U.S.), $11.16
3. Exxon (U.S.), $9.95
4. Mobil (U.S.), $8.67
5. Shell (U.K./Netherlands), $8.42
6. Caltex (U.S.), $6.87
7. General Motors (U.S.), $6.16
8. Xerox (U.S.), $4.20
9. Alcan (Canada), $3.03
10. Nestle (Switzerland), $2.52

Source: http:// 205.223.239.34/newscomm.html, January 17, 1997, p. 12.

★ **999** ★

TOP PUBLICLY TRADED CORPORATIONS IN JAPAN, 1995
Ranked by: Revenue, in millions of U.S. dollars. **Remarks:** Also notes net income, assets, market value, stock price, employees, and global rank. **Number listed:** 211
1. Mitsubishi with $184,510 million
2. Mitsui & Co., $181,661
3. Itochu, $169,300
4. Sumitomo, $167,662
5. Marubeni, $161,184
6. Toyota Motor, $111,139
7. Nissho Iwai, $97,963
8. Hitachi, $84,233
9. Nippon Tel. & Tel., $82,002
10. Matsushita Electric Indl., $70,454

Source: *Forbes,* Forbes Foreign Rankings (annual), July 15, 1996, p. 258.

Corporations – Korea, South

★ **1000** ★

LARGEST COMPANIES IN SOUTH KOREA BY REVENUE, 1995
Ranked by: Revenue, in millions of U.S. dollars. **Remarks:** Notes profits and global rank. **Number listed:** 12
1. Daewoo with $51,215.3 million

2. Samsung, $35,060.0
3. Ssangyong, $25,392.0
4. Sunkyong, $24,218.0
5. Samsung Electronics, $24,150.9
6. Hyundai, $23,221.2
7. Samsung Life, $16,448.8
8. Hyundai Motor, $13,726.5
9. LG International, $13,188.5
10. Korea Electric Power, $12,955.1

Source: *Fortune,* The Global 500: World's Biggest Corporations (annual), August 5, 1996, p. F-37.

★ **1001** ★

TOP PUBLICLY TRADED CORPORATIONS IN SOUTH KOREA, 1995
Ranked by: Revenue, in millions of U.S. dollars. **Remarks:** Also notes net income, assets, market value, stock price, employees, and global rank. **Number listed:** 15
1. Samsung with $24,964 million
2. Hyundai, $23,274
3. Samsung Electronics, $20,991
4. Daewoo, $19,480
5. Hyundai Motor, $13,757
6. LG International, $13,218
7. Korea Electric Power, $12,984
8. Yukong, $11,805
9. Pohang Iron and Steel, $11,206
10. LG Electronics, $8,547

Source: *Forbes,* Forbes Foreign Rankings (annual), July 15, 1996, p. 268.

Corporations – Latin America

★ **1002** ★

FOREIGN-OWNED COMPANIES IN LATIN AMERICA WITH THE MOST EMPLOYEES, 1994
Ranked by: Number of employees. **Remarks:** Notes country of origin. Autolatina Brasil, a joint venture between Ford and Volkswagen, was disbanded in 1995. **Number listed:** 9
1. General Motors Mexico with 76,426 employees
2. Autolatina Brasil, 47,000
3. Carrefour Comercial e Industrial, 22,658
4. General Motors do Brazil, 21,600
5. Fiat Automoveis, 17,701
6. Mercedes-Benz do Brasil, 16,536
7. Chrysler de Mexico, 10,445
8. Shell Brazil, 2,623
9. Esso Brasileira de Petroleo, 1,161

Source: *Business Latin America,* September 30, 1996, p. 8.

★ 1003 ★
TOP FOREIGN-OWNED COMPANIES IN LATIN AMERICA BY SALES, 1994
Ranked by: Sales, in millions of U.S. dollars. **Remarks:** Notes country of origin. Autolatina Brasil, a joint venture between Ford and Volkswagen, was disbanded in 1995. **Number listed:** 10
1. Autolatina Brasil with $9,660 million
2. Fiat Automoveis, $6,100
3. General Motors do Brasil, $5,873
4. Shell Brazil, $5,261
5. Chrysler de Mexico, $4,002
6. Carrefour Comercial e Industrial, $3,993
7. Ford Motors Company, $3,870
8. General Motors Mexico, $3,772
9. Mercedes-Benz do Brasil, $3,249
10. Esso Brasileira de Petroleo, $2,984

Source: *Business Latin America*, September 30, 1996, p. 8.

★ 1004 ★
TOP LATIN AMERICAN COMPANIES BY EMPLOYEES
Ranked by: Employees. **Number listed:** 1
1. Corporacion Venezolana de Transporte Silva CA with 333,333 employees
2. Contreras Morales Lucia, 160,018
3. Banco do Brasil SA, 119,380
4. Banco Bradesco SA, 74,580
5. Empresa Brasileira de Correios e Telegrafos, 70,000
6. Caixa Economica Federal, 65,000
7. Petroleo Brasileiro SA Petrobras, 51,399
8. General Motors de Mexico SA de CV, 50,000
9. Luguide Industria e Comercio de Confeccoes Ltda., 50,000
10. Petroleos de Venezuela SA, 49,218

Source: *Dun & Bradstreet's Latin America 25,000,* Top Businesses by Employees (annual), 1997, p. E1.

★ 1005 ★
TOP LATIN AMERICAN FIRMS BY PROFITS, 1995
Ranked by: Profits, in millions of U.S. dollars. **Number listed:** 10
1. PDVSA (Venezuela) with $2,922 million
2. Pemex (Mexico), $1,546
3. Telmex (Mexico), $1,475
4. Cemex (Mexico), $1,064
5. CFE (Mexico), $1,030
6. YPF (Argentina), $793
7. Codelco (Chile), $637
8. Industrial Min (Mexico), $607
9. Fiat (Brazil), $476
10. Telefonica (Argentina), $458

Source: *Business Latin America*, February 24, 1997, p. 8.

★ 1006 ★
TOP LATIN AMERICAN FIRMS BY SALES, 1995
Ranked by: Sales, in millions of U.S. dollars. **Number listed:** 10
1. PDVSA (Venezuela) with $26,463 million
2. Pemex (Mexico), $24,930
3. Petrobras (Brazil), $21,200
4. Petrobras Distribuidora (Brazil), $8,553
5. Volkswagen (Brazil), $7,222
6. Telmex (Mexico), $6,605
7. General Motors (Brazil), $6,391
8. Fiat (Brazil), $6,229
9. Souza Cruz (Brazil), $5,670
10. Shell (Brazil), $5,300

Source: *Business Latin America*, February 24, 1997, p. 8.

Corporations—Malaysia

★ 1007 ★
LARGEST COMPANIES IN MALAYSIA
Ranked by: Sales, in thousands of U.S. dollars. **Number listed:** 100
1. Sime Darby Bhd with $3,699,960 thousand
2. Tenaga Nasional Berhad, $2,700,000
3. Perlis Plantations Bhd., $2,404,987
4. Edaran Otomobil Nasional Bhd., $2,240,021
5. Telekom Malaysia Bhd., $2,068,846
6. Malaysian Airline System Bhd., $1,882,665
7. Federal Flour Mills Bhd., $1,677,680
8. Amsteel Corp. Bhd., $1,622,487
9. Perusahaan Otomobil Nasional Bhd., $1,460,582
10. Berjaya Group Bhd., $1,297,844

Source: *Asia's 7,500 Largest Companies* (annual), Dun & Bradstreet, 1997, p. 66+.

★ 1008 ★
LEADING COMPANIES IN MALAYSIA
Ranked by: Scores (1-7) based on a survey response of over 4,000 professionals throughout Asia. Respondents were asked to rate companies on their quality of services/products offered, long-term management vision, response to customer needs, and financial soundness. **Number listed:** 10
1. Genting with 5.93
2. Maybank, 5.62
3. Arab-Malaysian Merchant Bank, 5.56
4. Sime Darby, 5.55
5. Hong Leong Group, 5.34
6. Public Bank, 5.28
7. Petronas, 5.23
8. YTL Corp., 5.23
9. Rashid Hussain Berhad, 5.17

10. Hong Leong Bank, 4.99
Source: *Far Eastern Economic Review,* Review 200 (annual), January 2, 1997, p. 48.

Corporations – Mexico

★ 1009 ★
TOP COMPANIES IN MEXICO, 1996
Ranked by: Net sales, in U.S. dollars. **Remarks:** Includes data on profits, assets, profitability, efficiency, and international sales and notes the percent change over 1995 figures. **Number listed:** 100
1. Telefonos de Mexico with $6,936,501
2. Alfa, $3,661,884
3. Cemex, $3,489,388
4. Grupo Carso, $3,153,634
5. Cifra, $3,059,526
6. Valores Industriales, $2,573,917
7. FEMSA, $2,559,151
8. Vitro, $2,317,460
9. Grupo Industrial Bimbo, $1,983,591
10. Emprasas La Moderna, $1,894,199
Source: *Mexico Business,* July/August 1997, p. 44+.

★ 1010 ★
TOP PUBLICLY TRADED CORPORATIONS IN MEXICO, 1995
Ranked by: Revenue, in millions of U.S. dollars. **Remarks:** Also notes net income, assets, market value, stock price, employees, and global rank. **Number listed:** 2
1. Grupo Financiero Bancomer with $10,743 million
2. Telefonos de Mexico, $6,511
Source: *Forbes,* Forbes Foreign Rankings (annual), July 15, 1996, p. 274.

Corporations – Netherlands

★ 1011 ★
LARGEST COMPANIES IN THE NETHERLANDS
Ranked by: Sales, in thousands of U.S. dollars. **Number listed:** 100
1. Royal Dutch Petroleum Comapany (Shell) with $59,540,265 thousand
2. Unilever NV, $49,718,046
3. Philips Electronics NV, $40,210,841
4. Internationale Nederlanden Groep NV, $30,557,669
5. Koninklijke Ahold NV, $18,475,033
6. SHV Holdings NV, $16,195,184
7. Akzo Nobel NV, $13,404,029

8. Koninklijke PTT Nederland NV, $12,385,378
9. GEC Alsthom NV, $11,444,676
10. Nederlandse Gasunie NV, $10,601,584
Source: *Europe's 15,000 Largest Companies* (annual), Dun & Bradstreet, 1997, p. 82+.

★ 1012 ★
LARGEST COMPANIES IN THE NETHERLANDS BY REVENUE, 1995
Ranked by: Revenue, in millions of U.S. dollars. **Remarks:** Notes profits and global rank. **Number listed:** 8
1. Philips Electronics with $40,148.2 million
2. ING Group, $33,416.2
3. ABN AMRO Holding, $26,534.6
4. Koninklijke Ahold, $18,446.3
5. Rabobank, $13,428.6
6. Akzo Nobel, $13,383.2
7. Aegon, $13,066.1
8. Royal PTT Nederland, $12,186.7
Source: *Fortune,* The Global 500: World's Biggest Corporations (annual), August 5, 1996, p. F-36.

★ 1013 ★
TOP CORPORATIONS IN NETHERLANDS BY MARKET VALUE, 1996
Ranked by: Market value as of May, 31, 1996, in millions of U.S. dollars. **Remarks:** Also notes price per share, price to book value ratio, yield, sales, profits, assets, and return on equity. **Number listed:** 18
1. Royal Dutch Petroleum with $81,146 million
2. ING Groep, $24,035
3. Unilever NV, $21,729
4. ABN Amro Holdings, $17,340
5. Koninklijke PTT Nederland, $16,716
6. Aegon, $12,542
7. Philips Electronics, $12,216
8. Heineken, $11,353
9. Polygram, $10,516
10. Elsevier, $10,263
Source: *Business Week,* Global 1,000 (annual), July 8, 1996, p. 62.

★ 1014 ★
TOP PUBLICLY TRADED CORPORATIONS IN THE NETHERLANDS, 1995
Ranked by: Revenue, in millions of U.S. dollars. **Remarks:** Also notes net income, assets, market value, stock price, employees, and global rank. **Number listed:** 18
1. Royal Dutch/Shell Group with $109,853 million
2. Unilever, $49,638
3. Philips Group, $40,146
4. ING Group, $33,326
5. ABN-Amro Holding, $26,533

6. Fortis Group, $22,619
7. Ahold, $18,445
8. Akzo Nobel Group, $13,383
9. Aegon Insurance Group, $13,066
10. Royal PTT Nederlands, $11,929

Source: *Forbes,* Forbes Foreign Rankings (annual), July 15, 1996, p. 266.

Corporations – New Zealand

★ 1015 ★
TOP COMPANIES IN NEW ZEALAND, 1996
Ranked by: Turnover, in millions of New Zealand dollars (NZ$). **Remarks:** Also notes number of employees at each company. **Number listed:** 25

1. Fletcher Challenge Group with NZ$9,144 million
2. New Zealand Dairy Board, NZ$5,344
3. Telecom Corp. of New Zealand, NZ$3,220
4. Carter Holt Harvey, NZ$3,141
5. Brierley Investments, NZ$3,053
6. Air New Zealand, NZ$3,041
7. Lion Nathan, NZ$2,582
8. New Zealand Dairy Group, NZ$2,360
9. Progressive Enterprises, NZ$2,254
10. Bank of New Zealand, NZ$2,154

Source: *National Trade Data Bank*, February 20, 1997, p. IMI910220.

★ 1016 ★
TOP CORPORATIONS IN NEW ZEALAND BY MARKET VALUE, 1996
Ranked by: Market value as of May, 31, 1996, in millions of U.S. dollars. **Remarks:** Also notes price per share, price to book value ratio, yield, sales, profits, assets, and return on equity. **Number listed:** 2

1. Telecom Corp. of New Zealand with $7,678 million
2. Carter Holt Harvey, $3,773

Source: *Business Week,* Global 1,000 (annual), July 8, 1996, p. 62.

Corporations – Norway

★ 1017 ★
LARGEST COMPANIES IN NORWAY
Ranked by: Sales, in thousands of U.S. dollars. **Number listed:** 100

1. Den Norske Stats Oljeselskap AS Statoil with $15,600,607 thousand
2. Norsk Hydro AS, $12,623,612
3. Statoil Norge AS, $10,832,159

4. Kvaerner AS, $4,140,529
5. Orkla AS, $3,408,590
6. Norsk Hydro Produksjon AS, $3,141,812
7. Aker AS, $2,623,137
8. ABB Konsernet I Norge, $2,053,624
9. Siemens-Nixdorf Informasjonssystemer AS, $2,026,567
10. Norske Skogindustrier AS, $1,986,668

Source: *Europe's 15,000 Largest Companies* (annual), Dun & Bradstreet, 1997, p. 81+.

★ 1018 ★
LARGEST COMPANIES IN NORWAY BY REVENUE, 1995
Ranked by: Revenue, in millions of U.S. dollars. **Remarks:** Notes profits and global rank. **Number listed:** 2

1. Statoil with $13,648.2 million
2. Norsk Hydro, $12,577.8

Source: *Fortune,* The Global 500: World's Biggest Corporations (annual), August 5, 1996, p. F-37.

Corporations – Philippines

★ 1019 ★
PHILIPPINES' TOP CORPORATIONS BY SALES
Ranked by: Sales, in thousands of U.S. dollars. **Number listed:** 100

1. San Miguel Corp. with $3,021,104 thousand
2. Philippine Long Distance Telephone Co., $962,729
3. Philippine Airlines Inc., $931,188
4. Ayala Corporation, $928,631
5. Texas Instruments (Philippines) Inc., $489,091
6. Ayala Land Inc., $386,122
7. Toyota Motor Philippine Corporation, $332,048
8. Philippine Automotive Manufacturing Corp., $327,434
9. Pure Foods Corporation, $268,980
10. General Milling Corporation, $249,411

Source: *Asia's 7,500 Largest Companies* (annual), 1997, p. 67.

★ 1020 ★
TOP COMPANIES IN THE PHILIPPINES
Ranked by: Scores (1-7) based on a survey response of over 4,000 professionals throughout Asia. Respondents were asked to rate companies on their quality of services/products offered, long-term management vision, response to customer needs, and financial soundness. **Number listed:** 10

1. San Miguel with 6.42
2. Jollibee Foods, 6.26
3. Ayala Corp., 6.13

4. ShoeMart, 6.03
5. ABS-CBN Broadcasting, 5.79
6. Bank of Philippine Islands, 5.66
7. Metropolitan Bank & Trust, 5.46
8. Purefoods, 5.29
9. PCI Bank, 5.26
10. Far East Bank & Trust, 5.13

Source: *Far Eastern Economic Review,* Review 200 (annual), January 2, 1997, p. 48.

Corporations – Portugal

★ 1021 ★
LARGEST COMPANIES IN PORTUGAL

Ranked by: Sales, in thousands of U.S. dollars. **Number listed:** 100

1. Petrogal-Petroleos De Portugal SA with $4,652,362 thousand
2. Iglo - Industrias de Gelados Lda, $1,405,274
3. Transportes Aereos Portugueses SA, $1,084,732
4. Renault Portuguesa-Soc Ind e Comercial SA, $1,014,082
5. Shell Portuguesa SA, $916,927
6. Tabaqueira - Empresa Industrial De Tabacos SA, $916,479
7. Mobil Oil Portuguesa Lda, $689,089
8. Modelo Continente Hipermercados SA, $680,140
9. Telefones de Lisbona E Porto (TLP) SA, $634,859
10. General Motors De Portugal SA, $587,570

Source: *Europe's 15,000 Largest Companies* (annual), Dun & Bradstreet, 1997, p. 83+.

Corporations – Singapore

★ 1022 ★
SINGAPORE'S TOP CORPORATIONS BY SALES

Ranked by: Sales, in thousands of U.S. dollars. **Number listed:** 100

1. Singapore Airlines Ltd. with $4,634,782 thousand
2. Singapore Telecommunications Ltd., $2,485,683
3. Cycle & Carriage, $2,076,988
4. Fraser and Neave Ltd., $1,790,481
5. Keppel Corp. Ltd., $1,699,540
6. NatSteel Ltd., $1,464,368
7. City Developments Ltd., $1,394,132
8. Cycle & Carriage Ltd., $1,333,616
9. Neptune Orient Lines Ltd., $1,319,901

10. Singapore Petroleum Co. Ltd., $1,277,580

Source: *Asia's 7,500 Largest Companies* (annual), 1997, p. 68.

★ 1023 ★
TOP COMPANIES IN SINGAPORE

Ranked by: Scores (1-7) based on a survey response of over 4,000 professionals throughout Asia. Respondents were asked to rate companies on their quality of services/products offered, long-term management vision, response to customer needs, and financial soundness. **Number listed:** 10

1. Singapore Airlines with 6.44
2. Development Bank of Singapore, 5.41
3. Singapore Telecom, 5.35
4. United Overseas Bank, 5.33
5. Oversea-Chinese Banking Corp., 5.31
6. Shangri-La Hotel, 5.29
7. Overseas Union Bank, 5.06
8. Singapore MRT, 5.04
9. Asia Pacific Breweries, 5.01
10. Singapore Press Holdings, 5.01

Source: *Far Eastern Economic Review,* Review 200 (annual), January 2, 1997, p. 48.

★ 1024 ★
TOP CORPORATIONS IN SINGAPORE BY MARKET VALUE, 1996

Ranked by: Market value as of May, 31, 1996, in millions of U.S. dollars. **Remarks:** Also notes price per share, price to book value ratio, yield, sales, profits, assets, and return on equity. **Number listed:** 13

1. Singapore Telecommunications with $42,623 million
2. Singapore Airlines, $13,192
3. OCBC Overseas Chinese Bank, $11,608
4. United Overseas Bank, $8,279
5. Development Bank of Singapore, $8,050
6. Singapore Press Holdings, $6,335
7. City Developments, $6,037
8. Hongkong Land Holdings, $5,954
9. Jardine Matheson Holdings, $5,635
10. Overseas Union Bank, $4,823

Source: *Business Week,* Global 1,000 (annual), July 8, 1996, p. 62.

Corporations – South Africa

★ **1025** ★
LARGEST SOUTH AFRICAN FIRMS, 1996
Ranked by: Market capitalization, in millions of U.S. dollars. **Remarks:** Notes turnover and profits. **Number listed:** 50
1. Anglo American Corporation with $14,442.3 million
2. De Beers Consolidated Mines, $11,914.1
3. South African Breweries, $8,085.8
4. Liberty Life Association of Africa, $7,563.9
5. Sasol, $7,182.6
6. Gencor Ltd., $5,383.1
7. Standard Bank Investment Corp, $4,988.0
8. Rembrandt Group, $4,756.4
9. Liberty Holdings, $3,899.2
10. Anglo American Investment Trust, $3,244.7
Source: *Financial Times*, January 24, 1997, p. 43.

★ **1026** ★
TOP PUBLICLY TRADED CORPORATIONS IN SOUTH AFRICA, 1995
Ranked by: Revenue, in millions of U.S. dollars. **Remarks:** Also notes net income, assets, market value, stock price, employees, and global rank. **Number listed:** 3
1. South African Breweries with $8,189 million
2. Smith (CG), $6,386
3. AMIC-Anglo American Industries, $5,659
Source: *Forbes,* Forbes Foreign Rankings (annual), July 15, 1996, p. 274.

Corporations – Spain

★ **1027** ★
LARGEST COMPANIES IN SPAIN
Ranked by: Sales, in thousands of U.S. dollars. **Number listed:** 100
1. Empresa Nacional De Electricidad SA with $7,103,784 thousand
2. Iberdrola SA, $6,730,502
3. El Corte Ingles SA, $5,977,963
4. Fabricacion De Automoviles Renault Espana SA, $4,572,209
5. Autopistas Concesionaria Espanola SA, $4,285,226
6. SEAT SA, $3,763,553
7. Iberia - Lineas Aereas De Espana SA, $3,512,967
8. Fomento de Construcciones Y Contratas SA, $3,461,450
9. Citroen Hispania SA, $3,167,098

10. Sociedad Cooperativa De Consumo Eroski, $2,508,516
Source: *Europe's 15,000 Largest Companies* (annual), Dun & Bradstreet, 1997, p. 76.

★ **1028** ★
LARGEST COMPANIES IN SPAIN BY REVENUE, 1995
Ranked by: Revenue, in millions of U.S. dollars. **Remarks:** Notes profits and global rank. **Number listed:** 6
1. Teneo with $17,163.2 million
2. Repsol, $15,124.5
3. Santander Group, $13,966.9
4. Telefonica de Espana, $13,959.7
5. Banco Bibao Vizcaya, $11,914.8
6. Banco Central Hisp. Amer., $9,088.4
Source: *Fortune,* The Global 500: World's Biggest Corporations (annual), August 5, 1996, p. F-37.

★ **1029** ★
TOP CORPORATIONS IN SPAIN BY MARKET VALUE, 1996
Ranked by: Market value as of May, 31, 1996, in millions of U.S. dollars. **Remarks:** Also notes price per share, price to book value ratio, yield, sales, profits, assets, and return on equity. **Number listed:** 12
1. Telefonica Nacional de Espana with $16,833 million
2. Endesa, $16,033
3. Repsol, $10,239
4. Iberdrola, $9,399
5. Banco Bilbao Vizcaya, $8,480
6. Banco de Santander, $7,272
7. Gas Natural SDG, $6,570
8. Argentaria, Corp. Bancaria de Espana, $5,247
9. Banco Popular Espanol, $5,032
10. Pryca, $4,440
Source: *Business Week,* Global 1,000 (annual), July 8, 1996, p. 62.

★ **1030** ★
TOP PUBLICLY TRADED CORPORATIONS IN SPAIN, 1995
Ranked by: Revenue, in millions of U.S. dollars. **Remarks:** Also notes net income, assets, market value, stock price, employees, and global rank. **Number listed:** 9
1. Repsol with $14,586 million
2. Telefonica, $13,959
3. Banco Santander, $13,084
4. Banco Bibao Vizcaya, $11,327
5. Banco Central Hispanoamer, $8,770
6. Argentaria, $8,538
7. Endesa Group, $7,089
8. Iberdrola, $6,490

9. Cepsa-Cia Espanola de Pet, $6,332
Source: *Forbes,* Forbes Foreign Rankings (annual), July 15, 1996, p. 269.

Corporations – Sweden

★ 1031 ★
LARGEST COMPANIES IN SWEDEN
Ranked by: Sales, in thousands of U.S. dollars. **Number listed:** 100
1. Volvo AB with $25,879,077 thousand
2. AB Electrolux, $16,296,586
3. Ericssonkoncernen, $14,904,789
4. Volvo Personvagnar AB, $11,105,109
5. Svenska Cellulosa Aktiebolaget SCA, $9,855,599
6. Stora Kopparbergs Bergslags AB, $8,662,069
7. Volvo Latvagnar AB, $7,904,457
8. ICA Handlarnas AB, $6,227,766
9. Skanska AB, $6,151,281
10. ABB AB, $6,089,114
Source: *Europe's 15,000 Largest Companies* (annual), Dun & Bradstreet, 1997, p. 84+.

★ 1032 ★
LARGEST COMPANIES IN SWEDEN BY REVENUE, 1995
Ranked by: Revenue, in millions of U.S. dollars. **Remarks:** Notes profits and global rank. **Number listed:** 3
1. Volvo with $24,021.8 million
2. Electrolux, $16,219.0
3. L.M. Ericsson, $13,961.3
Source: *Fortune,* The Global 500: World's Biggest Corporations (annual), August 5, 1996, p. F-37.

★ 1033 ★
TOP CORPORATIONS IN SWEDEN BY MARKET VALUE, 1996
Ranked by: Market value as of May, 31, 1996, in millions of U.S. dollars. **Remarks:** Also notes price per share, price to book value ratio, yield, sales, profits, assets, and return on equity. **Number listed:** 19
1. Astra with $28,088 million
2. L.M. Ericsson, $21,415
3. Volvo, $9,826
4. ABB AB, $9,642
5. Sandvik, $6,166
6. Investor, $5,665
7. Scania, $5,647
8. Svenska Handelsbanken, $4,673
9. Stora Kopparbergs Bergslags, $4,267

10. Skandinaviska Enskilda Banken, $4,150
Source: *Business Week,* Global 1,000 (annual), July 8, 1996, p. 64.

★ 1034 ★
TOP PUBLICLY TRADED CORPORATIONS IN SWEDEN, 1995
Ranked by: Revenue, in millions of U.S. dollars. **Remarks:** Also notes net income, assets, market value, stock price, employees, and global rank. **Number listed:** 12
1. ABB Group with $33,667 million
2. Volvo Group, $24,044
3. Electrolux Group, $16,234
4. LM Ericsson, $13,848
5. SCA-Svenska Cellulosa, $9,157
6. Stora Group, $8,006
7. Skandia Insurance, $7,733
8. Svenska Handelsbanken, $5,834
9. Skandinaviska Enskilda Bk, $5,658
10. Skanska, $5,383
Source: *Forbes,* Forbes Foreign Rankings (annual), July 15, 1996, p. 269.

Corporations – Switzerland

★ 1035 ★
LARGEST COMPANIES IN SWITZERLAND
Ranked by: Sales, in thousands of U.S. dollars. **Number listed:** 79
1. Nestle SA with $49,086,642 thousand
2. ABB Asea Brown Boveri A.G., $35,381,941
3. Ciba Geigy Switzerland A.G., $17,988,181
4. Sandoz A.G., $13,247,588
5. Coop Switzerland A.G., $9,637,611
6. Societe Internationale Pirelli SA, $9,466,693
7. Holderbank Financiere Glarus A.G., $7,912,574
8. Alusuisse-Lonza Holding A.G., $6,516,902
9. Danzas A.G., $5,275,049
10. Sulzer A.G., $4,988,268
Source: *Europe's 15,000 Largest Companies* (annual), Dun & Bradstreet, 1997, p. 73+.

★ 1036 ★
LARGEST COMPANIES IN SWITZERLAND BY REVENUE, 1995
Ranked by: Revenue, in millions of U.S. dollars. **Remarks:** Notes profits and global rank. **Number listed:** 16
1. Metro Holding with $56,459.0 million
2. Nestle, $47,780.4
3. ABB Asea Brown Boveri, $33,738.0
4. Zurich Insurance, $24,823.2
5. CS Holding, $24,794.5

6. Winterthur Group, $21,324.6
7. Union Bank of Switzerland, $18.500.9
8. Ciba-Geigy, $17,509.5
9. Swiss Bank Corp., $14,404.2
10. Migros, $13,566.8

Source: *Fortune,* The Global 500: World's Biggest Corporations (annual), August 5, 1996, p. F-37.

★ 1037 ★

TOP CORPORATIONS IN SWITZERLAND BY MARKET VALUE, 1996

Ranked by: Market value as of May, 31, 1996, in millions of U.S. dollars. **Remarks:** Also notes price per share, price to book value ratio, yield, sales, profits, assets, and return on equity. **Number listed:** 18

1. Roche Holding with $73,313 million
2. Nestle, $44,052
3. Sandoz, $39,262
4. Ciba-Geigy, $31,862
5. Union Bank of Switzerland, $24,329
6. CS Holding, $16,268
7. Swiss Re., $13,565
8. Swiss Bank Corp., $13,502
9. Zurich Insurance Group, $11,992
10. ABB A.G., $10,879

Source: *Business Week,* Global 1,000 (annual), July 8, 1996, p. 64.

★ 1038 ★

TOP PUBLICLY TRADED CORPORATIONS IN SWITZERLAND, 1995

Ranked by: Revenue, in millions of U.S. dollars. **Remarks:** Also notes net income, assets, market value, stock price, employees, and global rank. **Number listed:** 17

1. Nestle with $47,767 million
2. ABB Group, $33,667
3. CS Holding Group, $24,788
4. Zurich Insurance Group, $23,994
5. Winterthur Group, $21,224
6. Union Bank of Switzerland, $18,496
7. Ciba-Geigy Group, $17,505
8. Swiss Bank, $14,400
9. Sandoz Group, $12,892
10. Roche Group, $12,450

Source: *Forbes,* Forbes Foreign Rankings (annual), July 15, 1996, p. 270.

Corporations – Taiwan

★ 1039 ★

LARGEST COMPANIES IN TAIWAN

Ranked by: Sales, in thousands of U.S. dollars. **Number listed:** 100

1. Nan Ya Plastics Corporation with $3,352,988 thousand
2. China Steel Corporation, $2,821,013
3. Tatung Co. Ltd., $1,497,746
4. Formosa Chemicals & Fibre Corporation, $1,481,731
5. Formosa Plastics Corporation, $1,327,738
6. Hualon Corporation, $1,263,678
7. Far Eastern Textile Ltd., $1,255,432
8. Taiwan Semiconductor Manufacturing Co. Ltd., $1,054,201
9. Yulon Motor Co. Ltd., $1,033,679
10. First International Computer Inc., $930,586

Source: *Asia's 7,500 Largest Companies* (annual), Dun & Bradstreet, 1997, p. 69+.

★ 1040 ★

TOP COMPANIES IN TAIWAN

Ranked by: Scores (1-7) based on a survey response of over 4,000 professionals throughout Asia. Respondents were asked to rate companies on their quality of services/products offered, long-term management vision, response to customer needs, and financial soundness. **Number listed:** 10

1. Acer with 6.37
2. Evergreen Marine, 5.92
3. Formosa Plastics, 5.85
4. EVA Airways, 5.83
5. President Enterprises, 5.52
6. Taiwan Semiconductor, 5.40
7. Nan Ya Plastics, 5.36
8. China Steel, 5.26
9. United Microelectronics, 5.08
10. Chinatrust Commercial Bank, 5.02

Source: *Far Eastern Economic Review,* Review 200 (annual), January 2, 1997, p. 48.

Corporations – Thailand

★ 1041 ★

LARGEST COMPANIES IN THAILAND

Ranked by: Sales, in thousands of U.S. dollars. **Number listed:** 100

1. Thai Airways International Plc with $2,976,736 thousand
2. Thai Oil Co. Ltd., $2,446,181
3. Seagate Technology (Thailand) Ltd., $1,278,895

4. MMC Sittipol Co. Ltd., $1,263,645
5. Sura Mahathip Co. Ltd., $836,014
6. Siam Nissan Automobile Co. Ltd., $816,825
7. Siam Makro Public Co. Ltd., $755,438
8. Bangkok Produce Merchandising Co. Ltd., $736,800
9. Boonrawd Trading Co. Ltd., $683,319
10. Charoen Pokphand Feedmill Public Ltd., $624,454

Source: *Asia's 7,500 Largest Companies* (annual), Dun & Bradstreet, 1997, p. 70+.

★ 1042 ★
TOP COMPANIES IN THAILAND
Ranked by: Scores (1-7) based on a survey response of over 4,000 professionals throughout Asia. Respondents were asked to rate companies on their quality of services/products offered, long-term management vision, response to customer needs, and financial soundness.
Number listed: 10
1. C.P. Group with 6.18
2. Thai Farmers Bank, 6.05
3. Bangkok Bank, 6.04
4. Siam Cement, 6.01
5. Siam Commercial Bank, 5.72
6. Italian-Thai Development, 5.66
7. Shinawatra Group, 5.61
8. Dusit Thani, 5.59
9. Petroleum Authority of Thailand, 5.54
10. TelecomAsia, 5.34

Source: *Far Eastern Economic Review,* Review 200 (annual), January 2, 1997, p. 48.

Corporations – United Kingdom

★ 1043 ★
LARGEST COMPANIES IN THE UNITED KINGDOM
Ranked by: Sales, in thousands of U.S. dollars. **Number listed:** 100
1. British Petroleum Co. Plc with $56,065,217 thousand
2. Shell Transport & Trading Co. Plc, $43,226,708
3. BAT Industries Plc, $36,298,136
4. Shell International Petroleum Co. Ltd., $26,274,844
5. BP International Ltd., $24,302,795
6. Sumitomo Corporation (U.K.) Plc, $22,616,459
7. British Telecommunications Plc, $22,431,677
8. J. Sainsbury Plc, $20,961,180
9. Mitsui & Co. U.K. Plc, $20,704,968
10. Tesco Plc, $18,779,503

Source: *Europe's 15,000 Largest Companies* (annual), Dun & Bradstreet, 1997, p. 78+.

★ 1044 ★
TOP BRITISH COMPANIES, 1997
Ranked by: Market capital based on closing share prices on May 9, 1997, in billions of U.S. dollars. **Number listed:** 10
1. HSBC Holdings with $76.40 billion
2. Glaxo Wellcome, $69.20
3. British Petroleum, $67.49
4. Shell Transport & Trading, $60.16
5. Lloyds TSB Group, $53.93
6. British Telecom, $46.54
7. SmithKline Beecham, $45.67
8. GMG Brands, $39.40
9. Barclays, $30.87
10. Zeneca Group, $29.56

Source: *The Guardian*, May 13, 1997, p. 17.

★ 1045 ★
TOP CORPORATIONS IN THE UNITED KINGDOM BY MARKET VALUE, 1996
Ranked by: Market value as of May, 31, 1996, in millions of U.S. dollars. **Remarks:** Also notes price per share, price to book value ratio, yield, sales, profits, assets, and return on equity. **Number listed:** 97
1. British Petroleum with $48,210 million
2. Shell Transport & Trading, $47,144
3. Glaxo Wellcome, $45,680
4. HSBC Holdings, $40,021
5. British Telecommunications, $34,343
6. SmithKline Beecham, $28,041
7. Lloyds TSB Group, $25,053
8. B.A.T. Industries, $24,796
9. Zeneca Group, $20,109
10. Marks & Spencer, $20,074

Source: *Business Week,* Global 1,000 (annual), July 8, 1996, p. 50.

★ 1046 ★
TOP PUBLICLY TRADED CORPORATIONS IN THE UNITED KINGDOM, 1995
Ranked by: Revenue, in millions of U.S. dollars. **Remarks:** Also notes net income, assets, market value, stock price, employees, and global rank. **Number listed:** 63
1. Royal Dutch/Shell Group with $109,853 million
2. British Petroleum, $56,992
3. Unilever, $49,638
4. HSBC, $26,682
5. National Westminster Bank, $23,533
6. Barclays, $23,202
7. British Telecom, $22,618
8. Prudential, $21,407
9. J. Sainsbury, $19,770

10.   B.A.T. Industries, $19,450
Source: *Forbes,* Forbes Foreign Rankings (annual), July 15, 1996, p. 272.

Cosmetics, Door – to – Door

★ 1047 ★
TOP DOOR-TO-DOOR COSMETIC RETAILERS IN JAPAN
Ranked by: Annual sales, in billions of yen (¥).
Remarks: Table shows only those companies listed on the Tokyo Stock Exchange. **Number listed:** 13
1.   Yakuruto Honsha Co., Ltd. with ¥159.00 billion
2.   Pola Cosmetics Inc., ¥102.00
3.   Noevir Co., Ltd., ¥43.00
4.   Avon Products Co., Ltd., ¥34.90
5.   Naris Cosmetics Co., Ltd., ¥21.25
6.   Oppen Cosmetics K.K., ¥20.00
7.   Arsor Co., Ltd., ¥14.00
8.   Furuberu K.K., ¥14.00
9.   Shanson Keshohin J.J., ¥7.20
10.   Belsereju K.K., ¥6.40
Source: *National Trade Data Bank,* March 5, 1997, p. IMI970224.

Cosmetics Industry
See Also: Perfumes; Personal Care Products

★ 1048 ★
JAPAN'S TOP COSMETICS MAKERS
Ranked by: Market share, in percent. **Number listed:** 6
1.   Shiseido with 26.0%
2.   Kao, 16.0%
3.   Kanebo, 10.1%
4.   Kose, 6.0%
5.   Pola Cosmetics, 5.9%
6.   Others, 35.4%
Source: *Nikkei Weekly,* August 5, 1996, p. 10.

★ 1049 ★
LARGEST SOAPS AND COSMETICS COMPANIES, 1995
Ranked by: Revenue, in millions of U.S. dollars.
Remarks: Notes profits and global rank. **Number listed:** 3
1.   Procter & Gamble (United States) with $33,434 million
2.   L'Oreal (France), $10,698
3.   Henkel (Germany), $9,907
Source: *Fortune,* The Global 500: World's Biggest Corporations (annual), August 5, 1996, p. F-25.

★ 1050 ★
LEADING SEGMENTS OF THE EGYPTIAN COSMETICS MARKET
Ranked by: Percent distribution. **Number listed:** 4
1.   Perfume and deodorant with 40%
2.   Make-up, 30%
3.   Hair care, 20%
4.   Skin care, 10%
Source: *National Trade Data Bank,* June 24, 1997, p. IMI970619.

★ 1051 ★
POPULAR COSMETICS BRANDS IN GERMANY, 1996
Ranked by: Women over the age of 14 who use each brand, in percent. **Number listed:** 19
1.   Jade with 20.5%
2.   Margaret Astor, 15.4%
3.   Ellen Betrix, 11.6%
4.   Yves Rocher, 10.1%
5.   Chicogo, 9.0%
6.   Avon, 8.6%
7.   Marbert, 6.4%
8.   Manhattan, 5.8%
9.   Elizabeth Arden, 4.7%
10.   Lancome, 4.5%
Source: *Marketing in Europe,* January 1997, p. 23.

★ 1052 ★
TOP COSMETICS BRANDS BY BRAND VALUE
Ranked by: Brand value, in millions of U.S. dollars.
Remarks: Value was calculated using capital, ratio of capital to company sales, earnings, and corporate tax rate of the country where the parent company is located. See source for details. **Number listed:** 15
1.   Avon (Avon Products) with $3,448 million
2.   L'Oreal (L'Oreal), $2,860
3.   Lancome (L'Oreal), $2,022
4.   Chanel (Chanel), $1,881
5.   Christian Dior (LVMH), $1,613
6.   Clinique (Estee Lauder), $1,246
7.   Estee Lauder (Este Lauder), $1,182
8.   Yves Sant Laurent (Sanofi), $880
9.   Revlon (Revlon), $668
10.   Elizabeth Arden (LVMH), $433
Source: *Financial World,* World's Most Valuable Brands (annual), July 8, 1996, p. 58.

★ 1053 ★
TOP COSMETICS FIRMS IN BRAZIL
Ranked by: Annual sales, in thousands of U.S. dollars.
Number listed: 10
1.   Gessy Lever with $1,268,027.96 thousand
2.   Johnsons & Johnsons, $226,152.69
3.   Colgate Palmolive, $213,168.06
4.   Gillete do Brasil, $157,152.69

5. Procter & Gamble, $97,836.56
6. IFF Essencias e Fragrancias, $53,129.03
7. L'Oreal, $37,769.89
8. O Boticario, $32,418.06
9. Memphis, $25,455.91
10. Natura, $20,578.49

Source: *National Trade Data Bank*, February 13, 1996, p. ISA9512.

Cost and Standard of Living

★ 1054 ★
COST OF BUSINESS ATTIRE IN SELECTED COUNTRIES

Ranked by: Cost for the same man's suit, shoes, and haircut, in U.S. dollars. **Number listed:** 5

1. Japan with $1,250.82
2. Germany, $673.93
3. Philippines, $637.03
4. Canada, $530.76
5. United States, $527.65

Source: *Canadian Business*, April 1997, p. 16.

Costa Rica – see under individual headings

Cotton

★ 1055 ★
LARGEST COTTON CONSUMERS, 1995

Ranked by: Share of consumption, in percent. **Number listed:** 7

1. Asia/Australia with 63%
2. North America, 15%
3. Central & South America, 7%
4. Western Europe, 7%
5. Africa, 4%
6. Former Soviet Union, 4%
7. Eastern Europe, 1%

Source: *Financial Times*, November 21, 1996, p. 26.

★ 1056 ★
TOP COTTON PRODUCERS IN LATIN AMERICA, 1996

Ranked by: Thousands of tons for the first nine months of 1996. **Number listed:** 7

1. Argentina with 375.0 thousand tons
2. Paraguay, 115.0
3. Colombia, 71.0
4. Peru, 63.0
5. Mexico, 19.0

6. Nicaragua, 8.0
7. Guatemala, 4.0

Source: *Latin American Economy & Business - Quarterly Update*, September 1996, p. 10.

Country Credit Risk

★ 1057 ★
COUNTRIES WITH THE BEST CREDIT RATING, ACCORDING TO EUROMONEY, 1997

Ranked by: Credit risk according to Euromoney. A score of "100" denotes the highest credit worthiness. **Number listed:** 131

1. Luxembourg with 99.30
2. United States, 97.09
3. Singapore, 96.16
4. United Kingdom, 95.73
5. Netherlands, 95.66
6. Denmark, 95.04
7. Norway, 94.74
8. Germany, 94.65
9. Canada, 94.40
10. Switzerland, 93.70

Source: *Euromoney*, Credit Risk Survey (biannual), March 1997, p. 164.

★ 1058 ★
COUNTRIES WITH THE BEST CREDIT RISK RATING, 1996-1997

Ranked by: Change in credit risk rating from March 1996 to March 1997, according to Institutional Investor. A high credit risk rating denotes good credit worthiness. **Remarks:** Notes 6 month changes in ratings. **Number listed:** 135

1. Switzerland with 92.5
2. Germany, 91.5
3. Japan, 91.3
4. United States, 91.2
5. Netherlands, 89.7
6. United Kingdom, 88.4
7. France, 88.2
8. Luxembourg, 87.3
9. Norway, 84.7
10. Austria, 84.6

Source: *Institutional Investor - International Edition*, March 1997, p. 184.

★ 1059 ★

COUNTRIES WITH THE LARGEST DECREASE IN CREDIT RISK RATING, 1996-1997

Ranked by: Change in credit risk rating from March 1996 to March 1997, according to Institutional Investor. A high credit risk rating denotes good credit worthiness. **Remarks:** Notes 6 month changes in ratings. **Number listed:** 16

1. Thailand with -2.3
2. Bahrain, -2.0
3. Pakistan, -1.8
4. Taiwan, -1.8
5. Senegal, -1.7
6. Qatar, -1.4
7. Saudi Arabia, -1.4
8. Libya, -1.2
9. Sierra Leone, -1.2
10. Austria, -1.1

Source: *Institutional Investor - International Edition*, March 1997, p. 183.

★ 1060 ★

COUNTRIES WITH THE LARGEST INCREASE IN CREDIT RISK RATING, 1996-1997

Ranked by: Change in credit risk rating from March 1996 to March 1997, according to Institutional Investor. A high credit risk rating denotes good credit worthiness. **Remarks:** Notes 6 month changes in ratings. **Number listed:** 16

1. Croatia with 7.9
2. Poland, 7.7
3. Slovenia, 6.2
4. Slovakia, 5.3
5. Lebanon, 5.0
6. Peru, 4.8
7. Estonia, 4.7
8. Latvia, 4.4
9. Philippines, 4.2
10. Hungary, 4.0

Source: *Institutional Investor - International Edition*, March 1997, p. 183.

Courier Services

★ 1061 ★

ASIA'S EXPRESS PACKAGE MARKET

Ranked by: Estimated share of the intra-Asia express package market, in percent. **Number listed:** 5

1. DHL with 36.0%
2. TNT, 27.0%
3. FedEx, 13.0%
4. United Parcel Service, 5.0%
5. Others, 19.0%

Source: *The Wall Street Journal*, January 22, 1997, p. B1.

★ 1062 ★

BULGARIA'S COURIER SERVICE MARKET

Ranked by: Market share, in percent. **Number listed:** 4

1. DHL with 60.0%
2. In Time, 10.0%
3. Other, 30.0%

Source: *National Trade Data Bank*, March 2, 1996, p. IMI950515.

★ 1063 ★

BULGARIAN NONDOCUMENTARY COURIER SERVICES

Ranked by: Market share, in percent. **Number listed:** 3

1. DHL with 48.0%
2. Despred, 20.0%
3. RSE-Worldwide, 20.0%
4. Other, 12.0%

Source: *National Trade Data Bank*, March 2, 1996, p. IMI950515.

Credit Cards

See Also: Bank Credit Cards

★ 1064 ★

CREDIT CARD CIRCULATION IN LATIN AMERICAN COUNTRIES, 1995

Ranked by: Cards in circulation, in thousands. **Remarks:** Notes cards per 1,000 inhabitants and 1991 circulation. **Number listed:** 6

1. Argentina with 15,864 thousand
2. Mexico, 14,210
3. Brazil, 13,285
4. Chile, 6,079
5. Colombia, 4,945
6. Venezuela, 2,002

Source: *Latin American Weekly Report*, September 2, 1997, p. 413.

★ 1065 ★

LEADING BANK CARD ISSUERS IN FRANCE, 1995

Ranked by: Cards, in millions. **Remarks:** Shows domestic and international figures. **Number listed:** 9

1. Credit Agricole with 6.5 million cards
2. Credit Mutuel, 3.2
3. Societe Generale, 2.4
4. BNP, 2.3
5. Credit Lyonnais, 2.3
6. La Poste, 2.1
7. Banques Populaires, 1.7
8. Caisses d'Epargne, 1.7
9. CCF, 0.2

Source: *Credit Card Management*, October 1996, p. 105.

★ 1066 ★
LEADING CREDIT CARDS IN MEXICO
Ranked by: Cards, in millions. **Remarks:** Figure for Maestro includes 4 million Banamex cards that are being converted to Maestro. **Number listed:** 5
1. Visa with 5.5 million cards
2. Maestro, 4.2
3. MasterCard, 4.0
4. Visa Check, 2.1
5. Private label, 2.8

Source: *Credit Card Management*, November 1996, p. 44.

★ 1067 ★
TOP CREDIT CARD ISSUERS IN EUROPE
Ranked by: Thousands of cards issued. **Number listed:** 10
1. Barclays Bank with 15,842 thousand cards
2. Lloyds/TSB Group, 11,774
3. National Westminster Bank, 11,711
4. Midland Bank, 9,517
5. Postbank, 8,210
6. Cetelem, 7,900
7. Credit Agricole, 6,950
8. Rabobank, 6,255
9. Marks & Spencer, 5,130
10. American Express, 4,900

Source: *The Banker*, July 1997, p. 95.

★ 1068 ★
TOP NON-BANK PAYMENT CARDS IN FRANCE
Ranked by: Cards issued, in millions. Issuers are shown in parentheses. **Number listed:** 6
1. Aurore (Cetelem) with 5.5 million cards
2. Cofinoga (Cofinoga), 3.5
3. Kangourou (Finaref), 3.2
4. 4 Etoile (Cofidis), 2.2
5. Carrefour (Cetelem), 1.0
6. Printemps (Finaref/Sovac), 1.0

Source: *Credit Card Management*, October 1996, p. 105.

Credit Cards – Asia

★ 1069 ★
TOP CREDIT CARD MARKETS IN ASIA, 1995
Ranked by: Cards issued, in millions. **Number listed:** 10
1. Korea with 32.4 million cards
2. China, 11.0
3. Taiwan, 4.0
4. Hong Kong, 3.0
5. Thailand, 1.9
6. Malaysia, 1.7
7. Singapore, 1.7
8. India, 1.4
9. Indonesia, 1.4

10. Philippines, 1.1

Source: *Impact21*, December 1996, p. 53.

Credit Cards – Great Britain

★ 1070 ★
TOP CREDIT CARDS IN THE UNITED KINGDOM
Ranked by: Brand value, in millions of British pounds (£). **Number listed:** 10
1. Barclaycard with £1,334 million
2. Halifax, £956
3. Abbey National, £518
4. Cheltenham & Gloucester, £182
5. Leeds, £154
6. Woolwich, £113
7. Direct Line, £24
8. Northern Rock, £24
9. Alliance & Leicester, £16
10. N&P, £13

Source: *Marketing*, February 13, 1997, p. 17.

Crime and Criminals

★ 1071 ★
INTELLECTUAL PROPERTY RIGHTS SEIZURES BY TRADING PARTNER, 1995
Ranked by: Domestic value of seizures, in millions of U.S. dollars. **Remarks:** Also notes number of seizures, percent of total, and change over 1994. **Number listed:** 20
1. China with $8,745,423 million
2. Korea, $7,039,467
3. Hong Kong, $3,697,090
4. Taiwan, $3,035,047
5. India, $1,187,775
6. Panama, $887,476
7. Mexico, $783,466
8. Indonesia, $659,578
9. Thailand, $659,200
10. Japan, $458,348

Source: *Columbia Journal of World Business*, Fall 1996, p. 36.

★ 1072 ★
LOSSES ATTRIBUTABLE TO SOFTWARE PIRACY, 1994
Ranked by: Distribution of $15.2 billion lost to piracy, in percent. **Number listed:** 5
1. Europe with 39%
2. Asia, 29%
3. North America, 21%
4. Latin America, 9%

5. Africa/Middle East, 2%
Source: *The Economist*, July 27, 1996, p. 58.

★ 1073 ★
TOP INDUSTRIAL PIRATES, 1995
Ranked by: Criteria such as well organized piracy networks, weak laws, and inadequate enforcement.
Remarks: No specific data were given. **Number listed:** 5
1. Turkey
2. China
3. Thailand
4. Italy
5. Colombia
Source: *The New York Times*, July 3, 1997, p. C1.

★ 1074 ★
TOP NATIONS FOR CD AND CASSETTE PIRACY, 1995
Ranked by: Number of copies, in millions. **Remarks:** Also notes shares of domestic market. **Number listed:** 10
1. Russia with 222.3 million copies
2. China, 145.0
3. India, 128.4
4. Pakistan, 75.4
5. Mexico, 70.0
6. Brazil, 62.4
7. United States, 26.6
8. Italy, 21.5
9. Romania, 21.5
10. Turkey, 16.4
Source: *The New York Times*, July 3, 1997, p. C1.

★ 1075 ★
TOP NATIONS FOR SOFTWARE PIRACY, 1994
Ranked by: Rate of software piracy, in percent. **Number listed:** 10
1. China with 98%
2. Russia, 94%
3. South Korea, 78%
4. Brazil, 77%
5. Japan, 67%
6. Italy, 58%
7. France, 57%
8. Germany, 50%
9. United Kingdom, 43%
10. United States, 35%
Source: *The Economist*, July 27, 1996, p. 58.

★ 1076 ★
TOP NATIONS FOR SOFTWARE PIRACY, 1996
Ranked by: Value of pirated software, in millions of U.S. dollars. **Remarks:** Also notes share of domestic market.
Number listed: 10
1. United States with $2,361 million
2. Japan, $1,190
3. China, $704

4. South Korea, $516
5. Germany, $498
6. France, $412
7. Russia, $383
8. Canada, $357
9. Brazil, $356
10. Italy, $341
Source: *The New York Times*, July 3, 1997, p. C1.

★ 1077 ★
TOP NATIONS FOR VIDEO PIRACY, 1995
Ranked by: Production of U.S. movies, in millions of U.S. dollars. **Number listed:** 5
1. Russia with $312 million
2. Italy, $294
3. China, $124
4. Britain, $112
5. Japan, $108
Source: *The New York Times*, July 3, 1997, p. C1.

Croatia – see under individual headings

Crown Corporations
See: **Government Ownership**

Cruise Lines

★ 1078 ★
LARGEST PASSENGER SHIPS
Ranked by: Tonnage. **Number listed:** 11
1. Carnival Destiny with 101,000 tons
2. Normandie, 88,000
3. Queen Mary, 84,000
4. Queen Elizabeth, 82,000
5. Sun Princess, 77,000
6. Norway, 76,000
7. Majesty of the Seas, 74,000
8. Monarch of the Seas, 74,000
9. Sovereign of the Seas, 74,000
10. QE2, 70,000
Source: *The European*, April 25, 1996, p. 17.

Cuba – see under individual headings

Curtains
See: **Drapery**

Cyprus – see under individual headings

Czech Republic – see under individual headings

Dairy Industry

★ 1079 ★
FRESH DAIRY PRODUCTS IN FRANCE, 1995
Ranked by: Value, in percent distribution. **Number listed:** 3
1. Yogurt with 45.7%
2. Chilled desserts, 27.2%
3. Fromage frais, 27.1%

Source: *Dairy Foods*, March 1997, p. 32.

★ 1080 ★
TOP DAIRY EXPORTERS, 1995
Ranked by: Milk equivalent trade units, in thousands of metric tons. **Remarks:** The European Free Trade Association is comprised of Iceland, Switzerland, and Norway. **Number listed:** 10
1. European Union with 15,190 thousand metric tons
2. New Zealand, 6,948
3. Eastern Europe, 4,378
4. Australia, 3,513
5. United States, 2,905
6. European Free Trade Association, 986
7. Latin America, 681
8. Asia, 610
9. Canada, 606
10. Middle East, 331

Source: *Dairy Foods*, December 1996, p. 13.

Dairy Products

★ 1081 ★
LEADING MILK AND DAIRY PROCESSORS IN COLOMBIA, 1996
Ranked by: Market share, in percent. **Number listed:** 14
1. Nestle de Colombia S.A. with 19.8%
2. Alpina S.A., 14.7%
3. Colanta S.A., 14.7%
4. Cicolac S.A., 9.0%
5. Proleche S.A., 6.9%
6. Coolechera, 5.2%
7. Meals de Colombia, 3.7%
8. La Alqueria S.A., 2.2%
9. Colpurace S.A., 2.1%

10. El Pomar S.A., 2.1%

Source: *National Trade Data Bank*, July 9, 1997, p. ISA970501.

★ 1082 ★
TOP SPREAD BRANDS IN THE UNITED KINGDOM, 1995
Ranked by: Estimated sales, in millions of British pounds (£). **Remarks:** Notes ad agency and spending. **Number listed:** 10
1. Flora (Van den Bergh) with £Over 128 million
2. Anchor (Anchor Foods), £105-110
3. Clover (Dairy Crest Foods), £55-60
4. Lurpak (Danish Diary Board), £55-60
5. Gold (St. Ivel), £50-55
6. Dairylea cheese spread (Kraft Jacob Suchard), £35-40
7. I Can't Believe It's Not Butter (Van den Bergh), £30-35
8. Golden Crown (Kraft Jacob Suchard), £25-30
9. Philadelphia cheese spread (Kraft Jacob Suchard), £25-30
10. Vitalite (Kraft Jacob Sucard), £25-30

Source: *Marketing*, July 4, 1996, p. 27.

Debt

★ 1083 ★
MOST INDEBTED BUSINESS GROUPS IN SOUTH KOREA
Ranked by: Ratio of debt to equity. **Remarks:** Includes each company's capital and debt in billions of won. Notes each company's primary industry. **Number listed:** 10
1. Sammi with 32.45
2. Halla, 26.50
3. Jinro, 24.05
4. Hanil, 9.36
5. New Core, 9.24
6. Hanbo, 6.59
7. Hanwha, 6.42
8. Hanjin, 6.36
9. Doosan, 6.25
10. Dongbu, 5.84

Source: *Far Eastern Economic Review*, April 3, 1997, p. 45.

Defense Industries

★ 1084 ★
TOP DEFENSE FIRMS WORLDWIDE
Ranked by: Sales, in billions of U.S. dollars. **Remarks:** Includes defense sales as percent of turnover, civil sales and group turnover. **Number listed:** 11

1. Boeing/McDonnell Douglas with $19 billion
2. Lockeed Martin/Loral, $19
3. Raytheon/Hughes, $13
4. British Aerospace, $9
5. Northrop Grumman, $6
6. GEC, $5
7. Thomson CSF, $4
8. United Technologies, $4
9. Aerospace/Dassault, $3
10. Daimler-Benz, $3

Source: *The Observer*, June 8, 1997, p. B5.

★ 1085 ★
TOP DEFENSE FIRMS WORLDWIDE, 1995
Ranked by: Defense revenue, in billions of U.S. dollars. **Number listed:** 20

1. Lockheed Martin with $19.39 billion
2. McDonnell Douglas, $10.08
3. Boeing/Rockwell, $7.82
4. British Aerospace, $6.47
5. Hughes Electronics, $5.95
6. Northrop Grumman, $5.70
7. Thomson, $4.68
8. GEC, $4.12
9. Raytheon, $4.00
10. United Technologies, $3.65

Source: *The Economist*, August 10, 1996, p. 46.

Denmark – see under individual headings

Dental Care Products

★ 1086 ★
POPULAR DENTAL CLEANING BRANDS IN GERMANY, 1996
Ranked by: People over the age of 14 who use each brand, in percent. **Remarks:** Data include multiple responses. **Number listed:** 7

1. Corega Tabs with 8.5%
2. Blend-a-dent 2-Phasen, 4.3%
3. Kukident aktiv 3, 4.1%
4. Kukident Die Blauen, 2.3%
5. Corega Raucher Tabs, 1.1%
6. Other brands, 0.3%

7. Do not use, 80.3%

Source: *Marketing in Europe*, March 1997, p. 17.

★ 1087 ★
POPULAR DENTAL RINSES IN GERMANY, 1996
Ranked by: People over the age of 14 who use each brand, in percent. **Remarks:** Data include multiple responses. **Number listed:** 7

1. Odol with 24.4%
2. Plax, 6.1%
3. Blendax, 6.0%
4. Dentagard, 5.9%
5. Nur 1 Tropfen, 5.1%
6. Odol-med 3 antiplaque, 4.3%
7. Do not use, 46.5%

Source: *Marketing in Europe*, March 1997, p. 17.

Deodorants and Antiperspirants

★ 1088 ★
POPULAR DEODORANT BRANDS USED IN GERMANY, 1996
Ranked by: People over the age of 14 who use each brand, in percent. **Remarks:** Data include multiple responses. **Number listed:** 22

1. 8x4 with 17.9%
2. Nivea, 10.7%
3. Bac, 9.5%
4. Axe, 9.3%
5. Credo, 8.2%
6. Fa, 6.2%
7. Cliff, 5.8%
8. Irischer Fruhling, 5.8%
9. CD, 4.9%
10. Mum, 4.7%

Source: *Marketing in Europe*, March 1997, p. 15.

Department Stores

★ 1089 ★
BRITAIN'S TOP DEPARTMENT STORES BY SALES PER SQUARE FOOT, 1995
Ranked by: Sales per square foot, in U.S. dollars. **Number listed:** 6

1. Harvey Nichols with $945
2. Harrods, $805
3. Bergdorf Goodman, $797
4. Nordstrom's, $397
5. Neiman Marcus, $368
6. Sak's Fifth Avenue, $363

Source: *The New York Times*, November 9, 1996, p. 20.

Department Stores – Canada

★ 1090 ★
CANADA'S TOP DEPARTMENT STORES
Ranked by: Revenue, in thousands of Canadian dollars.
Remarks: Includes figures on profits and return on capital. **Number listed:** 6
1. Hudson's Bay Co. with C$5,984,621 thousand
2. Sears Canada, C$3,925,600
3. Zellers Inc., C$3,536,600
4. Price Costco Canada, C$2,372,000
5. Jean Coutu Group, C$1,273,904
6. Kmart Canada, C$1,262,552

Source: *Globe and Mail's Report on Business Magazine*, July 1996, p. 159.

★ 1091 ★
TOP CANADIAN DEPARTMENT STORES, 1996
Ranked by: Market share, in percent. **Number listed:** 6
1. Wal-Mart with 24%
2. Zellers, 23%
3. Sears, 18%
4. Hudson's Bay, 15%
5. Eatons, 12%
6. Kmart, 8%

Source: *Globe and Mail*, April 29, 1997, p. B6.

Department Stores – Japan

★ 1092 ★
TOP DEPARMENT STORES IN JAPAN
Ranked by: Income, in millions of yen (¥). **Number listed:** 10
1. Marui with ¥28,501 million
2. Sogo, ¥4,907
3. Yokohama Takashimaya, ¥4,770
4. Daimaru, ¥4,450
5. Matsuzakaya, ¥3,842
6. Tokyu Department Store, ¥3,326
7. Tenmaya, ¥3,095
8. Daiwa, ¥2,970
9. Tsuruya Department Store, ¥2,525
10. Hankyu Department Stores, ¥2,061

Source: *Tokyo Business Today*, August 1995, p. 27.

Derivative Securities

★ 1093 ★
COUNTRIES WITH THE HIGHEST TURNOVER OF DERIVATIVES
Ranked by: Average daily turnover of over-the-counter and exchange-traded derivatives, in billions of U.S. dollars. **Number listed:** 17
1. United Kingdom with $360 billion
2. United States, $169
3. Japan, $138
4. Singapore, $79
5. Hong Kong, $60
6. France, $56
7. Germany, $56
8. Switzerland, $46
9. Belgium, $28
10. Australia, $26

Source: *World Business*, March - April 1996, p. 30.

Detergents

★ 1094 ★
INDIA'S DETERGENT MARKET
Ranked by: Market share, in percent. **Number listed:** 7
1. Nirma with 35.0%
2. Wheel, 25.0%
3. Surf Ultra, 10.0%
4. Ariel Supersoaker, 9.0%
5. Rin Power White, 6.0%
6. Ariel, 2.0%
7. Other, 14.0%

Source: *Business Today*, September 7, 1996, p. 165.

★ 1095 ★
SPAIN'S TOP DETERGENT MAKERS
Ranked by: Market share, in percent. **Number listed:** 5
1. Procter & Gamble with 24.5%
2. Lever Espana, 19.5%
3. Benickser, 18.0%
4. Henkel Iberica, 17.0%
5. Other, 21.0%

Source: *National Trade Data Bank*, March 2, 1996, p. IMI950403.

★ 1096 ★
TOP LAUNDRY DETERGENT BRANDS IN THE UNITED KINGDOM, 1995
Ranked by: Estimated sales, in millions of British pounds (£). **Remarks:** Notes ad agency and spending. **Number listed:** 10
1. Ariel (Procter & Gamble) with £Over 200 million

2. Persil (Lever Brothers), £180-185
3. Daz (Procter & Gamble), £100-105
4. Bold (Procter & Gamble), £90-95
5. Comfort (Lever Brothers), £55-60
6. Lenor (Procter & Gamble), £55-60
7. Fairy (Procter & Gamble), £40-45
8. Radion (Lever Brothers), £25-30
9. Surf (Lever Brothers), £20-25
10. Dreft (Procter & Gamble), £10-15

Source: *Marketing*, July 4, 1996, p. 283.

Development Banks

★ 1097 ★

TOP DEVELOPMENT BANKS WORLDWIDE

Ranked by: Total equity, in millions of U.S. dollars.
Remarks: Includes assets and gross disbursements.
Number listed: 50

1. World Bank with $28,300 million
2. European Investment Bank, $21,977
3. Export-Import Bank of Japan, $13,019
4. The Japan Development Bank, $10,407
5. Inter-American Development Bank, $9,910
6. Asian Development Bank, $9,653
7. European Bank for Reconstruction & Development, $3,750
8. Korea Development Bank, $2,460
9. Islamic Development Bank, $1,909
10. African Development Bank, $1,740

Source: *The Banker,* Top 50 Development Banks (annual), May 1997, p. 79.

Dhaka Stock Exchange

★ 1098 ★

LARGEST COMPANIES ON THE DHAKA STOCK EXCHANGE, 1996

Ranked by: Market capitalization for March 1996, in millions of U.S. dollars. **Number listed:** 20

1. Bangladesh Tobacco Company with $156.26 million
2. Singer Bangladesh, $80.18
3. Bangladesh Oxygen, $57.44
4. Shine Pukur Hotels, $50.29
5. Beximco Pharmaceuticals, $47.79
6. Square Pharmaceuticals, $37.33
7. Glaxo, $36.83
8. Bata Shoe (Bangladesh), $35.50
9. Padma Textile Mills, $28.75
10. Ctg. Cement, $27.94

Source: *GT Guide to World Equity Markets* (annual), Euromoney Publications, 1996, p. 428.

Diagnostic Kits

★ 1099 ★

BLOOD GLUCOSE-MONITORING MARKET WORLDWIDE, 1995

Ranked by: Market share, in percent. **Number listed:** 5

1. LifeScan (Johnson & Johnson) with 35.0%
2. Boehringer Mannheim, 32.0%
3. Bayer, 20.0%
4. MediSense (Abbott Labs), 8.0%
5. Other, 5.0%

Source: *Investor's Business Daily*, September 30, 1996, p. A4.

Diamonds, International

★ 1100 ★

LARGEST DIAMOND PRODUCING NATIONS

Ranked by: Value of diamonds produced, as a percent of the $7,286 million diamond market. **Remarks:** Includes production figures and average price per carat. **Number listed:** 12

1. Botswana with 24%
2. Russia, 19%
3. South Africa, 15%
4. Angola, 10%
5. Namibia, 6%
6. Zaire, 6%
7. Australia, 5%
8. South America, 5%
9. Illicit, 3%
10. Other, 7%

Source: *Financial Times*, February 11, 1997, p. 17.

★ 1101 ★

TOP DIAMOND-DEALING CITIES, 1996

Ranked by: Trade volume, in billions of U.S. dollars. **Remarks:** Figure for Bombay is for the year ended March 31, 1996. **Number listed:** 4

1. Antwerp with $22.87 billion
2. Tel Aviv, $9.55
3. New York, $8.01
4. Bombay, $7.80

Source: *The Wall Street Journal*, June 3, 1997, p. A8.

Diapers

★ 1102 ★

LEADING PRODUCERS OF DIAPERS IN POLAND

Ranked by: Market share, in percent. **Number listed:** 4

1. Procter & Gamble with 75%

2. Libero, 15%
3. Bella, 5%
4. Other, 5%

Source: *The Warsaw Voice*, August 31, 1997, p. 13.

★ 1103 ★
TOP DIAPER BRANDS IN FRANCE
Ranked by: Market share, in percent. **Number listed:** 4
1. Huggies with 33.7%
2. Pampers, 23.2%
3. Luvs, 17.3%
4. Other, 25.8%

Source: *Le Figaro*, September 2, 1996, p. 13.

Digital Signal Processors

★ 1104 ★
TOP PROGRAMMABLE DSP PRODUCERS, 1995
Ranked by: Company shares based on sales, in percent.
Remarks: "DSP" stands for digital signal processors.
Number listed: 6
1. TI with 44.1%
2. AT&T, 28.5%
3. Motorola, 12.1%
4. Analog Devices, 8.8%
5. NEC, 2.9%
6. Other, 3.5%

Source: *Electronic Business Today*, March 1996, p. 62.

Direct Marketing

★ 1105 ★
FASTEST GROWING CHANNELS FOR DIRECT MARKETING IN AUSTRALIA, 1996
Ranked by: Growth, in percent. **Number listed:** 4
1. Internet with 171% growth
2. Magazines (inserts and advertisements), 37%
3. Exhibitions, 25%
4. Telemarketing, 17%

Source: *National Trade Data Bank*, May 20, 1997, p. IMI970520.

Direct Marketing – United Kingdom

★ 1106 ★
LEADING DIRECT MARKETERS IN THE UNITED KINGDOM, 1996
Ranked by: Turnover, in thousands of British pounds (£). **Remarks:** Also notes pre-tax profits and total staff.
Number listed: 12
1. WWAV Rapp Collins with £56,900 thousand
2. Ogilvy & Mather Direct, £49,218
3. Brann, £42,000
4. Wunderman Cato Johnson, £41,146
5. Carlson, £36,737
6. McCann-Erickson Manchester, £34,000
7. Colleagues Direct Marketing, £32,000
8. TBWA Payne Stracey Direct, £30,456
9. Evans Hunt Scott, £28,239
10. Barraclough Hall Woolston Gray, £24,633

Source: *Marketing*, March 19, 1996, p. IX.

Disk Drive Industry

★ 1107 ★
GLOBAL RIGID DISK DRIVE SHIPMENTS, 1996
Ranked by: Market share, in percent. **Number listed:** 6
1. Seagate Technology with 27.5%
2. Quantum, 22.2%
3. Western Digital, 18.4%
4. IBM, 10.5%
5. Maxtor, 5.8%
6. Other, 15.6%

Source: *Computerworld*, January 27, 1997, p. 41.

★ 1108 ★
TOP CD-R VENDORS WORLDWIDE, 1996
Ranked by: Market share, in percent. **Number listed:** 12
1. Kodak with 16%
2. TDK, 15%
3. MCC/Verbatim, 10%
4. Sony, 9%
5. Philips, 7%
6. Traxdata, 7%
7. Mitsui Toatsu, 6%
8. Imation (3M), 5%
9. Kao, 5%
10. Pioneer, 5%

Source: *E-Media Professional*, August 1997, p. 28.

★ 1109 ★
TOP CD-ROM DRIVE VENDORS WORLDWIDE, 1996
Ranked by: Market share, in percent. **Number listed:** 11
1. Mitsui with 22.5%
2. Matsushita/Panasonic, 21.5%

---

3. Sony, 14.0%
4. Toshiba, 10.0%
5. Goldstar, 6.3%
6. NEC, 5.0%
7. Shinanno Kenshi/Plextor, 3.5%
8. Hitachi, 2.2%
9. Chinon, 1.5%
10. Philips, 1.5%

Source: *E-Media Professional*, September 1997, p. 56.

★ 1110 ★
VARIABLE SPEED DRIVE MARKET WORLDWIDE, 1995
Ranked by: Market share, in percent. **Number listed:** 10
1. ABB with 10.0%
2. Toshiba, 6.0%
3. Yaskawa, 6.0%
4. Hitachi, 5.0%
5. Mitsubishi, 5.0%
6. Siemens, 5.0%
7. Allen Bradley, 4.0%
8. Danfoss, 3.0%
9. Reliance, 3.0%
10. Others, 53.0%

Source: *National Trade Data Bank*, April 25, 1996, p. IMI960425.

Distilling Industry
See: **Liquor Industry**

Diversified Corporations – Asia

★ 1111 ★
MOST ADMIRED CONGLOMERATES IN ASIA, 1997
Ranked by: Score, based on a survey. **Remarks:** See source for specific criteria. Notes score for 1996.
Number listed: 10
1. Samsung with 8.47
2. Charoen Pokphand, 8.31
3. Astra International, 8.12
4. Hyundai Corporation, 7.84
5. LG Group (Lucky Goldstar), 7.72
6. Genting, 7.66
7. Cycle & Carriage, 7.60
8. Swire Pacific, 7.57
9. Sime Darby, 7.48
10. Hutchison Whampoa, 7.38

Source: *Asian Business,* Most Admired Companies in Asia (annual), May 1997, p. 30.

Djibouti – see under individual headings

Dog Food
See: **Pet Food**

Dominican Republic – see under individual headings

Drapery

★ 1112 ★
TOP BLINDS MAKERS IN JAPAN
Ranked by: Market share, in percent. **Number listed:** 4
1. Tachikawa Corporation with 40.0%
2. Nichibei Blind Mfg. Co., 35.0%
3. Toso Co., 10.0%
4. Other, 15.0%

Source: *National Trade Data Bank*, August 26, 1996, p. ISA9408.

Drug Industry

★ 1113 ★
ANALGESIC ANTIPYRETICS MARKET IN INDIA
Ranked by: Market share, in percent. **Number listed:** 6
1. Crocin with 12.10%
2. Calpol, 10.80%
3. Novalgin, 9.50%
4. Metacin, 5.23%
5. Disprin, 3.36%
6. Other, 59.01%

Source: *Business Today*, February 22, 1996, p. 62.

★ 1114 ★
ANIMAL HEALTH AND NUTRITION MARKET, 1996
Ranked by: Percent distribution. **Number listed:** 6
1. Nutritional food additives with 27%
2. Pesticides, 19%
3. Vaccines, 15%
4. Antibiotics, 14%
4. Medicinal food additives, 14%
6. Pharmaceuticals, 11%

Source: *Chemical Week*, July 16, 1997, p. 26.

★ 1115 ★
ANTIBIOTICS LEADERS IN INDIA
Ranked by: Market share, in percent. **Number listed:** 4
1. Alembic with 52.60%
2. Ranbaxy, 11.02%
3. Cipla, 10.11%
4. Other, 26.27%

Source: *Business Today*, April 7, 1996, p. 12.

★ 1116 ★
BEST SELLING BIOTECH DRUGS WORLDWIDE
Ranked by: Sales, in millions of U.S. dollars. **Number listed:** 6
1. Neupogen with $829 million
2. Epogen (EPO), $721
3. Humulin, $665
4. Procrit (EPO), $600
5. Intron A, $426
6. Activase (TPA), $251

Source: *Business Week*, October 21, 1996, p. 76.

★ 1117 ★
BEST SELLING DRUGS WORLDWIDE, 1996
Ranked by: Sales, in millions of U.S. dollars. **Number listed:** 5
1. Zantac with $1,760 million
2. Prilosec, $1,741
3. Prozac, $1,685
4. Epogen, $1,183
5. Zoloft, $1,097

Source: *Chemical Market Reporter*, February 24, 1997, p. 21.

★ 1118 ★
GERMANY'S FASTEST GROWING PHARMACEUTICAL CATEGORIES, 1996
Ranked by: Increase in value of sales over 1995 sales, in percent. **Remarks:** Also notes change in sales volume. **Number listed:** 10
1. Vaccines with 39% increase
2. Immune stimulators, 38%
3. Anti-thrombotics, 24%
4. Lipid reducers, 19%
5. Psycholeptics, 18%
6. Cytostatics, 13%
7. Cytotstatic hormones, 12%
8. Drugs for Parkinson disease, 11%
9. Anit-diabetic drugs, 11%
10. Beta blockers, 10%

Source: *Marketing in Europe*, March 1997, p. 6.

★ 1119 ★
GLOBAL PHARMACEUTICAL MARKET
Ranked by: Market share, in percent. **Number listed:** 5
1. North America, NAFTA with 32.6%
2. Europe, 28.9%
3. Japan, 21.6%
4. Asia, Africa, Australia, 10.1%
5. Latin America, 6.8%

Source: *The World in 1997*, 1997, p. 95.

★ 1120 ★
LARGEST DANISH PHARMACEUTICAL COMPANIES, 1995
Ranked by: Pharmacy purchase price, in millions of Danish krone (DKr). **Number listed:** 10
1. Nycomed-DAK with DKr532 million
2. Novo Nordisk, DKr255
3. Lundbeck, DKr193
4. Statens Seruminstitut, DKr163
5. Leo Pharmaceutical Products, DKr158
6. GEA, DKr122
7. Ercopharm, DKr120
8. Dumex Alpharma, DKr108
9. ALK, DKr9
10. Ferrosan, DKr9

Source: *National Trade Data Bank*, July 9, 1997, p. ISA970601.

★ 1121 ★
LARGEST DRUG FIRMS IN GREECE, 1994
Ranked by: Sales revenue, in billions of Greek drachma (GDr). **Number listed:** 17
1. Vianex SA with GDr22.06 billion
2. Ciba-Geigy Hellas SA, GDr19.80
3. Bristol-Myers Squidd SA, GDr19.17
4. Lavipharm SA, GDr18.20
5. Glaxo SA, GDr13.60
6. Abbott Laboratories Hellas SA, GDr11.49
7. Boehringer Ingelheim Hellas, GDr10.44
8. Pharmalex SA Pharmaceutical, GDr9.87
9. Sandoz Hellas SA, GDr8.70
10. Famar SA, GDr7.48

Source: *Trade With Greece*, December 1995, p. 47.

★ 1122 ★
LARGEST PHARMACEUTICAL PRODUCERS IN INDONESIA, 1995
Ranked by: Sales, in billions of rupiah (Rp). **Number listed:** 30
1. Kalbe Farma with Rp514.35 billion
2. Kimia Farma, Rp476.00
3. Tempo ScanPacific, Rp316.41
4. Bayer Ind., Rp229.99
5. Darya Varia, Rp136.31
6. Konimex, Rp135.80
7. Indonesia Farma, Rp97.73
8. Sandoz Biochemie, Rp92.24
9. Dankos Labs, Rp84.69
10. Warner Lambert Ind., Rp56.50

Source: *National Trade Data Bank*, March 17, 1997, p. IMI970317.

★ 1123 ★
LARGEST PHARMACEUTICALS COMPANIES, 1995
Ranked by: Revenues, in millions of U.S. dollars.
Remarks: Notes profits and global rank. **Number listed:** 10

1. Johnson & Johnson (United States) with $18,842 million
2. Merck (United States), $16,681
3. Bristol-Myers Squibb (United States), $13,767
4. American Home Products (United States), $13,376
5. Sandoz (Switzerland), $12,895
6. Roche Holding (Switzerland), $12,453
7. Glaxo Wellcome (United Kingdom), $12,054
8. SmithKline Beecham (United Kingdom), $11,065
9. Pfizer (United States), $10,021
10. Abbott Laboratories (United States), $10,012

Source: *Fortune,* The Global 500: World's Biggest Corporations (annual), August 5, 1996, p. F-24.

★ 1124 ★
LEADING PHARMACEUTICAL CORPORATIONS, 1996
Ranked by: Market share, in percent. **Remarks:** Also notes figures for 1994 and 1995. **Number listed:** 10

1. Glaxo Wellcome with 4.4%
2. Novartis (Ciba-Geigy/Sandoz), 4.4%
3. Merck & Co., 4.0%
4. Hoechst Marion Roussel, 3.3%
5. Bristol Myers Squibb, 3.2%
6. American Home, 3.1%
7. Johnson & Johnson, 3.1%
8. Pfizer, 3.1%
9. Roche, 2.7%
10. SmithKline Beecham, 2.7%

Source: *Financial Times*, April 24, 1997, p. I.

★ 1125 ★
MOST VALUABLE SEGMENTS OF SPAIN'S PHARMACEUTICALS MARKET
Ranked by: Value, as a percent of total market value.
Number listed: 13

1. Cardiovascular apparatus with 23.5%
2. Metabolism and digestive system, 15.2%
3. Anti-infectious via general, 12.3%
4. Central nervous system, 9.7%
5. Respiratory system, 8.2%
6. Blood and hemopoietic organs, 7.0%
7. Locomotor apparatus, 6.3%
8. Hormone (excluding sexual), 5.0%
9. Citostatics, 3.6%
10. Genitourinary products, 3.4%

Source: *National Trade Data Bank,* July 8, 1997, p. ISA970601.

★ 1126 ★
TOP ANIMAL HEALTH AND NUTRITION COMPANIES, 1996
Ranked by: Sales, in millions of U.S. dollars. **Number listed:** 19

1. Roche with $1,464 million
2. Merial, $1,415
3. Pfizer, $1,222
4. Bayer, $888
5. Rhone-Poulenc Animal Nutrition, $763
6. BASF, $730
7. American Home Products, $710
8. Novartis, $680
9. Schering-Plough, $666
10. DowElanco, $547

Source: *Chemical Week*, July 16, 1997, p. 26.

★ 1127 ★
TOP DRUG COMPANIES IN BRAZIL
Ranked by: Sales, in millions of U.S. dollars. **Number listed:** 10

1. Hoechst Marion Roussel with $424 million
2. Bristol-Meyers Squibb, $407
3. Ache, $380
4. Roche, $357
5. Biogalencia, $304
6. Lilly, $288
7. Schering-Plough, $250
8. Glaxo Wellcome, $243
9. Boehringer de Angeli, $220
10. Schering, $199

Source: *Chemical Week*, November 13, 1996, p. 44.

★ 1128 ★
TOP DRUG FIRMS IN INDIA, 1995
Ranked by: Market share, in percent. **Number listed:** 11

1. Glaxo-Burroughs Wellcome with 7.1%
2. Cipia, 4.3%
3. Hoechst Roussel, 3.8%
4. Ranbaxy, 3.5%
5. Cadilia Health Care, 3.3%
6. Knoll Pharma, 2.7%
7. Pfizer, 2.4%
8. Torrent, 2.4%
9. Alembia, 2.3%
10. Lupin Labs, 2.3%

Source: *Business India*, April 22, 1996, p. 85.

★ 1129 ★
TOP DRUG FIRMS IN PAKISTAN, 1995
Ranked by: Sales, in millions of rupees (Rs). **Number listed:** 10

1. Ciba Geigy Pakistan with Rs2,675.15 million
2. Sandoz Pakistan, Rs2,288.82
3. Hoechst Pakistan, Rs1,960.29
4. Abbott Pakistan, Rs1,463.83

5.　Wellcome Pakistan, Rs1,432.82
6.　Glaxo Pakistan, Rs1,391.18
7.　Cyanamid Pakistan, Rs1,125.42
8.　Reckitt & Colman, Rs992.45
9.　Parke Davis, Rs698.49
10.　Boots (Knoll) Pakistan, Rs597.61

Source: *Economic Review*, 1996, p. 35.

★ 1130 ★

TOP DRUG MAKERS WORLDWIDE, 1996

Ranked by: Sales, in millions of U.S. dollars. **Number listed:** 6
1.　Glaxo Wellcome with $5,802 million
2.　Johnson & Johnson, $5,275
3.　American Home, $5,250
4.　Bristol-Myers Squibb, $5,159
5.　Merck & Co., $5,025
6.　Pfizer, $4,511

Source: *Chemical Market Reporter*, February 24, 1997, p. 21.

★ 1131 ★

TOP FOREIGN COMPANIES IN THE POLISH PHARMACEUTICALS MARKET, 1996

Ranked by: Sales, in millions of U.S. dollars. **Remarks:** Also notes market share. **Number listed:** 8
1.　Rhone Poulenc Rorer with $42.3 million
2.　Servier, $35.5
3.　Eli Lilly, $35.2
4.　Glaxo, $33.1
5.　Krka, $30.4
6.　Bristol Myers Squibb, $21.3
7.　Bayer, $19.5
8.　Smith Kline Beecham, $17.4

Source: *National Trade Data Bank*, July 1, 1997, p. IMI970630.

★ 1132 ★

TOP LABORATORIES IN SPAIN, 1996

Ranked by: Market share based on sales, in percent. **Number listed:** 10
1.　Almirall with 3.62%
2.　Bayer, 3.47%
3.　Esteve, 3.38%
4.　Glaxo, 3.00%
5.　Merck Sharp & Dohme, 2.60%
6.　Beecham, 2.40%
7.　Pharmacia & Upjohn, 2.30%
8.　Schering Plough, 2.28%
9.　Astra, 2.10%
10.　Sandoz Pharma, 2.04%

Source: *National Trade Data Bank*, July 8, 1997, p. ISA970601.

★ 1133 ★

TOP PHARMACEUTICAL COMPANIES IN POLAND, 1996

Ranked by: Sales for the first half of 1996, in millions of zlotys (Zl). **Remarks:** Notes gross profits and net profits. **Number listed:** 9
1.　Polpharma SA Starogard Gdanski with Zl222.5 million
2.　Polfa Tarchomin SA, Zl165.8
3.　PZF Polfa SA Poznan, Zl143.4
4.　Polfa Krakow SA, Zl111.4
5.　Polfa Kutno SA, Zl104.1
6.　Polfa Pabianice, Zl77.9
7.　Jelfa SAPF Jelenia Gora, Zl75.0
8.　Polfa Grodzisk Mazowiecki, Zl58.4
9.　Polfa Rzeszow SA, Zl55.6

Source: *The Warsaw Voice*, March 9, 1997, p. 13.

★ 1134 ★

TOP PHARMACEUTICAL FIRMS IN ARGENTINA, 1995

Ranked by: Sales, in millions of U.S. dollars. **Number listed:** 9
1.　Roemmers with $239.0 million
2.　Bago, $183.0
3.　Roche, $161.4
4.　Sidus, $151.8
5.　Boehringer, $98.5
6.　Ciba, $96.6
7.　Montpellier, $87.7
8.　Bayer, $86.3
9.　Beta, $83.6

Source: *Business Latin America*, March 17, 1997, p. 3.

★ 1135 ★

TOP PHARMACEUTICAL FIRMS, 1996

Ranked by: Sales, in millions of U.S. dollars. **Remarks:** Also notes pre-tax profits. **Number listed:** 13
1.　Hoechst with $8,455 million
2.　Rhone-Poulenc, $5,464
3.　Bayer, $4,532
4.　Merck (Darmstadt), $2,300
5.　Akzo Nobel, $2,271
6.　BASF, $2,188
7.　Monsanto, $1,995
8.　Sumitomo Chemical, $1,645
9.　DuPont, $1,300
10.　Solvay, $1,250

Source: *Chemical Week*, April 16, 1997, p. 25.

★ 1136 ★

TOP PHARMACEUTICALS FIRMS IN SOUTH KOREA, 1996

Ranked by: Sales for the first six months of 1996, in hundred million won (W). **Number listed:** 22
1.　Dong-A Pharm. with W1,300.4 hundred million

2. Korea Green Cross, W966.1
3. Yuhan, W901.9
4. Chong Kun Dang, W653.7
5. Young Jin Pharm., W618.4
6. Choong Wae Pharm., W584.1
7. Han Dok Pharm., W468.5
8. Kwang Dong Pharm., W455.8
9. Boryung Pharm., W449.4
10. Hanmi Pharm., W382.6

Source: *Business Korea*, October 1996, p. 34.

★ 1137 ★
TOP PHARMACEUTICALS MAKERS IN HUNGARY
Ranked by: Market share, in percent, based on value of sales. **Number listed:** 7
1. Egis with 12.4%
2. Richter Gedeon, 8.8%
3. Biogal, 8.4%
4. Chinoin, 7.6%
5. Ciba, 6.3%
6. Sandoz, 4.0%
7. Other, 52.5%

Source: *European Chemical News*, April 29, 1996, p. 15.

★ 1138 ★
TOP SUPPLIERS OF HUMAN SPECIALTY PHARMACEUTICALS IN DENMARK, 1995
Ranked by: Pharmacy purchase price, in millions of Danish krone (DKr). **Number listed:** 25
1. Nycomed-DAK with DKr532 million
2. Glaxo, DKr369
3. Novo Nordisk, DKr255
4. Lundbeck, DKr193
5. Leo Pharmaceutical Products, DKr158
6. Sandoz/Novartis, DKr135
7. Janssen-Cilag, DKr131
8. Merck, Sharp & Dohme, DKr124
9. GEA, DKr122
10. Ercopharm, DKr120

Source: *National Trade Data Bank*, July 9, 1997, p. ISA970601.

★ 1139 ★
TOP SUPPLIERS OF VETERINARY SPECIALTY PHARMACEUTICALS IN DENMARK, 1995
Ranked by: Pharmacy purchase price, in millions of Danish krone (DKr). **Number listed:** 10
1. Mallinckrodt Veterinary with DKr43 million
2. Pfizer Animal Health, DKr34
3. Intervet Scandinavia A/S, DKr32
4. Bayer Danmark A/S, DKr31
5. Leo Pharmaceutical Products, DKr31
6. Ciba-Geigy A/S, DKr25
7. Ingelheim Agrovet A/S, DKr25
8. MSD-Agrovet A/S, DKr22
9. Medimerc A/S, DKr20

10. Hoechst Danmark A/S, DKr18

Source: *National Trade Data Bank*, July 9, 1997, p. ISA970601.

Drug Industry – Europe

★ 1140 ★
TOP DRUG FIRMS IN EUROPE
Ranked by: Revenue, in billions of U.S. dollars. **Remarks:** Includes net income and market capitalization. **Number listed:** 10
1. Ciba Geigy with $16.54 billion
2. Glaxo Wellcome, $15.84
3. Sandoz, $12.03
4. Roche, $11.74
5. Smithkline Beecham, $10.59
6. Zeneca, $7.40
7. Pharmacia & Upjohn, $6.94
8. Astra, $5.23
9. Sanofi, $4.43
10. Merck, $4.08

Source: *Financial Times*, June 17, 1996, p. 25.

Drug Industry – Japan

★ 1141 ★
LEADING DRUG GROUPS IN JAPAN, 1997
Ranked by: Sales for the year ending March 1997, in billions of yen (¥). **Remarks:** Also notes recurring profits. **Number listed:** 8
1. Takeda with ¥637.2 billion
2. Sanyo, ¥442.6
3. Yamanouchi, ¥312.6
4. Eisai, ¥257.9
5. Shionogi, ¥229.7
6. Daiichi, ¥229.1
7. Fujisawa, ¥224.6
8. Tanabe, ¥185.8

Source: *Financial Times*, May 28, 1997, p. 20.

★ 1142 ★
TOP PHARMACEUTICAL COMPANIES IN JAPAN
Ranked by: Sales, in billions of yen (¥). **Remarks:** Includes reoccuring profits. **Number listed:** 8
1. Takeda with ¥637.2 billion
2. Sankyo, ¥442.6
3. Yamanouchi, ¥312.4
4. Eisai, ¥257.9
5. Shionogi, ¥229.7
6. Daiichi, ¥229.1
7. Fujisawa, ¥224.6

8. Tanabe, ¥185.8
Source: *Financial Times*, May 28, 1997, p. 20.

Drug Stores

★ 1143 ★
LARGEST PHARMACY CHAINS IN THE UNITED KINGDOM, 1996
Ranked by: Number of pharmacies. **Number listed:** 7
1. AAH - Hills & Llyods with 1,270 outlets
2. Boots, 1,170
3. Unichem - Moss, 430
4. National Co-Op, 230
5. Tesco, 120
6. Superdrug, 100
7. Safeway, 75
Source: *National Trade Data Bank*, July 15, 1997, p. ISA970701.

Drug Trade

★ 1144 ★
LEADING OUTLETS FOR NON-PRESCRIPTION DRUGS IN BEIJING, 1996
Ranked by: Percent distribution. **Number listed:** 4
1. Retail drug store with 40%
2. Work unit, 33%
3. Hospital pharmacy, 15%
4. Other, 12%
Source: *China-Britain Trade Review*, April 1997, p. 10.

Drug Trade – Great Britain

★ 1145 ★
PRESCRIPTION MEDICINES MARKET IN THE UNITED KINGDOM BY THERAPEUTIC CLASS, 1995
Ranked by: Number of prescriptions, as a percentage of all prescriptions. **Remarks:** Also notes cost of prescriptions in each class. **Number listed:** 11
1. Cardiovascular system with 18%
2. Central nervous system, 18%
3. Infections, 11%
4. Respiratory system, 10%
5. Gastro-intestinal, 8%
6. Skin, 7%
7. Endocrine, 6%
8. Musculoskeletal and joint diseases, 5%
9. Nutrition and blood, 3%

10. Obstetrics, gynecology, and urinary tract, 3%
Source: *National Trade Data Bank*, July 15, 1997, p. ISA970701.

Drugs, Nonprescription

★ 1146 ★
GERMANY'S OVER-THE-COUNTER DRUG MARKET
Ranked by: Market share, in percent. **Number listed:** 7
1. Klosterfran with 5.8%
2. Abtei, 3.7%
3. Fink, 3.7%
4. Smithkline Beecham, 3.7%
5. Bayer, 3.6%
6. Procter & Gamble, 3.1%
7. Boehringer, 2.8%
Source: *National Trade Data Bank*, September 11, 1996, p. ISA960801.

Drugs, Nonprescription – United Kingdom

★ 1147 ★
TOP OVER-THE-COUNTER MEDICINE BRANDS IN THE UNITED KINGDOM, 1995
Ranked by: Estimated sales, in millions of British pounds (£). **Remarks:** Notes ad agency and spending. **Number listed:** 10
1. Seven Seas (Seven Seas) with £Over 64 million
2. Anadin (Whitehall Labs), £35-40
3. Benylin (Warner Wellcome), £25-30
4. Lemsip (Reckitt & Colman), £25-30
5. Beecham's cold treatments (SmithKline Beecham), £20-25
6. Nicorette (Pharmacia), £20-25
7. Nurofen (Crookes Healthcare), £20-25
8. Sanatogen (Roche), £20-25
9. Solpadeine (SmithKline Beecham), £20-25
10. Calpol (Warner Wellcome), £15-20
Source: *Marketing*, July 4, 1996, p. 27.

Drugstores
See: **Drug Stores**

Duty and Tax Free Retailing – Europe

★ 1148 ★
TAX AND DUTY FREE SALES IN EUROPE OF FRAGRANCES AND COSMETICS, 1994
Ranked by: Share, in percent. **Remarks:** Table ranks share of fragrances and cosmetics among all duty free sales for countries of the European Union. **Number listed:** 10
1. Germany with 37.7%
2. Austria, 35.7%
3. Greece, 35.4%
4. Belgium, 31.9%
5. Luxembourg, 31.7%
6. Spain, 31.6%
7. Portugal, 31.4%
8. Netherlands, 26.8%
9. United Kingdom, 26.0%
10. France, 24.9%
Source: *The European*, August 1-7, 1996, p. 4.

★ 1149 ★
TAX AND DUTY FREE SALES IN EUROPE OF TOBACCO GOODS, 1994
Ranked by: Share, in percent. **Remarks:** Table ranks countries of the European Union by share of tobacco goods among all duty free sales. **Number listed:** 9
1. Austria with 30.9%
2. Belgium, 26.7%
3. Germany, 26.7%
4. Portugal, 25.3%
5. Spain, 25.3%
6. United Kingdom, 21.9%
7. Denmark, 21.5%
8. Sweden, 21.2%
9. France, 20.1%
10. Ireland, 20.0%
Source: *The European*, August 1-7, 1996, p. 4.

★ 1150 ★
TAX AND DUTY FREE SALES IN EUROPE, 1994
Ranked by: Sales of tax and duty free merchandise for countries in European Union, in millions of U.S. dollars. **Number listed:** 10
1. United Kingdom with $1,393 million
2. Germany, $652.1
3. Finland, $626.4
4. Denmark, $589.8
5. France, $543.1
6. Sweden, $434.5
7. Netherlands, $361.7
8. Spain, $247.4
9. Italy, $235.7
10. Greece, $146.7
Source: *The European*, August 1-7, 1996, p. 4.

Duty Free Importation

★ 1151 ★
TOP DUTY FREE AIRPORTS
Ranked by: Annual sales, in millions of U.S. dollars.
Number listed: 10
1. Heathrow (London, England) with $524 million
2. Honolulu (HI), $420
3. Hong Kong, $400
4. Singapore, $359
5. Tokyo (Japan), $340
6. Amsterdam (Netherlands), $327
7. Manila (Philippines), $303
8. Frankfurt (Germany), $289
9. Paris (France), $283
10. Gatwick (London, England), $194
Source: *The World in 1997*, 1997, p. 108.

Duty Free Shops

★ 1152 ★
LARGEST DUTY FREE SHOPS WORLDWIDE, 1995
Ranked by: Sales estimates, in millions of U.S. dollars.
Number listed: 20
1. London (Heathrow, United Kingdom) with $524.1 million
2. Honolulu (International Airport, U.S.), $419.5
3. Silja (International, Finland), $401.9
4. Hong Kong (Kai Tak International Airport), $400.0
5. Singapore (Changi Airport, Singapore), $358.8
6. Tokyo (Narita Airport, Japan), $340.0
7. Amsterdam (Schipol Airport, Netherlands), $326.6
8. Viking line (Finland), $314.0
9. Manila (N. Aquino International Aiport and FCS, Philipines), $302.6
10. Frankfurt Main Airport (Germany), $289.4
Source: *Soap/Cosmetics/Chemical Specialties*, January 1997, p. 26.

Economic Conditions, International

★ 1153 ★
ECONOMIC GROWTH IN THE BIG EMERGING MARKETS, 1995
Ranked by: Estimated annual percentage change in real GDP. **Number listed:** 10
1. China with 9.0%
2. South Korea, 7.5%
3. Indonesia, 7.0%

4. Taiwan, 6.4%
5. India, 5.5%
6. Argentina, 5.5%
7. Hong Kong, 5.4%
8. Poland, 4.5%
9. Brazil, 4.0%
10. Turkey, 3.0%

Source: *U.S. Global Trade Outlook 1995-2000: Toward the 21st Century*, 1995, p. 14.

★ 1154 ★
GROSS DOMESTIC PRODUCT OF WORLD'S BIGGEST ECONOMIES, 1996
Ranked by: Estimates of the output of goods and services, in U.S. dollars. **Number listed:** 9

1. United States with $6,408 billion
2. Japan, $3,198
3. Germany, $1,827
4. France, $1,290
5. Italy, $1,194
6. Britain, $1,064
7. China, $685
8. Canada, $628
9. Brazil, $565

Source: *The Christian Science Monitor*, January 31, 1996, p. 8.

★ 1155 ★
MOST OPEN LATIN AMERICAN MARKETS
Ranked by: Countries rated 1 to 10 on market openness based on a survey of 300 Latin American businesses. A score of "1" denotes a less open market in which the government imposes heavy restrictions; a score of "5" is average; and a score of "10" would be given to an open market in which the government imposes few restrictions. **Number listed:** 10

1. Argentina with 6.2
2. Chile, 6.2
3. Uruguay, 6.2
4. Bolivia, 6.1
5. Paraguay, 5.9
6. Mexico, 5.7
7. Ecuador, 5.4
8. Colombia, 5.3
9. Venezuela, 3.9
10. Brazil, 2.8

Source: *Business Latin America*, December 2, 1996, p. 2.

Economy

★ 1156 ★
COUNTRIES WITH THE LEAST GROWTH POTENTIAL
Ranked by: Growth potential, based on expected absolute increase in total output. **Remarks:** No specific data were given. **Number listed:** 10

1. Russia
2. Italy
3. Ukraine
4. Iceland
5. Luxembourg
6. Hungary
7. Greece
8. Slovakia
9. Zimbabwe
10. Jordan

Source: *The New York Times*, May 21, 1997, p. C3.

★ 1157 ★
COUNTRIES WITH THE MOST GROWTH POTENTIAL
Ranked by: Growth potential, based on expected absolute increase in total output. **Remarks:** No specific data were given. **Number listed:** 10

1. United States
2. China
3. India
4. Japan
5. Indonesia
6. United Kingdom
7. Brazil
8. Mexico
9. Canada
10. Thailand

Source: *The New York Times*, May 21, 1997, p. C3.

Ecuador – see under individual headings

EFT
See: **Electronic Funds Transfer**

Eggs

★ 1158 ★
CHICKEN EGG PRODUCTION IN SOUTHEAST ASIA
Ranked by: Production, in millions of eggs. **Number listed:** 10
1. Indonesia with 9,697 million eggs
2. Thailand, 7,330
3. Malaysia, 6,445
4. Philippines, 5,501
5. Vietnam, 2,352
6. Myanmar, 825
7. Laos, 821
8. Singapore, 311
9. Cambodia, 266

Source: *Broiler Industry*, June 1996, p. 28.

★ 1159 ★
DUTCH EGG MARKET
Ranked by: Market share, in percent. **Number listed:** 4
1. Van den Burg Eiprodukten BV with 45.0%
2. G. Kwetters & Zn BV, 15.0%
3. Adriaan Goede BV, 10.0%
4. Other, 30.0%

Source: *Egg Industry*, September 1996, p. 36.

★ 1160 ★
TOP EGG PRODUCERS, 1995
Ranked by: Estimated millions of eggs produced. **Remarks:** Global production reached 616,998 million eggs. **Number listed:** 10
1. China with 285,000 million eggs
2. United States, 74,400
3. Japan, 42,850
4. Russia, 35,400
5. Mexico, 21,200
6. France, 15,800
7. Brazil, 14,940
8. Germany, 13,800
9. Italy, 11,655
10. United Kingdom, 10,600

Source: *Egg Industry*, January 1996, p. 17.

Egypt – see under individual headings

Electric Appliances, Domestic
See: **Household Appliances**

Electric Connectors

★ 1161 ★
WORLDWIDE ELECTRONIC CONNECTOR MARKET BY END USE, 1996
Ranked by: Purchases of electronic connectors, in millions of U.S. dollars. **Remarks:** Notes projections for 1997. **Number listed:** 11
1. Computer and peripherals with $5,704.6 million
2. Data/telecom, $3,305.2
3. Automotive, $3,104.3
4. Industrial, $2,712.1
5. Consumer, $1,355.1
6. Transportation, $1,165.6
7. Military, $1,164.8
8. Office equipment, $800.8
9. Medical equipment, $449.4
10. Instrumentation, $433.9

Source: *Electronic Business Today*, November 1996, p. 92.

Electric Industries

★ 1162 ★
PRIVATIZATION IN THE ELECTRICITY INDUSTRY, 1988-1995
Ranked by: Value of privatizations of electric utilities, in millions of U.S. dollars. **Number listed:** 10
1. United Kingdom with $13,515.7 million
2. Germany, East, $6,607.1
3. Argentina, $4,652.9
4. Australia, $4,276
5. Malaysia, $1,474.3
6. Germany, West, $1,350
7. Spain, $1,300
8. Hungary, $1,248.3
9. Brazil, $1,195.7
10. China, $987

Source: *Energy*, April 1996, p. 4.

Electric Power

★ 1163 ★
DENMARK'S ELECTRIC POWER GENERATION, 1995
Ranked by: Market share based on production, in percent. **Number listed:** 3
1. Heat power (solar) with 96.6%
2. Wind power, 3.3%
3. Power plant generated, 0.1%

Source: *Dagens Nyheter*, September 16, 1996, p. A11.

★ 1164 ★
NORWAY'S ELECTRIC POWER GENERATION, 1995
Ranked by: Market share based on production, in percent. **Number listed:** 3
1. Power plant generated with 99.50%
2. Heat power (solar), 0.50%
3. Wind power, 0.01%
Source: *Dagens Nyheter*, September 16, 1996, p. A11.

★ 1165 ★
SOURCES OF ELECTRIC POWER IN CHINA, 1996
Ranked by: Distribution, in percent. **Number listed:** 4
1. Coal with 74%
2. Hydroelectric, 19%
3. Oil, 5%
4. Nuclear, 2%
Source: *The World in 1997*, 1997, p. 94.

★ 1166 ★
USES OF ELECTRIC POWER IN CHINA, 1996
Ranked by: End use, in percent. **Number listed:** 6
1. Heavy Industry with 60%
2. Light Industry, 15%
3. Residential, 10%
4. Government, 7%
5. Agriculture, 6%
6. Transport and telecoms, 2%
Source: *The World in 1997*, 1997, p. 94.

Electric Utilities

★ 1167 ★
LARGEST ELECTRIC POWER FIRMS IN JAPAN, 1996
Ranked by: Sales estimated for the fiscal year, in millions of U.S. dollars. **Remarks:** Includes 1994 - 1995 figures. Data for EPDC are wholesale figures. **Number listed:** 12

1. Tokyo with $15,914 million
2. Kansai, $7,440
3. Chubu, $7,320
4. Tohoku, $5,146
5. Chugoku, $3,775
6. Kyushu, $3,740
7. EPDC, $2,480
8. Shikoku, $1,534
9. Hokuriku, $2,480
10. Hokkaido, $1,500
Source: *National Trade Data Bank*, June 1, 1996, p. ISA960601.

★ 1168 ★
TOP ELECTRIC COMPANIES IN THE UNITED KINGDOM
Ranked by: Market capital, in billions of British pounds (£). **Number listed:** 10
1. National Power with £6.441 billion
2. PowerGen, £4.150
3. Scottish Power, £3.500
4. National Grid, £3.436
5. London Electricity, £1.374
6. Scottish Hydro-Electricity, £1.364
7. Yorkshire Electricity, £1.310
8. East Midlands Electricity, £1.226
9. Northern Electricity, £0.677
10. N. Ireland Electricity, £0.632
Source: *Financial Times*, April 25, 1996, p. 27.

Electric Utilities – Canada

★ 1169 ★
CANADA'S TOP ELECTRIC UTILITIES
Ranked by: Revenue, in thousands of Canadian dollars. **Remarks:** Includes figures on profits and return on capital. **Number listed:** 14
1. Ontario Hydro with C$8,730,000 thousand
2. Hydro-Quebec, C$7,667,000
3. B.C. Hydro and Power, C$2,292,000
4. CanUtilities Holdings, C$1,694,800
5. Canadian Utilities, C$1,690,000
6. TransAlta Corp., C$1,658,500
7. TransAlta Utilities, C$1,431,500
8. New Brunswick Power Corp., C$1,067,756
9. Manitoba Hydro-Electric Board, C$998,700
10. Saskatchewan Power Corp, C$894,000
Source: *Globe and Mail's Report on Business Magazine*, July 1996, p. 159.

Electricity

★ 1170 ★
TOP NATIONS IN ASIA BY ELECTRIC CAPACITY
Ranked by: Capacity, in kilowatt hours. **Number listed:** 28
1. Japan with 205,140,000 kilowatt hours
2. China, 162,000,000
3. India, 81,200,000
4. South Korea, 26,940,000
5. Taiwan, 21,460,000
6. Iran, 19,080,000
7. Thailand, 12,810,000
8. Indonesia, 12,100,000
9. Pakistan, 10,800,000

10. North Korea, 9,500,000

Source: *The World Factbook 1995,* Information obtained from the Internet, http:// www.odci.gov.

★ 1171 ★

TOP NATIONS IN EUROPE BY ELECTRIC CAPACITY

Ranked by: Capacity, in kilowatt hours. **Number listed:** 33

1. Germany with 115,430,000 kilowatt hours
2. France, 105,250,000
3. United Kingdom, 65,360,000
4. Italy, 61,630,000
5. Spain, 43,800,000
6. Sweden, 34,560,000
7. Poland, 31,120,000
8. Norway, 27,280,000
9. Romania, 22,180,000
10. Netherlands, 17,520,000

Source: *The World Factbook 1995,* Information obtained from the Internet, http:// www.odci.gov.

★ 1172 ★

TOP NATIONS IN FORMER SOVIET COUNTRIES BY ELECTRIC PRODUCTION

Ranked by: Production, in kilowatt hours. **Number listed:** 10

1. Russia with 876,000 million kilowatt hours
2. Ukraine, 182,000
3. Kazakhstan, 65,100
4. Uzbekistan, 47,500
5. Belarus, 31,400
6. Lithuania, 18,900
7. Azerbaijan, 17,500
8. Tajikistan, 17,000
9. Kyrgyzstan, 12,700
10. Estonia, 11,300

Source: *The World Factbook 1995,* Information obtained from the Internet, http:// www.odci.gov.

★ 1173 ★

TOP NATIONS IN LATIN AMERICA AND THE CARIBBEAN BY ELECTRIC PRODUCTION

Ranked by: Production, in kilowatt hours. **Number listed:** 10

1. Brazil with 241,400 million kilowatt hours
2. Mexico, 122,000
3. Venezuela, 72,000
4. Argentina, 54,800
5. Colombia, 33,000
6. Paraguay, 26,500
7. Chile, 22,000
8. Puerto Rico, 15,600
9. Cuba, 12,000

10. Peru, 11,200

Source: *The World Factbook 1995,* Information obtained from the Internet, http:// www.odci.gov.

★ 1174 ★

TOP NATIONS IN THE NEAR EAST BY ELECTRIC PRODUCTION

Ranked by: Production, in kilowatt hours. **Number listed:** 10

1. Turkey with 71,000 million kilowatt hours
2. Saudi Arabia, 46,000
3. Iraq, 25,700
4. Israel, 23,000
5. United Arab Emirates, 16,500
6. Syria, 13,200
7. Kuwait, 11,000
8. Oman, 6,000
9. Qatar, 4,500
10. Jordan, 4,200

Source: *The World Factbook 1995,* Information obtained from the Internet, http:// www.odci.gov.

★ 1175 ★

TOP NATIONS OF ASIA BY ELECTRIC PRODUCTION

Ranked by: Production, in kilowatt hours. **Number listed:** 10

1. Japan with 840,000 million kilowatt hours
2. China, 746,000
3. India, 314,000
4. South Korea, 137,000
5. Taiwan, 108,000
6. Thailand, 56,800
7. Pakistan, 52,400
8. Iran, 50,800
9. North Korea, 50,000
10. Indonesia, 44,000

Source: *The World Factbook 1995,* Information obtained from the Internet, http:// www.odci.gov.

★ 1176 ★

TOP NATIONS OF EUROPE BY ELECTRIC PRODUCTION

Ranked by: Production, in kilowatt hours. **Number listed:** 10

1. Germany with 493,000 million kilowatt hours
2. France, 447,000
3. United Kingdom, 303,000
4. Italy, 209,000
5. Spain, 148,000
6. Sweden, 141,000
7. Poland, 124,000
8. Norway, 118,000
9. Netherlands, 72,400

10. Belgium, 66,000
Source: *The World Factbook 1995,* Information obtained from the Internet, http:// www.odci.gov.

★ 1177 ★
TOP NATIONS OF LATIN AMERICA/CARIBBEAN BY ELECTRIC CAPACITY
Ranked by: Capacity, in kilowatt hours **Number listed:** 25
1. Brazil with 55,130,000 kilowatt hours
2. Mexico, 28,780,000
3. Venezuela, 18,740,000
4. Argentina, 17,330,000
5. Colombia, 10,220,000
6. Paraguay, 6,530,000
7. Chile, 4,810,000
8. Puerto Rico, 4,230,000
9. Peru, 4,190,000
10. Cuba, 3,990,000
Source: *The World Factbook 1995,* Information obtained from the Internet, http:// www.odci.gov.

★ 1178 ★
TOP NATIONS OF NORTH AFRICA BY ELECTRIC CAPACITY
Ranked by: Capacity, in kilowatt hours. **Number listed:** 6
1. Egypt with 11,830,000 kilowatt hours
2. Algeria, 5,370,000
3. Libya, 4,600,000
4. Morocco, 2,620,000
5. Tunisia, 1,410,000
6. Sudan, 500,000
Source: *The World Factbook 1995,* Information obtained from the Internet, http:// www.odci.gov..

★ 1179 ★
TOP NATIONS OF THE FORMER SOVIET UNION BY ELECTRIC CAPACITY
Ranked by: Capacity, in kilowatt hours. **Number listed:** 15
1. Russia with 213,100,000 kilowatt hours
2. Ukraine, 54,380,000
3. Kazakhstan, 17,380,000
4. Uzbekistan, 11,690,000
5. Belarus, 7,010,000
6. Lithuania, 6,190,000
7. Azerbaijan, 4,900,000
8. Armenia, 4,620,000
9. Georgia, 4,410,000
10. Tajikistan, 3,800,000
Source: *The World Factbook 1995,* Information obtained from the Internet, http:// www.odci.gov.

★ 1180 ★
TOP NATIONS OF THE NEAR EAST BY ELECTRIC CAPACITY
Ranked by: Capacity, in kilowatt hours. **Number listed:** 10
1. Turkey with 18,710,000 kilowatt hours
2. Saudi Arabia, 17,550,000
3. Iraq, 7,170,000
4. Kuwait, 7,070,000
5. United Arab Emirates, 4,760,000
6. Syria, 4,160,000
7. Israel, 4,140,000
8. Oman, 1,540,000
9. Qatar, 1,520,000
10. Lebanon, 1,220,000
Source: *The World Factbook 1995,* Information obtained from the Internet, http:// www.odci.gov.

★ 1181 ★
TOP POWER MARKETS
Ranked by: Demand, in megawatts. **Remarks:** Notes number of projects and total capacity for solicitation and privatizations. **Number listed:** 20
1. China with 176,181 megawatts
2. India, 80,571
3. Brazil, 36,412
4. Turkey, 30,174
5. Pakistan, 19,119
6. Thailand, 15,970
7. Nigeria, 11,290
8. Philippines, 10,802
9. Argentina, 9,429
10. Venezuela, 8,496
Source: *Financial Times,* June 19, 1997, p. 4.

Electronic Funds Transfer

★ 1182 ★
ELECTRONIC DEBIT CARD TRANSACTIONS, 1994
Ranked by: Number of transactions per inhabitant. **Number listed:** 10
1. France with 26.100
2. Belgium, 18.000
3. Sweden, 8.800
4. Netherlands, 8.200
5. Canada, 6.300
6. Switzerland, 5.700
7. United States, 2.400
8. Germany, 1.280
9. Italy, 0.570
10. Japan, 0.006
Source: *Financial Times,* September 12, 1996, p. 6.

Electronic Industries

★ 1183 ★

FASTEST GROWING MARKETS FOR ELECTRICAL POWER SYSTEMS OUTSIDE THE U.S.

Ranked by: Average annual growth, in percent. **Number listed:** 10

1. Honduras with 75%
2. Philippines, 50%
3. South Korea, 50%
4. Venezuela, 30%
5. Argentina, 25%
6. Bulgaria, 25%
7. Egypt, 20%
8. Kuwait, 20%
9. Morocco, 20%
10. Romania, 20%

Source: *National Trade Data Bank*, March 21, 1995, p. BMR9404.

★ 1184 ★

GLOBAL WARFARE ELECTRONICS MARKET

Ranked by: Sales, in millions of U.S. dollars. **Remarks:** Includes market shares. **Number listed:** 9

1. Raytheon with $1,600 million
2. Lockheed Martin, $1,000
3. Northrup Grumman, $450
4. Thomson-Elettronica, $400
5. GEC-Marconi, $300
6. Israel, $300
7. DASA, $200
8. Other U.S., $850
9. Rest of world, $900

Source: *Interavia*, November 1996, p. 10.

★ 1185 ★

LARGEST ELECTRONIC COMPONENT MAKERS IN THAILAND, 1994

Ranked by: Revenue, in millions of bahts (Bt). **Remarks:** Includes profits and assets. **Number listed:** 31

1. Seagate Technology with Bt32,428.91 million
2. Alphatec Electronics, Bt9,995.39
3. Fujitsu, Bt9,204.45
4. Minebea Electronics, Bt7,479.35
5. Cal-Comp Electronics, Bt7,243.05
6. Philips Semiconductors, Bt5,731.08
7. Sony Semiconductor, Bt5,474.77
8. NS Electronics Bangkok, Bt4,120.70
9. Delta Electronics, Bt4,062.93
10. AT&T Microelectronics, Bt3,767.20

Source: *Business Review*, December 1995, p. 174.

★ 1186 ★

LARGEST ELECTRONICS BRANDS BY BRAND VALUE

Ranked by: Brand value, in millions of U.S. dollars. **Remarks:** Value was calculated using capital, ratio of capital to company sales, earnings, and corporate tax rate of the country where the parent company is located. See source for details. Brand values for BASF, Philips Electronic's Grundig brand, and Zenith were "not meaningful." **Number listed:** 8

1. Intel (Intel) with $10,499 million
2. Motorola (Motorola), $9,624
3. Sony (Sony), $8,800
4. Philips (Philips Electronics), $5,177
5. Siemens (Siemens), $4,256

Source: *Financial World*, World's Most Valuable Brands (annual), July 8, 1996, p. 61.

★ 1187 ★

LARGEST ELECTRONICS COMPANIES, 1995

Ranked by: Revenue, in millions of U.S. dollars. **Remarks:** Notes profits and global rank. **Number listed:** 30

1. Hitachi (Japan) with $84,167 million
2. Matsushita Elec. Indl. (Japan), $70,398
3. General Electric (United States), $70,028
4. Siemens (Germany), $60,674
5. Toshiba (Japan), $53,047
6. Daewoo (South Korea), $51,215
7. Sony (Japan), $47,581
8. NEC (Japan), $45,557
9. Philips Electronics (Netherlands), $40,148
10. Mitsubishi Electric (Japan), $36,380

Source: *Fortune*, The Global 500: World's Biggest Corporations (annual), August 5, 1996, p. F-18.

★ 1188 ★

LARGEST IMPORT MARKETS FOR ELECTRICAL POWER SYSTEMS OUTSIDE THE U.S.

Ranked by: Value of imports, in millions of U.S. dollars. **Number listed:** 10

1. Germany with $13,650.0 million
2. France, $5,600.0
3. Mexico, $3,341.3
4. Canada, $2,809.0
5. Singapore, $2,446.0
6. Belgium, $2,126.0
7. Italy, $1,950.0
8. South Korea, $1,850.0
9. Malaysia, $1,740.0
10. Spain, $1,450.0

Source: *National Trade Data Bank*, March 21, 1995, p. BMR9404.

★ 1189 ★

LARGEST MARKETS FOR ELECTRICAL POWER SYSTEMS OUTSIDE THE U.S.

Ranked by: Total market value, in millions of U.S. dollars. **Number listed:** 10

1. Germany with $90,000.0 million
2. Japan, $29,041.0
3. China, $12,400.0
4. France, $11,000.0
5. South Korea, $7,500.0
6. India, $6,500.0
7. Mexico, $6,201.2
8. Italy, $5,700.0
9. Canada, $4,769.0
10. Belgium, $3,188.0

Source: *National Trade Data Bank*, March 21, 1995, p. BMR9404.

★ 1190 ★

MOST RESPECTED EUROPEAN ELECTRONICS AND ELECTRICAL COMPONENTS FIRMS

Ranked by: Survey based on FT 500 list, as well as polls of investment analysts and chief executives of European companies. See source for details. **Number listed:** 3

1. Electrolux
2. Siemens
3. Ericsson

Source: *Financial Times,* Europe's Most Respected Companies (annual), September 24, 1997, p. 2.

★ 1191 ★

TOP ELECTRIC AND ELECTRONICS COMPANIES IN SOUTH KOREA, 1996

Ranked by: Sales for the first six months of 1996, in hundred million won (W). **Number listed:** 77

1. Samsung Electronics with W87,137.0 hundred million
2. LG Electronics, W36,769.2
3. Daewoo Electronics, W16,401.9
4. Samsung Display Devices, W11,814.2
5. LG Cable & Machinery, W7,404.6
6. Samsung Electro-Mechanics, W7,302.7
7. LG Ind. Systems, W7,211.8
8. Taihan Electric Wire, W6,120.8
9. Anam Ind., W5,450.8
10. Trigem Computer, W3,876.5

Source: *Business Korea*, October 1996, p. 37.

★ 1192 ★

TOP ELECTRONICS FIRMS IN THAILAND, 1994

Ranked by: Revenue, in millions of bahts (Bt). **Remarks:** Includes profits and assets. **Number listed:** 36

1. Siew - National with Bt9,241.54 million
2. Singer Thailand, Bt6,715.57
3. National Thai, Bt5,755.25
4. Sanyo Universal Electric, Bt5,287.74

5. Muramoto Electron, Bt4,253.42
6. Philips Electronics, Bt4,172.75
7. Kang Yong Watana, Bt3,602.36
8. Thai Yazaki Electric Wire, Bt3,324.79
9. Phelps Dodge Thailand, Bt2,777.48
10. Toshiba Thailand, Bt2,570.71

Source: *Business Review*, December 1995, p. 173.

Electronic Industries – Distributors

★ 1193 ★

TOP ELECTRONICS DISTRIBUTORS IN EUROPE, 1995

Ranked by: Sales, in millions of U.S. dollars. **Remarks:** Also notes 1994 sales. **Number listed:** 10

1. Arrow with $1,520 million
2. Avnet, $1,002
3. Farnell, $723
4. Sonepar (SEI), $689
5. Eurodis-Electron, $467
6. EBV, $412
7. Memec, $331
8. RS Components, $257
9. Tekelec, $228
10. IEC, $174

Source: *Electronic Business Today*, May 1996, p. 74.

Electronic Industries – Export-Import Trade

★ 1194 ★

HONG KONG'S TOP MARKETS FOR EXPORTS OF ELECTRONICS, 1996

Ranked by: Value of exports, in thousands of Hong Kong dollars (HK$). **Number listed:** 31

1. China with HK$90,066,828 thousand
2. United States, HK$88,171,826
3. Japan, HK$28,750,689
4. Singapore, HK$22,454,187
5. Germany, Federal Republic of, HK$17,454,428
6. United Kingdom, HK$14,882,900
7. Taiwan, HK$14,522,801
8. South Korea, HK$10,527,741
9. Netherlands, HK$9,777,000
10. France, HK$7,862,974

Source: http:// www.tdc.org.hk/hkstat/electron.htm, August 25, 1997, p. 2.

Electronic Industries – Japan

★ 1195 ★
TOP ELECTRONIC EQUIPMENT MAKERS IN JAPAN
Ranked by: Income, in millions of yen (¥). **Number listed:** 10
1. Hitachi with ¥67,891 million
2. Matsushita Electric Industries, ¥50,476
3. Mitsubishi Electric, ¥48,045
4. Toshiba, ¥47,012
5. Matsushita Electric Works, ¥45,421
6. Sharp, ¥43,909
7. Fuji Xerox, ¥38,198
8. NEC Corp., ¥34,647
9. Sanyo Electric, ¥34,329
10. Sony, ¥27,522
Source: *Tokyo Business Today*, August 1995, p. 26.

★ 1196 ★
TOP ELECTRONIC PARTS MAKERS IN JAPAN
Ranked by: Income, in millions of yen (¥). **Number listed:** 10
1. Kyocera with ¥39,906 million
2. Murata Mfg., ¥24,775
3. Matsushita Battery Ind., ¥24,042
4. Matsushita Electronics, ¥23,483
5. Matsushita Communication Ind., ¥18,436
6. TDK, ¥14,299
7. Rohm, ¥10,562
8. Hirose Electric, ¥8,182
9. Daikoku Denki, ¥7,971
10. Futaba Corp., ¥7,934
Source: *Tokyo Business Today*, August 1995, p. 26.

Elevators

★ 1197 ★
GLOBAL ELEVATOR MAKERS, 1995
Ranked by: Market share, in percent. **Remarks:** The market reached $21.7 billion in sales in 1995. **Number listed:** 6
1. Otis with 22.0%
2. Schindler, 15.0%
3. Kone, 10.0%
4. Mitsubishi, 8.0%
5. Thyssen, 7.0%
6. Other, 38.0%
Source: *The Economist*, March 16, 1996, p. 71.

El Salvador – see under individual headings

Employee Benefit Consultants

★ 1198 ★
LARGEST EMPLOYEE BENEFIT CONSULTANTS, 1996
Ranked by: Gross benefit consulting revenues, in millions of U.S. dollars. **Remarks:** Notes percent increase in revenues from 1995 to 1996 and number of U.S. offices. **Number listed:** 10
1. William M. Mercer Cos. Inc. with $790 million
2. Towers Perrin, $618
3. Watson Wyatt Worldwide, $537
4. Hewitt Associates L.L.C., $488
5. Coopers & Lybrand L.L.P., Human Resources Advisory Group, $363
6. Sedwick Noble Lowndes, $291
7. A. Foster Higgins & Co. Inc., $257
8. Buck Consultants Inc., $225
9. Aon Consulting, $209
10. Alexander Consulting Group Inc., $205
Source: *Business Insurance*, December 9, 1996, p. 3.

Employee Fringe Benefits

★ 1199 ★
DAYS OF SICK LEAVE TAKEN IN EUROPEAN COUNTRIES, 1994
Ranked by: Average number of sick days taken by a worker. **Number listed:** 9
1. Netherlands with 6.4 days
2. Germany, 5.5
3. Sweden, 5.3
4. Austria, 4.8
5. Belgium, 4.4
6. Finland, 4.4
7. Italy, 3.9
8. Ireland, 3.5
9. Britain, 3.2
Source: *The New York Times*, October 1, 1996, p. C3.

★ 1200 ★
SICK LEAVE IN EUROPEAN COUNTRIES, 1994
Ranked by: Minimum number of paid sick days to which a worker is entitled in countries cited. **Number listed:** 6
1. Italy with 3 months
2. Austria, 4-12 weeks
3. Germany, 6 weeks
4. Netherlands, 6 weeks
5. Sweden, 2 weeks
6. Finland, 7 days
Source: *The New York Times*, October 1, 1996, p. C3.

★ 1201 ★

SICK LEAVE PAY IN EUROPEAN COUNTRIES, 1994

Ranked by: Percent of gross wages paid. **Number listed:** 7

1. Germany with 100%
2. Austria, 100%
3. Belgium, 100%
4. Finland, 100%
5. Italy, 100%
6. Netherlands, 70%
7. Sweden, 75-90%

Source: *The New York Times*, October 1, 1996, p. C3.

Employee Vacations, International

★ 1202 ★

EMPLOYEE VACATION DAYS IN INDUSTRIALIZED COUNTRIES

Ranked by: Vacation days alloted employees with one year on the job. **Remarks:** Data are from a survey of 1,005 large employers. Figure for Norway is based on a six day workweek. **Number listed:** 15

1. Austria with 30 days
2. Brazil, 30
3. Finland, 25
4. Norway, 25
5. Sweden, 25
6. Germany, 24
7. Britain, 22
8. Australia, 20
9. Netherlands, 20
10. Switzerland, 20

Source: *The New York Times*, May 11, 1996, p. 12F.

★ 1203 ★

EMPLOYEE VACATION TIME IN EUROPEAN NATIONS

Ranked by: Employees taking more than 5 weeks vacation per year, as a percent of total workforce. **Number listed:** 5

1. Germany with 97%
2. Spain, 84%
3. Italy, 75%
4. France, 72%
5. United Kingdom, 22%

Source: *The Guardian*, June 26, 1997, p. 3.

★ 1204 ★

LONGEST EMPLOYEE VACATIONS BY CITY

Ranked by: Average number of paid vacation days per year. **Remarks:** Data are based on the weighted average of 11 professions in 55 cities. **Number listed:** 5

1. Berlin with 30.0 days
2. Frankfurt, 30.0

3. Helsinki, 26.9
4. Amsterdam, 26.6
5. Bombay, 26.6

Source: *The Christian Science Monitor*, September 15, 1997, p. 2.

★ 1205 ★

SHORTEST EMPLOYEE VACATIONS BY CITY

Ranked by: Average number of paid vacation days per year. **Remarks:** Data are based on the weighted average of 11 professions in 55 cities. **Number listed:** 5

1. Shanghai with 1.2 days
2. Mexico City, 8.7
3. Taipei, 9.0
4. Jakarta, 9.4
5. Bangkok, 9.8

Source: *The Christian Science Monitor*, September 15, 1997, p. 2.

★ 1206 ★

VACATION AND FREE TIME, 1994

Ranked by: Annual vacation and additional free time for negotiated scheduled work situations as of November 1, 1994. **Number listed:** 18

1. Finland with 37.5 work days
2. Italy, 35.0
3. Netherlands, 32.5
4. Federal Republic of Germany, 30.0
5. Luxembourg, 27.0
6. Austria, 26.5
7. Denmark, 25.0
8. France, 25.0
9. Sweden, 25.0
10. United Kingdom, 25.0

Source: *Foreign Labor Trends: Germany, 1994-95*, 1995, p. 10.

Employment

★ 1207 ★

ASIAN COUNTRIES WHERE JAPANESE ARE EMPLOYED

Ranked by: Numbers of Japanese staying more than 3 months in countries cited. **Number listed:** 6

1. Singapore with 20,179
2. Thailand, 18,170
3. Hong Kong, 17,548
4. China, 12,736
6. Taiwan, 8,047
5. South Korea, 8,718

Source: *Nikkei Weekly*, September 9, 1996, p. 20.

★ 1208 ★

COUNTRIES WHERE MEN PREFER FEMALE BOSSES

Ranked by: Percent of male respondents preferring female bosses. **Remarks:** A Gallup Poll inquired into the preference for male or female bosses; more than 22,000 people in 22 countries were interviewed. Table ranks selected countries by the percent of male respondents preferring female bosses. **Number listed:** 7

1. France with 26%
2. Germany, 17%
2. United States, 17%
3. Spain, 15%
4. Canada, 13%
5. Mexico, 11%
6. Japan, 10%
7. China, 9%

Source: *Working Woman*, September 1996, p. 16.

★ 1209 ★

COUNTRIES WHERE MEN PREFER MALE BOSSES

Ranked by: Percent of male respondents preferring male bosses. **Remarks:** A Gallup Poll inquired into the preference for male or female bosses; more than 22,000 people in 22 countries were interviewed. Table ranks selected countries by the percent of male respondents preferring male bosses. **Number listed:** 7

1. Japan with 77%
2. France, 53%
3. China, 43%
3. Mexico, 43%
4. United States, 37%
5. Germany, 35%
6. Spain, 28%
7. Canada, 27%

Source: *Working Woman*, September 1996, p. 16.

★ 1210 ★

COUNTRIES WHERE WOMEN PREFER FEMALE BOSSES

Ranked by: Percent of female respondents preferring female bosses. **Remarks:** A Gallup Poll inquired into the preference for male or female bosses; more than 22,000 people in 22 countries were interviewed. Table ranks selected countries. **Number listed:** 8

1. Mexico with 31%
2. United States, 22%
3. Japan, 21%
4. Spain, 19%
5. Germany, 15%
6. Canada, 14%
7. China, 14%
8. France, 14%

Source: *Working Woman*, September 1996, p. 16.

★ 1211 ★

COUNTRIES WHERE WOMEN PREFER MALE BOSSES

Ranked by: Percent of female respondents preferring male bosses. **Remarks:** A Gallup Poll inquired into the preference for male or female bosses; more than 22,000 people in 22 countries were interviewed. Table ranks selected countries. **Number listed:** 8

1. France with 77%
2. Japan, 71%
3. Germany, 56%
4. United States, 54%
5. Canada, 39%
6. Mexico, 35%
7. China, 33%
8. Spain, 23%

Source: *Working Woman*, September 1996, p. 16.

★ 1212 ★

GOVERNMENT SPENDING ON EMPLOYMENT PROGRAMS, 1995

Ranked by: Costs of employment in selected countries, as percent of GDP. **Number listed:** 17

1. Denmark with 7.00%
2. Finland, 6.73%
3. Sweden, 5.44%
4. Belgium, 4.33%
5. Ireland, 4.27%
6. Germany, 3.84%
7. Netherlands, 3.82%
8. Spain, 3.64%
9. France, 3.31%
10. Britain, 2.18%

Source: *The Wall Street Journal*, September 30, 1995, p. A16.

★ 1213 ★

JAPAN'S FASTEST GROWING EMPLOYMENT SECTORS, 1991-1996

Ranked by: Employee increase from 1991 through 1996, in percent. **Number listed:** 10

1. Convenience stores with 77.0% increase
2. Entertainment (Karaoke boxes, etc.), 74.3%
3. Welfare for elderly, 71.2%
4. Security, 45.3%
5. Pachinko parlors, 32.8%
6. Welfare for disabled people, 31.3%
7. Natural science institutes, 26.3%
8. Restaurants, 26.2%
9. Bars and beer halls, 25.3%
10. Construction, 21.8%

Source: *Look Japan*, September 1997, p. 16.

★ 1214 ★

LARGEST CHEMCIAL ENGINEER EMPLOYERS IN THE UNITED KINGDOM

Ranked by: Number of engineers. **Number listed:** 20

1. ICI with 663
2. British Petroleum, 647
3. Kvaerner John Brown, 356
4. Shell, 335
5. Exxon, 325
6. Foster Wheeler, 246
7. Unilever, 228
8. BNFL, 210
9. British Gas, 191
10. Zeneca, 185

Source: *Financial Times*, April 3, 1997, p. 25.

★ 1215 ★

LEADING COUNTRIES WHERE CHILDREN WORK FULL OR PART TIME, 1995

Ranked by: Children who work, in percent. **Remarks:** Figures are estimated for selected countries. **Number listed:** 16

1. Kenya with 42%
2. Bangladesh, 30%
3. Haiti, 25%
4. Turkey, 24%
5. Pakistan, 17%
6. Brazil, 16%
7. Guatemala, 16%
8. Thailand, 16%
9. India, 14%
10. China, 11%

Source: *The Wall Street Journal*, November 12, 1996, p. 2.

★ 1216 ★

TOP FIRMS BY FOREIGN EMPLOYMENT

Ranked by: Percent of employees employed in foreign countries. **Remarks:** Includes number of foreign and domestic employees. **Number listed:** 14

1. Nestle (Switzerland) with 97%
2. Philips Electronics (Netherlands), 82%
3. Unilever (Netherlands), 64%
4. Ford (U.S.), 54%
5. IBM (U.S.), 51%
6. Volkswagen (Germany), 40%
7. Matsushita Electric (Japan), 38%
8. Siemens (Germany), 38%
9. General Motors (U.S.), 36%
10. PepsiCo. (U.S.), 30%

Source: *The Wall Street Journal*, September 26, 1996, p. R6.

★ 1217 ★

WHERE WORKERS ARE MOST SATISFIED

Ranked by: Percentage of workers in selected countries satisfied with company that employs them. **Number listed:** 8

1. Switzerland with 82%
2. Mexico, 72%
3. Germany, 66%
4. United States, 65%
5. France, 58%
6. Singapore, 53%
7. Hong Kong, 43%
8. Japan, 31%

Source: *Business Week*, June 24, 1996, p. 28.

Employment Agencies

★ 1218 ★

TOP TEMP FIRMS WORLDWIDE, 1995

Ranked by: Systemwide sales, in billions of U.S. dollars. **Remarks:** Ecco and Aida have announced plans to merge. The top three firms have 15% of the market. **Number listed:** 6

1. Manpower Inc. with $6.88 billion
2. Ecco SA, $4.21
3. Adia SA, $3.15
4. Olsten Corp., $3.01
5. Randstand Holding, $2.94
6. Kelly Services Inc., $2.69

Source: *The Wall Street Journal*, May 9, 1996, p. A3.

Energy Consumption

★ 1219 ★

HOW ASIA CONSUMES ENERGY, 1995

Ranked by: Consumption, in percent. **Number listed:** 5

1. Coal with 46.0%
2. Oil, 39.0%
3. Gas, 9.0%
4. Nuclear, 5.0%
5. Hydro, 2.0%

Source: *Financial Times*, February 19, 1997, p. 26.

★ 1220 ★

ROMANIA'S ENERGY CONSUMPTION, 1994

Ranked by: Consumption, in percent. **Number listed:** 5

1. Gas with 40.0%
2. Petroleum, 26.0%
3. Heat, 20.0%
4. Electricity, 13.0%
5. Coal, 1.0%

Source: *The Times*, August 29, 1996, p. 14.

Energy Industries

★ 1221 ★
TOP FIVE GROWTH MARKETS FOR WIND ENERGY, 1995-2005
Ranked by: Projected capacity additions through 2005, in megawatts. **Number listed:** 4
1. United States with 2,730 megawatts
2. India, 2,500
3. China, 1,300
3. Germany, 1,300
4. Spain, 1,275
Source: *Energy*, April 1996, p. 15.

★ 1222 ★
TOTAL WIND ENERGY CAPACITY, 1995
Ranked by: Total installed wind energy capacity for selected countries, in megawatts. **Number listed:** 8
1. United States with 1,770 megawatts
2. Germany, 1,136
3. Denmark, 614
4. India, 565
5. Holland, 259
6. United Kingdom, 193
7. Spain, 145
8. China, 36
Source: *Energy*, April 1996, p. 15.

★ 1223 ★
WIND ENERGY PRODUCERS IN GERMANY
Ranked by: Share of wind energy production, in percent. **Number listed:** 9
1. Enercon (Germany) with 29.4%
2. Tacke (Germany), 15.1%
3. Vestas (Denmark), 13.6%
4. Micen (Denmark), 9.8%
5. AN Maschinenbau (Denmark), 8.4%
6. Nordtank (Denmark), 7.2%
7. Nordex (Denmark), 3.4%
8. HSW (Germany), 3.1%
9. Others, 10.0%
Source: *National Trade Data Bank*, January 30, 1996, p. IMI960130.

Engineering

★ 1224 ★
ENGINEERING GRADUATES BY COUNTRY
Ranked by: Number of annual graduates in Engineering in selected countries. **Number listed:** 9
1. China, Peoples Rep. with 113,000 graduates
2. Japan, 81,000
3. United States, 80,000

4. Germany, 38,000
5. Mexico, 30,000
6. India, 29,000
7. South Korea, 28,000
8. Czech Republic, 9,400
9. Taiwan, 8,900
Source: *Deutschland*, June 1995, p. 18.

Engineering Construction Companies

★ 1225 ★
LARGEST ENGINEERING CONSTRUCTION COMPANIES, 1995
Ranked by: Revenue, in millions of U.S. dollars. **Remarks:** Notes profits and global rank. **Number listed:** 13
1. Cie Generale des Eaux (France) with $32,665 million
2. Lyonnaise des Eaux (France), $21,117
3. Taisei (Japan), $19,762
4. Shimizu (Japan), $18,923
5. Kajima (Japan), $18,271
6. Takenaka (Japan), $15,368
7. Bouygues (France), $14,801
8. Sekisui House (Japan), $13,841
9. Obayashi (Japan), $12,891
10. Kumagai Gumi (Japan), $11,294
Source: *Fortune,* The Global 500: World's Biggest Corporations (annual), August 5, 1996, p. F-19.

★ 1226 ★
TOP DESIGN FIRMS IN AFRICA, 1995
Ranked by: Billings. **Remarks:** The top 10 firms billed $430.9 million of $907.2 million total billings. Specific dollar values were not provided. **Number listed:** 10
1. SNC-Lavalin International Inc.
2. Louis Berger Group
3. Nethconsult
4. Dar Al-Handasah Consultants
5. NEDECO
6. Brown & Root Inc.
7. Law Engineering & Environmental Services
8. Bechtel Group Inc.
9. ABB Lummus Global Inc.
10. Tractebel Engineering
Source: *ENR*, July 22, 1996, p. 34.

★ 1227 ★
TOP DESIGN FIRMS IN LATIN AMERICA, 1995
Ranked by: Billings. **Remarks:** The top 10 firms billed $492.1 million of $826.0 million total billings. No further data were provided for these rankings. **Number listed:** 10
1. Jaakko Poyry Group
2. Foster Wheeler Corp.

3. SNC-Lavalin International Inc.
4. Snamprogetti SPA
5. Louis Berger Group
6. Harza Engineering Co.
7. NEDECO
8. Nethconsult
9. AGRA Industries Ltd.
10. Bechetel Group Inc.
Source: *ENR*, July 22, 1996, p. 34.

★ 1228 ★
TOP DESIGN FIRMS IN THE MIDDLE EAST, 1995
Ranked by: Billings. **Remarks:** The top 10 firms billed $525.6 million of $1,045.0 million total billings. Specific dollar values were not provided. **Number listed:** 10
1. Dar Al-Handasah Consultants
2. ABB Lummus Global Inc.
3. Stone & Webster Engineering Corp.
4. Parsons Corp.
5. Snamprogetti SPA
6. Norconsult International AS
7. M.W. Kellogg Co.
8. Bechtel Group Inc.
9. Jacobs Engineering Group Inc.
10. Mott MacDonald
Source: *ENR*, July 22, 1996, p. 34.

★ 1229 ★
TOP ENGINEERING CONSTRUCTION COMPANIES IN THE U.K. AND GERMANY
Ranked by: Annual sales, in millions of U.S. dollars. **Remarks:** Notes number of employees, specialty, and year founded. **Number listed:** 20
1. Heidelberger Druckmaschinen (Germany) with $2,900 million
2. J.C. Bamford (U.K.), $1,200
3. Krones (Germany), $940
4. Knorr-Bremse (Germany), $890
5. Claas (Germany), $820
6. Trumpf (Germany), $530
7. Molins (U.K.), $490
8. Putzmeister (Germany), $411
9. Mayer (Germany), $400
10. Spirax Sarco (U.K.), $400
Source: *Financial Times*, May 19, 1997, p. 8.

★ 1230 ★
TOP INTERNATIONAL DESIGN FIRMS IN BUILDINGS, 1995
Ranked by: Billings. **Remarks:** Specific dollar value is not provided. **Number listed:** 10
1. Nikken Sekkei Ltd.
2. Hellmuth, Obata & Kassabaum Inc.
3. Nihon Sekkei Inc.
4. Kume Sekkei Co. Ltd.
5. Sverdrup Corp.

6. Ove Arup Partnership
7. Yamashita Sekkei Inc.
8. Gensler
9. Kajima Corp.
10. Holmes & Narver Inc.
Source: *ENR*, Top International Design Firms (annual), July 22, 1996, p. 36.

★ 1231 ★
TOP INTERNATIONAL DESIGN FIRMS IN HAZARDOUS WASTE, 1995
Ranked by: Billings. **Remarks:** Specific dollar value is not provided. **Number listed:** 10
1. International Technology Corp.
2. ICF Kaiser International Inc.
3. CH2M Hill Cos. Ltd.
4. ERM Group
5. Heidemij N.V.
6. Roy F. Weston Inc.
7. Dames & Moore
8. Jacobs Engineering Group Inc.
9. Brown & Root Inc.
10. Foster Wheeler Corp.
Source: *ENR*, Top International Design Firms (annual), July 22, 1996, p. 36.

★ 1232 ★
TOP INTERNATIONAL DESIGN FIRMS IN MANUFACTURING, 1995
Ranked by: Billings. **Remarks:** Specific dollar value is not provided. **Number listed:** 10
1. Raytheon Engineers & Constructors Intl.
2. CH2M Hill Cos. Ltd.
3. BE&K Inc.
4. Lockwood Greene Engineers Inc.
5. AGRA Industries Ltd.
6. Sverdrup Corp.
7. Samsung Engineering Co. Ltd.
8. Lester B. Knight & Associates Inc.
9. Kajima Corp.
10. General Physics Corp.
Source: *ENR*, Top International Design Firms (annual), July 22, 1996, p. 36.

★ 1233 ★
TOP INTERNATIONAL DESIGN FIRMS IN POWER, 1995
Ranked by: Billings. **Remarks:** Specific dollar value is not provided. **Number listed:** 10
1. Tractebel Engineering
2. Mitsubishi Heavy Industries Ltd.
3. Sargent & Lundy LLC
4. Stone & Webster Engineering Corp.
5. Raytheon Engineers & Constructors Intl.
6. Black & Veatch
7. Bechtel Group Inc.

8. Morrison Knudsen Corp.
9. The Parsons Corp.
10. Burns and Roe Enterprises Inc.

Source: *ENR,* Top International Design Firms (annual), July 22, 1996, p. 36.

★ 1234 ★

TOP INTERNATIONAL DESIGN FIRMS IN SEWER/ WASTE, 1995

Ranked by: Billings. **Remarks:** Specific dollar value is not provided. **Number listed:** 10

1. CH2M Hill Cos. Ltd.
2. Rust International Inc.
3. Metcalf & Eddy/AWT Cos.
4. Montgomery Watson Inc.
5. Camp Dresser & McKee Inc.
6. Nethconsult
7. Malcolm Pirnie Inc.
8. Roy F. Weston Inc.
9. The Parsons Corp.
10. Brown and Caldwell

Source: *ENR,* Top International Design Firms (annual), July 22, 1996, p. 36.

★ 1235 ★

TOP INTERNATIONAL DESIGN FIRMS IN TRANSPORTATION, 1995

Ranked by: Billings. **Remarks:** Specific dollar value is not provided. **Number listed:** 10

1. Parsons Brinckerhoff Inc.
2. The Parsons Corp.
3. The Louis Berger Group
4. HNTB Corp.
5. SYSTRA-SOFRETU-SOFRERAIL
6. ICF Kaiser International Inc.
7. Maunsell
8. NEDECO
9. Daniel, Mann, Johnson, & Mendenhall
10. Greiner Engineering Inc.

Source: *ENR,* Top International Design Firms (annual), July 22, 1996, p. 36.

★ 1236 ★

TOP INTERNATIONAL DESIGN FIRMS IN WATER, 1996

Ranked by: Billings. **Remarks:** Specific dollar value is not provided. **Number listed:** 10

1. Montgomery Watson Inc.
2. Nippon Koei Co. Ltd.
3. Camp Dresser & McKee Inc.
4. CH2M Hill Cos. Ltd.
5. CTI Engineering Co. Ltd.
6. NEDECO
7. Mott MacDonald
8. Nethconsult
9. Acer Consultants Ltd.

10. Yachiyo Engineering Co. Ltd.

Source: *ENR,* Top International Design Firms (annual), July 22, 1996, p. 36.

★ 1237 ★

TOP INTERNATIONAL DESIGN FIRMS, 1995

Ranked by: Total billings, in millions of U.S. dollars. **Remarks:** Also notes international billings. **Number listed:** 200

1. The Parsons Corp. with $927.7 million
2. Brown & Root Inc., $872.8
3. Raytheon Engrs. & Constructors Intl., $846.0
4. Fluor Daniel Inc., $786.0
5. Nethconsult, $760.9
6. CH2M Hill Cos. Ltd., $721.3
7. Jacobs Engineering Group Inc., $698.0
8. Stone & Webster Engineering Corp., $654.5
9. SNC-Lavalin International Inc., $636.7
10. Rust International Inc., $572.0

Source: *ENR,* Top International Design Firms (annual), July 22, 1996, p. 40+.

★ 1238 ★

TOP INTERNATIONAL INDUSTRIAL/PETROLEUM DESIGN FIRMS, 1995

Ranked by: Billings. **Remarks:** Specific dollar value is not provided. **Number listed:** 10

1. Fluor Daniel Inc.
2. ABB Lummus Global Inc.
3. Jacobs Engineering Group Inc.
4. Raytheon Engineers & Constructors Intl.
5. Brown & Root Inc.
6. Jaakko Poyry Group
7. Stone & Webster Engineering Corp.
8. Foster Wheeler Corp.
9. The Parsons Corp.
10. SNC-Lavalin International Inc.

Source: *ENR,* Top International Design Firms (annual), July 22, 1996, p. 36.

Engineering Construction Companies – Asia

★ 1239 ★

LARGEST ELECTRICAL, ENGINEERING, AND TRANSPORTATION COMPANIES IN ASIA

Ranked by: Sales, in thousands of U.S. dollars. **Remarks:** Notes profits as a percent of sales. **Number listed:** 100

1. Toyota Motor Corp. with $104,065,427 thousand
2. Hitachi Ltd., $78,871,941
3. Matsushita Electric Industrial Co. Ltd., $65,969,436
4. Nissan Motor Co. Ltd., $58,632,106
5. Toshiba Corp., $51,117,844

6. Sony Corp., $44,588,009
7. Honda Motor Co. Ltd., $41,283,980
8. NEC Corp., $36,395,699
9. Fujitsu Ltd., $36,523,941
10. Mitsubishi Motors, $34,339,980

Source: *Asia's 7,500 Largest Companies* annual, Dun & Bradstreet, 1997, p. 77.

★ 1240 ★
TOP DESIGN FIRMS IN ASIA, 1995
Ranked by: Billings. **Remarks:** The top 10 firms billed $1,197.0 million of $3,527.7 million total billings. No further data were provided for these rankings. **Number listed:** 10

1. Raytheon Engineers & Constructors International
2. Stone & Webster Engineering Corp.
3. Mott MacDonald
4. Maunsell
5. Louis Berger Group
6. Pacific Consultants International
7. Nethconsult
8. Ove Arup Partnership
9. ABB Lummus Global Inc.
10. SNC-Lavalin International Inc.

Source: *ENR*, July 22, 1996, p. 34.

Engineering Construction Companies – Canada

★ 1241 ★
TOP DESIGN FIRMS IN CANADA, 1995
Ranked by: Billings. **Remarks:** The top 10 firms billed $211.1 million of $254.5 million total billings. No further data were provided for these rankings. **Number listed:** 10

1. Fluor Daniel Inc.
2. Golder Associates Corp.
3. Philip Environmental Services Corp.
4. CH2M Hill Cos. Ltd.
5. SYSTRA-SOFRETU-SOFRERAIL
6. Eichleay Holdings Inc.
7. Brown & Root Inc.
8. Dames & Moore
9. Raytheon Engineers & Constructors International
10. Stone & Webster Engineering Corp.

Source: *ENR*, July 22, 1996, p. 34.

Engineering Construction Companies – Europe

★ 1242 ★
TOP DESIGN FIRMS IN EUROPE, 1995
Ranked by: Billings. **Remarks:** The top 10 firms billed $1,561.2 million of $3,419.5 million total billings. No further data were provided for these rankings. **Number listed:** 10

1. Brown & Root Inc.
2. ABB Lummus Global Inc.
3. Nethconsult
4. Fugro NV
5. Foster Wheeler Corp.
6. Jaakko Poyry Group
7. McDermott International Inc.
8. NEDECO
9. Rust International Inc.
10. Fluor Daniel Inc.

Source: *ENR*, July 22, 1996, p. 34.

Engines, Jets

★ 1243 ★
TOP AIRCRAFT-ENGINE PRODUCERS WORLDWIDE, 1995
Ranked by: Market share, in percent. **Number listed:** 11

1. General Electric (United States) with 26%
2. United Technologies (United States), 26%
3. Rolls Royce (United Kingdom), 16%
4. AlliedSignal (United States), 8%
5. Snecma (France), 7%
6. Ishikawajima-Harima Heavy Industries (Japan), 5%
7. Daimler-Benz (Germany), 4%
8. Fiat-Avio (Italy), 4%
9. Turbomeca (France), 2%
10. Kawasaki Heavy Industries (Japan), 1%

Source: *The Wall Street Journal*, June 19, 1997, p. A14.

Entertainers

★ 1244 ★
TOP MUSICAL ACTS WORLDWIDE, 1996
Ranked by: Concert grosses, in millions of U.S. dollars. **Number listed:** 10

1. The Eagles with $60.3 million
2. Kiss, $36.6
3. Garth Brooks, $33.6
4. Bob Seger, $26.3
5. Neil Diamond, $25.1
6. Rod Stewart, $23.0

7. Reba McEntire, $21.6
8. Alanis Morissette, $19.5
9. Jimmy Buffet, $18.4
10. Ozzy Osborne, $17.7

Source: *Entertainment Weekly*, January 10, 1996, p. 59.

Entertainment Industries

★ 1245 ★
ASIA'S TOP MEDIA/COMMUNICATIONS FIRMS, 1995
Ranked by: Sales, in millions of U.S. dollars. **Remarks:** Includes profits, profits as a percentage of sales and assets, and overall sales rank. **Number listed:** 20

1. Nippon Telegraph & Telephone with $84,080.1 million
2. Dentsu, $14,186.3
3. Dai Nippon Printing, $13,239.4
4. Toppan Printing, $12,615.3
5. Telstra, $11,289.9
6. News Corp., $10,705.9
7. Korea Telecom, $8,464.5
8. Tohan, $8,207.6
9. Nippon Shuppan Hanbai, $8,093.4
10. DDI Corp., $7,118.9

Source: *Asiaweek*, The Asiaweek 1,000, November 22, 1996, p. 161.

★ 1246 ★
LARGEST MEDIA GROUPS IN EUROPE
Ranked by: Turnover, in billions of U.S. dollars. **Remarks:** Includes figures on net income and market capitalization. **Number listed:** 10

1. Havas with $8.58 billion
2. Reed Elsevier, $5.51
3. Reuters, $4.08
4. Pearson, $2.76
5. Axel Springer, $2.70
6. Audiofina, $2.68
7. Carlton Comms, $2.39
8. WPP, $2.35
9. CEP Communication, $2.18
10. Canal, $1.95

Source: *Financial Times*, June 17, 1997, p. 24.

★ 1247 ★
TOP ENTERTAINMENT COMPANIES WORLDWIDE, 1996-1997
Ranked by: Revenue, in millions of U.S. dollars. **Remarks:** Also notes earnings, percent change, and figures from previous year. **Number listed:** 50

1. Time Warner with $20,925 million
2. Walt Disney, $18,730
3. Bertelsmann, $12,300

4. Viacom, $12,080
5. News Corp., $11,216
6. Sony Entertainment, $8,400
7. Havas, $8,200
8. Tele-Communications Inc., $8,022
9. Universal Studios, $6,514
10. Granada Group, $6,450

Source: *Variety*, August 31, 1997, p. 33.

Environmental Services Firms

★ 1248 ★
ENVIRONMENTAL CONSULTING MARKETS IN EUROPE, 1993-2000
Ranked by: Growth, in percent, of each environmental consulting market. **Number listed:** 7

1. Spain with 12.0% growth
2. France, 8.3%
3. Belgium, 7.7%
4. Italy, 7.4%
5. United Kingdom, 6.0%
6. Germany, 5.1%
7. Netherlands, 4.9%

Source: *Chemical Week*, January 15, 1997, p. 34.

Equipment Leasing
See: **Leasing and Renting of Equipment**

Equity Research, International

★ 1249 ★
ASIAN BANKS ISSUING THE MOST EQUITY, 1997
Ranked by: Value of issues for the 12 months to mid-1997, in millions of U.S. dollars. **Remarks:** Data do not include Japanese banks. Source notes number of issues. **Number listed:** 10

1. Overseas Union Bank (Singapore) with $492.98 million
2. Bank International Indonesia (Indonesia), $398.02
3. Bank Negara Indonesia (Indonesia), $396.68
4. State Bank of India (India), $369.95
5. Bank Dagang Negara (Indonesia), $367.47
6. Kookmin Bank (South Korea), $300.00
7. Equitable Banking Corporation (Philippines), $267.53
8. Bank of Baroda (India), $237.50
9. Chiao Tung Bank (Taiwan), $215.58

10. United World Chinese Commercial Bank (Taiwan), $207.02

Source: *Global Finance*, August 1997, p. 30.

★ **1250** ★
TOP EQUITY ISSUERS IN ASIA, 1997

Ranked by: Value of issues for the 12 months through June 1997, in millions of U.S. dollars. **Remarks:** Data do not include Japanese firms. Source notes number of issues. **Number listed:** 50

1. Singapore Telecom with $1,424.52 million
2. Henderson Land Development (Hong Kong), $767.27
3. Telekomunikasi Indonesia, $594.38
4. Ekran (Malaysia), $583.95
5. Cheung Kong Infrastructure (Hong Kong), $569.94
6. Videsh Sanchar Nigam (India), $526.55
7. Amoy Properties (Hong Kong), $445.03
8. Malaysian Resources, $419.77
9. Indofood Sukses Makmur (Indonesia), $414.47
10. Jakarta International Hotel & Development (Indonesia), $383.15

Source: *Global Finance*, August 1997, p. 29.

★ **1251** ★
TOP EQUITY ISSUERS IN CHINA, 1997

Ranked by: Value of issues for the 12 months ending June 1997, in millions of U.S. dollars. **Remarks:** Also notes number of issues and industry sector. **Number listed:** 20

1. Jiangsu Expressway with $491.01 million
2. Beijing Datang Power Generation, $466.00
3. Zhejiang Expressway, $440.56
4. Shanghai Industrial Investment, $355.96
5. China Overseas Land & Investment, $298.11
6. China Eastern Airlines, $281.16
7. Beijing Enterprises, $278.21
8. China Travel International Investment, $272.26
9. Beijing Yanhua Petrochemical, $232.71
10. Beijing North Star, $219.03

Source: *Global Finance*, August 1997, p. 33.

★ **1252** ★
TOP EQUITY RESEARCH REPORT PRODUCERS, 1996

Ranked by: Company specific reports, 2 pages or longer, added to the Nelson Research Database from January 1 through December 31, 1996. **Number listed:** 100

1. Merrill Lynch with 8,245
2. Morgan Stanley, 3,952
3. UBS, 3,086
4. Prudential Securities, 2,616
5. SBC Warburg, 2,575
6. Goldman, Sachs, 2,538
7. Smith Barney, 2,296

8. Oppenheimer & Co., 2,284
9. Alex Brown, 2,282
10. BZW Ltd., 2,238

Source: *Institutional Research Reports*, January 1997, p. 1.

Estonia – see under individual headings

Eurobond Market
See Also: Participation Loans; Security Underwriting

★ **1253** ★
LARGEST BOND UNDERWRITERS IN CHINA

Ranked by: Market share, in percent. **Number listed:** 10

1. Morgan Stanley with 39.54%
2. CS First Boston/Credit Suisse, 28.25%
3. HSBC Group, 8.77%
4. ING Barings, 8.47%
5. Long-Term Credit Bank of Japan, 6.78%
6. Seoulbank, 3.77%
7. Daiwa Securities, 2.99%
8. SBC Warburg, 2.54%
9. Korea Long Term Credit bank, 0.94%
10. Peregrine Capital, 0.94%

Source: *Euromoney*, December 1996, p. 28.

★ **1254** ★
LARGEST BOND UNDERWRITERS IN JAPAN

Ranked by: Market share, in percent. **Number listed:** 10

1. Nomura Securities with 9.94%
2. Daiwa Securities, 8.33%
3. Bank of Tokyo-Mitsubishi, 6.23%
4. Sanwa Bank, 6.09%
5. Merrill Lynch, 5.62%
6. Industrial Bank of Japan, 5.14%
7. Nikko Securities, 4.96%
8. Yamaichi Securities, 4.77%
9. Dai-Ichi Kangyo Bank, 4.62%
10. Other, 44.30%

Source: *Euromoney*, December 1996, p. 28.

★ **1255** ★
LARGEST BOND UNDERWRITERS IN PHILIPPINES

Ranked by: Market share, in percent. **Number listed:** 10

1. J.P. Morgan with 34.81%
2. Citicorp, 9.49%
3. Robert Fleming/Jardine, 9.49%
4. ING Barings, 9.38%
5. Goldman Sachs, 7.91%
6. Merrill Lynch, 7.44%
7. Lehman Brothers, 4.75%

8. Morgan Stanley, 4.75%
9. Nomura Securities, 3.71%
10. Other, 8.27%

Source: *Euromoney*, December 1996, p. 32.

★ **1256** ★

LARGEST BOND UNDERWRITERS IN SINGAPORE

Ranked by: Market share, in percent. **Number listed:** 10

1. Union Bank of Switzerland with 43.05%
2. Keppei Bank of Singapore, 15.43%
3. Schroders, 12.87%
4. Nomura Securities, 10.05%
5. Robert Fleming/Jardine, 8.61%
6. Deutsche Morgan Grenfell, 7.18%
7. Daiwa Securities, 1.44%
8. Bank of Tokyo-Mitsubishi, 1.38%

Source: *Euromoney*, December 1996, p. 32.

★ **1257** ★

LARGEST EQUITY UNDERWRITERS IN MALAYSIA

Ranked by: Market share, in percent. **Number listed:** 4

1. Rashid Hussain Securities with 64.59%
2. ING Barings, 23.06%
3. Daiwa Securities, 7.12%
4. Barcalys de Zoete Wedd, 5.24%

Source: *Euromoney*, December 1996, p. 32.

★ **1258** ★

LEADING EUROBOND MANAGERS, 1996

Ranked by: Amount, in millions of U.S. dollars. **Remarks:** Also includes number of issues and percentage of market. **Number listed:** 15

1. Merrill Lynch with $25,194.6 million
2. SBC Warburg, $23,652.7
3. Deutsche Morgan Grenfell, $23,490.9
4. Goldman Sachs, $21,724.2
5. ABN AMRO Hoare Govett, $20,361.4
6. Morgan Stanley, $18,614.8
7. J.P. Morgan, $18,126.9
8. BZW/Barclays, $16,795.1
9. UBS, $16,076.6
10. Credit Suisse First Boston, $15,927.3

Source: *Investment Dealers' Digest*, Underwriting Rankings (annual), January 13, 1997, p. 46.

★ **1259** ★

LEADING MANAGERS OF EUROBONDS BY U.S. ISSUERS, 1996

Ranked by: Amount, in millions of U.S. dollars. **Remarks:** Also includes number of issues and percentage of market. **Number listed:** 15

1. Merrill Lynch with $9,121.3 million
2. Goldman Sachs, $5,568.4
3. Lehman Brothers, $4,351.2
4. Morgan Stanley, $4,075.4
5. Salomon Brothers, $3,628.9

6. J.P. Morgan, $3,028.3
7. Deutsche Morgan Grenfell, $2,852.1
8. SBC Warburg, $2,820.1
9. Credit Suisse First Boston, $2,028.9
10. UBS, $2,027.0

Source: *Investment Dealers' Digest*, Underwriting Rankings (annual), January 13, 1997, p. 46.

★ **1260** ★

LEADING MANAGERS OF FIXED-RATE U.S. DOLLAR-DENOMINATED EUROBONDS, 1996

Ranked by: Amount, in millions of U.S. dollars. **Remarks:** Also includes number of issues and percentage of market. **Number listed:** 15

1. Goldman Sachs with $13,696.0 million
2. SBC Warburg, $10,497.8
3. Merrill Lynch, $9,657.1
4. J.P. Morgan, $8,084.4
5. Credit Suisse First Boston, $6,552.5
6. Morgan Stanley, $6,225.9
7. UBS, $5,185.5
8. Nomura Securities, $5,047.7
9. ABN AMRO Hoare Govett, $4,485.0
10. Salomon Brothers, $4,397.7

Source: *Investment Dealers' Digest*, Underwriting Rankings (annual), January 13, 1997, p. 46.

★ **1261** ★

TOP ASIAN EUROBOND RUNNERS, 1996

Ranked by: Amount, in millions of U.S. dollars. **Remarks:** Also notes number of deals. **Number listed:** 20

1. Nomura Securities with $2,719.20 million
2. CS First Boston/Credit Suisse, $2,494.65
3. J.P. Morgan, $2,345.00
4. Salomon Brothers, $2,260.59
5. Lehman Brothers, $1,475.00
6. Morgan Stanley, $1,335.00
7. Daiwa Securities, $1,235.00
8. Yamaichi Securities, $1,218.47
9. Merrill Lynch, $1,150.00
10. Nikko Securities, $717.05

Source: *Asiamoney*, Deals of the Year (annual), February 1997, p. 40.

★ **1262** ★

TOP BOOKRUNNERS OF ASIAN EUROCONVERTIBLE BONDS, 1996

Ranked by: Amount, in millions of U.S. dollars. **Remarks:** Also notes number of deals. **Number listed:** 20

1. Robert Fleming/Jardine Fleming with $1,257.66 million
2. Goldman Sachs, $659.60
3. Morgan Stanley, $658.50
4. Lehman Brothers, $540.00

5. Merrill Lynch, $475.00
6. Deutsche Morgan Grenfell, $446.50
7. Union Bank of Switzerland, $428.17
8. HSBC Group, $410.00
9. SBC Warburg, $408.97
10. ING Barings, $300.50

Source: *Asiamoney,* Deals of the Year (annual), February 1997, p. 59.

★ 1263 ★

TOP BOOKRUNNERS OF ASIAN SAMURAI BONDS, 1996
Ranked by: Amount, in millions of U.S. dollars.
Remarks: Also notes number of deals. **Number listed:** 6
1. Nomura Securities with $1,835.17 million
2. Yamaichi Securities, $1,218.47
3. Daiwa Securities, $1,004.11
4. Nikko Securities, $592.07
5. Industrial Bank of Japan, $143.02
6. Kokusai Securities, $44.82

Source: *Asiamoney,* Deals of the Year (annual), February 1997, p. 48.

★ 1264 ★

TOP BOOKRUNNERS OF ASIAN YANKEE BONDS, 1996
Ranked by: Amount, in millions of U.S. dollars.
Remarks: Also notes number of deals. **Number listed:** 9
1. Salomon Brothers with $1,060.59 million
2. J.P. Morgan, $780.00
3. Lehman Brothers, $700.00
4. Morgan Stanley, $610.00
5. Merrill Lynch, $600.00
6. CS First Boston/Credit Suisse, $400.00
7. Union Bank of Switzerland, $400.00
8. Goldman Sachs, $250.00
9. Bank of America, $75.00

Source: *Asiamoney,* Deals of the Year (annual), February 1997, p. 49.

★ 1265 ★

TOP UNDERWRITERS BY BONDS IN INDONESIA
Ranked by: Market share, in percent. **Number listed:** 11
1. Peregrine Capital with 20.22%
2. Morgan Stanley, 18.14%
3. Salomon Brothers, 7.18%
4. Merrill Lynch, 6.82%
5. SBC Warburg, 5.46%
6. J.P. Morgan, 4.76%
7. Bankers Trust, 4.13%
8. London Forfaiting Company, 3.44%
9. ING Barings, 2.54%
10. Other, 27.31%

Source: *Euromoney,* December 1996, p. 28.

★ 1266 ★

TOP UNDERWRITERS BY EQUITY IN HONG KONG
Ranked by: Market share, in percent. **Number listed:** 11
1. Morgan Stanley with 30.80%
2. Credit Lyonnais, 17.35%
3. HSBC Group, 12.45%
4. ING Barings, 10.20%
5. Goldman Sachs, 7.57%
6. CEF Capital, 6.76%
7. Merrill Lynch, 6.11%
8. Robert Fleming/Jardine, 4.69%
9. Union Bank of Switzerland, 1.59%
10. Others, 2.48%

Source: *Euromoney,* December 1996, p. 28.

Eurobonds

★ 1267 ★

TOP BOOKRUNNERS OF NON-YANKEE/SAMURAI GLOBAL BONDS
Ranked by: Amount, in billions of U.S. dollars.
Remarks: Also notes number of issues and percentage of market. **Number listed:** 10
1. Merrill Lynch with $51.80 billion
2. Morgan Stanley, $37.06
3. SBC Warburg, $36.50
4. Goldman Sachs, $34.14
5. J.P. Morgan, $33.77
6. CS First Boston/Credit Suisse, $28.23
7. Deutsche Morgan Grenfell, $28.03
8. Lehman Brothers, $27.12
9. Nomura Securities, $24.93
10. Union Bank of Switzerland, $24.67

Source: *Financial Times,* January 31, 1997, p. 10.

★ 1268 ★

TOP ISSUERS OF INTERNATIONAL BONDS, 1996
Ranked by: Amount issued, in billions of U.S. dollars.
Remarks: Also notes number of issues and percentage of market. **Number listed:** 10
1. European Investment Bank with $22.30 billion
2. Commerzbank, $14.50
3. International Bank for Reconstruction and Development, $14.36
4. United Mexican States, $13.52
5. Caisse d'Amortissement de la Dette Sociale (CAD), $10.88
6. Republic of Argentina, $10.15
7. Deutsche Siedlungs- und Landesrentenbank, $9.46
8. Kingdom of Sweden, $9.34
9. Deutsche Pfandbrief- und Hypothekenbank, $9.21

10. Abbey National, $8.86
Source: *Financial Times*, January 31, 1997, p. 10.

Euroloans
See Also: Participation Loans

★ **1269** ★
TOP ARRANGERS OF PROJECT FINANCE LOANS TO POWER PROJECTS IN ASIA, 1995
Ranked by: Loans, in millions of U.S. dollars. **Number listed:** 10
1. Citicorp with $511.20 million
2. Industrial Development Bank of India, $491.82
3. Barclays Bank, $468.86
4. Bank of America, $365.86
5. Bank Indosuez, $324.56
6. Banque Paribas, $324.56
7. HSBC Group, $294.95
8. Sanwa Bank, $253.96
9. Bank of Tokyo, $209.48
10. NationsBank, $157.50
Source: *Asiamoney*, January 1996, p. 54.

Europe – see under individual headings

Executive Search Consultants

★ **1270** ★
TOP HEADHUNTERS IN CENTRAL AND EASTERN EUROPE, 1995
Ranked by: Central and eastern European revenue, in millions of U.S. dollars. **Remarks:** Also notes worldwide revenue and number of offices. **Number listed:** 10
1. H. Neumann with $9.8 million
2. Ward Howell, $6.2
3. Korn/Ferry, $6.0
4. Amrop, $3.1
5. Accord, $2.9
6. Egon Zehnder, $2.8
7. Nicholson, $2.0
8. Transearch, $1.7
9. Heidrick & Struggles, $1.5
10. Spencer Stuart, $1.5
Source: *Financial Times*, November 1, 1996, p. I.

Executives

★ **1271** ★
COUNTRIES WHERE EXECUTIVES DELEGATE THE MOST AUTHORITY
Ranked by: Countries rated 1 to 10 on the willingness of management to delegate authority to subordinates. **Remarks:** Figures are from an international survey of more than 3,292 executives. **Number listed:** 58
1. Sweden with 8.23
2. Denmark, 7.55
3. Norway, 7.49
4. United States, 7.14
5. New Zealand, 6.90
6. Switzerland, 6.76
7. Hong Kong, 6.63
8. Australia, 6.51
9. Netherlands, 6.49
10. Canada, 6.46
Source: *World Business*, January - February 1996, p. 14.

★ **1272** ★
HIGHEST PAID CANADIAN EXECUTIVES, 1996
Ranked by: Total income for corporate years ending in 1996, in Canadian dollars. **Remarks:** Notes basic salary, bonus and incentive pay, exercised option gains, and other compensations. **Number listed:** 50
1. Laurent Beaudoin (Bombardier Inc.) with C$19,100,317
2. Michael Brown (Thomson Corp.), C$11,389,268
3. Francesco Bellini (BioChem Pharma Inc.), C$9,993,104
4. William Holland (United Dominion Industries Ltd.), C$8,925,640
5. Gerald Schwartz (Onex Corp.), C$8,375,505
6. William Stinson (Canadian Pacific Ltd.), C$8,301,983
7. Charles Childers (Potash Corp. of Saskatchewan Inc.), C$7,729,256
8. Pierre Lessard (Metro-Richelieu Inc.), C$7,345,600
9. Jean Monty (Northern Telecom Ltd.), C$6,437,804
10. Edward Newall (Nova Corp. of Alberta), C$6,350,750
Source: *Globe and Mail*, April 12, 1997, p. B6.

★ **1273** ★
TOP COUNTRIES TO WHICH U.S. EXECUTIVES TRANSFER, 1996
Ranked by: Number of executives transferring to each country. No specific data were given. **Number listed:** 10
1. England
2. Mexico

3. Belgium
4. Germany
5. Australia
6. Japan
7. Hong Kong
8. Singapore
9. France
10. India

Source: *The Wall Street Journal*, March 14, 1997, p. B8.

★ 1274 ★

TOP MILLIONAIRE EXECUTIVE DIRECTORS UNDER 40 IN THE UNITED KINGDOM, 1997

Ranked by: British pounds (£) as of January 23, 1997, in millions. Companies are shown in parentheses. **Number listed:** 20

1. Daniel Chiu (Fortune Oil) with £49.8 million
2. Daniel Wagner (MAID), £30.5
3. Daniel Harris (Alba), £18.7
4. Stanley Fink (ED&F Man Group), £9.1
5. Julian Schild (Huntleigh Technology), £6.5
6. Wayne Channon (Persona Group), £5.5
7. Bruno Kemoun (Aegis Group), £5.0
8. Luke Johnson (PizzaExpress), £4.3
9. Stephen Streater (Eidos), £4.0
10. Robert Laurence (Argent Group), £3.8

Source: *Director*, May 1997, p. 34.

Executives – Salaries, Pensions, etc.

★ 1275 ★

LARGEST COMPENSATION PACKAGES FOR MEDIA EXECUTIVES IN THE UNITED KINGDOM

Ranked by: Total compensation package, in British pounds (£). **Remarks:** Companies are shown in parentheses. Total compensation includes benefits, bonuses, and salaries, but excludes company contributions to pensions. Source also notes salary. **Number listed:** 9

1. Sam Chisholm (BSkyB) with £3,800,000
2. David Chance (BSkyB), £2,600,000
3. Michael Green (Carlton Communications), £727,000
4. Michal Grade (Channel 4), £464,000
5. Nigel Walmsley (Carlton Television), £364,000
6. John Birt (BBC), £354,000
7. Richard Eyre (Capital Radio), £332,000
8. Bruce Gyngell (Yorkshire TV), £308,000
9. Gus Macdonald (Scottish TV), £227,000

Source: *The Guardian*, July 7, 1997, p. 2.

Exercise Equipment Industry

★ 1276 ★

HOME EXERCISE EQUIPMENT MAKERS IN EGYPT, 1995

Ranked by: Market share, in percent. **Number listed:** 10

1. Taiwan with 40.0%
2. Local Production, 20.0%
3. Master, 10.0%
4. Rovera, 7.0%
5. Carnilli, 5.0%
6. Universal, 5.0%
7. Sven, 4.0%
8. Katler, 3.0%
9. Krist, 3.0%
10. Others, 3.0%

Source: *National Trade Data Bank*, August 29, 1995, p. ISA9506.

★ 1277 ★

TOP WORK OUT EQUIPMENT MAKERS IN EGYPT, 1995

Ranked by: Market share, in percent. **Number listed:** 10

1. Universal with 30.0%
2. Life Fitness, 18.0%
3. Power Sport, 17.0%
4. Sven, 8.0%
5. Katler, 6.0%
6. Krist, 5.0%
7. Nautilus, 4.0%
8. Wieder, 4.0%
9. A.A.I., 3.0%
10. Others, 5.0%

Source: *National Trade Data Bank*, August 29, 1995, p. ISA9506.

Expatriate Employees

★ 1278 ★

TOP LOCATIONS FOR CURRENT EXPATRIATES, 1995

Ranked by: Respondents who named the site as a current location of expatriate employees, in percent. **Remarks:** Data are based on a survey of 151 respondents from 138 companies; respondents were allowed to name three countries. **Number listed:** 10

1. United Kingdom with 46%
2. Hong Kong, 25%
3. Singapore, 20%
4. Japan, 19%
5. China, 15%
6. Germany, 15%
7. France, 12%

8. Belgium, 11%
9. Mexico, 11%
10. United States, 9%

Source: *Global Workforce*, October 1996, p. 8.

★ **1279** ★

TOP LOCATIONS FOR FUTURE EXPATRIATES, 1995

Ranked by: Respondents who named the site as a future location for expatriate employees, in percent. **Remarks:** Data are based on a survey of 151 respondents from 138 companies; respondents were allowed to name three countries. **Number listed:** 10

1. China with 45%
2. India, 21%
3. Mexico, 12%
4. Russia, 11%
5. Malaysia, 10%
6. Singapore, 9%
7. Vietnam, 9%
8. Argentina, 7%
9. South Africa, 7%
10. Thailand, 7%

Source: *Global Workforce*, October 1996, p. 8.

Export-Import Trade

★ **1280** ★

COUNTRIES WITH HIGHEST AVERAGE EXPORT GROWTH, 1990-1996

Ranked by: Average annual growth, in percent of U.S. dollar terms. **Number listed:** 11

1. Malaysia with 18% growth
2. Philippines, 17%
3. China, 16%
4. Thailand, 16%
5. Mexico, 15%
6. Singapore, 15%
7. Ireland, 13%
8. Argentina, 12%
9. Kuwait, 12%
10. Indonesia, 12%

Source: *Globe and Mail*, April 11, 1997, p. B7.

★ **1281** ★

COUNTRIES WITH THE HIGHEST AVERAGE IMPORT GROWTH, 1996

Ranked by: Average annual growth, in percent of U.S. dollar terms. **Number listed:** 11

1. Argentina with 34% growth
2. Poland, 22%
3. Malaysia, 18%
4. Philippines, 18%
5. Brazil, 17%

6. China, 17%
7. Colombia, 16%
8. Chile, 15%
9. United Arab Emirates, 15%
10. Mexico, 14%

Source: *Globe and Mail*, April 11, 1997, p. B7.

★ **1282** ★

ISRAEL'S TOP EXPORTS, 1996

Ranked by: Value of exports, in millions of U.S. dollars. **Number listed:** 10

1. Telecom equipment with $1,792 million
2. Organic and inorganic chemicals, $1,396
3. Electrical machinery, $1,318
4. Metalworking and industrial machinery, $1,301
5. ADP and office machines, $830
6. Clothing and apparel, $645
7. Scientific and controlling instruments, $572
8. Plastic products in non-primary form, $371
9. Pharmaceutical and medical supplies, $332
10. Fertilizers, $326

Source: *National Trade Data Bank*, April 15, 1997, p. IMI970415.

★ **1283** ★

ISRAEL'S TOP IMPORTS, 1996

Ranked by: Value of imports, in millions of U.S. dollars. **Number listed:** 12

1. Electrical machinery with $2,424 million
2. Automobiles, $2,324
3. Machinery under Channel 84, $2,383
4. Petroleum and derivatives, $1,824
5. Telecom and related equipment, $1,202
6. ADP and office equipment, $1,129
7. Steel and non-ferrous metals, $1,104
8. Chemicals, organic and inorganic, $780
9. Plastic products, $647
10. Scientific and controlling instruments, $607

Source: *National Trade Data Bank*, April 15, 1997, p. IMI970415.

★ **1284** ★

LARGEST SLOVENIAN EXPORTERS, 1995

Ranked by: Exports, in millions of tolars (To). **Number listed:** 101

1. Revoz Novo mesto with To84,750.0 million
2. Gorenjo G. A. Velenje, To33,624.1
3. Slovenske zelezarne, To32,539.1
4. Lek Ljubljana, To23,359.3
5. Sava Kranji, To22,764.9
6. Krka Novo mesto, To22,755.5
7. Talum Kidricevo, To16,613.2
8. IBN-JT, Ljubljana, To14,942.2
9. Mura Murska Sobota, To12,471.5
10. Iskraemeco Kranj, To11,600.0

Source: *Slovenian Business Report*, Summer 1996, p. 14.

★ 1285 ★

TOP COUNTRIES OF ORIGIN FOR IMPORTS TO INDIA, 1994-1995

Ranked by: Value of imports, in millions of U.S. dollars.
Number listed: 10
1. United States with $2,900 million
2. Germany, $2,180
3. Japan, $2,030
4. Saudi Arabia, $1,560
5. United Kingdom, $1,550
6. United Arab Emirates, $1,530
7. Kuwait, $1,480
8. Belgium, $1,200
9. Australia, $910
10. Singapore, $900

Source: *Chemtech*, July 1997, p. 56.

★ 1286 ★

TOP DESTINATIONS FOR SOUTH KOREAN EXPORTS, 1994

Ranked by: Distribution, in percent. **Number listed:** 7
1. G7 nations with 45.1%
2. Southeast Asia, 20.2%
3. China, 6.5%
4. Latin America, 3.2%
5. Northeast Asia, 2.8%
6. Indian subcontinent, 1.7%
7. Rest of world, 20.4%

Source: *Financial Times*, July 11, 1996, p. 4.

★ 1287 ★

TOP EXPORTING NATIONS, 1995

Ranked by: Market share, in percent, for exportation of merchandise trade excluding services. **Number listed:** 25
1. United States with 12%
2. Germany, 10%
3. Japan, 9%
4. France, 6%
5. United Kingdom, 5%
6. Italy, 5%
7. Netherlands, 4%
8. Canada, 4%
9. Hong Kong, 4%
10. Belgium-Luxembourg, 3%

Source: *American Shipper*, January 1997, p. 17.

★ 1288 ★

TOP EXPORTS CATEGORIES IN ISRAEL, 1996

Ranked by: Value, in millions of U.S. dollars. **Number listed:** 10
1. Telecom equipment with $1,792 million
2. Organic and inorganic chemicals, $1,396
3. Electrical machinery, $1,318
4. Metalworking and industrial machinery, $1,301
5. ADP and office machines, $830
6. Clothing and apparel, $645

7. Scientific and controlling instruments, $572
8. Plastic products in non-primary form, $371
9. Pharmaceutical and medical supplies, $332
10. Fertilizers, $326

Source: *National Trade Data Bank*, April 15, 1997, p. IMI970415.

★ 1289 ★

TOP IMPORTERS IN THE ASIA-PACIFIC REGION, 1995

Ranked by: Imports, as a percentage of world imports.
Remarks: Also notes rank among world's top importers.
Number listed: 14
1. Japan with 6.5%
2. Hong Kong, 3.8%
3. China, 2.6%
4. South Korea, 2.6%
5. Singapore, 2.4%
6. Taiwan, 2.0%
7. Malaysia, 1.5%
8. Thailand, 1.4%
9. Australia, 1.2%
10. Indonesia, 0.8%

Source: *Far Eastern Economic Review*, February 20, 1997, p. 69.

★ 1290 ★

TOP IMPORTING NATIONS, 1995

Ranked by: Market share, in percent, for importation of merchandise trade excluding services. **Number listed:** 25
1. United States with 15%
2. Germany, 9%
3. Japan, 7%
4. France, 5%
5. United Kingdom, 5%
6. Italy, 4%
7. Hong Kong, 4%
8. Netherlands, 3%
9. Canada, 3%
10. Belgium-Luxembourg, 3%

Source: *American Shipper*, January 1997, p. 17.

★ 1291 ★

TOP IMPORTS CATEGORIES IN ISRAEL, 1996

Ranked by: Value, in millions of U.S. dollars. **Number listed:** 12
1. Electrical machinery with $2,424 million
2. Machinery under Ch. 84, $2,383
3. Automobiles, $2,324
4. Petroleum and derivatives, $1,824
5. Telecom and related equipment, $1,202
6. ADP and office equipment, $1,129
7. Steel and non-ferrous metals, $1,104
8. Chemicals, organic and inorganic, $780
9. Plastic products, $647

10. Scientific and controlling instruments, $607
Source: *National Trade Data Bank*, April 15, 1997, p. IMI970415.

★ 1292 ★
TOP MARKETS FOR EXPORTS FROM INDIA, 1994-1995
Ranked by: Value of exports, in millions of U.S. dollars.
Number listed: 10
1. United States with $4,990 million
2. Japan, $2,020
3. Germany, $1,740
4. United Kingdom, $1,680
5. Hong Kong, $1,510
6. United Arab Emirates, $1,260
7. Belgium, $980
8. Italy, $860
9. Russia, $800
10. Singapore, $770
Source: *Chemtech*, July 1997, p. 56.

Export-Import Trade – China

★ 1293 ★
CHINA'S TOP TRADING PARTNERS, 1996
Ranked by: Trade distribution, in percent. **Number listed:** 9
1. Japan with 20.7%
2. United States, 14.8%
3. Hong Kong, 14.1%
4. European Union, 13.7%
5. Association of South East Asian Nations, 7.0%
6. South Korea, 6.9%
7. Taiwan, 6.5%
8. Russia, 2.4%
9. Other, 13.9%
Source: *The China Business Review*, June 1997, p. 37.

Export-Import Trade, International

★ 1294 ★
LEADING EXPORTERS OF ELECTRONIC PRODUCTS TO THE U.S., 1995
Ranked by: Value of exports, in billions of U.S. dollars.
Remarks: Also notes percent change. **Number listed:** 10
1. Japan with $41.8 billion
2. Singapore, $15.3
3. South Korea, $13.3
4. Malaysia, $13.2
5. Taiwan, $13.0
6. Mexico, $12.1
7. Canada, $9.6

8. China, $7.9
9. Thailand, $4.0
10. United Kingdom, $3.9
Source: *Electronic Business Today*, August 1996, p. 10.

★ 1295 ★
LEADING IMPORTERS OF ELECTRONIC PRODUCTS FROM THE U.S., 1995
Ranked by: Value of imports, in billions of U.S. dollars.
Number listed: 10
1. Canada with $19.3 billion
2. Japan, $13.6
3. United Kingdom, $9.1
4. Mexico, $8.8
5. Singapore, $7.4
6. Germany, $6.6
7. South Korea, $5.9
8. Malaysia, $5.6
9. Hong Kong, $4.6
10. Taiwan, $4.5
Source: *Electronic Business Today*, August 1996, p. 10.

Export-Import Trade – United Kingdom

★ 1296 ★
BRITAIN'S TRADE WITH FOREIGN MARKETS, 1995
Ranked by: Export and import share, as a percent of all exports and imports. **Remarks:** Asian Tigers include Hong Kong, Malaysia, Taiwan, Thailand, Singapore, and South Korea. **Number listed:** 10
1. Germany with 14.4%
2. United States, 11.9%
3. France, 9.8%
4. Netherlands, 7.3%
5. Asian tigers, 6.4%
6. Ireland, 4.6%
7. Japan, 4.2%
8. Latin America, 1.7%
9. Rest of European Union, 20.6%
10. Other, 19.1%
Source: *The Economist*, November 23, 1996, p. 60.

Fabrics

★ 1297 ★
LARGEST POLYESTER MAKERS, 1995
Ranked by: Production, in thousands of tons. **Number listed:** 20
1. Trevira with 1709 thousand tons
2. DuPont, 1105
3. Eastman, 1028

4. Nan Ya, 932
5. Teijin, 631
6. Far Eastern, 600
7. Yizheng, 600
8. Huston, 533
9. Wellman, 520
10. Toray, 490

Source: *Textile World*, March 1997, p. 128.

Facsimile Machines

★ 1298 ★
TOP FAX MACHINES IN JAPAN

Ranked by: Market share, in percent. Number listed: 6
1. Ricoh with 17.0%
2. Canon, 14.5%
3. Matsushita Graphic Communication Systems, 14.0%
4. NEC, 12.0%
5. TEC, 8.5%
6. Others, 34.0%

Source: *Nikkei Weekly*, July 22, 1996, p. 8.

Factories

★ 1299 ★
ELECTRONICS FACILITIES WITH THE LARGEST CAPITAL INVESTMENTS, 1990-1996

Ranked by: Capital investment, in millions of U.S. dollars. Remarks: Also notes industry sector. Number listed: 20
1. Hyundai Electronics Europe Ltd. (Dumfermline, United Kingdom) with $3.6 million
2. Motorola (Goochland, Virginia), $3.0
3. LF Group (Newport, England), $2.5
4. Micron Technology (Lehi, Utah), $2.5
5. Intel (Hillsboro, Oregon), $2.2
6. Chartered Semiconductor Mfg. (Singapore), $2.0
7. Texas Instruments (Dallas, Texas), $2.0
8. Chartered Semiconductor Mfg. (Singapore), $1.8
9. Siemens (Wallsend, England), $1.8
10. Intel (Kiryat Gat, Israel), $1.6

Source: *Site Selection*, May 1997, p. 447.

★ 1300 ★
ELECTRONICS FACILITIES WITH THE MOST EMPLOYEES, 1990-1996

Ranked by: Number of employees. Remarks: Also notes industry sector. Number listed: 20
1. LG Group (Newport, England) with 6,100 employees
2. Intel (Dupont, Washington), 6,000
3. Motorola (Goochland, Virgina), 5,000
4. Toshiba Corp. (Portland, Oregon), 5,000
5. Sun Microsystems (Santa Clara, California), 4,000
6. Micron Technology (Lehi, Utah), 3,500
7. Sun Microsystems (Broomfield, Colorado), 3,500
8. Motorola (Beloit, Wisconsin), 3,000
9. Motorola (Harvard, Illinois), 3,000
10. Packard Bell Electronics (Sacarmento, California), 3,000

Source: *Site Selection*, May 1997, p. 447.

★ 1301 ★
INDUSTRIAL FACILITIES WITH THE LARGEST CAPITAL INVESTMENTS, 1996

Ranked by: Capital investment, in billions of U.S. dollars. Remarks: Also notes industry sector. Power plants, resource-based locations, and speculative developments are not included. Number listed: 20
1. Hyundai Electronics Europe (Dumfermline, Scotland) with $3.6 billion
2. LG Group (Cardiff, Wales), $2.5
3. Ssangyong (Dalsung, South Korea), $2.4
4. Bayer (Taichung, Taiwan), $1.8
5. Charterd Semiconductor Mfg. (Singapore), $1.8
6. Volkswagen/First Automobile Corp. (Changchun, China), $1.2
7. Hewlett-Packard/WK Technology Fund (Taipei, Taiwan), $1.1
8. Hitachi Ltd./Nippon Steel (Singapore), $1.1
9. Hyundai Motor (New Delhi, India), $1.1
10. IBM (Corbeil Essonnes, France), $1.0

Source: *Site Selection*, February 1997, p. 91.

★ 1302 ★
INDUSTRIAL FACILITIES WITH THE LARGEST FLOOR AREA, 1996

Ranked by: Floor space, in square feet. Remarks: Also notes industry sector. Power plants, resource-based locations, and speculative developments are not included. Number listed: 20
1. Fujitsu (Akigawa, Japan) with 1,370,000 square feet
2. Sanyo Electric/Sumitomo (Bien Hoa, Vietnam), 1,080,000
3. Intel (Leixlip, Ireland), 750,000

4. Hewlett-Packard (Leixlip, Ireland), 495,000
5. Beijing Johnson Controls Automotive (Beijing, China), 420,000
6. Sara Lee (Autun, Burgundy, France), 330,000
7. U.K. Can (Merthyr Tydfil, Wales), 330,000
8. Packard Bell (Angers, France), 325,000
9. Magna International (St. Thomas, Canada), 308,000
10. Williams Lake Fibreboard Ltd. (Williams Lake, Canada), 300,000

Source: *Site Selection*, February 1997, p. 91.

★ 1303 ★

INDUSTRIAL FACILITIES WITH THE MOST EMPLOYEES, 1996
Ranked by: Number of employees. **Remarks:** Also notes industry sector. Power plants, resource-based locations, and speculative developments are not included. **Number listed:** 20
1. LG Group (Cardiff, Wales) with 6,100 employees
2. Hyundai Electronics Europe (Dumfermline, Scotland), 2,000
3. Siemens (Wallsend, England), 1,800
4. BMW (Wackersdorf, Germany), 1,600
5. Emerson Electric/Caterpillar (Belfast, Northern Ireland), 1,500
6. Siemens (Dresden, Germany), 1,450
7. Daewoo/Samcholli General (Nampo, North Korea), 1,300
8. Gateway 2000 (Dublin, Ireland), 1,200
9. Volkswagen (Nitra, Slovakia), 1,200
10. Delphi Packard Electric (Sinnicolaul, Romania), 1,000

Source: *Site Selection*, February 1997, p. 91.

★ 1304 ★

TOP EUROPEAN SITES FOR JAPANESE PRODUCTION BASES
Ranked by: Respondents from 296 Japanese companies who were asked to name up to two countries that would be good sites for a production base, distributed in percent. **Number listed:** 10
1. United Kingdom with 41.9%
2. Czech Republic/Slovakia, 23.6%
3. Spain, 16.9%
4. Poland, 16.2%
5. Hungary, 14.2%
6. Italy, 13.9%
7. Germany, 10.5%
8. Netherlands, 9.5%
9. France, 7.1%
10. Ireland, 6.4%

Source: *Financial Times*, October 3, 1996, p. 5.

Factoring (Finance)

★ 1305 ★

LARGEST FACTORING FIRMS IN MEXICO, 1995
Ranked by: Assets as of December 31, 1995, in millions of U.S. dollars. **Number listed:** 10
1. Factoraje Serfin with $224.3 million
2. Factoraje Bancomer, $197.5
3. Banamex Factoraje, $166.8
4. Factoraje Capital, $126.2
5. Factor Quadrum, $115.1
6. Empresarial, $105.3
7. Factoraje Invermexico, $91.1
8. Kapital Haus, $78.4
9. Factoraje Bancrecer, $74.7
10. Factoring Inverlet, $70.6

Source: *National Trade Data Bank*, September 9, 1996, p. ISA960801.

Fast Food Restaurants

★ 1306 ★

FAST FOOD MARKET IN THE UNITED KINGDOM, 1996
Ranked by: Segment value, in millions of U.S. dollars. **Number listed:** 7
1. Sandwiches with $3,000 million
2. Hamburgers, $2,500
3. Fish and chips, $1,600
4. Pizza and pasta, $1,300
5. Ethnic, $1,000
6. Chicken, $500
7. Other, $2

Source: *National Trade Data Bank*, June 16, 1997, p. IMI970604.

★ 1307 ★

HAMBURGER MARKET IN PHILIPPINES
Ranked by: Market share, in percent. **Number listed:** 3
1. Jollibee with 46.0%
2. McDonald's, 16.0%
3. Other, 38.0%

Source: *Business Week*, July 29, 1996, p. 77.

★ 1308 ★

TOP FAST FOOD CHAINS WORLDWIDE, 1996
Ranked by: Sales, in billions of U.S. dollars. **Number listed:** 10
1. McDonald's with $31.8 billion
2. Burger King, $9.3
3. KFC, $8.2
4. Pizza Hut, $7.4
5. Wendy's, $4.8

6. Taco Bell, $4.5
7. Subway, $3.2
8. Hardee's, $3.1
9. Dairy Queen, $2.9
10. Domino's Pizza, $2.8

Source: *The New York Times*, July 16, 1997, p. C1.

Feminine Hygiene Products

★ 1309 ★
TOP YEAST INFECTION REMEDIES IN CANADA, 1996
Ranked by: Market share based on sales, in percent.
Remarks: Notes 1995 figures. **Number listed:** 3
1. Monistat with 52%
2. Canesten, 35%
3. Gynecure, 12%

Source: *Marketing Magazine*, May 26, 1997, p. 12.

Fertilizer Industry

★ 1310 ★
TOP FERTILIZER MAKERS IN TURKEY, 1995
Ranked by: Market share, in percent. **Remarks:** Includes 1994 market share. **Number listed:** 9
1. Tugsas with 30.0%
2. Toros Gubre, 24.8%
3. Igsas, 18.0%
4. Bagfas, 13.1%
5. Gubretas, 9.0%
6. Ege Gubre, 4.4%
7. Isdemir, 0.3%
8. Erdemir, 0.2%
9. Kardemir, 0.2%

Source: *National Trade Data Bank*, May 27, 1996, p. IMI960510.

Fiber Industry, International

★ 1311 ★
TOP MAN-MADE FIBER PRODUCERS
Ranked by: Share of production, in percent. **Number listed:** 8
1. United States with 18.0%
2. Western Europe, 14.5%
3. China, 13.0%
4. Taiwan, 11.0%
5. Korea, 9.0%
6. Japan, 7.5%
7. Eastern Europe, 4.0%

8. Rest of world, 23.0%

Source: *Chemical Week*, June 4, 1997, p. 36.

★ 1312 ★
TOP PRODUCERS OF RAYON FIBER, 1996
Ranked by: Production, in thousands of tons per year.
Number listed: 13
1. Lenzing with 262 thousand tons
2. Grasim Industries, 174
3. Formosa Chemicals, 143
4. Courtaulds, 137
5. Indo Bharat Rayon, 73
6. Faserwerk Kelheim, 70
7. Thai Rayon, 64
8. Kemira, 60
9. Inti Indorayon, 60
10. Akzo Faser, 60

Source: *Chemistry & Industry*, July 7, 1997, p. 520.

Fiber Optics Industry

★ 1313 ★
TOP PRODUCERS OF OPTICAL FIBERS, 1995
Ranked by: Production, as a percent of 25.5 million fiber-kilometer. **Number listed:** 11
1. Corning with 32%
2. Lucent, 18%
3. Alcatel, 9%
4. Sumitomo, 7%
5. Fujikura, 5%
6. Pirelli, 5%
7. BICC, 4%
8. Furukawa, 4%
9. Siemens, 3%
10. Draka, 2%

Source: *Telephony*, May 19, 1997, p. 9.

Fibers

★ 1314 ★
TOP GLOBAL MAN-MADE FIBER PRODUCERS, 1995
Ranked by: Market share, in percent. **Number listed:** 11
1. United States with 19.0%
2. Western Europe, 15.0%
3. China, 11.0%
4. Taiwan, 11.0%
5. Japan, 8.0%
6. South Korea, 8.0%
7. Eastern Europe, 6.0%
8. Latin America, 5.0%
9. India, 4.0%

10. Other Southeast Asian Countries, 9.0%
Source: *European Chemical News*, May 20, 1996, p. 15.

Fiji – see under individual headings

Filling Stations
See: **Automobile Service Stations**

Film Distribution

★ 1315 ★
FILM DISTRIBUTION IN JAPAN
Ranked by: Market share, in percent. **Number listed:** 6
1. United International Pictures with 17.7%
2. Toho, 16.6%
3. 20th Century Fox, 13.4%
4. Toho-Towa, 9.8%
5. Toei, 9.3%
6. Other, 33.2%
Source: *Nikkei Weekly*, August 5, 1996, p. 10.

★ 1316 ★
TOP FILM DISTRIBUTORS IN GERMANY, 1996
Ranked by: Market share based on total box office from January 4 to October 13, 1996, in percent. **Remarks:** U.S. majors controlled 68.1% of the market. **Number listed:** 10
1. United Intl. Pictures with 22.0%
2. Buena Vista, 17.3%
3. Fox, 12.1%
4. Constantin Films, 10.7%
5. Warner Bros., 8.4%
6. Columbia/Tri-Star, 8.3%
7. Concorde, 5.7%
8. Delphi, 3.5%
9. Pandora, 1.7%
10. Kinowelt, 1.4%
Source: *Variety*, October 27, 1996, p. 104.

Films, Photographic
See: **Photography–Films**

Finance Companies

★ 1317 ★
TOP FINANCE COMPANIES IN THAILAND, 1996
Ranked by: Year-end assets, in billions of U.S. dollars.
Remarks: Notes foreign partners. **Number listed:** 5
1. Finance One with $5.5 billion
2. Phatra Thanakit, $3.1
3. National Finance, $2.8
4. Dhana Siam, $2.7
5. CMIC, $2.6
Source: *National Trade Data Bank*, April 1, 1997, p. 1.

Financial Analysts

★ 1318 ★
TOP FINANCIAL ANALYSTS COVERING AUSTRIA, 1997
Ranked by: Results of research undertaken by editorial staff of Institutional Investor. **Remarks:** Also contains a lengthy synopsis of reasons for selection of the individuals ranked. **Number listed:** 2
1. Chuck Mentcher (SBC Warburg)
2. Robin Horne (Dresdner Kleinwort Benson)
Source: *Institutional Investor - International Edition,* All-Europe Research Team (annual), February 1997, p. 115.

★ 1319 ★
TOP FINANCIAL ANALYSTS COVERING BELGIUM, 1997
Ranked by: Results of research undertaken by editorial staff of Institutional Investor. **Remarks:** Also contains a lengthy synopsis of reasons for selection of the individuals ranked. **Number listed:** 2
1. Jeffrey Taylor (Dillon, Read Securities)
2. Marc Debrouwer (Peterbroeck, Van Campenhout)
Source: *Institutional Investor - International Edition,* All-Europe Research Team (annual), February 1997, p. 115.

★ 1320 ★
TOP FINANCIAL ANALYSTS COVERING CZECH REPUBLIC, 1997
Ranked by: Results of research undertaken by editorial staff of Institutional Investor. **Remarks:** Also contains a lengthy synopsis of reasons for selection of the individuals ranked. **Number listed:** 3
1. Sandy Winthrop Chen (Credit Suisse First Boston)
2. Anna Bossong (ING Barings)
3. Vladimir Jaros (Wood & Co.)
Source: *Institutional Investor - International Edition,* All-Europe Research Team (annual), February 1997, p. 116.

★ 1321 ★
TOP FINANCIAL ANALYSTS COVERING FRANCE, 1997
Ranked by: Results of research undertaken by editorial staff of Institutional Investor. **Remarks:** Also contains a lengthy synopsis of reasons for selection of the individuals ranked. Cites 3 runners-up. **Number listed:** 3
1. Henri Chermont (Cheuvreux de Virieu)
2. Alain Galene (Societe Generale)
3. Peter Beck (Paribas Capital Markets)

Source: *Institutional Investor - International Edition,* All-Europe Research Team (annual), February 1997, p. 116.

★ 1322 ★
TOP FINANCIAL ANALYSTS COVERING GERMANY, 1997
Ranked by: Results of research undertaken by editorial staff of Institutional Investor. **Remarks:** Also contains a lengthy synopsis of reasons for selection of the individuals ranked. Cites 1 runner-up. **Number listed:** 3
1. Hans-Dieter Klein (Deutsche Morgan Grenfell)
2. Roger Hirst (Dresdner Kleinwort Benson Research)
3. Charalampos Christopoulous (BZW)

Source: *Institutional Investor - International Edition,* All-Europe Research Team (annual), February 1997, p. 117.

★ 1323 ★
TOP FINANCIAL ANALYSTS COVERING HUNGARY, 1997
Ranked by: Results of research undertaken by editorial staff of Institutional Investor. **Remarks:** Also contains a lengthy synopsis of reasons for selection of the individuals ranked. **Number listed:** 3
1. Gabor Sitanyi (ING Barings)
2. Spencer Jakab (Credit Suisse First Boston)
3. Katalin Danin (Creditanstalt Securities)

Source: *Institutional Investor - International Edition,* All-Europe Research Team (annual), February 1997, p. 118.

★ 1324 ★
TOP FINANCIAL ANALYSTS COVERING ITALY, 1997
Ranked by: Results of research undertaken by editorial staff of Institutional Investor. **Remarks:** Also contains a lengthy synopsis of reasons for selection of the individuals ranked. Cites 4 runners-up. **Number listed:** 3
1. Roberto Condulmari (Giubergia Warburg)
2. Gianpaolo Trasi (IMI Sigeco)
3. Francesco Conte (Schroder Securities)

Source: *Institutional Investor - International Edition,* All-Europe Research Team (annual), February 1997, p. 118.

★ 1325 ★
TOP FINANCIAL ANALYSTS COVERING POLAND, 1997
Ranked by: Results of research undertaken by editorial staff of Institutional Investor. **Remarks:** Also contains a lengthy synopsis of reasons for selection of the individuals ranked. Cites 2 runners-up. **Number listed:** 3
1. Andreas Wesemann (ING Barings)
2. Margot Galinska (Credit Suisse First Boston)
3. Timothy Drinkall (Creditanstalt Securities)

Source: *Institutional Investor - International Edition,* All-Europe Research Team (annual), February 1997, p. 120.

★ 1326 ★
TOP FINANCIAL ANALYSTS COVERING RUSSIA, 1997
Ranked by: Results of research undertaken by editorial staff of Institutional Investor. **Remarks:** Also contains a lengthy synopsis of reasons for selection of the individuals ranked. **Number listed:** 3
1. Par Mellstrom (Brunswick Brokerage)
2. Julia Dawson (ING Barings)
3. Stuart Amor (Credit Suisse First Boston)

Source: *Institutional Investor - International Edition,* All-Europe Research Team (annual), February 1997, p. 121.

★ 1327 ★
TOP FINANCIAL ANALYSTS COVERING SCANDINAVIA, 1997
Ranked by: Results of research undertaken by editorial staff of Institutional Investor. **Remarks:** Also contains a lengthy synopsis of reasons for selection of the individuals ranked. Cites 1 runner-up. **Number listed:** 3
1. Bjorn Jansson (Alfred Berg)
2. Fredrik Nygren (Enskilda Securities)
3. Jan Dworsky (FIBA Nordic Securities)

Source: *Institutional Investor - International Edition,* All-Europe Research Team (annual), February 1997, p. 120.

★ 1328 ★
TOP FINANCIAL ANALYSTS COVERING SOUTH AFRICA, 1997
Ranked by: Results of research undertaken by editorial staff of Institutional Investor. **Remarks:** Also contains a lengthy synopsis of reasons for selection of the individuals ranked. Cites 1 runner-up. **Number listed:** 3
1. Jerome O'Regan (Fleming Martin)
2. Dana Becker (ING Barings)
3. John Graham (SBC Warburg Securities)

Source: *Institutional Investor - International Edition,* All-Europe Research Team (annual), February 1997, p. 121.

★ 1329 ★

TOP FINANCIAL ANALYSTS COVERING SOUTH KOREA, 1997

Ranked by: Results of research undertaken by editorial staff of Institutional Investor. **Remarks:** Also contains a lengthy synopsis of reasons for selection of the individuals ranked. Cites 2 runners-up. **Number listed:** 3

1. Keunmo Lee (ING Barings)
2. David Kadarauch (Jardine Fleming Securities)
3. Namuh Rhee (Peregrine Securities International)

Source: *Institutional Investor - International Edition,* All-Asia Research Team (annual), April 1997, p. 112.

★ 1330 ★

TOP FINANCIAL ANALYSTS COVERING SPAIN, 1997

Ranked by: Results of research undertaken by editorial staff of Institutional Investor. **Remarks:** Also contains a lengthy synopsis of reasons for selection of the individuals ranked. Cites 2 runners-up. **Number listed:** 3

1. Ignacio Gomez Montejo (Merrill Lynch)
2. Mark Giacopazzi (Schroder Securities)
3. Pablo Diaz (SBC Warburg)

Source: *Institutional Investor - International Edition,* All-Europe Research Team (annual), February 1997, p. 122.

★ 1331 ★

TOP FINANCIAL ANALYSTS COVERING SWITZERLAND, 1997

Ranked by: Results of research undertaken by editorial staff of Institutional Investor. **Remarks:** Also contains a lengthy synopsis of reasons for selection of the individuals ranked. Cites 1 runner-up. **Number listed:** 3

1. Mirko Sangiorgio (Pictet & Cie)
2. Andreas Vogler (SBC Warburg)
3. Hans-Peter Ast (Union Bank of Switzerland)

Source: *Institutional Investor - International Edition,* All-Europe Research Team (annual), February 1997, p. 123.

★ 1332 ★

TOP FINANCIAL ANALYSTS COVERING THE NETHERLANDS, 1997

Ranked by: Results of research undertaken by editorial staff of Institutional Investor. **Remarks:** Also contains a lengthy synopsis of reasons for selection of the individuals ranked. Cites 3 runners-up. **Number listed:** 3

1. Heinie Hakker (BZW)
2. Frans van Schaik (ABN Amro Hoare Govett)
3. Ian Blackford (NatWest Securities)

Source: *Institutional Investor - International Edition,* All-Europe Research Team (annual), February 1997, p. 119.

★ 1333 ★

TOP FINANCIAL ANALYSTS COVERING TURKEY, 1997

Ranked by: Results of research undertaken by editorial staff of Institutional Investor. **Remarks:** Also contains a lengthy synopsis of reasons for selection of the individuals ranked. **Number listed:** 3

1. Atilla Yesilda (Global Securities)
2. Emre Yigit (UBS)
3. Atif Cezairli (ING Barings)

Source: *Institutional Investor - International Edition,* All-Europe Research Team (annual), February 1997, p. 123.

Financial Analysts – Asia

★ 1334 ★

FIRMS WITH THE MOST ANALYSTS ON THE ALL-ASIA RESEARCH TEAM, 1997

Ranked by: Total number of positions brokerage firm has on the team. **Remarks:** Also notes 1996 rank, number of analysts from each firm that made the first, second, and third All-Asia Research Teams, and the number of runners-up. Coverage does not include Japan. **Number listed:** 24

1. Jardine Fleming Securities with 16
2. ING Barings, 14
3. SBC Warburg, 11
4. Merrill Lynch, 9
5. Morgan Stanley Asia, 9
6. Credit Lyonnais Securities (Asia), 8
7. ABN Amro Hoare Govett Asia, 5
8. Indosuez W.I. Carr Securities, 5
9. Peregrine Securities International, 5
10. Deutsche Morgan Grenfell Securities, 4

Source: *Institutional Investor - International Edition,* All-Asia Research Team (annual), April 1997, p. 101.

★ 1335 ★

TOP FINANCIAL ANALYSTS COVERING AIRLINES IN ASIA, 1997

Ranked by: Results of research undertaken by editorial staff of Institutional Investor. **Remarks:** Also contains a lengthy synopsis of reasons for selection of the individuals ranked. Coverage does not include Japan. **Number listed:** 2

1. Viktor Shvets (Deutsche Morgan Grenfell Securities)
2. Chin Lim (Morgan Stanley Asia)

Source: *Institutional Investor - International Edition,* All-Asia Research Team (annual), April 1997, p. 114.

★ 1336 ★

TOP FINANCIAL ANALYSTS COVERING BANKS IN ASIA, 1997

Ranked by: Results of research undertaken by editorial staff of Institutional Investor. **Remarks:** Also contains a lengthy synopsis of reasons for selection of the individuals ranked. Cites 3 runners-up. Coverage does not include Japan. **Number listed:** 3

1. Roy Ramos (Goldman Sachs)
2. Robert Zielinski (Jardine Fleming Securities)
3. John Hobson (Morgan Stanley Asia)

Source: *Institutional Investor - International Edition,* All-Asia Research Team (annual), April 1997, p. 114.

★ 1337 ★

TOP FINANCIAL ANALYSTS COVERING ECONOMICS IN ASIA, 1997

Ranked by: Results of research undertaken by editorial staff of Institutional Investor. **Remarks:** Also contains a lengthy synopsis of reasons for selection of the individuals ranked. Cites 1 runner-up. Coverage does not include Japan. **Number listed:** 3

1. Jim Walker (Credit Lyonnais Securities)
2. Simon Ogus (SBC Warburg)
3. Annabel Betz (ING Barings)

Source: *Institutional Investor - International Edition,* All-Asia Research Team (annual), April 1997, p. 118.

★ 1338 ★

TOP FINANCIAL ANALYSTS COVERING EQUITY STRATEGY IN ASIA, 1997

Ranked by: Results of research undertaken by editorial staff of Institutional Investor. **Remarks:** Also contains a lengthy synopsis of reasons for selection of the individuals ranked. Cites 4 runners-up. Coverage does not include Japan. **Number listed:** 3

1. Russell Napier (Credit Lyonnais Securities)
2. Colin Bradbury (Jardine Fleming Securities)
3. Alan Butler-Henderson (ING Barings)

Source: *Institutional Investor - International Edition,* All-Asia Research Team (annual), April 1997, p. 119.

★ 1339 ★

TOP FINANCIAL ANALYSTS COVERING PROPERTY IN ASIA, 1997

Ranked by: Results of research undertaken by editorial staff of Institutional Investor. **Remarks:** Also contains a lengthy synopsis of reasons for selection of the individuals ranked. Cites 3 runners-up. Coverage does not include Japan. **Number listed:** 3

1. Michael Green (Salomon Brothers Hong Kong)
2. Peter Churchouse (Morgan Stanley Asia)
3. John So (Jardine Fleming Securities)

Source: *Institutional Investor - International Edition,* All-Asia Research Team (annual), April 1997, p. 115.

★ 1340 ★

TOP FINANCIAL ANALYSTS COVERING PUBLIC UTILITIES IN ASIA, 1997

Ranked by: Results of research undertaken by editorial staff of Institutional Investor. **Remarks:** Also contains a lengthy synopsis of reasons for selection of the individuals ranked. Cites 2 runners-up. Coverage does not include Japan. **Number listed:** 3

1. Hilary Judis (Goldman Sachs)
2. Angello Chan (Morgan Stanley Asia)
3. Timothy Andrew (Deutsche Morgan Grenfell Securities)

Source: *Institutional Investor - International Edition,* All-Asia Research Team (annual), April 1997, p. 115.

★ 1341 ★

TOP FINANCIAL ANALYSTS COVERING TECHNOLOGY IN ASIA, 1997

Ranked by: Results of research undertaken by editorial staff of Institutional Investor. **Remarks:** Also contains a lengthy synopsis of reasons for selection of the individuals ranked. Coverage does not include Japan. **Number listed:** 3

1. Peter Wolff (ING Barings)
2. Gurinder Kalra (Morgan Stanley Asia)
3. Lily Wu (Salomon Brothers Hong Kong)

Source: *Institutional Investor - International Edition,* All-Asia Research Team (annual), April 1997, p. 115.

★ 1342 ★

TOP FINANCIAL ANALYSTS COVERING TELECOMMUNICATIONS IN ASIA, 1997

Ranked by: Results of research undertaken by editorial staff of Institutional Investor. **Remarks:** Also contains a lengthy synopsis of reasons for selection of the individuals ranked. Cites 1 runner-up. Coverage does not include Japan. **Number listed:** 3

1. Adam Quinton (Merrill Lynch)
2. Dylan Tinker (Jardine Fleming Securities)
3. Viktor Shvets (Deutsche Morgan Grenfell Securities)

Source: *Institutional Investor - International Edition,* All-Asia Research Team (annual), April 1997, p. 117.

Financial Analysts – Australia

★ 1343 ★

TOP FINANCIAL ANALYSTS COVERING AUSTRALIA, 1997

Ranked by: Results of research undertaken by editorial staff of Institutional Investor. **Remarks:** Also contains a lengthy synopsis of reasons for selection of the individuals ranked. Cites 2 runners-up. **Number listed:** 3

1. Craig Drummond (J.B. Were & Son)

2. David Wilson (Ord Minnett Securities)
3. Malcom Sinclair (County NatWast Securities Australia)

Source: *Institutional Investor - International Edition,* All-Asia Research Team (annual), April 1997, p. 104.

Financial Analysts – China

★ 1344 ★

TOP FINANCIAL ANALYSTS COVERING CHINA, 1997

Ranked by: Results of research undertaken by editorial staff of Institutional Investor. **Remarks:** Also contains a lengthy synopsis of reasons for selection of the individuals ranked. Cites 5 runners up. **Number listed:** 3

1. Jing Ulrich (Credit Lyonnais Securities)
2. Graham Ormerod (Jardine Fleming Securities)
3. Kalina Ip (ABN Amro Hoare Govett Asia)

Source: *Institutional Investor - International Edition,* All-Asia Research Team (annual), April 1997, p. 105.

Financial Analysts – Europe

★ 1345 ★

FIRMS WITH THE MOST ANALYSTS ON THE ALL-EUROPE RESEARCH TEAM, 1997

Ranked by: Total number of positions brokerage firm has on the team. **Remarks:** Also notes 1996 rank, number of analysts from each firm that made the first, second, and third All-European Research Teams, and the number of runners-up. **Number listed:** 22

1. SBC Warburg with 43
2. UBS, 33
3. Merrill Lynch, 31
4. NatWest Securities, 29
5. HSBC James Capel, 22
6. BZW, 20
7. Dresdner Kleinwort Benson, 19
8. Goldman Sachs International, 19
9. Morgan Stanley International, 18
10. Deutsche Morgan Grenfell, 9

Source: *Institutional Investor - International Edition,* All-Europe Research Team (annual), February 1997, p. 72.

★ 1346 ★

LEADING BROKERAGE FIRMS COVERING CONTINENTAL SECTORS, 1997

Ranked by: Number of team positions. **Number listed:** 6

1. SBC Warburg
2. Morgan Stanley International
3. Goldman Sachs International
4. NatWest Securities

4. Merrill Lynch
4. UBS

Source: *Institutional Investor - International Edition,* All-Europe Research Team (annual), February 1997, p. 75.

★ 1347 ★

LEADING BROKERAGE FIRMS COVERING STRATEGY & ECONOMICS, 1997

Ranked by: Number of team positions. **Number listed:** 6

1. Merrill Lynch
2. Goldman Sachs International
3. Morgan Stanley International
4. SBC Warburg
5. J.P. Morgan
6. UBS

Source: *Institutional Investor - International Edition,* All-Europe Research Team (annual), February 1997, p. 75.

★ 1348 ★

LEADING BROKERAGE FIRMS IN THE FINANCIAL ANALYSIS OF U.K. SECTORS, 1997

Ranked by: Number of team positions. **Number listed:** 5

1. NatWest Securities
1. SBC Warburg
3. BZW
4. HSBC James Capel
4. UBS

Source: *Institutional Investor - International Edition,* All-Europe Research Team (annual), February 1997, p. 75.

★ 1349 ★

LEADING BROKERAGES COVERING CONTINENTAL COUNTRIES AND EMERGING MARKETS, 1997

Ranked by: Number of team positions. **Number listed:** 5

1. UBS
2. SBC Warburg
3. ING Barings
4. Credit Suisse First Boston
5. BZW

Source: *Institutional Investor - International Edition,* All-Europe Research Team (annual), February 1997, p. 75.

★ 1350 ★

TOP FINANCIAL ANALYSTS COVERING BANKS IN EUROPE, 1997

Ranked by: Results of research undertaken by editorial staff of Institutional Investor. **Remarks:** Also contains a lengthy synopsis of reasons for selection of the individuals ranked. **Number listed:** 3

1. Alan Broughton (SBC Warburg)
2. Christopher Williams (Fox-Pitt, Kelton)
3. Susan Leadem (Goldman and Sachs International)

Source: *Institutional Investor - International Edition,* All-Europe Research Team (annual), February 1997, p. 97.

★ 1351 ★

**TOP FINANCIAL ANALYSTS COVERING
ENGINEERING & MACHINERY IN EUROPE, 1997**

Ranked by: Results of research undertaken by editorial staff of Institutional Investor. **Remarks:** Also contains a lengthy synopsis of reasons for selection of the individuals ranked. **Number listed:** 3

1.　Christopher Heminway (Lehman Brothers)
2.　Graham Phillips (HSBC James Capel)
3.　Tim Youngman (SBC Warburg)

Source: *Institutional Investor - International Edition,* All-Europe Research Team (annual), February 1997, p. 98.

★ 1352 ★

**TOP FINANCIAL ANALYSTS COVERING
EUROPEAN BONDS, 1997**

Ranked by: Results of research undertaken by editorial staff of Institutional Investor. **Remarks:** Also contains a lengthy synopsis of reasons for selection of the individuals ranked. Cites 1 runner-up. **Number listed:** 3

1.　Jan Loeys (J.P. Morgan)
2.　David Knott (Deutsch Morgan Grenfell)
3.　Andrew Bevan (Goldman Sachs International)

Source: *Institutional Investor - International Edition,* All-Europe Research Team (annual), February 1997, p. 108.

★ 1353 ★

**TOP FINANCIAL ANALYSTS COVERING
EUROPEAN ECONOMICS, 1997**

Ranked by: Results of research undertaken by editorial staff of Institutional Investor. **Remarks:** Also contains a lengthy synopsis of reasons for selection of the individuals ranked. Cites 5 runners-up. **Number listed:** 3

1.　David Bowers (Merrill Lynch)
2.　Gavyn Davies (Goldman Sachs International)
3.　Richard Reid (UBS)

Source: *Institutional Investor - International Edition,* All-Europe Research Team (annual), February 1997, p. 110.

★ 1354 ★

**TOP FINANCIAL ANALYSTS COVERING
EUROPEAN EQUITY STRATEGY, 1997**

Ranked by: Results of research undertaken by editorial staff of Institutional Investor. **Remarks:** Also contains a lengthy synopsis of reasons for selection of the individuals ranked. Cites 2 runners-up. **Number listed:** 3

1.　David Bowers (Merrill Lynch)
2.　Richard Davidson (Morgan Stanley International)
3.　Mark Howdle (UBS)

Source: *Institutional Investor - International Edition,* All-Europe Research Team (annual), February 1997, p. 112.

★ 1355 ★

**TOP FINANCIAL ANALYSTS COVERING MEDIA &
ENTERTAINMENT IN EUROPE, 1997**

Ranked by: Results of research undertaken by editorial staff of Institutional Investor. **Remarks:** Also contains a lengthy synopsis of reasons for selection of the individuals ranked. Cites 2 runners-up. **Number listed:** 3

1.　Mark Beilby (Deutsche Morgan Grenfell)
2.　Guy Lamming (SBC Warburg)
3.　Neil Blackley (Merrill Lynch)

Source: *Institutional Investor - International Edition,* All-Europe Research Team (annual), February 1997, p. 102.

★ 1356 ★

**TOP FINANCIAL ANALYSTS COVERING PAPER &
PACKAGING IN EUROPE, 1997**

Ranked by: Results of research undertaken by editorial staff of Institutional Investor. **Remarks:** Also contains a lengthy synopsis of reasons for selection of the individuals ranked. Cites 2 runners-up. **Number listed:** 3

1.　Mads Asprem (Morgan Stanley International)
2.　Thomas Brodin (Salomon Brothers International)
3.　Denis Christie (Dresdner Kleinwort Benson)

Source: *Institutional Investor - International Edition,* All-Europe Research Team (annual), February 1997, p. 103.

★ 1357 ★

**TOP FINANCIAL ANALYSTS COVERING
PHARMACEUTICALS IN EUROPE, 1997**

Ranked by: Results of research undertaken by editorial staff of Institutional Investor. **Remarks:** Also contains a lengthy synopsis of reasons for selection of the individuals ranked. Cites 4 runners-up. **Number listed:** 3

1.　Mark Tracey (Goldman Sachs International)
2.　Stewart Adkins (Lehman Brothers)
3.　Janet Dyson (Merrill Lynch)

Source: *Institutional Investor - International Edition,* All-Europe Research Team (annual), February 1997, p. 103.

★ 1358 ★

**TOP FINANCIAL ANALYSTS COVERING
RETAILERS IN EUROPE, 1997**

Ranked by: Results of research undertaken by editorial staff of Institutional Investor. **Remarks:** Also contains a lengthy synopsis of reasons for selection of the individuals ranked. Cites 1 runner-up. **Number listed:** 3

1.　Claire Kent (Morgan Stanley International)
2.　Keith Wills (Goldman Sachs International)
3.　Didier Rabattu (Deustche Morgan Grenfell)

Source: *Institutional Investor - International Edition,* All-Europe Research Team (annual), February 1997, p. 104.

★ 1359 ★
TOP FINANCIAL ANALYSTS COVERING TELECOM EQUIPMENT IN EUROPE, 1997
Ranked by: Results of research undertaken by editorial staff of Institutional Investor. **Remarks:** Also contains a lengthy synopsis of reasons for selection of the individuals ranked. Cites 2 runners-up. **Number listed:** 3
1. Richard Kramer (Goldman Sachs International)
2. Russ Mould (SBC Warburg)
3. Nimrod Schwarzmann (HSBC James Capel)
Source: *Institutional Investor - International Edition,* All-Europe Research Team (annual), February 1997, p. 105.

★ 1360 ★
TOP FINANCIAL ANALYSTS COVERING TELECOM SERVICES IN EUROPE, 1997
Ranked by: Results of research undertaken by editorial staff of Institutional Investor. **Remarks:** Also contains a lengthy synopsis of reasons for selection of the individuals ranked. Cites 3 runners-up. **Number listed:** 3
1. Francis Woollen (UBS)
2. Patrick Earl (SBC Warburg)
3. James Golob (Deutsche Morgan Grenfell)
Source: *Institutional Investor - International Edition,* All-Europe Research Team (annual), February 1997, p. 105.

★ 1361 ★
TOP FINANCIAL ANALYSTS COVERING THE AUTO INDUSTRY IN EUROPE, 1997
Ranked by: Results of research undertaken by editorial staff of Institutional Investor. **Remarks:** Also contains a lengthy synopsis of reasons for selection of the individuals ranked. **Number listed:** 3
1. Nick Snee (J.P. Morgan)
2. Keith Hayes (Goldman Sachs International)
3. Stephen Reitman (Merrill Lynch)
Source: *Institutional Investor - International Edition,* All-Europe Research Team (annual), February 1997, p. 96.

★ 1362 ★
TOP FINANCIAL ANALYSTS COVERING THE BEVERAGE INDUSTRY IN EUROPE, 1997
Ranked by: Results of research undertaken by editorial staff of Institutional Investor. **Remarks:** Also contains a lengthy synopsis of reasons for selection of the individuals ranked. **Number listed:** 2
1. Sylvain Massot (Morgan Stanley International)
2. John Wakely (Lehman Brothers)
Source: *Institutional Investor - International Edition,* All-Europe Research Team (annual), February 1997, p. 97.

★ 1363 ★
TOP FINANCIAL ANALYSTS COVERING THE BUILDING INDUSTRY IN EUROPE, 1997
Ranked by: Results of research undertaken by editorial staff of Institutional Investor. **Remarks:** Also contains a lengthy synopsis of reasons for selection of the individuals ranked. **Number listed:** 2
1. Sandrine Naslin (SBC Warburg)
2. Ken Rumph (UBS)
Source: *Institutional Investor - International Edition,* All-Europe Research Team (annual), February 1997, p. 97.

★ 1364 ★
TOP FINANCIAL ANALYSTS COVERING THE CHEMICALS INDUSTRY IN EUROPE, 1997
Ranked by: Results of research undertaken by editorial staff of Institutional Investor. **Remarks:** Also contains a lengthy synopsis of reasons for selection of the individuals ranked. Cites 5 runners-up. **Number listed:** 3
1. Charles Brown (Goldman Sachs International)
2. Jenny Barker (UBS)
3. Campbell Gillies (NatWest Securities)
Source: *Institutional Investor - International Edition,* All-Europe Research Team (annual), February 1997, p. 98.

★ 1365 ★
TOP FINANCIAL ANALYSTS COVERING THE FOOD INDUSTRY IN EUROPE, 1997
Ranked by: Results of research undertaken by editorial staff of Institutional Investor. **Remarks:** Also contains a lengthy synopsis of reasons for selection of the individuals ranked. **Number listed:** 3
1. Sylvain Massot (Morgan Stanley International)
2. Mark Lynch (SBC Warburg)
3. David Atkinson (NatWest Securities)
Source: *Institutional Investor - International Edition,* All-Europe Research Team (annual), February 1997, p. 99.

★ 1366 ★
TOP FINANCIAL ANALYSTS COVERING THE INSURANCE INDUSTRY IN EUROPE, 1997
Ranked by: Results of research undertaken by editorial staff of Institutional Investor. **Remarks:** Also contains a lengthy synopsis of reasons for selection of the individuals ranked. Cites 1 runner-up. **Number listed:** 3
1. Robert Yates (Fox-Pitt, Kelton)
2. Katherine Moynes (SBC Warburg)
3. Stephen Dias (Goldman Sachs International)
Source: *Institutional Investor - International Edition,* All-Europe Research Team (annual), February 1997, p. 99.

★ 1367 ★
TOP FINANCIAL ANALYSTS COVERING THE OIL & GAS INDUSTRY IN EUROPE, 1997
Ranked by: Results of research undertaken by editorial staff of Institutional Investor. **Remarks:** Also contains a lengthy synopsis of reasons for selection of the individuals ranked. Cites 1 runner-up. **Number listed:** 3
1. Fergus MacLeod (NatWest Securities)
2. Gavin White (SBC Warburg)
3. Susan Graham (Merrill Lynch)

Source: *Institutional Investor - International Edition,* All-Europe Research Team (annual), February 1997, p. 102.

★ 1368 ★
TOP FINANCIAL ANALYSTS COVERING THE TECHNOLOGY INDUSTRY IN EUROPE, 1997
Ranked by: Results of research undertaken by editorial staff of Institutional Investor. **Remarks:** Also contains a lengthy synopsis of reasons for selection of the individuals ranked. Cites 1 runner-up. **Number listed:** 3
1. Charles Elliot (Goldman Sachs International)
2. Angela Dean (Morgan Stanley International)
3. Kevin Brau (Credit Suisse First Boston)

Source: *Institutional Investor - International Edition,* All-Europe Research Team (annual), February 1997, p. 104.

★ 1369 ★
TOP FINANCIAL ANALYSTS COVERING TRANSPORTATION IN EUROPE, 1997
Ranked by: Results of research undertaken by editorial staff of Institutional Investor. **Remarks:** Also contains a lengthy synopsis of reasons for selection of the individuals ranked. Cites 1 runner-up. **Number listed:** 3
1. Andrew Barker (SBC Warburg)
2. Mark McVicar (NatWest Securities)
3. Christopher Tarry (Dresdner Kleinwort Benson)

Source: *Institutional Investor - International Edition,* All-Europe Research Team (annual), February 1997, p. 106.

★ 1370 ★
TOP FINANCIAL ANALYSTS COVERING UTILITIES IN EUROPE, 1997
Ranked by: Results of research undertaken by editorial staff of Institutional Investor. **Remarks:** Also contains a lengthy synopsis of reasons for selection of the individuals ranked. **Number listed:** 3
1. Ricardo Barcelona (SBC Warburg)
2. John Willis (NatWest Securities)
3. Isabelle Hayen (Goldman Sachs International)

Source: *Institutional Investor - International Edition,* All-Europe Research Team (annual), February 1997, p. 107.

Financial Analysts – Hong Kong

★ 1371 ★
TOP FINANCIAL ANALYSTS COVERING HONG KONG, 1997
Ranked by: Results of research undertaken by editorial staff of Institutional Investor. **Remarks:** Also contains a lengthy synopsis of reasons for selection of the individuals ranked. Cites 4 runners-up. **Number listed:** 3
1. Steven Li (Jardine Fleming Securities)
2. Brian Parker (Credit Lyonnais Securities)
3. Mark Simpson (ING Barings)

Source: *Institutional Investor - International Edition,* All-Asia Research Team (annual), April 1997, p. 105.

Financial Analysts – India

★ 1372 ★
TOP FINANCIAL ANALYSTS COVERING INDIA, 1997
Ranked by: Results of research undertaken by editorial staff of Institutional Investor. **Remarks:** Also contains a lengthy sysnopsis of reasons for selection of the individuals ranked. Cites 2 runners-up. **Number listed:** 3
1. Sam Tully (Jardine Fleming Securities)
2. Pravin Shah (Morgan Stanley Asia)
3. Praween Napate (ING Barings)

Source: *Institutional Investor - International Edition,* All-Asia Research Team (annual), April 1997, p. 108.

Financial Analysts – Indonesia

★ 1373 ★
TOP FINANCIAL ANALYSTS COVERING INDONESIA, 1997
Ranked by: Results of research undertaken by editorial staff of Institutional Investor. **Remarks:** Also contains a lengthy synopsis of reasons for selection of the individuals ranked. Cites 2 runners-up. **Number listed:** 3
1. Charles Whitworth (Jardine Fleming Securities)
2. Thomas Inglis (ING Barings)
3. Jason Donville (Credit Lyonnais Securities)

Source: *Institutional Investor - International Edition,* All-Asia Research Team (annual), April 1997, p. 109.

Financial Analysts, International

★ 1374 ★
BEST FINANCIAL ANALYSTS COVERING CURRENCY FORECASTING
Ranked by: Results of research undertaken by editorial staff of Institutional Investor. **Remarks:** Also contains a lengthy synopsis of reasons for selection of the individuals ranked. Cites 3 runners-up. **Number listed:** 3
1. Terence O'Neill (Goldman Sachs International)
2. Avinash Persaud (J.P. Morgan)
3. Michael Rosenberg (Merrill Lynch)

Source: *Institutional Investor - International Edition*, All-Europe Research Team (annual), February 1997, p. 110.

★ 1375 ★
BEST FINANCIAL ANALYSTS COVERING GLOBAL ASSET ALLOCATION
Ranked by: Results of research undertaken by editorial staff of Institutional Investor. **Remarks:** Also contains a lengthy synopsis of reasons for selection of the individuals ranked. Cites 2 runners-up. **Number listed:** 3
1. Barton Biggs (Morgan Stanley International)
2. Charles Clough Jr. (Merrill Lynch)
3. Andrew Garthwaite (SBC Warburg)

Source: *Institutional Investor - International Edition*, All-Europe Research Team (annual), February 1997, p. 107.

★ 1376 ★
BEST FINANCIAL ANALYSTS COVERING GLOBAL BONDS
Ranked by: Results of research taken by editorial staff of Institutional Investor. **Remarks:** Also contains a lengthy synopsis of reasons for selection of the individuals ranked. **Number listed:** 3
1. Jan Loeys (J.P. Morgan)
2. Andrew Bevan (Goldman Sachs International)
3. Michael Rosenberg (Merrill Lynch)

Source: *Institutional Investor - International Edition*, All-Europe Research Team (annual), February 1997, p. 108.

★ 1377 ★
BEST FINANCIAL ANALYSTS COVERING GLOBAL ECONOMICS
Ranked by: Result of research undertaken by editorial staff of Institutional Investor. **Remarks:** Also contains a lengthy synopsis of reasons for selection of the individuals ranked. Cites 1 runner-up. **Number listed:** 3
1. Gavyn Davies (Goldman Sachs International)
2. William Brown (J.P. Morgan)
3. Donald Straszheim (Merrill Lynch)

Source: *Institutional Investor - International Edition*, All-Europe Research Team (annual), February 1997, p. 111.

★ 1378 ★
BEST FINANCIAL ANALYSTS COVERING GLOBAL EQUITY STRATEGY
Ranked by: Results of research undertaken by editorial staff of Institutional Investor. **Remarks:** Also contains a lengthy synopsis of reasons for selection of the individuals ranked. Cites 1 runner-up. **Number listed:** 3
1. Barton Biggs (Morgan Stanley International)
2. Andrew Garthwaite (SBC Warburg)
3. Charles Clough Jr. (Merrill Lynch)

Source: *Institutional Investor - International Edition*, All-Europe Research Team (annual), February 1997, p. 113.

★ 1379 ★
BEST FINANCIAL ANALYSTS COVERING QUANTITATIVE ANALYSIS
Ranked by: Results of research undertaken by editorial staff of Institutional Investor. **Remarks:** Also contains a lengthy synopsis of reasons for selection of the individuals ranked. **Number listed:** 3
1. Markus Barth (Merrill Lynch)
2. Alun Jones (UBS)
3. Michael Young (Goldman Sachs International)

Source: *Institutional Investor - International Edition*, All-Europe Research Team (annual), February 1997, p. 114.

Financial Analysts – Japan

★ 1380 ★
JAPAN'S LEADING INVESTMENT ANALYSIS COMPANIES, 1997
Ranked by: Total number of positions on the All-Asia Research Team. **Remarks:** Notes 1996 rank, number of analysts from each firm that made the first, second, and third All-Asia Research Teams, and the number of runners-up. **Number listed:** 13
1. Nomura with 25
2. Merrill Lynch Japan, 16
3. Salomon Brothers Asia, 12
4. Goldman Sachs (Japan), 11
5. Morgan Stanley Japan, 10
6. UBS Securities, 10
7. Daiwa Institute of Research, 7
8. HSBC James Capel Japan, 7
9. Nikko Research Center, 6
10. Dresdner Kleinwort Benson Research, 5

Source: *Institutional Investor - International Edition*, All-Asia Research Team (annual), April 1997, p. 123.

★ 1381 ★

**TOP ANALYSTS COVERING PHARMACEUTICALS
AND HEALTH CARE IN JAPAN, 1997**

Ranked by: Results of research undertaken by editorial
staff of Institutional Investor. **Remarks:** Also contains a
lengthy synopsis of reasons for selection of the
individuals ranked. Cites 1 runner-up. **Number listed:** 3

1. Yoshihiko Yamamoto (Salomon Brothers
   Asia)
2. Hiroshi Nakagawa (Merrill Lynch Japan)
3. Shigeru Mishima (UBS Securities)

Source: *Institutional Investor - International Edition,* All-
Asia Research Team (annual), April 1997, p. 132.

★ 1382 ★

**TOP ANALYSTS COVERING PRECISION
ELECTRONIC INSTRUMENTS IN JAPAN, 1997**

Ranked by: Results of research undertaken by editorial
staff of Institutional Investor. **Remarks:** Also contains a
lengthy synopsis of reasons for selection of the
individuals ranked. Cites 1 runner-up. **Number listed:** 3

1. Hiroshi Yoshihara (Salomon Brothers Asia)
2. Kimihide Takano (Dresdner Kleinwort Benson
   Research)
3. Yutaka Sugiyama (UBS Securities)

Source: *Institutional Investor - International Edition,* All-
Asia Research Team (annual), April 1997, p. 129.

★ 1383 ★

**TOP ANALYSTS IN SHIPBUILDING & PLANT
ENGINEERING IN JAPAN, 1997**

Ranked by: Results of research undertaken by editorial
staff of Institutional Investor. **Remarks:** Also contains a
lengthy synopsis of reasons for selection of the
individuals ranked. Cites 1 runner-up. **Number listed:** 3

1. Akira Sato (Nomura)
2. Minoru Kawahara (Smith Barney
   International)
3. Yutaka Asai (Daiwa Institute of Research)

Source: *Institutional Investor - International Edition,* All-
Asia Research Team (annual), April 1997, p. 136.

★ 1384 ★

**TOP FINANCIAL ANALYSTS COVERING AUTOS
AND AUTO PARTS IN JAPAN, 1997**

Ranked by: Results of research undertaken by editorial
staff of Institutional Investor. **Remarks:** Also contains a
lengthy synopsis of reasons for selection of the
individuals ranked. Cites 2 runners-up. **Number listed:** 3

1. Noriyuki Matsushima (Nikko Research
   Center)
2. Koji Endo (Lehman Brothers)
3. Takaki Nakanishi (Merrill Lynch Japan)

Source: *Institutional Investor - International Edition,* All-
Asia Research Team (annual), April 1997, p. 124.

★ 1385 ★

**TOP FINANCIAL ANALYSTS COVERING
CHEMICALS IN JAPAN, 1997**

Ranked by: Results of research undertaken by editorial
staff of Institutional Investor. **Remarks:** Also contains a
lengthy synopsis of reasons for selection of the
individuals ranked. Cites 2 runners-up. **Number listed:** 3

1. Toshihiko Ginbayashi (Morgan Stanley Japan)
2. Takao Kanai (Nomura)
3. Koichi Ishihara (UBS Securities)

Source: *Institutional Investor - International Edition,* All-
Asia Research Team (annual), April 1997, p. 125.

★ 1386 ★

**TOP FINANCIAL ANALYSTS COVERING
COMPUTER SOFTWARE IN JAPAN, 1997**

Ranked by: Results of research undertaken by editorial
staff of Institutional Investor. **Remarks:** Also contains a
lengthy synopsis of reasons for selection of the
individuals ranked. **Number listed:** 3

1. Mitsuko Morita (Morgan Stanley Japan)
2. Naoko Ito (Goldman Sachs)
3. Yoshinori Tanahashi (Nomura)

Source: *Institutional Investor - International Edition,* All-
Asia Research Team (annual), April 1997, p. 127.

★ 1387 ★

**TOP FINANCIAL ANALYSTS COVERING
CONSTRUCTION IN JAPAN, 1997**

Ranked by: Results of research undertaken by editorial
staff of Institutional Investor. **Remarks:** Also contains a
lengthy synopsis of reasons for selection of the
individuals ranked. Cites 1 runner-up. **Number listed:** 3

1. Etsusuke Masuda (HSBC James Capel Japan)
2. Rie Murayama (Goldman Sachs)
3. Takashi Hashimoto (Salomon Brothers Asia)

Source: *Institutional Investor - International Edition,* All-
Asia Research Team (annual), April 1997, p. 127.

★ 1388 ★

**TOP FINANCIAL ANALYSTS COVERING
CONSUMER ELECTRONICS IN JAPAN, 1997**

Ranked by: Results of research undertaken by editorial
staff of Institutional Investor. **Remarks:** Also contains a
lengthy synopsis of reasons for selection of the
individuals ranked. Cites 4 runners-up. **Number listed:** 3

1. Kiyotaka Teranishi (Nomura)
2. Takatoshi Yamamoto (Morgan Stanley Japan)
3. Hitoshi Kuriyama (Goldman Sachs)

Source: *Institutional Investor - International Edition,* All-
Asia Research Team (annual), April 1997, p. 128.

★ 1389 ★
TOP FINANCIAL ANALYSTS COVERING ECONOMICS IN JAPAN, 1997
Ranked by: Results of research undertaken by editorial staff of Institutional Investor. **Remarks:** Also contains a lengthy synopsis of reasons for selection of the individuals ranked. Cites 5 runners-up. **Number listed:** 3
1. Tetsufumi Yamakawa (Goldman Sachs)
2. Richard Koo (Nomura)
3. Robert Alan Feldman (Salomon Brothers Asia)

Source: *Institutional Investor - International Edition,* All-Asia Research Team (annual), April 1997, p. 139.

★ 1390 ★
TOP FINANCIAL ANALYSTS COVERING EQUITY STRATEGY IN JAPAN, 1997
Ranked by: Results of research undertaken by editorial staff of Institutional Investor. **Remarks:** Also contains a lengthy synopsis of reasons for selection of the individuals ranked. Cites 1 runner-up. **Number listed:** 3
1. Chisato Haganuma (Nomura)
2. Alexander Kinmont (Morgan Stanley Japan)
3. Peter Tasker (Dresdner Kleinwort Benson Research)

Source: *Institutional Investor - International Edition,* All-Asia Research Team (annual), April 1997, p. 140.

★ 1391 ★
TOP FINANCIAL ANALYSTS COVERING FIXED-INCOME STRATEGY IN JAPAN, 1997
Ranked by: Results of research undertaken by editorial staff of Institutional Investor. **Remarks:** Also contains a lengthy synopsis of reasons for selection of the individuals ranked. Cites 1 runner-up. **Number listed:** 3
1. Atsushi Mizuno (Nomura)
2. Tadashi Kikugawa (Goldman Sachs)
3. Kazuto Uchida (Tokyo-Mitsubishi Securities)

Source: *Institutional Investor - International Edition,* All-Asia Research Team (annual), April 1997, p. 140.

★ 1392 ★
TOP FINANCIAL ANALYSTS COVERING FOOD & BEVERAGES IN JAPAN, 1997
Ranked by: Results of research undertaken by editorial staff of Institutional Investor. **Remarks:** Also contains a lengthy synopsis of reasons for selection of the individuals ranked. **Number listed:** 3
1. Shuichi Shibanuma (Merrill Lynch Japan)
2. Masaaki Yamaguchi (Nomura)
3. Nobuyoshi Miura (Yamaichi Research Institute)

Source: *Institutional Investor - International Edition,* All-Asia Research Team (annual), April 1997, p. 130.

★ 1393 ★
TOP FINANCIAL ANALYSTS COVERING INDUSTRIAL ELECTRONICS IN JAPAN, 1997
Ranked by: Results of research undertaken by editorial staff of Institutional Investor. **Remarks:** Also contains a lengthy synopsis of reasons for selection of the individuals ranked. Cites 1 runner-up. **Number listed:** 3
1. Hideki Wakabayashi (Nomura)
2. Takatoshi Yamamoto (Morgan Stanley Japan)
3. Fumiaki Sato (Smith Barney International)

Source: *Institutional Investor - International Edition,* All-Asia Research Team (annual), April 1997, p. 128.

★ 1394 ★
TOP FINANCIAL ANALYSTS COVERING MACHINERY IN JAPAN, 1997
Ranked by: Results of research undertaken by editorial staff of Institutional Investor. **Remarks:** Also contains a lengthy synopsis of reasons for selection of the individuals ranked. Cites 3 runners-up. **Number listed:** 3
1. Fumihiko Nakazawa (Merrill Lynch Japan)
2. Ken Maruyama (UBS Securities)
3. Masayuki Mochizuki (Morgan Stanley Japan)

Source: *Institutional Investor - International Edition,* All-Asia Research Team (annual), April 1997, p. 132.

★ 1395 ★
TOP FINANCIAL ANALYSTS COVERING METALS IN JAPAN, 1997
Ranked by: Results of research undertaken by editorial staff of Institutional Investor. **Remarks:** Also contains a lengthy synopsis of reasons for selection of the individuals ranked. Cites 3 runners-up. **Number listed:** 3
1. Makoto Hiranuma (Nomura)
2. Masahiro Iwano (Goldman Sachs)
3. Toru Nagai (Morgan Stanley Japan)

Source: *Institutional Investor - International Edition,* All-Asia Research Team (annual), April 1997, p. 125.

★ 1396 ★
TOP FINANCIAL ANALYSTS COVERING QUANTITATIVE RESEARCH IN JAPAN, 1997
Ranked by: Results of research undertaken by editorial staff of Institutional Investor. **Remarks:** Also contains a lengthy synopsis of reasons for selection of the individuals ranked. Cites 1 runner-up. **Number listed:** 3
1. Takashi Ito (Nomura)
2. Kazuho Toyoda (Salomon Brothers Asia)
3. Patrick Mohr (Merrill Lynch Japan)

Source: *Institutional Investor - International Edition,* All-Asia Research Team (annual), April 1997, p. 142.

★ 1397 ★
TOP FINANCIAL ANALYSTS COVERING REAL ESTATE AND HOUSING JAPAN, 1997
Ranked by: Results of research undertaken by editorial staff of Institutional Investor. **Remarks:** Also contains a lengthy synopsis of reasons for selection of the individuals ranked. Cites 2 runners-up. **Number listed:** 3
1. Junichi Shiomoto (Nomura)
2. Takashi Hashimoto (Salomon Brothers Asia)
3. Keiko Otsuki (UBS Securities)

Source: *Institutional Investor - International Edition,* All-Asia Research Team (annual), April 1997, p. 134.

★ 1398 ★
TOP FINANCIAL ANALYSTS COVERING RETAILING IN JAPAN, 1997
Ranked by: Results of research undertaken by editorial staff of Institutional Investor. **Remarks:** Also contains a lengthy synopsis of reasons for selection of the individuals ranked. Cites 1 runner-up. **Number listed:** 3
1. Takayuki Suzuki (Merrill Lynch Japan)
2. Yukihiro Moroe (Goldman Sachs)
3. Hirokazu Ishii (Nomura)

Source: *Institutional Investor - International Edition,* All-Asia Research Team (annual), April 1997, p. 134.

★ 1399 ★
TOP FINANCIAL ANALYSTS COVERING SMALL AND OTC COMPANIES IN JAPAN, 1997
Ranked by: Results of research undertaken by editorial staff of Institutional Investor. **Remarks:** Also contains a lengthy synopsis of reasons for selection of the individuals ranked. Cites 2 runners-up. **Number listed:** 3
1. Kiyohisa Hirano (Daiwa Institute of Research)
2. Noboru Terashima (Goldman Sachs)
3. Ken Segawa (UBS Securities)

Source: *Institutional Investor - International Edition,* All-Asia Research Team (annual), April 1997, p. 137.

★ 1400 ★
TOP FINANCIAL ANALYSTS COVERING TELECOMMUNICATIONS IN JAPAN, 1997
Ranked by: Results of research undertaken by editorial staff of Institutional Investor. **Remarks:** Also contains a lengthy synopsis of reasons for selection of the individuals ranked. **Number listed:** 3
1. Kiyohisa Ota (Merrill Lynch Japan)
2. Eric Gan (Goldman Sachs)
3. Yoshio Ando (Nomura)

Source: *Institutional Investor - International Edition,* All-Asia Research Team (annual), April 1997, p. 137.

★ 1401 ★
TOP FINANCIAL ANALYSTS COVERING THE BANKING INDUSTRY IN JAPAN, 1997
Ranked by: Results of research undertaken by editorial staff of Institutional Investor. **Remarks:** Also contains a lengthy synopsis of reasons for selection of the individuals ranked. Cites 4 runners-up. **Number listed:** 3
1. Yoshinobu Yamada (Merrill Lynch Japan)
2. David Atkinson (Goldman Sachs)
3. Alicia Ogawa (Salomon Brothers Asia)

Source: *Institutional Investor - International Edition,* All-Asia Research Team (annual), April 1997, p. 129.

★ 1402 ★
TOP FINANCIAL ANALYSTS COVERING TRADING COMPANIES IN JAPAN, 1997
Ranked by: Results of research undertaken by editorial staff of Institutional Investor. **Remarks:** Also contains a lengthy synopsis of reasons for selection of the individuals ranked. Cites 1 runner-up. **Number listed:** 3
1. Tomoyasu Kato (Nomura)
2. Kenichiro Yoshida (Salomon Brothers Asia)
3. Tsuyoshi Ishisone (Daiwa Institute of Research)

Source: *Institutional Investor - International Edition,* All-Asia Research Team (annual), April 1997, p. 138.

★ 1403 ★
TOP FINANCIAL ANALYSTS COVERING TRANSPORTATION IN JAPAN, 1997
Ranked by: Results of research undertaken by editorial staff of Institutional Investor. **Remarks:** Also contains a lengthy synopsis of reasons for selection of the individuals ranked. Cites 1 runner-up. **Number listed:** 3
1. Naoto Hashimoto (Nomura)
2. Naoko Matsumoto (Merrill Lynch Japan)
3. Paul Smith (HSBC James Capel Japan)

Source: *Institutional Investor - International Edition,* All-Asia Research Team (annual), April 1997, p. 138.

★ 1404 ★
TOP FINANCIAL ANALYSTS COVERING UTILITIES IN JAPAN, 1997
Ranked by: Results of research undertaken by editorial staff of Institutional Investor. **Remarks:** Also contains a lengthy synopsis of reasons for selection of the individuals ranked. Cites 1 runner-up. **Number listed:** 3
1. Naoto Hashimoto (Nomura)
2. Paul Smith (HSBC James Capel Japan)
3. Yoshio Oe (Yamaichi Research Institute)

Source: *Institutional Investor - International Edition,* All-Asia Research Team (annual), April 1997, p. 139.

★ 1405 ★

TOP FINANCIAL ANALYSTS IN NONBANKING FINANCIAL INDUSTRIES IN JAPAN, 1997

Ranked by: Results of research undertaken by editorial staff of Institutional Investor. **Remarks:** Also contains a lengthy synopsis of reasons for selection of the individuals ranked. Cites 1 runner-up. **Number listed:** 3

1. Shin Maeda (Nomura)
2. Yuko Taniwaki (Nomura)
3. Ayako Sato (UBS Securities)

Source: *Institutional Investor - International Edition,* All-Asia Research Team (annual), April 1997, p. 130.

★ 1406 ★

TOP FINANCIAL ANALYSTS IN TECHNICAL ANALYSIS IN JAPAN, 1997

Ranked by: Results of research undertaken by editorial staff of Institutional Investor. **Remarks:** Also contains a lengthy synopsis of reasons for selection of the individuals ranked. **Number listed:** 3

1. Tatsuo Kurokawa (Nomura)
2. Hidenobu Sasaki (Nikko Research Center)
3. Yukiharu Abe (ING Barings)

Source: *Institutional Investor - International Edition,* All-Asia Research Team (annual), April 1997, p. 143.

Financial Analysts – Malaysia

★ 1407 ★

TOP FINANCIAL ANALYSTS COVERING MALAYSIA, 1997

Ranked by: Results of research undertaken by editorial staff of Institutional Investor. **Remarks:** Also contains a lengthy synopsis of reasons for selection of the individuals ranked. Cites 1 runner-up. **Number listed:** 3

1. Richard Jones (ING Barings)
2. Dominic Armstrong (Jardine Fleming Securities)
3. Yeo Kar Peng (UBS Securities)

Source: *Institutional Investor - International Edition,* All-Asia Research Team (annual), April 1997, p. 109.

Financial Analysts – New Zealand

★ 1408 ★

TOP FINANCIAL ANALYSTS COVERING NEW ZEALAND, 1997

Ranked by: Results of research undertaken by editorial staff of Institutional Investor. **Remarks:** Also contains a lengthy synopsis of reasons for selection of the individuals ranked. Cites 3 runners-up. **Number listed:** 3

1. Clark Perkins (J.B. Were & Sons)

2. Kevin Bennett (Doyle Paterson Brown)
3. Guy Hallwright (First NZ Capital Securities)

Source: *Institutional Investor - International Edition,* All-Asia Research Team (annual), April 1997, p. 110.

Financial Analysts – Philippines

★ 1409 ★

TOP FINANCIAL ANALYSTS COVERING THE PHILIPPINES, 1997

Ranked by: Results of research undertaken by editorial staff of Institutional Investor. **Remarks:** Also contains a lengthy synopsis of reasons for selection of the individuals ranked. Cites 1 runner-up. **Number listed:** 3

1. Alexander Pomento (ING Barings)
2. Edmund Brandt (Jardine Fleming Securities)
3. Scott Gibson (ABN Amro Hoare Govett Asia)

Source: *Institutional Investor - International Edition,* All-Asia Research Team (annual), April 1997, p. 110.

Financial Analysts – Singapore

★ 1410 ★

TOP FINANCIAL ANALYSTS COVERING SINGAPORE, 1997

Ranked by: Results of research undertaken by editorial staff of Institutional Investor. **Remarks:** Also contains a lengthy synopsis of reasons for selection of the individuals ranked. Cites 6 runners-up. **Number listed:** 3

1. Neil Payne (ING Barings)
2. Nels Friets (Credit Lyonnais Securities)
3. Lim Jit Soon (UBS Securities)

Source: *Institutional Investor - International Edition,* All-Asia Research Team (annual), April 1997, p. 111.

Financial Analysts – Taiwan

★ 1411 ★

TOP FINANCIAL ANALYSTS COVERING TAIWAN, 1997

Ranked by: Results of research undertaken by editorial staff of Institutional Investor. **Remarks:** Also contains a lengthy synopsis of reasons for selection of the individuals ranked. Cites 3 runners-up. **Number listed:** 3

1. Peter Kurz (ING Barings)
2. Ti-Sheng Young (SBC Warburg)
3. Jonathan Ross (ABN Amro Hoare Govett Asia)

Source: *Institutional Investor - International Edition,* All-Asia Research Team (annual), April 1997, p. 112.

Financial Analysts – Thailand

★ 1412 ★

TOP FINANCIAL ANALYSTS COVERING THAILAND, 1997

Ranked by: Results of research undertaken by editorial staff of Institutional Investor. **Remarks:** Also contains a lengthy synopsis of reasons for selection of the individuals ranked. Cites 2 runners-up. **Number listed:** 3

1. Andrew Houston (Jardine Fleming Securities)
2. Mark Faulkner (Credit Lyonnais Securities)
3. Robert Collins (Asia Equity Thailand)

Source: *Institutional Investor - International Edition,* All-Asia Research Team (annual), April 1997, p. 113.

Financial Analysts – United Kingdom

★ 1413 ★

TOP ANALYSTS COVERING DIVERSIFIED INDUSTRIALS IN THE UNITED KINGDOM, 1997

Ranked by: Results of research undertaken by editorial staff of Institutional Investor. **Remarks:** Also contains a lengthy synopsis of reasons for selection of the individuals ranked. Cites 3 runners-up. **Number listed:** 3

1. David Ireland (ABN Amro Hoare Govett)
2. Clyde Lewis (HSBC James Capel)
3. Andrew Hollins (Dresdner Kleinwort Benson)

Source: *Institutional Investor - International Edition,* All-Europe Research Team (annual), February 1997, p. 84.

★ 1414 ★

TOP ANALYSTS COVERING ELECTRONIC/ ELECTRICAL EQUIPMENT IN THE U.K., 1997

Ranked by: Results of research undertaken by editorial staff of Institutional Investor. **Remarks:** Also contains a lengthy synopsis of reasons for selection of the individuals ranked. **Number listed:** 3

1. Neil Steer (HSBC James Capel)
2. Andrew Bryant (NatWest Securities)
3. David Clayton (BZW)

Source: *Institutional Investor - International Edition,* All-Europe Research Team (annual), February 1997, p. 85.

★ 1415 ★

TOP ANALYSTS COVERING HEALTH AND HOUSEHOLD PRODUCTS IN THE U.K., 1997

Ranked by: Results of research undertaken by editorial staff of Institutional Investor. **Remarks:** Also contains a lengthy synopsis of reasons for selection of the individuals ranked. Cites 1 runner-up. **Number listed:** 3

1. Mark Clark (UBS)
2. Mark Lynch (SBC Warburg)

3. Steve Plag (BZW)

Source: *Institutional Investor - International Edition,* All-Europe Research Team (annual), February 1997, p. 87.

★ 1416 ★

TOP ANALYSTS COVERING PRINTING, PAPER, AND PACKAGING IN THE U.K., 1997

Ranked by: Results of research undertaken by editorial staff of Institutional Investor. **Remarks:** Also contains a lengthy synopsis of reasons for selection of the individuals ranked. Cites 1 runner-up. **Number listed:** 3

1. Alastair Irvine (Merrill Lynch)
2. Sonia Falaschi (UBS)
3. Francesca Raleigh (Panmure Gordon & Co.)

Source: *Institutional Investor - International Edition,* All-Europe Research Team (annual), February 1997, p. 90.

★ 1417 ★

TOP ANALYSTS COVERING SUPPORT SERVICES AND DISTRIBUTORS IN THE U.K., 1997

Ranked by: Results of research undertaken by editorial staff of Institutional Investor. **Remarks:** Also contains a lengthy synopsis of reasons for selection of the individuals ranked. Cites 1 runner-up. **Number listed:** 3

1. Mark Shepperd (UBS)
2. Andrew Ripper (Merrill Lynch)
3. Mike Murphy (SBC Warburg)

Source: *Institutional Investor - International Edition,* All-Europe Research Team (annual), February 1997, p. 93.

★ 1418 ★

TOP ANALYSTS COVERING TELECOMMUNICATIONS SERVICES IN THE U.K., 1997

Ranked by: Results of research undertaken by editorial staff of Institutional Investor. **Remarks:** Also contains a lengthy synopsis of reasons for selection of the individuals ranked. Cites 4 runners-up. **Number listed:** 3

1. Robert Millington (BZW)
2. Mark Lambert (NatWest Securities)
3. Martin Mabbutt (HSBC James Capel)

Source: *Institutional Investor - International Edition,* All-Europe Research Team (annual), February 1997, p. 94.

★ 1419 ★

TOP FINANCIAL ANALYSTS COVERING BANKS IN THE UNITED KINGDOM, 1997

Ranked by: Results of research undertaken by editorial staff of Institutional Investor. **Remarks:** Also contains a lengthy synopsis of reasons for selection of the individuals ranked. Cites 3 runners-up. **Number listed:** 3

1. Richard Coleman (Merrill Lynch)
2. Christopher Ellerton (SBC Warburg)
3. Michael Lever (HSBC James Capel)

Source: *Institutional Investor - International Edition,* All-Europe Research Team (annual), February 1997, p. 79.

★ 1420 ★

TOP FINANCIAL ANALYSTS COVERING BEVERAGES IN THE UNITED KINGDOM, 1997

Ranked by: Results of research undertaken by editorial staff of Institutional Investor. **Remarks:** Also contains a lengthy synopsis of reasons for selection of the individuals ranked. Cites 1 runner-up. **Number listed:** 3

1. John Spicer (SBC Warburg)
2. Ian Shackleton (HSBC James Capel)
3. Graeme Eadie (NatWest Securities)

Source: *Institutional Investor - International Edition*, All-Europe Research Team (annual), February 1997, p. 80.

★ 1421 ★

TOP FINANCIAL ANALYSTS COVERING BUILDING IN THE UNITED KINGDOM, 1997

Ranked by: Results of research undertaken by editorial staff of Institutional Investor. **Remarks:** Also contains a lengthy synopsis of reasons for selection of the individuals ranked. Cites 2 runners-up. **Number listed:** 3

1. Robert Donald (NatWest Securities)
2. Jamie Stevenson (Dresdner Kleinwort Benson)
3. Mark Stockdale (SBC Warburg)

Source: *Institutional Investor - International Edition*, All-Europe Research Team (annual), February 1997, p. 80.

★ 1422 ★

TOP FINANCIAL ANALYSTS COVERING CHEMICALS IN THE UNITED KINGDOM, 1997

Ranked by: Results of research undertaken by editorial staff of Institutional Investor. **Remarks:** Also contains a lengthy synopsis of reasons for selection of the individuals ranked. Cites 2 runners-up. **Number listed:** 3

1. Andrew Benson (BZW)
2. Charles Lambert (Merrill Lynch)
3. David Ingles (HSBC James Capel)

Source: *Institutional Investor - International Edition*, All-Europe Research Team (annual), February 1997, p. 84.

★ 1423 ★

TOP FINANCIAL ANALYSTS COVERING ECONOMICS IN THE UNITED KINGDOM, 1997

Ranked by: Results of research undertaken by editorial staff of Institutional Investor. **Remarks:** Also contains a lengthy synopsis of reasons for selection of the individuals ranked. Cites 7 runners-up. **Number listed:** 3

1. David Walton (Goldman Sachs International)
2. Geoffrey Dicks (NatWest Securities)
3. Paul Turnbull (Merrill Lynch)

Source: *Institutional Investor - International Edition*, All-Europe Research Team (annual), February 1997, p. 111.

★ 1424 ★

TOP FINANCIAL ANALYSTS COVERING ELECTRICITY IN THE UNITED KINGDOM, 1997

Ranked by: Results of research undertaken by editorial staff of Institutional Investor. **Remarks:** Also contains a lengthy synopsis of reasons for selection of the individuals ranked. **Number listed:** 3

1. Nick Pink (SBC Warburg)
2. Ian Graham (NatWest Securities)
3. Simon Williams (Deutsche Morgan Grenfell)

Source: *Institutional Investor - International Edition*, All-Europe Research Team (annual), February 1997, p. 85.

★ 1425 ★

TOP FINANCIAL ANALYSTS COVERING ENGINEERING IN THE UNITED KINGDOM, 1997

Ranked by: Results of research undertaken by editorial staff of Institutional Investor. **Remarks:** Also contains a lengthy synopsis of reasons for selection of the individuals ranked. Cites 1 runner-up. **Number listed:** 3

1. Charles Burrows (HSBC James Capel)
2. Colin Fell (Dresdner Kleinwort Benson)
3. Paul Ruddle (SBC Warburg Securities)

Source: *Institutional Investor - International Edition*, All-Europe Research Team (annual), February 1997, p. 86.

★ 1426 ★

TOP FINANCIAL ANALYSTS COVERING EQUITY STRATEGY IN THE U.K., 1997

Ranked by: Results of research undertaken by editorial staff of Institutional Investor. **Remarks:** Also contains a lengthy synopsis of reasons for selection of the individuals ranked. Cites 1 runner-up. **Number listed:** 3

1. Philip Wolstencroft (Merrill Lynch)
2. George Hodgson (SBC Warburg)
3. Richard Kersley (BZW)

Source: *Institutional Investor - International Edition*, All-Europe Research Team (annual), February 1997, p. 113.

★ 1427 ★

TOP FINANCIAL ANALYSTS COVERING FOOD IN THE UNITED KINGDOM, 1997

Ranked by: Results of research undertaken by editorial staff of Institutional Investor. **Remarks:** Also contains a lengthy synopsis of reasons for selection of the individuals ranked. Cites 3 runners-up. **Number listed:** 3

1. Mark Duffy (SBC Warburg)
2. Alan Erskine (NatWest Securities)
3. Charles Mills (UBS)

Source: *Institutional Investor - International Edition*, All-Europe Research Team (annual), February 1997, p. 86.

★ 1428 ★
TOP FINANCIAL ANALYSTS COVERING FOOD RETAILERS IN THE U.K., 1997
Ranked by: Results of research undertaken by editorial staff of Institutional Investor. **Remarks:** Also contains a lengthy synopsis of reasons for selection of the individuals ranked. Cites 2 runners-up. **Number listed: 3**
1. Andrew Fowler (UBS)
2. William de Winton (ABN Amro Hoare Govett)
3. Frank Davidson (HSBC James Capel)

Source: *Institutional Investor - International Edition,* All-Europe Research Team (annual), February 1997, p. 92.

★ 1429 ★
TOP FINANCIAL ANALYSTS COVERING GENERAL RETAILERS IN THE U.K., 1997
Ranked by: Results of research undertaken by editorial staff of Institutional Investor. **Remarks:** Also contains a lengthy synopsis of reasons for selection of the individuals ranked. **Number listed: 3**
1. Nicholas Hawkins (Merrill Lynch)
2. Tony Shiret (BZW)
3. John Richards (NatWest Securities)

Source: *Institutional Investor - International Edition,* All-Europe Research Team (annual), February 1997, p. 93.

★ 1430 ★
TOP FINANCIAL ANALYSTS COVERING GILTS IN THE UNITED KINGDOM, 1997
Ranked by: Results of research undertaken by editorial staff of Institutional Investor. **Remarks:** Also contains a lengthy synopsis of reasons for selection of the individuals ranked. **Number listed: 3**
1. Martin Brookes (Goldman Sachs International)
2. Kevin Adams (BZW)
3. Roger Bootle (HSBC Group)

Source: *Institutional Investor - International Edition,* All-Europe Research Team (annual), February 1997, p. 114.

★ 1431 ★
TOP FINANCIAL ANALYSTS COVERING INSURANCE IN THE UNITED KINGDOM, 1997
Ranked by: Results of research undertaken by editorial staff of Institutional Investor. **Remarks:** Also contains a lengthy synopsis of reasons for selection of the individuals ranked. Cites 1 runner-up. **Number listed: 3**
1. David Nisbet (NatWest Securities)
2. Roman Cizdyn (Merrill Lynch)
3. Roger Hill (SBC Warburg)

Source: *Institutional Investor - International Edition,* All-Europe Research Team (annual), February 1997, p. 87.

★ 1432 ★
TOP FINANCIAL ANALYSTS COVERING INVESTMENT TRUSTS IN THE U.K., 1997
Ranked by: Results of research undertaken by editorial staff of Institutional Investor. **Remarks:** Also contains a lengthy synopsis of reasons for selection of the individuals ranked. Cites 1 runner-up. **Number listed: 3**
1. Philip Middleton (Merrill Lynch)
2. Garth Milne (SBC Warburg)
3. Robbie Robertson (Dresdner Kleinwort Benson)

Source: *Institutional Investor - International Edition,* All-Europe Research Team (annual), February 1997, p. 88.

★ 1433 ★
TOP FINANCIAL ANALYSTS COVERING LEISURE & HOTELS IN THE U.K., 1997
Ranked by: Results of research undertaken by editorial staff of Institutional Investor. **Remarks:** Also contains a lengthy synopsis of reasons for selection of the individuals ranked. Cites 1 runner-up. **Number listed: 3**
1. Mark Finnie (NatWest Securities)
2. Paul Slattery (Dresdner Kleinwort Benson)
3. Simon Johnson (BZW)

Source: *Institutional Investor - International Edition,* All-Europe Research Team (annual), February 1997, p. 88.

★ 1434 ★
TOP FINANCIAL ANALYSTS COVERING MEDIA IN THE UNITED KINGDOM, 1997
Ranked by: Results of research undertaken by editorial staff of Institutional Investor. **Remarks:** Also contains a lengthy synopsis of reasons for selection of the individuals ranked. Cites 2 runners-up. **Number listed: 3**
1. Richard Dale (Salomon Brothers International)
2. Vighnesh Padiachy (BZW)
3. Neil Junor (NatWest Securities)

Source: *Institutional Investor - International Edition,* All-Europe Research Team (annual), February 1997, p. 89.

★ 1435 ★
TOP FINANCIAL ANALYSTS COVERING OIL AND GAS IN THE UNITED KINGDOM, 1997
Ranked by: Results of research undertaken by editorial staff of Institutional Investor. **Remarks:** Also contains a lengthy synopsis of reasons for selection of the individuals ranked. Cites 1 runner-up. **Number listed: 3**
1. Fergus MacLeod (NatWest Securities)
2. Alan Macdonald (SBC Warburg Securities)
3. Jeremy Elden (UBS)

Source: *Institutional Investor - International Edition,* All-Europe Research Team (annual), February 1997, p. 89.

★ 1436 ★

TOP FINANCIAL ANALYSTS COVERING PHARMACEUTICS IN THE U.K., 1997

Ranked by: Results of research undertaken by editorial staff of Institutional Investor. **Remarks:** Also contains a lengthy synopsis of reasons for selection of the individuals ranked. Cites 1 runner-up. **Number listed:** 3

1. Steve Plag (BZW)
2. James Culverwell (Merrill Lynch)
3. Ian Smith (Lehman Brothers)

Source: *Institutional Investor - International Edition,* All-Europe Research Team (annual), February 1997, p. 90.

★ 1437 ★

TOP FINANCIAL ANALYSTS COVERING PROPERTY IN THE UNITED KINGDOM, 1997

Ranked by: Results of research undertaken by editorial staff of Institutional Investor. **Remarks:** Also contains a lengthy synopsis of reasons for selection of the individuals ranked. Cites 3 runners-up. **Number listed:** 3

1. Alec Pelmore (Dresdner Kleinwort Benson)
2. Roger Moore (SBC Warburg Securities)
3. Alan Carter (BZW)

Source: *Institutional Investor - International Edition,* All-Europe Research Team (annual), February 1997, p. 92.

★ 1438 ★

TOP FINANCIAL ANALYSTS COVERING TOBACCO IN THE UNITED KINGDOM, 1997

Ranked by: Results of research undertaken by editorial staff of Institutional Investor. **Remarks:** Also contains a lengthy synopsis of reasons for selection of the individuals ranked. **Number listed:** 3

1. Mark Duffy (SBC Warburg)
2. Paul Beaufrere (HSBC James Capel)
3. Nyren Scott-Malden (BZW)

Source: *Institutional Investor - International Edition,* All-Europe Research Team (annual), February 1997, p. 94.

★ 1439 ★

TOP FINANCIAL ANALYSTS COVERING TRANSPORT IN THE UNITED KINGDOM, 1997

Ranked by: Results of research undertaken by editorial staff of Institutional Investor. **Remarks:** Also contains a lengthy synopsis of reasons for selection of the individuals ranked. Cites 2 runners-up. **Number listed:** 3

1. Clive Anderson (Merrill Lynch)
2. Richard Hannah (UBS)
3. Mark McVicar (NatWest Securities)

Source: *Institutional Investor - International Edition,* All-Europe Research Team (annual), February 1997, p. 95.

★ 1440 ★

TOP FINANCIAL ANALYSTS COVERING WATER IN THE UNITED KINGDOM, 1997

Ranked by: Results of research undertaken by editorial staff of Institutional Investor. **Remarks:** Also contains a lengthy synopsis of reasons for selection of the individuals ranked. Cites 1 runner-up. **Number listed:** 3

1. William Dale (SBC Warburg)
2. Lakis Athanasiou (UBS)
3. Jamie Tunnicliffe (HSBC James Capel)

Source: *Institutional Investor - International Edition,* All-Europe Research Team (annual), February 1997, p. 95.

Financial Companies

See: **Financial Institutions**

Financial Institutions

★ 1441 ★

LARGEST DIVERSIFIED FINANCIAL COMPANIES, 1995

Ranked by: Revenue, in millions of U.S. dollars. **Remarks:** Notes profits and global rank. **Number listed:** 4

1. Federal National Mortgage (United States) with $22,246 million
2. Cie de Suez (France), $19,272
3. American Express (United States), $16,942
4. Federal Home Loan Mtg. (United States), $9,519

Source: *Fortune,* The Global 500: World's Biggest Corporations (annual), August 5, 1996, p. F-18.

★ 1442 ★

LARGEST FINANCIAL-SECTOR COMPANIES BY MARKET CAPITALIZATION, 1997

Ranked by: Market capitalization, in billions of U.S. dollars. **Number listed:** 8

1. Bank of Tokyo-Mitsubishi with $87.0 billion
2. HSBC, $79.7
3. AIG, $73.1
4. Lloyds TSB, $66.3
5. Citicorp, $61.5
6. Allianz, $55.0
7. Travelers + Salomon, $53.9
8. BankAmerica, $51.6

Source: *The Economist,* September 27, 1997, p. 80.

★ 1443 ★
TOP FINANCIAL INFORMATION VENDORS, 1995
Ranked by: Market share, in percent. **Remarks:** Includes revenues and number of terminals. **Number listed:** 3
1. Reuters with 33%
2. Dow Jones Telerate, 14%
3. Bloomberg, 7%

Source: *Financial Times*, March 14, 1997, p. 15.

Financial Institutions – Asia

★ 1444 ★
TOP INVESTMENT COMPANIES IN ASIA
Ranked by: Assets, in thousands of U.S. dollars. **Remarks:** Companies include property companies, finance companies, and unit trusts. **Number listed:** 200
1. Mitsui Marine & Fire Insurance Co. Ltd. with $25,061,106 thousand
2. Daiichi Housing Loan Co. Ltd., $19,260,271
3. Tokyo Leasing Co. Ltd., $12,994,213
4. Guoco Group Ltd., $12,670,327
5. Central Leasing Co. Ltd., $7,958,233
6. Hong Leong Investment Holdings Pte. Ltd., $5,359,134
7. Affin Holdings Bhd., $4,989,787
8. Industrial Finance Corporation of Thailand, $4,699,444
9. Hong Leong Finance Ltd., $3,911,629
10. Arab-Malaysian Finance Bhd., $3,677,794

Source: *Asia's 7500 Largest Companies* (annual), Dun & Bradstreet, 1997, p. 310+.

Financial Institutions – Europe

★ 1445 ★
TOP FINANCIAL ADVISORS ON EUROPEAN CROSS BORDER TRANSACTIONS, 1996
Ranked by: Value of transactions, in millions of British pounds (£). **Remarks:** Includes number of deals conducted during this period. **Number listed:** 10
1. Lazard Houses with £12.0 million
2. Morgan Stanley, £11.0
3. Goldman Sachs, £10.1
4. Credit Suisse First Boston, £9.9
5. JP Morgan, £9.3
6. Merrill Lynch, £8.2
7. SBC Warburg, £5.8
8. Lehman Brothers, £4.2
9. Rothschild Group, £3.9
10. Societe Generale, £3.7

Source: *The Guardian*, January 23, 1997, p. 9.

Financial Services

★ 1446 ★
LARGEST FINANCIAL SERVICE FIRMS IN EUROPE
Ranked by: Market capitalization in billions of dollars. **Number listed:** 10
1. HSBC with $94 billion
2. Lloyds TSB, $64
3. Allianz, $56
4. ING, $40
5. Credit Suisse-Winterthur, $36
6. Barclays, $34
7. ABN Amro, $33
8. Deutsche Bank, $32
9. Halifax, $29
10. Muenchener Rueck, $28

Source: *The Wall Street Journal*, August 13, 1997, p. A10.

★ 1447 ★
TOP COUNTRIES FOR EXPORTED FINANCIAL SERVICES, 1995
Ranked by: Value of exported services, in billions of U.S. dollars. **Remarks:** Also notes figures for 1994. **Number listed:** 5
1. Germany with $11.1 billion
2. United Kingdom, $9.1
3. France, $8.1
4. United States, $7.5
5. Belgium-Luxembourg, $5.6

Source: *The Wall Street Journal*, September 19, 1997, p. A8.

★ 1448 ★
TOP COUNTRIES FOR IMPORTED FINANCIAL SERVICES, 1995
Ranked by: Value of imported services, in billions of U.S. dollars. **Number listed:** 5
1. Germany with $9.4 billion
2. France, $8.2
3. United States, $6.2
4. Belgium-Luxembourg, $4.0
5. United Kingdom, $0.7

Source: *The Wall Street Journal*, September 19, 1997, p. A8.

Financing

★ **1449** ★

TOP COUNTRIES FOR PROJECT FINANCING, 1996
Ranked by: Signed project finance deals, in billions of U.S. dollars. **Remarks:** Also notes number of projects.
Number listed: 20
1. United States with $46.7 billion
2. Hong Kong, $19.4
3. Indonesia, $14.1
4. United Kingdom, $13.2
5. Australia, $12.7
6. Thailand, $9.4
7. China, $8.4
8. India, $6.9
9. Germany, $6.2
10. Brazil, $5.8
Source: *Financial Times*, May 23, 1997, p. 5.

Finland – see under individual headings

Fire Detection Systems

★ **1450** ★

TOP SWISS FIRE ALARM MARKETS
Ranked by: Market share, in percent. **Number listed:** 4
1. Cerebrus with 58.0%
2. Securiton, 23.0%
3. Zettler, 15.0%
4. Other, 4.0%
Source: *National Trade Data Bank*, March 2, 1996, p. ISA9405.

Firearms Industry

★ **1451** ★

TOP RIFLE BRANDS IN FRANCE
Ranked by: Market share, in percent. **Remarks:** Includes data on cost of guns and hunting gear in France. Notes spending of hunters on such items as hunting licenses, outdoor gear, weaponry, and heavy apparel. **Number listed:** 11
1. Beretta with 15.0%
2. Verney-Carron, 13.0%
3. Merkel, 10.0%
4. Browning, 8.0%
5. Remington, 7.0%
6. Winchester, 6.0%
7. Baikal, 4.0%

8. Fabarm, 4.0%
9. Franchi, 3.0%
10. Other brands, 20.0%
Source: *National Trade Data Bank*, December 12, 1996, p. ISA961001.

Fisheries

★ **1452** ★

TOP FISH FARMING NATIONS
Ranked by: Fish harvested on fish farms, in millions of tons. **Number listed:** 11
1. China with 7.55 million tons
2. India, 1.52
3. Japan, 0.90
4. Indonesia, 0.61
5. United States, 0.45
6. Philippines, 0.43
7. South Korea, 0.42
8. Thailand, 0.40
9. France, 0.28
10. Taiwan, 0.28
Source: *Chicago Tribune*, September 2, 1996, p. 11.

Fishing

★ **1453** ★

CANADIAN SPORT FISHERS MOST FREQUENT CATCHES
Ranked by: Kind of fish, in percent distribution. **Number listed:** 5
1. Trout with 29%
2. Walleye, 15%
3. Pike, 11%
4. Bass, 10%
5. Smelt, 8%
6. Other, 27%
Source: *National Trade Data Bank*, July 2, 1997, p. IMI970630.

★ **1454** ★

LARGEST FISH PRODUCING NATIONS, 1993
Ranked by: Catch, in millions of tons. **Number listed:** 20
1. China with 19.3 million tons
2. Japan, 9.3
3. Peru, 9.2
4. Chile, 6.6
5. United States, 6.2
6. Russia, 4.9
7. India, 4.6
8. Indonesia, 4.0
9. Thailand, 3.7

10.　South Korea, 2.9
Source: *Chicago Tribune*, September 2, 1996, p. 2.

Fixtures

★ 1455 ★
TOP WATER CLOSET PRODUCERS IN KOREA, 1994
Ranked by: Production schedule, in thousands of units.
Remarks: Includes domestic and export schedules as well as production capacity for each company. **Number listed:** 8
1.　Kelim Toto Co. with 620 thousand units
2.　Daelim Ceramic Co., 450
3.　Dong Suh Ind. Co., 390
4.　Selim Co. Ltd., 200
5.　Chungja Ceramic Co., 180
6.　Duksan Ceramic Co., 120
7.　Selim Ceramic Co., 50
8.　Samjin Ceramic Co. Ltd., 12
Source: *National Trade Data Bank*, March 2, 1996, p. ISA9403.

Flavoring Essences Industry

★ 1456 ★
TOP FLAVOR AND FRAGRANCE FIRMS
Ranked by: Estimated annual sales, in millions of U.S. dollars. **Number listed:** 10
1.　IFF with $1,400 million
2.　Givaudan/Tastemaker, $1,320
3.　Takasago, $1,200
4.　Quest, $950
5.　Firmenich, $900
6.　H&R Florasynth, $730
7.　Bush Boake Allen, $450
8.　Dragoco, $300
9.　Universal Foods, $260
10.　Hasegawa, $240
Source: *Chemical Market Reporter*, February 10, 1997, p. 15.

Floor Coverings

★ 1457 ★
HARDWOOD FLOORING MARKET IN HONG KONG
Ranked by: Market share, in percent. **Remarks:** Ivory flooring is also known as Brazilian maple or Marfin.
Number listed: 4
1.　Maple with 60%
2.　Beech, 20%
3.　Red oak, 10%
4.　Ivory, 5%
Source: *National Trade Data Bank*, July 17, 1997, p. ISA970701.

★ 1458 ★
PVC FLOORING IN TURKEY
Ranked by: Market share, in percent. **Number listed:** 2
1.　Kaleflex with 70.0%
2.　Other, 30.0%
Source: *National Trade Data Bank*, May 27, 1996, p. ISA9311.

Food Chain Stores
See: **Grocery Trade**

Food Industry and Trade

★ 1459 ★
ETHNIC FOOD PURCHASED IN AUSTRALIAN SUPERMARKETS
Ranked by: Value, in millions of Australian dollars (A$).
Number listed: 4
1.　Italian with A$337 million
2.　Chinese, A$123
3.　Mexican, A$53
4.　Other, A$30
Source: *Sydney Morning Herald*, September 18, 1997, p. 14.

★ 1460 ★
LARGEST FOOD COMPANIES, 1995
Ranked by: Revenue, in millions of U.S. dollars.
Remarks: Notes profits and global rank. **Number listed:** 11
1.　Unilever (United Kingdom/Netherlands) with $49,738 million
2.　Nestle (Switzerland), $47,780
3.　Conagra (United States), $24,109
4.　Sara Lee (Italy), $17,719
5.　Ferruzzi Finanziaria (Italy), $16,085

6. RJR Nabisco Holdings (United States), $16,008
7. Danone Group (France), $15,925
8. Archer Daniels Midland (United States), $12,672
9. IBP (United States), $12,668

Source: *Fortune,* The Global 500: World's Biggest Corporations (annual), August 5, 1996, p. F-19.

★ 1461 ★
LARGEST FOOD PROCESSING COMPANIES IN BRAZIL, 1994
Ranked by: Sales, in millions of U.S. dollars. **Remarks:** Also notes 1993 sales figures, number of employees, and number of plants. **Number listed:** 10
1. Companhia Cervejaria Brahma with $3,313 million
2. Sadia Concordia S/A, $2,800
3. Compania Antarctica Paulista, $2,600
4. Nestle Industrial e Comercial, $2,200
5. Ceval Alimentos, $2,144
6. Industrias Gessy Lever, $1,400
7. Santista Alimentos S/A, $1,300
8. Perdigao Agroindustrial, $828
9. Refina es de Milho, $785
10. Cargill Agricola, $740

Source: *National Trade Data Bank,* March 22, 1996, p. ISA960301.

★ 1462 ★
LEADING FOOD AND DRINK COMPANIES WORLDWIDE
Ranked by: Food and drink sales, in billions of U.S. dollars. **Remarks:** Also notes total sales. **Number listed:** 100
1. Nestle SA with $38.80 billion
2. Philip Morris Companies Inc., $33.38
3. Unilever Plc/NV, $26.73
4. ConAgra Inc., $24.82
5. PepsiCo Inc., $19.09
6. Cargill Inc., $18.67
7. Coca-Cola Company, $18.02
8. Danone, $14.19
9. Archer Daniels Midland Co., $13.31
10. Mars Inc., $13.00

Source: *Food Engineering International,* June 1997, p. 39.

★ 1463 ★
LEADING FOOD COMPANIES IN SOUTH KOREA, 1996
Ranked by: Sales for the first six months of 1996, in hundred million won (W). **Remarks:** Also notes net profits. **Number listed:** 36
1. Cheil Foods & Chemicals with W8,640.7 hundred million
2. Lotte Confectionery, W3,727.4
3. Lotte Chilsung Beverage, W3,215.5

4. Miwon, W3,017.7
5. Dongwon Industries, W2,657.6
6. Ottogi Foods, W2,195.8
7. Taihan Sugar Industries, W2,155.5
8. Shin Dong Bang, W2,052.3
9. Chosun Brewery, W1,941.3
10. Tong Yang Confectionery, W1,891.7

Source: *Business Korea,* October 1996, p. 31.

★ 1464 ★
MOST RESPECTED EUROPEAN FOOD PROCESSING FIRMS
Ranked by: Survey based on FT 500 list, as well as polls of investment analysts and chief executives of European companies. See source for details. **Number listed:** 3
1. Nestle
2. Unilever
3. Tate & Lyle

Source: *Financial Times,* Europe's Most Respected Companies (annual), September 24, 1997, p. 2.

★ 1465 ★
TIME SPENT EATING IN SELECTED COUNTRIES
Ranked by: Average time spent eating, in minutes per day. **Remarks:** Notes breakdown for breakfast, lunch, and dinner. **Number listed:** 8
1. Germany with 92 minutes
2. Italy, 92
3. France, 86
4. United Kingdom, 78
5. United States, 71
6. Japan, 70
7. Spain, 69
8. Brazil, 57

Source: *Food Processing,* May 1997, p. 19.

★ 1466 ★
TOP DOOR-TO-DOOR DIETARY SUPPLEMENT AND HEALTH FOODS RETAILERS IN JAPAN
Ranked by: Annual sales, in billions of yen (¥). **Remarks:** Table shows only those companies listed on the Tokyo Stock Exchange. **Number listed:** 15
1. Miki Shoji with ¥121.2 billion
2. Japan Amway, ¥65.5
3. Japan Forever Living Products, ¥48.3
4. Japan Shaklee, ¥29.7
5. Nikkenso Honsha, ¥20.0
6. Japan Herususamitto K.K., ¥19.4
7. Sun Chlorella, ¥18.0
8. Koyo-sha K.K., ¥12.2
9. Advance Co., Ltd., ¥6.4
10. Fancl, ¥6.4

Source: *National Trade Data Bank,* March 5, 1997, p. IMI970224.

★ 1467 ★
TOP NON-STORE HEALTH FOOD DISTRIBUTORS IN JAPAN, 1996
Ranked by: Annual sales for November 30, 1996, in billions of yen (¥). **Number listed:** 15
1. Miki Shoji with ¥121.2 billion
2. Japan Amway, ¥65.5
3. Japan Forever Living Products, ¥48.3
4. Japan Shaklee, ¥29.7
5. Nikkenso Honsha, ¥20.0
6. Sun Chlorella, ¥18.0
7. Advance Co., Ltd., ¥6.4
8. Fancl, ¥6.4
9. Happy Family, ¥6.4
10. Global, ¥4.9

Source: *National Trade Data Bank*, February 20, 1997, p. IMI970215.

★ 1468 ★
TOP PREPARED FOOD BRANDS BY BRAND VALUE
Ranked by: Brand value, in millions of U.S. dollars. **Remarks:** Value was calculated using capital, ratio of capital to company sales, earnings, and corporate tax rate of the country where the parent company is located. See source for details. **Number listed:** 32
1. Kellogg's (Kellogg) with $11,409 million
2. Frito-Lay (Pepsico), $7,786
3. Campbell's (Campbell Soup), $6,464
4. Kraft (Philip Morris), $5,742
5. Nabisco (RJR Nabisco), $4,858
6. General Mills (General Mills), $3,433
7. Danone (Danone), $2,754
8. Purina (Ralston Purina), $2,645
9. Knorr (CPC International), $2,326
10. Quaker Oats (Quaker Oats), $2,240

Source: *Financial World*, World's Most Valuable Brands (annual), July 8, 1996, p. 60.

★ 1469 ★
TOP SHIPPED FOOD CATEGORIES IN JAPAN, 1994
Ranked by: Shipments, in billions of yen (¥). **Number listed:** 15
1. Stock farm products with ¥4,825.6 billion
2. Alcohol, ¥4,485.6
3. Breads and sweets, ¥4,265.3
4. Marine food products, ¥4,129.5
5. Soft drinks, ¥2,099.6
6. Spices, ¥1,772.2
7. Flour, ¥1,712.2
8. Noodles, ¥1,002.7
9. Animal feed, ¥984.6
10. Canned vegetables and fruit, ¥943.6

Source: *Journal of Japanese Trade & Industry*, 1997, p. 47.

Food Industry and Trade – Asia

★ 1470 ★
LEADING FOOD, BEVERAGE, AND TOBACCO COMPANIES IN ASIA
Ranked by: Sales, in thousands of U.S. dollars. **Remarks:** Also notes profits as a percent of sales. **Number listed:** 100
1. Kirin Brewery Co. Ltd. with $15,857,233 thousand
2. Snow Brand Milk Products Co. Ltd., $11,230,582
3. Asahi Breweries Ltd., $10,562,135
4. Maruha Corp., $9,223,466
5. Nippon Meat Packers Inc., $7,850,980
6. Ajinomoto Co. Inc., $7,289,747
7. Sapporo Breweries Ltd., $6,433,242
8. Yamazaki Baking Co. Ltd., $6,273,262
9. Hitachi Sales Co., $5,517,368
10. Nichirei Corp., $5,451,000

Source: *Asia's 7500 Largest Companies* (annual), Dun & Bradstreet, 1997, p. 73+.

Food Industry and Trade – Distributors – Canada

★ 1471 ★
LARGEST FOOD DISTRIBUTORS IN CANADA
Ranked by: Revenue, in thousands of Canadian dollars. **Remarks:** Includes profits and return on capital. **Number listed:** 7
1. George Weston Ltd. with C$12,966,000 thousand
2. Loblaw Cos., C$9,901,500
3. Oshawa Group, C$6,180,300
4. Provlgo, C$5,704,300
5. Canada Safeway, C$4,795,900
6. Metro-Richelieu Inc., C$3,160,200
7. Westfair Foods, C$3,035,713

Source: *Globe and Mail's Report on Business Magazine*, July 1996, p. 164.

Food Industry and Trade – Europe

★ 1472 ★
TOP EUROPEAN FOOD AND BEVERAGE PROCESSORS
Ranked by: Food and beverage sales, in millions of U.S. dollars. **Remarks:** Notes total sales and net profits. **Number listed:** 50
1. Nestle SA with $46,400 million
2. Unilever Plc/NV, $25,300

3. Danone, $12,560
4. Kraft Jacobs Sucard, $11,800
5. Grand Metropolitan, $10,659
6. Eridania Beghin-Say, $10,090
7. Dalgety Plc, $7,491
8. Cadbury Schweppes, $7,292
9. Guinness Plc, $7,147
10. Allied Domecq Plc, $6,790

Source: *Prepared Foods*, July 1996, p. 14.

★ 1473 ★
TOP FOOD AND KINDRED PRODUCTS COMPANIES IN EUROPE
Ranked by: Sales, in millions of European Currency Units (ECUs). **Remarks:** Also notes number of employees. **Number listed:** 422
1. Unilever Nederland BV with 37,524 million ECUs
2. Unilever NV, 37,524
3. Nestle SA, 36,418
4. Unilever Plc, 31,618
5. Danone (Groupe), 12,354
6. Allied Domecq Plc, 9,512
7. Grand Metropolitan Plc, 8,553
8. Kraft Jacobs Suchard SA, 7,463
9. Tchibo Holdings AG, 5,870
10. Saint-Louis, 5,313

Source: *Duns Europa,* (annual), vol. 4, Dun & Bradstreet, 1997, p. 210.

Food Industry and Trade – Latin America

★ 1474 ★
LEADING PREPARED FOOD AND BEVERAGE PROCESSORS IN LATIN AMERICA, 1994
Ranked by: Food and beverage sales, in millions of U.S. dollars. **Remarks:** Also notes data for 1993. **Number listed:** 50
1. Brahma with $3,313 million
2. Sadia, $2,800
3. Antarctica Paulista, $2,600
4. Ceval Alimentos, $2,144
5. FEMSA, $1,854
6. Grupo Modelo, $1,841
7. Bimbo, $1,819
8. Coca-Cola Argentina, $1,627
9. PANAMCO, $1,339
10. Santista Alimentos S.A., $1,300

Source: *Prepared Foods*, July 1996, p. 32.

Food Industry and Trade – United Kingdom

★ 1475 ★
BRITAIN'S TOP GROCERY ITEMS
Ranked by: Sales, in millions of British pounds (£).
Number listed: 10
1. Coca-Cola with £321.7 million
2. Walkers Crisps, £283.9
3. Nescafe, £245.0
4. Ariel, £216.8
5. Andrex toilet paper, £180.2
6. Persil, £176.7
7. Pampers Nappies, £163.1
8. Whiskas, £156.8
9. Robinsons Squash, £146.1
10. Silver Spoon Sugar, £137.7

Source: *The Observer*, December 15, 1996, p. 4.

★ 1476 ★
TOP INTERNATIONAL CUISINE BRANDS IN THE UNITED KINGDOM, 1995
Ranked by: Estimated sales, in millions of British pounds (£). **Remarks:** Note ad agencies and spending.
Number listed: 10
1. Dolmio pasta sauces with £37 million
2. Sharwood's Indian foods, £30
3. Ragu pasta sauces, £25
4. Sharwood's Chinese foods, £20
5. Buitoni dry pasta, £15
6. Dornay Food, £15
7. Patak's Indian Foods, £15
8. Old El Paso, £10
9. Napolina dry pasta, £5
10. Sacla, £5

Source: *Marketing*, July 4, 1996, p. 25.

Food Machinery

★ 1477 ★
BOTTLE-LABELING MACHINERY WORLDWIDE
Ranked by: Market share, in percent. **Number listed:** 2
1. Krones with 70.0%
2. Other, 30.0%

Source: *The Economist*, July 13, 1996, p. 59.

Food Processors – Europe

★ 1478 ★
TOP FOOD PROCESSORS IN EUROPE
Ranked by: Turnover, in billions of U.S. dollars.
Remarks: Includes figures on net income and market capitalization. **Number listed:** 20
1. Unilever with $47.59 billion
2. Nestle, $45.13
3. Danone, $15.28
4. Eridania Beghin Say, $9.77
5. Dalgety, $7.41
6. Association of British Foods, $7.39
7. Cadbury Schweppes, $7.21
8. Tate & Lyle, $6.81
9. Saint Louis, $6.78
10. Hillsdown Holdings, $5.21
Source: *Financial Times*, June 17, 1996, p. 24.

Food Service

★ 1479 ★
LARGEST FOOD SERVICES COMPANIES, 1995
Ranked by: Revenue, in millions of U.S. dollars.
Remarks: Notes profits and global rank. **Number listed:** 2
1. Pepsico (United States) with $30,421 million
2. McDonald's (United States), $9,795
Source: *Fortune,* The Global 500: World's Biggest Corporations (annual), August 5, 1996, p. F-20.

Food Stores
See: **Convenience Stores**

Foreign Exchange Brokers

★ 1480 ★
LARGEST FOREIGN EXCHANGE FIRMS IN MEXICO, 1995
Ranked by: Assets as of December 31, 1995, in millions of U.S. dollars. **Number listed:** 10
1. Euromex with $56.6 million
2. Inverlat, $37.6
3. Plus, $37.4
4. Consultoria International, $35.4
5. Monex, $18.9
6. Indicador y Operador Monetario, $16.8
7. Majapara, $13.2
8. C.B.I., $12.2

9. Aba Divisas, $11.9
10. Invermexico, $11.1
Source: *National Trade Data Bank*, September 9, 1996, p. ISA960801.

★ 1481 ★
TOP FOREIGN EXCHANGE TRADERS, 1996
Ranked by: Revenue, in millions of U.S. dollars.
Remarks: Notes 1995 revenues. **Number listed:** 15
1. Citibank with $932.0 million
2. HSBC Midland, $597.0
3. SBC Warburg, $594.0
4. Chase Manhattan, $444.0
5. UBS, $374.0
6. NatWest, $368.9
7. J.P. Morgan, $320.0
8. Bank of America, $316.0
9. Stanchart, $261.9
10. State Street, $126.0
Source: *Financial Times*, April 18, 1997, p. 2.

Foreign Investments
See: **Investments, Foreign**

Forest Products Industry

★ 1482 ★
LARGEST FOREST AND PAPER PRODUCTS COMPANIES, 1995
Ranked by: Revenue, in millions of U.S. dollars.
Remarks: Notes profits and global rank. **Number listed:** 5
1. International Paper (United States) with $19,797 million
2. Georgia-Pacific (United States), $14,292
3. Kimberly-Clark (United States), $13,789
4. Weyerhaeuser (United States), $11,788
5. Nippon Paper Industries (Japan), $11,043
Source: *Fortune,* The Global 500: World's Biggest Corporations (annual), August 5, 1996, p. F-20.

★ 1483 ★
LARGEST FOREST INDUSTRY COMPANIES IN EUROPE, 1995
Ranked by: Turnover, in millions of U.S. dollars.
Number listed: 11
1. UPM-Kymmene (Finland) with $10,036 million
2. SCA + PWA (Sweden), $8,648
3. Stora (Sweden), $6,791
4. Enso (Finland), $6,181
5. Jefferson Smurfit (Ireland), $4,892
6. KNP BT (Netherlands), $4,738

7. Metsa-Serla + Myllykoski Paper + MD Papier (Finalnd), $4,062
8. Arjo Wiggins Appleton (United Kingdom), $3,111
9. AssiDoman (Sweden), $2,948
10. MoDo (Sweden), $2,550

Source: *Unitas*, 1997, p. 6.

★ **1484** ★

TOP FOREST INDUSTRY COMPANIES OUTSIDE OF NORTH AMERICA, 1995

Ranked by: Pulp, paper and converting sales, in millions of U.S. dollars. **Remarks:** Also notes outputs of paper/board, market pulp, and converted products. **Number listed:** 25

1. UPM-Kymmene (Finland) with $10,282.60 million
2. KNP BT (Netherlands), $9,363.50
3. Nippon Paper Industries (Japan), $9,349.10
4. New Oji Paper (Japan), $7,054.10
5. Svenska Cellulosa (SCA) (Sweden), $6,693.30
6. Stora (Sweden), $6,561.80
7. Enso-Gutzeit (Finland), $5,630.60
8. Arjo Wiggins Appleton (U.K.), $5,352.50
9. Jefferson Smurfit Group (Ireland), $4,864.20
10. Honshu Paper (Japan), $4,802.20

Source: *North American Pulp & Paper Fact Book*, 1997, p. 137.

Forest Products Industry – Europe

★ **1485** ★

LARGEST FORESTRY GROUPS IN EUROPE

Ranked by: Turnover, in billions of U.S. dollars. **Remarks:** Includes net income and market capitalization. **Number listed:** 10

1. UPM-Kymenne with $11.48 billion
2. SCA, $9.60
3. KNP BT, $8.75
4. Stora, $8.39
5. Arjo Wiggins Appleton, $5.38
6. Smurfit, Jefferson, $4.72
7. Enso Gutzeit, $4.41
8. Rexam, $3.61
9. MoDo, $3.26
10. Assidoman, $3.21

Source: *Financial Times*, June 17, 1996, p. 25.

Forestry

★ **1486** ★

LEADING PLANTED FOREST OWNERS AND MANAGERS IN NEW ZEALAND, 1997

Ranked by: Percent distribution as of July 1997. **Number listed:** 13

1. Carter Holt Harvey Forests with 21%
2. Fletcher Challenge Forests, 19%
3. Rayonier New Zealand, 6%
4. Juken Nissho, 4%
5. Weyerhaeuser, 4%
6. Crown Lease Forests, 3%
7. Crown Forestry Management, 2%
8. Ernslaw One, 2%
9. Glenealy, 2%
10. Hawkes Bay Forests, 2%

Source: *National Trade Data Bank*, July 14, 1997, p. ISA970801.

Forwarding Companies

★ **1487** ★

LARGEST FREIGHT FORWARDERS WORLDWIDE, 1996

Ranked by: Gross revenues, in millions of U.S. dollars for the first six months of 1996. **Number listed:** 7

1. Danzas with $2,390 million
2. Kuhne & Nagel, $1,950
3. Fritz Companies, $1,043
4. AEI, $615
5. Ocean/MSAS Cargo, $614
6. Expeditors International, $304
7. Harper/Circle Group, $275

Source: *American Shipper*, November 1996, p. 28.

Foundations, Charitable and Educational

★ **1488** ★

LARGEST PRIVATE CHARITABLE FOUNDATIONS IN CANADA

Ranked by: Assets, in millions of Canadian dollars. **Number listed:** 10

1. J.W. McConnell Family Foundation with C$376 million
2. Chastell Foundation, C$133
3. Donner Canadian Foundation, C$108
4. Apotex Foundation, C$96
5. EJLB Foundation, C$91
6. Kahanoff Foundation, C$87
7. R. Howard Webster Foundation, C$87

8. Fondation Marcelle et Jean Coutu, C$65
9. Samuel and Saidye Bronfman Family Foundation, C$62
10. Fondation J.A. De Seve, C$56

Source: *Globe and Mail*, May 27, 1997, p. B2.

France – see under individual headings

Franchises (Retail Trade)

★ 1489 ★

LARGEST APPAREL FRANCHISES IN THE NETHERLANDS

Ranked by: Number of owned and associated outlets.
Number listed: 7

1. Mexx with 656 outlets
2. Steps (Dormael Vrijtijdsmode), 143
3. Didi Fahion, 85
4. Benetton (Colori Uniti Holding), 69
5. Vet, 62
6. Levi's shop in shop (Levi Straus Netherlands), 57
7. Original Levi's Store (Levi Strauss Netherlands), 55

Source: *National Trade Data Bank*, February 6, 1997, p. ISA961101.

★ 1490 ★

TOP EUROPEAN COUNTRIES FOR FRANCHISORS, 1995

Ranked by: Number of franchisors. **Remarks:** Also notes number of franchisees. **Number listed:** 5

1. France with 500
2. Germany, 420
3. United Kingdom, 396
4. Italy, 361
5. Netherlands, 330

Source: *National Trade Data Bank*, February 6, 1997, p. ISA961101.

Franchises (Retail Trade) – France

★ 1491 ★

TOP FRANCHISES IN FRANCE

Ranked by: Sales, in millions of U.S. dollars. **Remarks:** Includes number of outlets for each franchise and notes the type of operation. **Number listed:** 20

1. Champion with $5,466.0 million
2. Continent, $4,000.0
3. Mammouth, $3,000.0

4. Shopi, $2,000.0
5. But, $1,360.0
6. McDonalds, $1,333.2
7. Eurocar Interrent, $1,120.0
8. Huit Huit, $680.0
9. Connexion, $600.0
10. Comod, $500.0

Source: *National Trade Data Bank*, September 6, 1996, p. IMI960830.

Frankfurt Stock Exchange

★ 1492 ★

LARGEST COMPANIES ON THE FRANKFURT STOCK EXCHANGE, 1995

Ranked by: Market value, in billions of deustchmarks.
Number listed: 20

1. Allianz Holding AG with 58.57 billion
2. Siemens AG, 44.10
3. Daimler Benz AG, 37.10
4. Deutsche Bank AG, 32.29
5. Veba AG, 29.84
6. Bayer AB, 26.39
7. RWE AG, 24.88
8. Muench, Rueckv.-Ges. AG, 23.16
9. Hoechst AG, 22.93
10. SAP AG, 22.03

Source: *GT Guide to World Equity Markets* (annual), Euromoney Publications, 1996, p. 144.

★ 1493 ★

MOST ACTIVELY TRADED DOMESTIC SHARES ON THE FRANKFURT STOCK EXCHANGE, 1995

Ranked by: Trading value, in billions of deustchmarks (DM). **Remarks:** Also notes number of shares. **Number listed:** 20

1. Daimler Benz AG with DM159.17 billion
2. Siemens AG, DM155.32
3. Deutsche Bank AG, DM142.81
4. Volkswagen AG Ord, DM81.06
5. Bayer AG, DM76.72
6. Allianz AG Holding, DM71.97
7. Veba AG, DM71.42
8. Mannesmann AG, DM60.50
9. BASF AG, DM58.91
10. Hoechst AG, DM45.98

Source: *GT Guide to World Equity Markets* (annual), Euromoney Publications, 1996, p. 145.

Freezers, Home
See: **Home Freezers**

French Polynesia – see under individual headings

Frozen Food Industry

★ 1494 ★
AUSTRALIA'S TOP FROZEN FOOD MAKERS, 1995
Ranked by: Market share, in percent. **Number listed:** 7
1. Nestle with 21.0%
2. Edgells, 14.0%
3. Unilever, 13.0%
4. McCain, 7.0%
5. Goodman Fielder, 6.0%
6. Aust. Co-Op, 4.0%
7. Other, 35.0%
Source: *Quick Frozen Foods International*, April 1996, p. 132.

★ 1495 ★
FROZEN FOOD MARKET IN SWITZERLAND
Ranked by: Sector share, in percent. **Number listed:** 8
1. Poultry with 25
2. Vegetables, 20
3. Potato products, 20
4. Fish, seafood, and crustaceans, 11
5. Dough/bakery products, 10
6. Meat & game, 6
7. Pasta goods, 5
8. Fruit, berries, and juices, 3
Source: *National Trade Data Bank*, October 28, 1996, p. ISA961001.

★ 1496 ★
INDIA'S FROZEN DESSERT MARKET
Ranked by: Market share, in percent. **Remarks:** Leading brands include Kwality-Wall's, Dollops, Milkfood. **Number listed:** 2
1. Hindustan Lever Ltd. with 70.0%
2. Other, 30.0%
Source: *Business Today*, May 7, 1996, p. 87.

★ 1497 ★
THAILAND'S FROZEN FOOD MAKERS
Ranked by: Market share, in percent. **Number listed:** 6
1. Surapon with 7.0%
2. Thailand Fishery, 6.0%
3. Sea Horse, 6.0%
4. Pakpanang, 5.0%
5. Thai Agri Foods, 4.0%
6. Other, 72.0%
Source: *National Trade Data Bank*, May 27, 1996, p. ISA9408.

Fruit Juices

★ 1498 ★
LEADING JUICE AND NECTAR BRANDS IN SPAIN, 1995
Ranked by: Market share based on production, in percent. **Number listed:** 11
1. Juver with 12.0%
2. Don Simon, 11.1%
3. Zumosol, 10.1%
4. Kasfruit, 10.0%
5. Cofrutos, 8.5%
6. Mocitos, 5.0%
7. Campo Bello, 4.5%
8. La Verja, 3.4%
9. Zumley, 3.4%
10. Vida, 3.0%
Source: *Marketing in Europe*, January 1997, p. 91.

Fuel

★ 1499 ★
PANAMA'S FUEL LEADERS
Ranked by: Market share, in percent. **Number listed:** 5
1. Delta with 26.0%
2. Shell, 25.0%
3. Esso, 25.0%
4. Texaco, 22.0%
5. Accel, 2.0%
Source: *National Trade Data Bank*, March 2, 1996, p. ISA9308.

Furniture Industry

★ 1500 ★
LEADING FURNITURE EXPORTERS IN POLAND, 1995
Ranked by: Value, in millions of U.S. dollars. **Number listed:** 11
1. MM, Olsztyn with $160 million
2. Forte SA, Ostrow Mazowiecki, $95
3. BFM SA, Bydgoszcz, $63
4. SFM SA, Swarzedz, $40
5. Fameg SA, Jasienica, $36
6. Opole Furniture Plant, $35
7. WFM SA, Oborniki, $34
8. PP-H Black, Red, White, $31
9. Zefam SA, Zielona Gora, $27
10. Furnel Int., Warsaw, $25
Source: *The Warsaw Voice*, May 18, 1997, p. A3.

★ 1501 ★

POLAND'S LARGEST FURNITURE INVESTORS

Ranked by: Funds invested, in millions of U.S. dollars.
Number listed: 5
1. IKEA (Sweden) with $29.0 million
2. Schooner Capital Corporation (United States), $23.9
3. St. Lewandowski (Sweden), $19.0
4. MM Beteilgungen (Germany), $7.2
5. Karl-Heinz Klose (Germany), $4.5

Source: *National Trade Data Bank*, June 25, 1996, p. IMI96011.

★ 1502 ★

TOP FURNITURE MANUFACTURERS IN SOUTH KOREA, 1994

Ranked by: Sales, in millions of U.S. dollars. **Number listed:** 10
1. Borneo International Furniture with $144.5 million
2. Baroque Furniture, $83.0
3. Dongsuh Furniture, $80.0
4. Livart Furninture, $76.0
5. Lady Furniture, $72.0
6. Samick Furniture, $70.0
7. Sang-il, $52.5
8. Sunwood, $41.0
9. Raja, $40.0
10. Wooami, $37.5

Source: *National Trade Data Bank*, March 31, 1997, p. ISA970301.

★ 1503 ★

TOP PRODUCERS OF WOODEN FURNITURE IN JAPAN

Ranked by: Sales, in millions of yen (¥). **Number listed:** 8
1. Karimoku Furniture with ¥40,405 million
2. Maruni Furniture, ¥24,696
3. Tendo Mokko, ¥15,953
4. Seikosha, ¥11,665
5. Kosuga, ¥11,370
6. Kyowa Woodworking, ¥10,029
7. Asahi Industries, ¥8,870
8. Daimaru Woodworking, ¥6,784

Source: *National Trade Data Bank*, October 18, 1995, p. ISA9503.

Furniture Industry – Canada

★ 1504 ★

TOP FURNITURE BUYING GROUPS IN CANADA, 1995

Ranked by: Retail sales of furniture, bedding and decorative accessories, in millions of Canadian dollars.
Remarks: Shows number of members and number of stores for 1994 and 1995, as well as sales figures for 1994.
Number listed: 5
1. Cantrex Group with $533.0 million
2. Mega Group, $397.9
3. Allied-P.A.S., $280.0
4. Gest-Accor Group, $157.5
5. Home Furniture Stores, $30.9

Source: *Furniture/Today*, August 5, 1996, p. 21.

Furniture Industry – Europe

★ 1505 ★

TOP FURNITURE AND FIXTURE COMPANIES IN EUROPE

Ranked by: Sales, in millions of European Currency Units (ECUs). **Number listed:** 53
1. Sepawand BV with 765 million ECUs
2. Bertrand Faure Sitztechnik GmbH & Co. KG, 554
3. Keiper Recaro GmbH & Co., 495
4. Bertrand Faure Equipements SA, 476
5. Wagon Industrial Holdings PLC, 366
6. Umdasch Aktiengesellschaft, 353
7. Ahrend NV, 324
8. Wihuri Oy, 246
9. Lear Corporation Sweden AB, 242
10. Hygena Ltd., 230

Source: *Duns Europa*, (annual), vol. 4, Dun & Bradstreet, 1997, p. 219.

Furniture Stores

★ 1506 ★

TOP FURNITURE BUYING GROUPS IN CANADA, 1996

Ranked by: Sales of furniture, bedding, and accessories, in millions of Canadian dollars. **Remarks:** Also notes number of members, number of stores, and figures for 1995. **Number listed:** 4
1. Cantrex Group with C$496.1 million
2. Mega Group, C$365.4
3. Allied-P.A.S., C$287.0

4. G.A. Finance, C$133.0
Source: *Furniture/Today*, May 26, 1997, p. 9.

★ 1507 ★
TOP FURNITURE RETAILERS IN CANADA, 1996
Ranked by: Sales of furniture, bedding, and accessories, in millions of Canadian dollars. **Remarks:** Also notes unit sales and figures for 1995. **Number listed:** 10
1. Sears Canada with C$380.0 million
2. Leon's Furniture, C$279.2
3. Ikea Canada, C$253.8
4. Brick, C$233.0
5. Groupe BMTC, C$186.0
6. Eaton's, C$112.0
7. Maxi Muebles/Maxi Furniture, C$70.0
8. Bay, C$60.0
9. Bombay Company, C$51.9
10. Le Meubleur, C$38.2
Source: *Furniture/Today*, May 26, 1997, p. 9.

Gabon − see under individual headings

Gambling

★ 1508 ★
BRITAIN'S SCRATCHCARD MARKET
Ranked by: Market share, in percent. **Remarks:** Sales in Britain reached 1.4 billion pounds, making it the second largest market in the world. France lead the industry with sales over 2.1 billion pounds. **Number listed:** 2
1. Camelot with 93.0%
2. Other, 7.0%
Source: *The Guardian*, March 20, 1996, p. 6.

★ 1509 ★
GLOBAL LOTTERY SALES
Ranked by: Sales, in millions of British pounds (£). **Number listed:** 10
1. U.K. National Lottery with £5,217 million
2. Dai-Ichi (Japan), £5,111
3. ONLAE (Spain), £4,381
4. La Francaise des Jeux, £4,058
5. Lottomatica, £2,250
6. Texas, £1,993
7. New York, £1,988
8. Massachusetts, £1,840
9. Florida, £1,469
10. CONI (Italy), £1,445
Source: *The Times*, June 5, 1996, p. 31.

Gas Industry
See Also: Natural Gas

★ 1510 ★
HUNGARY'S GAS MARKET
Ranked by: Market share, in percent. **Number listed:** 9
1. Eastern with 25.0%
2. Business Gas, 24.0%
3. Alliance Gas, 20.0%
4. Accord, 6.0%
5. AGAS, 6.0%
6. Quadrant, 6.0%
7. Mobil, 4.0%
8. United Gas, 4.0%
9. Amerada Hess, 3.0%
10. Other, 2.0%
Source: *Financial Times*, April 29, 1996, p. 27.

★ 1511 ★
LEADING PRODUCERS OF LIQUIDS
Ranked by: Worldwide liquids production, in millions of barrels. **Number listed:** 20
1. Exxon Corp. with 614.0 million barrels
2. Chevron Corp., 365.0
3. Mobil Corp., 296.0
4. Texaco Inc., 290.0
5. ARCO (Atlantic Richfield Corp.), 237.0
6. Amoco Corp., 222.0
7. Shell Oil Co., 180.0
8. Conoco Inc., 121.0
9. Occidental Petroleum Corp., 101.0
10. Phillips Petroleum Co., 97.0
Source: *Oil & Gas Journal*, Oil & Gas Journal 200 (annual), September 2, 1996, p. 52.

★ 1512 ★
TOP COMPANIES IN GAS PRODUCTION
Ranked by: Worldwide gas production, in billions of cubic feet. **Number listed:** 20
1. Exxon Corp. with 2,383.0 billion
2. Mobil Corp., 1,662.0
3. Amoco Corp., 1,537.0
4. Chevron Corp., 888.0
5. Texaco Inc., 766.0
6. Unocal Corp., 681.0
7. Shell Oil Co., 666.0
8. ARCO (Atlantic Richfield Corp.), 568.0
9. Phillips Petroleum Co., 573.0
10. Conoco Inc., 453.0
Source: *Oil & Gas Journal*, Oil & Gas Journal 200 (annual), September 4, 1996, p. 54.

★ 1513 ★
TOP COMPANIES IN GAS RESERVES
Ranked by: Worldwide gas reserves, in billions of cubic feet. **Number listed:** 20
1. Exxon Corp. with 42,036.0 billion
2. Amoco Corp., 19,153.0
3. Mobil Corp., 17,968.0
4. Chevron Corp., 10,070.0
5. ARCO (Atlantic Richfield Corp.), 8,349.0
6. Unocal Corp., 6,765.0
7. Phillips Petroleum Co., 6,708.0
8. Texaco Inc., 6,095.0
9. Shell Oil Co., 6,063.0
10. Meridian Oil Inc., 5,507.0

Source: *Oil & Gas Journal,* Oil & Gas Journal 200 (annual), September 4, 1996, p. 54.

★ 1514 ★
TOP GAS COMPANIES BY LIQUIDS RESERVES
Ranked by: Worldwide liquids reserves, in millions of barrels. **Number listed:** 20
1. Exxon Corp. with 6,670.0 million barrels
2. Chevron Corp., 4,343.0
3. Mobil Corp., 3,419.0
4. Texaco Inc., 2,658.0
5. ARCO (Atlantic Richfield Corp.), 2,369.0
6. Amoco Corp., 2,322.0
7. Shell Oil Co., 2,208.0
8. Phillips Petroleum Co., 1,091.0
9. Conoco Inc., 977.0
10. Occidental Petroleum Corp., 968.0

Source: *Oil & Gas Journal,* Oil & Gas Journal 200 (annual), September 2, 1996, p. 52.

★ 1515 ★
TOP GAS FIRMS WORLDWIDE BY PRODUCTION, 1995
Ranked by: Production, in billions of cubic meters. **Number listed:** 10
1. Gazprom (Russia) with 559.5 billion cubic meters
2. RD-Shell (Netherlands/United Kingdom), 71.5
3. Exxon (United States), 61.7
4. Sonatrach (Algeria), 58.1
5. Mobil (United States), 48.2
6. Amoco (United States), 43.8
7. Saudi Aramco (Saudi Arabia), 40.3
8. NIOC (Iran), 35.1
9. Chevron (United States), 27.4
10. Pemex (Mexico), 26.6

Source: *Financial Times,* June 10, 1997, p. 9.

★ 1516 ★
TOP GAS FIRMS WORLDWIDE BY RESERVES, 1995
Ranked by: Reserves, in billions of cubic meters. **Number listed:** 10
1. Gazprom (Russia) with 49,270 billion cubic meters
2. NIOC (Iran), 20,963
3. QGPC (Qatar), 7,070
4. ADNOC (Abu Dhabi), 5,380
5. Saudi Aramco (Saudi Arabia), 5,341
6. PDVSA (Venezuela), 4,012
7. Sonatrach (Algeria), 3,690
8. Pertamina (Indonesia), 3,520
9. NNPC (Nigeria), 3,474
10. INOC (Iraq), 3,360

Source: *Financial Times,* June 10, 1997, p. 9.

★ 1517 ★
TOP NATURAL GAS PRODUCERS IN INDONESIA, 1996
Ranked by: Production, in billions of standard cubic feet. **Remarks:** Notes figures for 1994 and 1995. **Number listed:** 15
1. Mobil with 1,172 standard cubic feet
2. Vico, 585
3. Total, 410
4. Arco, 320
5. Pertamina, 279
6. Unocal, 112
7. Asamera, 48
8. CalTex, 46
9. Marathon, 35
10. Maxus, 21

Source: *National Trade Data Bank,* March 19, 1997, p. IMI970318.

★ 1518 ★
UKRAINE'S TOP GAS FIRMS, 1996
Ranked by: Government authorizations, in billions of cubic meters. **Number listed:** 6
1. United Energy Systems with 25.20 billion cubic meters
2. Itera, 18.46
3. Intergaz, 3.82
4. UkrGazProm, 3.70
5. Olgaz, 1.53
6. Other, 5.42

Source: *Financial Times,* August 7, 1996, p. 2.

★ 1519 ★
WORLDWIDE GAS MARKETS, 1996
Ranked by: Distribution, in percent. **Number listed:** 7
1. NAFTA with 32%
2. Europe, 28%
3. Pacific Rim, 13%
4. Japan, 12%

5. Africa, India, Mideast, 6%
6. South America, 6%
7. C.I.S., 3%
Source: *Chemical Week*, February 19, 1997, p. 26.

Gas Stations
See: **Automobile Service Stations**

Gas Utilities – Canada

★ 1520 ★
CANADA'S TOP GAS UTILITIES
Ranked by: Revenue, in thousands of Canadian dollars.
Remarks: Includes figures on profits and return on capital. **Number listed:** 11
1. Consumers' Gas Co. with C$1,845,425 thousand
2. Union Gas, C$1,325,500
3. BC Gas Inc., C$894,900
4. Progas Ltd., C$801,411
5. BC Gas Utility, C$732,100
6. Centra Gas Ontario, C$541,200
7. Northwestern Utilities, C$422,320
8. Canadian Western Nat. Gas Co., C$344,480
9. Centra Gas Manitoba, C$276,540
10. Gaz Metropolitain, C$132,069
Source: *Globe and Mail's Report on Business Magazine*, July 1996, p. 159.

Gases

★ 1521 ★
TOP GAS COMPANIES WORLDWIDE, 1996
Ranked by: Market share, in percent. **Number listed:** 9
1. Air Liquide with 17.9%
2. BOC, 15.6%
3. Praxair, 14.4%
4. Air Products, 8.4%
5. Aga, 6.8%
6. Linde, 5.4%
7. Messer Griesheim, 5.4%
8. NSC, 4.0%
9. Other, 21.9%
Source: *Chemical Week*, February 19, 1997, p. 26.

★ 1522 ★
TOP INDUSTRIAL GAS MAKERS WORLDWIDE
Ranked by: Market share, in percent. **Remarks:** Shares are of the $25 billion market. **Number listed:** 9
1. Air Liquide with 20.0%

2. BOC, 17.0%
3. Praxair, 12.0%
4. Air Products, 9.0%
5. Aga, 7.0%
6. Messer Griesheim, 7.0%
7. Linde, 7.0%
8. Nippon Sanso, 6.0%
9. Other, 15.0%
Source: *Chemical Week*, April 24, 1996, p. 22.

Gasoline

★ 1523 ★
JAPAN'S GASOLINE MARKET
Ranked by: Market share, in percent. **Number listed:** 10
1. Nippon Oil with 16.1%
2. Idemitsu, 14.2%
3. Showa Shell, 12.5%
4. Cosmo Oil, 11.8%
5. Japan Energy, 11.0%
6. Mitsubishi Oil, 8.4%
7. Mobil, 8.2%
8. Esso, 6.7%
9. General Seklyu, 5.6%
10. Other, 5.5%
Source: *Nikkei Weekly*, August 5, 1996, p. 10.

General Merchandise
See: **Retail Trade**

Georgia – see under individual headings

Germany – see under individual headings

Ghana – see under individual headings

Gifts (In Business)

★ 1524 ★
CORPORATE GIFT MARKET IN JAPAN, 1994
Ranked by: Sales, in billions of U.S. dollars. **Number listed:** 3
1. Sales promotion (premium incentives) with $12.0 billion

2. Business seasonal gifts, $8.0
3. Business occasional gifts, $3.0

Source: *National Trade Data Bank*, October 28, 1996, p. IMI961028.

Glass

★ 1525 ★
TOP PLATE GLASS MAKERS IN JAPAN
Ranked by: Market share, in percent. **Number listed:** 4
1. Asahi Glass with 40.5%
2. Nippon Sheet Glass, 31.9%
3. Central Glass, 17.5%
4. Other (imports), 4.1%

Source: *Nikkei Weekly*, July 29, 1996, p. 8.

Global Custodians

★ 1526 ★
TOP GLOBAL CUSTODIANS
Ranked by: Custody assests, in millions of U.S. dollars.
Remarks: Also notes custody as a percent of total assests held.
1. Chase Manhattan with $1,006,000 million
2. Citibank, $567,000
3. Bank of New York, $494,000
4. Deutsche Bank, $457,000
5. State Street, $369,900
6. Bankers Trust, $369,000
7. Bank of Tokyo Mitsubishi, $261,384
8. Brown Brothers Harriman, $250,000
9. Barclays Bank, $167,225
10. ABN Amro Bank, $152,000

Source: *Financial Times*, November 26, 1996, p. 7.

Gold

★ 1527 ★
AFRICAN COUNTRIES WITH THE GREATEST SUPPLY OF GOLD FROM FABRICATED OLD SCRAP, 1995
Ranked by: Total amount fabricated, in metric tons.
Remarks: Notes 1986-1994 totals. Data exclude dishoarding of investment bars. **Number listed:** 4
1. Libya with 7.0 metric tons
2. Morocco, 5.5
3. Algeria, 2.5
4. Other, 1.7

Source: *Gold 1997* (annual), Gold Fields Mineral Services, 1997, p. 35.

★ 1528 ★
AFRICAN COUNTRIES FABRICATING THE MOST GOLD FOR USE IN CARAT JEWELRY, 1995
Ranked by: Total amount fabricated, in metric tons.
Remarks: Totals include the use of scrap. 1986-1994 totals also noted. **Number listed:** 7
1. Morocco with 11.5 metric tons
2. South Africa, 5.2
3. Libya, 4.0
4. Algeria, 3.0
5. Zimbabwe, 2.0
6. Tunisia, 1.5
7. Other, 4.2

Source: *Gold 1997* (annual), Gold Fields Mineral Services, 1997, p. 45.

★ 1529 ★
AFRICAN COUNTRIES FABRICATING THE MOST GOLD, 1995
Ranked by: Total amount fabricated, in metric tons.
Remarks: Totals include the use of scrap. 1986-1994 totals also noted. **Number listed:** 7
1. Morocco with 11.5 metric tons
2. South Africa, 11.0
3. Libya, 4.0
4. Algeria, 3.0
5. Zimbabwe, 3.0
6. Tunisia, 1.5
7. Other, 4.2

Source: *Gold 1997* (annual), Gold Fields Mineral Services, 1997, p. 41.

★ 1530 ★
COUNTRIES OF THE FAR EAST WITH THE GREATEST SUPPLY OF GOLD FROM FABRICATED OLD SCRAP, 1995
Ranked by: Total amount fabricated, in metric tons.
Remarks: Notes 1986-1994 totals. Data exclude dishoarding of investment bars. **Number listed:** 11
1. Japan with 15.9 metric tons
2. Indonesia, 12.5
3. South Korea, 11.0
4. Thailand, 9.0
5. Hong Kong, 8.0
6. Taiwan, 7.0
7. Singapore, 4.5
8. Malaysia, 3.3
9. Vietnam, 3.0
10. Burma, Laos and Cambodia, 1.4

Source: *Gold 1997* (annual), Gold Fields Mineral Services, 1997, p. 35.

★ 1531 ★

COUNTRIES OF THE INDIAN SUBCONTINENT WITH THE GREATEST SUPPLY OF GOLD FROM FABRICATED OLD SCRAP, 1995

Ranked by: Total amount fabricated, in metric tons.
Remarks: Notes 1986-1994 totals. Data exclude dishoarding of investment bars. **Number listed:** 4

1. India with 97.0 metric tons
2. Pakistan and Afghanistan, 9.0
3. Bangladesh and Nepal, 1.4
4. Sri Lanka, 0.6

Source: *Gold 1997* (annual), Gold Fields Mineral Services, 1997, p. 35.

★ 1532 ★

EUROPEAN COUNTRIES FABRICATING THE MOST GOLD, 1995

Ranked by: Total amount fabricated, in metric tons.
Remarks: Totals include the use of scrap. 1986-1994 totals also noted. **Number listed:** 22

1. Italy with 457.9 metric tons
2. Germany, 70.4
3. Switzerland, 47.1
4. France, 43.1
5. United Kingdom and Ireland, 39.7
6. Austria, 32.8
7. Spain, 31.3
8. Portugal, 16.8
9. Greece, 13.3
10. Netherlands, 9.7

Source: *Gold 1997* (annual), Gold Fields Mineral Services, 1997, p. 40.

★ 1533 ★

EUROPEAN COUNTRIES WITH THE GREATEST SUPPLY OF GOLD FROM FABRICATED OLD SCRAP, 1995

Ranked by: Total amount fabricated, in metric tons.
Remarks: Notes 1986-1994 totals. Data exclude dishoarding of investment bars. **Number listed:** 23

1. Italy with 27.0 metric tons
2. Germany, 4.3
3. United Kingdom and Ireland, 3.8
4. Yugoslavia (former), 2.8
5. Belgium, 1.6
6. Spain, 1.5
7. Austria, 1.2
8. Czech and Slovak Republics, 1.1
9. France, 1.0
10. Romania, 0.8

Source: *Gold 1997* (annual), Gold Fields Mineral Services, 1997, p. 34.

★ 1534 ★

FAR EASTERN COUNTRIES FABRICATING THE MOST GOLD FOR USE IN CARAT JEWELRY, 1995

Ranked by: Total amount fabricated, in metric tons.
Remarks: Totals include the use of scrap. 1986-1994 totals also noted. **Number listed:** 11

1. Indonesia with 133.0 metric tons
2. Taiwan, 102.0
3. Hong Kong, 82.0
4. Japan, 78.0
5. Malaysia, 77.8
6. Thailand, 76.2
7. South Korea, 62.0
8. Singapore, 19.0
9. Vietnam, 16.0
10. Burma, Laos and Cambodia, 10.5

Source: *Gold 1997* (annual), Gold Fields Mineral Services, 1997, p. 45.

★ 1535 ★

FAR EASTERN COUNTRIES FABRICATING THE MOST GOLD, 1995

Ranked by: Total amount fabricated, in metric tons.
Remarks: Totals include the use of scrap. 1986-1994 totals also noted. **Number listed:** 11

1. Japan with 187.2 metric tons
2. Indonesia, 133.0
3. Taiwan, 110.0
4. Hong Kong, 86.9
5. South Korea, 80.9
6. Thailand, 79.1
7. Malaysia, 77.8
8. Singapore, 21.7
9. Vietnam, 16.0
10. Burma, Laos and Cambodia, 10.5

Source: *Gold 1997* (annual), Gold Fields Mineral Services, 1997, p. 41.

★ 1536 ★

LARGEST EUROPEAN FABRICATORS OF GOLD FOR USE IN CARAT JEWELRY, 1995

Ranked by: Total amount fabricated, in metric tons.
Remarks: Totals include the use of scrap. 1986-1994 totals also noted. **Number listed:** 22

1. Italy with 446.0 metric tons
2. Germany, 38.9
3. France, 29.9
4. Switzerland, 29.8
5. Spain, 29.4
6. United Kingdom and Ireland, 27.2
7. Portugal, 16.6
8. Greece, 13.3
9. Poland, 4.7
10. Austria, 3.2

Source: *Gold 1997* (annual), Gold Fields Mineral Services, 1997, p. 44.

★ 1537 ★

LARGEST FABRICATORS OF GOLD FOR USE IN CARAT JEWELRY ON THE INDIAN SUBCONTINENT, 1995

Ranked by: Total amount fabricated, in metric tons.
Remarks: Totals include the use of scrap. 1986-1994 totals also noted. **Number listed:** 5
1. India with 400.6 metric tons
2. Pakistan and Afghanistan, 39.2
3. Bangladesh and Nepal, 9.4
4. Sri Lanka, 4.0
5. Mauritius, 0.9
Source: *Gold 1997* (annual), Gold Fields Mineral Services, 1997, p. 44.

★ 1538 ★

LARGEST GOLD FABRICATORS ON THE INDIAN SUBCONTINENT, 1995

Ranked by: Total amount fabricated, in metric tons.
Remarks: Totals include the use of scrap. 1986-1994 totals also noted. **Number listed:** 5
1. India with 426.1 metric tons
2. Pakistan and Afghanistan, 40.7
3. Bangladesh and Nepal, 9.4
4. Sri Lanka, 4.0
5. Mauritius, 0.9
Source: *Gold 1997* (annual), Gold Fields Mineral Services, 1997, p. 40.

★ 1539 ★

LARGEST GOLD MARKETS WORLDWIDE, 1996

Ranked by: Consumption, in tons. **Number listed:** 10
1. India with 508
2. U.S., 345
3. China, 208
4. Saudi Arabia, 185
5. Japan, 170
6. Turkey, 153
7. Indonesia, 129
8. South Korea, 126
9. Taiwan, 123
10. Thailand, 106
Source: *Financial Times*, February 27, 1997, p. 24.

★ 1540 ★

LARGEST GOLD PRODUCING COUNTRIES, 1995

Ranked by: Production, in millions of ounces. **Number listed:** 5
1. South Africa with 18.4 million ounces
2. United States, 11.3
3. Australia, 8.9
4. Canada, 5.3
5. China, 4.9
Source: *The New York Times*, February 18, 1997, p. C6.

★ 1541 ★

LARGEST NORTH AMERICAN FABRICATORS OF GOLD FOR USE IN CARAT JEWELRY, 1995

Ranked by: Total amount fabricated, in metric tons.
Remarks: Totals include the use of scrap. 1986-1994 totals also noted. **Number listed:** 2
1. United States with 148.3 metric tons
2. Canada, 17.2
Source: *Gold 1997* (annual), Gold Fields Mineral Services, 1997, p. 44.

★ 1542 ★

LATIN AMERICAN COUNTRIES WITH THE GREATEST SUPPLY OF GOLD FROM FABRICATED OLD SCRAP, 1995

Ranked by: Total amount fabricated, in metric tons.
Remarks: Notes 1986-1994 totals. Data exclude dishoarding of investment bars. **Number listed:** 9
1. Mexico with 16.0 metric tons
2. Brazil, 4.8
3. Argentina, 4.3
4. Venezuela, 2.3
5. Dominican Republic, 1.4
6. Colombia, 1.2
7. Peru, 0.8
8. Ecuador, 0.5
9. Other, 1.2
Source: *Gold 1997* (annual), Gold Fields Mineral Services, 1997, p. 34.

★ 1543 ★

LEADING FABRICATORS OF GOLD CARAT JEWELRY EXCLUDING THE USE OF SCRAP IN THE FAR EAST, 1995

Ranked by: Total amount fabricated, in metric tons.
Remarks: 1986-1994 totals also noted. **Number listed:** 11
1. Indonesia with 120.5 metric tons
2. Taiwan, 95.0
3. Malaysia, 74.5
4. Hong Kong, 74.0
5. Japan, 68.4
6. Thailand, 67.2
7. South Korea, 51.0
8. Singapore, 15.0
9. Vietnam, 13.0
10. Burma, Laos and Cambodia, 9.6
Source: *Gold 1997* (annual), Gold Fields Mineral Services, 1997, p. 49.

★ 1544 ★

LEADING FABRICATORS OF GOLD CARAT JEWELRY EXCLUDING THE USE OF SCRAP ON THE INDIAN SUBCONTINENT, 1995

Ranked by: Total amount fabricated, in metric tons.
Remarks: 1986-1994 totals also noted. **Number listed:** 5
1. India with 303.6 metric tons

2. Pakistan and Afghanistan, 30.2
3. Bangladesh and Nepal, 8.0
4. Sri Lanka, 3.4
5. Mauritius, 0.8

Source: *Gold 1997* (annual), Gold Fields Mineral Services, 1997, p. 48.

★ 1545 ★

LEADING FABRICATORS OF GOLD FOR USE IN DENTISTRY, 1995

Ranked by: Total amount fabricated, in metric tons.
Remarks: Totals include the use of scrap. 1986-1994 totals also noted. **Number listed:** 26

1. Japan with 18.0 metric tons
2. Germany, 14.9
3. United States, 11.1
4. Italy, 4.3
5. Switzerland, 3.9
6. South Korea, 3.0
7. Netherlands, 1.9
8. Brazil, 0.8
9. Austria, 0.8
10. Czech and Slovak Republics, 0.5

Source: *Gold 1997* (annual), Gold Fields Mineral Services, 1997, p. 55.

★ 1546 ★

LEADING FABRICATORS OF GOLD FOR USE IN ELECTRONICS, 1995

Ranked by: Total amount fabricated, in metric tons.
Remarks: Totals include the use of scrap. 1986-1994 totals also noted. **Number listed:** 20

1. Japan with 76.0 metric tons
2. United States, 53.0
3. South Korea, 11.0
4. Germany, 8.7
5. United Kingdom and Ireland, 6.8
6. Switzerland, 6.7
7. Taiwan, 6.4
8. France, 5.2
9. Netherlands, 4.1
10. Singapore, 2.3

Source: *Gold 1997* (annual), Gold Fields Mineral Services, 1997, p. 54.

★ 1547 ★

LEADING GOLD FABRICATORS IN LATIN AMERICA, 1995

Ranked by: Total amount fabricated, in metric tons.
Remarks: Totals include the use of scrap. 1986-1994 totals also noted. **Number listed:** 10

1. Mexico with 20.1 metric tons
2. Brazil, 19.7
3. Peru, 9.0
4. Dominican Republic, 8.1
5. Chile, 6.1

6. Colombia, 3.2
7. Argentina, 2.3
8. Ecuador, 2.3
9. Venezuela, 1.1
10. Other, 11.1

Source: *Gold 1997* (annual), Gold Fields Mineral Services, 1997, p. 40.

★ 1548 ★

LEADING LATIN AMERICAN FABRICATORS OF GOLD FOR USE IN CARAT JEWELRY, 1995

Ranked by: Total amount fabricated, in metric tons.
Remarks: Totals include the use of scrap. 1986-1994 totals also noted. **Number listed:** 10

1. Mexico with 18.9 metric tons
2. Brazil, 16.0
3. Peru, 9.0
4. Dominican Republic, 8.1
5. Chile, 6.1
6. Colombia, 2.9
7. Ecuador, 2.2
8. Argentina, 2.1
9. Venezuela, 1.0
10. Other, 11.1

Source: *Gold 1997* (annual), Gold Fields Mineral Services, 1997, p. 44.

★ 1549 ★

LEADING MIDDLE EASTERN FABRICATORS OF GOLD CARAT JEWELRY EXCLUDING THE USE OF SCRAP, 1995

Ranked by: Total amount fabricated, in metric tons.
Remarks: 1986-1994 totals also noted. **Number listed:** 9

1. Saudi Arabia and Yemen with 74.1 metric tons
2. Turkey, 63.4
3. Arabian Gulf States, 33.4
4. Iran, 22.0
5. Iraq, Syria and Jordan, 19.3
6. Israel, 15.0
7. Egypt, 11.0
8. Lebanon, 10.4
9. Kuwait, 9.1

Source: *Gold 1997* (annual), Gold Fields Mineral Services, 1997, p. 48.

★ 1550 ★

LEADING NORTH AMERICAN FABRICATORS OF GOLD CARAT JEWELRY EXCLUDING THE USE OF SCRAP, 1995

Ranked by: Total amount fabricated, in metric tons.
Remarks: 1986-1994 totals also noted. **Number listed:** 2

1. United States with 129.8 metric tons
2. Canada, 13.5

Source: *Gold 1997* (annual), Gold Fields Mineral Services, 1997, p. 48.

★ 1551 ★

**MIDDLE EASTERN COUNTRIES FABRICATING
THE MOST GOLD FOR USE IN CARAT JEWELRY,
1995**

Ranked by: Total amount fabricated, in metric tons.
Remarks: Totals include the use of scrap. 1986-1994
totals also noted. **Number listed:** 9
1. Saudi Arabia and Yemen with 153.1 metric
   tons
2. Turkey, 110.4
3. Egypt, 60.5
4. Arabian Gulf States, 41.2
5. Iraq, Syria and Jordan, 35.7
6. Iran, 30.0
7. Kuwait, 23.1
8. Israel, 18.5
9. Lebanon, 11.9
Source: *Gold 1997* (annual), Gold Fields Mineral
Services, 1997, p. 44.

★ 1552 ★

**MIDDLE EASTERN COUNTRIES FABRICATING
THE MOST GOLD, 1995**

Ranked by: Total amount fabricated, in metric tons.
Remarks: Totals include the use of scrap. 1986-1994
totals also noted. **Number listed:** 9
1. Saudi Arabia and Yemen with 156.1 metric
   tons
2. Turkey, 125.6
3. Egypt, 60.7
4. Arabian Gulf States, 44.2
5. Iraq, Syria and Jordan, 37.7
6. Iran, 37.0
7. Kuwait, 23.3
8. Israel, 18.9
9. Lebanon, 12.0
Source: *Gold 1997* (annual), Gold Fields Mineral
Services, 1997, p. 40.

★ 1553 ★

**MIDDLE EASTERN COUNTRIES WITH THE
GREATEST SUPPLY OF GOLD FROM FABRICATED
OLD SCRAP, 1995**

Ranked by: Total amount fabricated, in metric tons.
Remarks: Notes 1986-1994 totals. Data exclude
dishoarding of investment bars. **Number listed:** 9
1. Saudi Arabia and Yemen with 97.0 metric tons
2. Turkey, 47.0
3. Egypt, 40.0
4. Kuwait, 17.8
5. Iraq, Syria and Jordan, 15.2
6. Iran, 10.0
7. Israel, 3.5
8. Arabian Gulf States, 3.0

9. Lebanon, 2.2
Source: *Gold 1997* (annual), Gold Fields Mineral
Services, 1997, p. 34.

★ 1554 ★

**NORTH AMERICAN COUNTRIES FABRICATING
THE MOST GOLD, 1995**

Ranked by: Total amount fabricated, in metric tons.
Remarks: Totals include the use of scrap. 1986-1994
totals also noted. **Number listed:** 2
1. United States with 250.3 metric tons
2. Canada, 28.1
Source: *Gold 1997* (annual), Gold Fields Mineral
Services, 1997, p. 40.

★ 1555 ★

**NORTH AMERICAN COUNTRIES WITH THE
GREATEST SUPPLY OF GOLD FROM FABRICATED
OLD SCRAP, 1995**

Ranked by: Total amount fabricated, in metric tons.
Remarks: Notes 1986-1994 totals. Data exclude
dishoarding of investment bars. **Number listed:** 2
1. United States with 54.9 metric tons
2. Canada, 4.8
Source: *Gold 1997* (annual), Gold Fields Mineral
Services, 1997, p. 34.

★ 1556 ★

**TOP AFRICAN FABRICATORS OF GOLD CARAT
JEWELRY EXCLUDING THE USE OF SCRAP, 1995**

Ranked by: Total amount fabricated, in metric tons.
Remarks: 1986-1994 totals also noted. **Number listed:** 7
1. Morocco with 6.5 metric tons
2. South Africa, 5.2
3. Libya, 3.5
4. Zimbabwe, 2.0
5. Tunisia, 1.5
6. Algeria, 0.5
7. Other, 2.9
Source: *Gold 1997* (annual), Gold Fields Mineral
Services, 1997, p. 49.

★ 1557 ★

**TOP EUROPEAN FABRICATORS OF GOLD CARAT
JEWELRY EXCLUDING THE USE OF SCRAP, 1995**

Ranked by: Total amount fabricated, in metric tons.
Remarks: 1986-1994 totals also noted. **Number listed:** 22
1. Italy with 419.0 metric tons
2. Germany, 36.1
3. Switzerland, 29.8
4. France, 29.1
5. Spain, 27.9
6. United Kingdom and Ireland, 25.3
7. Portugal, 16.3
8. Greece, 12.6
9. Poland, 4.0

10. Cyprus and Malta, 2.3
Source: *Gold 1997* (annual), Gold Fields Mineral Services, 1997, p. 48.

★ 1558 ★
TOP FABRICATORS OF GOLD FOR MISCELLANEOUS INDUSTRIAL AND DECORATIVE USES, 1995
Ranked by: Total amount fabricated, in metric tons.
Remarks: Totals include the use of scrap. 1986-1994 totals also noted. **Number listed:** 26
1. United States with 19.0 metric tons
2. India, 17.5
3. Japan, 14.8
4. Germany, 7.4
5. France, 7.1
6. Switzerland, 6.0
7. Italy, 5.5
8. South Korea, 4.4
9. Hong Kong, 3.9
10. South Africa, 3.7
Source: *Gold 1997* (annual), Gold Fields Mineral Services, 1997, p. 56.

★ 1559 ★
TOP FABRICATORS OF GOLD FOR USE IN MEDALS AND IMITATION COINS, 1995
Ranked by: Total amount fabricated, in metric tons.
Remarks: Totals include the use of scrap. 1986-1994 totals also noted. **Number listed:** 21
1. Turkey with 13.6 metric tons
2. India, 7.0
3. Arabian Gulf States, 3.0
4. Saudi Arabia and Yemen, 3.0
5. Iraq, Syria and Jordan, 2.0
6. Pakistan and Afghanistan, 1.5
7. Italy, 0.9
8. Switzerland, 0.6
9. Germany, 0.5
10. South Korea, 0.5
Source: *Gold 1997* (annual), Gold Fields Mineral Services, 1997, p. 57.

★ 1560 ★
TOP FABRICATORS OF GOLD FOR USE IN OFFICIAL COINS, 1995
Ranked by: Total amount fabricated, in metric tons.
Remarks: Totals include the use of scrap. 1986-1994 totals also noted. **Number listed:** 27
1. Austria with 28.8 metric tons
2. United States, 18.9
3. Canada, 10.5
4. Australia, 10.1
5. Iran, 7.0
6. United Kingdom and Ireland, 4.0
7. South Africa, 2.3

8. Mexico, 1.7
9. Turkey, 1.3
10. Norway, 0.9
Source: *Gold 1997* (annual), Gold Fields Mineral Services, 1997, p. 58.

★ 1561 ★
TOP GOLD PRODUCERS IN CANADA
Ranked by: Revenue, in thousands of Canadian dollars.
Remarks: Includes profits and return on capital. **Number listed:** 18
1. Barrick Gold with C$1,307,200 thousand
2. Placer Dome Inc., C$1,098,000
3. Teck Corp., C$714,217
4. Placer Dome Canada, C$466,000
5. Echo Bay Mines, C$375,900
6. Homestake Canada, C$366,484
7. Camblor Inc., C$347,846
8. Pegasus Gold, C$259,164
9. Royal Oak Mines, C$234,457
10. TVX Gold, C$175,584
Source: *Globe and Mail's Report on Business Magazine*, July 1996, p. 160.

★ 1562 ★
TOP GOLD PRODUCERS WORLDWIDE, 1995
Ranked by: Output, in millions of troy ounces. **Number listed:** 7
1. Anglo American with 7.56 million troy ounces
2. Gold Fields of South Africa, 3.38
3. Barrick Gold, 3.15
4. Newmont/Santa Fe Pacific, 2.71
5. Gencor, 2.03
6. Newmont Mining, 1.86
7. Placer Dome, 1.86
Source: *The New York Times*, December 6, 1996, p. C1.

★ 1563 ★
TOP LATIN AMERICAN FABRICATORS OF GOLD CARAT JEWELRY EXCLUDING THE USE OF SCRAP, 1995
Ranked by: Total amount fabricated, in metric tons.
Remarks: 1986-1994 totals also noted. **Number listed:** 9
1. Brazil with 11.3 metric tons
2. Peru, 8.7
3. Dominican Republic, 8.1
4. Mexico, 7.5
5. Chile, 6.1
6. Colombia, 2.1
7. Ecuador, 2.0
8. Venezuela, 0.8
9. Other, 9.9
Source: *Gold 1997* (annual), Gold Fields Mineral Services, 1997, p. 48.

Gold Mines and Mining

★ 1564 ★
INDONESIA'S TOP GOLD MINES
Ranked by: Production, in millions of ounces. **Number listed:** 8
1. Grasberg with 82.3 million ounces
2. Busang, 46.9
3. Batu Hijau, 15.1
4. Kelian, 5.8
5. G. Pongkor, 3.3
6. Cabang Kiri, 2.5
7. Mesel, 2.0
8. Mt. Muro, 1.3
Source: *Engineering & Mining Journal*, May 1997, p. WW-13.

★ 1565 ★
TOP GOLD PRODUCING COMPANIES, 1995
Ranked by: Beneficial production, in tons. **Remarks:** South African firms are ranked by managed production. Also notes 1994 production. 15
1. Anglo American (South Africa) with 235 tons
2. GFSA (South Africa), 105
3. Barrick Gold (Canada), 98
4. Gencor (South Africa), 63
5. Newmont (United States), 58
6. Placer Dome (Canada), 58
7. RTZ-CRA (United Kingdom), 53
8. Homestake (United States), 51
9. JCI (South Africa), 47
10. Freeport-McMoRan (United States), 41
Source: *Gold 1996* (annual), Gold Fields Mineral Services, 1996, p. 18.

Golf

★ 1566 ★
LEADING CANADIAN PROVINCES FOR SALES OF GOLF EQUIPMENT
Ranked by: Sales, in percent distribution. **Remarks:** Atlantic Provinces include Newfoundland, Prince Edward Island, Nova Scotia and New Brunswick. **Number listed:** 5
1. Ontario with 44%
2. Quebec, 20%
3. Alberta, Saskatchewan, and Manitoba, 20%
4. British Columbia, 12%
5. Atlantic Provinces, 4%
Source: *National Trade Data Bank*, June 27, 1997, p. IMI970625.

Government Bonds

★ 1567 ★
OUTSTANDING GOVERNMENT BONDS WORLDWIDE, 1995
Ranked by: Bonds outstanding at the end of 1995, as a percent of global total. **Number listed:** 7
1. United States with 47%
2. Japan, 18%
3. Germany, 7%
4. Italy, 7%
5. France, 6%
6. Britain, 3%
7. Other, 12%
Source: *The Economist*, September 14, 1996, p. 76.

Government Ownership

★ 1568 ★
LARGEST STATE-OWNED ENTERPRISES IN SOUTH KOREA
Ranked by: Assets, in billions of U.S. dollars. **Remarks:** Includes net profits, market value, return on equity and government holding. **Number listed:** 6
1. Korea Development Bank with $53 billion
2. Korea Electric Power Corporation, $35
3. Industrial Bank of Korea, $32
4. Korea Housing Bank, $32
5. Pohang Iron & Steel, $17
6. Korea Telecom, $16
Source: *The Economist*, December 2, 1996, p. 66.

Government Ownership – Canada

★ 1569 ★
LARGEST CROWN CORPORATIONS IN CANADA, 1995
Ranked by: Revenue, in thousands of Canadian dollars. **Remarks:** Also lists figures for return on capital, profit, assets, and number of employees. **Number listed:** 10
1. Canada Post Corp. with C$4,747,972 thousand
2. Canada Mortgage and Housing, C$1,580,505
3. Export Development Corp., C$965,000
4. Canadian Commercial Corp., C$892,620
5. Atomic Energy of Canada, C$469,665
6. Canadian Broadcasting Corp., C$411,232
7. Farm Credit Corp., C$385,940
8. Business Development Bank Canada, C$342,840
9. Royal Canadian Mint, C$310,600

10. Marine Atlantic, C$258,800
Source: *Globe and Mail,* Globe and Mail Report on Business 1000 (annual), July 1996, p. 153.

Grain

★ 1570 ★
LEADERS IN THE CANADIAN GRAIN HANDLERS MARKET, 1996
Ranked by: Market share, in percent. **Number listed:** 7
1. Saskatchewan Wheat Pool with 31%
2. Alberta Wheat Pool, 17%
3. United Grain Growers, 17%
4. Cargill Inc., 10%
5. Pioneer, 10%
6. Manitoba Pool Elevators, 7%
7. Other, 8%
Source: *Globe and Mail's Report on Business Magazine,* June 1997, p. 36.

★ 1571 ★
TOP COARSE GRAIN PRODUCING NATIONS IN CENTRAL AND EASTERN EUROPE, 1996
Ranked by: Production, in millions of tons. **Number listed:** 8
1. Poland with 16.5 millin tons
2. Romania, 10.9
3. Hungary, 7.1
4. Yugoslavia Federal Republic, 5.4
5. Czech Republic, 2.9
6. Bulgaria, 1.6
7. Slovakia, 1.5
8. Other, 3.4
Source: *Financial Times,* August 1, 1997, p. 30.

Greece – see under individual headings

Greenland – see under individual headings

Greenmail
See: **Stocks – Repurchase**

Grocery Store Chains
See: **Grocery Trade**

Grocery Stores
See: **Convenience Stores**

Grocery Trade
See Also: **Supermarkets**

★ 1572 ★
AUSTRALIA'S GROCERY MARKET
Ranked by: Market share, in percent. **Number listed:** 5
1. Woolworths with 33.4%
2. Coles, 24.3%
3. Davids, 22.6%
4. Franklins, 14.0%
5. FAL, 5.7%
Source: *IGA GROCERGRAM,* July 1996, p. 10.

★ 1573 ★
BEST-SELLING GROCERY STORE BRANDS IN CANADA, 1996
Ranked by: Sales, in millions of U.S. dollars. **Number listed:** 10
1. Pepsi-Cola with $392.1 million
2. Coca-Cola, $391.8
3. Campbell's soups, $231.3
4. Tide laundry detergent, $137.3
5. Tropicana chilled juices, $125.3
6. Christie cookies, $121.6
7. Kraft cheese slices, $109.1
8. Christie crackers, $106.8
9. Minute Maid frozen juices and drinks, $94.6
10. Kraft cheddar, $91.3
Source: *Macleans,* February 3, 1996, p. 12.

★ 1574 ★
TOP GROCERY BRANDS IN IRELAND
Ranked by: Market share, as a percent of total sales for each brand's category. **Remarks:** Data do not include cigarettes and alcohol. **Number listed:** 10
1. Coca-Cola with 34.0%
2. 7-Up, 22.0%
3. Lyons Tea, 22.0%
4. Pampers Nappies, 21.0%
5. Dairygold Spread, 16.0%
6. Tayto Crisps, 16.0%
7. Siucra, 15.0%
8. Yoplait Yogurt, 15.0%
9. Barry's Tea, 14.0%
10. Club Soft Drinks, 13.0%
Source: *Irish Times,* May 1, 1997, p. 2.

★ 1575 ★

TOP GROCERY STORES IN CANADA, 1996

Ranked by: Market share based on sales, in percent.
Remarks: Notes 1995 figures. **Number listed:** 10
1. Loblaw Companies with 18.7%
2. Non-grocery stores, 12.1%
3. Canada Safeway, 8.7%
4. IGA, 7.5%
5. Membership Club Stores, 7.5%
6. Metro-Richelieu, 6.6%
7. Provigo, 6.5%
8. Corporate A&P, 4.9%
9. Co-Op, 4.8%
10. Other, 22.7%
Source: *Marketing Magazine*, May 26, 1997, p. 12.

★ 1576 ★

TOP SUPERMARKETS IN CHILE

Ranked by: Market share, in percent. **Number listed:** 3
1. Santa Isabel with 15.0%
2. Almarc, 14.0%
3. Other, 71.0%
Source: *Investor's Business Daily*, July 31, 1996, p. A4.

★ 1577 ★

TOP SUPERMARKETS IN GERMANY, 1995

Ranked by: Turnover, in millions of deutschmarks
(DM). **Number listed:** 10
1. Metro-Gruppe with DM61.5 million
2. Rewe-Gruppe, DM44.4
3. Edeka/AVA-Gruppe, DM40.6
4. Aldi-Gruppe, DM32.0
5. Tengelmann-Gruppe, DM25.2
6. Karstadt/Hertie-Gruppe, DM24.5
7. Lidl & Schwartz-Gruppe, DM17.0
8. Spar AG, DM13.9
9. Allkauf, DM6.5
10. Schlecker, DM5.5
Source: *Der Spiegel*, 1995, p. 95.

Gross Domestic Product

★ 1578 ★

LARGEST ECONOMIES WORLDWIDE, 1996

Ranked by: Nominal gross domestic product, in billions
of U.S. dollars. **Remarks:** Also notes gross domestic
product per capita. **Number listed:** 8
1. United States with $7,260.0 billion
2. Japan, $4,600.0
3. Germany, $2,360.0
4. France, $1,550.0
5. Italy, $1,200.0
6. United Kingdom, $1,140.0
7. Canada, $577.8

8. Russia, $551.0
Source: *Globe and Mail*, June 19, 1997, p. B12.

Gross National Product

★ 1579 ★

POOREST NATIONS WORLDWIDE

Ranked by: Gross national product per capita. No
specific data provided. **Number listed:** 10
1. Mozambique
2. Tanzania
3. Ethiopia
4. Eritrea
5. Somalia
6. Sierra Leone
7. Vietnam
8. Bhutan
9. Uganda
10. Burundi
Source: *The European Magazine*, April 10, 1997, p. 30.

★ 1580 ★

RICHEST NATIONS WORLDWIDE

Ranked by: Gross national product per capita. No
specific data provided. **Number listed:** 10
1. Luxembourg
2. Switzerland
3. Japan
4. Denmark
5. Norway
6. Iceland
7. Sweden
8. United States
9. Germany
10. Austria
Source: *The European Magazine*, April 10, 1997, p. 30.

Guatemala − see under individual headings

Guinea − see under individual headings

Hair Care Products

★ 1581 ★
BEST-SELLING BRANDS OF CHILDREN'S HAIR PRODUCTS IN FRANCE, 1996
Ranked by: No specific dollar values provided. **Remarks:** Company names are shown in parentheses. **Number listed:** 5
1. P'Tit Dop (Lascad)
2. Mixa Enfant (Lascad)
3. Palmolive Junior (Colgate Palmolive)
4. Corine de Farme for Kids (Corine de Farme)
5. Ultra Doux (Laboratoires Garnier)
Source: *National Trade Data Bank*, May 23, 1997, p. IMI970508.

★ 1582 ★
BEST-SELLING BRANDS OF CONDITIONERS IN FRANCE, 1996
Ranked by: No specific dollar values provided. **Remarks:** Company names are shown in parentheses. **Number listed:** 8
1. Elseve Performance (L'Oreal)
2. Dessange (J. Dessange)
3. Ultra Rich (Laboratoires Garnier)
4. Ultra Doux (Laboratoires Garnier)
5. Organics (Elida)
6. Timotei (Laboratoires Garnier)
7. Fructis (Laboratoires Garnier)
8. Jean Louis David (J.L. David)
Source: *National Trade Data Bank*, May 23, 1997, p. IMI970508.

★ 1583 ★
BEST-SELLING BRANDS OF HAIR COLOR PRODUCTS IN FRANCE, 1996
Ranked by: No specific dollar values provided. **Remarks:** Company names are shown in parentheses. **Number listed:** 9
1. Belle Color (Laboratoires Garnier)
2. Excellence (L'Oreal)
3. Dedicace (L'Oreal)
4. Movida (Laboratoires Garnier)
5. Recital (L'Oreal)
6. Cristal Color (Laboratoires Garnier)
7. Casting (L'Oreal)
8. Eclat et Douceur (Laboratoires Eugene)
Source: *National Trade Data Bank*, May 23, 1997, p. IMI970508.

★ 1584 ★
TAIWAN'S HAIR CARE MARKET
Ranked by: Market share, in percent. **Number listed:** 4
1. Procter & Gamble with 40.0%
2. Kao, 15.0%

3. Mavibel, 15.0%
4. Other, 30.0%
Source: *National Trade Data Bank*, May 27, 1996, p. ISA9503.

Haiti – see under individual headings

Hardware Stores

★ 1585 ★
TOP HARDWARE STORES IN CANADA, 1996
Ranked by: Market share based on sales, in percent. **Number listed:** 11
1. Canadian Tire Corp. with 29.4%
2. Home Hardware, 10.6%
3. Home Depot, 6.2%
4. Beaver Lumber, 4.3%
5. Rere Depot, 2.7%
6. Revelstoke Home Centres, 2.4%
7. Cashway Building Centres, 1.7%
8. Kent Building Supplies, 0.9%
9. Lansing Buildall, 0.9%
10. Lumberland Building Materials, 0.8%
Source: *Marketing Magazine*, May 26, 1997, p. 12.

Hawaii – see under individual headings

Health and Beauty Aid Products
See: **Personal Care Products**

Health Clubs

★ 1586 ★
LARGEST FITNESS COMPANIES IN JAPAN, 1994
Ranked by: Sales, in millions of U.S. dollars. **Remarks:** Notes growth rates and number of clubs. The name of the club has been included if it is different from the company name. **Number listed:** 10
1. Central Sports with $262 million
2. People (Exas), $258
3. Nippon Athletic Service, $121
4. Tipness, $100
5. JSS, $86
6. Dic Renaissance, $76
7. Daiei Leisure Land (Orange One), $68
8. Jusco (The Space), $46

9. Levene (Sporting World Levene), $45
10. Nissin Seito (Do Sports Plaza), $37
Source: *National Trade Data Bank*, August 1, 1996, p. ISA960601.

Health Food Industry
See: **Food Industry and Trade**

Heating and Cooling Industry
See: **Air Conditioning Industry**

Heating Pads
See: **Household Appliances**

Helsinki Stock Exchange

★ 1587 ★
LARGEST COMPANIES ON THE HELSINKI STOCK EXCHANGE, 1995
Ranked by: Market capitalization, in thousands of Finnish marks (FM). **Number listed:** 20
1. Oy Nokia Ab with FM51,332,424 thousand
2. Repola Oy, FM12,511,243
3. Kymmene Oy, FM9,430,000
4. Outukumpu Oy, FM8,592,539
5. Neste Oy, FM7,684,800
6. Enso-Gutzeit Oy, FM7,029,307
7. Orion-Yhtyma Oy, FM6,150,475
8. Unitas Oy, FM5,317,217
9. Metra Oy Ab, FM4,862,923
10. Valmet Oy, FM4,638,028
Source: *GT Guide to World Equity Markets* (annual), Euromoney Publications, 1996, p. 124.

★ 1588 ★
MOST ACTIVELY TRADED SHARES ON THE HELSINKI STOCK EXCHANGE, 1995
Ranked by: Turnover, in thousands of Finnish marks (FM). **Number listed:** 20
1. Oy Nokia Ab A with FM29,764,989 thousand
2. Oy Nokia Ab K, FM10,771,154
3. Repola Oy, FM5,765,246
4. Kymmene Oy, FM5,229,057
5. Enso-Gutzeit Oy R, FM2,997,422
6. Outukumpu Oy A, FM1,819,494
7. Merita A, FM1,664,552
8. Metsa-Serla Oy B, FM1,426,206
9. Valmet Oy, FM1,368,812

10. Metra Oy Ab B, FM1,234,128
Source: *GT Guide to World Equity Markets* (annual), Euromoney Publications, 1996, p. 124.

High Technology Industries

★ 1589 ★
JAPANESE HIGH-TECH COMPANIES POSTING THE HIGHEST GROWTH, 1994-1995
Ranked by: Sales growth, in percent. **Number listed:** 5
1. Advantest with 81.8% growth
2. Tokyo Electron, 59.6%
3. I-O Data Devices, 43.6%
4. Tamura Electric Works, 37.0%
5. Melco, 30.5%
Source: *Electronic Business Today*, October 1996, p. 20.

★ 1590 ★
JAPANESE HIGH-TECH COMPANIES POSTING THE LOWEST GROWTH, 1994-1995
Ranked by: Sales growth, in percent. **Number listed:** 5
1. Uniden with -20.0% growth
2. Nintendo, -14.8%
3. Akai, -11.0%
4. Hosiden, -8.8%
5. Toyo Communications, -4.4%
Source: *Electronic Business Today*, October 1996, p. 20.

Hogs

★ 1591 ★
HOG POPULATION BY COUNTRY, 1995
Ranked by: Hog population as of January 1, 1995. **Number listed:** 10
1. China with 401,000 thousand
2. United States, 60,500
3. Former U.S.S.R., 42,600
4. Brazil, 32,100
5. Germany, 25,400
6. Poland, 19,000
7. Spain, 18,200
8. Netherlands, 14,100
9. France, 13,000
10. Canada, 11,650
Source: *World Agricultural Production.*, March 1995, p. 45.

★ 1592 ★
TOP HOG MARKETS IN CANADA'S PRAIRIE REGION
Ranked by: Number of hogs brought to market, in millions. **Remarks:** Data are estimated. **Number listed:** 3
1. Manitoba with 2.8 million hogs
2. Alberta, 2.6
3. Saskatchewan, 1.1

Source: *National Trade Data Bank*, June 5, 1997, p. IMI970604.

Holding Companies

★ 1593 ★
TOP WORLDWIDE HOLDING COMPANIES, 1996
Ranked by: Revenues, in thousands of U.S. dollars. **Number listed:** 15
1. WPP Group PLC with $3,419,900 thousand
2. Omnicom Group, $3,035,450
3. Interpublic Group of Companies, Inc., $2,873,790
4. Dentsu, $1,909,200
5. Young & Rubicam, $1,356,418
6. Cordiant PLC, $1,177,600
7. True North, $1,086,042
8. Havas Advertising, $976,939
9. Grey Advertising, $920,200
10. Leo Burnett Co., $866,301

Source: *Adweek*, April 7, 1997, p. 49.

Holding Companies – Europe

★ 1594 ★
TOP EUROPEAN COMPANIES IN HOLDINGS AND OTHER INVESTMENTS
Ranked by: Sales, in millions of European Currency Units (ECUs). **Remarks:** Also notes the number of employees. **Number listed:** 89
1. Metro Holding A.G. with 35,204 million ECUs
2. Metro International A.G., 35,204
3. Philips Domestic Appl. & Personal Care Int. BV., 30,349
4. Metro A.G., 27,490
5. ABB Asea Brown Boveri Ltd., 26,061
6. Thyssen A.G., 17,758
7. Telefon AB L.M. Ericsson, 12,151
8. Saint Gobain (Compagnie De), 11,124
9. Compagnie Financiere Michelin, 10,604
10. Sandoz A.G., 10,158

Source: *Duns Europa* (annual), vol. 4, Dun & Bradstreet, 1997, p. 279+.

Home Building Industry
See: **Construction Industry**

Home Electronics

★ 1595 ★
TOP MINIDISC PLAYERS IN JAPAN
Ranked by: Market share, in percent. **Number listed:** 6
1. Sony with 47.0%
2. Sharp, 26.0%
3. Kenwood, 15.6%
4. Nippon Columbia, 5.0%
5. Onkyo, 3.1%
6. Other, 3.3%

Source: *Nikkei Weekly*, July 22, 1996, p. 8.

Home Freezers

★ 1596 ★
TOP FREEZER MANUFACTURERS IN CHINA, 1995
Ranked by: Units shipped. **Number listed:** 8
1. Aukema with 656,400 units
2. XingXing, 332,600
3. Haier, 331,500
4. Baixue, 289,700
5. Xiangxuehai, 238,900
6. Bingxiong, 179,800
7. Huamei, 176,200
8. Xileng, 171,300

Source: *Appliance Manufacturer*, February 1997, p. G-17.

Home Improvement Centers

★ 1597 ★
BEST-SELLING HOME CENTER ITEMS IN JAPAN
Ranked by: Market share based on annual sales, in percent. **Number listed:** 16
1. Housewares with 18.5%
2. Home improvement items, 12.0%
3. Household electric appliances, 11.1%
4. Car items, 9.7%
5. Horticulture items, 8.2%
6. Interior items, 7.0%
7. Pet items, 5.9%
8. Exterior items, 3.9%
9. Leisure sports items, 3.8%
10. Watches, cameras, etc., 3.6%

Source: *National Trade Data Bank*, May 8, 1997, p. IMI970507.

★ 1598 ★
HOME RENOVATION SPENDING IN CANADA, 1995
Ranked by: Spending, in billions of U.S. dollars.
Remarks: Atlantic Provinces include New Brunswick, Newfoundland, Nova Scotia, and Prince Edward Island.
Number listed: 7
1. Ontario with $5.0 billion
2. Quebec, $3.0
3. British Columbia, $1.9
4. Alberta, $1.0
5. Atlantic Provinces, $1.0
6. Manitoba, $0.4
7. Saskatchewan, $0.3
Source: *National Trade Data Bank*, January 16, 1997, p. ISA961201.

★ 1599 ★
TOP HOME CENTERS IN JAPAN
Ranked by: Annual sales, in billions of yen (¥). **Number listed:** 40
1. Keiyo with ¥136.06 billion
2. Nafco, ¥134.16
3. Tostemviva, ¥105.81
4. Cainz, ¥105.31
5. Kahma, ¥101.15
6. Homack, ¥89.24
7. Shimachu, ¥87.72
8. Tokyo Hands, ¥80.81
9. Komeri, ¥64.80
10. Kohnan Shoji, ¥49.31
Source: *National Trade Data Bank*, May 27, 1997, p. IMI970522.

Home Textiles
See: **Household Linens**

Honduras – see under individual headings

Hong Kong – see under individual headings

Hong Kong Stock Exchange

★ 1600 ★
LARGEST COMPANIES LISTED ON THE HONG KONG STOCK EXCHANGE, 1995
Ranked by: Market value, in billions of Hong Kong dollars (HK$). **Number listed:** 20
1. HSBC Holdings with HK$306.112 billion

2. Hutchison Whampoa, HK$170.254
3. HK Telecommunications, HK$153.908
4. Sun Hung Kai Properties, HK$147.027
5. Hang Seng Bank, HK$133.756
6. Cheung Kong (Holdings), HK$103.504
7. Swire Pacific, HK$87.890
8. Henderson Land Development Co., HK$74.373
9. China Light & Power Co., HK$70.867
10. New World Development Co., HK$56.697
Source: *GT Guide to World Equity Markets* (annual), Euromoney Publications, 1996, p. 161.

★ 1601 ★
MOST ACTIVELY TRADED SHARES ON THE HONG KONG STOCK EXCHANGE, 1995
Ranked by: Trading value, in billions of Hong Kong dollars (HK$). **Number listed:** 20
1. HSBC Holdings with HK$81.208 billion
2. Cheung Kong (Holdings), HK$44.846
3. Hutchison Whampoa, HK$42.600
4. Hong Kong Telecom, HK$37.571
5. Sun Hung Kai Properties, HK$34.905
6. Swire Pacific A, HK$28.340
7. Hang Seng Bank, HK$27.318
8. China Light, HK$25.384
9. Henderson Land Development, HK$22.375
10. New World Development, HK$21.247
Source: *GT Guide to World Equity Markets* (annual), Euromoney Publications, 1996, p. 161.

Hosiery

★ 1602 ★
LARGEST HOSIERY PRODUCERS WORLDWIDE, 1995
Ranked by: Turnover, in millions of U.S. dollars.
Remarks: Notes subsidiaries and brands. **Number listed:** 10
1. Sara Lee Corp with $1,714 million
2. Kunert AG, $378
3. Kayser-Roth Corp., $330
4. Golden Lady, $329
5. Valter Gruppe, $316
6. DIM, $262
7. Falke, $258
8. Wolford, $148
9. Ergee Gruppe, $147
10. CSP Internationale Industria, $134
Source: *Hosiery News*, May 1997, p. 31.

Hotels and Motels

★ 1603 ★

BEST HOTELS IN ASIA PACIFIC REGION

Ranked by: Survey of executives from 23 countries rating hotels on a score of 1 to 100. Scores were averaged. To qualify for ranking, hotels had to receive a substantial number of favorable reviews and have a minimum score of 75.7. **Remarks:** Notes global ranking. **Number listed:** 24

1. Oriental (Bangkok) with 91.5
2. Peninsula (Hong Kong), 89.4
3. Raffles (Singapore), 88.0
4. Mandarin Oriental (Hong Kong), 87.6
5. Regent (Hong Kong), 87.5
6. Shangri-La (Bangkok), 87.2
7. Grand Hyatt (Hong Kong), 86.2
8. Imperial (Tokyo), 86.0
9. Okura (Tokyo), 85.7
10. Shangri-La (Singapore), 85.7

Source: *Institutional Investor,* Best Hotels Worldwide (annual), September 1996, p. 203.

★ 1604 ★

BEST HOTELS WORLDWIDE, 1997

Ranked by: Results of a survey of assistants and in-house travel agents about their bosses' business trips over the past year. They were asked to nominate the top three hotels in individual cities. **Remarks:** See source for details on scoring. Notes best hotels by region. **Number listed:** 16

1. Mandarin Oriental (Hong Kong) with 70
2. Imperial (Tokyo), 49
3. Grand (Stockholm), 47
4. Arabella Grand (Frankfurt), 40
5. Principe di Savoia (Milan), 40
6. Shangri-La (Kuala Lumpur), 40
7. Okura (Tokyo), 38
8. Grand Hyatt (Jakarta), 36
9. Le Royal (Luxembourg), 36
10. Ritz (Madrid), 36

Source: *Euromoney*, Business Travel Survey (biannual), April 1997, p. 141.

★ 1605 ★

LARGE HOTEL CHAINS WORLDWIDE

Ranked by: Number of rooms. **Number listed:** 15

1. HFS with 509,500
2. Holiday Inn Worldwide, 369,738
3. Best Western International, 282,062
4. Accor, 268,256
5. Choice Hotels International, 249,926
6. Marriott International, 198,000
7. ITT Sheraton, 129,201
8. Hilton Hotels, 90,879

9. Promus, 88,117
10. CarlsonRadissonSAS, 84,607

Source: *Financial Times*, January 31, 1997, p. 19.

★ 1606 ★

TEMPORARY LODGINGS MARKET IN SOUTH AFRICA

Ranked by: Percent distribution, based on a total of 334,000 beds. **Number listed:** 10

1. Holiday flats and hostels with 23.1%
2. Resorts, 22.5%
3. Graded hotels, 15.9%
4. Non-graded hotels, 9.6%
5. Guest houses and farms, 9.0%
6. Game and hunting lodges, 7.1%
7. Timeshare, 6.6%
8. National and provincial parks, 2.9%
9. Bed and breakfasts, 2.4%
10. Executive apartments, 0.9%

Source: *Hotels*, August 1997, p. 6.

★ 1607 ★

TOP HOTELS BY REVENUES IN THAILAND, 1994

Ranked by: Revenue, in millions of bahts (Bt). **Remarks:** Includes profits and assets. **Number listed:** 8

1. Dusit Thani with Bt1,162.23 million
2. Shangri-La Hotel, Bt1,101.02
3. Oriental Hotel, Bt1,023.20
4. New Imperial Hotel, Bt942.88
5. Cental Plaza Hotel, Bt711.81
6. Turismo Thai, Bt692.59
7. Royal Orchid Hotel, Bt670.84
8. American Express, Bt636.21

Source: *Business Review*, December 1995, p. 182.

★ 1608 ★

TOP HOTELS IN LATIN AMERICA

Ranked by: Number of rooms. **Number listed:** 20

1. Fiesta Americana (Mexico City) with 7,996 rooms
2. Allegro Resorts (Domincan Republic), 7,880
3. Inter-Continental (London), 7,850
4. Best Western (Phoenix), 6,043
5. Holiday Inn Worldwide (Atlanta), 5,677
6. ITT Sheraton (Boston), 5,495
7. Former Situr Hotels (Mexico), 4,752
8. Westin-Caesar Parks (Seattle), 4,277
9. Camino Real (Mexico City), 3,561
10. Othon (Rio de Janeiro), 3,306

Source: *Hotel & Motel Management*, June 16, 1997, p. 28.

Hotels and Motels – Asia

★ 1609 ★
LARGEST HOTEL AND RESTAURANT COMPANIES IN ASIA
Ranked by: Sales, in thousands of U.S. dollars. **Remarks:** Also notes profit as a percent of sales. **Number listed:** 100

1. Skylark Co. Ltd. with $2,398,495 thousand
2. New World Development Co. Ltd., $2,257,575
3. Dia Kensetsu Co. Ltd., $2,103,174
4. Genting Bhd., $983,064
5. Denny's Japan Co. Ltd., $962,135
6. Fujita Kanko Inc., $944,669
7. Royal Co. Ltd., $900,223
8. Uehara Sei Shoji Co. Ltd., $770,922
9. Kentucky Fried Chicken Japan Ltd., $747,252
10. Resorts World Bhd., $735,328

Source: *Asia's 7,500 Largest Companies* (annual), Dun & Bradstreet, 1997, p. 91+.

★ 1610 ★
MOST ADMIRED HOTELS IN ASIA, 1997
Ranked by: Results of a questionnaire sent to more than 9,000 managers and CEOs chosen from the magazine's circulation and evaluated by Asia Market Intelligence, a research firm. **Remarks:** Respondents scored each company in terms of overall admirability, then on six attributes: quality of products, quality of management, contribution to local economy, record as an employer, growth potential and reputation for ethics. Also notes 1996 figures. **Number listed:** 10

1. Shangri-La Hotels with 7.93
2. Mandarin Oriental, 7.80
3. Dusit Thani Hotel, 7.45
4. Hyatt Hotels, 7.42
5. Resorts World, 7.29
6. Marriott, 7.22
7. Westin Hotels, 7.10
8. Sheraton Hotels, 7.05
9. New World Development, 7.04
10. Hilton International, 7.00

Source: *Asian Business,* Most Admired Companies in Asia (annual), May 1997, p. 30.

Hotels and Motels – Europe

★ 1611 ★
BEST HOTELS IN EUROPE, 1996
Ranked by: Survey of executives from 23 countries rating hotels on a score of 1 to 100. Scores were averaged. To qualify for ranking, hotels had to receive a substantial number of favorable reviews and have a minimum score of 75.7. **Remarks:** Notes global ranking. **Number listed:** 38

1. Ritz (Paris) with 90.6
2. Connaught (London), 90.5
3. Bristol (Paris), 87.1
4. Claridge's (London), 86.2
5. Schlosshotel Kronberg (Frankfurt), 86.1
6. Dolder Grand (Zurich), 85.8
7. Vier Jahreszeiten (Hamburg), 85.6
8. Le Richemond (Geneva), 85.2
9. Hyde Park (London), 85.0
10. Crillon (Paris), 84.8

Source: *Institutional Investor,* Best Hotels Worldwide (annual), September 1996, p. 202.

★ 1612 ★
TOP HOTELS AND RESTAURANTS IN EUROPE BY SALES, 1995
Ranked by: Sales, in thousands of U.S. dollars. **Remarks:** Notes percent change. **Number listed:** 100

1. Accor with $6,844,289 thousand
2. The Rank Organisation Plc., $4,059,006
3. Forte Plc., $2,777,950
4. Compass Group Plc., $2,338,509
5. Sodexho S.A., $2,337,383
6. McDonald's Deutschland Inc., $2,082,722
7. Toshiba International Finance (U.K.) Plc., $1,664,635
8. Club Mediterranee, $991,717
9. Generale De Restauration, $708,312
10. Queen's Moat Houses Plc., $704,968

Source: *Europe's 15,000 Largest Companies* (annual), Dun & Bradstreet, 1997, p. 682.

Hotels and Motels, International

★ 1613 ★
BEST HOTELS WORLDWIDE, 1996
Ranked by: Survey of executives from 23 countries rating hotels on a score of 1 to 100. Scores were averaged. To qualify for ranking, hotels had to receive a substantial number of favorable reviews and have a minimum score of 75.7. **Remarks:** Notes global ranking and 1995 scores. **Number listed:** 100

1. Bel-Air (Los Angeles) with 91.9

2. Oriental (Bangkok), 91.5
3. Mansion on Turtle Creek (Dallas), 91.3
4. Ritz (Paris), 90.6
5. Connaught (London), 90.5
6. Al Bustan Palace Inter-Continental (Muscat), 89.8
7. Mandarin Oriental (San Francisco), 89.6
8. Peninsula (Hong Kong), 89.4
9. Four Seasons (Boston), 88.5
10. Raffles (Singapore), 88.0

Source: *Institutional Investor,* Best Hotels Worldwide (annual), September 1997, p. 201.

Hours of Labor – Europe

★ 1614 ★

COUNTRIES WITH THE LONGEST WORK WEEK IN EUROPE, 1995

Ranked by: Average hours worked per week. **Remarks:** Data include only basic hours. Only figure for Greece includes overtime. **Number listed:** 14

1. United Kingdom with 43.8 hours
2. Portugal, 41.9
3. Greece, 40.8
4. Sweden, 40.7
5. Spain, 40.6
6. Ireland, 40.1
7. France, 40.1
8. Germany, 39.9
9. Luxembourg, 39.8
10. Netherlands, 39.6

Source: *Dawn*, September 15, 1996, p. 16.

★ 1615 ★

LENGTH OF WORKWEEK IN EUROPEAN NATIONS

Ranked by: Employees working more than 40 hours a week, as a percent of total workforce. **Number listed:** 5

1. United Kingdom with 47%
2. Italy, 41%
3. Spain, 31%
4. Germany, 14%
5. France, 10%

Source: *The Guardian*, June 26, 1997, p. 3.

Household Appliances

★ 1616 ★

BEST-SELLING APPLIANCES IN SINGAPORE

Ranked by: Market size, in millions of U.S. dollars. **Number listed:** 5

1. Refrigerators with $30.0 million

2. Washers, $21.9
3. Cookers, $11.3
4. Microwave Ovens, $5.0
5. Dishwashers, $0.6

Source: *National Trade Data Bank*, December 13, 1995, p. ISA9512.

★ 1617 ★

LEADING HOUSEHOLD APPLIANCE MANUFACTURERS IN WESTERN EUROPE, 1996

Ranked by: Market share, in percent. **Number listed:** 9

1. Electrolux with 21%
2. Bosch-Siemens, 17%
3. Whirlpool, 9%
4. Miele, 7%
5. El. Fi, 6%
6. Candy, 5%
7. Merloni, 5%
8. GDA, 3%
9. Other, 27%

Source: *Financial Times*, July 2, 1997, p. 13.

★ 1618 ★

MAJOR APPLIANCE DEMAND WORLDWIDE, 1995

Ranked by: Distribution, in percent. **Number listed:** 5

1. Cooking with 43.0%
2. Laundry, 22.5%
3. Refrigeration, 22.2%
4. Microwave ovens, 8.0%
5. Dishwashers, 4.3%

Source: *Appliance Manufacturer*, February 1997, p. G-2.

★ 1619 ★

TOP APPLIANCE BRANDS BY BRAND VALUE

Ranked by: Brand value, in millions of U.S. dollars. **Remarks:** Value was calculated using capital, ratio of capital to company sales, earnings, and corporate tax rate of the country where the parent company is located. See source for details. Brand value for Moulinex's Krups brand was "not meaningful." **Number listed:** 9

1. GE (General Electric) with $9,304 million
2. Black & Decker (Black & Decker), $2,282
3. Braun (Gillette), $1,756
4. Whirlpool (Whirlpool), $1,700
5. Electrolux (Electrolux), $805
6. Hoover (Maytag), $485
7. Mr. Coffee (Health o meter Products), $112
8. Moulinex (Moulinex), $68

Source: *Financial World,* World's Most Valuable Brands (annual), July 8, 1996, p. 56.

★ 1620 ★

TOP APPLIANCE MAKERS IN ECUADOR

Ranked by: Market share, in percent. **Number listed:** 4

1. Electrodomesticos Durex C.A. with 40.0%
2. Indurama, 30.0%

3. Ecasa, 18.0%
4. Fibroacero, 12.0%

Source: *National Trade Data Bank*, September 1995, p. ISA9509.

★ 1621 ★
TOP APPLIANCE MARKETS WORLDWIDE, 1995
Ranked by: Market volume, in millions of units. **Number listed:** 11
1. China with 74.1 million units
2. United States, 39.8
3. Japan, 22.8
4. Germany, 12.3
5. France, 9.5
6. United Kingdom, 9.3
7. Brazil, 8.4
8. Italy, 6.2
9. Spain, 5.4
10. India, 5.3

Source: *Appliance Manufacturer*, February 1997, p. G-4.

★ 1622 ★
TOP KITCHEN APPLIANCE MAKERS IN PANAMA
Ranked by: Market share, in percent. **Number listed:** 10
1. Black and Decker with 50.0%
2. Hamilton Beach, 10.0%
3. Oster, 7.0%
4. Sankey, 7.0%
5. Proctor Silex, 5.0%
6. Sunbeam, 5.0%
7. Daewoo, 3.0%
8. Hitachi, 3.0%
9. Toastmaster, 3.0%
10. Other, 7.0%

Source: *National Trade Data Bank*, March 2, 1996, p. ISA9407.

★ 1623 ★
TOP SELLING GAS APPLIANCES IN SPAIN, 1995
Ranked by: Sales, in millions of U.S. dollars. **Remarks:** Includes unit sales. **Number listed:** 11
1. Water heaters with $236.0 million
2. Heating boilers, $229.0
3. Cooking tops, $125.0
4. Ranges, $70.8
5. Vitroceramic tops, $22.5
6. Portable stoves, $5.3
7. Ovens, $4.0
8. Room heaters, $3.9
9. Dishwashers, $1.2
10. Dryers, $1.2

Source: *National Trade Data Bank*, December 4, 1995, p. IMI951204.

Household Cleaning Products Industry
See: **Cleaning Products Industry**

Household Income
See: **Income**

Household Linens

★ 1624 ★
BEST-SELLING LINEN IN FRANCE
Ranked by: Consumption, in thousands of items. **Number listed:** 12
1. Flannels with 37,209 thousand items
2. Hand towels, 30,999
3. Dusters, 23,454
4. Sheets, 23,339
5. Pillow cases, 16,483
6. Napkins, 9,635
7. Duvet covers, 5,585
8. Duvets, eiderdown, 4,848
9. Blankets, 4,131
10. Tablecloths and sets of linen, 3,885

Source: *National Trade Data Bank*, March 2, 1996, p. ISA9406.

★ 1625 ★
LEADING PRODUCERS OF BED AND BATH LINEN IN SOUTH AFRICA
Ranked by: No specific criteria provided. **Number listed:** 6
1. Romoatex Home Textiles
2. Berg River Textiles
3. David Whitehead
4. Da Gama
5. Frame Textiles
6. Mooi River Textiles

Source: *National Trade Data Bank*, April 14, 1997, p. IMI970411.

Household Products
See: **Housewares**

Housewares

★ 1626 ★
TOP HOUSEHOLD PRODUCTS BRANDS BY BRAND VALUE

Ranked by: Brand value, in millions of U.S. dollars. **Remarks:** Value was calculated using capital, ratio of capital to company sales, earnings, and corporate tax rate of the country where the parent company is located. See source for details. **Number listed:** 19

1. Tupperware (Tupperware) with $1,634 million
2. Rubbermaid (Rubbermaid), $1,504
3. Clorox (Clorox), $1,451
4. Tide (Procter & Gamble), $978
5. Kleenex (Kimberly-Clark), $685
6. Ajax (Colgate-Palmolive), $585
7. Tefal (Groupe SEB), $583
8. Reynolds (Reynolds Metals), $527
9. Cheer (Procter & Gamble), $463
10. WD-40 (WD-40), $216

Source: *Financial World,* World's Most Valuable Brands (annual), July 8, 1996, p. 62.

Hungary – see under individual headings

Ice Cream, Ices, etc.

★ 1627 ★
ICE CREAM MARKET IN THE PHILIPPINES

Ranked by: Market share, in percent. **Number listed:** 4

1. Magnolia (San Miguel) with 47.6%
2. Selecta, 31.2%
3. Purefoods, 12.8%
4. Presto, 8.4%

Source: *Asiaweek*, May 10, 1996, p. 52.

★ 1628 ★
JAPAN'S TOP ICE CREAM MAKERS

Ranked by: Market share, in percent. **Number listed:** 6

1. Meiji Milk Products with 13.6%
2. Morinaga Milk Industry, 13.0%
3. Ezaki Glico, 12.7%
4. Snow Brand Milk Products, 9.9%
5. Lotte, 9.7%
6. Other, 41.1%

Source: *Nikkei Weekly*, August 5, 1996, p. 10.

★ 1629 ★
TOP CHILDREN'S IMPULSE BRANDS IN THE UNITED KINGDOM, 1996

Ranked by: Top brands. **Remarks:** The source provides no criteria for these rankings. **Number listed:** 12

1. Twister
2. Rowntree's Fruit Pastil-Lolly
3. Calippo
4. Toppit
5. Fab
6. Nobbly Bobbly
7. Mr. Men
8. Mister Long
9. Nerds
10. Kick Off

Source: *The Sunday Post*, June 29, 1997, p. 27.

★ 1630 ★
TOP ICE CREAM MAKERS IN NORWAY

Ranked by: Market share, in percent. **Number listed:** 4

1. Norske Iskrem (NI) with 50.0%
2. Henning Olsen, 34.0%
3. Drammen, 14.0%
4. Other, 2.0%

Source: *National Trade Data Bank*, May 27, 1996, p. IMI950406.

★ 1631 ★
TOP ICE CREAM MAKERS IN PUNJAB

Ranked by: Installed capacity, in millions of liters. **Number listed:** 9

1. Lever Brothers Ltd. with 5.0 million liters
2. Pakistan Industrial Promoters, 5.0
3. Kaghan Food Products, 2.4
4. Shah Shams Ltd., 1.8
5. Yummy Milk Products, 1.2
6. Pixie Ice Cream Ltd., 0.7
7. Happy Ice Cream Ltd., 0.2
8. Hotels and restaurants, 1.0
9. Unorganized sectors, 3.2

Source: *Economic Review* no. 1, 1996, p. 37.

★ 1632 ★
TOP ICE CREAM MANUFACTURERS IN THE UNITED KINGDOM, 1996

Ranked by: Market share, in percent. **Number listed:** 4

1. Wall's with 42%
2. Nestle Lyons Maid, 10%
3. Mars, 7%
4. Others, 41%

Source: *The Sunday Post*, June 29, 1997, p. 27.

★ 1633 ★
TOP MULTI-PACKS IN THE UNITED KINGDOM, 1996
Ranked by: Top brands. **Remarks:** The source provides no criteria for these rankings. **Number listed:** 10
1. Magnum
2. Mars Bar
3. Cornetto
4. Solero
5. Fab
6. Feast
7. Rowntree's Fruit Pastil-Lolly
8. Mini Juice
9. Mini Milk
10. Snickers
Source: *The Sunday Post*, June 29, 1997, p. 27.

Iceland – see under individual headings

Illinois – see under individual headings

Imaging Systems

★ 1634 ★
ALGERIA'S IMAGING MARKET
Ranked by: Market share, in percent. **Number listed:** 3
1. Siemens/TUR with 45.0%
2. Medicor, 25.0%
3. Other, 30.0%
Source: *National Trade Data Bank*, May 27, 1996, p. ISA9311.

★ 1635 ★
TOP IMAGING BRANDS BY BRAND VALUE
Ranked by: Brand value, in millions of U.S. dollars. **Remarks:** Value was calculated using capital, ratio of capital to company sales, earnings, and corporate tax rate of the country where the parent company is located. See source for details. Brand value for Nikon was "not meaningful." **Number listed:** 6
1. Kodak (Eastman Kodak) with $13,267 million
2. Canon (Canon), $4,079
3. Xerox (Xerox), $2,920
4. Fuji (Fuji Photo Film), $1,991
5. Polaroid (Polaroid), $477
Source: *Financial World*, World's Most Valuable Brands (annual), July 8, 1996, p. 62.

Income

★ 1636 ★
PER CAPITA INCOME IN FIVE BEST CITIES FOR WORK AND FAMILY
Ranked by: Per capita income, in U.S. dollars. **Remarks:** Table shows ranking based on Arthur Andersen's Survey of Major Cities. **Number listed:** 5
1. Toronto, Canada with $21,000
2. Paris, France, $17,320
3. London, England, $14,535
4. Singapore, $8,782
5. Hong Kong, $8,000
Source: *Fortune*, November 11, 1996, p. 133.

★ 1637 ★
WORLD'S WEALTHIEST COUNTRIES
Ranked by: Per-capita income, in U.S. dollars. **Remarks:** A new ranking (shown in parentheses after country name) represents the recalculated wealth according to the World Bank's additional criteria: including natural resources; machinery, building, highways, and other produced assets; human resources; and so-called social capital-- the value added by families and communities. **Number listed:** 15
1. Luxembourg (3) with $36,650
2. Switzerland (4), $36,330
3. Japan (5), $29,770
4. Sweden (6), $27,600
5. Denmark (10), $26,470
6. Norway (11), $25,510
7. Iceland (7), $24,550
8. Austria (16), $23,330
9. United States (12), $23,260
10. France (13), $22,800
Source: *USA TODAY*, September 18, 1995, p. 4B.

India – see under individual headings

Indonesia – see under individual headings

Industrial Designers – United Kingdom

★ 1638 ★

LEADING INDUSTRIAL DESIGN CONSULTANTS IN THE UNITED KINGDOM, 1995

Ranked by: Turnover, in thousands of British pounds (£). **Remarks:** Also notes 1994 turnover, percentage change, and staff numbers. **Number listed:** 111

1. Landor Associates with £32,000 thousand
2. IDEO, £24,153
3. Imagination, £22,281
4. Fitch, £15,933
5. Dragon International, £13,400
6. Siegel & Gale Worldwide, £13,050
7. Interbrand, £12,160
8. Carre Noir, £11,448
9. Holmes & Marchant Design Companies, £11,269
10. Wolff Olins, £10,248

Source: *Marketing*, Design Consultancies (annual), July 25, 1996, p. 23.

★ 1639 ★

TOP CORPORATE IDENTITY DESIGN CONSULTANTS IN THE UNITED KINGDOM, 1995

Ranked by: Corporate identity turnover, in thousands of British pounds (£). **Remarks:** Also notes total turnover. **Number listed:** 45

1. Siegel & Gale Worldwide with £13,050 thousand
2. Wolff Olins, £10,248
3. Sampsons Tyrrell Enterprise, £8,550
4. Interbrand, £7,296
5. Landor Associates, £7,200
6. Newell & Sorrell, £4,400
7. Lambie Nairn/Tutssels, £4,016
8. Carre Noir, £3,263
9. Dragon International, £3,082
10. Coley Porter Bell, £2,489

Source: *Marketing*, Design Consultancies (annual), July 25, 1996, p. 27.

★ 1640 ★

TOP CORPORATE LITERATURE DESIGN CONSULTANTS IN THE UNITED KINGDOM, 1995

Ranked by: Literature turnover, in thousands of British pounds (£). **Remarks:** Also notes total turnover. **Number listed:** 34

1. Holmes & Marchant Design Companies with £7,776 thousand
2. Landor Associates, £7,200
3. Pauffley PRL, £5,275
4. Minale Tattersfield Design Strategy, £3,300
5. Wunderman Cato Johnson, £2,947
6. The Tayburn Group, £2,759

7. Stocks Austin Sice, £2,710
8. Basten Greenhill Andrews, £2,268
9. Imagination, £2,228
10. Dragon International, £2,144

Source: *Marketing*, Design Consultancies (annual), July 25, 1996, p. 29.

★ 1641 ★

TOP INTERIOR DESIGN CONSULTANTS IN THE UNITED KINGDOM, 1995

Ranked by: Design turnover, in thousands of British pounds (£). **Remarks:** Also notes total turnover. **Number listed:** 28

1. Fitch with £5,258 thousand
2. Morgan Lovell, £5,170
3. Landor Associates, £4,800
4. Imagination, £3,788
5. Checkland Kindleysides, £2,544
6. Carre Noir, £1,949
7. Design House, £1,530
8. RPA Europe, £1,501
9. Crabtree Hall/Plan Creatif, £1,370
10. Din Associates, £1,211

Source: *Marketing*, Design Consultancies (annual), July 25, 1996, p. 25.

★ 1642 ★

TOP PACKAGING DESIGN CONSULTANTS IN THE UNITED KINGDOM, 1995

Ranked by: Packaging turnover, in thousands of British pounds (£). **Remarks:** Also notes total turnover. **Number listed:** 31

1. Landor Associates with £11,200 thousand
2. Dragon International, £6,968
3. Design Bridge, £6,139
4. Carre Noir, £5,152
5. Wickens Tutt Southgate, £3,522
6. Holmes & Marchant Design Companies, £3,493
7. Coley Porter Bell, £3,438
8. Jones Knowles Ritchie, £3,367
9. PI Design International, £3,188
10. Ziggurat, £2,462

Source: *Marketing*, Design Consultancies (annual), July 25, 1996, p. 25.

Industrial Equipment Industry

★ 1643 ★

ASIA'S TOP HEAVY EQUIPMENT FIRMS, 1995

Ranked by: Sales, in millions of U.S. dollars. **Remarks:** Includes profits, profits as a percentage of sales and assets, and overall sales rank. **Number listed:** 20

1. Mitsubishi Heavy Industries with $32,066.4 million
2. Kawasaki Heavy Industries, $11,548.4
3. Ishikawajima-Harima, $11,536.6
4. Hitachi Zosen, $6,356.1
5. Kinden, $5,974.4
6. Kandenko, $5,487.3
7. Sumitomo Heavy Industries, $5,315.6
8. Hyundai Heavy Industries, $5,070.1
9. Chiyoda Corp., $4,142.8
10. Mitsui Engineering & Shipbuilding, $4,046.9

Source: *Asiaweek*, The Asiaweek 1,000, November 22, 1996, p. 160.

★ 1644 ★

ASIA'S TOP INDUSTRIAL/FARM EQUIPMENT MAKERS, 1995

Ranked by: Sales, in millions of U.S. dollars. **Remarks:** Includes profits, profits as a percentage of sales and assets, and overall sales rank. **Number listed:** 20

1. Kubota with $11,393.6 million
2. Komatsu Ltd., $10,624.4
3. Fuji Electric, $9,466.4
4. Omron, $5,584.6
5. Toyoda Automatic Loom, $5,308.7
6. Ebara Corp., $5,219.7
7. Daewoo Heavy Industries, $5,138.3
8. NSK, $4,677.9
9. Daikin Industries, $4,515.6
10. Koyo Seiko, $3,430.5

Source: *Asiaweek*, The Asiaweek 1,000, November 22, 1996, p. 160.

★ 1645 ★

CANADA'S FORKLIFT MARKET, 1995

Ranked by: Market share, in percent. **Number listed:** 5

1. Toyota with 25.0%
2. Hyster, 23.0%
3. Nissan, 13.0%
4. Caterpillar, 10.0%
5. Komatsu, 5.0%

Source: *National Trade Data Bank*, March 5, 1996, p. ISA9607.

★ 1646 ★

LARGEST INDUSTRIAL AND FARM EQUIPMENT COMPANIES, 1995

Ranked by: Revenue, in millions of U.S. dollars. **Remarks:** Notes profits and global rank. **Number listed:** 8

1. Mitsubishi Heavy Industries (Japan) with $31,249 million
2. Mannesmann (Germany), $22,395
3. Caterpillar (United States), $16,072
4. BTR (United Kingdom), $15,431
5. Ishikawajima-Harima (Japan), $11,243
6. Kubota (Japan), $11,103
7. Komatsu (Japan), $10,354
8. Deere (United States), $10,291

Source: *Fortune,* The Global 500: World's Biggest Corporations (annual), August 5, 1996, p. F-21.

★ 1647 ★

LEADING DOMESTIC MANUFACTURERS OF FORKLIFTS IN JAPAN, 1996

Ranked by: Market share, in percent. **Number listed:** 6

1. Toyota Motor with 35%
2. Komatsu Lift, 19%
3. Nippon Yusoki, 10%
4. Nissan Motor, 10%
5. Toyo Unpanki, 10%
6. Other, 16%

Source: *National Trade Data Bank*, May 29, 1997, p. IMI970529.

★ 1648 ★

TOP INDUSTRIAL EQUIPMENT MAKERS IN JAPAN

Ranked by: Income, in millions of yen (¥). **Number listed:** 10

1. Nippon Motorola with ¥11,888 million
2. Tokyo Electron, ¥8,730
3. Intel Japan, ¥7,973
4. J.S.T. Mfg., ¥6,458
5. Ryosan, ¥6,302
6. Inaba Denkisangyo, ¥6,040
7. Nippon Totor, ¥4,915
8. Fujitsu Business Systems, ¥4,576
9. Ryoyo Electro, ¥4,403
10. Applied Materials Japan, ¥4,397

Source: *Tokyo Business Today*, August 1995, p. 27.

★ 1649 ★

TOP INDUSTRIAL MACHINERY PRODUCERS IN SOUTH KOREA, 1996

Ranked by: Sales for the first six months of 1996, in hundred million won (W). **Number listed:** 21

1. Daewoo Heavy Ind. with W25,421.9 hundred million
2. Halla Climate Control Company, W2,338.5

3. Hanwha Machinery, W2,282.9
4. Dae Dong Ind., W2,013.1
5. Ssangyong Heavy Ind., W1,494.3
6. Tong Yang Mool San, W1,352.3
7. Hyundai Elevator Company Ltd., W1,163.6
8. Doosan Machinery, W851.6
9. Soosan Heavy Ind., W602.6
10. Kyung Dong Boiler, W490.9

Source: *Business Korea*, October 1996, p. 37.

Industrial Gases
See: **Gases**

Industries
See: **Industry**

Industries, Manufacturing
See: **Manufacturing Industries**

Industry

★ 1650 ★
TOP INDUSTRIES BY ASSETS, 1995
Ranked by: Assets, in millions of U.S. dollars. **Remarks:** Notes number of companies in industry. **Number listed:** 45

1. Commercial banks with $15,566,920 million
2. Insurance: life and health (mutual), $2,377,808
3. Insurance: property and casualty (stock), $1,877,120
4. Motor vehicles and parts, $1,184,635
5. Electronics, electrical equipment, $1,089,473
6. Insurance: life and health (stock), $1,071,648
7. Telecommunications, $916,297
8. Petroleum refining, $846,264
9. Electric and gas utilities, $796,869
10. Diversified financials, $689,855

Source: *Fortune,* The Global 500: World's Biggest Corporations (annual), August 5, 1996, p. F-27.

★ 1651 ★
TOP INDUSTRIES BY EMPLOYEES, 1995
Ranked by: Number of employees **Remarks:** Notes number of companies in industry. **Number listed:** 45

1. Electronics, electrical equipment with 4,008,030
2. Motor vehicles and parts, 3,471,164
3. Telecommunications, 2,425,249
4. Commercial banks, 2,417,587

5. General merchandisers, 2,348,856
6. Mail, package, and freight delivery, 2,330,622
7. Food and drug stores, 2,243,297
8. Chemicals, 1,123,225
9. Petroleum refining, 1,063,294
10. Food, 1,028,762

Source: *Fortune,* The Global 500: World's Biggest Corporations (annual), August 5, 1996, p. F-27.

★ 1652 ★
TOP INDUSTRIES BY PROFITS, 1995
Ranked by: Profits, in millions of U.S. dollars. **Remarks:** Notes number of companies in industry. **Number listed:** 45

1. Petroleum refining with $34,814 million
2. Electronics, electrical equipment, $24,336
3. Commercial banks, $24,074
4. Pharmaceuticals, $21,302
5. Motor vehicles and parts, $20,080
6. Chemicals, $17,840
7. Insurance: life and health (mutual), $15,686
8. Insurance: property and casualty (stock), $14,108
9. Telecommunications, $13,793
10. Electric and gas utilities, $9,951

Source: *Fortune,* The Global 500: World's Biggest Corporations (annual), August 5, 1996, p. F-27.

★ 1653 ★
TOP INDUSTRIES BY REVENUE, 1995
Ranked by: Revenue, in millions of U.S. dollars. **Remarks:** Notes number of companies in industry. **Number listed:** 45

1. Trading with $1,378,179 million
2. Commercial banks, $1,173,039
3. Motor vehicles and parts, $1,087,251
4. Electronics, electrical equipment, $889,206
5. Petroleum refining, $849,039
6. Insurance: life and health (mutual), $520,962
7. Telecommunications, $513,285
8. Insurance: property and casualty (stock), $452,661
9. Food and drug stores, $429,485
10. General merchandisers, $386,074

Source: *Fortune,* The Global 500: World's Biggest Corporations (annual), August 5, 1996, p. F-27.

★ 1654 ★
TOP INDUSTRIES BY STOCKHOLDERS' EQUITY, 1995
Ranked by: Stockholders' equity, in millions of U.S. dollars. **Remarks:** Notes number of companies in industry. **Number listed:** 45

1. Commercial banks with $611,218 million
2. Petroleum refining, $327,694
3. Electronics, electrical equipment, $267,171

4. Telecommunications, $252,682
5. Motor vehicles and parts, $233,468
6. Electric and gas utilities, $177,473
7. Insurance: property and casualty (stock), $140,449
8. Chemicals, $117,013
9. Metals, $68,295
10. Computers, office equipment, $68,026

Source: *Fortune,* The Global 500: World's Biggest Corporations (annual), August 5, 1996, p. F-27.

Infants' Food

★ 1655 ★
TOP PRODUCERS OF CEREAL FOR INFANTS IN ST. PETERSBURG, RUSSIA
Ranked by: Market share, in percent. **Number listed:** 6
1. Baby-papa with 20.0%
2. Nestle, 18.0%
3. Danone, 15.0%
4. Heinz, 15.0%
5. Hipp, 9.0%
6. Other, 23.0%

Source: *National Trade Data Bank,* March 20, 1997, p. IMI970318.

★ 1656 ★
TOP PRODUCERS OF FRUIT PUREES FOR INFANTS IN ST. PETERSBURG, RUSSIA
Ranked by: Market share, in percent. **Number listed:** 7
1. Nestle with 18.0%
2. Hipp, 14.0%
3. Danone, 13.0%
4. Nutrisia, 11.0%
5. Heinz, 9.0%
6. Bona, 26.0%
7. Other, 26.0%

Source: *National Trade Data Bank,* March 20, 1997, p. IMI970318.

★ 1657 ★
TOP PRODUCERS OF MILK FOR INFANTS IN ST. PETERSBURG, RUSSIA
Ranked by: Market share, in percent. **Number listed:** 7
1. Nutrisia with 20.0%
2. Bona, 10.0%
3. Danone, 10.0%
4. Nestle, 10.0%
5. Valio, 10.0%
6. Hipp, 9.0%
7. Other, 31.0%

Source: *National Trade Data Bank,* March 20, 1997, p. IMI970318.

Infants' Supplies – United Kingdom

★ 1658 ★
TOP BABY PRODUCTS IN THE UNITED KINGDOM, 1995
Ranked by: Estimated sales, in millions of British pounds (£). **Remarks:** Notes ad agency and spending. **Number listed:** 10
1. Pampers nappies (Procter & Gamble) with £Over 197 million
2. Huggies nappies (Kimberly-Clarke), £40-50
3. Heinz baby foods (SMA Nutrition), £35-40
4. SMA Milks (HJ Heinz), £35-40
5. Cow & Gate infant milks (Cow & Gate Nutricia), £25-30
6. Cow & Gate baby meals (Cow & Gate Nutricia), £15-20
7. Farleys foods (HJ Heinz), £10-15
8. Milupa baby foods (Cow & Gate), £10-15
9. Baby Fresh Wipes (Kimberly-Clark), £5-10
10. Pampers Baby Wipes (Procter & Gamble), £5-10

Source: *Marketing,* July 4, 1996, p. 26.

Information Technology

★ 1659 ★
ASIA'S TOP I.T. FIRMS, 1995
Ranked by: Sales, in millions of U.S. dollars. **Remarks:** Includes profits, profits as a percentage of sales and assets, and overall sales rank. **Number listed:** 20
1. Hitachi Ltd. with $86,368.4 million
2. Toshiba Corp., $54,434.3
3. NEC Corp., $46,748.8
4. Fujitsu Ltd., $39,995.4
5. Mitsubishi Electric Corp., $37,331.1
6. Canon, $23,023.9
7. IBM Japan, $13,913.8
8. Ricoh, $11,833.2
9. Fuji Xerox, $8,413.4
10. OKI Electric Industry, $7,955.9

Source: *Asiaweek,* The Asiaweek 1,000, November 22, 1996, p. 161.

★ 1660 ★
LEADING I.T. MULTINATIONALS IN INDIA
Ranked by: Revenue, in millions of rupees (Rs). **Number listed:** 40
1. HP with Rs5,780 million
2. IBM, Rs3,560
3. Acer, Rs3,200
4. Intel, Rs2,700
5. Digital, Rs2,590

6. Compaq, Rs2,000
7. Sun, Rs1,700
8. Microsoft, Rs1,120
9. Apple, Rs1,100
10. Citizen, Rs810

Source: *Financial Times*, November 6, 1996, p. FT3.

Infrastructure (Economics), International

★ 1661 ★
COST OF AIR CONNECTIONS IN LATIN AMERICAN COUNTRIES

Ranked by: Countries rated 1 to 10 on the cost to make air connections. A rating of "1" denotes very expensive connections; "5" is average; "10" is least expensive. **Number listed:** 7

1. Argentina with 7
2. Colombia, 7
3. Mexico, 7
4. Peru, 7
5. Brazil, 6
6. Venezuela, 6
7. Chile, 4

Source: *Business Latin America*, October 7, 1996, p. 8.

★ 1662 ★
COST OF FREIGHT CONNECTIONS IN LATIN AMERICAN COUNTRIES

Ranked by: Countries rated 1 to 10 on the cost to make freight connections. A rating of "1" denotes very expensive connections; "5" is average; "10" is least expensive. **Number listed:** 7

1. Argentina with 8
2. Colombia, 8
3. Venezuela, 7
4. Mexico, 6
5. Peru, 6
6. Brazil, 6
7. Chile, 5

Source: *Business Latin America*, October 7, 1996, p. 8.

★ 1663 ★
QUALITY OF RAIL SERVICE IN LATIN AMERICAN COUNTRIES

Ranked by: Countries rated 1 to 10 on the quality of rail service. A rating of "1" denotes low quality; "5" is average; "10" is high. **Number listed:** 7

1. Argentina with 5
2. Colombia, 5
3. Mexico, 3
4. Brazil, 2
5. Chile, 2
6. Peru, 1

7. Venezuela, 1

Source: *Business Latin America*, October 7, 1996, p. 8.

Insecticides

★ 1664 ★
LEADING INSECTICIDE COMPANIES

Ranked by: Sales, in millions of dollars. **Remarks:** Figure for American Cyanamid was unavailable. **Number listed:** 9

1. Bayer with $1,065 million
2. AgrEvo, $699
3. Rhone-Poulenc, $670
4. Dow Elanco, $520
5. Zeneca, $510
6. FMC, $500
7. DuPont, $230
8. Ciba, $180
9. BASF, $80

Source: *Chemical Week*, August 7, 1996, p. 29.

★ 1665 ★
TOP HOUSEHOLD INSECTICIDES SALES IN SPAIN, 1995

Ranked by: Market share, in percent. **Number listed:** 5

1. Cruz Verde with 31.2%
2. Zelnova, 13.9%
3. Johnson's Wax, 13.4%
4. Benckiser, 10.5%
5. Bayer, 9.5%
6. Other, 21.5%

Source: *National Trade Data Bank*, June 25, 1996, p. IMI960618.

Institutional Investments

★ 1666 ★
LARGEST INSTITUTIONAL INVESTORS BASED IN THE UNITED KINGDOM

Ranked by: Funds under management, in billions of British pounds (£). **Number listed:** 10

1. Prudential with £91 billion
2. Schroder, £88
3. Mercury, £86
4. Morgan Grenfell, £69
5. Commercial Union, £68
6. Fleming, £58
7. Invesco, £58
8. PDFM, £57
9. Gartmore, £51
10. Standard Life, £48

Source: *Financial Times*, May 28, 1997, p. 7.

★ 1667 ★

LARGEST INSTITUTIONAL INVESTORS IN SOUTH KOREA, 1995

Ranked by: Assets, in millions of U.S. dollars. **Remarks:** Notes foreign and domestic bonds and equities. **Number listed:** 30

1. Korea Investment Trust Co. with $29,811 million
2. Samsung Life Insurance Co., $29,024
3. Daehan Investment Trust Co., $27,466
4. Kyobo Life Insurance Co., $17,396
5. Citizens Investment Trust Management Co., $15,962
6. Cho Hung Bank, $15,614
7. National Pension Corp., $15,500
8. Korea First Bank, $14,611
9. Korea Exchange Bank, $14,337
10. Commercial Bank of Korea, $14,052

Source: *Institutional Investor,* Asia's Biggest Institutional Investors (annual), September 1996, p. 144.

★ 1668 ★

LARGEST INVESTMENT TRUST FUND MANAGERS BASED IN THE UNITED KINGDOM

Ranked by: Investment trusts, in billions of British pounds (£). **Number listed:** 10

1. Henderson with £5.1 billion
2. Fleming, £4.4
3. 3i, £4.1
4. Foreign & Colonial, £4.0
5. Edinburgh Fund Managers, £3.3
6. Baillie Gifford, £2.2
7. Martin Currie, £2.0
8. Alliance Trust, £1.8
9. Murray Johnstone, £1.7
10. John Govett, £1.7

Source: *Financial Times*, May 28, 1997, p. 7.

★ 1669 ★

TOP FUND MANAGING CITIES

Ranked by: Funds, in billions of U.S. dollars, managed by companies in international financial centers. **Number listed:** 20

1. Tokyo with $1,524.4 billion
2. London, $1,016.5
3. New York, $896.4
4. Boston, $603.8
5. Zurich, $411.0
6. San Francisco, $289.0
7. Geneva, $264.0
8. Paris, $261.1
9. Los Angeles, $242.6
10. Chicago, $179.4

Source: *The European*, September 19, 1996, p. 32.

★ 1670 ★

WHERE OFFSHORE FUNDS ARE BASED

Ranked by: Location of offshore accounts, in percent. **Remarks:** An estimated $3,000 billion is invested offshore. **Number listed:** 11

1. Luxembourg with 55%
2. Guernsey, 8%
3. Jersey, 6%
4. Bermuda, 5%
5. British Virgin Islands, 5%
6. Cayman Islands, 5%
7. Isle of Man, 5%
8. Republic of Ireland, 5%
9. Hong Kong, 4%
10. Bahamas, 1%

Source: *The European*, October 2, 1996, p. 24.

Institutional Investments – Australia

★ 1671 ★

LARGEST INSTITUTIONAL INVESTORS IN AUSTRALIA, 1995

Ranked by: Assets, in millions of U.S. dollars. **Remarks:** Notes foreign and domestic bonds and equities. Data includes New Zealand. **Number listed:** 8

1. AMP Group with $64,277 million
2. Bankers Trust Funds Management, $22,128
3. Lend Lease Investment Management, $19,736
4. National Mutual Funds Management, $17,292
5. State Superannuation Investment & Management Corp., $12,795
6. CBA Financial Services, $10,386
7. Colonial Investment Management, $9,921
8. Macquarie Investment, $9,512

Source: *Institutional Investor,* Asia's Biggest Institutional Investors (annual), September 1996, p. 138.

Institutional Investments – China

★ 1672 ★

LARGEST INSTITUTIONAL INVESTORS IN CHINA, 1995

Ranked by: Total assets, in millions of U.S. dollars. **Number listed:** 10

1. Industrial & Commercial Bank of China with $11,241 million
2. People's Insurance Co. of China, $7,950
3. Bank of China, $1,640
4. China International Trust & Investment Corp., $1,629
5. Shenyin and Wanguo Securities Co., $1,428
6. China Pacific Insurance Co., $1,008

7. Southern Securities Co., $981
8. Ping An Insurance Co. of China, $916
9. Shanghai Haitong Securities Co., $829
10. China Xuaxia Securities Co., $805

Source: *Institutional Investor - International Edition,* Asia's Biggest Institutional Investors (annual), September 1996, p. 183.

Institutional Investments – Hong Kong

★ 1673 ★
LARGEST INSTITUTIONAL INVESTORS IN HONG KONG, 1995
Ranked by: Total assets, in millions of U.S. dollars. **Number listed:** 15

1. Hong Kong Government SAR Land Fund with $13,000 million
2. Hong Kong Housing Authority, $3,045
3. Grant/Subsidised Schools Provident Fund, $2,500
4. HSBC Life (International), $2,069
5. Royal Hong Kong Jockey Club, $1,552
6. Lloyd George Management (Hong Kong), $1,268
7. CEF Investment Management, $802
8. Swire Group, $801
9. University of Hong Kong, $783
10. Hongkong & Shanghai Banking Corp., $744

Source: *Institutional Investor - International Edition,* Asia's Biggest Institutional Investors (annual), September 1996, p. 182.

Institutional Investments – India

★ 1674 ★
LARGEST INSTITUTIONAL INVESTORS IN INDIA, 1995
Ranked by: Total assets, in millions of dollars. **Number listed:** 10

1. Life Insurance Corp. of India Group with $18,170 million
2. Unit Trust of India, $16,648
3. Employees' Provident Fund, $13,057
4. Coal Miners Provident Fund, $2,706
5. General Insurance Corp. of India Group, $1,252
6. Canbank Investment Management Services, $1,094
7. SBI Funds Management, $868
8. Industrial Credit & Investment Corp. of India, $736
9. BOI Asset Management Co., $357

10. Housing Development Finance Corp., $274

Source: *Institutional Investor - International Edition,* Asia's Biggest Institutional Investors (annual), September 1996, p. 182.

Institutional Investments – Indonesia

★ 1675 ★
LARGEST INSTITUTIONAL INVESTORS IN INDONESIA, 1995
Ranked by: Total assets, in millions of dollars. **Number listed:** 15

1. Astek (Employees Social Security System) with $1,428 million
2. Taspen, $1,399
3. PLN Pension Fund, $590
4. Bank Negara Indonesia 1946 Pension Fund, $437
5. Bank Indonesia Pension Fund, $431
6. Danareksa Fund Management, $386
7. Pertamina Pension Fund, $376
8. Asuransi Jiwasraya, $365
9. Bank Exim Pension Fund, $306
10. Telkom Pension Fund, $261

Source: *Institutional Investor - International Edition,* Asia's Biggest Institutional Investors (annual), September 1996, p. 186.

Institutional Investments – Japan

★ 1676 ★
LARGEST INSTITUTIONAL INVESTORS IN JAPAN, 1995
Ranked by: Assets, in millions of U.S. dollars. **Remarks:** Notes foreign and domestic bonds and equities. **Number listed:** 40

1. Kampo with $865,422 million
2. Nippon Life Insurance Co. Group, $362,412
3. Dai-ichi Mutual Life Insurance Group, $261,783
4. Zenkyoren, $238,250
5. Sumitomo Mutual Life Insurance Group, $223,134
6. Nempuku, $204,588
7. Meiji Mutual Life Insurance Group, $160,606
8. Nomura Securities Group, $121,516
9. Asahi Mutual Life Insurance Group, $120,007
10. Nikko Securities Group, $103,554

Source: *Institutional Investor,* Asia's Biggest Institutional Investors (annual), September 1996, p. 136.

★ 1677 ★
LARGEST INSTITUTIONAL INVESTORS IN JAPAN, 1995
Ranked by: Total assets, in millions of dollars. **Remarks:** Also notes domestic equities, other asian equities, other foreign equities, domestic bonds, property, cash, and other assets. **Number listed:** 40
1. Kampo (Postal Life Insurance Bureau) with $865,422 million
2. Nippon Life Insurance Co. Group, $362,412
3. Dai-ichi Mutual Life Insurance Group, $261,783
4. Zenkyoren, $238,250
5. Sumitomo Mutual Life Insurance Group, $223,134
6. Nempuku (Pension Welfare Public Service Corp.), $204,588
7. Meiji Mutual Life Insurance Group, $160,606
8. Nomura Securities Group, $121,516
9. Asahi Mutual Life Insurance Group, $120,007
10. Nikko Securities Group, $103,554
Source: *Institutional Investor - International Edition,* Asia's Biggest Institutional Investors (annual), September 1996, p. 168.

Institutional Investments – Malaysia

★ 1678 ★
LARGEST INSTITUTIONAL INVESTORS IN MALAYSIA, 1995
Ranked by: Total assets, in millions of dollars. **Remarks:** Figures for Lembaga Urusan & Tabung Hagi and Khazanah Nasional are estimated. Also notes domestic equities, Japan equities, other asian equities, foreign equities, domestic bonds, property, cash, and other assets. **Number listed:** 15
1. Employees Provident Fund with $37,785 million
2. Permodalan Nasional, $13,561
3. Lembaga Urusan & Tabung Haji (Pilgrims Fund Board), $2,500
4. Pension Trust Fund, $2,330
5. Social Security Organization, $1,758
6. Lembaga Tabung Angkatan Tentera (Armed Forces Fund), $1,229
7. Khazanah Nasional, $1,200
8. Kuala Lumpur Mutual Fund, $838
9. Rashid Hussain Asset Management, $827
10. Perbadanan Johor Group, $690
Source: *Institutional Investor - International Edition,* Asia's Biggest Institutional Investors (annual), September 1996, p. 179.

Institutional Investments – Philippines

★ 1679 ★
LARGEST INSTITUTIONAL INVESTORS IN THE PHILIPPINES, 1995
Ranked by: Total assets, in millions of dollars. **Number listed:** 15
1. Social Security System with $4,893 million
2. Government Service Insurance System, $2,903
3. Bank of the Philippine Islands, $1,282
4. Far East Bank & Trust Co., $1,164
5. Metropolitan Bank & Trust Co., $761
6. Philippine Commercial International Bank, $727
7. Philippine National Bank, $631
8. Insular Life Assurance Co., $564
9. United Coconut Planters Bank, $540
10. Rizal Commercial Banking Corp., $538
Source: *Institutional Investor - International Edition,* Asia's Biggest Institutional Investors (annual), September 1996, p. 215.

Institutional Investments – Singapore

★ 1680 ★
LARGEST INSTITUTIONAL INVESTORS IN SINGAPORE, 1995
Ranked by: Total assets, in millions of dollars. **Remarks:** Figures for Government of Singapore Investment Corp. and Temasek Holdings are estimated. **Number listed:** 10
1. Central Provident Fund with $46,417 million
2. Government of Singapore Investment Corp., $30,400
3. Temasek Holdings, $12,000
4. Post Office Savings Bank of Singapore, $11,898
5. Great Eastern Life Assurance Co., $3,331
6. DBS Asset Management, $2,655
7. Port of Singapore Authority Group, $2,156
8. OUB Asset Management, $1,548
9. OCBC Asset Management, $1,403
10. NTUC Income Insurance Co-operative, $1,396
Source: *Institutional Investor - International Edition,* Asia's Biggest Institutional Investors (annual), September 1996, p. 174.

Institutional Investments—Taiwan

★ 1681 ★
LARGEST INSTITUTIONAL INVESTORS IN TAIWAN, 1995
Ranked by: Total assets, in millions of U.S. dollars.
Number listed: 20
1. Cathay Life Insurance Co. with $21,486 million
2. Shin Kong Life Insurance Co., $9,130
3. Taiwan Provincial Labor Insurance Bureau, $4,800
4. Central Trust of China, $4,252
5. Kuo Hua Life Insurance, $1,959
6. Kwang Hua Securities Investment & Trust Co., $1,459
7. China Life Insurance, $1,351
8. National Investment Trust Co., $1,265
9. Central Investment Holding Co., $1,216
10. China Securities Investment Trust Corp., $1,185

Source: *Institutional Investor - International Edition,* Asia's Biggest Institutional Investors (annual), September 1996, p. 180.

Institutional Investments—Thailand

★ 1682 ★
LARGEST INSTITUTIONAL INVESTORS IN THAILAND, 1995
Ranked by: Total assets, in millions of U.S. dollars.
Remarks: Also notes value of domestic bonds, cash, and other assets. **Number listed:** 15
1. Mutual Fund Public Co. with $3,588 million
2. SCB Asset Management Co., $1,645
3. Thai Farmers Asset Management, $1,197
4. Thai Investment & Securities Co., $1,120
5. Thai Life Insurance Co., $1,117
6. G.S. Asset Management Co., $1,059
7. One Asset Management, $852
8. BBL Asset Management Co., $783
9. Phatra Thanakit, $476
10. Thai Capital Management Co., $437

Source: *Institutional Investor - International Edition,* Asia's Biggest Institutional Investors (annual), September 1996, p. 184.

Instrument Industry—Europe

★ 1683 ★
TOP MEASURING, ANALYZING & CONTROLLING INSTRUMENTS COMPANIES IN EUROPE
Ranked by: Sales, in millions of European Currency Units (ECUs). Data also covers producers of photographic, medical, and optical instruments, as well as watch and clock makers. **Number listed:** 62
1. Philips Medical Systems International B.V. with 30,349 million ECUs
2. Rank Xerox Ltd., 4,411
3. Thomson C.S.F., 2,440
4. Carl Zeiss, 2,326
5. Stork Kwant BV, 1,940
6. Stork-Veco BV, 1,940
7. Hewlett-Packard Ltd., 1,820
8. Blancpain SA, 1,704
9. SMH Societe Suisse de Microelectronique et d'Horlogerie, 1,704
10. Swatch AG, 1,704

Source: *Duns Europa,* (annual), vol. 4, Dun & Bradstreet, 1997, p. 242.

Insurance Brokers

★ 1684 ★
LEADING GLOBAL BUSINESS INSURANCE BROKERS, 1995
Ranked by: Gross revenue, in U.S. dollars. **Remarks:** Also employees, revenues per employee, and figures for 1994. **Number listed:** 20
1. Marsh & McLennan Cos. Inc. with $3,788,000,000
2. Aon Group Inc., $1,701,000,000
3. Sedgwick Group P.L.C., $1,469,907,000
4. Alexander & Alexander Services Inc., $1,282,400,000
5. Willis Corroon Group P.L.C., $1,114,699,200
6. Johnson & Higgins, $1,082,700,000
7. Acordia Inc., $555,064,000
8. Arthur J. Gallagher & Co., $411,998,000
9. Minet Group, $370,910,000
10. JIB Group P.L.C., $359,784,000

Source: *Business Insurance,* July 22, 1996, p. 1.

★ 1685 ★
TOP BROKERS WORLDWIDE, 1995
Ranked by: Gross revenues, in millions of U.S. dollars. **Number listed:** 10
1. Marsh & McLennan Cos. Inc. with $3,788.0 million
2. Aon Group Inc., $1,701.0

3.　Sedgwick Group, $1,469.9
4.　Alexander & Alexander Services Inc., $1,282.4
5.　Willis Corroon Group, $1,114.6
6.　Johnson & Higgins, $1,082.7
7.　Acordia Inc., $555.0
8.　Arthur J. Gallagher & Co., $411.9
9.　Minet Group, $370.9
10.　JIB Group, $359.7

Source: *Business Insurance*, July 22, 1996, p. 1.

Insurance Business

★ 1686 ★
TOP CLASSES OF GROSS WRITTEN PREMIUMS IN THE UNITED KINGDOM

Ranked by: Share of premiums written, in percent. **Remarks:** Figures include Llyod's. PMI stands for private mortgage insurance. **Number listed:** 5

1.　Property with 33%
2.　Motor, 30%
3.　Personal accident and PMI, 14%
4.　Liability, 11%
5.　Pecuniary loss, 11%

Source: *Financial Times*, March 24, 1997, p. 2.

★ 1687 ★
TOP INSURANCE MARKETS

Ranked by: Market share, in percent. **Remarks:** Includes volume of non-life business in billions of dollars. **Number listed:** 10

1.　U.S. with 39.6%
2.　Japan, 13.9%
3.　Germany, 10.2%
4.　U.K., 6.1%
5.　France, 5.3%
6.　Italy, 2.6%
7.　Canada, 2.3%
8.　Netherlands, 1.8%
9.　Spain, 1.7%
10.　South Korea, 1.4%

Source: *National Underwriter*, July 2, 1997, p. 31.

Insurance Companies

★ 1688 ★
BRITAIN'S LARGEST COMPOSITE INSURERS, 1995

Ranked by: Premium income, in billions of British pounds (£). **Number listed:** 6

1.　Royal Sun Alliance with £9.38 billion
2.　Commercial Union, £8.64
3.　General Accident, £5.91
4.　Norwich Union, £4.10

5.　Guardian, £3.77
6.　Eagle Star, £2.88

Source: *The Guardian*, January 6, 1996, p. 24.

★ 1689 ★
LARGEST INSURANCE FIRMS IN GREECE, 1994

Ranked by: Profits, in millions of Greek drachmas (GDr). **Number listed:** 10

1.　Alico with GDr3,345 million
2.　Interamerican Life, GDr1,426
3.　National, GDr1,352
4.　Agrotiki Aega, GDr1,341
5.　Nat. - Nederlanden, GDr1,318
6.　Aspis Pronoia, GDr522
7.　Commercial, GDr489
8.　Hellenic - British Life, GDr488
9.　European Trust, GDr437
10.　Metrolife Life, GDr430

Source: *Trade With Greece*, Spring 1996, p. 28.

★ 1690 ★
LARGEST INSURERS IN ARGENTINA

Ranked by: Market share, in percent. **Number listed:** 6

1.　Caja de Seguros de Vida with 6.4%
2.　Omega, 6.1%
3.　Buenos Aires, 4.5%
4.　Caja de Seguros, 4.0%
5.　San Cristobal, 3.4%
6.　Other, 75.6%

Source: *Latin Trade*, October 1996, p. 79.

★ 1691 ★
LARGEST INSURERS IN COLOMBIA

Ranked by: Market share, in percent. **Number listed:** 6

1.　Colsguros with 15.5%
2.　Suramericana, 14.4%
3.　Bolivar, 7.4%
4.　La Previsora, 6.2%
5.　Colmena, 5.0%
6.　Other, 51.5%

Source: *Latin Trade*, October 1996, p. 79.

★ 1692 ★
LARGEST INSURERS IN PERU

Ranked by: Market share, in percent. **Number listed:** 6

1.　Pacifico Peruano-Suiza with 29.0%
2.　Rimac Nacional, 12.0%
3.　Condor, 10.0%
4.　Popular y Porvenir, 10.0%
5.　La Positiva, 9.0%
6.　Other, 30.0%

Source: *Latin Trade*, October 1996, p. 79.

★ 1693 ★
LARGEST INSURERS WORLDWIDE, 1995
Ranked by: Assets, in billions of U.S. dollars. **Number listed:** 10

1. AXA/UAP with $450.0 billion
2. Nippon Life, $354.7
3. Dai-Ichi Mutual Life, $251.5
4. Prudential Ins. Co. of America, $219.4
5. Sumitomo Life, $217.8
6. Allianz, $200.0
7. Meiji Mutual Life, $151.5
8. Metropolitan Life, $142.1
9. AIG, $134.1
10. Prudential, $116.3

Source: *The Wall Street Journal*, November 13, 1996, p. A3.

★ 1694 ★
LARGEST MUTUAL LIFE AND HEALTH INSURANCE COMPANIES, 1995
Ranked by: Revenue, in millions of U.S. dollars. **Remarks:** Notes profits and global rank. **Number listed:** 21

1. Nippon Life (Japan) with $83,207 million
2. Dai-Ichi Mutual Life (Japan), $58,052
3. Sumitomo Life (Japan), $50,711
4. Prudential of America (United States), $41,330
5. Meiji Mutual Life (Japan), $38,047
6. Metropolitan Life (United States), $27,977
7. Asahi Mutual Life (Japan), $25,322
8. Mitsui Mutual Life (Japan), $23,084
9. Yasuda Mutual Life (Japan), $21,631
3. Taiyo Mutual Life (Japan), $16,662

Source: *Fortune*, The Global 500: World's Biggest Corporations (annual), August 5, 1996, p. F-21.

★ 1695 ★
LARGEST NON-LIFE INSURANCE FIRMS IN POLAND, 1994
Ranked by: Market share, in percent. **Remarks:** Includes income for 1994 and 1993. **Number listed:** 18

1. PZU with 60.6%
2. Warta, 19.0%
3. Polisha, 3.2%
4. Hestia Insurance, 3.0%
5. GRYF, 2.7%
6. Polonia, 2.3%
7. TUK, 1.6%
8. Compensa, 1.4%
9. Hestja, 1.2%
10. Fenix, 1.1%

Source: *National Trade Data Bank*, June 24, 1995, p. ISA9507.

★ 1696 ★
LARGEST STOCK LIFE AND HEALTH INSURANCE COMPANIES, 1995
Ranked by: Revenue, in millions of U.S. dollars. **Remarks:** Notes profits and global rank. **Number listed:** 11

1. ING Group (Netherlands) with $33,416 million
2. Fortis (Belgium/Netherlands), $22,695
3. Assur, Generales de France, $21,883
4. Prudential (United Kingdom), $21,503
5. CIGNA (United States), $18,955
6. CNP Assurances (France), $16,891
7. Samsung Life (South Korea), $16,449
8. Aegon (Netherlands), $13,066
9. Aetna Life & Casualty (United States), $12,978
10. Kyoei Life (Japan), $12,408

Source: *Fortune*, The Global 500: World's Biggest Corporations (annual), August 5, 1996, p. F-21.

★ 1697 ★
LATIN AMERICAN INSURANCE MARKET, 1995
Ranked by: Premiums, in billions of U.S. dollars. **Remarks:** Figures do not include insurance pruchased outside the region. Premiums for all Latin American countries reached $30.06 billion in 1994. **Number listed:** 5

1. Brazil with $14.3 billion
2. Argentina, $5.0
3. Mexico, $3.7
4. Chile, $2.0
5. Colombia, $1.7

Source: *Latin Trade*, October 1996, p. 80.

★ 1698 ★
MOST RESPECTED EUROPEAN INSURANCE FIRMS
Ranked by: Survey based on FT 500 list, as well as polls of investment analysts and chief executives of European companies. See source for details. **Number listed:** 3

1. ING
2. Allianz
3. AXA-UAP

Source: *Financial Times*, Europe's Most Respected Companies (annual), September 24, 1997, p. 2.

★ 1699 ★
TOP GLOBAL BUSINESS INSURERS, 1995
Ranked by: Non-life net premiums written, in millions of U.S. dollars. **Remarks:** Also notes adjusted shareholders funds. **Number listed:** 100

1. Tokio Marine & Fire Insurance Ltd. with $13,858 million
2. Yasuda Fire & Marine Insurance Ltd., $9,867
3. Continental Casualty/Continental Insurance Group (CNA), $9,218
4. American International Group, $8,753

5. Travelers/Aetna Insurance Group, $7,863
6. Mitsui Marine & Fire Insurance Ltd., $6,733
7. Royal & Sun Alliance Insurance Group, $5,871
8. Sumitomo Marine & Fire Ltd., $5,838
9. Hartford Fire Group, $5,674
10. Zurich Versicherung AG, $5,402

Source: *Business Insurance,* Standard & Poor's Top Global Business Insurers (annual), November 18, 1996, p. 48.

★ 1700 ★

TOP INSURANCE COMPANIES IN LONDON, 1995

Ranked by: Net premiums, in thousands of British pounds (£). **Remarks:** Notes combined ratio. **Number listed:** 10

1. Mercantile & General Reinsurance Co. with £1,262,900 thousand
2. CNA International Reinsurance Co. Ltd., £342,164
3. Zurich Re (U.K.) Ltd., £268,025
4. Eagle Star Reinsurance Co. Ltd., £263,134
5. General Re Europe Ltd., £230,735
6. Sphere Drake Insurance P.L.C., £227,400
7. St. Paul Reinsurance Co. (U.K.) Ltd., £176,569
8. Swiss Reinsurance Co. (U.K.) Ltd., £128,131
9. Terra Nova Insurance Co. Ltd., £107,138
10. Everest Reinsurance Ltd., £90,934

Source: *Business Insurance*, September 2, 1996, p. 24.

★ 1701 ★

TOP INSURANCE FIRMS IN BRAZIL

Ranked by: Market share, in percent. **Number listed:** 10

1. Sul America with 16.6%
2. Bradesco, 14.1%
3. Itau, 6.8%
4. Bamerindus, 6.5%
5. Porto Seguro, 5.9%
6. Unibanco/Nacional, 5.2%
7. Paulista, 3.2%
8. Golden Cross, 2.7%
9. Real, 2.6%
10. Sasse, 2.5%

Source: *National Trade Data Bank*, June 26, 1996, p. IMI960626.

★ 1702 ★

TOP INSURANCE FIRMS IN QUEBEC, 1996

Ranked by: Market share, in percent. **Remarks:** Includes sales figures and number of employees in Quebec and Canada. **Number listed:** 12

1. AXA Canada with 13.9%
2. ING Canada, 11.2%
3. Desjardins, 9.6%
4. General Accident, 5.3%
5. Assurance Royale, 4.2%
6. Promutuel, 4.2%

7. Guardian, 3.4%
8. Unindal, 2.8%
9. Lloyds, 2.6%
10. Zurich, 2.6%

Source: *Le Devoir*, March 9, 1997, p. B12.

★ 1703 ★

TOP INSURERS IN MEXICO, 1996

Ranked by: Market share, in percent, for the first six months of 1996. **Number listed:** 47

1. Comercial America with 17.46%
2. Nacional Provincial, 17.06%
3. Asemex, 14.16%
4. Moneterrey Aetna, 12.23%
5. Inbursa, 5.03%
6. Tepeyac, 3.95%
7. Interamericana, 2.18%
8. Genesis, 2.17%
9. Atlas, 1.72%
10. Banamex, 1.57%

Source: *National Trade Data Bank*, September 12, 1996, p. ISA960801.

★ 1704 ★

TOP INSURERS WORLDWIDE, 1995

Ranked by: Assets, in millions of dollars as of December 31, 1995. **Remarks:** Notes change from 1994, capital, and net income. **Number listed:** 50

1. Nippon Life (Japan) with $354,707 million
2. Zenkyoren (Japan), $256,864
3. Dai-Ichi Mutual Life (Japan), $251,507
4. Prudential Insurance (U.S.), $219,380
5. Sumitomo Life (Japan), $217,831
6. Allianz Holding (Germany), $199,952
7. Axa (France), $193,738
8. Compagnie UAP (France), $183,577
9. Meiji Mutual Life (Japan), $151,451
10. Metropolitan Life (U.S.), $142,132

Source: *The Wall Street Journal*, September 26, 1996, p. R27.

★ 1705 ★

TOP NON-LIFE INSURERS IN KOREA, 1995

Ranked by: Capital, in billions of won (W). **Number listed:** 17

1. Hankuk Fidelity & Surety with W1,031 billion
2. Hyundai Fire & Mairne, W447
3. The Oriental Fire & Marine, W429
4. Korean Reinsurance Company, W340
5. Shin Dongah Fire & Marine, W333
6. Dong Bu Fire & Marine, W300
7. Ssangyong Fire & Marine, W274
8. LG Fire & Marine, W217
9. Daehan Fire & Marine, W195

10.   First Fire & Marine, W172
Source: *National Trade Data Bank*, November 20, 1996, p. ISA961001.

★ **1706** ★
TOP PERSONAL INSURANCE FIRMS IN QUEBEC, 1996
Ranked by: Market share, in percent. **Remarks:** Includes sales figures and number of employees in Quebec and Canada. **Number listed:** 12
1.   Desjardins-Laurentienne with 17.7%
2.   Industrielle-Alliance, 9.4%
3.   Sun Life, 6.8%
4.   SSQ-Vie, 6.0%
5.   Standard Life, 5.4%
6.   La Mutuelle, 4.7%
7.   La Metropolitaine, 4.4%
8.   Prudentielle, 4.2%
9.   ManuVie, 3.6%
10. Canada-Vie, 3.5%
Source: *Le Devoir*, March 9, 1997, p. B12.

Insurance Companies – Asia

★ **1707** ★
LARGEST INSURANCE COMPANIES IN ASIA, 1995
Ranked by: Assets, in thousands of U.S. dollars. **Remarks:** Notes percent change on previous year. **Number listed:** 50
1.   Tokio Marine & Fire Insurance Co. Ltd. with $48,741,145 thousand
2.   Yasuda Fire & Marine Insurance Co. Ltd., $34,359,757
3.   Sumitomo Marine & Fire Insurance Co. Ltd., $23,876,611
4.   Cathay Life Insurance Co. Ltd., $20,827,556
5.   Nichido Fire & Marine Insurance Co. Ltd., $15,986,155
6.   Fuji Fire & Marine Insurance Co. Ltd., $12,157,757
7.   Chiyoda Fire & Marine Insurance Co. Ltd., $11,928,669
8.   Dowa Fire & Marine Insurance Co. Ltd., $10,076,757
9.   Nissan Fire & Marine Insurance Co. Ltd., $8,716,613
10. Nisshin Fire & Marine Insurance Co. Ltd., $5,495,669
Source: *Asia's 7,500 Largest Companies* annual, Dun & Bradstreet, 1997, p. 306.

Insurance Companies – Europe

★ **1708** ★
LARGEST EUROPEAN INSURANCE GROUPS
Ranked by: Premiums, in billions of U.S. dollars. **Remarks:** Includes figures on net income and market capitalization. **Number listed:** 10
1.   Allianz with $45.58 billion
2.   Generali, $21.86
3.   AXA, $19.27
4.   Zurich Insurance, $19.07
5.   Munich RE, $18.86
6.   Prudential, $12.86
7.   ING, $12.52
8.   Aegon, $11.28
9.   UAP, $6.17
10. Commercial Union, $5.55
Source: *Financial Times*, June 17, 1996, p. 24.

★ **1709** ★
TOP EUROPEAN INSURERS BY TURNOVER, 1995
Ranked by: Turnover, in millions of French francs (FFr). **Number listed:** 10
1.   Axa-UAP (France) with FFr313 million
2.   Allianz (Germany), FFr231
3.   Zurich (Switzerland), FFr112
4.   Generali (Italy), FFr105
5.   Winterthur (Switzerland), FFr94
6.   CNP (France), FFr84
7.   AGF (France), FFr77
8.   Commercial Union (United Kingdom), FFr72
9.   Ing (Netherlands), FFr65
10. GAN (France), FFr51
Source: *L'Expansion*, March 6, 1997, p. 70.

Insurance Companies – Germany

★ **1710** ★
TOP INSURANCE COMPANIES IN GERMANY, 1995
Ranked by: Premium income, in millions of deutsche marks (DM). **Remarks:** Also notes pre-tax profit, net profit, claims, net interest income, and reserves. **Number listed:** 25
1.   Allianz A.G. Holding with DM70,548 million
2.   Munchener Ruckversicherungs-Gesellschaft, DM29,100
3.   AMB Aachener und Munchener Beteiligungs-A.G., DM15,101
4.   Allianz Versicherungs-A.G., DM14,081
5.   Allianz Lebensversicherungs-A.G., DM11,519
6.   CKAG (Colonia Konzern A.G.), DM9,741
7.   R + V Insurance Group, DM8,443

8. HDI Haftpflichtverband der Deutschen Industrie V.a.G., DM8,377
9. Debeka Versicherungen und Bausparkasse, DM7,635
10. Vereinte Versicherungen, DM7,605

Source: *Germany's Top 500: A Handbook of Germany's Largest Corporations* (annual), 1997, p. 537.

Insurance Companies – Japan

★ 1711 ★
TOP NON-LIFE INSURANCE PROVIDERS IN JAPAN
Ranked by: Income, in millions of yen (¥). **Number listed:** 10
1. Tokio Marine & Fire with ¥85,734 million
2. Yasuda Fire & Marine, ¥41,042
3. Mitsui Marine & Fire, ¥34,503
4. Sumitomo Marine & Fire, ¥29,300
5. Dai-Tokyo Fire & Marine, ¥26,351
6. Nippon Fire & Marine, ¥25,076
7. Nichido Fire & Marine, ¥23,402
8. Chiyoda Fire & Marine, ¥20,966
9. Fuji Fire & Marine, ¥19,620
10. AIU, ¥14,033

Source: *Tokyo Business Today*, August 1995, p. 27.

Insurance Companies – Russia

★ 1712 ★
TOP INSURANCE FIRMS IN RUSSIA, 1995
Ranked by: Receipts, in millions of U.S. dollars. **Remarks:** Notes the types of insurance issued by each firm. **Number listed:** 10
1. Rosno (Moscow) with $149.9 million
2. Energogarant (Moscow), $132.8
3. Maks (Moscow), $109.0
4. Ingosstrakh (Moscow), $93.3
5. Voenno-Strakhovaya Kompaniya (Moscow), $71.8
6. Rogosstrakha (Moscow), $57.8
7. Kuzbass (Kernerovo), $57.6
8. Zashchita (Moscow), $57.4
9. Sibirskaya Strakhovaya Kompaniya (Krasnoyarsk), $48.1
10. Rosenergo (Barnaul), $47.6

Source: *The Russian*, February 1997, p. 18.

Insurance, Disaster

★ 1713 ★
COSTLY INSURED DISASTERS, 1970-1996
Ranked by: Insured loss, in billions of U.S. dollars.
Number listed: 15
1. Hurricane Andrew, United States (1992) with $17.95 billion
2. Northridge earthquake, United States (1994), $13.28
3. Tornado Mireille, Japan (1991), $6.42
4. Winter storm Daria, Europe (1990), $5.53
5. Hurricane Hugo, Puerto Rico (1989), $5.33
6. Autumn storm in Europe (1987), $4.15
7. Winter storm Vivian, Europe (1990), $3.84
8. Piper Alpha explosion, Europe (1988), $2.66
9. Great Hanshin earthquake, Japan (1995), $2.55
10. Hurricane Opal, United States (1995), $2.17

Source: *The Economist*, April 19, 1997, p. 103.

Insurance, Health

★ 1714 ★
LEADING HEALTH INSURERS IN ITALY, 1994
Ranked by: Market share, in percent. **Number listed:** 8
1. Assitalia with 11.71%
2. Assicurazioni Generali, 10.21%
3. Sai, 9.31%
4. Fondiaria Assicurazioni, 5.06%
5. Toro Assicurazioni, 4.31%
6. Milano Assicurazioni, 3.77%
7. Unipol, 2.94%
8. Societa Reale Mutua, 2.70%

Source: *National Trade Data Bank*, March 2, 1996, p. ISA9506.

★ 1715 ★
TOP PRIVATE HEALTH INSURERS IN SPAIN
Ranked by: Market share, in percent. **Number listed:** 20
1. Asisa with 21.5%
2. Sanitas, 13.8%
3. Adeslas, 13.2%
4. Asistencia Sanitaria, 5.4%
5. Previasa, 4.8%
6. Ig. Med. Quir rgico, 4.2%
7. Aresa, 2.5%
8. Fiatc, 2.3%
9. Caja Salud, 2.1%
10. Mapfre Vida, 1.3%

Source: *National Trade Data Bank*, March 26, 1997, p. IMI970326.

Insurance, Life

★ 1716 ★
**COUNTRIES WITH THE LARGEST LIFE
INSURANCE PREMIUMS, 1994**
Ranked by: Life insurance premiums, in millions of U.S.
dollars. **Remarks:** Notes share of global market for each
country. **Number listed:** 15
1. Japan with $477,016 million
2. United States, $251,419
3. United Kingdom, $74,786
4. France, $69,741
5. Germany, $51,400
6. South Korea, $34,766
7. Canada, $16,687
8. Switzerland, $15,419
9. Netherlands, $15,092
10. South Africa, $12,578
Source: *National Underwriter*, August 5, 1996, p. 1.

★ 1717 ★
GREECE'S LIFE INSURANCE PROVIDERS, 1995
Ranked by: Market share, in percent. **Remarks:** Includes
percent changed and rankings from 1994. **Number listed:**
10
1. Interamerican with 24.2%
2. Nation. - Nederlanden, 14.7%
3. National, 13.1%
4. Alico, 11.1%
5. Agrotiki Life, 5.1%
6. Aspis Pronoia, 4.5%
7. AGF Kosmos, 3.3%
8. Astir, 2.6%
9. Metrolife, 2.5%
10. Hellenic - British, 2.4%
Source: *Trade With Greece*, Spring 1996, p. 26.

★ 1718 ★
**LARGEST WRITERS OF INSURANCE IN ITALY,
1995**
Ranked by: Direct premiums, in billions of lire (L).
Remarks: Notes market share for 1993, 1994, and 1995.
Number listed: 5
1. INA with L2,971 billion
2. Alleanza, L2,720
3. Generali, L2,399
4. Fideuram Vita, L1,211
5. RAS, L945
Source: *International Insurance Monitor*, 4th Quarter
1996, p. 23.

Insurance, Life – Canada

★ 1719 ★
TOP LIFE INSURANCE FIRMS IN CANADA
Ranked by: Revenue, in thousands of Canadian dollars.
Remarks: Includes figures on profits and return on
capital. **Number listed:** 9
1. Sun Life Assurance of Canada with
C$10,615,000 thousand
2. Manulife Financial, C$8,874,000
3. Great-West Lifeco, C$6,306,763
4. Great-West Life Assurance, C$6,305,926
5. London Insurance Group, C$5,282,000
6. Canada Life Assurance, C$4,670,660
7. Mutual Life Assurance, C$4,422,000
8. London Life Insurance, C$4,218,000
9. Desjardins-Laurentian Life Group,
C$2,235,076
Source: *Globe and Mail's Report on Business Magazine*,
July 1996, p. 159.

Insurance, Life, International

★ 1720 ★
WORLDWIDE LIFE INSURANCE MARKET, 1994
Ranked by: Global market share based on premiums, in
percent. **Number listed:** 15
1. Japan with 42.55%
2. United States, 22.42%
3. United Kingdom, 6.67%
4. France, 6.22%
5. Germany, 4.58%
6. South Korea, 3.10%
7. Canada, 1.49%
8. Switzerland, 1.38%
9. Netherlands, 1.35%
10. South Africa, 1.12%
Source: *National Underwriter*, August 5, 1996, p. 1.

Insurance, Life – Japan

★ 1721 ★
TOP LIFE INSURANCE PROVIDERS IN JAPAN
Ranked by: Income, in millions of yen (¥). **Number
listed:** 10
1. Nippon Life with ¥85,809 million
2. Sumitomo Life, ¥72,995
3. Meiji Mutual Life, ¥68,558
4. Dai-ichi Mutual Life, ¥50,338
5. Yasuda Mutual Life, ¥32,477
6. Mitsui Mutual Life, ¥25,819
7. Taiyo Mutual Life, ¥25,227

8. Daido Mutual Life, ¥24,686
9. American Life, ¥19,456
10. Kyoei Life, ¥17,493

Source: *Tokyo Business Today*, August 1995, p. 27.

Insurance, Property and Casualty

★ 1722 ★

GREECE'S DAMAGE INSURANCE PROVIDERS, 1995

Ranked by: Market share, in percent. **Remarks:** Includes percent changed and rankings from 1994. **Number listed:** 10

1. National with 14.6%
2. Astir, 6.5%
3. Phoenix, 6.1%
4. Interamerican, 5.7%
5. Agrotiki, 5.5%
6. AGF Kosmos, 4.1%
7. Nordstern Colonia, 2.8%
8. Commercial Union, 2.2%
9. European Trust, 2.1%
10. International Union, 2.0%

Source: *Trade With Greece*, Spring 1996, p. 26.

★ 1723 ★

LARGEST PROPERTY & CASUALTY INSURANCE MARKETS, 1994

Ranked by: Premiums, in billions of U.S. dollars. **Remarks:** Also notes world market share. **Number listed:** 10

1. United States with $342.7 billion
2. Japan, $129.0
3. Germany, $77.0
4. United Kingdom, $42.1
5. France, $40.7
6. Italy, $22.8
7. Canada, $17.4
8. Netherlands, $14.3
9. Spain, $13.9
10. Australia, $11.8

Source: *National Underwriter,* World's Largest P&C Insurance Markets (annual), September 9, 1996, p. 49.

★ 1724 ★

TOP INTERNATIONAL PROPERTY & CASUALTY INSURANCE COMPANIES, 1995

Ranked by: Foreign premium volume, in thousands of U.S. dollars. **Remarks:** Notes percent change, employees in non-U.S. locations, and total employees. **Number listed:** 10

1. Allianz A.G. Holding with $15,166,144 thousand
2. Zurich Insurance Group, $14,620,000

3. Assicurazioni Generali S.p.A., $8,804,086
4. AIU, $6,441,000
5. Commercial Union P.L.C., $6,278,862
6. Gourp UAP, $5,125,500
7. Wintethur Swiss Insurance Co. Ltd., $3,995,000
8. Royal Insurance Holdings P.L.C., $3,542,610
9. CIGNA International, $2,050,032
10. The Chubb Corp., $1,045,381

Source: *Business Insurance*, November 18, 1996, p. 36.

Insurance – Reinsurance
See: **Reinsurance**

Internet (Computer Network)

★ 1725 ★

GROWTH OF INTERNET HOSTS, 1995

Ranked by: Growth in annual number of hosts for countries, in percent. **Number listed:** 10

1. New Zealand with 441% growth
2. Denmark, 181%
3. Czech Republic, 153%
4. South Africa, 147%
5. Spain, 141%
6. Belgium, 125%
7. Poland, 121%
8. United Kingdom, 112%
9. Finland, 103%
10. South Korea, 101%

Source: *Sloan Management Review*, Spring 1996, p. 60.

★ 1726 ★

GROWTH OF INTERNET HOSTS, 1995-1996

Ranked by: Growth from previous year of internet hosts as of July 1996, in percent. **Number listed:** 10

1. China with 1,003% growth
2. Russian Federation, 462%
3. Singapore, 368%
4. Brazil, 305%
5. Japan, 211%
6. Finland, 148%
7. Italy, 147%
8. Poland, 145%
9. Mexico, 142%
10. Greece, 128%

Source: *The Wall Street Journal*, September 26, 1996, p. B6.

★ 1727 ★
HOW FIRMS ACCESS THE INTERNET IN FRANCE, 1996
Ranked by: Market share, distributed as a percent of 131 survey respondents. **Remarks:** Multiple answers were allowed. **Number listed:** 12
1. Compuserve with 37.0%
2. France Telecom, 26.0%
3. Oleane, 20.0%
4. America Online, 13.0%
5. Internet-Way, 12.0%
6. FranceNet, 9.0%
7. Grolier Interactive, 8.0%
8. WorldNet, 8.0%
9. EUNet, 7.0%
10. Others, 11.0%

Source: *Nouvel Economiste*, December 24, 1996, p. 49.

★ 1728 ★
INTERNET CONNECTIONS BY COUNTRY
Ranked by: Number of computers with Internet linkage as of January 1995. **Number listed:** 10
1. United States with 2,860,439
2. United Kingdom, 241,191
3. Germany, 207,717
4. Canada, 186,722
5. Australia, 161,166
6. Japan, 96,632
7. France, 93,041
8. South Africa, 27,040
9. South Korea, 18,049
10. Hong Kong, 12,437

Source: *World Business*, Spring 1995, p. 20.

★ 1729 ★
INTERNET DOMAINS WORLDWIDE
Ranked by: Share for country of all Internet sites, in percent. **Number listed:** 8
1. United States with 56.1%
2. Canada, 9.5%
3. France, 4.0%
4. Australia, 3.7%
5. Japan, 3.6%
6. Germany, 3.5%
7. United Kingdom, 2.8%
8. Others, 16.9%

Source: *Investor's Business Daily*, May 16, 1996, p. A8.

★ 1730 ★
LEADING TOPICS OF INTERNET INFORMATION SEARCHES IN SOUTH KOREA
Ranked by: Topics, in percent. **Remarks:** Data are based on a survey of 320 office workers. Multiple responses were allowed. **Number listed:** 6
1. Education and culture with 38.3%
2. Market and company news, 19.0%

3. Economy and industry, 18.8%
4. Policies, 11.6%
5. Entertainment, 7.3%
6. Information and telecommunications, 5.0%

Source: *Business Korea*, April 1997, p. 55.

★ 1731 ★
NATIONS LEAST-WIRED TO THE INTERNET
Ranked by: People per Internet server. **Number listed:** 19
1. India with 1,200,000
2. China, 561,000
3. Indonesia, 87,000
4. Thailand, 15,000
5. Brazil, 8,000
6. South Korea, 1,550
7. South Africa, 930
8. Taiwan, 850
9. Japan, 470
10. Hong Kong, 310

Source: *Fortune*, October 28, 1996, p. 132.

★ 1732 ★
TOP INTERNET HOSTS BY COUNTRY
Ranked by: Hosts per thousands of people. **Number listed:** 14
1. Finland with 62 hosts
2. Iceland, 42
3. United States, 31
4. Norway, 30
5. Australia, 24
6. Canada, 23
7. New Zealand, 23
8. Sweden, 23
9. Singapore, 18
10. Switzerland, 18

Source: *The New York Times*, January 20, 1997, p. C6.

Investment Banking

★ 1733 ★
TOP INVESTMENT BANKS BY MARKET VALUE, 1997
Ranked by: Market value as of February 1997, in billions of U.S. dollars. **Number listed:** 11
1. HSBC Holdings with $62.3 billion
2. American International Group, $54.6
3. Citicorp, $51.4
4. Chase Manhattan, $40.8
5. BankAmerica, $38.1
6. Travelers Group, $32.8
7. NationsBank, $30.6
8. American Express Co., $28.4
9. Deutschebank, $24.4

10.   Union Bank of Switzerland, $20.6
Source: *Forbes*, February 10, 1997, p. 150.

★ 1734 ★
TOP INVESTMENT BANKS IN ASIA BY INTERNATIONAL EQUITY OFFERINGS, 1996
Ranked by: International equity offerings, in millions of U.S. dollars. **Remarks:** Figures do not include Japan. **Number listed:** 10
1.   Peregrine with $2,352.95 million
2.   Morgan Stanley, $1,157.20
3.   Goldman Sachs, $998.02
4.   Credit Lyonnais, $772.62
5.   Merrill Lynch, $705.02
6.   ING Barings, $660.47
7.   Flemings, $574.83
8.   HSBC Investment, $570.75
9.   BZW, $545.38
10.   Bear Stearns, $543.89
Source: *Far Eastern Economic Review*, January 23, 1997, p. 55.

★ 1735 ★
TOP INVESTMENT BROKERS IN ASIA
Ranked by: Market share, in percent. **Number listed:** 11
1.   Jardine Fleming with 14.2%
2.   Merrill Lynch, 13.3%
3.   BZW, 10.0%
4.   Goldman Sachs, 7.1%
5.   Kleinwort Benson, 6.8%
6.   SBC Warburg, 5.8%
7.   NatWest Markets, 4.5%
8.   Credit Lyonnais, 4.4%
9.   Morgan Stanley, 4.2%
10.   SocGen Crosby, 3.7%
Source: *South China Morning Post*, February 11, 1997, p. 1.

★ 1736 ★
TOP MUTUAL FUND MANAGERS IN CANADA, 1997
Ranked by: Market share based on assets as of March 31, 1997, in percent. **Number listed:** 11
1.   Investors Group with 11.4%
2.   Trimark Investment Management, 9.7%
3.   Royal Mutual Funds, 9.0%
4.   Mackenzie Financial, 7.4%
5.   TD Asset Management, 5.2%
6.   Templeton Management, 5.1%
7.   AGF Management, 4.5%
8.   CIBC Securities, 4.4%
9.   Fidelity Investments Canada, 3.8%
10.   Bank of Montreal, 3.7%
Source: *Marketing Magazine*, May 26, 1997, p. 18.

★ 1737 ★
WORLDWIDE INVESTMENT FUNDS BY REGION, 1996
Ranked by: Distribution based on assets under management, in percent. **Number listed:** 7
1.   United States with 57.1%
2.   Europe, 28.4%
3.   Japan, 6.8%
4.   Canada, 2.5%
5.   Brazil, 1.7%
6.   South Korea, 1.4%
7.   Others, 2.1%
Source: *The European*, July 2, 1997, p. 24.

Investment Management Firms – Rating

★ 1738 ★
TOP MANAGERS OF ACTIVE U.S. ASSETS INVESTED ABROAD, 1996
Ranked by: Total assets under non-U.S. management, in millions of U.S. dollars. **Remarks:** Also notes equity and bond value. **Number listed:** 25
1.   Capital Guardian Trust with $28,289 million
2.   Brinson Partners, $18,146
3.   Schroders, $17,643
4.   Morgan Stanley Asset, $16,677
5.   J.P. Morgan, $16,431
6.   Grantham, Mayo, Van Otterloo, $14,541
7.   Scudder, Stevens & Clark, $13,499
8.   Rowe Price-Fleming, $11,321
9.   Putnam Investments, $10,780
10.   Morgan Grenfell Asset, $9,901
Source: *Pensions & Investments,* Largest Money Managers Issue (annual), May 12, 1997, p. 64.

★ 1739 ★
TOP MONEY MANAGERS OUTSIDE THE UNITED STATES
Ranked by: Total funds under management, in billions of U.S. dollars. **Remarks:** Also includes figures for domestic and foreign management. **Number listed:** 250
1.   Kampo (Japan) with $844,266 billion
2.   Nippon Life (Japan), $366,586
3.   BZW Asset Management (United Kingdom), $351,359
4.   Union Bank of Switzerland (Switzerland), $351,145
5.   Swiss Bank Corporation (Switzerland), $337,957
6.   Groupe Axa (France), $275,000
7.   Zenkyoren (Japan), $259,124
8.   Dai-Ichi Mutual Life (Japan), $257,922
9.   Mitsubishi Trust & Banking (Japan), $253,841

10. Credit Suisse (Switzerland), $253,645
Source: *Euromoney,* Intersec 250 (annual), August 1996, p. 53.

Investment Management Firms – Rating – Asia

★ 1740 ★
TOP INVESTMENT MANAGEMENT FIRMS IN ASIA
Ranked by: Assets, in millions of U.S. dollars. Remarks: Does not include firms in Japan. Number listed: 100
1. Jardine Fleming Investment Mgmt. Ltd. (Hong Kong) with $16,684 million
2. HSBC Asset Mgmt. Hong Kong Ltd., $12,300
3. AIG Investment Corp Ltd (Hong Kong), $11,600
4. Baring Asset Mgmt. Ltd. (Hong Kong), $11,000
5. Fidelity Investments Mgmt. Ltd. (Hong Kong), $9,500
6. Scudder, Stevens & Clark Asia Ltd. (Hong Kong), $8,400
7. Schroder Investment Mgmt. Group (Singapore, Hong Kong), $8,400
8. Franklin Templeton Group (Hong Kong, Singapore), $8,000
9. LGT Asset Mgmt. Group (Hong Kong, Singapore), $6,400
10. Mercury Asset Mgmt. Group (Singapore), $4,500
Source: *Pensions & Investments*, April 14, 1997, p. 16.

Investment Management Firms – Rating – Canada

★ 1741 ★
TOP INVESTMENT MANAGERS IN CANADA BY TAX-EXEMPT FUNDS
Ranked by: Tax-exempt funds under management, in thousands of U.S. dollars. Number listed: 61
1. Caisse de Depot et Placement du Quebec with $38,007,864 thousand
2. Phillips, Hager & North, Investment Management, Ltd., $10,744,004
3. T.A.L. Investment Counsel, Ltd., $10,682,590
4. Perigee Investment Counsel, Inc., $10,350,874
5. Altamira Management, Ltd., $9,389,300
6. RT Capital Management Inc., $9,109,658
7. Sceptre Investment Counsel, Ltd., $7,935,073
8. Beutel, Goodman & Company, Ltd., $7,649,000
9. Kinght, Bain, Seath & Holbrook Capital Management, Inc., $7,289,000
10. Jarislowsky, Fraser Limited, $6,917,139
Source: *Money Market Directory of Pension Funds and Their Investment Managers* (annual), 1997, p. 1799.

Investment Management Firms – Rating – Europe

★ 1742 ★
TOP EUROPEAN FUND MANAGERS BY ASSET GROWTH
Ranked by: Asset growth, in percent. of U.S. dollars. Remarks: Notes assets in local currency. Number listed: 18
1. Axa Group with 389.8% growth
2. Asset Management Group, 355.8%
3. Foreign & Colonial Mgmt., 145.3%
4. ING Group, 50.5%
5. Dresdner Bank Group, 47.2%
6. J.P. Morgan Inv. Mgmt., 40.5%
7. NatWest Group, 30.7%
8. Invesco, 29.0%
9. Schroder Inv. Mgmt., 28.5%
10. Banque Cantonale Vaudoise, 24.0%
Source: *Institutional Investor,* The Euro 150 (annual), November 1996, p. 93.

★ 1743 ★
TOP EUROPEAN FUND MANAGERS BY ASSETS UNDER MANAGEMENT
Ranked by: Total assets under management, in millions of U.S. dollars. Remarks: Also notes the value of domestic equities, foreign equities, domestic fixed income, foreign fixed income, property, cash, and other assets. Number listed: 100
1. Union Bank of Switzerland with $390,800 million
2. Asset Management Group, $319,826
3. Credit Suisse, $308,300
4. Swiss Bank Corp., $301,300
5. AXA Group, $275,432
6. Deutsche Bank, $200,245
7. Allianz Holding, $197,035
8. Caisse des Depots Group, $190,441
9. Dresdner Bank Group, $179,278
10. Union des Assurances de Paris, $144,472
Source: *Institutional Investor,* The Euro 150 (annual), November 1996, p. 78.

Investment Trusts
See: **Mutual Funds**

Investments

★ 1744 ★
HOW THE CZECH REPUBLIC ALLOCATES FOREIGN AID, 1990-1996
Ranked by: Distribution, in percent. **Number listed:** 6
1. Transport & communications with 22.1%
2. Transport equipment, 15.0%
3. Consumer goods & tobacco, 13.9%
4. Chemicals, 8.5%
5. Construction, 8.3%
6. Others, 32.2%

Source: *Financial Times*, May 14, 1997, p. IV.

★ 1745 ★
INVESTMENT RISK IN EMERGING MARKETS
Ranked by: Order of increased risk for economic investment, based on a study analyzing over 50 criteria. **Remarks:** No specific figures were provided. **Number listed:** 10
1. Argentina
2. Poland
3. Mexico
4. Turkey
5. India
6. Brazil
7. Russia
8. Indonesia
9. China
10. South Africa

Source: *The Christian Science Monitor*, June 3, 1997, p. 3.

★ 1746 ★
LEADING INVESTORS IN THE CZECH REPUBLIC, 1990-1996
Ranked by: Distribution, in percent. **Number listed:** 6
1. Germany with 27.5%
2. Netherlands, 14.5%
3. United States, 14.4%
4. Switzerland, 12.1%
5. France, 7.8%
6. Others, 23.8%

Source: *Financial Times*, May 14, 1997, p. IV.

Investments, Foreign

★ 1747 ★
FOREIGN INVESTMENTS IN CUBA, 1997
Ranked by: Number of deals by sector. **Number listed:** 7
1. Industry with 85 deals
2. Tourism, 45
3. Mining (non-nickel), 33
4. Oil extraction/exploration, 30

5. Transportation and communication, 12
6. Mining (nickel), 5
7. Other, 50

Source: *Financial Times*, March 12, 1997, p. 6.

★ 1748 ★
TOP FOREIGN INVESTORS IN INDIA, 1996
Ranked by: Investments, in billions of rupees (Rs). **Number listed:** 10
1. United States with Rs254.78 billion
2. United Kingdom, Rs53.22
3. Mauritius, Rs48.01
4. Japan, Rs43.24
5. Israel, Rs41.64
6. Germany, Rs37.51
7. South Korea, Rs37.17
8. Australia, Rs28.37
9. Netherlands, Rs26.94
10. Thailand, Rs24.26

Source: *Nikkei Weekly*, April 28, 1997, p. 24.

★ 1749 ★
TOP LATIN AMERICAN REGIONS FOR INVESTMENT, 1996
Ranked by: Direct foreign investment, estimated in millions of U.S. dollars. **Remarks:** Notes percent change over 1995. **Number listed:** 15
1. Brazil with $8,000 million
2. Mexico, $7,000
3. Peru, $3,400
4. Argentina, $3,200
5. Chile, $2,800
6. Colombia, $2,550
7. Venezuela, $1,350
8. Bolivia, $560
9. Dominican Republic, $430
10. Ecuador, $320

Source: *Latin Trade*, June 1997, p. 13A.

★ 1750 ★
TOP TAIWANEESE INVESTORS IN CHINA
Ranked by: Investments, in millions of U.S. dollars. **Remarks:** Notes categories and locations of key investments. **Number listed:** 4
1. President Enterprises with $300 million
2. Cheng Hsin, $100
3. Taiwan Glass, $100
4. Walsin Lihwa, $100

Source: *Business Week*, June 9, 1997, p. 62.

Investments, Foreign – China

★ 1751 ★
LEADING DIRECT INVESTORS IN CHINA, 1995
Ranked by: Actual investment, in billions of U.S. dollars.
Remarks: Also notes pledged investment. **Number listed:** 10
1. Hong Kong with $20.060 billion
2. Taiwan, $3.762
3. Japan, $3.108
4. United States, $3.083
5. Singapore, $1.851
6. South Korea, $1.043
7. United Kingdom, $0.914
8. Macao, $0.439
9. Germany, $0.386
10. Virgin Islands, $0.304

Source: *Accountancy - International Edition*, July 1996, p. 30.

★ 1752 ★
TOP INVESTORS IN CHINA, 1979-1995
Ranked by: Cumulative investments, in billions of U.S. dollars. **Number listed:** 5
1. Hong Kong/Macao with $241.4 billion
2. Taiwan, $29.4
3. United States, $28.3
4. Japan, $21.3
5. Singapore, $17.3

Source: *Financial Times*, May 1, 1997, p. 6.

★ 1753 ★
TOP INVESTORS IN CHINA, 1996
Ranked by: Investment distribution based on amount contracted, in percent. **Number listed:** 5
1. Hong Kong & Macao with 39%
2. United States, 9%
3. Japan, 7%
4. Taiwan, 7%
5. Others, 38%

Source: *The China Business Review*, June 1997, p. 12.

Investments, Foreign – Hong Kong

★ 1754 ★
HONG KONG INVESTMENTS BY CHINESE PROVINCE, 1996
Ranked by: Number of investments as of March 1996.
Number listed: 18
1. Guangdong with 150
2. Shanghai, 87
3. Beijing, 44
4. Fujian, 20

5. Hubei, 19
6. Tianjin, 15
7. Liaoning, 14
8. Shandong, 10
9. Sichuan, 10
10. Jiangsu, 7

Source: *Financial Times*, June 16, 1997, p. 11.

★ 1755 ★
TOP FOREIGN INVESTORS IN HONG KONG
Ranked by: Investments, in millions of Hong Kong dollars (HK$). **Number listed:** 10
1. New World Development with HK$24,962 million
2. Hopewell Holdings, HK$21,296
3. Henderson Land, HK$13,751
4. Hutchison Whampoa, HK$9,592
5. Cons Elec Power, HK$8,767
6. China Light, HK$7,700
7. New World Infrastructure, HK$7,370
8. Hang Lung Development, HK$4,812
9. Sun Hung Kai Property, HK$3,822
10. Citic Pacific, HK$3,714

Source: *Financial Times*, June 16, 1997, p. 11.

★ 1756 ★
TOP INVESTORS IN HONG KONG, 1996
Ranked by: Investments, in millions of Hong Kong dollars (HK$). **Number listed:** 10
1. New World Development with HK$24,962 million
2. Hopewell Holdings, HK$21,296
3. Henderson Land, HK$13,751
4. Hutchison Whampoa, HK$9,592
5. Cons Elec Power (CEPA), HK$8,767
6. China Light, HK$7,700
7. New World Infrastructure, HK$7,370
8. Hang Lung Development, HK$4,812
9. Sun Hung Kai Property, HK$3,822
10. Citic Pacific, HK$3,714

Source: *Accountancy - International Edition*, July 1997, p. 27.

Iowa – see under individual headings

Iran – see under individual headings

Iraq – see under individual headings

Ireland – see under individual headings

Irish Stock Exchange

★ 1757 ★
LARGEST COMPANIES ON THE IRISH STOCK EXCHANGE, 1995
Ranked by: Market value, in millions of Irish pounds (IR£). **Number listed:** 20
1. Allied Irish Banks with IR£2,281 million
2. Bank of Ireland, IR£2,182
3. CRH, IR£1,672
4. Smurfit, IR£1,573
5. Elan Corporation, IR£1,150
6. Kerry Group, IR£803
7. Irish Life, IR£730
8. Greencore, IR£502
9. Independent, IR£478
10. Waterford Wedgwood, IR£428
Source: *GT Guide to World Equity Markets* (annual), Euromoney Publications, 1996, p. 187.

★ 1758 ★
MOST ACTIVELY TRADED SHARES ON THE IRISH STOCK EXCHANGE, 1995
Ranked by: Turnover, in millions of Irish pounds (IR£). **Number listed:** 20
1. Bank of Ireland with IR£1,349.3 million
2. Smurfit, IR£1,240.9
3. CRH, IR£1,211.4
4. AIB, IR£1,132.2
5. Irish Life, IR£649.4
6. Tullow, IR£386.3
7. Greencore, IR£288.2
8. Irish Permanent, IR£210.6
9. Waterford Wedgwood, IR£202.3
10. Aran Energy, IR£193.5
Source: *GT Guide to World Equity Markets* (annual), Euromoney Publications, 1996, p. 187.

Iron Ore

★ 1759 ★
LEADING NATIONS IN IRON ORE EXPORTS, 1996
Ranked by: Exports, in millions of metric tons. **Remarks:** Notes figures for 1985, 1990, and 1993-1995. **Number listed:** 8
1. Australia with 135.7 million metric tons
2. Brazil, 129.7
3. India, 31.7
4. Former Soviet Union, 30.3

5. Canada, 27.9
6. South Africa, 19.3
7. Sweden, 16.1
8. Other, 44.2
Source: *Skillings Mining Review*, August 2, 1997, p. 10.

★ 1760 ★
LEADING NATIONS IN IRON ORE IMPORTS, 1996
Ranked by: Imports, in millions of metric tons. **Remarks:** Notes figures for 1985, 1990, and 1993-1995. **Number listed:** 8
1. Japan with 119.2 million metric tons
2. China, 43.9
3. Germany, 39.4
4. South Korea, 34.4
5. United Kingdom, 20.4
6. France, 18.4
7. United States, 18.4
8. Other, 136.7
Source: *Skillings Mining Review*, August 2, 1997, p. 10.

★ 1761 ★
LEADING NATIONS IN IRON ORE PRODUCTION, 1996
Ranked by: Production, in millions of metric tons. **Remarks:** Notes figures for 1985, 1990, and 1993-1995. **Number listed:** 8
1. Brazil with 179.9 million metric tons
2. Australia, 147.2
3. Former Soviet Union, 128.5
4. China, 116.2
5. India, 66.6
6. United States, 62.1
7. Canada, 36.8
8. Other, 143.5
Source: *Skillings Mining Review*, August 2, 1997, p. 10.

Isle of Man – see under individual headings

Israel – see under individual headings

Istanbul Stock Exchange

★ 1762 ★
HIGHEST CAPITALIZATION COMPANIES ON THE ITALIAN STOCK EXCHANGE, 1995
Ranked by: Market value, in billions of Turkish lire (TL). **Number listed:** 20
1. Petkim with TL93,000 billion
2. Turk Hava Yollari, TL81,000

3. Akbank, TL69,000
4. T. Is Bank, TL57,288
5. Koc Holding, TL52,200
6. Tupras, TL47,187
7. T. Garanti Bankasi, TL40,800
8. Ege Biracilik, TL33,107
9. Eregli Demir Celik, TL31,680
10. Aksa, TL32,944

Source: *GT Guide to World Equity Markets* (annual), Euromoney Publications, 1996, p. 346.

★ **1763** ★

MOST ACTIVELY TRADED SHARES ON THE ISTANBUL STOCK EXCHANGE, 1995

Ranked by: Turnover value, in billions of Turkish lire (TL). **Number listed:** 20

1. Eregli Dernir Celik with TL234,784 billion
2. Cukurova Elektrik, TL149,805
3. Ihlas Holding, TL104,805
4. Petkim, TL88,676
5. Yapi Kredi Bankasi, TL75,378
6. Tupras, TL69,741
7. Ic Bankas (C), TL61,284
8. Ic Bankas (B), TL51,621
9. Kepez Elektrik, TL50,879
10. Transturk Holding, TL43,519

Source: *GT Guide to World Equity Markets* (annual), Euromoney Publications, 1996, p. 347.

Italian Stock Exchange

★ **1764** ★

HIGHEST CAPITALIZATION ON THE ITALIAN STOCK EXCHANGE, 1995

Ranked by: Market value, in billions of Italian lire (L). **Number listed:** 20

1. ENI with L43,955.6 billion
2. Generali, L30,619.7
3. Telecom Italia Mobile, L18,456.7
4. Stet, L17,139.4
5. Fiat, L16,848.8
6. Telcom Italia, L16,279.1
7. Ina, L8,360.0
8. Allianza Ass, L8,299.0
9. San Paolo Torino, L7,337.8
10. IMI, L5,994.6

Source: *GT Guide to World Equity Markets* (annual), Euromoney Publications, 1996, p. 202.

★ **1765** ★

MOST ACTIVELY TRADED SHARES ON THE ITALIAN STOCK EXCHANGE, 1995

Ranked by: Trading value, in billions of Italian lira (L). **Number listed:** 20

1. Fiat with L17,734.4 billion
2. Telecom Italia, L12,187.7
3. Generali Assicurazioni, L11,022.9
4. Stet, L9,427.7
5. Montedison, L7,539.3
6. Stet rsp, L4,894.2
7. Telecom Italia Mobile, L4,632.4
8. Olivetti, L4,417.3
9. Banca Commerciale Italiana, L3,780.6
10. Credito Italiano, L3,724.6

Source: *GT Guide to World Equity Markets* (annual), Euromoney Publications, 1996, p. 202.

Italy – see under individual headings

Ivory Coast – see under individual headings

Jakarta Stock Exchange

★ **1766** ★

LARGEST COMPANIES ON THE JAKARTA STOCK EXCHANGE, 1995

Ranked by: Market value, in billions of rupiah (Rp). **Number listed:** 20

1. Telekomunikasi Indonesia with Rp28,000 billion
2. Gudang Garam, Rp11,496
3. HM Sampoerna, Rp10,710
4. Indocement Tunggal Perkarsa, Rp9,265
5. Indosat, Rp8,595
6. Indofood Sukses Makmur, Rp8,393
7. Astra International, Rp4,127
8. Semen Gresik, Rp3,796
9. Bank International Indonesia, Rp2,396
10. Barito Pacific Timber, Rp2,345

Source: *GT Guide to World Equity Markets* (annual), Euromoney Publications, 1996, p. 179.

★ **1767** ★

MOST ACTIVE SHARES ON THE JAKARTA STOCK EXCHANGE, 1995

Ranked by: Trading value, in billions of rupiah (Rp). **Number listed:** 20

1. H.M. Sampoerna with Rp2,218 billion
2. Telekomunikasi Indonesia, Rp1,903

3. Astra International, Rp1,668
4. Indocement Tunggal Perkasa, Rp1,193
5. Indosat, Rp1,055
6. Semen Gresik, Rp1,040
7. Barito Pacific Timber, Rp1,009
8. Indah Kiat Paper & Pulp, Rp878
9. BDNI, Rp813
10. Putra Surya Perkasa, Rp732

Source: *GT Guide to World Equity Markets* (annual), Euromoney Publications, 1996, p. 179.

Jamaica – see under individual headings

Jamaica Stock Exchange

★ 1768 ★
LARGEST COMPANIES ON THE JAMAICA STOCK EXCHANGE, 1995
Ranked by: Market value, in millions of Jamaican dollars (J$). **Number listed:** 20

1. Telecommunications of Jamaica with J$10,236 million
2. Bank of Nova Scotia, J$9,733
3. CIBC Holdings, J$4,432
4. Carreras Group, J$4,065
5. NCB Group, J$2,735
6. Desnoes and Geddes, J$2,007
7. CIBC, J$1,739
8. Kingston Wharves, J$1,719
9. Lascelles, J$1,660
10. Grace Kennedy, J$1,293

Source: *GT Guide to World Equity Markets* (annual), Euromoney Publications, 1996, p. 401.

★ 1769 ★
MOST ACTIVELY TRADED ISSUES ON THE JAMAICA STOCK EXCHANGE, 1995
Ranked by: Trading value, in millions of Jamaican dollars (J$). **Number listed:** 20

1. Telecommunications of Jamaica with J$7,598.30 million
2. Lacelles, J$426.62
3. Bank of Nova Scotia, J$416.61
4. NCB Group, J$367.14
5. Jamaica Producers, J$366.10
6. Carreras, J$281.70
7. NCC Group, J$259.83
8. Jamaica Broilers, J$203.53
9. Grace Kennedy, J$191.39
10. Dyoll Group, J$126.17

Source: *GT Guide to World Equity Markets* (annual), Euromoney Publications, 1996, p. 401.

Japan – see under individual headings

Jeans (Clothing)

★ 1770 ★
LEADING JEANS BRANDS IN FRANCE, 1996
Ranked by: Sales. **Remarks:** Source provides no specific dollar value. **Number listed:** 19

1. Levi's
2. Complices
3. Ober
4. Lee Cooper
5. Oboush
6. Lee
7. Rica Lewis
8. Naf Naf
9. Teddy Smith
10. Chipie

Source: *National Trade Data Bank*, May 23, 1997, p. IMI970507.

★ 1771 ★
TOP JEANS BRANDS IN GERMANY
Ranked by: Market share, in percent. **Number listed:** 7

1. Levi's (U.S.) with 10.0%
2. Mustang (Germany), 9.0%
3. Diesel (Italy), 7.0%
4. Edwin (Japan), 7.0%
5. Lee (U.S.), 7.0%
6. Wrangler (U.S.), 5.0%
7. Others, 55.0%

Source: *National Trade Data Bank*, October 18, 1995, p. ISA9508.

★ 1772 ★
TOP JEANS MAKERS IN SPAIN
Ranked by: Market share, in percent. **Number listed:** 9

1. Levi Strauss & Co. with 40.0%
2. Lee, 12.0%
3. Liberto, 12.0%
4. Pepe Jean so London, 12.0%
5. El Charro, 4.0%
6. Solido, 4.0%
7. Caroche, 3.0%
8. Grins, 3.0%
9. Other, 10.0%

Source: *National Trade Data Bank*, March 2, 1996, p. ISA9402.

Jewelry

★ 1773 ★
BEST-SELLING JEWELRY ITEMS IN JAPAN
Ranked by: Market share, in percent. **Number listed:** 8
1. Fashion rings with 45%
2. Necklaces, 15%
3. Engagement rings, 12%
4. Pendants, 8%
5. Earrings, 7%
6. Wedding rings, 4%
7. Bracelets, 2%
8. Other, 7%
Source: *National Trade Data Bank*, June 4, 1997, p. ISA970501.

★ 1774 ★
HONG KONG'S TOP MARKETS FOR EXPORTS OF JEWELRY, 1996
Ranked by: Value of exports, in thousands of Hong Kong dollars (HK$). **Number listed:** 31
1. United States with HK$4,017,102 thousand
2. Japan, HK$1,745,239
3. Germany, Federal Republic of, HK$603,462
4. Singapore, HK$489,705
5. France, HK$486,858
6. Switzerland, HK$463,525
7. United Kingdom, HK$443,578
8. Taiwan, HK$400,462
9. China, HK$196,369
10. Australia, HK$139,156
Source: http:// www.tdc.org.hk/hkstat/jeweller.htm, August 25, 1997, p. 2.

Jewelry, Costume

★ 1775 ★
COSTUME JEWELRY MARKET IN FRANCE
Ranked by: Market share, in percent. **Number listed:** 5
1. Earrings with 45%
2. Necklaces, bracelets, 20%
3. Rings, 16%
4. Brooches, 15%
5. Others, 4%
Source: *National Trade Data Bank*, December 12, 1996, p. ISA961101.

Jewelry Industry

★ 1776 ★
TOP JEWELRY MAKERS IN THAILAND, 1994
Ranked by: Revenue, in millions of bahts (Bt). **Remarks:** Includes profits and assets. **Number listed:** 9
1. General Diamond with Bt1,532.35 million
2. Pranda Jewelry, Bt1,488.22
3. Gold Associate, Bt1,222.39
4. Beauty Gems Factory, Bt1,214.46
5. Sawang Export, Bt876.42
6. Oriental Lapidary, Bt752.09
7. Ronda, Bt726.26
8. Oriental Diamond Trading, Bt663.80
9. Essex International, Bt645.79
Source: *Business Review*, December 1995, p. 185.

Job Satisfaction

★ 1777 ★
WORKER SATISFACTION WORLDWIDE
Ranked by: Workers satisfied with their company as an employer, in percent. **Remarks:** Data are based on a survey of 1,500 of the world's largest companies. **Number listed:** 8
1. Switzerland with 82%
2. Mexico, 72%
3. Germany, 66%
4. U.S., 65%
5. France, 58%
6. Singapore, 53%
7. Hong Kong, 43%
8. Japan, 31%
Source: *Business Week*, June 24, 1996, p. 28.

Johannesburg Stock Exchange

★ 1778 ★
LARGEST COMPANIES ON THE JOHANNESBURG STOCK EXCHANGE, 1995
Ranked by: Market value, in millions of South African rands (SAr). **Number listed:** 20
1. Anglo American Corporation of South Africa Limited with SAr51,333 million
2. De Beers Consolidated Mines Limited, SAr42,012
3. South African Breweries Limited, SAr39,566
4. Liberty Life Association of Africa Limited, SAr28,710
5. Richemont Securities AG, SAr27,561
6. Minorco Societe Anonyme, SAr23,827

7. Gencor Limited, SAr20,957
8. Sasol Limited, SAr18,270
9. Johannesburg Consolidated Investment Company Limited, SAr17,776
10. Rembrandt Group Limited, SAr17,617

Source: *GT Guide to World Equity Markets* (annual), Euromoney Publications, 1996, p. 297.

★ 1779 ★

MOST ACTIVELY TRADED SHARES ON THE JOHANNESBURG STOCK EXCHANGE, 1995

Ranked by: Trading value, in millions of South African rands (SAr). **Number listed:** 20

1. De Beers Consolidated Mines Limited with SAr2,354 million
2. Anglo American Corporation of South Africa Limited, SAr2,279
3. Richemont Securities AG, SAr1,970
4. South African Breweries Limited, SAr1,935
5. Sasol Limited, SAr1,899
6. Iscor Limited, SAr1,815
7. Barlows Limited, SAr1,422
8. Gencor Limited, SAr1,361
9. Liberty Life Association of Africa Limited, SAr1,302
10. Rembrandt Group Limited, SAr1,196

Source: *GT Guide to World Equity Markets* (annual), Euromoney Publications, 1996, p. 297.

Jordan – see under individual headings

Kaolin

★ 1780 ★

WORLD KAOLIN CONSUMPTION BY END USE, 1995

Ranked by: End use, in percent. **Number listed:** 8

1. Paper with 45%
2. Refactories, 17%
3. Ceramics, 8%
4. Cement, 5%
5. Fiberglass, 5%
6. Rubber, 5%
7. Paint, 3%
8. Other, 12%

Source: *Chemical Marketing Reporter*, October 14, 1996, p. 18.

Karachi Stock Exchange

★ 1781 ★

LARGEST LISTED COMPANIES ON THE KARACHI STOCK EXCHANGE, 1995

Ranked by: Market value, in billions of rupees (Rp).
Number listed: 20

1. Hub Power Company with Rp20.39 billion
2. Pakistan Telecommunication, Rp18.33
3. Fauji Fertilizer Company, Rp13.70
4. Pakistan State Oil, Rp12.73
5. ICI Pakistan, Rp11.39
6. Sui Southern Gas Company, Rp10.12
7. Dewan Salman Fibre, Rp8.70
8. Engro Chemical, Rp8.29
9. Lever Brothers Pakistan, Rp6.99
10. Sui Northern Gas, Rp6.95

Source: *GT Guide to World Equity Markets* (annual), Euromoney Publications, 1996, p. 432.

★ 1782 ★

MOST ACTIVELY TRADED STOCKS ON THE KARACHI STOCK EXCHANGE, 1995

Ranked by: Share volume, in millions of shares. **Number listed:** 20

1. Pakistan Telecommunications with 4,513.36 million shares
2. Hub Power Company, 405.61
3. Dhan Fibres, 187.69
4. Dewan Salman Fibre, 165.92
5. Pakistan Synthetic, 117.81
6. Kohinoor Power, 52.74
7. ICI (Pak), 44.88
8. LTV Capital Modaraba, 35.14
9. Bank of Punjab, 21.95
10. DG Khan Cement, 20.31

Source: *GT Guide to World Equity Markets* (annual), Euromoney Publications, 1996, p. 433.

Kazakhstan – see under individual headings

Kenya – see under individual headings

Ketchup

★ 1783 ★

INDIA'S KETCHUP MARKET

Ranked by: Market share, in percent. **Number listed:** 3

1. Kissan with 45.0%

Kitchenware

★ 1784 ★
GREAT BRITAIN'S OVENWARE MARKET
Ranked by: Market share, in percent. **Number listed:** 4
1. George Wilkinson with 20.0%
2. Prestige, 20.0%
3. Wilkinson Housewares, 20.0%
4. Other, 40.0%

Source: *National Trade Data Bank*, March 2, 1996, p. ISA9406.

Korea Stock Exchange

★ 1785 ★
LARGEST COMPANIES ON THE SOUTH KOREAN STOCK EXCHANGE, 1995
Ranked by: Market value, in millions of won (W). **Number listed:** 20
1. Korea Electric Poser Corporation with W19,213,264 million
2. Samsung Electronics, W11,216,867
3. Pohand Iron & Steel, W4,760,822
4. Korea Mobile Telecommunications, W3,332,398
5. Daewoo Heavy Industry, W3,085,827
6. LG Electronics, W2,680,351
7. Shinan Bank, W1,862,640
8. Hyundai Motor, W1,806,158
9. Hyundai Engineering & Construction, W1,775,777
10. Dacom Corporation, W1,762,771

Source: *GT Guide to World Equity Markets* (annual), Euromoney Publications, 1996, p. 221.

★ 1786 ★
MOST ACTIVELY TRADED SHARES ON THE SOUTH KOREAN STOCK EXCHANGE, 1995
Ranked by: Trading value, in billions of won (W). **Number listed:** 20
1. Samsung Electronics with W7,556.12 billion
2. LG Electronics, W2,750.75
3. Pohang Iron and Steel, W2,371.51
4. Korea Electric Power, W2,296.35
5. Korea Mobile Telecom, W1,897.83
6. Bank of Seoul, W1,426.71
7. Hyundai Motors, W1,315.37
8. Samsung Electronics (I preferred), W1,262.28

Opening of list:
2. Maggi, 40.0%
3. Other, 15.0%
Source: *Business Today*, August 7, 1996, p. 50.

9. Korea First Bank, W1,167.81
10. Commerical Bank of Korea, W1,163.55
Source: *GT Guide to World Equity Markets* (annual), Euromoney Publications, 1996, p. 222.

Kuala Lumpur Stock Exchange

★ 1787 ★
LARGEST COMPANIES ON THE KUALA LUMPUR STOCK EXCHANGE, 1995
Ranked by: Market value, in millions of Malaysian ringgits (MR). **Number listed:** 20
1. Telekom with MR39,440.17 million
2. TNB, MR30,749.89
3. Maybank, MR24,469.05
4. PGas, MR15,570.00
5. Genting, MR14,886.58
6. Resorts, MR14,849.07
7. Sime Darby, MR14,262.57
8. UE (M), MR8,906.16
9. MISC, MR6,580.00
10. Renong, MR6,289.24

Source: *GT Guide to World Equity Markets* (annual), Euromoney Publications, 1996, p. 236.

★ 1788 ★
MOST ACTIVELY TRADED SHARES ON THE KUALA LUMPUR STOCK EXCHANGE, 1995
Ranked by: Share volume, in thousands of shares. **Number listed:** 20
1. Renong with 964,022 thousand shares
2. Mulpha, 677,741
3. D BHD, 675,949
4. MPHB, 608,414
5. Aokam, 540,375
6. Kel'Mas, 492,368
7. S Darby, 445,013
8. Idris, 404,134
9. Granite, 402,655
10. Promet, 391,745

Source: *GT Guide to World Equity Markets* (annual), Euromoney Publications, 1996, p. 237.

Kuwait – see under individual headings

Labor Costs – Europe

★ 1789 ★

EUROPEAN NATIONS WITH THE LOWEST COSTS FOR LABOR

Ranked by: Hourly wage, in U.S. dollars. **Number listed:** 5

1. Portugal with $5.35 per hour
2. Greece, $8.95
3. Spain, $12.70
4. United Kingdom, $13.77
5. Ireland, $13.83

Source: *Site Selection*, September 1997, p. 656.

Labor Costs, International

★ 1790 ★

COUNTRIES WITH THE HIGHEST LABOR COSTS IN MANUFACTURING, 1995

Ranked by: Hourly rates for manufacturing labor, in U.S. dollars. **Remarks:** Includes figures for 1985. **Number listed:** 27

1. Germany with $31.88
2. Japan, $23.66
3. France, $19.34
4. United States, $17.20
5. Italy, $16.48
6. Canada, $16.03
7. Australia, $14.40
8. United Kingdom, $13.77
9. Spain, $12.70
10. South Korea, $7.40

Source: *The Economist*, November 2, 1996, p. 77.

Labor Supply

★ 1791 ★

LABOR FORCE IN ASIA

Ranked by: Number in labor force. **Number listed:** 25

1. China with 583,600,000
2. India, 314,751,000
3. Indonesia, 67,000,000
4. Japan, 65,870,000
5. Bangladesh, 50,100,000
6. Pakistan, 36,000,000
7. Vietnam, 32,700,000
8. Thailand, 30,870,000
9. Philippines, 24,120,000
10. South Korea, 20,000,000

Source: *The World Factbook 1995,* Information obtained from the Internet, http:// www.odci.gov.

★ 1792 ★

LABOR FORCE IN EUROPE

Ranked by: Number in labor force. **Number listed:** 36

1. Germany with 36,750,000
2. United Kingdom, 28,048,000
3. France, 24,170,000
4. Italy, 23,988,000
5. Poland, 17,321,000
6. Spain, 14,621,000
7. Romania, 11,300,000
8. Netherlands, 6,400,000
9. Hungary, 5,400,000
10. Czech Republic, 5,389,000

Source: *The World Factbook 1995,* Information obtained from the Internet, http:// www.odci.gov.

★ 1793 ★

LABOR FORCE IN FORMER SOVIET COUNTRIES

Ranked by: Number in labor force. **Number listed:** 15

1. Russia with 85,000,000
2. Ukraine, 23,550,000
3. Uzbekistan, 8,234,000
4. Kazakhstan, 7,356,000
5. Belarus, 4,887,000
6. Azerbaijan, 2,789,000
7. Georgia, 2,763,000
8. Moldova, 2,030,000
9. Tajikistan, 1,950,000
10. Kyrgyzstan, 1,836,000

Source: *The World Factbook 1995,* Information obtained from the Internet, http:// www.odci.gov.

★ 1794 ★

LABOR FORCE IN LATIN AMERICA AND THE CARIBBEAN

Ranked by: Number in labor force. **Number listed:** 41

1. Brazil with 57,000,000
2. Mexico, 26,200,000
3. Colombia, 12,000,000
4. Argentina, 10,900,000
5. Peru, 8,000,000
6. Venezuela, 7,600,000
7. Chile, 4,728,000
8. Cuba, 46,20,800
9. Bolivia, 3,540,000
10. Guatemala, 3,200,000

Source: *The World Factbook 1995,* Information obtained from the Internet, http:// www.odci.gov.

★ 1795 ★

LABOR FORCE IN NEAR EAST

Ranked by: Number in labor force. **Number listed:** 13

1. Turkey with 20,400,000
2. Saudi Arabia, 5,000,000
3. Iraq, 4,400,000
4. Syria, 4,300,000

5. Israel, 1,900,000
6. Lebanon, 650,000
7. Jordan, 600,000
8. United Arab Emirates, 580,000
9. Kuwait, 566,000
10. Oman, 430,000

Source: *The World Factbook 1995,* Information obtained from the Internet, http:// www.odci.gov.

★ 1796 ★
LABOR FORCE IN NORTH AFRICA
Ranked by: Number in labor force. **Number listed:** 6
1. Egypt with 16,000,000
2. Morocco, 7,400,000
3. Sudan, 6,500,000
4. Algeria, 6,200,000
5. Tunisia, 2,250,000
6. Libya, 1,000,000

Source: *The World Factbook 1995,* Information obtained from the Internet, http:// www.odci.gov.

★ 1797 ★
LABOR FORCE IN NORTH AMERICA
Ranked by: Number in labor force. **Number listed:** 5
1. United States with 131,056,000
2. Canada, 13,380,000
3. Bermuda, 32,000
4. Greenland, 22,800
5. Saint Pierre and Miquelon, 2,850

Source: *The World Factbook 1995,* Information obtained from the Internet, http:// www.odci.gov.

★ 1798 ★
LABOR FORCE IN OCEANIA
Ranked by: Number in labor force. **Number listed:** 12
1. Australia with 8,630,000
2. New Zealand, 1,603,500
3. Fiji, 235,000
4. French Polynesia, 76,630
5. New Caledonia, 50,469
6. Guam, 46,930
7. American Samoa, 14,400
8. Kiribati, 7,870
9. Northern Mariana Islands, 7,476
10. Cook Islands, 5,810

Source: *The World Factbook 1995,* Information obtained from the Internet, http:// www.odci.gov.

★ 1799 ★
LABOR FORCE IN SUB-SAHARAN AFRICA
Ranked by: Number in labor force. **Number listed:** 36
1. Nigeria with 42,844,000
2. Ethiopia, 18,000,000
3. Zaire, 15,000,000
4. South Africa, 13,400,000
5. Cote d'Ivoire, 5,718,000

6. Uganda, 4,500,000
7. Ghana, 3,700,000
8. Rwanda, 3,600,000
9. Zambia, 3,400,000
10. Zimbabwe, 3,100,000

Source: *The World Factbook 1995,* Information obtained from the Internet, http:// www.odci.gov.

★ 1800 ★
LABOR FORCE PARTICIPATION RATE OF WOMEN, AGES 15 AND OVER
Ranked by: Percent of population of specified gender and age group. **Remarks:** Rate represents percent of poulation of specified gender and age group in labor force of the seven countries cited. **Number listed:** 7
1. Thailand with 76%
2. China, 70%
3. Sweden, 61%
4. United States, 56%
5. The Philippines, 48%
6. South Korea, 47%
7. India, 23%

Source: *The China Business Review,* February 1996, p. 23.

Laboratory Instruments

★ 1801 ★
FASTEST GROWING LABORATORY INSTRUMENTS IMPORT MARKETS OUTSIDE THE U.S., 1993-1995
Ranked by: Average annual growth, in percent. **Number listed:** 10
1. Chile with 30%
2. Czech Republic, 25%
3. Belgium, 20%
4. Honduras, 20%
5. India, 20%
6. Portugal, 20%
7. Taiwan, 20%
8. Argentina, 15%
9. Ecuador, 15%
10. Egypt, 15%

Source: *National Trade Data Bank,* March 21, 1995, p. BMR9405.

★ 1802 ★
FASTEST GROWING LABORATORY INSTRUMENTS MARKETS OUTSIDE THE U.S., 1993-1995
Ranked by: Average annual growth, in percent. **Number listed:** 10
1. Chile with 30%
2. Belgium, 20%

3. Honduras, 20%
4. India, 20%
5. Peru, 20%
6. Portugal, 20%
7. Taiwan, 18%
8. Argentina, 15%
9. Czech Republic, 15%
10. Ecuador, 15%

Source: *National Trade Data Bank*, March 21, 1995, p. BMR9405.

★ 1803 ★
LARGEST LABORATORY INSTRUMENTS IMPORT MARKETS OUTSIDE THE U.S.
Ranked by: Value of imports, in millions of U.S. dollars.
Number listed: 10
1. Germany with $3,600.0 million
2. France, $1,999.0
3. Singapore, $1,217.0
4. Italy, $870.0
5. Canada, $814.0
6. Netherlands, $705.0
7. South Korea, $656.4
8. Spain, $620.0
9. Japan, $600.0
10. United Kingdom, $593.0

Source: *National Trade Data Bank*, March 21, 1995, p. BMR9405.

★ 1804 ★
LARGEST LABORATORY INSTRUMENTS MARKETS OUTSIDE THE U.S.
Ranked by: Total market value, in millions of U.S. dollars. **Number listed:** 10
1. Germany with $5,500.0 million
2. Japan, $5,000.0
3. France, $2,140.0
4. United Kingdom, $1,607.0
5. Italy, $1,100.0
6. Singapore, $932.0
7. Canada, $863.0
8. Spain, $800.0
9. Netherlands, $725.0
10. South Korea, $689.7

Source: *National Trade Data Bank*, March 21, 1995, p. BMR9405.

Land – Ownership

★ 1805 ★
FOREIGN PURCHASES OF REAL ESTATE IN POLAND, 1996
Ranked by: Number of permits to purchase land.
Number listed: 6
1. Germany with 336
2. Netherlands, 140
3. United States, 123
4. Sweden, 46
5. Italy, 36
6. United Kingdom, 36

Source: *National Trade Data Bank*, June 30, 1997, p. IMI970625.

★ 1806 ★
TOP LAND OWNERS IN SCOTLAND
Ranked by: Acres owned. **Number listed:** 10
1. Forestry Commn. with 1,600,000 acres
2. Duke of Buccleuch, 270,000
3. Scottish Office, 260,000
4. National Trust, 190,000
5. Alcan Highland Estates, 135,000
6. Duke of Atholl, 130,000
7. Capt. Alwyn Farquharson, 125,000
8. Duchess of Westminster, 120,000
9. Earl of Seafield, 105,000
10. Crown Estate, 100,000

Source: *The Guardian*, June 9, 1997, p. 3.

Laos – see under individual headings

Latin America – see under individual headings

Latvia – see under individual headings

Law Firms

★ 1807 ★
BRITAIN'S TOP LAW FIRMS, 1995
Ranked by: Gross fees, in millions of U.S. dollars.
Number listed: 5
1. Clifford Chance with $1,348 million
2. Linklaters & Paines, $862
3. Freshfields, $755
4. Allen & Overy, $646

5. Slaughter and May, $578
Source: *The Economist*, November 23, 1996, p. 78.

★ 1808 ★
LARGEST LAW FIRMS IN MEXICO
Ranked by: Lawyers in Mexico. **Number listed:** 10
1. Baker & Botts, L.L.P. with 428 lawyers
2. Santamarina y Steta, S.C., 57
3. Basham, Ringe y Correa, S.C., 55
4. Goodrich, Riquelme y Asociados, S.C., 50
5. Baker & Mckenzie, S.C., 40
6. Barrera, Siquieros y Torres Landa, S.C., 30
7. Jauregui, Navarrete, Nader y Rojas, S.C., 24
8. Noriega y Escobedo, S.C., 24
9. Ritch, Heather y Mueller, S.C., 14
10. Gardere & Wynne, Arena, Arce, Robles, Yarza, S.C., 7
Source: *Mexico Business*, May 1996, p. 52.

Lawn and Garden Equipment

★ 1809 ★
LAWN/GARDEN TOOL MARKET IN DENMARK
Ranked by: Market share, in percent. **Number listed:** 5
1. Electrolux Group with 40.0%
2. Ginge, 23.0%
3. Fiskars, 10.0%
4. Murray, 10.0%
5. Other, 17.0%
Source: *National Trade Data Bank*, March 2, 1996, p. ISA9406.

Lead

★ 1810 ★
TOP LEAD CONSUMING COUNTRIES, 1995
Ranked by: Consumption, in thousands of tons. **Number listed:** 5
1. United States with 1,472 thousand tons
2. Germany, 368
3. Japan, 334
4. United Kingdom, 283
5. France, 265
Source: *Japanese Finance and Industry*, 1997, p. 5.

★ 1811 ★
TOP LEAD PRODUCERS IN JAPAN, 1995
Ranked by: Market share based on sales of 217,000 tons, in percent. **Number listed:** 7
1. Toho Zinc with 27.4%
2. Mitsui Mining & Smelting, 25.6%
3. Mitsubishi Materials, 21.3%

4. Sumitomo Metal Mining, 11.4%
5. Dowa Mining, 9.5%
6. Nippon Mining and Metals, 4.5%
7. Others, 0.4%
Source: *Japanese Finance and Industry*, 1997, p. 24.

★ 1812 ★
TOP LEAD PRODUCING COUNTRIES, 1995
Ranked by: Production, in thousands of tons. **Number listed:** 5
1. United States with 1,346 thousand tons
2. China, 421
3. United Kingdom, 321
4. Germany, 314
5. France, 297
6. Japan, 287
Source: *Japanese Finance and Industry*, 1997, p. 5.

Leasing and Renting of Equipment

★ 1813 ★
LARGEST LEASING FIRMS IN MEXICO, 1995
Ranked by: Assets as of December 31, 1995, in millions of U.S. dollars. **Number listed:** 10
1. Internacional with $508.5 million
2. Bancomer, $401.4
3. Banamex, $228.6
4. Invermexico, $228.4
5. Serfin, $209.8
6. Inverlat, $153.4
7. Inbursa, $134.8
8. Capital, $132.4
9. Atlas, $119.8
10. Banobras, $81.3
Source: *National Trade Data Bank*, September 9, 1996, p. ISA960801.

★ 1814 ★
LARGEST LEASING FIRMS IN POLAND, 1995
Ranked by: Market share, in percent. **Remarks:** Includes company ranking by capital. **Number listed:** 14
1. Europejski Fundusz Leasingowy with 17.47%
2. Carcade Invest, 12.03%
3. Centralne Towarzystwo Leasingowe, 11.62%
4. BEL Leasing, 9.00%
5. BRE Services, 5.69%
6. Centrum Leasingu i Finansow CLiF, 3.70%
7. ASC Ltd., 3.56%
8. Towarzystwo Finansowo Leasingowe, 3.56%
9. Lubelskie Towarzystwo Leasingowe, 3.39%
10. BG Leasing, 3.31%
Source: *National Trade Data Bank*, October 9, 1996, p. ISA960901.

★ 1815 ★
TOP MARKETS FOR NEW EQUIPMENT LEASING, 1996
Ranked by: Sales, in billions of ECUs (European Currency Units). **Remarks:** Includes figures for 1993-95. **Number listed:** 15
1. United Kingdom with 24.28 billion ECUs
2. Germany, 22.89
3. France, 9.97
4. Italy, 8.94
5. Spain, 3.74
6. Holland, 2.64
7. Sweden, 2.42
8. Switzerland, 2.34
9. Ireland, 2.18
10. Austria, 2.09

Source: *Financial Times*, July 24, 1997, p. 2.

Leather Finishing

★ 1816 ★
TOP LEATHER GOODS PRODUCED IN FRANCE
Ranked by: Sales, in millions of U.S. dollars. **Number listed:** 7
1. Handbags with $380 million
2. Luggage, $200
3. Small leather goods, $149
4. Briefcases, $109
5. Belts, $73
6. Wrist watches, $70
7. Other, $77

Source: *National Trade Data Bank*, March 2, 1996, p. IMI951214.

Leather Goods

★ 1817 ★
LEATHER FOOTWEAR MARKET IN INDIA
Ranked by: Market share, in percent. **Number listed:** 4
1. Liberty with 36.00%
2. Bata, 24.28%
3. Carona, 1.18%
4. Other, 38.54%

Source: *Business Today*, April 22, 1996, p. 64.

Leather Industry – Europe

★ 1818 ★
TOP LEATHER AND LEATHER PRODUCTS COMPANIES IN EUROPE
Ranked by: Sales, in millions of European Currency Units (ECUs). **Remarks:** Also notes the number of employees. **Number listed:** 36
1. Lafarge with 5,165 million ECUs
2. R.M.C. Group Plc, 4,387
3. Pilkington Plc, 2,852
4. Heidelberger Zement A.G., 2,741
5. Redland Plc, 2,668
6. C.R.H. Plc, 2,438
7. Schott Glaswerke, 2,326
8. T & N Plc, 2,229
9. Ciments Francais, 1,955
10. Blue Circle Industries Plc, 1,891

Source: *Duns Europa* (annual), vol. 4, Dun & Bradstreet, 1997, p. 229+.

Lebanon – see under individual headings

Leisure

★ 1819 ★
TOP LEISURE BRANDS BY BRAND VALUE
Ranked by: Brand value, in millions of U.S. dollars. **Remarks:** Value was calculated using capital, ratio of capital to company sales, earnings, and corporate tax rate of the country where the parent company is located. See source for details. **Number listed:** 7
1. Disney (Walt Disney) with $15,358 million
2. Blockbuster (Viacom), $2,376
3. Hilton (Hilton Hotels), $690
4. Holiday Inn (Bass), $635
5. Sheraton (ITT), $443
6. Marriott (Marriott International), $308
7. Four Seasons (Four Seasons Hotels), $53

Source: *Financial World*, World's Most Valuable Brands (annual), July 8, 1996, p. 62.

Lesotho – see under individual headings

Liberia – see under individual headings

Libraries

★ 1820 ★
PUBLIC LIBRARIES IN THE FIVE BEST CITIES FOR WORK AND FAMILY
Ranked by: Number of libraries. **Remarks:** Table shows ranking based on Arthur Andersen's Survey of Major Cities. **Number listed:** 5
1. London, England with 443 libraries
2. Paris, France, 400
3. Toronto, Canada, 178
4. Hong Kong, 61
5. Singapore, 11
Source: *Fortune*, November 11, 1996, p. 133.

Libya – see under individual headings

Light Bulbs

★ 1821 ★
TOP LIGHT BULB FACTORIES IN EAST JAVA, 1997
Ranked by: Projected annual production, in millions of light bulbs. **Remarks:** Data include flourescent and incandescent bulbs. **Number listed:** 5
1. General Electric Lighting Indonesia with 232 million
2. Philips Ralin Electronics, 231
3. Sinar Angkasa Rungkut, 172
4. Matsushita Lighting Indonesia, 47
5. TFC Maspion Indonesia, 15
Source: *National Trade Data Bank*, June 4, 1997, p. IMI970602.

Lima Stock Exchange

★ 1822 ★
LARGEST COMPANIES ON THE LIMA STOCK EXCHANGE, 1995
Ranked by: Market value, in millions of U.S. dollars. **Number listed:** 20
1. Telefonica del Peru with $2,958.02 million
2. Credicorp Ltd., $885.77
3. Banco de Credito, $669.28
4. Buenaventura, $583.59
5. Backus, $473.02
6. Banco Wiese, $384.90
7. Banco Continental, $366.72
8. Telefonica del Peru (A1), $352.33
9. Backus (E), $277.29

10. Cementos Lima, $275.46
Source: *GT Guide to World Equity Markets* (annual), Euromoney Publications, 1996, p. 410.

★ 1823 ★
MOST ACTIVELY TRADED SHARES ON THE LIMA STOCK EXCHANGE, 1995
Ranked by: Value, in millions of U.S. dollars. **Number listed:** 20
1. Banco de Credito with $2,454.37 million
2. Telefonica del Peru (B), $1,597.21
3. Southern Peru (E), $474.78
4. Backus (E), $382.39
5. El Pacifico - Peruano Suiza, $381.95
6. Cementos Lima, $293.06
7. Minsur (E), $291.76
8. Telefonica del Peru (A), $265.31
9. Buenaventura, $191.42
10. Banco Wiese, $106.54
Source: *GT Guide to World Equity Markets* (annual), Euromoney Publications, 1996, p. 411.

Linens, Household
See: **Household Linens**

Lingerie

★ 1824 ★
JAPAN'S TOP LINGERIE MAKERS
Ranked by: Market share, in percent. **Number listed:** 6
1. Wacoal with 24.0%
2. Cecile, 10.7%
3. Charle, 7.2%
4. Triumph International, 6.2%
5. Gunze, 5.6%
6. Other, 46.3%
Source: *Nikkei Weekly*, August 5, 1996, p. 10.

Liquid Crystal Displays

★ 1825 ★
TOP LIQUID CRYSTAL DISPLAY MAKERS IN JAPAN
Ranked by: Market share, in percent. **Number listed:** 6
1. Sharp with 32.3%
2. Toshiba, 16.5%
3. NEC, 12.4%
4. Hitachi, 9.9%
5. Sanyo Electric Group, 8.7%

6. Other, 20.2%
Source: *Nikkei Weekly*, July 22, 1996, p. 8.

Liquor Industry
See Also: Vodka

★ 1826 ★
GLOBAL ALCOPOP MARKET
Ranked by: Market share, in percent. **Number listed:** 2
1. Bass with 70.0%
2. Other, 30.0%
Source: *Newsweek*, September 30, 1996, p. 8.

★ 1827 ★
LEADING SPIRITS BRANDS BY BRAND VALUE
Ranked by: Brand value, in millions of U.S. dollars.
Remarks: Value was calculated using capital, ratio of capital to company sales, earnings, and corporate tax rate of the country where the parent company is located. See source for details. **Number listed:** 40
1. Bacardi (Bacardi) with $4,409 million
2. Hennessy (LVMH), $3,400
3. Johnnie Walker Black (Guinness), $2,724
4. Johnnie Walker Red (Guinness), $2,406
5. Ballantine's (Allied Domecq), $1,974
6. Chivas Regal (Seagram), $1,935
7. J&B (Grand Metropolitan), $1,668
8. Smirnoff (Grand Metropolitan), $1,537
9. Jack Daniels (Brown-Forman), $1,484
10. Martini & Rossi (Barcadi), $1,430
Source: *Financial World,* World's Most Valuable Brands (annual), July 8, 1996, p. 57.

★ 1828 ★
LOCALLY PRODUCED LIQUOR MARKET IN COLOMBIA, 1996
Ranked by: Market share, in percent. **Number listed:** 5
1. Pedro Domecq S.A. with 31.6%
2. Casa Grajales S.A., 12.3%
3. Internacional de Licres S.A., 5.3%
4. Jave Licores S.A., 7.3%
5. Bodegas del Rhin Ltda., 6.7%
Source: *National Trade Data Bank*, July 9, 1997, p. ISA970501.

★ 1829 ★
TOP CHAMPAGNES AND WINES BY BRAND VALUE
Ranked by: Brand value, in millions of U.S. dollars.
Remarks: Value was calculated using capital, ratio of capital to company sales, earnings, and corporate tax rate of the country where the parent company is located. See source for details. **Number listed:** 5
1. Moet & Chandon (LVMH) with $536 million

2. Dom Perignon (LVMH), $163
3. Cinzano (Grand Metropolitan), $137
4. Mumm (Seagram), $103
5. Sandeman (Seagram), $99
Source: *Financial World,* World's Most Valuable Brands (annual), July 8, 1996, p. 57.

★ 1830 ★
TOP GINS WORLDWIDE, 1996
Ranked by: Cases sold, in millions. **Remarks:** Also notes data for 1990. **Number listed:** 7
1. Ginebra San Miguel with 26.0 million cases
2. Gordon's, 5.4
3. Seagram's, 4.1
4. Larios, 2.7
5. Gilbey's, 2.6
6. Beefeater, 2.1
7. Tanqueray, 1.6
Source: *The European*, May 15, 1997, p. 19.

★ 1831 ★
TOP SCOTCH WHISKIES WORLDWIDE, 1996
Ranked by: Cases sold, in millions. **Remarks:** Also notes data for 1990. **Number listed:** 10
1. Johnnie Walker Red Label with 7.6 million cases
2. J&B Rare, 6.0
3. Ballantines, 4.9
4. William Grants, 3.9
5. Chivas Regal, 3.7
6. Johnnie Walker Black Label, 3.4
7. Bell's, 2.9
8. Dewar's White Label, 2.8
9. Famous Grouse, 2.3
10. Passport, 2.3
Source: *The European*, May 15, 1997, p. 19.

★ 1832 ★
TOP SPIRIT BRANDS IN THE UNITED KINGDOM, 1995
Ranked by: Estimated sales, in millions of British pounds (£). **Remarks:** Notes ad agency and sales. **Number listed:** 10
1. Bell's (United Distillers) with Over £143 million
2. Gordon's Gin (United Distillers), £95-100
3. Smirnoff Red Label (IDV), £95-100
4. Famous Grouse (Highland Distilleries), £85-90
5. Teacher's Highland Cream (Allied Distillers), £65-70
6. Bacardi (Bacardi & Co.), £60-65
7. Grant's (William Grant & Sons), £45-50
8. Claymore (Whyte & Mackay), £35-40
9. Martell 3 Star (Seagram), £35-40
10. Whyte & Mackay (Whyte & Mackay), £35-40
Source: *Marketing*, July 4, 1996, p. 28.

★ 1833 ★
TOP SPIRITS BRANDS WORLDWIDE, 1995
Ranked by: Bottles consumed, in millions. **Remarks:** Includes growth rate from 1990 to 1995. **Number listed:** 20
1. Bacardi with 234.0 million bottles
2. Smirnoff, 182.4
3. Ricard, 88.8
4. Johnnie Walker Red, 87.6
5. J&B Rare, 72.0
6. Jim Bean, 66.0
7. Gordon's Gin, 63.6
8. Ballantine's, 61.2
9. Jack Daniel's Black, 57.6
10. Absolut Vodka, 56.4

Source: *The Observer*, December 15, 1996, p. 4.

★ 1834 ★
TOP SPIRITS MARKETERS WORLDWIDE BY UNIT SALES, 1996
Ranked by: Estimated sales volume, in millions of 9 liter cases. **Number listed:** 10
1. Grand Metropolitan with 38 million cases
2. Guiness, 30
3. Allied Domecq, 26
4. Seagram, 25
5. Polmos, 23
6. Bacardi-Martini, 22
7. Brown-Forman, 15
8. Pernod-Ricard, 15
9. Suntory, 12
10. LVMH Moet Hennessy, 3

Source: *The New York Times*, May 13, 1997, p. C10.

★ 1835 ★
TOP SPIRITS MARKETERS WORLDWIDE, 1996
Ranked by: Estimated sales volume, in billions of U.S. dollars. **Number listed:** 10
1. Guinness with $5.5 billion
2. Grand Metropolitan, $4.8
3. Seagram, $4.7
4. Allied Domecq, $3.7
5. Suntory, $3.0
6. Pernod-Ricard, $2.1
7. Polmos, $2.1
8. Bacardi-Martini, $2.0
9. Brown-Forman, $1.8
10. LVMH Moet Hennessy, $1.5

Source: *The New York Times*, May 13, 1997, p. C10.

★ 1836 ★
TOP VODKAS WORLDWIDE, 1996
Ranked by: Cases sold, in millions. **Remarks:** Also notes data for 1990. **Number listed:** 10
1. Smirnoff with 15.0 million cases
2. Wyborowa, 7.5

3. Zytnia, 6.7
4. Absolut, 5.3
5. Krakus, 3.8
6. Popov, 2.8
7. Premium, 2.3
8. Gordon's, 2.0
9. Finlandia, 1.8
10. Koskenkorva, 1.8

Source: *The European*, May 15, 1997, p. 19.

★ 1837 ★
VENEZUELA'S LIQUOR SALES, 1995
Ranked by: Sales estimates, in thousands of cases. **Number listed:** 8
1. Rum with 3,000 thousand cases
2. Locally produced hard liquors, cordials, 2,000
3. Imported cordials, brandies, 600
4. Imported whisky, 500
5. Imported gin, vodka, cognac, 300
6. Locally bottled whisky, 250
7. Locally produced whisky, 250
8. Pousse-cafes, imported, 200

Source: *National Trade Data Bank*, May 27, 1996, p. IMI1960118.

Lisbon Stock Exchange

★ 1838 ★
LARGEST COMPANIES ON THE LISBON STOCK EXCHANGE, 1995
Ranked by: Market value, in millions of escudos (Esc). **Number listed:** 20
1. Banco Portugues do Atlantico with Esc231,550 million
2. Banco Comercial Portugues, Esc223,211
3. Banco Espirito Santo, Esc185,048
4. Modelo Continente SGPS, Esc151,937
5. Portugal Telecom, Esc145,817
6. BTA, Esc129,812
7. Sonae Investimentos, Esc127,960
8. Jeronimo Martins, Esc109,462
9. Soporcel, Esc99,403
10. BPI, Esc98,505

Source: *GT Guide to World Equity Markets* (annual), Euromoney Publications, 1996, p. 280.

★ 1839 ★
MOST ACTIVELY TRADED SHARES ON THE LISBON STOCK EXCHANGE, 1995
Ranked by: Turnover, in millions of escudos (Esc). **Number listed:** 20
1. Modelo SGPS with Esc68,105 million
2. Sonae Investimentos, Esc46,455
3. Banco Comercial Portugues, Esc44,053

4.   Portucel Telecom, Esc41,135
5.   Banco Portugues do Atlantico, Esc34,546
6.   Banco Totta & Acores, Esc31,002
7.   Banco Portugues de Investimento, Esc30,359
8.   Radio Marconi, Esc28,012
9.   Cimentos Portugal, Esc25,566
10. BESCL, Esc22,843

Source: *GT Guide to World Equity Markets* (annual), Euromoney Publications, 1996, p. 281.

Lithuania – see under individual headings

Ljubljana Stock Exchange

★ 1840 ★
LARGEST COMPANIES ON THE LJUBLJANA STOCK EXHCANGE, 1995
Ranked by: Market value, in millions of tolars (To). **Number listed:** 10

1.   SKB Bank with To14,086.41 million
2.   Blag Trgovinski Centre, To4,391.93
3.   GPG, To3,866.18
4.   Salus, To2,184.25
5.   Nika, To2,068.80
6.   Dadas, To1,968.60
7.   Probanka, To1,699.80
8.   Hmezad Banka, To1,557.00
9.   MK Zalozba, To1,531.08
10. Finmedia, To1,301.98

Source: *GT Guide to World Equity Markets* (annual), Euromoney Publications, 1996, p. 536.

★ 1841 ★
MOST ACTIVELY TRADED SHARES ON THE LJUBLJANA STOCK EXCHANGE, 1995
Ranked by: Turnover, in millions of tolars (To). **Number listed:** 9

1.   Dadas with To9,457.51 million
2.   SKB Bank, To8,884.53
3.   Blag Trgovinski Centre, To3,653.80
4.   MK Zalozba, To3,425.36
5.   Nika, To2,816.14
6.   Probanka, To2,408.01
7.   Salus, To1,691.19
8.   Terme Catez, To1,188.04
9.   Finmedia, To1,113.24

Source: *GT Guide to World Equity Markets* (annual), Euromoney Publications, 1996, p. 536.

Loans

★ 1842 ★
LARGEST BANK LOAN PROVIDERS
Ranked by: Share of commercial bank loans, in percent. **Remarks:** Notes loans in millions of baht. **Number listed:** 15

1.   Bangkok Bank with 21.95%
2.   Krung Thai Bank, 14.20%
3.   Thai Farmers Bank, 12.73%
4.   Siam Commercial Bank, 10.74%
5.   Bank of Ayudhya, 8.52%
6.   Thai Military Bank, 6.56%
7.   First Bangkok City Bank, 5.26%
8.   Siam City Bank, 4.38%
9.   Bangkok Metropolitan Bank, 3.83%
10. Bangkok Bank of Commerce, 3.73%

Source: *Bangkok Post*, March 3, 1997, p. 14.

★ 1843 ★
TOP CORPORATE LOAN ARRANGERS IN ARGENTINA, 1996
Ranked by: Market share, in percent. **Remarks:** Shares are shown based on total loans of $3.86 billion. Notes number of deals conducted by each firm. Offshore issues were credited to countries where issues are located. Sovereign issues were excluded. Data calculated using equal apportionments. **Number listed:** 20

1.   Bank of America with 11.70%
2.   ABN-AMRO Bank NV, 9.58%
3.   Societe Generale SA, 8.67%
4.   Chase Manhattan Bank NA, 8.03%
5.   ING Barings, 5.87%
6.   Banco de Santander, 5.18%
7.   BHF-Bank, 5.18%
8.   Dresdner Bank AG, 4.44%
9.   Union Bank of Switzerland, 4.19%
10. Goldman Sachs International Ltd., 4.14%

Source: *Latin Corporate Finance Handbook* (annual), 1997, p. 26.

★ 1844 ★
TOP CORPORATE LOAN ARRANGERS IN CHILE, 1996
Ranked by: Market share, in percent. **Remarks:** Shares are shown based on total loans of $2.89 billion. Notes number of deals conducted by each firm. Offshore issues were credited to countries where issues are located. Sovereign issues were excluded. Data calculated using equal apportionments. **Number listed:** 20

1.   Chase Manhattan Bank NA with 25.12%
2.   Dresdner Bank AG, 17.10%
3.   Citicorp, 11.56%
4.   Bank of Nova Scotia, 7.76%
5.   Union Bank of Switzerland, 7.45%

6. Banco de Santander, 4.53%
7. Bank of Boston, 4.53%
8. J.P. Morgan & Co., 3.55%
9. ABN-AMRO Bank NV, 3.45%
10. CIBC Wood Gundy, 3.45%

Source: *Latin Corporate Finance Handbook* (annual), 1997, p. 26.

★ 1845 ★
TOP LOAN ARRANGERS IN AUSTRALIA
Ranked by: Loans, as a percent of all loans arranged.
Number listed: 6
1. Commonwealth with 18.9%
2. National Australia Bank, 18.2%
3. Westpac, 15.4%
4. Regionals, 23.0%
5. Other, 11.4%

Source: *Financial Times*, March 25, 1997, p. 19.

★ 1846 ★
TOP LOAN ARRANGERS IN CZECHOSLOVAKIA
Ranked by: Market share, in percent. **Number listed:** 6
1. Komercni Banka with 25.8%
2. Ceska Sportitelna, 14.5%
3. Investicni A Postovni Banka, 12.7%
4. Ceskoslovenska Obchodni Banka, 9.9%
5. Agrobanka, 5.0%
6. Other, 32.0%

Source: *Global Finance*, July 1996, p. 69.

★ 1847 ★
TOP NATIONS FOR LOAN ARRANGEMENT TO LATIN AMERICA, 1995
Ranked by: Value of loans, in millions of U.S. dollars.
Number listed: 36
1. United States with $4,306 million
2. Australia, $3,760
3. United Kingdom, $2,839
4. Indonesia, $2,056
5. Colombia, $1,557
6. Philippines, $1,097
7. Hong Kong, $954
8. Italy, $940
9. Argentina, $735
10. Netherlands, $532

Source: *Financial Times*, December 3, 1996, p. 3.

★ 1848 ★
WORLD BANK'S TOP BORROWERS, 1996
Ranked by: Amount of new loans during fiscal year 1996, in billions of U.S. dollars. **Number listed:** 6
1. China with $3.0 billion
2. India, $2.1
3. Russia, $1.8
4. Argentina, $1.5
5. Indonesia, $1.0

6. Brazil, $0.9

Source: *The Journal of Commerce*, August 2, 1996, p. 1.

Locksets

★ 1849 ★
SWEDEN'S LOCK SET MARKET
Ranked by: Market share, in percent. **Number listed:** 2
1. Assa Abloy with 75.0%
2. Other, 25.0%

Source: *National Trade Data Bank*, May 27, 1996, p. ISA9408.

Logging

★ 1850 ★
LARGEST LOGGING FIRMS IN GABON
Ranked by: Capital, in millions of C.F.A. francs (CFA).
Number listed: 8
1. Leroy Gabon with CFA2,080 million
2. Societe De Mise En Valeur Du Bois, CFA1,555
3. Rougier Ocean Gabon, CFA1,202
4. Lutexfo/Soforga, CFA375
5. Societe D'Exploitation Gabonaise, CFA254
6. Gabexfo, CFA100
7. Societe Des Bois De Lastourville, CFA50
8. Forestieres Des Bois D'Otoumbi, CFA10

Source: *National Trade Data Bank*, May 5, 1996, p. IMI950505.

London Stock Exchange

★ 1851 ★
LARGEST COMPANIES ON THE LONDON STOCK EXCHANGE, 1995
Ranked by: Market value, in millions of British pounds (£). **Number listed:** 20
1. Glaxo Wellcome with £23,552.1 million
2. British Petroleum, £23,443.8
3. Shell Transport & Trading, £23,068.9
4. HSBC Holdings, £20,204.1
5. British Telecommunications, £18,193.2
6. SmithKline Beecham, £13,619.3
7. BAT Industries, £13,313.6
8. Lloyds TSB, £12,075.5
9. Marks & Spencer, £11,781.3
10. BTR, £11,097.3

Source: *GT Guide to World Equity Markets* (annual), Euromoney Publications, 1996, p. 355.

★ 1852 ★

MOST ACTIVELY TRADED SHARES ON THE LONDON STOCK EXCHANGE, 1995

Ranked by: Turnover value, in millions of British pounds (£). **Number listed:** 20
1. HSBC Holdings with £19,253.1 million
2. Glaxo Wellcome, £19,201.6
3. Shell Transport & Trading Co., £15,490.5
4. SmithKline Beecham, £15,323.4
5. British Petroleum Co., £14,772.7
6. British Telecommunications, £12,931.8
7. Hanson, £11,193.0
8. BTR, £10,882.3
9. British Gas, £9,003.3
10. Cable & Wireless, £8,945.1

Source: *GT Guide to World Equity Markets* (annual), Euromoney Publications, 1996, p. 356.

Long Distance Telephone Calls

★ 1853 ★

TOP LONG-DISTANCE PHONE SERVICES IN CANADA, 1996

Ranked by: Market share based on revenue, in percent. **Remarks:** Notes 1995 figures. **Number listed:** 6
1. Stentor Group of Cos. with 72.0%
2. Sprint Canada Inc., 9.5%
3. AT&T Canada Long Distance Services Co., 8.0%
4. Fonorola, 3.8%
5. ACC Telenterprises Ltd., 2.2%
6. Others, 4.5%

Source: *Marketing Magazine*, May 26, 1997, p. 14.

Lotteries

★ 1854 ★

LEADING CONTINENTS FOR LOTTERY SALES, 1996

Ranked by: Sales, in millions of dollars. **Number listed:** 6
1. Europe with $56,274.4 million
2. North America, $42,394.3
3. Asia and Middle East, $14,900.0
4. Central America, South America, and the Caribbean, $3,951.9
5. Australia and New Zealand, $2,888.7
6. Africa, $289.0

Source: *Gaming & Wagering Business* (annual), June 1997, p. 49.

★ 1855 ★

LEADING COUNTRIES FOR LOTTERY SALES, 1996

Ranked by: Sales, in billions of dollars. **Number listed:** 10
1. United States with $36.4 billion
2. Spain, $10.3
3. Germany, $9.7
4. United Kingdom, $9.6
5. Japan, $7.6
6. France, $6.6
7. Italy, $6.4
8. Canada, $5.1
9. Australia, $2.5
10. Malaysia, $2.5

Source: *Gaming & Wagering Business* (annual), June 1997, p. 49.

★ 1856 ★

TOP GROSSING LOTTERY ORGANIZATIONS, 1996

Ranked by: Sales, in billions of dollars. **Number listed:** 10
1. The National Lottery (United Kingdom) with $8.1 billion
2. Dai-Ichi Kangyo Bank Lottery (Japan), $7.6
3. Organismo Nacional de Loterias y Apuestas (Spain), $7.2
4. La Francaise des Jeux (France), $6.6
5. Amministrazione Autonoma dei Monopoli di Stato (Italy), $4.2
6. New York State Lottery (United States), $3.6
7. Texas State Lottery (United States), $3.4
8. Massachusetts State Lottery (United States), $3.0
9. Organizacion Nacional de Ciegos de Espana (Spain), $3.0
10. Ohio State Lottery (United States), $2.4

Source: *Gaming & Wagering Business* (annual), June 1997, p. 49.

Lubrication and Lubricants

★ 1857 ★

PANAMA'S LUBRICANT MAKERS

Ranked by: Market share, in percent. **Number listed:** 5
1. Texaco with 30.0%
2. Esso, 27.0%
3. Shell, 20.0%
4. Delta, 19.0%
5. Accel, 4.0%

Source: *National Trade Data Bank*, March 2, 1996, p. ISA9308.

Luggage – Export-Import Trade

★ 1858 ★
HONG KONG'S TOP MARKETS FOR EXPORTS OF TRAVEL GOODS AND HANDBAGS, 1996
Ranked by: Value of exports, in thousands of Hong Kong dollars (HK$). **Number listed:** 31
1. United States with HK$11,464,805 thousand
2. Japan, HK$4,773,082
3. Germany, Federal Republic of, HK$2,828,428
4. United Kingdom, HK$2,654,569
5. France, HK$1,866,402
6. Netherlands, HK$1,167,053
7. Australia, HK$1,006,829
8. Italy, HK$1,004,924
9. Singapore, HK$965,438
10. Canada, HK$944,306
Source: http:// www.tdc.org.hk/hkstat/handbags.htm, August 25, 1997, p. 2.

Lumber Trade – Europe

★ 1859 ★
TOP LUMBER AND WOOD PRODUCTS COMPANIES
Ranked by: Sales, in millions of European Currency Units (ECUs). **Remarks:** Also notes the number of employees. **Number listed:** 47
1. Rugby Group Plc with 1,218 million ECUs
2. Danske Traelast A/S Aktieselskab, 972
3. Glunz A.G., 948
4. Fort Bouw BV, 765
5. Metsalitto Osuuskunta, 704
6. Tarkett AB, 561
7. Fritz Egger Gesellschaft M.B.H., 534
8. Lapeyre, 452
9. Hornitex-Werke Gebr. Kuennemeyer GmbH & Co. Kg., 422
10. Alno A.G., 395
Source: *Duns Europa* (annual), vol. 4, Dun & Bradstreet, 1997, p. 219+.

Luxembourg – see under individual headings

Luxembourg Stock Exchange

★ 1860 ★
LARGEST DOMESTIC COMPANIES ON THE LUXEMBOURG STOCK EXCHANGE, 1995
Ranked by: Market value, in millions of Luxembourg francs (LFr). **Number listed:** 20
1. Minorca with LFr189,377.21 million
2. Vendome Luxury Group, LFr171,468.72
3. Audiofina, LFr95,354.96
4. Exor Group, LFr55,366.00
5. Safra Republic Holdings, LFr46,932.90
6. Kredietbank SA Luxembourg, LFr34,343.47
7. Banque Generale du Luxembourg, LFr32,541.93
8. Millicom International Cellular, LFr31,449.45
9. Quilmes Industrial (Quinsa), LFr31,424.33
10. Banque Internationale a Luxembourg, LFr28,049.79
Source: *GT Guide to World Equity Markets* (annual), Euromoney Publications, 1996, p. 229.

★ 1861 ★
MOST ACTIVELY TRADED SHARES ON THE LUXEMBOURG STOCK EXCHANGE, 1995
Ranked by: Number of deals. **Number listed:** 15
1. Quilmes Industrial (Quinsa) with 1,537 deals
2. Banque Internationale a Luxembourg, 1,363
3. Banque Generale de Luxembourg, 1,151
4. Arbed, 711
5. Socfinasia, 634
6. Cegedel, 462
7. Socfinal, 457
8. Audiofina, 444
9. Selangor, 422
10. Kredietbank SA Luxembourg (ord), 397
Source: *GT Guide to World Equity Markets* (annual), Euromoney Publications, 1996, p. 229.

Macedonia – see under individual headings

Machine Tools

★ 1862 ★
DICING SAW MARKET WORLDWIDE
Ranked by: Market share, in percent. **Number listed:** 2
1. Disco Corp. with 80.0%
2. Other, 20.0%
Source: *Look Japan*, June 1996, p. 22.

★ 1863 ★
TOP MACHINE TOOL FIRMS WORLDWIDE
Ranked by: Sales, in millions of U.S. dollars. **Number listed:** 10
1. Fanuc (Japan) with $1,138 million
2. Amada (Japan), $1,104
3. Yamazaki (Japan), $1,021
4. Fuji Machine (Japan), $893
5. Okuma (Japan), $723
6. Giddings & Lewis (U.S.), $659
7. Trumpf (Germany), $646
8. Mori Seiki (Japan), $622
9. W Atlas (U.S.), $558
10. Comau (Italy), $547

Source: *Financial Times*, September 27, 1996, p. 9.

★ 1864 ★
TOP NC LATHE MAKERS IN JAPAN, 1995
Ranked by: Market share, in percent. **Number listed:** 6
1. Yamazaki Mazak with 22.3%
2. Okuma, 21.3%
3. Mori Selki, 20.1%
4. Citizen Watch, 8.6%
5. Hitachi Selki, 7.0%
6. Others, 20.7%

Source: *Nikkei Weekly*, July 29, 1996, p. 8.

Machinery – Europe

★ 1865 ★
TOP NON-ELECTRICAL MACHINERY COMPANIES IN EUROPE
Ranked by: Sales, in millions of European Currency Units (ECUs). **Remarks:** Also notes the number of employees. **Number listed:** 274
1. Mannesmann A.G. with 14,567 million ECUs
2. Fried, Krupp AG Hoesch - Krupp, 10,683
3. IBM Deutschland GmbH, 5,551
4. I.B.M. United Kingdom Holdings Ltd., 4,897
5. IBM France (Compagnie), 4,829
6. IBM Semea S.P.A., 4,619
7. I.B.M. United Kingdom Ltd., 4,337
8. Asea Brown Boveri A.G., 4,262
9. Hewlett-Packard GmbH, 3,975
10. IBM Deutschland Informationssysteme GmbH, 3,885

Source: *Duns Europa* (annual), vol. 4, Dun & Bradstreet, 1997, p. 234+.

Madagascar – see under individual headings

Madrid Stock Exchange
See: **Bolsa de Madrid**

Magazine Advertising
See: **Advertising, Magazine**

Magazines

★ 1866 ★
BRITAIN'S LEADING MAGAZINES FOR TEENS, 1996
Ranked by: Circulation for the first six months of 1996. **Number listed:** 10
1. Sugar with 361,764
2. It's Bliss, 322,063
3. TV Hits, 204,152
4. Smash Hits, 202,202
5. Top of the Pops, 192,674
6. Big!, 175,049
7. Just Seventeen, 162,490
8. Sky, 154,281
9. Mizz, 150,889
10. Live & Kicking, 141,833

Source: *The Guardian*, August 5, 1996, p. 15.

★ 1867 ★
CONSUMER MAGAZINES BY AD REVENUES IN CANADA, 1996
Ranked by: Market share based on advertising revenues, in percent. **Remarks:** Notes 1995 figures. **Number listed:** 11
1. Maclean's with 9.2%
2. Chatelaine, 8.9%
3. Canadian Living, 6.5%
4. TV Guide, 5.8%
5. Time, 5.1%
6. Reader's Digest, 4.7%
7. TV Times, 3.9%
8. Report On Business Magazine, 3.2%
9. Homemaker's, 3.1%
10. Flare, 2.9%

Source: *Marketing Magazine*, May 26, 1997, p. 15.

★ 1868 ★
MOST READ MAGAZINES IN FINLAND, 1996
Ranked by: Circulation, in thousands. **Remarks:** Includes 1995 figures. **Number listed:** 14
1. Se og Hor with 1442 thousand
2. Hjemmet, 992
3. Norsk Ukeblad, 856
4. Familien, 641

5. Allers, 616
6. Vi Menn, 608
7. Illustrert Vitenskap, 580
8. Villmarksliv, 440
9. Bonytt, 390
10. KK, 390

Source: *Aftenposten*, March 11, 1997, p. 24.

★ 1869 ★

TOP MAGAZINE PUBLISHERS IN BRITAIN, 1995

Ranked by: Market share based on circulation, in percent. **Number listed:** 10

1. IPC Weeklies with 13.53%
2. BBC, 7.59%
3. Bauer, 7.51%
4. IPC Southbank, 7.19%
5. National Mags, 4.63%
6. EMAP Elan, 4.44%
7. IPC Specialists, 4.26%
8. Reader's Digest, 3.73%
9. DC Thomson, 3.05%
10. Others, 44.07%

Source: *The Guardian*, August 5, 1996, p. 15.

Mail Order Business

★ 1870 ★

MAIL ORDER MARKETS IN WESTERN EUROPE

Ranked by: Turnover, in millions of U.S. dollars.
Remarks: Also notes turnover per capita. **Number listed:** 12

1. Germany with $22,992 million
2. France, $8,403
3. United Kingdom, $6,195
4. Switzerland, $1,404
5. Italy, $1,397
6. Austria, $1,338
7. Sweden, $1,337
8. Netherlands, $1,223
9. Belgium, $706
10. Denmark, $673

Source: *National Trade Data Bank*, December 1995, p. ISA9512.

★ 1871 ★

TOP MAIL ORDER COMPANIES WORLDWIDE, 1995

Ranked by: Mail order sales, in millions of U.S. dollars.
Number listed: 25

1. Otto Versand with $11,800 million
2. United Services Automobile Association, $6,634
3. Quelle, $6,078
4. Time Warner, $5,596

5. Tele-Communications Inc., $4,465
6. J.C. Penney, $4,216
7. Dell Computer Corp., $4,042
8. American Association of Retired Persons, $3,936
9. Gateway 2000, $3,500
10. Great Universal Stores, $3,236

Source: *Direct Marketing*, August 1996, p. 56.

Mail Order Business – Netherlands

★ 1872 ★

DUTCH MAIL ORDER MARKET, 1994

Ranked by: Turnover, in millions of U.S. dollars per product. **Number listed:** 8

1. Textiles with $418 million
2. Consumer electronics, $170
3. Books, $113
4. Insurances, $104
5. Furniture, $77
6. Domestic appliances, $74
7. Other, $228

Source: *National Trade Data Bank*, February 9, 1996, p. ISA9512.

Mail Order Business – United Kingdom

★ 1873 ★

MAIL ORDER COMPANIES BY SALES IN THE UNITED KINGDOM

Ranked by: Sales, in millions of U.S. dollars. **Number listed:** 7

1. Great Universal Stores Plc with $3,334 million
2. Littlewoods Plc, $1,601
3. Freemans Plc, $870
4. Grattan, $754
5. Empire Stores, $409
6. N. Brown, $378
7. Other, $6,454

Source: *Catalog Age*, July 1997, p. 6.

★ 1874 ★

MAIL ORDER MARKET IN THE UNITED KINGDOM

Ranked by: Market share, in percent. **Number listed:** 7

1. Great Universal Stores Plc with 24%
2. Littlewoods Plc, 12%
3. Freemans Plc, 6%
4. Grattan, 5%
5. Empire Stores, 3%
6. N. Brown, 3%

7. Other, 47%
Source: *Catalog Age*, July 1997, p. 6.

Malawi – see under individual headings

Malaysia – see under individual headings

Malta – see under individual headings

Management Consultants
See: **Business Consultants**

Managers
See: **Executives**

Manufacturing Industries

★ 1875 ★
CANADIAN INDUSTRIES WITH THE LARGEST INCREASE IN MANUFACTURING PRICES, 1996
Ranked by: Change in manufacturing prices from 1995 to 1996, in percent. **Remarks:** Notes figures for change from 1994 to 1995. **Number listed:** 22
1. Petroleum and coal products with + 11.5% change
2. Food, + 4.1%
3. Tobacco, + 3.3%
4. Machinery, + 2.9%
5. Wood, + 2.8%
6. Leather, + 2.7%
7. Transport equipment, + 2.6%
8. Clothing, + 2.5%
9. Beverage, + 2.4%
10. Textile products, + 2.1%
Source: *Globe and Mail*, April 4, 1997, p. B8.

★ 1876 ★
LARGEST COMMERCIAL SECTORS IN COLOMBIA
Ranked by: Percent distribution, based on 132,000 enterprises. **Number listed:** 6
1. Food, beverage, and tobacco (retail and wholesale) with 28.5%
2. Restaurants, cafeterias, and hotels, 15.2%
3. Textiles and garments, 10.6%

4. Plastics, 7.5%
5. Vehicles and accessories, 5.0%
6. Drugs, medecine, cosmetics, and chemical products, 4.7%
Source: *National Trade Data Bank*, June 24, 1997, p. ISA970501.

★ 1877 ★
LEAST PROFITABLE SECTORS IN POLAND, 1996
Ranked by: Loss for the first four months of 1996, in percent. **Number listed:** 12
1. Masonry with -22.81% profit
2. Inland water transportation, -21.36%
3. Retail outlets, except for retail chains, -17.86%
4. Guns and ammunition, -17.15%
5. Mining, -14.66%
6. Construction infrastructure, -13.63%
7. Furs and fur products, -11.85%
8. Libraries, archives, and museums, -11.84%
9. Leather clothing, -10.22%
10. Building stone production, -9.64%
Source: *National Trade Data Bank*, September 11, 1996, p. IMI960906.

★ 1878 ★
MOST PROFITABLE SECTORS IN POLAND, 1996
Ranked by: Profit for the first four months of 1996, in percent. **Remarks:** During this period, 119 sectors were profitable. Operating costs of 186 sectors ranged from 39.9% to 115.9%. The average cost indicator amounted to 92.5%. **Number listed:** 12
1. Chemical products with 31.70% profit
2. Telecommunications, 20.26%
3. Fruit and vegetable processing, 16.52%
4. Agriculture and forestry machinery, 16.35%
5. Cement, lime, and clay, 12.76%
6. Ceramic tiles, 12.65%
7. Financial services, 11.48%
8. Radio and television broadcasting, 10.54%
9. Data processing, 10.36%
10. Surveillance and security, 10.01%
Source: *National Trade Data Bank*, September 11, 1996, p. IMI960906.

★ 1879 ★
TOP MANUFACTURING COMPANIES WORLDWIDE, 1996
Ranked by: Revenues, in millions of U.S. dollars. **Remarks:** Also notes earnings per share, profit margin, profit growth, total equity, and debt to equity ratio. **Number listed:** 1000
1. General Motors Corp. with $164,069.0 million
2. Ford Motor Co., $146,991.0
3. Royal Dutch Petroleum Co., $139,082.9
4. Exxon Corp., $134,249.0
5. Mobil Corp., $81,503.0

6. General Electric Co., $79,179.0
7. International Bus. Machines Corp., $75,947.0
8. British Petroleum Co. PLC, $75,796.7
9. Hitachi Ltd., $70,677.2
10. Toyota Motor Corp., $70,652.5

Source: *IndustryWeek,* IndustryWeek 1000 (annual), June 9, 1997, p. 50.

Manufacturing Industries – Asia

★ 1880 ★
MOST ADMIRED LIGHT MANUFACTURING COMPANIES IN ASIA, 1997

Ranked by: Results of a questionnaire sent to more than 9,000 managers and CEOs chosen from the magazine's circulation and evaluated by Asia Market Intelligence, a research firm. **Remarks:** Respondents scored each company in terms of overall admirability, then on six attributes: quality of products, quality of management, contribution to local economy, record as an employer, growth potential and reputation for ethics. Also notes 1996 figures. **Number listed:** 5

1. NEC with 32.0%
2. Fujitsu, 21.9%
3. IBM, 11.9%
4. Apple, 11.0%
5. Toshiba, 5.4%

Source: *Asian Business,* Most Admired Companies in Asia (annual), May 1997, p. 30.

Manufacturing Industries – Europe

★ 1881 ★
TOP MISCELLANEOUS MANUFACTURING COMPANIES IN EUROPE

Ranked by: Sales, in millions of European Currency Units (ECUs). **Remarks:** Also notes the number of employees. **Number listed:** 39

1. Comadur S.A. with 1,704 million ECUs
2. Tiedemanns - Joh.H. Andresen Ans, 608
3. Lego Systems A/S, 597
4. Pelikan Holding A.G., 527
5. Tefal S.A., 468
6. Artsana S.P.A., 409
7. ADP Gauselmann GmbH, 394
8. Salomon S.A., 346
9. Engel Automatisierungstechnik Gesellschaft M.B.H., 334
10. Rosy Blue NV, 332

Source: *Duns Europa* (annual), vol. 4, Dun & Bradstreet, 1997, p. 243+.

★ 1882 ★
TOP STONE, CLAY, GLASS, AND CONCRETE MANUFACTURING COMPANIES IN EUROPE

Ranked by: Sales, in millions of European Currency Units (ECUs). **Remarks:** Also notes the number of employees. **Number listed:** 117

1. Lafarge with 5,165 million ECUs
2. R.M.C. Group Plc, 4,387
3. Pilkington Plc, 2,852
4. Heidelberger Zement A.G., 2,741
5. Redland Plc, 2,668
6. C.R.H. Plc, 2,438
7. Schott Glaswerke, 2,326
8. T & N Plc, 2,229
9. Ciments Francais, 1,955
10. Blue Circle Industries Plc, 1,891

Source: *Duns Europa* (annual), vol. 4, Dun & Bradstreet, 1997, p. 229+.

Maquiladoras

★ 1883 ★
MAQUILADORAS WITH THE MOST EMPLOYEES IN YUCATAN

Ranked by: Number of employees. **Remarks:** Also notes products manufactured. **Number listed:** 25

1. Createx, S.A. de C.V. with 1,940
2. Monty Industries, S.A. de C.V., 1,050
3. Balmex, S.A. de C.V., 998
4. Industrias Oxford de Merida, S.A. de C.V., 600
5. Manufacturera Lee de Izamal, S.A. de C.V., 530
6. Falco Electronics Mexico, S.A., 510
7. Joyas de Exportacion, S.A. de C.V., 500
8. Ormex, S.A. de C.V., 460
9. Doulton de Mexico, S.A. de C.V., 420
10. Tejidos de Henequen, 350

Source: *Business Mexico,* February 1997, p. 40.

Marinas

★ 1884 ★
SPAIN'S MARINAS BY REGION

Ranked by: Number of sports boats held in each region. **Remarks:** Spain currently has an estimated 270 marinas to serve 127,000 sports boats. **Number listed:** 10

1. Catalonia with 33,020 sports boats
2. Balearic Islands, 31,750
3. Levante, 19,050
4. Andaluzia, 16,510
5. Galicia, 7,620
6. Canary Islands, 5,715

7. Cantabria, 3,810
8. Basque Region, 3,175
9. Asturias, 2,540
10. Others, 3,810

Source: *National Trade Data Bank*, June 14, 1996, p. IMI960612.

Market Research Firms

★ **1885** ★

TOP GLOBAL RESEARCH ORGANIZATIONS, 1996
Ranked by: Research revenue, in millions of U.S. dollars. **Remarks:** Also notes number of full-time employees, percent change, and revenues from outside home country. **Number listed:** 25
1. ACNielsen Corp. (United States) with $1,358.6 million
2. Cognizant Corp. (United States), $1,223.8
3. The Kantar Group Ltd. (United Kingdom), $472.9
4. Information Resources Inc. (United States), $405.6
5. GfK AG (Germany), $317.6
6. SOFRES Group S.A. (France), $276.0
7. Infratest Burke AG (Germany), $167.5
8. IPSOS Group S.A. (France), $161.4
9. The Arbitron Company (United States), $153.1
10. PMSI/Source Informatics (United States), $152.2

Source: *Marketing News*, August 18, 1997, p. 44.

Massachusetts – see under individual headings

Mauritania – see under individual headings

Mauritius – see under individual headings

Meat Industry

★ **1886** ★

CHINA'S LEADING MEAT PRODUCING SECTORS, 1996
Ranked by: Percent distribution. **Number listed:** 4
1. Pork with 67%
2. Poultry, 17%
3. Beef, 10%

4. Mutton, 6%

Source: *China-Britain Trade Review*, July 1997, p. 10.

★ **1887** ★

LAMB AND GOAT MEAT PRODUCTION BY COUNTRY
Ranked by: Production, in metric tons. **Number listed:** 10
1. China with 1,700 thousand metric tons
2. Australia, 656
3. India, 620
4. Former U.S.S.R., 501
5. New Zealand, 492
6. Turkey, 370
7. Russia, 280
8. Spain, 240
9. Saudi Arabia, 199
10. Kazakhstan, 195

Source: *World Agricultural Production*, March 1995, p. 46.

★ **1888** ★

PROCESSED MEAT MARKET IN THE PHILIPPINES
Ranked by: Market share, in percent. **Number listed:** 4
1. Purefoods with 50.0%
2. RFM, 25.0%
3. San Miguel, 11.0%
4. Other, 14.0%

Source: *Asiaweek*, May 10, 1996, p. 52.

★ **1889** ★

TOP BROILER MEAT PRODUCERS, 1994
Ranked by: Metric tons of meat. **Number listed:** 15
1. North America with 12,222 thousand metric tons
2. European Union, 5,004
3. Asia, 4,941
4. South America, 4,371
5. Russia, 1,030
6. Africa, 855
7. Middle East, 802
8. Eastern Europe, 517
9. Oceania, 437
10. Other Western Europe, 98

Source: *Poultry: World Markets and Trade* U.S. Department of Agriculture, January 1994, p. 17.

Meat Industry – Canada

★ 1890 ★

TOP CANADIAN MEAT AND POULTRY COMPANIES, 1995

Ranked by: Sales, in millions of Canadian dollars.
Remarks: Also notes number of employees, plants, and subsidiaries. **Number listed:** 8

1. Maple Leaf Foods, Inc. with $3,067 million
2. Schneider Corp., $826
3. Olymel and Co. Ltd., $605
4. Flamingo Foods, $349
5. Intercontinental Packers Ltd., $335
6. Lilydale Poultry, $299
7. Maple Lodge Farms Ltd., $273
8. Fletcher's Fine Foods Ltd., $270

Source: *Meat & Poultry Magazine,* July 1996, p. 42.

Meat Industry – Export-Import Trade

★ 1891 ★

TOP MARKETS FOR U.K. BEEF AND CALF EXPORTS, 1995

Ranked by: Value, in millions of British pounds (£).
Number listed: 6

1. France with £179.0 million
2. Italy, £126.0
3. Ireland, £52.0
4. Netherlands, £49.0
5. Rest of European Union, £50.7
6. Others, £39.2

Source: *Financial Times,* September 19, 1997, p. 9.

Meat Packing Industry

See: **Meat Industry**

Mechanical Contractors

See: **Contractors**

Media Companies

★ 1892 ★

CANADA'S TOP MEDIA BUYING FIRMS, 1996

Ranked by: Projected media billings, in millions of U.S. dollars. **Remarks:** Clients are shown for each firm.
Number listed: 11

1. McKim Media Group with $360.0 million

2. Initiative Media, $324.0
3. Alliance HYPN/Strategem, $312.0
4. Media Buying Services Ltd./Publicite MBS, $275.0
5. WPP Alliance, $245.0
6. Cossette Communication-Marketing, $216.0
7. Young & Rubicam Ltd., $210.0
8. Genesis Media Inc., $176.0
9. Optimedia Canada, $155.0
10. Leo Burnett Company Ltd., $145.0

Source: *Marketing Magazine,* Annual Agency Issue, December 9, 1996, p. 24.

Media – Europe

★ 1893 ★

TOP MEDIA FIRMS IN EUROPE, 1994

Ranked by: Media revenue, in thousands of U.S. dollars.
Remarks: Also notes total revenues. **Number listed:** 15

1. Reed Elsevier with $3,187.3 thousand
2. Fininvest, $3,122.2
3. Bertelsmann, $3,065.7
4. Havas, $2,815.3
5. CLT, $2,805.0
6. Axel Springer, $2,420.3
7. Matra Hachette, $2,160.9
8. Bauer, $1,956.0
9. Canal+, $1,577.6
10. WAZ, $1,573.4

Source: *Advertising Age International,* Special Issue: Europe, May 1997, p. I3.

Medical Equipment and Supplies, International

★ 1894 ★

GLOBAL MAMMOGRAPHY MARKET, 1995

Ranked by: Market share, in percent. **Number listed:** 7

1. Trex Medical with 41.0%
2. GE, 21.0%
3. Instrumentarium, 10.0%
4. Siemens, 10.0%
5. Acoma, 4.0%
6. Fischer, 4.0%
7. Other, 10.0%

Source: *Investor's Business Daily,* September 24, 1996, p. A6.

★ 1895 ★
GLOBAL STEREOTACTIC NEEDLE BIOPSY MARKET, 1995
Ranked by: Market share, in percent. **Number listed:** 7
1. Trex Medical with 47.0%
2. Fischer, 19.0%
3. Philips, 14.0%
4. GE, 13.0%
5. Siemens, 6.0%
6. Other, 1.0%

Source: *Investor's Business Daily*, September 24, 1996, p. A6.

★ 1896 ★
TOP X-RAY/FLUROSCOPY MAKERS WORLDWIDE, 1995
Ranked by: Market share, in percent. **Number listed:** 7
1. GE with 24.0%
2. Philips, 22.0%
3. Siemens, 19.0%
4. Toshiba, 16.0%
5. Picker, 10.0%
6. Trex Medical, 4.0%
7. Other, 5.0%

Source: *Investor's Business Daily*, September 24, 1996, p. A6.

Medical Technology, International

★ 1897 ★
LEADING MEDICAL TECHNOLOGY CONSUMERS IN EMERGING MARKETS
Ranked by: Consumption growth, in percent. **Number listed:** 15
1. China with 28% growth
2. Thailand, 19%
3. Malaysia, 18%
4. Taiwan, 18%
5. India, 16%
6. Chile, 15%
7. Indonesia, 15%
8. Korea, 13%
9. Argentina, 8%
10. Brazil, 8%

Source: *The Journal of Commerce*, March 19, 1997, p. 1.

★ 1898 ★
TOP MEDICAL TECHNOLOGY PRODUCERS
Ranked by: Production, in billions of U.S. dollars. **Number listed:** 6
1. United States with $61.2 billion
2. Western Europe, $36.8
3. Japan, $18.9
4. Canada, $1.5

5. Australia, $0.3
6. Other, $10.8

Source: *The Journal of Commerce*, March 19, 1997, p. 1.

Meeting Sites

★ 1899 ★
TOP SITES FOR INTERNATIONAL MEETINGS, 1995
Ranked by: Distribution, in percent. **Remarks:** Japan is the only Asian country in the top 15. **Number listed:** 15
1. United States with 9.03%
2. France, 6.43%
3. United Kingdom, 5.25%
4. Germany, 4.76%
5. Italy, 4.10%
6. Switzerland, 2.98%
7. Belgium, 2.97%
8. Netherlands, 2.82%
9. Austria, 2.75%
10. Spain, 2.32%

Source: *Meeting News*, May 26, 1997, p. 54.

Men's Clothing
See: **Clothing and Dress – Men**

Merchant Banking
See Also: **Investment Banking**

★ 1900 ★
TOP MERCHANT BANKS IN INDIA, 1996-1997
Ranked by: Sum managed, in Rupees crore (RCr). **Number listed:** 10
1. SBI Capital Markets with RCr7,773
2. JM Financial Services, RCr7,222
3. Kotak Mahindra Finance, RCr7,132
4. DSP Consultants, RCr6,768
5. Enam Financials, RCr3,830
6. R.R. Financial, RCr2,237
7. Lodha Capital, RCr2,037
8. ANZ Grindlays, RCr1,800
9. IDBI, RCr1,661
10. ICICI Securities, RCr1,602

Source: *Business Today*, June 21, 1997, p. 21.

Mergers
See: **Corporate Acquisitions and Mergers**

Metal Industry

★ 1901 ★
ASIA'S TOP METALS FIRMS, 1995
Ranked by: Sales, in millions of U.S. dollars. **Remarks:** Includes profits, profits as a percentage of sales and assets, and overall sales rank. **Number listed:** 20

1. Nippon Steel Corp. with $31,414.7 million
2. NKK Corp., $19,200.4
3. Kobe Steel, $15,702.4
4. Sumitomo Metal Industries, $15,217.8
5. Kawasaki Steel, $12,379.2
6. Sumitomo Electric Industries, $12,340.6
7. Pohang Iron & Steel, $11,206.0
8. Toyo Seikant Metal, $7,842.9
9. Furukawa Electric, $7,477.3
10. Nippon Light Metal, $6,472.5

Source: *Asiaweek*, The Asiaweek 1,000, November 22, 1996, p. 162.

★ 1902 ★
LARGEST METALS COMPANIES, 1995
Ranked by: Revenue, in millions of U.S. dollars. **Remarks:** Notes profits and global rank. **Number listed:** 15

1. Nippon Steel (Japan) with $30,614 million
2. Thyssen (Germany), $28,032
3. NKK (Japan), $18,711
4. Fried, Krupp (Germany), $16,423
5. Usinor-Sacilor (France), $15,719
6. Kobe Steel (Japan), $15,302
7. Sumitomo Metal Industries (Japan), $14,830
8. Broken Hill Proprietary (Australia), $13,746
9. Alcoa (United States), $12,655
10. Kawasaki Steel (Japan), $12,064

Source: *Fortune,* The Global 500: World's Biggest Corporations (annual), August 5, 1996, p. F-22.

Metal Industry – Europe

★ 1903 ★
TOP EUROPEAN COMPANIES IN PRIMARY METAL INDUSTRIES
Ranked by: Sales, in millions of European Currency Units (ECUs). **Remarks:** Also notes number of employees. **Number listed:** 125

1. Viag A.G. with 19,033 million ECUs
2. Usinor Sacilor, 12,195
3. Thyssen Stahl A.G., 5,418
4. British Steel Plc, 5,099
5. Engelhard Ltd., 5,038
6. Pechiney International, 4,934
7. Alusuisse-Lonza Holding A.G., 4,794

8. Ilva Laminati Piani S.P.A., 4,752
9. Sollac, 4,362
10. Koninklijke Hoogovens NV, 3,813

Source: *Duns Europa* (annual), vol. 4, Dun & Bradstreet, 1997, p. 230+.

Metal Industry – France

★ 1904 ★
TOP BASIC METALS PRODUCERS IN SOUTH KOREA, 1996
Ranked by: Sales for the first six months of 1996, in hundred million won (W). **Number listed:** 33

1. Pohang Iron & Steel with W41,739.9 hundred million
2. LG Metals, W8,271.5
3. Inchon Iron & Steel, W7,591.2
4. Dong Kuk Steel Mill, W5,395.7
5. Dongbu Steel, W4,929.3
6. Sammi Steel, W4,503.6
7. Poongsan, W3,879.3
8. Han Bo Steel, W3,326.4
9. Union Steel Mfg., W2,998.5
10. Korea Iron & Steel, W2,685.2

Source: *Business Korea*, October 1996, p. 36.

Metal Products

★ 1905 ★
ALUMINUM WINDOW/DOOR FRAME MAKERS IN TURKEY
Ranked by: Market share, in percent. **Number listed:** 5

1. Fenis-Istanbul with 13.0%
2. Aksan-Istanbul, 11.0%
3. Aykim-Kocarli, 11.0%
4. Alcin-Istanbul, 8.0%
5. Other, 57.0%

Source: *National Trade Data Bank*, May 27, 1996, p. ISA9311.

★ 1906 ★
LEADING FABRICATED METAL PRODUCTS COMPANIES IN SOUTH KOREA, 1996
Ranked by: Sales for the first six months of 1996, in hundred million won (W). **Number listed:** 12

1. Kum Kang Ind. with W911.7 hundred million
2. Korea Tungsten, W705.2
3. Daelim Trading, W506.4
4. Tae Yang Metal, W471.7
5. Hyundai Metal, W335.2
6. Cho Sun Steel Wire, W269.1
7. San Nae Dle Insu, W256.0

8. Samick Ind., W243.9
9. Sam Hwa Crown & Closure, W240.6
10. Eusung Ind., W220.0

Source: *Business Korea*, October 1996, p. 36.

Metal Products – Europe

★ 1907 ★

**TOP EUROPEAN COMPANIES IN FABRICATED
METAL PRODUCTS**
Ranked by: Sales, in millions of European Currency
Units (ECUs). **Remarks:** Does not include machinery
and transportation equipment. Also notes number of
employees. **Number listed:** 165

1. Framatome with 1,885 million ECUs
2. Koninklijke Emballage Industrie Van Leer NV,
   1,873
3. Schmalbach-Lubeca A.G., 1,872
4. T.I. Group Plc, 1,815
5. Williams Holdings Plc, 1,704
6. Adolf Wuerth GmbH & Co. KG, 1,618
7. Diehl GmbH & Co., 1,425
8. Buderus A.G., 1,412
9. Georg Fischer A.G., 1,365
10. Glynwed International Plc, 1,334

Source: *Duns Europa* (annual), vol. 4, Dun & Bradstreet,
1997, p. 232+.

Metals – Asia

★ 1908 ★

TOP METALS COMPANIES ASIA
Ranked by: Sales, in thousands of U.S. dollars. **Remarks:**
Also notes profit as a percent of sales. **Number listed:**
100

1. Kobe Steel Ltd. with $14,339,495 thousand
2. Sumitomo Metal Industries, $13,896,941
3. Kawasaki Steel Corp., $11,304,699
4. Sumitomo Electric Industries Ltd., $11,269,446
5. NKK Corp., $11,259,631
6. Mitsubishi Materials Corp., $10,948,883
7. Furukawa Electric Co. Ltd., $6,828,320
8. Nippon Light Metal Co. Ltd., $5,910,718
9. Sumitomo Metal Mining Co. Ltd., $4,969,776
10. Hitachi Metals Ltd., $4,597,951

Source: *Asia's 7,500 Largest Companies* (annual), Dun &
Bradstreet, 1997, p. 79.

Mexico – see under individual headings

Mexico Stock Exchange

★ 1909 ★

**LARGEST COMPANIES ON THE MEXICAN STOCK
EXCHANGE, 1995**
Ranked by: Market value, in billions of U.S. dollars.
Number listed: 20

1. Telmex with $16.504 billion
2. Gcarso, $5.932
3. Cemex, $5.575
4. Gmodelo, $4.162
5. Cifra, $4.064
6. Kimber, $3.540
7. Gmexico, $3.401
8. Banacci, $3.371
9. Alfa, $2.677
10. TTolmex, $2.163

Source: *GT Guide to World Equity Markets* (annual),
Euromoney Publications, 1996, p. 245.

★ 1910 ★

**MOST ACTIVELY TRADED ISSUES ON THE
MEXICAN STOCK EXCHANGE, 1995**
Ranked by: Trading value, in millions of U.S. dollars.
Remarks: Also notes stock volume. **Number listed:** 20

1. Telmex L with $6,926.3 million
2. Gcarso A1, $2,387.4
3. Cemex B, $2,311.4
4. Ttolmex B2, $1,414.5
5. Cemex CPO, $1,154.7
6. Cifra C, $1,143.7
7. Gmexico G, $1,109.6
8. Kimber A, $1,051.1
9. Femsa B, $1,000.7
10. Alfa A, $981.8

Source: *GT Guide to World Equity Markets* (annual),
Euromoney Publications, 1996, p. 245.

Microcomputers
See Also: Computer Industry

★ 1911 ★

**LEADING PRODUCERS OF DESKTOP AND
NOTEBOOK PERSONAL COMPUTERS, 1996**
Ranked by: Market size, in millions of units. **Remarks:**
Notes figures for 1995 and estimates for 1997. **Number
listed:** 6

1. Compaq with 7.1 million
2. IBM, 6.0
3. Apple, 4.0
4. NEC, 3.5
5. Hewlett-Packard, 3.2

6. Packard Bell, 2.9
Source: *Electronic News*, January 6, 1997, p. 46.

★ 1912 ★
TOP MICROCOMPUTER MAKERS IN FRANCE, 1996
Ranked by: Market share, in percent. **Number listed:** 11
1. Compaq with 14.3%
2. Hewlett-Packard, 10.9%
3. IBM, 10.4%
4. Apple, 6.5%
5. ZDS, 5.9%
6. Packard Bell, 5.5%
7. Toshiba, 4.3%
8. Dell, 4.0%
9. Olivetti, 3.7%
10. SNI, 2.3%
Source: *Nouvel Economiste*, February 14, 1997, p. 49.

Microprocessors

★ 1913 ★
LEADING PRODUCERS OF MICROCHIPS IN JAPAN, 1996
Ranked by: Output, in billions of Japanese yen (¥). **Number listed:** 6
1. NEC Corp. with ¥330 billion
2. Hitachi Ltd., ¥302
3. Toshiba Corp., ¥267
4. Mitsubishi Electric Corp., ¥182
5. Fujitsu Ltd., ¥181
6. Oki Electric Industry Co., ¥108
Source: *Nikkei Weekly*, July 14, 1997, p. 7.

★ 1914 ★
WORLDWIDE MICROPROCESSOR MARKET, 1996
Ranked by: Market share, in percent. **Remarks:** Notes manufacturers. **Number listed:** 6
1. X86 with 92.8%
2. PowerPC, 3.3%
3. MIPS, 2.1%
4. Sparc, 1.2%
5. 68000, 0.4%
6. Alpha, 0.1%
Source: *Business Week*, April 1997, p. 95.

Microwave Ovens

★ 1915 ★
TOP MICROWAVE OVEN MANUFACTURERS IN CHINA, 1995
Ranked by: Units shipped. **Number listed:** 6
1. Xianhua with 800,000 units
2. Gelanshi, 200,000
3. Shangling, 150,000
4. Xinbao, 100,000
5. Kaige, 80,000
6. Haier, 20,000
Source: *Appliance Manufacturer*, February 1997, p. G-17.

★ 1916 ★
TOP MICROWAVE OVENS IN JAPAN, 1996
Ranked by: Market share as of September 1996, in percent. **Remarks:** Data are based on sales in large department stores in 35 major cities. **Number listed:** 5
1. Galanz with 46.1%
2. SMC, 11.5%
3. Hulbao, 10.5%
4. Matsushita, 7.9%
5. Shanghai Matsushita, 5.8%
Source: *South China Morning Post*, February 13, 1997, p. B7.

Milk

★ 1917 ★
GERMANY'S MILK MARKET
Ranked by: Market share, in percent. **Number listed:** 7
1. Ehrmann with 15.1%
2. Sudmilch, 12.9%
3. Bauer, 11.8%
4. Zott, 10.1%
5. Gervais Danone, 7.8%
6. Nestle, 5.7%
7. Other, 36.6%
Source: *Wirtschaftswoche*, May 23, 1996, p. 66.

★ 1918 ★
GREAT BRITAIN'S MILK MARKET
Ranked by: Market share, in percent. **Number listed:** 5
1. Northern Foods with 25.0%
2. Unigate, 16.0%
3. Dairy Crest, 10.0%
4. Other, 49.0%
Source: *The Observer*, February 18, 1996, p. 4.

★ 1919 ★
TOP MILK PRODUCERS IN SPAIN
Ranked by: Production, in millions of liters. **Number listed:** 11
1. Corporacion Alimentaria Penasanta with 820 million liters
2. Pascual, 532
3. Grupo Leyma, 490
4. Nestle, 310
5. Danone e Iparlat, 300
6. Ilas, 290
7. Lagasa, 250
8. Puleva, 230
9. Kraft, 210
10. Clesa, 200
Source: *El Pais*, June 22, 1997, p. 12.

Millionaires – United Kingdom

★ 1920 ★
TOP EXECUTIVE DIRECTORS UNDER 40 IN THE UNITED KINGDOM, 1997
Ranked by: Net worth, in millions of British pounds (£).
Remarks: Also notes company. **Number listed:** 20
1. Daniel Chiu with £49.8 million
2. Daniel Wagner, £30.5
3. Daniel Harris, £18.7
4. Stanley Fink, £9.1
5. Julian Schild, £6.5
6. Wayne Channon, £5.5
7. Bruno Kemoun, £5.0
8. Luke Johnson, £4.3
9. Stephen Streater, £4.0
10. Robert Laurence, £3.8
Source: *Director*, May 1997, p. 34.

Mineral Industry
See: **Mining Industry**

Mining Industry

★ 1921 ★
BRAZIL'S TOP MINING PRODUCTS, 1995
Ranked by: Reserves, in millions of tons. **Remarks:** Notes Brazil's rank in world market. **Number listed:** 10
1. Iron with 20,0000.0 million tons
2. Aluminum, 3,910.0
3. Kaolin, 1,700.0
4. Magnesite, 180.0
5. Manganese, 69.0

6. Graphite, 56.0
7. Vermiculite, 15.0
8. Flourite, 8.0
9. Niobium, 4.5
10. Gold, 0.8
Source: *The Wall Street Journal*, January 22, 1997, p. A10.

★ 1922 ★
LARGEST MINING AND CRUDE OIL PRODUCTION COMPANIES, 1995
Ranked by: Revenue, in millions of U.S. dollars.
Remarks: Notes profits and global rank. **Number listed:** 3
1. Pemex (Mexico) with $22,330 million
2. Ruhrkohle (Germany), $17,233
3. Statoil (Norway), $13,648
Source: *Fortune,* The Global 500: World's Biggest Corporations (annual), August 5, 1996, p. F-23.

★ 1923 ★
MINERAL EXPLORATION SPENDING IN AUSTRALIA, 1995-1996
Ranked by: Expenditures on mineral exploration by region for July 1995 to June 1996, distributed in percent.
Number listed: 7
1. Western Australia with 54.0%
2. Queensland, 19.0%
3. Tasmania, 9.0%
4. New South Wales, 8.0%
5. Northern Territories, 5.0%
6. Victoria, 4.0%
7. South Australia, 3.0%
Source: *Financial Times*, November 8, 1996, p. 24.

★ 1924 ★
TOP MINING COMPANIES IN SOUTH KOREA, 1996
Ranked by: Sales for the first six months of 1996, in hundred million won (W). **Remarks:** Also notes net profits. **Number listed:** 3
1. Young Poong Mining & Construction with W870.5 hundred million
2. Daesung Resources, W160.5
3. Dong Won, W123.3
Source: *Business Korea*, October 1996, p. 31.

★ 1925 ★
TOP NON-METAL MINERAL COMPANIES IN SOUTH KOREA, 1996
Ranked by: Sales, in hundred million won (W) for the first six months of 1996. **Number listed:** 25
1. Ssangyong Cement Mfg. with W6,696.2 hundred million
2. Tong Yan G Cement, W3,306.2
3. Keumkang, W2,491.0
4. Halla Cement, W2,026.0

5. Hanil Cement, W1,730.9
6. Sungshin Cement Mfg., W1,620.7
7. Hyundai Cement, W1,597.8
8. Hankuk Glass, W1,521.4
9. Hankuk Electric Glass, W1,403.6
10. Asia Cement Mfg., W1,054.5
Source: *Business Korea*, October 1996, p. 35.

★ 1926 ★
TOP NONFUEL MINING COMPANIES IN THE WESTERN WORLD, 1995
Ranked by: Market share, in percent. **Number listed:** 20
1. Anglo American Corp of South Africa Ltd. with 7.78%
2. RTZ Corporation PLC (United Kingdom), 5.70%
3. Broken Hill Pty Co. Ltd. (Australia), 3.43%
4. State of Brazil, 3.18%
5. State of Chile, 2.90%
6. Gencor Ltd. (South Africa), 1.92%
7. Phelps Dodge Corp. (United States), 1.72%
8. ASARCO Inc. (United States), 1.64%
9. Freeport McMoran Copper & Gold (United States), 1.48%
10. Inco Ltd. (Canada), 1.47%
Source: *Fortune*, July 7, 1997, p. B46.

Mining Industry – Europe

★ 1927 ★
TOP MINING COMPANIES IN EUROPE
Ranked by: Sales, in millions of European Currency Units (ECUs). **Remarks:** Also notes the number of employees. **Number listed:** 45
1. NV Kon. Nederlandse Petroleum Maatschappij with 86,900 million ECUs
2. British Petroleum Co. Plc, 38,482
3. Britoil Plc, 35,295
4. Elf Aquitaine, 32,604
5. Ruhrkohle A.G., 11,210
6. Den Norske Stats Oljeselskap A.S., 8,298
7. Gaz de France, 7,659
8. Deutsche BP Holding A.G., 6,449
9. Shell Nederland BV, 5,917
10. Shell U.K. Ltd., 5,784
Source: *Duns Europa* (annual), vol. 4, Dun & Bradstreet, 1997, p. 206+.

Minnesota – see under individual headings

Missouri – see under individual headings

Modems

★ 1928 ★
HOUSEHOLDS WITH MODEMS IN SELECTED COUNTRIES
Ranked by: Estimated modem penetration within a country, as a percentage of all households. **Number listed:** 7
1. United States with 20%
2. Australia, 6%
3. Sweden, 5%
4. Singapore, 4%
5. France, 2%
6. United Kingdom, 2%
7. Japan, 1%
Source: *Financial Times*, August 23, 1996, p. 6.

Monaco – see under individual headings

Mongolia – see under individual headings

Montreal Exchange

★ 1929 ★
LARGEST COMPANIES ON THE MONTREAL EXCHANGE, 1995
Ranked by: Market value, in millions of Canadian dollars. **Number listed:** 20
1. Seagram Ltd. with C$17,572 million
2. BCE Inc., C$15,518
3. Northern Telecom Ltd., C$14,738
4. Barrick Gold Corporation, C$12,842
5. Royal Bank of Canada, C$11,588
6. Thomson Corporation, C$11,227
7. Bank of Commerce, C$10,009
8. Canadian Imperial, C$10,009
9. Alcan Aluminium, C$9,793
10. Imperial Oil Ltd., C$9,396
Source: *GT Guide to World Equity Markets* (annual), Euromoney Publications, 1996, p. 88.

★ 1930 ★
MOST ACTIVELY TRADED SHARES ON THE MONTREAL EXCHANGE, 1995
Ranked by: Trading value, in millions of Canadian dollars. **Number listed:** 20
1. Alcan Aluminium Ltd. with C$1,528 million
2. BCE Inc., C$1,502
3. BioChem Pharma Inc., C$1,310
4. Royal Bank of Canada, C$1,237
5. Inco Ltd., C$1,158
6. Toronto Dominion Bank, C$1,108
7. Seagram Inc., C$913
8. Canadian Imperial Bank of Commerce, C$890
9. Bank of Montreal, C$858
10. Bombardier Inc. Class B, C$816

Source: *GT Guide to World Equity Markets* (annual), Euromoney Publications, 1996, p. 89.

Morocco – see under individual headings

Mortality

★ 1931 ★
TOP CAUSES OF DEATH FOR MEN IN ENGLAND AND WALES
Ranked by: Frequency, as a percentage of total deaths among men. **Number listed:** 6
1. Cancer with 27%
2. Heart attack, 27%
3. Respiratory diseases and pneumonia, 15%
4. Stroke, 8%
5. Other circulatory diseases, 8%
6. Other, 15%

Source: *The World in 1997*, 1997, p. 128.

★ 1932 ★
TOP CAUSES OF DEATH FOR WOMEN IN ENGLAND AND WALES
Ranked by: Frequency, as a percentage of total deaths among women. **Number listed:** 6
1. Cancer with 23%
2. Heart attack, 21%
3. Respiratory diseases and pneumonia, 17%
4. Stroke, 13%
5. Other circulatory diseases, 10%
6. Other, 16%

Source: *The World in 1997*, 1997, p. 128.

Mortgage Loans
See: **Mortgages**

Mortgages

★ 1933 ★
LARGEST BUILDING SOCIETIES IN THE U.K.
Ranked by: Loans, in billions of British pounds (£). **Number listed:** 20
1. Halifax with £77.2 billion
2. Abbey National, £48.0
3. Cheltenham & Glouchester, £37.4
4. Nationwide, £26.3
5. Woolwich, £21.8
6. Alliance & Leicester, £16.0
7. National Westminster Bank, £15.0
8. Barclays Bank, £14.0
9. Bradford & Bingley, £11.6
10. National & Provincial, £10.4

Source: *Financial Times*, December 14, 1996, p. 8.

Motels
See: **Hotels and Motels**

Motion Picture Industry

★ 1934 ★
COUNTRIES WITH THE HIGHEST CINEMA BOX OFFICE GROSSES, 1996
Ranked by: Box office receipts, in millions of U.S. dollars. **Remarks:** Notes average ticket price, number of yearly cinema visits per capita, and number of movie screens per capita. **Number listed:** 4
1. United States with $5,659 million
2. Japan, $1,514
3. France, $915
4. Germany, $852

Source: *The Hollywood Reporter*, October 8, 1996, p. 1.

★ 1935 ★
MOVIE SPENDING BY COUNTRY
Ranked by: Consumer spending on feature films, in millions of U.S. dollars. **Number listed:** 10
1. United States with $21,329.0 million
2. Japan, $6,565.0
3. France, $3,078.0
4. U.K./Ireland, $2,971.0
5. Germany, $1,959.0
6. Canada, $1,941.0
7. Italy, $1,338.0
8. Spain, $1,125.0
9. Netherlands, $328.0
10. Belgium, $257.0

Source: *EuroBusiness*, June 1994, p. 30.

★ 1936 ★
TOP FILMS IN AUSTRALIA, 1995
Ranked by: Box office revenue, in millions of U.S. dollars. **Remarks:** Attendance grew from 52.7 million in 1993 to 63.9 million in 1994 to 69.9 million in 1995. Box office revenues grew from $369 million in 1993 to $440.8 million in 1994 to $470.3 million in 1995. **Number listed:** 10
1. Batman Forever with $16.9 million
2. Casper, $16.8
3. Dumb and Dumber, $16.4
4. Forrest Gump, $13.3
5. Apollo 13, $12.4
6. Die Hard With A Vengeance, $12.0
7. Braveheart, $11.9
8. Babe, $10.9
9. While You Were Sleeping, $10.7
10. Ace Ventura: When Nature Calls, $10.4
Source: *Sydney Morning Herald*, January 1, 1996, p. 41.

★ 1937 ★
TOP MOTION PICTURES IN THE UNITED KINGDOM, 1995-1996
Ranked by: Box office gross takings for December 1, 1995-November 29, 1996, in milions of British pounds (£). **Number listed:** 10
1. Independence Day with £36.8 million
2. Toy Story, £22.1
3. Babe, £20.2
4. Seven, £19.5
5. Mission: Impossible, £18.6
6. Twister, £15.0
7. Sense and Sensibility, £13.6
8. Jumanji, £13.4
9. GoldenEye, £12.7
10. Trainspotting, £12.4
Source: *The Guardian*, December 20, 1996, p. 9.

Motion Picture Theaters

★ 1938 ★
POLAND'S MOVIE THEATERS, 1994
Ranked by: Audience attendance. **Remarks:** Includes number of seats. **Number listed:** 6
1. Luna with 504,896
2. Relax, 383,873
3. Muranow, 305,608
4. Bajika, 269,289
5. Moskwa, 245,042
6. Atlantic, 228,744
Source: *The Warsaw Voice*, April 9, 1995, p. 12.

Motor Oil

★ 1939 ★
TOP MOTOR OIL MAKERS IN TURKEY, 1994
Ranked by: Market share, in percent. **Remarks:** Notes sales figures and production capacity. **Number listed:** 5
1. PO with 36.7%
2. Shell, 20.4%
3. Mobil, 16.1%
4. BP, 15.0%
5. Turcas, 10.8%
Source: *National Trade Data Bank*, March 12, 1996, p. IMI960312.

Motorcycle Industry

★ 1940 ★
BRITAIN'S TOP MOTORCYCLE MAKERS
Ranked by: Market share, in percent. **Number listed:** 9
1. Honda with 25.6%
2. Yamaha, 16.6%
3. Suzuki, 16.3%
4. Kawasaki, 12.8%
5. Piaggio, 5.8%
6. Triumph, 4.7%
7. BMW, 3.4%
8. Harley Davidson, 2.9%
9. Others, 11.9%
Source: *Financial Times*, September 10, 1996, p. 7.

★ 1941 ★
JAPAN'S MOTORCYCLE MARKET LEADERS, 1995
Ranked by: Market share, in percent. **Number listed:** 4
1. Honda Motor with 53.1%
2. Yamaha Motor, 29.9%
3. Suzuki Motor, 13.7%
4. Kawasaki Heavy Industries, 3.3%
Source: *Nikkei Weekly*, July 29, 1996, p. 8.

Mousses, Hair
See: **Hair Care Products**

Mozambique – see under individual headings

Multimedia Equipment

★ 1942 ★
GLOBAL MULTIMEDIA MARKET, 1995
Ranked by: Market share, in percent. **Number listed:** 10
1. Apple with 22.9%
2. Packard Bell, 19.2%
3. Compaq, 11.9%
4. IBM, 8.0%
5. NEC, 4.3%
6. Acer, 2.7%
7. Escom, 0.7%
8. Fujitsu, 0.6%
9. Highscreen, 0.6%
10. Other, 29.1%
Source: *Investor's Business Daily*, June 13, 1996, p. A8.

Multinational Corporations

★ 1943 ★
MULTINATIONAL CORPORATIONS BASED IN DEVELOPING COUNTRIES, 1995
Ranked by: International exposure. **Remarks:** Rankings are based on the average of ratios of foreign assets to total assets, foreign sales to total sales and foreign employment to total employment. See source for details. **Number listed:** 10
1. Panamerican Beverages (Mexico)
2. First Pacific (Hong Kong)
3. Gruma (Mexico)
4. Creative Technology (Singapore)
5. Guangdong Investment (Hong Kong)
6. Fraser & Neave (Singapore)
7. Jardine Matheson Holdings (Bermuda)
8. Cemex (Mexico)
9. Daewoo (South Korea)
10. Dairy Farm International Holdings (Hong Kong)
Source: *Financial Times*, October 3, 1997, p. 10.

★ 1944 ★
TOP INTERNATIONAL CORPORATIONS BASED IN DEVELOPING COUNTRIES
Ranked by: Foreign assets. **Remarks:** The source provides no further data. **Number listed:** 25
1. Daewoo (South Korea)
2. Hutchison Whampoa (Hong Kong)
3. Cemex (Mexico)
4. Jardine Matheson Holdings (Hong Kong)
5. China State Construction (China)
6. China Chemicals Imports & Exports (China)
7. Samsung Co. (South Korea)
8. LG Group (South Korea)
9. Grupo Televisia (Mexico)
10. Hyundai (South Korea)
Source: *Far Eastern Economic Review*, October 31, 1996, p. 5.

★ 1945 ★
TOP MULTINATIONAL COMPANIES IN DEVELOPING COUNTRIES
Ranked by: Foreign assets, in billions of U.S. dollars. **Remarks:** Also notes total assets, sales, and employment. **Number listed:** 25
1. Cemex S.A. (Mexico) with $3,603 billion
2. Hutchison Whampoa Limited (Hong Kong), $2,743
3. Hyundai Motor Co. (South Korea), $1,105
4. Grupo Televisa S.A. de C.V. (Mexico), $948
5. Souza Cruz S.A. (Brazil), $770
6. Genting Berhad (Malaysia), $752
7. Dong Ah Construction Industrial Co. (South Korea), $706
8. Tatung Co. Ltd. (Taiwan), $703
9. New World Development Co. Ltd. (Hong Kong), $624
10. Keppel Corporation Ltd. (Singapore), $565
Source: *Transnational Corporations*, December 1995, p. 122.

★ 1946 ★
TOP MULTINATIONALS IN LATIN AMERICA, 1995
Ranked by: Revenues, in millions of U.S. dollars. **Remarks:** Includes countries of operation for each company. **Number listed:** 25
1. Petrobas with $16,387 million
2. YPF, $4,954
3. Odebrecht, $3,820
4. Cisneros, $3,100
5. Techint, $2,800
6. Cemex, $2,564
7. Enersis, $1,809
8. Panamco, $1,609
9. Bimbo, $1,321
10. Televisa, $1,149
Source: *Latin Trade*, October 1996, p. 68.

Museums and Parks

★ 1947 ★
MUSEUMS IN THE FIVE BEST CITIES FOR WORK AND FAMILY
Ranked by: Number of museums. **Remarks:** Table shows ranking based on Arthur Andersen's Survey of Major Cities. **Number listed:** 5
1. Singapore with 400 museums
2. London, England, 300

3. Paris, France, 97
4. Toronto, Canada, 90
5. Hong Kong, 15

Source: *Fortune*, November 11, 1996, p. 133.

Music, Prerecorded

★ 1948 ★
TOP DOMESTIC RECORD COMPANIES IN JAPAN
Ranked by: Market share, in percent. **Number listed:** 6
1. Sony Music Entertainment with 17.5%
2. Toshiba EMI, 14.7%
3. Pony Canyon, 8.3%
4. Polydor, 8.0%
5. Victor Entertainment, 7.7%
6. Others, 43.8%

Source: *National Trade Data Bank*, October 6, 1995, p. ISA9508.

★ 1949 ★
TOP LATIN AMERICAN MUSIC MARKETS, 1995
Ranked by: Sales, in millions of U.S. dollars. **Remarks:** Figures include estimated piracy sales. **Number listed:** 10
1. Brazil with $1,171.9 million
2. Mexico, $384.3
3. Argentina, $310.5
4. Colombia, $218.3
5. Chile, $86.6
6. Venezuela, $48.0
7. Peru, $25.9
8. Uruguay, $22.1
9. Paraguay, $20.1
10. Ecuador, $10.7

Source: *Latin Trade*, November 1996, p. 15.

Music Trade

★ 1950 ★
MUSIC PIRACY IN SELECTED COUNTRIES
Ranked by: Piracy level, as a percentage of domestic market for CDs and tapes. **Number listed:** 10
1. Russia with 70%
2. China, 54%
3. Mexico, 50%
4. Brazil, 45%
5. Argentina, 30%
6. India, 30%
7. Saudi Arabia, 30%
8. Greece, 25%
9. Italy, 22%
10. Malaysia, 20%

Source: *Financial Times*, September 19, 1997, p. 6.

★ 1951 ★
TOP MARKETS FOR ILLICIT SALES OF MUSIC, 1995
Ranked by: Sales, in millions of U.S. dollars. **Number listed:** 5
1. Europe with $945 million
2. Asia, $434
3. North America, $304
4. Latin America, $298
5. Rest of world, $168

Source: *Financial Times*, August 24, 1997, p. 7.

★ 1952 ★
TOP MARKETS FOR LEGAL SALES OF MUSIC, 1995
Ranked by: Sales, in billions of U.S. dollars. **Number listed:** 5
1. Europe with $13.39 billion
2. North America, $13.22
3. Asia, $9.62
4. Latin America, $2.05
5. Rest of world, $1.41

Source: *Financial Times*, August 24, 1997, p. 7.

★ 1953 ★
TOP-SELLING FEMALE MUSICIANS
Ranked by: Table ranks performers by worldwide sales. **Number listed:** 4
1. Madonna with $80.0 million
2. Houston, Whitney, $79.5
3. Carey, Mariah, $60.0
4. Jackson, Janet, $25.5

Source: *Entertainment Weekly*, October 6, 1995, p. 8.

Mutual Funds

★ 1954 ★
LARGEST MUTUAL FUND FIRMS IN CANADA, 1997
Ranked by: Assets as of February 1997, in billions of Canadian dollars (C$). **Number listed:** 55
1. Investors Group with C$26.9 billion
2. Trimark, C$22.4
3. Royal, C$20.9
4. Mackenzie, C$17.1
5. TD, C$11.6
6. Templeton, C$11.5
7. AGF, C$10.7
8. CIBC, C$10.1
9. Fidelity, C$8.8
10. Canada Trust, C$8.2

Source: *Toronto Star*, March 18, 1997, p. B3.

★ 1955 ★

LARGEST MUTUAL FUNDS IN FRANCE

Ranked by: Total amount invested, in billions of U.S. dollars. **Number listed:** 13
1. Societe Generale with $38.1 billion
2. Credit Agricole, $36.0
3. Credit Lyonnais, $32.0
4. BNP, $31.8
5. La Poste, $23.2
6. CDC/Tresor Public, $22.9
7. La Caisse d'Epargne, $20.3
8. CIC Banques, $18.1
9. Banques Populaires, $16.9
10. Banque Paribas, $11.4

Source: *National Trade Data Bank*, October 18, 1996, p. IMI960912.

★ 1956 ★

MOSCOW'S TOP MUTUAL FUNDS FOR FOREIGNERS

Ranked by: Assets, in millions of U.S. dollars. **Remarks:** Also lists Moscow's top mutual funds for Russian citizens. **Number listed:** 6
1. First NIS Regional with $193 million
2. Morgan Stanley Russia, $141
3. Regent Russian Debt, $130
4. Templeton Russia, $113
5. Fleming Russia, $107
6. Regent White Tiger, $104

Source: *Business Week*, March 10, 1997, p. 101.

★ 1957 ★

MUTUAL FUNDS BY TYPE IN GREECE, 1996

Ranked by: Market share as of October 1996, in percent. **Remarks:** Includes figures for December 1994. **Number listed:** 6
1. Money market with 59.0%
2. Fixed income, 35.0%
3. International fixed, 2.0%
4. Stockmarket-linked, 2.0%
5. Other, 2.0%

Source: *Trade With Greece*, Spring 1996, p. 32.

★ 1958 ★

TOP GLOBAL MUTUAL FUNDS BY RETURN, 1996

Ranked by: Rate of return, in percent. **Remarks:** Includes each fund's assets in millions of dollars. **Number listed:** 10
1. Artisan: International with 34.37% return
2. Harbor: International Growth, 32.04%
3. Janus Overseas, 28.83%
4. Oakmark International, 28.02%
5. Oakmark International Emerging Value, 25.01%
6. Franklin International: Small Companies, 24.18%
7. Principal Sp. Market International, 24.12%
8. Princor World A, 23.76%
9. N&B International, 23.69%
10. Aetna International Group Select, 23.23%

Source: *The Wall Street Journal*, March 6, 1997, p. B4.

★ 1959 ★

TOP GLOBAL MUTUAL FUNDS, 1996

Ranked by: Rate of return, in percent. **Number listed:** 10
1. Nicholas-Applegate Emerging Country Institutional with 26.80%
2. Nicholas-Applegate Emerging Country Qualified, 26.45%
3. Nicholas-Applegate Emerging Country: A, 26.31%
4. Nicholas-Applegate Emerging Country: B, 25.45%
5. Nicholas-Applegate Emerging Country: C, 25.36%
6. Eaton-Vance Traditional Emerging Markets, 24.90%
7. Eaton-Vance Marathon Emerging Markets, 24.68%
8. Robertson Stephens Developing Country, 22.69%
9. Putnam Emerging Markets: A, 22.41%
10. Lazard Emerging Market, 22.30%

Source: *World Trade*, March 1997, p. 76.

★ 1960 ★

TOP MUTUAL FUND FIRMS IN POLAND, 1997

Ranked by: Assets as of the end of March 1997, in millions of zlotys (Zl). **Number listed:** 3
1. Pioneer with Zl1,680.6 million
2. Korona, Zl155.0
3. Przymierze, Zl42.4

Source: *The Warsaw Voice*, May 11, 1997, p. 12.

★ 1961 ★

TOP REGIONS FOR RETURN ON MUTUAL FUNDS, 1995-1997

Ranked by: Average return with dividends reinvested, in percent. **Remarks:** Also notes funds' average monthly volatility. **Number listed:** 25
1. United States with 58.1% return
2. North America, 55.7%
3. Britain, 54.3%
4. Canada, 48.7%
5. Malaysia, 47.7%
6. Taiwan, 40.8%
7. Hong Kong, 39.1%
8. Malaysia & Singapore, 35.8%
9. Europe, 32.0%
10. China, 25.5%

Source: *Far Eastern Economic Review*, April 24, 1997, p. 37.

Mutual Funds – United Kingdom

★ 1962 ★
BEST PERFORMING UNIT TRUSTS IN THE UNITED KINGDOM, 1995
Ranked by: Value of 1,000 British pounds (£) invested, after 1 year. **Number listed:** 20
1. Johnson Fry Slater Growth with £1,456.77
2. Gartmore U.K. Smaller Companies, £1,312.37
3. NatWest U.K. Smaller Cos., £1,263.06
4. Schroder Smaller Companies Inc., £1,259.62
5. TU European, £1,250.49
6. River & Mercantile 1st Growth, £1,233.34
7. BWD U.K. Smaller Cos., £1,230.93
8. Abtrust Property Share, £1,230.21
9. Mercury Recovery, £1,218.25
10. INVESCO U.K. Smaller Companies, £1,218.23

Source: *Investors Chronicle*, April 18, 1997, p. 59.

★ 1963 ★
TOP INVESTMENT TRUST PERSONAL EQUITY PLANS IN THE UNITED KINGDOM, 1996
Ranked by: Value of 1,000 British pounds (£) invested, after 1 years. **Number listed:** 20
1. Scottish National Cap with £2,095.24
2. Primadona, £1,683.85
3. Jupiter Extra Income, £1,555.36
4. Foreign & Col Enterprise, £1,543.77
5. Murray Split Capital Cap, £1,500.00
6. TR European Growth, £1,473.80
7. Dunedin Enterprise, £1,463.97
8. Fleming Income & Growth Cap, £1,463.64
9. Johnson Fry European Utilities, £1,451.95
10. Jupiter Geared Pfd. Cap, £1,448.98

Source: *Investors Chronicle*, April 18, 1997, p. 59.

★ 1964 ★
TOP INVESTMENT TRUSTS IN THE U.K. BY ONE-YEAR PERFORMANCE, 1996
Ranked by: Value of 1,000 British pounds (£) invested, after 1 year. **Number listed:** 15
1. Exmoor Dual Inc. with £1,559.67
2. Jove Inc., £1,456.04
3. M&G Recovery Inc., £1,453.23
4. Framlington Dual Inc., £1,447.91
5. MCIT Inc., £1,369.02
6. Derby Inc., £1,352.41
7. Abtrust Convertible Income, £1,345.06
8. Rights & Issues Inc., £1,334.57
9. Danae Inc., £1,316.91
10. Yeoman Inc., £1,299.07

Source: *Investors Chronicle*, April 11, 1997, p. 44.

★ 1965 ★
TOP INVESTMENT TRUSTS IN THE U.K. BY THREE-YEAR PERFORMANCE, 1996
Ranked by: Value of 1,000 British pounds (£) invested, after 3 years. **Number listed:** 15
1. Rights & Issues Inc. with £1,894.29
2. Derby Inc., £1,589.33
3. MCIT Inc., £1,549.58
4. Jove Inc., £1,486.24
5. Value and Income, £1,459.88
6. TR City of London, £1,443.57
7. Murray International, £1,408.64
8. M&G Recovery Inc., £1,394.76
9. Dartmoor, £1,383.61
10. City Merchants High Yield, £1,361.37

Source: *Investors Chronicle*, April 11, 1997, p. 44.

Myanmar – see under individual headings

Namibia – see under individual headings

Nationalization of Industry
See: **Government Ownership**

Natural Gas
See Also: **Gas Industry**

★ 1966 ★
TOP GAS CONSUMERS WORLDWIDE, 1995
Ranked by: Consumption, in billions of cubic meters. **Number listed:** 10
1. United States with 605.59 billion
2. Former Soviet Union, 586.91
3. Germany, 88.56
4. Canada, 80.29
5. United Kingdom, 76.24
6. Japan, 60.02
7. Italy, 55.39
8. Netherlands, 40.98
9. Saudi Arabia, 40.34
10. France, 37.07

Source: *Petroleum Economist,* World Gas Conference Issue, May 1997, p. 9.

★ 1967 ★

TOP GAS FIELDS WORLDWIDE

Ranked by: Reserves, in billions of cubic meters.
Number listed: 10
1. North Field (Qatar) with 8,000 billion
2. Urengoi (Russia), 6,611
3. Yamburg (Russia), 4,588
4. Bovanenkov (Russia), 4,375
5. Zapolyarnoye (Russia), 3,532
6. South Pars (Iran), 2,800
7. Shtokmanov (Russia), 2,762
8. Astrakhan (Russia), 2,592
9. Hassi R'mel, 2,400
10. Groningen (Netherlands), 2,300

Source: *Petroleum Economist,* World Gas Conference Issue, May 1997, p. 8.

★ 1968 ★

TOP GAS PRODUCERS WORLDWIDE

Ranked by: Production, in billions of cubic meters.
Number listed: 20
1. Former Soviet Union with 704.2 billion
2. United States, 529.9
3. Canada, 158.6
4. Netherlands, 78.4
5. United Kingdom, 75.4
6. Indonesia, 63.1
7. Algeria, 58.1
8. Saudi Arabia, 40.3
9. Iran, 35.1
10. Norway, 30.4

Source: *Petroleum Economist,* World Gas Conference Issue, May 1997, p. 9.

★ 1969 ★

TOP GAS PRODUCERS, 1995

Ranked by: Production, in billions of cubic feet. **Number listed:** 10
1. C.I.S. with 24,893.3 billion cubic feet
2. United States, 19,652.0
3. Canada, 6,197.0
4. Netherlands, 2,729.5
5. United Kingdom, 2,649.6
6. Indonesia, 2,170.8
7. Algeria, 1,834.0
8. Mexico, 1,372.1
9. Saudi Arabia, 1,335.0
10. Iran, 1,127.8

Source: *Oil & Gas Journal,* July 1, 1996, p. 52.

★ 1970 ★

TOP GAS RESERVES WORLDWIDE

Ranked by: Reserves, in billions of cubic meters.
Number listed: 10
1. Former Soviet Union with 58,500 billion
2. Iran, 20,963

3. Qatar, 7,070
4. Abu Dhabi, 5,380
5. Saudi Arabia, 5,341
6. United States, 4,653
7. Venezuela, 4,012
8. Algeria, 3,690
9. Indonesia, 3,520
10. Nigeria, 3,474

Source: *Petroleum Economist,* World Gas Conference Issue, May 1997, p. 8.

★ 1971 ★

TOP NATURAL GAS IMPORTERS

Ranked by: Trillions of cubic feet of gas imported.
Remarks: Figures include gas shipped by pipeline and by ship. **Number listed:** 10
1. United States with 2.82 trillion cubic feet
2. Germany, 2.45
3. Japan, 2.04
4. Italy, 1.25
5. France, 1.21
6. Czech Republic/Slovakia, 0.53
7. Belgium, 0.45
8. South Korea, 0.33
9. Spain, 0.30
10. Poland, 0.25

Source: *The New York Times,* July 23, 1997, p. C6.

★ 1972 ★

TOP NATURAL GAS LIQUIDS PRODUCERS, 1995

Ranked by: Market share, in percent, based on 205,975,400 gallons per day produced worldwide.
Number listed: 11
1. United States with 36.19%
2. Canada, 20.90%
3. Mexico, 9.14%
4. C.I.S., 6.64%
5. Indonesia, 4.53%
6. Algeria, 2.95%
7. Qatar, 2.76%
8. Australia, 2.41%
9. Venezuela, 2.04%
10. Kuwait, 1.71%

Source: *Oil & Gas Journal,* July 1, 1996, p. 52.

★ 1973 ★

TOP PRODUCERS OF NATURAL GAS LIQUIDS, 1996

Ranked by: Production, in thousands of gallons per day.
Remarks: Also notes percent of worldwide production.
Number listed: 10
1. United States with 76,172.9 thousand gallons
2. Canada, 42,103.8
3. Mexico, 17,738.0
4. Indonesia, 10,271.7
5. Former Soviet Union, 8,065.7

6. Venezuela, 7,312.9
7. Algeria, 6,082.0
8. Qatar, 5,677.0
9. Australia, 5,012.2
10. Kuwait, 3,513.8

Source: *Oil & Gas Journal*, June 2, 1997, p. 52.

Nauru – see under individual headings

Nepal – see under individual headings

Netherlands – see under individual headings

Netherlands Antilles – see under individual headings

New Caledonia – see under individual headings

New Jersey – see under individual headings

New Zealand Stock Exchange

★ 1974 ★

LARGEST COMPANIES ON THE NEW ZEALAND STOCK EXCHANGE, 1995

Ranked by: Market value, in millions of New Zealand dollars (NZ$). **Number listed:** 20

1. Telecom Corporation of NZ with NZ$12,471.4 million
2. Carter Holt Harvey, NZ$5,699.4
3. Fletcher Challenge, NZ$5,442.2
4. Brierley Investments, NZ$3,227.0
5. Lion Nathan, NZ$1,999.0
6. Flecther Challenge - Forests Division, NZ$1,784.4
7. Air New Zealand A, NZ$1,095.4
8. Trust Bank New Zealand, NZ$915.8
9. Wilson & Horton, NZ$900.3
10. Natural Gas Corporation, NZ$848.4

Source: *GT Guide to World Equity Markets* (annual), Euromoney Publications, 1996, p. 259.

★ 1975 ★

MOST ACTIVELY TRADED SHARES ON THE NEW ZEALAND STOCK EXCHANGE, 1995

Ranked by: Trading value, in millions of New Zealand dollars (NZ$). **Number listed:** 20

1. Carter Holt Harvey with NZ$2,407.0 million
2. Telecom Corporation of NZ, NZ$1,390.4
3. Fletcher Challenge, NZ$1,182.5
4. Brierley Investments, NZ$591.9
5. Fletcher Challenge - Forests Division, NZ$537.3
6. Lion Nathan, NZ$233.1
7. Fisher & Paykel Industries, NZ$128.4
8. St. Luke's Group, NZ$119.9
9. Power New Zealand, NZ$105.1
10. Fernz Corporation Holdings, NZ$97.1

Source: *GT Guide to World Equity Markets* (annual), Euromoney Publications, 1996, p. 259.

Newspaper Publishers and Publishing

★ 1976 ★

TOP NEWSPAPER PUBLISHERS IN SOUTH AFRICA

Ranked by: Share of the newspaper market, in percent. **Number listed:** 6

1. Nasionale with 21.0%
2. Times Media, 21.0%
3. Independent (Foreign), 18.0%
4. Perskor, 10.0%
5. Natal Witness, 1.0%
6. Other, 29.0%

Source: *The Observer*, February 16, 1997, p. 7.

Newspapers

See Also: Newspapers – Editions

★ 1977 ★

COUNTRIES WITH LARGE CIRCULATIONS OF DAILY NEWSPAPERS

Ranked by: Circulation. **Number listed:** 10

1. Japan with 71,690,000
2. United States, 60,164,000
3. Russia, 57,367,000
4. China, 50,520,000
5. India, 27,500,000
6. Germany, 25,952,000
7. United Kingdom, 22,100,000
8. South Korea, 19,000,000
9. France, 11,695,000
10. Mexico, 10,231,000

Source: *Look Japan*, May 1997, p. 35.

★ 1978 ★

DAILY NEWSPAPER GROUPS BY AD REVENUES IN CANADA, 1996

Ranked by: Market share based on advertising revenues, in percent. **Number listed:** 9

1. Southam Newspapers with 31.8%
2. Thomson Newspapers, 12.3%
3. Sun Media, 11.2%
4. Hollinger, 9.6%
5. Quebecer, 8.6%
6. Power Corporation, 5.7%
7. Irving Group, 2.6%
8. Newfoundland Capital Corp., 1.0%
9. Independents, 17.2%

Source: *Marketing Magazine*, May 26, 1997, p. 15.

★ 1979 ★

MOST READ NEWSPAPERS IN FINLAND, 1996

Ranked by: Circulation, in thousands. **Remarks:** Includes 1995 figures. **Number listed:** 16

1. VG with 1354 thousand
2. Dagbladet, 925
3. Aftenposten mrg, 789
4. Aftenposten Aften, 457
5. Bergens Tidende, 273
6. Adresseavisen, 255
7. Dagens Naeringsliv, 250
8. Stavanger Aft., 190
9. Arbelderbladet, 176
10. DT/BB, 123

Source: *Aftenposten*, March 11, 1997, p. 24.

Newspapers – Editions

★ 1980 ★

LARGEST NATIONAL NEWSPAPERS IN GERMANY

Ranked by: Daily circulation. **Number listed:** 5

1. Suddeutsche Zeitung with 408,573
2. Frankfurter Allgemeine Zeitung, 383,588
3. Die Welt, 217,358
4. Frankfurter Rundschau, 185,756
5. Handelsblatt, 126,969

Source: *Deutschland*, April 1997, p. 39.

★ 1981 ★

LARGEST NEWSPAPERS IN SOUTH AFRICA, 1996

Ranked by: Circulation for the first six months of 1996. **Remarks:** Includes 1986 figures. **Number listed:** 13

1. Rapport with 398,852
2. City Press, 271,228
3. Sowetan, 211,688
4. The Citizen, 138,071
5. Ilanga, 119,657
6. Beeld, 118,220
7. Burger, 97,630
8. Daily Dispatch, 39,147
9. Business Day, 38,146
10. P. Herald, 31,629

Source: *Mail & Guardian*, January 24, 1997, p. B7.

★ 1982 ★

LARGEST NEWSSTAND DAILIES IN GERMANY

Ranked by: Daily circulation. **Number listed:** 5

1. Bild Zeitung with 4,772,392
2. Express (Cologne), 368,066
3. B.Z. (Berlin), 316,314
4. Abendzeitung (Munich), 198,566
5. Berliner Kurier, 173,758

Source: *Deutschland*, April 1997, p. 39.

★ 1983 ★

LARGEST REGIONAL SUBSCRIPTION NEWSPAPERS IN GERMANY

Ranked by: Daily circulation. **Number listed:** 5

1. Westdeutsche Allgemeine Zeitung (Essen) with 1,141,066
2. Hannoverische Allgemeine Zeitung, 556,234
3. Sachsiche Zeitung ((Dresden), 526,792
4. Freie Presse (Chemnitz), 474,133
5. Rheinishce Post (Dusseldorf), 398,522

Source: *Deutschland*, April 1997, p. 39.

★ 1984 ★

LARGEST SUNDAY NEWSPAPERS IN AUSTRALIA, 1996

Ranked by: Circulation for the last six months of 1996. **Remarks:** Includes circulation for last six months of 1995. **Number listed:** 33

1. The Sunday Telegraph with 701,651
2. The Sunday Mail (Qld), 581,000
3. The Sun-Herald, 548,393
4. The Sunday Herald Sun, 506,082
5. The Sunday Times (WA), 347,961
6. Sunday Mail (SA), 337,615
7. The Sunday Age, 200,000
8. The Sunday Tasmanian, 53,205
9. The Canberra Times, 39,597
10. The Sun Territorian (NT), 25,117

Source: *Sydney Morning Herald*, January 27, 1997, p. 29.

★ 1985 ★

POPULAR RUSSIAN NEWSPAPERS

Ranked by: Circulation, in thousands. **Remarks:** Figures for Argumenti i Fakti and Moskovsky Novosti show weekly circulation. **Number listed:** 12

1. Argumenti i Fakti with 3,100 thousand
2. Komsomolskaya Pravda, 1,250
3. Trud, 1,250
4. Moskovsky Komsomolets, 800

6. Rossiiskaya Gazeta, 530
7. Moskovsky Novosti, 139
8. Kommersant Daily, 100
9. Selskaya Zhzin, 102
10. Pravda, 60

Source: *The Economist*, September 20, 1997, p. 60.

Newsprint – Manufacture

★ 1986 ★

TOP NEWSPRINT MAKERS WORLDWIDE

Ranked by: Share of total production capacity, in percent. **Number listed:** 8

1. Fletcher Challenge (New Zealand) with 5.1%
2. UPM-Kymmene (Finland), 5.1%
3. Stora (Sweden), 4.1%
4. Abitlbi-Price (Canada), 4.0%
5. Donohue (Canada), 3.8%
6. Stone-Consolidated (Canada), 3.6%
7. Bowater (U.S.), 3.5%
8. Norske Skog (Norway), 3.5%

Source: *The Wall Street Journal*, February 18, 1997, p. B4.

New Zealand – see under individual headings

Nicaragua – see under individual headings

Nigeria – see under individual headings

Nonferrous Metal Industries

★ 1987 ★

TOP NONFERROUS METALS COMPANIES IN JAPAN

Ranked by: Income, in millions of yen (¥). **Number listed:** 10

1. Shin-Etsu Handotai with ¥4,523 million
2. Ryobi, ¥4,016
3. Mitsubishi Materials, ¥3,824
4. Japan Nuclear Fuel, ¥2,959
5. Mitsubishi Nuclear Fuel, ¥2,691
6. Nuclear Fuel Industries, ¥2,131
7. Dowa Mining, ¥2,127
8. Mitsui Mining & Smelting, ¥1,819
9. Showa Aluminum, ¥1,688

10. Asahi Chemical Laboratory, ¥917

Source: *Tokyo Business Today*, August 1995, p. 26.

Nonwoven Fabrics Industry

★ 1988 ★

BELGIUM'S NONWOVEN PRODUCTS MARKET

Ranked by: Market share, in percent. **Number listed:** 10

1. Coverstock with 54.1%
2. Liquid, air, and gas filtration, 7.0%
3. Wipes, 6.9%
4. Civil engineering and construction, 6.1%
5. Household decoration, furnishing, and bedding, 6.0%
6. Medical and surgical, 3.7%
7. Interlinings, 3.4%
8. Garments, 1.7%
9. Shoes and leather goods, 1.5%
10. Other, 9.6%

Source: *National Trade Data Bank*, January 14, 1997, p. ISA961201.

★ 1989 ★

NONWOVEN FABRICS PRODUCTION, 1995

Ranked by: Distribution, in percent. **Number listed:** 9

1. Dry-laid with 35.9%
2. Spun-bond, 25.1%
3. Needle-punch, 15.5%
4. Wet-laid, 6.2%
5. Stitch-bond, 5.9%
6. Melt-blown, 4.3%
7. Spunlace, 3.9%
8. Extruded nets, 2.1%
9. Scrim, 1.1%

Source: *Textile World*, August 1996, p. 77.

★ 1990 ★

TOP NONWOVENS PRODUCERS BY ROLL GOODS SALES

Ranked by: Worldwide sales of roll goods, in millions of U.S. dollars. **Remarks:** Also notes U.S. sales. **Number listed:** 40

1. Freudenberg with $1,270 million
2. DuPont, $880
3. BBA Nonwovens, $530
4. PGI Nonwovens, $500
5. Kimberly-Clark, $488
6. Japan Vilene, $298
7. Dexter Nonwovens, $295
8. Veratec, $265
9. Hoechst Trevira, $218
10. Asahi Chemical, $182

Source: *Nonwoven Industry* (annual), September 1996, p. 34.

Nonwoven Fabrics Industry – Japan

★ 1991 ★
LEADING NEEDLEPUNCHED NONWOVEN FABRICS MANUFACTURERS IN JAPAN
Ranked by: Sales, in millions of U.S. dollars. **Remarks:** Figures for Nippon Felt, Toyobo, and Nippon Felt Industries are estimated. **Number listed:** 11
1. Inchikawa Woolen Textile with $92.9 million
2. Nippon Felt, $78.7
3. Sun Chemical, $63.1
4. Fujiko, $57.5
5. Toyobo, $55.1
6. Dynic, $50.4
7. Kureha Tec (Toyobo), $48.9
8. Ohtsuka, $35.4
9. Toa Wool Spinning & Weaving, $32.6
10. Nippon Felt Industries, $29.9

Source: *National Trade Data Bank*, October 12, 1995, p. ISA9508.

★ 1992 ★
LEADING SPUNBONDED NONWOVEN FABRICS MANUFACTURERS IN JAPAN
Ranked by: Sales, in millions of U.S. dollars. **Remarks:** Figures for Mitsui Petrochemical Ind. and Nippon Lutravil are estimated. **Number listed:** 11
1. Asahi Chemical Industry with $135.8 million
2. Unitika, $86.6
3. Mitsui Petrochemical Ind., $43.3
4. Toyobo, $35.4
5. Du Pont Japan, $23.6
6. Toray Industries, $22.0
7. Nimura Chemical Industry, $13.4
8. Nippon Lutravil, $13.4
9. Idemitsu Petrochemical, $9.4
10. Kureha Tec (Toyobo), $8.4

Source: *National Trade Data Bank*, October 12, 1995, p. ISA9508.

★ 1993 ★
LEADING THERMALBONDED NONWOVEN FABRICS MANUFACTURERS IN JAPAN
Ranked by: Sales, in millions of U.S. dollars. **Remarks:** Figures for Kuraray, Shinwa, Rengo Nonwoven, Kanaboshi Paper are estimated. **Number listed:** 11
1. Japan Vilene with $137.8 million
2. Kuraray, $31.5
3. Shinwa, $19.7
4. Rengo Nonwoven, $19.7
5. Fukuron, $17.3
6. Kurashiki Textile Kako, $14.2
7. Mitsubishi Rayon, $12.6
8. Aoyama, $7.5
9. Kanaboshi Paper, $7.1

10. Havix, $6.4

Source: *National Trade Data Bank*, October 12, 1995, p. ISA9508.

Norway – see under individual headings

Office Furniture

★ 1994 ★
OFFICE FURNITURE MAKERS IN JAPAN
Ranked by: Sales, in millions of yen (¥). **Number listed:** 8
1. Kokuyo with ¥303,700 million
2. Okamura, ¥188,200
3. Uchida Yoko, ¥172,500
4. Itoki, ¥143,762
5. Kurogane, ¥41,660
6. Kotobuki, ¥33,000
7. Hotoku, ¥9,520

Source: *National Trade Data Bank*, October 18, 1995, p. ISA9503.

Office Supplies

★ 1995 ★
LEADING OFFICE SUPPLY BRANDS BY BRAND VALUE
Ranked by: Brand value, in millions of U.S. dollars. **Remarks:** Value was calculated using capital, ratio of capital to company sales, earnings, and corporate tax rate of the country where the parent company is located. See source for details. **Number listed:** 8
1. Duracell (Duracell International) with $3,467 million
2. Scotch (Minnesota, Mining & Mfg.), $2,279
3. Eveready (Ralston Purina), $2,031
4. Post-It (Minnesota, Mining & Mfg.), $1,165
5. Parker (Gillette), $488
6. Mont Blanc (Vendome Luxury), $394
7. Waterman (Gillette), $120
8. Cross (A.T. Cross), $119

Source: *Financial World,* World's Most Valuable Brands (annual), July 8, 1996, p. 63.

Office Workers, International

★ 1996 ★

AVERAGE MONTHLY SALARIES OF OFFICE MANAGERS

Ranked by: Average monthly salary, in U.S. dollars. **Number listed:** 4
1. Japan with $7,135
2. Germany, $5,629
3. United States, $3,325
4. Indonesia, $1,313

Source: *Business Week*, September 2, 1996, p. 8.

Offices – Leasing and Renting

★ 1997 ★

CITIES WITH THE HIGHEST OCCUPANCY COSTS

Ranked by: Occupancy costs, in U.S. dollars per square foot. **Remarks:** Occupancy costs include basic rent, real estate taxes and operating expenses. **Number listed:** 5
1. Bombay (India) with $143.30
2. Hong Kong (China), $106.60
3. London - West End (United Kingdom), $97.32
4. London - City (United Kingdom), $94.87
5. Tokyo (Japan), $94.79

Source: *Globe and Mail*, June 17, 1997, p. B5.

★ 1998 ★

CITIES WITH THE HIGHEST OPERATING EXPENSES

Ranked by: Operating expenses, in U.S. dollars per square foot. **Number listed:** 5
1. Tokyo (Japan) with $11.54
2. Moscow (Russia), $11.15
3. London - West End (United Kingdom), $10.98
4. Nagoya (Japan), $10.41
5. London - City (United Kingdom), $10.14

Source: *Globe and Mail*, June 17, 1997, p. B5.

★ 1999 ★

CITIES WITH THE LOWEST OCCUPANCY COSTS

Ranked by: Occupancy costs, in U.S. dollars per square foot. **Remarks:** Occupancy costs include basic rent, real estate taxes and operating expenses. **Number listed:** 5
1. Houston (United States) with $14.85
2. Calgary (Canada), $16.70
3. Montreal (Canada), $16.90
4. Dallas (United States), $17.52
5. Atlanta (United States), $18.36

Source: *Globe and Mail*, June 17, 1997, p. B5.

★ 2000 ★

CITIES WITH THE LOWEST OPERATING EXPENSES

Ranked by: Operating expenses, in U.S. dollars per square foot. **Number listed:** 4
1. Milan (Italy) with $0.56
2. Zurich (Switzerland), $2.06
3. Amsterdam (Netherlands), $2.68
4. Shanghai (China), $3.00

Source: *Globe and Mail*, June 17, 1997, p. B5.

★ 2001 ★

MOST EXPENSIVE CITIES FOR INDUSTRIAL SPACE RENTAL

Ranked by: Cost per square foot, in U.S. dollars. **Number listed:** 10
1. Hong Kong with $18.37 per square foot
2. Moscow, $13.94
3. Seoul, $12.45
4. Delhi, $10.72
5. Bombay, $10.46

Source: *Electronic Business Today*, February 1997, p. 15.

★ 2002 ★

OFFICE RENTS IN LATIN AMERICAN CITIES, 1996

Ranked by: Base rental rates per month for selected cities, in U.S. dollars per square meter. **Remarks:** Also notes figures for 1995. **Number listed:** 8
1. Mexico City with $38.0
2. Sao Paulo (Brazil), $37.0
3. Buenos Aires (Argentina), $31.0
4. Bogota (Colombia), $30.0
5. Rio de Janeiro (Brazil), $26.0
6. Lima (Peru), $24.0
7. Santiago (Chile), $24.0
8. Caracas (Venezuela), $23.0

Source: *Latin Trade*, August 1997, p. 40.

★ 2003 ★

TOP OFFICE RENTS, 1996

Ranked by: Rent, in U.S. dollars per square meter. **Number listed:** 19
1. Bombay with $1,840
2. Tokyo, $1,600
3. Hong Kong, $1,300
4. Beijing, $970
5. New Delhi, $880
6. Shanghai, $880
7. London (West End), $730
8. Paris, $670
9. Singapore, $670
10. Frankfurt, $570

Source: *The World In 1996*, Special Issue, 1996, p. 112.

Offices – Leasing and Renting, International

★ 2004 ★
VACANCY RATES IN PRIME OFFICE SPACE, 1996
Ranked by: Vacancy rate, in percent. **Number listed:** 5
1. New York, United States with 11.8%
2. London, England, 10.2%
3. Paris, France, 8.9%
4. Tokyo, Japan, 8.4%
5. Frankfurt, Germany, 8.0%
Source: *The Economist*, August 10, 1996, p. 54.

Oil and Gas Well Drilling Contractors – Canada

★ 2005 ★
OIL & GAS FIELD SERVICE FIRMS IN CANADA
Ranked by: Revenue, in thousands of Canadian dollars.
Remarks: Includes figures on profits and return on capital. **Number listed:** 6
1. Nowsco Well Service with C$483,036 thousand
2. Canadian Fracmaster, C$333,479
3. Ensign Resource Service Group, C$180,665
4. Precision Drilling, C$179,315
5. Enserv Corp., C$174,686
6. Dreco Energy Services, C$90,461
Source: *Globe and Mail's Report on Business Magazine*, July 1996, p. 159.

Oil Companies
See: **Petroleum Industry**

Oils and Fats Industry

★ 2006 ★
GREAT BRITAIN'S TOP SPREAD BRANDS, 1996
Ranked by: Market share for the first quarter of 1996, in percent. **Number listed:** 5
1. I Can't Believe It's Not Butter with 26.8%
2. Clover, 25.2%
3. Utterly Butterly, 19.8%
4. Golden Crown, 13.0%
5. Other, 15.2%
Source: *The Guardian*, May 30, 1996, p. 20.

★ 2007 ★
SOYBEAN OIL MAKERS IN BRAZIL
Ranked by: Market share, in percent. **Number listed:** 3
1. Ceval with 25.0%

2. Cargill, 19.0%
3. Other, 56.0%
Source: *National Trade Data Bank*, May 27, 1996, p. ISA960301.

Olive Oil

★ 2008 ★
LARGEST OLIVE OIL CONSUMERS IN EUROPE, 1996-97
Ranked by: Consumption, in thousands of tons.
Remarks: Includes consumption by liters per person.
Number listed: 14
1. Italy with 500.0 thousand tons
2. Spain, 400.0
3. Greece, 187.0
4. France, 44.5
5. U.K., 17.5
6. Germany, 14.5
7. Belgium/Luxembourg, 5.5
8. Netherlands, 2.8
9. Austria, 1.5
10. Denmark, 1.5
Source: *The European*, July 3, 1997, p. 4.

Oman – see under individual headings

On-Line Computer Services

★ 2009 ★
JAPAN'S ON-LINE SERVICES MARKET
Ranked by: Market share, in percent. **Number listed:** 6
1. Nifty-Serve with 39.5%
2. PC-VAN, 38.5%
3. Asahi-Net/People, 12.1%
4. Microsoft Network, 3.1%
5. Ascii Net, 2.7%
6. Other, 4.1%
Source: *Nikkei Weekly*, July 15, 1996, p. 8.

★ 2010 ★
LARGEST ON-LINE SERVICES WORLDWIDE, 1996
Ranked by: Subscribers, in millions. **Number listed:** 6
1. America Online with 6.2 million subscribers
2. CompuServe, 3.2
3. NEC-PCVAN, 1.9
4. Nifty-Serve, 1.7
5. Microsoft, 1.2
6. Prodigy, 1.2
Source: *Computer Reseller News*, August 26, 1996, p. 66.

★ 2011 ★
ON-LINE SERVICE LEADERS IN FRANCE, 1996
Ranked by: Number of users as of October 18, 1996.
Number listed: 6
1. Compuserve with 75,000 users
2. America Online, 35,000
3. Microsoft Network, 20,000
4. Wanadoo (France Telecom), 20,000
5. Club Internet (Grolier), 17,000
6. Infonie, 16,000
Source: *Le Figaro*, January 8, 1997, p. 7.

Ophthalmic Supplies

★ 2012 ★
FIELD GLASS MAKERS WORLDWIDE
Ranked by: Market share, in percent. **Number listed:** 2
1. Steiner Optik with 80.0%
2. Other, 20.0%
Source: *The Economist*, July 13, 1996, p. 59.

★ 2013 ★
**LARGEST EYEGLASS FRAME MAKERS
WORLDWIDE**
Ranked by: Sales, in millions of U.S. dollars. **Number
listed:** 3
1. Luxottica Group with $1,700 million
2. Safilo, $270
3. Marcolin, $75
Source: *Forbes*, April 22, 1996, p. 68.

Optical Stores

★ 2014 ★
**LEADING OPTICAL GOODS STORES IN
GERMANY, 1994**
Ranked by: Total business, in millions of deutschmarks
(DM). **Number listed:** 10
1. Fielmann with DM960 million
2. Apollo Optik, DM282
3. Krane Optik, DM79
4. Abele-Optik, DM70
5. Ruhnke Optik, DM70
6. Binder Optik, DM55
7. Karstadt, DM53
8. Optiker Bode, DM49
9. Optik Matt, DM41
10. Becker + Floge, DM30
Source: *Wirtschaftswoche*, April 25, 1996, p. 86.

Oregon – see under individual headings

Oslo Stock Exchange

★ 2015 ★
**LARGEST COMPANIES ON THE OSLO STOCK
EXCHANGE, 1995**
Ranked by: Market value, in millions of Norwegian
krone (NKr). **Number listed:** 20
1. Norsk Hydro with NKr60,933 million
2. Hafslund Nycomed, NKr16,438
3. Orkla, NKr15,235
4. Saga Petroleum, NKr11,163
5. UNI Storebrand, NKr10,854
6. Den norske Bank, NKr10,632
7. Kvaerner, NKr9,594
8. Christiania Bank og Kreditkasse, NKr8,141
9. Bergesen dy, NKr7,125
10. Norske Skogindustrier, NKr5,999
Source: *GT Guide to World Equity Markets* (annual),
Euromoney Publications, 1996, p. 267.

★ 2016 ★
**MOST ACTIVELY TRADED SHARES ON THE OSLO
STOCK EXCHANGE, 1995**
Ranked by: Trading value, in millions of Norwegian
krone (Nkr). **Number listed:** 20
1. Norsk Hydro with NKr18,591 million
2. Kvaerner A, NKr7,257
3. Hafslund Nycomed A, NKr6,168
4. Orkla A, NKr5,282
5. Hafslund Nycomed B, NKr5,206
6. UNI Storebrand Ordinary, NKr4,853
7. Chr. Bank og Kreditkasse, NKr4,542
8. Saga Petroleum A, NKr4,130
9. Norske Skogindustrier, NKr3,802
10. Elkem, NKr3,536
Source: *GT Guide to World Equity Markets* (annual),
Euromoney Publications, 1996, p. 268.

Over-the-Counter Drugs
See: **Drugs, Nonprescription**

Packaging

★ 2017 ★
GLOBAL PACKAGING MARKET FOR NON-ALCOHOLIC DRINKS, 1995
Ranked by: Packaging share, in percent. **Number listed:** 4

1. Plastic with 45.8%
2. Metal, 18.6%
3. Glass, 18.4%
4. Carton, 17.1%

Source: *Prepared Foods*, November 1996, p. 93.

Packaging Industry
See: **Container Industry**

Paging Systems
See: **Radio Paging Systems**

Paint Industry

★ 2018 ★
MEXICAN PAINT MARKET, 1994
Ranked by: Market share, estimated in percent. **Number listed:** 7

1. Trade sales with 58.9%
2. Solvents, 16.6%
3. Industrial, 6.4%
4. Auto refinish, 5.5%
5. Wood finishes, 5.1%
6. Auto OEM, 4.9%
7. Maintenance, 2.7%

Source: *L'Actualite Chimique Canadienne*, May 1997, p. 16.

★ 2019 ★
TOP PAINT FIRMS IN INDIA, 1996
Ranked by: Sales for the year ending March 31, 1996, in millions of rupees (Rs). **Remarks:** Also notes percent growth. **Number listed:** 4

1. Asian Paints with Rs8,830 million
2. Goodlass Nerolac, Rs3,960
3. Berger Paints, Rs2,760
4. ICI (Paints), Rs2,310

Source: *Chemical Week*, September 11, 1996, p. 50.

★ 2020 ★
WORLD PAINT PRODUCTION, 1995
Ranked by: Production, in millions of tons. **Number listed:** 11

1. North America with 6.4 million
2. Western Europe, 6.2
3. Japan, 2.0
4. Eastern Europe, 1.7
5. China & South Korea, 1.7
6. Latin America, 1.5
7. Africa, 0.8
8. Southeast Asia, 0.8
9. South Asia, 0.6
10. Australia/New Zealand, 0.3

Source: *Modern Paint and Coatings*, March 1997, p. 30.

Pakistan – see under individual headings

Panama – see under individual headings

Panama Stock Exchange

★ 2021 ★
LARGEST COMPANIES ON THE PANAMA SECURITIES EXCHANGE, 1995
Ranked by: Market value, in millions of U.S. dollars. **Number listed:** 10

1. Empresa General de Inversiones with $199.02 million
2. Grupo Assa, $118.03
3. Cerveceria Nacional, $103.28
4. Primer Banco de Ahorros, $85.00
5. Capitales Nacionales, $62.67
6. Minamerica Corporation, $46.08
7. Cerveceria Baru-Panama, $45.59
8. Coca Cola de Panama, $39.10
9. Financiera Automotriz, $35.94
10. Banco Internacional de Panama, $34.00

Source: *GT Guide to World Equity Markets* (annual), Euromoney Publications, 1996, p. 405.

★ 2022 ★
MOST ACTIVELY TRADED SHARES ON THE PANAMA SECURITIES EXCHANGE, 1995
Ranked by: Turnover, in thousands of U.S. dollars. **Number listed:** 10

1. Golden Forest with $1,557 thousand
2. Cerveceria Nacional, $1,171
3. Empresa General de Inversiones, $752
4. Financiera Automotriz, $719

5. Geofino International, $666
6. Capatales Nacionales, $646
7. Coca Cola de Panama, $490
8. Cerveceria Baru-Panama, $216
9. Minamerica Corporation, $199
10. Grupo Assa, $161

Source: *GT Guide to World Equity Markets* (annual), Euromoney Publications, 1996, p. 405.

Paper Industry

★ 2023 ★

LARGEST PAPER AND PAPERBOARD PRODUCERS WORLDWIDE, 1995

Ranked by: Output, in thousands of tons. **Number listed:** 13

1. International Paper with 8,175 thousand
2. UPM-Kymmene, 6,733
3. Stone Container, 6,257
4. Georgia-Pacific, 6,054
5. SCA, 5,927
6. Oji Paper, 5,767
7. Stora, 5,263
8. Nippon Paper, 5,014
9. Kimberly-Clark, 4,800
10. Champion International, 4,765

Source: *Unitas,* no. 1, 1997, p. 7.

★ 2024 ★

PAPER & PAPERBOARD PRODUCTION IN RUSSIA, 1995

Ranked by: Distribution, in percent. **Number listed:** 6

1. Newsprint with 36.8%
2. Packaging boards, 27.0%
3. Packaging papers, 12.3%
4. Printings & writings, 12.3%
5. Tissue, 2.0%
6. Other, 9.8%

Source: *Paperboard Packaging,* August 1996, p. 13.

★ 2025 ★

PAPER AND PAPERBOARD CONSUMPTION IN SPAIN, 1996

Ranked by: Consumption, in thousands of metric tons. **Remarks:** Also notes figures for 1994 and 1995. **Number listed:** 7

1. Corrugated paperboard with 1,993 thousand metric tons
2. Writing paper, 1,507
3. Newsprint, 535
4. Paperboard, 365
5. Sanitary paper, 303
6. Kraft sacks, 134

7. Other, 588

Source: *National Trade Data Bank,* January 13, 1997, p. ISA961201.

★ 2026 ★

TOP COUNTRIES IN PER CAPITA PAPER & PAPERBOARD CONSUMPTION, 1995

Ranked by: Apparent per capita consumption, in kilograms per year. **Number listed:** 30

1. United States with 332.0 kilograms
2. Finland, 304.3
3. Belgium, 256.7
4. Japan, 239.1
5. Canada, 229.7
6. Singapore, 228.2
7. Taiwan, 223.7
8. Switzerland, 216.2
9. Denmark, 213.9
10. New Zealand, 212.6

Source: *North American Pulp & Paper Fact Book,* 1997, p. 136.

★ 2027 ★

TOP OFFICE PAPER PRODUCERS IN JAPAN

Ranked by: Market share, in percent. **Number listed:** 6

1. Nippon Paper Industries with 20.0%
2. New Oji Paper, 19.3%
3. Daishowa Paper Mfg., 12.4%
4. Daio Paper, 7.3%
5. Mitsubishi Paper Mills, 7.1%
6. Other, 33.9%

Source: *Nikkei Weekly,* July 29, 1996, p. 8.

★ 2028 ★

TOP PAPER & PAPER PRODUCTS FIRMS IN SOUTH KOREA, 1996

Ranked by: Sales for the first six months of 1996, in hundred million won (W). **Remarks:** Also notes net profits. **Number listed:** 22

1. Hansol Paper with W4,951.6 hundred million
2. Ssangyong Paper, W1,493.8
3. Hankuk Paper Manufacturing, W1,208.8
4. Sepoong, W1,204.4
5. Dae Han Pulp, W1,173.2
6. Woongjin Publishing, W1,161.4
7. Dong Hae Pulp, W607.8
8. Han Chang Paper Manufacturing, W487.1
9. Asia Paper, W468.9
10. Monalisa, W402.9

Source: *Business Korea,* October 1996, p. 33.

★ 2029 ★

TOP PAPER & PAPERBOARD CONSUMERS, 1995

Ranked by: Consumption, in thousands of metric tons.
Remarks: Notes percent change from 1994 to 1995.
Number listed: 30

1. United States with 87,409 thousand
2. Japan, 30,019
3. China, 26,499
4. Germany, 15,834
5. United Kingdom, 11,288
6. France, 9,631
7. Italy, 8,077
8. Canada, 6,730
9. South Korea, 6,580
10. Brazil, 5,433

Source: *North American Pulp & Paper Fact Book*, 1997, p. 138.

★ 2030 ★

TOP PAPER & PAPERBOARD PRODUCING NATIONS, 1995

Ranked by: Production, in thousands of metric tons.
Remarks: Notes percent change from 1994 to 1995.
Number listed: 30

1. United States with 81,000 thousand metric tons
2. Japan, 29,663
3. China, 24,000
4. Canada, 18,705
5. Germany, 14,827
6. Finland, 10,910
7. Sweden, 9,169
8. France, 8,615
9. South Korea, 6,877
10. Italy, 6,802

Source: *North American Pulp & Paper Fact Book*, 1997, p. 138.

★ 2031 ★

TOP PULP PRODUCING COUNTRIES, 1995

Ranked by: Production, in thousands of metric tons.
Remarks: Notes percent change from 1994 to 1995.
Number listed: 30

1. United States with 59,682 thousand metric tons
2. Canada, 25,388
3. China, 13,840
4. Japan, 11,120
5. Sweden, 10,187
6. Finland, 10,089
7. Brazil, 5,909
8. C.I.S., 5,220
9. Russia, 5,067
10. France, 2,819

Source: *North American Pulp & Paper Fact Book*, 1997, p. 138.

Paper Industry – Asia

★ 2032 ★

LARGEST PAPER, PRINTING, AND PUBLISHING COMPANIES IN ASIA

Ranked by: Sales, in thousands of U.S. dollars. **Remarks:** Also notes profit as a percent of sales. **Number listed:** 100

1. Dai Nippon Printing Co. Ltd. with $12,090,291 thousand
2. Toppan Printing Co. Ltd., $11,520,300
3. Nippon Paper Industries, $10,347,864
4. New Oji Paper Co. Ltd., $5,858,349
5. Honshu Paper Co. Ltd., $4,564,873
6. Daishowa Paper Manufacturing Co. Ltd., $3,581,893
7. Kokuyo Co. Ltd., $3,048,970
8. Rengo Co. Ltd., $2,786,883
9. Daio Paper Corp., $2,602,873
10. Mitsubishi Paper Mills Ltd., $2,147,252

Source: *Asia's 7,500 Largest Companies* (annual), Dun & Bradstreet, 1997, p. 83+.

Paper Industry – Canada

★ 2033 ★

TOP PAPER COMPANIES IN CANADA, 1995

Ranked by: Sales, in millions of Canadian dollars.
Number listed: 10

1. MacMillan Bloedel with C$5,254 million
2. Avenor, C$2,825
3. Domtar, C$2,795
4. Abitibi-Price, C$2,782
5. Noranda Forest, C$2,407
6. Cascades, C$2,270
7. Fletcher Challenge Canada, C$2,154
8. Repap Enterprises, C$2,077
9. Canfor, C$1,932
10. Stone-Consolidated, C$1,728

Source: *North American Pulp & Paper Fact Book*, 1997, p. 88.

Paper Industry – Europe

★ 2034 ★

TOP PAPER AND ALLIED PRODUCTS COMPANIES IN EUROPE

Ranked by: Sales, in millions of European Currency Units (ECUs). **Remarks:** Also notes the number of employees. **Number listed:** 103

1. GP Holding BV with 7,078 million ECUs

2. KNP BT Nederland BV, 7,078
3. KNP BT Solid Board Division BV, 7,078
4. NV Koninkijke KNP BT, 7,078
5. Jefferson Smurfit Group Plc, 3,870
6. Arjo Wiggins Appleton Plc, 3,801
7. MO OCH Domsjo AB, 2,764
8. PWA Papierwerke Waldhof-Aschaffenburg A.G., 2,356
9. FPB Holding A.G., 2,337
10. Van Leer Metallized Products BV, 1,873

Source: *Duns Europa* (annual), vol. 4, Dun & Bradstreet, 1997, p. 220+.

★ 2035 ★

TOP PAPER AND CARDBOARD PRODUCERS IN EUROPE

Ranked by: Production, in millions of tons. **Number listed:** 5

1. UPM-Kymmene (Finland) with 6,600 million tons
2. SCA-PWA (Sweden), 5,900
3. Stora (Sweden), 5,600
4. Enso-Veitsiluoto (Finland), 5,500
5. KNP-BT (Netherlands), 3,200

Source: *National Trade Data Bank*, May 28, 1997, p. ISA970301.

★ 2036 ★

WESTERN EUROPE'S TOP PAPER & BOARD PRODUCERS, 1996

Ranked by: Production for the first six months of 1996, in thousands of tons. **Number listed:** 15

1. Germany with 7,184 thousand tons
2. Finland, 4,945
3. Sweden, 4,413
4. France, 4,305
5. Italy, 3,524
6. U.K., 3,069
7. Spain, 1,955
8. Austria, 1,783
9. Netherlands, 1,494
10. Norway, 1,059

Source: *PIMA's Papermaker*, February 1997, p. 34.

Paper Industry – France

★ 2037 ★

PAPER PRODUCTION IN FRANCE

Ranked by: Percent distribution. **Number listed:** 7

1. Corrugated paper with 30.6%
2. Newsprint, 10.3%
3. Cardboard, 8.6%
4. Sanitary paper, 5.7%
5. Packaging and conditioning, 4.8%

6. Industrial and special paper, 3.0%
7. Other graphical uses, 37.0%

Source: *National Trade Data Bank*, May 28, 1997, p. ISA970301.

Papua New Guinea – see under individual headings

Paraguay – see under individual headings

Paris Stock Exchange

See: **Bourse de Paris**

Participation Loans

★ 2038 ★

GLOBAL LEAD ARRANGER LOANS BY SECTOR, 1995

Ranked by: Loans, in millions of U.S. dollars. **Number listed:** 9

1. Power with $8,742 million
2. Telecoms, $5,492
3. Oil and gas, $2,399
4. Infrastructure, $1,992
5. Industrial, $1,490
6. Mining, $1,137
7. Petrochemicals, $923
8. Leisure, $734
9. Others, $417

Source: *Financial Times*, December 3, 1996, p. 111.

★ 2039 ★

TOP SYNDICATED LOAN ARRANGERS IN LATIN AMERICA, 1996

Ranked by: Loans, in millions of U.S. dollars. **Remarks:** Also notes number of deals and share of loans. **Number listed:** 20

1. Chase Manhattan with $8,507.54 million
2. Bank of America, $4,235.75
3. J.P. Morgan, $1,858.50
4. ING Barings, $1,574.44
5. ABN-AMRO Bank, $1,507.14
6. Citicorp, $1,484.50
7. Dresdner Bank, $1,309.56
8. Banco Santander, $1,058.60
9. WestLB, $914.50
10. Societe Generale, $800.54

Source: *Investment Dealers' Digest*, June 2, 1997, p. 21.

Participation Loans – Asia

★ 2040 ★
TOP SYNDICATED LOAN ARRANGERS IN ASIA, 1996
Ranked by: Loans, in millions of U.S. dollars. **Remarks:** Also notes number of deals. **Number listed:** 120
1. ABN-AMRO Bank with $3,330.81 million
2. Citicorp, $3,023.16
3. Societe Generale, $2,903.73
4. Chase Manhattan Bank, $2,731.72
5. Sumitomo Bank, $2,429.10
6. Sanwa Bank, $2,279.26
7. HSBC Group, $2,254.25
8. Deutsche Morgan Grenfell, $2,235.76
9. Dai-Ichi Kangyo Bank, $2,098.29
10. Sakura Bank, $1,794.50

Source: *Asiamoney,* Deals of the Year (annual), February 1997, p. 81+.

Pasta, International

★ 2041 ★
PASTA CONSUMPTION IN SELECTED COUNTRIES
Ranked by: Annual per capita consumption, in pounds. **Number listed:** 10
1. Italy with 61.7 pounds
2. Venezuela, 27.9
3. Argentina, 26.4
4. Tunisia, 26.4
5. Switzerland, 20.1
6. United States, 19.8
7. Chile, 19.8
8. Greece, 19.4
9. Portugal, 15.6
10. Russia, 15.4

Source: *The New York Times,* October 28, 1995, p. 17.

Peanut Products

★ 2042 ★
GLOBAL PEANUT PRODUCTION
Ranked by: Production, in millions of metric tons. **Number listed:** 10
1. China with 8.42 million metric tons
2. India, 7.63
3. United States, 1.54
4. Indonesia, 0.87
5. Senegal, 0.62
6. Myanmar, 0.45
7. Sudan, 0.39

8. Zaire, 0.38
9. Vietnam, 0.27
10. Nigeria, 0.25

Source: *World Agricultural Production*, March 1995, p. 23.

Pension Fund Investments

★ 2043 ★
TOP EUROPEAN NATIONS FOR PENSION FUND ASSETS, 1996
Ranked by: Assets as of June 30, 1996, in billions of U.S. dollars. **Number listed:** 14
1. United Kingdom with $862 billion
2. Netherlands, $482
3. Germany, $360
4. Switzerland, $320
5. Sweden, $196
6. France, $168
7. Denmark, $136
8. Italy, $133
9. Finland, $39
10. Norway, $36

Source: *The European*, July 30, 1997, p. 35.

★ 2044 ★
TOP FUND MANAGERS IN THE UNITED KINGDOM
Ranked by: Assets managed, in billions of British pounds (£). **Number listed:** 10
1. Mercury Asset Management with £72 billion
2. Prudential Portfolio Managers, £58
3. Gartmore, £55
4. PDFM, £52
5. Schroders, £48
6. Standard Life, £44
7. Norwich Union, £36
8. Legal & General, £33
9. Morgan Grenfell Asset Management, £33
10. Hill Samuel, £28

Source: *The Guardian*, September 3, 1996, p. 18.

★ 2045 ★
TOP PENSION FUND MANAGERS IN AUSTRALIA
Ranked by: Market share, in percent. **Remarks:** Notes funds under management in millions of dollars. **Number listed:** 10
1. AMP with 13.02%
2. Citicorp, 9.27%
3. Commonwealth FM, 9.23%
4. MLC, 7.44%
5. National Mutual, 5.61%
6. Norwich, 4.82%
7. Bankers Trust, 4.66%

8. ANZ, 4.25%
9. AM, 4.14%
10. Colonial, 3.96%

Source: *Sydney Morning Herald*, February 13, 1997, p. 33.

★ 2046 ★

TOP PENSION FUNDS IN JAPAN

Ranked by: Assets, in trillions of yen (¥). **Remarks:** Rankings are for public pension funds only. Notes Japanese investment in foreign securities. **Number listed:** 6

1. Pension Fund Association of Local Government Officials with ¥70.9 trillion
2. Pension Fund Association for Government Officials, ¥66.6
3. Public School Teachers Pension Fund, ¥61.9
4. Retirement Pension Assoc., ¥24.0
5. Private School Teachers Pension Fund, ¥21.5
6. Pension Fund Assoc. for NTT Officials, ¥19.1

Source: *Euromoney*, September 1996, p. 46.

Pension Plan Administrators – United Kingdom

★ 2047 ★

BRITAIN'S TOP SEGREGATED PENSION FUND MANAGERS, 1996

Ranked by: Value of segregated funds, in millions of British pounds (£). **Remarks:** Also notes number of individual funds and number of funds managed. **Number listed:** 25

1. Mercury Asset Management with £54,171 million
2. PDFM, £48,049
3. Schroder Investment Management, £43,000
4. Gartmore Investment Management, £30,177
5. Barclays Global Investors, £22,992
6. Morgan Grenfell Asset Management, £16,254
7. Hill Samuel Investment Management, £10,945
8. Prudential Portfolio Management, £9,544
9. Fleming Investment Management, £9,118
10. Baillie Gifford, £6,492

Source: *Financial Times*, May 9, 1996, p. 2.

Pension Plans

★ 2048 ★

LARGEST PENSION FUNDS WORLDWIDE, 1995

Ranked by: Assets, in millions of U.S. dollars. **Number listed:** 300

1. Stichting Pensioenfonds ABP (Netherlands) with $141,038 million

2. California Public Employees (United States), $92,620
3. Allmanna Pensionsfonden (Sweden), $85,318
4. Local Government Officers (Japan), $82,162
5. General Motors (United States), $72,000
6. New York State & Local (United States), $71,456
7. National Public Service Personnel (Japan), $69,759
8. Public School Teachers (Japan), $64,814
9. California State Teachers (United States), $58,343
10. AT&T (United States), $57,097

Source: *Pensions & Investments,* Top 300 (annual), September 16, 1996, p. 24.

★ 2049 ★

MEXICAN PENSION FUNDS WITH THE MOST CONTRIBUTORS

Ranked by: Thousands of contributors. **Number listed:** 5

1. Bancomer with 1,103 thousand
2. Banamex, 804
3. Santander-Mexicano, 620
4. Profuturo-GNP, 568
5. Bital, 506

Source: *Latin American Economy & Business*, August 1997, p. 11.

Pension Plans – Brazil

★ 2050 ★

TOP PENSION FUNDS IN BRAZIL

Ranked by: Number of participants, in thousands. **Remarks:** Includes figures on pensioners and company assets. **Number listed:** 10

1. Preve with 89 thousand participants
2. Sistel, 76
3. Funcef, 55
4. Petros, 52
5. Fundacao Cesp, 35
6. Aerus, 34
7. Itaubanco, 34
8. Valia, 19
9. Forluz, 15
10. Centrus, 7

Source: *Latin American Economy & Business*, January 1997, p. 11.

Pension Plans – Europe

★ 2051 ★
TOP EUROPEAN PENSION FUND MANAGERS
Ranked by: Assets of European pension funds, in millions of U.S. dollars. **Remarks:** Figure for Barclays Global includes pooled assets. **Number listed:** 25
1. Mercury Asset Mgmt. with $74,018 million
2. PDFM and UBSII, $72,353
3. Schroder Investment Mgmt., $64,227
4. Barclays Global, $52,369
5. Gartmore, $47,556
6. Morgan Grenfell Asset Mgmt., $31,978
7. Danske Capital Mgmt., $29,902
8. Foreign & Colonial, $22,967
9. Dresdner Bank Group, $22,520
10. Hill Samuel Asset Mgmt., $17,302

Source: *Pensions & Investments*, March 31, 1997, p. 48.

Pension Plans – United Kingdom

★ 2052 ★
LARGEST EXTERNAL PENSION FUND MANAGERS IN THE U.K., 1995
Ranked by: Fund size, in millions of British pounds (£). **Number listed:** 10
1. Mercury with £37,393 million
2. PDFM, £33,914
3. Schroder, £26,370
4. Gartmore, £15,301
5. BZW, £12,473
6. Morgan Grenfell, £8,073
7. Baring, £7,950
8. Prudential, £6,925
9. Fleming, £6,577
10. Baillie Gifford, £5,253

Source: *The Guardian*, January 18, 1997, p. 3.

Perfumes

★ 2053 ★
TOP FRAGRANCES FOR MEN IN THE UNITED KINGDOM, 1995
Ranked by: Estimated sales, in millions of British pounds (£). **Remarks:** Notes ad agency and spending. **Number listed:** 10
1. Jazz (Yves St. Laurent) with £Over 14 million
2. Aramis Classic (Aramis), £10-14
3. Kouros (Yves St. Laurent), £10-14
4. Lynx Black (Elida Faberge), £10-14
5. Old Spice (Procter & Gamble), £10-14

6. Brut (Elida Faberge), £5-10
7. Eternity (Calvin Klein), £5-10
8. Fahrenheit (Christian Dior), £5-10
9. Obsession (Calvin Klein), £5-10
10. Paco Rabanne (Creative Fragrances), £5-10

Source: *Marketing*, July 4, 1996, p. 27.

★ 2054 ★
TOP FRAGRANCES FOR WOMEN IN THE UNITED KINGDOM, 1995
Ranked by: Estimated sales, in millions of British pounds (£). **Remarks:** Notes ad agency and spending. **Number listed:** 10
1. Anais Anais (Prestige Collection) with £Over 14 million
2. Channel No. 5 (Chanel), £10-14
3. Loulou (Prestige Collection), £10-14
4. Charlie (Revlon), £5-10
5. Dune (Christian Dior), £5-10
6. Eternity (Calvin Klein), £5-10
7. Giorgio (Giorgio Beverly Hills), £5-10
8. Paris (Yves St. Laurent), £5-10
9. Poison (Christian Dior), £5-10
10. Opium (Yves St. Laurent), £5-10

Source: *Marketing*, July 4, 1996, p. 29.

★ 2055 ★
TOP PERFUME ADVERTISERS IN HONG KONG, 1995
Ranked by: Ad spending, in thousands of U.S. dollars. **Remarks:** Notes spending by medium. **Number listed:** 12
1. Christian Dior with $591 thousand
2. Chanel, $351
3. Lancome, $145
4. Estee Lauder, $126
5. Elizabeth Arden, $64
6. Guerlain, $35
7. Shiseido, $27
8. Borghese, $17
9. Clarins, $15
10. YSL, $13

Source: *National Trade Data Bank*, August 1, 1996, p. ISA960701.

Periodicals – Germany

★ 2056 ★
LEADING MAGAZINES IN GERMANY, 1996
Ranked by: Millions of readers in the third quarter of 1996. **Number listed:** 5
1. Stern with 1,231 million readers
2. Der Spiegel, 1,034
3. Focus, 802
4. Die Zeit, 469

5. Die Woche, 119
Source: *The Economist*, January 11, 1997, p. 47.

Personal Care Products

★ 2057 ★
POPULAR BATH PRODUCTS USED IN GERMANY, 1996
Ranked by: People over the age of 14 who use each brand, in percent. **Remarks:** Data include multiple responses. **Number listed:** 20
1. Nivea with 18.4%
2. Litamin, 13.4%
3. Badedas, 13.0%
4. Aldi, 11.1%
5. Fa, 8.3%
6. Irischer Fruhling, 8.2%
7. Cliff, 8.0%
8. CD, 7.5%
9. Fenjala, 8.0%
10. Palmolive, 6.0%

Source: *Marketing in Europe*, March 1997, p. 16.

★ 2058 ★
POPULAR SHOWER PRODUCTS USED IN GERMANY, 1996
Ranked by: People over the age of 14 who use each brand, in percent. **Remarks:** Data include multiple responses. **Number listed:** 20
1. Nivea with 18.8%
2. Duschdas, 17.6%
3. Aldi (Ombra, Mildren, Caribic), 12.6%
4. Cliff, 12.4%
5. Doppeldusch, 10.8%
6. Litamin, 9.0%
7. Fa, 7.6%
8. CD, 6.5%
9. Irischer Fruhling, 6.5%
10. Axe, 5.8%

Source: *Marketing in Europe*, March 1997, p. 16.

★ 2059 ★
TOP PERSONAL CARE PRODUCTS BRANDS BY BRAND VALUE
Ranked by: Brand value, in millions of U.S. dollars. **Remarks:** Value was calculated using capital, ratio of capital to company sales, earnings, and corporate tax rate of the country where the parent company is located. See source for details. **Number listed:** 63
1. Gillette (Gillette) with $10,292 million
2. Pampers (Procter & Gamble), $5,731
3. Colgate (Colgate-Palmolive), $3,899
4. Bic (Bic), $1,959
5. Tampax (Tambrands), $1,539

6. Huggies (Kimberly-Clark), $1,492
7. Bausch & Lomb (Bausch & Lomb), $1,469
8. Tylenol (Johnson & Johnson), $1,418
9. Nivea (Beiersdorf), $1,354
10. Crest (Procter & Gamble), $1,022

Source: *Financial World*, World's Most Valuable Brands (annual), July 8, 1996, p. 63.

Personal Care Products – United Kingdom

★ 2060 ★
TOP PERSONAL CARE BRANDS IN THE UNITED KINGDOM, 1995
Ranked by: Estimated sales, in millions of British pounds (£). **Remarks:** Notes ad agencies and spending. **Number listed:** 10
1. Tampax with £81 million
2. Colgate toothpaste, £80
3. Always, £70
4. Lynx deodorants/body spray, £55
5. Sure, £55
6. Sensor razors and blades, £50
7. Oil of Ulay, £45
8. Lil-lets, £40
9. Macleans toothpaste, £40
10. Pantene shampoo, £40

Source: *Marketing*, July 4, 1996, p. 24.

Personal Computers
See: **Microcomputers**

Personal Income
See: **Income**

Pesticides Industry

★ 2061 ★
LEADING PESTICIDES PRODUCERS, 1996
Ranked by: Estimated sales, in millions of U.S. dollars. **Number listed:** 20
1. Novartis with $4,175 million
2. DuPont, $2,500-2,900
3. Monsanto, $2,500-2,900
4. Zeneca, $2,500-2,900
5. AgrEvo, $2,200-2,500
6. Bayer, $2,200-2,500
7. DowElanco, $2,000-2,200
8. Rhone-Poulenc, $2,000-2,200

9.   American Cyanamid, $1,900-2,000
10. BASF, $1,500-1,600
Source: *Chemical Week*, April 9, 1997, p. 29.

Pet Food

★ 2062 ★
GERMANY'S PET FOOD MARKET
Ranked by: Market share, in percent. **Number listed:** 2
1.   Mars with 80.0%
2.   Other, 20.0%
Source: *Pet Product News*, December 1995, p. 21.

★ 2063 ★
GREAT BRITAIN'S CAT FOOD MARKET
Ranked by: Market share, in percent. **Number listed:** 3
1.   Felix with 25.2%
2.   Whiskas, 25.0%
3.   Other, 49.8%
Source: *The Times*, May 2, 1996, p. 6.

★ 2064 ★
TOP DRY CAT FOOD MAKERS IN FRANCE, 1995
Ranked by: Market share for the first nine months of 1995, in percent. **Number listed:** 5
1.   Nestle with 53.02%
2.   Unisabi, 15.09%
3.   Spillers, 8.06%
4.   Royal Canin, 0.50%
5.   Others, 23.33%
Source: *National Trade Data Bank*, January 19, 1996, p. IMI960119.

★ 2065 ★
TOP DRY DOG FOOD MAKERS IN FRANCE, 1995
Ranked by: Market share for the first nine months of 1995, in percent. **Number listed:** 4
1.   Unisabi with 29.0%
2.   Royal Canin, 15.5%
3.   Nestle, 13.0%
4.   Others, 42.5%
Source: *National Trade Data Bank*, January 19, 1996, p. IMI960119.

★ 2066 ★
TOP PET FOOD BRANDS IN THE UNITED KINGDOM, 1995
Ranked by: Estimated sales, in millions of British pounds (£). **Remarks:** Notes ad agency and spending. **Number listed:** 10
1.   Whiskas (Pedigree Petfoods) with £Over 154 million
2.   Felix (Spillers), £105-110
3.   Pedigree Chum (Pedigree Petfoods), £105-110

4.   Arthur's (Spillers), £40-45
5.   Kit-e-Kat (Pedigree Petfoods), £35-40
6.   Butcher's (Butcher's Pet Care), £25-30
7.   Cesar (Pedigree Petfoods), £25-30
8.   Choosy (Spillers), £25-30
9.   Friskies (Nestle), £25-30
10. Pal (Pedigree Petfoods), £25-30
Source: *Marketing*, July 4, 1996, p. 26.

★ 2067 ★
TOP WET CAT FOOD MAKERS IN FRANCE, 1995
Ranked by: Market share for the first nine months of 1995, in percent. **Number listed:** 4
1.   Unisabi with 50.60%
2.   Nestle, 16.60%
3.   Spillers, 13.90%
4.   Others, 18.09%
Source: *National Trade Data Bank*, January 19, 1996, p. IMI960119.

★ 2068 ★
TOP WET DOG FOOD MAKERS IN FRANCE, 1995
Ranked by: Market share for the first nine months of 1995, in percent. **Number listed:** 4
1.   Unisabi with 65.1%
2.   Spillers, 10.7%
3.   Nestle, 3.0%
4.   Others, 21.2%
Source: *National Trade Data Bank*, January 19, 1996, p. IMI960119.

Petrochemical Industry

★ 2069 ★
TOP PETROCHEMICAL PRODUCERS IN THAILAND
Ranked by: Revenue, in millions of bahts (Bt). **Remarks:** Includes profits and assets. **Number listed:** 64
1.   Thai Petrochemical Industry with Bt11,377.07 million
2.   National Petrochemical, Bt6,840.12
3.   Thai Central Chemical, Bt6,153.78
4.   Thai Polyethylene, Bt5,936.12
5.   TPI Polene, Bt5,424.85
6.   Thai Plastic and Chemical, Bt5,109.90
7.   Vin Ythai, Bt3,697.34
8.   TOA, Bt3,172.22
9.   HMC Polymers, Bt2,613.75
10. Polymers Marketing, Bt2,481.78
Source: *Business Review*, December 1995, p. 162+.

Petroleum Industry

★ 2070 ★
CRUDE PRODUCTION IN TRINIDAD
Ranked by: Market share based on production, in percent. **Number listed:** 4
1. Amoco with 45%
2. Trinmar, 24%
3. Petrotrin, 23%
4. Enron, 5%

Source: *National Trade Data Bank*, June 13, 1997, p. IMI970613.

★ 2071 ★
LARGEST CRUDE OIL CONSUMERS, 1993
Ranked by: Consumption by less industrialized, non-OECD member countries, in thousands of barrels per day. **Number listed:** 21
1. Saudi Arabia with 198.0 thousand barrels
2. Brazil, 180.6
3. Venezuela, 179.9
4. South Africa, 152.5
5. Iran, 136.0
6. Indonesia, 128.4
7. Colombia, 125.6
8. Argentina, 123.5
9. Taiwan, 121.1
10. Nigeria, 118.3

Source: *Asiaweek*, October 18, 1996, p. 8.

★ 2072 ★
LARGEST OIL EXPORTERS, 1996
Ranked by: Exports for the first 10 months of 1996, in thousands of barrels per day. **Number listed:** 15
1. Saudi Arabia with 6,520 thousand barrels
2. Norway, 2,825
3. Iran, 2,700
4. Russia, 2,425
5. Venezuela, 2,000

Source: *The Wall Street Journal*, April 3, 1997, p. A15.

★ 2073 ★
LEADING NATIONS IN CRUDE OIL RESERVES, 1995
Ranked by: Reserves as of January 1, 1995, in millions of barrels. **Remarks:** Also notes for 1993-1994. **Number listed:** 20
1. Saudi Arabia with 258,703 million barrels
2. Iraq, 100,000
3. United Arab Emirates, 97,700
4. Kuwait, 94,000
5. Iran, 89,250
6. Venezuela, 64,477
7. Former Soviet Union, 57,000
8. Mexico, 50,776

9. China, 24,000
10. United States, 22,957

Source: *National Petroleum News*, Mid-July 1996, p. 72.

★ 2074 ★
LEADING OIL COMPANIES BY PROFITS PER EMPLOYEE, 1996
Ranked by: Profits per employee, in thousands of U.S. dollars. **Remarks:** Also notes sales, assets, and number of employees. **Number listed:** 5
1. Exxon with $93.3 thousand
2. Texaco, $70.6
3. Amoco, $67.1
4. Mobil, $63.5
5. Chevron, $62.2

Source: *Forbes,* Forbes 500s Annual Directory, April 21, 1997, p. 232.

★ 2075 ★
MOST APPEALING LOCATIONS FOR NEW VENTURES, 1997
Ranked by: Level of appeal, based on a survey of 111 international oil companies regarding new upstream ventures for the forthcoming year in 146 countries outside North America. **Remarks:** Criteria such as the availability of opportunities, technical merit, and commercial environment were considered. No specific data were given. Provides rankings for 1995 and 1996. **Number listed:** 25
1. United Kingdom
2. Venezuela
3. Indonesia
4. Algeria
5. Australia
6. Colombia
7. Argentina
8. Peru
9. Angola
10. Iraq

Source: *Petroleum Economist*, April 1997, p. 19.

★ 2076 ★
MOST PROFITABLE OIL COMPANIES
Ranked by: 5-year average return on capital, in percent. **Remarks:** Also notes sales, earnings per share, net income, profit margin, and debt to capital ratio. **Number listed:** 7
1. Exxon with 10.3%
2. Royal Dutch Petroleum, 9.6%
3. Mobil, 8.9%
4. Amoco, 8.6%
5. Texaco, 7.1%
6. Chevron, 6.9%
7. British Petroleum, 6.6%

Source: *Forbes*, January 13, 1997, p. 142.

★ 2077 ★
RUSSIA'S TOP OIL FIRMS, 1996
Ranked by: Oil reserves, in millions of barrels as of January 1, 1996. **Remarks:** Includes figures on production and refining. **Number listed:** 14
1. Yukos with 14,875 million barrels
2. Sidanco (Siberian & Far East Oil), 13,465
3. Lukoil, 13,460
4. Tyumen Oil, 13,220
5. Rosneft, 10,825
6. Surgutneftegaz, 8,500
7. Tatneft, 5,595
8. Sibneft, 4,850
9. Eastern Oil, 3,000
10. Slavneft, 2,800

Source: *Petroleum Economist*, February 1997, p. 8.

★ 2078 ★
TOP CRUDE OIL MINING COMPANIES, 1995
Ranked by: Revenue, in millions of U.S. dollars. **Remarks:** Also notes profits. **Number listed:** 3
1. Pemex with $22,330 million
2. Ruhrkohle, $17,233
3. Statoil, $13,648

Source: *Fortune,* The Global 500: World's Biggest Corporations (annual), August 5, 1996, p. 123.

★ 2079 ★
TOP OIL FIRMS BY PROFITS IN JAPAN, 1996
Ranked by: Operating profits for the year ended March 1996, in billions of yen (¥) **Number listed:** 8
1. Mitsubishi Oil with ¥20.7 billion
2. General, ¥19.8
3. Showa Shell, ¥19.0
4. Tonen, ¥13.0
5. Cosmo, ¥11.9
6. Nippon Oil, ¥10.9
7. Idemitsu Kosan, ¥8.5
8. Japan Energy, ¥5.8

Source: *The Economist*, October 26, 1996, p. 83.

★ 2080 ★
TOP OIL PRODUCERS IN BRAZIL, 1995
Ranked by: Barrels produced daily per employee. **Remarks:** Includes figures on oil and gas reserves for each company. **Number listed:** 10
1. Sonatrach with 35.8 barrels
2. Chevron, 24.8
3. Pertamina, 22.7
4. Royal Dutch/Shell, 20.7
5. Texaco, 20.6
6. Exxon, 19.9
7. Amoco, 15.9
8. Mobil, 14.5
9. Petrobas, 13.9

10. Elf Aquitaine, 7.5

Source: *The Wall Street Journal*, February 25, 1997, p. A18.

★ 2081 ★
TOP PETROLEUM COMPANIES IN JAPAN
Ranked by: Income, in millions of yen (¥). **Number listed:** 10
1. Nippon Oil with ¥47,962 million
2. Cosmo Oil, ¥40,913
3. General Sekiyu, ¥27,921
4. Esso Sekiyu, ¥27,522
5. Idemitsu Kosan, ¥22,824
6. Mitsubishi Oil, ¥20,287
7. Mobil Sekiyu, ¥18,296
8. Itochu Fuel, ¥8,444
9. Kyushu Oil, ¥7,998
10. Mitsuuroko, ¥4,659

Source: *Tokyo Business Today*, August 1995, p. 27.

★ 2082 ★
TOP PRODUCERS OF OIL AND PETROLEUM PRODUCTS, 1996
Ranked by: Market capitalization at September 30, 1996, in millions of U.S. dollars. **Number listed:** 10
1. Royal Dutch/Shell with $135,350.2 million
2. Exxon Corp., $103,384.0
3. British Petroleum, $58,197.6
4. Mobil Corp., $45,602.6
5. ENI, $41,006.3
6. Chevron Corp., $40,878.3
7. Amoco, $35,048.2
8. Texaco, $24,313.0
9. Elf Aquitaine, $21,513.7
10. Atlantic Richfield, $20,506.2

Source: *Financial Times*, January 7, 1997, p. VI.

★ 2083 ★
TOP STATE-OWNED OIL COMPANIES BY PRODUCTION
Ranked by: Production, in millions of barrels. **Number listed:** 20
1. Saudi Arabian Oil Co. with 2,944.5 million barrels
2. National Iranian Oil Co., 1,318.4
3. Petroleos Mexicanos, 1,119.0
4. China National Petroleum Co., 1,097.6
5. Petroleos de Venezuela SA, 952.3
6. Royal Dutch/Shell, 790.0
7. Kuwait Petroleum Corp., 730.0
8. Nigerian National Petroleum Corp., 688.8
9. Abu Dhabi National Oil Co., 683.6
10. Pertamina (Indonesia), 546.8

Source: *Oil & Gas Journal,* Oil & Gas Journal 200 (annual), September 2, 1996, p. 68.

★ 2084 ★
TOP STATE-OWNED OIL COMPANIES BY RESERVES
Ranked by: Reserves, in millions of barrels. **Number listed:** 20
1. Saudi Arabian Oil Co. with 258,703.0 million barrels
2. Iraq National Oil Co., 100,000.0
3. Kuwait Petroleum Corp., 94,000.0
4. Abu Dhabi National Oil Co., 92,200.0
5. National Iranian Oil Co., 88,200.0
6. Petroleos de Venezuela SA, 64,477.0
7. Petroleos Mexicanos, 48,796.0
8. National Oil Corp. (Libya), 29,500.0
9. China National Petroleum Co., 24,000.0
10. Nigerian National Petroleum Corp., 20,828.0
Source: *Oil & Gas Journal,* Oil & Gas Journal 200 (annual), September 2, 1996, p. 68.

Petroleum Industry – Canada

★ 2085 ★
LARGEST OIL AND GAS FIRMS IN CANADA
Ranked by: Revenue, in thousands of Canadian dollars. **Remarks:** Includes figures on profits and return on capital. **Number listed:** 8
1. Amoco Canada Petroleum with C$3,619,000 thousand
2. Imperial Oil Resources, C$2,297,000
3. PanCanadian Petroleum, C$2,013,200
4. Norcen Energy Resources, C$1,409,900
5. Chevron Canada Resources, C$1,359,205
6. Cdn. Occidental Petroleum, C$1,228,000
7. Talisman Energy, C$1,082,563
8. Gulf Canada Resources, C$752,000
Source: *Globe and Mail's Report on Business Magazine,* July 1996, p. 159.

Petroleum Industry – Europe

★ 2086 ★
EUROPE'S TOP OIL FIRMS
Ranked by: Turnover, in billions of U.S. dollars. **Number listed:** 10
1. Royal Dutch/Shell with $105.09 billion
2. British Petroleum, $54.52
3. Elf Aquitaine, $40.07
4. ENI, $35.91
5. Total, $26.13
6. Repsol, $19.87
7. Petrofina, $17.82
8. Norsk Hydro, $12.07
9. Cepsa, $7.53
10. OMV, $6.78
Source: *Financial Times,* June 17, 1996, p. 25.

Petroleum Refineries

★ 2087 ★
LARGEST REFINERS WORLDWIDE
Ranked by: Capacity, in millions of barrels per day. **Number listed:** 10
1. Royal Dutch/Shell with 4.68 million barrels
2. Exxon Corp., 3.43
3. Sinopec, 2.85
4. Petreleos de Venezuela SA, 2.50
5. Mobil Corp., 2.04
6. Saudi Aramco, 1.78
7. BP, 1.72
8. Petroleos Mexicanos, 1.64
9. Chevron Corp., 1.53
10. Petreleo Brasilero, 1.25
Source: *Oil & Gas Journal,* December 23, 1996, p. 42.

★ 2088 ★
LARGEST REFINING FIRMS
Ranked by: Capacity, in barrels per day. **Number listed:** 10
1. Yukong Ltd. with 769,500 barrels
2. Lagoven, 571,000
3. Chinese Petroleum Corp., 570,000
4. Hess Oil Virgin Islands, 545,000
5. Ssangyong Oil Ref. Co., 500,000
6. Amoco Oil Co., 433,000
7. Exxon Co., 424,000
8. Kuwait National Petr. Co., 415,000
9. Amoco Oil Co., 410,000
10. Shell Eastern, 405,000
Source: *Oil & Gas Journal,* December 23, 1996, p. 42.

★ 2089 ★
TOP PETROLEUM REFINING COMPANIES IN SOUTH KOREA, 1996
Ranked by: Sales for the first six months of 1996, in hundred million won (W). **Number listed:** 6
1. Yukong with W39,472.0 hundred million
2. Ssangyong Oil Refining, W19,638.8
3. Hanwha Energy, W10,868.1
4. Mi Chang Oil, W330.7
5. Han Kook Shell Oil, W281.2
6. Kukdong Oil & Chemical, W166.3
Source: *Business Korea,* October 1996, p. 34.

Petroleum Refineries – Europe

★ 2090 ★
TOP PETROLEUM REFINING COMPANIES IN EUROPE
Ranked by: Sales, in millions of European Currency Units (ECUs). **Remarks:** Also notes the number of employees. **Number listed:** 21
1. RWE A.G. with 28,861 million ECUs
2. Agip Petroli S.P.A., 19,637
3. RWE-DEA A.G. Fuer Mineraloel und Chemie, 10,822
4. Deutsche Shell A.G., 9,857
5. Esso A.G., 8,619
6. Italiana Petroli S.P.A., 8,295
7. Dea Mineraloel A.G., 8,238
8. Total Raffinage Distribution S.A., 7,973
9. Veba Oel A.G., 7,419
10. Esso Italiana S.P.A., 6,509

Source: *Duns Europa* (annual), vol. 4, Dun & Bradstreet, 1997, p. 226+.

Pharmaceutical Industry
See: **Drug Trade**

Philippines – see under individual headings

Photographic Industry

★ 2091 ★
GLOBAL FILM MARKET
Ranked by: Market share, in percent. **Number listed:** 3
1. Fuji with 40.0%
2. Kodak, 40.0%
3. Other, 20.0%

Source: *Advertising Age International*, January 1997, p. I36.

★ 2092 ★
PHOTOGRAPHIC FILM MARKET OUTSIDE JAPAN & THE UNITED STATES
Ranked by: Distribution, in percent. **Number listed:** 3
1. Kodak with 36%
2. Fujifilm, 33%
3. Other, 31%

Source: *Financial Times*, April 18, 1997, p. 9.

★ 2093 ★
TOP PHOTOGRAPHIC FILM MANUFACTURERS IN JAPAN
Ranked by: Market share, in percent. **Remarks:** Provides U.S. figures. **Number listed:** 3
1. Fujifilm with 70%
2. Kodak, 10%
3. Other, 20%

Source: *Financial Times*, April 18, 1997, p. 9.

Photographic Supply Stores

★ 2094 ★
LEADING OUTLETS FOR CAMERA SALES IN THE UNITED KINGDOM, 1995
Ranked by: Value of sales, in percent. **Number listed:** 3
1. Camera shops with 57.8%
2. Multiples, 41.2%
3. Chemists, 1.0%

Source: *Photo Marketing*, August 1997, p. 80.

Photography – Films

★ 2095 ★
EUROPE'S FILM MARKET
Ranked by: Market share, in percent. **Remarks:** Shares are estimated. **Number listed:** 3
1. Kodak with 50.0%
2. Fuji, 30.0%
3. Other, 20.0%

Source: *Advertising Age International*, January 1997, p. I36.

Pipeline Companies

★ 2096 ★
LEADING REGIONS IN EUROPE FOR PIPELINE CONSTRUCTION
Ranked by: Miles of pipeline planned or currently under construction. **Remarks:** Figures refer to all forms of products. **Number listed:** 10
1. Former Soviet Union with 10,605 miles
2. Germany, 2,375
3. Denmark, 2,298
4. North Sea, 1,993
5. Italy, 1,628
6. Spain, 1,476
7. Yugoslavia, 824
8. United Kingdom, 777
9. France, 675

10. Norway, 633
Source: *Pipeline & Gas Industry*, November 1996, p. 23.

Plastic Containers

★ 2097 ★
GREAT BRITAIN'S PLASTICWARE MARKET
Ranked by: Market share, in percent. **Number listed:** 3
1. Addis with 45.0%
2. Plysu, 10.0%
3. Other, 45.0%

Source: *National Trade Data Bank*, March 2, 1996, p. ISA9406.

Plastics Industry

★ 2098 ★
ENGINEERING PLASTICS MARKET
Ranked by: Market share, in percent. **Number listed:** 12
1. G.E. Plastics with 22%
2. DuPont, 12%
3. Hoechst, 11%
4. Bayer, 9%
5. BASF, 5%
6. Mitsubishi Gas Chemical, 4%
7. Asahi, 3%
7. Dow Chemical, 3%
7. Toray, 3%
10. Allied Signal, 2%

Source: *Chemical Week*, May 28, 1997, p. 28.

★ 2099 ★
INDIA'S HIGH DENSITY POLYETHYLENE MARKET, 1996-1997
Ranked by: Market share, in percent. **Number listed:** 3
1. Reliance with 50%
2. IPCL, 25%
3. NOCIL, 25%

Source: *Business Today*, July 22, 1997, p. 53.

★ 2100 ★
LEADING CONSUMERS OF PLASTICS, 1996
Ranked by: Consumption, in percent. **Number listed:** 8
1. Western Europe with 25%
2. United States, 24%
3. Japan, 9%
4. Latin America, 5%
5. Canada, 2%
6. Mexico, 2%
7. Rest of Asia, 25%

8. Other, 8%

Source: *Chemical & Engineering News*, May 26, 1997, p. 15.

★ 2101 ★
LEADING PLASTICS FACILITIES OUTSIDE THE U.S., 1990-1995
Ranked by: Production, in millions of U.S. dollars.
Number listed: 11
1. Hong Kong Petrochemical Co. Limited (Hong Kong) with $1,000 million
2. General Electric Co. (Spain), $750
3. British Petroleum (Indonesia), $230
4. Nissho Iwai Corp./British Petroleum (Indonesia), $148
5. Venture Holdings Trust (Australia), $110
6. Zimmer GmbH/Bangkok Cable Co. (Thailand), $102
7. Norsk Hydro A.S. (Norway), $85
8. Occidental Chemical Co./Thai Plastic & Chemical Co. (Thailand), $61
9. Ectona Fibres Ltd. (United Kingdom), $58
10. Dow Chemicals (Indonesia), $30

Source: *Site Selection*, August 1996, p. 646.

★ 2102 ★
LEADING POLYPROPYLENE PRODUCERS IN INDIA, 1996-1997
Ranked by: Market share, in percent. **Number listed:** 2
1. IPCL with 59%
2. Reliance, 41%

Source: *Business Today*, July 22, 1997, p. 53.

★ 2103 ★
LEADING POLYVINYL CHLORIDE PRODUCERS IN INDIA, 1996-1997
Ranked by: Market share, in percent. **Number listed:** 7
1. Reliance with 36%
2. Finolex, 23%
3. IPCL, 13%
4. DCW, 10%
5. Chemplast, 8%
6. DCM Shriram, 6%
7. NOCIL, 4%

Source: *Business Today*, July 22, 1997, p. 53.

★ 2104 ★
MOST WIDELY USED PLASTICS
Ranked by: Distribution, in percent. **Remarks:** ABS/SAN stands for acrylonitrile-butadiene-styrene/styrene-acrylonitrile. **Number listed:** 5
1. Polyethylene with 41%
2. Polyvinyl chloride, 23%
3. Polypropylene, 21%
4. Polystyrene, 11%

5. ABS/SAN, 4%

Source: *Chemical & Engineering News*, May 26, 1997, p. 15.

★ **2105** ★

PVC FRAME MAKERS IN TURKEY

Ranked by: Market share, in percent. **Number listed:** 3

1. Pimapen with 40.0%
2. Ege Pen, 30.0%
3. Other, 30.0%

Source: *National Trade Data Bank*, May 27, 1996, p. ISA9311.

★ **2106** ★

TOP LOW-DENSITY POLYETHYLENE PRODUCERS IN JAPAN

Ranked by: Production, in thousands of metric tons. **Number listed:** 7

1. Mitsubishi Kagaku with 327 thousand metric tons
2. Japan Polyolefin, 236
3. Sumitomo Chemical, 196
4. DuPont-Mitsui, 168
5. Nippon Unicar, 125
6. Asahi, 111
7. Tosoh, 99

Source: *Chemical Week*, May 21, 1997, p. 31.

★ **2107** ★

TOP POLYSTYRENE PRODUCERS IN JAPAN

Ranked by: Capacity, in thousands of metric tons. **Number listed:** 8

1. Asahi Chemical with 433 thousand metric tons
2. Sumitomo Chemical-Mitsui Toatsu, 242
3. Denki Kagaku, 203
4. Mitsubishi Kagaku, 200
5. Idemitsu Petrochemical, 180
6. Nippon Steel Chemical, 136
7. Dainippon Ink and Chemical, 95
8. Daicel Chemical, 93

Source: *Chemical Week*, July 11, 1997, p. 8.

Point-of-Sale Systems

★ **2108** ★

TOP SUPPLIERS OF POINT-OF-SALE TERMINALS IN SOUTH KOREA, 1995

Ranked by: Units sold as of the end of June 1995. **Number listed:** 6

1. IBM Korea with 4,795 units
2. IPC Korea, 3,393
3. Korea AT&T GIS, 2,985
4. Hyundai-Tech System, 3,082
5. Fujitsu Korea, 2,502

6. Other, 4,854

Source: *National Trade Data Bank*, October 19, 1995, p. ISA9509.

Poland − see under individual headings

Pollution

★ **2109** ★

LEADING PRODUCERS OF CHLOROFLUOROCARBON FOR TRADE

Ranked by: Global market share of production capacity, in percent. **Number listed:** 7

1. Russia with 47%
2. China, 28%
3. India, 7%
4. South Korea, 7%
5. Venezuela, 5%
6. Brazil, 3%
7. Mexico, 3%

Source: *Financial Times*, September 5, 1997, p. 2.

Pollution Control Industries

★ **2110** ★

FASTEST GROWING MARKETS FOR POLLUTION CONTROL EQUIPMENT OUTSIDE THE U.S.

Ranked by: Average annual growth, in percent. **Number listed:** 10

1. Chile with $50 million
2. Czech Republic, $40
3. Egypt, $40
4. Greece, $35
5. Poland, $30
6. Turkey, $30
7. Taiwan, $28
8. Malaysia, $27
9. Bulgaria, $25
10. India, $23

Source: *National Trade Data Bank*, March 21, 1995, p. BMR9403.

★ **2111** ★

LARGEST IMPORT MARKETS FOR POLLUTION CONTROL EQUIPMENT OUTSIDE THE U.S.

Ranked by: Value of imports, in millions of U.S. dollars. **Number listed:** 10

1. Germany with $7,150.0 million
2. France, $2,950.0
3. Mexico, $1,700.0

4.   Canada, $1,517.0
5.   United Kingdom, $1,000.0
6.   Taiwan, $940.0
7.   Austria, $780.5
8.   Italy, $780.0
9.   Australia, $773.0
10.   Singapore, $693.0

Source: *National Trade Data Bank*, March 21, 1995, p. BMR9403.

★ 2112 ★
LARGEST MARKETS FOR POLLUTION CONTROL EQUIPMENT OUTSIDE THE U.S.
Ranked by: Total market value, in millions of U.S. dollars. **Number listed:** 10

1.   Germany with $28,000.0 million
2.   France, $12,000.0
3.   Japan, $8,000.0
4.   Canada, $4,140.0
5.   United Kingdom, $4,000.0
6.   Austria, $3,978.4
7.   Italy, $3,770.0
8.   Mexico, $2,000.0
9.   Australia, $1,300.0
10.   Spain, $1,250.0

Source: *National Trade Data Bank*, March 21, 1995, p. BMR9403.

Pork Industry

★ 2113 ★
TOP PORK PRODUCING NATIONS IN THE EUROPEAN UNION, 1996
Ranked by: Production, in millions of metric tons. **Number listed:** 11

1.   Germany with 3,411 million metric tons
2.   France, 2,149
3.   Spain, 2,104
4.   Netherlands, 2,084
5.   Denmark, 1,532
6.   Italy, 1,194
7.   Belgium-Luxembourg Economic Union, 1,049
8.   United Kingdom, 980
9.   Portugal, 303
10.   Ireland, 209

Source: http:// www.mhr-viandes.com/en/docu/ d0000148.html, August 22, 1997, p. 1.

Ports

★ 2114 ★
ASIAN COUNTRIES WITH THE MOST PORTS
Ranked by: Number of ports. **Number listed:** 11

1.   Japan with 20
2.   China, 18
3.   Malaysia, 17
4.   Philippines, 15
5.   India, 12
6.   North Korea, 12
7.   South Korea, 9
8.   Indonesia, 8
9.   Thailand, 7
10.   Vietnam, 6

Source: *Far Eastern Economic Review*, January 30, 1997, p. 13.

★ 2115 ★
LEADING MEDITERRANEAN PORTS, 1995
Ranked by: Transaction volume, in thousands of twenty-foot equivalent units (TEUs). **Number listed:** 9

1.   Algeciras (Spain) with 1,155 thousand TEUs
2.   La Spezia (Italy), 965
3.   Barcelona (Spain), 685
4.   Valencia (Spain), 672
5.   Genoa (Italy), 615
6.   Piraeus (Greece), 598
7.   Dumyat (Egypt), 570
8.   Marsaxlokk (Malta), 515
9.   Marseille (France), 498

Source: *Neve Zurcher Zeitung*, October 6, 1996, p. 15.

★ 2116 ★
TOP CONTAINER PORTS, 1994
Ranked by: Cargo handled, in twenty-foot equivalent units (TEUs). **Remarks:** Data for Singapore, Kaohsiung, Busan, Kobe, Antwerp are estimated. **Number listed:** 11

1.   Hong Kong with 11,265,984 TEUs
2.   Singapore, 10,600,000
3.   Long Beach/Los Angeles, 5,091,845
4.   Rotterdam, 4,899,879
5.   Kaohsiung, 4,500,000
6.   Pusan, 3,754,000
7.   Kobe, 2,787,000
8.   Hamburg, 2,725,715
9.   Yokohama, 2,390,000
10.   Antwerp, 2,250,000

Source: *Economic Development Horizons*, April 1996, p. 24.

Portugal – see under individual headings

Postal Service

★ 2117 ★
**LARGEST MAIL, PACKAGE, AND FREIGHT
DELIVERY COMPANIES, 1995**
Ranked by: Revenue, in millions of U.S. dollars.
Remarks: Also notes profits. **Number listed:** 8
1. U.S. Postal Service with $54,294 million
2. Japan Postal Service, $22,498
3. United Parcel Service, $21,045
4. Nippon Express, $17,767
5. Deutsche Post, $17,486
6. La Poste, $16,642
7. British Post Office, $9,720
8. Federal Express, $9,392
Source: *Forbes* Global 500 (annual), August 5, 1996, p.
F-22.

Postal Service, International

★ 2118 ★
TYPES OF MAIL DISTRIBUTED IN BRITAIN
Ranked by: Types of mail, in percent. **Remarks:** In the
United Kingdom, 70 million letters a day are transported
to 25 million premises. Data show 62% are sent second
class and 38% are sent first class. **Number listed:** 4
1. Financial mail with 47.2%
2. Commercial mail, 28.7%
3. Direct mail, 14.9%
4. Social mail, 9.2%
Source: *The Observer*, June 30, 1996, p. 8.

Potash

★ 2119 ★
TOP POTASH PRODUCERS, 1996
Ranked by: Production of potash equivalent, in
thousands of metric tons. **Number listed:** 16
1. Canada with 8,200 thousand metric tons
2. Germany, 3,200
3. Russia, 2,700
4. Belarus, 2,600
5. United States, 1,380
6. Israel, 1,250
7. Jordan, 1,000
8. France, 760
9. Spain, 700
10. United Kingdom, 570
Source: *Engineering & Mining Journal*, 1997
Commodities Review Issue (annual), March 1997, p. 38-
WW.

Poultry

★ 2120 ★
TOP CHICKEN CONSUMING NATIONS
Ranked by: Consumption per person, in pounds.
Number listed: 6
1. United States with 80.1 pounds
2. Canada, 56.8
3. Brazil, 49.7
4. Argentina, 41.8
5. Venezuela, 36.1
6. Mexico, 35.0
Source: *The Wall Street Journal*, September 19, 1997, p.
A8.

Poultry Industry

★ 2121 ★
BRAZIL'S TOP POULTRY SLAUGHTERS
Ranked by: Market share, in percent. **Remarks:** The
majority of poultry producers reside in Santa Catarina,
Parana, and Rio Grande do Sul. **Number listed:** 10
1. Sadia with 14.88%
2. Perdigao, 7.04%
3. Ceval, 4.68%
4. Frangosul, 4.67%
5. Avipal, 3.71%
6. Chapeco, 3.03%
7. Pena Branca, 2.79%
8. Dagranja, 2.24%
9. Aurora, 1.76%
10. Minuano, 1.61%
Source: *National Trade Data Bank*, August 30, 1995, p.
ISA9411.

★ 2122 ★
**CHICKEN/LIVESTOCK MARKET IN THE
PHILIPPINES**
Ranked by: Market share, in percent. **Number listed:** 6
1. Vitarich with 24.3%
2. Swift Foods, 23.6%
3. San Miguel, 19.4%
4. Purefoods, 12.0%
5. Universal Robina, 8.0%
6. Other, 12.1%
Source: *Asiaweek*, May 10, 1996, p. 52.

★ 2123 ★
POULTRY MARKET IN SOUTH AFRICA
Ranked by: Market share, in percent. **Number listed:** 11
1. Rainbow with 37.5%
2. DOC producers, 21.9%
3. Early bird, 12.7%

4. Country Fair, 6.5%
5. Agrichick, 6.3%
6. Fouries, 2.4%
7. Country Bird, 2.3%
8. Crown, 2.1%
9. Tydstroom, 1.7%
10. Other, 6.5%

Source: *World Poultry*, Volume 13, No. 5, 1997, p. 13.

★ 2124 ★
TOP POULTRY PRODUCING REGIONS, 2000
Ranked by: Percent of estimated production. **Remarks:** Forecast data are estimates based on a total of 21.623 billion broilers produced by 2000. **Number listed:** 5

1. North America with 28.0%
2. Europe, 22.0%
3. Asia, 20.0%
4. Latin America, 17.0%
5. Middle East/Africa, 13.0%

Source: *World Poultry*, 1995, p. 35.

Poultry Industry – Canada

★ 2125 ★
TOP POULTRY COMPANIES IN CANADA, 1996
Ranked by: Sales, in millions of Canadian dollars. **Remarks:** Notes number of plants, employees, and subsidiaries. **Number listed:** 8

1. Maple Leaf Foods, Inc. with C$3,067 million
2. Schneider Corp., C$826
3. Olymel and Co. Ltd., C$605
4. Flamingo Foods, C$349
5. Intercontinental Packers Ltd., C$335
6. Lilydale Poultry, C$299
7. Maple Lodge Farms Ltd., C$273
8. Fletcher's Fine Foods Ltd., C$270

Source: *Meat & Poultry Magazine*, July 1996, p. 42.

Power Generation Equipment

★ 2126 ★
GLOBAL POWER/TRANSMISSION EQUIPMENT MAKERS
Ranked by: Market share, in percent. **Number listed:** 6

1. ABB with 16.2%
2. GEC Alsthom, 8.5%
3. Siemens, 7.6%
4. Schneider, 5.9%
5. AEG T&D, 5.0%
6. Others, 56.8%

Source: *Financial Times*, July 15, 1997, p. 5.

Printers, Computer
See: **Computer Printers**

Printing Industry, Commercial

★ 2127 ★
TOP PRINTERS IN JAPAN
Ranked by: Market share, in percent. **Number listed:** 6

1. Dai Nippon Printing with 13.0%
2. Toppan Printing, 10.8%
3. Toppan Moore, 1.7%
4. Kyodo Printing, 1.4%
5. Toyo Shigyo Printing, 0.8%
6. Other, 72.3%

Source: *Nikkei Weekly*, August 5, 1996, p. 10.

Printing Industry – Europe

★ 2128 ★
TOP COMPANIES IN PRINTING, PUBLISHING, AND ALLIED INDUSTRIES IN EUROPE
Ranked by: Sales, in millions of European Currency Units (ECUs). **Remarks:** Also notes number of employees. **Number listed:** 117

1. Bertelsmann A.G. with 9,329 million ECUs
2. Reed Elsevier Plc., 3,889
3. Reuters Holdings Plc., 2,881
4. Rexam Plc., 2,548
5. Pearson Plc., 1,951
6. Axel Springer Verlag A.G., 1,882
7. RCS Editori Spa, 1,462
8. NV Verenigd Bezit VNU, 1,437
9. VNU International BV, 1,437
10. VNU Verenigde Nederl. Uitgeversbedrijven BV, 1,437

Source: *Duns Europa*, (annual), vol. 4, Dun & Bradstreet, 1997, p. 221.

Private Brands

★ 2129 ★
JAPAN'S PRIVATE BRAND SALES IN DEPARTMENT STORES, 1995
Ranked by: Private brand sales at department stores, in millions of yen (¥). **Number listed:** 10

1. Mitsukoshi with ¥36,313 million
2. Seibu, ¥29,100
3. Sogo, ¥28,000
4. Daimaru, ¥17,100

5.　Matsuzakaya, ¥11,000
6.　Kintesu, ¥7,630
7.　Marui, ¥6,000
8.　Tokyu, ¥3,655
9.　Odakyu, ¥3,050
10.　Meitetsu, ¥2,058

Source: *National Trade Data Bank*, September 20, 1996, p. IMI960920.

★ 2130 ★

JAPAN'S PRIVATE BRAND SALES IN SUPERMARKETS, 1995

Ranked by: Private brand sales at supermarkets, in millions of yen (¥). **Number listed:** 9

1.　Daiei with ¥311,373 million
2.　Jusco, ¥82,600
3.　Seiyu, ¥40,800
4.　Nagasakiya, ¥33,000
5.　Yuni, ¥31,750
6.　Yaohan Japan, ¥27,000
7.　Izumiya, ¥14,570
8.　Daimaru Peacock, ¥9,517
9.　Kotobukiya, ¥8,000

Source: *National Trade Data Bank*, September 20, 1996, p. IMI960920.

Privatization

★ 2131 ★

LARGEST PRIVATIZATIONS IN BRAZIL

Ranked by: Value, in billions of U.S. dollars. **Number listed:** 10

1.　CVRD with $3.1 billion
1.　Telesp, $3.1
3.　Sao Paulo Cellular Telephone, $2.4
4.　Cesp, $2.0
4.　CPFL, $2.0
4.　CVRD, $2.0
4.　Embratel, $2.0
8.　Electrosull, $1.5
8.　Fumas, $1.5
10.　Petrobras, $1.0

Source: *Financial Times*, August 20, 1997, p. 9.

★ 2132 ★

TOP NATIONS IN WESTERN EUROPE FOR PRIVATIZATIONS, 1996

Ranked by: Share of total privatizations for 1996, in percent. **Number listed:** 17

1.　Germany with 31.5%
2.　Italy, 24.0%
3.　United Kingdom, 12.1%
4.　France, 10.7%
5.　Spain, 5.9%

6.　Portugal, 4.3%
7.　Netherlands, 2.4%
8.　Sweden, 2.1%
9.　Austria, 1.8%
10.　Finland, 1.8%

Source: *Financial Times*, January 31, 1997, p. 13.

★ 2133 ★

TOP PRIVATIZATIONS WORLDWIDE, 1996

Ranked by: Proceeds, in billions of U.S. dollars. **Remarks:** Deutsche Telekom and ENI's figures are estimated. **Number listed:** 10

1.　Deutsche Telekom (Germany) with $9.8 billion
2.　ENI (Italy), $3.4
3.　Railtrack (United Kingdom), $3.0
4.　British Energy (United Kingdom), $2.2
5.　INA (Italy), $2.1
6.　AGF (France), $1.7
7.　DBKom (Germany), $1.4
8.　Argentaria (Spain), $1.1
9.　Repsol (Spain), $1.1
10.　DSM (Netherlands), $1.0

Source: *The Economist*, October 26, 1996, p. 7.

Professional Sports Clubs

See: **Sports Clubs**

Public Relations Firms

★ 2134 ★

FRANCE'S TOP PUBLIC RELATIONS FIRMS, 1995

Ranked by: Gross profits, in millions of francs (FFr). **Number listed:** 10

1.　Euro RSCG France with FFr1,473 million
2.　Publicis Conseil, FFr1,014
3.　BDDP Groupe, FFr659
4.　DDB Needham, FFr633
5.　Young & Rubicam, FFr350
6.　Ogilvy & Mather, FFr334
7.　Compagnie BBDO, FFr318
8.　McCann-Erickson, FFr312
9.　Ammirati Puris Lintas, FFr290
10.　DMB & B, FFr197

Source: *Nouvel Economiste*, March 29, 1996, p. 41.

Public Utilities
See Also: Electric Utilities

★ 2135 ★
LARGEST ELECTRIC AND GAS UTILITIES, 1995
Ranked by: Revenue, in millions of U.S. dollars. **Remarks:** Notes profits and global rank. **Number listed:** 16

1. Tokyo Electric Power (Japan) with $52,362 million
2. Electricite de France, $43,508
3. RWE Group (Germany), $37,233
4. Kansai Electric Power (Japan), $26,736
5. Enel (Italy), $22,225
6. Chubu Electric Power (Japan), $21,850
7. Tohoku Electric Power (Japan), $15,848
8. Kyushu Electric Power (Japan), $14,829
9. British Gas (United Kingdom), $13,574
10. Korea Electirc Power (South Korea), $12,955

Source: *Fortune,* The Global 500: World's Biggest Corporations (annual), August 5, 1996, p. F-18.

★ 2136 ★
TOP ELECTRICITY & GAS COMPANIES IN SOUTH KOREA, 1996
Ranked by: Sales for the first six months of 1996, in hundred million won (W). **Number listed:** 5

1. Korea Electric Power with W53,418.0 hundred million
2. Samchully, W2,182.9
3. Seoul Gas, W1,979.8
4. Daehan City Gas, W1,448.7
5. Kyung Nam Energy, W360.5

Source: *Business Korea,* October 1996, p. 40.

★ 2137 ★
TOP EUROPEAN UTILITIES
Ranked by: Turnover, in billions of U.S. dollars. **Remarks:** Includes net income and market capitalization. **Number listed:** 20

1. RWE with $34.41 billion
2. Gen des Eaux, $31.24
3. Lyonnaise des Eaux, $18.89
4. British Gas, $12.99
5. Tractebel, $10.19
6. Endesa Empresa, $6.90
7. Electrabel, $6.83
8. Iberdrola, $6.30
9. National Power, $5.97
10. Vereinigte Elekt, $5.56

Source: *Financial Times,* June 17, 1996, p. 25.

Publishers and Publishing

★ 2138 ★
LARGEST MEDIA ENTERTAINMENT FIRMS IN THAILAND, 1994
Ranked by: Revenue, in millions of bahts (Bt). **Remarks:** Includes profits and assets. **Number listed:** 16

1. Bangkok Broadcasting & TV with Bt3,034.52 million
2. Vacharaphol, Bt2,613.73
3. Wattachak, Bt1,683.98
4. Si-Phya Publishing, Bt1,602.91
5. Bangkok Entertainment, Bt1,527.78
6. Great Luck Equity, Bt1,498.63
7. Matichon, Bt1,301.18
8. Nation Publishing Group, Bt1,240.60
9. Post Publishing, Bt1,180.57
10. Shinawatra Directories, Bt1,123.34

Source: *Business Review,* December 1995, p. 188.

★ 2139 ★
LARGEST PUBLISHING AND PRINTING COMPANIES, 1995
Ranked by: Revenue, in millions of U.S. dollars. **Remarks:** Notes profits and global rank. **Number listed:** 5

1. Bertelsmann (Germany) with $13,747 million
2. Dai Nippon Printing (Japan), $12,902
3. Toppan Printing (Japan), $12,294
4. Lagardere Groupe (France), $10,539
5. News Corp. (Australia), $9,039

Source: *Fortune,* The Global 500: World's Biggest Corporations (annual), May 8, 1996, p. F-24.

★ 2140 ★
POLAND'S LEADING PUBLISHERS, 1996
Ranked by: Sales, in millions of U.S. dollars. **Remarks:** Includes number of titles published. **Number listed:** 14

1. WSiP with $51.8 million
2. PWN, $45.1
3. Swiat Ksiazki, $20.7
4. Muza, $9.8
5. PPWK, $8.5
6. Egmont, $5.7
7. Amber, $4.4
8. Arkady, $3.8
9. BGW, $3.6
10. Wiedza Powszechna, $3.6

Source: *National Trade Data Bank,* May 15, 1997, p. IMI970515.

Puerto Rico – see under individual headings

Qatar – see under individual headings

Quality of Life

★ 2141 ★
QUALITY OF LIFE PERCEPTION
Ranked by: Citizens' perception of a long and happy life, in number of years. **Number listed:** 27
1. Iceland with 62.04 years
2. Netherlands, 61.66
3. Sweden, 61.52
4. Switzerland, 59.80
5. Ireland, 59.24
6. Denmark, 59.24
7. Belgium, 58.83
8. United Kingdom, 57.91
9. Norway, 57.17
10. Northern Ireland, 56.49
Source: *The European*, January 8, 1997, p. 3.

★ 2142 ★
TOP 10 COUNTRIES WITH HIGHEST PERCENTAGE OF SATISFIED CITIZENS
Ranked by: Percent of satisfied citizens. **Number listed:** 10
1. Iceland with 82%
2. Canada, 75%
3. Germany, 74%
4. Thailand, 74%
5. United States, 72%
6. France, 45%
7. Japan, 42%
8. United Kingdom, 42%
9. Costa Rica, 41%
10. Chile, 40%
Source: *Health*, January/February 1996, p. 22.

Radio Advertising

★ 2143 ★
CANADA'S TOP RADIO ADVERTISING, 1995
Ranked by: Ad spending, in millions of U.S. dollars. **Number listed:** 10
1. Eaton's of Canada Ltd. with $8.11 million
2. Government of Canada, $7.69
3. Government of Ontario, $5.41
4. John Labatt Ltd., $5.08
5. Dairy Farmers of Canada, $4.73
6. BCE Inc., $4.32
7. The Molson Companies, $3.91
8. Government of Quebec, $3.43

9. Government of B.C., $3.01
10. Royal Bank of Canada, $2.94
Source: *Marketing Magazine*, January 6, 1997, p. 11.

Radio Broadcasting

★ 2144 ★
GLOBAL RADIO SERVICE
Ranked by: Direct program hours per week. **Number listed:** 5
1. China Radio International with 1,620 hours
2. World Service, 1,036
3. Voice of America, 992
4. Voice of Russia, 726
5. Deutsche Welle, 655
Source: *The Guardian*, July 18, 1996, p. 9.

★ 2145 ★
RADIO LISTENERSHIP IN SOUTH AFRICA
Ranked by: Percentage of daily listenership by province. **Number listed:** 4
1. Mpumalanga with 83.7%
2. KwaZulu-Natal, 82.1%
3. Gauteng, 77.1%
4. Western Cape, 68.9%
Source: *Mail & Guardian*, June 14, 1996, p. B7.

★ 2146 ★
TOP RADIO BROADCASTING GROUPS IN CANADA, 1996
Ranked by: Market share, in percent. **Remarks:** Figures are based on an autumn 1996 survey of 516,108,000 hours tuned in by listeners of English language radio stations. **Number listed:** 8
1. Standard Broadcasting with 8.5%
2. CHUM Ltd., 6.7%
3. Rogers, 6.6%
4. WIC, 6.5%
5. Shaw, 4.3%
6. Rawlco, 3.2%
7. Telemedia, 3.2%
8. Others, 61.0%
Source: *Marketing Magazine*, May 26, 1997, p. 16.

Radio Paging Systems

★ 2147 ★
LARGEST PAGING SERVICES IN TAIWAN
Ranked by: Number of subscribers. **Number listed:** 6
1. Shinawatra Paging with 450,000 subscribers
2. Lenso Paging, 180,000
3. PacLink (Thailand), 170,000

4. Hutchinson Telecommunications (Thailand), 120,000
5. Samart Paging, 110,000
6. WorldPage, 50,000

Source: *Bangkok Post*, January 27, 1997, p. B1.

★ **2148** ★

TOP PAGING MARKETS

Ranked by: Subscribers, in millions. **Remarks:** Notes market penetration, date paging began, signalling formats, and address of communications authority. **Number listed:** 20

1. United States with 43.10 million subscribers
2. China, 33.00
3. South Korea, 12.70
4. Japan, 10.80
5. Taiwan, 2.20
6. Hong Kong, 1.50
7. Canada, 1.30
8. Germany, 1.05
9. Singapore, 1.00
10. Thailand, 1.00

Source: *RCR*, January 13, 1997, p. 12.

Railroads

★ **2149** ★

LARGEST RAILROAD COMPANIES, 1995

Ranked by: Revenue, in millions of U.S. dollars. **Remarks:** Notes profits and global rank. **Number listed:** 8

1. East Japan Railway (Japan) with $25,624 million
2. Deutsche Bahn (Germany), $20,811
3. SNCF (France), $13,785
4. West Japan Railway (Japan), $12,218
5. Central Japan Railway (Japan), $11,528
6. CSX (United States), $10,504
7. Kinki Nippon Railway (Japan), $9,466
8. Union Pacific (United States), $8,942

Source: *Fortune,* The Global 500: World's Biggest Corporations (annual), August 5, 1996, p. F-24.

Razor Blades

See: **Razors**

Razors

★ **2150** ★

EUROPE'S RAZOR MARKET

Ranked by: Market share, in percent. **Number listed:** 2

1. Gillette with 73.0%
2. Other, 27.0%

Source: *Fortune*, October 14, 1996, p. 210.

★ **2151** ★

RAZOR MARKET IN LATIN AMERICA

Ranked by: Market share, in percent. **Number listed:** 2

1. Gillette with 91.0%
2. Other, 9.0%

Source: *Fortune*, October 14, 1996, p. 210.

Real Estate Business

★ **2152** ★

JAPAN'S CONDOMINIUM MARKET

Ranked by: Market share, in percent. **Number listed:** 6

1. Daikyo with 6.1%
2. Dai Kensetsu, 3.4%
3. Mitsui Fudosan, 3.2%
4. Towa Real Estate Development, 2.9%
5. Marubeni, 2.5%
6. Other, 81.9%

Source: *Nikkei Weekly*, August 5, 1996, p. 10.

★ **2153** ★

LARGEST REAL ESTATE DEVELOPERS IN MEXICO

Ranked by: Number of employees. **Number listed:** 10

1. Colliers Lomelin with 75 employees
2. Re/Max Mexico, 75
3. ERA Mexico, 60
4. Cushman & Wakefield/GCI, 53
5. CB Comercial de Mexico, 52
6. Century 21 Mexico, 40
7. Staubach/CMI Mexico, 35
8. Mexico Real Estate Affiliates, Inc., 30
9. LaSalle Partners, 12
10. Trammell Crow Internacional de Mexico, 12

Source: *Mexico Business*, May 1996, p. 52.

★ **2154** ★

TOP EUROPEAN PROPERTY GROUPS IN EUROPE

Ranked by: Market capitalization, in billions of U.S. dollars. **Number listed:** 10

1. Land Securities with $4.82 billion
2. Rodamco, $4.47
3. British Land, $2.65
4. MEPC, $2.64

5. Hammerson, $1.62
6. Capital Shopping Centres, $1.58
7. Simco, $1.34
8. Slough Estates, $1.30
9. Sefimeg, $1.04
10. Intershop, $0.71

Source: *Financial Times*, June 17, 1996, p. 25.

★ 2155 ★

TOP PROPERTY DEVELOPERS IN THAILAND, 1994
Ranked by: Revenue, in millions of bahts (Bt). **Remarks:** Includes profits and assets. **Number listed:** 21
1. Land and Houses with Bt7,509.79 million
2. Bangkok Land, Bt6,050.97
3. Tanayong, Bt2,277.37
4. Rich Property, Bt1,992.60
5. Quality Houses, Bt1,807.90
6. Somprasong Land Development, Bt1,800.81
7. Property Perfect, Bt1,778.77
8. Travel Lodge Asia, Bt1,727.23
9. Univest Land, Bt1,425.35
10. Krisda Mahanakorn, Bt1,421.43

Source: *Business Review*, December 1995, p. 190.

★ 2156 ★

TOP REAL ESTATE FIRMS IN CANADA
Ranked by: Revenue, in thousands of Canadian dollars. **Remarks:** Includes figures on profits and return on capital. Trizec Corp's figure is in thousands of U.S. dollars. **Number listed:** 8
1. Brookfield Properties with C$809,261 thousand
2. Trizec Corp., C$554,000
3. Royal LePage Ltd., C$382,623
4. Brookfield Homes, C$368,452
5. Cambridge Shopping Centres, C$308,971
6. Markborough Properties., C$259,163
7. Tridel Enterprises, C$251,602
8. Intrawest Corp, C$194,711

Source: *Globe and Mail's Report on Business Magazine*, July 1996, p. 159.

★ 2157 ★

TOP REAL ESTATE FIRMS IN JAPAN, 1996
Ranked by: Sales for the fiscal year, in billions of yen (¥). **Remarks:** Also notes estimated 1997 sales, pretax profits, and vacancy rates.
1. Mitsui Fudosan Co. with ¥687.7 billion
2. Mitsubishi Estate, ¥401.9
3. Tokyu Land Corp., ¥264.2
4. Sumitomo Realty & Development Co., ¥223.8

Source: *Nikkei Weekly*, May 19, 1997, p. 8.

Recreational Vehicle Industry

★ 2158 ★

GERMANY'S TOP RV MAKERS
Ranked by: Market share, in percent. **Number listed:** 10
1. Roh with 20.3%
2. Knaus, 17.6%
3. Tabbert, 10.5%
4. Dethleffs, 9.8%
5. Burstner, 7.9%
6. Hymer, 6.8%
7. X. Fendt, 6.3%
8. LMC, 5.0%
9. Cl. Wilk, 4.0%
10. Other, 10.9%

Source: *Wirtschaftswoche*, May 30, 1996, p. 64.

Recruiting of Employees

★ 2159 ★

MOST PREVALENT RECRUITING METHODS IN POLAND
Ranked by: Percent of respondents using each method, based on a survey of 129 employers. **Number listed:** 6
1. Private contacts with 63.2%
2. Job center offers, 44.0%
3. Placing press ads, 40.8%
4. Reading press ads, 8.8%
5. Recruitment agencies, 4.0%
6. Job fairs, 2.4%

Source: *The Warsaw Voice*, August 24, 1997, p. 11.

Refrigerators

★ 2160 ★

TOP REFRIGERATOR BRANDS IN JAPAN, 1996
Ranked by: Market share as of September 1996, in percent. **Remarks:** Data are based on sales in large department stores in 35 major cities. **Number listed:** 5
1. Haier with 30.6%
2. Rongsheng, 14.0%
3. Meiling, 12.1%
4. Shangling, 9.9%
5. Xinfei, 9.1%

Source: *South China Morning Post*, February 13, 1997, p. B7.

★ 2161 ★

TOP REFRIGERATOR MAKERS IN JAPAN
Ranked by: Market share, in percent. **Number listed:** 6
1. Matsushita Electric Industrial with 20.3%

2. Sanyo Electric, 14.9%
3. Sharp, 14.4%
4. Hitachi, 14.2%
5. Toshiba, 14.0%
6. Others, 22.2%

Source: *Nikkei Weekly*, July 22, 1996, p. 8.

★ **2162** ★
TOP REFRIGERATOR MANUFACTURERS IN CHINA, 1995
Ranked by: Units shipped. **Number listed:** 10
1. Kelong with 1,221,900 units
2. Qindao Haier, 1,000,400
3. Shangling, 852,500
4. Meiling, 753,500
5. Yangzi, 750,200
6. Xinfei, 718,400
7. Changling, 626,200
8. Wanbao, 568,800
9. Xileng, 505,200
10. Shuanglu, 365,500

Source: *Appliance Manufacturer*, February 1997, p. G-17.

Reinsurance

★ **2163** ★
LARGEST REINSURERS IN GERMANY
Ranked by: Net premium income, in millions of deutschmarks (DM). **Remarks:** Also notes underwriting result before fluctuation funds. **Number listed:** 15
1. Munich Re with DM16,283 million
2. Allianz Holding, DM6,007
3. Cologne Re, DM3,329
4. Gerling-Konzern Globale Re, DM3,091
5. Hannover Re, DM2,702
6. Frankona Re, DM2,463
7. Bavarian Re, DM2,352
8. E+S Re, DM1,317
9. Deutsche Re, DM459
10. R+V Versicherung, DM446

Source: *Financial Times*, September 5, 1997, p. 2.

★ **2164** ★
LARGEST REINSURERS WORLDWIDE, 1995
Ranked by: Net reinsurance premiums, in thousands of U.S. dollars. **Number listed:** 20
1. Munich Re with $11,075,759 thousand
2. Swiss Re Group, $8,890,670
3. Employers Re, $6,967,000
4. General Re/Cologne Re Group, $6,102,000
5. Generali, $3,815,975
6. Hannover Re Group, $3,542,467
7. Lincoln National Re, $2,888,400
8. Gerling, $2,460,647

9. SCOR Group, $2,097,636
10. Tokio Marine & Fire, $1,133,930

Source: *Business Insurance*, September 2, 1996, p. 3.

★ **2165** ★
REINSURANCE MARKET WORLDWIDE
Ranked by: Market share based on premiums written, in percent. **Number listed:** 7
1. Germany with 37%
2. United States, 23%
3. Bermuda, 10%
4. Switzerland, 10%
5. France, 6%
6. United Kingdom, 4%
7. Others, 10%

Source: *Best's Review*, June 1997, p. 53.

★ **2166** ★
TOP LIFE REINSURANCE GROUPS WORLDWIDE, 1996
Ranked by: Life net premiums, estimated in millions of U.S. dollars. **Number listed:** 10
1. Munich Re with $1,900 million
2. Lincoln National, $1,850
3. Mercantile & General Re, $1,600
4. Swiss Re, $1,000
5. Employers Reassurance, $925
6. Cologne Re, $700
7. Gerling Global Re, $600
8. Transamerica Occidental Life, $550
9. Reins. Group of America, $525
10. SCOR, $475

Source: *National Underwriter*, August 26, 1996, p. S22.

Rental Housing

★ **2167** ★
TOP APARTMENT RENTS IN FOREIGN EXPATRIATE NEIGHBORHOODS
Ranked by: Monthly rent, in U.S. dollars, for luxury four-bedroom apartments in expatriate neighborhoods. **Remarks:** Data for Beijing and Shanghai show the monthly rent for three-bedroom, furnished apartments. **Number listed:** 10
1. Beijing with $13,200
2. Hong Kong, $13,000
3. Tokyo, $12,800
4. Shanghai, $10,000
5. Moscow, $9,000
6. Seoul, $8,500
7. London, $7,800
8. Ho Chi Minh City, $7,200
9. Singapore, $7,100

10.　New York, $6,000
Source: *The Wall Street Journal*, January 24, 1997, p. B8.

Research, Commercial

★ **2168** ★
TOP JAPANESE FIRMS FOR R&D, 1995
Ranked by: Total research expenditures for Japanese fiscal year 1995, in billions of U.S. dollars. **Remarks:** Notes top firms by research dollars as a percentage of sales. **Number listed:** 10
1.　Matsushita Electric Industrial with $4.2 billion
2.　Toyota Motor Corp., $4.2
3.　Hitachi, $3.9
4.　NEC, $3.2
5.　Fujitsu, Ltd., $3.0
6.　Toshiba Corp., $3.0
7.　Sony Corp., $2.5
8.　Honda Motor Co. Ltd., $2.2
9.　Mitsubishi Electric Corp., $1.8
10.　Nissan Motor Co., Ltd., $1.8
Source: *Automotive Engineering*, December 1996, p. 52.

★ **2169** ★
TOP NATIONS FOR MARKET RESEARCH, 1995
Ranked by: Market share, in percent. **Remarks:** World turnover reached $10,163 million. **Number listed:** 8
1.　United States with 38%
2.　Germany, 11%
3.　Japan, 10%
4.　United Kingdom, 9%
5.　France, 8%
6.　Italy, 3%
7.　Other European countries, 14%
8.　Other, 11%
Source: *Nikkei Weekly*, April 21, 1997, p. 16.

Research, Industrial

★ **2170** ★
TOP NON-U.S. RESEARCH AND DEVELOPMENT SPENDERS, 1995
Ranked by: Spending, in millions of U.S. dollars. **Number listed:** 50
1.　Hitachi Ltd. with $6,415.257 million
2.　Siemens AG, $5,149.911
3.　Matsushita Electric, $4,857.361
4.　Nippon Telegraph & Tele, $4,321.294
5.　Fujitsu Ltd., $4,045.979
6.　NEC Corp., $3,511.861
7.　Daimler-Benz AG, $3,341.236
8.　Sony Corp., $3,171.833

9.　Honda Motor Ltd., $2,705.095
10.　Bayer AG, $2,271.849
Source: *R&D Magazine*, October 1996, p. 13A.

Research, Industrial – Canada

★ **2171** ★
TOP CORPORATE R&D SPENDERS IN CANADA, 1995
Ranked by: Research and development expenditures, in millions of Canadian dollars. **Remarks:** Also notes revenues and primary industry sector. Figures for AECL and CAE Inc. are for the fiscal year ended March 31, 1995. **Number listed:** 100
1.　Northern Telecom Limited with C$2,332.1 million
2.　Pratt & Whitney Canada, Inc., C$247.0
3.　IBM Canada Ltd., C$225.0
4.　AECL, C$159.3
5.　Merck Frosst Canada Inc., C$154.6
6.　Hydro-Quebec, C$148.2
7.　Ericsson Communications Inc., C$126.8
8.　Ontario Hydro, C$117.0
9.　Alcan Aluminium Limited, C$104.3
10.　CAE Inc., C$99.0
Source: http:// www.evert.com/sub_aces/top-100c.htm, June 18, 1997, p. 1.

★ **2172** ★
TOP R&D COMPANIES IN CANADA, 1995
Ranked by: Spending, in thousands of Canadian dollars. **Number listed:** 100
1.　Northern Telecom Ltd. with C$2,332,050 thousand
2.　IBM Canada Ltd., C$225,000
3.　AECL, C$159,319
4.　Hydro-Quebec, C$148,200
5.　Ericsson Communications Inc., C$126,751
6.　Alcan Aluminium Ltd., C$104,318
7.　CAE Inc., C$99,000
8.　Newbridge Networks Corp., C$91,397
9.　Bombardier Inc., C$81,914
10.　Imperial Oil Ltd., C$74,000
Source: *Globe and Mail's Report on Business Magazine*, July 1996, p. 110.

Restaurants

★ 2173 ★

LARGEST RESTAURANT CHAINS BY BRAND VALUE

Ranked by: Brand value, in millions of U.S. dollars.
Remarks: Value was calculated using capital, ratio of capital to company sales, earnings, and corporate tax rate of the country where the parent company is located. See source for details. **Number listed:** 8
1. McDonald's (McDonald's) with $18,920 million
2. Burger King (Grand Metropolitan), $2,124
3. Pizza Hut (PepsiCo.), $1,736
4. Taco Bell (PepsiCo.), $1,237
5. KFC (PepsicoCo.), $1,125
6. Wendy's (Wendy's International), $874
7. Red Lobster (Darden Restaurants), $801
8. Olive Garden (Darden Restaurants), $100

Source: *Financial World,* World's Most Valuable Brands (annual), July 8, 1996, p. 64.

★ 2174 ★

LEADING FAST FOOD RESTAURANT CHAINS IN CANADA, 1995

Ranked by: Market share based on sales, in percent.
Number listed: 11
1. McDonald's Restaurants of Canada with 18.7%
2. Cara Operations Ltd., 11.3%
3. KFC Canada, 7.0%
4. Pizza Hut Canada, 4.6%
5. Subway Sandwiches and Salads, 3.6%
6. A&W Food Services of Canada, 3.4%
7. Dairy Queen of Canada, 2.9%
8. Burger King, 2.7%
9. Wendy's Restaurants of Canada, 2.6%
10. Les Rotisseries St-Hubert, 2.0%

Source: *Marketing Magazine,* May 26, 1997, p. 12.

★ 2175 ★

TOP PIZZA RESTAURANTS IN SPAIN, 1995

Ranked by: Sales, in millions of pesetas (Ptas). **Remarks:** Includes number of outlets. **Number listed:** 3
1. TelePizza with Ptas13,700 million
2. Pizza Hut, Ptas7,800
3. Pizza World, Ptas5,600

Source: *Cambio,* December 30, 1996, p. 16.

Retail Trade
See Also: Department Stores

★ 2176 ★

LARGEST CO-OPS IN THE UNITED KINGDOM

Ranked by: Retail sales, in millions of British pounds (£). **Number listed:** 10
1. CWS with £2,177 million
2. CRS, £1,686
3. Midlands, £631
4. United Norwest, £624
5. Yorkshire, £283
6. Anglia Regional, £260
7. Ipswich & Norwich, £229
8. Oxford, Swindon & Glos, £209
9. Portsea Island, £199
10. Lincoln, £170

Source: *The Sunday Times,* February 16, 1997, p. 3.

★ 2177 ★

LARGEST GENERAL MERCHANDISERS WORLDWIDE, 1995

Ranked by: Revenue, in millions of U.S. dollars.
Remarks: Also notes profits. **Number listed:** 17
1. Wal-Mart Stores with $93,627 million
2. Sears Roebuck, $35,181
3. Kmart, $34,654
4. Daiei, $33,149
5. Dayton Hudson, $23,516
6. J.C. Penney, $21,419
7. Nichii, $17,738
8. Karstadt, $16,811
9. Pinault-Printemps, $15,594
10. Federated Department Stores, $15,049

Source: *Fortune,* The Global 500: World's Biggest Corporations (annual), August 5, 1996, p. F-20.

★ 2178 ★

LEADING RETAIL FIRMS IN FRANCE

Ranked by: Market share, in percent. **Remarks:** Also notes share of the retail food market. **Number listed:** 5
1. Promedes-Casino with 18.5%
2. Carrefour-CM, 15.9%
3. Leclerc, 15.3%
4. Intermarche, 15.1%
5. Auchan-DDF, 12.5%

Source: *Financial Times,* September 2, 1997, p. 20.

★ 2179 ★

LEADING RETAILERS IN AUSTRALIA, 1995

Ranked by: Market share, in percent. **Number listed:** 4
1. Woolworths with 32.4%
2. Coles, 24.3%
3. Franklins, 14.0%

4. Independents, 29.3%
Source: *Quick Frozen Foods International*, April 1996, p. 132.

★ 2180 ★
MOST RESPECTED EUROPEAN RETAILERS
Ranked by: Survey based on FT 500 list, as well as polls of investment analysts and chief executives of European companies. See source for details. **Number listed: 3**
1. Tesco
2. Carrefour
3. Ahold
Source: *Financial Times,* Europe's Most Respected Companies (annual), September 24, 1997, p. 2.

★ 2181 ★
SHANGHAI'S RETAIL MARKET BY SEGMENT
Ranked by: Percentage of retail market. **Number listed: 8**
1. Food with 53.4%
2. Clothing, 10.4%
3. Entertainment & education, 7.5%
4. Household goods, 9.9%
5. Housing & utilities, 6.4%
6. Transport & communications, 6.0%
7. Medical, 1.8%
8. Others, 4.6%
Source: *Far Eastern Economic Review*, October 3, 1996, p. 48.

★ 2182 ★
TOP BRAZILIAN RETAILERS BY INTEREST/SALES RATIO, 1995
Ranked by: Interest result to sales ratio, in percent. **Remarks:** The interest to sales ratio is an indicator of financing-related profits or losses. **Number listed: 7**
1. Lojas Arapua with 13.7%
2. Lojas Renner, 10.4%
3. Lojas Riachuelo, 7.6%
4. Grazziotin, 1.7%
5. Lojas Americanas, 1.3%
6. Mesbla, 0.1%
7. Casa Anglo, - 0.3%
Source: *Business Latin America*, October 7, 1996, p. 7.

★ 2183 ★
TOP BRAZILIAN RETAILERS BY SALES, 1995
Ranked by: Sales, in millions of U.S. dollars. **Number listed: 7**
1. Lojas Americanas with $1,975 million
2. Mesbla, $1,165
3. Casa Anglo, $1,067
4. Lojas Arapua, $960
5. Lojas Riachuelo, $188
6. Lojas Renner, $159
7. Grazziotin, $93
Source: *Business Latin America*, October 7, 1996, p. 7.

★ 2184 ★
TOP FOREIGN RETAILERS WITH U.S. OPERATIONS, 1996
Ranked by: Sales, in billions of U.S. dollars. **Number listed: 10**
1. Ito Yokado (Japan) with $43,550 billion
2. Metro Group (Germany), $40,268
3. Tengelmann (Germany), $32,906
4. Aldi Group (Germany), $30,769
5. Auchan (France), $25,860
6. J. Sainsbury (United Kingdom), $21,640
7. Ahold (Netherlands), $20,966
8. Jusco (Japan), $19,480
9. Delhaize (Belgium), $12,977
10. Casino (France), $12,880
Source: *Discount Merchandiser*, May 1997, p. 72.

★ 2185 ★
TOP RETAILERS WORLDWIDE, 1996
Ranked by: Sales, in billions of dollars. **Remarks:** Notes figures for 1994 and 1995. **Number listed: 25**
1. Wal-Mart Stores (U.S.) with $104.44 billion
2. Ito Yokado (Japan), $43.55
3. Metro Group (Germany), $40.27
4. Rewe AG (Germany), $36.59
5. Edeka/AVA Group (Germany), $35.35
6. Carrefour (France), $33.85
7. Sear Roebuck (U.S.), $33.81
8. Tengelmann (Germany), $32.91
9. Kmart (U.S.), $31.44
10. Aldi Group (Germany), $30.77
Source: *Discount Merchandiser*, May 1997, p. 66.

Retail Trade – Asia

★ 2186 ★
ASIA'S TOP RETAILERS, 1995
Ranked by: Sales, in millions of U.S. dollars. **Remarks:** Includes profits, profits as a percentage of sales and assets, and overall sales rank. **Number listed: 20**
1. Daiei with $33,563.4 million
2. Ito-Yokado, $30,747.0
3. Jusco, $22,272.3
4. Mycal Corp., $17,959.6
5. Seiyu, $13,743.4
6. Coles Myer, $13,046.1
7. Takashimaya, $12,738.0
8. Mitsukoshi, $10,602.1
9. Woolworths, $9,688.4

10.   UNY, $8,439.4
Source: *Asiaweek*, The Asiaweek 1,000, November 22, 1996, p. 168.

★ **2187** ★
LARGEST RETAIL AND WHOLESALE COMPANIES IN ASIA
Ranked by: Sales, in thousands of U.S. dollars. **Number listed:** 100
1.   Mitsubishi Corp. with $172,766,300 thousand
2.   Mitsui & Co. Ltd., $170,098,873
3.   Sumitomo Corp., $156,990,893
4.   Marubeni Corp., $151,381,631
5.   Nissho Iwai Corp., $91,728,106
6.   Tomen Corp., $63,493,067
7.   Nichimen Corp., $47,643,291
8.   Kanematsu Corp., $46,702,990
9.   Daiei Inc., $30,650,252
10.   Ito-Yokado Co. Ltd., $28,078,271
Source: *Asia's 7500 Largest Companies* (annual), Dun & Bradstreet, 1997, p. 87.

★ **2188** ★
MOST ADMIRED COMPANIES IN RETAIL/ CONSUMER GOODS, 1997
Ranked by: Results of a questionnaire sent to more than 9,000 managers and CEOs chosen from the magazine's circulation and evaluated by Asia Market Intelligence, a research firm. **Remarks:** Respondents scored each company in terms of overall admirability, then on six attributes: quality of products, quality of management, contribution to local economy, record as an employer, growth potential and reputation for ethics. Also notes 1996 figures. **Number listed:** 10
1.   San Miguel Corp. with 8.51
2.   Jollibee, 8.37
3.   McDonald's, 8.32
4.   Unilever, 8.15
5.   Coca-Cola, 8.05
6.   Procter & Gamble, 7.68
7.   Nestle, 7.59
8.   PepsiCo, 7.50
9.   Colgate-Palmolive, 7.45
10.   Fraser & Neave, 7.44
Source: *Asian Business,* Most Admired Companies in Asia (annual), May 1997, p. 30.

Retail Trade – Europe

★ **2189** ★
TOP RETAIL TRADE COMPANIES IN EUROPE
Ranked by: Sales, in millions of European Currency Units (ECUs). **Number listed:** 444
1.   Carrefour with 22,487 million ECUs

2.   Koninklijke Ahold NV, 13,944
3.   J. Sainsbury PLC, 13,458
4.   Tesco PLC, 12,890
5.   Karstadt Aktiengesellschaft, 10,935
6.   Tesco Stores Ltd., 10,073
7.   Migros-Genossenschafts-Bund, 10,002
8.   Pinault-Printemps-Redoute, 9,843
9.   Otto-Versand (GmbH & Co.), 8,738
10.   Carrefour France, 8,571
Source: *Duns Europa,* (annual), vol. 4, Dun & Bradstreet, 1997, p. 266.

Retail Trade – Germany

★ **2190** ★
LARGEST HAIR STUDIO SALONS IN GERMANY
Ranked by: Average annual sales per outlet, in thousands of U.S. dollars. **Remarks:** Includes number of outlets for each company for 1993-95 and estimates for 1996-98. **Number listed:** 5
1.   Jacques Dess. with $625 thousand
2.   Mod's Hair, $438
3.   Axel Weiss AG, $313
4.   Essanelle, $250
5.   Kerz Haarmode, $231
Source: *National Trade Data Bank,* August 18, 1995, p. ISA9503.

★ **2191** ★
LARGEST PERSONAL CARE RETAILERS IN GERMANY
Ranked by: Average annual sales per outlet, in thousands of U.S. dollars. **Remarks:** Includes number of outlets for each company for 1993-95 and estimates for 1996-98. **Number listed:** 8
1.   Body Shop with $1,125 thousand
2.   Spinnrad, $500
3.   Lazartique, $469
4.   Aloette, $406
5.   Nectar Body Shop, $313
6.   Yves Rocher, $313
7.   Lanature, $156
8.   Dr. Babor, $150
Source: *National Trade Data Bank,* August 18, 1995, p. ISA9503.

★ **2192** ★
LARGEST TANNING SALONS IN GERMANY
Ranked by: Average annual sales per outlet, in thousands of U.S. dollars. **Remarks:** Includes number of outlets for each company for 1993-95 and estimates for 1996-98. **Number listed:** 5
1.   Sun Point with $356 thousand
2.   EHV, $344

3.   Eteson, $281
4.   Dermatech, $250
5.   Movie Sun, $250

Source: *National Trade Data Bank*, August 18, 1995, p. ISA9503.

Retail Trade – Japan

★ 2193 ★
TOP GENERAL MERCHANDISE RETAILERS IN JAPAN
Ranked by: Sales, in billions of yen (¥). **Number listed:** 10

1.   Daiei with ¥2,073 billion
2.   Ito-Yokado, ¥1,536
3.   Jusco, ¥1,061
4.   Seiyu, ¥1,050
5.   Nichii, ¥822
6.   Uny, ¥577
7.   Izumiya, ¥401
8.   Nagasakiya, ¥394
9.   Tokyu Store, ¥275
10. Life Corp., ¥188

Source: *National Trade Data Bank*, October 18, 1995, p. ISA9503.

★ 2194 ★
TOP RETAIL FIRMS IN JAPAN
Ranked by: Sales, in billions of yen (¥). **Number listed:** 10

1.   Mitsukoshi with ¥801 billion
2.   Takashimaya, ¥724
3.   Seibu, ¥681
4.   Daimaru, ¥543
5.   Marui, ¥507
6.   Matsuzakaya, ¥459
7.   Isetan, ¥421
8.   Tokyu, ¥339
9.   Hankyu, ¥326
10. Kintetsu, ¥281

Source: *National Trade Data Bank*, October 18, 1995, p. ISA9503.

Retail Trade – Spain

★ 2195 ★
TOP RETAILERS IN SPAIN
Ranked by: Turnover, in millions of pesetas (Ptas). **Remarks:** Also notes number of outlets. **Number listed:** 20

1.   El Corte Ingles with Ptas1,065,000 million
2.   Pryca, Ptas520,283

3.   Continente, Ptas429,957
4.   Alcampo, Ptas273,500
5.   Eroski, Ptas267,172
6.   Mercadona, Ptas192,000
7.   DIA, Ptas191,596
8.   Makro, Ptas89,837
9.   Unide, Ptas87,000
10. Sabeco, Ptas67,758

Source: http:// www.templeton.ox.ac.uk/www/insts/ oxirm/digest/wint9596/featsp.htm, June 9, 1997, p. 2.

Retail Trade – United Kingdom

★ 2196 ★
LARGEST RETAILERS IN THE UNITED KINGDOM
Ranked by: Estimated sales, in millions of U.S. dollars. **Number listed:** 10

1.   J. Sainsbury with $19.5 million
2.   Tesco, $18.8
3.   Marks & Spencer, $11.0
4.   Argyll (Safeway), $9.5
5.   ASDA, $9.3
6.   Kingfisher, $8.1
7.   Boots, $5.7
8.   Somerfield, $5.0
9.   Kwik Save, $4.7
10. John Lewis, $3.9

Source: *Stores*, November 1996, p. 76.

Reunion – see under individual headings

Rice

★ 2197 ★
LEADING RICE PRODUCERS PER HECTARE, 1995-1996
Ranked by: Estimated yield of rice production per hectare, in metric tons. **Number listed:** 10

1.   Australia with 6.129 metric tons
2.   United States, 4.828
3.   Republic of Korea, 4.792
4.   Japan, 4.779
5.   China, 4.300
6.   Indonesia, 2.888
7.   India, 1.929
8.   Pakistan, 1.900
9.   Philippines, 1.848
10. Burma, 1.832

Source: *Foreign Agricultural Service*, November 13, 1996, p. 14.

★ 2198 ★
LEADING RICE PRODUCERS, 1995-1996
Ranked by: Estimated rice production, million metric tons. **Number listed:** 10
1. China with 132.000 million metric tons
2. India, 82.000
3. Indonesia, 33.500
4. Bangladesh, 18.000
5. Thailand, 14.200
6. Burma, 10.440
7. Japan, 9.400
8. Philippines, 7.300
9. Brazil, 7.000
10. United States, 5.682

Source: *Foreign Agricultural Service*, November 13, 1996, p. 14.

★ 2199 ★
TOP RICE EXPORTERS IN THAILAND
Ranked by: Share of total rice exports. **Remarks:** Includes volume of total rice exports. **Number listed:** 10
1. Soon Hua Seng with 19.6%
2. STC (Capital Rice), 12.5%
3. Chaiyaporn Rice, 9.1%
4. Puay Heng Long, 4.2%
5. Bang Sue Chia Meng, 4.1%
6. Thai Fah, 4.1%
7. Uthai Produces, 4.1%
8. Siam Rice, 3.8%
9. Huay Chuan, 3.4%
10. Kamolkjj, 3.2%

Source: *Bangkok Post*, June 27, 1997, p. 8.

★ 2200 ★
TOP RICE EXPORTERS, 1996-1997
Ranked by: Exports, in millions of metric tons. **Number listed:** 7
1. Thailand with 4.5 million metric tons
2. United States, 2.6
3. Vietnam, 1.9
4. Pakistan, 1.4
5. China, 0.8
6. Burma, 0.9
7. India, 0.6

Source: *Rice Journal*, May 15, 1995, p. 31.

Robotics Industry – Japan

★ 2201 ★
TOP INDUSTRIAL ROBOT MAKERS IN JAPAN
Ranked by: Market share, in percent. **Number listed:** 6
1. Matsushita Electric Industrial with 23.0%
2. Fuji Machine Manufacturing, 15.5%
3. Fanuc, 10.8%

4. Yasukawa Electric, 7.0%
5. Kawasaki Heavy Industries, 4.0%
6. Others, 38.8%

Source: *Nikkei Weekly*, July 29, 1996, p. 8.

Romania – see under individual headings

Rubber Industry

★ 2202 ★
TOP RUBBER AND PLASTICS FIRMS IN SOUTH KOREA, 1996
Ranked by: Sales for the first six months of 1996, in hundred million won (W). **Number listed:** 14
1. Kumho Tire with W6,085.6 hundred million
2. Hankook Tire Mfg., W4,938.2
3. STC, W1,206.0
4. H.S. Chemical, W818.1
5. Youl Chon Chemical, W675.5
6. Dong Ah Tire, W590.5
7. Dong Il Rubber Belt, W561.9
8. Heung Ah Tire & Rubber, W480.3
9. Sam Young Chemical, W430.3
10. National Plastic, W363.9

Source: *Business Korea*, October 1996, p. 35.

Rubber Industry – Europe

★ 2203 ★
TOP EUROPEAN COMPANIES IN RUBBER AND MISCELLANEOUS PLASTICS
Ranked by: Sales, in millions of European Currency Units (ECUs). **Remarks:** Also notes number of employees. **Number listed:** 111
1. Neste Oy with 4,714 million ECUs
2. Continental A.G., 4,654
3. Re-Tech BV, 4,624
4. Carnaudmetalbox, 3,825
5. Michelin (Manufacturing Francaise des Pneumatiques), 2,852
6. Pirelli Tyre Holding NV, 2,505
7. Freudenberg & Co., 2,278
8. Ruetgers A.G., 2,262
9. Perstorp AB, 1,585
10. Dow Deutschland Inc., Zweigniederlassung Stade, 1,278

Source: *Duns Europa* (annual), vol. 4, Dun & Bradstreet, 1997, p. 227.

Russia – see under individual headings

Rwanda – see under individual headings

Sales Promotion Agencies – United Kingdom

★ 2204 ★
TOP SALES PROMOTION AGENCIES IN THE UNITED KINGDOM, 1995
Ranked by: Turnover, in thousands of British pounds (£). **Remarks:** Also notes pre-tax profits and total staff.
Number listed: 71
1. Wunderman Cato Johnson with £39,200 thousand
2. IMP, £31,692
3. Carlson, £30,078
4. Holmes & Marchant Group, £23,958
5. KLP Marketing, £23,647
6. Marketing Store, £22,860
7. Purchasepoint, £20,750
8. Interfocus, £12,207
9. Option One, £12,200
10. Grey Integrated, £12,176

Source: *Marketing*, July 25, 1996, p. XI.

Salt

★ 2205 ★
GLOBAL SALT PRODUCTION, 1995
Ranked by: Production, in metric tons. **Number listed:** 10
1. United States with 36.400 metric tons
2. China, 28.370
3. Soviet Union, 14.000
4. Canada, 11.099
5. Germany, 10.366
6. India, 9.500
7. Australia, 7.693
8. Mexico, 7.395
9. France, 6.516
10. United Kingdom, 6.250

Source: *Industrial Minerals*, September 1995, p. 81.

Santiago Stock Exchange

★ 2206 ★
LARGEST COMPANIES ON THE SANTIAGO STOCK EXCHANGE, 1995
Ranked by: Market value, in millions of U.S. dollars.
Number listed: 20
1. Endesa with $2,419.52 million
2. Copec, $2,261.75
3. CTC-A, $1,553.18
4. Enersis, $1,394.09
5. CMPC, $1,060.00
6. Andina, $853.19
7. Emos, $787.03
8. Melon, $719.96
9. Chilectra, $690.58
10. Esval, $689.30

Source: *GT Guide to World Equity Markets* (annual), Euromoney Publications, 1996, p. 102.

★ 2207 ★
MOST ACTIVELY TRADED SHARES ON THE SANTIAGO STOCK EXCHANGE, 1995
Ranked by: Trading value, in thousands of U.S. dollars.
Number listed: 20
1. Endesa with $527,784 thousand
2. CTC-A, $398,081
3. Enersis, $330,183
4. Copec, $272,393
5. Chilgener, $250,498
6. Entel, $162,336
7. Iansa, $159,694
8. Soquimich A&B, $155,920
9. Andina, $130,882
10. CMPC, $119,466

Source: *GT Guide to World Equity Markets* (annual), Euromoney Publications, 1996, p. 102.

Sao Paolo Stock Exchange

★ 2208 ★
LARGEST COMPANIES ON THE SAO PAULO STOCK EXCHANGE, 1995
Ranked by: Market value, in millions of U.S. dollars.
Number listed: 20
1. Eletrobras with $14,536.06 million
2. Telebras, $13,723.20
3. Vale do Rio Doce, $10,786.75
4. Telesp, $7,423.90
5. Petrobras, $6,465.08
6. Bradesco, $5,213.59
7. Light, $3,322.93
8. Itaubanco, $3,261.47

9. Brahma, $2,901.68
10. Cemig, $2,741.69

Source: *GT Guide to World Equity Markets* (annual), Euromoney Publications, 1996, p. 75.

★ 2209 ★
MOST ACTIVELY TRADED SHARES ON THE SAO PAULO STOCK EXCHANGE, 1995
Ranked by: Trading value, in millions of U.S. dollars. **Number listed:** 20

1. Telebras pn with $25,401.61 million
2. Electrobras pnb, $3,471.81
3. Petrobras pn, $3,240.92
4. Eletrobras on, $2,519.66
5. Vale do Rio Doce pn, $2,216.72
6. Usiminas pn, $1,525.31
7. Cemig pn, $940.56
8. Telesp pn, $797.72
9. Aracruz pnb, $668.94
10. Telebras on, $636.39

Source: *GT Guide to World Equity Markets* (annual), Euromoney Publications, 1996, p. 76.

Sauces

★ 2210 ★
TOP PASTA SAUCE MAKERS IN NEW ZEALAND
Ranked by: Market share, in percent. **Number listed:** 4

1. Dolmio with 48.0%
2. Watties/Heinz, 27.0%
3. Unifoods Raguletto, 12.9%
4. Other, 12.1%

Source: *National Trade Data Bank*, March 2, 1996, p. IMI951004.

Saudi Arabia – see under individual headings

Scandinavia – see under individual headings

Scotland – see under individual headings

Seaports
See: **Ports**

Secretaries

★ 2211 ★
ANNUAL GROSS SALARIES OF SECRETARY/ ASSISTANTS
Ranked by: Average annual salaries in Central European countries. **Number listed:** 6

1. Hungary with $14-16 thousand
2. Slovakia, $12-26
3. Poland, $6-14
4. Czech Republic, $5-15
5. Romania, $3-5
6. Russia, $2-7

Source: *Business Central Europe*, November 1995, p. IV.

Securities Exchange of Thailand

★ 2212 ★
LARGEST COMPANIES ON THE SECURITIES EXCHANGE OF THAILAND, 1995
Ranked by: Market value, in millions of U.S. dollars. **Number listed:** 20

1. Bangkok Bank with $8,651.02 million
2. Telecomasia Corporation, $6,802.38
3. Siam Cement, $6,412.80
4. Krung Thai Bank, $6,154.72
5. Thai Farmers Bank, $5,504.00
6. Advanced Info Service, $4,174.56
7. Siam Commercial Bank, $3,771.59
8. Shinawatra & Communications, $3,437.28
9. PTT Exploration & Production, $3,273.60
10. United Communication Industry, $3,013.43

Source: *GT Guide to World Equity Markets* (annual), Euromoney Publications, 1996, p. 337.

★ 2213 ★
MOST ACTIVELY TRADED SHARES ON THE SECURITIES EXCHANGE OF THAILAND, 1995
Ranked by: Trading volume, in lots. **Remarks:** One lot is 100 shares. **Number listed:** 20

1. Siam City Bank with 7,499,116 lots
2. Krung Thai Bank, 5,880,238
3. Thai Petrochemical Industry, 5,207,870
4. Telecomasia Corporation, 4,796,206
5. National Finance and Securities, 4,777,161
6. Bangkok Bank of Commerce, 4,701,493
7. Electricity Generating, 4,333,582
8. First Bangkok City Bank, 3,969,211
9. Cmic Finance and Securities, 3,820,528
10. Industrial Finance Corp. of Thailand Warrant, 3,514,406

Source: *GT Guide to World Equity Markets* (annual), Euromoney Publications, 1996, p. 337.

Security Services

★ 2214 ★

TOP SECURITY SERVICES IN JAPAN, 1995

Ranked by: Annual sales, in millions of U.S. dollars.
Number listed: 10
1. SECOM with $1,800 million
2. Sogo Keibi Hosho (General Security Guard Services), $1,400
3. Asahi Security Systems, $214
4. Senon, $181
5. Central Keibi Hosho, $166
6. Zen Nikkei, $159
7. Toyo Tech, $116
8. Nishi Nihon Keibi Hosho, $107
9. SECOM Joshinetsu, $107
10. Teikoku Keibi Hosho, $106

Source: *National Trade Data Bank*, January 2, 1997, p. IMI970102.

Security Underwriting

★ 2215 ★

LARGEST SECURITIES FIRMS, 1995

Ranked by: Capital, in millions of U.S. dollars as of December 31, 1995. **Remarks:** Notes change from 1994, assets, and net income. **Number listed:** 25
1. Nomura Securities (Japan) with $20,784 million
2. Merrill Lynch (U.S.), $17,864
3. Goldman Sachs (U.S.), $17,453
4. Salomon Bros (U.S.), $14,705
5. Morgan Stanley (U.S.), $14,345
6. Lehman Brothers Holdings (U.S.), $13,702
7. Daiwa Securities (Japan), $11,023
8. Nikko Securities (Japan), $10,794
9. Dean Witter, Discover (U.S.), $10,299
10. Yamaichi Securities (Japan), $9,577

Source: *The Wall Street Journal*, September 26, 1996, p. R29.

★ 2216 ★

LEADING GLOBAL UNDERWRITERS BY WORLDWIDE OFFERINGS, 1996

Ranked by: All debt and equity, in millions of U.S. dollars. **Remarks:** Notes number of issues. **Number listed:** 15
1. Merrill Lynch with $187,702.6 million
2. Goldman Sachs, $124,661.6
3. Lehman Brothers, $112,239.7
4. Salomon Brothers, $110,293.6
5. Morgan Stanley, $105,484.0
6. J.P. Morgan, $87,178.9
7. Credit Suisse First Boston, $83,534.5

8. Bear Stearns, $45.891.9
9. Donaldson Lufkin & Jenrette, $35,615.1
10. Deutsche Morgan Grenfell, $33,517.1

Source: *Investment Dealers' Digest*, Underwriting Rankings (annual), January 13, 1997, p. 47.

★ 2217 ★

LEADING GLOBAL UNDERWRITERS OF INTERNATIONAL DEBT, 1996

Ranked by: International debt, in millions of U.S. dollars. **Remarks:** Data excludes issues by U.S. and foreign companies in their home markets; data includes Eurobonds, Yankee bonds, and foreign bonds. Also notes number of issues. **Number listed:** 15
1. Merrill Lynch with $44,858.2 million
2. Goldman Sachs, $34,664.7
3. J.P. Morgan, $28,449.7
4. Lehman Brothers, $28,063.3
5. SBC Warburg, $27,168.3
6. Deutsche Morgan Grenfell, $25,926.8
7. Credit Suisse First Boston, $24,983.2
8. Morgan Stanley, $24,916.7
9. Salomon Brothers, $22,177.5
10. ABN AMRO Hoare Govett, $21,513.7

Source: *Investment Dealers' Digest*, Underwriting Rankings (annual), January 13, 1997, p. 47.

★ 2218 ★

LEADING MANAGERS OF EURO COMMON STOCK, 1996

Ranked by: Dollar amount, in millions of U.S. dollars. **Remarks:** Notes number of issues. **Number listed:** 12
1. SBC Warburg with $4,536.3 million
2. Goldman Sachs, $4,316.1
3. Merrill Lynch, $3,838.4
4. Morgan Stanley, $2,840.1
5. Credit Suisse First Boston, $1,985.1
6. Peregrine Brokerage, $1,826.0
7. Lehman Brothers, $1,291.3
8. Banque Paribas, $1,193.9
9. BZW/Barclays, $1,124.1
10. Salomon Brothers, $881.6

Source: *Investment Dealers' Digest*, Underwriting Rankings (annual), January 13, 1997, p. 48.

★ 2219 ★

LEADING MANAGERS OF YANKEE BONDS, 1996

Ranked by: Dollar amount, in millions of U.S. dollars. **Remarks:** Data refer to all debt issued by foreign firms in the U.S. Also notes number of issues. **Number listed:** 12
1. Lehman Brothers with $18,372.5 million
2. Merrill Lynch, $18,282.6
3. Goldman Sachs, $12,940.4
4. J.P. Morgan, $10,282.5
5. Salomon Brothers, $10,059.0

6. Morgan Stanley, $6,208.8
7. Credit Suisse First Boston, $3,542.2
8. Deutsche Morgan Grenfell, $1,873.8
9. UBS, $1,307.5
10. NationsBank, $997.9

Source: *Investment Dealers' Digest,* Underwriting Rankings (annual), January 13, 1997, p. 48.

★ **2220** ★

LEADING MANAGERS OF YANKEE COMMON, 1996

Ranked by: Dollar amount, in millions of U.S. dollars.
Remarks: Data refer to all common issued by foreign firms in the U.S. Also notes number of issues. **Number listed:** 12

1. Goldman Sachs with $6,587.0 million
2. Merrill Lynch, $2,126.4
3. Morgan Stanley, $1,899.9
4. Credit Suisse First Boston, $1,866.6
5. Lehman Brothers, $1,122.3
6. Donaldson Lufkin & Jenrette, $905.4
7. Alex. Brown & Sons, $555.0
8. J.P. Morgan, $424.4
9. · PaineWebber, $419.7
10. Salomon Brothers, $368.0

Source: *Investment Dealers' Digest,* Underwriting Rankings (annual), January 13, 1997, p. 48.

★ **2221** ★

LEADING U.S. UNDERWRITERS BY WORLDWIDE OFFERINGS, 1996

Ranked by: All debt and equity, in millions of U.S. dollars. **Remarks:** Notes number of issues. **Number listed:** 15

1. Merrill Lynch with $144,378.8 million
2. Salomon Brothers, $89,997.7
3. Lehman Brothers, $85,458.2
4. Goldman Sachs, $85,095.6
5. Morgan Stanley, $81,506.8
6. J.P. Morgan, $61,223.6
7. Credit Suisse First Boston, $57,081.0
8. Bear Stearns, $43,313.6
9. Donaldson Lufkin & Jenrette, $33,433.9
10. Smith Barney, $29,061.8

Source: *Investment Dealers' Digest,* Underwriting Rankings (annual), January 13, 1997, p. 47.

★ **2222** ★

TOP MANAGERS OF DOMESTIC EQUITY IN SOUTH KOREA, 1996

Ranked by: Amount underwritten, in millions of U.S. dollars. **Remarks:** Also notes number of issues. **Number listed:** 10

1. Dongwon with $128.0 million
2. Dongsuh, $98.5
3. LG Securities, $94.2
4. Daewoo Securities, $71.6

5. Ssangyong Securities, $69.8
6. Hyundai Securities, $62.8
7. Daishin Securities, $41.8
8. Sunkyong Securities, $23.5
9. First Securities, $9.4
10. Seoul Securities, $9.4

Source: *Asiamoney,* Deals of the Year (annual), February 1997, p. 84.

Security Underwriting – Canada

★ **2223** ★

TOP 10 UNDERWRITERS BY BONUS CREDIT IN CANADA

Ranked by: Value of total financings, in millions of U.S. dollars. **Remarks:** Notes number of deals. **Number listed:** 10

1. RBC Dominion Securities with $3,134 million
2. CIBC Wood Gundy Securities, $2,839
3. ScotiaMcLeod, $2,141
4. Nesbitt Burns, $1,997
5. Goldman, Sachs & Co., $1,987
6. Merrill Lynch & Co., $1,700
7. First Marathon Securities, $846
8. Levesque Beaubien Geoffrion, $765
9. Midland Walwyn Capital, $570
10. Toronto Dominion Securities, $449

Source: *Financial Post,* January 25, 1997, p. 21.

Security Underwriting – Hong Kong

★ **2224** ★

TOP MANAGERS OF DOMESTIC EQUITY IN HONG KONG, 1996

Ranked by: Amount underwritten, in millions of U.S. dollars. **Remarks:** Also notes number of issues. **Number listed:** 10

1. HSBC Investment Bank Asia with $566.9 million
2. Bear Stearns Asia, $468.1
3. CEF Capital, $321.7
4. Morgan Stanley Asia, $238.4
5. Credit Lyonnais Securities Asia, $177.5
6. SBC Warburg, $169.2
7. Goldman Sachs (Asia), $162.8
8. Peregrine Capital, $160.9
9. Wheelock NatWest, $153.5
10. Jardine Fleming Securities, $141.2

Source: *Asiamoney,* Deals of the Year (annual), February 1997, p. 84.

Security Underwriting – Indonesia

★ 2225 ★
TOP MANAGERS OF DOMESTIC EQUITY IN INDONESIA, 1996
Ranked by: Amount underwritten, in millions of U.S. dollars. **Remarks:** Also notes number of issues. **Number listed:** 10
1. Danareksa Sekuritas with $190.0 million
2. Pentasena Arthasentosa, $139.5
3. Lippo, $139.0
4. WI Carr, $108.0
5. Bahana Sekuritas, $97.3
6. BNI Securities, $97.3
7. ING Barings, $82.3
8. Usaha Bersama Sekuritas, $28.0
9. Pratama Penaga, $28.0
10. Asjaya Indosurya, $24.7
Source: *Asiamoney,* Deals of the Year (annual), February 1997, p. 84.

Security Underwriting – Japan

★ 2226 ★
TOP SECURITY UNDERWRITERS IN JAPAN
Ranked by: Income, in millions of yen (¥). **Number listed:** 10
1. Daiwa Securities with ¥57,899 million
2. Nomura Securities, ¥56,141
3. Nikko Securities, ¥49,070
4. Goldman Sachs (Japan), ¥7,811
5. Japan Bond Trading, ¥3,972
6. Paribas Capital Markets, ¥3,601
7. Jitsuei Securities, ¥2,581
8. Tachibana Securities, ¥2,333
9. Baring Securities Japan, ¥1,277
10. Utsumiya Securities, ¥1,115
Source: *Tokyo Business Today*, August 1995, p. 27.

Security Underwriting – Malaysia

★ 2227 ★
TOP MANAGERS OF DOMESTIC EQUITY IN MALAYSIA, 1996
Ranked by: Amount underwritten, in millions of U.S. dollars. **Remarks:** Also notes number of issues. **Number listed:** 10
1. Arab-Malaysian Merchant Bankers with $357.8 million
2. MIMB, $272.6
3. Aseambankers, $232.4

4. CIMB, $194.1
5. Amanah Merchant Bank, $112.6
6. DCB Sakura, $104.3
7. Utama Wardley, $94.9
8. Perdana, $56.2
9. Perwira Affin, $41.6
10. Bumiputra Merchant Bankers, $39.5
Source: *Asiamoney,* Deals of the Year (annual), February 1997, p. 85.

Security Underwriting – New Zealand

★ 2228 ★
TOP MANAGERS OF DOMESTIC EQUITY IN NEW ZEALAND, 1996
Ranked by: Amount underwritten, in millions of U.S. dollars. **Remarks:** Also notes number of issues. **Number listed:** 4
1. FR Partners with $526.6 million
2. JB Were, $70.8
3. BZW, $39.7
4. NZSE 10 Index Management, $25.3
Source: *Asiamoney,* Deals of the Year (annual), February 1997, p. 85.

Security Underwriting – Philippines

★ 2229 ★
TOP MANAGERS OF DOMESTIC EQUITY IN THE PHILIPPINES, 1996
Ranked by: Amount underwritten, in millions of U.S. dollars. **Remarks:** Also notes number of issues. **Number listed:** 9
1. PCI Capital with $255.6 million
2. RCBC Capital, $224.8
3. AB Capital, $217.8
4. Philippine National Bank, $122.1
5. Philippine Commercial Capital, $69.6
6. Urbancorp Investments, $31.2
7. All Asia Capital, $29.1
8. Belson-PrimeEast Capital, $28.6
9. FEB Investment, $22.0
Source: *Asiamoney,* Deals of the Year (annual), February 1997, p. 85.

Security Underwriting – Singapore

★ 2230 ★
TOP MANAGERS OF DOMESTIC EQUITY IN SINGAPORE, 1996
Ranked by: Amount underwritten, in millions of U.S. dollars. **Remarks:** Also notes number of issues. **Number listed:** 8
1. DBS Bank with $324.30 million
2. United Overseas Bank, $111.20
3. Overseas Union Bank, $81.01
4. OCBC, $52.20
5. NM Rothschild, $40.00
6. Vickers Ballas, $24.30
7. Deutsche Bank, $17.20
8. Nomura, $2.30

Source: *Asiamoney,* Deals of the Year (annual), February 1997, p. 85.

Security Underwriting – Taiwan

★ 2231 ★
TOP MANAGERS OF DOMESTIC EQUITY IN TAIWAN, 1996
Ranked by: Amount underwritten, in millions of U.S. dollars. **Remarks:** Also notes number of issues. **Number listed:** 10
1. China Development Corp. with $976.53 million
2. Taiwan Securities, $900.39
3. Grand Cathay, $894.63
4. Taiwan International, $415.47
5. Capital Securities, $381.50
6. National Securities, $270.72
7. President Securities, $201.14
8. Chinatrust, $179.75
9. Fubon Securities, $99.73
10. Jih Sun Securities, $70.80

Source: *Asiamoney,* Deals of the Year (annual), February 1997, p. 85.

Security Underwriting – Thailand

★ 2232 ★
TOP MANAGERS OF DOMESTIC EQUITY IN THAILAND, 1996
Ranked by: Amount underwritten, in millions of U.S. dollars. **Remarks:** Also notes number of issues. **Number listed:** 10
1. TISCO with $140.6 million
2. Asia Securities Trading, $127.8
3. Securities One, $79.9

4. Dhana Siam Finance & Securities, $71.0
5. National Finance & Securities, $54.5
6. Krungthai Thanakit, $51.2
7. Nithipat Capital, $49.2
8. IFCT Finance, $37.8
9. Ekkapat Finance & Securities, $37.5
10. Phatra Thanakit, $32.2

Source: *Asiamoney,* Deals of the Year (annual), February 1997, p. 85.

Semiconductor Equipment Industry

★ 2233 ★
JAPANESE SEMICONDUCTOR EQUIPMENT SUPPLIERS WITH THE HIGHEST CUSTOMER SATISFACTION
Ranked by: Results of a survey in which respondents were asked to rate their suppliers in eight categories: product performance, uptime, quality of results, process support, software support, technical leadership, after-sales service and overall support of customers' needs.
Number listed: 10
1. Disco with 8.29
2. Kaijo, 8.08
3. Shinkawa, 8.02
4. Tokyo Seimitsu, 7.71
5. Advantest, 7.70
6. Nikon, 7.42
7. Tokyo Electron, 7.35
8. Dainippon Screen Mfg., 7.28
9. Hitachi, 7.22
10. Canon, 6.73

Source: *Electronic Business Today*, January 1997, p. 15.

★ 2234 ★
TOP CHIP MAKERS, 1996
Ranked by: Revenues, in millions of U.S. dollars.
Remarks: Also notes market share and percent growth.
Number listed: 10
1. Intel with $16,938 million
2. NEC, $10,582
3. Motorola, $8,437
4. Hitachi, $8,056
5. Toshiba, $7,981
6. Texas Instruments, $7,090
7. Samsung, $6,196
8. Fujitsu, $4,507
9. Mitsubishi, $4,200
10. SGS-Thomson, $4,200

Source: *Electronic Business Today*, March 1997, p. 25.

★ 2235 ★
TOP SEMICONDUCTOR EQUIPMENT MANUFACTURERS, 1996
Ranked by: Sales, in millions of U.S. dollars. **Number listed:** 10
1. Applied Materials with $4,000 million
2. Tokyo Electron, $3,275
3. Nikon, $2,072
4. Lam Research, $1,247
5. Canon, $1,213
6. Advantest, $1,199
7. Hitachi, $867
8. Dainippon Screen, $815
9. ASM Lithography, $778
10. Teradyne, $759

Source: *Electronic News*, February 24, 1997, p. 8.

Semiconductor Industry

★ 2236 ★
4-MEGABIT DRAM MAKERS IN JAPAN, 1995
Ranked by: Market share, in percent. **Number listed:** 6
1. Hitachi with 19.5%
2. NEC, 16.0%
3. Toshiba, 15.5%
4. Samsung Electronics, 14.5%
5. Fujitsu, 9.5%
6. Other, 25.0%

Source: *Nikkei Weekly*, July 15, 1996, p. 8.

★ 2237 ★
EMBEDDED MICROCONTROLLER MARKET
Ranked by: Market share, in percent. **Number listed:** 5
1. Motorola with 13.0%
2. NEC, 11.0%
3. Intel, 10.0%
4. Hitachi, 6.0%
5. Texas Instruments, 6.0%
6. Other, 54.0%

Source: *Solid State Technology*, April 1996, p. 54.

★ 2238 ★
GLOBAL DRAM MARKET, 1996
Ranked by: Sales, in millions of U.S. dollars. **Remarks:** DRAM stands for dynamic random access memory. **Number listed:** 10
1. Samsung with $6,200.0 million
2. NEC, $2,950.0
3. Hitachi, $2,598.8
4. Hyundai, $2,100.0
5. Toshiba, $1,900.4
6. Texas Instruments, $1,740.0
7. LG Semicon (Goldstar), $1,542.6
8. Micron, $1,515.0

9. Fujitsu, $1,150.0
10. Mitsubishi, $1,043.0

Source: *Electronic Business Today*, May 1997, p. 50.

★ 2239 ★
GLOBAL MCU MARKET, 1996
Ranked by: Sales, in millions of U.S. dollars. **Remarks:** MCU stands for microprocessor control unit. **Number listed:** 10
1. Motorola with $2,061.0 million
2. NEC, $1,757.3
3. Hitachi, $1,208.6
4. Texas Instruments, $1,150.0
5. Intel, $752.0
6. Mitsubishi, $688.1
7. Lucent (AT&T), $679.8
8. Philips, $575.0
9. Toshiba, $308.0
10. Siemens, $304.0

Source: *Electronic Business Today*, May 1997, p. 54.

★ 2240 ★
GLOBAL MPU MARKET, 1996
Ranked by: Sales, in millions of U.S. dollars. **Remarks:** MPU stands for microprocessor unit. **Number listed:** 10
1. Intel with $14,742.4 million
2. Motorola, $1,223.2
3. Advanced Micro Devices, $672.2
4. IBM, $406.5
5. Texas Instruments, $240.0
6. NEC, $202.2
7. NKK, $200.0
8. LSI Logic, $174.3
9. Cyrix, $166.0
10. Hitachi, $146.2

Source: *Electronic Business Today*, May 1997, p. 54.

★ 2241 ★
GLOBAL PLD MARKET, 1996
Ranked by: Sales, in millions of U.S. dollars. **Remarks:** PLD stands for programmable logic devices. **Number listed:** 10
1. Xilinx with $566.1 million
2. Altera, $497.3
3. Advanced Micro Devices, $298.0
4. Lattice, $200.8
5. Actel, $148.8
6. Lucent (AT&T), $89.1
7. Cypress, $50.1
8. Philips, $32.0
9. Atmel, $25.3
10. Quick Logic, $22.6

Source: *Electronic Business Today*, May 1997, p. 54.

★ 2242 ★
GLOBAL SRAM MARKET, 1996
Ranked by: Sales, in millions of U.S. dollars. **Remarks:** SRAM stands for static random access memory. **Number listed:** 10

1. Samsung with $660.0 million
2. Hitachi, $623.8
3. Motorola, $518.0
4. NEC, $404.0
5. IDT, $354.0
6. Toshiba, $306.9
7. Cypress, $205.0
8. Mitsubishi, $200.0
9. Winbond, $140.0
10. Sony, $120.0

Source: *Electronic Business Today*, May 1997, p. 50.

★ 2243 ★
SEMICONDUCTOR MARKET LEADERS, 1996
Ranked by: Sales, in billions of U.S. dollars. **Remarks:** Notes 1995 sales and includes market shares for 1995 and 1996. **Number listed:** 25

1. Intel with $17.5 billion
2. NEC, $9.0
3. Toshiba, $8.5
4. Motorola, $7.9
5. Hitachi, $7.9
6. Texas Instruments, $7.0
7. Samsung, $6.2
8. Mitsubishi, $4.3
9. Philips, $4.1
10. SGS/Thomson, $4.1

Source: *Investor's Business Daily*, June 2, 1997, p. A6.

★ 2244 ★
TOP CHIP SUPPLIERS IN THE ASIA/PACIFIC REGION, 1996
Ranked by: Market share, in percent. **Remarks:** Includes 1995 - 96 revenues. **Number listed:** 10

1. Intel with 10.5%
2. Samsung, 6.8%
3. Toshiba, 6.0%
4. Texas Instruments, 5.8%
5. Motorola, 5.5%
6. Philips, 4.5%
7. NEC, 4.1%
8. LG Semicon, 4.0%
9. Hitachi, 3.9%
10. SGS-Thmopson, 3.9%

Source: *Investor's Business Daily*, April 1, 1997, p. A6.

★ 2245 ★
TOP JAPANESE SEMICONDUCTOR EQUIPMENT SUPPLIERS' SATISFACTION RATING
Ranked by: Average customer satisfaction rating. Users were asked to rate their suppliers in the following categories: product performance, uptime, quality of results, process support, software support, technical leadership, after-sales service and overall customer support. **Number listed:** 10

1. Disco with 8.29
2. Kaijo, 8.08
3. Shinkawa, 8.02
4. Tokyo Seimitsu, 7.71
5. Advantest, 7.70
6. Nikon, 7.42
7. Tokyo Electron, 7.35
8. Dainippon Screen Mfg., 7.28
9. Hitachi, 7.22
10. Canon, 6.73

Source: *Electronic Business Today*, January 1997, p. 15.

★ 2246 ★
TOP PRODUCERS OF GATE ARRAY AND CELL-BASED ASIC, 1996
Ranked by: Sales, in millions of U.S. dollars. **Remarks:** Notes 1995 figures and percent change. ASIC stands for application specific integrated circuits. **Number listed:** 11

1. NEC with $1,285.0 million
2. LSI Logic, $1,240.0
3. Lucent, $1,080.0
4. Toshiba, $1,050.0
5. Fujitsu, $900.0
6. Motorola, $900.0
7. Texas Instruments, $800.0
8. Hitachi, $555.2
9. VLSI, $551.8
10. IBM, $430.0

Source: *Electronic Business Today*, May 1997, p. 52.

★ 2247 ★
TOP PRODUCERS OF NON-VOLATILE MEMORY, 1996
Ranked by: Sales, in millions of U.S. dollars. **Remarks:** Notes 1995 figures and percent change. **Number listed:** 11

1. Intel with $923.0 million
2. Atmel, $735.0
3. Advanced Micro Devices, $664.0
4. SGS-Thomson, $643.0
5. Sharp, $520.0
6. NEC, $324.0
7. Macronix, $313.4
8. Fujitsu, $273.2
9. Samsung, $210.0
10. Texas Instruments, $172.0

Source: *Electronic Business Today*, May 1997, p. 52.

★ 2248 ★
TOP SEMICONDUCTOR MAKERS, 1996
Ranked by: Market share, in percent. **Remarks:** Includes company sales. **Number listed:** 10
1. Intel with 12.0%
2. NEC, 7.5%
3. Motorola, 6.0%
4. Hitachi, 5.7%
5. Toshiba, 5.7%
6. Texas Instruments, 5.0%
7. Samsung Electronics, 4.4%
8. Fujitsu, 3.2%
9. Mitsubishi Electric, 3.0%
10. SGS-Thomson, 3.0%

Source: *Nikkei Weekly*, February 17, 1997, p. 1.

Semiconductor Industry – Europe

★ 2249 ★
TOP CHIP MAKERS IN EUROPE, 1996
Ranked by: Semiconductor sales, in millions of U.S. dollars. **Number listed:** 12
1. Intel with $15,625 million
2. NEC, $10,800
3. Toshiba, $9,610
4. Motorola, $9,100
5. Hitachi, $8,545
6. Texas Instruments, $7,065
7. Samsung, $6,735
8. IBM, $5,435
9. Phillips, $4,475
10. Mitsubishi, $4,460

Source: *The European*, December 11, 1996, p. 23.

Senegal – see under individual headings

Service Industries

★ 2250 ★
TOP EMPLOYMENT SECTORS IN HONG KONG'S SERVICE INDUSTRIES, 1995
Ranked by: Employees, in thousands. **Number listed:** 5
1. Import/export trade with 535.8 thousand emloyees
2. Retailing, 196.1
3. Restaurants, 182.1
4. Finance, 155.0
5. Business services, 148.2

Source: *The Wall Street Journal*, May 15, 1997, p. A18.

Service Industries – Europe

★ 2251 ★
TOP SERVICE COMPANIES IN EUROPE
Ranked by: Sales, in millions of European Currency Units (ECUs). **Remarks:** Includes transportation, communication, power generation and distribution, and other services. Also notes number of employees. **Number listed:** 568
1. Veba A.G. with 32,850 million ECUs
2. Deutsche Telekom A.G., 30,019
3. Electricite de France, 28,509
4. France Telecom, 20,106
5. Enel S.P.A., 18,219
6. Telecom Italia S.P.A., 15,881
7. British Telecommunications Plc, 15,397
8. Deutsche Bahn A.G., 13,537
9. La Poste, 12,504
10. Deutsche Post A.G., 11,260

Source: *Duns Europa* (annual), vol. 4, Dun & Bradstreet, 1997, p. 244+.

★ 2252 ★
TOP SERVICE COMPANIES IN EUROPE, 1995
Ranked by: Sales, in thousands of U.S. dollars. **Remarks:** Also notes previous year's rank, type of industry, percent change in sales, and percent change in local currencies. **Number listed:** 300
1. Deutsche Telekom A.G. with $46,206,246 thousand
2. Shell Transport & Trading Co. Plc, $43,226,708
3. Internationale Nederlanden Groep NV, $30,557,669
4. France Telecom, $26,438,400
5. British Telecommunications Plc, $22,431,677
6. Deutsche Post A.G., $18,640,396
7. Altus Finance, $17,441,979
8. Glaxo Wellcome Plc, $16,288,819
9. SIP Soc. Ital. Per l'Esercizo Telecomnicz S.P.A., $14,757,012
10. Guichard Perrachon Et Cie (Casino), $12,884,142

Source: *Europe's 15,000 Largest Companies* (annual), Dun & Bradstreet, 1997, p. 688 I.

Service Stations
See: **Automobile Service Stations**

Shampoos

★ 2253 ★
BEST-SELLING SHAMPOO BRANDS IN FRANCE, 1996
Ranked by: No specific dollar values provided. **Remarks:** Company names are shown in parentheses. **Number listed:** 10
1. Elseve/Performance (L'Oreal)
2. Ultra Doux (Laboratoires Garnier)
3. Dessange (J. Dessange)
4. Dop (Lascad)
5. JL David (J.L. David)
6. Palmolive (Colgate Palmolive)
7. Petrole Hahn (Procter & Gamble)
8. Organics (Elida)
9. Timotei (Elida Faberge)
10. Ushuaia (Lanete Ushuaia)

Source: *National Trade Data Bank*, May 23, 1997, p. IMI970508.

★ 2254 ★
TOP SHAMPOO ADVERTISERS IN VIETNAM, 1996
Ranked by: Television ad expenditures for the first six months of 1996, in U.S. dollars. **Number listed:** 5
1. Sunsilk with $213,363
2. Rejoice, $196,880
3. Pantene, $188,880
4. Clear, $182,250
5. Head & Shoulders, $83,855

Source: *Vietnam Business Journal*, October 1996, p. 38.

Shanghai Stock Exchange

★ 2255 ★
LARGEST B SHARES ON THE SHANGHAI STOCK EXCHANGE, 1995
Ranked by: Market value, in millions of U.S. dollars. **Number listed:** 20
1. Yaohua Pilkington with $145.31 million
2. Shanghai Lujiazui Development, $113.60
3. Shanghai Chlor Chem, $85.34
4. Erdos Cashmere, $84.52
5. Shanghai Outer Gaoqiao, $60.66
6. Shanghai Dazhong Taxi, $57.72
7. Shanghai Jinqiao, $53.48
8. Shanghai New Asia, $52.80
9. Shanghai Shangling Electric, $45.90
10. Shanghai Tyre and Rubber, $45.53

Source: *GT Guide to World Equity Markets* (annual), Euromoney Publications, 1996, p. 109.

★ 2256 ★
MOST ACTIVELY TRADED B SHARES ON THE SHANGHAI STOCK EXCHANGE, 1995
Ranked by: Average daily volume, in millions of B shares. **Number listed:** 20
1. Shanghai Phoenix Bicycle with 0.29 million shares
2. Shanghai Refrigerator, 0.24
3. Shanghai Lujiazui Dev, 0.21
4. Shanghai Diesel Engine, 0.20
5. Shanghai New Asia (Group), 0.20
6. Shanghai Jinjiang, 0.18
7. Shanghai Lianhua, 0.17
8. Shanghai Narcissus, 0.16
9. Shanghai Tyre and Rubber, 0.16
10. Yaohua Pilkington, 0.14

Source: *GT Guide to World Equity Markets* (annual), Euromoney Publications, 1996, p. 110.

Shenzhen Stock Exchange

★ 2257 ★
LARGEST B SHARES ON THE SHENZHEN STOCK EXCHANGE, 1995
Ranked by: Market value, in millions of Hong Kong dollars (HK$). **Number listed:** 20
1. Guangdong Electric with HK$878.75 million
2. Shenzhen Chiwan Petroleum, HK$545.92
3. Jiangling Motor, HK$534.60
4. Shenzhen Konka Elt, HK$460.99
5. Shenzhen Jianshe Motorcycles, HK$384.00
6. Shenzhen China Bicycle, HK$369.66
7. China International Marine, HK$359.36
8. China Southern Glass, HK$277.57
9. Foshan Electric, HK$260.00
10. Xiamen Cankuen, HK$222.00

Source: *GT Guide to World Equity Markets* (annual), Euromoney Publications, 1996, p. 110.

Shipbuilding

★ 2258 ★
TOP SHIP BUILDERS IN JAPAN
Ranked by: Market share, in percent. **Number listed:** 6
1. Mitsubishi Heavy Industries with 13.4%
2. Hitachi Zosen, 10.5%
3. Imabari Shipbuilding, 6.8%
4. Mitsui Engineering & Shipbuilding, 6.0%
5. Ishikawajima-Harima Heavy Industries, 6.0%
6. Others, 57.3%

Source: *Nikkei Weekly*, July 29, 1996, p. 8.

Shipping

★ 2259 ★
LARGEST MERCHANT FLEETS IN THE WORLD
Ranked by: Deadweight, in deadweight tons. **Remarks:**
Also notes number of ships. **Number listed:** 12
1. Panama with 119,150 deadweight tons
2. Liberia, 95,405
3. Greece, 48,628
4. Cyprus, 39,841
5. Bahamas, 37,654
6. Malta, 31,628
7. Norway, 29,115
8. China, 23,411
9. Singapore, 23,409
10. Japan, 21,554
Source: *Marine Log,* Yearbook and Marine Review
(annual), June 1997, p. 22.

★ 2260 ★
LARGEST OCEAN CARRIERS, 1996
Ranked by: Cargo handled during the first nine months
of 1996, in millions of twenty-foot equivalent units
(TEUs). **Number listed:** 25
1. Sea-Land with 3.08 million TEUs
2. Evergreen, 2.54
3. Maersk, 2.06
4. Hanjin, 1.71
5. American President Lines, 1.43
6. COSCO, 1.22
7. NYK, 1.18
8. OOCL, 1.12
9. Hyundai, 1.08
10. "K" Line, 1.00
Source: *World Trade,* April 1997, p. 53.

★ 2261 ★
**LARGEST SHIPPING COMPANIES WORLDWIDE,
1995**
Ranked by: Revenues, in millions of U.S. dollars.
Remarks: Also notes profits. **Number listed:** 2
1. Peninsular & Oriental with $10,370 million
2. Nippon Yuson, $9,239
Source: *Fortune,* The Global 500: World's Biggest
Corporations (annual), August 5, 1996, p. F-25.

★ 2262 ★
TOP CONTAINER SHIPPING LEADERS, 1995
Ranked by: Revenue, in billions of U.S. dollars.
Remarks: Lists main activity for each conglomerate,
name of liner operation and liner shipping revenues.
Number listed: 10
1. Itochu with $178.4 billion
2. Mitsui & Co., $168.8
3. Mitsubishi Shoji, $154.6

4. Hyundai Group, $21.6
5. Hanjin Group, $11.7
6. P&O Group, $10.3
7. A.P. Moller, $5.2
8. Bollore Technologies, $4.5
9. Hapag-Loyd Group, $3.1
10. SAFREN Group, $1.6
Source: *American Shipper,* June 1996, p. 64.

Shoe Industry

★ 2263 ★
U.K. FOOTWEAR SALES BY OUTLET
Ranked by: Retail distribution, in percent. **Remarks:**
Total sales reached £4.336 billion. **Number listed:** 7
1. Shoe stores with 68.1%
2. Variety stores, 7.6%
3. Mail order, 7.3%
4. Sports shops, 7.2%
5. Department stores, 3.4%
6. Clothing shops, 3.3%
7. Other, 3.0%
Source: *Sunday Telegraph,* July 7, 1996, p. B5.

Shrimp Industry, International

★ 2264 ★
TOP SHRIMP PRODUCING NATIONS, 1996
Ranked by: Production, in tons. **Remarks:** Notes
percentage farmed and percentage fished. **Number
listed:** 10
1. China with 450,000 tons
2. India, 290,000
3. Indonesia, 240,000
4. Thailand, 240,000
5. United States, 131,000
6. Ecuador, 125,000
7. Greenland, 85,000
8. Philippines, 75,000
9. Vietnam, 70,000
10. Mexico, 67,000
Source: *Quick Frozen Foods International,* January 1997,
p. 39.

Sierra Leone – see under individual headings

Silver Mines and Mining

★ 2265 ★
TOP SILVER PRODUCERS, 1995
Ranked by: Mine production, in metric tons. **Number listed:** 5
1. Mexico with 2,495 metric tons
2. Peru, 1,871
3. United States, 1,464
4. Canada, 1,254
5. Australia, 915
Source: *Financial Times*, March 21, 1996, p. 19.

★ 2266 ★
TOP SILVER PRODUCING COMPANIES, 1995
Ranked by: Production, in millions of ounces. **Number listed:** 10
1. KGHM with 31.0 million ounces
2. Penoles, 29.7
3. Noranda, 15.7
4. Centromin, 14.7
5. Echo Bay, 11.9
6. MIM Holdings, 11.6
7. Frisco, 11.0
8. IMMSA, 10.8
9. Prime Resources, 10.0
10. Buenaventura, 9.1
Source: *World Silver Survey*, 1996, p. 16.

★ 2267 ★
TOP SILVER PRODUCING NATIONS, 1995
Ranked by: Production, in millions of ounces. **Remarks:** Also notes 199 figures. **Number listed:** 10
1. Mexico with 74.7 million ounces
2. Peru, 61.4
3. United States, 49.8
4. C.I.S., 45.2
5. Canada, 38.8
6. Chile, 33.5
7. Poland, 31.6
8. Australia, 29.6
9. China, 27.0
10. Bolivia, 11.9
Source: *World Silver Survey*, 1996, p. 16.

Singapore – see under individual headings

Singapore Stock Exchange

★ 2268 ★
LARGEST COMPANIES ON THE STOCK EXCHANGE OF SINGAPORE, 1995
Ranked by: Market value, in billions of Singapore dollars (S$). **Number listed:** 20
1. Singapore Telecom with S$47.83 billion
2. Singapore Airlines, S$10.32
3. OCBC, S$10.15
4. United Overseas Bank, S$8.39
5. City Developments, S$8.08
6. DBS, S$7.02
7. Keppel Corporation, S$6.51
8. Singapore Press Holdings, S$4.73
9. Overseas Union Bank, S$4.49
10. DBS Land, S$4.39
Source: *GT Guide to World Equity Markets* (annual), Euromoney Publications, 1996, p. 289.

★ 2269 ★
MOST ACTIVELY TRADED SHARES ON THE STOCK EXCHANGE OF SINGAPORE, 1995
Ranked by: Trading volume, in millions of shares. **Number listed:** 20
1. Amcol Holdings with 748.88 million shares
2. RF-JAMA Warrant 96, 705.32
3. Guthrie GTS, 687.41
4. DBS Land, 650.06
5. Hong Kong Land, 595.77
6. Tuan Sing, 468.06
7. DBS Land B Warrant 95, 445.90
8. LBS Land A Warrant 95, 410.40
9. IPC Corporation, 383.17
10. Dairy Farm Holdings, 346.63
Source: *GT Guide to World Equity Markets* (annual), Euromoney Publications, 1996, p. 289.

Skin Care Products

★ 2270 ★
LEADING FACIAL CARE BRANDS IN THAILAND, 1996
Ranked by: Market share, in percent. **Number listed:** 5
1. Pond's with 38%
2. Oil of Ulan, 29%
3. Plenitude, 4%
4. Nivea, 3%
5. Others, 26%
Source: *Bangkok Post*, May 9, 1997, p. 12.

★ 2271 ★
THAILAND'S SKIN CARE MARKET
Ranked by: Market share, in percent. Number listed: 5
1. Lever with 27.0%
2. Procter & Gamble, 22.0%
3. Beiersdorf, 13.0%
4. Johnson's, 11.0%
5. Other, 27.0%
Source: *Bangkok Post*, March 26, 1996, p. 30.

Slovakia – see under individual headings

Slovenia – see under individual headings

Smoke Detectors
See: **Fire Detection Systems**

Snacks – United Kingdom

★ 2272 ★
TOP SNACK BRANDS IN THE UNITED KINGDOM, 1995
Ranked by: Estimated sales, in millions of British pounds (£). Remarks: Also notes ad agency and spending. Number listed: 10
1. Walker Crisps (Pepsico) with £Over 299 million
2. Hula Hoops (KP Foods), £60-65
3. Pringles (Procter & Gamble), £50-55
4. Golden Wonder Crisps (Dalgety), £45-50
5. Quavers (Pepsico), £45-50
6. Doritos (Walkers), £30-35
7. Monster Munch (Pepsico), £25-30
8. Skips (KP Foods), £25-30
9. Wotsits (Dalgety), £25-30
10. KP Peanuts (KP Foods), £20-25
Source: *Marketing*, July 4, 1996, p. 24.

Soap Industry

★ 2273 ★
INDIA'S TOILET SOAP MARKET
Ranked by: Market share, in percent. Remarks: Leading brands include Lifebuoy, Lux, Rexona, Haman, and Jai. Number listed: 2
1. Hindustan Lever Ltd. with 76.8%

2. Other, 23.2%
Source: *Business Today*, May 7, 1996, p. 87.

★ 2274 ★
LARGEST SOAP/COSMETICS COMPANIES, 1995
Ranked by: Revenues, in millions of dollars. Remarks: Also notes profits. Number listed: 3
1. Procter & Gamble with $33,434 million
2. L'Oreal, $10,698
3. Henkel, $9,907
Source: *Fortune,* The Global 500: World's Biggest Corporations (annual), August 5, 1996, p. F-25.

★ 2275 ★
PERSONAL SOAP MARKET IN CANADA, 1997
Ranked by: Market share for the year ending March 31, 1997, in percent. Remarks: Notes figures for 1996. Number listed: 9
1. Dove with 21.6%
2. Oil of Olay, 12.0%
3. Ivory, 10.5%
4. Jergens, 8.8%
5. Lever 2000, 8.0%
6. Zest, 6.9%
7. Irish Spring, 6.0%
8. Dial, 3.9%
9. Others, 22.3%
Source: *Marketing Magazine*, June 9, 1997, p. 4.

★ 2276 ★
TOP PERSONAL SOAP BRANDS IN THE UNITED KINGDOM, 1995
Ranked by: Market share, in percent. Number listed: 15
1. Lynx with 11.5%
2. Boots, 11.0%
3. Imperial Leather, 9.5%
4. Radox Showerfresh, 9.5%
5. Avon, 9.0%
6. Palmolive, 6.0%
7. Badedas, 4.0%
8. Dove, 3.0%
9. Cussons for Men, 2.5%
10. Aquaspar, 2.0%
Source: *Inside Cosmetics*, December 1996, p. 15.

★ 2277 ★
TOP TOILET SOAP MAKERS IN KOREA
Ranked by: Market share, in percent. Number listed: 5
1. Lucky with 50.0%
2. Pacific, 20.0%
3. Dongsan, 12.0%
4. Aekyung, 10.0%
5. Othr, 8.0%
Source: *National Trade Data Bank*, March 2, 1996, p. ISA9312.

Soccer

★ 2278 ★
LEADING CANADIAN CITIES FOR SALES OF SOCCER EQUIPMENT
Ranked by: Sales, in percent distribution. **Number listed:** 4
1. Toronto with 17%
2. Montreal, 10%
3. Vancouver, 7%
4. Others, 66%

Source: *National Trade Data Bank*, July 2, 1997, p. IMI970630.

★ 2279 ★
LEADING CANADIAN PROVINCES FOR SALES OF SOCCER EQUIPMENT
Ranked by: Sales, in percent distribution. **Remarks:** Atlantic Provinces include Newfoundland, Prince Edward Island, Nova Scotia and New Brunswick. **Number listed:** 5
1. Ontario with 40%
2. Alberta, Saskatchewan, and Manitoba, 18%
3. Quebec, 17%
4. British Columbia, 14%
5. Atlantic Provinces, 9%

Source: *National Trade Data Bank*, July 2, 1997, p. IMI970630.

★ 2280 ★
LEADING PRODUCERS OF SOCCER BALLS IN CANADA
Ranked by: Market share, in percent. **Number listed:** 5
1. Umbro with 13%
2. Mitre, 10%
3. Cooper, 9%
4. Spalding, 9%
5. Other, 59%

Source: *National Trade Data Bank*, July 2, 1997, p. IMI970630.

Soft Drink Industry

★ 2281 ★
GLOBAL SOFT DRINK MARKET, 1995
Ranked by: Market share, in percent. **Number listed:** 3
1. Coca-Cola with 47.0%
2. PepsiCo., 23.0%
3. Other, 30.0%

Source: *Financial Times*, September 29, 1996, p. 9.

★ 2282 ★
LEADING BRANDS IN THE INDIAN SOFT DRINK INDUSTRY
Ranked by: Market share, in percent. **Remarks:** Coca-Cola brands control 50.5% of the market, with Pepsi controlling 43.5% of the market. Coke brands not listed include Bislen Club Soda, Rim Zim and Maaza. Pepsi brands include 7-Up, Mangola, Slice, Duke's Soda, and Duke's Lemonade. Cadbury Schweppes includes Crush, Canada Dry, Campa-Cola, and Campa Lemon. **Number listed:** 11
1. Pepsi with 26.5%
2. Thums-Up, 14.6%
3. Coca-Cola, 12.5%
4. Lithica, 8.2%
5. Mirinda, 7.2%
6. Fanta, 6.7%
7. Gold Spot, 2.1%
8. Cadbury Schweppes, 1.8%
9. Other Pepsi brands, 9.8%
10. Others, 10.6%

Source: *Business Today*, December 7, 1996, p. 66.

★ 2283 ★
LEADING SOFT DRINKS IN ITALY, 1995
Ranked by: Market share, in percent. **Number listed:** 8
1. Coca-Cola with 43.0%
2. Sogeam, 9.0%
3. San Benedetto, 8.0%
4. San Pellegrino, 6.5%
5. Pepsi-Cola, 4.5%
6. Terme di Crodo, 3.0%
7. Spumador, 2.5%
8. Other, 23.5%

Source: *Marketing in Europe*, January 1997, p. 35.

★ 2284 ★
SOFT DRINK MAKERS IN ARGENTINA, 1994
Ranked by: Market share, in percent. **Number listed:** 3
1. Coca-Cola with 57.4%
2. Pepsi, 36.0%
3. Other, 6.6%

Source: *The New York Times*, August 21, 1996, p. C1.

★ 2285 ★
SOFT DRINK MAKERS IN BOLIVIA, 1994
Ranked by: Market share, in percent. **Number listed:** 3
1. Coca-Cola with 54.4%
2. Pepsi, 18.3%
3. Other, 27.3%

Source: *The New York Times*, August 21, 1996, p. C1.

★ 2286 ★
SOFT DRINK MAKERS IN BRAZIL, 1994
Ranked by: Market share, in percent. **Number listed:** 3
1. Coca-Cola with 54.9%

2. Pepsi, 8.0%
3. Other, 37.1%
Source: *The New York Times*, August 21, 1996, p. C1.

★ 2287 ★
SOFT DRINK MAKERS IN COLOMBIA, 1994
Ranked by: Market share, in percent. **Number listed:** 3
1. Coca-Cola with 43.6%
2. Pepsi, 11.2%
3. Other, 45.2%
Source: *The New York Times*, August 21, 1996, p. C1.

★ 2288 ★
SOFT DRINK MAKERS IN ECUADOR, 1994
Ranked by: Market share, in percent. **Number listed:** 3
1. Coca-Cola with 55.5%
2. Pepsi, 17.4%
3. Other, 27.1%
Source: *The New York Times*, August 21, 1996, p. C1.

★ 2289 ★
SOFT DRINK MAKERS IN PERU, 1994
Ranked by: Market share, in percent. **Number listed:** 3
1. Coca-Cola with 42.1%
2. Pepsi, 23.5%
3. Other, 34.4%
Source: *The New York Times*, August 21, 1996, p. C1.

★ 2290 ★
SOFT DRINK MAKERS IN URUGUAY, 1994
Ranked by: Market share, in percent. **Number listed:** 3
1. Coca-Cola with 67.0%
2. Pepsi, 30.3%
3. Other, 2.7%
Source: *The New York Times*, August 21, 1996, p. C1.

★ 2291 ★
TOP CARBONATED DRINK BRANDS IN THE UNITED KINGDOM, 1995
Ranked by: Estimated sales, in millions of British pounds (£) **Remarks:** Also notes ad agency and spending. **Number listed:** 10
1. Coca-Cola (Coca-Cola) with £Over 483 million
2. Pepsi-Cola (PepsiCo.), £175-180
3. Lucozade (SmithKline Beecham), £100-105
4. Tango (Britvic Soft Drinks), £95-100
5. Lilt (Coca-Cola), £50-55
6. Schweppes mixers (Schweppes), £50-55
7. Irn-Bru (AG Barr), £45-50
8. 7-Up (PepsiCo.), £30-35
9. Sunkist Schweppes, £20-25
10. Virgin Cola (Virgin Cola), £20-25
Source: *Marketing*, July 4, 1996, p. 24.

★ 2292 ★
TOP SOFT DRINK PROVIDERS IN SOUTH AFRICA
Ranked by: Market share, in percent. **Number listed:** 3
1. Coca-Cola Co. with 75.0%
2. Cadbury Schweppes, 11.0%
3. Other, 14.0%
Source: *Beverage World's Periscope*, December 31, 1995, p. 8.

Solar Cells

★ 2293 ★
TOP REGIONS FOR THE PRODUCTION OF SOLAR CELLS, 1996
Ranked by: Storage capacity of cells produced, in millions of watts. **Number listed:** 4
1. United States with 38.9 million watts
2. Japan, 21.2
3. Europe, 18.8
4. Other, 9.7
Source: *The New York Times*, August 16, 1997, p. C1.

Somalia – see under individual headings

Sorghum

★ 2294 ★
SORGHUM PRODUCTION WORLDWIDE
Ranked by: Production, in millions of metric tons. **Number listed:** 8
1. United States with 13.57 million metric tons
2. India, 11.52
3. China, 5.00
4. Nigeria, 3.70
5. Sudan, 2.40
6. Argentina, 2.27
7. Mexico, 2.04
8. Ethiopia, 1.20
Source: *World Agricultural Production*, March 1995, p. 18.

Soup

★ 2295 ★
INDIA'S NOODLE MARKET
Ranked by: Market share, in percent. **Number listed:** 2
1. Maggi with 80.0%

2. Top Ramen, 20.0%
Source: *Business Today*, August 7, 1996, p. 50.

South Africa – see under individual headings

Soybean Industry

★ 2296 ★

TOP SOYBEAN PRODUCERS, 1996
Ranked by: Production, in billions of bushels. **Remarks:**
Data for Brazil and Argentina are estimates. **Number listed:** 9
1. United States with 2.400 billion bushels
2. Brazil, .970
3. Argentina, .500
4. China, .480
5. Iowa, .416
6. Illinois, .404
7. Minnesota, .224
8. Indiana, .210
9. Missouri, .158
Source: *Soybean Digest*, February 1997, p. 102.

★ 2297 ★

WORLD'S TOP SOYBEAN PRODUCERS, 1995
Ranked by: Production, in millions of metric tons
Remarks: Total world prodcution is 123.7 million metric tons. **Number listed:** 4
1. United States with 68.5 million metric tons
2. Brazil, 23.2
3. China, 13.5
4. Argentina, 12.6
Source: *Latin Trade*, November 1996, p. 69.

Spain – see under individual headings

Spices

★ 2298 ★

TOP CONDIMENT AND SPICE BRANDS BY BRAND VALUE
Ranked by: Brand value, in millions of U.S. dollars.
Remarks: Value was calculated using capital, ratio of capital to company sales, earnings, and corporate tax rate of the country where the parent company is located.
See source for details. **Number listed:** 10
1. Heinz (H.J. Heinz) with $3,758 million
2. Nutrasweet (Monsanto), $909

3. Hellman's (CPC International), $803
4. McCormick (McCormick), $630
5. Mazola (CPC International), $350
6. Morton (Morton International), $309
7. Smuckers (J.M. Smucker), $241
8. Colman's (Unilever), $206
9. Skippy (CPC International), $101
10. Lea & Perrins (Danona), $53
Source: *Financial World,* World's Most Valuable Brands (annual), July 8, 1996, p. 60.

Sport Utility Vehicles

★ 2299 ★

TOP SELLING SPORTS UTILITY MODELS IN THAILAND, 1997
Ranked by: Units sold, for the first four months of 1997.
Number listed: 5
1. Honda CR-V with 746 units
2. Jeep Cherokee, 668
3. Kia Sportage, 406
4. Jeep Grand Cherokee, 393
5. Suzuki Vitara, 271
Source: *Bangkok Post*, May 22, 1997, p. D1.

Sporting Goods

★ 2300 ★

FASTEST GROWING SPORTING GOODS IMPORT MARKETS OUTSIDE THE U.S., 1993-1995
Ranked by: Average annual growth, in percent. **Number listed:** 10
1. India with 25% growth
2. Portugal, 25%
3. Romania, 25%
4. Bulgaria, 20%
5. Honduras, 20%
6. South Korea, 20%
7. Argentina, 18%
8. Turkey, 18%
9. Taiwan, 18%
10. China, 16%
Source: *National Trade Data Bank*, March 21, 1995, p. BMR9404.

★ 2301 ★

FASTEST GROWING SPORTING GOODS MARKETS OUTSIDE THE U.S., 1993-1995
Ranked by: Average annual growth, in percent. **Number listed:** 10
1. Portugal with 25% growth
2. Bulgaria, 20%

3. Honduras, 20%
4. India, 20%
5. Philippines, 20%
6. Argentina, 17%
7. Malaysia, 17%
8. Algeria, 15%
9. China, 15%
10. Hungary, 15%

Source: *National Trade Data Bank*, March 21, 1995, p. BMR9404.

★ 2302 ★

LARGEST SPORTING GOODS MARKETS OUTSIDE THE U.S.

Ranked by: Total market value, in millions of U.S. dollars. **Number listed:** 10

1. Japan with $15,400.0 million
2. Germany, $5,720.0
3. Italy, $5,200.0
4. Canada, $1,153.0
5. Switzerland, $983.0
6. United Kingdom, $850.0
7. Belgium, $800.0
8. Argentina, $776.0
9. Brazil, $775.0
10. Taiwan, $640.0

Source: *National Trade Data Bank*, March 21, 1995, p. BMR9404.

★ 2303 ★

LEADING MANUFACTURERS OF INLINE SKATES, 1996

Ranked by: No specific criteria provided. **Number listed:** 6

1. Rollerblade
2. Ultra Wheels
3. Roces
4. Bauer
5. K2
6. Oxygen

Source: *National Trade Data Bank*, May 15, 1997, p. IMI970514.

Sporting Goods Industry

★ 2304 ★

COUNTRIES WITH THE MOST SWIMMING POOLS

Ranked by: Units, in thousands. **Remarks:** Data are estimated. **Number listed:** 14

1. United States with 6,000 thousand units
2. Australia, 1,500
3. Brazil, 600
4. Canada, 600
5. Spain, 330

6. France, 300
7. South Africa, 300
8. Germany, 225
9. Rest of South America, 60
10. Japan, 40

Source: *Swimming Pool/Spa Age*, June 1996, p. 22.

★ 2305 ★

LARGEST SPORTING GOODS IMPORT MARKETS OUTSIDE THE U.S.

Ranked by: Value of import market, in millions of U.S. dollars. **Number listed:** 10

1. Japan with $3,150.0 million
2. Germany, $2,690.0
3. Switzerland, $886.0
4. Italy, $800.0
5. United Kingdom, $625.0
6. Canada, $489.0
7. Netherlands, $484.0
8. Belgium, $375.0
9. France, $348.0
10. Hong Kong, $344.0

Source: *National Trade Data Bank*, March 21, 1995, p. BMR9404.

★ 2306 ★

SOUTH AFRICA'S TOP 10 GROWTH SPORTS, 1986-1994

Ranked by: Average growth for 1986 - 1994, in percent. **Remarks:** Includes the number of participants in each sport. **Number listed:** 10

1. Cycling with 39.0% growth
2. Basketball, 21.7%
3. Volleyball, 21.0%
4. Gym fitness training, 19.0%
5. Athletics, 16.9%
6. Triathlons, 14.0%
7. Baseball/softball, 14.0%
8. Karate, 12.1%
9. Cricket, 9.5%
10. Aerobics, 9.2%

Source: *National Trade Data Bank*, November 27, 1996, p. ISA950701.

★ 2307 ★

TOP EQUESTRIAN EQUIPMENT MAKERS IN SWEDEN

Ranked by: Turnover, in millions of Swedish krona (SKr). **Number listed:** 4

1. Borjes with SKr30 million
2. Hooks Sadelmakeri, SKr30
3. PIAB, SKr25
4. Kjellquists, SKr24

Source: *National Trade Data Bank*, May 27, 1996, p. ISA9410.

★ 2308 ★
TOP KITE MAKERS IN FRANCE
Ranked by: Market share, in percent. **Number listed:** 4
1. Paimpol with 60.0%
2. Voilerie LeNohan, 18.0%
3. Trucs, 9.0%
4. Other, 13.0%

Source: *National Trade Data Bank*, March 2, 1996, p. ISA9412.

★ 2309 ★
TOP POOL TABLE MAKERS IN EGYPT, 1995
Ranked by: Market share, in percent. **Number listed:** 9
1. AMF Play Master with 35.0%
2. Alamein, 20.0%
3. Ayman El-Azazi, 10.0%
4. Murrey International, 10.0%
5. Small Workshops, 10.0%
6. Brunswick, 5.0%
7. Allhausen, 4.0%
8. Thurston, 4.0%
9. Others, 2.0%

Source: *National Trade Data Bank*, August 29, 1995, p. ISA9506.

★ 2310 ★
TOP SWIMMING POOL MAKERS IN EGYPT, 1995
Ranked by: Market share, in percent. **Number listed:** 19
1. Hayward Pools with 20.0%
2. Astral, 18.0%
3. Sta-Rite, 18.0%
4. American Products, 7.0%
5. Kripsol, 7.0%
6. Aqua-tech, 6.0%
7. Back Fab, 5.0%
8. Bio-labs, 3.0%
9. Laseco, 3.0%
10. Culligan Filter, 2.0%

Source: *National Trade Data Bank*, June 14, 1995, p. ISA9502.

Sports Clothes
See: **Sportswear**

Sports Clubs

★ 2311 ★
MOST POPULAR SPORTS IN SOUTH KOREA
Ranked by: Percentage of respondents who are fans of each sport, based on a survey. **Remarks:** Data include multiple responses. **Number listed:** 9
1. Soccer with 59%

2. Baseball, 46%
3. Basketball, 28%
4. Volleyball, 15%
5. Tennis, 6%
6. Korean wrestling, 3%
7. Marathon, 3%
8. Golf, 2%
9. Others, 38%

Source: *Business Korea*, March 1997, p. 41.

★ 2312 ★
POPULAR PRO SPORTS IN JAPAN
Ranked by: Percent of 1,422 respondents indicating this their favorite professional sport. **Number listed:** 8
1. Baseball with 56.3%
2. Sumo, 47.5%
3. Soccer (junior league), 18.1%
4. Golf, 12.5%
5. Boxing, 9.4%
6. Auto racing, 7.7%
7. Wrestling, 5.5%
8. Other, 4.2%

Source: *Look Japan*, August 1996, p. 6.

Sportswear

★ 2313 ★
FRANCE'S JOGGING SALES BY SEGMENT, 1995
Ranked by: Segment, distributed in percent. **Number listed:** 4
1. Boys with 36%
2. Men, 29%
3. Women, 19%
4. Girls, 16%

Source: *National Trade Data Bank*, January 31, 1997, p. ISA970101.

★ 2314 ★
FRANCE'S SHORTS AND BERMUDAS SALES BY SEGMENT, 1995
Ranked by: Segment, distributed in percent. **Number listed:** 4
1. Women with 35%
2. Men, 31%
3. Boys, 23%
4. Girls, 11%

Source: *National Trade Data Bank*, January 31, 1997, p. ISA970101.

Steel Industry and Trade

★ 2315 ★
FRANCE'S SWEATSHIRTS SALES BY SEGMENT, 1995
Ranked by: Segment, distributed in percent. **Number listed:** 4
1. Men with 34%
2. Boys, 25%
3. Women, 24%
4. Girls, 17%
Source: *National Trade Data Bank*, January 31, 1997, p. ISA970101.

★ 2316 ★
FRANCE'S SWIMSUITS SALES BY SEGMENT, 1995
Ranked by: Segment, distributed in percent. **Number listed:** 4
1. Women with 58%
2. Men, 19%
3. Girls, 15%
4. Boys, 8%
Source: *National Trade Data Bank*, January 31, 1997; p. ISA970101.

★ 2317 ★
FRANCE'S WINDBREAKERS SALES BY SEGMENT, 1995
Ranked by: Segment, distributed in percent. **Number listed:** 4
1. Women with 36%
2. Men, 31%
3. Boys, 20%
4. Girls, 13%
Source: *National Trade Data Bank*, January 31, 1997, p. ISA970101.

Sri Lanka – see under individual headings

Stationery

★ 2318 ★
ARGENTINA'S STATIONERY MAKERS, 1994
Ranked by: Market share, in percent. **Number listed:** 5
1. Domestic with 43.0%
2. Estrada, 10.0%
3. Grafex, 9.5%
4. Della Penna, 17.0%
5. Others, 20.0%
Source: *National Trade Data Bank*, November 26, 1996, p. ISA950701.

★ 2319 ★
FRANCE'S TOP STEEL FIRMS, 1996
Ranked by: Sales for the first nine months of 1996, in billions of French francs (FFr). **Remarks:** Data for Usinor Sacilor show sales during the third quarter of 1996; Moulinex data show sales during the first half of 1996. Notes percent change. **Number listed:** 10
1. Alcatel Alsthom with FFr111.5 billion
2. Bouygues, FFr49.8
3. Schneider, FFr45.6
4. Lagardere, FFr37.6
5. Lafarge, FFr26.0
6. Usinor Sacilor, FFr16.0
7. Bull, FFr15.67
8. Moulinex, FFr3.35
9. Eurotunnel, FFr2.92
10. CGIP, FFr1.37
Source: *Financial Times*, November 14, 1996, p. 19.

★ 2320 ★
LARGEST STEEL PRODUCING NATIONS, 1996
Ranked by: Estimated production, in millions of metric tons. **Remarks:** Notes production figures for 1990 - 95. **Number listed:** 39
1. China with 100.4 million metric tons
2. Japan, 98.8
3. United States, 94.6
4. Russia, 49.2
5. Germany, 39.8
6. South Korea, 38.9
7. Brazil, 25.2
8. Italy, 24.5
9. Ukraine, 22.1
10. India, 21.8
Source: *Skillings Mining Review*, February 8, 1997, p. 11.

★ 2321 ★
STEELWORKER PRODUCTIVITY, 1995
Ranked by: Hours of work. **Remarks:** Numbers represent the hours of work required for each metric ton of cold-rolled steel sheet shipped by selected countries. **Number listed:** 5
1. United States with 4.42 hours
2. Japan, 4.49
3. France, 4.61
4. Germany, 4.69
5. Britain, 4.71
Source: *The New York Times*, April 16, 1996, p. 6A.

★ 2322 ★
TOP STEEL COMPANIES IN JAPAN
Ranked by: Income, in millions of yen (¥). **Number listed:** 10
1. Maruichi Steel Tube with ¥13,871 million
2. Bridgestone Metalpha, ¥8,113
3. Yodogawa Steel Works, ¥7,426
4. Toyo Kohan, ¥6,889
5. Hitachi Metals, ¥5,707
6. Kobe Steel, ¥5,027
7. Osaka Steel, ¥3,781
8. Oji Steel, ¥3,326
9. Aichi Steel Works, ¥2,350
10. Nishi Nippon Steel, ¥1,624

Source: *Tokyo Business Today*, August 1995, p. 26.

★ 2323 ★
TOP STEEL PRODUCERS IN INDIA
Ranked by: Market share, in percent. **Number listed:** 6
1. SAIL with 51.0%
2. Tisco, 15.0%
3. RINL, 11.0%
4. Secondary, 23.0%

Source: *The Hindu*, August 21, 1996, p. 25.

★ 2324 ★
TOP STEEL PRODUCERS IN JAPAN
Ranked by: Market share, in percent. **Number listed:** 6
1. Nippon Steel with 26.2%
2. NKK, 10.9%
3. Kawasaki Steel, 10.1%
4. Sumitomo Metal Ind., 10.0%
5. Kobe Steel, 5.9%
6. Others, 36.9%

Source: *Nikkei Weekly*, July 29, 1996, p. 8.

★ 2325 ★
TOP STEEL PRODUCERS WORLDWIDE, 1996
Ranked by: Production, in millions of tons. **Number listed:** 10
1. Nippon Steel (Japan) with 25.3 million tons
2. Posco (South Korea), 24.3
3. British Steel (United Kingdom), 18.1
4. Usinor-Sacilor (France), 15.0
5. Thyssen/Krupp (Germany), 14.2
6. Riva (Italy), 13.1
7. Arbed (Luxembourg), 11.5
8. Sall (India), 11.0
9. NKK (Japan), 10.5
10. U.S. Steel (United States), 10.4

Source: *Der Spiegel*, 1997, p. 100.

Steel Industry and Trade–Europe

★ 2326 ★
TOP STEEL MAKERS IN EUROPE, 1996
Ranked by: Output, in billions of tons of slab equivalent. **Number listed:** 10
1. British Steel (United Kingdom) with 16.12 billion tons
2. Usinor Sacilor (France), 14.96
3. Riva (Italy), 13.10
4. Arbed (Luxembourg), 11.50
5. Thyssen (Germany), 9.30
6. Cockerill Sambre (Belgium), 6.40
7. Hoogovens (Netherlands), 6.15
8. Krupp Hoesch (Germany), 4.92
9. Huta Katowice (Poland), 4.36
10. CSI (Spain), 4.30

Source: *Financial Times*, March 20, 1997, p. 17.

Stock Exchanges

★ 2327 ★
AFRICAN STOCK EXCHANGES
Ranked by: Market value, in billions of U.S. dollars. **Remarks:** Provides date founded, trading times, and number of listed companies. **Number listed:** 14
1. Johannesburg Stock Exchange with $241.6 billion
2. Cairo Stock Exchange, $14.2
3. Casablanca Stock Exchange, $8.7
4. Tunis Stock Exchange, $4.3
5. Nigerian Stock Exchange, $3.6
6. Zimbabwe Stock Exchange, $3.6
7. Nairobi Stock Exchange, $1.8
8. Mauritius Stock Exchange, $1.7
9. Swaziland Stock Exchange, $1.6
10. Ghana Stock Exchange, $1.5

Source: *USA TODAY*, May 23, 1997, p. 4B.

★ 2328 ★
LARGEST STOCK BROKERAGES IN MEXICO, 1995
Ranked by: Assets as of December 31, 1995, in millions of U.S. dollars. **Number listed:** 10
1. Operadora de Bolsa Serfin with $4,536.7 million
2. Inverlat, $2,983.2
3. G.B.M., $2,546.9
4. Invermexico, $1,957.1
5. BBV - Probursa, $1,427.4
6. Invex, $1,010.9
7. Acciones y Valores, $905.1
8. Multivalores, $899.2
9. Inversora, $788.6

10.　Abaco, $750.7

Source: *National Trade Data Bank*, September 9, 1996, p. ISA960801.

★ 2329 ★

LARGEST STOCK EXCHANGES, 1995

Ranked by: Turnover, in billions of U.S. dollars for the year ended December 1995. **Remarks:** Includes market capitalization figures. **Number listed:** 20

1.　New York with $3,082.9 billion
2.　Nasdaq, $2,398.2
3.　London, $1,138.4
4.　Paris, $931.1
5.　Tokyo, $888.4
6.　Germany, $606.5
7.　Taiwan, $389.2
8.　Switzerland, $320.0
9.　Osaka, $261.9
10.　Korca, $185.4

Source: *Financial Times*, October 17, 1996, p. 21.

★ 2330 ★

LARGEST STOCK MARKETS IN CHINA, 1996

Ranked by: Year-end capitalization, in millions of U.S. dollars. **Remarks:** Also notes monthly turnover. **Number listed:** 3

1.　Shanghai with $66,000 million
2.　Shenzhen, $52,600
3.　Zibo, $300

Source: *The New York Times*, September 16, 1997, p. A18.

★ 2331 ★

LEADING ASIAN STOCK EXCHANGES, 1997

Ranked by: Value of Datastream total market index on April 21, 1997, in millions of U.S. dollars. **Number listed:** 10

1.　Japan with $2,660,829 million
2.　Hong Kong, $365,387
3.　Taiwan, $213,459
4.　Malaysia, $182,083
5.　Singapore, $123,529
6.　China, $83,203
7.　South Korea, $74,388
8.　Indonesia, $71,311
9.　Philippines, $60,911
10.　Thailand, $57,602

Source: *Financial Times*, May 9, 1997, p. 1.

★ 2332 ★

LEADING LATIN AMERICAN STOCK MARKETS, 1996

Ranked by: Returns, in percent change from January 1 through August 20, 1996. **Number listed:** 7

1.　Venezuela with 63.7% returns
2.　Brazil, 43.8%

3.　Mexico, 25.9%
4.　Colombia, 6.4%
5.　Peru, 5.5%
6.　Argentina, - 0.9%
7.　Chile, - 2.9%

Source: *Business Latin America*, September 26, 1996, p. 8.

Stock Exchanges – Europe

★ 2333 ★

TOP STOCK EXCHANGES IN EUROPE, 1996

Ranked by: Total market capitalization, in billions of U.S. dollars. **Remarks:** Also notes number of listings. **Number listed:** 10

1.　London Stock Exchange with $1,723.7 billion
2.　Deutsche Borse, $664.6
3.　Bourse de Paris, $585.2
4.　Amsterdam Exchanges, $452.2
5.　Consiglio di Borsa, $255.8
6.　Stockholms Fondbors, $239.6
7.　Sociedad Rectora de la Bolsa de Valores de Madrid, $204.7
8.　Societe de la Bourse de Valeurs Mobilieres de Bruxelles, $133.8
9.　Kobenhavns Fondbors, $74.2
10.　Helsinki Stock Exchanges, $61.5

Source: *Institutional Investor*, May 1997, p. 25.

Stock Exchanges, International

★ 2334 ★

LEADING STOCK MARKETS BY PRICE TO EARNINGS RATIO

Ranked by: Ratio of price to earnings. **Number listed:** 26

1.　Japan with 85.4
2.　Switzerland, 76.9
3.　Germany, 29.7
4.　Taiwan, 25.2
5.　Milan, 24.6
6.　Canada, 23.5
7.　United States, 23.0
8.　Australia, 21.8
9.　Spain, 21.5
10.　Portugal, 21.4

Source: *Globe and Mail*, August 28, 1997, p. B15.

Stock Market, International

★ 2335 ★
STOCK MARKET CAPITALIZATION, 1995
Ranked by: Capitalization, as a percent of GDP.
Number listed: 8
1. Switzerland with 127%
2. Britain, 122%
3. United States, 90%
4. Japan, 87%
5. Sweden, 70%
6. France, 32%
7. Germany, 24%
8. Italy, 18%

Source: *Financial Times*, October 22, 1996, p. 13.

★ 2336 ★
STOCK MARKET RETURNS, 1986-1996
Ranked by: Average total return for the ten years ending March 31, 1996, in percent. **Number listed:** 10
1. Hong Kong with 25.79% return
2. Singapore, 21.77%
3. Netherlands, 17.55%
4. Sweden, 16.94%
5. Switzerland, 16.20%
6. Belgium, 16.10%
7. Denmark, 13.16%
8. United States, 12.85%
9. United Kingdom, 12.76%
10. Australia, 12.47%

Source: *Newsweek*, May 6, 1996, p. 4.

Stockholm Stock Exchange

★ 2337 ★
LARGEST COMPANIES ON THE STOCKHOLM STOCK EXCHANGE, 1995
Ranked by: Market value, in billions of Swedish krona (Skr). **Number listed:** 20
1. Astra with Skr163.1 billion
2. Ericsson, Skr125.1
3. Volvo, Skr63.1
4. ASEA, Skr58.9
5. Investor, Skr33.9
6. Pharmacia & Upjohn, Skr33.9
7. Sandvik, Skr31.8
8. Svenska Handelsbanken, Skr31.6
9. SE Banken, Skr28.8
10. Skanska, Skr26.6

Source: *GT Guide to World Equity Markets* (annual), Euromoney Publications, 1996, p. 313.

★ 2338 ★
MOST ACTIVELY TRADED SHARES ON THE STOCKHOLM STOCK EXCHANGE, 1995
Ranked by: Trading value, in billions of Swedish krona (Skr). **Number listed:** 20
1. Ericsson with Skr86.7 billion
2. Astra, Skr82.0
3. Volvo, Skr55.1
4. Pharmacia, Skr31.7
5. ASEA, Skr26.8
6. Investor, Skr25.0
7. Electrolux, Skr19.5
8. Mo & Domsjo, Skr18.8
9. Stora Kopparberg, Skr17.8
10. Trelleborg, Skr17.1

Source: *GT Guide to World Equity Markets* (annual), Euromoney Publications, 1996, p. 313.

Stocks

★ 2339 ★
LARGEST PUBLIC COMPANIES WORLDWIDE, 1996
Ranked by: Market value, in millions of U.S. dollars.
Remarks: Also notes profits and sales. **Number listed:** 100
1. General Electric with $136,515 million
2. Royal Dutch/Shell, $128,206
3. Coca-Cola, $117,258
4. NTT, $113,609
5. Exxon, $102,161
6. Bank of Tokyo-Mitsubishi, $98,191
7. Toyota Motor, $91,519
8. Philip Morris, $86,424
9. AT&T, $83,960
10. Merck, $78,163

Source: *The Wall Street Journal*, September 26, 1996, p. R27.

Stocks – Buybacks
See: **Stocks – Repurchase**

Stocks – Repurchase

★ 2340 ★
STOCK BUYBACKS IN EUROPE, 1985-1996
Ranked by: Number of buybacks. **Number listed:** 11
1. United Kingdom with 196 buybacks
2. Italy, 26
3. France, 20
4. Spain, 20

5. Holland, 10
6. Belgium, 7
7. Greece, 7
8. Ireland, 5
9. Germany, 3
10. Switzerland, 2

Source: *The Wall Street Journal*, January 10, 1997, p. A8.

Stores

See: **Clothing Stores; Computer Stores; Convenience Stores; Department Stores**

Strikes

★ 2341 ★
COUNTRIES WITH THE HIGHEST AVERAGE STRIKE RATES, 1990-1994

Ranked by: Days of labor lost per 1,000 workers. **Number listed:** 13

1. Greece with 3,500 days lost
2. Spain, 492
3. Italy, 240
4. Ireland, 135
5. Belgium, 57
6. United States, 43
7. Portugal, 39
8. Denmark, 37
9. United Kingdom, 37
10. France, 30

Source: *The Times*, March 28, 1997, p. 29.

Subsidies

★ 2342 ★
INDIAN OIL PRODUCTS RECEIVING THE MOST SUBSIDIES, 1996-1997

Ranked by: Subsidy, in billions of Indian rupees (Rs). **Number listed:** 5

1. Diesel with Rs83.4 billion
2. Kerosene, Rs63.5
3. Cooking gas, Rs19.5
4. Naphtha, Rs9.8
5. Other, Rs8.2

Source: *Financial Times*, September 3, 1997, p. 10.

Sudan – see under individual headings

Sugar

★ 2343 ★
GLOBAL SUGAR PRODUCTION, 1994-1995

Ranked by: Share of total global production, in percent. **Remarks:** Numbers shown for selected countries express percent of total global production. **Number listed:** 10

1. India with 15.0%
2. Brazil, 11.0%
3. United States, 7.8%
4. China, 6.5%
5. Australia, 5.2%
6. Thailand, 4.9%
7. France, 4.5%
8. Mexico, 4.2%
9. Germany, 4.2%
10. Ukraine, 4.0%

Source: *World Agricultural Production*, December 1994, p. 44.

★ 2344 ★
SUGAR PRODUCTION IN SPAIN

Ranked by: Market share, in percent. **Number listed:** 2

1. Ebro Agricolas Cla. de Alimentacion with 78.0%
2. Other, 22.0%

Source: *The Wall Street Journal*, September 26, 1996, p. A6.

Sun Care Products

★ 2345 ★
LEADING SUN CARE BRANDS IN THE UNITED KINGDOM, 1995

Ranked by: Market share, in percent. **Number listed:** 14

1. Ambre Solaire (L'Oreal) with 22.9%
2. Boots (Boots), 19.4%
3. Nivea (Beiersdorf), 13.9%
4. Piz Buin (Zyma), 7.4%
5. Avon (Avon), 5.6%
6. Hawaiian Tropic (Warner Lambert), 4.0%
7. Uvistat (Windsor Pharmaceuticals), 3.4%
8. Superdrug (Superdrug), 1.8%
9. E45 (Crookes), 1.7%
10. Bergasol (Chefarol), 1.5%

Source: *The Observer*, June 8, 1997, p. B10.

★ 2346 ★
TOP SUN TAN LOTIONS IN GERMANY, 1995

Ranked by: Market share, in percent. **Remarks:** Includes market share for 1993-94. **Number listed:** 6

1. Nivea Sun with 21.3%
2. Ambre Solaire, 20.1%

3. Delial, 14.7%
4. Piz Buin, 7.5%
5. Zeozon, 4.2%
6. Ellen Betrix, 4.4%

Source: *Nordamerikanische Wochen-Post*, August 17, 1996, p. 9.

Sunscreens
See: **Sun Care Products**

Suntan Lotion
See: **Sun Care Products**

Supermarkets
See Also: **Convenience Stores; Grocery Trade**

★ 2347 ★
LEADING ARGENTINE SUPERMARKETS, 1996
Ranked by: Sales for the first six months of 1996, in millions of U.S. dollars. **Number listed:** 6
1. Carrefour with $1,692 million
2. Norte, $879
3. Coto, $871
4. Disco, $804
5. Tia, $698
6. Jumbo, $657

Source: *Business Latin America*, February 10, 1997, p. 3.

Supermarkets – Europe

★ 2348 ★
TOP SUPERMARKET OPERATORS IN EUROPE
Ranked by: Turnover, in billions of U.S. dollars. **Remarks:** Includes figures on net income and market capitalization. **Number listed:** 10
1. Carrefour with $27.82 billion
2. Promodes, $19.24
3. Karstadt, $17.51
4. Asko, $17.38
5. J. Sainsbury, $17.15
6. Ahold, $16.86
7. Tesco, $15.25
8. Pinault Printemps, $14.97
9. Kauphof, $13.81
10. Casino, $12.33

Source: *Financial Times*, June 17, 1996, p. 25.

Supermarkets – United Kingdom

★ 2349 ★
BRITAIN'S LEADING SUPERMARKETS
Ranked by: Market share, in percent. **Number listed:** 13
1. Tesco with 15.3%
2. J. Sainsbury, 11.8%
3. Asda, 7.8%
4. Safeway, 7.8%
5. Co-op (food), 5.8%
6. Kwik Save, 4.0%
7. Somerfield, 3.6%
8. Marks & Spencer, 3.2%
9. Morrisons, 2.7%
10. Iceland, 1.7%

Source: *The Guardian*, January 27, 1997, p. 14.

Suriname – see under individual headings

Swaziland – see under individual headings

Sweden – see under individual headings

Switzerland – see under individual headings

Syria – see under individual headings

Taiwan – see under individual headings

Taiwan Stock Exchange

★ 2350 ★
LARGEST COMPANIES ON THE TAIWAN STOCK EXCHANGE, 1995
Ranked by: Market value, in billions of New Taiwan dollars (NT$). **Number listed:** 20
1. Cathay Life Insurance Company with NT$331.46 billion
2. Hua Nan Commercial Bank, NT$183.50
3. First Commercial Bank, NT$181.54
4. Chang Hwa Commercial Bank, NT$162.71

5. China Steel Corporation, NT$157.73
6. TSMC Co. Ltd., NT$122.32
7. International Commercial Bank of China, NT$120.16
8. China Development Corporation, NT$107.73
9. Shin Kong Life Insurance Company, NT$102.58
10. Nan Ya Plastics Corporation, NT$100.88

Source: *GT Guide to World Equity Markets* (annual), Euromoney Publications, 1996, p. 329.

★ 2351 ★

MOST ACTIVELY TRADED SHARES ON THE TAIWAN STOCK EXCHANGE, 1995

Ranked by: Trading volume, in millions of shares. **Number listed:** 20

1. Hualon Corporation with 10,091 million shares
2. China Steel Corporation, 8,208
3. Shin Kong Synthetic Fiber, 6,821
4. China Petrochemical, 4,449
5. Chung Shing Textile Company, 4,267
6. Walsin Lihwa Electric Wire and Cable, 4,094
7. Grand Pacific Petrochemical, 4,001
8. International Bills Finance Group, 3,983
9. Yang Ming Marine Transport Corporation, 3,315
10. Chinatrust Commercial Bank, 3,154

Source: *GT Guide to World Equity Markets* (annual), Euromoney Publications, 1996, p. 329.

Talc

★ 2352 ★

LEADING TALCUM POWDER BRANDS IN INDIA

Ranked by: Market share, in percent. **Number listed:** 7

1. Ponds with 65.0%
2. Cinthol, 4.0%
3. Liril, 4.0%
4. Lakme, 3.0%
5. Gokul Santol, 3.0%
6. Heaven's Gardens, 1.0%
7. Other, 20.0%

Source: *Business Today*, September 7, 1996, p. 166.

Tanzania – see under individual headings

Taxation

★ 2353 ★

COUNTRIES WITH THE HIGHEST TAXES AS A PERCENT OF GDP, 1993

Ranked by: Tax revenue, as a percent of gross domestic product. **Number listed:** 25

1. Denmark with 49.9%
2. Sweden, 49.9%
3. Netherlands, 48.0%
4. Belgium, 45.7%
5. Finland, 45.7%
6. Norway, 45.7%
7. Luxembourg, 44.6%
8. France, 43.9%
9. Italy, 43.8%
10. Austria, 43.6%

Source: *Government Finance Review*, October 1996, p. 5.

★ 2354 ★

RUSSIA'S LARGEST TAX DEBTORS, 1997

Ranked by: Tax debt as of January 1, 1997, in millions of U.S. dollars. **Number listed:** 7

1. Avtovaz with $504.1 million
2. Noyabrskneftegaz, $252.1
3. Nizhevartovskneftegaz, $198.1
4. Uraltransgaz, $180.0
5. Norilskgazprom, $144.0
6. Volgotransgaz, $144.0
7. Orenburgneft, $126.0

Source: *The New York Times*, February 19, 1997, p. A6.

★ 2355 ★

TOP TAX PAYERS IN INDIA, 1995-1996

Ranked by: Income tax paid for the assessment year 1995-1996, in rupees crore (RCr). **Number listed:** 10

1. State Bank of India, Mumbai with RCr962.97
2. MTNL, RCr458.94
3. Life Insurance Corporation of India, RCr456.81
4. Indian Oil Corporation Ltd., RCr351.39
5. Hindustan Petroleum Corporation, RCr201.00
6. IDBI, RCr198.20
7. CITI Bank Ltd., RCr170.52
8. Bharat Petroleum Corporation, RCr169.59
9. RCF, RCr156.29
10. ITC Ltd., RCr136.00

Source: *The Hindustan Times*, May 3, 1997, p. 15.

Telecommunications

★ 2356 ★
FRANCE'S MICRO-INFORMATION EQUIPMENT SALES
Ranked by: Sales, in thousands of units. **Number listed:** 4
1. Micro-ordinators with 2,350 thousand units
2. Monitors, 2,100
3. Imprinters, 1,750
4. Scanners, 250

Source: *Le Figaro*, January 23, 1997, p. C5.

★ 2357 ★
LARGEST TELECOMMUNICATIONS COMPANIES, 1995
Ranked by: Revenue, in millions of U.S. dollars. **Remarks:** Notes profits and global rank. **Number listed:** 22
1. Nippon Tel. & Tel. (Japan) with $81,937 million
2. AT&T (United States), $79,609
3. Deutsche Telekom (Germany), $46,149
4. IRI (Italy), $41,903
5. France Telecom (France), $30,060
6. BT (United Kingdom), $22,612
7. GTE (United States), $19,957
8. BellSouth (United States), $17,886
9. MCI Communications (United States), $15,265
10. L.M. Ericsson (Sweden), $13,961

Source: *Fortune,* The Global 500: World's Biggest Corporations (annual), August 5, 1996, p. F-25.

★ 2358 ★
TOP TELECOMMUNICATIONS COMPANIES IN JAPAN
Ranked by: Income, in millions of yen (¥). **Number listed:** 10
1. Nippon Telegraph & Telephone with ¥123,613 million
2. Kokusai Denshin Denwa, ¥29,532
3. DDI, ¥24,008
4. Kansai Cellular Telephone, ¥19,375
5. Japan Telecom, ¥17,502
6. NTT Kansai Mobile Comm. Network, ¥10,628
7. NTT Tokai Mobile Comm. Network, ¥10,368
8. NTT Mobile Comm. Network, ¥6,988
9. Kyushu Cellular Telephone, ¥6,420
10. Chugoku Cellular Telephone, ¥3,104

Source: *Tokyo Business Today*, August 1995, p. 26.

★ 2359 ★
WORLDWIDE SMART CARD MARKET BY SEGMENT, 2000
Ranked by: Market share, in percent. **Remarks:** An estimated 3.8 billion cards are estimated to be in circulation by the year 2000. GSM stands for Global System for Mobile telephones, an industry standard for digital mobile telephones. **Number listed:** 9
1. Phonecard with 36.84%
2. Bank and loyalty, 13.16%
3. Health, 10.53%
4. Identity, 10.53%
5. Access control/vending, 5.26%
6. Transportation, 5.26%
7. Pay-TV, 2.63%
8. GSM, 1.47%
9. Other, 14.32%

Source: *World of Banking*, Spring 1996, p. 21.

Telecommunications – Asia

★ 2360 ★
MOST ADMIRED TELECOMMUNICATIONS AND MEDIA FIRMS IN ASIA, 1997
Ranked by: Results of a questionnaire sent to more than 9,000 managers and CEOs chosen from the magazine's circulation and evaluated by Asia Market Intelligence, a research firm. **Remarks:** Respondents scored each company in terms of overall admirability, then on six attributes: quality of products, quality of management, contribution to local economy, record as an employer, growth potential and reputation for ethics. Also notes 1996 figures. **Number listed:** 10
1. Hongkong Telecom with 8.07
2. AT&T (Telecom), 7.81
3. Indosat, 7.79
4. Singapore Telecom, 7.78
5. ABS-CBN, 7.45
6. Dacom, 7.13
7. Post Publishing, 7.10
8. NTT Corporation, 6.46
9. Globe Telecom, 6.34
10. Telekom Malaysia, 6.20

Source: *Asian Business,* Most Admired Companies in Asia (annual), May 1997, p. 30.

Telecommunications – Equipment

★ 2361 ★
FRAME RELAY ACCESS DEVICE MARKET, 1995
Ranked by: Market share based on revenue, in percent.
Number listed: 7
1. Motorola with 18.7%
2. Cisco, 14.5%
3. Ascom Timeplex, 14.3%
4. Act Networks, 12.8%
5. Sync Research, 7.8%
6. Hypercom, 6.2%
7. Others, 25.7%

Source: *Computerworld*, August 12, 1996, p. 20.

★ 2362 ★
LEADING ISDN OPERATORS WORLDWIDE
Ranked by: Market penetration, in percent. National markets are shown in parentheses. **Number listed:** 13
1. Deutsche Telkom (Germany) with 4.93%
2. France Telecom (France), 4.75%
3. Swiss Telecom (Switzerland), 2.79%
4. Enterprise des P&T (Luxembourg), 1.59%
5. PTT Telecom (Netherlands), 1.28%
6. NTT (Japan), 1.16%
7. Telekom Austria (Austria), 0.95%
8. Belgacom (Belgium), 0.93%
9. British Telecom (United Kingdom), 0.63%
10. Portugal Telecom (Portugal), 0.62%

Source: *Electronic Business Today*, February 1997, p. 22.

★ 2363 ★
LEADING MOBILE EQUIPMENT SUPPLIERS IN EUROPE
Ranked by: Market share, in percent. **Number listed:** 10
1. Nokia with 22.8%
2. Motorola, 22.1%
3. Ericsson, 21.3%
4. Alcatel, 6.4%
5. Siemens, 4.7%
6. Philips, 4.1%
7. Italtel, 2.7%
8. NEC, 2.7%
9. Nortel Matra, 2.7%
10. Matsushita, 2.6%

Source: *The World in 1997*, 1997, p. 95.

Telecommunications, International

★ 2364 ★
INTERNATIONAL TELECOMMUNICATIONS ROUTES AMONG DEVELOPING COUNTRIES, 1994
Ranked by: Incoming and outgoing traffic, in millions of minutes. **Number listed:** 10
1. Hong Kong/China with 1,528.00 million minutes
2. Ukraine/Russia, 753.12
3. Singapore/Malaysia, 349.80
4. Taiwan-China/China, 204.68
5. Hong Kong/Taiwan-China, 151.61
6. Saudi Arabia/Egypt, 147.78
7. United Arab Emirates/India, 116.01
8. Hong Kong/Singapore, 97.00
9. India/Saudi Arabia, 95.45
10. Hong Kong/Macao, 90.67

Source: *Financial Times*, September 19, 1996, p. XXII.

★ 2365 ★
TOP INTERNATIONAL TELECOMMUNICATIONS ROUTES, 1994
Ranked by: Incoming and outgoing traffic on international telecommunications routes, in millions of minutes. **Number listed:** 10
1. United States/Canada with 4,582.28 million minutes
2. United States/Mexico, 2,401.44
3. Hong Kong/China, 1,528.00
4. United States/United Kingdom, 1,488.36
5. United States/Germany, 901.29
6. United States/Japan, 764.26
7. Switzerland/Germany, 755.16
8. Ukraine/Russia, 753.12
9. Germany/Austria, 733.60
10. Germany/France, 670.69

Source: *Financial Times*, September 19, 1996, p. XXII.

★ 2366 ★
TOP NATIONS BY TELECOM REVENUE, 1995
Ranked by: Service revenue per inhabitant for the top 10 economies, in U.S. dollars. **Number listed:** 10
1. Switzerland with $1,262.7
2. Singapore, $816.6
3. United States, $749.6
4. Norway, $719.9
5. Denmark, $713.4
6. Hong Kong, $704.5
7. Sweden, $651.9
8. Australia, $635.6
9. Japan, $588.1
10. Germany, $563.7

Source: *Financial Times*, September 19, 1996, p. XXII.

Telecommunications – United Kingdom

★ 2367 ★
TOP MOBILE PHONE NETWORKS IN THE UNITED KINGDOM, 1996
Ranked by: Subscribers at the end of 1996. **Number listed:** 4
1. Vodafone with 2,800,000 subscribers
2. Cellnet, 2,680,000
3. Orange, 785,000
4. One 2 One, 545,000
Source: *The Guardian*, January 7, 1997, p. 15.

Telemarketing

★ 2368 ★
TOP TELEMARKETING FIRMS IN JAPAN, 1995
Ranked by: Sales, in millions of U.S. dollars. **Number listed:** 20
1. Bell System 24 with $191 million
2. NTT Telemarketing, $157
3. Moshi Moshi Hotline, $153
4. Telemarketing Japan, $59
5. Densan, $38
6. Office Japan, $24
7. NTT Telephone Assist, $24
8. NTT Telemate, $23
9. Nihon Telecommax, $18
10. Nihon Telecomedia, $17
Source: *National Trade Data Bank*, December 3, 1996, p. IMI961201.

Telemarketing – United Kingdom

★ 2369 ★
TOP TELEMARKETERS IN THE UNITED KINGDOM BY INBOUND, 1996
Ranked by: Personal answering, in thousands of British pounds (£). **Number listed:** 30
1. Sitel Europe with £30,484 thousand
2. Merchants Group, £8,195
3. McIntyre & King, £7,853
4. Brann (Contact), £6,286
5. Subscription Services Ltd. (SSL), £5,861
6. Teledata, £4,208
7. InTelMark, £3,100
8. Mailcom, £2,586
9. ADS Telemarketing, £2,556
10. ABC Promotional Mktg. Services, £2,357
Source: *Marketing*, April 10, 1997, p. X.

★ 2370 ★
TOP TELEMARKETERS IN THE UNITED KINGDOM BY OUTBOUND, 1996
Ranked by: Outbound, in thousands of British pounds (£). **Number listed:** 25
1. Sitel Europe with £11,954 thousand
2. ADS Telemarketing, £2,840
3. Teledynamics, £2,430
4. Merchants Group, £1,875
5. InTelMark, £1,860
6. BPS Teleperformance, £1,769
7. Brann (Contact), £1,620
8. Procter & Procter - Protel, £1,246
9. Direct Dialog, £1,061
10. Teledata, £1,052
Source: *Marketing*, April 10, 1997, p. XII.

★ 2371 ★
TOP TELEMARKETERS IN THE UNITED KINGDOM, 1996
Ranked by: Turnover, in thousands of British pounds (£). **Remarks:** Also notes pre-tax profits, number of staff, and maximum lines. **Number listed:** 44
1. Sitel Europe with £59,772 thousand
2. Merchants Group, £18,754
3. Broadsystem, £15,225
4. IMS Group, £12,434
5. McIntyre & King, £11,448
6. Brann (Contact), £10,800
7. Teledata, £9,811
8. Subscription Services Ltd., £7,400
9. Mailcom, £7,389
10. ADS Telemarketing, £7,100
Source: *Marketing*, April 10, 1997, p. VII.

Telephone Calls

★ 2372 ★
INTERNATIONAL TELEPHONE TRAFFIC, 1995
Ranked by: Outgoing international telephone traffic, in millions of minutes. **Number listed:** 10
1. United States with 15,110 million minutes
2. Germany, 5,244
3. United Kingdom, 4,111
4. Canada, 2,870
5. France, 2,630
6. Italy, 1,908
7. Switzerland, 1,739
8. Hong Kong, 1,692
9. Japan, 1,599
10. Netherlands, 1,459
Source: *Financial Times*, September 19, 1996, p. XXII.

★ 2373 ★

MOST-EXPENSIVE PLACES TO CALL FROM THE UNITED STATES

Ranked by: Average charge for a phone call from the United States, in U.S. dollars per minute. **Remarks:** Notes millions of minutes of phone calls from the U.S. **Number listed:** 10

1. Cape Verde with $5.64 per minute
2. Mongolia, $3.94
3. Myanmar, $3.38
4. Laos, $3.36
5. Sao Tome and Principe, $3.31
6. Georgia, $3.22
7. Nauru, $2.97
8. Bhutan, $2.83
9. Vanuatu, $2.70
10. Chad, $2.57

Source: *The New York Times*, February 17, 1997, p. 30.

★ 2374 ★

TOP COUNTRIES FOR PHONE CALLS FROM THE UNITED STATES

Ranked by: Phone calls, in millions of minutes, from the U.S. **Remarks:** Notes average charge per minute. **Number listed:** 20

1. Canada with 3,049.37 million minutes
2. Mexico, 2,012.28
3. Britain, 1,025.04
4. Germany, 662.21
5. Japan, 576.25
6. Dominican Republic, 410.48
7. France, 363.83
8. South Korea, 319.30
9. Hong Kong, 316.81
10. Philippines, 296.71

Source: *The New York Times*, February 17, 1997, p. 30.

Telephone Companies

★ 2375 ★

LARGEST PHONE COMPANIES IN THE PHILIPPINES

Ranked by: Thousands of telephones in service. **Remarks:** There are 1.41 million phones in service in the Philippines, a ratio of 2.2 telephones to every 10 Filipinos. **Number listed:** 5

1. PLDT with 1,220.0 thousand phones
2. Digitel, 45.0
3. Piltel, 42.0
4. Cruztelco, 26.1
5. Other, 76.6

Source: *Manila Chronicle*, August 19, 1996, p. 20.

★ 2376 ★

PHONE COMPANY STOCK OFFERINGS, 1995-1996

Ranked by: International stock offerings by phone companies, in millions of U.S. dollars. **Number listed:** 10

1. Deutsche Telekom (Germany) with $10,000 million
2. STET (Italy), $8,000
3. KPN (Netherlands), $4,000
4. Turk Telekom (Turkey), $3,000
5. PT Telkom (Indonesia), $2,500
6. Telstra (Australia), $2,000
7. Telefonica (Spain), $1,500
8. TOT (Thailand), $1,000
8. Korea Telecom (Korea), $1,000
8. Telebras (Brazil), $1,000

Source: *The Wall Street Journal*, October 2, 1995, p. A10.

★ 2377 ★

TOP INTERNATIONAL CARRIERS, 1995

Ranked by: Millions of minutes of outgoing public voice traffic. **Remarks:** Includes 1994 figures and percent increase in traffic from 1994 to 1995. **Number listed:** 10

1. AT&T with 8,482 million minutes
2. Deutsche Telekom, 5,244
3. MCI, 4,452
4. BT, 2,909
5. France Telecom, 2,805
6. Telecom Italia, 1,908
7. Swiss PTT, 1,778
8. Sprint, 1,765
9. Hong Kong Telecom, 1,692
10. Stentor, 1,457

Source: *Network World*, November 25, 1996, p. 41.

★ 2378 ★

TOP PHONE COMPANIES, 1994

Ranked by: Revenue, in billions of U.S. dollars. **Number listed:** 10

1. NTT with $71.2 billion
2. AT&T, $50.2
3. Deutsche Telekom, $37.7
4. France Telecom, $25.7
5. British Telecom, $21.6
6. Telecom Italia, $18.0
7. BellSouth, $16.8
8. GTE, $15.9
9. Bell Atlantic, $13.8
10. MCI, $13.3

Source: *Advertising Age International*, January 15, 1996, p. 122.

★ 2379 ★

TOP TELEPHONE COMPANIES IN MEXICO

Ranked by: Market share, in percent. **Number listed:** 4

1. Telmex with 74.2%
2. Alestra, 14.3%

3. Avantel, 10.7%
4. Others, 0.7%
Source: *Financial Times*, August 19, 1997, p. 4.

★ 2380 ★
TOP TELEPHONE COMPANIES WORLDWIDE
Ranked by: Turnover, in millions of U.S. dollars.
Number listed: 10
1. NTT (Japan) with $84.0 million
2. AT&T (United States), $47.2
3. Deutsche Telekom (Germany), $46.1
4. France Telecom (France), $29.6
5. British Telecom (United Kingdom), $22.7
6. Telecom Italia (Italy), $18.4
7. Bell South (United States), $17.9
8. GTE (United States), $17.3
9. MCI (United States), $15.2
10. Sprint (United States), $13.5
Source: *L'Express*, April 24, 1997, p. 76.

Telephone Companies – Canada

★ 2381 ★
CANADA'S TELEPHONE FIRMS
Ranked by: Revenue, in thousands of Canadian dollars.
Remarks: Includes figures on profits and return on capital. **Number listed:** 10
1. BCE Inc. with C$24,968,000 thousand
2. Bell Canada, C$8,183,400
3. Anglo-Canadian Telephone, C$2,717,600
4. BC Telephone, C$2,453,500
5. BC Tel, C$1,999,000
6. Telus Corp., C$1,715,469
7. Sask. Telecommunications, C$774,911
8. Maritime Tel. and Tel. Company, C$572,809
9. Manitoba Telephone System, C$551,264
10. Maritime Tel & Tel, C$462,637
Source: *Globe and Mail's Report on Business Magazine*, July 1996, p. 159.

Telephone Equipment Industry

★ 2382 ★
TELEPHONE SWITCH MARKET IN EGYPT
Ranked by: Market share, in percent. **Number listed:** 6
1. Alcatel with 25%
2. Siemens, 20%
3. AT&T, 20%
4. Ericsson, 16%
5. Siemens/Arento, 6%

6. Others, 11%
Source: *National Trade Data Bank*, March 2, 1996, p. IMI950725.

Telephone Lines, International

★ 2383 ★
LEADING NATIONS FOR TELEPHONE LINES, 1995
Ranked by: Penetration of main telephone lines, in percent. **Number listed:** 10
1. Sweden with 68.11 per 100 inhabitants
2. United States, 62.71
3. Switzerland, 61.34
4. Denmark, 61.29
5. Canada, 59.24
6. Norway, 55.85
7. France, 55.80
8. Finland, 54.93
9. Hong Kong, 52.79
10. Netherlands, 52.52
Source: *Financial Times*, September 19, 1996, p. XXII.

★ 2384 ★
TELEPHONE LINES IN SERVICE IN LATIN AMERICA, 1996
Ranked by: Number of lines in service, in millions. **Number listed:** 7
1. Brazil with 14.3 million lines
2. Mexico, 9.4
3. Argentina, 6.3
4. Colombia, 4.5
5. Venezuela, 2.7
6. Chile, 2.1
7. Peru, 1.4
Source: *Latin Trade*, October 1996, p. 50.

Television Advertising

★ 2385 ★
RUSSIA'S LARGEST TV ADVERTISERS
Ranked by: Expenditures on TV airtime for May 1996, in millions of U.S. dollars. **Number listed:** 10
1. Procter & Gamble with $6.592 million
2. Mars-Russia, $2.641
3. Stimorol, $1.795
4. Wrigley, $1.343
5. Nestle, $1.322
6. Ferrero, $1.222
7. Unilever, $1.209
8. Polaroid, $1.065
9. Samsung Electronics, $1.043

10.   C Pro, $1.040

Source: *National Trade Data Bank*, August 26, 1996, p. IMI960805.

Television Advertising – Canada

★ **2386** ★

TOP CANADIAN SPECIALTY TELEVISION SERVICES BY AD REVENUE, 1996

Ranked by: Ad revenue, in millions of Canadian dollars. **Remarks:** Also notes figures for 1994 and 1995. **Number listed:** 18

1.   Sports Network (TSN) with C$41.25 million
2.   YTV, C$23.54
3.   MuchMusic, C$15.42
4.   CBC Newsworld, C$10.95
5.   Fairchild Television, C$8.45
6.   MusiquePlus, C$7.72
7.   Reseau des Sports (RDS), C$7.61
8.   Discovery Channel, C$7.15
9.   Life Network, C$5.19
10.   Country Music Television Canada, C$3.88

Source: *Marketing*, May 12, 1997, p. 25.

Television Broadcasting

★ **2387** ★

LARGEST BROADCASTERS IN CANADA

Ranked by: Revenue, in thousands of Canadian dollars. **Remarks:** Includes profits and return on capital. **Number listed:** 11

1.   Rogers Communications with C$2,576,596 thousand
2.   Groupe Videotron, C$817,954
3.   Shaw Communications, C$442,338
4.   WIC Western Int'l. Commun., C$423,511
5.   Canadian Broadcasting Corp., C$411,232
6.   CanWest Global Communications, C$339,353
7.   Baton Broadcasting, C$262,412
8.   Standard Broadcasting Corp., C$239,560
9.   CHUM Ltd., C$221,251
10.   CFCF Inc., C$220,035

Source: *Globe and Mail's Report on Business Magazine*, July 1996, p. 164.

★ **2388** ★

TOP TELEVISION BROADCASTING GROUPS IN CANADA, 1996

Ranked by: Market share, in percent. **Remarks:** Figures are based on a spring 1996 survey of 445,425,000 hours tuned in by viewers. **Number listed:** 11

1.   CTV with 27.3%

2.   TVA, 15.6%
3.   CBC, 12.8%
4.   SRC, 10.4%
5.   BBS, 9.7%
6.   Global, 7.0%
7.   TQS, 5.3%
8.   BCTV, 4.6%
9.   ATV, 2.5%
10.   Tele-Quebec, 1.1%

Source: *Marketing Magazine*, May 26, 1997, p. 16.

Television Programs

★ **2389** ★

NATIONS WITH QUALITY TV PROGRAMS

Ranked by: Adult consumers worldwide who ranked country as having the best television programming, in percent. **Number listed:** 6

1.   United States with 32.0%
2.   China, 7.0%
3.   India, 6.0%
4.   Japan, 5.0%
5.   United Kingdom, 5.0%
6.   Other, 45.0%

Source: *The Journal of Commerce*, October 24, 1995, p. 1.

★ **2390** ★

TOP U.S. SHOWS OVERSEAS, 1996

Ranked by: Viewers from March to August, 1996, in millions. **Remarks:** Data include 21 countries. Notes distributor for each show. **Number listed:** 10

1.   Renegade with 24 million viewers
2.   X-Files, 23
3.   Dr. Quinn, 21
4.   Beverly Hills 90210, 20
5.   ER, 18
6.   Lois & Clark, 17
7.   Columbo, 14
8.   Cosby Show, 9
9.   Walker, Texas Ranger, 9
10.   The Bold & The Beautiful, 8

Source: *Fortune*, November 25, 1996, p. 42.

Television Receivers

★ 2391 ★
ASIA'S TOP TV SET MAKERS, 1997
Ranked by: Output, in millions of units. **Remarks:** Includes 1996 output figures. Companies shown are located in Japan, except for Samsung, which is in South Korea, and Tatung, which is in Taiwan. **Number listed:** 8
1. Sony with 1.6 million units
2. Matsushita, 1.3
3. Samsung, 0.7
4. Toshiba, 0.8
5. JVC, 0.4
6. Mitsubishi, 0.4
7. Hitachi, 0.3
8. Tatung, 0.3

Source: *Financial Times*, April 16, 1997, p. 11.

★ 2392 ★
TOP TV BRANDS IN JAPAN, 1996
Ranked by: Market share as of September 1996, in percent. **Remarks:** Data are based on sales in large department stores in 35 major cities. **Number listed:** 5
1. Changhong with 22.6%
2. Konka, 18.1%
3. Matsushita, 9.6%
4. Beijing, 7.5%
5. TCL, 7.0%

Source: *South China Morning Post*, February 13, 1997, p. B7.

★ 2393 ★
TOP TV MAKERS IN GERMANY
Ranked by: Market share, in percent. **Number listed:** 12
1. Grundig with 18.5%
2. Philips, 14.0%
3. Sony, 10.2%
4. Loewe, 9.4%
5. Telefunken, 7.9%
6. Panasonic, 4.9%
7. Metz, 4.6%
8. Nokia, 4.5%
9. Nordmende, 3.8%
10. Blaupunkt, 3.6%

Source: *Wirtschaftswoche*, June 13, 1996, p. 68.

★ 2394 ★
TOP TV MAKERS IN JAPAN
Ranked by: Market share, in percent. **Number listed:** 5
1. Matsushita Electric Industrial with 16.3%
2. Sharp, 11.0%
3. Toshiba, 11.9%
4. Sanyo Electric, 8.7%
5. Others, 39.5%

Source: *Nikkei Weekly*, July 22, 1996, p. 8.

★ 2395 ★
TOP TV MAKERS IN RUSSIA BY REVENUES, 1996
Ranked by: Market share based on revenue, in percent.
Number listed: 4
1. Philips with 18.5%
2. Sony, 18.5%
3. Samsung, 16.4%
4. Other, 46.6%

Source: *The Russian*, May 1997, p. 44.

Television Sets
See: **Television Receivers**

Temporary Help Service Agencies

★ 2396 ★
LEADING TEMPORARY SERVICES COMPANIES IN FRANCE
Ranked by: No specific criteria provided. **Number listed:** 7
1. Adecco
2. Manpower
3. Vedior-Bis
4. Synergie
5. Olsten/Sogica
6. Randstad
7. Kelly

Source: *National Trade Data Bank*, July 7, 1997, p. ISA970601.

Tennessee − see under individual headings

Texas − see under individual headings

Textile Industry

★ 2397 ★
BELGIUM'S TECHNICAL TEXTILES MARKET
Ranked by: Market share, in percent. **Number listed:** 9
1. Industrial applications with 17.0%
2. Medical and healthcare, 16.0%
3. Vehicles, 16.0%
4. Transport and packing, 15.0%
5. Building and light structures, 11.0%
6. Geo-textiles, 7.0%
7. Protection and safety, 7.0%

8. Public sector, 5.0%
9. Agriculture, 4.0%
Source: *National Trade Data Bank*, January 14, 1997, p. ISA961201.

★ **2398** ★
HOURLY LABOR COSTS FOR TEXTILE MANUFACTURING IN SELECT COUNTRIES, 1996
Ranked by: Hourly cost of labor, in U.S. dollars.
Remarks: Data include benefits. **Number listed:** 17
1. Japan with $24.31
2. Australia, $13.91
3. New Zealand, $8.00
4. Taiwan, $6.38
5. South Korea, $5.65
6. Hong Kong, $4.90
7. Singapore, $4.78
8. Malaysia, $2.52
9. Thailand, $1.56
10. Philippines, $0.91
Source: *Textile World*, August 1997, p. 96.

★ **2399** ★
LEADING TEXTILE & APPAREL PRODUCERS IN SOUTH KOREA, 1996
Ranked by: Sales for the first six months of 1996, in hundred million won (W). **Remarks:** Also notes net profits. **Number listed:** 61
1. Tong Yang Nylon with W5,426.7 hundred million
2. Tae Kwang Ind., W5,284.0
3. Kolon Ind., W4,586.1
4. Cheil Ind., W4,342.0
5. Kohap, W4,003.9
6. Cheil Synthetics, W3,809.7
7. Sunkyong Ind., W3,525.3
8. Tongkook, W2,544.8
9. Shin Won, W2,411.2
10. Daehan Synthetic Fiber, W2,329.2
Source: *Business Korea*, October 1996, p. 31.

★ **2400** ★
TOP TEXTILE EMPLOYERS IN FRANCE
Ranked by: Employees by region. **Remarks:** Includes data on the textile export market in Europe. Notes sales of textile equipment in Europe. **Number listed:** 10
1. Nord-Pas-de-Calais with 50,000 employees
2. Rhone River Valley, 46,000
3. Paris Area, 40,000
4. Loire River Valley, 19,000
5. Champagne, 14,000
6. Mediterranean & SW, 13,000
7. Alsace, 12,000
8. Centre, 12,000
9. Lorraine, 12,000

10. Picardy, 11,000
Source: *http:// www.textile.fr/extern_a.htm*, February 10, 1997, p. 1.

Textile Industry – Asia

★ **2401** ★
LARGEST TEXTILE, CLOTHING, AND FOOTWEAR COMPANIES IN ASIA
Ranked by: Sales, in thousands of U.S. dollars. **Remarks:** Also notes profit as a percent of sales. **Number listed:** 100
1. Toyobo Co. Ltd. with $4,477,165 thousand
2. Unitika Ltd., $3,329,776
3. Daiwabo Co. Ltd., $2,375,368
4. Nisshinbo Industries Inc., $2,104,087
5. Onward Kashiyama Co. Ltd., $1,971,038
6. Gunze Ltd., $1,924,116
7. World Co. Ltd., $1,816,864
8. Nitto Boseki Co. Ltd., $1,485,038
9. Formosa Chemicals & Fibre Corporation, $1,481,731
10. Kurabo Industries Co. Ltd., $1,445,291
Source: *Asia's 7,500 Largest Companies* (annual), Dun & Bradstreet, 1997, p. 81+.

Textile Industry – Europe

★ **2402** ★
TOP TEXTILE MILL PRODUCTS COMPANIES IN EUROPE
Ranked by: Sales, in millions of European Currency Units (ECUs). **Remarks:** Also notes the number of employees. **Number listed:** 121
1. Coats Viyella Plc with 2,621 million ECUs
2. DuPont de Nemours G.m.b.H., 1,359
3. Coats Patons Plc, 1,349
4. Tootal Group Plc, 905
5. DLW A.G., 693
6. Courtaulds Textiles (Holdings) Ltd., 679
7. Koninklijke Ten Cate NV, 630
8. Ten Cate Nederland BV, 630
9. Gamma Holding NV, 606
10. Manifatture Lane Gaetano Marzotto & Figli S.P.A., 554
Source: *Duns Europa* (annual), vol. 4, Dun & Bradstreet, 1997, p. 216+.

Textile Industry – Export-Import Trade

★ 2403 ★
TOP DESTINATIONS FOR ITALY'S TEXTILE MACHINERY EXPORTS
Ranked by: Textile machinery exports, in millions of U.S. dollars. **Number listed:** 10
1. China with $337 million
2. Turkey, $230
3. United States, $194
4. Germany, $118
5. France, $110
6. Brazil, $104
7. India, $93
8. Switzerland, $81
9. South Korea, $78
10. Taiwan, $72

Source: *Textile World*, January 1997, p. 41.

Thailand – see under individual headings

Thailand Stock Exchange
See: **Securities Exchange of Thailand**

Thrift Institutions

★ 2404 ★
LARGEST SAVINGS INSTITUTIONS, 1995
Ranked by: Revenue, in millions of U.S. dollars.
Remarks: Notes profits and global rank. **Number listed:** 3
1. Groupe des Caisses (France) with $15,852 million
2. Abbey National (United Kingdom), $11,073
3. Halifax Building Society (United Kingdom), $10,991

Source: *Fortune,* The Global 500: World's Biggest Corporations (annual), August 5, 1996, p. F-24.

Tiles

★ 2405 ★
FIBER CEMENT TILE MARKET IN THAILAND
Ranked by: Market share, in percent. **Number listed:** 4
1. Siam Fibre Cement with 55.0%
2. Mahaphant, 20.0%
3. Oran Vanich, 16.0%
4. Siam City Cement, 9.0%

Source: *Bangkok Post*, May 31, 1996, p. 26.

Tire Industry

★ 2406 ★
BEST-SELLING TIRES WORLDWIDE, 1995
Ranked by: Global sales, in billions of U.S. dollars. **Number listed:** 10
1. Michelin with $9,500 billion
2. Goodyear, $8,900
3. Bridgestone, $8,500
4. Dunlop, $4,600
5. Firestone, $4,400
6. Yokohama, $2,800
7. Pirelli, $2,250
8. Continental, $1,870
9. General, $1,329
10. Toyo, $1,300

Source: *Tire Business*, December 9, 1996, p. 15.

★ 2407 ★
LARGEST TIRE BRANDS BY BRAND VALUE
Ranked by: Brand value, in millions of U.S. dollars.
Remarks: Value was calculated using capital, ratio of capital to company sales, earnings, and corporate tax rate of the country where the parent company is located. See source for details. **Number listed:** 7
1. Michelin (Michelin) with $5,348 million
2. Goodyear (Goodyear Tire & Rubber), $5,313
3. Bridgestone (Bridgestone), $4,488
4. Firestone (Bridgestone), $2,498
5. Pirelli (Pirelli), $490
6. Cooper (Cooper Tire & Rubber), $374
7. Continental (Continental), $280

Source: *Financial World,* World's Most Valuable Brands (annual), July 8, 1996, p. 64.

★ 2408 ★
LARGEST TIRE MAKERS IN SOUTH AFRICA, 1996
Ranked by: Employees. **Number listed:** 4
1. Firestone S.A. Pty. Ltd. with 2,600 employees
2. BTR Dunlop, 2,200
3. GenTyre Industries Ltd., 2,050
4. Goodyear S.A. Pty. Ltd., 2,000

Source: *Rubber & Plastics News*, January 27, 1997, p. 1.

★ 2409 ★
TOP TIRE BRANDS IN PANAMA
Ranked by: Market share, in percent. **Number listed:** 11
1. Bridgestone with 27.0%
2. Goodyear, 20.0%
3. Sumitomo, 10.0%
4. B.F. Goodrich, 8.0%

5.   Hankook, 6.0%
6.   Michelin, 5.0%
7.   Pirelli, 5.0%
8.   Dunlop, 3.0%
9.   Firestone, 3.0%
10. Other, 13.0%

Source: *National Trade Data Bank*, March 2, 1996, p. ISA9409.

★ 2410 ★

TOP TIRE FIRMS BY SALES PER EMPLOYEE, 1995

Ranked by: Sales per employee, in U.S. dollars.
Remarks: Includes capital investment and research and development figures. **Number listed:** 12

1.   Bridgestone with $17,552.2
2.   Michelin, $13,362.3
3.   Goodyear, $13,165.9
4.   Continental, $7,036.0
5.   Sumitomo, $5,679.5
6.   Yokohama, $4,034.2
7.   Pirelli (PTH), $3,319.5
8.   Toyo, $2,626.5
9.   Cooper, $1,493.6
10. Kumho, $1,398.2

Source: *European Rubber Journal,* Global Tyre Report, 1996-97, p. 6.

★ 2411 ★

TOP TIRE FIRMS WORLDWIDE, 1995

Ranked by: Tire sales, in millions of U.S. dollars.
Number listed: 63

1.   Bridgestone with $13,000 million
2.   Michelin, $12,278
3.   Goodyear, $10,105
4.   Continental, $4,928
5.   Sumitomo, $4,137
6.   Pirelli, $2,987
7.   Yokohama, $2,860
8.   Toyo, $1,524
9.   Cooper, $1,267
10. Kumho, $1,147

Source: *European Rubber Journal*, September 1996, p. 37.

★ 2412 ★

TOP TIRE MAKERS IN EASTERN EUROPE, 1995

Ranked by: Turnover, in millions of U.S. dollars.
Remarks: Notes turnover for 1993 and 1994. **Number listed:** 5

1.   Barum-Continental (Czech Republic) with $345 million
2.   Matador (Slovakia), $196
3.   Stomil Olsztyn (Poland), $196
4.   TC Debica (Poland), $196

5.   Sava Semperit (Slovenia), $159

Source: *European Rubber Journal,* Global Tyre Report, 1996-97, p. 26.

★ 2413 ★

TOP TIRE MAKERS IN GERMANY, 1995

Ranked by: Market share, in percent. **Number listed:** 7

1.   Continental with 25.0%
2.   Goodyear, 20.0%
3.   Michelin, 17.0%
4.   Bridgestone, 9.0%
5.   Sumitomo (Dunlop), 8.0%
6.   Pirelli, 5.0%
7.   Other, 16.0%

Source: *Wirtschaftswoche*, May 9, 1996, p. 78.

★ 2414 ★

TOP TIRE MANUFACTURERS IN BRAZIL

Ranked by: Annual sales, in millions of U.S. dollars.
Remarks: Notes each company's net worth. Figure for Firestone NE was unavailable. **Number listed:** 3

1.   Goodyear with $860,000.0 million
2.   Pirelli Pneus, $590,923.3
3.   Jo o Maggion, $9,974.0

Source: *National Trade Data Bank*, June 19, 1997, p. ISA970601.

Tire Industry – Europe

★ 2415 ★

EUROPE'S TOP TIRE MAKERS, 1995

Ranked by: Sales, in thousands of U.S. dollars. **Remarks:** Includes market shares. Figures for Hankook and Yokohama were unavailable. **Number listed:** 22

1.   Michelin with $6,760 thousand
2.   Conti Group, $3,670
3.   Goodyear, $2,850
4.   Pirelli, $1,858
5.   BS/FS, $1,800
6.   SP/Dunlop, $1,650
7.   Hankook, $n.a.
8.   Yokohama, $n.a.
9.   Vredestein, $253
10. Nokian, $230

Source: *European Rubber Journal,* Global Tyre Report, 1996-97, p. 14.

Tire Industry, International

★ 2416 ★
PRODUCTION OF TRUCK/BUS TIRES, 1995
Ranked by: Production, in thousands of units. **Number listed:** 10
1. United States with 45,027 thousand units
2. Japan, 44,525
3. South Korea, 15,639
4. India, 8,870
5. Russia/CIS, 6,900
6. Germany, 6,065
7. France, 5,713
8. Brazil, 4,501
9. Canada, 4,448
10. Spain, 3,558
Source: *Rubber & Plastics News*, August 26, 1996, p. 25.

★ 2417 ★
TOP PRODUCERS OF TIRES FOR PASSENGER CARS, 1995
Ranked by: Production, in thousands of units. **Number listed:** 10
1. United States with 210,127 thousand units
2. Japan, 104,935
3. France, 53,560
4. Germany, 41,867
5. South Korea, 36,898
6. Italy, 29,151
7. United Kingdom, 28,698
8. Canada, 26,954
9. Brazil, 26,227
10. Spain, 22,872
Source: *Rubber & Plastics News*, August 26, 1996, p. 25.

Tobacco Industry
See Also: Cigarette Industry

★ 2418 ★
LARGEST TOBACCO COMPANIES, 1995
Ranked by: Revenue, in millions of U.S. dollars. **Remarks:** Notes profits and global rank. **Number listed:** 3
1. Philip Morris (United States) with $53,139 million
2. B.A.T. Industries (United Kingdom), $24,033
3. Japan Tobacco (Japan), $20,538
Source: *Fortune,* The Global 500: World's Biggest Corporations (annual), August 5, 1996, p. F-25.

★ 2419 ★
LARGEST TOBACCO PRODUCING NATIONS
Ranked by: Production, in tons. **Remarks:** Includes production figures for African countries. C.I.S. stands for Commonwealth of Independent States. **Number listed:** 5
1. China with 2,886,150 tons
2. U.S., 697,400
3. India, 445,150
4. Brazil, 440,000
5. C.I.S., 242,000
Source: *East African Standard Business & Finance*, October 8, 1996, p. 10.

★ 2420 ★
LEADING TOBACCO BRANDS BY BRAND VALUE
Ranked by: Brand value, in millions of U.S. dollars. **Remarks:** Value was calculated using capital, ratio of capital to company sales, earnings, and corporate tax rate of the country where the parent company is located. See source for details. **Number listed:** 20
1. Marlboro (Philip Morris) with $44,614 million
2. Winston (RJR Nabisco), $6,077
3. Benson & Hedges (BAT, American Brands, Phillip Morris), $4,813
4. Camel (RJR Nabisco), $4,339
5. Newport (Loews, BAT Industries), $3,541
6. Merit (Philip Morris), $1,991
7. Salem (RJR Nabisco), $1,958
8. Virginia Slims (Philip Morris), $1,708
9. Copenhagen (UST), $1,670
10. Skoal (UST), $1,565
Source: *Financial World,* World's Most Valuable Brands (annual), July 8, 1996, p. 65.

★ 2421 ★
TOP TOBACCO FIRMS, 1995
Ranked by: Market share, in percent. **Number listed:** 8
1. Philip Morris with 15.08%
2. British-American Tobacco, 12.40%
3. R.J. Reynolds, 5.65%
4. Japan Tobacco, 5.16%
5. Rothman's, 2.98%
6. Korea Tobacco & Ginseng, 1.89%
7. Tekel, 1.62%
8. Other, 55.22%
Source: *World Watch*, July/August 1997, p. 22.

Tobacco Industry – Europe

★ 2422 ★
TOP TOBACCO COMPANIES IN EUROPE
Ranked by: Sales, in millions of European Currency Units (ECUs). **Remarks:** Also notes the number of employees. **Number listed:** 9
1. BAT Industries with 24,914 million ECUs
2. Hanson Plc, 11,920
3. Gallaher Ltd., 4,949
4. Tabacalera, S.A., 4,808
5. Philip Morris G.m.b.H., 4,722
6. Reemtsma Cigarettenfabriken G.m.b.H., 4,273
7. Imperial Tobacco Ltd., 3,802
8. British-American Tobacco Co. Ltd., 2,903
9. H.F. & Ph.F. Reemtsma G.m.b.H. & Co., 2,780
Source: *Duns Europa* (annual), vol. 4, Dun & Bradstreet, 1997, p. 216+.

Togo – see under individual headings

Toilet Goods

★ 2423 ★
TOP MARKETS FOR MEN'S PER CAPITA SPENDING ON TOILET GOODS, 1996
Ranked by: Per capita spending, in U.S. dollars. **Number listed:** 7
1. France with $51.31
2. Germany, $40.27
3. United Kingdom, $38.06
4. Italy, $32.01
5. Spain, $31.09
6. Japan, $31.06
7. United States, $29.96
Source: *Business Week*, September 8, 1997, p. 6.

Tokyo Stock Exchange

★ 2424 ★
LARGEST COMPANIES ON THE TOKYO STOCK EXCHANGE, 1995
Ranked by: Market value, in millions of yen (¥). **Number listed:** 20
1. Toyota Motor with ¥8,191,711 million
2. Industrial Bank of Japan, ¥7,360,077
3. Mitsubishi Bank, ¥7,000,000
4. Sumitomo Bank, ¥6,878,926
5. Fuji Bank, ¥6,605,861

6. Dai-ichi Kangyo Bank, ¥6,335,027
7. Sanwa Bank, ¥6,092,091
8. Nippon Telegraph & Telephone, ¥4,599,180
9. Sakura Bank, ¥4,485,654
10. Nomura Securities, ¥4,416,698
Source: *GT Guide to World Equity Markets* (annual), Euromoney Publications, 1996, p. 212.

★ 2425 ★
MOST ACTIVELY TRADED SHARES ON THE TOKYO STOCK EXCHANGE, 1995
Ranked by: Trading value, in millions of yen (¥). **Number listed:** 20
1. Fudo Construction with ¥1,396,471 million
2. Nippon Telegraph and Telephone, ¥1,332,430
3. NEC, ¥1,098,257
4. Nomura Securities, ¥981,979
5. Sony, ¥976,879
6. Hitachi, ¥919,581
7. Fujitsu, ¥888,132
8. Toshiba, ¥882,584
9. Oki Electric Industry, ¥875,777
10. Tokyo Motors, ¥856,389
Source: *GT Guide to World Equity Markets* (annual), Euromoney Publications, 1996, p. 212.

★ 2426 ★
TOKYO STOCK EXCHANGE LEADERS, 1996
Ranked by: Share of Tokyo Stock Exchange traded value. **Remarks:** Includes 1995 figures. **Number listed:** 4
1. Nomura with 10.3%
2. Nikko, 8.5%
3. Daiwa, 8.8%
4. Yamaichi, 6.4%
Source: *The Wall Street Journal*, July 30, 1996, p. A10.

Tools

★ 2427 ★
POWER TOOL MARKET IN DENMARK
Ranked by: Market share, in percent. **Number listed:** 5
1. Bosch with 30.0%
2. Black & Decker, 25.0%
3. Metabo, 20.0%
4. AEG, 15.0%
5. Other, 10.0%
Source: *National Trade Data Bank*, March 2, 1996, p. ISA9403.

Toothbrushes

★ 2428 ★
**POPULAR TOOTHBRUSH BRANDS USED IN
GERMANY, 1996**
Ranked by: People over the age of 14 who use each
brand, in percent. **Remarks:** Data include multiple
responses. **Number listed:** 8
1. Dr. Best with 30.4%
2. Blend-a-dent, 23.7%
3. Colgate, 13.0%
4. Oral B, 11.2%
5. Fuchs, 8.7%
6. Mentadent, 6.3%
7. Sensodyne, 3.3%
8. Reach, 1.7%
Source: *Marketing in Europe*, March 1997, p. 16.

Toothpaste

★ 2429 ★
LEADING TOOTHPASTES IN GERMANY, 1995
Ranked by: Market share, in percent. **Number listed:** 12
1. Blend-A-Mend (P&G) with 12.1%
2. Med3 (Linger & Fischer), 10.3%
3. Colgate (Colgate), 8.5%
4. Dentagard (Colgate), 8.3%
5. Thera-med (Henkel), 8.2%
6. Elmex (Wybert), 8.1%
7. Signal (Elida-Gibbs), 8.0%
8. Antibelag (Procter & Gamble), 6.8%
9. Sensodyne (Block Drug), 6.0%
10. Aronal (Wybert), 3.7%
Source: *Wirtschaftswoche*, March 14, 1996, p. 81.

★ 2430 ★
LEADING TOOTHPASTES IN INDIA
Ranked by: Brand shares, in percent. **Number listed:** 8
1. Colgate Dental Cream with 45.8%
2. Close-Up, 18.0%
3. Colgate Gel, 10.2%
4. Pepsodent, 9.3%
5. Cibaca Top, 2.9%
6. Promise, 1.5%
7. Babool, 0.5%
8. Others, 11.8%
Source: *Business Today*, April 22, 1997, p. 27.

★ 2431 ★
TOP TOOTHPASTE BRANDS IN CANADA, 1996
Ranked by: Market share based on sales, in percent.
Remarks: Notes 1995 figures. **Number listed:** 9
1. Colgate with 35.4%

2. Crest, 33.7%
3. Aqua Fresh, 14.3%
4. Close-Up, 4.4%
5. Macleans, 4.3%
6. Aim, 2.4%
7. Arm & Hammer, 2.3%
8. Pepsodent, 0.3%
9. Others, 3.0%
Source: *Marketing Magazine*, May 26, 1997, p. 12.

Toronto Stock Exchange

★ 2432 ★
**LARGEST COMPANIES ON THE TORONTO STOCK
EXCHANGE, 1995**
Ranked by: Market value, in millions of Canadian
dollars. **Number listed:** 20
1. Wal-Mart Stores Inc. with C$70,096 million
2. Mobil Corporation, C$67,456
3. General Motors Corporation, C$52,334
4. Amoco Corporation, C$48,585
5. Citicorp, C$35,956
6. Dow Chemical Co., C$31,363
7. British Gas plc, C$29,424
8. Chrysler Corporation, C$27,314
9. Travelers Group Inc., C$26,911
10. Seagram Company, C$17,566
Source: *GT Guide to World Equity Markets* (annual),
Euromoney Publications, 1996, p. 88.

★ 2433 ★
**MOST ACTIVELY TRADED SHARES ON THE
TORONTO STOCK EXCHANGE, 1995**
Ranked by: Trading value, in millions of Canadian
dollars. **Number listed:** 20
1. Alcan Aluminium with C$7,274 million
2. Barrick Gold, C$6,608
3. Inco Ltd., C$5,856
4. Placer Dome, C$5,739
5. Canadian Imperial Bank, C$5,503
6. Royal Bank, C$5,107
7. Seagram Co., C$4,903
8. Bank of Montreal, C$4,710
9. Bank of Nova Scotia, C$4,631
10. BCE Inc., C$4,483
Source: *GT Guide to World Equity Markets* (annual),
Euromoney Publications, 1996, p. 89.

Tourist Trade

★ **2434** ★

BRITAIN'S TOP TOUR OPERATORS, 1996

Ranked by: Market share for the end of summer 1996, in percent. **Remarks:** Spain was the leading packaged holiday destination. **Number listed:** 11

1. Thomson Holidays with 27.0%
2. Airtours, 16.5%
3. First Choice, 12.5%
4. Cosmos/Avro, 5.5%
5. Thomas Cook/Sunworld, 4.5%
6. Inspirations, 4.1%
7. Flying Colours, 3.9%
8. Unijet, 3.5%
9. Virgin Holidays, 1.5%
10. Others, 21.0%

Source: *The Observer*, December 8, 1996, p. B6.

★ **2435** ★

CHINA'S TOP DESTINATIONS FOR FOREIGN TOURISTS, 1995

Ranked by: Number of visitors. **Number listed:** 14

1. Beijing with 1,665,246 visitors
2. Shanghai, 1,075,439
3. Guangzhou, 489,599
4. Xian, 383,242
5. Shenzhen, 353,152
6. Kunming, 304,616
7. Guilin, 285,025
8. Hangzhou, 249,418
9. Suzhou, 182,679
10. Qingdao, 130,178

Source: *The China Business Review*, December 1996, p. 43.

★ **2436** ★

LEADING HOME COUNTRIES OF VISITORS TO GREECE, 1996

Ranked by: Number of visitors by nationality. **Number listed:** 43

1. Germany with 1,664,634 visitors
2. United Kingdom, 1,633,873
3. Italy, 488,635
4. France, 446,400
5. Holland, 377,964
6. Sweden, 348,939
7. Austria, 266,638
8. Denmark, 247,897
9. Former Yugoslavia, 202,974
10. Belgium-Luxembourg, 191,046

Source: *Trade With Greece*, Spring 1996, p. 96.

★ **2437** ★

LEADING TOURISM DESTINATIONS BY INTERNATIONAL ARRIVALS, 1995

Ranked by: International tourist arrivals, in millions. **Remarks:** Notes percent change. **Number listed:** 10

1. France with 60.6
2. Spain, 45.1
3. United States, 44.7
4. Italy, 29.2
5. China, 23.4
6. United Kingdom, 22.7
7. Hungary, 22.1
8. Mexico, 19.9
9. Poland, 19.2
10. Austria, 17.8

Source: *World Trade*, August 1996, p. 10.

★ **2438** ★

TOP "LONG-HAUL" VACATION DESTINATIONS FOR TRAVELERS FROM THE UNITED KINGDOM, 1997

Ranked by: Travelers, in thousands. **Remarks:** Also notes figures for 1993, market share, and percent change. **Number listed:** 12

1. United States with 2,150 thousand travelers
2. Canada, 325
3. India, 250
4. Australia, 160
5. Thailand, 150
6. South Africa, 130
7. Israel, 100
8. Kenya, 100
9. Jamaica, 90
10. Barbados, 85

Source: *National Trade Data Bank*, June 16, 1997, p. ISA970601.

★ **2439** ★

TOP DESTINATIONS FOR JAPANESE TRAVELERS

Ranked by: Percent of travelers visiting each region, based on a survey. **Number listed:** 10

1. United States with 40%
2. Europe, 21%
3. Southeast Asia, 10%
4. Australia, 9%
5. Canada, 5%
6. Hong Kong, 5%
7. China, 4%
8. New Zealand, 2%
9. South Korea, 2%
10. Taiwan, 2%

Source: *Travel Weekly*, May 26, 1997, p. 25.

★ 2440 ★

TOP NATIONS FOR TOURISM, 1996

Ranked by: Receipts, in billions of U.S. dollars.
Remarks: Includes ranking for 1995. **Number listed:** 10

1. United States with $64.4 billion
2. Spain, $28.4
3. France, $28.2
4. Italy, $27.3
5. United Kingdom, $20.4
6. Austria, $15.1
7. Germany, $13.2
8. Hong Kong, $11.2
9. China, $10.5
10. Switzerland, $9.9

Source: *Financial Times*, January 29, 1997, p. 8.

★ 2441 ★

TOP TOURISM NATIONS, 1995

Ranked by: Receipts, in billions of dollars. **Number listed:** 10

1. United States with $58.37 billion
2. France, $27.32
3. Italy, $27.07
4. Spain, $25.07
5. United Kingdom, $17.47
6. Austria, $12.50
7. Germany, $11.92
8. Hong Kong, $9.08
9. China, $8.25
10. Singapore, $7.55

Source: *The Straits Times*, March 23, 1996, p. 19.

★ 2442 ★

TOP TOURISM PROMOTERS, 1995

Ranked by: Advertising spending, in millions of U.S. dollars. **Number listed:** 9

1. Australia with $87.9 million
2. United Kingdom, $78.7
3. Spain, $78.6
4. France, $72.9
5. Singapore, $53.6
6. Thailand, $51.2
7. Netherlands, $49.7
8. Ireland, $37.8
9. Portugal, $37.3

Source: *Travel Weekly*, March 13, 1997, p. 19.

Toy Industry

★ 2443 ★

LEADING TOYS AND GAMES BRANDS BY BRAND VALUE

Ranked by: Brand value, in millions of U.S. dollars.
Remarks: Value was calculated using capital, ratio of capital to company sales, earnings, and corporate tax rate of the country where the parent company is located. See source for details. **Number listed:** 11

1. Nintendo (Nintendo) with $3,466 million
2. Barbie (Mattel), $2,456
3. Fisher-Price (Mattel), $1,128
4. Sega (Sega Enterprises), $802
5. Playskool (Hasbro), $264
6. Monopoly (Hasbro), $215
7. Matchbox (Tyco Toys), $127
8. Hot Wheels (Mattel), $115
9. Scrabble (Hasbro), $76
10. Trivial Pursuit (Hasbro), $43

Source: *Financial World*, World's Most Valuable Brands (annual), July 8, 1996, p. 65.

★ 2444 ★

TOP LATIN AMERICAN TOY MARKETS, 1995

Ranked by: Market value, in millions of U.S. dollars.
Remarks: Includes 1991 sales. Notes sales growth and leading producers in such market segments as dolls, action figures, and video games. **Number listed:** 8

1. Brazil with $696.6 million
2. Mexico, $222.6
3. Argentina, $181.8
4. Chile, $112.1
5. Venezuela, $106.2
6. Colombia, $79.4
7. Peru, $77.8
8. Ecuador, $28.6

Source: *World Trade*, May 1997, p. 12.

Toy Industry – Export-Import Trade

★ 2445 ★

EXPORT TOY MARKET IN FRANCE, 1995

Ranked by: Exported items, in percent. **Number listed:** 11

1. Plastic toys with 29.4%
2. Patience games, 11.6%
3. Dolls/stuffed animals, 7.9%
4. Pushers for dolls, 6.3%
5. Baby's rollers, 5.1%
6. Electronic games, 4.9%
7. Metal games, 4.4%
8. Electric trains, 4.4%

9.   Small cars, 4.4%
10.   Entertainment items, 3.6%

Source: *National Trade Data Bank*, February 27, 1997, p. IMI970227.

★ 2446 ★
IMPORT TOY MARKET IN FRANCE, 1995
Ranked by: Imported items, in percent. **Number listed:** 11

1.   Plastic toys with 19.2%
2.   Patience games, 12.5%
3.   Dolls, 12.1%
4.   Electronic games, 7.5%
5.   Plastic construction toys, 6.0%
6.   Stuffed animals, 6.0%
7.   Cycles, baby's rollers, 2.5%
8.   Small cars, 2.3%
9.   Musical games, 1.8%
10.   Electric trains, 1.5%

Source: *National Trade Data Bank*, February 27, 1997, p. IMI970227.

Tractors

★ 2447 ★
INDIA'S TRACTOR MARKET
Ranked by: Market share, in percent, for the 31-40 HP segment. **Remarks:** The 21-30 HP segment was led by Eicher with a 40.73% share; the 41-50 HP segment was led by Escorts with a 54% share. **Number listed:** 6

1.   TAFE with 30.22%
2.   M&M, 26.49%
3.   Punjab Tractors, 18.51%
4.   Escorts, 13.30%
5.   HMT, 7.73%
6.   Eicher, 3.62%

Source: *Business Today*, September 7, 1996, p. 76.

Trade Deficit
See: **Balance of Trade**

Trade Surplus
See: **Balance of Trade**

Trading Companies – Europe

★ 2448 ★
LARGEST TRADING COMPANIES IN EUROPE
Ranked by: Sales, in thousands of U.S. dollars. **Remarks:** Also notes previous year's rank, type of industry, percent change in sales, and percent change in local currencies. **Number listed:** 3

1.   Mercedes-Benz A.G. with $50,324,879 thousand
2.   Edeka Group, $37,169,007
3.   Tengelmann Group, $34,863,410
4.   Rewe Group, $30,134,143
5.   Shell International Petroleum Co. Ltd., $26,274,844
6.   Carrefour SA, $25,172,272
7.   ALDI Group, $22,357,297
8.   J. Sainsbury Plc, $20,961,180
9.   Promodes Sa, $20,565,586
10.   Tesco Plc, $18,779,503

Source: *Europe's 15,000 Largest Companies* (annual), Dun & Bradstreet, 1997, p. 494+.

Trading Companies, International

★ 2449 ★
ASIA'S LARGEST TRADING FIRMS, 1995
Ranked by: Sales, in millions of U.S. dollars. **Remarks:** Includes profits, profits as a percentage of sales and assets, and overall sales rank. **Number listed:** 20

1.   Mitsubishi Corp. with $189,187.0 million
2.   Mitsui & Co., $186,266.0
3.   Itochu Corp., $173,588.9
4.   Sumitomo Corp., $171,912.2
5.   Marubeni Corp., $165,269.6
6.   Nissho Iwai Corp., $100,446.5
7.   Tomen Corp., $69,527.8
8.   Nichimen Corp., $52,171.6
9.   Kanematsu Corp., $51,141.9
10.   Samsung Co., $24,963.8

Source: *Asiaweek*, The Asiaweek 1,000, November 22, 1996, p. 168.

★ 2450 ★
LARGEST TRADING COMPANIES, 1995
Ranked by: Revenue, in millions of U.S. dollars. **Remarks:** Notes profits and global rank. **Number listed:** 21

1.   Mitsubishi (Japan) with $184,365 million
2.   Mitsui (Japan), $181,519
3.   Itochu (Japan), $169,165
4.   Sumitomo (Japan), $167,531
5.   Marubeni (Japan), $161,057

6. Nissho Iwai (Japan), $97,886
7. Tomen (Japan), $67,756
8. Nichimen (Japan), $50,842
9. Kanematsu (Japan), $50,842
10. Veba Group (Germany), $46,280

Source: *Fortune,* The Global 500: World's Biggest Corporations (annual), August 5, 1996, p. F-26.

★ 2451 ★

TOP TRADING COMPANIES IN JAPAN
Ranked by: Income, in millions of yen (¥). **Number listed:** 10

1. Mitsui & Co. with ¥63,059 million
2. Mitsubishi Corp., ¥56,978
3. Sumitomo Corp., ¥33,346
4. Itochu Corp., ¥31,498
5. Nichimen Corp., ¥15,772
6. Nagase & Co., ¥12,606
7. Toyota Tsusho, ¥10,260
8. Kowa, ¥10,200
9. Yazaki Corp., ¥9,842
10. Toshoku Ltd., ¥7,347

Source: *Tokyo Business Today*, August 1995, p. 27.

★ 2452 ★

TOP TRADING FIRMS IN THAILAND
Ranked by: Revenue, in millions of bahts (Bt). **Remarks:** Includes profits and assets. **Number listed:** 21

1. Mitsui with Bt7,571.79 million
2. Mitsiam International, Bt7,351.20
3. Thai-MC, Bt6,066.59
4. Mitsubishi, Bt6,024.17
5. Berli Jucker, Bt5,794.32
6. F.E. Zuellig, Bt4,700.91
7. Charoen Pokphand Group, Bt4,657.48
8. SCT, Bt3,963.26
9. East Asiatic, Bt3,854.19
10. Loxley, Bt3,722.97

Source: *Business Review*, December 1995, p. 164.

Transportation – Asia

★ 2453 ★

ASIA'S LARGEST TRANSPORTATION FIRMS, 1995
Ranked by: Sales, in millions of U.S. dollars. **Remarks:** Includes profits, profits as a percentage of sales and assets, and overall sales rank. **Number listed:** 20

1. East Japan Railway with $26,293.9 million
2. Nippon Express, $18,231.8
3. Japan Airlines, $15,405.5
4. Central Japan Railway, $13,190.0
5. West Japan Railway, $12,537.9
6. All Nippon Airways, $10,283.9
7. Kinki Nippon Railway, $9,714.0

8. Nippon Yusen, $9,480.4
9. Mitsui O.S.K. Lines, $7,038.5
10. Yamato Transport, $6,969.2

Source: *Asiaweek*, The Asiaweek 1,000, November 22, 1996, p. 169.

★ 2454 ★

LARGEST TRANSPORT AND ALLIED SERVICES COMPANIES IN ASIA
Ranked by: Sales, in thousands of U.S. dollars. **Remarks:** Also notes profit as a percent of sales. **Number listed:** 100

1. East Japan Railway Co. Ltd. with $24,011,650 thousand
2. Nippon Express Co. Ltd., $16,649,310
3. Japan Airlines Co. Ltd., $14,068,359
4. Kinki Nippon Railway Co. Ltd., $8,870,864
5. Nippon Yusen, $8,657,563
6. All Nippon Airways Co. Ltd., $7,372,077
7. Swire Pacific Ltd., $6,939,023
8. Mitsui O.S.K. Lines Ltd., $6,427,631
9. Yamato Transport Co. Ltd., $5,863,679
10. Odakyu Electric Railway Co. Ltd., $5,568,058

Source: *Asia's 7,500 Largest Companies* (annual), Dun & Bradstreet, 1997, p. 89+.

Transportation – Equipment and Supplies – Europe

★ 2455 ★

TOP TRANSPORTATION EQUIPMENT COMPANIES IN EUROPE
Ranked by: Sales, in millions of European Currency Units (ECUs). **Remarks:** Also notes the number of employees. **Number listed:** 112

1. Daimler-Benz A.G. with 47,001 million ECUs
2. Volkswagen A.G., 39,997
3. Mercedes-Benz A.G., 32,694
4. Peugeot S.A., 24,170
5. Bayerische Motorenwerke A.G., 20,945
6. Renault S.A. (Regie Nationale des Usines), 20,534
7. Robert Bosch GmbH., 16,270
8. Peugeot (Automobiles), 13,756
9. Fiat Auto S.P.A., 12,396
10. Adam Opel A.G., 11,760

Source: *Duns Europa* (annual), vol. 4, Dun & Bradstreet, 1997, p. 241+.

Transportation – Europe

★ 2456 ★
LARGEST TRANSPORTATION COMPANIES IN EUROPE
Ranked by: Sales, in thousands of U.S. dollars. **Remarks:** Also notes previous year's rank, type of industry, percent change in sales, and percent change in local currencies. **Number listed:** 300
1. Deutsche Bahn A.G. with $20,837,001 thousand
2. Deutsche Lufthansa A.G., $13,903,702
3. British Airways Plc, $12,049,689
4. SNCF-Ste National des Chemins de Fers Francais, $10,619,555
5. Cie Nationale Air France, $10,017,390
6. John Swire & Sons Ltd., $6,793,478
7. S.A.S., $5,565,681
8. Danzas A.G., $5,275,049
9. Koninklijke Luchtvaart Maatschappij NV, $5,167,487
10. Bilspedition AB, $4,545,221

Source: *Europe's 15,000 Largest Companies* (annual), Dun & Bradstreet, 1997, p. 662+.

Travel

★ 2457 ★
TOP TRAVEL INDUSTRY BRANDS BY BRAND VALUE
Ranked by: Brand value, in millions of U.S. dollars. **Remarks:** Value was calculated using capital, ratio of capital to company sales, earnings, and corporate tax rate of the country where the parent company is located. See source for details. **Number listed:** 12
1. American (AMR Corp.) with $2,656 million
2. Northwest (NWA), $1,723
3. United (UAL Corp.), $1,548
4. Delta (Delta Air Lines), $1,102
5. Hertz (Ford Motor), $594
6. Continental (Continental Airlines), $526
7. America West (America West Airlines), $228
8. Avis (Avis), $180
9. National (National Car Rental), $65
10. USAir (USAir Group), $33

Source: *Financial World,* World's Most Valuable Brands (annual), July 8, 1996, p. 65.

Travel Agencies

★ 2458 ★
TOP HOLIDAY DESTINATIONS FOR BRITS, 1995
Ranked by: Thousands of British travellers to the most popular holiday destinations. **Number listed:** 10
1. Balearic Islands with 1,877 thousand travellers
2. Greek Islands, 1,311
3. Mainland Spain, 1,074
4. Canary Islands, 951
5. Turkey, 624
6. United States, 473
7. France, 466
8. Cyprus, 416
9. Portugal, 413
10. Italy, 314

Source: *The Guardian*, August 16, 1996, p. 10.

★ 2459 ★
TOP JAPANESE TRAVEL AGENTS AND WHOLESALERS FOR OVERSEAS TRAVEL, 1996
Ranked by: Annual sales for overseas travel, in thousands of yen (¥). **Remarks:** Also notes figures for 1995. **Number listed:** 50
1. Japan Travel Bureau with ¥575,277,910 thousand
2. Kinki Nippon Tourist, ¥292,648,299
3. Nippon Travel Agency, ¥183,988,713
4. Hankyu Express International, ¥146,630,872
5. JALpack, ¥139,559,455
6. Nippon Express, ¥135,345,679
7. H.I.S., ¥116,398,218
8. Tokyu Tourist, ¥93,191,865
9. JTB World Vacations, ¥76,409,111
10. JTB World Vacations Western Japan, ¥76,169,470

Source: *National Trade Data Bank*, April 22, 1997, p. IMI970407.

★ 2460 ★
TOP TRAVEL AGENCIES IN GERMANY, 1994-1995
Ranked by: Market share, in percent. **Number listed:** 10
1. TUI with 24.4%
2. NUR, 15.6%
3. LTU, 13.2%
4. DER, 6.3%
5. ITS, 4.3%
6. Air Tours, 4.2%
7. Jahn, 4.2%
8. Oger, 3.4%
9. Hetzel, 1.6%
10. Other, 24.4%

Source: *Der Spiegel*, 1996, p. 69.

★ 2461 ★
TOP TRAVEL AGENCIES IN JAPAN
Ranked by: Market share, in percent. **Number listed:** 6
1. Japan Travel Bureau with 13.7%
2. Kinki Nippon Tourist, 7.7%
3. Nippon Travel Agency, 4.7%
4. Nippon Express, 3.5%
5. Hankyu Express International, 3.4%
6. Other, 67.0%
Source: *Nikkei Weekly*, August 5, 1996, p. 10.

Trinidad and Tobago – see under individual headings

Trinidad and Tobago Stock Exchange

★ 2462 ★
LARGEST COMPANIES ON THE TRINIDAD AND TOBAGO STOCK EXCHANGE, 1995
Ranked by: Market capitalization, in Trinidad and Tobagoan dollars (TT$). **Number listed:** 5
1. Republic Bank with TT$1,189,008,338
2. Trinidad Cement, TT$998,000,000
3. Royal Bank T&T, TT$946,335,428
4. Bank of Nova Scotia, TT$664,335,000
5. CIBC (WI) Holdings, TT$611,718,061
Source: *GT Guide to World Equity Markets* (annual), Euromoney Publications, 1996, p. 415.

★ 2463 ★
MOST ACTIVE SHARES ON THE TRINIDAD AND TOBAGO STOCK EXCHANGE, 1995
Ranked by: Trading value, in millions of Trinidad and Tobagoan dollars (TT$). **Number listed:** 20
1. Royal Bank T&T with TT$207.3 million
2. Trinidad Cement, TT$149.3
3. Republic Bank, TT$125.9
4. Guardian Life of the Caribbean, TT$85.4
5. Lever Brothers (WI), TT$71.9
6. Bank of Nova Scotia, TT$37.5
7. Angostura Holdings, TT$34.4
8. Neal & Massy Holdings, TT$23.2
9. West Indian Tobacco Company, TT$16.2
10. Ansa McAl Group, TT$15.3
Source: *GT Guide to World Equity Markets* (annual), Euromoney Publications, 1996, p. 416.

Truck Industry

★ 2464 ★
TOP FOREIGN COMPANIES IN VIETNAM'S COMMERCIAL VEHICLE MARKET
Ranked by: Market share, in percent. **Remarks:** Data refer to foreign manufacturers of trucks and minibuses. Figure for Toyota represents minibuses only. **Number listed:** 6
1. Toyota with 40.0%
2. Kia/Mazda, 23.0%
3. Mitsubishi, 18.0%
4. Iveco, 10.0%
5. Mercedes-Benz, 10.0%
6. Other, 7.0%
Source: *Financial Times*, October 4, 1996, p. 4.

★ 2465 ★
TOP TRUCK MARKETS IN AFRICA, 1996
Ranked by: Units sold. **Remarks:** Also notes 1995 figures. **Number listed:** 20
1. South Africa with 149,200 units
2. Egypt, 32,300
3. Libya, 11,300
4. Kenya, 9,500
5. Morocco, 9,500
6. Algeria, 7,600
7. Nigeria, 4,600
8. Reunion, 4,300
9. Tunisia, 3,900
10. Uganda, 3,500
Source: *Automotive News*, Market Data Fact Book (annual), 1997, p. 22.

★ 2466 ★
TOP TRUCK MARKETS IN LATIN AMERICA, 1996
Ranked by: Units sold. **Remarks:** Also notes 1995 figures. **Number listed:** 20
1. Brazil with 308,600 units
2. Chile, 75,700
3. Argentina, 57,000
4. Venezuela, 48,500
5. Colombia, 46,600
6. Ecuador, 24,100
7. Peru, 12,400
8. El Salvador, 8,700
9. Uruguay, 7,500
10. Panama, 7,100
Source: *Automotive News*, Market Data Fact Book (annual), 1997, p. 22.

★ 2467 ★
TOP TRUCK MARKETS IN THE ASIA-PACIFIC REGION, 1996
Ranked by: Units sold. **Remarks:** Also notes 1995 figures. **Number listed:** 20
1. Japan with 2,386,900 units
2. China, 983,200
3. South Korea, 413,900
4. Indonesia, 378,400
5. Thailand, 369,400
6. India, 246,400
7. Australia, 164,200
8. Taiwan, 131,300
9. Philippines, 58,400
10. Malaysia, 51,800

Source: *Automotive News*, Market Data Fact Book (annual), 1997, p. 22.

★ 2468 ★
TOP TRUCK PRODUCERS IN JAPAN, 1995
Ranked by: Market share, in percent. **Number listed:** 4
1. Hino Motors with 28.4%
2. Mitsubishi Motors, 27.5%
3. Isuzu Motors, 24.5%
4. Nissan Diesel Motor, 19.6%

Source: *Nikkei Weekly*, July 29, 1996, p. 8.

★ 2469 ★
TRUCK MARKET IN NEW ZEALAND, 1997
Ranked by: Market share for the year ending April 1997, in percent. **Number listed:** 8
1. Mitsubishi with 22%
2. Hino, 21%
3. Isuzu, 16%
4. Nissan, 10%
5. Ford, 5%
6. Freightliner, 4%
7. Daihatsu, 4%
8. Others, 18%

Source: *National Trade Data Bank*, July 14, 1997, p. ISA970801.

★ 2470 ★
TRUCK REGISTRATIONS IN THE UNITED KINGDOM, 1996
Ranked by: Trucks registered. **Remarks:** Also notes percent change and share of registrations. **Number listed:** 9
1. Iveco Group (Fiat) with 10,909 trucks
2. Leyland DAF (DAF Trucks), 10,088
3. Daimler-Benz, 8,414
4. Volvo, 6,293
5. Scania (Investor), 5,592
6. MAN, 3,219
7. ERF, 2,247
8. Renault, 1,872

9. Imports, 30,507
Source: *Financial Times*, January 14, 1997, p. 8.

Truck Plants

★ 2471 ★
TOP MANUFACTURERS OF TRUCK CABS IN BRAZIL
Ranked by: Annual sales, in millions of U.S. dollars. **Remarks:** Notes each company's net worth. **Number listed:** 11
1. Randon with $145,807.0 million
2. Recrusul, $69,366.0
3. A. Guerra, $49,991.0
4. Iderol, $37,754.0
5. Antonini, $16,542.0
6. Refrisa, $11,793.0
7. Nova Kabi, $4,316.0
8. Cimasa, $2,656.0
9. Altari, $1,427.0
10. Carroceria Brasil, $1,283.3

Source: *National Trade Data Bank*, June 19, 1997, p. ISA970601.

Trucks

★ 2472 ★
SPORTS UTILITY VEHICLE SALES IN CANADA, 1996
Ranked by: Market share based on unit sales, in percent. **Number listed:** 11
1. General Motors SU/Blazer/Jimmy with 16.9%
2. Chrysler Jeep Grand Cherokee, 16.5%
3. Ford Explorer, 15.9%
4. General Motors Blazer/Yukon, 8.8%
5. Nissan Pathfinder, 7.7%
6. GM Suburban, 5.3%
7. Toyota 4Runner, 5.2%
8. Chrysler Jeep YJ/TJ, 4.9%
9. Suzuki Sidekick, 4.4%
10. Ford Expedition, 2.7%

Source: *Marketing Magazine*, May 26, 1997, p. 17.

Tunisia – see under individual headings

Turbines and Generators

★ 2473 ★
WORLDWIDE GAS TURBINE MARKET
Ranked by: Market share, in percent. **Number listed:** 5
1. GE Technology with 50.0%
2. Westinghouse/Mitsubishi Heavy Industries/ Fiat, 18.0%
3. ABB, 14.0%
4. Siemens/Ansaldo, 14.0%
5. Other, 4.0%
Source: *Financial Times*, June 19, 1997, p. 6.

★ 2474 ★
WORLDWIDE STEAM TURBINE MARKET
Ranked by: Market share, in percent. **Number listed:** 7
1. Chinese state enterprises with 21.0%
2. GE Technology, 20.0%
3. Westinghouse/Mitsubishi Heavy Industries, 14.0%
4. GEC/Alsthom, 11.0%
5. ABB, 10.0%
6. Siemens, 5.0%
7. Other, 19.0%
Source: *Financial Times*, June 19, 1997, p. 6.

Turkey – see under individual headings

Uganda – see under individual headings

Underwriting of Securities
See: **Security Underwriting**

Unemployment

★ 2475 ★
UNEMPLOYMENT RATE IN EUROPE, 1996
Ranked by: Unemployment rate at the end of 1996, in percent. **Number listed:** 15
1. Spain with 22.2% unemployment
2. Finland, 15.0%
3. France, 12.4%
4. Italy, 11.9%
5. Ireland, 11.8%
6. Sweden, 10.6%
7. Greece, 10.0%
8. Belgium, 9.5%

9. Germany, 9.3%
10. United Kingdom, 7.5%
Source: *The Guardian*, March 6, 1997, p. 16.

Unit Trusts
See: **Mutual Funds**

United Arab Emirates – see under individual headings

United Kingdom – see under individual headings

Uranium Industry

★ 2476 ★
TOP URANIUM PRODUCTION CENTERS, 1996
Ranked by: Production, in millions of pounds. **Number listed:** 10
1. Key Lake (Canada) with 13.5 million pounds
2. Rabbit Lake (Canada), 11.2
3. Ranger (Australia), 8.9
4. Krasnokamensk (Russia), 7.2
5. Rossing (Namibia), 6.2
6. Akouta (Niger), 5.0
7. Olympic Dam (Australia), 3.6
8. Cluff Lake (Canada), 3.2
9. Arlit (Niger), 2.6
10. Vaal Reefs (South Africa), 2.4
Source: *Engineering & Mining Journal*, 1997 Commodities Review Issue (annual), March 1997, p. 42-WW.

Uruguay – see under individual headings

Utah – see under individual headings

Utilities, Public
See: **Public Utilities**

Valves

★ 2477 ★

LEADING INDUSTRIAL VALVE MAKERS IN FRANCE, 1995

Ranked by: Sales, in millions of U.S. dollars. **Remarks:** Includes principal activities of each company. **Number listed:** 9

1. Trouvay and Cauvin with $212.0 million
2. Dresser Produits, $187.0
3. AMRI-KSB, $101.0
4. FMC Europe, $77.0
5. Fisher Controls, $72.0
6. GEC Alsthom-Sapag, $70.0
7. Cooper Oil Tool, $63.0
8. Legris S.A., $62.0
9. Malbranque, $62.0

Source: *National Trade Data Bank*, March 2, 1996, p. ISA9503.

Venture Capital – Europe

★ 2478 ★

TOP EUROPEAN COUNTRIES FOR VENTURE CAPITAL, 1995

Ranked by: Funds raised, as a percent of European total. **Number listed:** 6

1. United Kingdom with 43.3%
2. France, 21.3%
3. Germany, 9.5%
4. Italy, 7.7%
5. Netherlands, 3.8%
6. Other, 14.4%

Source: *The Economist*, September 28, 1996, p. 90.

★ 2479 ★

TOP EUROPEAN NATIONS FOR VENTURE CAPITAL INVESTMENT, 1996

Ranked by: Investment, in millions of ECUs (European Currency Units). **Number listed:** 17

1. U.K. with 2,973 million ECUs
2. France, 849
3. Germany, 715
4. Netherlands, 593
5. Italy, 510
6. Sweden, 420
7. Spain, 193
8. Switzerland, 127
9. Belgium, 109
10. Norway, 83

Source: *The Guardian*, June 17, 1997, p. 19.

Video Cassettes
See: **Video Tapes**

Video Games

★ 2480 ★

TOP VIDEO GAME MACHINE MAKERS IN JAPAN, 1995

Ranked by: Market share, in percent. **Number listed:** 6

1. Nintendo with 32.9%
2. Sega Enterprises, 29.9%
3. Sony Computer Entertainment, 29.2%
4. Matsushita Electric Industrial, 4.4%
5. NEC Home Electronics, 2.5%
6. Other, 1.1%

Source: *Nikkei Weekly*, July 15, 1996, p. 8.

Video Tapes

★ 2481 ★

JAPAN'S PRERECORDED VIDEO TAPE MARKET

Ranked by: Market share, in percent. **Number listed:** 6

1. Victor Entertainment with 17.2%
2. Buena Vista Japan, 15.4%
3. Pony Canyon, 12.8%
4. Time Warner Entertainment Japan, 8.0%
5. Toei Video, 5.8%
6. Others, 40.8%

Source: *Nikkei Weekly*, July 15, 1996, p. 8.

★ 2482 ★

MOST POPULAR VIDEO RENTALS FOR SOUTH KOREAN MEN

Ranked by: Market share, in percent. **Number listed:** 8

1. Action adventure with 60%
2. Comic, 6%
3. Family, 6%
4. Sci-fi, 6%
5. Kung Fu, 5%
6. Melodrama, 5%
7. Adult only, 3%
8. Other, 9%

Source: *Business Korea*, February 1997, p. 75.

★ 2483 ★

MOST POPULAR VIDEO RENTALS FOR SOUTH KOREAN WOMEN

Ranked by: Market share, in percent. **Number listed:** 8

1. Action Adventure with 34%
2. Family, 17%
3. Melodrama, 17%

4. Comic, 11%
5. Adult only, 4%
6. Kung Fu, 3%
7. Sci-fi, 3%
8. Other, 11%

Source: *Business Korea*, February 1997, p. 75.

Vienna Stock Exchange

★ 2484 ★
LARGEST COMPANIES ON THE VIENNA STOCK EXCHANGE, 1995
Ranked by: Market value, in millions of Austrian schillings (AS). **Number listed:** 20
1. OMV with AS23,625 million
2. Bank Austria, AS23,328
3. Creditanstalt, AS22,414
4. EA-Generali, AS22,273
5. VA Technologie, AS19,200
6. Weinerberger Baustoff, AS13,810
7. EVN, AS13,157
8. Flughafen Wien, AS10,557
9. VA Stahl, AS9,537
10. Verbund, AS9,151

Source: *GT Guide to World Equity Markets* (annual), Euromoney Publications, 1996, p. 53.

★ 2485 ★
MOST ACTIVELY TRADED SHARES ON THE VIENNA STOCK EXCHANGE, 1995
Ranked by: Turnover, in millions of Austrian schillings (AS). **Number listed:** 20
1. OMV with AS38,899 million
2. VA Technologie, AS34,788
3. EVN, AS30,466
4. Verbund Kat. A, AS19,462
5. CA Vz, AS19,148
6. Weinerberger, AS18,875
7. Flughafen Wien, AS12,705
8. CA St, AS10,905
9. Mayr-Melnhof, AS5,912
10. EA-Generali St, AS5,282

Source: *GT Guide to World Equity Markets* (annual), Euromoney Publications, 1996, p. 53.

Vietnam – see under individual headings

Virginia – see under individual headings

Vodka

★ 2486 ★
TOP VODKA BRANDS WORLDWIDE
Ranked by: Cases sold per year, in millions. **Number listed:** 10
1. Smirnoff with 15.1 million cases
2. Kremlyovskaia, 6.3
3. Zytnia, 6.0
4. Absolut, 5.5
5. Wyborowa, 5.0
6. Popov, 3.6
7. Polonaise, 3.5
8. Gordon's, 2.1
9. Koskenkorva, 2.0
10. Stolichnaya, 1.9

Source: *The Guardian*, December 12, 1995, p. 3.

Wages and Salaries

★ 2487 ★
LEADING EXPORTERS OF CHEMICALS TO MEXICO, 1996
Ranked by: Share of export market from January to August, in percent. **Number listed:** 6
1. North America with 52%
2. Latin American Integration Association, 19%
3. European Union, 9%
4. Central America, 6%
5. Asia, 5%
6. Others, 9%

Source: *Chemical Week*, January 8, 1997, p. 31.

Warehousing

★ 2488 ★
LARGEST WAREHOUSING FIRMS IN MEXICO, 1995
Ranked by: Assets as of December 31, 1995, in millions of U.S. dollars. **Number listed:** 10
1. Almacenes Nacionales de Dep sito with $206.7 million
2. Almacenadora, $39.4
3. Almacenadora Bancomer, $33.4
4. Almacenadora Serfin, $14.1
5. Almacenadora Invermexico, $8.9
6. Almacenadora Tihuana, $8.5
7. Almacenadora Gomez, $7.3
8. Almacenadora Bital, $6.3
9. Almacenadora Comercial America, $5.6

10.   Almacenadara Inter Americana, $5.2
Source: *National Trade Data Bank*, September 9, 1996, p. ISA960801.

Warsaw Stock Exchange

★ 2489 ★
LARGEST COMPANIES ON THE WARSAW STOCK EXCHANGE, 1995
Ranked by: Market value, in millions of U.S. dollars.
Number listed: 10
1.   BSK with $540.17 million
2.   BPH, $301.11
3.   Stomil Olsztyn, $254.51
4.   Elektrim, $227.08
5.   BRE, $221.04
6.   Zywiec, $207.32
7.   Wedel, $192.46
8.   Gorazdze, $191.02
9.   Bgdanski, $183.36
10.   Debica, $152.73
Source: *GT Guide to World Equity Markets* (annual), Euromoney Publications, 1996, p. 521.

★ 2490 ★
MOST ACTIVELY TRADED SHARES ON THE WARSAW STOCK EXCHANGE, 1995
Ranked by: Turnover, in millions of zloty (Zl). **Number listed:** 10
1.   Universal with Zl753.12 million
2.   BSK, Zl705.05
3.   Budimex, Zl668.71
4.   BPH, Zl637.17
5.   Stalexport, Zl616.47
6.   Debica, Zl545.14
7.   Elektrim, Zl443.82
8.   Rolimpex, Zl432.46
9.   BRE, Zl420.84
10.   Kabelbfk, Zl380.42
Source: *GT Guide to World Equity Markets* (annual), Euromoney Publications, 1996, p. 521.

★ 2491 ★
TOP COMPANIES ON THE WARSAW STOCK EXCHANGE
Ranked by: Growth, in percent. **Number listed:** 20
1.   ComputerLand with 396% growth
2.   WBK, 273%
3.   Agros, 270%
4.   Chemiskor, 229%
5.   Domplast, 229%
6.   Elektrim, 211%
7.   BIG, 205%
8.   Polfa Kutno, 193%

9.   Indykpol, 191%
10.   Animex, 187%
Source: *The Warsaw Voice*, April 27, 1997, p. 13.

Washing Machines

★ 2492 ★
TOP WASHER MANUFACTURERS IN CHINA, 1995
Ranked by: Units shipped. **Number listed:** 10
1.   Rongshida with 1,277,200 units
2.   Weili, 1,268,100
3.   Shuixian, 1,063,200
4.   Little Swan (Xiotianer), 808,300
5.   Haier, 643,400
6.   Jinyu, 607,400
7.   Tianyang (Tianjin Xinbao), 598,100
8.   Jinling, 388,200
9.   Changfeng, 363,600
10.   Jinan Xaoya, 332,000
Source: *Appliance Manufacturer*, February 1997, p. G-17.

★ 2493 ★
TOP WASHING MACHINE BRANDS IN JAPAN, 1996
Ranked by: Market share as of September 1996, in percent. **Remarks:** Data are based on sales in large department stores in 35 major cities. **Number listed:** 5
1.   Little Swan with 25.7%
2.   Xiaoya, 14.7%
3.   Haier, 13.0%
4.   Rongshida, 9.9%
5.   Shuixian, 7.7%
Source: *South China Morning Post*, February 13, 1997, p. B7.

Washington – see under individual headings

Waste Management Industry

★ 2494 ★
TOP INCINERATOR MAKERS IN JAPAN
Ranked by: Market share, in percent. **Number listed:** 6
1.   NKK with 17.5%
2.   Kawasaki Heavy Industries, 16.2%
3.   Takuma, 15.5%
4.   Hitachi, 12.9%
5.   Ishikawajima-Harima, 7.2%
6.   Other, 30.7%
Source: *Nikkei Weekly*, August 5, 1996, p. 10.

Water Services

★ 2495 ★
TOP WATER SANITATION AND SUPPLY COMPANIES IN SPAIN
Ranked by: Market share based on consumer volume, in percent. **Number listed:** 7
1. Aguas de Barcelona with 20.0%
2. Canal de Isabel II, 12.5%
3. Saur Internacional, 7.50%
4. Sociedad Mediterranea de Aguas, 5.00%
5. Enamesa, 3.75%
6. Consorcio de Aguas del Gran Bibao, 2.50%
7. Others, 48.70%

Source: *National Trade Data Bank*, February 24, 1997, p. IMI970224.

Wealth
See Also: Billionaires

★ 2496 ★
RICHEST STOCK-BASED BUSINESSMEN IN THAILAND
Ranked by: Value of stock assets, in millions of baht (Bt). **Number listed:** 10
1. Paiboon Damrongchaitham with Bt7,724.52 million
2. Pojamarn Shinawatra, Bt3,754.10
3. Thaksin Shinawatra, Bt3,553.20
4. Premchai Karnasuta, Bt3,420.23
5. Anant Asvabhosin, Bt2,808.13
6. Adisai Bhotaramik, Bt2,732.17
7. Yuwaree Uakarnchanawilai, Bt2,052.07
8. Pitch Bhotaramik, Bt1,920.29
9. Nijaporn Jaranachit, Bt1,919.06
10. Viroj Preechawongwaikul, Bt1,580.00

Source: *Bangkok Post*, May 21, 1997, p. B1.

Western Samoa – see under individual headings

Wheat

★ 2497 ★
LEADING WHEAT PRODUCING NATIONS IN CENTRAL AND EASTERN EUROPE, 1996
Ranked by: Production, in millions of tons. **Number listed:** 8
1. Poland with 8.5 million tons

2. Hungary, 3.9
3. Czech Republic, 3.7
4. Romania, 3.2
5. Slovakia, 1.9
6. Bulgaria, 1.8
7. Yugoslavia Federal Republic, 1.5
8. Other, 1.7

Source: *Financial Times*, August 1, 1997, p. 30.

Whiskey Industry
See: **Liquor Industry**

Wholesale Trade

★ 2498 ★
BRITAIN'S LARGEST GASOLINE WHOLESALERS, 1996
Ranked by: Market share during January 1996, in percent. **Remarks:** Hypermarkets had a 4.0% share of the market. **Number listed:** 16
1. Esso with 12.4%
2. Shell, 12.4%
3. BP, 8.3%
4. Texaco, 7.4%
5. Save, 5.9%
6. Conoco, 5.4%
7. Mobil, 4.1%
8. Elf, 3.9%
9. Fina, 3.3%
10. Total, 3.3%

Source: *The Guardian*, July 26, 1996, p. 21.

★ 2499 ★
GASOLINE SALES IN FINLAND, 1996
Ranked by: Market share, in percent. **Number listed:** 6
1. Statoil with 28.0%
2. Esso, 22.9%
3. Shell, 19.5%
4. Hydro Texaco, 18.6%
5. Fina, 8.0%
6. Jet, 2.9%

Source: *Aftenposten*, January 21, 1997, p. 1.

★ 2500 ★
LARGEST WHOLESALERS, 1995
Ranked by: Revenue, in millions of U.S. dollars. **Remarks:** Notes profits and global rank. **Number listed:** 7
1. Fleming (United States) with $17,502 million
2. Franz Haniel (Germany), $16,883
3. Supervalu (United States), $16,486
4. McKesson (United States), $13,719

5. Sysco (United States), $12,118
6. Edeka Zentrale (Germany), $10,906
7. Alco Standard (Germany), $9,892

Source: *Fortune,* The Global 500: World's Biggest Corporations (annual), August 5, 1996, p. F-26.

★ 2501 ★

PERIODICAL DISTRIBUTION IN POLAND

Ranked by: Number of sales outlets. **Remarks:** 60 private distributors are registered in Poland. **Number listed:** 9

1. Ruch with 27,800 outlets
2. Kolporter SA, 8,100
3. Bur Press, 1,500
4. Jard Press, 1,400
5. Garmond, 1,200
6. Goniec Podlaski, 1,000
7. Rolkon, 650
8. Fran-Press, 300
9. Other, 450

Source: *The Warsaw Voice,* January 7, 1996, p. 9.

★ 2502 ★

TOP VET EQUIPMENT DISTRIBUTORS IN SWITZERLAND

Ranked by: Market share, in percent. **Number listed:** 3

1. AB G.L. Jacoby with 48.0%
2. SweVet-Piab, 48.0%
3. Medexa AB, 4.0%

Source: *National Trade Data Bank,* May 27, 1996, p. ISA9411.

Wholesale Trade – Computers

★ 2503 ★

TOP COMPUTER DISTRIBUTORS, 1996

Ranked by: Sales, in billions of U.S. dollars. **Remarks:** Includes 1995 sales. **Number listed:** 7

1. Ingram Micro with $12.00 billion
2. Tech Data, $4.60
3. Computer 2000, $4.30
4. Merisel, $3.44
5. Intelligent Electronics, $2.70
6. MicroAge, $2.10
7. Inacom, $1.70

Source: *Computer Reseller News,* June 2, 1997, p. 98.

Wholesale Trade – Electronics

★ 2504 ★

SWEDEN'S WHOLESALE ELECTRONICS MARKET

Ranked by: Market share, in percent. **Number listed:** 6

1. ABB Asea Skandia with 30.0%
2. Selga, 20.0%
3. Ahlsell, 15.0%
4. Skoogs Elektriska, 15.0%
5. Storel AB, 15.0%
6. Other, 5.0%

Source: *National Trade Data Bank,* February 26, 1996, p. IMI960226.

Wholesale Trade – Europe

★ 2505 ★

TOP WHOLESALERS OF DURABLE GOODS IN EUROPE

Ranked by: Sales, in millions of European Currency Units (ECUs). **Remarks:** Also notes the number of employees. **Number listed:** 646

1. Sumitomo Corporation (U.K.) Plc with 15,523 million ECUs
2. Mitsui & Co. U.K. Plc, 14,211
3. Preussag A.G., 11,961
4. Franz Haniel & Cie. GmbH., 10,982
5. B.T.R. Plc, 10,421
6. Mitsubishi Corporation (U.K.) Plc, 9,269
7. Thyssen Handelsunion A.G., 8,291
8. Metallgesellschaft A.G., 8,008
9. Degussa A.G., 6,292
10. Thomson Multimedia, 5,676

Source: *Duns Europa* (annual), vol. 4, Dun & Bradstreet, 1997, p. 249+.

★ 2506 ★

TOP WHOLESALERS OF NON-DURABLE GOODS IN EUROPE

Ranked by: Sales, in millions of European Currency Units (ECUs). **Remarks:** Also notes the number of employees. **Number listed:** 672

1. Shell International Petroleum Co. Ltd. with 18,034 million ECUs
2. Glencore A.G., 17,923
3. Glencore International A.G., 17,923
4. Promodes, 15,640
5. Rewe & Co. OHG, 12,540
6. SHV Holdings NV, 12,223
7. Teranol A.G., 9,440
8. Vitol Holding BV, 9,290
9. SHV Makro NV, 8,941

10. Stinnes Vermoegensverwaltungs-A.G., 8,913
Source: *Duns Europa* (annual), vol. 4, Dun & Bradstreet, 1997, p. 257+.

Wine Industry

★ 2507 ★
CHILE'S WINE EXPORTS
Ranked by: Shipments, shown in millions of U.S. dollars.
Number listed: 5
1. United States with $41.0 million
2. United Kingdom, $26.0
3. Canada, $20.0
4. Denmark, $7.0
5. Holland, $7.0

Source: *Wines & Vines*, August 1996, p. 30.

★ 2508 ★
SPARKLING WINE MARKET IN ITALY, 1995
Ranked by: Market share based on volume, in percent.
Number listed: 7
1. Cepage (vitigno) with 19.1%
2. Prosecco, 14.2%
3. DOCG Asti Spumanti, 13.5%
4. Classic method, 10.6%
5. Champagne, 5.1%
6. Other sweet wines, 26.2%
7. Other dry wines, 11.3%

Source: *Marketing in Europe*, March 1997, p. 39.

★ 2509 ★
TOP WINE PRODUCING COUNTRIES, 1995
Ranked by: Production, in millions of gallons. **Number listed:** 13
1. Italy with 1,554 million gallons
2. France, 1,408
3. Spain, 544
4. Argentina, 433
5. United States, 428
6. Germany, 275
7. South Africa, 251
8. Former U.S.S.R., 227
9. Yugoslavia, 196
10. Portugal, 172

Source: *Wines & Vines*, May 1997, p. 22.

Wine Industry – Europe

★ 2510 ★
TOP WINE CONSUMING NATIONS IN THE EUROPEAN UNION
Ranked by: Consumption, in liters per capita. **Number listed:** 15
1. Italy with 61.9 liters
2. France, 60.7
3. Portugal, 57.4
4. Luxembourg, 53.7
5. Spain, 37.4
6. Austria, 31.1
7. Greece, 29.1
8. Denmark, 23.8
9. Germany, 23.1
10. Netherlands, 13.0

Source: *Europe*, August 1997, p. 32.

★ 2511 ★
TOP WINE PRODUCING NATIONS IN THE EUROPEAN UNION
Ranked by: Production, in hectoliters per year. **Number listed:** 10
1. Italy with 56,294,000 hectoliters
2. France, 55,610,000
3. Spain, 21,140,000
4. Germany, 8,361,000
5. Portugal, 7,255,000
6. Greece, 3,875,000
7. Austria, 2,229,000
8. Luxembourg, 150,000
9. United Kingdom, 13,000
10. Belgium, 2,000

Source: *Europe*, August 1997, p. 32.

Wine Industry – Export-Import Trade

★ 2512 ★
LARGEST WINE MARKETS IN ASIA, 1996
Ranked by: Market size, in thousands of U.S. dollars.
Remarks: Notes figures for 1995. **Number listed:** 7
1. Japan with $31,578 thousand
2. Hong Kong, $5,667
3. Taiwan, $5,239
4. Thailand, $4,993
5. South Korea, $3,390
6. Singapore, $2,749
7. China, $1,072

Source: *Wines & Vines*, May 1997, p. 19.

★ 2513 ★

**LEADING MARKETS FOR EXPORTS OF
BORDEAUX WINES, 1996**

Ranked by: Value of exports during the first six months
of 1996, in percent. **Remarks:** Also notes 1995 figures.
Number listed: 10

1. Germany with 18.8%
2. United States, 14.3%
3. United Kingdom, 12.9%
4. Switzerland, 12.0%
5. Belgium, 10.1%
6. Japan, 9.3%
7. Canada, 3.6%
8. Holland, 3.3%
9. Denmark, 3.2%
10. Rest of world, 12.5%

Source: *Financial Times*, May 25, 1997, p. 20.

★ 2514 ★

**TOP DESTINATIONS FOR AUSTRALIAN WINE
EXPORTS**

Ranked by: Distribution based on metric volume, in
percent. **Number listed:** 7

1. United Kingdom with 46.0%
2. United States, 13.0%
3. New Zealand, 11.0%
4. Canada, 5.0%
5. Sweden, 5.0%
6. Ireland, 3.0%
7. Others, 17.0%

Source: *Financial Times*, July 2, 1996, p. 18.

★ 2515 ★

**TOP DESTINATIONS FOR CHILEAN WINE
EXPORTS BY DOLLAR VALUE, 1995**

Ranked by: Value, in millions of U.S. dollars. **Number
listed:** 5

1. United States with $41 million
2. United Kingdom, $26
3. Canada, $20
4. Denmark, $7
5. Holland, $7

Source: *Wines & Vines*, August 1996, p. 30.

★ 2516 ★

**TOP DESTINATIONS FOR CHILEAN WINE
EXPORTS BY METRIC VOLUME, 1995**

Ranked by: Volume, in millions of liters. **Number listed:**
5

1. Canada with 24 million liters
2. United States, 24
3. United Kingdom, 14
4. Denmark, 5
5. Holland, 3

Source: *Wines & Vines*, August 1996, p. 30.

★ 2517 ★

TOP WINE EXPORTERS, 1995

Ranked by: Exports, in millions of gallons. **Number
listed:** 11

1. Italy with 462 million gallons
2. France, 309
3. Spain, 177
4. Germany, 66
5. Bulgaria, 50
6. Portugal, 42
7. United States, 37
8. Chile, 34
9. Hungary, 34
10. Australia, 29

Source: *Wines & Vines*, May 1997, p. 22.

★ 2518 ★

TOP WINE IMPORTERS, 1995

Ranked by: Imports, in millions of gallons. **Number
listed:** 13

1. Germany with 251 million gallons
2. United Kingdom, 185
3. France, 169
4. United States, 74
5. Belgium-Luxembourg, 63
6. Former U.S.S.R., 63
7. Spain, 63
8. Netherlands, 50
9. Switzerland, 50
10. Canada, 40

Source: *Wines & Vines*, May 1997, p. 22.

Wireless Communication Systems

★ 2519 ★

PHS SERVICE IN JAPAN

Ranked by: Market share, in percent. **Remarks:** PHS
stands for Personal Handyphone System. PHS has more
than 3.2 million subscribers in Japan. **Number listed:** 3

1. DDI Pocket Telephone with 51.5%
2. NTT Personal Communications, 25.9%
3. Astel, 22.6%

Source: *RCR*, August 26, 1996, p. 11.

Wisconsin – see under individual headings

Women – Employment

★ 2520 ★

EARNED INCOME OF WOMEN IN LATIN AMERICA

Ranked by: Share of earned income, in percent.
Remarks: Notes figures for United States, Central African Republic, and Japan. **Number listed:** 8

1. Colombia with 32%
2. Uruguay, 32%
3. Brazil, 29%
4. Venezuela, 26%
5. Mexico, 24%
6. Peru, 22%
7. Guatemala, 19%
8. Ecuador, 17%

Source: *Business Latin America*, November 4, 1996, p. 8.

★ 2521 ★

FEMALE ADMINISTRATORS AND MANAGERS IN LATIN AMERICA

Ranked by: Female administrators and managers as a percent of all administrators and managers. **Remarks:** Notes figures for United States, Central African Republic, and Japan. **Number listed:** 8

1. Ecuador with 32%
2. Guatemala, 32%
3. Colombia, 27%
4. Uruguay, 25%
5. Mexico, 20%
6. Peru, 20%
7. Venezuela, 18%
8. Brazil, 17%

Source: *Business Latin America*, November 4, 1996, p. 8.

★ 2522 ★

FEMALE PROFESSIONAL AND TECHNICAL WORKERS IN LATIN AMERICA

Ranked by: Female professional and technical workers as a percent of all professional and technical workers. **Remarks:** Notes figures for United States, Central African Republic, and Japan. **Number listed:** 8

1. Uruguay with 63%
2. Brazil, 57%
3. Venezuela, 55%
4. Ecuador, 48%
5. Guatemala, 45%
6. Mexico, 44%
7. Colombia, 42%
8. Peru, 41%

Source: *Business Latin America*, November 4, 1996, p. 8.

Women Executives

★ 2523 ★

TOP FEMALE FASHION DESIGNERS

Ranked by: Sales, in millions of U.S. dollars. **Remarks:** Includes country of origin. **Number listed:** 10

1. Donatella Versace Beck (Versace) with $730 million
2. Donna Karan (Donna Karan), $500
3. Muiccia Prada (Prada), $500
4. Hanae Mori (Hanae Mori), $450
5. Carole Little (Carole Little), $375
6. Agnes Trouble (Agnes B.), $248
7. Josephine Chaus (Bernard Chaus), $206
8. Paloma Picasso (Lopez-Cambil), $200
9. Jil Sander (Jil Sander), $200
10. Lea Gottlieb (Gottex), $60

Source: *World Business*, April 1996, p. 30.

Women-Owned Business Enterprises

★ 2524 ★

LARGEST WOMEN-OWNED FIRMS IN SLOVENIA, 1995

Ranked by: Gross turnover, in millions of U.S. dollars. **Remarks:** Includes name of chief executives for each firm. **Number listed:** 30

1. Kompas Mejni turisticni servis, d.d. with $59.101 million
2. Fructual, d.d., $53.125
3. Magistrat International, d.o.o., $50.000
4. Slovenijales Stanovanjska oprema, d.o.o., $50.000
5. Zdruzena HKS Novo mesto, p.o., $47.376
6. Trimo, d.d., $37.745
7. SZI FI PROM, d.o.o., $35.000
8. Gorenjska mlekarna, d.d., $28.979
9. Kras Commerce, d.d., $28.760
10. Prehrana TP, d.d., $27.393

Source: *Slovenian Business Report*, Winter 1996, p. 54.

Women's Apparel Industry
See: **Clothing Trade**

Wood Products

★ 2525 ★
LARGEST MEDIUM DENSITY FIBERBOARD MILLS, 1995
Ranked by: Production, in million square feet for a 3/4 inch basis. **Remarks:** Includes figures on production by company and future industry expansion. **Number listed:** 10

1. Fantoni SpA (Italy) with 328 million square feet
2. Bipan SpA (Avellino), 192
3. CSR Wood Panels (Australia), 170
4. Medite of Europe (Tripperary), 170
5. Kronospan (Luxembourg), 141
6. Kronotex (Germany), 141
7. Louisiana-Pacific Corp. (U.S.), 135
8. Caberboard Ltd. (U.K.), 130
9. Egger (Germany), 130
10. G-P Flakeboard Ltd. (Canada), 130

Source: *Wood & Wood Products*, January 1997, p. 88.

★ 2526 ★
LARGEST MEDIUM DENSITY FIBERBOARD PRODUCERS, 1995
Ranked by: Production, in million square feet for a 3/4 inch basis. **Remarks:** Includes figures on production by company and future industry expansion. **Number listed:** 10

1. United States with 1,508 million square feet
2. Germany, 814
3. Italy, 685
4. South Korea, 584
5. China, 521
6. Australia, 417
7. Malaysia, 392
8. Canada, 367
9. New Zealand, 367
10. Spain, 334

Source: *Wood & Wood Products*, January 1997, p. 88.

★ 2527 ★
LARGEST PARTICLEBOARD PRODUCERS, 1995
Ranked by: Production, in million square feet for a 3/4 inch basis. **Remarks:** Includes figures on production by company and future industry expansion. **Number listed:** 10

1. Germany with 5,282 million square feet
2. United States, 5,037
3. Russia, 3,087
4. Italy, 2,479
5. Belgium, 1,960
6. France, 1,832
7. Turkey, 1,494
8. Canada, 1,278

9. United Kingdom, 1,197
10. Poland, 1,007

Source: *Wood & Wood Products*, January 1997, p. 88.

★ 2528 ★
TOP WOOD PROCESSING COMPANIES IN SLOVENIA BY EXPORTS, 1996
Ranked by: Value of exports, in tolars (To). **Remarks:** Also notes imports for 1996, as well as import and export plans for 1997. **Number listed:** 39

1. Inles Holding, d.d. with To5,607,598,000
2. Javor, d.d., To4,386,367,000
3. LIP Lesna industrija Bled., d.d., To4,236,984,450
4. Inles Hrast, d.d., To4,094,151,000
5. Slovenijales Stanovanjska oprema, d.d., To3,686,845,440
6. Marles Hise, d.o.o., To3,216,000,000
7. Jelovica, d.d., To2,591,779,000
8. KLI Logatec, p.o., To2,541,388,235
9. Brest Pohistivo, d.o.o., To2,313,660,000
10. Liko, d.d., To2,306,727,000

Source: *Slovenian Business Report*, Summer 1997, p. 43.

★ 2529 ★
TOP WOODEN DOOR MAKERS IN JAPAN, 1995
Ranked by: Market share, in percent. **Remarks:** Production reached 310 billion yen. **Number listed:** 7

1. Houtech with 3.9%
2. Eidai Industries, 2.3%
3. Matsushita Electric Works, 1.9%
4. Nihon Flush, 1.9%
5. Daiken Kogyo, 1.8%
6. Dantani Industries, 1.5%
7. Juken Industries, 1.3%

Source: *National Trade Data Bank*, June 4, 1996, p. ISA960501.

Workstations (Office Automation)

★ 2530 ★
TOP WORKSTATION MAKERS IN THE NETHERLANDS, 1995
Ranked by: Market share, in percent. **Number listed:** 6

1. Sun Microsystems with 41.0%
2. Hewlett Packard, 20.0%
3. Silicon Graphics, 14.0%
4. IBM, 9.0%
5. Digital, 8.0%
6. Other, 8.0%

Source: *National Trade Data Bank*, August 19, 1996, p. IMI960815.

★ 2531 ★
TOP WORKSTATION PRODUCERS WORLDWIDE
Ranked by: Market share, in percent. **Number listed:** 8
1. Sun with 20.4%
2. Hewlett-Packard, 17.5%
3. IBM, 15.6%
4. Silicon Graphics, 7.1%
5. DEC, 6.9%
6. Fujitsu, 2.5%
7. Intergraph, 1.9%
8. Others, 28.1%
Source: *Business Today*, May 22, 1996, p. 77.

★ 2532 ★
UNIX WORKSTATION MARKET, 1995
Ranked by: Market share, in percent. **Number listed:** 10
1. Sun with 35.0%
2. HP, 20.0%
3. SGI, 13.0%
4. IBM, 12.0%
5. DEC, 9.0%
6. Other, 11.0%
Source: *Investor's Business Daily*, June 13, 1996, p. A8.

Workstations (Office Automation), Japan

★ 2533 ★
JAPAN'S WORKSTATION MAKERS
Ranked by: Market share, in percent. **Number listed:** 6
1. Nihon Sun Microsystems with 29.9%
2. Hewlett-Packard Japan, 23.4%
3. NEC, 13.2%
4. Fujitsu, 9.3%
5. Hitachi, 6.4%
6. Others, 17.8%
Source: *Nikkei Weekly*, July 15, 1996, p. 8.

Yemen – see under individual headings

Yugoslavia – see under individual headings

Zaire – see under individual headings

Zambia – see under individual headings

Zimbabwe – see under individual headings

Zimbabwe Stock Exchange

★ 2534 ★
LARGEST COMPANIES ON THE ZIMBABWE STOCK EXCHANGE, 1995
Ranked by: Market value, in millions of Zimbabwe dollars (Z$). **Number listed:** 20
1. Delta with Z$4,034.03 million
2. Bindura Nickel, Z$1,576.91
3. Barclays Bank of Zimbabwe, Z$1,243.24
4. Zimbabwe Sun, Z$1,157.52
5. Hippo Valley Estates, Z$1,075.82
6. Tobacco Sales, Z$779.98
7. Portland Holdings, Z$702.39
8. Rio Tinto Zimbabwe, Z$618.75
9. National Foods, Z$579.94
10. Plate Glass Industries, Z$563.54
Source: *GT Guide to World Equity Markets* (annual), Euromoney Publications, 1996, p. 498.

★ 2535 ★
MOST ACTIVELY TRADED SHARES ON THE ZIMBABWE STOCK EXCHANGE, 1995
Ranked by: Trading value, in millions of Zimbabwe dollars (Z$). **Number listed:** 15
1. Delta with Z$593.09 million
2. Bindura Nickel, Z$85.36
3. TA Holdings, Z$61.22
4. Wankie Colliery, Z$45.07
5. Portland Holdings, Z$44.75
6. Colcom Holdings, Z$38.39
7. Zimbabwe Sun, Z$33.76
8. Hippo Valley Estates, Z$28.16
9. National Foods, Z$22.42
10. Barclays Bank of Zimbabwe, Z$20.86
Source: *GT Guide to World Equity Markets* (annual), Euromoney Publications, 1996, p. 498.

Zinc

★ 2536 ★
LARGEST ZINC PLANTS WORLDWIDE
Ranked by: Capacity, in metric tons. **Remarks:** Notes the location of each facility. **Number listed:** 12
1. San Juan de Nieva (AZSA) with 320,000 metric tons
2. Trail (Cominco), 272,000
3. Valteyfield (Noranda), 250,000
4. Ust-Kamenogorsk (Estado), 240,000

5. Auby (Union Miniere), 230,000
6. Ruludao (Estado), 230,000
7. Burdel (Pasminco), 220,000
8. Risdon (Pasminco), 220,000
9. Balen (Union Miniere), 200,000
10. Onsan (Korea Zinc), 200,000

Source: *El Pais*, March 2, 1997, p. 7.

★ **2537** ★
TOP ZINC CONSUMING COUNTRIES, 1995
Ranked by: Production, in thousands of tons. **Number listed:** 5
1. United States with 1,202 thousand tons
2. China, 887
3. Japan, 752
4. Germany, 503
5. Italy, 345

Source: *Japanese Finance and Industry*, 1997, p. 5.

★ **2538** ★
TOP ZINC PRODUCERS IN JAPAN, 1995
Ranked by: Market share based on sales of 666,000 tons, in percent. **Number listed:** 7
1. Mitsui Mining & Smelting with 25.0%
2. Toho Zinc, 16.8%
3. Nippon Mining and Metals, 15.0%
4. Sumitomo Metal Mining, 14.7%
5. Dowa Mining, 14.5%
6. Mitsubishi Materials, 13.1%
7. Others, 0.9%

Source: *Japanese Finance and Industry*, 1997, p. 24.

★ **2539** ★
TOP ZINC PRODUCING NATIONS, 1995
Ranked by: Production of refined zinc, in thousands of metric tons. **Number listed:** 8
1. Europe with 2,147 thousand metric tons
2. Canada, 720
3. Japan, 664
4. United States, 363
5. Australia, 322
6. Mexico, 219
7. Peru, 160
8. Other, 879

Source: *Engineering & Mining Journal*, 1997 Commodities Review Issue (annual), March 1997, p. WW-45.

Zurich Stock Exchange

★ **2540** ★
LARGEST SWISS COMPANIES ON THE ZURICH STOCK EXCHANGE, 1995
Ranked by: Market value, in millions of Swiss francs (SFr). **Number listed:** 20
1. Roche GS with SFr64,073.72 million
2. Sandoz N, SFr36,791.22
3. SBG I, SFr26,069.72
4. Ciba-GY N, SFr25,441.25
5. CS Holding, SFr21,704.08
6. Rueckv N, SFr18,825.08
7. Zuerich N, SFr15,562.67
8. SBV I, SFr11,241.31
9. BBC I N, SFr10,355.49
10. SBV N, SFr6,511.05

Source: *GT Guide to World Equity Markets* (annual), Euromoney Publications, 1996, p. 320.

★ **2541** ★
MOST ACTIVELY TRADED SHARES ON THE ZURICH STOCK EXCHANGE, 1995
Ranked by: Trading value, in millions of Swiss francs (SFr). **Number listed:** 20
1. Roche GS with SFr4,710.72 million
2. Nestle N, SFr3,333.00
3. Ciba-Gy N, SFr2,794.09
4. Rueckv N, SFr2,792.35
5. SBV I, SFr2,371.40
6. SBG I, SFr1,776.65
7. Sandoz N, SFr1,708.07
8. W'thur N, SFr1,683.30
9. CS Holding N, SFr1,219.41
10. SBV N, SFr1,195.87

Source: *GT Guide to World Equity Markets* (annual), Euromoney Publications, 1996, p. 321.

Index

AIG
  Advertising Expenditures
    103
  Captive Insurance
    Companies – Bermuda
  Financial Institutions 1442
  Insurance Companies 1693
  Investment Management
    Firms – Rating – Asia 1740
Aim
  Toothpaste 2431
Air Canada
  Airlines 133
Air France
  Advertising Expenditures
    102
  Air Freight Service 127, 128
  Airlines 135, 136, 138
  Airlines – Europe 140
Air fresheners
  Cleaning Products Industry
    656
Air Liquide
  Bourse de Paris 456
  Gases 1521, 1522
Air New Zealand
  Corporations – New Zealand
    1015
  New Zealand Stock
    Exchange 1974
Air Products
  Gases 1521, 1522
Air Tours
  Tourist Trade 2434
  Travel Agencies 2460
Airborne
  Air Freight Service 123
Airlines
  Air Freight Service 123
  Corporations 876
Airtel
  Cellular Radio Service
    Companies 590, 591
  Cellular Telephones 596
Aisin AV
  Automobile Parts 230
Aisin AW
  Automobile Parts 224
Aisin Seiki
  Automobile Parts 224, 229,
    230
Aite
  Air Conditioning Industry
    120
Aitken Spence
  Colombo Stock Exchange
    690, 691
AIU
  Insurance Companies –
    Japan 1711
  Insurance, Property and
    Casualty 1724
Ajax
  Housewares 1626
Ajinomoto Co. Inc.
  Food Industry and Trade –
    Asia 1470
Akai
  High Technology Industries
    1590
Akbank
  Banks and Banking – Turkey
    401

  Istanbul Stock Exchange
    1762
Aker AS
  Corporations – Norway 1017
Akira Sato
  Financial Analysts – Japan
    1383
Akouta
  Uranium Industry 2476
Aksa
  Istanbul Stock Exchange
    1762
Aksan-Istanbul
  Metal Products 1905
Aktiva PZDU Ljublana
  Corporations 870
Aktor A.T.E.
  Construction Industry 786
Akzo Faser
  Fiber Industry, International
    1312
Akzo Nobel
  Amsterdam Stock Exchange
    161
  Chemical Industries 619
  Chemical Industries –
    Europe 628, 629
  Chemical Industries –
    Western Europe 633
  Corporations – Netherlands
    1011, 1012, 1014
  Drug Industry 1135
**Al Bustan Palace Inter-
  Continental**
  Hotels and Motels,
    International 1613
**Al Rajhi Banking and
  Investment Corp.**
  Banks and Banking 266
Alain Galene
  Financial Analysts 1321
Alamein
  Sporting Goods Industry
    2309
Alan Broughton
  Financial Analysts – Europe
    1350
Alan Butler-Henderson
  Financial Analysts – Asia
    1338
Alan Carter
  Financial Analysts – United
    Kingdom 1437
Alan Erskine
  Financial Analysts – United
    Kingdom 1427
Alan Macdonald
  Financial Analysts – United
    Kingdom 1435
Alanis Morissette
  Entertainers 1244
Alastair Irvine
  Financial Analysts – United
    Kingdom 1416
Alba
  Executives 1274
Albacomp
  Computer Industry 716
Albarus
  Automobile Parts 240
Alberta
  Coal Industry 675
  Golf 1566

  Hogs 1592
  Home Improvement
    Centers 1598
  Soccer 2279
Alberta Wheat Pool
  Grain 1570
Alcampo
  Retail Trade – Spain 2195
Alcan (Canada)
  Corporations – Japan 998
Alcan Aluminium
  Corporations – Canada 947,
    949, 950, 952
  Corporations – France 977
  Montreal Exchange 1929,
    1930
  Research, Industrial –
    Canada 2171, 2172
  Toronto Stock Exchange
    2433
Alcatel Alsthom
  Bourse de Paris 456, 457
  Corporations – Europe 959
  Corporations – France 975,
    976
  Steel Industry and Trade
    2319
Alcin-Istanbul
  Metal Products 1905
Alco Standard
  Wholesale Trade 2500
Alcoa
  Metal Industry 1902
Alcoholic Beverages
  Advertising 67
  Beer 414, 421, 423, 424, 425
  Beverage Industry 426
  Liquor Industry 1826, 1833,
    1837
Alcopops
  Liquor Industry 1826
Aldi Group
  Coffee Industry 680, 681
  Convenience Stores 814
  Grocery Trade 1577
  Personal Care Products
    2057, 2058
  Retail Trade 2184, 2185
  Trading Companies –
    Europe 2448
Alec Pelmore
  Financial Analysts – United
    Kingdom 1437
Alem Bank Kazakhstan
  Banks and Banking –
    Kazakhstan 346
Alembia
  Drug Industry 1128
Alembic
  Drug Industry 1115
Alestra
  Telephone Companies 2379
Alex Brown
  Equity Research,
    International 1252
Alex. Brown & Sons
  Security Underwriting 2220
**Alexander & Alexander
  Services Inc.**
  Insurance Brokers 1684,
    1685

**Alexander Consulting Group
  Inc.**
  Employee Benefit
    Consultants 1198
**Alexander Insurance
  Managers Ltd.**
  Captive Insurance
    Companies – Bermuda
Alexander Kinmont
  Financial Analysts – Japan
    1390
Alexander Pomento
  Financial Analysts –
    Philippines 1409
Alfa
  Corporations 874, 890
  Corporations – Mexico 1009
  Mexico Stock Exchange
    1909, 1910
Alfa Romeo
  Automobile Industry and
    Trade 189
  Automobile Industry and
    Trade – Europe 211
Alfred Berg
  Financial Analysts 1327
Algeciras, Spain
  Ports 2115
Alger, Algeria
  Airports 146
Algeria
  Automobile Industry and
    Trade 200
  Banks and Banking 269
  Banks and Banking – Algeria
    277
  Chocolate Industry 639
  Electricity 1178
  Gas Industry 1515, 1516
  Gold 1527, 1528, 1529, 1556
  Labor Supply 1796
  Natural Gas 1968, 1969,
    1970, 1972, 1973
  Petroleum Industry 2075
  Sporting Goods 2301
  Truck Industry 2465
Alicia Ogawa
  Financial Analysts – Japan
    1401
Alico
  Insurance Companies 1689
  Insurance, Life 1717
Alicorp
  Corporations 891
Alitalia
  Airlines – Europe 140
ALK
  Drug Industry 1120
All Asia
  Brokers – Philippines 521,
    523, 524
  Security Underwriting –
    Philippines 2229
All Nippon Airways
  Airlines 134
  Airlines – Asia 139
  Transportation – Asia 2453,
    2454
All Star
  Amusement Parks – Latin
    America 162
Allard et associes
  Advertising Agencies –

Index

Index

Index

277
Banque Nationale de Mauritanie
Banks and Banking – Mauritania 364
Banque Nationale pour le Commerce
Banks and Banking – Madagascar 359
Banque Nationale pour le Developpement Economique Sarl
Banks and Banking – Burundi 299
Banque Nat'l de Paris (Canada)
Banks and Banking, Foreign – Canada 321
Banque Paribas
Banks and Banking 262
Euroloans 1269
Mutual Funds 1955
Security Underwriting 2218
Banque pour le Commerce et l'Industrie-Mer Rouge
Banks and Banking – Djibouti 312
Banque Sengalo-Tunisienne
Banks and Banking – Senegal 382
Banque Togolaise de Developpement
Banks and Banking – Togo 398
Banques Populaires
Credit Cards 1065
Mutual Funds 1955
Bansud
Banks and Banking – Argentina 278
Barbados
Tourist Trade 2438
Barbie
Toy Industry 2443
Barcadi
Liquor Industry 1827
Barcalys de Zoete Wedd
Eurobond Market 1257
Barcelona, Spain
Automobile Plants 241
Ports 2115
Barclaycard
Credit Cards – Great Britain 1070
Barclays
Banks and Banking 265
Banks and Banking – Europe 318
Corporations – United Kingdom 1044, 1046
Financial Services 1446
Barclays Bank
Banks and Banking 262
Banks and Banking, Foreign 319
Cigarette Industry 649, 650
Credit Cards 1067
Euroloans 1269
Global Custodians 1526
Mortgages 1933
Barclays Bank Kenya
Corporations 872

Barclays Bank of Botswana Limited
Banks and Banking – Botswana 294
Barclays Bank of Sierra Leone Limited
Banks and Banking – Sierra Leone 383
Barclays Bank of Swaziland Limited
Banks and Banking – Swaziland 392
Barclays Bank of Unganda Limited
Banks and Banking – Uganda 402
Barclays Bank of Zimbabwe
Corporations 872
Zimbabwe Stock Exchange 2534, 2535
Barclays Global
Pension Plan Administrators – United Kingdom 2047
Pension Plans – Europe 2051
Barclays Plc
Banks and Banking – Europe 317
Charities – United Kingdom 614
Barilla SpA
Advertisers – Italy 49
Baring
Brokers – Indonesia 494, 495, 496, 497, 498
Pension Plans – United Kingdom 2052
Baring Asset Mgmt. Ltd.
Investment Management Firms – Rating – Asia 1740
Baring Brothers & Co., Ltd
Corporate Acquisition and Merger Services 827
Baring Brothers & Co., Ltd.
Corporate Acquisitions and Mergers 832, 834
Baring Securities Japan
Security Underwriting – Japan 2226
Barings/Dillon Read
Corporate Acquistions and Mergers – Germany 838
Barito Pacific Timber
Jakarta Stock Exchange 1766, 1767
Barlows Limited
Johannesburg Stock Exchange 1779
Barnardos
Charities – United Kingdom 615
Baroque Furniture
Furniture Industry 1502
Barraclough Hall Woolston Gray
Direct Marketing – United Kingdom 1106
Barrera, Siquieros y Torres Landa, S.C.
Law Firms 1808
Barrick Gold
Corporations – Canada 950
Gold 1561, 1562

Gold Mines and Mining 1565
Montreal Exchange 1929
Toronto Stock Exchange 2433
Barry's Tea
Grocery Trade 1574
Barton Biggs
Financial Analysts, International 1375, 1378
Barum-Continental (Czech Republic)
Tire Industry 2412
Baseball
Sporting Goods Industry 2306
Sports Clubs 2311, 2312
BASF
Chemical Industries 619, 621, 622, 623, 624
Chemical Industries – Canada 627
Chemical Industries – Europe 628, 629
Chemical Industries – Western Europe 633
Corporations – Germany 979, 981
Drug Industry 1126, 1135
Electronic Industries 1186
Frankfurt Stock Exchange 1493
Insecticides 1664
Pesticides Industry 2061
Plastics Industry 2098
Basham, Ringe y Correa, S.C.
Law Firms 1808
Basketball
Sporting Goods Industry 2306
Sports Clubs 2311
Basque Region
Marinas 1884
Bass
Beer 414, 419
Beverage Industry – Europe 435
Fishing 1453
Leisure 1819
Liquor Industry 1826
Bass Brewers
Brewing Industry – United Kingdom 466
Bass Taverns
Bars and Barrooms – Great Britain 411
Bassat
Advertising Agencies – Spain 93
Basten Greenhill Andrews
Industrial Designers – United Kingdom 1640
Bastow Charleton
Accounting Firms – Ireland 17
BAT Industries
Corporations – Europe 966
Corporations – United Kingdom 1043, 1045, 1046
London Stock Exchange 1851
Tobacco Industry 2418, 2420
Tobacco Industry – Europe

2422
Bata
Athletic Shoes 168
Leather Goods 1817
Bata Shoe (Bangladesh)
Dhaka Stock Exchange 1098
Bates Advertising Holding
Advertising Agencies – Spain 93
Bates Centrade Saatchi & Saatchi
Advertising Agencies – Romania 92
Bates Dorland
Advertising Agencies – United Kingdom 98
Bates Gruppen
Advertising Agencies – Norway 90
Bates Gruppen Denmark
Advertising Agencies – Denmark 76
Bates Hong Kong
Advertising Agencies – Hong Kong 82
Bates Ireland
Advertising Agencies – Ireland 84
Bates Malaysia
Advertising Agencies – Malaysia 88
Bates Saatchi & Saatchi Advertising
Advertising Agencies – Costa Rica 75
Batey Ads Malaysia
Advertising Agencies – Malaysia 88
Batman Forever
Motion Picture Industry 1936
Baton Broadcasting
Television Broadcasting 2387
Batu Hijau
Gold Mines and Mining 1564
Bau Holding A.G.
Corporations – Austria 938
Bauer
Magazines 1869
Media – Europe 1893
Milk 1917
Sporting Goods 2303
Bausch & Lomb
Accessories 1
Contact Lenses 792
Personal Care Products 2059
Bavaria
Beer 417
Corporations 885
Bavarian Re
Reinsurance 2163
Baxters of Speyside
Canned Food Industry 575
Baxters Soup
Canned Food Industry 575
BAY
Automated Teller Machines 172
Furniture Stores 1507

World Business Rankings Annual

Index

Index

Index

Hardee's
Fast Food Restaurants 1308
Harley Davidson
Motorcycle Industry 1940
Harper/Circle Group
Forwarding Companies 1487
Harpic
Cleaning Products Industry
657
Harrods
Department Stores 1089
Hartford Fire Group
Insurance Companies 1699
**Hartsfield Atlanta
International**
Airports 149
Harvest Advertising Co., Ltd.
Advertising Agencies –
Taiwan 95
Harvey Nichols
Department Stores 1089
Harza Engineering Co.
Engineering Construction
Companies 1227
Hasbro
Toy Industry 2443
Hasegawa
Flavoring Essences Industry
1456
Haseko
Corporations – Asia 920
Haseko Corp.
Corporations – Asia 918
Hassi R'mel
Natural Gas 1967
Hatton National Bank
Banks and Banking – Sri
Lanka 390
Colombo Stock Exchange
690, 691
Havas
Advertising Agencies 70
Advertising Agencies –
Europe 77
Entertainment Industries
1246, 1247
Holding Companies 1593
Media – Europe 1893
Havix
Nonwoven Fabrics
Industry – Japan 1993
Hawaii
Duty Free Importation 1151
Hawaiian Tropic
Sun Care Products 2345
Hawkes Bay Forests
Forestry 1486
Hayes Wheel
Corporate Acquisitions and
Mergers 829
Hayles
Colombo Stock Exchange
690, 691
Hayward Pools
Sporting Goods Industry
2310
Hazama Corp.
Contractors 801
Haze
Cleaning Products Industry
657
HB
Beer 425

Cigarette Industry –
Germany 654
**HBG, Hollandsche Beton
Groep N.V.**
Contractors 797, 802
Contractors, Foreign –
Africa 805
Contractors, Foreign –
Europe 808
HCL Consulting
Computer Software Industry
749
HCL Corporation Ltd.
Computer Software Industry
769
HCL HP
Computer Networks 739
**HDI Haftpflichtverband der
Deutschen Industrie
V.a.G.**
Insurance Companies –
Germany 1710
Head & Shoulders
Shampoos 2254
Health Clubs
Health Clubs 1586
Health o meter Products
Household Appliances 1619
Health services
Corporate Acquisitions and
Mergers – International
Aspects 843
**Heathrow Airport (London,
England)**
Airports 149, 152
Duty Free Importation 1151
Duty Free Shops 1152
Heaven's Gardens
Talc 2352
Hebros Bank
Banks and Banking –
Bulgaria 297
Hector
Computer Industry 710
**Heidelberger
Druckmaschinen**
Engineering Construction
Companies 1229
Heidelberger Zement A.G.
Leather Industry – Europe
1818
Manufacturing Industries –
Europe 1882
Heidemij N.V.
Engineering Construction
Companies 1231
Heidrick & Struggles
Executive Search
Consultants 1270
Heineken
Advertising Expenditures
101
Amsterdam Stock Exchange
160
Beer 413, 418, 419, 421, 423,
425
Beverage Industry – Europe
435
Brewing Industry – United
Kingdom 466
Corporations – Netherlands
1013

Heinie Hakker
Financial Analysts 1332
Heinz
Canned Food Industry 575
Infants' Food 1655, 1656
Infants' Supplies – United
Kingdom 1658
Spices 2298
Heiwado
Convenience Stores 813
Helicopters
Aerospace Industries –
Export-Import Trade 113
Hella
Automobile Parts 228
Hellenic Bank Limited
Banks and Banking – Cyprus
308
Hellenic Bottling Co.
Athens Stock Exchange 165,
166
Hellenic - British Life
Insurance Companies 1689
Insurance, Life 1717
Hellenic Sugar Industry SA
Athens Stock Exchange 166
Hellman's
Spices 2298
**Hellmuth, Obata &
Kassabaum Inc.**
Engineering Construction
Companies 1230
Help The Aged
Charities – United Kingdom
615
Helsinki, Finland
Employee Vacations,
International 1204
Helsinki Stock Exchanges
Stock Exchanges – Europe
2333
Hem-Hamburg
Automobile Service Stations
248
Henderson Land Development
Corporations – Asia 922
Corporations – Hong Kong
984
Equity Research,
International 1250
Hong Kong Stock Exchange
1600, 1601
Institutional Investments
1668
Investments, Foreign – Hong
Kong 1755, 1756
Hendry Hay McIntosh
Brokers – New Zealand 510,
511, 512, 513, 514
Henkel
Advertisers – Germany 48
Chemical Industries 622
Chemical Industries –
Europe 628
Cosmetics Industry 1049
Detergents 1095
Soap Industry 2274
Toothpaste 2429
Hennessy
Liquor Industry 1827
Henning Olsen
Ice Cream, Ices, etc. 1630

Henri Chermont
Financial Analysts 1321
Heracles General Cement Co.
Athens Stock Exchange 165
Hering Nordeste
Clothing Trade 672
Hering Textil
Clothing Trade 669
Hermes
Accessories 1
Hermes Plus, D.D.
Computer Industry 712
Heroux Inc.
Aerospace Industries 110
Hershey Foods
Confectionery 781
Hertz
Automobile Leasing and
Rental Companies 222
Travel 2457
Hess Oil Virgin Islands
Petroleum Refineries 2088
Hestia Insurance
Insurance Companies 1695
Hestja
Insurance Companies 1695
Hetzel
Travel Agencies 2460
Heung Ah Tire & Rubber
Rubber Industry 2202
Hewitt Associates L.L.C.
Employee Benefit
Consultants 1198
Hewlett-Packard
Computer Industry 701, 703,
704, 705, 706, 707, 709,
714, 716, 717, 718, 719,
720
Hewlett Packard
Computer Industry 725
Hewlett-Packard
Computer Industry 726
Computer Industry – Canada
729
Computer Networks 735,
736, 737, 738
Computer Printers 741, 742,
743, 744, 745
Corporations 851
Corporations – Asia 913,
914, 919, 921, 924, 929
Corporations, Foreign 974
Factories 1301, 1302
Information Technology
1660
Instrument Industry –
Europe 1683
Machinery – Europe 1865
Manufacturing Industries –
Asia 1880
Microcomputers 1911, 1912
Hewlett Packard
Workstations (Office
Automation) 2530
Hewlett-Packard
Workstations (Office
Automation) 2531, 2532
Workstations (Office
Automation), Japan 2533
**H.F. & Ph.F. Reemtsma
G.m.b.H. & Co.**
Tobacco Industry – Europe
2422

925, 928, 930
Corporations – Japan 998
Disk Drive Industry 1107
Employment 1216
Factories 1301
Information Technology
1660
Manufacturing Industries
1879
Manufacturing Industries –
Asia 1880
Microcomputers 1911, 1912
Multimedia Equipment 1942
Research, Industrial –
Canada 2171, 2172
Semiconductor Industry
2240, 2246
Semiconductor Industry –
Europe 2249
Workstations (Office
Automation) 2530, 2531,
2532
IBM Deutschland GmbH
Corporations, Foreign 974
Machinery – Europe 1865
IBM France (Compagnie)
Machinery – Europe 1865
IBM Japan
Computer Industry 702
Information Technology
1659
IBM Korea
Point-of-Sale Systems 2108
IBM Semea S.P.A.
Machinery – Europe 1865
IBM Slovenija, D.O.O.
Computer Industry 712, 713
IBM Turk Ltd
Computer Software Industry
755
**IBM United Kingdom
Holdings Ltd.**
Machinery – Europe 1865
IBP
Corporations 854
Food Industry and Trade
1460
ICA Handlarnas AB
Corporations – Sweden 1031
ICBC
Bank Credit Cards 255
ICCI
Cobalt 678
Icebank Ltd.
Banks and Banking – Iceland
332
Iceland
Economy 1156
Gross National Product
1580
Income 1637
Internet (Computer
Network) 1732
Quality of Life 2141, 2142
Supermarkets – United
Kingdom 2349
ICF Kaiser International Inc.
Contractors 798
Engineering Construction
Companies 1231, 1235
Ichitaro Office
Computer Software Industry
750

ICI
Chemical Industries –
Canada 627
Chemical Industries –
Europe 628
Chemical Industries –
Western Europe 633
Corporate Acquisitions and
Mergers 833
Employment 1214
Karachi Stock Exchange
1781, 1782
Paint Industry 2019
ICICI Securities
Merchant Banking 1900
**ICL Poland Operators
(Warsaw/London)**
Computer Industry 704
IDBI
Merchant Banking 1900
Taxation 2355
Ideal Bike
Bicycles 437
Ideal Standard
Ceramics 609
Idee (Darboven)
Coffee Industry 680
Idemitsu
Gasoline 1523
Idemitsu Kosan
Petroleum Industry 2079,
2081
Idemitsu Petrochemical
Nonwoven Fabrics
Industry – Japan 1992
Plastics Industry 2107
IDEO
Industrial Designers –
United Kingdom 1638
Ideology Advertising Agency
Advertising Agencies –
Taiwan 95
Iderol
Truck Plants 2471
IDO
Cellular Telephones 597
Idris
Kuala Lumpur Stock
Exchange 1788
IDT
Semiconductor Industry
2242
IDV
Beverage Industry 433
Liquor Industry 1832
IEC
Electronic Industries –
Distributors 1193
IFAC
Accounting Firms – Ireland
17
IFCT Finance
Security Underwriting –
Thailand 2232
IFF
Cosmetics Industry 1053
Flavoring Essences Industry
1456
IGA
Grocery Trade 1575
Igal Brightman
Accounting Firms 4

Igasa
Automobile Parts 235
**Iglo - Industrias de Gelados
Lda**
Corporations – Portugal
1021
Ignacio Gomez Montejo
Financial Analysts 1330
Igsas
Fertilizer Industry 1310
Iguaza
Airports 145
Ihlas Holding
Istanbul Stock Exchange
1763
IKEA
Furniture Industry 1501
Furniture Stores 1507
Ilanga
Newspapers – Editions 1981
Ilas
Milk 1919
Illinois
Soybean Industry 2296
Illustrert Vitenskap
Magazines 1868
Ilva Laminati Piani S.P.A.
Metal Industry – Europe
1903
Imabari Shipbuilding
Shipbuilding 2258
Imagination
Industrial Designers –
United Kingdom 1638,
1640, 1641
Imasco Ltd.
Corporations – Canada 946
Imation (3M)
Disk Drive Industry 1108
Imhoff
Chocolate Industry 640
IMI
Financial Analysts 1324
Italian Stock Exchange 1764
Immex
Biotechnology Industries
440
IMMSA
Silver Mines and Mining
2266
IMP
Sales Promotion Agencies –
United Kingdom 2204
Imperial
Banks and Banking – Russia
(Republic) 380, 381
Hotels and Motels 1603,
1604
**Imperial Cancer Reserach
Fund**
Charities – United Kingdom
615
Imperial Chemical Industries
Chemical Industries 619, 621
Chemical Industries –
Europe 629
Imperial Leather
Soap Industry 2276
Imperial Oil
Charitable Contributions
613
Chemical Industries –
Canada 627

Corporations – Canada 950
Montreal Exchange 1929
Petroleum Industry –
Canada 2085
Research, Industrial –
Canada 2172
Imperial Tobacco Ltd.
Tobacco Industry – Europe
2422
IMPREGILO S.P.A.
Contractors 803
Contractors, Foreign –
Africa 805
Contractors, Foreign – Latin
America 809
IMS Group
Telemarketing – United
Kingdom 2371
IMSA
Corporations 903
In Time
Courier Services 1062
INA
Insurance, Life 1718
Italian Stock Exchange 1764
Privatization 2133
Inaba Denkisangyo
Industrial Equipment
Industry 1648
Inacom
Wholesale Trade –
Computers 2503
Inbursa
Insurance Companies 1703
Leasing and Renting of
Equipment 1813
Inchikawa Woolen Textile
Nonwoven Fabrics
Industry – Japan 1991
Inchon Iron & Steel
Metal Industry – France
1904
Inco Ltd.
Cobalt 678
Mining Industry 1926
Montreal Exchange 1930
Toronto Stock Exchange
2433
Indah Kiat Paper & Pulp
Corporations – India 987
Jakarta Stock Exchange
1767
Independence Day
Motion Picture Industry
1937
India
Air Pollution 130
Airplanes 141
Airports – Asia 153
Automobile Industry and
Trade 202
Banks and Banking 264
Capital Market 576
Chocolate Industry 639
Coal Industry 676
Competitiveness 694
Computer Programmers,
International 746
Computer Software Industry
747, 748, 763
Corporations 882
Credit Cards – Asia 1069
Crime and Criminals 1071,

Index

Jardine International Motor Holdings Ltd.
Corporations – Hong Kong 982

Jardine Matheson Holdings
Corporations – Asia 923
Corporations – Hong Kong 985
Corporations – Singapore 1024
Multinational Corporations 1943, 1944

Jardine Strategic Holdings Ltd.
Corporations – Asia 934

Jarislowsky, Fraser Limited
Investment Management Firms – Rating – Canada

Jason Donville
Financial Analysts – Indonesia 1373

Jauregui, Navarrete, Nader y Rojas, S.C.
Law Firms 1808

Jave Licores S.A.
Liquor Industry 1828

Javor, d.d.
Wood Products 2528

Jaya Real Property
Corporations – Asia 926

Jazz
Perfumes 2053

JB Were
Brokers – Australia 474, 475, 476, 477, 478
Brokers – New Zealand 511, 512, 513, 514
Financial Analysts – Australia 1343
Financial Analysts – New Zealand 1408
Security Underwriting – New Zealand 2228

JBR McCann
Advertising Agencies – Norway 90

J.C. Bamford
Engineering Construction Companies 1229

J.C. Penney
Mail Order Business 1871
Retail Trade 2177

JCB
Construction Equipment Industry 784

JCI
Gold Mines and Mining 1565

J.D. Edwards
Computer Software Industry 753

J.E. Teixeira
Automobile Parts 234

Jean Coutu Group
Department Stores – Canada 1090

Jean Louis David
Hair Care Products 1582

Jean Monty (Northern Telecom Ltd.)
Executives 1272

Jeep Cherokee
Sport Utility Vehicles 2299

Jeep-Eagle
Automobile Dealers – Canada 175

Jeep Grand Cherokee
Sport Utility Vehicles 2299

Jefferson Smurfit Group Plc
Corporations – Ireland 991
Forest Products Industry 1483, 1484
Paper Industry – Europe 2034

Jeffrey Taylor
Financial Analysts 1319

Jeffreys Henry International
Accounting Firms – Japan 18

Jelfa SAPF Jelenia Gora
Drug Industry 1133

Jell-O
Brand Name Goods 463

Jelovica, d.d.
Wood Products 2528

Jenny Barker
Financial Analysts – Europe 1364

Jeremy Elden
Financial Analysts – United Kingdom 1435

Jergens
Soap Industry 2275

Jerome O'Regan
Financial Analysts 1328

Jeronimo Martins
Lisbon Stock Exchange 1838

Jersey
Institutional Investments 1670

Jet
Wholesale Trade 2499

Jetform
Computer Software Industry – Canada 777

JGC Corp.
Contractors 804
Contractors, Foreign – Africa 805
Contractors, Foreign – Asia 806

Jiangling Motor
Shenzhen Stock Exchange 2257

Jiangsu, China
Investments, Foreign – Hong Kong 1754

Jiangsu Expressway
Equity Research, International 1251

Jiangsu Supplies & Marketing Co-op.
Corporations – Asia 923

JIB Group
Insurance Brokers 1684, 1685

Jif
Cleaning Products Industry 657

Jih Sun Securities
Security Underwriting – Taiwan 2231

Jil Sander (Jil Sander)
Women Executives 2523

Jim Bean
Liquor Industry 1833

Jim Walker
Financial Analysts – Asia 1337

Jimenez & Fernandez
Coffee Industry 683

Jimenez, Blanco & Quiros
Advertising Agencies – Costa Rica 75

Jimmy Buffet
Entertainers 1244

Jinan Xaoya
Washing Machines 2492

Jindal Iron
Corporations – India 986

Jing Ulrich
Financial Analysts – China 1344

Jinling
Washing Machines 2492

Jinro
Debt 1083

Jinyu
Washing Machines 2492

Jitsuei Securities
Security Underwriting – Japan 2226

J.L. David
Hair Care Products 1582
Shampoos 2253, 2253

JM Financial Services
Merchant Banking 1900

J.M. Smucker
Spices 2298

Jo o Maggion
Tire Industry 2414

Johannesburg Consolidated Investment Company Limited
Johannesburg Stock Exchange 1778

Johannesburg, South Africa
Airports 146

Johannesburg Stock Exchange
Stock Exchanges 2327

John Birt
Executives – Salaries, Pensions, etc. 1275

John Deere
Construction Equipment Industry 784

John Govett
Institutional Investments 1668

John Graham
Financial Analysts 1328

John Hobson
Financial Analysts – Asia 1336

John Keels Holdings
Colombo Stock Exchange 690, 691

John Labatt Ltd.
Radio Advertising 2143

John Lewis
Retail Trade – United Kingdom 2196

John Richards
Financial Analysts – United Kingdom 1429

John So
Financial Analysts – Asia 1339

John Spicer
Financial Analysts – United Kingdom 1420

John Swire & Sons Ltd.
Transportation – Europe 2456

John Wakely
Financial Analysts – Europe 1362

John West Foods
Canned Food Industry 575

John West Salmon
Canned Food Industry 575

John West Tuna
Canned Food Industry 575

John Willis
Financial Analysts – Europe 1370

Johnnie Walker Black
Liquor Industry 1827, 1831

Johnnie Walker Red
Liquor Industry 1827, 1831, 1833

Johnson & Higgins
Captive Insurance Companies – Bermuda
Captive Insurance Companies – Cayman Islands 578
Insurance Brokers 1684, 1685

Johnson & Johnson
Contact Lenses 792
Corporations 854
Cosmetics Industry 1053
Diagnostic Kits 1099
Drug Industry 1123, 1124, 1130
Personal Care Products 2059

Johnson Controls
Corporate Acquisitions and Mergers 829

Johnson Fry European Utilities
Mutual Funds – United Kingdom 1963

Johnson Fry Slater Growth
Mutual Funds – United Kingdom 1962

Johnson's Wax
Agricultural Chemicals 114
Insecticides 1665

Jollibee
Corporations – Asia 924
Corporations – Philippines 1020
Fast Food Restaurants 1307
Retail Trade – Asia 2188

Jolly
Automobile Parts 238

Jonathan Ross
Financial Analysts – Taiwan 1411

Jones Knowles Ritchie
Industrial Designers – United Kingdom 1642

Jordan
Banks and Banking 269
Economy 1156
Electricity 1174
Gold 1549, 1551, 1553, 1559
Labor Supply 1795

Index

Index

1007
Malaysian Resources
  Equity Research,
    International 1250
Malbranque
  Valves 2477
Malcolm Pirnie Inc.
  Engineering Construction
    Companies 1234
Malcom Sinclair
  Financial Analysts –
    Australia 1343
Mallinckrodt Veterinary
  Drug Industry 1139
Malta
  Gold 1557
  Ports 2115
  Shipping 2259
Malterias de Colombia S.A.
  Beer 417
Malterias Unidas S.A.
  Beer 417
Maltesers
  Candy Industry 571
Malwee
  Clothing Trade 669
Mammouth
  Franchises (Retail Trade) –
    France 1491
MAN
  Automobile Industry and
    Trade 188
  Truck Industry 2470
Manajans-Thompson
  Advertising Agencies –
    Turkey 97
Mancera, S.C. Ernst & Young
  Accounting Firms 5
**Manchster Airport, United
    Kingdom**
  Airports 150
Mandarin Oriental
  Hotels and Motels 1603,
    1604
  Hotels and Motels – Asia
    1610
  Hotels and Motels,
    International 1613
Manganese
  Mining Industry 1921
Manhattan, NY
  Cosmetics Industry 1051
**Manifatture Lane Gaetano
    Marzotto & Figli S.P.A.**
  Textile Industry – Europe
    2402
Manila, Philippines
  Duty Free Importation 1151
  Duty Free Shops 1152
Manitoba, Canada
  Coal Industry 675
  Golf 1566
  Hogs 1592
  Home Improvement
    Centers 1598
  Soccer 2279
**Manitoba Hydro-Electric
    Board**
  Electric Utilities – Canada
    1169
Manitoba Pool Elevators
  Grain 1570

Manitoba Telephone System
  Telephone Companies –
    Canada 2381
Mannesmann
  Automobile Parts 228
  Frankfurt Stock Exchange
    1493
  Industrial Equipment
    Industry 1646
  Machinery – Europe 1865
Manpa
  Caracas Stock Exchange 580
Manpower Inc.
  Employment Agencies 1218
  Temporary Help Service
    Agencies 2396
Mansion on Turtle Creek
  Hotels and Motels,
    International 1613
Mantex
  Caracas Stock Exchange 580
  Corporations 896
Manufacturas de Papel
  Caracas Stock Exchange 579
**Manufacturera Lee de Izamal,
    S.A. de C.V.**
  Maquiladoras 1883
Manulife Financial
  Closely Held Corporations –
    Canada 660
  Insurance, Life – Canada
    1719
ManuVie
  Insurance Companies 1706
Map-trade d.o.o.
  Corporations 860
Mapfre Vida
  Insurance, Health 1715
Maple Leaf Foods, Inc.
  Meat Industry – Canada
    1890
  Poultry Industry – Canada
    2125
Maple Lodge Farms Ltd.
  Meat Industry – Canada
    1890
  Poultry Industry – Canada
    2125
Mar del Plata
  Airports 145
Mar lia
  Automobile Parts 232
Marathon
  Gas Industry 1517
  Sports Clubs 2311
Marbert
  Cosmetics Industry 1051
Marc Debrouwer
  Financial Analysts 1319
Marcolin
  Ophthalmic Supplies 2013
Marcopolo
  Buses 546
Margaret Astor
  Cosmetics Industry 1051
Margot Galinska
  Financial Analysts 1325
Marine Atlantic
  Government Ownership –
    Canada 1569
Marisol
  Clothing Trade 669

Maritime Tel & Tel
  Telephone Companies –
    Canada 2381
Mark Beilby
  Financial Analysts – Europe
    1355
Mark Clark
  Financial Analysts – United
    Kingdom 1415
Mark Duffy
  Financial Analysts – United
    Kingdom 1427, 1438
Mark Faulkner
  Financial Analysts –
    Thailand 1412
Mark Finnie
  Financial Analysts – United
    Kingdom 1433
Mark Giacopazzi
  Financial Analysts 1330
Mark Howdle
  Financial Analysts – Europe
    1354
Mark Lambert
  Financial Analysts – United
    Kingdom 1418
Mark Lynch
  Financial Analysts – Europe
    1365
  Financial Analysts – United
    Kingdom 1415
Mark McVicar
  Financial Analysts – Europe
    1369
  Financial Analysts – United
    Kingdom 1439
Mark Shepperd
  Financial Analysts – United
    Kingdom 1417
Mark Simpson
  Financial Analysts – Hong
    Kong 1371
Mark Stockdale
  Financial Analysts – United
    Kingdom 1421
Mark Tracey
  Financial Analysts – Europe
    1357
Markborough Properties.
  Real Estate Business 2156
Marketel
  Advertising Agencies –
    Quebec 91
Marketing Store
  Sales Promotion Agencies –
    United Kingdom 2204
Markkinointi Viherjuuri Oy
  Advertising Agencies –
    Costa Rica 75
Marks & Spencer
  Charities – United Kingdom
    614
  Corporations – United
    Kingdom 1045
  Credit Cards 1067
  London Stock Exchange
    1851
  Retail Trade – United
    Kingdom 2196
  Supermarkets – United
    Kingdom 2349
Mark's Work Wearhouse
  Clothing Stores 666

Marlboro
  Advertising, Magazine 105
  Brand Name Goods 465
  Cigarette Industry 648, 649,
    650, 651
  Cigarette Industry –
    Germany 654
  Cigarette Industry – Spain
    655
  Tobacco Industry 2420
Marlboro "Red" KS
  Cigarette Industry 653
Marlboro Lights
  Cigarette Industry 650, 653
  Cigarette Industry –
    Germany 654
Marles Hise, d.o.o.
  Wood Products 2528
Marocaine
  Cigarette Industry 649
Marriott
  Hotels and Motels – Asia
    1610
  Leisure 1819
Marriott International
  Hotels and Motels 1605
  Leisure 1819
Mars
  Advertisers 25
  Advertisers – Europe 46
  Advertisers – Germany 48
  Brand Choice 458, 459
  Candy Industry 571
  Chocolate Industry 635, 636,
    637
  Confectionery Industry –
    United Kingdom 783
  Food Industry and Trade
    1462
  Ice Cream, Ices, etc. 1632
  Pet Food 2062
Mars Bar
  Candy Industry 571
  Ice Cream, Ices, etc. 1633
Mars-Russia
  Television Advertising 2385
Marsaxlokk, Malta
  Ports 2115
Marseille, France
  Ports 2115
Marsh & McLennan
  Captive Insurance
    Companies – Bermuda
  Captive Insurance
    Companies – Cayman
    Islands 578
  Insurance Brokers 1684,
    1685
Martell 3 Star
  Liquor Industry 1832
Martin Brookes
  Financial Analysts – United
    Kingdom 1430
Martin Currie
  Institutional Investments
    1668
Martin Mabbutt
  Financial Analysts – United
    Kingdom 1418
Martini & Rossi
  Liquor Industry 1827
Marubeni Corp.
  Bonds 445

Index

Index

Index

Nurofen
Drugs, Nonprescription –
United Kingdom 1147
Nutrasweet
Spices 2298
Nutrine
Confectionery 780
Nutrisia
Infants' Food 1656, 1657
Nutritional food additives
Drug Industry 1114
NV Kon. Nederlandse
Petroleum Maatschappij
Corporations – Europe 968
Mining Industry – Europe
1927
NV Koninkijke KNP BT
Paper Industry – Europe
2034
NV Verenigd Bezit VNU
Printing Industry – Europe
2128
NWA
Airlines 134
Travel 2457
Nycomed-DAK
Drug Industry 1120, 1138
NYK
Shipping 2260
Nynex
Cable Broadcasting 562
Corporate Acquisitions and
Mergers 831
NYNEX CableComms
Corporate Acquisitions and
Mergers 830
Nyren Scott-Malden
Financial Analysts – United
Kingdom 1438
NZI Corp.
Banks and Banking –
Australia 285
NZSE 10 Index Management
Security Underwriting – New
Zealand 2228

O

O & K
Construction Equipment
Industry 784
O Boticario
Cosmetics Industry 1053
O Estado de Sao Paulo
newspaper
Advertisers – Latin America
52
O Estado de Sao Paulo
Newspaper
Advertising Expenditures
104
Oakmark International
Mutual Funds 1958
Obayashi Corp.
Building Materials Industry
544
Construction Industry – Asia
788, 789
Contractors 796
Engineering Construction
Companies 1225
Ober
Jeans (Clothing) 1770

Oberbank
Banks and Banking – Austria
289
Object Design
Computer Software Industry
759
Objectivity
Computer Software Industry
759
Oboush
Jeans (Clothing) 1770
Obsession
Perfumes 2053
OCBC
Security Underwriting –
Singapore 2230
Singapore Stock Exchange
2268
OCBC Asset Management
Institutional Investments –
Singapore 1680
OCBC Bank (Malaysia)
Banks and Banking –
Malaysia 362
OCBC Overseas Chinese
Bank
Corporations – Singapore
1024
OCBC Sikap
Brokers – Indonesia 494
Occidental Chemical Co./
Thai Plastic & Chemical
Co.
Plastics Industry 2101
Occidental Petroleum Corp.
Gas Industry 1511, 1514
Ocean/MSAS Cargo
Forwarding Companies 1487
Oceania
Meat Industry 1889
O'Connor & O'Sullivan
Advertising Agencies –
Ireland 84
Odakyu
Private Brands 2129
Odakyu Electric Railway Co.
Ltd.
Transportation – Asia 2454
Odebrecht
Contractors 803
Contractors, Foreign – Latin
America 809
Corporations 887
Multinational Corporations
1946
Office equipment
Advertising 61, 64
Electric Connectors 1161
Office Japan
Telemarketing 2368
Oger
Travel Agencies 2460
Ogilvy & Mather
Advertising 68
Advertising Agencies –
Denmark 76
Advertising Agencies –
France 78
Advertising Agencies –
Germany 79
Advertising Agencies –
Hong Kong 82
Advertising Agencies – India

83
Advertising Agencies –
Malaysia 88
Advertising Agencies –
Netherlands 89
Advertising Agencies –
Norway 90
Advertising Agencies –
Romania 92
Advertising Agencies –
Thailand 96
Advertising Agencies –
United Kingdom 98
Direct Marketing – United
Kingdom 1106
Public Relations Firms 2134
Oh Henry!
Chocolate Industry 636
O'Hare International Airport
Airports 149, 152
Ohbayashi Corp.
Construction Industry –
Japan 791
Ohio State Lottery
Lotteries 1856
Ohne Gleichen VM
Cookies and Crackers 815
Ohtsuka
Nonwoven Fabrics
Industry – Japan 1991
Oil of Olay
Personal Care Products –
United Kingdom 2060
Skin Care Products 2270
Soap Industry 2275
Oji Paper
Paper Industry 2023
Oji Steel
Steel Industry and Trade
2322
Okamura
Office Furniture 1994
Okanagan Cider
Beverage Industry 434
Okasan
Brokers – Japan 504
Oki Electric Industry
Computer Printers 741, 742
Information Technology
1659
Microprocessors 1913
Tokyo Stock Exchange 2425
Oktiabri Cannery
Canned Food Industry 574
Okuma
Machine Tools 1863, 1864
Okumura Corp.
Construction Industry –
Japan 791
Okura
Hotels and Motels 1603,
1604
Old El Paso
Food Industry and Trade –
United Kingdom 1476
Old Spice
Perfumes 2053
Oldham Estate Company Plc
Corporations – Europe 965
Oleane
Internet (Computer
Network) 1727

Olgaz
Gas Industry 1518
Olive Garden
Brand Name Goods 464
Restaurants 2173
Olivetti
Computer Industry 697, 708,
714
Copying Machines 823
Italian Stock Exchange 1765
Microcomputers 1912
Olsten Corp.
Employment Agencies 1218
Olsten/Sogica
Temporary Help Service
Agencies 2396
Olymel and Co. Ltd.
Meat Industry – Canada
1890
Poultry Industry – Canada
2125
Olympic DDB/Needham
Advertising Agencies –
Greece 80
Olympus
Cameras 566
Oman
Electricity 1174, 1180
Labor Supply 1795
Oman Arab Bank SAO
Banks and Banking – Oman
372
Oman Development Bank
SAO
Banks and Banking – Oman
372
Oman International Bank
SAOG
Banks and Banking – Oman
372
Ombra
Personal Care Products
2058
Omega
Insurance Companies 1690
OMG
Cobalt 678
Omnicom Group
Advertising Agencies 70
Holding Companies 1593
Omron
Industrial Equipment
Industry 1644
OMV
Corporations – Austria 938,
939
Petroleum Industry –
Europe 2086
Vienna Stock Exchange
2484, 2485
ONA
Casablanca Stock Exchange
583, 584
One-2-One
Cellular Telephones 601
Telecommunications –
United Kingdom 2367
One Asset Management
Institutional Investments –
Thailand 1682
Onex Corp.
Executives 1272

Index

Steel Industry and Trade
2319
Scholz & Friends
Advertising Agencies –
Germany 79
Schooner Capital Corporation
Furniture Industry 1501
Schott Glaswerke
Leather Industry – Europe
1818
Manufacturing Industries –
Europe 1882
Schroder Investment Mgmt.
Institutional Investments
1666
Investment Management
Firms – Rating – Asia 1740
Investment Management
Firms – Rating – Europe
Pension Plan
Administrators – United
Kingdom 2047
Pension Plans – Europe 2051
Pension Plans – United
Kingdom 2052
Schroder Securities
Financial Analysts 1324,
1330
**Schroder Smaller Companies
Inc.**
Mutual Funds – United
Kingdom 1962
Schroders
Brokers – Japan 499
Corporate Acquisition and
Merger Services 827
Eurobond Market 1256
Investment Management
Firms – Rating 1738
Pension Fund Investments
2044
Schwartau
Chocolate Industry 637
**Schweizerischer
Bankgesellschaft**
Banks and Banking –
Europe 317
Schweizerischer Bankverein
Banks and Banking –
Europe 317
Schweppes
Beverage Industry 431
Soft Drink Industry 2291
SCIB
Automated Teller Machines
172
Scope
Charities – United Kingdom
615
SCOR
Reinsurance 2164, 2166
Scorro
Automobile Parts 238
Scotch
Office Supplies 1995
ScotiaMcLeod
Security Underwriting –
Canada 2223
Scott Gibson
Financial Analysts –
Philippines 1409
Scottish & Newcastle
Bars and Barrooms – Great

Britain 411
Beverage Industry – Europe
435
Brewing Industry – United
Kingdom 466
Scottish Courage
Beer 414
Scottish Hydro-Electricity
Electric Utilities 1168
Scottish National Cap
Mutual Funds – United
Kingdom 1963
Scottish Power
Electric Utilities 1168
Scottish TV
Executives – Salaries,
Pensions, etc. 1275
Scrabble
Toy Industry 2443
Scrim
Nonwoven Fabrics Industry
1989
SCT
Trading Companies,
International 2452
Scudder, Stevens & Clark
Investment Management
Firms – Rating 1738
Investment Management
Firms – Rating – Asia 1740
SE Banken
Stockholm Stock Exchange
2337
Se og Hor
Magazines 1868
Sea Containers
Container Industry 794
Sea Horse
Frozen Food Industry 1497
Sea-Land
Shipping 2260
Seagate Technology
Corporations – Asia 921
Corporations – Thailand
1041
Disk Drive Industry 1107
Electronic Industries 1185
Seagram
Beverage Industry 428, 431,
433
Charitable Contributions
613
Corporations 854, 855
Corporations – Canada 947,
949, 950, 952
Corporations – France 977
Liquor Industry 1827, 1829,
1830, 1832, 1834, 1835
Montreal Exchange 1929,
1930
Toronto Stock Exchange
2432, 2433
Sealand
Container Industry 793
Seanix
Computer Industry – Canada
729
Sears Canada
Department Stores – Canada
1090, 1091
Furniture Stores 1507
Sears Roebuck
Retail Trade 2177, 2185

SEAT
Automobile Industry and
Trade 190, 194, 195
Automobile Industry and
Trade – Europe 211
Automobile Plants 241
Corporations – Spain 1027
SECOM
Security Services 2214
Securitest
Automobile Service Stations
245
Securities One
Security Underwriting –
Thailand 2232
Securiton
Fire Detection Systems 1450
Sedgwick Group
Insurance Brokers 1684,
1685
**Sedgwick Management
Services Ltd.**
Captive Insurance
Companies – Bermuda
Sedwick Noble Lowndes
Employee Benefit
Consultants 1198
Sefimeg
Real Estate Business 2154
Sega Enterprises
Brand Choice 459, 462
Brand Name Goods 464
Corporations – Japan 996
Toy Industry 2443
Video Games 2480
Segafredo Zanetti
Coffee Industry 682
Seibu
Private Brands 2129
Retail Trade – Japan 2194
Seiko Epson
Computer Printers 740
Seikosha
Furniture Industry 1503
Seiler DDB
Advertising Agencies –
Switzerland 94
Seiyu
Convenience Stores 813
Private Brands 2130
Retail Trade – Asia 2186
Retail Trade – Japan 2193
Sekisui Chemical
Chemical Industries – Asia
626
Chemical Industries – Japan
632
Construction Industry – Asia
788
Corporations 856
Sekisui House
Building Materials Industry
544
Construction Industry – Asia
788, 789
Construction Industry –
Japan 791
Engineering Construction
Companies 1225
Selangor
Luxembourg Stock
Exchange 1861

Select
Cigarette Industry 649
Selecta
Ice Cream, Ices, etc. 1627
Selene
Clothing Trade 670
Selga
Wholesale Trade –
Electronics 2504
Selim Ceramic Co.
Fixtures 1455
Selim Co. Ltd.
Fixtures 1455
Selonda Aquaculture
Athens Stock Exchange 166
Selskaya Zhzin
Newspapers – Editions 1985
Selva Magica
Amusement Parks – Latin
America 162
Sema Group
Business Consultants 549
Semapa
Cement Industry 606
Semen Gresik
Jakarta Stock Exchange
1766, 1767
Semi-Tech Corp.
Corporations – Canada 946
Sen Tai
Bicycles 437
Senegal
Country Credit Risk 1059
Peanut Products 2042
Senon
Security Services 2214
Sense and Sensibility
Motion Picture Industry
1937
Sensodyne
Toothbrushes 2428
Toothpaste 2429
Seoul Bank
Banks and Banking – Korea,
South 348, 349, 350
Eurobond Market 1253
Seoul Gas
Public Utilities 2136
Seoul, South Korea
Air Freight Service 129
Airports 152
Offices – Leasing and
Renting 2001
Rental Housing 2167
Sepawand BV
Furniture Industry – Europe
1505
Sepoong
Paper Industry 2028
Serfin
Banks and Banking – Latin
America 352
Banks and Banking – Mexico
366
Leasing and Renting of
Equipment 1813
Servair/Ogden
Catering 588
Servier
Drug Industry 1131
Sevel
Corporations 886

Index

756

Springer & Jacoby
Advertising Agencies –
Germany 79

Sprint
Telephone Companies 2377,
2380

Sprint Canada Inc.
Long Distance Telephone
Calls 1853

Sprite
Beverage Industry 431

SPT Telecom
Corporations 868

Spumador
Soft Drink Industry 2283

Square D Software Ltd.
Computer Software Industry
769

Square Pharmaceuticals
Dhaka Stock Exchange 1098

Squash
Food Industry and Trade –
United Kingdom 1475

Sri Lanka
Gold 1531, 1537, 1538, 1544

Sri Trang Agro-Industry
Agriculture 115

SSA
Computer Software Industry
753, 772

Ssangyong
Automobile Plants 242
Brokers 469, 471, 472
Corporations – Korea, South
1000
Factories 1301

Ssangyong Cement Mfg.
Mining Industry 1925

Ssangyong Fire & Marine
Insurance Companies 1705

Ssangyong Heavy Ind.
Industrial Equipment
Industry 1649

Ssangyong Oil Refining
Petroleum Refineries 2088,
2089

Ssangyong Paper
Paper Industry 2028

Ssangyong Securities
Security Underwriting 2222

SSKI
Brokers – India 490, 491, 493

SSQ-Vie
Insurance Companies 1706

Sta-Rite
Sporting Goods Industry
2310

Stakis
Casinos 585

Stalexport
Warsaw Stock Exchange
2490

Stampeder Exploration
Corporations – Canada 944,
945, 951

Stanbic
Banks and Banking – Africa
276
Banks and Banking – South
Africa 388, 389

**Stanbic Bank Botswana
Limited**
Banks and Banking –
Botswana 294

Stanbic Bank Lesotho Limited
Banks and Banking –
Lesotho 355

**Stanbic Bank Swaziland
Limited**
Banks and Banking –
Swaziland 392

Stanchart
Foreign Exchange Brokers
1481

**Standard Bank Investment
Corp**
Corporations – South Africa
1025

**Standard Bank Isle of Man
Limited**
Banks and Banking – Isle of
Man 338

Standard Bank Namibia Ltd.
Banks and Banking –
Namibia 368

Standard Broadcasting Corp.
Radio Broadcasting 2146
Television Broadcasting
2387

Standard Chartered Bank
Bank Credit Cards 255
Banks and Banking – India
333
Banks and Banking –
Malaysia 362
Corporations – Asia 915

**Standard Chartered Bank
(Channel Island) Limited**
Banks and Banking –
Channel Islands 304

**Standard Chartered Bank
Botswana Limited**
Banks and Banking –
Botswana 294

**Standard Chartered Bank
Sierra Leone Limited**
Banks and Banking – Sierra
Leone 383

**Standard Chartered Bank
Swaziland Limited**
Banks and Banking –
Swaziland 392

**Standard Chartered Bank
Uganda Limited**
Banks and Banking –
Uganda 402

Standard Life
Institutional Investments
1666
Insurance Companies 1706
Pension Fund Investments
2044

Standard, O&M
Advertising Agencies –
Brazil 73

Standard Oil Co.
Corporate Acquisitions and
Mergers – International
Aspects 847

Stanford Telecommunications
Aerospace Industries 110

Stanley Fink
Executives 1274

Millionaires – United
Kingdom 1920

Stanley Leisure
Casinos 585

Star
Computer Printers 741, 743,
744

Star Chinese
Cable Television –
Advertising 565

Star Prime
Cable Television –
Advertising 565

Staroup
Clothing Trade 672

State Bank International
Banks and Banking –
Mauritius 365

State Bank of India
Banks and Banking 272
Banks and Banking – India
334
Bombay Stock Exchange
443, 444
Equity Research,
International 1249
Taxation 2355

State Bank of Mauritius
Banks and Banking –
Mauritius 365

State of Brazil
Mining Industry 1926

State of Chile
Mining Industry 1926

State Savings Bank
Banks and Banking –
Bulgaria 296

State Street Bank and Trust
Banks and Banking, Foreign
319
Foreign Exchange Brokers
1481
Global Custodians 1526

**State Superannuation
Investment &
Management Corp.**
Institutional Investments –
Australia 1671

Statens Seruminstitut
Drug Industry 1120

Statoil
Corporations – Norway 1017,
1018
Mining Industry 1922
Petroleum Industry 2078
Wholesale Trade 2499

Staubach/CMI Mexico
Real Estate Business 2153

Stavanger Aft.
Newspapers 1979

STC
Rubber Industry 2202

Steel Authority of India
Bombay Stock Exchange
443

Steiner Optik
Ophthalmic Supplies 2012

Steinlager
Beer 413

Stella Artois
Beer 413
Brewing Industry – United
Kingdom 466

Stentor
Long Distance Telephone
Calls 1853
Telephone Companies 2377

Stephen Dias
Financial Analysts – Europe
1366

Stephen Reitman
Financial Analysts – Europe
1361

Stephen Streater
Executives 1274
Millionaires – United
Kingdom 1920

Stereotactic needles
Medical Equipment and
Supplies, International
1895

Sterling Chemicals
Chemical Industries 624

Stern
Periodicals – Germany 2056

STET
Corporations – Italy 993, 994
Italian Stock Exchange
1764, 1765
Telephone Companies 2376

Steve Plag
Financial Analysts – United
Kingdom 1415, 1436

Steven Li
Financial Analysts – Hong
Kong 1371

Stewart Adkins
Financial Analysts – Europe
1357

Stichting Pensioenfonds ABP
Pension Plans 2048

Stiebel Eltron
Air Conditioning Industry
121

Stimorol
Television Advertising 2385

**Stinnes
Vermoegensverwaltungs-
A.G.**
Wholesale Trade – Europe
2506

Stock Exchanges
Tokyo Stock Exchange 2426

Stockholm, Sweden
Hotels and Motels 1604

Stockholms Fondbors
Stock Exchanges – Europe
2333

Stocks Austin Sice
Industrial Designers –
United Kingdom 1640

Stolichnaya
Vodka 2486

Stollwerck
Chocolate Industry 638

Stomil Olsztyn
Tire Industry 2412
Warsaw Stock Exchange
2489

**Stone & Webster Engineering
Corp.**
Engineering Construction
Companies 1228, 1233,
1237, 1238
Engineering Construction
Companies – Asia 1240

Index

Index

Index

Index

Geographical Index

Geographical Index

Steel Industry and Trade
2320
Stock Exchanges 2331
Telephone Calls 2374
Telephone Companies 2376
Textile Industry 2398
Textile Industry – Export-
Import Trade 2403
Tire Industry, International
2416, 2417
Tourist Trade 2439
Truck Industry 2467
Video Tapes 2482, 2483
Wine Industry – Export-
Import Trade 2512
South Pars, Iran
Natural Gas 1967
Southeast Asia
Automobile Industry and
Trade 197
Export-Import Trade 1286
Paint Industry 2020
Tourist Trade 2439
Soviet Union
Iron Ore 1759, 1761
Salt 2205
Spain
Advertising Agencies –
Spain 93
Agricultural Chemicals 114
Air Freight Service 126
Automated Teller
Machines, Europe 173
Automobile Industry and
Trade 190, 204
Automobile Plants 243
Automobile Service Stations
244
Beverage Industry 429
Book Industries and Trade
449
Brand Choice 462
Cable Broadcasting 558
Candy Industry 573
Catering 587
Cellular Radio Service
Companies 590, 591
Cellular Telephones 595,
596
Chemical Industries 618
Cigarette Industry – Spain
655
Clock and Watch Industry –
Export-Import Trade 659
Clothing and Dress – Men
662
Clothing and Dress –
Women 665
Coffee Industry 687
Collectors and Collecting
689
Computer Industry 714
Computer Software Industry
762
Corporate Acquisitions and
Mergers 828, 836
Corporations 859
Corporations – Spain 1027,
1028, 1029, 1030
Detergents 1095
Drug Industry 1125, 1132
Duty and Tax Free
Retailing – Europe 1148,

1149, 1150
Electric Industries 1162
Electricity 1171, 1176
Electronic Industries 1188
Employee Vacations,
International 1203
Employment 1208, 1209,
1210, 1211, 1212
Energy Industries 1221, 1222
Environmental Services
Firms 1248
Factories 1304
Financial Analysts 1330
Food Industry and Trade
1465
Fruit Juices 1498
Gambling 1509
Gold 1532, 1533, 1536, 1557
Hogs 1591
Hours of Labor – Europe
1614, 1615
Household Appliances 1621,
1623
Insecticides 1665
Insurance Business 1687
Insurance, Health 1715
Insurance, Property and
Casualty 1723
Internet (Computer
Network) 1725
Jeans (Clothing) 1772
Labor Costs – Europe 1789
Labor Costs, International
1790
Labor Supply 1792
Laboratory Instruments
1803, 1804
Leasing and Renting of
Equipment 1815
Lotteries 1855
Marinas 1884
Meat Industry 1887
Meeting Sites 1899
Milk 1919
Motion Picture Industry
1935
Paper Industry 2025
Paper Industry – Europe
2036
Pipeline Companies 2096
Plastics Industry 2101
Pollution Control Industries
2112
Pork Industry 2113
Potash 2119
Privatization 2132, 2133
Restaurants 2175
Retail Trade – Spain 2195
Sporting Goods Industry
2304
Steel Industry and Trade –
Europe 2326
Stock Exchanges,
International 2334
Stocks – Repurchase 2340
Strikes 2341
Sugar 2344
Telephone Companies 2376
Tire Industry, International
2416, 2417
Toilet Goods 2423
Tourist Trade 2437, 2440,
2441, 2442

Travel Agencies 2458
Unemployment 2475
Venture Capital – Europe
2479
Water Services 2495
Wine Industry 2509
Wine Industry – Europe
2510, 2511
Wine Industry – Export-
Import Trade 2517, 2518
Sri Lanka
Banks and Banking – Sri
Lanka 390
Gold 1531, 1537, 1538, 1544
Stockholm, Sweden
Stockholm Stock Exchange
2337, 2338
Stuttgart, Germany
Airports 147
Suadi Arabia
Natural Gas 1970
Sudan
Electricity 1178
Labor Supply 1796
Peanut Products 2042
Sorghum 2294
Suriname
Banks and Banking –
Suriname 391
Suzhou, China
Tourist Trade 2435
Swaziland
Banks and Banking –
Swaziland 392
Sweden
Advertisers 38
Airports – Europe 154
Arts Funding 164
Automobile Industry and
Trade 193, 204
Automobile Industry and
Trade – Sweden 218
Automobile Leasing and
Rental Companies 223
Business Ethics 552
Cable Broadcasting 559, 560
Candy Industry 570
Cellular Telephones 595,
603
Collecting of Accounts 688
Computer Software Industry
760, 761, 762
Corporate Acquisitions and
Mergers 828, 836
Corporate Acquisitions and
Mergers – International
Aspects 839
Corporations 859
Corporations – Europe 961
Corporations – Sweden 1032,
1033, 1034
Duty and Tax Free
Retailing – Europe 1149,
1150
Electricity 1171, 1176
Electronic Funds Transfer
1182
Employee Fringe Benefits
1199, 1200, 1201
Employee Vacations,
International 1202, 1206
Employment 1212
Executives 1271

Forest Products Industry
1484
Furniture Industry 1501
Gross National Product
1580
Hours of Labor – Europe
1614
Income 1637
Internet (Computer
Network) 1732
Iron Ore 1759
Labor Supply 1800
Land – Ownership 1805
Leasing and Renting of
Equipment 1815
Locksets 1849
Modems 1928
Newsprint – Manufacture
1986
Paper Industry 2030, 2031
Paper Industry – Europe
2035, 2036
Pension Fund Investments
2043
Privatization 2132
Quality of Life 2141
Stock Market, International
2335, 2336
Taxation 2353
Telecommunications 2357
Telecommunications,
International 2366
Telephone Lines,
International 2383
Tourist Trade 2436
Unemployment 2475
Venture Capital – Europe
2479
Wholesale Trade 2502
Wholesale Trade –
Electronics 2504
Wine Industry – Export-
Import Trade 2514
Switzerland
Automated Teller
Machines, Europe 173
Automobile Leasing and
Rental Companies 223
Business Ethics 552
Cable Broadcasting 559
Candy Industry 569
Chemical Industries 618, 619
Chemical Industries –
Western Europe 633
Clock and Watch Industry –
Export-Import Trade 659
Coffee Industry 687
Collecting of Accounts 688
Competitiveness 695, 696
Computer Software Industry
760, 761, 762
Corporate Acquisitions and
Mergers 828, 836
Corporate Acquisitions and
Mergers – International
Aspects 839, 840, 846
Corporations 859, 869
Corporations – Europe 960,
961, 962
Corporations – Japan 998
Corporations – Switzerland
1036, 1037, 1038
Country Credit Risk 1057,

398
Tokyo, Japan
Advertising Agencies 70
Air Freight Service 129
Airports 149
Business Travel 557
Duty Free Importation 1151
Institutional Investments
  1669
Offices – Leasing and
  Renting 1997, 1998, 2003
Offices – Leasing and
  Renting, International
  2004
Rental Housing 2167
Tokyo Stock Exchange 2424,
  2425
Toronto, Canada
Business Travel 556
Income 1636
Libraries 1820
Museums and Parks 1947
Soccer 2278
Toronto Stock Exchange
  2432, 2433
Trebnje, Slovenia
Corporations 905
Trinidad and Tobago
Banks and Banking –
  Trinidad and Tobago 399
Petroleum Industry 2070
Trinidad and Tobago Stock
  Exchange 2462, 2463
Tunis, Tunisia
Airports 146
Tunisia
Automobile Industry and
  Trade 200
Banks and Banking 269
Banks and Banking – Tunisia
  400
Chocolate Industry 639
Electricity 1178
Gold 1528, 1529, 1556
Labor Supply 1796
Pasta, International 2041
Truck Industry 2465
Turin-Mirafiori, Italy
Automobile Plants 241
Turkey
Advertising Agencies –
  Turkey 97
Automated Teller
  Machines, Europe 173
Automobiles 251
Banks and Banking – Turkey
  401
Bicycles 438
Capital Market 576
Computer Software Industry
  755
Crime and Criminals 1073,
  1074
Economic Conditions,
  International 1153
Electricity 1174, 1180, 1181
Employment 1215
Fertilizer Industry 1310
Financial Analysts 1333
Floor Coverings 1458
Gold 1539, 1549, 1551, 1552,
  1553, 1559, 1560
Investments 1745

Labor Supply 1795
Meat Industry 1887
Metal Products 1905
Motor Oil 1939
Plastics Industry 2105
Pollution Control Industries
  2110
Sporting Goods 2300
Telephone Companies 2376
Textile Industry – Export-
  Import Trade 2403
Travel Agencies 2458
Wood Products 2527
Turkmenistan
Airports, International 155

U

Uganda
Banks and Banking –
  Uganda 402
Gross National Product
  1579
Labor Supply 1799
Truck Industry 2465
Ukraine
Air Pollution 130
Airports, International 155
Banks and Banking –
  Ukraine 403
Competitiveness 694
Economy 1156
Electricity 1172, 1179
Labor Supply 1793
Steel Industry and Trade
  2320
Sugar 2343
Telecommunications,
  International 2364, 2365
United Arab Emirates
Banks and Banking 269
Banks and Banking – United
  Arab Emirates 404
Clock and Watch Industry –
  Export-Import Trade 659
Electricity 1174, 1180
Export-Import Trade 1281,
  1285, 1292
Labor Supply 1795
Petroleum Industry 2073
Telecommunications,
  International 2364
United Kindgom
Banks and Banking 274
United Kingdom
Accounting Firms – United
  Kingdom 22
Advertisers 25, 31
Advertising 67
Advertising Agencies –
  United Kingdom 98
Advertising, Magazine 105
Aerosols 107
Aerospace Industries 108
Air Freight Service 126
Air Pollution 130
Airplanes 142, 143
Airports – Europe 154
Arts Funding 164
Automated Teller
  Machines, Europe 173
Automobile Industry and
  Trade 191, 193, 204

Automobile Industry and
  Trade – United Kingdom
  219
Automobile Leasing and
  Rental Companies 223
Automobile Plants 243
Banks and Banking 270
Bars and Barrooms – Great
  Britain 411
Beer 414
Book Industries and Trade
  449
Brewing Industry – United
  Kingdom 466
Business Consultants –
  United Kingdom 551
Cable Broadcasting 562
Cable Television 564
Cameras 568
Candy Industry 569, 570,
  571, 572, 573
Canned Food Industry 575
Carpet Industry – United
  Kingdom 581
Casinos 585
Cellular Telephones 595,
  601, 603
Cereal Products – United
  Kingdom 611
Champagne 612
Charities – United Kingdom
  614, 615
Chemical Industries 618, 619
Chemical Industries –
  Western Europe 633
Chocolate Industry 635
Cleaning Products Industry
  657
Clock and Watch Industry –
  Export-Import Trade 659
Clothing and Dress – Men
  662
Clothing and Dress –
  Women 665
Clothing Trade 667
Coffee Industry 687
Collecting of Accounts 688
Computer Industry 697
Computer Industry,
  International 730
Computer Programmers,
  International 746
Computer Software Industry
  756, 760, 761, 762
Computer Stores 778
Confectionery Industry –
  United Kingdom 783
Contractors – United
  Kingdom 811
Corporate Acquisitions and
  Mergers 828, 836
Corporate Acquisitions and
  Mergers – International
  Aspects 839, 840, 841, 842,
  846, 847
Corporations 859, 865, 866,
  867, 869, 883
Corporations – Europe 960,
  961, 962
Corporations, Foreign 973
Corporations – Japan 998
Corporations – United
  Kingdom 1043, 1044,

1045, 1046
Country Credit Risk 1057,
  1058
Credit Cards – Great Britain
  1070
Crime and Criminals 1075,
  1077
Dairy Products 1082
Department Stores 1089
Derivative Securities 1093
Detergents 1096
Direct Marketing – United
  Kingdom 1106
Drug Industry 1123
Drug Stores 1143
Drug Trade – Great Britain
  1145
Drugs, Nonprescription –
  United Kingdom 1147
Duty and Tax Free
  Retailing – Europe 1148,
  1149, 1150
Duty Free Shops 1152
Economic Conditions,
  International 1154
Economy 1157
Eggs 1160
Electric Industries 1162
Electric Utilities 1168
Electricity 1171, 1176
Electronic Industries –
  Export-Import Trade
  1194
Employee Fringe Benefits
  1199
Employee Vacations,
  International 1202, 1203,
  1206
Employment 1212, 1214
Energy Industries 1222
Engineering Construction
  Companies 1229
Environmental Services
  Firms 1248
Executives 1274
Executives – Salaries,
  Pensions, etc. 1275
Expatriate Employees 1278
Export-Import Trade 1285,
  1287, 1290, 1292
Export-Import Trade,
  International 1294, 1295
Export-Import Trade –
  United Kingdom 1296
Factories 1304
Fast Food Restaurants 1306
Financial Analysts – Europe
  1348
Financial Analysts – United
  Kingdom 1413, 1414,
  1415, 1416, 1417, 1418,
  1419, 1420, 1421, 1422,
  1423, 1424, 1425, 1426,
  1427, 1428, 1429, 1430,
  1431, 1432, 1433, 1434,
  1435, 1436, 1437, 1438,
  1439, 1440
Financial Services 1447,
  1448
Financing 1449
Food Industry and Trade
  1460, 1465
Food Industry and Trade –

Zurich, Switzerland
　Hotels and Motels – Europe
　　1611
　Institutional Investments
　　1669
　Offices – Leasing and
　　Renting 2000
　Zurich Stock Exchange 2540

SIC Index

SIC Index

SIC Index

Kingdom 2047
Pension Plans 2048, 2049
Pension Plans – Brazil 2050
Pension Plans – Europe 2051
Pension Plans – United
Kingdom 2052

INSURANCE AGENTS, BROKERS, & SERVICE

6411 Insurance agents, brokers, & service
Brokers – Japan 504
Insurance Brokers 1684, 1685
Insurance Companies 1699

REAL ESTATE

6512 Nonresidential building operators
Offices – Leasing and Renting 1997, 1998, 1999, 2000, 2001, 2002, 2003
Offices – Leasing and Renting, International 2004
Rental Housing 2167
6531 Real estate agents and managers
Real Estate Business 2152, 2153, 2154, 2155, 2156, 2157

HOLDING AND OTHER INVESTMENT OFFICES

6710 Holding Offices
Holding Companies – Europe 1594
6719 Holding companies, nec
Holding Companies 1593
6794 Patent owners and lessors
Franchises (Retail Trade) 1490
Franchises (Retail Trade) – France 1491
6799 Investors, nec
Investments 1744, 1746
Investments, Foreign – China 1751
Venture Capital – Europe 2478, 2479

HOTLES AND OTHER LODGING PLACES

7011 Hotels and motels
Business Travel 557
Hotels and Motels 1603, 1604, 1605, 1606, 1607, 1608
Hotels and Motels – Asia 1609, 1610
Hotels and Motels – Europe 1611, 1612
Hotels and Motels, International 1613

PERSONAL SERVICES

7231 Beauty shops
Retail Trade – Germany 2190
7299 Miscellaneous personal services, nec
Retail Trade – Germany 2192

BUSINESS SERVICES

7310 Advertising
Advertisers – Japan 50
Advertisers – Latin America 53
Advertising 55, 56, 57, 61, 62, 63, 64, 65, 66, 67
Advertising – Canada 99
Advertising Expenditures 100, 101, 102, 103, 104
Bank Advertising 254
7311 Advertising agencies
Advertisers 23, 24, 25
Advertisers – Brazil 44, 45
Advertisers – Europe 46
Advertisers – France 47
Advertisers – Germany 48
Advertisers – Italy 49
Advertisers – Japan 51
Advertisers – Taiwan 54
Advertising 58, 59, 68
Advertising Agencies 69, 70
Advertising Agencies – Australia 71
Advertising Agencies – Belgium 72
Advertising Agencies – Brazil 73
Advertising Agencies – Chile 74
Advertising Agencies – Costa Rica 75
Advertising Agencies – Denmark 76
Advertising Agencies – Europe 77
Advertising Agencies – France 78
Advertising Agencies – Germany 79
Advertising Agencies – Greece 80
Advertising Agencies – Guatemala 81
Advertising Agencies – Hong Kong 82
Advertising Agencies – India 83
Advertising Agencies – Ireland 84
Advertising Agencies – Italy 85
Advertising Agencies – Japan 86, 87
Advertising Agencies – Malaysia 88
Advertising Agencies – Netherlands 89
Advertising Agencies – Norway 90
Advertising Agencies – Quebec 91

Advertising Agencies – Romania 92
Advertising Agencies – Spain 93
Advertising Agencies – Switzerland 94
Advertising Agencies – Taiwan 95
Advertising Agencies – Thailand 96
Advertising Agencies – Turkey 97
Advertising Agencies – United Kingdom 98
Television Advertising 2385
7313 Radio, TV, publisher representatives
Advertising 60
Advertising, Magazine 105
Television Advertising – Canada 2386
7319 Advertising, nec
Advertisers 26, 27, 28, 29, 30, 31, 32, 33, 34, 35, 36, 37, 38, 39, 40, 41, 42, 43
Advertisers – Latin America 52
Cable Television – Advertising 565
7331 Direct mail advertising services
Direct Marketing 1105
Direct Marketing – United Kingdom 1106
Sales Promotion Agencies – United Kingdom 2204
7350 Misc. Equipment Rental & Leasing
Leasing and Renting of Equipment 1814, 1815
7353 Heavy construction equipment rental
Container Industry 794
7361 Employment agencies
Executive Search Consultants 1270
7363 Help supply services
Employment Agencies 1218
Temporary Help Service Agencies 2396
7372 Prepackaged software
CD-ROM 589
Client Server Computing 658
Computer Software Industry 747, 748, 749, 750, 751, 752, 753, 754, 756, 757, 758, 759, 760, 761, 762, 763, 764, 765, 766, 767, 768, 769, 770, 771, 772, 773, 774, 775, 776
Computer Software Industry – Canada 777
Information Technology 1660
7373 Computer integrated systems design
Computer Networks 735, 736, 737, 738, 739
Telecommunications – Equipment 2362

7375 Information retrieval services
Information Technology 1659
Internet (Computer Network) 1725, 1726, 1727, 1728, 1729, 1730, 1731, 1732
On-Line Computer Services 2009, 2010, 2011
7378 Computer maintenance & repair
Computer Software Industry 755
7381 Detective & armored car services
Art Organizations 163
7382 Security systems services
Security Services 2214
7384 Photofinishing laboratories
Photographic Supply Stores 2094
7389 Business services, nec
Corporate Acquisition and Merger Services 825, 826, 827
Corporate Acquisitions and Mergers 828, 830, 831, 832, 833, 834, 835, 836
Corporate Acquisitions and Mergers – Europe 837
Corporate Acquisitions and Mergers – Germany 838
Corporate Acquisitions and Mergers – International Aspects 839, 840, 841, 842, 843, 844, 845, 846, 847
Meeting Sites 1899
Packaging 2017
Telemarketing 2368
Telemarketing – United Kingdom 2369, 2370, 2371

AUTO REPAIR, SERVICES, AND PARKING

7514 Passenger car rental
Automobile Leasing and Rental Companies 222
7515 Passenger car leasing
Automobile Leasing and Rental Companies 223
7530 Automotive Repair Shops
Automobile Service Stations 245

MOTION PICTURES

7812 Motion picture & video production
Motion Picture Industry 1934, 1935, 1936, 1937
Television Programs 2389, 2390
Video Tapes 2481
7822 Motion picture and tape distribution
Film Distribution 1315, 1316
7832 Motion picture theaters, ex drive-in
Motion Picture Theaters

BIBLIOGRAPHY

ACCOUNTANCY
Institute of Chartered Account-
ants in England and Wales
PO Box 433
London EC2P 2BJ, England
071-833-3291
Monthly
ISSN: 0001-4664

THE ACCOUNTANT
Lafferty Publications Ltd.
IDA Tower, Pearse Street
Dublin 2, Ireland
(353-1) 671-8022
Fax: (353-1) 671-8520,
Published: monthly.

ADVERTISING AGE
Crain Communications Inc.
220 E. 42nd St.
New York, NY 10017
(212)210-0100
Fax: (212)210-0111
Toll Free: (800)678-9595
Weekly
Subscription Rate: $99
ISSN: 0001-8899

Special Issue:
  Ad Age 300 (annual)

ADVERTISING AGE
INTERNATIONAL
Crain Communications, Inc.
220 E. 42nd St.
New York, NY 10017
(212) 210-0725
Fax: (212) 210-0111,
Weekly.

ADWEEK
Eastern Edition
BPI Communications Inc.
1515 Broadway
New York, NY 10036
(212)536-5336
Fax: (212)536-1416
Toll Free: (800)722-6658
Weekly
Subscription Rate: $105
ISSN: 0199-286

AFTENPOSTEN
Akersgaten 51, 0180
Oslo, Norway.

AGEXPORTER
U.S. Department of Agriculture
USGPO
Washington D.C. 20402
 (202) 783-3238.

AGRI FINANCE
Century Communications Inc.
6201 W. Howard St.
Niles, IL 60714
(708)647-1200
Fax: (708)647-7055
Toll Free: (800)322-5510
10x/yr
Subscription Rate: $45
ISSN: 0002-1164

AIR CARGO WORLD
Communication Channels, Inc.
6255 Barfield Rd.
Atlanta, GA 30328
Telephone: (404) 256-9800
Fax: (404) 256-3116

AIR TRANSPORT WORLD
Penton Publishing Co.
PO Box 1361
Stamford, CT 06904
(203)348-7531
Fax: (203)348-4023
Toll Free (800)321-7003
Monthly
Subscription Rate: $50
ISSN: 0002-2543

AMERICAN BANKER
American Banker Bond Buyer
1 State Street Plaza
New York, NY 10004
(212)803-8200
Fax: (800)235-5552
Toll Free: (800)221-1809
Daily
Subscription Rate: $750
ISSN: 1064-5349

AMERICAN SHIPPER
Howard Publications Inc.
33 South Hogan Street
P.O. Box 4728
Jacksonville, FL 32201
(904) 365-2601.
Monthly
Price: $35 per year; $3 per single
copy.

AMUSEMENT BUSINESS
BPI Communications Inc.
Box 24970
Nashville, TN 37202
(615) 321-4250
Fax: (615) 327-1575.
Published: weekly

**APPLIANCE
MANUFACTURER**
BusinessNews Publishing
5900 Harper Rd., Ste. 105
Solon, OH 44139
(216)349-3060
Fax: (216)498-9121
Monthly
Subscription Rate: $55
ISSN: 0003-679X

ASIA INC.
Asia Inc. Ltd.
8/F Kinwick Centre
32 Hollywood Road
Central, Hong Kong,
Monthly
Cost: $59 for one year in the U.S.;
HK$349 in Hong Kong; U.S. $83
in rest of world.

**ASIA'S 7,500 LARGEST
COMPANIES**
E.L.C. Publishing Ltd.
109 Uxbridge Rd., Eating
London W5STL, England
081-566-2288
Fax: 081-566-4931
Annual

ASIAMONEY
Euromoney Publications PLC
Trust Tower, 20th Floor
68 Johnston Rd.
Wanchai, Hong Kong
852-529-5009
Fax: 852-866-9046
10x/yr

Special Issues:
    Deals of the Year (annual)
    Stockbrokers Poll (annual)

ASIAN BUSINESS
Far East Trade Press Ltd.
2-F Kai Tak Commercial Bldg.
317 Des Voeux Rd., Central
Hong Kong
545-7200
Fax: 544-6979
Monthly
Subscription Rate: $105
ISSN: 0254-3729

Special Issue:
    *Most Admired Companies
    (annual)*

ASIAWEEK
20th Floor, Trust Tower
58 Johnston Road
Wanchal, Hong Kong,
Weekly

**AUTOMOTIVE
ENGINEERING**
Society of Automotive Engineers
400 Commonwealth Drive
Warrendale, PA 15096
(412) 776-4841
Fax: (412) 776-9765,
Monthly
Cost: $48 U.S. and Canada.

AUTOMOTIVE INDUSTRIES
Capital Cities/ABC/Chilton Co.
Chilton Way
Radnor PA 19089
(215) 964-4255
Fax: (215) 964-4251.

AUTOMOTIVE NEWS
Crain Communications Inc.
1400 Woodbridge Ave.
Detroit, MI 48207
(313)446-6000
Fax: (313)446-0383
Weekly
Subscription Rate: $85
ISSN: 0005-1551

Special Issue:
    *Automotive News Market Data
    Book (annual)*

AVIATION WEEK & SPACE TECHNOLOGY
McGraw-Hill Inc.
1221 Avenue of the Americas
New York, NY 10020
(212)512-2000
Toll Free: (800)525-5003
Weekly
Subscription Rate: $105
ISSN: 0005-2175

Special Issue:
   Industry Report on Competitiveness (annual)

BANGKOK POST
Post Publishing Company Ltd.
Bankok Post Building
136 Na Ranong Road,
Office Kosa Road
Klong Toei, Bangkok, Thailand 10110,
Published: daily.

THE BANKER
Financial Times Business Information Ltd.
2 Greystoke Pl., Fetter Ln.
London EC4A IND, England
171-405-6969
Fax: 171-405-5276
Monthly
Subscription Rate: $197
ISSN: 0005-5395

Special Issues:
   Asian Top 200 (annual)
   Europe Top 500 (annual)
   Global Banking (annual)
   Latin American 100 (annual)
   Top European Savings Banks by Country (annual)
   Top African Banks - By Country (annual)
   Top 100 Arab Financial Institutions (annual)

   Top 100 Central European (annual)
   Top 100 Japanese Banks (annual)
   Top 100 Russians
   World Top 1,000 (annual)

BANKERS' ALMANAC WORLD RANKING
Reed Information Services
Windsor Court, East Grinstead House
East Grinstead, W. Sussex, RH19 1XA, England
342-326972
Fax: 342-335612
Annual
Price: $229

BEST'S REVIEW
A.M. Best Co.
Ambest Rd.
Oldwick, NJ 08858
(908)439-2200
Fax: (908)439-3363
Monthly
Subscription Rate: $21

Special Issues:
   Life/Health Edition
   Property/Casualty Edition

BEVERAGE INDUSTRY
Stagnito Publishing
1935 Shermer Rd., Ste. 100
Northbrook, IL 60062
(708)205-5660
Fax: (708)205-5680
Monthly
Subscription Rate: $55
ISSN: 0148-6187

BEVERAGE WORLD
Keller International Publishing Corp.
150 Great Neck Rd.
Great Neck, NY 11021
(516)829-9210
Fax: (516)829-5414
Monthly
Subscription Rate: $39.95
ISSN: 0098-2318

Special Issue:
   Top 50 (annual)

BEVERAGE WORLD'S PERISCOPE
Keller International Publishing Corp.
150 Great Neck Rd.
Great Neck, NY 11021
(516)829-9210
Fax: (516)829-5414
Monthly
Subscription Rate: $39.95
ISSN: 0098-2318

BROILER INDUSTRY
Watt Publishing Co.
122 S. Wesley Ave.
Mount Morris, IL 61054-1497
(815) 734-4171
Fax: (815) 734-4201.
Published: monthly.

BUSINESS/CENTRAL EUROPE
The Economist Bldg
111 W. 57th St.
New York, NY 10019
(212) 541-5730
Fax: (212) 541-9378,
Published: monthly.

BUSINESS IN RUSSIA
U.I. Profsoyuznaya 73
Moscow 117342, Russia
(7-095) 333-3340
Fax: (7-095) 3301568.

BUSINESS INDIA
Living Media India
Connaught Place
New Delhi, India 11001.

BUSINESS INSURANCE
Crain Communications Inc.
965 E. Jefferson
Detroit, MI 48207
(313)446-0619
Fax: (313)446-6777
Toll Free: (800)678-9595
Weekly
Subscription Rate: $80
ISSN: 0007-6864

Special Issue:
   Lloyd's of London (annual)

BUSINESS KOREA
Marston Webb International
60 Madison Ave.
New York, NY 10010
(212) 684-660011
Fax: (212) 725-4709,
Published: monthly.

BUSINESS LATIN AMERICA
The Economist Bldg
111 W. 57th St.
New York, NY 10019
(212) 541-5730
Fax: (212) 541-9378,

BUSINESS MEXICO
Reference Press Inc.
6448 Hwy. 290 E., E-104
Austin, TX 78723
(512)454-7778
Fax: (512)454-9401
Toll Free: (800)486-8666
Price: $24.95

BUSINESS REVIEW
Thanachi Theerapatvong
44 Moo 10 Banga-Trat Road Km
4.5
banga, Prakanong, Bangkok
10260

BUSINESS TODAY
Living Media India Ltd.
Connaught Place
New Delhi 110001
3315801-4
Fax: 3316180

BUSINESS TRAVEL NEWS
Miller Freeman Inc.
1515 Broadway
New York, NY 10036
(212)869-1300
Fax: (212)279-3945
Toll Free: (800)447-0138
29x/yr
Subscription Rate: $95

Special Issues:
   Business Travel Survey (annual)
   Corporate Travel 100 (annual)

BUSINESS WEEK
McGraw-Hill Inc.
1221 Ave. of the Americas
New York, NY 10020
Toll Free: (800)635-1200
Fax: (212)512-4025
Weekly
Subscription Rate: $37.95
ISSN: 0007-7135

Special Issues:
   Business Week 1000 (annual)
   Global 1,000 (annual)

CABLE WORLD
Cowles Business Media
1905 Sherman St., Ste. 1000
Denver, CO 80203
(303)837-0900
Fax: (303)837-0915
Weekly
Subscription Rate: $60
ISSN: 1042-7228

CALIFORNIA MANAGEMENT REVIEW
University of California, Berkley
School of Business Administration
350 Barrows Hall
Berkley, CA 94720

CAMBIO
08750 Molins de Rei
Barcelona
418 47 49.

CANADIAN BUSINESS
CB Media Ltd.
777 Bay St., 5th Fl.
Toronto, ON, Canada M5W 1A7
(416)596-5151
Fax: (416)596-5152
Monthly
ISSN: 0008-3100

Special Issue:
Canadian Business 500 (an-nual)

CANADIAN CHEMICAL NEWS
Chemical Publishers Ltd.
130 Slater St
Ste. 550
Ottawa ON Canada K 1 P 652.

CANADIAN FORUM
804-251 Laurier Ave.
W. Ottawa, ON Canada K1P 5J6
(613) 230-3078
Fax: (613) 233-1458.

CANDY INDUSTRY
Advanstar Communications
7500 Old Oak Blvd.
Cleveland, OH 44130
(216)826-2866
Fax: (216)891-2733
Monthly
Subscription Rate: $39
ISSN: 0745-1032

Special Issue:
State of the Industry Report (annual)

CATALOG AGE
Cowles Business Media Inc.
911 Hope St., Bldg. 6
Stamford, CT 06907-0949
(203)358-9900
Fax: (203)348-5792
Monthly
Subscription Rate: $74
ISSN: 0740-3119

Special Issue:
The Catalog Age 100 (annual)

CERAMIC FORUM INTERNATIONAL
Bauverlag GmbH
Am Klingenweg 4, D-65396
Wallurf, Germany

CHEMICAL & ENGINEERING NEWS
American Chemical Society
1155 16th St. N.W.
Washington, DC 20036
(202)872-4600
Fax: (202)872-4615
Weekly
Subscription Rate: $132
ISSN: 0009-2347

Special Issues:
Facts & Figures for Chemical R & D (annual)
Facts & Figures for the Chemical Industry (annual)

CHEMICAL MARKET REPORTER (FORMERLY CHEMICAL MARKETING REPORTER)
Schnell Publishing Co., Inc.
80 Broad St.
New York, NY 1004-2203
(212) 248-4177
Fax: (212) 248-4903,
Weekly.

CHEMICAL WEEK
ChemicalWeek Associates
888 7th Ave., 26th Fl.
New York, NY 10106
(212)621-4900
Fax: (212)621-4900
Weekly
Subscription Rate: $115
ISSN: 0009-272X

CHEMISTRY & INDUSTRY
15 Belgrave Square
London SW1X 8PS U.K.
0171 235 3681
Fax: 0171 235 9140.

CHEMTECH
Smerican Chemical Society
1155 16th St. NW
Washington D.C. 20036
(202) 872-4600
Fax: (202) 872-6060

CHICAGO TRIBUNE
435 N. Michigan Ave.
Chicago, IL 60611
(312) 222-3232.
Published: daily.

CHINA-BRITAIN TRADE REVIEW
Abford House
15 Wilton Road
London SW1V 1LT
Telephone: 0171-828 5176.

THE CHINA BUSINESS REVIEW
China Business Forum
1818 N St., NW Ste. 500
Washington D.C., 20036
(202) 429-0340
Fax: (202) 775-2476,
6x/yr.

THE CHRISTIAN SCIENCE MONITOR
Christian Science Publishing Society
One Norway St., Boston, MA 02115
(800) 456-2220
Daily, except weekends and holidays.

COAL
Maclean Hunter Publishing Co.
29 N. Wcker Drive
Chicago, IL 60606
(312) 726-2802
Fax: (312) 726-2574

COLUMBIA JOURNAL OF WORLD BUSINESS
Columbia University
Columbia University Business School
315 Uris Hall
New York, NY 10027
(212) 854-3431
Fax: (212) 854-5315.

COMPUTER RESELLER NEWS
CMP Media Inc.
One Jericho Plaza
Jericho, New York 11753,
Published: $199; Canada $224.

COMPUTERWORLD
Computerworld Inc.
500 Old Connecticut Path
Framingham, MA 01701
(508)879-0700
Fax: (508)875-8931
Toll Free: (800)343-6474
Weekly
Subscription Rate: $39.95
ISSN: 0010-4841

Special issue:
Premier 100 (annual)

COMPUTING JAPAN
Hiroo AK Bldg. 4th Floor
5-25-2 Hiroo, Shibuya-ku
Tokyo 150, Japan
03-3445-2616
Fax: 03-3447-4925.

CORNELL HOTEL AND RESTAURANT ADMINISTRATION QUARTERLY
Cornell University of School of Hotel Administration
Statlet Hall
Ithaca, NY 14853
(607) 255-5093
Fax: (607) 257-1204
6x/yr.
Subscription Rate $62; $102 institutions; $90 foreign.

CREDIT CARD MANAGEMENT
Faulkner & Gray Inc.
300 S. Wacker Dr., 18th Fl.
Chicago, IL 60606
(312)913-1334
Fax: (312)913-1365
Monthly
Subscription Rate: $78
ISSN: 0896-9329

Special Issue:
CCM's Credit Card Industry Annual Report

DAGENS NYHETER
Gjorwellsgatan 30
Stockholm, Sweden,
Published: daily.

DAIRY FOODS
Cahners Publishing Co.
1350 E. Touhy Ave.
Des Plaines, IL 60018-3358
(708)635-8800
Fax: (708)299-8622
Monthly
Subscription Rate: $88
ISSN: 0888-0050

DAWN
Pakistan Herald Ltd. Press
Pakistan,
Daily.

LE DEVOIR
L'Imprimiere Populaire
211 du SAT
Sacremento, Montreal, PQ Canada H2Y 1X1
Telephone: (514) 985-3333.

DIRECT MARKETING
Hoke Communications Inc.
224 7th St.
Garden City, NY 11530
(516) 746-6700
Fax: (516) 294-8141,
Monthly
Subscription Rate: $56.

THE DIRECTOR
11121 W Oklahoma Ave
Milwaukee WI 53227-4096.

DISCOUNT MERCHANDISER
233 Park Ave. S., 6th Fl.
New York, NY 10003
(212)979-4860
Fax: (212)979-7431
Monthly
Subscription Rate: $55

DUN & BRADSTREET LATIN AMERICA'S 25,000
Dun & Bradstreet
3 Sylvan way
Parsippany, NJ 07054-3896
(201)605-600
Fax: (201)605-6911
Toll Free: (800)526-0651

DUN'S EUROPA
Dun & Bradstreet
3 Sylvan way
Parsippany, NJ 07054-3896
(201)605-600
Fax: (201)605-6911
Toll Free: (800)526-0651
Annual
Price: $650

E-MEDIA PROFESSIONAL
Online Inc.
462 Danbury Road
Wilton, CT 06897-2126
Monthly
Subscription Rate: $55

EAST AFRICAN STANDARD BUSINESS & FINANCE
P.O. Box 30080
Nairobi, Kenya
540280/1/2/3/5/6/7
Fax: 553939.

ECONOMIC DEVELOPMENT HORIZONS
3821 E. Guasti Road, Ste. 275
Ontario, CA 91764

ECONOMIC REVIEW
3718 Locust Walk
Philadelphia, PA 19104-6297.

THE ECONOMIST
The Economist Bldg
111 W. 57th St.
New York, NY 10019
(212) 541-5730
Fax: (212) 541-9378
Weekly
Cost: $110; $3.50 per single issue.

EGG INDUSTRY
Watt Publishing Co.
122 S. Wesley Ave.
Mount Morris, IL 61054-1497
(815) 734-4171
Fax: (815) 734-4201,
Bimonthly.

EL MERCURIO
Cassilla 13-D Stgo, Spain
330144.

EL PAIS
Miguel Yeste 40
28037 Madrid, Spain
(91) 337 82 00,
Daily.

ELECTRONIC BUSINESS TODAY
CMP Publications Inc.
8773 South Ridgeline Blvd.
Highlands Ranch, CO, 80126-2329
(516) 562-5000
Fax: (516) 562-5409,
Monthly.

ELECTRONIC NEWS
Electronic News Publishing Corp.
488 Madison Ave.
New York, NY 10022
(212) 909-5924,
Weekly, except last week of Dec.

ENERGY
Pergamon Press, Inc.
660 White Plains Rd.
Tarrytown, NY 10591-5153
(914) 524-9200
Fax: (914) 333-2444.

**ENGINEERING & MINING
JOURNAL**
Maclean Hunter Publishing Co.
29 Wacker Dr.
Chicago, IL 60606
Fax: (312) 726-2574,
Published: monthly.

ENR
McGraw-Hill Inc.
1221 Ave. of the Americas
New York, NY 10020
(212)512-2000
Fax: (212)512-2820
Toll Free: (800)635-1200
Weekly
Subscription Rate: $69
ISSN: 0891-9526

Special Issues:
   Top CM Firms (annual)
   Top 500 Design Firms (annual)
   Top 400 Contractors (annual)
   Top International Design Firms (annual)
   Top Owners (annual)
   Top Specialty Contractors (annual)
   Top 225 International Contractors (annual)

ENTERTAINMENT WEEKLY
Time-Warner Inc.
1675 Broadway
New York, NY 10019,
Published: weekly.

ENTREPENEUR
Entrepeneur Group
2392 Morse Ave.
Irvine, CA 92714-6234

(714) 261-2325
Fax: (714) 755-4211
Monthly
ISSN: 0163-3341

EUROBUSINESS
Transnational Business Magazines Ltd.
Stratton House, Stratton St.
London W1X 5FE, England
ISSN: 0953-0711
Note: No longer published

EUROMONEY
Euromoney Publications PLC
c/o World Publications Service
19 Union Ave., Ste. 202
Rutherford, NJ 07070
(201)531-0760
Monthly
Subscription Rate: $395
ISSN: 0014-2433

Special Issues:
   Intersec 250 (annual)
   Business Travel (annual)
   Credit Risk Survey (annual)

EUROPE
Delegation of the European Commission
2300 M Street NW
Washington DC 20037.

**EUROPE'S 15,000 LARGEST
COMPANIES**
Dun & Bradstreet
3 Sylvan Way
Parsippany, NJ 07054-3896

(201)605-6000
Fax: (201)605-6911
Toll Free: (800)526-0651
Annual
Price: $475

THE EUROPEAN
P.O. Box 14, Harold Hill
Romford RM3 8EQ, England
Published: weekly
Cost: $135 for one year.

**EUROPEAN CHEMICAL
NEWS**
Reed Business Publishing Group
Quadrant House
Sutton, Surrey SM2 5AS, U.K.
081-6613500
Weekly.

**EUROPEAN RUBBER
JOURNAL**
Crain Communications Ltd.
20-22 Bedford Row
London WC1R 4EW, UK
(071) 831-9511
Fax: (071) 430-2176,
Published: monthly, except August.

Special Issue:
   Global Tyre Report (annual)

L'EXPANSION
482 F. Grupe Expansion
25 Rue Leblanc, F-75842
Paris Cedex 15.

L'EXPRESS
67 Ave. de Wagram
75017 Paris, France
(1) 47 63 12 11,
Biweekly.

**FAR EASTERN ECONOMIC
REVIEW**
Review Publishing Co.
c/o Datamovers
36 W. 36th St., 4th Fl.
New York, NY 10018
(212)564-5040
Fax: (212)564-5139
Weekly
Subscription Rate: $199

Special Issue:
Review 200 (annual)

FINANCIAL POST
Financial Post Co. Ltd.
333 King St. E
Toronto, ON, Canada M5A 4N2
(416)350-6176
Fax: (416)350-6171
Annual
ISSN: 0829-1640

FINANCIAL TIMES
1 Southwark Bridge
London SE1 9HL, England
171-873-3000
Fax: 171-263-9764
Daily

Special Issue:
FT Top 500 (annual)

FINANCIAL WORLD
Financial World Partners
1328 Broadway, 3rd Fl.
New York, NY 10001-2132

(212)594-5030
Fax: (212)629-0021
Biweekly
Subscription Rate: $37.50
ISSN: 0015-2064
Special Issue:
*World's Most Valuable
Brands*

**FOOD ENGINEERING
INTERNATIONAL**
Chilton Co.
One Chilton Way
Radnor, PA 19089
(215) 964-4000.
Monthly
Price: solicited only from professionals in field:
$55 per year, $100 for 2 years;
educational rate: $28 per year.

FOOD PROCESSING
Putnam Publishing Co.
301 E. Erie St.
Chicago, IL 60611-3059
(312)644-2020
Fax: (312)644-7870
Monthly
Subscription Rate: $35
ISSN: 0015-6523

FORBES
60 5th Ave.
New York, NY 10011
(212)620-2200
Biweekly
Subscription Rate: $57
ISSN: 0015-6914

Special Issues:
*Forbes 500S (annual)
Forbes Foreign Rankings (annual)
Super 40 (annual)*

**FOREIGN AGRICULTURAL
SERVICES**
USGPO
Washington D.C. 20230.

**FOREIGN LABOR TRENDS
GERMANY: 1994-95**
USGPO
Washington D.C. 20230.

FORTUNE
Time Inc.
Time & Life Bldg.
Rockefeller Center
New York, NY 10020-1393
(212)586-1212
Fax: (212)522-0601
Biweekly
Subscription Rate: $57
ISSN: 0015-8259

Special Issues:
*Global 500: World's Biggest
Industrial Corporations (annual)
Global Service 500 (annual)
1995 Investor's Guide Issue
(annual)*

FRANCHISING WORLD
International Franchise Association
1350 New York Ave., NW, Ste. 900
Washington, DC 20005
(202)628-8000
Fax: (202)628-0812
Bimonthly
Subscription Rate: $12

FURNITURE/TODAY
Cahners Publishing Co.
7025 Albert Pick Rd., Ste. 200
Greensboro, NC 27409
(910)605-0121
Fax: (910)605-1143
Weekly
Subscription Rate: $94.97
ISSN: 0194-360X

GAMING & WAGERING BUSINESS
BMT Publications Inc.
7 Penn Plaza, 12th Fl.
New York, NY 10001-3900
(212)594-4120
Fax: (212)714-0514
Monthly
Subscription Rate: $86
ISSN: 8750-8222

GERMANY'S TOP 500: A HANDBOOK OF GERMANY'S TOP CORPORATIONS
World Publications Service
19 Union Ave., Ste. 202
Rutherford, NJ 07070
(201)531-0760
Annual

THE GLEANER
7 North St.
P.O. Box 40
Kingston, Jamaica W.I.
(876) 922-3400
Fax: (876) 922-6223.

GLOBAL FINANCE
McGraw-Hill Inc.
11 W. 19th St.
New York, NY 10011

(212)337-5900
Fax: (212)337-5055
Monthly
Subscription Rate: $255
ISSN: 0896-4181

GLOBAL WORKFORCE
P.O. Box
55695
Boulder, CO 80322-5695
(800) 444-6485.

THE GLOBE AND MAIL
The Globe and Mail Newspaper
444 Front St. W.
Toronto, ON, Canada M5V 2S9
(416)585-5316
Fax: (416)585-5641
Monthly
Price: $1/copy

Special Issue:
Globe and Mail Report on Business 1000 (annual)

GOLD 1997
Gold Institute
Administrative Office
1112 16th St. NW Ste. 240
Washington D.C. 20036
(202) 835-0185
Fax: (202) 835-0155
Annual
Price: $95.

GOVERNMENT FINANCE REVIEW
Government Finance Officers Assn.
180 N. Michigan Ave. Ste. 800
Chicago, IL 60601
(312) 977-9700
Fax: (312) 977-4806.

GT GUIDE TO WORLD EQUITY MARKETS
World Publications Service
19 Union Ave., Ste. 202
Rutherford, NJ 07070
(201)531-0760
Annual
Price: $260

THE GUARDIAN
Guardian Newspapers Ltd.
119 Farrington Road
London EC1R 3ER
0171-278-2332,
Daily.

HEALTH
Hippocrates Partners
301 Howard St., Ste. 1800
San Francisco, CA 94121-0056
(415) 512-9100
Fax: (415) 512-9600.

THE HINDU
National Press
Kasturi Buildings
Madras 6000002.

THE HINDUSTAN TIMES
Hindustan Times Press
18-20 Kasturba Gahndi
Marg, New Delhi 11001.

THE HOLLYWOOD REPORTER
H.R. Industries Inc.
5055 Wilshire Blvd.
Los Angeles, CA 90036-4396,
Published: weekly
Subscription Rate: $90.

HOSIERY NEWS
National. Assoc. of Hosiery
Manufacturers
200 N Sharon Amity Rd.
Charlotte, NC 28211, (704) 365-
0913

**HOTEL & MOTEL
MANAGEMENT**
Advanstar Communications Inc.
7500 Old Oak Blvd.
Cleveland, OH 44130
(216)243-8100
Fax: (216)891-3120
Toll Free: (800)225-4569
21x/yr
Subscription Rate: $55
ISSN: 0018-6082

Special Issue:
   *Top 25 Management Compa-
   nies (annual)*

HOTELS
Cahners Publishing Co.
1350 Touhy Ave.
P.O. Box 5080
Des Plaines, IL 60017-5080
Telephone: (708) 635-8800

**HUMAN RESOURCES
MANAGEMENT**
John Wiley & Sons Inc.
605 3rd Ave.
New York, NY 10158
(212)850-6000
Fax: (212)850-8888
Toll Free: (800)225-5945
Quarterly
Subscription Rate: $58
ISSN: 0090-4848

ICAO JOURNAL
International Civil Aviation Or-
ganization
1000 Sherbrooke St. W., Ste 652
Montreal, PQ, Canada H3A 2R2
(514) 285-8219
Fax: (514) 288-4772
10x/yr.
Subscription Rate: $20
ISSN: 0018-8778

IGA GROCERGRAM
Pace Communications Inc.
1301 Carolina St.
Greensboro, NC 27401
(910)378-6065
Fax: (910)275-2864
Monthly
Subscription Rate: $40
ISSN: 0018-9766

IMPACT21
PHP Institute of America
420 Lexington AVe., Suite 646
New York, NY 10170
(212) 949-8050
Fax: (212) 949-0263,
Monthly.

INBOUND LOGISTICS
Thomas Publishing Co.
5 Penn Plaza
New York, NY 10001
(212) 629-1560
Fax: (212) 629-1584.

INDIA ABROAD
43 West 24th Street
New York, NY 10010,
Published: weekly
Cost: $35.

INDIA TODAY
Nike & Mackenzie Ltd.
13 John Prince's Street
London W1M 9HB
071-493 0351.

INDUSTRIAL MINERALS
220 Fifth Ave.
New York, NY 10001
(212) 213-6619.

INDUSTRY WEEK
Penton Publishing
1100 Superior Ave.
Cleveland, OH 44114
(216)696-7000
Fax: (216)696-7670
Bimonthly
Subscription Rate: $60
ISSN: 0039-0895

INFORMATIONWEEK
CMP Publications, Inc.
P.O. Box 1093
Skokie, IL 60076-8093,
Weekly, except double issue in
the last two weeks of December
Price: U.S./Canada: $120 per
year; free to qualified persons in
field of information management.

INSIDE COSMETICS
Morgan Grampian Ltd.
30 Calderwood St.
Woolrich, London SE18 6QH
UK

INSTITUTIONAL INVESTOR
Capital Cities Media
488 Madison Ave.
New York, NY 10022-5751
(212)303-3300
Fax: (212)224-3171
Monthly
Subscription Rate: $405
ISSN: 0020-3580

Special Issues:
Best Hotels Worldwide
The Euro 100 (annual)

INSTITUTIONAL INVESTOR INTERNATIONAL EDITION
Capital Cities Media
488 Madison Ave.
New York, NY 10022-5751
(212)303-3300
Fax: (212)303-3171
Monthly
Subscription Rate: $430
ISSN: 0192-5660

Special Issues:
All-Asia Research Team (annual)
All-Europe Research Team (annual)
All-Latin America Research Team (annual)

INSTITUTIONAL RESEARCH
Research Services Inc.
2201 3rd St.,
San Francisco, CA 94107
(415) 621-0220

INTERAVIA
Aerospace Media Publishing
Swiss Air Centre
31 rte. de l'Aeroport
Case Postale 437

CH-1215 Geneva 15, Switzerland
Fax: 22 7882726
Monthly
Subscription Rate: $128
ISSN: 0983-1592

INTERNATIONAL BUSINESS
IB Communications Inc.
9 E. 40th St., 10th Fl.
New York, NY 10016
(212)683-2426
Fax: (212)683-3426
Monthly
Subscription Rate: $48
ISSN: 1060-4073

INTERNATIONAL INSURANCE MONITOR
Chase Communciations Group Ltd.
P.O. Box 9001
Mount Vernon, NY10552-9001,
(914) 699-2020,
Fax: (914) 699-2025.

INVESTMENT DEALERS' DIGEST
100 Enterprises
2 World Trade Center, 18th Fl.
New York, NY 10048
(212)227-1200
Fax: (212)321-3805
Weekly
Subscription Rate: $495
ISSN: 0021-0080

Special Issues:
Fees (annual)
M & A Rankings (annual)
Medium-Term Notes Rankings (annual)
Private Placement Sweepstakes (annual)

Underwriter Rankings (annual)

INVESTOR'S BUSINESS DAILY
P.O. Box 661750
Los Angeles, CA 90066-8950,
Published: daily, except weekends and holidays
Subscription Rate: $128 per year.

INVESTOR'S CHRONICLE
Financial Times Business Information Ltd.
2 Greystoke Pl.
Fetter Ln.
London, EC4A 1ND, England
171-405-6969
Fax: 171-405-5276
Weekly
Subscription Rate: 115
ISSN: 0261-3115

IRISH TIMES
11-15 D'Olier
Dublin, Ireland.

JAPANESE FINANCE & INDUSTRY
Industrial Bank of Japan
1251 Avenue of the Americas
New York, NY 10020-1104
Telephone: 1-212-282-3000.

JEUNE AFRIQUE ECONOMIE
30 Avenue of the Messine
75008 Paris
(1) 49 53 06 02.

JOURNAL OF COMMERCE
Journal of Commerce, Inc.,
Two World Trade Center, 27th
Floor
New York, NY 10048
(212) 837-7000
Fax: (212) 837-7035.

**JOURNAL OF JAPANESE
TRADE & INDUSTRY**
Japan Economic Foundation
11th Floor
Fukoku Seimei Bldg, 2-2-2
Uchisawai-cho, Chiyoda-ku, To-
kyo.
Monthly.

**LATIN AMERICAN
ECONOMY & BUSINESS**
Latin American Newsletters
61 Old Street
London EC1V 9hX, England
(4471) 251 0012,
Monthly.

**LATIN AMERICAN
ECONOMY & BUSINESS -
QUARTERLY UPDATE**
Latin American Newsletters
61 Old Street
London EC1V 9hX, England
(4471) 251 0012,
Quarterly.

**LATIN AMERICAN WEEKLY
REPORT**
Latin American Newsletters
61 Old Street
London EC1V 9hX, England
(4471) 251 0012,

**LATIN CORPORATE
FINANCE HANDBOOK**
Reed Busines Publishing
205 E. 42nd St., Ste. 1705
New York, NY 10017
Telephone: 9212) 867-2080.

LATIN TRADE
Freedom Communications Inc.
200 South Bicauyne Blvd.
Suite 1150, Miami, FL 33131,
Published: monthly.
Special Issue:
   *Top 100 Publicly Traded Com-
   panies (annual)*

LOOK JAPAN
Look Japan Ltd.
Asahiseimei Hibiya Bldg
1-5-1 Yurakucho Chiyoda-ku
Tokyo 100 Japan
(03) 5511-7111
Fax: (03) 5511-7110.

MACLEANS
Maclean Hunter Ltd.
777 Bay St.
Toronto, ON Canada M5W 1A7,
Telephone: (416) 596-5311.

MACWEEK
JCI Co.
301 Howard St., 15th Fl.
San Francisco, CA 94015
(415) 243-3500
Fax: (415) 243-3651.

MAIL & GUARDIAN
M&G Media
139 Smit Street
Braamfontein, Johannesburg,
South Africa
(011) 403-7111,
Daily
Cost: South Africa 1 year: R140,
Rest ofthe world: airmail, 1 year,
R960; surface mail, 1 year, R260.

MANAGEMENT TODAY
Haymarket Management Maga-
zine
22 Lancaster Gate
London W2 3LY, England
171-413-4288
Fax: 171-413-4138
Monthly
ISSN: 0025-1925

Special Issue:
   *Britain's Most Admired Cor-
   porations (annual)*

MANILA CHRONICLE
Chronicle Securities Corp.
371 A. Bonifacio Drive
Port Area, Manila,
Daily.

**THE MANUFACTURING
CONFECTIONER**
The Manufacturing Confectioner
Publishing Company
175 Rock Rd.
Glen Rock, NJ 07452
(201) 652-2655
Fax: (201) 652-3419,
Monthly
Price: $25 per year, single copies
$10 each, except $25 for April
and July issues.

Bibliography

MARINE LOG
Simmons-Boardman Publishing
345 Hudson St.
New York, NY 10014
(212) 620-7200
Fax: (212) 633-1165,
Monthly.

MARKETING
Haymarket Business Publications
Ltd.
30 Lancaster Gate
London W2 3LY, England
Weekly
Subscription Rate: 75
ISSN: 0025-3650

Special Issues:
  Britain's Biggest Brands (an-nual)
  Top Agencies (annual)

MARKETING IN EUROPE
Corporate Intelligence on REtail-ing
51 Doughty Street
London WC 1N 2LSS
Telephone: (0171) 696-9006.

MARKETING MAGAZINE
Maclean Hunter Ltd.
Maclean Hunter Bldg.
777 Bay St.
Toronto, ON, Canada M5W 1A7
(416)596-5835
Weekly
Subscription Rate: C$116
ISSN: 0025-3642

MARKETING NEWS
American Marketing Association
250 S. Wacker Dr., Ste. 200
Chicago, IL 60606

(312)648-0536
Fax: (312)993-7540
Toll Free: (800)262-1150
Biweekly
Subscription Rate: $60
ISSN: 0025-3790

MEAT & POULTRY
Oman Publishing Inc.
PO Box 1059
Mill Valley, CA 94942
(415)388-7575
Fax: (415)388-4961
Monthly
Free to industry
ISSN: 0892-6077

Special Issue:
  Top 100 (annual)

MEED
Meed House
21 John Street
GB-London, WCIN2BP.

MEETING NEWS
Miller Freeman Inc.
1515 Broadway
New York, NY 10036
(212)626-2380
Fax: (212)944-7164
Toll Free: (800)950-1314
Monthly
Subscription Rate: $65

**MERGERS &
ACQUISITIONS**
IDD Enterprises
2 World Trade Center, 18th Fl.
New York, NY 10048

(212)227-1200
Fax: (212)321-2336
Bimonthly
Subscription Rate: $325
ISSN: 0026-0010

MERGERSTAT REVIEW
Houlihan Lokey Howard &
Zukin
1930 Century Park West
Los Angeles, CA 90067
(310)553-8871
Fax: (310)553-2173
Toll Free: (800)455-8871
Annual
Price: $235

MEXICO BUSINESS
3033 Chimey Rd., Suite 300
Houston, TX 77056
Published: monthly, combined is-sues in Jan./Feb. and July/Aug.

MIDDLE EAST
IC Publications Limited
7 Coldbath Square
London EC1R 4LQ, United
Kingdom
(0171) 713 7711
Fax: (0171) 713 789

MINING ENGINEERING
Society for Mining, Metallurgy
and Exploration Inc.
8307 Shaffer Pkwy.
P.O. Box 625002
Littleton, CO 80127
Telephone: (303) 973-9550
Fax: (303) 973-3845.

MODERN PAINT AND COATINGS

Communciations Channels Inc.
6255 Barfield Rd., Atlanta, GA
30328
(404) 256-9800
Fax: (404) 256-3116,
Monthly.

MONEY MARKET DIRECTORY OF PENSION FUNDS AND THEIR INVESTMENT MANAGERS

Money Market Directories
320 E. Main St.
Charlottesville, VA 22902-5234
(804)977-1450
Fax: (804)971-8738
Annual
Price: $945

NATIONAL PETROLEUM NEWS

Adams/Hunter Publishing Ltd.
2101 S. Arlington Heights Rd.,
Ste. 115
Arlington Heights, IL 60005
(708)427-9512
Fax: (708)427-2006
13x/yr.
ISSN: 0149-5267

Special Issue:
 NPN Market Facts (annual)

NATIONAL TRADE DATA BANK

STAT-USA
U.S. Department of Commerce
Washington D.C., 20230
(202) 482-1986
Fax: (202) 482-2164.

NATIONAL UNDERWRITER LIFE & HEALTH/FINANCIAL SERVICES

National Underwriter Co.
505 Gest St.
Cincinnati, OH 45203-1716
(513)721-2140
Fax: (513)721-0126
Toll Free: (800)543-0874
Weekly
Subscription Rate: $80
ISSN: 0028-033X

NATIONAL UNDERWRITER PROPERTY & CASUALTY/RISK & BENEFITS MANAGEMENT

National Underwriter Co.
505 Gest St.
Cincinnati, OH 45203-1716
(513)721-2140
Fax: (513)721-0126
Toll Free: (800)543-0874
Weekly
Subscription Rate: $85
ISSN: 1042-6841

Special Issue:
 World Reinsurance Report

NETWORK WORLD

Network World, Inc.
161 Worcester Rd.
Framingham, MA 01701-9172
(508) 875-6400,
Weekly.

NEUE ZURCHER ZEITUNG

Falkenstrasse 11, Postfach
CH-8021 Zurich
(01) 258-1111
Fax: (01) 252 1329.

THE NEW YORK TIMES

The New York Times Co.
229 W. 43rd St.
New York, NY 10036-3913
(212)556-1234
Fax: (212)727-4833
Toll Free: (800)631-2500
Daily
Subscription Rate: $442
ISSN: 0362-4331

NEWSWEEK

The Newsweek Building
Livingston, NJ 07039-1666
(800) 631-1040,
Weekly
Price: U.S.: $41.08 per year; Canada: $61.88 per year (send to P.O. Box 4012, Postal Station A, Toronto, ON M5W 2K1).

NIKKEI WEEKLY

1-9-5 Otemachi, Chiyoda-ku
Tokyo 100-66 Japan.

NONWOVENS INDUSTRY

Rodman Publishing Co.
17 S Franklin Tpke
Box 555
Ramsey NJ 07446
Telephone: (201) 825-2552.

NORTH AMERICAN PULP & PAPER FACT BOOK

Miller Freeman Inc.
P.O. Box 1065
Skokie, IL 60076-8065.

Bibliography

NOUVEL ECONOMISTE
10 Rue Guynemer 92136
Issy les Moulineaux
(1) 41 09 30 00.

THE OBSERVER
Guardian Newspapers Ltd.
119 Farrington Road
London ECR1R ER
(0171) 278-2332,
Sundays.

OIL & GAS JOURNAL
Penn Well Publishing Co.
3050 Post Oak Blvd., Ste. 200
Houston, TX 77056
(713)621-9720
Fax: (713)963-6285
Weekly
Subscription Rate: $79
ISSN: 0030-1388

Special Issue
   Oil & Gas Journal 200 (annual)

PAPERBOARD PACKAGING
Advanstar Communications Inc.
131 West First Street
Duluth, MN 55802
(218) 723-9477
Fax: (218) 723-9437,
Published: monthly
Price: U.S.: $39 per year, $58 for
2 years; Canada: $59 per year,
$88
for 2 years.

PC TODAY
131 West Grand Drive
Lincoln, NE 68521
Monthly

PC WEEK
Ziff-Davis Publishing Company
L.P.
Customer Service Dept.,
P.O. Box 1770, Riverton, NJ
08077-7370
(609) 461-210,
Weekly, except combined issue at
year-end
Subscription Rate: U.S.: $160 per
year; Canada/Mexico: $200 per
year.

**PENSIONS &
INVESTMENTS**
Crain Communications Inc.
220 E. 42nd St.
New York, NY 10017-5806
(212)210-0114
Fax: (212)210-0117
Biweekly
Subscription Rate: $205
ISSN: 1050-4974

PET PRODUCT NEWS
Fancy Publications, Inc.
P.O. Box 6050
Mission Viejo, CA 92690
(714) 855-8822
Fax: (714) 855-3045,
Monthly.

PETROLEUM ECONOMIST
Hart Publications Inc.
1900 Grant St, Suite 400
P.O. Box 1917
Denver, CO 80201,
Monthly.

PHOTO MARKETING
Photo Marketing Association International
3000 Picture Place
Jackson, MI 49201
(517) 788-8100
Fax: (517) 788-8371.
Monthly
Price: U.S.: $35 per year/with
Newsline $50, $55 for 2
years/$65 with Newsline; Canada: $35 per year/$50 with
Newsline, $55 for 2 years/$70
with Newsline (payable in Canadian funds plus GST).

PIMA'S PAPERMAKER
2400 East Oakston Street, Arlington Heights
Arlington Heights, IL 6005.

PIPELINE & GAS JOURNAL
Oildom Publishing Co. of Texas,
Inc.
3314 Mercer St.
Houston, TX 77027
(713) 622-0676
Fax: (713) 623-4768,
Monthly
Price: free to qualitifed subscribers; all others $15 per year.
Subscription Rate: $75
ISSN: 0032-0188

Special Issue:
   *Pipeline & Gas Journal 500
   (annual)*

*POULTRY: WORLD
MARKETS AND TRADE*
USGPO
Washington D.C. 20402.

PREPARED FOODS
Cahners Publishing Co.
1350 E. Touhy Ave.
Des Plaines, IL 60018-5080
(708)635-8800
Fax: (708)299-8622
Toll Free: (800)637-6079
13x/yr.
Subscription Rate: $89.90
ISSN: 0747-2536

Special Issue:
   *The Leading 200 Prepared
   Food & Beverage Processors
   (annual)*

*QUICK FROZEN FOODS
INTERNATIONAL*
E.W. Williams Publications Co.
2125 Center Ave., Ste. 305
Fort Lee, NJ 07024
(201) 592-7007
Fax: (201) 592-7171,
Quarterly.

R & D MAGAZINE
Cahners Publishing Co.
1350 E. Touhy Ave.
Des Plaines, IL 60018-5080
(708)635-8800
Fax: (708)299-8622
Toll Free: (800)637-6079
13x/yr.
Subscription Rate: $79.90
ISSN: 0746-9179

RCR
RCR Publications
777 East Speer Blvd.
Denver, CO 80203.

RICE JOURNAL
Specialized Agricultural Publica-
tions
3000 Highwoods Blvd, Suite 300
Raleigh, NC 27604
(919) 872-5040
Fax: (919) 876-6531,
Published: 6x/yr.

RUBBER & PLASTICS NEWS
Crain Communications
1725 Merriman Road, Ste. 300
Akron, OH 44313
(330) 836-9180
Fax: (33) 836-1005,
Published: weekly.

THE RUSSIAN
Russian Business Press
8621 Wilshire Blvd.
Beverly Hills, CA 90211
(213) 462-7005,
Monthly
Subscription Rate: U.S.: $48; for-
eign: $108.

SITE SELECTION
Conway Data Inc.
40 Technology Park, Ste. 200
Norcross, GA 30092-9990
(404)446-6996
Fax: (404)263-8825
Bimonthly
Subscription Rate: $75

*SKILLINGS MINING
REVIEW*
1st Bank Place
Ste. 278
130 W Superioe St.
Duluth, MN 55802
(218) 722-2310
Monthly.

*SLOAN MANAGEMENT
REVIEW*
Massachusetts Institue of Technology
292 Main St. E38-120
Cambridge, MA 02139
(617) 253-7170
4x/yr.

*SLOVENIAN BUSINESS
REPORT*
GV
Dunajska 5
Ljublijana, Slovenia
386 61 13212 30
Fax: 386 61 1321 012.

SMART COMPUTING
Sandhills Publishing
12o W Harvest Drive
Lincoln, NE 68521
Monthly.

*SOAP/COSMETIC/CHEMICAL
SPECIALTIES*
455 Broad Hollow Road
Melville, NY 11747-4722.

Bibliography

SOFTWARE MAGAZINE
Sentry Publishing Co.
One Research Drive, Suite 400B
Westborough, MA 01581
(508) 366-2031.
Monthly.

**SOLID STATE
TECHNOLOGY**
PennWell Publishing Company
1421 S. Sheridan Road
Tulsa, OK 74112
(603) 891-0123.

**SOUTH CHINA MORNING
POST**
Morning Post Bldg.
Tong Chong St.
P.O. Box 47
Quarry Bay, Hong Kong
(5) 620161.

SOYBEAN DIGEST
American Soybean Association
540 Maryville Centre Drive
P.O. Box 411007
Saint Louis, MO 63141-1007
(314) 576-2788
Fax: (314) 576-2786.

**SPRAY TECHNOLOGY &
MARKETING**
Industry Publications, Inc.
389 Passaic Ave.
Fairfield, NJ 07004
(201) 227-5151
Fax: (201) 227-921,
Monthly.

THE STATESMAN
Statesman Printing Press
Statesman House
4 Chowringhee Square
Calcutta, India.

STORES
National Retail Federation Enter-
prises
325 7th St. NW, Ste. 1000
Washington, DC 20004
(202)783-7971
Fax: (202)737-2849
Monthly
Subscription Rate: $49
ISSN: 0039-1867

THE STRAITS TIMES
390 Kim Seng Road
Singapore 239455
Fax: 65-732-0131.

THE SUNDAY POST
D.C. Thomson & Co.
144 Port Dundas Rd.
Glasgow, G4 OHZ,
Daily.

THE SUNDAY TELEGRAPH
1 Canada Aquare
Canary Wharf
London E14 5AR,
Daily.

THE SUNDAY TIMES
Times Newspapers
P.O. Box 495
Virginia Street
London E19XY.

SUPERMARKET NEWS
Fairchild Publications
7 W. 34th St.
New York, NY 10001-8191
(212)630-4750
Fax: (212)630-4760
Toll Free: (800)204-4515
Weekly
Subscription Rate: $185
ISSN: 0039-5803

SWIMMING POOL/SPA AGE
Intersec Publishing Co.
6151 Powers Ferry Rd., NW
Atlanta, GA 30339
(770) 955-2500
Monthly.

**SYDNEY MORNING
HERALD**
John Fairfax Holdings & Co.
Sydney, Australia
Fax: (612) 9282 3800.

**TEA & COFFEE TRADE
JOURNAL**
Lockwood Trade Journal Co.
130 W. 42nd St., Ste. 2200
New York, NY 10036-7802
(212) 391-2060
Fax: (212) 827-0945,
Monthly
Subscription Rate: $29 per year.

TELEPHONY
Interec Publishing Corp
9800 Metcalf
Overland Park, KS 66210
(913) 341-1300

TEXTILE WORLD
Tak Yan Commercial Bldg., 11th
Fl.
30-32 D'Aguilar St.
Hong Kong
(5) 247467,
Monthly.

TIME
Time, Inc.
Time & Life Bldg.
Rockefeller Center
New York, NY 10020-1393
(800) 843-8463

THE TIMES
Times Newspapers
P.O. Box 495
Virginia Street, London E1 9XY
0171-782-5000.

THE WORLD IN 1996
Economist Bldg
111 West 57th Street
New York, NY 10019
(212) 541-5730.

THE WORLD IN 1997
Economist Bldg
111 West 57th Street
New York, NY 10019
(212) 541-5730.

TIRE BUSINESS
Crain Communications, Inc.
1725 Merriman Rd., Ste. 300
Akron, OH 44313-5251
(216) 836-9180
Fax: (216) 836-1005.

TOBACCO INTERNATIONAL
Lockwood Trade Journal Co. Inc.
130 W. 42nd St.
New York, NY 10036-7802
(212)391-2060
Fax: (212)827-0945
Monthly
Subscription Rate: $36
ISSN: 0049-3945

TOKYO BUSINESS TODAY
1-2-1, Nihonbashi Hongokucho
Chuo-ku, Tokyo 103, Japan.
(212) 949-6737.

THE TORONTO STAR
One Yong Street
Toronto, Ontario M5E 1E6
(416) 367-2000,
Daily.

TRADE WITH GREECE
26-28 G. Averof Str.
142 32 Perissos - Athens, Greece.

TRAVEL WEEKLY
Reed Travel Group
500 Plaza Dr.
Secaucus, NJ 07096
(201) 902-2000
Fax: (201) 319-1947
Published: 2 times/week (Mon.
and Thurs.).

UNITAS
Oy Pohjoismaiden Yhdyspankki
AB Nordiska Forensingsbanken
Finland
Quarterly

U.S. GLOBAL TRADE OUTLOOK
USGPO
Washington D.C. 20602.

USA TODAY
Gannett Co., Inc.
1000 Wilson Blvd.
Arlington, VA 22229
(703) 276-3400.
Mon.-Fri.

VARIETY
475 Park Ave., South
New York, NY 10016
(212) 779-1100
Fax: (212) 779-0026.
Weekly.

VIETNAM BUSINESS JOURNAL
VIAM Communications Group
Inc.
114 East 32nd, Suite 1010
New York, NY 10016
(212) 725-1717
Fax: (212) 725-8160.

THE WALL STREET JOURNAL
Dow Jones & Co. Inc.
200 Liberty St.
New York, NY 10281
(212)416-2000
Fax: (212)416-2658
Daily
ISSN: 0099-9660

Special Issue:
  Annual Global Ranking

Bibliography

WARD'S AUTOMOTIVE INTERNATIONAL
Ward's Communications
28 W. Adams
Detroit, MI 48226
(313) 962-4456.
Published: monthly.

THE WARSAW VOICE
413 B Logan Blvd., Lakemont
Altoona, PA 16602
(1-800) 488-2939.
Weekly

WINES & VINES
The Hiaring Co.
1800 Lincoln Ave.
San Rafael, CA 94901
(415)453-9700
Fax: (415)453-2517
Monthly
Subscription Rate: $32.50
ISSN: 0043-583X

WIRTSCHAFTSWOCHE
40045 Dusseldorf
Postfach 1054 65 Kaserman-
strabe
Germany 67 40213.

WOOD & WOOD PRODUCTS
Vance Publishing Corp.
400 Knightsbridge Pkway.
Lincolnshire, IL 60069
(708) 634-4347
Fax: (708) 634-4379,
Monthly, except semimonthly in
March.

WORLD AGRICULTURAL PRODUCTION
USGPO
Washington, DC 20402
(202) 783-3238.

WORLD AIR TRANSPORT STATISTICS
International Air Transport Asso-
ciation
2000 Peel St.
Montreal, pQ, Canada H3A 2R4
Fax: (514)844-7711
Annual
Price: $130

WORLD OF BANKING
FIA Financial Publishing Co.
582 Oakwood Ave., Suite 203
Lake Forest, IL 60045,
6x/yr.
Subscription Rate: $80 for one
year.

WORLD SILVER SURVEY
The Silver Institute
112 16th St., Ste. 240
Washington, DC 20036
(202)835-0185
Annual
Price: $40

WORLD POULTRY
Misset International
P.O. Box 4
7000 BA
Doetinchem the Netherlands
31 8340-49562
Fax: 31 8340-40515
Subscription Rate: U.S.: $79 per
year, $123 for 2 years, $155 for 3
years.

WORLD TRADE
Freedom Magazines Inc.
17702 Cowan, Ste. 100
Irvine, CA 92714
(714)640-7070
Fax: (714)798-3501
Monthly
Subscription Rate: $24
ISSN: 1054-8637

WORLD WATCH
Worldwatch Institute
1776 Massachusetts Ave NW,
Washington DC 20036
(202) 452-1991
Fax: (202) 296-7365.